Microsoft

Microsoft® Office Access 2003 Inside Out

D1088868

John L. Viescas

PUBLISHED BY
Microsoft Press
A Division of Microsoft Corporation
One Microsoft Way
Redmond, Washington 98052-6399

Library of Congress Cataloging-in-Publication Data
Viescas, John, 1947-
    Microsoft Office Access 2003 Inside Out / John L. Viescas.
        p. cm.
    Includes index.
    ISBN 0-7356-1513-6
        1. Database management.   2. Microsoft Access.   I. Title.

    QA76.9.D3V545   2003
    005.75'65--dc21   2003056160

Printed and bound in the United States of America.

10 11 12 13 14   QWT   8 7 6

Distributed in Canada by H.B. Fenn and Company Ltd.

A CIP catalogue record for this book is available from the British Library.

Microsoft Press books are available through booksellers and distributors worldwide. For further information about international editions, contact your local Microsoft Corporation office or contact Microsoft Press International directly at fax (425) 936-7329. Visit our Web site at www.microsoft.com/mspress. Send comments to *mspinput@microsoft.com*.

ActiveX, FoxPro, FrontPage, InfoPath, Microsoft, Microsoft Internet Explorer (logo only), Microsoft Press, MSDN, MS-DOS, MSN, the Office logo, OpenType, Outlook, PivotChart, PivotTable, PowerPoint, SharePoint, Visual Basic, Visual C# , Visual C++ , Visual FoxPro, Visual J#, Visual Studio, the Microsoft Visual Tools eMbedded logo, Windows, and Windows NT are either registered trademarks or trademarks of Microsoft Corporation in the United States and/or other countries. Other product and company names mentioned herein may be the trademarks of their respective owners.

The example companies, organizations, products, domain names, e-mail addresses, logos, people, places, and events depicted herein are fictitious. No association with any real company, organization, product, domain name, e-mail address, logo, person, place, or event is intended or should be inferred.

Acquisitions Editor: Alex Blanton
Project Editor: Sandra Haynes
Series Editor: Sandra Haynes
Technical Editor: Curt Philips

Body Part No. X09-71422

For my bestest pal in the whole wide world. Without your love and support, we wouldn't have made this project happen.

And for mom. I finished this book just in time for your 90th birthday. I hope I've made you proud.

Contents at a Glance

v

Contents at a Glance

Table of Contents

Part 1
Understanding Microsoft Access

Chapter 1
What Is Microsoft Access?   3

Chapter 2
The Many Faces of Microsoft Access   17

Chapter 3
Designing Your Database Application   53

Part 2
Building a Microsoft Access Desktop Application

Chapter 4
Creating Your Database and Tables   85

Chapter 7
Creating and Working with Simple Queries   219

Chapter 8
Building Complex Queries 277

Chapter 9
Modifying Data with Action Queries 337

Chapter 13
Advanced Form Design   481

Chapter 23
Automating Your Application with Visual Basic   857

Chapter 27
Building Data Access Pages   1015

Chapter 28
Working with XML and SharePoint   1095

Part 7
After Completing Your Application

Table of Contents

Part 8
Appendix

Appendix
Installing Microsoft Office   1223

Part 9
Articles

Article 1
Understanding SQL   A1

Article 2
Exporting Data   A45

Article 3
Visual Basic Function Reference   A49

Article 4
Internet Explorer Web Page Color Names   A59

Acknowledgments

The folks on the Microsoft Access development team provided invaluable technical support as I worked with the beta software and tried to figure out some of the challenging technical details in Microsoft Office Access 2003. Special thanks to Bill Ramos, Mike Wachal, Tim Getsch, and Clint Covington. You guys make an author's job so much easier. But any errors or omissions in this book are ultimately mine.

This book wouldn't have happened without the outstanding efforts of Sandra Haynes, my project editor; Curt Phillips, the excellent technical editor on the book; and Andrea Fox, who kept all my commas in order. Thanks also to the entire production team at Microsoft Press. Special thanks to Alex Blanton, who talked me into "running the gauntlet" again.

Thanks also to G. L. Sanders, my "partner in crime" at LawTrack, who thought it would be a neat idea to include our contact and sales tracking database as one of the main examples in this book. Including a real production database in the book helps readers see the true value of using Microsoft Access. And last, but certainly not least, thanks to my son, Michael, who wrote major portions of five of the chapters in this book. He's really turning into a database expert in his own right (maybe it's genetic)—not bad for someone who majored in psychology in college.

John Viescas
Austin, Texas
August 2003

We'd Like to Hear from You!

Our goal at Microsoft Press is to create books that help you find the information you need to get the most out of your software.

The *Inside Out* series was created with you in mind. As part of our ongoing effort to ensure that we're creating the books that meet your learning needs, we'd like to hear from you. Let us know what you think. Tell us what you like about this book and what we can do to make it better. When you write, please include the title and author of this book in your e-mail message, as well as your name and contact information. We look forward to hearing from you!

How to Reach Us

E-Mail: nsideout@microsoft.com

Mail: Inside Out Series Editor
            Microsoft Press
            One Microsoft Way
            Redmond, WA 98052

Note: Unfortunately, we can't provide support for any software problems you might experience. Please go to *http://support.microsoft.com* for help with any software issues.

About the CD

The companion CD that ships with this book contains many tools and resources to help you get the most out of your *Inside Out* book.

What's On the CD

Your *Inside Out* CD includes the following:

- **Complete eBook.** In this section you'll find the an electronic version of *Microsoft Office Access 2003 Inside Out*. The eBook is in PDF format.
- **Insider Extras.** This section includes sample files referenced in the book. Use these files to follow along with the examples in the book; you can also use them to form the basis for your own work. See also "Sample Applications," later in this section for more detail.
- **Microsoft Resources.** In this section, you'll find information about additional resources from Microsoft that will help you get the most out of the Microsoft Office System. Building on the familiar tools that many people already know, the Microsoft Office System includes servers, services, and desktop programs to help address a broad array of business needs.
- **Extending Access.** In this section, you'll find great information about third-party utilities and tools you use to further enhance your experience with Access 2003.
- *Computer Dictionary, Fifth Edition* **eBook.** Here you'll find the full electronic version of the *Microsoft Computer Dictionary, Fifth Edition*. Suitable for home and office, the dictionary contains more than 10,000 entries.

The companion CD provides detailed information about the files on this CD and links to Microsoft and third-party sites on the Internet. All the files on this CD are designed to be accessed through Microsoft Internet Explorer (version 5.01 or higher).

> **Note** Please note that the links to third-party sites are not under the control of Microsoft Corporation, and Microsoft is therefore not responsible for their content, nor should their inclusion on this CD be construed as an endorsement of the product or the site.
>
> Software provided on this CD is in English language only and may be incompatible with non-English language operating systems and software.

Sample Applications

Throughout this book, you'll see examples from three sample Access applications included on the companion CD. These are located in the Insider Extras area of the CD.

- **Wedding List (*WeddingList.mdb*).**   This application is an example of a simple database that you might build for your personal use. It has a single main table where you can track the names and addresses of wedding invitees, whether they've said that they will attend, the description of any gift they sent, and whether a thank you note has been sent. Although you might be tempted to store such a simple list in an Excel spreadsheet or a Word document, this application demonstrates how storing the information in Access makes it easy to search and sort the data and produce reports.

- **Housing Reservations (*Housing.mdb*).**   This application demonstrates how a company housing department might track and manage reservations in company-owned housing facilities for out-of-town employees and guests. This application includes data access pages that could be published on a company intranet for use by employees logging in from remote locations. You'll also find *HousingDataCopy.mdb* and *HousingDataCopy2.mdb* files that contain many of the query, form, and report examples. The *Housing2BSecured.mdb* and *HousingSecured.mdb* files demonstrate how to design an application that works with Microsoft Access desktop security.

- **LawTrack Contacts (*Contacts.mdb*, *ContactsData.mdb*, *Contacts.adp*, and *ContactsSQL.mdf*).**   This is a real application that I developed as part of a partnership with LawTrack Software Development (*http://www.lawtrack.net/*). It is both a contacts management and order entry database—two samples for the price of one! This sample database demonstrates how to build a client/server application using only desktop tools as well as how to "upsize" an application to create an Access project and related SQL Server tables, views, stored procedures, and functions. You will need to install the desktop version of SQL Server from your Microsoft Office 2003 Setup discs to be able to fully use the project version of this database. (See the Appendix for instructions.) You'll also find a *ContactsDataCopy.mdb* file that contains additional query, form, and report examples.

Please note that the person names, company names, e-mail addresses, and Web site addresses in these databases are all fictitious. Although I preloaded both databases with sample data, the Housing Reservations and LawTrack Contacts databases also include a special form (*zfrmLoadData*) that has code to load random data into the sample tables based on parameters that you supply.

The examples in this book assume you have installed Microsoft Office 2003, not just Access 2003. Several examples also assume that you have installed all optional features of Access through the Office 2003 setup program. If you have not installed these additional features, your screen might not match the illustrations in this book or you might not be able to run some of the samples from the companion CD. A list of the additional features you will need to run all the samples in this book is included in the Appendix. The dialog boxes illustrated in this book were captured with the Office Assistant turned off.

Using the CD

To use this companion CD, insert it into your CD-ROM. Accept the license agreement that is presented to access the starting menu. If AutoRun is not enabled on your system, run StartCD.exe in the root of the CD or refer to the Readme.txt file.

System Requirements

Following are the minimum system requirements necessary to run the CD:

- Microsoft Windows XP or later or Windows 2000 Professional with Service Pack 3 or later.
- 266-MHz or higher Pentium-compatible CPU
- 64 megabytes (MB) RAM
- 8X CD-ROM drive or faster
- Microsoft Windows–compatible sound card and speakers
- Microsoft Internet Explorer 5.01 or higher
- Microsoft Mouse or compatible pointing device

> **Note** System requirements may be higher for the add-ins available on the CD. Individual add-in system requirements are specified on the CD. An Internet connection is necessary to access the some of the hyperlinks. Connect time charges may apply.

Support Information

Every effort has been made to ensure the accuracy of the book and the contents of this companion CD. For feedback on the book content or this companion CD, please contact us by using any of the addresses listed in the "We'd Like to Hear From You" section.

Microsoft Press provides corrections for books through the World Wide Web at *http://www.microsoft.com/mspress/support/*. To connect directly to the Microsoft Press Knowledge Base and enter a query regarding a question or issue that you may have, go to *http://www.microsoft.com/mspress/support/search.asp*.

For support information regarding Office 2003, you can connect to Microsoft Technical Support on the Web at *http://support.microsoft.com/*.

Conventions and Features Used in This Book

This book uses special text and design conventions to make it easier for you to find the information you need.

Text Conventions

Convention	Meaning
Abbreviated menu commands	For your convenience, this book uses abbreviated menu commands. For example, "Click Tools, Track Changes, Highlight Changes" means that you should click the Tools menu, point to Track Changes, and click the Highlight Changes command.
Boldface type	**Boldface** type is used to indicate text that you enter or type.
Initial Capital Letters	The first letters of the names of menus, dialog boxes, dialog box elements, and commands are capitalized. Example: the Save As dialog box.
Italicized type	*Italicized* type is used to indicate new terms.
Plus sign (+) in text	Keyboard shortcuts are indicated by a plus sign (+) separating two key names. For example, Ctrl+Alt+Delete means that you press the Ctrl, Alt, and Delete keys at the same time.

Design Conventions

 This icon identifies a new or significantly updated feature in this version of the software

 Inside Out

This statement illustrates an example of an "Inside Out" problem statement

These are the book's signature tips. In these tips, you'll get the straight scoop on what's going on with the software—inside information about why a feature works the way it does. You'll also find handy workarounds to deal with software problems.

Tip   Tips provide helpful hints, timesaving tricks, or alternative procedures related to the task being discussed.

Troubleshooting

This statement illustrates an example of a "Troubleshooting" problem statement

Look for these sidebars to find solutions to common problems you might encounter. Troubleshooting sidebars appear next to related information in the chapters. You can also use the Troubleshooting Topics index at the back of the book to look up problems by topic.

Cross-references point you to other locations in the book that offer additional information about the topic being discussed.

   This icon indicates information or text found on the companion CD.

Caution   Cautions identify potential problems that you should look out for when you're completing a task or problems that you must address before you can complete a task.

Note   Notes offer additional information related to the task being discussed.

Sidebars

The sidebars sprinkled throughout these chapters provide ancillary information on the topic being discussed. Go to sidebars to learn more about the technology or a feature.

Syntax Conventions

The following conventions are used in the syntax descriptions for Visual Basic statements in Chapter 22, SQL statements in the "Understanding SQL" article on the companion CD, and other chapters where you find syntax displayed. These conventions do not apply to code examples listed within the text; all code examples appear exactly as you'll find them in the sample databases.

You must enter all other symbols, such as parentheses and colons, exactly as they appear in the syntax line. Much of the syntax shown in the Visual Basic chapter has been broken into multiple lines. You can format your code all on one line, or you can write a single line of code on multiple lines using the Visual Basic line continuation character (_).

Convention	Meaning
Bold	Bold type indicates keywords and reserved words that you must enter exactly as shown. Microsoft Visual Basic understands keywords entered in uppercase, lowercase, and mixed case type. Access stores SQL keywords in queries in all uppercase, but you can enter the keywords in any case.
Italic	Italicized words represent variables that you supply.
Angle brackets < >	Angle brackets enclose syntactic elements that you must supply. The words inside the angle brackets describe the element but do not show the actual syntax of the element. Do not enter the angle brackets.
Brackets [ ]	Brackets enclose optional items. If more than one item is listed, the items are separated by a pipe character (|). Choose one or none of the elements. Do not enter the brackets or the pipe; they're not part of the element. Note that Visual Basic and SQL in many cases require that you enclose names in brackets. When brackets are required as part of the syntax of variables that you must supply in these examples, the brackets are italicized, as in [MyTable].[MyField].
Braces { }	Braces enclose one or more options. If more than one option is listed, the items are separated by a pipe character (|). Choose one item from the list. Do not enter the braces or the pipe.
Ellipsis ...	Ellipses indicate that you can repeat an item one or more times. When a comma is shown with an ellipsis (,...), enter a comma between items.
Underscore _	You can use a blank space followed by an underscore to continue a line of Visual Basic code to the next line for readability. You cannot place a continuation underscore in the middle of a string literal. You do not need an underscore for continued lines in SQL, but you cannot break a literal across lines.

Introduction

Once upon a time, in a far-off corner of a land renowned for its wizards and inventors, there lived a Great Wizard. Like other great wizards before him (the names of Eli Whitney, Orville and Wilbur Wright, and Thomas Edison still ring throughout the land), this Great Wizard devoted his life to inventing products that would improve the lives of people throughout the known world.

One beautiful spring day under blue skies laced with wispy clouds (and there was great rejoicing throughout the realm, for such fine days are rare in this far-north land), the Great Wizard declared to all his wizard assistants: "We should create a new invention that will help all people store and manage information more easily. In honor of this fine day, I name the new invention *Cirrus*." And so it came to pass that the wizard assistants, toiling ever-diligently over their keyboards, created the new invention.

When the new invention was almost finished, the Great Wizard declared: "We must fully test this new invention before we can send it out to compete with products from the realms of Borland or Ashton-Tate. Call forth people from around the world, and we shall dub them *beta testers*." The beta testers marveled at the capabilities of the new invention. They exclaimed: "We can assemble new applications to manage our data in record time! We can store our information in tables, ask questions with queries, edit the data with forms, summarize the information with reports, and automate the entire process with macros and Basic. We can even access information we already have stored in text files, spreadsheets, or even other data storage systems!"

The Great Wizard studied the information provided by the beta testers with great care and declared, "I think our new invention is ready to enter world competition, but we need to give it a new name: *ACCESS*! We should also make it easy for everyone to acquire and use our great invention, so we will ask only for the small sum of $99 to obtain the fruits of our wizardry."

And so the new invention was sent out into the world, and it immediately became a great success. But the wizards were not finished with their work. In the many years hence (and a year is a long time in the world of such inventions), the wizards toiled on and produced not one but seven new versions of their original invention. They made queries faster and forms and reports more powerful. They enhanced the original Access Basic language (renaming it Visual Basic for Applications) and made it compatible with other inventions in the group of products they came to call Office. They created a way to directly link the powerful forms, reports, and Visual Basic capabilities of Access to another invention of the wizards: Microsoft SQL Server.

Meanwhile, another great invention—the Internet (or World Wide Web)—was taking the world by storm. Although this new invention was not directly the work of these wizards of the north, the Great Wizard quickly realized its value and declared that all new inventions or enhancements to old inventions must work with the Internet. In response, the wizards working on Access created new tools to make it easy to design Web pages that can display or update information stored in an Access or SQL Server database. They made it possible for Access applications to exchange information with Web servers by adding the ability for Access to understand the new data storage language of the Web—Extensible Markup Language (XML). And in the latest version they have made it possible for Access queries, forms, and reports to work directly with data stored on a Web server.

Ignoring the man behind the curtain (please pardon the mixed metaphor), we now return to the real world to continue our story.

Microsoft Access Today

Access is just one part of Microsoft's overall data management product strategy. Like all good relational databases, it allows you to link related information easily—for example, customer and order data that you enter. But Access also complements other database products because it has several powerful connectivity features. As its name implies, Access can work directly with data from other sources, including many popular PC database programs (such as dBASE and Paradox); with many SQL (structured query language) databases on the desktop, on servers, on minicomputers, or on mainframes; and with data stored on Internet or intranet Web servers. Access also fully supports Microsoft's ActiveX technology, so an Access application can be either a client or a server for all the other Office applications, including Microsoft Word, Excel, PowerPoint, Outlook, FrontPage, Publisher, and the new Microsoft OneNote.

Access provides a very sophisticated application development system for the Microsoft Windows operating system. This helps you build applications quickly, whatever the data source. In fact, you can build simple applications by defining forms and reports based on your data and linking them with a few Visual Basic statements; there's no need to write complex code in the classic programming sense. Because Access uses Visual Basic, you can use the same set of skills with other applications in Microsoft Office or with Microsoft Visual Basic.

For small businesses (and for consultants creating applications for small businesses), the Access desktop development features are all that's required to store and manage the data used to run a typical small business. Access coupled with Microsoft SQL Server—on the desktop or on a server—is an ideal way for many medium-size companies to build new applications for Windows quickly and inexpensively. For large corporations with a big investment in mainframe relational database applications as well as a proliferation of desktop applications that rely on PC databases, Access provides the tools to easily link mainframe and PC data in a single Windows-based application.

Microsoft Access can also act as a direct source of information published on an intranet or the World Wide Web. Data access pages let you quickly create and deploy intranet applications using pages that you create directly from Access much like you would create an Access application form. Data access pages can retrieve and update data stored either in an Access database or in Microsoft SQL Server. Microsoft Access 2003 includes new and enhanced features to allow you to export or import data in XML format (the lingua franca of data stored on the Web) or to directly link to an XML data source on a Microsoft SharePoint Services Web site. You can export data (or subsets of data) stored in a Microsoft Access or SQL Server database to a SharePoint server and then link those files back into your original application.

About This Book

If you're developing a database application with the tools in Microsoft Access, this book gives you a thorough understanding of "programming without pain." It provides a solid foundation for designing databases, forms, and reports and getting them all to work together. You'll learn that you can quickly create complex applications by linking design elements with Visual Basic. This book will also show you how to take advantage of some of the more advanced features of Microsoft Access. You'll learn how to build an Access project that links directly to a Microsoft SQL Server database. You'll also learn how to use Access tools to link to your Access data from the Web or link your Access application to data stored on the Web.

If you're new to developing applications, particularly database applications, this probably should not be the first book you read about Microsoft Access. I recommend that you first take a look at *Microsoft Office Access 2003 Step by Step* or *Faster Smarter Microsoft Office Access 2003*.

Microsoft Office Access 2003 Inside Out is divided into seven major parts:

- Part 1 provides an overview of Access and discusses work you must do before you write a single line of code.
    - Chapter 1 explains the major features that a database should provide, explores those features in Access, and discusses some of the main reasons why you should consider using database software.
    - Chapter 2 describes the architecture of Microsoft Access, gives you an overview of the major objects in an Access database by taking you on a tour through two of the sample databases, and explains the many ways you can use Access to create an application.
    - Chapter 3 explains a simple technique that you can use to design a good relational database application with little effort. Even if you're already familiar with Access or creating database applications in general, getting the table design right is so important that this chapter is a "must read" for everyone. Starting with a good design is the key to building easy-to-use and easy-to-modify applications.
- Part 2 shows you how to create your desktop application database and tables and build queries to analyze and update data in your tables.
    - Chapter 4 teaches you how to create databases, tables, and the indexes for those tables.
    - Chapter 5 shows you the ins and outs of modifying tables even after you've already begun to load data and build other parts of your application.
    - Chapter 6 explains how to link to or import data from other sources.
    - Chapter 7 shows you how to build simple queries and how to work with data in Datasheet view.

- Chapter 8 discusses how to design queries to work with data from multiple tables, summarize information, build queries that require you to work in SQL view, and work with the PivotTable and PivotChart views of queries.
- Chapter 9 focuses on modifying sets of data with action queries—updating data, inserting new data, deleting sets of data, or creating a new table from a selection of data from existing tables.

- Part 3 discusses how to build and work with forms and reports in a desktop application.
  - Chapter 10 introduces you to forms—what they look like and how they work.
  - Chapters 11, 12, and 13 teach you all about form design in a desktop application, from simple forms you build with a wizard to complex, advanced forms that incorporate embedded forms, multiple pages, PivotCharts, or ActiveX controls.
  - Chapter 14 leads you on a guided tour of reports and explains their major features as well as how to print them.
  - Chapters 15 and 16 teach you how to design, build, and implement both simple and complex reports in your desktop application.

- Part 4 expands on what you learned in Parts 2 and 3 by teaching you the additional skills you need to create client/server applications in an Access project.
  - Chapter 17 shows you how to build a new Access project file and explains how to define SQL Server tables for the project.
  - Chapter 18 teaches you how to design views, stored procedures, and functions—the Access project equivalent of Access desktop queries.
  - Chapter 19 builds on what you learned in Chapters 11, 12, and 13 and shows you how forms work differently in an Access project.
  - Chapter 20 leverages what you learned in Chapters 15 and 16 and teaches you how to design reports in an Access project.

- Part 5 shows you how to use the programming facilities in Visual Basic to integrate your database objects and make your application "come alive."
  - Chapter 21 discusses the concept of event processing in Access, provides a comprehensive list of events, and briefly discusses the macro design facility.
  - Chapter 22 is a comprehensive reference to the Visual Basic language and object models implemented in Access. The final section of the chapter presents two complex coding examples with a line-by-line discussion of the code.
  - Chapter 23 thoroughly discusses some of the most common tasks that you might want to automate with Visual Basic. Each section describes a problem, shows you specific form or report design techniques you must use to solve the problem, and walks you through the code from one or more of the sample databases that implements the solution.
  - Chapter 24, appropriately titled "Finishing Touches," teaches you how to build custom command bars (menus and toolbars), how to use the Performance Analyzer tool, how to design a switchboard, and how to set Startup properties.

- Part 6 is all about using Access tools with the Web.

  - Chapter 25 provides an overview of the ways you can publish data on a Web site.

  - Chapter 26 discusses specific ways to publish either static or dynamic data from your Access applications.

  - Chapter 27 teaches you how to design, automate, and publish data access pages.

  - Chapter 28 covers the features in Access that handle XML, including publishing data to and linking data from a Microsoft SharePoint server.

- Part 7 covers tasks you might want to perform after completing your application.

  - Chapter 29 discusses ways to implement an Access application in a client/server environment and considerations for converting your application from a desktop database (.mdb) file to a project (.adp) file linked to SQL Server.

  - Chapter 30 shows you how to secure a desktop application file and how to deal with the new macro security features.

  - Chapter 31 shows you how to set up your application so that you can distribute it to others.

The book also includes an Appendix that explains how to install Microsoft Office, including which options you should choose for Microsoft Access to be able to open all the samples in this book. It also discusses how to install the SQL Server desktop engine (MSDE), and how to define Open Database Connectivity (ODBC) connections to remote data.

Four articles that provide important supplementary information are included on the companion CD in Adobe PDF format:

- "Understanding SQL" is a complete reference to SQL as implemented in Access desktop databases. It also contains notes about differences between SQL supported natively by Access and SQL implemented in SQL Server.

- "Exporting Data" discusses how to export data and objects from your Access application to such data formats as a spreadsheet, Word mail-merge document, text file, SQL table, or a dBASE or Paradox file.

- "Visual Basic Function Reference" lists the functions most commonly used in an Access application and the equivalent functions you can use when creating queries in SQL Server.

- "Internet Explorer Web Page Color Names" lists all the Internet Explorer color names (as well as their corresponding hexadecimal codes) so you can designate your colors by name instead of in hexadecimal code when creating Web pages.

Understanding Microsoft Access

What Is Microsoft Access?

If you're a serious user of a personal computer, you've probably been using word processing or spreadsheet applications to help you solve problems. You might have started a long time ago with character-based products running under MS-DOS but subsequently upgraded to software that runs under the Microsoft Windows operating system. You might also own some database software, either as part of an integrated package such as Microsoft Works or as a separate program.

Database programs have been available for personal computers for a long time. Unfortunately, many of these programs have been either simple data storage managers that aren't suitable for building applications or complex application development systems that are difficult to learn and use. Even many computer-literate people have avoided the more complex database systems unless they have been handed a complete, custom-built database application. The introduction of Microsoft Access, however, represented a significant turnaround in ease of use. Many people are drawn to it to create both simple databases and sophisticated database applications.

Now that Access is in its seventh release and has become an even more robust product in the fifth edition designed for 32-bit versions of Windows, perhaps it's time to take another look at how you work with your personal computer to get the job done. If you've previously shied away from database software because you felt you needed programming skills or because it would take you too much time to become a proficient user, you'll be pleasantly surprised at how easy it is to work with Access. But how do you decide whether you're ready to move up to a database system such as Access? To help you decide, let's take a look at the advantages of using database application development software.

What Is a Database?

In the simplest sense, a *database* is a collection of records and files that are organized for a particular purpose. You might keep the names and addresses of all your friends or customers on your computer system. Perhaps you collect all the letters you write and organize them by recipient. You might have another set of files in which you keep all your financial data—accounts payable and accounts receivable or your checkbook entries and balances. The word processor documents that you organize by topic are, in the broadest sense, one type of database. The spreadsheet files that you organize according to their uses are another type of database. Shortcuts to all your programs on your Windows Start menu are a kind of database. Internet shortcuts organized in your Favorites folder are a database.

If you're very organized, you can probably manage several hundred spreadsheets or shortcuts by using folders and subfolders. When you do this, *you're* the database manager. But what do you do when the problems you're trying to solve get too big? How can you easily collect information about all customers and their orders when the data might be stored in several document and spreadsheet files? How can you maintain links between the files when you enter new information? How do you ensure that data is being entered correctly? What if you need to share your information with many people but don't want two people to try updating the same data at the same time? How do you keep duplicate copies of data proliferating when people can't share the same data at the same time? Faced with these challenges, you need a *database management system (DBMS)*.

Relational Databases

Nearly all modern database management systems store and handle information using the *relational* database management model. In a relational database management system, sometimes called an *RDBMS*, the system manages all data in *tables*. Tables store information about a single subject (such as customers or products) and have *columns* (or *fields*) that contain the different kinds of information about the subject (for example, customers' addresses or phone numbers) and *rows* (or *records*) that describe all the attributes of a single instance of the subject (for example, data on a specific customer or product). Even when you *query* the database (fetch information from one or more tables), the result is always something that looks like another table.

The term *relational* stems from the fact that each table in the database contains information related to a single subject and only that subject. If you study the relational database management model, you'll find the term *relation* applied to a set of rows (a table) about a single subject. Also, data about two classes of information (such as customers and orders) can be manipulated as a single entity based on related data values. For example, it would be redundant to store customer name and address information with every order that the customer places. In a relational database system, the information about orders contains a field that stores data, such as a customer number, which can be used to connect each order with the appropriate customer information.

You can also *join* information on related values from multiple tables or queries. For example, you can join company information with contact information to find out the contacts for a particular company. You can join employee information with department information to find out the department in which an employee works.

Some Relational Database Terminology

Relation   Information about a single subject such as customers, orders, employees, products, or companies. A relation is usually stored as a *table* in a relational database management system.

Attribute   A specific piece of information about a subject, such as the address for a customer or the dollar amount of an order. An attribute is normally stored as a data *column*, or *field*, in a table.

Instance   A particular member of a relation—an individual customer or product. An instance is usually stored in a table as a *record*, or *row*.

Relationship   The way information in one relation is related to information in another relation. For example, customers have a *one-to-many* relationship with orders because one customer can place many orders, but any order belongs to only one customer. Companies might have a *many-to-many* relationship with contacts because there might be multiple contacts for a company, and a contact might be associated with more than one company.

Join   The process of linking tables or queries on tables via their related data values. For example, customers might be joined to orders by matching customer ID in a customers table and an orders table.

Database Capabilities

An RDBMS gives you complete control over how you define your data, work with it, and share it with others. The system also provides sophisticated features that make it easy to catalog and manage large amounts of data in many tables. An RDBMS has three main types of capabilities: data definition, data manipulation, and data control.

Data definition   You can define what data is stored in your database, the type of data (for example, numbers or characters), and how the data is related. In some cases, you can also define how the data should be formatted and how it should be validated.

Data manipulation   You can work with the data in many ways. You can select which data fields you want, filter the data, and sort it. You can join data with related information and summarize the data. You can select a set of information and ask the RDBMS to update it, delete it, copy it to another table, or create a new table containing the data.

Data control   You can define who is allowed to read, update, or insert data. In many cases, you can also define how data can be shared and updated by multiple users.

All this functionality is contained in the powerful features of Microsoft Access. Let's take a look at how Access implements these capabilities and compare them to what you can do with spreadsheet or word processing programs.

Microsoft Access as an RDBMS

A Microsoft Access desktop database (which uses the .mdb file extension) is a fully functional RDBMS. It provides all the data definition, data manipulation, and data control features you need to manage large volumes of data.

You can use an Access desktop database (.mdb) either as a stand-alone RDBMS on a single workstation or in a shared client/server mode across a network. A desktop database can also act as the data source for data displayed on Web pages on your company intranet. When you build an application with an Access desktop database, Access is the RDBMS. You can also use Access to build applications in a project file (which uses the .adp file extension) connected to Microsoft SQL Server, and you can share the server data with other applications or with users on the Web. When you create a Microsoft Access project file (.adp), SQL Server (or the Microsoft SQL Server Desktop Engine—MSDE) is the RDBMS.

Data Definition and Storage

As you work with a document or a spreadsheet, you generally have complete freedom to define the contents of the document or each cell in the spreadsheet. Within a given page in a document, you might include paragraphs of text, a table, a chart, or multiple columns of data displayed with multiple fonts. Within a given column on a spreadsheet, you might have text data at the top to define a column header for printing or display, and you might have various numeric formats within the same column, depending on the function of the row. You need this flexibility because your word processing document must be able to convey your message within the context of a printed page, and your spreadsheet must store the data you're analyzing as well as provide for calculation and presentation of the results.

This flexibility is great for solving relatively small, well-defined business problems. But a document becomes unwieldy when it extends beyond a few dozen pages, and a spreadsheet becomes difficult to manage when it contains more than a few hundred rows of information. As the amount of data grows, you might also find that you exceed the data storage limits of your word processing or spreadsheet program or of your computer system. If you design a document or spreadsheet to be used by others, it's difficult (if not impossible) to control how they will use the data or enter new data. For example, on a spreadsheet, even though one cell might need a date and another a currency value to make sense, a user might easily enter character data in error.

Some spreadsheet programs allow you to define a "database" area within a spreadsheet to help you manage the information you need to produce the desired result. However, you are still constrained by the basic storage limitations of the spreadsheet program, and you still don't have much control over what's entered in the rows and columns of the database area. Also, if you need to handle more than number and character data, you might find that your spreadsheet program doesn't understand such data types as pictures or sounds.

An RDBMS allows you to define the kind of data you have and how the data should be stored. You can also usually define rules that the RDBMS can use to ensure the integrity of your data. In its simplest form, a *validation rule* might ensure that the user can't accidentally store alphabetic characters in a field that should contain a number. Other rules might define valid values or ranges of values for your data. In the most sophisticated systems, you can define the relationship between collections of data (usually tables or files) and ask the RDBMS to ensure that your data remains consistent. For example, you can have the system automatically check to ensure that every order entered is for a valid customer.

With an Access desktop database (.mdb), you have complete flexibility to define your data (as text, numbers, dates, times, currency, Internet hyperlinks, pictures, sounds, documents, and spreadsheets), to define how Access stores your data (string length, number precision, and date/time precision), and to define what the data looks like when you display or print it. You can define simple or complex validation rules to ensure that only accurate values exist in your database. You can request that Access check for valid relationships between files or tables in your database. When you connect an Access project (.adp) to an SQL Server database, SQL Server provides all these capabilities.

Because Access is a state-of-the-art application for Microsoft Windows, you can use all the facilities of ActiveX objects and ActiveX custom controls. ActiveX is an advanced Windows technology that, in part, allows you to link objects to or embed objects in your Access desktop database or SQL Server. Objects include pictures, graphs, spreadsheets, and documents from other Windows-based applications that also support ActiveX. Figure 1-1 shows a form with embedded object data from the sample Northwind Traders database that ships with Access. You can see a product category record that not only has the typical name and descriptive information but also has a picture to visually describe each category. Microsoft Office Access 2003 can also act as an ActiveX *server*, allowing you to open and manipulate Access database objects (such as tables, queries, and forms) from other Windows-based applications.

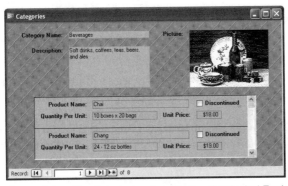

Figure 1-1. The Categories form in the Northwind Traders sample database.

Within your Access forms and reports, you can include ActiveX custom controls to enhance the operation of your application. ActiveX controls provide sophisticated design objects that allow you to present complex data in a simpler, more graphical way. Most ActiveX controls provide a rich set of "actions" (called *methods* in object terminology) that you can call from a procedure and properties you can set to manage how the control looks and behaves. For example, you might want to let your user enter a date by selecting from a calendar picture. One of the ActiveX controls that you can use in an Access application is the calendar control that provides just such a graphical interface. This control is used in a pop-up form in the LawTrack Contacts sample database that is included with this book. You can see this form in Figure 1-2.

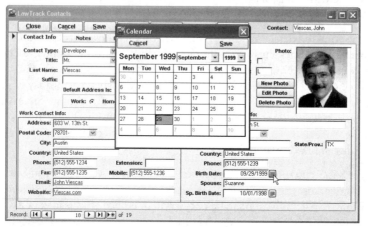

Figure 1-2. Choosing a date using the ActiveX calendar control.

The user can type in dates anywhere in the application or click a button next to any date value to open the ActiveX calendar control as a pop-up form. The user can choose a different month or year from the drop-down boxes on the control, and the control displays the appropriate month. When the user clicks a specific date on the calendar and then clicks Save on the pop-up form, the control passes the date back to the form to update the date field in the record. If you purchase Microsoft Office Access 2003 Developer Extensions, you will have several additional ActiveX controls available to use in your applications. Many third-party software vendors have built libraries of ActiveX controls that you can purchase for use with Microsoft Access.

Access can also understand and use a wide variety of other data formats, including many other database file structures. You can export data to and import data from word processing files or spreadsheets. You can directly access Paradox, dBASE III, dBASE IV, Microsoft Fox-Pro, and other database files. You can also import data from these files into an Access table. In addition, Access can work with most popular databases that support the Open Database Connectivity (ODBC) standard, including SQL Server, Oracle, and DB2.

Data Manipulation

Working with data in an RDBMS is very different from working with data in a word processing or spreadsheet program. In a word processing document, you can include tabular data and perform a limited set of functions on the data in the document. You can also search for text strings in the original document and, with ActiveX, include tables, charts, or pictures from other applications. In a spreadsheet, some cells contain functions that determine the result you want, and in other cells you enter the data that provides the source information for the functions. The data in a given spreadsheet serves one particular purpose, and it's cumbersome to use the same data to solve a different problem. You can link to data in another spreadsheet to solve a new problem, or you can use limited search capabilities to copy a selected subset of the data in one spreadsheet to use in problem solving in another spreadsheet.

An RDBMS provides you with many ways to work with your data. You can, for example, search a single table for information or request a complex search across several related tables. You can update a single field or many records with a single command. You can write programs that use RDBMS commands to fetch data you want to display and allow the user to update.

Access uses the powerful SQL database language to process data in your tables. (SQL is an acronym for Structured Query Language.) Using SQL, you can define the set of information that you need to solve a particular problem, including data from perhaps many tables. But Access simplifies data manipulation tasks. You don't even have to understand SQL to get Access to work for you. Access uses the relationship definitions you provide to automatically link the tables you need. You can concentrate on how to solve information problems without having to worry about building a complex navigation system that links all the data structures in your database. Access also has an extremely simple yet powerful graphical query definition facility that you can use to specify the data you need to solve a problem. Using point and click, drag and drop, and a few key strokes, you can build a complex query in a matter of seconds.

 Figure 1-3 shows a complex query used in the desktop database version of the LawTrack Contacts application. You can find this query in the *Contacts.mdb* sample database on the companion CD included with this book. Access displays field lists from selected tables in the upper part of the window; the lines between field lists indicate the automatic links that Access will use to solve the query.

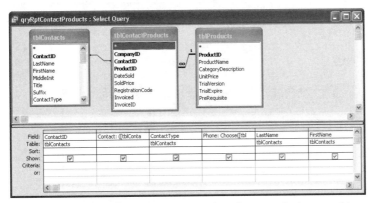

Figure 1-3. A query to retrieve information about products owned by contacts in the Law-Track Contacts sample application.

To create the query, you add the tables containing the data you need to the top of the query design grid, select the fields you want from each table, and drag them to the design grid in the lower part of the window. Choose a few options, type in any criteria, and you're ready to have Access select the information you want.

 Figure 1-4 on the next page shows the same query in the project file version of the LawTrack Contacts application, *Contacts.adp*. You can see that the design interface is similar but also provides an SQL pane so that you can watch Access build the SQL for your query as you work. You don't need to be an expert to correctly construct the SQL syntax you need to solve your problem, but you can learn a lot about SQL in Chapter 18, "Building Queries in an Access Project," and in Article 1, "Understanding SQL." For certain advanced types of queries, you'll need to learn the basics of SQL.

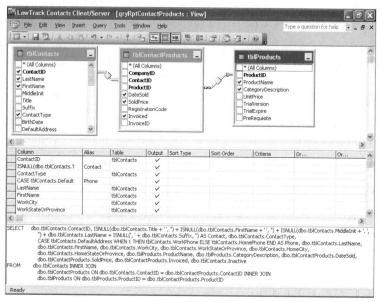

Figure 1-4. The project file version of a query to retrieve information about products owned by contacts.

Figure 1-5 shows the result of asking the query to return its data.

Last Name	First Name	Work City	State/Provin	Home City	State/Provin	Product Name	Product Type
Groncki	Douglas	Waterville	NY	Vernon	NY	Demo Edition, Single User	Single User
Wruck	David	Rutherford	TN	Pinson	TN	Demo Edition, Multi-User	Multi-User
Delmarco	Stefan	Rutherford	TN	Ramer	TN	Demo Edition, Single User	Single User
Sullivan	Michael	Rutherford	TN	Reagan	TN	Demo Edition, Multi-User	Multi-User
Sullivan	Michael	Rutherford	TN	Reagan	TN	Single User	Single User
Sullivan	Michael	Rutherford	TN	Reagan	TN	Multi-User	Multi-User
Sullivan	Michael	Rutherford	TN	Reagan	TN	Remote User	Remote User
Fakhouri	Fadi	Elgin	TN	Eagan	TN	Demo Edition, Multi-User	Multi-User
Cannon	Chris	Harpursville	NY	Harpursville	NY	Demo Edition, Single User	Single User
Cannon	Chris	Harpursville	NY	Harpursville	NY	Remote User	Remote User
Casselman	Kevin	Tyler Hill	PA	Waverly	PA	Single User	Single User
Gray	Chris	Tyler Hill	PA	Waymart	PA	Demo Edition, Single User	Single User
Gray	Chris	Tyler Hill	PA	Waymart	PA	Multi-User	Multi-User
Knopf	Steve	Philadelphia	PA	Philadelphia	PA	Remote User	Remote User
Playstead	Craig	Tickfaw	LA	Talisheek	LA	Multi-User	Multi-User
Playstead	Craig	Tickfaw	LA	Talisheek	LA	Remote User	Remote User
Ajenstat	François	Elberfeld	IN	Grandview	IN	Single User	Single User
Ajenstat	François	Elberfeld	IN	Grandview	IN	Multi-User	Multi-User
Ajenstat	François	Elberfeld	IN	Grandview	IN	Remote User	Remote User
Deniut	Bruno	Elberfeld	IN	Grandview	IN	Demo Edition, Single User	Single User
Deniut	Bruno	Elberfeld	IN	Grandview	IN	Single User	Single User

Record: 1 of 29

Figure 1-5. A list of contacts and the products they own.

Data Control

Spreadsheets and word processing documents are great for solving single-user problems, but they are difficult to use when more than one person needs to share the data. Although spreadsheets are useful for providing templates for simple data entry, they don't do the job well if you need to perform complex data validation. For example, a spreadsheet works well as a template for an invoice for a small business with a single proprietor. But if the business expands and a number of salespeople are entering orders, the company needs a database. Likewise, a spreadsheet can assist employees with expense reports in a large business, but the data eventually must be captured and placed in a database for corporate accounting.

When you need to share your information with others, true relational database management systems allow you to make your information secure so that only authorized users can read or update your data. An RDBMS that is designed to allow data sharing also provides features to ensure that no two people can change the same data at the same time. The best systems also allow you to group changes (a series of changes is sometimes called a *transaction*) so that either all of the changes or none of the changes appear in your data. For example, while confirming a new order for a customer, you probably want to know that both the inventory for ordered products is updated and the order confirmation is saved or, if you encounter an error, that none of the changes are saved. You probably also want to be sure that no one else can view any part of the order until you have entered all of it.

Because you can share your Access data with other users, Access has excellent data security and data integrity features. You can define which users or groups of users can have access to objects (such as tables, forms, and queries) in your database. Access automatically provides locking mechanisms to ensure that no two people can update an object at the same time. Access also understands and honors the locking mechanisms of other database structures (such as Paradox, FoxPro, and SQL databases) that you attach to your database.

Microsoft Access as an Application Development System

Being able to define exactly what data you need, how it should be stored, and how you want to access it solves the data management part of the problem. However, you also need a simple way to automate all the common tasks you want to perform. For example, each time you need to enter a new order, you don't want to have to run a query to search the Customers table, execute a command to open the Orders table, and then create a new record before you can enter the data for the order. And after you've entered the data for the new order, you don't want to have to worry about scanning the table that contains all your products to verify the order's sizes, colors, and prices.

Advanced word processing software lets you define templates and macros to automate document creation, but it's not designed to handle complex transaction processing. In a spreadsheet, you enter formulas that define what automatic calculations you want performed. If you're an advanced spreadsheet user, you might also create macros or Visual Basic procedures to help automate entering and validating data. If you're working with a lot of data, you've probably figured out how to use one spreadsheet as a "database" container and use references to selected portions of this data in your calculations.

Although you can build a fairly complex application using spreadsheets, you really don't have the debugging and application management tools you need to easily construct a robust data management application. Even something as simple as a wedding guest invitation and gift list is much easier to handle in a database. (See the Wedding List sample database included with this book.) Database systems are specifically designed for application development. They give you the data management and control tools that you need and also provide facilities to catalog the various parts of your application and manage their interrelationships. You also get a full programming language and debugging tools with a database system.

When you want to build a more complex database application, you need a powerful relational database management system and an application development system to help you automate your tasks. Virtually all database systems include application development facilities to allow programmers or users of the system to define the procedures needed to automate the creation and manipulation of data. Unfortunately, many database application development systems require that you know a programming language, such as C or Xbase, to define procedures. Although these languages are very rich and powerful, you must have experience before you can use them properly. To really take advantage of some database systems, you must learn programming, hire a programmer, or buy a ready-made database application (which might not exactly suit your needs) from a software development company.

Fortunately, Microsoft Access makes it easy to design and construct database applications without requiring that you know a programming language. Although you begin in Access by defining the relational tables and the fields in those tables that will contain your data, you will quickly branch out to defining actions on the data via forms, reports, data access pages, macros, and Microsoft Visual Basic.

You can use forms and reports to define how you want the data displayed and what additional calculations you want performed—very much like spreadsheets. In this case, the format and calculation instructions (in the forms and reports) are separate from the data (in the tables), so you have complete flexibility to use your data in different ways without affecting the data. You simply define another form or report using the same data.

When you want to automate actions in a simple application, Access provides a macro definition facility to make it easy to respond to events (such as clicking a button to open a related report) or to link forms and reports together. When you want to build something a little more complex (like the Housing Reservations database included with this book), you can quickly learn how to create simple Visual Basic event procedures for your forms and reports. If you want to create more sophisticated applications, such as contact tracking, order processing, and reminder systems (see the LawTrack Contacts sample database), you can employ more advanced techniques using Visual Basic and module objects.

Access 2003 includes features to make it easy to provide access to your data over your company's local intranet or on the Internet. You can create data access pages that allow users to view and browse the data in your Access database from Microsoft Internet Explorer. You can share and link to data on a Microsoft SharePoint Team Services site. You can also export selected data as a static HTML Web page or link a Microsoft Active Server Page from the Web to your database.

Access provides advanced database application development facilities to process not only data in its own database structures but also information stored in many other popular database formats. Perhaps Access's greatest strength is its ability to handle data from spreadsheets, text files, dBASE files, Paradox and FoxPro databases, and any SQL database that supports the ODBC standard. This means you can use Access to create a Windows-based application that can process data from a network SQL server or from a mainframe SQL database.

For advanced developers, Access provides the ability to create an Access application in a project file (.adp) that links directly to Microsoft SQL Server (version 6.5 and later). You store your tables and queries (as views, functions, or stored procedures) directly in SQL Server and create forms, reports, and data access pages in Access.

Deciding to Move to Database Software

When you use a word processing document or a spreadsheet to solve a problem, you define both the data and the calculations or functions you need at the same time. For simple problems with a limited set of data, this is an ideal solution. But when you start collecting lots of data, it becomes difficult to manage in many separate document or spreadsheet files. Adding one more transaction (another contact or a new investment in your portfolio) might push you over the limit of manageability. It might even exceed the memory limits of your system or the data storage limits of your software program. Because most spreadsheet programs must be able to load an entire spreadsheet file into memory, running out of memory will probably be the first thing that forces you to consider switching to a database.

If you need to change a formula or the way certain data is formatted, you might find you have to make the same change in many places. When you want to define new calculations on existing data, you might have to copy and modify an existing document or create complex links to the files that contain the data. If you make a copy, how do you keep the data in the two copies synchronized?

Before you can use a database such as Microsoft Access to solve problems that require a lot of data or that have complex and changing requirements, you must change the way you think about solving problems with word processing or spreadsheet applications. In Access, you store a single copy of the data in the tables you design. Perhaps one of the hardest concepts to grasp is that you store only your basic data in database tables. For example, in a database, you would store the quantity of items ordered and the price of the items, but you would not usually store the extended cost (a calculated value). You use a query, a form, or a report to define the quantity-times-price calculation.

You can use the query facility to examine and extract the data in many ways. This allows you to keep only one copy of the basic data, yet use it over and over to solve different problems. In a sales database, you might create one form to display vendors and the products they supply. You can create another form to enter orders for these products. You can use a report defined on the same data to graph the sales of products by vendor during specified time periods. You don't need a separate copy of the data to do this, and you can change either the forms or the report independently, without destroying the structure of your database. You can also add new product or sales information easily without having to worry about the impact on any of your forms or reports. You can do this because the data (tables) and the routines you define to operate on the data (queries, forms, reports, macros, or modules) are completely independent of each other. Any change you make to the data via one form is immediately reflected by Access in any other form or query that uses the same data.

Reasons to Switch to a Database

Reason 1 You have too many separate files or too much data in individual files. This makes it difficult to manage the data. Also, the data might exceed the limits of the software or the capacity of the system memory.

Reason 2 You have multiple uses for the data—detailing transactions (invoices, for example), and analyzing summaries (such as quarterly sales summaries) and "what if" scenarios. Therefore, you need to be able to look at the data in many different ways, but you find it difficult to create multiple "views" of the data.

Reason 3 You need to share data. For example, numerous people are entering and updating data and analyzing it. Only one person at a time can update a word processing document, and although an Excel 2003 spreadsheet can be shared among several people, there is no mechanism to prevent two users from updating the same row simultaneously on their local copies of the spreadsheet, requiring the changes to be reconciled later. In contrast, Access locks the row of a table being edited by one person so that no conflicting changes can be made by another user, while still permitting many other users to access or update the remaining rows of the database table. In this way each person is working from the same data and always sees the latest saved updates made by any other user.

Reason 4 You must control the data because different users access the data, because the data is used to run your business, and because the data is related (such as data for customers and orders). This means you must secure access to data and control data values, and you must ensure data consistency.

If you're wondering how you'll make the transition from word processing documents and spreadsheets to Access, you'll be pleased to find features in Access to help you out. You can use the import facilities to copy the data from your existing text or spreadsheet files. You'll find that Access supports most of the same functions you have used in your spreadsheets, so defining calculations in a form or a report will seem very familiar. Within the Help facility, you can find "how do I" topics that walk you through key tasks you need to learn to begin working with a database and "tell me about" and reference topics that enhance your knowledge. In addition, Access provides powerful wizard facilities to give you a jump-start on moving your spreadsheet data to an Access database, such as the Import Spreadsheet Wizard and the Table Analyzer Wizard to help you design database tables to store your old spreadsheet data.

> **Tip   A very common problem: Ignoring table design when converting from a spreadsheet to a database**
>
> You can obtain free assistance from me and many other Microsoft MVPs (Most Valuable Professionals) in the Microsoft Access newsgroups. Some of the most difficult problems arise in databases that have been created by directly copying spreadsheet data into an Access table. The typical advice in this situation is to design the database tables first, and then import and split up the spreadsheet data.
>
> You can access the newsgroups using Microsoft Outlook Express, or you can go to *http://support.microsoft.com/newsgroups/default.aspx*, and in the Community Newsgroups column on the left, expand the Office category and then the Access category to see the available newsgroups. Click one of the links to go to that newsgroup within your Web browser where you can post questions and read answers to questions posted by others.

Take a long look at the kind of work you're doing today. The preceding sidebar, "Reasons to Switch to a Database," summarizes some of the key reasons why you might need to move to Access. Is the number of files starting to overwhelm you? Do you find yourself creating copies of old files when you need to answer new questions? Do others need to share the data and update it? Do you find yourself exceeding the limits of your current software or the memory on your system? If the answer to any of these is *yes*, you should be solving your problems with a relational database management system like Microsoft Access.

In the next chapter, "The Many Faces of Microsoft Access," you'll learn about the internal architecture of an Access application. You'll also open the Housing Reservations and Law-Track Contacts sample databases to explore some of the many features and functions of Access. Finally, you'll discover some of the ways you can use Microsoft Access as an application solution.

The Many Faces of Microsoft Access

Before you explore the many features of Microsoft Access, it's worth spending a little time looking it over and "kicking the tires." This chapter helps you understand the relationships between the main components in Access and shows you how to move around within the database management system.

The Architecture of Microsoft Access

Microsoft Access calls anything that can have a name an *object*. Within an Access database, the main objects are tables, queries, forms, reports, data access pages, macros, and modules.

If you have worked with other database systems on desktop computers, you might have seen the term *database* used to refer to only those files in which you store data. In Access, however, a desktop database file, which uses the .mdb file extension, also includes all the major objects related to the stored data, including objects you define to automate the use of your data. You can also create an Access application using a project file (with the .adp file extension) that contains the objects that define your application linked to an SQL Server database that stores the tables and queries. Here is a summary of the major objects in an Access database:

- **Table** An object you define and use to store data. Each table contains information about a particular subject, such as customers or orders. Tables contain *fields* (or *columns*) that store different kinds of data, such as a name or an address, and *records* (or *rows*) that collect all the information about a particular instance of the subject, such as all the information about a department named Housing Administration. You can define a *primary key* (one or more fields that have a unique value for each record) and one or more *indexes* on each table to help retrieve your data more quickly.

- **Query** An object that provides a custom view of data from one or more tables. In Access, you can use the graphical query by example (QBE) facility or you can write SQL statements to create your queries. You can define queries to select, update, insert, or delete data. You can also define queries that create new tables from data in one or more existing tables. When your Access application is a project file connected to an SQL Server database, you can create special types of queries—functions and stored procedures—that can perform complex actions directly on the server.

- **Form**   An object designed primarily for data input or display or for control of application execution. You use forms to customize the presentation of data that your application extracts from queries or tables. You can also print forms. You can design a form to run a *macro* or a Visual Basic *procedure* in response to any of a number of events—for example, to run a procedure when the value of data changes.

- **Report**   An object designed for formatting, calculating, printing, and summarizing selected data. You can view a report on your screen before you print it.

- **Data access page**   An object that links to an HTML file containing special code and an ActiveX control that makes it easy to display and edit your data from Microsoft Internet Explorer. You can publish these files on your company intranet to allow other users on your network who also have Microsoft Office and Internet Explorer version 5 or later to view, search, and edit your data.

- **Macro**   An object that is a structured definition of one or more actions that you want Access to perform in response to a defined event. For example, you might design a macro that opens a second form in response to the selection of an item on a main form. You can include simple conditions in macros to specify when one or more actions in the macro should be performed or skipped. You can use macros to open and execute queries, to open tables, or to print or view reports. You can also run other macros or Visual Basic procedures from within a macro.

- **Module**   An object containing custom procedures that you code using Visual Basic. Modules provide a more discrete flow of actions and allow you to trap errors—something you can't do with macros. Modules can be stand-alone objects containing functions that can be called from anywhere in your application, or they can be directly associated with a form or a report to respond to events on the associated form or report.

For a list of events on forms and reports, see Chapter 21, "Understanding Event Processing."

Figure 2-1 shows a conceptual overview of how objects in Access are related. Tables store the data that you can extract with queries and display in reports or that you can display and update in forms or data access pages. Notice that forms, reports, and data access pages can use data either directly from tables or from a filtered view of the data created by using queries. Queries can use Visual Basic functions to provide customized calculations on data in your database. Access also has many built-in functions that allow you to summarize and format your data in queries.

Events on forms and reports can trigger either macros or Visual Basic procedures. An *event* is any change in state of an Access object. For example, you can write macros or Visual Basic procedures to respond to opening a form, closing a form, entering a new row on a form, or changing data either in the current record or in an individual *control* (an object on a form or report that contains data). You can even design a macro or a Visual Basic procedure that responds to the user pressing individual keys on the keyboard when entering data!

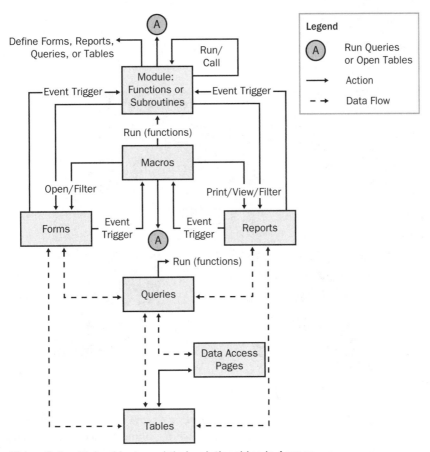

Figure 2-1. Main objects and their relationships in Access.

For more information about using Visual Basic within Access, see Chapter 22, "Understanding Visual Basic Fundamentals," and Chapter 23, "Automating Your Application with Visual Basic."

Using macros and modules, you can change the flow of your application; open, filter, and change data in forms and reports; run queries; and build new tables. Using Visual Basic, you can create, modify, and delete any Access object; manipulate data in your database row by row or column by column; and handle exceptional conditions. Using module code you can even call Windows Application Programming Interface (API) routines to extend your application beyond the built-in capabilities of Access.

Exploring a Desktop Database— Housing Reservations

Now that you know something about the major objects that make up a Microsoft Access database, a good next step is to spend some time exploring the Housing Reservations

Microsoft Office Access 2003 Inside Out

database (*Housing.mdb*) that comes with this book. First, follow the instructions at the beginning of this book for installing the sample files on your hard drive. When you start Access, it displays the Getting Started page in the task pane open to the right, as shown in Figure 2-2.

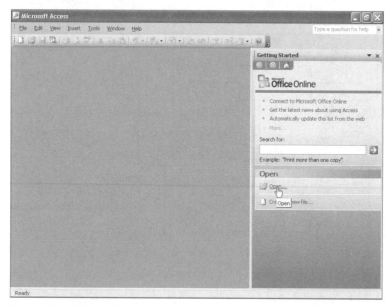

Figure 2-2. The Getting Started page in the Access task pane.

Click the Open link to see the Open dialog box, shown in Figure 2-3. In the Open dialog box, select the file *Housing.mdb* from the folder to which you installed the sample databases, and then click Open. By default, the companion CD setup program will place *Housing.mdb* in *C:\Microsoft Press\Access 2003 Inside Out*. You can also double-click the file name to open the database. (If you haven't set options in Windows Explorer to show file name extensions for registered applications, you won't see the .mdb extension for your database files.)

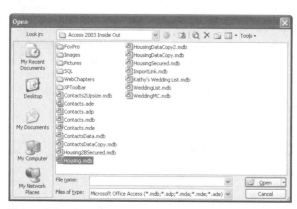

Figure 2-3. The Open dialog box for databases.

Inside Out

I get a Security Warning dialog box when I try to open a database. What should I do?

In response to growing threats from viruses and worms, Microsoft launched a security initiative in early 2002, called Trustworthy Computing, to focus on making all its products safer to use. In an e-mail sent to all employees, Bill Gates summed up the seriousness of the initiative.

"In the past, we've made our software and services more compelling for users by adding new features and functionality, and by making our platform richly extensible. We've done a terrific job at that, but all those great features won't matter unless customers trust our software. So now, when we face a choice between adding features and resolving security issues, we need to choose security. Our products should emphasize security right out of the box, and we must constantly refine and improve that security as threats evolve."

Prior to Microsoft Access 2003, it was quite possible for a malicious person to send you a database file that contained code that could damage your system. As soon as you opened the database, the harmful code would run—perhaps without your knowledge. Or, the programmer could embed dangerous code in a query, form, or report, and your computer would be damaged as soon as you opened that object.

Access 2003 provides enhanced security by offering you three levels of macro security on your system. You can set your security level by choosing Macro from the Tools menu and then Security on the submenu. The three levels are as follows:

- **Low**   With this setting, you are running with the same level of security as was available in Access 2002. Access will not prompt you to verify whether you want to open and run potentially unsafe code.

- **Medium**   This is the default setting. Access prompts you to verify that you want to open an Access database that is not signed by a trusted source. If you have installed JET 4.0 Service Pack 8, you can enable "sandbox" mode to prevent most harmful Visual Basic functions from being executed from queries or table validation rules. You can download the service pack by selecting Windows Update from the Start menu or from *http://windowsupdate.microsoft.com*. To read more about what the service pack does, go to *http://support.microsoft.com/?kbid=282010*.

- **High**   When you choose this setting, Access lets you open only Access databases that have been digitally signed by the author, and you or your system administrator have registered the author as a trusted source. See Chapter 30, "Securing Your Database," for details about how to digitally sign an Access database.

I did not digitally sign any of the sample databases (they would become unsigned as soon as you change any of the queries or sample code), so you won't be able to open them if your system is set to run in high macro security mode. I do not recommend that you change your macro security setting to low unless you never open any database except ones that you create. If you have installed the JET service pack, you can leave your macro security setting at medium and be assured that you can open most databases with very little risk. I have designed all the sample applications to run successfully in "sandbox" mode. You can click the Open button in the Security Warning dialog box to open and run any database.

Chapter 2

The Housing Reservations application will start, and you'll see the Database window for the Housing Reservations database, as shown in Figure 2-4. (Note: This database contains data access pages. When the database opens for the first time, Visual Basic code that corrects the links to the pages runs. Click OK to any prompts until the procedure completes.)

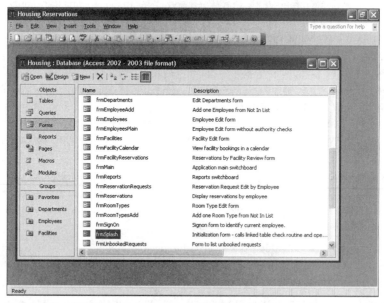

Figure 2-4. The Database window for the Housing Reservations sample database.

For an existing database, the Database window always remains where you last placed it on your screen. The title bar of the window shows the name of the database that you have open. As you'll learn later in this book, you can set options in the database to change the title bar of the main Access window to show the name of your application instead of displaying *Microsoft Access*—the sample database has been modified to display a custom icon and the title *Housing Reservations* on the title bar.

As you explore Access, you'll see that it provides more than a dozen built-in toolbars. Normally, Access shows you the toolbar most appropriate for the work you're doing. However, you can control which toolbars are active, and you can customize which buttons appear on each toolbar. You can define custom toolbars and menu bars that display all the time. You can also open and close toolbars from macros or modules. In fact, the Housing Reservations application includes a custom form toolbar and a custom menu bar that are open for all the forms in the application. You'll learn how to build custom toolbars and menu bars in Chapter 24, "The Finishing Touches."

Tip You can pause your mouse pointer over any toolbar button (without clicking the button), and Access displays a ToolTip to help you discover the purpose of the button.

Down the left side of the Database window is the Object bar, which allows you to choose one of the seven major object types: tables, queries, forms, reports, data access pages, macros, and modules. In the lower part of the Object bar, you can define custom groups to help organize your work. You'll see how to work with groups later in this chapter.

At the upper left corner of the Database window you can see three toolbar buttons. The first button changes depending on the type of object you select in the database window, but, in general, this button allows you to open or run the object. For example, you can select a table in the Database window and then click the Open button to see the data stored in the table (Datasheet view). The Design button allows you to view and modify the object's definition (Design view). The New button allows you to begin defining a new object. When the Database window is active, you can choose any of these command buttons from the keyboard by pressing the first letter of the button name while holding down the Alt key.

To the right of these three buttons, you can see the Delete button that you can click to delete the currently selected object, and four buttons to change the view of objects in the Database window to large icons, small icons, list, or detail view. (I personally prefer detail view, as shown in Figure 2-4.)

Tables

Click Tables on the Database window Object bar to see the list of tables defined in the Housing Reservations database, as shown in Figure 2-5.

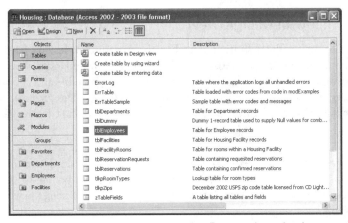

Figure 2-5. The tables in the Housing Reservations database.

At the top of the tables list in the Database window are three special shortcuts for creating a new table. You can double-click any of these shortcuts to begin defining a new table.

> **Note** You can remove the new object shortcuts from the Database window by choosing Options from the Tools menu, and then clearing the New object shortcuts option on the View tab.

You can also open a table in Datasheet view to see the data in the table by double-clicking the table name in the Database window; or you can open the table in Design view by holding down the Ctrl key and double-clicking the table name. If you right-click a table name, Access displays a shortcut menu, as shown in Figure 2-6, that lets you perform a number of handy operations on the item you selected. Choose one of the options on the shortcut menu, or left-click anywhere else in the Access window to dismiss the menu.

Figure 2-6.   The shortcut menu for a table in the Database window.

The Table Window in Design View

When you want to change the definition of a table (the structure or design of a table, as opposed to the data in a table), you must open the Table window in Design view. With the Housing Reservations database open, right-click the *tblEmployees* table and choose Design View from the shortcut menu; this opens the tblEmployees table in Design view, as shown in Figure 2-7. You'll learn about creating table definitions in Chapter 4, "Creating Your Database and Tables."

> **Tip**   If you choose the option to use the Windows taskbar for each document (choose Options from the Tools menu, and then choose Windows in Taskbar on the View tab), you can switch between the Database window and the Table window by clicking the window buttons on the taskbar.

In Design view, each row in the top portion of the Table window defines a different field in the table. You can use the mouse to select any field that you want to modify. You can also use the Tab key to move left to right across the screen from column to column, or Shift+Tab to move right to left. Use the Up and Down Arrow keys to move from row to row in the field list. As you select a different row in the field list in the top portion of the window, you can see the property settings for the selected field in the bottom portion of the window. Press F6 to move between the field list and the field property settings portions of the Table window in Design view.

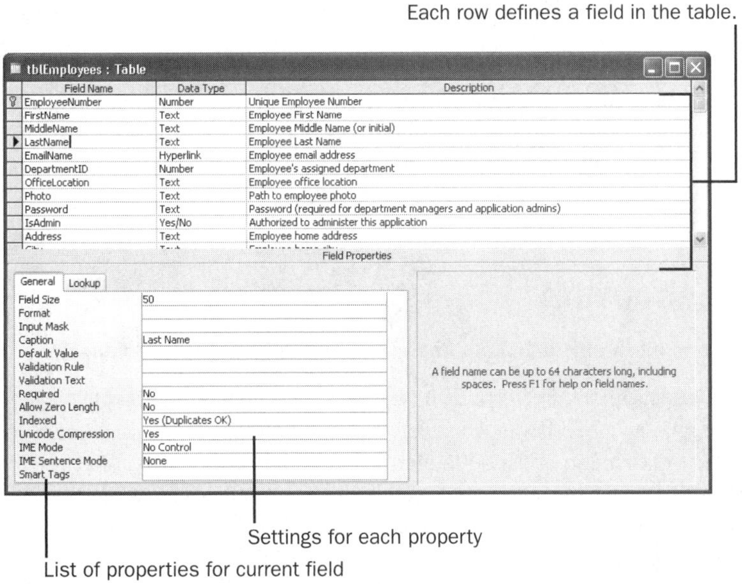

The Many Faces of Microsoft Access

Each row defines a field in the table.

Figure 2-7. A table open in Design view.

List of properties for current field

Settings for each property

> **Note** If you have the task pane open, pressing F6 jumps to the task pane. Press F6 again to move back to a different portion of the Table window in Design view.

Access has many convenient features. Wherever you can choose from a limited list of valid values, Access provides a drop-down list box to assist you in selecting the proper value. For example, when you tab to the Data Type column in the field list, a down arrow button appears at the right of the column. Click the button or press Alt+Down Arrow to see the list of valid data types, as shown in Figure 2-8.

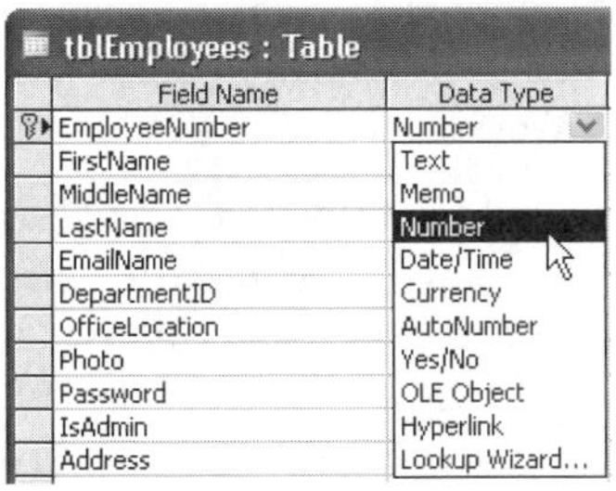

Figure 2-8. The Data Type drop-down list box.

You can open as many as 254 tables (fewer if you are limited by your computer's memory). You can minimize any of the windows to an icon by clicking the Minimize button in the upper right corner of the window, or you can maximize the window to fill the Access workspace by clicking the Maximize/Restore button in that same corner. If you don't see a window

Chapter 2

you want, you can select it from the list of active windows on the Window menu to bring the window to the front. If you choose the option to use the Windows taskbar for each document, you can also select the window you want by clicking the window's button on the taskbar. You can choose the Hide command on the Window menu to make selected windows temporarily disappear, or choose the Unhide command to make visible any windows that you've previously hidden. Choose the Close command from the File menu or click the window's Close button to close any window.

Troubleshooting

Why can't I see all the available commands when I open a menu in Access?

By default, all applications in Office 2003 use adaptive menus that display only the most commonly or recently used items when you first open a menu. For this reason, you might not see some of the menu options mentioned in this book right away. After the menu has been displayed for a few seconds, it will expand to display all available options. You can display the seldom-used commands immediately by clicking the down arrow at the bottom of the menu. If you prefer to see full menus without any delay, choose Customize from the Tools menu, click the Options tab, and select the Always show full menus option.

The Table Window in Datasheet View

To view, change, insert, or delete data in a table, you can use the table's Datasheet view. A datasheet is a simple way to look at your data in rows and columns without any special formatting. You can open a table's Datasheet view by selecting the name of the table you want in the Database window and clicking the Open button. When you open a table in Design view, such as the tblEmployees table shown in Figure 2-7, you can switch to the Datasheet view of this table, shown in Figure 2-9, by clicking the View button on the toolbar. Likewise, when you're in Datasheet view, you can return to Design view by clicking the View button. You can also list all available views by clicking the small down arrow button to the right of the View button and then choosing the view you want by clicking its name. You'll read more about working with data in Datasheet view in Chapter 7, "Creating and Working with Simple Queries."

As in Design view, you can move from field to field in the Table window in Datasheet view using the Tab key, and you can move up and down through the records using the arrow keys. You can also use the scroll bars along the bottom and on the right side of the window to move around in the table. To the left of the bottom scroll bar, Access shows you the current record number and the total number of records in the currently selected set of data. You can select the Record Number box with your mouse (or by pressing F5), type a new number, and then press Enter to go to that record. You can use the arrows on either side of the Record Number box to move up or down one record or to move to the first or last record in the table. You can start entering data in a new record by clicking the New Record button on the right.

The Many Faces of Microsoft Access

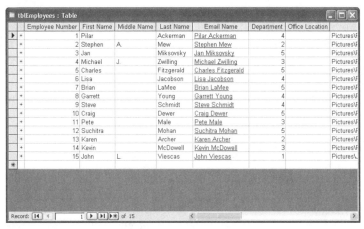

Figure 2-9. A Table window in Datasheet view.

Close the *tblEmployees* table now by clicking the window's Close button or by choosing the Close command from the File menu. You should now be back in the Database window for the Housing Reservations database.

Queries

You probably noticed that the Datasheet view of the tblEmployees table gave you all the fields and all the records in the table. But what if you want to see only the employee names and addresses? Or maybe you'd like to see in one view information about employees and all of their confirmed room reservations. To fill these needs, you can create a query. Click Queries on the Object bar in the Database window to see the list of queries available in the Housing Reservations database, as shown in Figure 2-10.

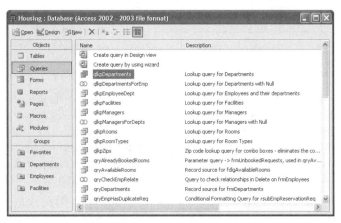

Figure 2-10. A list of queries in the Housing Reservations database.

Microsoft Office Access 2003 Inside Out

At the upper left corner of the Database window, you can see the same three toolbar buttons that you saw for tables. At the top of the queries list in the Database window, you can see two special shortcuts for creating a new query. You can double-click either of these shortcuts to begin defining a new query.

You can also open a query in Datasheet view by double-clicking the query name, or you can open the query in Design view by holding down the Ctrl key and double-clicking the query name. You can right-click a query name and choose an option from the shortcut menu.

The Query Window in Design View

When you want to change the definition of a query (the structure or design, as opposed to the data represented in the query), you must open the query in Design view. Take a look at one of the more complex queries in the Housing Reservations query list by scrolling to the query named *qryFacilityReservations*. Hold down the Ctrl key and double-click the query name to see the query in Design view, as shown in Figure 2-11.

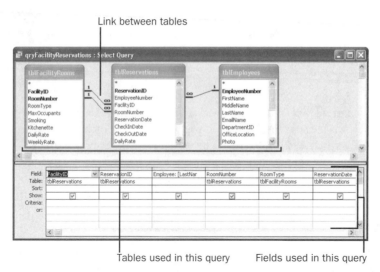

Figure 2-11. A Query window in Design view showing data from three tables being linked.

In the upper part of a Query window in Design view, you can see the field lists of the tables or other queries that this query uses. The lines connecting the field lists show how Access links the tables to solve your query. If you define relationships between tables in your database design, Access draws these lines automatically. See Chapter 4, "Creating Your Database and Tables," for details. You can also define relationships when you build the query by dragging a field from one field list and dropping it on the appropriate field of another field list.

In the lower part of the Query window, you can see the design grid. The design grid shows fields that Access uses in this query, the tables or queries from which the fields come (when the Table Names command on the View menu has a check mark next to it), any sorting criteria, whether fields show up in the result, and any selection criteria for the fields. You can use the horizontal scroll bar to bring other fields in this query into view. As in the Design view of

The Many Faces of Microsoft Access

tables, you can use F6 to move between the top and bottom portions of the Query window.

You can learn how to build this type of complex multiple-table query in Chapter 8, "Building Complex Queries." You can find this query used in the Housing Reservations database as the source of data for the *fsubFacilityReservations* form.

The Query Window in Datasheet View

Click the View button on the toolbar to run the query and see the query results in Datasheet view, as shown in Figure 2-12.

The Query window in Datasheet view is similar to a Table window in Datasheet view. Even though the fields in the query datasheet shown in Figure 2-12 are from three different tables, you can work with the fields as if they were in a single table. If you're designing an Access application for other users, you can use queries to hide much of the complexity of the database and make the application simpler to use. Depending on how you designed the query, you might also be able to update some of the data in the underlying tables simply by typing in new values in the Query window as you would in a Table window in Datasheet view. Close the Query window to see only the Database window.

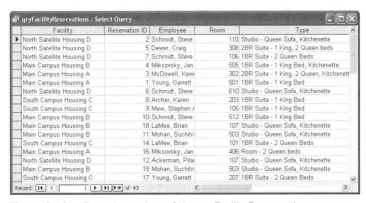

Figure 2-12. Datasheet view of the qryFacilityReservations query.

Forms

Datasheets are useful for viewing and changing data in your database, but they're not particularly attractive or simple to use. If you want to format your data in a special way or automate how your data is used and updated, you need to use a form. Forms provide a number of important capabilities.

● You can control and enhance the way your data looks on the screen. For example, you can add color and shading or add number formats. You can add controls such as drop-down list boxes and check boxes. You can display ActiveX objects such as pictures and graphs directly on the form. And you can calculate and display values based on data in a table or a query.

- You can perform extensive editing of data using macros or Visual Basic procedures.

- You can link multiple forms or reports by using macros or Visual Basic procedures that are run from buttons on a form. In addition, you can customize the menu bar by using macros associated with your form.

Click Forms on the Object bar in the Database window to see the list of forms in the Housing Reservations database, shown in Figure 2-13.

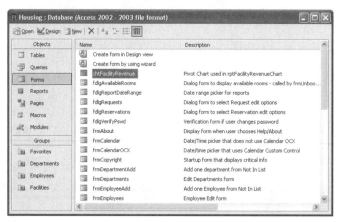

Figure 2-13. The list of forms in the Database window.

At the upper left corner of the Database window you can see three toolbar buttons to open the selected form in Form view or Design view or to begin creating a new form. At the top of the list of forms in the Database window, you can also find two special shortcuts for creating a new form. Double-clicking either of these shortcuts will let you begin defining a new form.

You can also open a form in Form view by double-clicking the form name in the window, or you can open the form in Design view by holding down the Ctrl key and double-clicking the form name. Finally, you can right-click a form name and choose a command from the shortcut menu.

The Form Window in Design View

When you want to change the definition of a form (the structure or design, as opposed to the data displayed in the form), you generally must open the form in Design view. As you'll learn in Chapter 12, you can also set a form property to allow you to make changes from Form view while you are designing the form. Take a look at the *frmEmployeesPlain* form in the Housing Reservations database. (To open the form in Design view, scroll through the list of forms in the Database window and then hold down the Ctrl key and double-click the *frmEmployees-Plain* form.) This form, shown in Figure 2-14, is designed to display all data from the tblEmployees table. Don't worry if what you see on your screen doesn't exactly match Figure 2-14. In this figure, I moved a few items around and selected several options so that you can see all the main features of the Form window in Design view.

The Many Faces of Microsoft Access

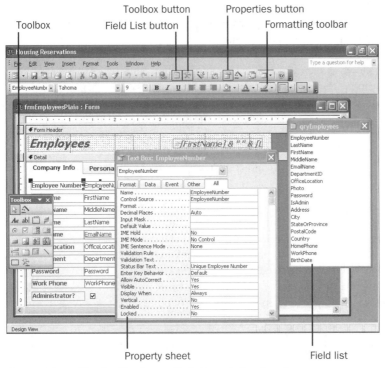

Figure 2-14. The frmEmployeesPlain form in Design view.

The large window in the background is the form design window where you create the design of the form. When you first open this form in Design view, you should see the toolbox in the lower left area of the screen. If you don't see it, choose the Toolbox command from the View menu or click the Toolbox button (the crossed hammer and wrench symbol) on the toolbar. This is the action center of form design—you'll use the tools here to add the design elements you want. You can click the title bar of the toolbox and drag it to another location.

In the lower right of the window shown in Figure 2-14, you can see a field list labeled qryEmployees. This query selects all the fields in the tblEmployees table and then sorts the records by last name and first name. You might see the field list near the top of the Form window when you first open the form. If you don't see the field list, choose the Field List command from the View menu or click the Field List button (the mini-datasheet symbol) on the toolbar. You can move the field list by dragging its title bar, and you can resize it by dragging its corners, sides, or bottom. When you read about form design in Chapter 11, "Building a Form," you'll see that you can choose a tool from the toolbox and then drag a field from the field list to place a control on the form that displays the contents of the selected field.

After you place all the controls on a form, you might want to customize some of them. You do this by opening the Properties window, which is shown in the lower center of Figure 2-14. To see the Properties window, choose the Properties command from the View menu or click the Properties button (a datasheet with a pointing-finger symbol) on the toolbar. The Properties window always shows the property values for the control selected in the Form window. (The Properties window can also display the properties for the form or any section on the form.) Click the All tab in the Properties window to display all the properties in a single list, or display subsets of the available properties by clicking Format, Data, Event, or Other. In the example shown in Figure 2-14, I clicked the text box named EmployeeNumber, near the top of the form, to select it. As you might guess, you can use a text box control to display text as well as to input text into the database. If you click this text box and select the All tab in the Properties window, you can scroll down the list of properties for this text box and see the wide range of properties you can set to customize this control. As you learn to build applications using Access, you'll soon discover that you can customize the way your application works by simply setting form and control properties—you don't have to write any code.

If you scroll to the bottom of the property list, or click the Event tab, you'll see a number of properties that you can set to define the macros or Visual Basic procedures that Access runs whenever the associated event occurs on this control. For example, you can use the Before Update event property to perform additional validation before Access saves any changes typed in this control. You can use the On Click or On Dbl Click event properties to perform actions when the user clicks or double-clicks the control. If you need to, you can even look at every individual character the user types in a control with the On Key event properties. As you'll discover later, Access provides a rich set of events that you can detect for the form and all controls on the form.

You might have noticed that Access made available all the boxes and buttons on the Formatting toolbar when you selected the EmployeeNumber control. When you select a text box on a form in Design view, Access enables the drop-down list boxes on this toolbar to make it easy to select a font and font size, and it also enables Bold, Italic, and Underline buttons that let you set the text display properties. To the right of these buttons are three buttons that set text alignment: Align Left, Center, and Align Right. You can also set the foreground, background, and border colors; border width; and special effects from buttons on this toolbar.

If all of this looks just a bit too complex, don't worry! Building a simple form is really quite easy. In addition, Access provides form wizards that you can use to automatically generate a number of standard form layouts based on the table or query you choose. You'll find it simple to customize a form to your needs once the form wizard has done most of the hard work. You'll learn more about form design in Chapter 11, "Building a Form"; Chapter 12, "Customizing a Form"; and Chapter 13, "Advanced Form Design."

The Form Window in Form View

To view, change, insert, or delete data via a form, you can use Form view. Depending on how you've designed the form, you can work with your data in an attractive and clear context, have the form validate the information you enter, or use the form to trigger other forms or reports based on actions you take while viewing the form. You can open a form in Form view by selecting the form's name in the Database window and then clicking the Open button. Because you have the *frmEmployeesPlain* form open in Design view, you can go directly to Form view by clicking the View button on the toolbar.

The Many Faces of Microsoft Access

Figure 2-15 shows a complex form that brings together data from three tables and loads the related employee picture from a file on your hard drive and displays it in a way that's easy to use and understand. This form includes all the fields from the tblEmployees table. You can tab or use the arrow keys to move through the fields. You can click the Personal Info tab to see additional information about the current employee. You can experiment with the Filter By Form and Filter By Selection toolbar buttons to see how easy it is to select only the records you want to see. For example, you can click in the Department field on the Company Info tab and then click the Filter By Selection button to display records only for the current department.

Chapter 2

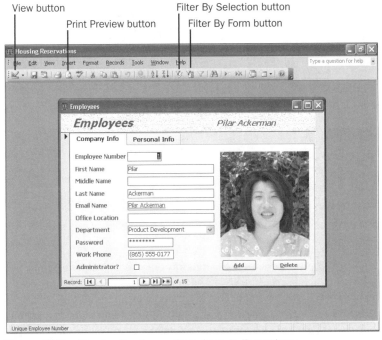

Figure 2-15. The frmEmployeesPlain form in Form view.

> **Note** The frmEmployeesPlain form is the only form in the Housing Reservations data-base that you can open to see a built-in Form view menu bar and toolbar. All the other forms in the Housing Reservations sample database have form properties set to use a custom menu bar and toolbar.

There are four other ways to look at a form: in Datasheet view, PivotTable view, PivotChart view, and Print Preview. You can select Datasheet View from the View button drop-down list to see all the fields in the form arranged in a datasheet—similar to a datasheet for a table or a query. When a form has been designed to display data in a PivotTable (similar to a spread-sheet) or graphed in a PivotChart, you can select these views from the View button drop-down list. You can click the Print Preview button on the toolbar to see what the form will look like on a printed page. You'll read more about Print Preview in the next section. For now, close the *frmEmployeesPlain* window so that only the Database window is visible on your screen.

Reports

If your primary need is to print data, you should use an Access report. Click Reports on the Object bar in the Database window to see the list of reports available in the Housing Reservations database, as shown in Figure 2-16.

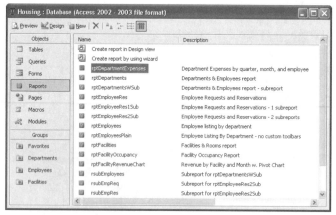

Figure 2-16.   A list of reports in the Database window.

Although you can print information in a datasheet or a form, neither of these formats provides the flexibility that reports do when you need to produce complex printed output (such as invoices or summaries) that might include many calculations and subtotals. Formatting in datasheets is limited to sizing the rows and columns, specifying fonts, and setting the colors and gridline effects. You can do a lot of formatting in a form, but because forms are designed primarily for viewing and entering data on the screen, they are not suited for extensive calculations, grouping of data, or multiple totals and subtotals in print. Also, a form that is designed to be attractive on screen might not print attractively on paper.

At the upper left corner of the Database window are three toolbar buttons to open the selected report in Print Preview or Design view or to begin creating a new report. At the top of the list of reports in the Database window, you can also find two special shortcuts for creating a new report. You can double-click either of these shortcuts to begin defining a new report.

You can also view the report in Print Preview by double-clicking the report name in the window, or you can open the report in Design view by holding down the Ctrl key and double-clicking the report name. Finally, you can right-click any report name and choose Design View from the shortcut menu.

The Many Faces of Microsoft Access

The Report Window in Design View

When you want to change the definition of a report, you must open the report in Design view. In the report list for Housing Reservations, hold down the Ctrl key and double-click the *rptEmployeesPlain* report to see the design for the report, as shown in Figure 2-17. Don't worry if what you see on your screen doesn't exactly match Figure 2-17. In this figure, I moved a few things and selected several options so that you can see all the main features of the Report window in Design view.

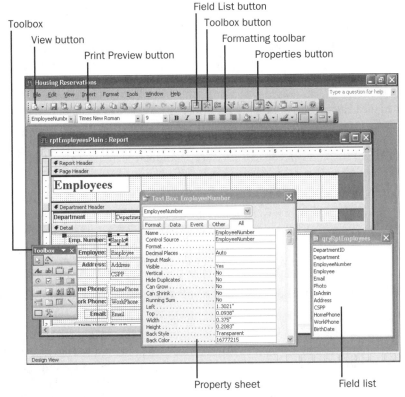

Figure 2-17. The rptEmployeesPlain report in Design view.

The large window in the background is the report design window where you create the design of the report. This report is designed to display all the information about employees by department. You can see that the Design view for reports is similar to the Design view for forms. (For comparison, see Figure 2-14 on page 31.) Reports provide additional flexibility, allowing you to group items and to total them (either across or down). You can also define header and footer information for the entire report, for each page, and for each subgroup on the report.

When you first open this report in Design view, the toolbox should appear in the lower left area of the screen. If you don't see the toolbox, choose the Toolbox command from the View menu or click the Toolbox button on the toolbar. You can click the title bar of the toolbox and drag it to another location.

In the lower right of Figure 2-17, you can see a window titled qryRptEmployees. This is a field list containing all the fields from the tblEmployees table and related fields from the tblDepartments table that provide the data for this report. You might see this list near the top of the report's Design view when you first open it. If you don't see the field list, choose the Field List command from the View menu or click the Field List button on the toolbar. You can move the field list by dragging its title bar.

After you place all the controls on a report, you might want to customize some of them. Do this by opening the Properties window, which you can see in the lower center of Figure 2-17. To see the Properties window, choose the Properties command from the View menu or click the Properties button on the toolbar. The Properties window always shows the property settings for the control selected in the Report window. (The Properties window can also display the properties for the report or any section on the report.) In the example shown in Figure 2-17, I clicked the text box named EmployeeNumber to select it. If you click this text box and click the All tab or the Data tab in the Properties window, you can see in the Control Source property box that Access displays the EmployeeNumber field from the tblEmployees table as the input data for this control. You can also specify complex formulas that calculate additional data for report controls.

You might have noticed that Access made available some additional list boxes and buttons on the Formatting toolbar when you selected the EmployeeNumber control. When you click a text box in a report in Design view, Access enables drop-down list boxes on the Formatting toolbar that make it easy to select a font and font size. Access also enables Bold, Italic, and Underline buttons that let you set the text properties. To the right of these buttons are three buttons that set text alignment: Align Left, Center, and Align Right. You can also set the foreground, background, and border colors; border width; and special effects from buttons on this toolbar.

Reports can be even more complex than forms, but building a simple report is really quite easy. Access provides report wizards that you can use to automatically generate a number of standard report layouts based on the table or query you choose. You'll find it simple to customize a report to suit your needs after the report wizard has done most of the hard work. You'll learn how to customize a report in Chapter 15, "Constructing a Report," and in Chapter 16, "Advanced Report Design."

The Report Window in Print Preview

Reports do not have a Datasheet or Form view. To see what the printed report will look like, click the Print Preview button (shown in Figure 2-17) on the toolbar when you're in the Report window in Design view. From the Database window, you can also select the report name and then click the Preview button or right-click the report name and choose Print Preview from the shortcut menu. Figure 2-18 shows a Report window in Print Preview.

The Many Faces of Microsoft Access

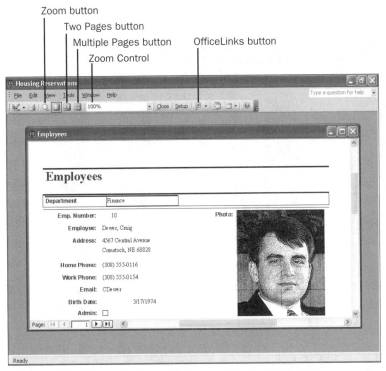

Figure 2-18. The rptEmployeesPlain report in Print Preview.

Access initially shows you the upper left corner of the report. To see the report centered in full-page view in Print Preview, click the Zoom button on the toolbar. To see two pages side-by-side, click the Two Pages button. This gives you a reduced picture of two pages, as shown in Figure 2-19 on the next page, and an overall idea of how Access arranges major areas of data on the report. Unless you have a large monitor, however, you won't be able to read the data. Click the Multiple Pages button to see more than two pages. When you move the mouse pointer over the window in Print Preview, the pointer changes to a magnifying glass icon. To zoom in, place this icon in an area that you want to see more closely and then press the left mouse button. You can also click the Zoom button on the toolbar again to see a close-up view of the report and then use the scroll bars to move around in the magnified report. Use the Zoom box on the toolbar to magnify or shrink your view. Access also provides an OfficeLinks button on the standard Print Preview toolbar to let you output the report to Microsoft Office Word or Microsoft Office Excel.

Microsoft Office Access 2003 Inside Out

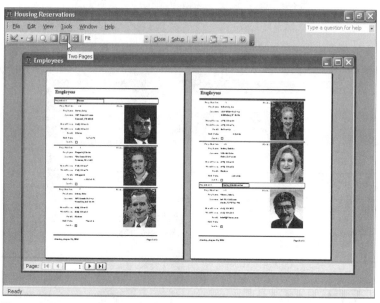

Figure 2-19. Two pages of the rptEmployeesPlain report in Print Preview.

Close the Report window to return to the Database window.

Data Access Pages

A feature first introduced in Access 2000 is the capability to easily publish your data as Web pages on your company's intranet using data access pages that you design from within Access. Click Pages on the Object bar in the Database window to see the list of data access pages available in the Housing Reservations database, as shown in Figure 2-20.

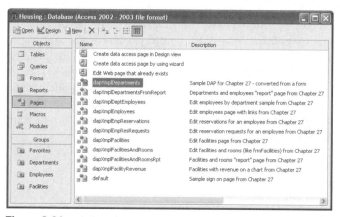

Figure 2-20. A list of data access pages in the Database window.

As you'll learn in Part 6, "Linking Access and the Web," Access 2003 provides many ways to help you make your Access application data available on a Web site. Data access pages are special Web pages (.htm files) that contain an Office ActiveX control that allows your users to display, search, and update the data in your database. As long as your Web users have Microsoft Office installed, they can open your data access pages directly from their client machines.

At the upper left corner of the Database window are three toolbar buttons to open the selected page in Page view or Design view or to begin creating a new page. At the top of the list of pages in the Database window, you can also find two special shortcuts for creating a new page and a third shortcut to link an existing page into your database. You can double-click any of these shortcuts to begin defining a new page or link an existing one.

You can also view the data access page in Page view by double-clicking the data access page name in the window, or you can open the data access page in Design view by holding down the Ctrl key and double-clicking the data access page name. Finally, you can right-click any data access page name and choose Design View from the shortcut menu.

The Data Access Page Window in Design View

When you want to change the definition of a data access page, you must open the page in Design view. In the page list for Housing Reservations, hold down the Ctrl key and double-click the *dapXmplFacilitiesAndRooms* page to see the design for the page, as shown in Figure 2-21 on the next page. Don't worry if what you see on your screen doesn't exactly match Figure 2-21. In this figure, I moved a few things around and selected several options so that you can see all the main features of the Page window in Design view.

The large window in the background is the page design window where you create the design of the page. This page is designed to display information about facilities and the rooms in each facility, bringing together information from several tables. You can see that the Design view for pages is similar to the Design view for forms and reports. (For comparison, see Figure 2-14 on page 31 and Figure 2-17 on page 35.) While a form's data is edited in Access, you can allow users to edit your page data using Microsoft Internet Explorer. You can group and sort data and make it easy for users to drill down into details about a particular topic—as you can on a report. On the *dapXmplFacilitiesAndRooms* page, users can browse through the information by facility, and then review and edit the details about rooms for the facility they choose.

When you first open this page in Design view, the toolbox should appear in the lower left area of the screen. If you don't see the toolbox, choose the Toolbox command from the View menu or click the Toolbox button on the toolbar. You can click the title bar of the toolbox and drag it to another location.

Microsoft Office Access 2003 Inside Out

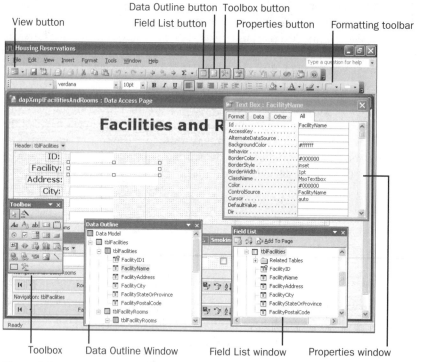

Figure 2-21. The dapXmplFacilitiesAndRooms data access page in Design view.

Caution Data access pages are connected to the location of your database file. If you move the database file, you must also change the connection properties of the data access page. For example, if you do not install the sample files for this book to C:\Microsoft Press\Access 2003 Inside Out, the data access page examples might not work. As noted earlier, Visual Basic code executes when you first open the database that verifies and attempts to correct the data access page connection properties. See Chapter 27, "Building Data Access Pages," for details about changing the connection properties.

In the lower right of Figure 2-21, you can see the Field List window. In this window, you can choose any table or query in the database that provides data for this page and drag any field onto the page to show the data. To see the field list, choose the Field List command from the View menu or click the Field List button on the toolbar. Click the plus sign next to the database name to see the Tables and Queries folders. Click the plus sign next to the Queries folder to see the list of queries. You can move the field list by dragging its title bar.

In the lower center of Figure 2-21, you can see the Data Outline window. In this window, Access displays the groups, record sources (the queries and tables providing the data for the page), and fields that you have defined to be used on the page. To see this window, choose Data

Outline from the View menu or click the Data Outline button on the toolbar. When Access understands the relationship between the record sources, it displays the record sources as a hierarchy. For example, in the figure you can see that Access understands that fields from the tblFacilities table are in a grouping level above the remaining fields that display the room data.

After you place all the controls on a page, you might want to customize some of them. You do this by opening the Properties window, which you can see in the right center of Figure 2-21. To see the Properties window, choose the Properties command from the View menu or click the Properties button on the toolbar. The Properties window always shows the property settings for the control selected in the Data Access Page window. (The Properties window can also display the properties for the page or any section on the page.) In the example shown in Figure 2-21, I clicked the text box named FacilityName to select it. If you click this text box and select the Data tab or the All tab in the Properties window, you can see that the Control-Source property specifies that the FacilityName field provides the data that the data access page will display in the FacilityName control. You can also specify complex formulas that calculate additional data for page controls.

You might have noticed that Access made available some additional list boxes and buttons on the Formatting toolbar when you selected the FacilityName control. When you click a text box in a page in Design view, Access enables drop-down list boxes on the Formatting toolbar that make it easy to select a font and font size. Access also enables Bold, Italic, and Underline buttons that let you set the text properties. To the right of these buttons are three buttons that set text alignment: Align Left, Center, and Align Right. You can also set the foreground, background, and border colors; border width; and special effects from buttons on this toolbar.

Data access pages can be even more complex than forms or reports, but building a simple page is really quite easy. Access provides data access page wizards that you can use to automatically generate a number of standard page layouts based on the table or query you choose. You'll find it simple to customize a page to suit your needs after the data access page wizard has done most of the hard work. You'll learn how to design data access pages in Chapter 27, "Building Data Access Pages."

The Data Access Page Window in Page View

To see what the finished page looks like, click the View button (shown in Figure 2-21) on the toolbar when you're in the Data Access Page window in Design view. From the Database window, you can also select the page name and then click the Open button, or right-click the page name and choose Web Page Preview from the shortcut menu. Figure 2-22 on the next page shows a Data Access Page window in Page view.

You can experiment with this page to see how it works. Use the buttons on the Facilities navigation bar to move to the facility you want. Use the buttons on the Rooms navigation bar to see the rooms defined for the selected facility in groups of five. Note that you can also click in the facility name and then click options on the Facilities navigation bar to sort or filter what you see.

Microsoft Office Access 2003 Inside Out

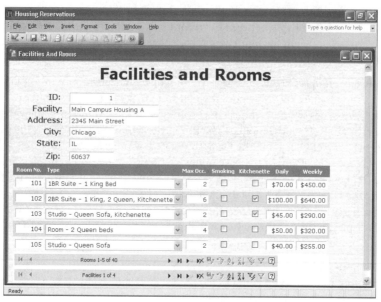

Figure 2-22. The dapXmplFacilitiesAndRooms data access page in Page view.

You can also test this page to see how it works in Internet Explorer. Close the data access page in Access and find the *dapXmplFacilitiesAndRooms.htm* file in the \WebChapters\DataAccessPages subfolder of your sample files in Windows Explorer. Double-click the file to open it in Internet Explorer. You should see a result, as shown in Figure 2-23.

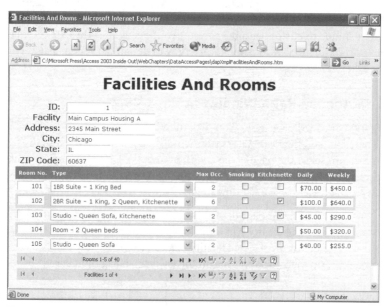

Figure 2-23. The dapXmplFacilitiesAndRooms data access page displayed in Internet Explorer.

The Many Faces of Microsoft Access

Close Internet Explorer and return to the Housing Reservations database in Microsoft Access to continue the tour.

> **Note** If you open a table in the Housing Reservations database in Design view, Access locks the table so no other user or program can reference or change the data or object designs. If you try to display a data access page that uses data from the table in Internet Explorer while the table is still open in Design view, you will see no data because Access has the data locked.

Macros

You can make working with your data within forms and reports much easier by triggering a macro action. Microsoft Access provides more than 40 actions that you can include in a macro. They perform tasks such as opening tables and forms, running queries, running other macros, selecting options from menus, and sizing open windows. You can also group multiple actions in a macro and specify conditions that determine when each set of actions will or will not be executed by Access.

In the Database window, click Macros on the Object bar to see the list of macros in the Housing Reservations database, shown in Figure 2-24. At the upper left corner of the Database window you can see three toolbar buttons to run the selected macro, open the selected macro in Design view, or begin creating a new macro.

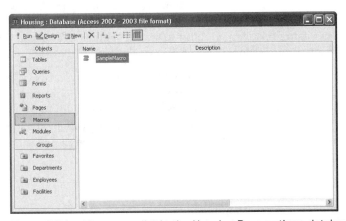

Figure 2-24. The macro list in the Housing Reservations database.

Macros are a great way to learn about the basics of responding to events and automating actions in an Access database. However, for any application that you intend to distribute to others, you should use Visual Basic to handle events and automate actions. Nearly all the sample databases use Visual Basic exclusively. You can take a look at the design of the single macro example in the Housing Reservations database, shown in Figure 2-25 on the next page, by selecting it and then clicking the Design button on the Database window toolbar.

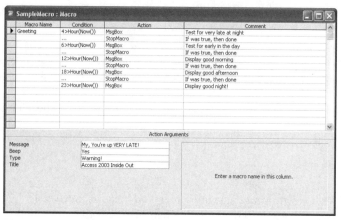

Figure 2-25. The design of the SampleMacro macro object in the Housing Reservations database.

You can design multiple macro actions within a single macro object and give each one a name in the first column. Any unnamed lines following a named line all belong to the named macro. In the second column, you can optionally specify a condition test that must be true for the macro command on that line to execute. You can use a continuation indicator (...) on subsequent lines to specify additional commands that should also execute when the condition is true. You select the action you want to run from a drop-down list in the Action column and set the arguments required for the action in the Action Arguments area in the bottom part of the design window. Some of the limitations of macros include the lack of handling any errors that might occur, limited ability to branch to other actions, and very limited ability to loop through a set of actions.

If you want to see what this macro does, click the Run button (the exclamation point) on the toolbar to execute it. You should see a greeting message appropriate to the time of day on your machine. To learn more about events and the macro design facility, see Chapter 21, "Understanding Event Processing." You can find one sample application on the companion CD that is automated entirely using macros—*WeddingListMC.mdb*. Close the macro design window to return to the Database window.

Modules

You might find that you keep coding the same complex formula over and over in some of your forms or reports. Although you can build a complete Microsoft Access application using only forms, reports, and macros, some actions might be difficult or impossible to define in a macro. If that is the case, you can create a Visual Basic procedure that performs a series of calculations and then use that procedure in a form or report.

If your application is so complex that it needs to deal with errors (such as two users trying to update the same record at the same time), you must use Visual Basic. Because Visual Basic is a complete programming language with complex logic and the ability to link to other appli-

The Many Faces of Microsoft Access

cations and files, you can solve unusual or difficult application problems by using Visual Basic procedures.

Version 2 of Access introduced the ability to code Basic routines in special modules attached directly to the forms and reports that they support. You can create these procedures from Design view for forms or reports by requesting the Code Builder in any event property. You can make Visual Basic the default for form and report events by choosing Options from the Tools menu and selecting Always use event procedures on the Form/Reports tab. You can also edit this code behind forms and reports by choosing Code from the View menu in Design view. See Chapter 22, "Understanding Visual Basic Fundamentals," and Chapter 23, "Automating Your Application with Visual Basic," for details. In fact, after you learn a little bit about Visual Basic, you might find that coding small event procedures for your forms and reports is much more efficient and convenient than trying to keep track of many macro objects. You'll also soon learn that you can't fully respond to some sophisticated events, such as KeyPress, in macros because macros can't access special additional parameters (such as the value of the key pressed) generated by the event. You can fully handle these events only in Visual Basic.

Click Modules on the Object bar in the Database window to display the list of modules in the Housing Reservations database, as shown in Figure 2-26. The Housing Reservations database has several module objects that contain procedures that can be called from any query, form, report, or other procedure in the database. For example, the *modMedian* module contains a function to calculate the median value of a column in any table or query. The *modUtility* module contains several functions that you might find useful in your applications.

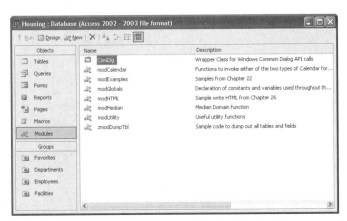

Figure 2-26. The Visual Basic modules in the Housing Reservations database.

From the Database window, you can create a new module by clicking the New button or you can open the design of an existing module by clicking the Design button. In a module, you can define procedures that you can call from a macro, a form, or a report. You can also use some procedures (called functions) in expressions in queries and in validation rules that you create for a table or a form. You'll learn how to create procedures in Chapter 22.

Microsoft Office Access 2003 Inside Out

Select the *modUtility* module and click the Design button to open the Visual Basic Editor window containing the Visual Basic code in the module. The Visual Basic Editor is a separate program that runs tightly coupled with Access to manage your code. It's the same program you'll see when you create code in other Office programs such as Word or Excel. Use the Procedure drop-down list box (in the upper right of the Code window) to look at the procedure names available in the sample. One of the functions in this module, IsFormLoaded, checks all forms open in the current Access session to see whether the form name, passed as a parameter, is one of the open forms. This function is useful in macros or in other modules to direct the flow of an application based on which forms the user has open. You can click on IsFormLoaded in the Procedure list box to scroll the Code window to this function, as shown in Figure 2-27.

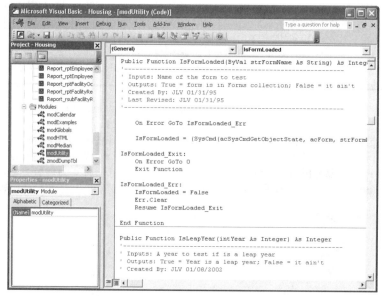

Figure 2-27. The IsFormLoaded function in the modUtility module displayed in the Visual Basic Editor window.

Click the View Microsoft Office Access button on the far left of the toolbar to easily return to the Access window.

Organizing Your Objects

Although you might not have created any objects yet yourself, it's useful to know that you can create special groups in your database to help you organize related tables, queries, forms, reports, data access pages, macros, and modules. You can save shortcuts in each of these groups that are pointers to the objects in the group.

In the Housing Reservations sample database, you can find groups defined for each of the main subjects in the database: the company departments, the employees in each department, and the housing facilities available for employees to book room reservations. In the Database window, click the Departments group button to see all the shortcuts to objects related to departments, as shown in Figure 2-28.

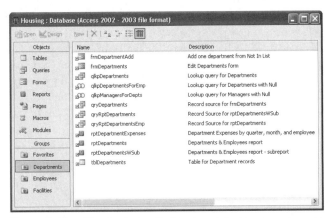

Figure 2-28. Shortcuts to all objects related to departments.

To add an object to a group, use the Object bar to find the object you want in the Database window. Right-click the object to display the shortcut menu, as shown in Figure 2-29. Choose Add To Group in the shortcut menu, and then select the group or choose New Group to define a new group of shortcuts. After you have defined groups, you can also drag an object from an object listing onto one of the group names in the lower left of the Database window to add a shortcut to the object to the group.

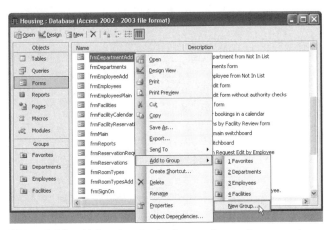

Figure 2-29. Using the shortcut menu to create a new group.

This completes the tour of the objects in the Housing Reservations sample database. Close the Visual Basic Editor window if you still have it open, return to the Access window, and close the database.

Exploring a Project File—LawTrack Contacts

Microsoft Access 2000 introduced an advanced facility that allows you to create a project file (with an .adp extension) that contains only your forms, reports, data access pages, macros, and modules. When you create a new project file, you can specify a Microsoft SQL Server database to support the project. SQL Server stores the tables and queries that you use in the application that you design in the project. You can connect your project file to a Microsoft SQL Server version 6.5 database on a server or to a version 7.0 or later database on a server or on your desktop. Included with Microsoft Office 2003 is a special edition of SQL Server 2000, the Microsoft SQL Server Desktop Engine (MSDE), that you can install to run on your desktop computer. An Access project file is ideal for designing mission-critical applications or applications that need to support dozens of users. SQL Server provides more robust data integrity and data sharing features than a desktop database.

You will see available tables in the server database as table objects in your project. You will also see views, functions, and stored procedures as query objects. Access 2003 includes special table and query editors to allow you to work directly with the objects in SQL Server. Your project file also contains forms, reports, macros, and modules that are virtually identical to those you develop in a desktop database (.mdb).

To see the differences in tables and queries in a project file, start Microsoft Access and then open the *Contacts.adp* sample project file.

Tip   Opening the sample project file

To be able to open the *Contacts.adp* file successfully, you must first install MSDE or have access to an SQL Server that allows you Create authority. You'll need to attach the sample database files to a server and possibly modify the connection properties of the sample project so that Access knows where to find the tables and queries required by the project. See the Appendix, "Installing Microsoft Office," for details about how to install and start MSDE. See Chapter 17, "Building Tables in an Access Project," for details about setting project connection properties. If you are unable to perform these steps at this time, you can still read through this section to gain an understanding of some of the differences in project files.

Tables

Click Tables on the Object bar in the Database window to see all the tables defined in the SQL Server database connected to the project. Figure 2-30 shows you the tables in the Contacts-SQL database that are connected to the LawTrack Contacts project file.

As you can see, the Database window in a project file looks very similar to the one in a desktop database. You can see one additional object type—Database Diagrams. SQL Server allows you to create a diagram of all the tables in your database, and the diagram shows you the relationships that you have defined between the tables.

The Many Faces of Microsoft Access

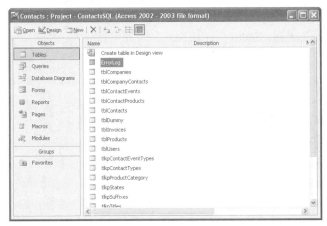

Figure 2-30. The SQL Server tables that you can view in the Database window in the sample LawTrack Contacts project file.

Select the tblContacts table in the Database window and click the Design button on the Database window toolbar to see the table in Design view, as shown in Figure 2-31.

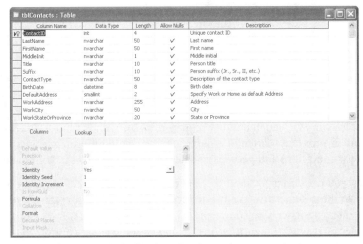

Figure 2-31. A table in Design view in an Access project.

As you can see, the table designer in an Access project is very similar to the one in a desktop database. (See Figure 2-7 on page 25.) In an SQL Server database, fields are called columns. SQL Server supports a wider variety of data types than does an Access desktop database. Many of the data types are identical, but they have different names in SQL Server. For example, the int data type in SQL Server is the same as the Long Integer data type in a desktop database. If you want, you can click the View button to switch to Datasheet view, but you'll find that Datasheet view in an Access project is identical to that in a desktop database. You can learn all the details for creating tables in a project in Chapter 17, "Building Tables in an Access Project." Close the table design window to return to the Database window.

Chapter 2

Views, Functions, and Stored Procedures

Although all query objects in a desktop database are called simply "queries," you'll find that SQL Server stores three different types of objects—views, functions, and stored procedures—that Access displays when you click the Queries button on the Object bar in the Database window, as shown in Figure 2-32.

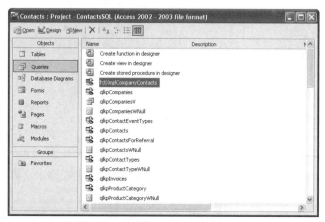

Figure 2-32. The list of views, functions, and stored procedures displayed as queries in the *Contacts.adp* sample project file.

A view returns a filtered view of data from one or more tables. A function can return a table, or it can perform a calculation and return a single value, much like a Visual Basic function. The difference is that a function you see in the queries list in a project file Database window executes on SQL Server, and the server returns the result to your project. A stored procedure can be as simple as an SQL statement that returns rows from one or more tables, or it can contain a complex program written in Transact-SQL (the programming language for SQL Server) that tests conditions and perhaps updates one or more tables in your database.

In many cases, you can design a view, function, or stored procedure using a query designer that is similar to the designer you use in a desktop database. To see an example of a query in a project file's query designer, scroll down the list of queries in the LawTrack Contacts sample project file, select *qryContactProductsForInvoice*, and click the Design button on the Database window toolbar. Access displays the query in Design view, as shown in Figure 2-33.

As you can see on the title bar, this query is a function that returns columns from three tables. The query designer in an Access project is similar in some ways to the designer in an Access desktop database. (See Figure 2-11 on page 28.) You can see the tables used in the query in the top pane of the designer window. In the center pane, you can see the columns (fields) used in the query, but the columns are listed vertically in this designer instead of horizontally as in the desktop database query designer. In the bottom pane, you can see the SQL statement that defines this query on the server. You can close this pane if you like and work exclusively in the

The Many Faces of Microsoft Access

design grid. Access reflects any change you make in the design grid by modifying the displayed SQL. When you become more expert in SQL, you can also modify the SQL statement, and Access changes the top two panes accordingly.

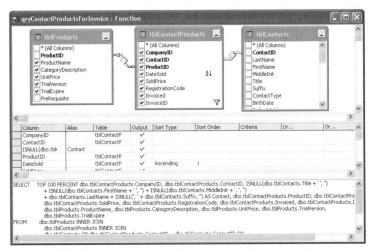

Figure 2-33. A query opened in the query designer in an Access project.

You can learn about the details of creating a query in an Access project in Chapter 18, "Building Queries in an Access Project." For details about the SQL database language, see Article 1, "Understanding SQL," on the companion CD.

You can close the query design window and the Database window. As noted earlier, the forms, reports, macros, and modules in a project file are virtually identical to those in a desktop database. You can learn about the minor differences for forms and reports in Chapter 19, "Designing Forms in an Access Project," and Chapter 20, "Building Reports in an Access Project."

The Many Faces of Microsoft Access

Access is not only a powerful, flexible, and easy-to-use database management system, it is also a complete database application development facility. You can use Access to create and run, under the Microsoft Windows operating system, an application tailored to your data management needs. Access lets you limit, select, and total your data by using queries. You can create forms for viewing and changing your data. You can also use Access to create simple or complex reports. Forms, reports, and data access pages inherit the properties of the underlying table or query, so in most cases you need to define such properties as formats and validation rules only once. You can create data access pages bound to your data to make it easy to share your information over your company's intranet. Figure 2-34 on the next page gives you an overview of all the ways you can use Access to implement an application.

Microsoft Office Access 2003 Inside Out

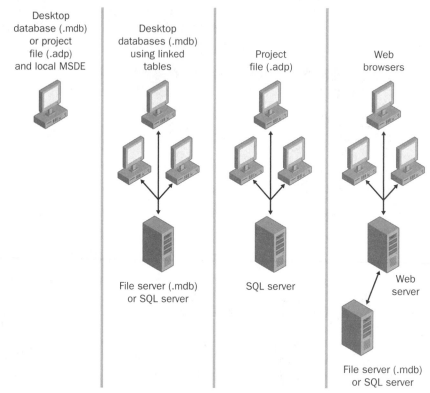

Figure 2-34. Implementation architectures for Access applications.

The four panes in the figure illustrate ways you can implement an Access application, as follows:

- Using the desktop database facility or an Access project file linked to a local copy of MSDE, you can create a stand-alone application used by a single person.

- You can place a data-only desktop database on a file server or in a database in SQL Server and link the tables over a network into multiple desktop databases so that several users can share the same application.

- You can design your database in SQL Server and connect to the server over a network from multiple Access project files running on different computers.

- You can create Web pages that connect to data that you designed using Access.

At the risk of using a cliché, the possibilities are endless...

In this chapter, you've had a chance to look at the major objects in the Housing Reservations and LawTrack Contacts sample databases. You've also been introduced to the architecture of Access and the wide range of ways that you can use Access. You should be feeling comfortable that you can learn to use Access at the level appropriate to solve your database application needs. Perhaps the most important aspect of building an application is designing the database that will support your application. The next chapter describes how you should design your database application and its data structures. Building a solid foundation makes creating the forms and reports for your application easy.

Chapter 3

Designing Your Database Application

You could begin building a database in Microsoft Access much as you might begin creating a simple single-sheet solution in a spreadsheet application such as Microsoft Excel—by simply organizing your data into rows and columns and then inserting formulas where you need calculations. If you've ever worked extensively with a database or a spreadsheet application, you already know that this unplanned approach works in only the most trivial situations. Solving real problems takes some planning; otherwise, you end up building your application over and over again. One of the beauties of a relational database system such as Access is that it's much easier to make midcourse corrections. However, it's well worth spending time up front designing the tasks you want to perform, the data structures you need to support those tasks, and the flow of tasks within your database application.

You don't have to go deeply into application and database design theory to build a solid foundation for your database project. You'll read about the fundamentals of application design in the next section of this chapter, and then you'll apply those fundamentals in the succeeding sections, "An Application Design Strategy" and "Data Analysis." The section "Database Design Concepts" teaches you a basic method for designing the tables you'll need for your application and for defining relationships between those tables.

Application Design Fundamentals

Methodologies for good computer application design were first devised in the 1960s by recognized industry consultants such as James Martin, Edward Yourdon, and Larry Constantine. At the dawn of modern computing, building an application or fixing a broken one was so expensive that the experts often advised spending 60 percent or more of the total project time getting the design right before writing a single line of code.

Today's application development technologies make building an application much cheaper and quicker. In fact, the pace of computing is several orders of magnitude faster than it was just a decade ago. An experienced user can sit down with Microsoft Access on a PC and build in an afternoon what took months to create on an early mainframe system (if it was even possible).

Today's technologies also give you the power to build very complex applications. But even with powerful tools, creating a database application (particularly a moderately complex one) without first spending some time determining what the application should do and how it

Microsoft Office Access 2003 Inside Out

should operate invites a lot of expensive time reworking the application. Even though it's easier than ever to go back and fix mistakes or to redesign "on the fly," if your application design is not well thought out it will be expensive and time-consuming later to track down any problems or to add new functionality.

The following is a brief overview of the typical steps involved in building a database application.

Step 1: Identifying Tasks

Before you start building an application, you should have some idea of what you want it to do. It is well worth your time to make a comprehensive list of all the major tasks you want to accomplish with the application—including those that you might not need right away but might want to implement in the future. By major tasks, I mean application functions that will ultimately be represented in a form or a report in your Access database. For example, "Enter customer orders" is a major task that you would accomplish by using a form created for that purpose, while "Calculate extended price" is most likely a subtask of "Enter customer orders" that you would accomplish by using the same form.

Step 2: Charting Task Flow

To be sure your application operates smoothly and logically, you should group the major tasks by topic and then order those tasks within groups on the basis of the sequence in which the tasks must be performed. For example, you should separate employee-related tasks and sales-related tasks into two topic groups. Within sales, an order must be entered into the system before you can print the order or examine commission totals.

You might discover that some tasks are related to more than one group or that completing a task in one group is a prerequisite to performing a task in another group. Grouping and charting the flow of tasks helps you discover a natural flow that you can ultimately reflect in the way you link the forms and reports in your finished application. Later in this chapter, you'll see how I laid out the tasks performed in one of the sample applications included with this book.

 Inside Out

Understand the work process

When you're designing an application for someone else, these first two steps are absolutely the most important. Learning the work process of the business is critical to building an application that works correctly for the user. These first two steps help you understand how the business is run. Remember, your application is trying to make life easier for the users by automating some critical process that they're doing some other way.

I tend to do a lot of work for small businesses or small departments within larger businesses. Walking the user through this process often helps them understand their own business, and often leads to new efficiencies even before I start to write a line of code!

Designing Your Database Application

Step 3: Identifying Data Elements

After you develop your task list, perhaps the most important design step is to list the bits of data—the data elements—required by each task and the changes that will be made to that data. A given task will require some input data (for example, a price to calculate an extended amount owed on an order); the task might also update the data. The task might delete some data elements (remove invoices paid, for example) or add new ones (insert new order details). Or the task might calculate some data and display it, but not save the data anywhere in the database.

Step 4: Organizing the Data

After you determine all the data elements you need for your application, you must organize the data elements by subject and then map the subjects into tables in your database. A subject is a person, place, thing, or action that you need to track in your application. Each subject normally requires several data elements—individual fields such as name or address—to fully define the subject. With a relational database system such as Access, you use a process called *normalization* to help you design the most efficient and most flexible way to store the data.

> See the section "Database Design Concepts," page 67, for a simple method of creating a normalized design.

Step 5: Designing a Prototype and a User Interface

After you build the table structures needed to support your application, you can easily mock up the application flow in forms and tie the forms together using simple macros or Microsoft Visual Basic event procedures. You can build the actual forms and reports for your application "on screen," switching to Form View or Print Preview periodically to check your progress. If you're building the application to be used by someone else, you can easily demonstrate and get approval for the "look and feel" of your application before you spend time writing complex code that's needed to actually accomplish the tasks. (Parts 3 and 4 of this book show you how to design and construct forms and reports for desktop applications and client/server (project) applications, respectively; Part 5 shows you how to use Visual Basic to link forms and reports to build an application.)

Step 6: Constructing the Application

For very simple applications, you might find that the prototype *is* the application. Most applications, however, will require that you write code to fully automate all the tasks you identified in your design. You'll probably also need to create certain navigation forms that facilitate moving from one task to another. For example, you might need to construct forms that provide the road map for your application. You might also need to build dialog forms to gather user input to allow users to easily filter the data they want to use in a particular task. You might also want to build custom menus for most, if not all, of the forms in the application.

Step 7: Testing, Reviewing, and Refining

As you complete various components of your application, you should test each option that you provide. When you automate your application using Visual Basic, you'll have many debugging tools at your disposal to verify correct application execution and to identify and fix errors.

> **Tip** Get feedback from your users
>
> If at all possible, you should provide completed portions of your application to users so that they can test your code and provide feedback about the flow of the application. Despite your best efforts to identify tasks and lay out a smooth task flow, users will invariably think of new and better ways to approach a particular task after they've seen your application in action. Also, users often discover that some features they asked you to include are not so useful after all. Discovering a required change early in the implementation stage can save you a lot of time reworking things later.

The refinement and revision process continues even after the application is put into use. Most software developers recognize that after they've finished one "release," they often must make design changes and build enhancements. For major revisions, you should start over at Step 1 to assess the overall impact of the desired changes so that you can smoothly integrate them into your earlier work.

> ## Summary of the Typical Application Development Steps
>
> 1 Identifying tasks
> 2 Charting task flow
> 3 Identifying data elements
> 4 Organizing the data
> 5 Designing a prototype and a user interface
> 6 Constructing the application
> 7 Testing, reviewing, and refining

An Application Design Strategy

The two major schools of thought on designing databases are *process-driven design* (also known as *top-down design*), which focuses on the functions or tasks you need to perform, and *data-driven design* (also known as *bottom-up design*), which concentrates on identifying and organizing all the bits of data you need. The method I describe here incorporates some of the best ideas from both philosophies.

Designing Your Database Application

The method I like to use starts by identifying and grouping tasks to decide whether you need only one database or more than one database. (This is a top-down approach.) As explained previously, databases should be organized around a group of related tasks, or functions. For each task, you choose the individual elements of data you need. Next, you gather all the data fields for all related tasks and begin organizing them into subjects. (This is a bottom-up approach.) Each subject forms the foundation for the individual tables in your database. Finally, you apply the rules you will learn in the "Database Design Concepts" section of this chapter to create your tables.

Note　The examples in the rest of this chapter are based on the LawTrack Contacts sample database application from the companion CD. Later in this book, you'll learn how to build various parts of the application as you explore the architecture and features of Microsoft Access. LawTrack Contacts is not only a contacts management application (companies, people, events, and reminders) but also an order entry application (products, sales, and invoices). As such, it is considerably more complex than the Northwind Traders application that is included with Access. It also employs many techniques not found in the product documentation.

Chapter 3

Oh No! Not Another Order-Entry Example!

You might have noticed that when you study database design—whether in a seminar, by reading a book, or by examining sample databases—nearly all the examples (including the one presented here) seem to be order-entry applications. There are several good reasons why you encounter this sort of example over and over again.

1　A large percentage of business-oriented database applications use the common order-entry model. If you build a database, it's likely to use this model.

2　Using the order-entry model makes it easy to demonstrate good database design techniques.

3　At the core of the model, you'll find a "many-to-many" relationship example. (An order might be for many products, and any one product can appear in many orders.) Many-to-many relationships are common to most database applications yet often trip up even the most seasoned database designer.

You might argue, "Wait a minute, I'm building a hospital patient tracking system, not an order-entry system!" Or perhaps you're creating a database to reserve rooms in corporate housing for employees visiting from out of town. (The Housing Reservations sample database that I included with this book does this.) Aren't you "selling" hospital beds to patients? Isn't reserving a room for an employee "selling" that room? If you look at your business applications from this viewpoint, you'll be able to compare your project to the order-entry example with ease. Even if you're writing a personal application to keep track of your wine collection, you're "selling" a rack position in your cellar to your latest bottle purchase, and you're probably also tracking the "supplier" of your purchases.

Microsoft Office Access 2003 Inside Out

The concept of data subjects related to each other in a "many-to-many" fashion is important in all but the simplest of database applications. This type of data relationship can be found in nearly all business or personal database applications. For example, a particular patient might need many different medications, and any one medication is administered to many patients. A movie in your home collection has many starring actors, and any one actor appears in many movies. As you'll discover, a well-designed order-entry database contains several many-to-many relationships.

Analyzing the Tasks

Let's assume that you've been hired by the owner of LawTrack Software Development to build a Contacts and Sales Tracking database. The database application must allow the owner to enter companies or organizations, the people in these companies, and the various types of contacts a user within LawTrack made while marketing several software products. If the contact results in a sale, the application should track the sale and print invoices.

The first design step you should perform is to list all the major tasks that this database application must implement. A partial list might include the following:

- Enter company/organization data.
- Enter person data.
- Link persons with companies/organizations.
- Indicate the primary contact person for a company and the primary company for a person.
- Enter product information.
- Perform a company search.
- Perform a person search.
- Log a contact event with a person.
- Sell a product during a contact event.
- Create an invoice for products ordered.
- Print an invoice.
- Log contact events after the sale.

Figure 3-1 shows a blank application design worksheet that you should fill out for each task.

Designing Your Database Application

APPLICATION DESIGN WORKSHEET #1 = TASKS			
Task Name:			
Brief Description:			
Related Tasks:			
Data Name	**Usage**	**Description**	**Subject**

Figure 3-1. An application design worksheet for describing tasks.

Note You can find the Application Design Worksheet #1 in the Documents subfolder of the files you install from the companion CD, in the file *Chap3-01.doc*. Worksheet #2 is in the file *Chap3-02.doc*.

Chapter 3

Microsoft Office Access 2003 Inside Out

Consider the task of logging a new contact event (such as a letter received). For this task, the user might need to search for the person or the person's company. If the search is by company, then the user should be able to look at a list of people who are contacts for that company and select the specific person. The user should then be able to directly enter the details about the letter received and schedule a follow-up if necessary. In this particular application, LawTrack also wants to be able to log a sale as a contact event and be able to easily specify the product sold as part of entering the event. The program must also automatically create the related product sale record for the contact when this happens.

> **Note** Some of the terminology I'm using here may be a bit confusing. A "contact" might either be a person (the person contacted) or an event (the telephone call or letter or what have you). Throughout the rest of this book, I'll use *contact* to refer to the person and *contact event* to refer to the action.

Data or Information?

You need to understand the difference between data and information before you start building your data design. This bit of knowledge makes it easier for you to determine what you need to store in your database.

Data is the set of static values you store in the tables of the database, while *information* is data that is retrieved and organized in a way that is meaningful to the person viewing it. You *store* data and you *retrieve* information. The distinction is important because of the way that you construct a database application. You first determine the tasks that are necessary (what *information* you need to be able to retrieve), and then you determine what must be stored in the database to support those tasks (what *data* you need in order to construct and supply that information).

Whenever you refer to or work with the structure of your database or the items stored in the tables, queries, macros, or code, you're dealing with data. Likewise, whenever you refer to or work with query records, filters, forms, or reports, you're dealing with information. The process of designing a database and its application becomes clearer once you understand this distinction. Unfortunately, these two terms are ones that folks in the computer industry have used interchangeably. But armed with this new knowledge, you're ready to tackle data design.

Selecting the Data

After you identify all the tasks, you must list the data items you need in order to perform each task. On the task worksheet, you enter a name for each data item, a usage code, and a brief description. In the Usage column, you enter one or more usage codes—I, O, U, D, and C—which stand for input, output, update, delete, and calculate. A data item is an *input* for a task if you need to read it from the database (but not update it) to perform the task. For example, a contact person name and address are some of the inputs needed to create a contact event. Likewise, data is an *output* for a task if it is new data that you enter as you perform the task or that the task calculates and stores based on the input data. For example, the payment due date of an invoice is an output; quantity sold and the selling price for a product in a new order are outputs as well. When an identifier needs to be fetched from one subject table and stored as a linking value in another subject table, a data item may be *input* from one table but *output* to another.

You *update* data in a task if you read data from the database, change it, and write it back. A task such as recording a company's change of address would input the old address, update it, and write the new one back to the database. As you might guess, a task *deletes* data when it removes the data from the database. In the Contacts database, you might have a task to remove a product from the list of products owned by a contact person if that person decides to return the product. Finally, *calculated* data creates new values from input data to be displayed or printed but not written back to the database.

In the Subject column of the task worksheet, you enter the name of the subject to which you think each data element belongs. For example, an address might belong to a Contact. A completed application design worksheet for the Enter a Contact Event task might look like the one shown in Figure 3-2 on the next page.

You might be wondering why I appear to have duplicate data here—ContactEventRequires-FollowUp and ContactFollowUp or ContactEventFollowUpDays and ContactFollowUpDate. The two ContactEvent data elements define the default actions that should occur for a particular type of event, and the ContactFollowUp and ContactFollowUpDate fields are items that should be calculated by the application whenever the user chooses an event that requires a follow-up. The latter is something I call *point in time* data, which I'll discuss later in this chapter. You might not be able to spot this sort of subtle distinction as you first start to document your tasks, but you'll sort it out later in the design process as you finalize your table design following the rules I list in the section "Normalization Is the Solution."

Chapter 3

Microsoft Office Access 2003 Inside Out

APPLICATION DESIGN WORKSHEET #1 = TASKS			
Task Name:	Enter a contact event		
Brief Description:	Search for contact person		
	Add event to person		
Related Tasks:	Company add / edit, Contact person add / edit		
	Contact event type add / edit, Contact product add / edit*		
	Product add / edit		
Data Name	**Usage**	**Description**	**Subject**
ContactID	I, O	ID of the contact for the event	Contacts
ContactDateTime	O	Date and time of the contact event	ContactEvents
ContactEventTypeID	I, O	ID of the type of contact event	ContactEventTypes
ContactEventTypeDesc	I	Description of the contact type	ContactEventTypes
ContactEventRequires-FollowUp	I	Follow-up flag	ContactEventTypes
ContactEventFollowUp-Days	I	Default number of days in future for follow-up	ContactEventTypes
ContactEventProduct-Sold	I	Flag indicating a product sale event	ContactEventTypes
ContactEventProductID	I	Unique ID of the product sold	Products
ContactNotes	O	Notes about the contact event	ContactEvents
ContactFollowUp	O	Flag indicating follow-up required	ContactEvents
ContactFollowUpDate	O	Date the follow-up should occur	ContactEvents
*Additional items if ContactEventProduct-Sold is true.			
CompanyID	I, O	ID of the default company for this contact person	Companies
ProductID	I, O	ID of the product sold	Products
DateSold	O	Date the product was sold	ContactProducts
SoldPrice	O	Price charged for the product	ContactProducts

Figure 3-2. A completed worksheet for the Enter a Contact Event task.

Designing Your Database Application

Organizing Tasks

You should use task worksheets as a guide in laying out an initial structure for your application. Part of the planning you do on these worksheets is to consider usage—whether a piece of data might be needed as input, for updating, or as output of a given task.

Wherever you have something that is required as input, you should have a *precedent* task that creates that data item as output. For example, for the worksheet shown in Figure 3-2, you must gather company, contact, and product data before you can record a contact event. Similarly, you need to create the contact event type data in some other task before you can use that data in this task. Therefore, you should have a task for gathering basic company data, a task for entering basic contact person data, a task for creating product data, and a task for defining contact event types. It's useful to lay out all your defined tasks in a relationship diagram. You can see relationships among the tasks in the LawTrack Contacts database in Figure 3-3. When one task is optionally precedent to another task, the two tasks are linked with dashed lines. For example, you do not have to define all products before you define simple contact event types. You can create an event for a contact (but you can't sell a product in that event) before you define the default company for a contact.

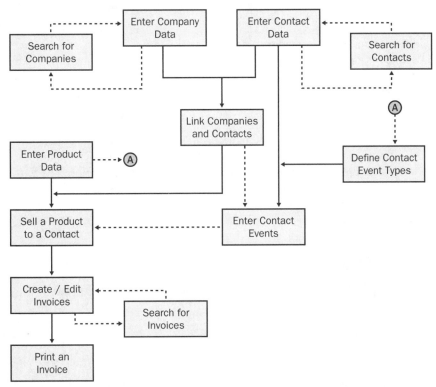

Figure 3-3. The relationships among tasks in the LawTrack Contacts database.

Chapter 3

Data Analysis

Now you're ready to begin a more thorough analysis of your data and to organize the individual elements into data subjects. These subjects become candidates for tables in your database design.

Choosing the Database Subjects

If you've been careful in identifying the subject for each data item you need, the next step is very easy. You create another worksheet, similar to the worksheet shown in Figure 3-4, to help you collect all the data items that belong to each subject. In the top part of the worksheet, you list the related subjects that appear in any given task and indicate the kind of relationship.

If there are potentially many instances of the related subject for one instance of the current subject (for example, there might be many contacts within a company), enter Many in the relationship column. If there is potentially only one instance of the related subject to one instance of the current subject (for example, a company is referred by only one contact), enter One in the relationship column. For details about relationship types, see the section "Efficient Relationships Are the Result," page 77.

It's important to understand these relationships because they have a significant effect on the database structure and on how you work with two related subject tables in Access. If you take care in filling out and revising your worksheets, you can ultimately use each worksheet to create a table in Access. You'll learn more about these relationships later in this chapter.

You can see a completed worksheet for the Companies subject in Figure 3-5 on page 66.

As you copy each data item to the subject worksheet, you designate the data type (text, number, currency, memo, and so on) and the data length in the Data Type column. You can enter a short descriptive phrase for each data item in the Description column. When you create your table from the worksheet, the description is the default information that Access will display on the status bar at the bottom of the screen whenever the field is selected on a datasheet or in a form or a report.

Finally, in the Validation Rule column, you should make a note of any validation rules or input mask restrictions that always apply to the data field. Later, you can define these rules in Access, and Access will check each time you create new data to ensure that you haven't violated any of the rules. Validating data can be especially important when you create a database application for other people to use.

Designing Your Database Application

APPLICATION DESIGN WORKSHEET #2 = SUBJECTS			
Subject Name:			
Brief Description:			
Related Subjects:	Name	Relationship	
Data Name	**Data Type**	**Description**	**Validation Rule**

Figure 3-4. An application design worksheet for identifying related subjects.

Chapter 3

Microsoft Office Access 2003 Inside Out

APPLICATION DESIGN WORKSHEET #2 = SUBJECTS			
Subject Name:	Companies		
Brief Description:	Information about companies / organizations to which contact persons are related.		
Related Subjects:	**Name**	**Relationship**	
	CompanyContacts	Many	
	Invoices	Many	
	Contacts	One (contact referring this Company)	
Data Name	**Data Type**	**Description**	**Validation Rule**
CompanyID	Autonumber	Company identifier	Required (P Key)
CompanyName	Text (50)	Name of the company or organization	Is Not Null
Department	Text (50)	Optional department name	
Address	Text (255)	Street address	
City	Text (50)	City	
County	Text (50)	County	
StateOrProvince	Text (20)	State or province	
PostalCode	Text (20)	Postal code	00000\-9999
Country	Text (50)	Country	
PhoneNumber	Text (30)	Phone	!\(999") "000\-0000
FaxNumber	Text (30)	Phone	!\(999") "000\-0000
WebSite	Hyperlink	Website address	
ReferredBy	Number, Long	Contact who referred this company / organization.	RI rule – child of Contacts

Figure 3-5. A completed worksheet for the Companies subject.

Mapping Subjects to Your Database

After you fill out all of the subject worksheets, each worksheet becomes a candidate to be a table in your database. For each table, you must confirm that all the data you need is included. You should also be sure that you don't include any unnecessary data.

For example, if any customers need more than one line for an address, you should consider adding a second data field. If you expect to have more than one type of product category (in LawTrack's case, they sell Single, Multi-User, and Remote versions of their software as well as

Designing Your Database Application

support for each), you should create a separate worksheet for product categories that you'll use to define a table that contains records for each product type. In the next section, you'll learn how to use four simple rules to create a flexible and logical set of tables from your subject worksheets.

Database Design Concepts

When using a relational database system such as Microsoft Access, you should begin by designing each database around a specific set of tasks or functions. For example, you might design one database for customers and orders that contains data about each customer, the products available for sale, the orders for each customer, and the product sales history. You might have another database that handles human resources for your company. It would contain all relevant data about the employees and their dependents, such as names, job titles, employment histories, departmental assignments, insurance information, and the like.

> **Tip** If you have filled out the Subject worksheets for your application before you start this process, it's a good idea to go back and make any necessary corrections to those worksheets as you follow the rules in this section to refine your table structure. At the end of the process, each Subject worksheet should map to exactly one table.

At this point, you face your biggest design challenge: How do you organize data within each task-oriented database so that you take advantage of the relational capabilities of Access and avoid inefficiency and waste? If you followed the steps outlined earlier in this chapter for analyzing application tasks and identifying database subjects, you're well on your way to creating a logical, flexible, and usable database design. But what if you just dove in and started laying out your tables without first analyzing tasks and subjects? The rest of this chapter shows you how to apply some rules to transform a makeshift database design into one that is robust and efficient.

Waste Is the Problem

A *table* stores the data you need for the tasks you want to perform. A table is made up of columns, or *fields,* each of which contains a specific kind of data (such as a customer name or a credit rating), and rows, or *records,* that collect all the data about a particular person, place, or thing. You can see this organization in the Companies table in the LawTrack Contacts database, as shown in Figure 3-6.

Company ID	Company / Organization	Department	Billing Address	City	County	State/Province	Postal
1	Waterville City Police Dept.	K-9	3456 3rd Street	Waterville	Oneida	NY	13480
2	Tennessee State Highway Patrol	K-9	6789 4th Boulevard	Rutherford	Gibson	TN	38369
3	C, P and L K-9 Training	Training	2345 Central Avenue	Elgin	Scott	TN	37732
4	Harpursville City Police Dept.	K-9	7890 4th Avenue	Harpursville	Broome	NY	13787
5	Tyler Hill City Police Dept.	K-9	1234 1st Street	Tyler Hill	Wayne	PA	18469
6	Philadelphia City Police Dept.	K-9	6789 Church Drive	Philadelphia	Philadelphia	PA	19135
7	Tickfaw City Police Dept.	K-9	3456 Lincoln Street	Tickfaw	Tangipahoa	LA	70466
8	Fabrikam K-9 Training	Training	6789 3rd Parkway	Elberfeld	Warrick	IN	47613
9	Calhoun County Sheriff	K-9	2345 Central Parkway	Leary	Calhoun	GA	31762
10	Saint Croix County Sheriff	K-9	7890 3rd Avenue	St Croix	Saint Croix	VI	00820

Figure 3-6. The Companies table in Datasheet view.

Microsoft Office Access 2003 Inside Out

> **Note** The example companies, organizations, products, domain names, e-mail addresses, logos, people, places, and events depicted herein are fictitious. No association with any real company, organization, product, domain name, e-mail address, logo, person, place, or event is intended or should be inferred.

For the purposes of this design exercise, let's say you want to build a new database (named Contacts) for tracking contacts, contact events, and products sold during contact events without the benefit of first analyzing the tasks and subjects you'll need. You might be tempted to put all the data about the task you want to do—keeping track of customers and their contacts with you and the products they might buy during a contact—in a single Contact Events table, whose fields are represented in Figure 3-7.

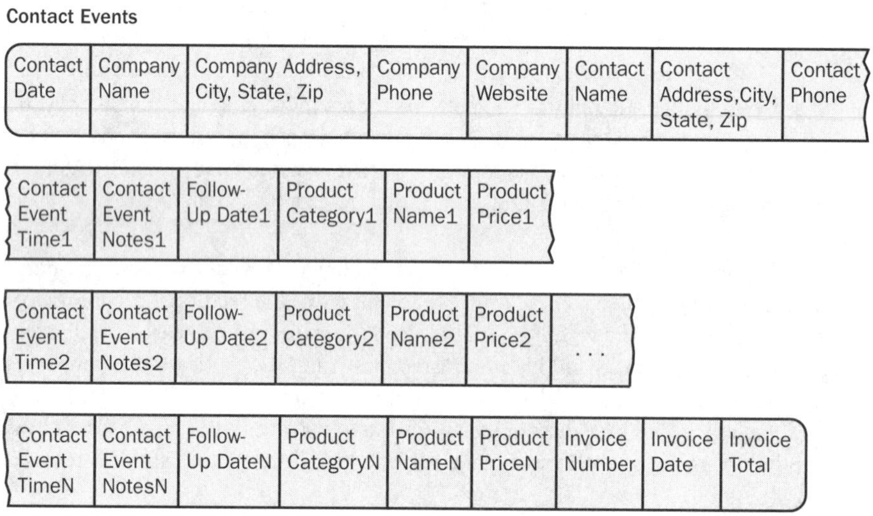

Contact Events

Figure 3-7. The design for the Contacts database using a single Contact Events table.

There are many problems with this technique. For example:

- Every day that a contact calls you, you have to duplicate the Company Name, Company Address, Contact Name, and Contact Address fields in another record for the new contact event. Repeatedly storing the same name and address in your database wastes a lot of space—and you can easily make mistakes if you have to enter basic information about a contact more than once.

Designing Your Database Application

- You have no way of predicting how many contact events you'll have in a given day or how many products might be ordered. If you keep track of each day's contact events in a single record, you have to guess the largest number of individual events and products and leave space for Event Time 1, Event Time 2, Event Time 3, Product Name 1, Product Name 2, and so on, all the way to the maximum number. Again you're wasting valuable space in your database. If you guess wrong, you'll have to change your design just to accommodate a day when a contact calls you (or you call them) more times than you have allocated in your record. And later, if you want to find out what products were sold to which contacts, you'll have to search each Product Name field in every record.

- You have to waste space in the database storing data that can easily be calculated when it's time to print a report. For example, you'll certainly want to calculate the total invoice amount, but you do not need to keep the result in a field.

- Designing one complex field to contain all the parts of simple data items (for example, lumping together Street Address, City, State, and Postal Code) makes it difficult to search or sort on part of the data. In this example, it would be impossible to sort on company or contact postal code because that piece of information might appear anywhere within the more complex single address fields.

Normalization Is the Solution

You can minimize the kinds of problems noted above (although it might not always be desirable to eliminate all duplicate values), by using a process called *normalization* to organize data fields into a group of tables. The mathematical theory behind normalization is rigorous and complex, but the tests you can apply to determine whether you have a design that makes sense and that is easy to use are quite simple—and can be stated as rules.

Field Uniqueness

Because wasted space is one of the biggest problems with an unnormalized table design, it makes sense to remove redundant fields from a table. So the first rule is about field uniqueness.

Rule 1: Each field in a table should represent a unique type of information. This means that you should break up complex compound fields and get rid of repeating groups of information. In this example, the complex address fields should be separated into simple fields and new tables designed to eliminate the repeating contact event and product information. When you create separate tables for the repeating data, you include some "key" information from the main table to create a link between the new tables and the original one. One possible result might look like the diagram in Figure 3-8 on the next page.

Microsoft Office Access 2003 Inside Out

Contacts

Company Name	Company Address	Company City	Company State	Company Postal Code	Company Phone	Company Website

Contact Name	Contact Address	Contact City	Contact State	Contact Postal Code	Contact Phone	Contact Email

Contact Events

Company Name	Contact Name	Contact Date	Contact Event Time	Contact Event Notes	Follow-Up Date	Product Category	Product Name	Product Price	Invoice Number

Invoices

Invoice Number	Invoice Date	Company Name	Invoice Total

Figure 3-8. This design for the Contacts database eliminates redundant fields.

These tables are much simpler because you can store one record per contact event. Also, you don't have to reserve room in your records to hold a large number of events per day per contact. All the lengthy address information is now in a separate table so you don't have to repeat it for each event. Because an invoice might cover multiple products purchased, there's also a separate table for that. Notice that the Contact Events table includes certain key information to link it to the Contacts table (Company Name and Contact Name) and to the Invoices table (Invoice Number).

Searching and sorting the information will now also be easier. You can sort the Contact records on postal code or do a search on the separate city and state fields. Can you spot a field that I failed to break up into separate elements? If your answer is the Contact Name field, you're correct! As you'll see in the final solution, we need to break this field into at least separate First Name and Last Name fields.

The duplicate data problem is now somewhat worse because you are repeating the Company Name and Contact Name fields in each Contact Events record. This duplicate data is necessary, however, to maintain the links between the tables. The potentially long Product Name field is also redundant in the Contact Events table—when you sell the same product more than once, the product name will appear in multiple rows. (Maybe products should have a separate table?) What happens if you misspell a product name in one of the rows? Will you be able to find all contacts who bought the same product? You can solve this problem by following the second rule.

Designing Your Database Application

Primary Keys

In a good relational database design, each record in any table must be uniquely identified. That is, some field (or combination of fields) in the table must yield a unique value for each record in the table. This unique identifier is called the *primary key*.

Rule 2: Each table must have a unique identifier, or primary key, that is made up of one or more fields in the table.   Whenever possible, you should use the simplest data that naturally provides unique values. You should always be able to find a field or some combination of fields whose values are unique across all rows. (In relational design terminology, these are called *candidate keys*.) You should consider the simplest combination of fields as the best candidate to be your primary key. However, in the case of the Contacts table as currently designed in Figure 3-8, you would probably need a combination of Company Name, Contact Name, and perhaps one of the contact address or contact city fields to guarantee uniqueness. When this happens, it is preferable to generate an artificial unique ID field to use as the primary key (Contact ID). However, you might want to add code in your final application that checks for a potential duplicate name (another record previously saved that has the same name as the new record about to be saved) and warns the user before inserting a new unique record. You'll learn in the next chapter that Access provides a handy data type called *AutoNumber* to make it easy to create a unique ID field like Contact ID.

Once we assign Contact ID as the primary key of the Contacts table, it becomes much easier to link a contact with a contact event by substituting Contact ID for the Company Name and Contact Name fields in the Contact Events table. Although Contact ID in the Contact Events table perhaps looks like duplicate information, it's really the link that you can use to associate or *relate* the rows from the two tables. Relational databases are equipped to support this design technique by giving you powerful tools to bring related information back together easily. You'll take a first look at some of these tools in Chapter 7, "Creating and Working with Simple Queries."

A common mistake would be to create another ID field to uniquely identify the rows in Contact Events. Now with the addition of Contact ID, it's easy to see that the combination of Contact ID, Contact Date, and Contact Event Time are most likely unique to each row, so you should use this combination of elements as a natural primary key. For the new Invoices table, the choice is simple. Invoice Number might be an AutoNumber ID field, but it is probably a unique number entered by the user when creating a new invoice record. Some companies like to use a year prefix combined with a unique sequence number within the year as an invoice number. The Invoice Number field is still in the Contact Events table to identify which products were billed on what invoice number. You can see the result of adding primary keys in Figure 3-9 on the next page.

Chapter 3

Microsoft Office Access 2003 Inside Out

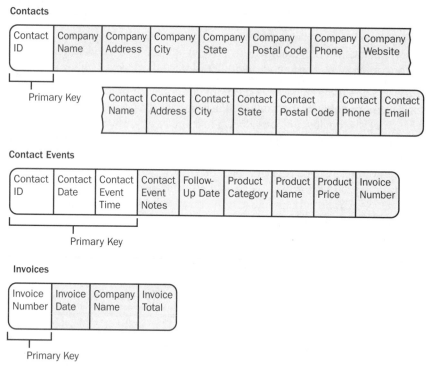

Figure 3-9. The LawTrack Contacts database tables with primary keys defined.

Functional Dependence

Defining a primary key helps you better identify the true subject of the table. Now, you can check to see whether you included all the data relevant to the subject of the table and whether each of the fields in the table describes an attribute of the subject (and not some other subject). In relational terminology, you should check to see whether each field is *functionally dependent* on the primary key that defines the subject of the table.

Rule 3: For each unique primary key value, the values in the data columns must be relevant to, and must completely describe, the subject of the table. This rule works in two ways. First, you shouldn't have any data in a table that is not relevant to the subject (as defined by the primary key) of the table. Second, the data in the table should completely describe the subject.

Let's start by looking at the Contacts table as defined in Figure 3-9. The subject of this table is the people who are our contacts. We certainly need to know the company or organization with which a person is associated. What if a person has more than one such association?

For example, a person might work for a company but also be a member of one or more professional organizations. We certainly do not want to repeat the contact name and personal address information multiple times for each different association. Is the Company information in a Contact row unique to the individual defined by that row? Probably not. Even if we're certain that a person is associated with only one company or organization, we'll have to duplicate the company information in multiple rows when a company has more than one person associated with it.

The solution is to identify companies (organizations) as a separate subject with its own unique identifier. If a person is related to one and only one company, we can place a linking copy of the Company ID in the Contacts table. In this case, let's assume that a person can be related to more than one company or organization. A company has many persons, and a person might belong to many companies or organizations. In relational terminology, this is called a *many-to-many relationship*, which you can read more about later in this chapter. To define this in our table design, we need what I call a *linking table* that stores the multiple relationships of the companies and people—a table called Company Contacts. While we're at it, let's refine the Contact Name field by splitting it into separate First Name and Last Name fields (so we can sort and search by just the last name), and let's complete the Company Contacts table by adding an indicator field that defines which company is the primary one for the contact.

Now, we should turn our attention to the Contact Events table. In the table shown in Figure 3-9, we have not only information about the event but also information about a product that might be sold during the event. In fact, the user of this database might make many calls or mail out many brochures or letters before actually selling a product. The product information isn't fully *functionally dependent* on the subject of this table, so it needs to be in a separate subject table. In fact, a product is not going to be purchased by an individual contact—it will be bought by the contact's primary company or organization.

So, we also need to create a separate Contact Products table to store the products a contact might purchase after dozens of contacts. This table should have all the information relevant to a company purchasing a product for an employee, but nothing extra. This moves the extra product information from the old Contact Events table and makes the fields in that table relevant only to events and nothing else.

Finally, we should completely define the Invoices subject by adding other relevant information such as the purchasing company's purchase order number, the date the invoice payment is due, and an indicator field to mark when the invoice has been paid. You can see the result of applying Rule 3 in Figure 3-10 on the next page.

Microsoft Office Access 2003 Inside Out

Companies

Company ID	Company Name	Company Address	Company City	Company State	Company Postal Code	Company Phone	Company Website

Company Contacts

Company ID	Contact ID	Position	Primary for Contact

Contacts

Contact ID	Contact Last Name	Contact First Name	Contact Address	Contact City	Contact State	Contact Postal Code	Contact Phone	Contact Email

Contact Events

Contact ID	Contact Date	Contact Event Time	Contact Event Notes	Follow-Up Date

Contact Products

Company ID	Contact ID	Product Name	Product Category	Date Sold	Product Price	Invoice Number

Invoices

Invoice Number	Invoice Date	Company ID	PO Number	Invoice Due	Invoice Paid	Invoice Total

Figure 3-10. Creating additional subject tables in the LawTrack Contacts database ensures that all fields in a table are functionally dependent on the primary key of the table.

Field Independence

The last rule checks to see whether you'll have any problems when you make changes to the data in your tables.

Rule 4: You must be able to make a change to the data in any field (other than to a field in the primary key) without affecting the data in any other field. Take a look again at the Contact Products table in Figure 3-10. As we applied the second and third rules, we left Product information with the Contact Products information because it seems reasonable that you need to know about the product sold to a contact. Note that if you need

Designing Your Database Application

to correct the spelling of a product name, you can do so without affecting any other fields in that record. If you misspelled the same product name for many contact products, however, you might have to change many records. Also, if you entered the wrong product (for example, an order is actually for a Single-User edition, not a Multi-User edition), you can't change the product name without also changing that record's category and pricing information.

The Product Category, Product Name, and Product Price fields are not independent of one another. In fact, Product Category and Product Price are functionally dependent on Product Name. (See Rule 3.) Although it wasn't obvious at first, Product Name describes another subject that is different from the subject of contact products. You can see how carefully applying this fourth rule helps you identify changes that you perhaps should have made when applying earlier rules. This situation calls for another table in your design: a separate Products table, as shown in Figure 3-11 on the next page.

Now, if you misspell a product name, you can simply change the product name in the Products table. Also, instead of using the Product Name field (which might be 40 or 50 characters long) as the primary key for the Products table, you can create a shorter Product ID field (perhaps a five-digit number) to minimize the size of the relational data you need in the Contact Products table.

Note also that I removed the Invoice Total field from the Invoices table because any change to a price in Contact Products would make this value incorrect. The database is not going to maintain this calculated value for you, so you would have to write extra code in your application to recalculate and update the value each time a contact ordered another product. As you'll see later when you learn about building queries, it's a simple matter to build a query to sum the product prices for the records related to an invoice to calculate the total owed. You can also calculate the total invoice value when the invoice is complete—perhaps as part of the report that prints the invoice.

An alternative (but less rigorous) way to check for field independence is to see whether you have the same data repeated in your records. In the previous design, whenever you created a sale for a particular product during a contact event, you had to enter the product's name, category, and price in the record. With a separate Products table, if you need to correct a product name spelling or change a list price or product category, you have to make the change only in one field of one record in the Products table. If you entered the wrong product in a contact product record, you have to change only the Product ID to fix the problem.

Note that I added a new field, a separate Product Sold Price in the Contact Products table. Why not link to the new Products table to find out the price? Why isn't this duplicate data that violates Rule 1? This is an example of why it is very important to understand how the business runs. In this case, LawTrack sometimes offers a discount off "list price" to a company that purchases multiple copies of LawTrack's products. The price in the Contact Products table is the actual sales price that the user enters when the company buys the product. You can learn more about the concept of such point-in-time data later in this chapter.

Companies

Company ID	Company Name	Company Address	Company City	Company State	Company Postal Code	Company Phone	Company Website

Company Contacts

Company ID	Contact ID	Position	Primary for Contact

Contacts

Contact ID	Contact Last Name	Contact First Name	Contact Address	Contact City	Contact State	Contact Postal Code	Contact Phone	Contact Email

Contact Events

Contact ID	Contact Date	Contact Event Time	Contact Event Notes	Follow-Up Date

Contact Products

Company ID	Contact ID	Product ID	Date Sold	Product Sold Price	Invoice Number

Products

Product ID	Product Category	Product Name	Product Price

Invoices

Invoice Number	Invoice Date	Company ID	PO Number	Invoice Due	Invoice Paid

Figure 3-11. This design for the LawTrack Contacts database follows all the design rules.

The actual LawTrack Contacts sample database includes 10 tables, which are all shown in the Relationships window in Figure 3-12 on the next page. Notice that additional fields were created in each table to fully describe the subject of each table and that other tables were added to support some of the other tasks identified earlier in this section. For example, many fields were added to both the Companies and Contacts tables to fully capture all the pertinent information about those subjects. There are also three *lookup tables* to help ensure accurate data entry and to provide additional information about the nature of some classification codes. A lookup table helps you restrict the list of values that are valid for a field in a main

Designing Your Database Application

table, and they may also contain additional fields that help further define the meaning of each value in the list. You'll learn more about defining lookup properties in Chapter 4, "Creating Your Database and Tables."

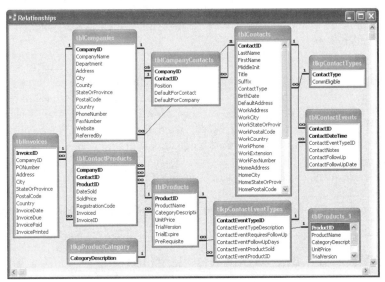

Figure 3-12. Tables in the LawTrack Contacts sample database shown in the Relationships window.

The Four Rules of Good Table Design

Rule 1: Each field in a table should represent a unique type of information.

Rule 2: Each table must have a unique identifier, or primary key, that is made up of one or more fields in the table.

Rule 3: For each unique primary key value, the values in the data columns must be relevant to, and must completely describe, the subject of the table.

Rule 4: You must be able to make a change to the data in any field (other than to a field in the primary key) without affecting the data in any other field.

Efficient Relationships Are the Result

When you apply good design techniques, you end up with a database that efficiently links your data. You probably noticed that when you normalize your data as recommended, you tend to get many separate tables. Before relational databases were invented, you had to either compromise your design or manually keep track of the relationships between files or tables. For example, you had to put company data in your contacts and invoices table or write your program to first open and read a record from one table and then search for the matching record in the related table. Relational databases solve these problems. With a good design you don't have to worry about how to bring the data together when you need it.

Chapter 3

Foreign Keys

You might have noticed as you followed the LawTrack Contacts design example that each time I created a new table, I left behind in the other table a field that could link the two, such as the Company ID, Contact ID, and Product ID fields in the Contact Products table. The Invoice Number field in Contact Products is also a link to the Invoices table. These "linking" fields are called *foreign keys*.

In a well-designed database, foreign keys result in efficiency. You keep track of related foreign keys as you lay out your database design. When you define your tables in Access, you link primary keys to foreign keys to tell Access how to join the data when you need to retrieve information from more than one table. You can also ask Access to maintain the integrity of your table relationships—for example, Access will ensure that you don't create a contact event for a contact that doesn't exist. When you ask Access to maintain this *referential integrity*, Access automatically creates indexes for you. As you'll learn in the next chapter, indexes help Access find data more quickly when you're searching, filtering, or linking data.

For details about referential integrity and defining indexes, see Chapter 4, "Creating Your Database and Tables."

One-to-Many and One-to-One Relationships

In most cases, the relationship between any two tables is one-to-many. That is, for any one record in the first table, there can be many related records in the second table; but for any record in the second table, there is exactly one matching record in the first table. You can see several instances of this type of relationship in the design of the LawTrack Contacts database. For example, each company might have several invoices, but a single invoice record applies to only one company.

Occasionally, you might want to break down a table further because you use some of the data in the table infrequently or because some of the data in the table is highly sensitive and should not be available to everyone. For example, you might want to keep track of certain company data for marketing purposes, but you don't need access to that data all the time. Or you might have data about credit ratings that should be accessible only to authorized people. In either case, you can create a separate table that also has a primary key of Company ID. The relationship between the original Companies table and the Company Info or Company Credit table is one-to-one. That is, for each record in the first table, there is exactly one record in the second table.

Creating Table Links

The last step in designing your database is to create the links between your tables. For each subject, identify those for which you wrote *Many* under Relationship on the worksheet. Be sure that the corresponding relationship for the other table is *One*. If you see *Many* in both places, you must create a separate **linking table** to handle the relationship. (Access won't let you define a many-to-many relationship directly between two tables.) In the example of the

Add/Edit a Contact task, a contact might be associated with *many* companies or organizations, and a company most likely has *many* contacts. The Company Contacts table in the LawTrack Contacts database is a linking table that clears up this many-to-many relationship between companies and contacts. Contact Products is another table that works as an intersection table because it has a one-to-many relationship with both Contacts and Products. (A contact might purchase several products, and a product is most likely owned by many contacts.)

After you straighten out the many-to-many relationships and create additional subject worksheets to reflect the linking tables, you need to create the links between subjects. To complete the links, you should place a copy of the primary key from the *one* subject in a field in the *many* subject. For example, by looking at the worksheet for Companies shown in Figure 3-5, you can surmise that the primary key for the Companies subject, Company ID, also needs to be a field in the Company Contacts and Invoices subjects.

When to Break the Rules

As a starting point for every application that you build, you should always analyze the tasks you need to perform, decide on the data required to support those tasks, and create a well-designed (also known as *normalized*) database table structure. After you have a design that follows all the rules, you might discover changes that you need to make either to follow specific business rules or to make your application more responsive to the needs of your users. In every case for which you decide to "break the rules," you should know the specific reason for doing so, document your actions, and be prepared to add procedures to your application to manage the impact of those changes. The following sections discuss some of the reasons why you might need to break the rules.

Improving Performance of Critical Tasks

The majority of cases for breaking the rules involve manipulating the design to achieve better performance for certain critical tasks. For example, although modern relational database systems (like Microsoft Access) do a good job of linking many related tables to perform complex tasks, you might encounter situations in which the performance of a multiple-table link (also called a *joined query*—see Chapter 8 for details) is not fast enough. Sometimes if you *denormalize* selected portions of the design, you can achieve the required performance. For example, instead of building a separate table of product category codes that requires a link, you might place the category descriptions directly in the products table. If you choose to do this, you will need to add procedures to the forms you provide to enter these categories to make sure that any similar descriptions aren't duplicate entries. I chose to do this in the LawTrack Contacts database, and I solved the problem by using a combo box that allows the user to choose a value only from a validated list in another table. You'll learn more about working with combo box controls in Chapter 11, "Building a Form."

Another case for breaking the rules is the selective inclusion of calculated values in your database. For example, if a critical management report needs the calculated totals for all orders in a month, but the data is retrieved too slowly when calculating the detailed values for thousands of product purchase records per order and thousands of orders, you might want to add

Microsoft Office Access 2003 Inside Out

a field for order total in the Orders or Invoices table. Of course, this also means adding procedures to your order-entry forms to ensure that any change in an order detail record is reflected immediately in the calculated order total. Your application will spend a few extra fractions of a second processing each order so that month-end totals can be obtained quickly.

Capturing Point-In-Time Data

Sometimes you need to break the rules to follow known business rules. In the previous design exercise, we considered removing the Price field from the Contact Products table because it duplicated the price information in the Products table. However, if your business rules say that the price of a product can change over time, you might need to include the price in your order details to record the price at the *point in time* that the order was placed. If your business rules dictate this sort of change, you should add procedures to your application to automatically copy the "current" price to any new order detail row.

You can see another case in the LawTrack Contacts database. Some of the billing address information in the Invoices table looks like it duplicates information in the Companies table. If you examine the way the database works, you'll find some code that copies the company information to the invoice information when you create a new invoice. Again, this address information in the Invoice is point-in-time data. It is the address that was current at the time the invoice was created. The company address might change later, but we will always know where we mailed a particular invoice.

 Note You can find the Housing Reservations sample application on the companion CD.

There's yet another example in the Housing Reservations database. In this database, the user creates room reservation requests that indicate an employee needs a specific type of room over a range of dates. Some of this request information gets copied to the actual reservation record at the time the housing manager confirms the reservation. It is also company policy to honor the quoted rate at the time the reservation is made so that the manager who approves the reservation knows exactly what will be charged. (Likewise, if this were a commercial hotel, you would expect to pay the rate quoted at the time of the reservation, not the current rate at the time you check in three months later!) If you look at the database design for the Housing Reservations database, shown in Figure 3-13, you'll see what looks like duplicate information in the Reservation Requests and the Reservations tables. In this case, check-in and check-out information is copied from Reservation Requests to Reservations when a reservation is confirmed. Likewise, the daily and weekly rates that are current at the time the reservation is made are copied to the reservation by code in the application.

Designing Your Database Application

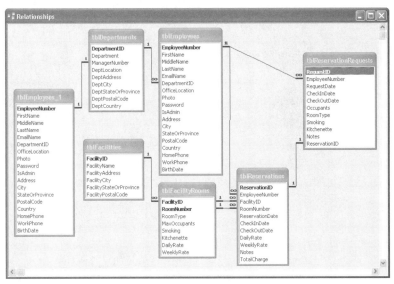

Figure 3-13. The design for the Housing Reservations database includes duplicate point-in-time pricing information in the Reservations table.

Note also that there's a Total Charge field in the record that must be calculated by code within the application. The application spends a little computing time for each change to the records in the table to save processing time in reports that might need to work with hundreds of rows. If you look behind the Reservations form in the Housing Reservations database, you'll find lots of code to accomplish both the rate copy and the total calculation.

Creating Report Snapshot Data

One additional case for breaking the rules involves accumulating data for reporting. As you'll see in Chapter 16, "Advanced Report Design," the queries required to collect data for a complex report can be quite involved. If you have a lot of data required for your report, running the query could take an unacceptably long time, particularly if you need to run several large reports from the same complex collection of data. In this case, it's acceptable to create temporary but "rule-breaking" tables that you load once with the results of a complex query in order to run your reports. I call these tables "snapshots" because they capture the results of a complex reporting query for a single moment in time. You can look in Chapter 9, "Modifying Data with Action Queries," for some ideas about how to build action queries that save a complex data result to a temporary table. If you use the resulting "snapshot" data from these tables, you can run several complex reports without having to run long and complex queries more than once.

Now that you understand the fundamentals of good database design, you're ready to do something a little more fun with Access—build a database. The next chapter, "Creating Your Database and Tables," shows you how to create a new database and tables; Chapter 5, "Modifying Your Table Design," shows you how to make changes later if you discover that you need to modify your design.

Part 2

Building a Microsoft Access Desktop Application

Creating Your Database and Tables

After you design the tables for your database, defining them in a Microsoft Access desktop database (.mdb file) is incredibly easy. This chapter shows you how it's done. You'll learn how to

- Create a new database application using a database template
- Create a new empty database for your own custom application
- Create a simple table by entering data directly in the table

Get a jump start on defining custom tables by using the Table Wizard to

- Define your own tables from scratch by using table Design view
- Select the best data type for each field
- Define the primary key for your table
- Set validation rules for your fields and tables
- Tell Access what relationships to maintain between your tables
- Optimize data retrieval by adding indexes
- Set options that affect how you work in table Design view
- Print a table definition

> **Note** All the screen images in this chapter were taken on a Windows XP system with the display theme set to Windows XP.

Creating a New Database

When you first start Microsoft Access, you see a blank work area on the left and the Home task pane on the right as shown in Figure 4-1. If you've previously opened other databases, such as the Northwind Traders sample database that is included with Access, you also see a most recently used list of up to nine database selections under Open in the top part of the task pane.

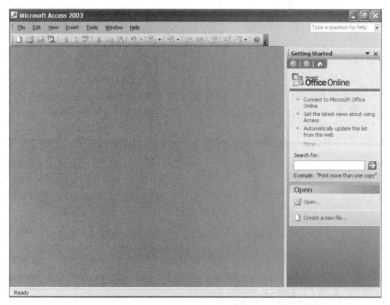

Figure 4-1. When you first start Access, you see the Home task pane.

Using a Database Template to Create a Database

Just for fun, let's explore the built-in database templates first. If you're a beginner, you can use the templates included with Access to create one of several common applications without needing to know anything about designing database software. You might find that one of these applications meets most of your needs right off the bat. As you learn more about Access, you can build on and customize the basic application design and add new features.

Even if you're an experienced developer, you might find that the application templates save you lots of time in setting up the basic tables, queries, forms, and reports for your application. If the application you need to build is covered by one of the templates, the wizard that builds an application with one of the templates can take care of many of the simpler design tasks.

When you start Access, you can access the built-in templates by clicking More under New on the Home task pane and then clicking the On my computer option under Other Templates on the New File task pane. You can also open the New File task pane by clicking the New button at the far left of the toolbar or by selecting New from the File menu. You can see the New File task pane in Figure 4-2.

New button

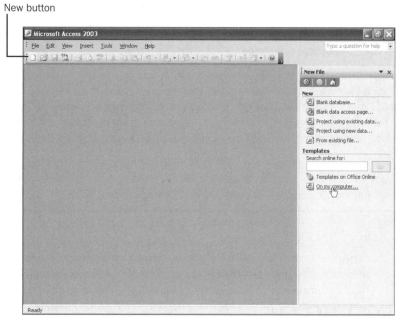

Figure 4-2. You can access the built-in templates by clicking On my computer in the New File task pane.

When you click the On my computer option, Access opens the Templates dialog box. Click the Databases tab of this dialog box to see a list of the 10 available templates, as shown in Figure 4-3. You work with all the templates in the Database Wizard in the same way. This example will show you the steps that are needed to build an Asset Tracking database.

Chapter 4

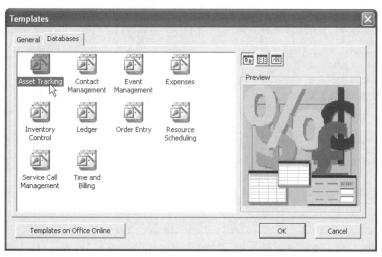

Figure 4-3. Choosing one of the Database Wizard templates.

87

Inside Out

Where to find database templates

In addition to the 10 templates supplied with Microsoft Access, you can find dozens of database examples at *http://officeupdate.microsoft.com/templategallery*. You can go directly to this Web site by clicking on the Templates home page link on the New File task pane shown in Figure 4-2 or by clicking the Templates on Microsoft.com link shown in Figure 4-1. To find all the database examples, perform a search on the word *Access* on this Web site.

Note that the examples you find on the Web site are completed .mdb files, not template files that require the Database Wizard to build a sample database.

Scan the list of available templates on the Databases tab of the Templates dialog box. When you click a template icon, Access shows a preview graphic to give you another hint about the purpose of the template. You start the Database Wizard by selecting a template and then clicking OK. You can also double-click a template icon. Access opens the File New Database dialog box and suggests a name for your new database file. You can modify the name and then click Create to launch the wizard.

The wizard takes a few moments to initialize and to create a blank file for your new database application. The wizard first displays a window with a few more details about the capabilities of the application you are about to build. If this isn't what you want, click Cancel to close the wizard and delete the database file. You can click Finish to have the wizard quickly build the application with all the default options. Click Next to proceed to a window that provides options for customizing the tables in your application, as shown in Figure 4-4.

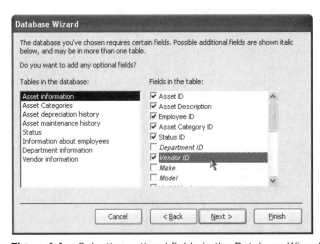

Figure 4-4.   Selecting optional fields in the Database Wizard.

In this window, you can see the names of the tables the wizard plans to build. As you select each table name in the list on the left, the wizard shows you the fields it will include in that table in the list on the right. For many of the tables, you can have the wizard include or exclude certain optional fields (which appear in *italic*). In the Asset Tracking application, for example, you might be interested in keeping track of the vendor for each asset. When you click the optional Vendor ID field in the Asset information table, you'll be able to specify from which vendor you acquired the asset. Click Next when you finish selecting optional fields for your application.

In the next window, shown in Figure 4-5, you select one of several styles for the forms in your database. As you recall from Chapter 1, "Microsoft Access Overview," forms are objects in your database that are used to display and edit data on your screen. As you click each style name, the Database Wizard shows you a sample of that style on the left. Some of the styles, such as Expedition or Ricepaper, are quite whimsical. The Standard style has a very business-like gray-on-gray look. In this case, I chose the Sumi Painting style that has a bit more character but is still businesslike.

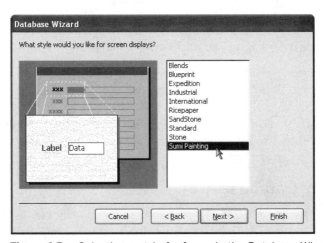

Figure 4-5. Selecting a style for forms in the Database Wizard.

After you select a form style, click Next to proceed to the window to select a report style. You might want to select Bold, Casual, or Compact for personal applications. Corporate, Formal, and Soft Gray are good choices for business applications. Again, you can see a sample of the style on the left as you click on each available style on the right. Select an appropriate report style, and then click Next.

In the next window of the Database Wizard, you specify the title that will appear on the Access title bar when you run the application. You can also include a picture file such as a company logo in your reports. This picture file can be a bitmap (.bmp), a Windows metafile (.wmf), or an icon file (.ico). Click Next after you supply a title for your application.

In the final window, you can choose to start the application immediately after the wizard finishes building it. You can also choose to open a special set of help topics to guide you through using a database application. Select the Yes, Start the database option and click Finish to create and then start your application. Figure 4-6 shows the Main Switchboard form for the Asset Tracking database application.

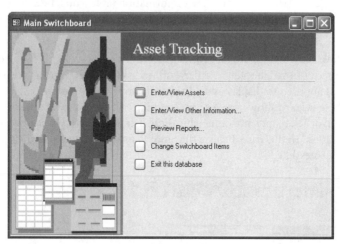

Figure 4-6. The Main Switchboard form for the Asset Tracking database application.

> **Tip** Once you use one of the built-in templates, Access lists that template under Recently used templates on the New File task pane in case you want to use that template again.

Creating a New Empty Database

To begin creating a new empty database when you start Access, go to the New File task pane (as shown in Figure 4-2) and click Blank Database. This opens the File New Database dialog box, shown in Figure 4-7. Select the drive and folder you want from the Save in drop-down list. In this example, I selected the My Documents folder on my computer. Finally, go to the File name box and type the name of your new database. Access appends an .mdb extension to the file name for you. (Access uses a file with an .mdb extension to store all your database objects, including tables, queries, forms, reports, data access pages, macros, and modules.) For this example, create a new sample database named Kathy's Wedding List to experiment with one way to create a database and tables. Click the Create button to create your database.

Figure 4-7. Defining the name of a new database in the File New Database dialog box.

Access takes a few moments to create the system tables in which to store all the information about the tables, queries, forms, reports, data access pages, macros, and modules that you might create. When Access completes this process, it displays the Database window for your new database, shown in Figure 4-8.

Figure 4-8. The Database window for a new database.

When you open a database (unless the database includes special startup settings), Access selects the button under Objects that you last chose in the Database window for that database. For example, if the last time you were in this database you worked on queries, Access highlights the Queries button on the left and shows you the last query you selected in the pane on the right the next time you open the database. Each button under objects displays the available objects of that type.

Because this is a new database and no tables or special startup settings exist yet, you see a Database window with no objects defined. The items you see under Tables are simply shortcuts to three ways to create a table. The following sections show you how to use each of these.

Troubleshooting

Wait a minute! Why do I see "(Access 2000 file format)" at the top of the Database window? I thought I was working in Microsoft Access 2003!

Microsoft Access 2003 fully supports two different file formats to provide you maximum flexibility if your organization still has some users who have Microsoft Access 2000 (version 9) or Microsoft Access 2002 (version 10) installed. By default, any new database you create is in the "lowest common denominator" format—Access 2000. See the section, "Setting Table Design Options," page 133, for information about how to change this default.

Creating Your First Simple Table by Entering Data

If you've been following along to this point, you should still have your new Kathy's Wedding List database open with the Database window displaying the Tables pane, as shown in Figure 4-8. (You can also follow these steps in any open database.) Make sure the Tables button under Objects is selected, and then click the New button in the Database window to open the New Table dialog box, shown in Figure 4-9.

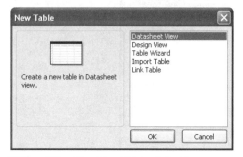

Figure 4-9.   The New Table dialog box.

Select Datasheet View in the list, and then click OK to get started. (You can also just double-click Datasheet View in the list.) What you see next is an empty datasheet, which looks quite similar to a spreadsheet. Note that you also could have double-clicked Create table by entering data as shown in Figure 4-8—there's usually more than one way to accomplish a task in Access. You can enter just about any type of data you want—text, dates, numbers, currency. But unlike in a spreadsheet, in a datasheet you can't enter any calculated expressions. As you'll see later in the chapters about queries, you can easily display a calculated result using data from one or more tables by entering an expression in a query.

Because we're starting a list of wedding invitees, we'll need columns containing information such as title, first name, middle initial, last name, street address, city, state, postal code, number of guests invited, number of guests confirmed, gift received, and a gift acknowledged indicator. Be sure that each column contains the same type of data in every row. For example, enter the city name in the sixth column for every row.

You can see some of the data entered for the wedding invitee list in Figure 4-10. When you start to type in a field within a row, Access displays a pencil icon on the row selector at the far left to indicate that you're adding or changing data in that row. Use the Tab key to move from column to column. When you move to another row, Access saves what you typed. If you make a mistake in a particular row or column, you can click the data you want to change and type over it or delete it.

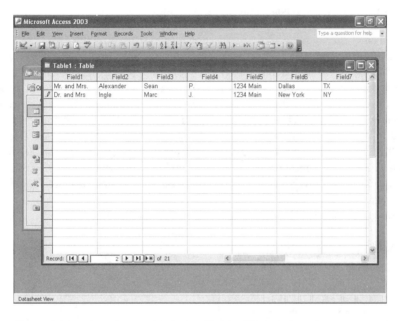

Figure 4-10.   Creating a table in the Kathy's Wedding List database by entering data.

If you create a column of data that you don't want, click anywhere in the column and choose Delete Column from the Edit menu. If you want to insert a blank column between two columns that already contain data, click anywhere in the column to the right of where you want to insert the new column and then choose Column from the Insert menu. To move a column to a different location, click the field name at the top of the column to highlight the entire column, and then click again and drag the column to a new location. You can also click an unselected column and drag your mouse pointer through several adjacent columns to highlight them all. You can then move the columns as a group.

You probably noticed that Access named your columns Field1, Field2, and so forth—not very informative. You can enter a name for each column by double-clicking the column's field name. You can also click anywhere in the column and then choose Rename Column from the Format menu. In Figure 4-11 on the next page, I have already renamed one of the columns and am in the process of renaming the second one.

Chapter 4

93

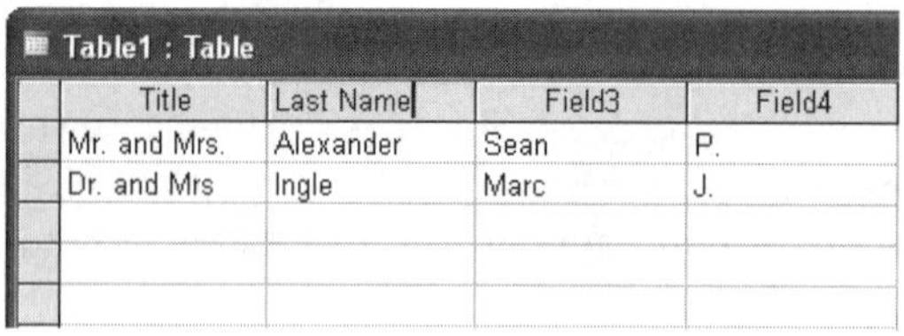

Figure 4-11.   Renaming a column in Datasheet view.

After you enter several rows of data, it's a good idea to save your table. You can do this by clicking the Save button on the toolbar or by choosing Save from the File menu. Access displays a Save As dialog box, as shown in Figure 4-12. Type an appropriate name for your table, and then click OK. Access displays a message box warning you that you have no primary key defined for this table and offering to build one for you. If you accept the offer, Access adds a field called ID and assigns it a special data type named AutoNumber that automatically generates a unique number for each new row you add. See "Understanding Field Data Types," page 102, for details about the AutoNumber feature. If one or more of the data columns you entered would make a good primary key, click No in the message box. In Chapter 5, "Modifying Your Table Design," you'll learn how to use the Design view of a table to define your own primary key(s) or to change the definition of an existing primary key. In this case, click Yes to build a field called ID that will serve as the primary key.

Figure 4-12.   Saving your new table.

Creating a Table Using the Table Wizard

If you look in the Wedding List sample database (*WeddingList.mdb*) included on the companion CD with this book, you'll find it very simple, with one main table and a few supporting tables for data such as titles, cities, and postal codes. Most databases are usually quite a bit more complex. For example, the Proseware Housing Reservations sample database, also included on the companion CD, contains six main tables, and the LawTrack Contacts sample database contains more than a dozen tables. If you had to create every table "by hand," it could be quite a tedious process.

Fortunately, Microsoft Access comes with a Table Wizard to help you build many common tables. Let's move on to a more complex task—building tables like those you find in Law-Track Contacts (and like those you designed in Chapter 3). For this exercise, create a new blank database and give it the name Contact Tracking, as shown in Figure 4-13. You'll use this database to start building tables like some of those you saw in Chapter 3.

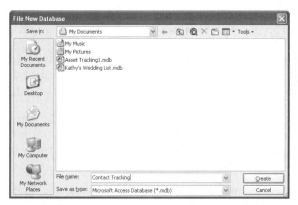

Figure 4-13. Creating a blank database named Contract Tracking.

To build a table using the Table Wizard, go to the Database window, click the Tables button, and then click the New button. In the New Table dialog box (see Figure 4-9), select Table Wizard from the list and click OK. You can also double-click the Create table by using wizard shortcut shown near the top of the Database window in Figure 4-8. You'll see the opening window of the Table Wizard, shown in Figure 4-14.

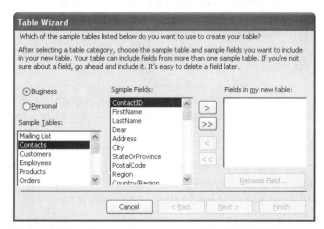

Figure 4-14. The opening window of the Table Wizard.

Toward the middle left of the window are two option buttons—Business (to select business-oriented tables) and Personal (to select personal tables). You can find an entry for a Contacts sample table in the Business category. When you select this table, the wizard displays all the fields from the Contacts sample table in the Sample Fields list. (You will change the table you create now in Chapter 5, "Modifying Your Table Design," so that it is more like the final tbl-Contacts table in the LawTrack Contacts database.)

To select a field, click its name in the Sample Fields list, and then click the single right arrow (>) button to move it to the Fields in my new table list. (You can also select a field by double-clicking its name.) You define the sequence of fields in your table on the basis of the

95

sequence in which you select them from the Sample Fields list. If you add a field that you decide you don't want, select it in the Fields in my new table list and click the single left arrow (<) button to remove it. If you want to start over, you can remove all fields by clicking the double left arrow (<<) button. If you pick fields in the wrong sequence, you must remove the field that is out of sequence, click the field above where you want the field inserted, and then select the field again.

Many of the fields in the Contacts sample table are fields you'll need in the Contacts table for your Contact Tracking database. You can pick ContactID, FirstName, LastName, Address, City, StateOrProvince, PostalCode, Country/Region, WorkPhone, WorkExtension, and EmailName directly from the Contacts sample table.

In this Contact Tracking database, you want to track some home contact information, so you need to find a second set of address fields in another sample table to use in your new Contacts table. You also need a field for middle name or middle initial. In the Sample Tables list, select the Employees sample table. You can see a MiddleName field here that you can use, and some more address fields while you're about it. Click the LastName field in the Fields in my new table list to indicate that you want to insert a field after LastName, and then double-click the MiddleName field to insert it after LastName. Similarly, click the WorkExtension field in the Fields in my new table list, and then add Address from the Sample Fields list (which the wizard will rename Address1 because you already have an Address field), City, StateOrProvince, PostalCode, and Country/Region—you'll use these fields to store the contact's home address information. Also, below EmailName, add Photograph, Notes, SpouseName, and two copies of the Birthdate field from the Employees sample table. (The wizard will name the second one Birthdate1 for now.)

Note The sequence of FirstName, LastName, and MiddleName might not seem exactly logical, but I did it this way on purpose so I could show you how to move fields in a table design in the next chapter.

Now you need to rename some of the fields. Rename the first Address field to WorkAddress by clicking that field in the Fields in my new table list and then clicking the Rename Field button. The Table Wizard opens a dialog box to allow you to type in a new name. You need to rename the rest of the first set of address fields with a "Work" prefix and then correct the names of the second set of fields to use as home address information by adding a "Home" prefix. While you're at it, also remove "/Region" from the Country/Region fields. Figure 4-15 shows how to rename the second Birthdate field to SpouseBirthDate. As you can see, it's easy to mix and match fields from various sample tables and then rename the fields to get exactly what you want.

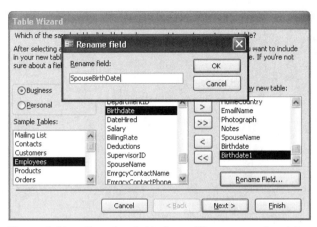

Figure 4-15. Choosing fields from different sample tables and renaming fields.

Click the Next button to see the window shown in Figure 4-16. In this window, you can specify a name for your new table. (Because you started by choosing fields from the Contacts
sample table, the wizard suggests that you name the table "Contacts," which is just fine.) You
can also ask the wizard to set a primary key for you, or you can define your own primary key.
In many cases, the wizard chooses the most logical field or fields to be the primary key, but
you can ensure that it picks the right one by specifying that you want to select it (No, I'll set
the primary key). If the wizard can't find an appropriate field to be the primary key, it creates a new primary key field that uses a special data type called AutoNumber. As you'll learn
later in this chapter, the AutoNumber data type ensures that each new row in your table will
have a unique value as its primary key.

Inside Out

Why you should always pick the primary key in the Table Wizard

The wizard might pick the wrong field as the primary key, particularly when you're using the
Table Wizard to define a table that contains both an identifier field for the table as well as
fields that you'll use to link to other tables. For example, if you build an Employees table
and include both the EmployeeNumber field (that you intend to use as the primary key) and
the DepartmentID field (to link later to a Departments table), the wizard incorrectly picks
DepartmentID as the primary key of the table. It seems to prefer fields that end in ID over
ones that end in Number.

Chapter 4

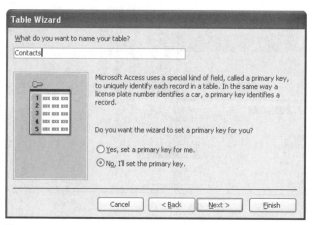

Figure 4-16.   Specifying a table name and selecting a primary key option in the Table Wizard.

Go ahead and choose the option to pick your own primary key and then click Next. The Table Wizard displays the window shown in Figure 4-17. You can open the list at the top of the window to select any field that you defined. This is a Contacts table, so ContactID is the appropriate field to choose. If you choose the first option for the type of key, the wizard uses an AutoNumber data type that I've already mentioned. The second option causes the wizard to create a number field into which you must enter a number for each record, and the third option gives you a text field for each record. In this case, pick the first option.

For details about the different data types that you can assign to fields in your tables, see "Defining Fields," page 100.

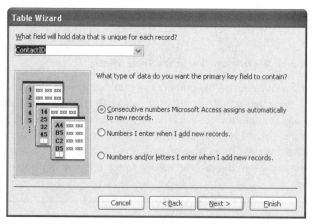

Figure 4-17.   Identifying the field you want as the primary key.

Click the Next button to move to the next window. If you have other tables already defined in your database, the Table Wizard shows you a list of those tables and tells you whether it thinks your new table is related to any of the existing tables. If the wizard finds a primary key in another table with the same name and data type as a field in your new table (or vice versa),

Chapter 4

it assumes that the tables are related. If you think the wizard has made a mistake, you can tell it not to create a relationship (a link) between your new table and the existing table. You'll learn how to define your own relationships between tables later in this chapter.

Because this is the first and only table in this database, you won't see the Relationships window in the Table Wizard. Instead, the wizard shows you a final window in which you can choose to modify the table design, open it as a datasheet, or call another wizard to build a form to edit your data as shown in Figure 4-18.

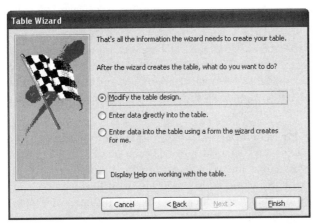

Figure 4-18. The final window in the Table Wizard offers you three options.

Select the Modify the table design option and click Finish to let the wizard build your table. The table will open in Design view, as shown in Figure 4-19. In the next chapter, you'll learn how to modify this table in Design view to exactly match the tblContacts table in the Law-Track Contacts database. For now, close the Table window so that you can continue building other tables that you need.

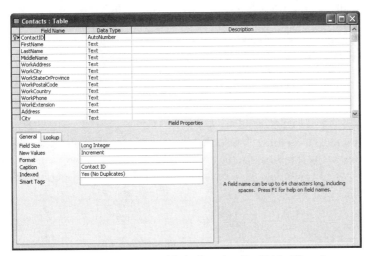

Figure 4-19. The Contacts table built using the Table Wizard.

Creating a Table in Design View

You could continue to use the Table Wizard to build some of the other tables in the Contact Tracking database to mimic those in LawTrack Contacts. For example, you could use the Customers sample table from the Business samples to build the Companies table or the Products sample table to get a jump-start on the Products table you need. However, you'll find it very useful to learn the mechanics of building a table from scratch, so now is a good time to explore Design view and learn how to build tables without using the Table Wizard. You'll also see many additional features that you can use to customize the way your tables (and any queries, forms, or reports built on these tables) work.

To design a new table in a database, go to the Database window (shown in Figure 4-8). Click the Tables button under Objects, and then click the New button. Access shows you the New Table dialog box you saw in Figure 4-9. Select Design View and click OK. You can also double-click the Create table in Design view shortcut in the Database window. Access displays a blank Table window in Design view.

In Design view, the upper part of the Table window displays columns in which you can enter the field names, the data type for each field, and a description of each field. After you select a data type for a field, Access allows you to set field properties in the lower left area of the Table window. In the lower right area of the Table window is a box in which Access displays information about fields or properties. The contents of this box change as you move from one location to another within the Table window.

> For details about data type values, see "Understanding Field Data Types" on page 102.

For details about data type values, see "Understanding Field Data Types" on page 102.

Defining Fields

Now you're ready to begin defining the fields for the Companies table as we designed it in Chapter 3. Be sure the insertion point is in the first row of the Field Name column, and then type the name of the first field, **CompanyID**. Press the Tab key once to move to the Data Type column. A button with a down arrow appears on the right side of the Data Type column. Here and elsewhere in Microsoft Access, this type of button signifies the presence of a drop-down list. Click the down arrow or press Alt+Down arrow to open the list of data types, shown in Figure 4-20. In the Data Type column, you can either type a valid value or select from the list of values in the drop-down list. Select AutoNumber as the data type for CompanyID.

In the Description column for each field, you can enter a descriptive phrase. Access displays this description on the status bar (at the bottom of the Access window) whenever you select this field in a query in Datasheet view or in a form in Form view or Datasheet view.

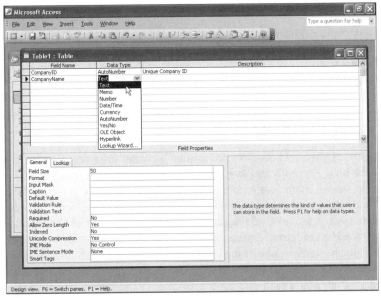

Figure 4-20. The drop-down list of data types.

Inside Out

Why setting the Description property is important

Entering a Description property for every field in your table helps document your application. Because Access also displays the description on the status bar, paying careful attention to what you type in the Description field can later pay big dividends as a kind of mini-help for the users of your database. Also, since this data propagates automatically, you probably don't want to type something nonsensical or silly. Typing **I don't have a clue what this field does** is probably not a good idea—it will show up later on the status bar!

Tab down to the next line, enter **CompanyName** as a field name, and then choose Text as the data type. After you select a data type, Access displays some property boxes in the Field Properties area in the lower part of the Table window. These boxes allow you to set *properties*—settings that determine how Access handles the field—and thereby customize a field. The properties Access displays depend on the data type you selected; the properties appear with some default values in place, as shown in Figure 4-20.

For details about the values for each property, see "Setting Field Properties," page 104.

Chapter 4

101

Understanding Field Data Types

Access supports nine types of data, each with a specific purpose. You can see the details about each data type in Table 4-1. Access also gives you a tenth option, Lookup Wizard, to help you define the characteristics of foreign key fields that link to other tables. You'll learn about the Lookup Wizard (and why you shouldn't use it) in the next chapter.

Choosing Field Names

Microsoft Access gives you lots of flexibility when it comes to naming your fields. A field name can be up to 64 characters long, can include any combination of letters, numbers, spaces, and special characters except a period (.), an exclamation point (!), an accent grave (`), and brackets ([ ]); however, the name cannot begin with a space and cannot include control characters (ANSI values 0 through 31). In general, you should give your fields meaningful names and should use the same name throughout for a field that occurs in more than one table. You should avoid using field names that might also match any name internal to Microsoft Access or Visual Basic. For example, all objects have a Name property, so it's a good idea to qualify a field containing a name by calling it CustomerName or CompanyName. You should also avoid names that are the same as built-in functions, such as Date, Time, Now, or Space. See Microsoft Access Help for a list of all the built-in function names.

Although you can use spaces anywhere within names in Access, you should try to create field names and table names *without* embedded spaces. Most SQL databases to which Access can attach do not support spaces within names. If you ever want to move your application to a client/server environment and store your data in an SQL database such as Microsoft SQL Server or Oracle, you'll have to change any names in your database tables that have an embedded space character. As you'll learn later in this book, table field names propagate into the queries, forms, reports, and data access pages that you design using these tables. So any name you decide to change later in a table must also be changed in all your queries, forms, reports, and data access pages. See "Setting Table Design Options," page 133, for details about options to automatically propagate changes.

Table 4-1. Access Data Types

Data Type	Usage	Size
Text	Alphanumeric data	Up to 255 characters
Memo	Alphanumeric data—sentences and paragraphs	Up to about 1 gigabyte (but controls to display a memo are limited to the first 65,535 characters)
Number	Numeric data	1, 2, 4, 8, or 16 bytes
Date/Time	Dates and times	8 bytes

Table 4-1. **Access Data Types**

Data Type	Usage	Size
Currency	Monetary data, stored with 4 decimal places of precision	8 bytes
AutoNumber	Unique value generated by Access for each new record	4 bytes (16 bytes for Replication ID)
Yes/No	Boolean (true/false) data; Access stores the numeric value zero (0) for false, and minus one (-1) for true.	1 bit
OLE Object	Pictures, graphs, or other ActiveX objects from another Windows-based application	Up to about 2 gigabytes
Hyperlink	A link "address" to a document or file on the World Wide Web, on an intranet, on a local area network (LAN), or on your local computer	Up to about 1 gigabyte

For each field in your table, select the data type that is best suited to how you will use that field's data. For character data, you should normally select the Text data type. You can control the maximum length of a Text field by using a field property, as explained later. Use the Memo data type only for long strings of text that might exceed 255 characters or that might contain formatting characters such as tabs or line endings (carriage returns).

When you select the Number data type, you should think carefully about what you enter as the Field Size property because this property choice will affect precision as well as length. (For example, integer numbers do not have decimals.) The Date/Time data type is useful for calendar or clock data and has the added benefit of allowing calculations in seconds, minutes, hours, days, months, or years. For example, you can find out the difference in days between two Date/Time values.

Inside Out

Understanding what's inside the Date/Time data type

Use the Date/Time data type to store any date, time, or date and time value. It's useful to know that Access stores the date as the integer portion of the Date/Time data type and the time as the fractional portion—the fraction of a day, measured from midnight, that the time represents, accurate to seconds. For example, 6:00:00 AM internally is 0.25. The day number is actually the number of days since December 30, 1899 (there will be a test on that later!) and can be a negative number for dates prior to that date. When two Date/Time fields contain only a date, you can subtract one from the other to find out how many days are between the two dates.

Chapter 4

You should generally use the Currency data type for storing money values. Currency has the precision of integers, but with exactly four decimal places. When you need to store a precise fractional number that's not money, use the Number data type and choose Decimal for the Field Size property.

The AutoNumber data type is specifically designed for automatic generation of primary key values. Depending on the settings for the Field Size and New Values properties you choose for an AutoNumber field, you can have Access create a sequential or random long integer. You can include only one field using the AutoNumber data type in any table. If you define more than one AutoNumber field, Access displays an error message when you try to save the table.

Use the Yes/No data type to hold Boolean (true or false) values. This data type is particularly useful for flagging accounts paid or not paid or orders filled or not filled.

The OLE Object data type allows you to store complex data, such as pictures, graphs, or sounds, which can be edited or displayed through a dynamic link to another Windows-based application. For example, Access can store and allow you to edit a Microsoft Word document, a Microsoft Excel spreadsheet, a Microsoft PowerPoint presentation slide, a sound file (.wav), a video file (.avi), or pictures created using the Paint or Draw application.

The Hyperlink data type lets you store a simple or complex "link" to an external file or document. (Internally, Hyperlink is a memo data type with a special flag set to indicate that it is a link.) This link can contain a Uniform Resource Locator (URL) that points to a location on the World Wide Web or on a local intranet. It can also contain the Universal Naming Convention (UNC) name of a file on a server on your local area network (LAN) or on your local computer drives. The link can point to a file that is in Hypertext Markup Language (HTML) or in a format that is supported by an ActiveX application on your computer.

Setting Field Properties

You can customize the way Access stores and handles each field by setting specific properties. These properties vary according to the data type you choose. Table 4-2 lists all the possible properties that can appear on a field's General tab in a table's Design view, and the data types that are associated with each property.

Table 4-2. **Field Properties on the General Tab**

Data Type	Options, Description
Field Size Property	
Text	Text can be from 0 through 255 characters long, with a default length of 50 characters.
Number	**Byte.** A single-byte integer containing values from 0 through 255.

Table 4-2. Field Properties on the General Tab

Data Type	Options, Description
	Integer. A 2-byte integer containing values from –32,768 through +32,767.
	Long Integer. A 4-byte integer containing values from –2,147,483,648 through +2,147,483,647.
	Single.* A 4-byte floating-point number containing values from –3.4 $\times$ 10^{38} through +3.4 $\times$ 10^{38} and up to seven significant digits.
	Double.* An 8-byte floating-point number containing values from –1.797 $\times$ 10^{308} through +1.797 $\times$ 10^{308} and up to 15 significant digits.
	Replication ID.† A 16-byte globally unique identifier (GUID).
	Decimal. A 12-byte integer with a defined decimal precision that can contain values from –10^{28} through +10^{28}. The default precision (number of decimal places) is 0 and the default scale is 18.
AutoNumber	**Long Integer.** A 4-byte integer containing values from –2,147,483,648 through +2,147,483,647 when New Values is Random or from 1 to +2,147,483,647 when New Values is Increment.
	Replication ID. A 16-byte globally unique identifier (GUID).
New Values Property	
AutoNumber only	**Increment.** Values start at 1 and increment by 1 for each new row.
	Random. Access assigns a random long integer value to each new row.
Format Property	
Text, Memo	You can specify a custom format that controls how Access displays the data. For details about custom formats, see "Setting Control Properties" on page 451 or the Access Help topic "Format Property—Text and Memo Data Types."
Number (except Replication ID), Currency, AutoNumber	**General Number (default).** No commas or currency symbols; the number of decimal places shown depends on the precision of the data.
	Currency.‡ Currency symbol (from the regional settings in Windows Control Panel) and two decimal places.
	Euro. Euro currency symbol (regardless of Control Panel settings) and two decimal places.

Table 4-2. **Field Properties on the General Tab**

Data Type	Options, Description
	Fixed. At least one digit and two decimal places.
	Standard. Two decimal places and separator commas.
	Percent. Percentage—moves displayed decimal point two places to the right and appends a percentage (%) symbol.
	Scientific. Scientific notation (for example, 1.05E+06 represents 1.05×10^6).
	You can specify a custom format that controls how Access displays the data. For details about custom formats, see "Setting Control Properties" on page 451 or the Access Help topic "Format Property—Number and Currency Types."
Date/Time**	**General Date (default).** Combines Short Date and Long Time format (for example, 4/15/2003 5:30:10 PM).
	Long Date. Uses Long Date Style from the regional settings in Windows Control Panel (for example, Tuesday, April 15, 2003).
	Medium Date. 15-Apr-2003.
	Short Date.†† Uses Short Date Style from the regional settings in Windows Control Panel (for example, 4/15/2003).
	Long Time. Uses Time Style from the regional settings in Windows Control Panel (for example, 5:30:10 PM).
	Medium Time. 5:30 PM.
	Short Time. 17:30.
	You can specify a custom format that controls how Access displays the data. For details about custom formats, see "Setting Control Properties" on page 451 or the Access Help topic "Format Property—Date/Time Data Type."
Yes/No	**Yes/No (default).**
	True/False.
	On/Off.
	You can specify a custom format that controls how Access displays the data. For details about custom formats, see "Setting Control Properties" on page 451 or the Access Help topic "Format Property—Yes/No Data Type."
Precision Property	
Number, Decimal	You can specify the maximum number of digits allowed. The default value is 18, and you can specify an integer value between 1 and 28.
Scale Property	
Number, Decimal	You can specify the number of decimal digits stored. This value must be less than or equal to the value of the Precision property.

Table 4-2. Field Properties on the General Tab

Data Type	Options, Description
Decimal Places Property	
Number (except Replication ID), Currency	You can specify the number of decimal places that Access displays. The default specification is Auto, which causes Access to display two decimal places for the Currency, Fixed, Standard, and Percent formats and the number of decimal places necessary to show the current precision of the numeric value for General Number format. You can also request a fixed display of decimal places ranging from 0 through 15.
Input Mask Property	
Text, Number (except Replication ID), Date/Time, Currency	You can specify an editing mask that the user sees while entering data in the field. For example, you can have Access provide the delimiters in a date field such as __/__/__, or you can have Access format a U.S. phone number as (###) 000-0000. See "Defining Input Masks," page 114, for details.
Caption Property	
All	You can enter a more fully descriptive field name that Access displays in form labels and in report headings. (Tip: If you create field names with no embedded spaces, you can use the Caption property to specify a name that includes spaces for Access to use in labels and headers associated with this field in queries, forms, and reports.)
Default Value Property	
Text, Memo, Date/Time, Hyperlink, Yes/No	You can specify a default value for the field that Access automatically uses for a new row if no other value is supplied. If you don't specify a Default Value, the field will be Null if the user fails to supply a value. (See also the Required property.)
Number, Currency	Access sets the property to 0. You can change the setting to a valid numeric value. You can also remove the setting, in which case the field will be Null if the user fails to supply a value. (See also the Required property.)
Validation Rule Property	
All (except OLE Object, Replication ID, and AutoNumber)	You can supply an expression that must be true whenever you enter or change data in this field. For example, **<100** specifies that a number must be less than 100. You can also check for one of a series of values. For example, you can have Access check for a list of valid cities by specifying **"Chicago" Or "New York" Or "San Francisco"**. In addition, you can specify a complex expression that includes any of the built-in functions in Access. See "Defining Simple Field Validation Rules," page 111, for details.

Chapter 4

107

Table 4-2. Field Properties on the General Tab

Data Type	Options, Description
Validation Text Property	
All (except OLE Object, Replication ID, and Auto-Number)	You can specify a custom message that Access displays whenever the data entered does not pass your validation rule.
Required Property	
All (except AutoNumber)	If you don't want to allow a Null value for the field, set this property to Yes.
Allow Zero Length Property	
Text, Memo	You can set the field equal to a zero-length string ("") if you set this property to Yes. See the sidebar titled "Nulls and Zero-Length Strings" on page 110 for more information.
Indexed Property	
All except OLE Object.	You can ask that an index be built to speed access to data values. You can also require that the values in the indexed field always be unique for the entire table. See "Adding Indexes," page 130, for details.
Unicode Compression Property	
Text, Memo, Hyper-link	As of version 2000, Access stores character fields in an .mdb file using a double-byte (Unicode) character set to support extended character sets in languages that require them. The Latin character set required by most Western European languages (such as English, Spanish, French, or German) requires only one byte per character. When you set Unicode Compression to Yes for character fields, Access stores compressible characters in one byte instead of two, thus saving space in your database file. However, Access will not compress Memo or Hyperlink fields that will not compress to fewer than 4,096 bytes. The default for new tables is Yes in all countries where the standard language character set does not require two bytes to store all the characters.
IME Mode Property, IME Sentence Mode Property	
Text, Memo, Hyperlink	On machines with an Asian version of Windows and appropriate Input Method Editor (IME) installed, these properties control conversion of characters in kanji, hiragana, katakana, and hangul character sets.

Table 4-2. **Field Properties on the General Tab**

Data Type	Options, Description
Smart Tags	
All data types except Yes/No, OLE Object, and Replication ID	Indicates the registered smart tag name and action that you want associated with this field. When the user views this field in a table datasheet, a query datasheet, or a form, Access displays a smart tag available indicator next to the field. The user can click on the indicator and select the smart tag action to perform. For an example using a smart tag, see Chapter 12, "Customizing a Form."

* Single and Double field sizes use an internal storage format called floating point that can handle very large or very small numbers, but that is somewhat imprecise. If the number you need to store contains more than 7 significant digits for a Single or more than 15 significant digits for a Double, the number will be rounded. For example, if you try to save 10,234,567 in a Single, the actual value stored will be 10,234,570. Likewise, Access stores 10.234567 as 10.23457 in a Single. If you want absolute fractional precision, use Decimal field size or Currency data type instead.

† In general, the Replication ID field size should be used only in a database that is managed by the Replication Manager.

‡ Note that Currency, Euro, Fixed, and Standard formats always display two decimal places regardless of the number of actual decimal places in the underlying data. Access rounds any number to two decimal places for display if the number contains more than two decimal places.

**You can also specify a custom format in addition to the built-in ones described here. See Chapter 11 for details.

††To help alleviate problems with dates spanning the start of the century, I recommend that you select the Use Four-Digit Year Formatting option in Access. Choose Options from the Tools menu, and then click the General tab to find this option. You should also be sure that your Short Date Style in the regional settings in Windows Control Panel uses a four-digit year. (This is the default in Windows XP.)

Inside Out

Don't specify a validation rule without validation text

If you specify a validation rule but no validation text, Access generates an ugly and cryptic message that your users might not understand:

"One or more values are prohibited by the validation rule '*<your expression here>*' set for '*<table name.field name>*'. Enter a value that the expression for this field can accept."

Unless you like getting lots of support calls, I recommend that you always enter a custom validation text message whenever you specify a validation rule.

For details about the properties on the Lookup tab, see "Taking a Look at Lookup Properties," page 171.

Chapter 4

Completing the Fields in the Companies Table

You now know enough about field data types and properties to finish designing the Companies table in this example. (You can also follow this example using the tblCompanies table from the LawTrack Contacts sample database.) Use the information listed in Table 4-3 to design the table shown in Figure 4-21.

Nulls and Zero-Length Strings

Relational databases support a special value in fields, called a *Null*, that indicates an unknown value. In contrast, you can set Text or Memo fields to a *zero-length string* to indicate that the value of a field is known but the field is empty.

Why is it important to differentiate Nulls (unknown values) from zero-length strings? Here's an example: Suppose you have a database that stores the results of a survey about automobile preferences. For questionnaires on which there is no response to a color-preference question, it is appropriate to store a Null. You don't want to match responses based on an unknown response, and you don't want to include the row in calculating totals or averages. On the other hand, some people might have responded "I don't care" for a color preference. In this case, you have a known "no preference" answer, and a zero-length string is appropriate. You can match all "I don't care" responses and include the responses in totals and averages.

Another example might be fax numbers in a customer database. If you store a Null, it means you don't know whether the customer has a fax number. If you store a zero-length string, you know the customer has no fax number. Access gives you the flexibility to deal with both types of "empty" values.

You can join tables on zero-length strings, and two zero-length strings will compare to be equal. However, for Text, Memo, and Hyperlink fields, you must set the Allow Zero Length property to Yes to allow users to enter zero-length strings. (*Yes* became the default in Microsoft Access 2002.) Otherwise, Access converts a zero-length or all-blank string to a Null before storing the value. If you also set the Required property of the Text field to Yes, Access stores a zero-length string if the user enters either " " (two double quotes with no space) or blanks in the field.

Nulls have special properties. A Null value cannot be equal to any other value, not even to another Null. This means you cannot join (link) two tables on Null values. Also, the question "Is A equal to B?" when A, B, or both A and B contain a Null, can never be answered "yes." The answer, literally, is "I don't know." Likewise, the answer to the question "Is A not equal to B?" is also "I don't know." Finally, Null values do not participate in aggregate calculations involving such functions as Sum or Avg. You can test a value to determine whether it is a Null by comparing it to the special keyword NULL or by using the IsNull built-in function.

Table 4-3. Field Definitions for the Companies Table

Field Name	Data Type	Description	Field Size
CompanyID	AutoNumber	Unique Company ID	
CompanyName	Text	Company Name	50
Department	Text	Department	50
Address	Text	Address	255
City	Text	City	50
County	Text	County	50
StateOrProvince	Text	State or Province	20
PostalCode	Text	Postal/Zip Code	10
PhoneNumber	Text	Phone Number	15
FaxNumber	Text	Fax Number	15
WebSite	Hyperlink	Web site address	
ReferredBy	Number	Contact who referred this company	Long Integer

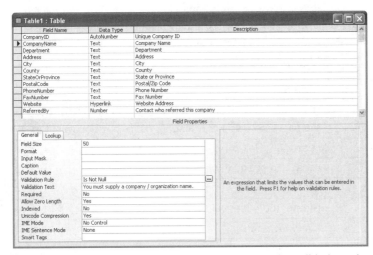

Figure 4-21. The fields in the Companies table and a validation rule on the CompanyName field.

Defining Simple Field Validation Rules

To define a simple check on the values that you allow in a field, enter an expression in the Validation Rule property box for the field. Access won't allow you to enter a field value that violates this rule. Access performs this validation for data entered in a Table window in Datasheet view, in an updateable query, or in a form. You can specify a more restrictive

111

validation rule in a form, but you cannot override the rule defined for the field in the table by specifying a completely different rule in the form. For more information on using validation rules in forms, see Chapter 12, "Customizing a Form."

In general, a field validation expression consists of an operator and a comparison value. If you do not include an operator, Access assumes you want an "equals" (=) comparison. You can specify multiple comparisons separated by the Boolean operators OR and AND.

It is good practice to always enclose text string values in quotation marks. If one of your values is a text string containing blanks or special characters, you must enclose the entire string in quotation marks. For example, to limit the valid entries for a City field to the two largest cities in the state of California, enter **"Los Angeles" Or "San Diego"**. If you are comparing date values, you must enclose the date constants in pound sign (#) characters, as in #01/15/2004#.

You can use the comparison symbols to compare the value in the field to a value or values in your validation rule. Comparison symbols are summarized in Table 4-4. For example, you might want to ensure that a numeric value is always less than 1000. To do this, enter **<1000**. You can use one or more pairs of comparisons to ask Access to check that the value falls within certain ranges. For example, if you want to verify that a number is in the range of 50 through 100, enter either **>=50 And <=100** or **Between 50 And 100**. Another way to test for a match in a list of values is to use the IN comparison operator. For example, to test for states surrounding the U.S. capital, enter **In ("Virginia", "Maryland")**. If all you need to do is ensure that the user enters a value, you can use the special comparison phrase **Is Not Null**.

Table 4-4. Comparison Symbols Used in Validation Rules

Operator	Meaning
NOT	Use before any comparison operator except IS NOT NULL to perform the converse test. For example, NOT > 5 is equivalent to <=5.
<	Less than
<=	Less than or equal to
>	Greater than
>=	Greater than or equal to
=	Equal to
<>	Not equal to
IN	Test for *equal to* any member in a list; comparison value must be a comma-separated list enclosed in parentheses
BETWEEN	Test for a range of values; comparison value must be two values (a low and a high value) separated by the AND operator
LIKE	Test a Text or Memo field to match a pattern string
IS NOT NULL	Requires the user to enter a value in the field

Inside Out

A more friendly way to require a field value

When you set the Required property to Yes and the user fails to enter a value, Access displays an unfriendly message:

"The field '<tablename.fieldname>' cannot contain a Null value because the Required property for this field is set to True. Enter a value in this field."

I recommend that you use the Validation Rule property to require a value in the field and then use the Validation Text property to generate your own more specific message.

If you need to validate a Text, Memo, or Hyperlink field against a matching pattern (for example, a postal code or a phone number), you can use the LIKE comparison operator. You provide a text string as a comparison value that defines which characters are valid in which positions. Access understands a number of *wildcard characters*, which you can use to define positions that can contain any single character, zero or more characters, or any single number. These characters are shown in Table 4-5.

Table 4-5. LIKE Wildcard Characters

Character	Meaning
?	Any single character
*	Zero or more characters; used to define leading, trailing, or embedded strings that don't have to match any specific pattern characters
#	Any single digit

You can also specify that any particular position in the Text or Memo field can contain only characters from a list that you provide. You can specify a range of characters within a list by entering the low value character, a hyphen, and the high value character, as in [A-Z] or [3-7]. If you want to test a position for any characters *except* those in a list, start the list with an exclamation point (!). You must enclose all lists in brackets ([ ]). You can see examples of validation rules using LIKE here.

Validation Rule	Tests For
LIKE "#####" or	A U.S. 5-digit ZIP Code
LIKE "#####-####"	A U.S. 9-digit ZIP+ Code
LIKE "[A-Z]#[A-Z] #[A-Z]#"	A Canadian postal code
LIKE "###-##-####"	A U.S. Social Security Number
LIKE "Smith*"	A string that begins with *Smith**
LIKE "*smith##*"	A string that contains *smith* followed by two numbers, anywhere in the string

Chapter 4

Validation Rule	Tests For
LIKE "??00####"	An eight-character string that contains any first two charac-ters followed by exactly two zeros and then any four digits
LIKE "[!0-9BMQ]*####"	A string that contains any character other than a number or the letter B, M, or Q in the first position and ends with exactly four digits

* Character string comparisons in Microsoft Access are case-insensitive. So, *smith*, *SMITH*, and *Smith* are all equal.

Defining Input Masks

To assist you in entering formatted data, Access allows you to define an *input mask* for Text, Number (except Replication ID), Date/Time, and Currency data types. You can use an input mask to do something as simple as forcing all letters entered to be uppercase or as complex as adding parentheses and hyphens to phone numbers. You create an input mask by using the special mask definition characters shown in Table 4-6. You can also embed strings of characters that you want displayed for formatting or stored in the data field.

Table 4-6. **Input Mask Definition Characters**

Mask Character	Meaning
0	A single digit must be entered in this position.
9	A digit or a space can be entered in this position. If the user skips this position by moving the cursor past the position without entering anything, Access stores nothing in this position.
#	A digit, a space, or a plus or minus sign can be entered in this position. If the user skips this position by moving the cursor past the position without entering anything, Access stores a space.
L	A letter must be entered in this position.
?	A letter can be entered in this position. If the user skips this position by moving the cursor past the position without entering anything, Access stores nothing.
A	A letter or a digit must be entered in this position.
a	A letter or a digit can be entered in this position. If the user skips this position by moving the cursor past the position without entering anything, Access stores nothing.
&	A character or a space must be entered in this position.
C	Any character or a space can be entered in this position. If the user skips this position by moving the cursor past the position without entering any-thing, Access stores nothing.

Table 4-6. Input Mask Definition Characters

Mask Character	Meaning
.	Decimal placeholder (depends on the setting in the regional settings in Windows Control Panel).
,	Thousands separator (depends on the setting in the regional settings in Windows Control Panel).
: ; - /	Date and time separators (depends on the settings in the regional settings in Windows Control Panel).
<	Converts to lowercase all characters that follow.
>	Converts to uppercase all characters that follow.
!	Causes the mask to fill from right to left when you define optional characters on the left end of the mask. You can place this character anywhere in the mask.
\	Causes the character immediately following to be displayed as a literal character rather than as a mask character.
"literal"	You can also enclose any literal string in double quotation marks rather than use the \ character repeatedly.

An input mask consists of three parts, separated by semicolons. The first part defines the mask string using mask definition characters and embedded literal data. The optional second part indicates whether you want the embedded literal characters stored in the field in the database. Set this second part to 0 to store the characters or to 1 to store only the data entered. The optional third part defines a single character that Access uses as a placeholder to indicate positions where data can be entered. The default placeholder character is an underscore (_).

Perhaps the best way to learn to use input masks is to take advantage of the Input Mask Wizard. In the Companies table of the Contact Tracking database, the PhoneNumber field could benefit from the use of an input mask. Click the PhoneNumber field in the upper part of the Table window in Design view, and then click in the Input Mask property box in the lower part of the window. You should see a small button with three dots on it (called the *Build* button) to the right of the property box.

Click the Build button to start the Input Mask Wizard. If you haven't already saved the table, the wizard will insist that you do so. Save the table and name it "Companies." When Access warns you that you have not defined a primary key and asks if you want to create a primary key now, click No. We'll define a primary key in the next section. In the first window of the Input Mask Wizard, you have a number of choices for standard input masks that can be generated for you. In this case, click the first one in the list—Phone Number, as shown in Figure 4-22 on the next page. Note that you can type something in the Try It box below the Input Mask selection box to try out the mask.

Chapter 4

Figure 4-22. Selecting an input mask in the Input Mask Wizard.

Click the Next button to go to the next window. In this window, shown in Figure 4-23, you can see the mask name, the proposed mask string, a drop-down list from which you select the placeholder character, and another Try It box. The default underscore character (_) works well as a placeholder character for phone numbers.

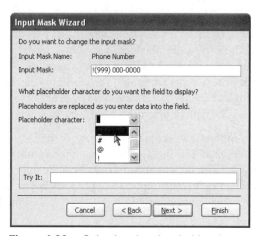

Figure 4-23. Selecting the placeholder character in the Input Mask Wizard.

Click Next to go to the next window, where you can choose whether you want the data stored without the formatting characters (the default) or stored with the parentheses, spaces, and hyphen separator. In Figure 4-24, we're indicating that we want the data stored with the formatting characters. Click Next to go to the final window, and then click the Finish button in that window to store the mask in the property setting. Figure 4-25 shows the resulting mask in the PhoneNumber field. You'll find this same mask handy for any text field that is meant to contain a U.S. phone number (such as the phone number fields in the Contacts table).

Chapter 4

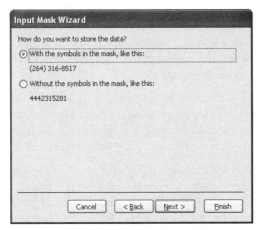

Figure 4-24. Opting to store formatting characters.

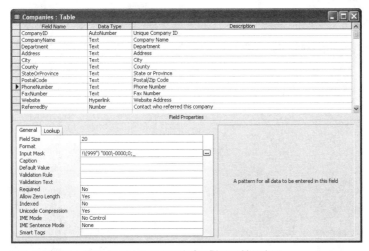

Figure 4-25. The field input mask for PhoneNumber.

Caution Although an input mask can be very useful to help guide the user to enter valid data, if you define an input mask incorrectly or do not consider all possible valid values, you can prevent the user from entering necessary data. For example, I just showed you how to build an input mask for a U.S. telephone number, but that mask would prevent someone from entering a European phone number correctly.

Defining a Primary Key

Every table in a relational database should have a primary key. If you use the procedure outlined in Chapter 3, "Designing Your Database Application," you should know what fields must make up the primary key for each of your tables.

Telling Microsoft Access how to define the primary key is quite simple. Open the table in Design view, and then select the first field for the primary key by clicking the row selector to the left of that field's name. If you need to select multiple fields for your primary key, hold down the Ctrl key and click the row selector of each additional field you need.

After you select all the fields you want for the primary key, click the Primary Key button on the toolbar or choose the Primary Key command from the Edit menu. Access displays a key symbol to the left of the selected field(s) to acknowledge your definition of the primary key. To eliminate all primary key designations, see the section titled "Adding Indexes," page 130. When you've finished creating the Companies table for the Contact Tracking database, the primary key should be the CompanyID field, as shown in Figure 4-26.

Be sure to click the Save button on the toolbar to save this latest change to your table definition.

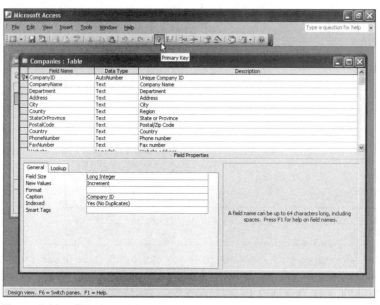

Figure 4-26. The Companies table with a primary key defined.

Defining a Table Validation Rule

The last detail to define is any validation rules that you want Microsoft Access to apply to any fields in the table. Although field validation rules get checked as you enter each new value, Access checks a table validation rule only when you save or add a row. Table validation rules are handy when the values in one field are dependent on what's stored in another field. You need to wait until the entire row is about to be saved before checking one field against another.

One of the tables in the Contact Tracking database—Products—needs a table validation rule. Define that table now using the specifications in Table 4-7. Be sure to define ProductID as the primary key and then save the table and name it Products.

Table 4-7. Field Definitions for the Products Table

Field Name	Data Type	Description	Field Size
ProductID	AutoNumber	Unique product identifier	
ProductName	Text	Product description	100
CategoryDescription	Text	Description of the category	50
UnitPrice	Currency	Price	
TrialVersion	Yes/No	Is this a trial version?	
TrialExpire	Number	If trial version, number of days before expiration	Long Integer

To define a table validation rule, be sure that the table is in Design view, and then click the Properties button on the toolbar or choose the Properties command from the View menu to open the Table Properties window, shown in Figure 4-27.

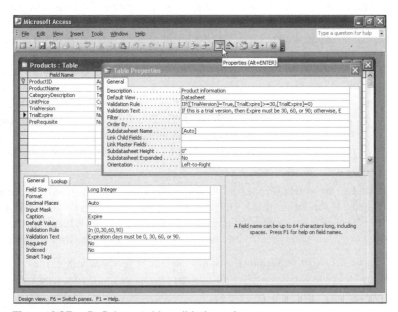

Figure 4-27. Defining a table validation rule.

To learn more about expressions, see "Using the Expression Builder," page 240.

On the Validation Rule line in the Table Properties window, you can enter any valid comparison expression, or you can use one of the built-in functions to test your table field values. In the Products table, we want to be sure that any trial version of the software expires in 30, 60, or 90 days. Zero is also a valid value if this particular product isn't a trial version. As you can see in Figure 4-27, I've already entered a *field* validation rule for TrialExpire on the General tab to make sure the TrialExpire value is always 0, 30, 60, or 90—IN (0, 30, 60, 90). But how do we make sure that TrialExpire is zero if TrialVersion is False, or one of the other values if TrialVersion is True? For that, we need to define a *table-level* validation rule in the Table Properties window.

To refer to a field name, enclose the name in brackets ([ ]), as shown in Figure 4-27. You'll use this technique whenever you refer to the name of an object anywhere in an expression. In this case, we're using a special built-in function called *Immediate If* (or *IIF* for short) in the table validation rule to perform the test on the TrialExpire and TrialVersion fields. The IIF function can evaluate a test in the first argument and then return the evaluation of the second argument if the first argument is true or the evaluation of the third argument if the first argument is false. As you will learn in Chapter 22, "Understanding Visual Basic Fundamentals," you must separate the arguments in a function with commas. Note that I said *evaluation of the argument*—this means I can enter additional tests, even another IIF, in the second and third arguments.

So, the first argument uses IIF to evaluate the expression [**TrialVersion**] = **True**—is the value in the field named TrialVersion True? If this is true (this is a trial version that must have a nonzero number of expiration days), IIF returns the evaluation of the second argument. If this is not a trial version, IIF evaluates the third argument. Now all we need to do is type in the appropriate test based on the true or false result on TrialVersion. If this is a trial version, the TrialExpire field must be 30 or greater (we'll let the field validation rule make sure it's exactly 30, 60, or 90), so we need to test for that by entering [**TrialExpire**] >= **30** in the second argument. If this is not a trial version, we need to make sure TrialExpire is zero by entering [**TrialExpire**] = **0** in the third argument. Got it? If TrialVersion is True, then [**TrialExpire**] >= 30 must be true or the validation rule will fail. If TrialVersion is False, then [**TrialExpire**] = 0 must be true. As you might imagine, once you become more familiar with building expressions and with the available built-in functions, you can create very sophisticated table validation rules.

On the fourth line in the Table Properties window, enter the text that you want Access to display whenever the table validation rule is violated. You should be careful to word this message so that the user clearly understands what is wrong. If you enter a table validation rule and fail to specify validation text, Access displays the following message when the user enters invalid data.

One or more values are prohibited by the validation rule '< your validation rule expression here >' set for '<table name>'. Enter a value that the expression for this field can accept.

Not very pretty, is it? And you can imagine what the user will say about your IIF expression!

Understanding Other Table Properties

As you can see in Figure 4-27, Access provides several additional table properties that you can set in Design view. You can enter a description of the table on the first line, and you'll see this description in the Database window if you select the details view. For Default View, you can choose from Datasheet (the default), PivotTable, or PivotChart. You can read more about PivotTable and PivotChart views in Chapter 13, "Advanced Form Design."

The Filter property lets you predefine criteria to limit the data displayed in the Datasheet view of this table. You can use Order By to define one or more fields that define the default display sequence of rows in this table when in Datasheet view. If you don't define an Order By property, Access displays the rows in primary key sequence.

The next five properties—Subdatasheet Name, Link Child Fields, Link Master Fields, Subdatasheet Height, and Subdatasheet Expanded—are all related. Microsoft Access 2000 introduced a feature that lets you see information from related tables when you view the datasheet of a table. For example, in the Contacts Tracking database you have been building, you can set the Subdatasheet properties in the definition of Contacts to also show you related information from ContactEvents or ContactProducts. In the Proseware Housing Reservations sample database, you can see Departments and their Employees or Employees and their Reservation Requests. Figure 4-28 shows you the Departments table in *Housing.mdb* open in Datasheet view. For this table, I defined a subdatasheet to show related Employee information for each department.

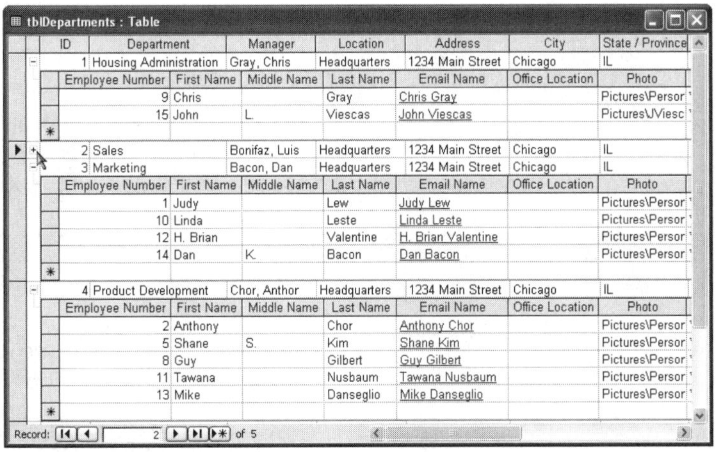
tblDepartments : Table

ID	Department	Manager	Location	Address	City	State / Province
1	Housing Administration	Gray, Chris	Headquarters	1234 Main Street	Chicago	IL
Employee Number	First Name	Middle Name	Last Name	Email Name	Office Location	Photo
9	Chris		Gray	Chris Gray		Pictures\Persor
15	John	L.	Viescas	John Viescas		Pictures\JViesc
2	Sales	Bonifaz, Luis	Headquarters	1234 Main Street	Chicago	IL
3	Marketing	Bacon, Dan	Headquarters	1234 Main Street	Chicago	IL
Employee Number	First Name	Middle Name	Last Name	Email Name	Office Location	Photo
1	Judy		Lew	Judy Lew		Pictures\Persor
10	Linda		Leste	Linda Leste		Pictures\Persor
12	H. Brian		Valentine	H. Brian Valentine		Pictures\Persor
14	Dan	K.	Bacon	Dan Bacon		Pictures\Persor
4	Product Development	Chor, Anthor	Headquarters	1234 Main Street	Chicago	IL
Employee Number	First Name	Middle Name	Last Name	Email Name	Office Location	Photo
2	Anthony		Chor	Anthony Chor		Pictures\Persor
5	Shane	S.	Kim	Shane Kim		Pictures\Persor
8	Guy		Gilbert	Guy Gilbert		Pictures\Persor
11	Tawana		Nusbaum	Tawana Nusbaum		Pictures\Persor
13	Mike		Danseglio	Mike Danseglio		Pictures\Persor

Record: 2 of 5

Figure 4-28. The datasheet for the Departments table in the Proseware Housing Reservations sample database shows expanded subdatasheets.

Notice the small plus and minus signs at the beginning of each department row. Click on a plus sign to expand the subdatasheet to show related employees. Click on the minus sign to shrink the subdatasheet and show only department information. Table 4-8 on the next page explains each of the Table Property settings that you can specify to attach a subdatasheet to a table.

Chapter 4

Table 4-8. Table Properties for Defining a Subdatasheet

Property Name	Setting	Description
Subdatasheet Name	[Auto]	Creates a subdatasheet using the first table that has a *many* relationship defined with this table.
	[None]	Turns off the subdatasheet feature.
	Table.*name* or Query.*name*	Uses the selected table or query as the subdatasheet.
Link Child Fields	Name(s) of the foreign key field(s) in the related table, separated by semicolons	Defines the fields in the subdatasheet table or query that match the primary key fields in this table. When you choose a table or query for the Subdatasheet Name property, Access uses an available relationship definition or matching field names and data types to automatically set this property for you. You can correct this setting if Access has guessed wrong.
Link Master Fields	Name(s) of the primary key field(s) in this table, separated by semicolons	Defines the primary key fields that Access uses to link to the subdatasheet table or query. When you choose a table or query for the Subdatasheet Name property, Access uses an available relationship definition or matching field names and data types to automatically set this property for you. You can correct this setting if Access has guessed wrong.
Subdatasheet Height	A measurement in inches	If you specify zero (the default), each subdatasheet expands to show all available rows when opened. When you specify a nonzero value, the subdatasheet window opens to the height you specify. If the height is insufficient to display all rows, a scroll bar appears to allow you to look at all the rows.
Subdatasheet Expanded	Yes or No	If you specify Yes, all subdatasheets appear expanded when you open the table datasheet. No is the default.

Inside Out

Don't set subdatasheet properties in a table

For a production application, it's a good idea to set Subdatasheet Name in all your tables to [None]. First, when Access opens your table, it must not only fetch the rows from the table but also fetch the rows defined in the subdatasheet. Adding a subdatasheet to a large table can negatively impact performance.

Also, any production application should not allow the user to see table or query datasheets because you cannot enforce complex business rules. Any data validation in a table or query datasheet depends entirely on the validation and referential integrity rules defined for your tables because you cannot define any Visual Basic code behind tables or queries.

However, you might find the table and query subdatasheets feature useful in your own personal databases. I'll show you how to build a query with a subdatasheet in Chapter 8, "Building Complex Queries," and a form that uses a subdatasheet in Chapter 13, "Advanced Form Design."

The last property available in the Table Properties window is Orientation. The default in most versions of Microsoft Access is Left-to-Right. In versions that support a language that is normally read right to left, the default is Right-to-Left. When you use Right-to-Left, field and table captions appear right-justified, the field order is right to left, and the tab sequence proceeds right to left.

Defining Relationships

After you have defined two or more related tables, you should tell Microsoft Access how the tables are related. You do this so that Access will be able to link all your tables when you need to use them in queries, forms, data access pages, or reports.

Thus far in this chapter, you have seen how to build the main subject tables of the Contact Tracking database—Companies, Contacts, and Products. Before we define the relationships in the sample database you've been building, you need to create a couple of *linking* tables that define the many-to-many relationships between Companies and Contacts and between Products and Contacts. Table 4-9 on the next page shows you the fields you need for the Company Contacts table that forms the "glue" between the Companies and Contacts tables.

Table 4-9. Field Definitions for the Company Contacts Table

Field Name	Data Type	Description	Field Size
CompanyID	Number	Company/organization	Long Integer
ContactID	Number	Person within company	Long Integer
Position	Text	Person's position within the company	50
DefaultForContact	Yes/No	Is this the default company for this contact?	

Define the combination of CompanyID and ContactID as the primary key for this table by clicking the selection button next to CompanyID and then holding down the Ctrl key and clicking the button next to ContactID. Click the Primary Key button on the toolbar to define the key and save the table as CompanyContacts.

Table 4-10 shows you the fields you need to define the Contact Products linking table between the Contacts and Products tables.

Table 4-10. Field Definitions for the Contact Products Table

Field Name	Data Type	Description	Field Size
CompanyID	Number	Company/organization	Long Integer
ContactID	Number	Related contact	Long Integer
ProductID	Number	Related product	Long Integer
DateSold	Date/Time	Date product sold	
SoldPrice	Currency	Price paid	

As you might remember from Chapter 3, the primary key of the Contact Products table is the combination of CompanyID, ContactID, and ProductID. You can click CompanyID to select it, then hold down the Shift key while you click ProductID (if you defined the fields in sequence) to select all three fields. Click the Primary Key button on the toolbar to define the key, and save the table as ContactProducts.

You need one last table, the Contact Events table, to define all the major tables you'll need for Contact Tracking as we designed it in Chapter 3. Table 4-11 shows you the fields you need. The primary key for this table is the combination of ContactID and ContactDateTime. Note that we took advantage of the fact that a Date/Time data type in Access can store both a date and a time, so we don't need two separate date and time fields.

Table 4-11. Field Definitions for the Contact Events Table

Field Name	Data Type	Description	Field Size
ContactID	Number	Related contact	Long Integer
ContactDateTime	Date/Time	Date and time of the contact	
ContactNotes	Memo	Description of the contact	
ContactFollowUpDate	Date/Time	Follow-up date	

Now you're ready to start defining relationships. To define relationships, you need to return to the Database window by closing any Table windows that are open and then clicking in the Database window to make it active. Choose the Relationships command from the Tools menu to open the relationships definition window. If this is the first time you have defined relationships in this database, Access opens a blank Relationships window and opens the Show Table dialog box, shown in Figure 4-29.

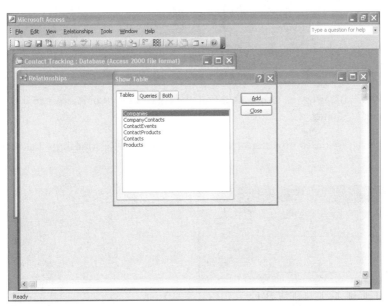

Figure 4-29. The Show Table dialog box.

In the Show Table dialog box, select each table and click the Add button in turn. Click Close to dismiss the Show Table dialog box.

Defining Your First Relationship

If you remember the design work you did in Chapter 3, "Designing Your Database Application," you know that a company can have several contacts, and any contact can belong to several companies or organizations. This means that companies have a many-to-many relationship with contacts. You should also recall that defining a many-to-many relationship between two tables requires a linking table. Let's link the Companies and Contacts tables by defining the first half of the relationship—the one between Companies and the linking table, CompanyContacts. You can see that for the CompanyID primary key in the Companies table, there is a matching CompanyID foreign key in the CompanyContacts table. To create the relationship you need, click in the CompanyID field in the Companies table and drag it to the CompanyID field in the CompanyContacts table, as shown in Figure 4-30.

Figure 4-30. Dragging the linking field from the "one" table (Companies) to the "many" table (CompanyContacts).

When you release the mouse button, Access opens the Edit Relationships dialog box, shown in Figure 4-31.

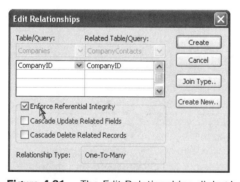

Figure 4-31. The Edit Relationships dialog box.

Tip You can also choose Edit Relationship from the Relationships menu to create a new relationship, but you have to fill in the table and field names yourself. Dragging and dropping does some of this work for you.

You'll notice that Access has filled in the field names for you. If you need to define a multiple-field relationship between two tables, use the additional blank lines to define those fields (we'll do that in just a second). Because you probably don't want any rows created in CompanyContacts for a nonexistent company, click the Enforce Referential Integrity check box. When you do this, Access ensures that you can't add a row in the CompanyContacts table containing an invalid CompanyID. Also, Access won't let you delete any records from the Companies table if they have contacts still defined.

Note that after you click the Enforce Referential Integrity check box, Access makes two additional options available: Cascade Update Related Fields and Cascade Delete Related Records. If you select Cascade Delete Related Records, Access deletes child rows (the related rows in the *many* table of a one-to-many relationship) when you delete a parent row (the related row in the *one* table of a one-to-many relationship). For example, if you removed a company from the database, Access would remove the related Company Contact rows. In this database design, the CompanyID field has the AutoNumber data type, so it cannot be changed once it is set. However, if you build a table with a primary key that is Text or Number (perhaps a ProductID field that could change at some point in the future), it might be a good idea to select Cascade Update Related Fields. This option requests that Access automatically update any foreign key values in the *child* table (the *many* table in a one-to-many relationship) if you change a primary key value in a *parent* table (the *one* table in a one-to-many relationship).

You might have noticed that the Show Table dialog box, shown earlier in Figure 4-29, gives you the option to include queries as well as tables. Sometimes you might want to define relationships between tables and queries or between queries so that Access knows how to join them properly. You can also define what's known as an *outer join* by clicking the Join Type button in the Relationships dialog box and selecting an option in the Join Properties dialog box. With an outer join, you can find out, for example, which companies have no contacts or which products haven't been sold.

For details about outer joins, see "Using Outer Joins," page 287.

Inside Out

Avoid defining a relationship with an outer join

I recommend that you do not define an outer join relationship between two tables. As you'll learn in Chapter 8, "Building Complex Queries," Access automatically links two tables you include in a query design using the relationships you have defined. In the vast majority of cases, you will want to include only the matching rows from both tables. If you define the relationship as an outer join, you will have to change the link between the two tables every time you include them in a query.

I also do not recommend that you define relationships between queries or between a table and a query. If you have done a good job of naming your fields in your tables, the query designer will recognize the natural links and define the joins for you automatically. Defining extra relationships adds unnecessary overhead in your database application.

Click the Create button to finish your relationship definition. Access draws a line between the two tables to indicate the relationship. Notice that when you ask Access to enforce referential integrity, Access displays a 1 at the end of the relationship line, next to the *one* table, and an infinity symbol (∞) next to the *many* table. If you want to delete the relationship, click the line and press the Delete key.

You now know enough to define the additional one-to-many simple relationships that you need. Go ahead and define a relationship on ContactID between the Contacts and Company-Contacts tables to complete the other side of the many-to-many relationship between Companies and Contacts, a relationship on ContactID between the Contacts and Contact Events tables, and a relationship on ProductID between the Products and ContactProducts tables.

Creating a Relationship on Multiple Fields

There's one last relationship you need to define in the Contact Tracking database between CompanyContacts and ContactProducts. The relationship between these two tables requires multiple fields from each table. You can start by dragging the CompanyID field from the CompanyContacts table to the ContactProducts table. Access opens the Edit Relationships dialog box.

When you first see the Edit Relationships dialog box for the relationship you are defining between CompanyContacts and ContactProducts, Access shows you only the CompanyID field in the two lists. To complete the relationship definition on the combination of CompanyID and ContactID, you must click in the second line under both tables and select ContactID as the second field for both tables, as shown in Figure 4-32. Select Enforce Referential Integrity as shown and click Create to define the compound relationship.

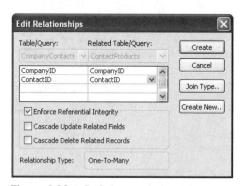

Figure 4-32. Defining a relationship between two tables using multiple fields.

Figure 4-33 shows the Relationships window for all the main tables in your Contact Tracking database. Notice that there are two linking lines that define the relationship between CompanyContacts and ContactProducts.

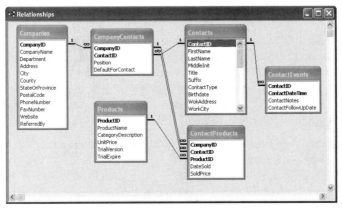

Figure 4-33. The Relationships window showing all the main tables in your Contact Tracking database.

If you want to edit or change any relationship, double-click the line to open the Edit Relationships dialog box again. If you want to remove a relationship definition, click on the line linking two tables to select the relationship (the line appears highlighted) and press the Delete key. Access presents a warning dialog box in case you are asking it to delete a relationship in error.

Note that once you define a relationship, you can delete the table or query field lists from the Relationships window without affecting the relationships. To do this, click the table or query list header and press the Delete key. This can be particularly advantageous in large databases that have dozens of tables. You can also display only those tables that you're working with at the moment. To see the relationships defined for any particular table or query, include it in the Relationships window by using the Show Table dialog box, and then click the Show Direct Relationships button on the toolbar or choose Show Direct from the Relationships menu. To redisplay all relationships, click the Show All Relationships button on the toolbar or choose Show All from the Relationships menu.

When you close the Relationships window, Access asks whether you want to save your layout changes. Click Yes to save the relationships you've defined. That's all there is to it. Later, when you use multiple tables in a query in Chapter 7, "Creating and Working with Simple Queries," you'll see that Access builds the links between tables based on these relationships.

Tip Additional features in the Relationships window

You can right-click any table in the Relationships window and then choose Table Design from the shortcut menu to open that table in Design view. You can also choose Print Relationships from the File menu while viewing the Relationships window to create a report that prints what you laid out in the window.

Chapter 4

Adding Indexes

The more data you include in your tables, the more you need indexes to help Microsoft Access search your data efficiently. An *index* is simply an internal table that contains two columns: the value in the field or fields being indexed and the physical location of each record in your table that contains that value. Access uses an index similarly to how you use the index in this book—you find the term you want and jump directly to the pages containing that term. You don't have to leaf through all the pages to find the information you want.

Let's assume that you often search your Contacts table by city. Without an index, when you ask Access to find all the Contacts who live in the city of Chicago, Access has to search every record in your table. This search is fast if your table includes only a few contacts but very slow if the table contains thousands of contact records collected over many years. If you create an index on the HomeCity field, Access can use the index to find more rapidly the records for the contacts in the city you specify.

Single Field Indexes

Most of the indexes you'll need to define will probably contain the values from only a single field. Access uses this type of index to help narrow down the number of records it has to search whenever you provide search criteria on the field—for example, *HomeCity = Chicago* or *HomePostalCode = 60633*. If you have defined indexes for multiple fields and provided search criteria for more than one of the fields, Access uses the indexes together (using a technology called Rushmore from Microsoft FoxPro) to find the rows you want quickly. For example, if you have created one index on HomeCity and another on LastName and you ask for *HomeCity = Austin* and *LastName = Viescas*, Access uses the entries in the HomeCity index that equal *Austin* and matches those with the entries in the LastName index that equal *Viescas*. The result is a small set of pointers to the records that match both criteria.

Creating an index on a single field in a table is easy. Open the Contacts table in Design view, and select the field for which you want an index—in this case, WorkStateOrProvince. Click the Indexed property box in the lower part of the Table window, and then click the down arrow to open the list of choices, as shown in Figure 4-34.

When you create a table from scratch (as you did earlier in this chapter for the Companies table), the default Indexed property setting for all fields except the primary key is No. If you use the Table Wizard to create a table (as you did for the Contacts table in this chapter), the wizard indexes fields that might benefit from an index. If you followed along earlier using the Table Wizard to build the Contacts table, you will find that the wizard built indexes for the EmailName, LastName, WorkPostalCode, and HomePostalCode fields.

130

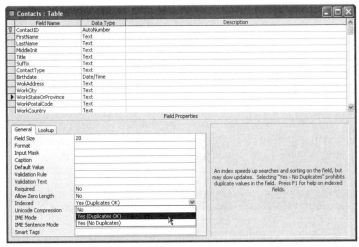

Figure 4-34. Using the Indexed property box to set an index on a single field.

If you want to set an index for a field, Access offers two possible Yes choices. In most cases, a given field will have multiple records with the same value—perhaps you have multiple contacts in a particular state or province or multiple products in the same product category. You should select Yes (Duplicates OK) to create an index for this type of field. By selecting Yes (No Duplicates) you can use Access to enforce unique values in any field by creating an index that doesn't allow duplicates. Access always defines the primary key index with no duplicates because, as you learned in Chapter 3, all primary key values must be unique.

> **Note** You cannot define an index using an OLE Object field.

Multiple-Field Indexes

If you often provide multiple criteria in searches against large tables, you might want to consider creating a few multiple-field indexes. This helps Access narrow the search quickly without having to match values from two separate indexes. For example, suppose you often perform a search for contacts by last name, first name, and middle name. If you create an index that includes all these fields, Access can satisfy your query more rapidly.

To create a multiple-field index, you must open the Table window in Design view and open the Indexes window by clicking the Indexes button on the toolbar or by choosing the Indexes command from the View menu. You can see the primary key index and the index that you defined on the WorkStateOrProvince field in the previous section as well as the indexes defined by the Table Wizard. Each of these indexes comprises exactly one field.

To create a multiple-field index, move the cursor to an empty row in the Indexes window and type a unique name. In this example, you want a multiple-field index using the LastName, FirstName, and MiddleName fields, so *FullName* might be a reasonable index name. Select the LastName field in the Field Name column of this row. To add the other fields, skip down to the next row and select another field without typing a new index name. When you're done, your Indexes window should look like the one shown in Figure 4-35.

> **Tip**   To insert a row in the middle of the list in the Indexes window, right-click in the Index Name column and then choose Insert Rows from the shortcut menu. Do not click the Insert Rows button on the main toolbar—that inserts rows into the main table design.

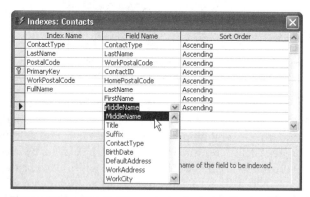

Figure 4-35.   The FullName index includes the LastName, FirstName, and MiddleName fields.

You can remove an existing single-field index by changing the Indexed property of a field to No. The only way to remove a multiple-field index is via the Indexes window. To remove a multiple-field index, highlight the rows (by holding down the Ctrl key as you click each row selector) that define the index and then press the Delete key. Access saves any index changes you make when you save the table definition.

Access can use a multiple-field index in a search even if you don't provide search values for all the fields, as long as you provide search criteria for consecutive fields starting with the first field. Therefore, with the FullName multiple-field index shown in Figure 4-35, you can search for last name; for last name and first name; or for last name, first name, and middle name. There's one additional limitation on when Access can use multiple-field indexes: only the last search criterion you supply can be an inequality, such as >, >=, <, or <=. In other words, Access can use the index shown in Figure 4-35 when you specify searches such as these:

```
LastName = "Smith"
LastName > "Franklin"
LastName = "Buchanan" And FirstName = "Steven"
LastName = "Viescas" And FirstName >= "Bobby"
```

But Access will not use the FullName index shown in Figure 4-35 if you ask for

```
LastName > "Davolio" And FirstName > "John"
```

because only the last field in the search string (FirstName) can be an inequality. Access also will not use this index if you ask for

```
FirstName = "John"
```

because the first field of the multiple-field index (LastName) is missing from the search criterion.

Setting Table Design Options

Now that you understand the basic mechanics of defining tables in your desktop database, it's useful to take a look at a few options you can set to customize how you work with tables in Design view. Close any open tables so that all you see is the Database window. From the Tools menu, choose Options to take a look at all the custom settings offered.

You can find the first options that affect table design on the General tab, as shown in Figure 4-36. One option that I highly recommend you use is four-digit year formatting. When you set four-digit year formatting, Access displays all year values in date/time formats with four digits instead of two. This is important because when you see a value (in two-digit medium date format) such as 15 MAR 12, you won't be able to easily tell whether this is March 15, 1912 or March 15, 2012. Although you can affect the display of some formats in your regional settings in Windows Control Panel, you won't affect them all unless you set four-digit formatting in Access.

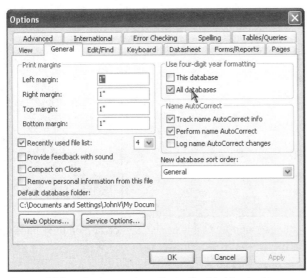

Figure 4-36. Some settings that affect table design are on the General tab of the Options dialog box.

Chapter 4

As you can see in Figure 4-36, you have two options under Use four-digit year formatting on the General tab. If you choose This database, the setting creates a property in the database you currently have open and affects only that database. If you choose All databases, the setting creates an entry in your Windows registry that affects all databases that you open on your machine.

On this tab, you can also choose a feature that was introduced in Access 2000 called Name AutoCorrect that asks Access to track and correct field name references in queries, forms, and reports. If you choose Track name AutoCorrect info, Access maintains a unique internal ID number for all field names. This allows you to use the new Object Dependencies feature explained in the next chapter. It also allows you to select the next option, Perform name AutoCorrect.

If you choose Perform name AutoCorrect, when you change a field name in a table, Access automatically propagates the name change to other objects (queries, forms, reports, and pages) that use the field. However, Track name AutoCorrect requires some additional overhead in all your objects, so it's a good idea to carefully choose names as you design your tables so that you won't need to change them later. Finally, if you choose Log name AutoCorrect changes, Access logs all changes it makes in a table called AutoCorrect Log. You can open this table to verify the changes made by this feature. (Access doesn't create the table until it makes some changes.)

The next tab that contains useful settings that affect table design is the Tables/Queries tab. Click that tab to see the settings shown in Figure 4-37.

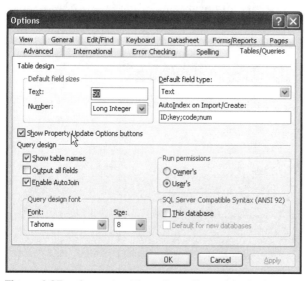

Figure 4-37.   Several settings that affect table design are located on the Tables/Queries tab of the Options dialog box.

In the upper left corner of this tab, you can set the default field sizes for Text and Number fields. When you choose a data type of Text, Access will automatically fill in the length you choose. When you choose a data type of Number, Access sets the number size to your choice of Byte, Integer, Long Integer, Single, Double, Decimal, or Replication ID. In the upper right corner, you can choose the default data type that Access selects when you type in a new field name in table design and then tab to the Data Type column. Use the AutoIndex on Import/ Create field to define a list of field name prefixes or suffixes for which Access automatically sets the Index property to Yes (Duplicates OK). In the default list, for example, any field that you define with a name that begins or ends with "ID" will automatically have an index.

The last item on this tab that affects how you work in table Design view is Show Property Update Options buttons. If you choose this option, a smart tag appears that offers to automatically update related properties in queries, forms, and reports when you change certain field properties in a table design. You can see more details about this option in the next chapter.

You can find the last option that affects how your tables are stored (and, in fact, all objects in your database) on the Advanced tab shown in Figure 4-38. When you create a new database in Microsoft Access 11, you actually have a choice of two different file formats. You would think that you would see this option in the File New Database dialog box, but it's actually buried away in the Options dialog box. You should use the Access 2000 format if others with whom you might share this database are still using Microsoft Access version 9 (2000). Choosing the Access 2002 format ensures maximum compatibility of what you build in Access with future versions of the product.

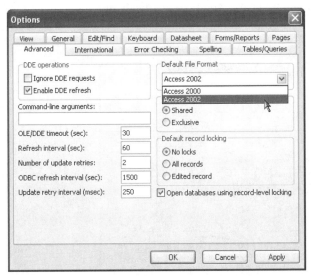

Figure 4-38. Choosing your default database file format.

Printing a Table Definition

After you create several tables, you might want to print out their definitions to provide a permanent paper record. You can do this by selecting Analyze on the Tools menu and then choosing Documenter from the submenu. Microsoft Access displays several options in the Documenter dialog box, as shown in Figure 4-39.

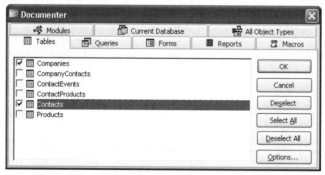

Figure 4-39. The Documenter dialog box.

You can select not only the type of object you want to document but also which objects you want to document. Click the Options button to select what you want reported. For example, you can ask for the properties, relationships, and permissions for a table; the names, data types, sizes, and properties for fields; and the names, fields, and properties for indexes. Click OK in the Documenter dialog box to produce the report and view it in Print Preview, as shown in Figure 4-40.

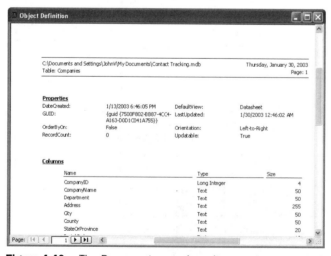

Figure 4-40. The Documenter previews its reports on your screen.

Database Limitations

As you design your database, you should keep in mind the following limitations:

- A table can have up to 255 fields.
- A table can have up to 32 indexes.

> **Important** Keep in mind that defining relationships with Referential Integrity turned on creates one additional index in each participating table that counts toward the 32-index limit per table.

- A multiple-field index can have up to 10 fields. The sum of the lengths of the fields cannot exceed 255 bytes.
- A row in a table, excluding memo fields and ActiveX objects, can be no longer than approximately 4 kilobytes.
- A memo field can store up to 1 gigabyte of characters,[1] but you can't display a memo larger than 64 kilobytes in a form or a datasheet.
- An ActiveX object can be up to 2 gigabytes in size.
- There is no limit on the number of records in a table, but an Access database cannot be larger than 2 gigabytes. If you have several large tables, you might need to define each one in a separate Access database and then attach them to the database that contains the forms, reports, macros, and modules for your applications. See Chapter 6, "Importing and Linking Data," for details.

Now that you've started to get comfortable with creating databases and tables, you can read the next chapter to learn how to make modifications to existing tables in a database.

Chapter 4

---

1. Clearly, if you try to store a 1-gigabyte memo (which requires 2 gigabytes of storage because of double-byte character set support) or a 2-gigabyte ActiveX object in your database file, your file will be full with the data from one record.

Modifying Your Table Design

No matter how carefully you design your database, you can be sure that you'll need to change it at some later date. Here are some of the reasons you might need to change your database.

- You no longer need some of the tables.

- You need to perform some new tasks that require not only creating new tables but also inserting some linking fields in existing tables.

- You find that you use some fields in a table much more frequently than others, so it would be easier if those fields appeared first in the table design.

- You no longer need some of the fields.

- You want to add some new fields that are similar to fields that already exist.

- You discover that some of the data you defined would be better stored as a different data type. For example, a field that you originally designed to be all numbers (such as a U.S. ZIP Code) must now contain some letters (as in a Canadian postal code).

- You have a number field that needs to hold larger values or needs a different number of decimal places than you originally planned.

- You can improve your database design by splitting an existing table into two or more tables using the Table Analyzer Wizard.

- You discover that the field you defined as a primary key isn't always unique, so you need to change the definition of your primary key.

- You find that some of your queries take too long to run and might execute faster if you add an index to your table.

Note The examples in this chapter are based on the tables and data in *Housing.mdb*, *Contact Tracking.mdb*, and *Contacts.mdb* on the companion CD included with this book. The results you see from the samples you build in this chapter may not exactly match what you see in this book if you have changed the sample data in the files. Also, all the screen images in this chapter were taken on a Windows XP system with the display theme set to Windows XP, and Use Windows Themed Controls on Forms has been turned on in the sample databases.

This chapter takes a look at how you can make these changes easily and relatively painlessly with Microsoft Access. If you want to follow along with the examples in this chapter, you should first create the Contact Tracking database described in Chapter 4, "Creating Your Database and Tables."

> **Note** You might have noticed that the Contacts table you defined for the Contact Tracking database in Chapter 4 is different from the tblContacts table in the LawTrack Contacts database on the companion CD that comes with this book. In this chapter, you'll modify the Contacts table you built in Chapter 4 so that it is more like the one on the companion CD. You'll also learn how to use the Table Analyzer Wizard to help you normalize an existing table that contains data from several subjects.

Before You Get Started

Microsoft Access makes it easy for you to change the design of your database, even when you already have data in your tables. You should, however, understand the potential impact of any changes you plan and take steps to ensure that you can recover your previous design if you make a mistake. Here are some things to consider before you make changes.

- Access does not automatically propagate changes that you make in tables to any queries, forms, reports, macros, data access pages, or modules. You must make changes to dependent objects yourself, or choose Options from the Tools menu and then select the option on the General tab to ask Access to autocorrect table field name changes for you. See "Setting Table Design Options," page 133, for more details.

- You cannot change the data type of a field that is part of a relationship between tables. You must first delete the relationship, and then change the field's data type and redefine the relationship.

- You cannot change the definition of any table that you have open in a query, a form, a data access page, or a report. You must close any objects that refer to the table you want to change before you open that table in Design view. If you give other users access to your database over a network, you won't be able to change the table definition if someone else has the table (or a query or form based on the table) open.

> **Tip** Before saving any changes that permanently alter or delete data in your database, Access always prompts you for confirmation and gives you a chance to cancel the operation.

Making a Backup Copy

The safest way to make changes to the design of your database is to make a backup copy of the database before you begin. If you expect to make extensive changes to several tables in your database, you should also make a copy of the .mdb file that contains your database. You could use a utility such as Windows Explorer, but Microsoft Office Access 2003 includes a handy new feature for making backups easily. When you have the database open that you want to back up, choose Back Up Database from the File menu. Access offers to create a copy of your database with the current date appended in the file name.

If you want to change a single table, you can easily make a backup copy of that table right in your database. Use the following procedure to copy any table—structure and the data together.

1   Open the database containing the table you want to copy. If the database is already open, click the Tables button in the Database window.

2   Select the table you want to copy by clicking the table's name or icon in the Database window. The table name will be highlighted.

3   Choose the Copy command from the Edit menu (as shown in Figure 5-1), or click the Copy button on the toolbar. This copies the entire table (structure and data) to the Clipboard.

Figure 5-1.   Using the Copy command to copy a table from the Tables list.

4   Choose the Paste command from the Edit menu, or click the Paste button on the toolbar. Access opens the Paste Table As dialog box, shown in Figure 5-2. Type in a new name for your table. (When naming a backup copy, you might simply add *Backup* and the date to the original table name, as shown in Figure 5-2.) The default option is to copy both the structure and the data. (You also have the option of copying only the table's structure or of appending the data to another table.)

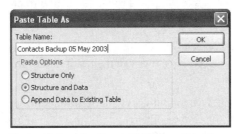

Figure 5-2.   The Paste Table As dialog box.

Checking Object Dependencies

If you're just starting out and learning Microsoft Access by reading this book through from the beginning, you probably haven't built anything but tables yet. The new Object Dependency tool in Microsoft Access won't provide very interesting results in a database with nothing but tables, but you'll find this tool invaluable later after you have built dozens of objects and then need to make some changes to your tables.

As you learned in the previous chapter, you can turn on features to track and perform Name AutoCorrect for objects by choosing Options from the Tools menu and then selecting these features on the General tab. Microsoft Access 2003 uses this AutoCorrect information not only to automatically correct names but also to provide you with detailed information about which objects depend on one another. If you're about to make a change to a field in a table, wouldn't it be good to know which queries, forms, and reports use that table before you make the change? The Perform name AutoCorrect feature will help you out if you have enabled it, but it can't always detect and fix field names when you have used them in an expression. You'll learn more about creating expressions in Chapter 7, "Creating and Working with Simple Queries," and in the chapters on using Visual Basic later in this book.

If you would like to see the Object Dependencies feature in action on your machine, open one of your own databases that contains tables, queries, forms, and reports, or open the LawTrack Contacts sample database (*Contacts.mdb*) that you installed from the companion CD. You can find out which other objects depend on a particular object (such as a table) by selecting the object that you're planning to change in the Database window and then choosing Object Dependencies from the View menu. You can also select an object, right-click, and choose Object Dependencies from the shortcut menu. If you haven't turned on Track name AutoCorrect info (or have turned it off), Access shows you the dialog box in Figure 5-3.

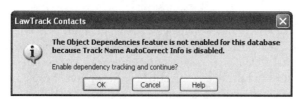

Figure 5-3. The Object Dependencies feature tells you it needs to turn on Track name AutoCorrect info and examine all objects in your database.

Click OK to turn on Name AutoCorrect—the Object Dependencies feature will take a few seconds to examine all your objects. Access shows you the result in the Object Dependencies task pane as shown in Figure 5-4.

Notice that in many cases you will have to follow a chain of dependencies to find all the objects that might be affected by the change of a field name in a table. For example, in the LawTrack Contacts sample database, I use a query (qryContacts) rather than the table (tblContacts) to provide records to the form that edits contact information (frmContacts). If I were to scroll further down the Object Dependencies window looking for forms dependent on tblContacts, I would not find the form frmContacts listed.

Task pane

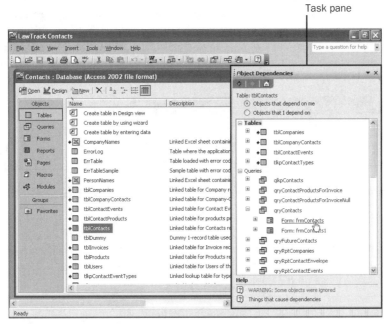

Figure 5-4. Examining the list of objects in the task pane that depend on an object selected in the Database window.

You can click the plus sign next to any object name to open an expanded list of dependent objects as I did with qryContacts in Figure 5-4. Notice that we find frmContacts listed there as a dependent object of qryContacts, which is ultimately dependent on the table we're thinking about changing. When you find an object that you want to investigate further, you can click the object name to open it in Design view.

As you can imagine, this new tool can make maintaining your application much easier. Even if you have the Perform name AutoCorrect feature enabled, you can use this tool after you have modified your table to verify that the changes you expect were made.

Deleting Tables

You probably won't need to delete an entire table very often. However, if you set up your application to collect historical information—for example, total product sales by year— you'll eventually want to delete information that you no longer need. You also might want to delete a table if you've made extensive changes that are incorrect and it would be easier to delete your work and restore the table from a backup.

To delete a table, select it in the Database window and press the Delete key (or choose the Delete command from the Edit menu). Access opens the dialog box shown in Figure 5-5 on the next page, which asks you to confirm or cancel the delete operation.

Chapter 5

Tip Even if you mistakenly confirm the table deletion, you can select the Undo command from the Edit menu to get your table back. In fact, you can undo up to the last 20 changes that you made in the Database window. You can also undo up to 20 changes in table Design view; however, once you save changes to a table design, you will not be able to undo those changes.

Figure 5-5. This dialog box gives you the option of canceling the deletion of a table.

Tip You can use the Cut command on the Edit menu or the Cut button on the toolbar to delete a table. Both of these methods place a copy of the table on the Clipboard. After you close the database in which you've been working, you can open another database and paste the table that's on the Clipboard into it.

If the warning dialog box doesn't look exactly like Figure 5-5, it might be because you turned on the Microsoft Office Assistant. If you chose the option to have it display alerts, the Office Assistant will respond with any Access warning message, as shown in Figure 5-6. In this message, the Links character stuck its nose forward and yowled at me as part of its animation.

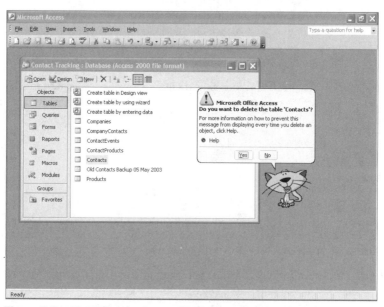

Figure 5-6. The Office Assistant displaying the same table deletion warning as shown in Figure 5-5.

> **Tip** Although the Office Assistant can be fun at first blush, it can get a bit annoying if you're working hard on a development project and getting several error messages. If you want to turn on the Assistant, choose Show the Office Assistant from the Help menu. Once the character appears, you can right-click it and choose Options from the shortcut menu to customize how it works. When the Assistant is visible, you can choose Hide the Office Assistant on the Help menu to make it go away.

If you have defined relationships between the table you want to delete and other tables, Access displays another dialog box that alerts you and asks whether you want to also delete the relationships. If you click Yes, Access deletes all relationships between any other table and the table you want to delete and then deletes the table. (You can't have a relationship defined to a nonexistent table.) Even at this point, if you find you made a mistake, you can choose Undo from the Edit menu or click the Undo button on the toolbar to restore both the table and all simple relationships.

> **Caution** When you undo a table deletion, Access may not restore all the previously defined relationships between the table and other tables. You should verify the table relationships in the Relationships window.

Renaming Tables

If you keep transaction data (such as receipts, deposits, or checks written), you might want to save that data at the end of each month in a table with a unique name. One way to save your data is to rename the existing table (perhaps by adding a date to the name). You can then create a new table (perhaps by making a copy of the backup table's structure) to start collecting information for the next month.

To rename a table, select it in the Database window and choose the Rename command from the Edit menu. Access places the name in an edit mode in the Database window so that you can type in a new name, as shown in Figure 5-7. Type in the new name, and press Enter to save it.

Figure 5-7. Renaming a table in the Database window.

> **Tip** You can also edit the name of the object by selecting it in the Database window, waiting a second, and then clicking the name again. This works just like renaming a file in Windows Explorer.

If you enter the name of a table that already exists, Access displays a dialog box that asks whether you want to replace the existing table, as shown in Figure 5-8. If you click Yes, Access deletes the old table before performing the renaming operation. Even if you replace an existing table, you can undo the renaming operation by choosing the Undo command from the Edit menu.

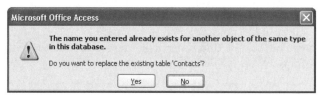

Figure 5-8. This dialog box asks whether you want to replace an existing table with the same name.

> **Tip** You can use the techniques you just learned for copying, renaming, and deleting tables to copy, rename, and delete queries, forms, reports, data access pages, macros, or modules.

Changing Field Names

Perhaps you misspelled a field name when you first created one of your tables. Or perhaps you've decided that one of the field names isn't descriptive enough. As you learned in Chapter 4, you can change the displayed name for a field by setting its Caption property. But you won't necessarily want the hassle of giving the field a caption every time it appears in a query, a form, or a report. Fortunately, Microsoft Access makes it easy to change a field name in a table—even if you already have data in the table.

> **Note** The next several examples in this chapter show you how to change the Contacts table that you created in the previous chapter to more closely match the tblContacts table in the LawTrack Contacts sample database.

Chapter 5

You created the first draft of the Contacts table by using a wizard. Now you need to make a few changes so that it will hold all the data fields that you need for your application. You bypassed your chance in the wizard to rename all sample fields when you originally selected them, but now you decide to rename one of the fields before beginning work on the rest of your application.

Renaming a field is easy. For example, you chose the field MiddleName in the wizard, but you've decided that you need only the contact's middle initial in this database. It makes sense to change the field name to reflect the actual data you intend to store in the field. (Later in this chapter, you'll see how to shorten the length of the field.) Open the Contacts table in the Contact Tracking database in Design view, and then move the cursor to the MiddleName field. Use the mouse to highlight the characters *Name* at the end of the field name, and then type **Init**. You can also click in the field name, use the arrow keys to position the cursor just before the letter *N*, press the Delete key to remove the characters you don't want, and type in the new ones. While you're at it, press F6 to jump down to the Field Properties area of the window, tab to the Caption property, and change the field caption. Your result should look something like Figure 5-9.

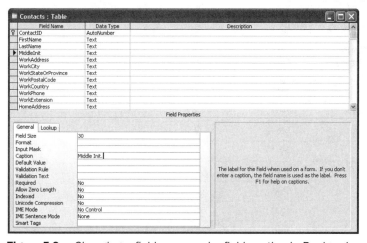

Figure 5-9.   Changing a field name and a field caption in Design view.

Comparing the Two Contacts Tables

As you follow along with the examples in this chapter, it might be useful to compare the structure of the Contacts table you built in Chapter 4 and the actual tblContacts table in the LawTrack Contacts sample database. If you exactly followed the instructions in Chapter 4, your Contacts table in the Contact Tracking database should look like Table 5-1. You can see the actual design of tblContacts in Table 5-2.

Table 5-1. Contacts

Field Name	Type	Length
ContactID	Auto Number	
FirstName	Text	50
LastName	Text	50
MiddleName	Text	30
WorkAddress	Text	255
WorkCity	Text	50
WorkStateOrProvince	Text	20
WorkPostalCode	Text	20
WorkCountry	Text	50
WorkPhone	Text	30
WorkExtension	Text	20
HomeAddress	Text	255
HomeCity	Text	50
HomeStateOrProvince	Text	20
HomePostalCode	Text	20
HomeCountry	Text	50
EmailName	Text	50
Photograph	OLE Object	
Notes	Memo	
SpouseName	Text	50
BirthDate	Date/Time	8
SpouseBirthDate	Date/Time	8

Table 5-2. tblContacts

Field Name	Type	Length
ContactID	Auto Number	
LastName	Text	50
FirstName	Text	50
MiddleInit	Text	1
Title	Text	10
Suffix	Text	10
ContactType	Text	50
BirthDate	Date/Time	
DefaultAddress	Integer	
WorkAddress	Text	255
WorkCity	Text	50
WorkStateOrProvince	Text	20
WorkPostalCode	Text	20
WorkCountry	Text	50
WorkPhone	Text	30
WorkExtension	Text	20
WorkFaxNumber	Text	30
HomeAddress	Text	255
HomeCity	Text	50
HomeStateOrProvince	Text	20
HomePostalCode	Text	20
HomeCountry	Text	50
HomePhone	Text	30
MobilePhone	Text	30
EmailName	Hyperlink	
Website	Hyperlink	
Photo	OLE Object	
SpouseName	Text	75
SpouseBirthDate	Date/Time	
Notes	Memo	
CommissionPercent	Number	Double

As you can see, we have a lot of work to do—renaming fields, moving fields, inserting fields, and changing data types and lengths—to make the two tables identical.

Chapter 5

Moving Fields

You might want to move a field in a table definition for a number of reasons. Perhaps you made an error as you entered or changed the information in a table. Or perhaps you've discovered that you're using some fields you defined at the end of a table quite frequently in forms or reports, in which case it would be easier to find and work with those fields if they were nearer the beginning of your table definition.

Inside Out

Is the sequence of fields in your table important?

The actual sequence of field definitions in a table is not all that important. In the relational database model, there really is no defined sequence of fields in a row or rows in a table. Microsoft Access, like most databases that implement the relational model, does allow you to define a field order when you create a table. This order or sequence of fields becomes the default order you see in a table datasheet or in a list of field names when you're designing a query, form, or report.

I like to at least group fields together in some reasonable order so they're easy to find, and I like to place the primary key fields at the top of the list. There's really no hard and fast rule that you must follow for your database to work efficiently.

You can use the mouse to move one or more rows. Simply follow these steps.

1 To select a row you want to move, click its row selector.

   If you want to move multiple contiguous rows, click the row selector for the first row in the group and scroll until you can see the last row in the group. Hold down the Shift key and click the row selector for the last row in the group. The first and last rows and all rows in between will be selected. Release the Shift key.

2 Click and drag the row selector(s) for the highlighted row(s) to a new location. A small shaded box attaches to the bottom of the mouse pointer while you're dragging, and a highlighted line will appear, indicating the position to which the row(s) will move when you release the mouse button.

In the design for the tblContacts table in the LawTrack Contacts database, the LastName field appears before the FirstName field. Let's assume you want the LastName field to appear first by default in all datasheets (and it makes more sense to sort first on LastName and then First-Name). Select the LastName field by clicking its row selector. Click the row selector again, and drag up until the line between the ContactID field and the FirstName field is highlighted, as shown in Figure 5-10.

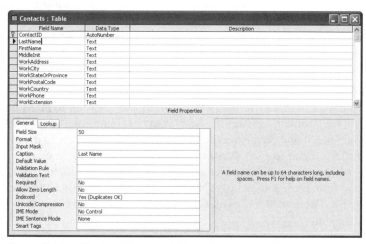

Figure 5-10. The LastName field is being dragged to its new position between the ContactID and FirstName fields.

Inside Out

Using the keyboard instead of the mouse in table design

When it comes to moving fields, you might find it easier to use a combination of mouse and keyboard methods. Use the mouse to select the row or rows you want to move. Then activate Move mode by pressing Ctrl+Shift+F8, and use the arrow keys to position the row(s). Press Esc to deactivate Move mode. As you experiment with Access, you'll discover more than one way to perform many tasks, and you can choose the techniques that work the best for you.

In Figure 5-11, the fields are positioned correctly.

Figure 5-11. The LastName field is now correctly placed.

Chapter 5

In this exercise, there's one additional field you need to move to make the design of Contacts more similar to tblContacts. Near the bottom of the field list, grab the Birthdate field and move it up just after MiddleInit. It makes more sense to have the contact's birth date field close to the contact name fields and not stuck down at the bottom with the spouse information. Also, grab the Notes field and move it to the end after SpouseBirthDate. After you've done this, your table should now look like Figure 5-12.

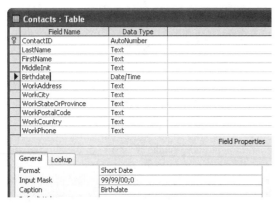

Figure 5-12. The Contacts table after moving the Birthdate field.

Inserting Fields

Perhaps one of the most common changes you'll make to your database is to insert a new field in a table. Up until now, we've renamed and moved the available fields to more closely match tblContacts. If you take a look at the comparison of the two tables again (Tables 5-1 and 5-2 on page 148 and 149), you can see that we need to add a few more fields. Now you're ready to insert fields to store the contact title, suffix, contact type, default address indicator, and more.

First, you must select the row or move your cursor to the row that defines the field *after* the point where you want to insert the new field. In this case, if you want to insert fields for the title (Mr., Mrs., etc.), suffix (Jr., Sr., etc.), and contact type (customer, sales prospect, etc.) between the MiddleInit and Birthdate fields, place the cursor anywhere in the row that defines the Birthdate field. You can also select the entire row by using the arrow keys to move to the row and then pressing Shift+Spacebar or by clicking the row selector. Next, choose the Rows command from the Insert menu (as shown in Figure 5-13) or click the Insert Row button on the toolbar. (You can also click a field row and press the Insert key to insert a row above your selection.)

Inset Row button

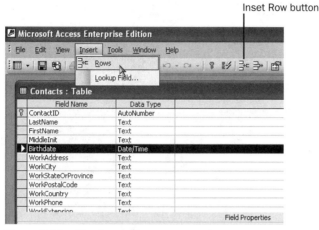

Figure 5-13. The Insert Rows command inserts a new row above a selected row or above the row in which the cursor is located.

Microsoft Access adds a blank row that you can use to define your new field. Type in the definition for the Title field. Choose the Text data type, and set the Field Size property to **10**. Move down to the Birthdate field again, and insert another row above it. Enter a Suffix field that has the Text data type with a field size of **10**. Do it one more time and enter a Contact-Type field, data type Text, and length **50**. Insert a field between Birthdate and WorkAddress, name it DefaultAddress, set its data type to Number, and set the Field Size to Integer. The actual LawTrack Contacts application uses this field to indicate whether the work or home address is the default mailing address.

Move down to Photo and insert a field above it. Enter a field name of Website, and set its data type to Hyperlink. Finally, move down to the blank row beyond Notes (you can use an existing blank row to add a field at the end), and create a field named CommissionPercent that has the Number data type and a field size of Double. When you finish, your Table window in Design view should look something like the one shown in Figure 5-14 on the next page. Don't worry about setting other properties just yet.

Chapter 5

Figure 5-14. The Contacts table with additional fields inserted.

> **Tip** You can move the cursor between the upper part and the lower part of any Table or Query window in Design view by pressing F6.

Copying Fields

As you create table definitions, you might find that several fields in your table are similar. Rather than enter each of the field definitions separately, you can enter one field definition, copy it, and then paste it as many times as necessary.

To finish defining our Contacts table, we need three additional fields—WorkFaxNumber, HomePhone, and MobilePhone. You could certainly insert a new row and type in all the properties as you just did in the previous section, but why not copy a field that is similar and make minor changes to it?

For this part of the exercise, select the row for the WorkPhone field definition by clicking the row selector at the far left of the row. Choose the Copy command from the Edit menu, or click the Copy button on the toolbar, as shown in Figure 5-15. Move the insertion point to the row that should follow the row you'll insert. (In this case, move the insertion point to the HomeAddress field, which should follow your new field.) Insert a blank row by choosing Rows from the Insert menu or by clicking the Insert Row button on the toolbar. Select the new row by clicking the row selector. Choose the Paste command from the Edit menu or click the Paste button on the toolbar to insert the copied row, as shown in Figure 5-16 on page 156.

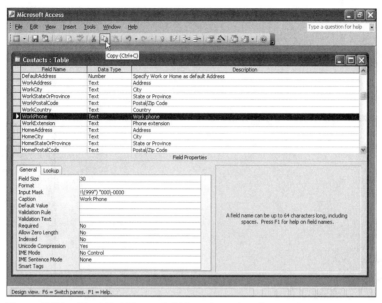

Figure 5-15. The WorkPhone field is selected and copied.

Caution If you choose the Paste command when a row containing data is selected, the copied row will *replace* the selected row. Should you make this replacement in error, choose the Undo command from the Edit menu to restore the original row.

You can use the Paste command repeatedly to insert a copied row more than once. Remember to change both the name and the description of the resulting field or fields before you save the modified table definition. In this case, it's a simple matter to change the name of the copied row from WorkPhone to WorkFaxNumber and to correct the description and caption accordingly. Note that this procedure also has the benefit of copying any formatting, default value, or validation rule information.

Chapter 5

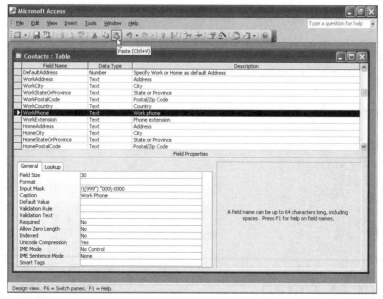

Figure 5-16. The copied WorkPhone field can be pasted into a new blank row.

If you're careful, you don't actually have to insert a blank row to paste a field definition from the Clipboard. After you fix the WorkFaxNumber field name and description in the upper part of the window, and Caption in the lower part of the window, scroll down to the Email-Name field and click in the row but *do not select the row*. Click the Paste button on the toolbar twice to insert two more copies of WorkPhone just above EmailName. Change the name of the first one to HomePhone and the second to MobilePhone, and correct the descriptions and captions. You should now have a table that's almost identical to the tblContacts table in the LawTrack Contacts sample database. Be sure to save your changed table.

Deleting Fields

Removing unwanted fields is easy. With the Table window open in Design view, select the field that you want to delete by clicking the row selector. You can extend the selection to multiple contiguous fields by holding down the Shift key and using the up and down arrow keys to select multiple rows. You can also select multiple contiguous rows by clicking the row selector of the first row and, without releasing the mouse button, dragging up or down to select all the rows you want. After you select the appropriate fields, choose Delete or Delete Rows from the Edit menu or press the Delete key to delete the selected fields.

If a table contains one or more rows of data, Access displays a warning message when you delete field definitions in Design view, as shown in Figure 5-17. Click No if you think you made a mistake. Click Yes to proceed with the deletion of the fields and the data in those fields. Keep in mind that you can still undo this change up to the point that you save the table.

Figure 5-17.   This dialog box asks you to confirm a field deletion.

If you want to test this out in the sample table you have been building, make sure you have saved your latest changes and then switch to Datasheet view by clicking the View button on the far left end of the toolbar. Type your name in the Last Name and First Name fields and switch back to Design view by clicking the View button again. Try deleting any field in the design, and Access will warn you that you might be deleting some data as well.

Changing Data Attributes

As you learned in the previous chapter, Microsoft Access provides a number of different data types. These data types help Access work more efficiently with your data and also provide a base level of data validation; for example, you can enter only numbers in a Number or Currency field.

When you initially design your database, you should match the data type and length of each field to its intended use. You might discover, however, that a field you thought would contain only numbers (such as a U.S. ZIP Code) must now contain some letters (perhaps because you've started doing business in Canada). You might find that one or more number fields need to hold larger values or a different number of decimal places. Access allows you to change the data type and length of many fields, even after you've entered data in them.

Changing Data Types

Changing the data type of a field in a table is simple. Open the table in Design view, click in the Data Type column of the field definition you want to change, click the down arrow button at the right to see the available choices, and select a new data type. You cannot convert an OLE Object or a Replication ID data type to another data type. With several limitations, Access can successfully convert every other data type to any other data type, even when you have data in the table. Table 5-3 on the next page shows you the possible conversions and potential limitations when the table contains data.

> **Warning**   When the field contents don't satisfy the limitations noted in Table 5-3, Access *deletes* the field contents (sets it to Null) when you save the changes.

Chapter 5

Table 5-3. Limitations on Converting One Data Type to Another

Convert To:	From:	Limitations:
Text	Memo	Access truncates text longer than 255 characters.
	Hyperlink	Might lose some data if the hyperlink string is longer than 255 characters.
	Number, except Replication ID	No limitations.
	AutoNumber	No limitations except Replication ID.
	Currency	No limitations.
	Date/Time	No limitations.
	Yes/No	Yes (-1) converts to Yes; No (0) converts to No.
Memo	Text	No limitations.
	Hyperlink	No limitations.
	Number, Except Replication ID	No limitations.
	AutoNumber	No limitations.
	Currency	No limitations.
	Date/Time	No limitations.
	Yes/No	Yes (-1) converts to Yes; No (0) converts to No.
Hyperlink	Text	If the text contains a valid Hyperlink string consisting of a display name, a # delimiter, a valid link address, a # delimiter, and optional bookmark and screen tip, Access changes the data type without modifying the text. If the text contains only a valid link address, Access surrounds the address with # delimiters to form the Hyperlink field. Access recognizes strings beginning with *http://, ftp://, mailto:, news:, \\servername*, and *d:* as link addresses. If Access does not recognize the text as a link, it converts the text to *[text]#http://[text]#*, where *[text]* is the original contents of the field; the result is probably not a valid link address.
	Memo	Same restrictions as converting from Text.
	Number, except Replication ID	Possible, but Access converts the number to a text string in the form *[number]#http://[number]#, where [number]* is the text conversion of the original numeric value; the result is probably not a valid link address.

Table 5-3. Limitations on Converting One Data Type to Another

Convert To:	From:	Limitations:
Hyperlink	AutoNumber	Possible, but Access converts the AutoNumber to a text string in the form *[number]#http://[number]*, where *[number]* is the text conversion of the original AutoNumber; the result is probably not a valid link address.
	Currency	Possible, but Access converts the currency value to a text string in the form *[currency]#http://[currency]*, where *[currency]* is the text conversion of the original currency value; the result is probably not a valid link address.
	Date/Time	Possible, but Access converts the date/time to a text string in the form *[date/time]#http://[date/time]#*, where *[date/time]* is the text conversion of the original date or time value; the result is probably not a valid link address.
	Yes/No	Possible, but Access converts the yes/no to a text string in the form *[yes/no]#http://[yes/no]#*, where *[yes/no]* is the text conversion of the original yes (-1) or no (0) value; the result is probably not a valid link address.
Number	Text	Text must contain only numbers and valid separators. The number value must be within the range for the Field Size.
	Memo	Memo must contain only numbers and valid separators. The number value must be within the range for the Field Size.
	Hyperlink	Not possible.
	Number (different field size or precision)	Number must not be larger or smaller than can be contained in the new field size. If you change precision, Access might round the number.
	AutoNumber	The number value must be within the range for the Field Size.
	Currency	Number must not be larger or smaller than can be contained in the Field Size.
	Date/Time	If the new Field Size is Byte, the date must be between April 18, 1899*, and September 11, 1900. If the new Field Size is Integer, the date must be between April 13, 1810, and September 16, 1989. For all other Field Sizes, there are no limitations.
	Yes/No	Yes (-1) converts to -1; No (0) converts to 0.

Chapter 5

Table 5-3. Limitations on Converting One Data Type to Another

Convert To:	From:	Limitations:
AutoNumber	Text	Not possible if the table contains data.
	Memo	Not possible if the table contains data.
	Hyperlink	Not possible.
	Number	Not possible if the table contains data.
	Currency	Not possible if the table contains data.
	Date/Time	Not possible if the table contains data.
	Yes/No	Not possible if the table contains data.
Currency	Text	Text must contain only numbers and valid separators.
	Memo	Memo must contain only numbers and valid separators.
	Hyperlink	Not possible.
	Number, except Replication ID	No limitations.
	AutoNumber	No limitations.
	Date/Time	No limitations, but value might be rounded.
	Yes/No	Yes (-1) converts to $1; No (0) converts to $0.
Date/Time	Text	Text must contain a recognizable date and/or time, such as 11-Nov-04 5:15 PM.
	Memo	Memo must contain a recognizable date and/or time, such as 11-Nov-04 5:15 PM.
	Hyperlink	Not possible.
	Number, except Replication ID	Number must be between -657,434 and 2,958,465.99998843.
	AutoNumber	Value must be less than 2,958,466 and greater than -657,433.
	Currency	Number must be between -$657,434 and $2,958,465.9999.
	Yes/No	Yes (-1) converts to 12/29/1899; No (0) converts to 12:00:00 AM.
Yes/No	Text	Text must contain only one of the following values: Yes, True, On, No, False, or Off.
	Memo	Memo must contain only one of the following values: Yes, True, On, No, False, or Off.
	Hyperlink	Not possible.

Table 5-3. **Limitations on Converting One Data Type to Another**

Convert To:	From:	Limitations:
Yes/No	Number, except Replication ID	Zero or Null converts to No; any other value converts to Yes.
	AutoNumber	All values evaluate to Yes.
	Currency	Zero or Null converts to No; any other value converts to Yes.
	Date/Time	12:00:00 AM or Null converts to No; any other value converts to Yes.

* Remember, Access stores a date/time value as an integer date offset and fraction of a day. April 18, 1899 happens to be ⁻256 internally, which is the smallest number you can store in a Byte.

If you want to see how this works in the Contacts table you have been building, open the table in Datasheet view and enter any last name and first name in one or two rows. We want to change the EmailName field from the Text data type that the Table Wizard provided to Hyperlink. Scroll right on one of the rows and enter an email address in one of the rows in the form: myname@proseware.com. In another row, add the correct URL prefix in the form: mailto:myname@proseware.com.

Now, switch to Design view and change the data type of the EmailName field from Text to Hyperlink and save the change. Notice that Access gives you no warning about any conversion problems because it knows it can store any text field that is not larger than 255 characters in a Hyperlink, which can be up to 2 gigabytes. Switch back to Datasheet view and scroll to the right to find the changed field. You should see a result something like Figure 5-18.

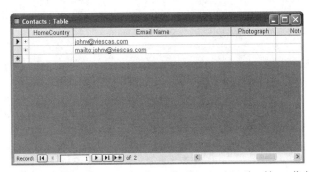

Figure 5-18. The result of converting text to the Hyperlink data type.

Both entries look fine. However, if you click the first one, Access attempts to open your browser because the full text stored in the Hyperlink is *johnv@viescas.com#http://johnv@viescas.com/#*. Because the link address portion indicates the http protocol, your browser opens instead of your email program. When you click the second link, it should open a blank message in your email program with the To: line filled in correctly. Access recognized the mailto: prefix and converted the text correctly.

You can read more about working with Hyperlinks in Chapter 10, "Using Forms." I show you how to make sure that Access correctly recognizes an e-mail name typed into a hyperlink field in Chapter 23, "Automating Your Application with Visual Basic."

Changing Data Lengths

For text and number fields, you can define the maximum length of the data that can be stored in the field. Although a text field can be up to 255 characters long, you can restrict the length to as little as 1 character. If you don't specify a length for text, Access normally assigns the length you specify on the Tables/Queries tab of the Options dialog box. (The default length is 50.) Access won't let you enter text field data longer than the defined length. If you need more space in a text field, you can increase the length at any time; but if you try to redefine the length of a text field so that it's shorter, you will get a warning message (like the one shown in Figure 5-19) stating that Access will truncate any data field that contains data longer than the new length when you try to save the changes to your table. Note also that it warns you that any validation rules you have designed might fail on the changed data.

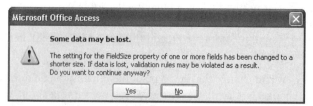

Figure 5-19. This dialog box informs you of possible data truncation problems.

Tip Remember, you can change the default data type for a new field and the default length of new text and number fields by choosing Options from the Tools menu and then clicking the Tables/Queries tab of the Options dialog box.

If you want to try this in your Contacts table, open it in Datasheet view and type more than one character in MiddleInit. The last two changes you need to make to this table so that it is exactly like tblContacts in the LawTrack Contacts database are to set the length of MiddleInit to 1 and the length of SpouseName to 75. Switch to Design view and make those two changes. When you try to save the changes, you should see the error message in Figure 5-19 (because you're shortening the length of the MiddleInit field). Click Yes to allow the changes and then switch back to Datasheet view. You should find one truncated character in MiddleInit.

Sizes for numeric data types can vary from a single byte (which can contain a value from 0 through 255) to 2 or 4 bytes (for larger integers), 8 bytes (necessary to hold very large floating-point or currency numbers), or 16 bytes (to hold a unique ReplicationID or decimal number). Except for ReplicationID, you can change the size of a numeric data type at any time, but you might generate errors if you make the size smaller. Access also rounds numbers when converting from floating-point data types (Single or Double) to integer or currency values.

Dealing with Conversion Errors

When you try to save a modified table definition, Access always warns you if any changes to the data type or length will cause conversion errors. For example, if you change the Field Size property of a number field from Integer to Byte, Access warns you if any of the records contain a number larger than 255. (Access deletes the contents of any field it can't convert at all.) If you examine Table 5-3, you'll see that you should expect some data type changes to always cause problems. For example, if you change a field from Hyperlink to Date/Time, you can expect all data to be deleted. You'll see a dialog box similar to the one shown in Figure 5-20 warning you about fields that Access will set to a Null value if you proceed with your changes. Click the Yes button to proceed with the changes. You'll have to examine your data to correct any conversion errors.

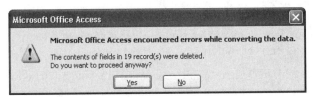

Figure 5-20. This dialog box informs you of conversion errors.

If you click the No button, Access opens the dialog box shown in Figure 5-21. If you deleted any fields or indexes, added any fields, or renamed any fields, Access will save those changes. Otherwise, the database will be unchanged. You can correct any data type or length changes you made, and then try to save the table definition again.

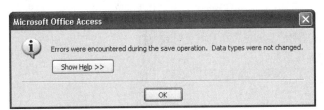

Figure 5-21. This dialog box appears if you decide not to save a modified table definition.

Changing Other Field Properties

As you learned in Chapter 4, you can set a number of other properties that define how Access displays or validates a field that have nothing to do with changing the data type. These properties include Description, Format, Input Mask, Caption, Default Value, Validation Rule, Validation Text, Required, Allow Zero Length, and Indexed.

If you have data in your table, changing some of these properties might elicit a warning from Access. If you change or define a validation rule, or set Required to Yes, Access offers to check the new rule or requirement that a field not be empty against the contents of the table when you try to save the change. If you ask Access to test the data, it checks all the rows in your table and opens a warning dialog box if it finds any rows that fail. However, it doesn't tell you *which* rows failed—I'll show you how to do that in Chapter 7. If you changed the rules for more than one field, you'll see the error dialog box once for each rule that fails.

As you'll learn later, when you define queries, forms, and reports, these objects inherit several of the properties that you define for your table fields. In previous versions of Access, the catch was that once you defined and saved another object that used table fields, any subsequent change that you made to properties in table design didn't change automatically in other dependent objects. You had to go find those properties yourself and fix them (or use a tool such as the Black Moshannon Systems—*http://www.moshannon.com*—Speed Ferret product). You would get the new property settings in any new objects you created, but the old ones remained unchanged.

 The good news is there's a new feature in Microsoft Access 2003 that takes care of this problem for some properties. To see how this works, you must first make sure that you have this feature turned on in Options as I showed you in the previous chapter. Choose Options from the Tools menu, select the Tables/Queries tab, and verify that you have selected the Show Property Update Options buttons option.

Next, open the Contacts table in Design view in the Contact Tracking database you have been building. You haven't defined a description for any of the fields yet. Remember from the previous chapter that Access displays the description on the status bar when the focus is on this field in any datasheet or form. Click in the Description column next to the ContactID field and enter a useful description such as "Unique contact ID" and press Tab. As soon as you do this, you'll see a little AutoCorrect Smart Tag appear that looks like a lightning bolt. If you hover near the Smart Tag, it tells you that it offers property update options. Click on the down arrow next to the tag to see the option you can choose as shown in Figure 5-22. Access offers you this option whenever you change the Description, Format, or Input Mask properties.

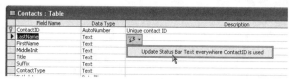

Figure 5-22. The Property Update Options Smart Tag feature in action.

You can click the option to ask Access to also change this property wherever the ContactID field is used in other objects. Of course, you don't have anything but tables in your sample database right now, so choosing the option won't do anything.

> **Caution** You must choose the option shown on the Property Update Option button immediately after you make the change in your table definition. If you move to another field or move to another property and make another change, the button disappears. You can get it back by returning to the property you changed and changing it again. If you ask it to make changes, Access opens an Update Properties dialog box that lists all the objects it plans to change. You can reject all changes or selectively apply the change to only some of the objects.

Reversing Changes

If you make several changes and then decide you don't want any of them, you can close the Table window without saving it. When you do this, Access opens the dialog box shown in Figure 5-23. Simply click the No button to reverse all your changes. Click the Cancel button to return to the Table window without saving or reversing your changes.

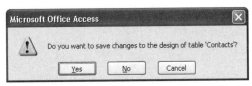

Figure 5-23. This dialog box gives you the option of reversing unsaved changes to a table.

> **Tip** You can always reverse up to the last 20 changes you made since you last saved the table design by clicking the Undo button. You can also open the list next to the Undo button to selectively undo a series of changes.

Using the Table Analyzer Wizard

Even if you follow all the recommendations in Chapter 3, "Designing Your Database Application," and build a normalized database, you might not arrive at the best design. In fact, you often cannot fully evaluate a database design until you use the database and store data. Access includes the Table Analyzer Wizard that can examine data in your tables (or data you import from another source) and recommend additional refinements and enhancements to your database design.

You'll recall from Chapter 3 that one of the key elements of good database design is the elimination of redundant data. The Table Analyzer Wizard is particularly good at scanning data in your tables, identifying data repeated in one or more columns, and recommending alterations to your design that break out the redundant data into separate tables. You can find an example of such redundant data in the LawTrack Contacts database (*Contacts.mdb*). Imagine that a customer sent you a file containing company and contact information. Sounds like a good, easy place to start collecting or adding to your contact data. However, when you open the file, you see that most companies are listed several times because the original data isn't normalized. You'll find just such a table, saved as tblContacts4Analyzer, in the LawTrack Contacts sample database.

You can see how the Table Analyzer Wizard works by using it on the tblContacts4Analyzer table. First, open the LawTrack Contacts database. Choose Analyze from the Tools menu and then choose Table from the submenu. Access starts the Table Analyzer Wizard and displays the first window, shown in Figure 5-24 on the next page.

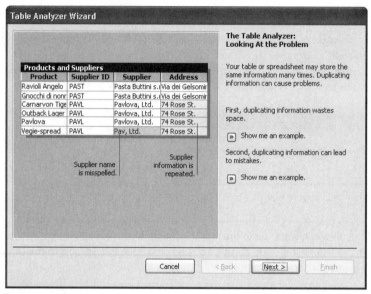

Figure 5-24.   The opening window of the Table Analyzer Wizard.

This first window is one of two introductory windows that explain what the wizard can do. Click the Show Me buttons to get a better understanding of the kinds of problems the wizard can solve and to see how the wizard works. Click Next twice to get to the first "action" window of the wizard, shown in Figure 5-25.

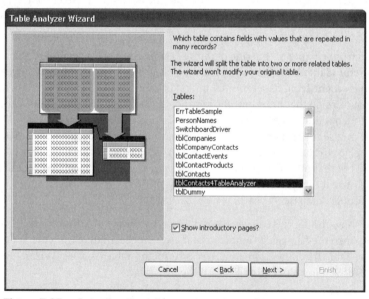

Figure 5-25.   Selecting the table you want to analyze.

In this window, you select the table you want to analyze. For this exercise, select the tblContacts4Analyzer table. (Note that you have an option in this window to continue to show the two introductory windows each time you start the wizard. If you think you understand how the wizard works, you can clear the check box to skip the introductory windows the next time you start the wizard.) Click Next.

In the next window, the wizard asks if you want to rearrange the fields in the target table or if you want the wizard to decide the arrangement for you. If you know which fields contain redundant data, you can make the decision yourself. Because the wizard handles all the "grunt work" of splitting out lookup data, you might choose the latter option in the future to further normalize tables in your application. For now, select the Yes, let the wizard decide option to see how effective it is. Click Next to start the analysis of your table. Figure 5-26 shows the result of the wizard's analysis. (I've shifted the contents of this figure to fit the result in a single window.)

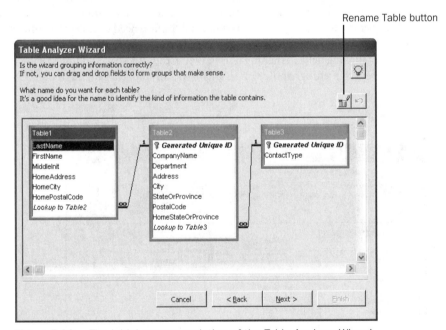

Figure 5-26. The initial recommendation of the Table Analyzer Wizard.

In this case, the wizard did a pretty good job of identifying the separate company and contact information and splitting the fields into two tables. It also recognized that ContactType has lots of repeating values and perhaps should be in a separate lookup table, but it incorrectly related that table to the company information. There isn't enough data (only 18 rows—and each contact is related to only one company) in the table for the wizard to have noticed a many-to-many relationship between companies and contacts. It probably kept the HomeStateOrProvince field with the company data because it didn't see a different value across multiple rows for the same company. It also incorrectly used the Department field as the primary key for the table containing the ContactType lookup field.

We really don't need to do much work to fix this if we're happy with the one-to-many relationship. First, click HomeStateOrProvince in Table2 and drag and drop it into Table1 between HomeCity and HomePostalCode. Also move the Lookup to Table3 field from Table2 to Table1 to correctly relate the contact type lookup information to contacts instead of companies, and move the Department field from Table3 to Table2 between CompanyName and Address.

Once you have adjusted the way the wizard split your tables, the next step is to give each of the new tables a new name. To rename a table, first click the table name and then click the Rename Table button in the upper part of the window. (You can also double-click the table's title bar.) The wizard opens a dialog box in which you can enter a new name. You should change Table1 to **Contacts**, Table2 to **Companies**, and Table3 to **ContactTypes**. Click Next when you are finished.

The next window asks you to verify the primary key fields for these tables. You can select new fields for the primary key of each table or add fields to the primary key. The wizard couldn't identify any naturally occurring unique value, so it generated a unique ID (which will be an AutoNumber in the final tables) for two of the tables. You need to select the Contacts table and click the Add Generated Key button to create a primary key for that table. Figure 5-27 shows the result of moving fields, assigning new names to the tables, and adding a primary key. Click Next to accept the settings and go on to an analysis of duplicate values in the lookup tables.

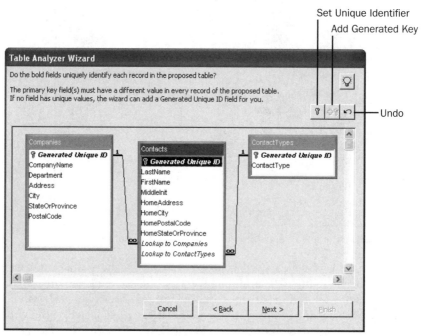

Figure 5-27. The result after moving fields and renaming the new tables.

The Table Analyzer Wizard looks at values in the new tables to try to eliminate any possible duplicates created by typing errors. Figure 5-28 shows the result of this analysis on the sample table. Because the wizard sees several rows with *Training* or *Police Dept.* in them, it suggests that some of these values might, in fact, be the same. You can use this window to tell the wizard any correct values for actual mistyped duplicates. This could be extremely useful if your incoming data had the same company listed several times but with a slightly different spelling or address. The wizard will store only unique values in the final table. You could, if necessary, tell the wizard to substitute one set of similar values for another to eliminate the near duplicates. In this case, you should tell the wizard to use the original value for all the values listed as duplicates by selecting the (Leave as is) option as shown in Figure 5-28. Click Next when you are finished to go on to the next window.

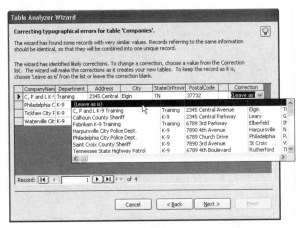

Figure 5-28. Looking at potentially duplicate lookup values.

Finally, the wizard offers to create a new query that has the same name as the original table. (See Figure 5-29 on the next page.) If you've already been using the old table in queries, forms, reports, and data access pages, creating a new query that integrates the new tables into the original data structure means you won't have to change any other objects in your database. In most cases, the new query will look and operate just like the original table. Old queries, forms, reports, and data access pages based on the original table will now use the new query and won't know the difference.

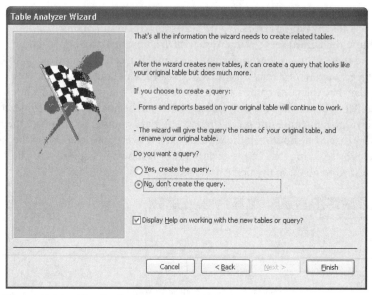

Figure 5-29.   The final window of the Table Analyzer Wizard.

This is only an example, so select No, don't create the query. Click Finish to build your new tables. The wizard also creates relationships among the new tables to make sure you can easily re-create the original data structure in queries. Figure 5-30 shows the three new tables built by the wizard.

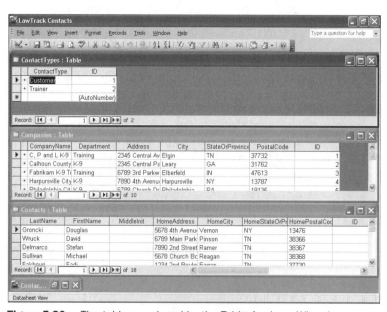

Figure 5-30.   The tables produced by the Table Analyzer Wizard.

Notice that the wizard left behind an ID field in the Contacts table as a link to the Contact-Types table. The values in the ContactTypes table are actually unique, so there's no reason not to use the actual value as the primary key instead of an artificial ID. I'll show you how to change the primary key in a later section in this chapter.

Taking a Look at Lookup Properties

As you have been working in table design, you've probably noticed that there's a Lookup tab available in the lower part of the Design window. You might have also noticed that Access offers you a Lookup Wizard entry in the drop-down list of data types and a Lookup Field option on the Insert menu.

Microsoft Access for Windows 95 (version 7) introduced this feature to allow you to pre-define how you want the field displayed in a datasheet, form, or report. For example, if you have a DepartmentID field in an Employees table that stores the primary key value of the department for which the employee works, you might want to display the department name rather than the number value when you look at the data. If you're displaying a Yes/No field, you might want to provide a drop-down list that shows options for *invoiced* and *not invoiced* instead of *yes* and *no* or *true* and *false*.

In the sample databases, I defined Lookup properties for only a few fields—ones for which I knew that I would later need a drop-down list (combo box) on one or more forms or reports. One such example is in the Proseware Housing sample database (*Housing.mdb*). Open the database, view the Table objects, select tblEmployees, and open it in Design view. Click the DepartmentID field and then click the Lookup tab to see the settings as shown in Figure 5-31.

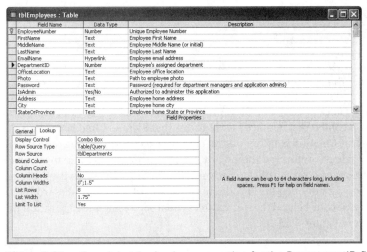

Figure 5-31. Examining the Lookup properties for the DepartmentID field in tblEmployees in the Proseware Housing sample database.

As you can see, I have set the Display Control property to Combo Box. You see combo boxes in Windows applications all the time—sometimes called drop-down lists. It's a box that you can type in with a button on the right that you can click to drop down a list of values to select. In Access, you tell the combo box what type of list you want (Row Source Type) and specify the source of the list (Row Source). Access is a bit unusual because it lets you define a list that contains more than one column that you can display (Column Count), and it requires you to specify which of the columns (Bound Column) actually supplies the value to be stored when you pick an item from the list. This means that you might see a text value, but the combo box stores a number.

You can see this combo box in action by switching to Datasheet view. You can click in the Department field and type a name from the list, or click the drop-down arrow on the right and choose an item from the list as shown in Figure 5-32. Remember, DepartmentID is actually a number. If you didn't define the special settings on the Lookup tab, you would see a list of numbers in the Department column. For details about these settings, see Table 5-4 on page 174.

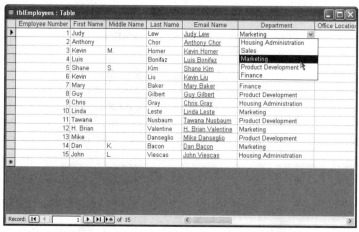

Figure 5-32. The Lookup tab settings show you a combo box in Datasheet view.

I decided to go ahead and define these properties in this table because I knew I was probably going to use a combo box in one or more forms that I would build later to display related Department information while editing an employee record. By setting the values in the table, I can avoid having to define the combo box settings again when I build my forms. If you want to see how this works on a form, you can open frmEmployeesPlain in the Proseware Housing database. (You cannot open the "production" version of frmEmployees from the Database window because code behind that form forces you to sign on to the application first.) You can see the result in Figure 5-33.

Figure 5-33.   The table Lookup tab properties were inherited by the combo box on frmEmployeesPlain.

Inside Out

Lookup tab settings: for *advanced* users only!

I recommend that only experienced users set the Lookup tab properties of a field in table Design view. Unless you are fully aware of what the settings do, you can have problems later when you look at the information in a datasheet or try to build a query on the table. For example, if you look at the data in tblEmployees, you could mistakenly decide that "Housing Administration" is a valid value in the DepartmentID field. If you try to build a query and filter the DepartmentID field looking for that department name, your query won't run.

Table 5-4 on the next page gives you an overview of what the lookup settings mean. When you study combo box controls later, in Chapter 11, "Building a Form," you'll see how you can also use lookup properties to display lists from related tables in a form. I'll also show you in that chapter the Combo Box Wizard that makes it easy to correctly define these settings.

Table 5-4. Lookup Properties

Lookup Property	Setting	Meaning
Display Control	Check Box (Yes/No fields only), Text Box, List Box, or Combo Box	Setting this property to Text Box or Check Box disables lookups. List Box shows a list of values in an open window. Combo Box shows the selected value when closed and shows the available list of values when opened.
Properties Available When You Set Display Control to List Box or Combo Box		
Row Source Type	Table/Query, Value List, or Field List	Table/Query specifies that you want rows from a table or query to fill the list. If you select Value List, you must enter the values you want displayed in the Row Source property, separated by semicolons. The Field List setting shows the names of the fields from the table or query you enter in Row Source—not the data in its rows.
Row Source	Table Name, Query Name, or a list of values separated by semicolons	Use a table name, query name, or enter the text of the query (in SQL) that provides the list values when Row Source Type is Table/Query. See Chapters 7 and 8 for details about building queries, and Article 1 on the companion CD for details about SQL. Enter a list of values separated by semicolons when Row Source Type is Value List. Use a table or query name when Row Source Type is Field List.
Bound Column	An integer value from 1 to the number of columns in the Row Source	Specify the column in the Row Source that provides the value stored by the list box or combo box.
Column Count	An integer value from 1 to 255	This determines the number of columns available to display. (See Column Widths below.) When the Row Source Type is a Value List, this setting determines how many consecutive values you enter in Row Source make up a logical row.
Column Heads	No (default) or Yes	Choose Yes to display the field name at the top of any displayed column when you open the list.

Table 5-4. Lookup Properties

Lookup Property	Setting	Meaning
Column Widths	One width value per column, separated by semicolons	Specify a zero width if you do not want the combo box or list box to display the column. It is common to not display an AutoNumber ID field, but you might need that field in the Row Source as the bound column.
Properties That Apply to Combo Boxes Only		
List Rows	An integer value between 1 and 255 (Default is 8)	Determines how many rows the combo box displays when you open the list. If this setting is less than the number of rows in the Row Source, the combo box makes a scroll bar available to move through the list.
List Width	Auto or a specific width	Specifies the width of the list when you open it. Auto opens the list the width of the field display.
Limit To List	No (default) or Yes	Specifies whether the user can enter a value that's not in the list. When the bound column is not the first displayed column, the combo box acts as though Limit To List is Yes regardless of the setting.

Tip When I'm designing a combo box that displays multiple columns when dropped down, I always specify a List Width value that's the sum of the Column Width values plus 0.25 inches to allow for the vertical scroll bar.

Troubleshooting

Why you should not use the Lookup Wizard

Wait a minute! What about the Lookup Wizard entry under Data Types? I recommend that you *never* use this wizard. It often builds strange SQL for the Row Source property, it always defines a relationship between the table you're editing and the lookup table, and it defines indexes on both fields. If the lookup table contains only a few rows, the index is a waste of time and resources. As you learned in Chapter 4, there's a limit of 32 indexes on a table. I have seen some cases where I haven't been able to build all the indexes I need because the Lookup Wizard built these unnecessary indexes.

Chapter 5

Changing the Primary Key

Chapter 3, "Designing Your Database Application," discussed the need to have one or more fields that provide a unique value to every row in your table. This field or group of fields with unique values is identified as the *primary key*. If a table doesn't have a primary key, you can't define a relationship between it and other tables, and Microsoft Access has to guess how to link tables for you. Even if you define a primary key in your initial design, you might discover later that it doesn't actually contain unique values. In that case, you might have to define a new field or fields to be the primary key.

Let's go back to the three tables we built earlier with the Table Analyzer Wizard. Suppose you discover that users are becoming confused by the fact that ContactTypes_ID is a number instead of the actual text. (See my comments about using the Lookup Table Wizard in the previous section.) You could keep the lookup table to help avoid duplicate values, but there's no reason not to store the actual text value in the Contacts table instead of a linking ID.

To fix this, you need to perform the following steps. Be sure to save your work at the end of each step.

1 Open the Contacts table in Design view and insert a new field named ContactType, data type Text, length 50.

2 Update the new ContactType field with related information from the ContactTypes table. I'll show you how to do this easily with an update query in Chapter 9. For now, you can switch to Datasheet view and copy what you see in the Lookup to Contact-Types field to your new ContactType field. (There are only 18 rows, so this shouldn't take you very long.)

3 Open the Relationships window and click the Show All Relationships button so that you can see the additional relationships that the Table Analyzer Wizard built. Click on the line between Contacts and ContactTypes and press the Delete key to remove the relationship. (You must delete any relationship involving the primary key of a table before you can change the key.)

4 Open the Contacts table in Design view and delete the ContactTypes_ID field.

5 Open the ContactTypes table in Design view and change the primary key from ID to ContactType. (You can also select the ID field and delete it if you like.)

Access provides several ways for you to accomplish this task. You could open the Indexes window (as you learned in Chapter 4), delete the primary key definition, and build a new one. A simpler way is to select the new field you want as the primary key and then click the Primary Key button on the toolbar, as shown in Figure 5-34.

6 Finally, reopen the Relationships window and define a new relationship between ContactType in the ContactTypes table and your new ContactType field in the Contacts table.

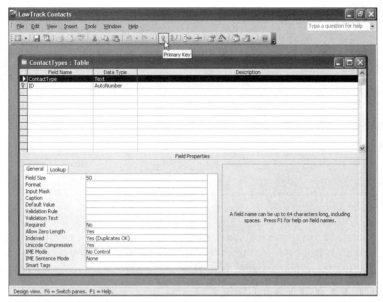

Figure 5-34. Highlighting the new field that will become the primary key.

Keep in mind that you can directly change the primary key for any table that does not have any relationships defined. Also, when the table contains data, the new fields that you choose for a primary key must have unique values in all the rows.

Compacting Your Database

As you delete old database objects and add new ones, the space within your .mdb file can become fragmented. The result is that, over time, your database file can grow larger than it needs to be to store all your definitions and data.

To remove unused space, you should compact your database periodically. No other users should be accessing the database you intend to compact. You can compact the database you currently have open by choosing Database Utilities from the Tools menu and then choosing Compact and Repair Database from the submenu. If you want to compact another database, you must close your current database and then choose the Compact and Repair Database command. Access opens the dialog box shown in Figure 5-35 on the next page.

Chapter 5

177

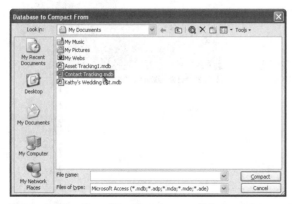

Figure 5-35. The dialog box for specifying a database to compact.

Select the database you want to compact, and then click Compact. Access asks you for a name for the compacted database. You can enter the same name as the database you are compacting, or you can use a different name. If you use the same name, Access warns you that the original database of the same name will be replaced. If you proceed, Access compacts your database into a temporary file. When compaction is successfully completed, Access deletes your old database and gives its name to the new compacted copy.

> **Tip** You can also set an option to compact the database each time you close it. Choose Options from the Tools menu, click the General tab, and select Compact on Close. If multiple users are sharing the same database, Access compacts the database when the last user closes it.

You now have all the information you need to modify and maintain your database table definitions. In the next chapter, you'll explore importing data from other sources and linking to data in other files.

Importing and Linking Data

You can certainly build all your tables, design queries, forms, and reports, and then enter from scratch all the data into your empty tables. However, in many cases you'll have some of the data you need lying around in other files. For example, you might have a customer list in a spreadsheet or a text file. Your list of products might be in another non-Access database file. Microsoft Access provides tools to help you bring the data into your new application.

Although you can use Microsoft Access as a self-contained database and application system, one of its primary strengths is that it allows you to work with many kinds of data in other databases, in spreadsheets, or in text files. In addition to using data in your local Access database, you can *import* (copy in) or *link* (connect to) data that's in text files, spreadsheets, other Access databases, dBASE, Paradox, and any other SQL database that supports the Open Database Connectivity (ODBC) software standard (including Microsoft Visual FoxPro). As you'll learn later in Chapter 28, "Working with XML and SharePoint," Access also supports files in eXtensible Markup Language (XML), which is the standard format for defining and storing data on the Web.

A Word About Open Database Connectivity (ODBC)

If you look under the hood of Access, you'll find that it uses a database language called *SQL (Structured Query Language)* to read, insert, update, and delete data. SQL grew out of a relational database research project conducted by IBM in the 1970s. It has been adopted as the official standard for relational databases by organizations such as the American National Standards Institute (ANSI) and the International Organization for Standardization (ISO). When you're viewing a query in Design view, you can see the SQL statements that Access uses by choosing the SQL View command from the View menu or by selecting SQL View from the View toolbar button.

 Article 1 on the companion CD, "Understanding SQL," provides more details about how Access uses SQL. The Appendix, on page 1223, provides details about installing and managing ODBC connections on your computer.

In an ideal world, any product that "speaks" SQL should be able to "talk" to any other product that understands SQL. You should be able to build an application that can work with the data in several relational database management systems using the same database language.

Although standards exist for SQL, most software companies have implemented variations on or extensions to the language to handle specific features of their products. Also, several products evolved before standards were well established, so the companies producing those products invented their own SQL syntaxes, which differ from the official standard. An SQL statement intended to be executed by Microsoft SQL Server might require modification before it can be executed by other databases that support SQL, such as DB2 or Oracle, and vice versa.

To solve this problem, a group of influential hardware and software companies—more than 30 of them, including Microsoft Corporation—formed the SQL Access Group. The group's goal was to define a common base SQL implementation that its members' products could all use to "talk" to one another. The companies jointly developed the *Common Language Interface (CLI)* for all the major variants of SQL, and they committed themselves to building CLI support into their products. About a dozen of these companies jointly demonstrated this capability in early 1992.

In the meantime, Microsoft formalized the CLI for workstations and announced that Microsoft products—especially those designed for the Microsoft Windows operating system—would use this interface to access SQL databases. Microsoft calls this formalized interface the *Open Database Connectivity (ODBC) standard*. In the spring of 1992, Microsoft announced that more than a dozen database and application software vendors had committed to providing ODBC support in their products by the end of 1992. With Access, Microsoft provides the basic ODBC Driver Manager and the driver to translate ODBC SQL to the SQL understood by Microsoft SQL Server. Microsoft has also worked with several database vendors to develop drivers for other databases. You can see a diagram of the ODBC architecture in Figure 6-1.

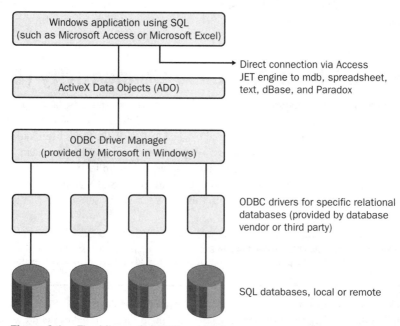

Figure 6-1. The Microsoft ODBC architecture.

Access was one of Microsoft's first ODBC-compliant products, and the ODBC Driver Manager is a standard part of Microsoft's operating systems. Microsoft has further refined this architecture with the introduction of ActiveX Data Objects (ADO). ADO is a special library of objects that you can use to fetch and update data from any database, including Microsoft Access. Once you've added the drivers for the other SQL databases that you want to work with, you can use Access to build an application using data from any of these databases.

> **Note** You can use ADO as a "universal interface" to both databases that support ODBC as well as to those that do not. See Chapter 22, "Understanding Visual Basic Fundamentals," for details about working with ADO using Visual Basic.

Importing vs. Linking Database Files

You have the choice of importing or linking data from other databases, but how do you decide which type of access is best? Here are some guidelines.

You should consider *importing* another database file when any of the following is true:

- The file you need is relatively small and is not changed frequently by users of the other database application.
- You don't need to share the data you create with users of the other database application.
- You're replacing the old database application, and you no longer need the data in the old format.
- You need to load data (such as customers or products as I mentioned earlier) from another source to begin populating your Access tables.
- You need the best performance while working with the data from the other database (because Access performs best with a local copy of the data in Access's native format).

On the other hand, you should consider *linking* another database file when any of the following is true:

- The file is larger than the maximum capacity of a local Access database (2 gigabytes).
- The file is changed frequently by users of the other database application.
- You must share the data on a network with users of the other database application.
- You'll be distributing your application to several individual users, and you will need to make changes to the queries, forms, reports, and modules in the application without disturbing data already entered in the tables.

Chapter 6

Inside Out

Using linked tables in a complex application is a good idea

Even when I'm building an application that I know will be run by only a single user, I usually create a separate .mdb file that contains all the tables and link those tables back into the .mdb file that contains all my queries, forms, reports, and code. If I've been careful creating my original table design, I rarely have to change it. But users are always thinking up some new feature that they would like to have. I can add a new form or report and send the user an update without having to disturb all the data they've already entered.

If you look closely at the tables in the LawTrack Contacts sample database (*Contacts.mdb*), you can see that most of the tables have a little arrow next to the table icon in the Database window, like this:

This indicates that these tables are linked from another data source.

 Note The samples in this chapter use data you can find in files on the companion CD. You can import the data into or export the data from the LawTrack Contacts or Proseware Housing Reservations databases. You might want to work from a copy of these databases to follow along with the examples in this chapter. You can find the result of following many of these examples in the ImportLink sample database, which contains a Companies table that has columns using nearly every available data type in Access.

Importing Data and Databases

You can copy data from a number of different file formats to create a Microsoft Access table. In addition to copying data from a number of popular database file formats, Access can also create a table from data in a spreadsheet or a text file. When you copy data from another database, Access uses information stored by the source database system to convert or name objects in the target Access table. You can import data not only from other Access databases but also from dBASE, Paradox, and—using ODBC—any SQL database that supports the ODBC standard (including Microsoft Visual FoxPro).

Importing dBASE Files

To import a dBASE file, do the following:

1 Open the Access database that will receive the dBASE file. If that database is already open, switch to the Database window.

Chapter 6

2 Choose the Get External Data command from the File menu, and then choose Import from the submenu. Access opens the Import dialog box, as shown here.

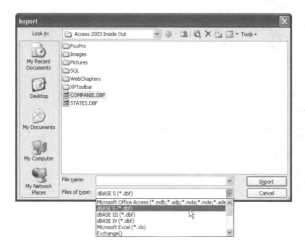

3 Select dBASE III, dBASE IV, or dBASE 5, as appropriate, in the Files of type drop-down list. Select the source file folder from the Look in drop-down list, and then select or type in the file name in the File name text box. If you're having difficulty finding the file you want, click the Tools button on the Import window toolbar and choose Search to open a search dialog box.

4 Click the Import button to import the dBASE file you selected. Access displays a message that informs you of the result of the import procedure, as shown here.

If the import procedure is successful, the new table will have the name of the dBASE file (without the file extension). If Access finds a duplicate table name, it will generate a new name by adding a unique integer to the end of the name. For example, if you import a file named COMPANY.dbf and you already have tables named Company and Company1, Access creates a table named COMPANY2.

5 Click OK to dismiss the message that confirms the import procedure. Access returns to the Import dialog box. You can select another file to import, or you can click the Close button to dismiss the Import dialog box.

You'll find a dBASE 5 file named COMPANIE.DBF on the companion CD included with this book. Follow the procedure described above to import this file into the LawTrack Contacts sample database or into a new blank database. When you open the table that Access creates from this dBASE format data, you'll see data for the sample companies, as shown in Figure 6-2 on the next page.

Chapter 6

183

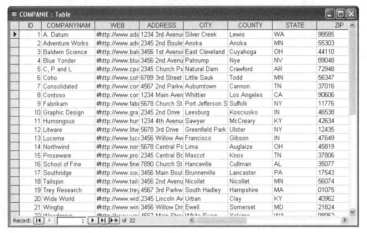

Figure 6-2. An imported dBASE file.

When you look at a table imported from dBASE in Design view, you'll find that Access has converted the data types, as shown in Table 6-1.

Table 6-1. dBASE-to-Access Data Type Conversions

dBASE Data Type	Converts to Access Data Type
Character	Text
Numeric	Number, Field Size property set to Double
Float	Number, Field Size property set to Double
Logical	Yes/No
Date	Date/Time
Memo	Memo

As I noted earlier, I created the COMPANIE dBASE file from the Companies table you can find in the ImportLink sample database. You can open these two tables side by side to see the differences. First, dBASE doesn't support field names longer than 10 characters. So, Company-Name in the original file is shortened to COMPANYNAM, and LastOrderDate appears as LASTORDERD. Also, dBASE doesn't support HyperLink, Currency, or Decimal data types, so it stores HyperLink as Memo, and Currency and Decimal as Number, Double.

Importing Paradox Files

The procedure for importing Paradox files is similar to the procedure for importing dBASE files. To import a Paradox file, do the following:

1   Open the Access database that will receive the Paradox file. If that database is already open, switch to the Database window.

2   Choose the Get External Data command from the File menu, and then choose Import from the submenu. Access opens the Import dialog box, as shown earlier on page 183.

3   Select Paradox in the Files of type drop-down list, and then select the folder and the name of the Paradox file that you want to import.

4   Click the Import button to import the Paradox file you selected.

5   If the Paradox file is encrypted, Access opens a dialog box that asks for the password. Type the correct password and click OK to proceed, or click Cancel to start over.

  When you proceed, Access responds with a message that indicates the result of the import procedure. If the import procedure is successful, the new table will have the name of the Paradox file (without the file extension). If Access finds a duplicate table name, it will generate a new name by adding a unique integer to the end of the name as explained earlier about dBASE files.

6   Click OK to dismiss the message that confirms the import procedure. Access returns to the Import dialog box. You can select another file to import, or you can click Close to dismiss the Import dialog box.

You can try this procedure using the *Companie.db* file that's included on the companion CD.

When you look at a table imported from Paradox in Design view, you'll find that Access has converted the data types, as shown in Table 6-2.

Table 6-2. Paradox-to-Access Data Type Conversions

Paradox Data Type	Converts to Access Data Type
Alphanumeric	Text
Number	Number, Field Size property set to Double
Money	Number, Field Size property set to Double
Short Number	Number, Field Size property set to Integer
Long Integer	Number, Field Size property set to Long Integer
Binary Coded Decimal	Number, Field Size property set to Double
Date	Date/Time
Time	Date/Time
Timestamp	Date/Time
Memo	Memo
Formatted Memo	Not supported
Graphic	Not supported
OLE	OLE Object (but Access won't be able to activate the object)
Logical	Yes/No
AutoIncrement	AutoNumber
Binary	Not supported
Bytes	Not supported

Chapter 6

Importing SQL Tables

To import a table from another database system that supports ODBC SQL, you must first have the ODBC driver for that database installed on your computer. Your computer must also be linked to the network that connects to the SQL server from which you want to import data, and you must have an account on that server. Check with your system administrator for information about correctly connecting to the SQL server.

 If you installed the Microsoft SQL Server Desktop Engine or MSDE that comes with Microsoft Access, you already have an SQL server at your disposal. See the Appendix for instructions about how to install MSDE. One of the best ways to be sure SQL Server is running on your machine is to use the SQL Server Service Manager. Look for the icon of the Service Manager in the notification area of your Windows taskbar. If you don't see it running, start C:\Program Files\Microsoft SQL Server\80\Tools\Binn\sqlmangr.exe. Click the Start/Continue button, check the option to Auto-start service when OS starts, and close the manager. The little green arrow means your server is running. If you see a red block, double-click the icon to open the Manager and click Start/Continue.

To import data from an SQL table, do the following:

1 Open the Access database that will receive the SQL data. If that database is already open, switch to the Database window.

2 Choose the Get External Data command from the File menu, and then choose Import from the submenu. Access opens the Import dialog box, as shown earlier on page 183.

3 Select ODBC Databases in the Files of type drop-down list. Access opens the Select Data Source dialog box, shown in the following illustration, from which you can select the data source that maps to the SQL server containing the table you want to import.

You can select a data source name (.dsn) file that you created previously, or click the Machine Data Source tab, as shown here, to see data sources that are already defined for your computer.

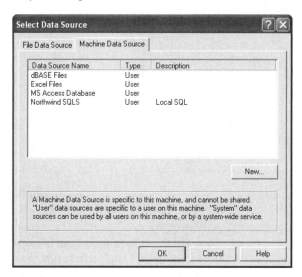

To create a new data source name file, click the New button and follow the instructions to pick an available ODBC driver and locate the data source. A data source is simply a named set of ODBC driver parameters that provide the information the driver needs to dynamically link to the data. If you're familiar with the parameters required by the driver, you can create a data source name file like the one listed here for SQL Server.

```
[ODBC]
DRIVER=SQL Server
UID=JohnV
Trusted_Connection=Yes
WSID=JVXPTEST
APP=Microsoft Open Database Connectivity
SERVER=(local)
Description=SQL Server Local
```

Once you select a data source, click OK.

4 For SQL Server or MSDE, you might need to enter a login ID and password. On a Windows 2000 or Windows XP system, MSDE configures to use your Windows logon to authenticate you, so you do not need to log on to your server. If you connect to a server that uses SQL Server authentication, the driver displays the SQL Server Login dialog box as shown on the next page. You must supply a login ID and password with sufficient authority to read the table you want to import.

Chapter 6

For a server database using SQL Server authentication, enter your login ID and your password, and click OK. If you are authorized to connect to more than one database on the server and you want to connect to a database other than your default database, enter your login ID and password and then click the Options button to open the lower part of the dialog box. When you click in the Database text box, Access logs on to the server and returns a list of available database names. Select the one you want, and click OK. If you don't specify a database name and if multiple databases exist on the server, you'll be connected to the default database for your login ID.

When Access connects to the server, you'll see the Import Objects dialog box, which lists the available tables on that server, as shown next.

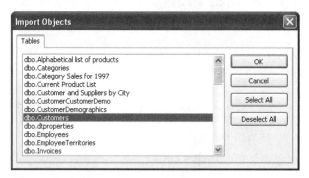

For a Microsoft FoxPro database or file, the ODBC driver displays the ODBC Visual FoxPro Setup dialog box, as shown next. Enter a Data Source Name and optional Description. Select the Database type, and specify the database name or table folder location in the Path box. Click Browse to navigate to the file or folder you want.

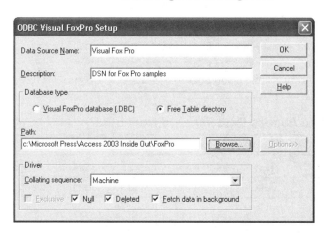

5   From the list of tables or list of files, select the ones you want to import. In the Import
    Objects dialog box for SQL Server, if you select a table name in error, you can click it
    again to deselect it or you can click the Deselect All button to start over. Click OK to
    import the SQL tables you selected.

6   If the import procedure is successful, the new table will have the name of the SQL or
    FoxPro table. If Access finds a duplicate table name, it will generate a new name by
    adding a unique integer to the end of the name as explained earlier about dBASE files.

Troubleshooting

Access won't use ODBC for all file types

Notice that the Machine Data Source tab lists installed sources for dBASE, Excel, Access,
and Visual FoxPro Files. Access will not let you use ODBC for dBASE, Excel, and Access
because it uses its own more efficient direct connection via its database engine. Access
2003 uses ODBC to import and link to Microsoft Visual FoxPro, but you must have FoxPro
installed on your machine to be able to work with FoxPro tables from Access.

Troubleshooting

Connecting to a specific database using trusted authentication

When you connect to a server using Trusted Authentication (your Windows user ID), you automatically connect to the database specified in the data source. You might need to create
more than one data source if you need to connect to more than one database on that server.
See the Appendix, "Installing Microsoft Office," for details about defining ODBC data sources.

Chapter 6

> **Note** You've no doubt noticed by now that the different databases use different style conventions (dbo.newstore, Newstore, NEWSTORE) for table names.

In general, Access converts SQL and FoxPro data types to Access data types, as shown in Tables 6-3 and 6-4.

Table 6-3. SQL-to-Access Data Type Conversions

SQL Data Type	Converts to Access Data Type
CHAR[ACTER]	Text, or Memo if more than 255 characters in length
VARCHAR	Text, or Memo if more than 255 characters in length
TEXT	Memo
TINYINT	Number, Field Size property set to Byte
SMALLINT	Number, Field Size property set to Integer
INT	Number, Field Size property set to Long Integer
REAL	Number, Field Size property set to Double
FLOAT	Number, Field Size property set to Double
DOUBLE	Number, Field Size property set to Double
DATE	Date/Time
TIME	Date/Time
TIMESTAMP	Binary*
IMAGE	OLE Object

* The JET database engine supports a Binary data type (raw hexadecimal), but the Access user interface does not. If you link to a table that has a data type that maps to Binary, you will be able to see the data type in the table definition, but you won't be able to successfully edit this data in a datasheet or form. You can manipulate Binary data in Visual Basic.

Table 6-4. FoxPro-to-Access Data Type Conversions

FoxPro Data Type	Converts to Access Data Type
Character	Text
Numeric	Number, Field Size property set to Integer
Float	Number, Field Size property set to Double
Date	Date/Time
Logical	Yes/No
Memo	Memo
General	OLE Object

Importing Access Objects

If the database from which you want to import data is another Access database, you can import any of the seven major types of Access objects: tables, queries, forms, reports, data access pages, macros, or modules. To achieve the same result, you can also open the source database, select the object you want, choose the Copy command from the Edit menu, open the target database, and then choose the Paste command from the Edit menu. Using the Import command, however, allows you to copy several objects without having to switch back and forth between the two databases.

To import an object from another Access database, take the following steps:

1 Open the Access database that will receive the object. If that database is already open, switch to the Database window.

2 Choose the Get External Data command from the File menu, and then choose Import from the submenu. Access opens the Import dialog box, as shown earlier on page 183.

3 Select Microsoft Access in the Files of type drop-down list, and then select the folder and the name of the .mdb, .adp, .mda, .mde, or .ade[1] file containing the object that you want to import.

4 Click the Import button. Access opens the Import Objects dialog box, shown here, which is a representation of the source database's Database window. First click the tab for the object type, and then select the specific object you want to import.

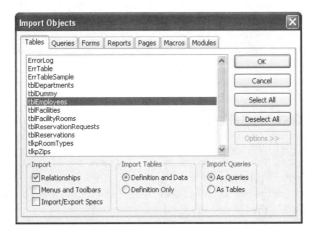

If you select an object in error, you can click the name again to deselect it. If you want to import all objects of a particular type, click the Select All button. You can import multiple objects of different types by clicking each object tab in turn and selecting the objects you want to import.

---

1. Microsoft Access provides a database utility to create a compiled version of an .mdb desktop application or adp project file that contains no source code. The compiled versions have .mde and .ade extensions, respectively. You cannot import forms, reports, macros, or modules from an .mde or .ade file. For details about creating a compiled version of your application, see Chapter 31, "Distributing Your Application."

You can also click the Options button (which has been clicked in the preceding illustration) to select additional options. If you import any tables from the source database, you can select the option to import the table relationships (if any) defined for those tables in the source database. If the object is a table, you can select the option to import the table structure (the table definition) only or to import the structure *and* the stored data. You can also select special options to import all custom menus and toolbars (all command bars) from the source database (see Chapter 24, "The Finishing Touches") or all import/export specifications. (See the sidebar titled "Defining an Import Specification," page 207, for details.) You can also choose to import a query object (the definition of the query) by choosing As Queries under Import Queries, or you can ask Access to run the query and import the data results into a table by choosing As Tables. (See Chapter 7, "Creating and Working with Simple Queries," for details about building and using queries.) Click OK to copy the objects you selected to the current database.

5   If the import procedure is successful, the new object will have the name of the object you selected. If Access finds a duplicate name, it will generate a new name by adding a unique integer to the end of the name as explained previously. Because objects such as queries, forms, reports, macros, and modules might refer to each other or to tables you're importing, you should carefully check name references if Access has to rename an imported object.

> **Note**   If the source Access database is secured, you must have at least read permission for the database, read data permission for the tables, and read definition permission for all other objects in order to import objects. Once you import the objects into your database, you will own the copies of those objects in the target database. See Chapter 30, "Securing Your Database," for details on Access security.

Importing Spreadsheet Data

Access also allows you to import data from spreadsheet files created by Lotus 1-2-3, Lotus 1-2-3 for Windows, and Microsoft Excel versions 3 and later. You can specify a portion of a spreadsheet or the entire spreadsheet file to import into a new table or to append to an existing table. If the first row of cells contains names suitable for field names in the resulting Access table, as shown in the Companies.xls spreadsheet in Figure 6-3, you can tell Access to use these names for your fields.

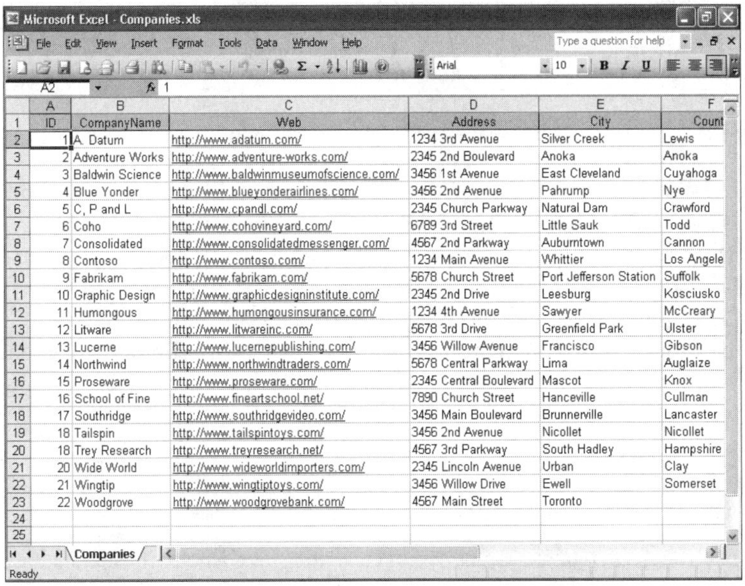

	A	B	C	D	E	F
1	ID	CompanyName	Web	Address	City	Count
2	1	A. Datum	http://www.adatum.com/	1234 3rd Avenue	Silver Creek	Lewis
3	2	Adventure Works	http://www.adventure-works.com/	2345 2nd Boulevard	Anoka	Anoka
4	3	Baldwin Science	http://www.baldwinmuseumofscience.com/	3456 1st Avenue	East Cleveland	Cuyahoga
5	4	Blue Yonder	http://www.blueyonderairlines.com/	3456 2nd Avenue	Pahrump	Nye
6	5	C, P and L	http://www.cpandl.com/	2345 Church Parkway	Natural Dam	Crawford
7	6	Coho	http://www.cohovineyard.com/	6789 3rd Street	Little Sauk	Todd
8	7	Consolidated	http://www.consolidatedmessenger.com/	4567 2nd Parkway	Auburntown	Cannon
9	8	Contoso	http://www.contoso.com/	1234 Main Avenue	Whittier	Los Angele
10	9	Fabrikam	http://www.fabrikam.com/	5678 Church Street	Port Jefferson Station	Suffolk
11	10	Graphic Design	http://www.graphicdesigninstitute.com/	2345 2nd Drive	Leesburg	Kosciusko
12	11	Humongous	http://www.humongousinsurance.com/	1234 4th Avenue	Sawyer	McCreary
13	12	Litware	http://www.litwareinc.com/	5678 3rd Drive	Greenfield Park	Ulster
14	13	Lucerne	http://www.lucernepublishing.com/	3456 Willow Avenue	Francisco	Gibson
15	14	Northwind	http://www.northwindtraders.com/	5678 Central Parkway	Lima	Auglaize
16	15	Proseware	http://www.proseware.com/	2345 Central Boulevard	Mascot	Knox
17	16	School of Fine	http://www.fineartschool.net/	7890 Church Street	Hanceville	Cullman
18	17	Southridge	http://www.southridgevideo.com/	3456 Main Boulevard	Brunnerville	Lancaster
19	18	Tailspin	http://www.tailspintoys.com/	3456 2nd Avenue	Nicollet	Nicollet
20	18	Trey Research	http://www.treyresearch.net/	4567 3rd Parkway	South Hadley	Hampshire
21	20	Wide World	http://www.wideworldimporters.com/	2345 Lincoln Avenue	Urban	Clay
22	21	Wingtip	http://www.wingtiptoys.com/	3456 Willow Drive	Ewell	Somerset
23	22	Woodgrove	http://www.woodgrovebank.com/	4567 Main Street	Toronto	
24						
25						

Figure 6-3. The data in the first row of this Excel spreadsheet can be used as field names when you import the spreadsheet into a new Access table.

Preparing a Spreadsheet

Access determines the data type for the fields in a new table based on the values it finds in the first few rows of data being imported (excluding the first row if that row contains field names). When you import a spreadsheet into a new table, Access stores alphanumeric data as the Text data type with an entry length of 255 characters, numeric data as the Number type with the Field Size property set to Double, numeric data with currency formatting as the Currency type, and any date or time data as the Date/Time type. If Access finds a mixture of data in any column in the first few rows, it imports that column as the Text data type.

> **Tip** If you want to append all or part of a spreadsheet to a target table, you should import or link the entire spreadsheet as a new table and then use an append query to edit the data and move it to the table you want to update. You can learn about Append queries in Chapter 9, "Modifying Data With Action Queries."

If the first several rows are not representative of all the data in your spreadsheet (excluding a potential field names row), you might want to insert a single "dummy" row at the beginning of your spreadsheet with data values that establish the data type you want to use for each column. You can easily delete that row from the table after you import the spreadsheet. For example, if you scroll down in the spreadsheet shown in Figure 6-3 above, you'll find that the last entry is a Canadian address, as shown in Figure 6-4 on the next page.

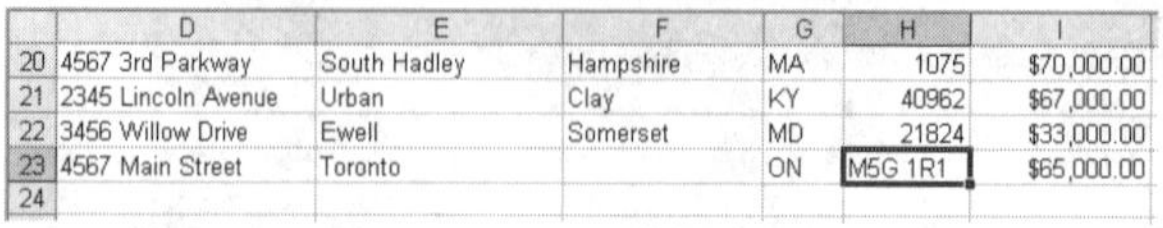

	D	E	F	G	H	I
20	4567 3rd Parkway	South Hadley	Hampshire	MA	1075	$70,000.00
21	2345 Lincoln Avenue	Urban	Clay	KY	40962	$67,000.00
22	3456 Willow Drive	Ewell	Somerset	MD	21824	$33,000.00
23	4567 Main Street	Toronto		ON	M5G 1R1	$65,000.00
24						

Figure 6-4. Zip field entry contains data that can't be stored in numeric format.

Because Access sees only numbers in the first few rows of the Zip column, it will use a Number data type for the Zip field. However, the entry for the Canadian address has letters and spaces, which requires the field to be defined as text. As you'll see later, if you attempt to import this spreadsheet without fixing this problem, Access generates an error for each row that contains nonnumeric data. Access sets the contents of fields that it cannot import to Null. You can solve this by inserting a dummy row at the top with the proper data types in each column, moving the row to the top, or fixing the one bad row after you import the file.

Importing a Spreadsheet

To import a spreadsheet into an Access database, do the following:

1   Open the Access database that will receive the spreadsheet. If that database is already open, switch to the Database window.

2   Choose the Get External Data command from the File menu, and then choose Import from the submenu. Access opens the Import dialog box, as shown earlier on page 183.

3   Select the type of spreadsheet you want to import (Excel or Lotus 1-2-3) in the Files of type drop-down list. Select the folder and the name of the spreadsheet file that you want to import. If you want to follow along with this example, select the *Companies.xls* file on the companion CD.

4   Click the Import button. If your spreadsheet is from Excel version 5.0 or later, it can contain multiple worksheets. If the spreadsheet contains multiple worksheets or any named ranges, Access shows you the first window of the Import Spreadsheet Wizard, as shown in the following illustration. (If you want to import a range that isn't yet defined, exit the wizard, open your spreadsheet to define a name for the range you want, save the spreadsheet, and then restart the import process in Access.) Select the worksheet or the named range that you want to import, and click Next to continue.

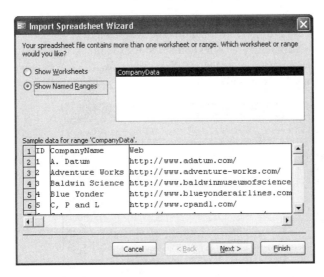

5   After you select a worksheet or a named range, or if your spreadsheet file contains only a single worksheet, the wizard displays the window shown next.

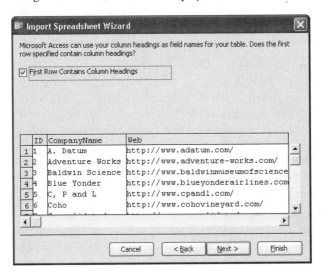

Select the First Row Contains Column Headings check box if you've placed names at the tops of the columns in your spreadsheet. Click Next to go to the next step.

6   In the window that appears, you can specify whether you want to import the data to a new table or append it to an existing one. Click Next to go to the next window.

7 If you choose to create a new table, you can scroll left and right to the various fields and tell the wizard which fields should be indexed in the new table. Your indexing choices are identical to the ones you'll find for the Indexed property of a table field in Design view. In this case, for the ID field, select Yes (No Duplicates) from the Indexed drop-down list box, as shown here, and for the Zip field, select Yes (Duplicates OK).

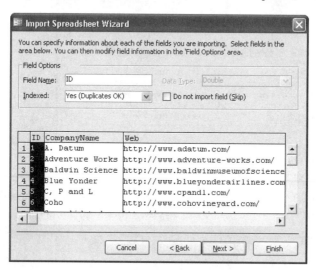

As you move from field to field, the Data Type combo box displays the data type that the wizard picks for each field (based on the data it finds in the first few rows). If what you see here is incorrect, you should exit the wizard and edit your spreadsheet to correct the data in the column. Notice that the Data Type box appears dimmed so you can't change it here. You can also choose to eliminate certain columns that you don't want to appear in the final table. For example, it's quite common to have intervening blank columns to control spacing in a spreadsheet that you print. You can eliminate blank columns by scrolling to them and selecting the Do Not Import Field (Skip) check box. Click Next to go to the next step.

In the window shown next, you can designate a field as the primary key of the new table. If you want, you can tell the wizard to build an ID field for you that will use the AutoNumber data type. (It so happens that this sample spreadsheet already has a numeric ID field that we'll attempt to use as the primary key.) If multiple fields form a unique value for the primary key, you can tell the wizard not to create a primary key. Later, you can open the resulting table in Design view to set the primary key.

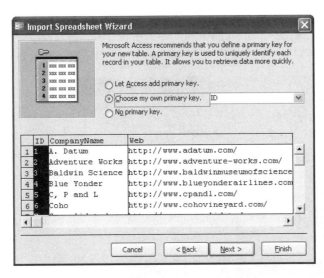

8 Click Next to go to the final window of the wizard. In this window, you can change the name of your new table. (The wizard chooses the name of the spreadsheet or the named range you picked in step 4.) You can also select the option to start the Table Analyzer Wizard to analyze your new table if you like. See Chapter 4, "Creating Your Database and Tables," for details about the Table Analyzer Wizard. If you enter the name of an existing table, Access asks if you want to replace the old table.

9 Click Finish in the last window to import your data. Access opens a message box that indicates the result of the import procedure. If the procedure is successful, the new table will have the name you entered in the last step. If you asked to append the data to an existing table and Access found errors, you can choose to complete the import with errors or go back to the wizard to attempt to fix the problem (such as incorrectly defined columns). You might need to exit the wizard and correct data in the original spreadsheet file as noted in the following section.

Fixing Errors

Earlier in this chapter, in the section titled "Preparing a Spreadsheet," you learned that Access determines data types for the fields in a new table based on the values it finds in the first several rows being imported from a spreadsheet. Figures 6-3 and 6-4, shown earlier, show a spreadsheet whose first few rows would generate a wrong data type for the Zip column in a new Access table. The Number data type that Access would generate for that field, based on the first several entries, would not work for the last row that contains character data. In addition, one of the rows has a duplicate value in the ID column. If you attempt to use this column as the primary key when you import the spreadsheet, you'll get an additional error.

If you were to import that spreadsheet, Access would first display an error message similar to the one shown in Figure 6-5 on the next page. This indicates that the wizard found a problem with the column that you designated as the primary key. If you have duplicate values, the wizard will also inform you. When the wizard encounters any problems with the primary key column, it imports your data but does not define a primary key. This gives you a chance to correct the data in the table and then define the primary key yourself.

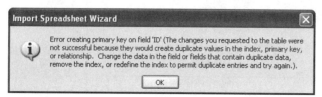

Figure 6-5. Access displays this error message when it encounters a problem with your primary key values.

In addition, if the wizard has any problems with data conversion, it displays a message similar to the one shown in Figure 6-6.

Figure 6-6. Access displays this message if it encounters data conversion errors while importing a spreadsheet.

When the wizard has problems with data conversion, it creates an import errors table in your database (with the name of the spreadsheet in the title) that contains a record for each error. Figure 6-7 shows the import errors table that Access creates when you import the spreadsheet shown in Figure 6-3. Notice that the table lists not only the type of error but also the field and row in the spreadsheet in which the error occurred. In this case, it lists the one row in the source spreadsheet that contains the Canadian Postal Code. The row number listed is the relative row number in the source spreadsheet, not the record number in the resulting table.

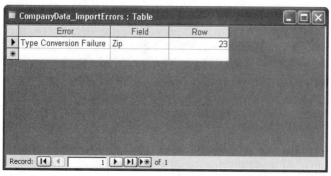

Figure 6-7. The import errors table that results from importing the spreadsheet shown in Figure 6-3.

Figure 6-8 shows the table that results from importing the spreadsheet shown in Figure 6-3. You can find one row that has no entry in the Zip column. If you switch to Design view, you can see that the Import Spreadsheet Wizard selected the Number data type for the Zip field. If you want to be able to store values that include letters, the Zip field must be a text field. Notice that in Design view there is no primary key defined.

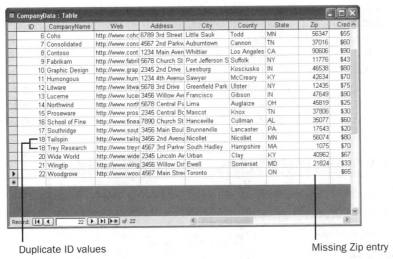

Duplicate ID values   Missing Zip entry

Figure 6-8. After importing the spreadsheet shown in Figure 6-3, one row is missing a postal code entry, and there is a duplicate value in the ID column.

You can correct some of the errors in the table in Design view. For example, you can change the data type of the Zip field to Text (and perhaps change the name to PostalCode), save the table, and then enter the missing value. For either of the rows that have a duplicate ID (18), you can switch to Datasheet view and either delete one of the rows or supply a unique value. You can then set ID as the primary key in Design view.

Importing Text Files

You can import data from a text file into Microsoft Access even though, unlike the data in a spreadsheet, the data in a text file isn't arranged in columns and rows in an orderly way. You make the data in a text file understandable to Access either by creating a *delimited text file*, in which special characters delimit the fields in each record, or by creating a *fixed-width text file*, in which each field occupies the same location in each record.

Preparing a Text File

You might be able to import some text files into Access without changing them, particularly if a text file was created by a program using standard field delimiters. However, in many cases, you'll have to modify the contents of the file, define the file for Access with an import specification, or do both before you can import it. See the sidebar later in this chapter for details about creating an import specification.

Setting Up Delimited Data

Access needs some way to distinguish where fields start and end in each incoming text string. Access supports four standard separator characters: a comma, a tab, a semicolon, and a space. When you use a comma as the separator (a very common technique), the comma (or the carriage return at the end of the record) indicates the end of each field, and the next field begins with the first nonblank character. The commas are not part of the data. To include a comma within a text string as data, you must enclose all text strings within single or double quotation marks (the text qualifier). If any of your text strings contain double quotation marks, you must enclose the strings within single quotation marks, and vice versa. Access accepts only single or double quotation marks (but not both) as the text qualifier, so all embedded quotes in a file that you want to import into Access must be of the same type. In other words, you can't include a single quotation mark in one field and a double quotation mark in another field within the same file. Figure 6-9 shows a sample comma-separated and double-quote–qualified text file. You can find this file (*CompaniesCSV.txt*) on the sample CD.

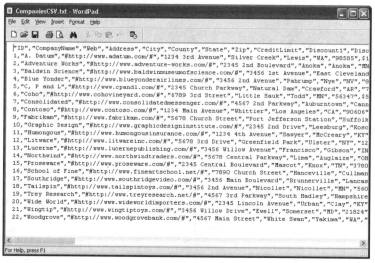

Figure 6-9. A comma-separated and double-quote–qualified text file.

Another common way to separate data is to use the tab character between fields. In fact, when you save a spreadsheet file as text in most spreadsheet programs, the program stores the columns with tab characters between them. Figure 6-10 shows one of the worksheets from the Companies spreadsheet from Microsoft Excel saved as text in Microsoft WordPad. (You can see the tab alignment marks that I placed on the Ruler to line up the columns.) Notice that Excel added double quotation marks around only one of the text fields—the company name that contains a comma. Because this file is tab delimited, Access accepts the text fields without quotation marks. However, if all or part of your incoming data contains a text qualifier surrounding some of the fields, you should specify that qualifier when you import the data. If you do not do that, Access imports the qualifier characters as well.

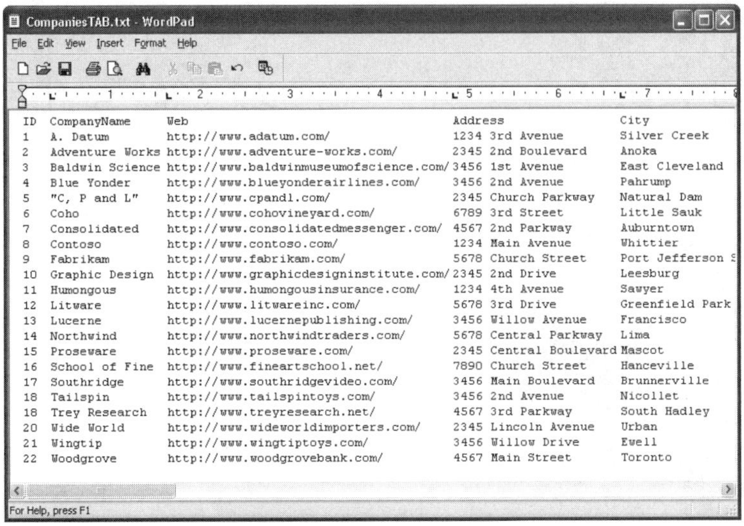

ID	CompanyName	Web	Address	City
1	A. Datum	http://www.adatum.com/	1234 3rd Avenue	Silver Creek
2	Adventure Works	http://www.adventure-works.com/	2345 2nd Boulevard	Anoka
3	Baldwin Science	http://www.baldwinmuseumofscience.com/	3456 1st Avenue	East Cleveland
4	Blue Yonder	http://www.blueyonderairlines.com/	3456 2nd Avenue	Pahrump
5	"C, P and L"	http://www.cpandl.com/	2345 Church Parkway	Natural Dam
6	Coho	http://www.cohovineyard.com/	6789 3rd Street	Little Sauk
7	Consolidated	http://www.consolidatedmessenger.com/	4567 2nd Parkway	Auburntown
8	Contoso	http://www.contoso.com/	1234 Main Avenue	Whittier
9	Fabrikam	http://www.fabrikam.com/	5678 Church Street	Port Jefferson S
10	Graphic Design	http://www.graphicdesigninstitute.com/	2345 2nd Drive	Leesburg
11	Humongous	http://www.humongousinsurance.com/	1234 4th Avenue	Sawyer
12	Litware	http://www.litwareinc.com/	5678 3rd Drive	Greenfield Park
13	Lucerne	http://www.lucernepublishing.com/	3456 Willow Avenue	Francisco
14	Northwind	http://www.northwindtraders.com/	5678 Central Parkway	Lima
15	Proseware	http://www.proseware.com/	2345 Central Boulevard	Mascot
16	School of Fine	http://www.fineartschool.net/	7890 Church Street	Hanceville
17	Southridge	http://www.southridgevideo.com/	3456 Main Boulevard	Brunnerville
18	Tailspin	http://www.tailspintoys.com/	3456 2nd Avenue	Nicollet
18	Trey Research	http://www.treyresearch.net/	4567 3rd Parkway	South Hadley
20	Wide World	http://www.wideworldimporters.com/	2345 Lincoln Avenue	Urban
21	Wingtip	http://www.wingtiptoys.com/	3456 Willow Drive	Ewell
22	Woodgrove	http://www.woodgrovebank.com/	4567 Main Street	Toronto

Figure 6-10. A tab-separated text file.

As with data type analysis, Access examines the first few rows of your file to determine the delimiter and the text qualifier. Notice in Figure 6-10 that tabs are clearly the delimiter, but only one of the text fields ("C, P and L" in the fifth line) is qualified with double quotes. As you'll see later, if you want to import a file that is delimited differently, you can specify different delimiters and separators in the Import Text Wizard. The important thing to remember is that your data should have a consistent data type in all the rows for each column—just as it should in spreadsheet files. If your text file is delimited, the delimiters must be consistent throughout the file.

Setting Up Fixed-Width Data

Access can also import text files when the fields appear in fixed locations in each record in the file. You might encounter this type of file if you download a print output file from a host computer. Figure 6-11 on the next page shows a sample fixed-width text file. Notice that each field begins in exactly the same location in all the records. (To see this sort of fixed spacing on your screen, you must display the file using a monospaced font such as Courier New.) Unlike delimited files, to prepare this type of file for importing, you must first remove any heading or summary lines from the file. The file must contain only records, with the data you want to import in fixed locations.

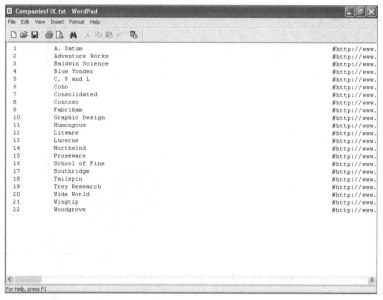

Figure 6-11. A fixed-width text file.

Importing a Text File

Before you can import a text file, you'll probably need to prepare the data or define the file for Access with an import specification, or both, as discussed earlier in the section titled "Preparing a Text File." After you do that, you can import the text file into an Access database by doing the following:

1 Open the Access database that will receive the text data. If that database is already open, switch to the Database window.

2 Choose the Get External Data command from the File menu, and then choose Import from the submenu. Access opens the Import dialog box, as shown earlier on page 183.

3 Select Text Files in the Files of type drop-down list, and then select the folder and the name of the file you want to import. (For these examples, I used the CompaniesTAB.txt and CompaniesFIX.txt files that you can find on the companion CD.) Access starts the Import Text Wizard and displays the first window of the wizard, as shown here.

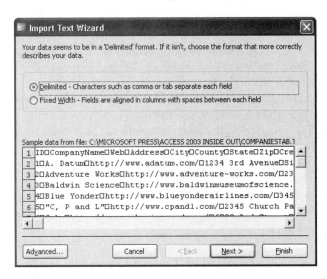

4   In this window, the wizard makes its best guess about whether the data is delimited or fixed-width. It displays the first several rows of data, which you can examine to confirm the wizard's choice. (The square characters you see in this window are the tab characters.) If the wizard has made the wrong choice, your data is probably formatted incorrectly. You should exit the wizard and fix the source file as suggested in the section "Preparing a Text File." If the wizard has made the correct choice, click Next to go to the next step.

5   If your file is delimited, the Import Text Wizard displays the window shown in the next illustration.

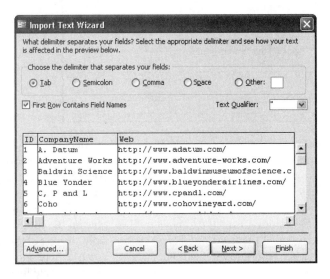

Here you can verify the character that delimits the fields in your text file and the qualifier character that surrounds text strings. Remember that usually when you save a delimited text file from a spreadsheet program, the field delimiter is a tab character and you'll find quotation marks only around strings that contain commas. If the wizard doesn't find a text field with quotation marks in the first few lines, it might assume that no text is surrounded by quotes, and therefore it might set the Text Qualifier field to {none}. You might need to change the Text Qualifier field from {none} to " if this is the case. (You'll need to do this with the *CompaniesTab.txt* sample file.)

> **Note** The *CompaniesTab.txt* file has a date field that Excel formatted as dd-mmm-yy (28-Mar-03). Access correctly identified this as a date/time field, but it won't import it correctly. You must click the Advanced button and change the Date Order to DMY and the Date Delimiter to – to be able to import this file correctly. See "Defining an Import Specification" later in this chapter for details.

If your file is in fixed-width format, the wizard displays the window shown in the following illustration. (I have scrolled to the right to show one of the problems.)

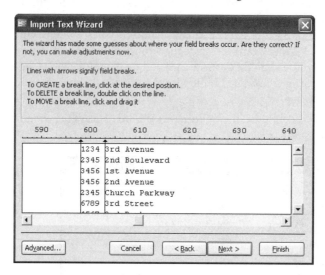

Instead of showing delimiting characters, the wizard offers a graphic representation of where it thinks each field begins. To change the definition of a field, you can drag any line to move it. You can also create an additional field by clicking at the position on the display where fields should be separated. If the wizard creates too many fields, you can double-click any extra delimiting lines to remove them. In the example shown in the preceding illustration (using the *CompaniesFIX.txt* file on the companion CD), the wizard assumes that the street number is separate from the rest of the address. It also assumes that the State and Zip fields are one field because there's no space between them. Because many of the spaces in the sample Comments field line up, it splits this field into several fields. You can double-click the line following the street number to remove it. You can click between the state and zip data to separate those into two fields. Finally, you can double-click all the extra lines the wizard inserted in Comments to turn that into one field.

After you finish in this window, click Next to go to the next step.

6 In the next window, shown here, you specify whether you want to import the text into a new table or append the data to an existing table.

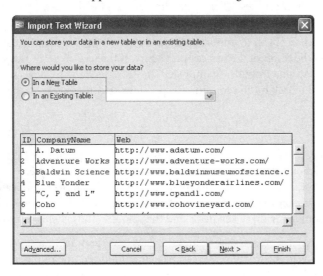

If you decide to create a new table, the wizard displays the window shown next. Here you can specify or confirm field names (you can change field names even if the first row in the text file contains names), select field data types, and set indexed properties. If you're working in a fixed-width text file, you should provide the field names; otherwise, Access names the fields Field1, Field2, and so on.

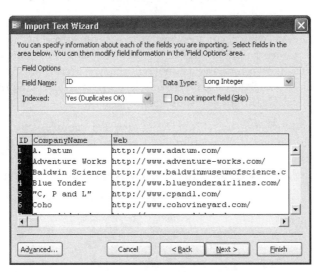

If you decide to append the data to an existing table, either the columns must exactly match both the count and the data type of the columns in the target table (left to right) or the file must be a delimited file with column names in the first row that match column names in the target table.

7   Click Next to go to the next window, where you can select a primary key, much as you did for spreadsheet files. Click Next when you are finished setting a primary key.

8   In the final window of the wizard, you confirm the name of the new table or the target table and click Finish to import your data. Access displays a confirmation message to show you the result of the import procedure. If the wizard encounters an error that prevents any data from being imported, it will reopen the final wizard window. You can click the Back button to return to previous settings to correct them.

Fixing Errors

While importing text files, you might encounter errors that are similar to those described earlier in the section titled "Importing Spreadsheet Data." For example, when you append a text file to an existing table, some rows might be rejected because of duplicate primary keys. Unless the primary key for your table is an AutoNumber field, the rows you append from the text file must contain primary key fields and the values in those fields must be unique.

For delimited text files, Access determines the data type (and delimiter and text qualifier) based on the fields in the first several records being imported. If a number appears in a field in the first several records but subsequent records contain text data, you must enclose that field in quotation marks in at least one of the first few rows so that Access will use the Text data type for that field. If a number first appears without decimal places, Access will use the Number data type with the Field Size property set to Long Integer. This setting will generate errors later if the numbers in other records contain decimal places. You can also explicitly tell Access the data type to use by defining a custom import specification. See "Defining an Import Specification" for details.

Access displays a message if it encounters any errors. As with errors that are generated when you import a spreadsheet, Access creates an import errors table. The table contains a record for each error. The import errors table lists not only the type of error but also the column and row in the text file in which the error occurred. The errors you can encounter with a text file are similar to those described for a spreadsheet file earlier.

You can correct some errors in the table in Design view. For example, you can change the data type of fields if the content of the fields can be converted to the new data type. With other errors, you must either add missing data in Datasheet view or delete the imported records and import the table again after correcting the values in the text file that originally caused the errors.

Defining an Import Specification

If you are likely to import the same fixed-width file often (for example, a text file you receive from a mainframe once a month) or if you want to be able to use a macro or a Visual Basic procedure to automate importing a text file, you can use the Import Text Wizard to save an import specification for use by your automation procedures. To do so, use the wizard to examine your file, and verify that the wizard identifies the correct fields. Click the Advanced button to see an Import Specification window like the one shown here.

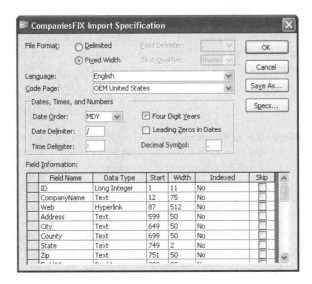

For fixed-width specifications, you can define the field names, data types, start column, width, indexed properties, and whether or not to skip a field. You can identify the language in the Language combo box and the character set in the Code Page combo box. You can also specify the way Access recognizes date and time values and numeric fractions. (For example, for a file coming from a non-U.S. machine, the Date Order value might be DMY, and the Decimal Symbol character might be a comma.) Click the Save As button to save your specification, and give it a name. You can also click the Specs button to load and edit other previously saved specifications. The loaded specification is the one Access uses to import the current file.

For details about modifying your table design, see Chapter 5, "Modifying Your Table Design." See Table 5-3 in Chapter 5 for data conversion limitations.

Modifying Imported Tables

When you import data from an external source, Microsoft Access often has to use default data types or lengths that can accommodate all the incoming data. You will then need to correct these default settings for your needs. For example, Access assigns a maximum length of 255 characters to text data imported from a spreadsheet or a text file. Even when the source of the data is another database, Access might choose numeric data types that can accept the data but that might not be correct. For example, numeric data in dBASE might be of the Integer type, but Access stores all numeric data from dBASE with a Field Size setting of Double.

Unless you're importing data from an SQL or Paradox database that has a primary key defined, Access does not define a primary key in the new table, so you must do that yourself. Also, if you did not include field names when importing a text or spreadsheet file, you'll probably want to enter meaningful names in the resulting table.

Linking Files

You can link tables from other Microsoft Access databases—whether the other databases are local or on a network—and work with the data as if these tables were defined in your current Access database. If you want to work with data stored in another database format supported by Access (dBASE, Paradox, or any SQL database that supports ODBC, including Microsoft FoxPro), you can link the data instead of importing it.

> **Note** Although you can *import* queries, forms, reports, macros, and modules from another Access database file, you cannot link these types of objects. Any object that Access needs to run (rather than simply be a container for data) must be in your local database.

In most cases, you can read data, insert new records, delete records, or change data just as if the linked file were an Access table in your database. You can also link text and spreadsheet format data so that you can process it with queries, forms, and reports in your Access database. You can update and insert new rows in spreadsheets, but you can't delete rows. You can only read the data in linked text files.

This ability to link data is especially important when you need to access data on a host computer or share data from your application with many other users.

> **Note** Microsoft Access 2003 supports linking to dBASE or Paradox versions 5.0 and earlier, and it allows full update if it can find the associated index files. If you need to work with later versions, you must install the Borland Database Engine (BDE).

Security Considerations

If you attempt to link a file or a table from a database system that is protected, Access asks you for a password. If the security information you supply is correct and Access success-fully links the secured data, Access optionally stores the security information with the linked table entry so that you do not have to enter this information each time you or your application opens the table. Access stores this information in the hidden Connect property of a linked table, so a knowledgeable person might be able to retrieve it by writing code to examine this property. Therefore, if you have linked sensitive information to your Access database and have supplied security information, you should consider encrypting your database. Consult Chapter 30, "Securing Your Database," for information about securing and encrypting your Access database.

If you are linking your database to Microsoft SQL Server tables and are using Microsoft Windows domain security, you can set options in SQL Server to accept the Windows domain user ID if the user logs on correctly to the network. Therefore, you won't need to store secu-rity information with the link. If your server contains particularly sensitive information, you can disable this option to guard against unauthorized access from logged on but unattended network workstations.

Performance Considerations

Access always performs best when working with its own files on your local machine. If you link tables or files from other databases, you might notice slower performance. In particular, you can expect slower performance if you connect over a network to a table or a file in another database, even if the remote table is an Access table. You won't see any performance difference if you link to Access tables in another .mdb file on your local machine.

When sharing data over a network, you should consider how you and other people can use the data in a way that maximizes performance. For example, instead of working directly with the tables, you should work with queries on the shared data whenever possible to limit the amount of data you need at any one time. When inserting new data in a shared table, you should use an Access form that is set only for data entry so that you don't have to access the entire table to add new data.

> See Chapter 7, "Creating and Working with Simple Queries," Chapter 12, "Customizing a Form," Chapter 18, "Building Views, Functions, and Stored Procedures," Chapter 23, "Automating Your Application with Visual Basic," and Chapter 31, "Distributing Your Application," for more information.

You can view and set options for multiple users sharing data by choosing Options from the Tools menu and clicking the Advanced tab of the Options dialog box, as shown in Figure 6-12 on the next page. The original settings for these options are often appropriate when you share data over a network, so it's a good idea to consult your system administrator before making changes.

Chapter 6

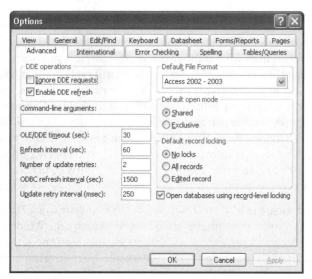

Figure 6-12. The Options dialog box with the Advanced tab selected.

One very important consideration is record locking. When Access needs to update data in a shared file, it must lock the data to ensure no other machine is trying to write the same data at the same time. You should set options so that records are not locked if you are simply browsing through data. Even if your application frequently updates and inserts data, you should leave Default record locking set to No locks. With this setting, Microsoft Access 2003 locks individual records only for the short period of time that it is writing the row, so the chance of receiving an update error while two users are trying to update the same row at the exact same time is very small.

If you want to ensure that no one else can change a record that you have begun to update, you should set Default record locking to Edited record. Note, however, that no other user will be able to edit a record that another has begun to change. If a user begins to type a change in a record and then goes off for lunch, no one else will be able to change that record from another machine until that user either saves the row or clears the edit.

Inside Out

Leave default record locking alone

I never set either All records or Edited record as the default. Either one can cause extra overhead while updating data and can lock out other users unnecessarily. In the rare case that an update conflict occurs with No locks, Access gives the second user the opportunity to refresh the data and reenter the blocked update. Also, you can set record locking individually in forms and reports. See Chapter 12, "Customizing a Form," and Chapter 16, "Advanced Report Design," for details.

You can set options to limit the number of times Access will retry an update to a locked record and how long it will wait between retries. You can also control how often Access reviews updates made by other users to shared data by setting the refresh interval. If this setting is very low, Access will waste time performing this task repeatedly.

Microsoft Access 97 (version 8) and earlier locked an entire 2-KB page each time you updated, inserted, or deleted rows. This meant that only one user at a time could update any of the rows stored physically within the page. The page size in Access 2000 increased to 4 KB, but Access 2000 (version 9) and later also support record-level locking that eliminates locking collisions when two users attempt to update different rows stored on the same data storage page. Unless you are designing an application that frequently needs to update hundreds of rows at a time (for example, with action queries), you should leave the Open databases using record-level locking check box selected.

Linking Access Tables

To link a table from another Access database to your database, do the following:

1   Open the Access database to which you want to link the table. If that database is already open, switch to the Database window.

2   Choose the Get External Data command from the File menu, and then choose Link Tables from the submenu. Access opens the Link dialog box, which is similar to the Import dialog box shown earlier on page 183 and which lists the types of databases you can link.

3   Select Microsoft Access in the Files of type drop-down list, and then select the folder and the name of the .mdb, .mda, or .mde file that contains the table you want to link. (You cannot link tables from an .adp or .ade file because those are actually tables in SQL Server—use an ODBC link to the server directly as explained in "Linking SQL Tables," page 215.) If you're connecting over a network, select the logical drive that is assigned to the network server containing the database you want. If you want Access to automatically connect to the network server each time you open the table, type the full network location (also known as the UNC or Universal Naming Convention name) in the File name box instead of selecting a logical drive. For example, on a Microsoft Windows network you might enter a network location such as:

    `\\dbsvr\access\shared\northwind.mdb`

    After you select the Access database file you want, click the Link button to see the tables in that database.

4   Access opens the Link Tables dialog box, shown next, which lists the tables available in the database you selected. Select one or more tables, and click OK to link the tables to the current database. If the link procedure is successful, the new table will have the name of the table you selected.

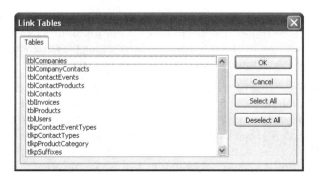

Access marks the icon for linked tables in the Database window with an arrow, as shown in the next illustration. If Access finds a duplicate name, it generates a new name by adding a unique integer to the end of the name as described earlier. Because objects such as forms, reports, macros, and modules might refer to the linked table by its original name, you should carefully check name references if Access has to rename a linked table.

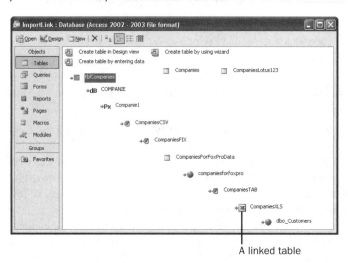

A linked table

Inside Out

Keeping the Connect property current

One problem with using linked data in an application that you're going to distribute to someone else is the location of the linked files on your machine might not be exactly the same as it is on your user's machine. For example, the internal Connect property might point to D:\MyDatabases\MyData.mdb, but your user installs the application on the C: drive. You might have noticed that a form always opens when you open the LawTrack Contacts sample database and that it takes a few seconds before it returns you to the Database window. I wrote code behind this initial form that verifies the table links and fixes them. You can learn how I built this code in Chapter 31, "Distributing Your Application."

Linking dBASE and Paradox Files

Linking files from a foreign database is almost as easy as linking an Access table. To link to a file from dBASE or Paradox, do the following:

1 Open the Access database to which you want to link the file. If that database is already open, switch to the Database window.

2 Choose the Get External Data command from the File menu, and then choose Link Tables from the submenu. Access opens the Link dialog box, which lists the types of databases you can link.

3 Select dBASE III, dBASE IV, dBASE 5, or Paradox, as appropriate, in the Files of type drop-down list, and then select the folder and the name of the database file that you want to link. If you're connecting over a network, select the logical drive that is assigned to the network server that contains the database you want. If you want Access to automatically connect to the network server each time you open the linked file, type the full network location in the File name box instead of selecting a logical drive. For example, on a Windows network you might enter a network location such as:

```
\\dbsvr\dbase\shared\newstore.dbf
```

4 Click the Link button to link the selected dBASE or Paradox file.

> **Note** If you have Microsoft JET 4.0 Service Pack 5 or later installed on your machine (you should be running Service Pack 8 or later with Microsoft Office 2003), Access locates any required index for your dBase or Paradox file as long as the index resides in the same folder as the file. If you have an earlier version of JET installed, Access prompts you for the location of the index file. If Access cannot locate the index file, you might not be able to update data in the file from Access. To check for the latest updates, go to *http://windows-update.microsoft.com/*.

5 If you have selected an encrypted Paradox file, Access opens a dialog box that asks you for the correct password. Type the correct password and click OK to proceed, or click Cancel to start over. If the link procedure is successful, the new table will have the name of the file you selected (without the file extension). If Access finds a duplicate name, it will generate a new name by adding a unique integer to the end of the name.

6 Click OK to dismiss the message that confirms the link action. Access returns you to the Link dialog box. You can select another file to link, or you can click Close to dismiss the dialog box.

Linking Text and Spreadsheet Files

Linking a text file or an Excel spreadsheet file is almost identical to importing these types of files, as discussed earlier in this chapter. (You cannot link Lotus 1-2-3 files, you can only import them.) As noted, you can only read linked text files, but you can update and add new rows (but not delete rows) in Excel spreadsheet files.

Chapter 6

To link a spreadsheet file or a text file, do the following:

1 Open the Access database to which you want to link the file. If that database is already open, switch to the Database window.

2 Choose the Get External Data command from the File menu, and then choose Link Tables from the submenu. Access opens the Link dialog box, which lists the types of files you can link.

3 Select Microsoft Excel or Text Files, as appropriate, in the Files of type drop-down list, and then select the folder and the name of the file that you want to link. If you're connecting over a network, select the logical drive that is assigned to the network server that contains the database you want. If you want Access to automatically connect to the network server each time you open the linked file, type the full network location in the File name box instead of choosing a logical drive, path, and file name. For example, on a Windows network you might enter a network location such as:

```
\\filesvr\excel\shared\companies.xls
```

4 Click the Link button to start the Link Spreadsheet Wizard or the Link Text Wizard.

5 Follow the steps in the wizard, which are identical to the steps for importing a spreadsheet or text file, as described earlier in this chapter.

> **Caution** You can have the same problems with delimiters, text qualifiers, and data types noted under importing. You might need to correct or reformat the data in your text or spreadsheet file to be able to successfully link it. For example, if Access guesses the wrong data type for a column in an Excel file, you will see #Error in fields that have the incorrect data type and you will not be able to edit the data.

Linking SQL Tables

To link a table from another database system that supports ODBC SQL, you must have the ODBC driver for that database installed on your computer. Your computer must also be linked to the network that connects to the SQL server from which you want to link a table, and you must have an account on that server. Check with your system administrator for information about correctly connecting to the SQL server.

 If you installed the Microsoft SQL Server Desktop Engine, or MSDE, that comes with Microsoft Access, you already have an SQL server at your disposal. See the Appendix for instructions about how to install MSDE. One of the best ways to be sure SQL Server is running on your machine is to use the SQL Server Service Manager. Look for the icon of the Service Manager in the notification area of your Windows taskbar. If you don't see it running, start C:\Program Files\Microsoft SQL Server\80\Tools\Binn\sqlmangr.exe. The little green arrow means your server is running. If you see a red block, double-click the icon to open the Manager and click Start/Continue. It's also a good idea to select Auto-start service when OS starts.

To link an SQL table, do the following:

1 Open the Access database to which you want to link the SQL table. If that database is already open, switch to the Database window.

2 Choose the Get External Data command from the File menú, and then choose Link Tables from the submenu. Access opens the Link dialog box, which lists the types of files you can link.

3 Select ODBC Databases in the Files of type drop-down list. Access opens the Select Data Source dialog box, shown earlier on page 88, in which you can select the data source that maps to the SQL server containing the table you want to link. Select a data source, and click OK. The ODBC driver displays the SQL Server Login dialog box for the SQL data source that you selected if the server is not set up to accept your Windows login. If you are linking to a Microsoft FoxPro database or file, the ODBC driver displays the Configure Connection dialog box.

4 When you are required to enter a login ID and password and if you are authorized to connect to more than one database on the server and you want to connect to a database other than your default database, enter your login ID and password. Then click the Options button to open the lower part of the dialog box. When you click in the Database combo box, Access logs on to the server and returns a list of available database names. Select the one you want, and click OK. If you don't specify a database name and if multiple databases exist on the server, Access will connect you to the default database for your login ID.

For Microsoft FoxPro, specify the database name or FoxPro file folder and click OK.

When Access connects to the server or FoxPro database, you'll see the Link Tables dialog box, similar to the Import Objects dialog box shown earlier on page 183, which lists the available tables on that server.

5 From the list of tables, select the ones you want to link. If you select a table name in error, you can click it again to deselect it, or you can click the Deselect All button to start over. Click OK to link to the tables you selected.

6 If the link procedure is successful, the new table will have the name of the SQL table or FoxPro file (without the file extension). If Access finds a duplicate name, it will generate a new name by adding a unique integer to the end of the name.

Troubleshooting

You can't connect to a specific database using trusted authentication because you use more than one data source

When you connect to a server using Trusted Authentication (your Windows user ID), you automatically connect to the database specified in the data source. You might need to create more than one data source if you need to connect to more than one database on that server. See the Appendix, "Installing Microsoft Office," for details about defining ODBC data sources.

Chapter 6

215

Modifying Linked Tables

You can make some changes to the definitions of linked tables to customize them for use in your Access environment. When you attempt to open the table in Design view, Access opens a dialog box to warn you that you cannot modify certain properties of a linked table. You can still click OK to open the linked table in Design view.

You can open a linked table in Design view to change the Format, Decimal Places, Caption, Description, and Input Mask property settings for any field. You can set these properties to customize the way you look at and update data in Access forms and reports. You can also give any linked table a new name for use within your Access database (although the table's original name remains unchanged in the source database) to help you better identify the table or to enable you to use the table with the queries, forms, and reports that you've already designed.

Changing a table's design in Access has no effect on the original table in its source database. However, if the design of the table in the source database changes, you must relink the table to Access. You must also unlink and relink any table if your user ID or your password changes.

Unlinking Linked Tables

It is easy to unlink tables that are linked to your Access database. In the Database window, simply select the table you want to unlink and then press the Delete key or choose Delete from the Edit menu. Access displays the confirmation message shown in Figure 6-13. Click the Yes button to unlink the table. Unlinking the table does not delete the table; it simply removes the link from your table list in the Database window.

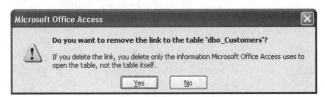

Figure 6-13. The confirmation message that appears when you unlink a table.

Using the Linked Table Manager

If you move some or all of your linked tables to a different location, you must either delete your linked tables and relink them or update the location information before you can open the tables. You can easily update the location information in the table links by using the Linked Table Manager. To use this handy utility, open the database that contains linked tables that need to be relinked, choose Database Utilities from the Tools menu, and then choose Linked Table Manager from the submenu. The utility opens a dialog box that displays all the linked tables in your database, as shown in Figure 6-14. Simply select the ones that you think need to be verified and updated, and then click OK. If any of the linked tables have been moved to a different location, the Linked Table Manager prompts you with a dialog box so that you can specify the new file location. You can also select the Always prompt for new location check box to verify the file location for all linked tables.

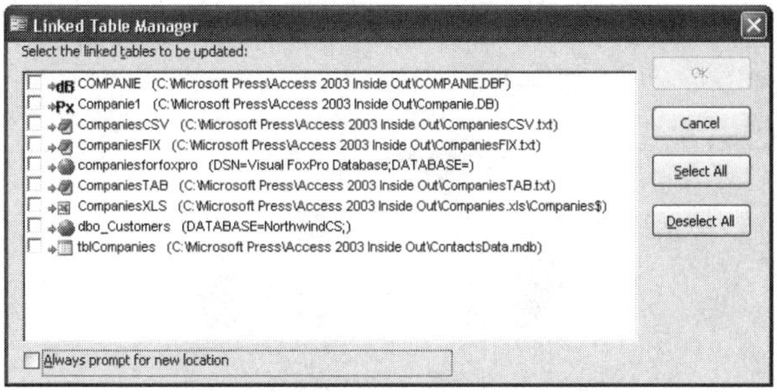

Figure 6-14. The Linked Table Manager dialog box.

Now you have all the information you need to import and link data using Access. For information on how to export data, see Article 2. Now that you know how to build tables, modify them, and import/link them, it's time to move on to more fun stuff—building queries on your tables—in the next chapter.

Creating and Working with Simple Queries

In the last three chapters, you learned how to create tables, modify them, and link or import tables from other data sources. Although you can certainly build forms and reports that get their data directly from your tables, most of the time you will want to sort or filter your data or display data from more than one table. For these tasks, you need queries.

When you define and run a *select query*, which selects information from the tables and queries in your database, Microsoft Access creates a *recordset* of the selected data. In most cases, you can work with a recordset in the same way that you work with a table: You can browse through it, select information from it, print it, and even update the data in it. But unlike a real table, a recordset doesn't actually exist in your database. Access creates a recordset from the data in the source tables of your query at the time you run the query. *Action queries*—which insert, update, or delete data—will be covered in Chapter 9, "Modifying Data with Action Queries."

As you learn to design forms and reports later in this book, you'll find that queries are the best way to focus on the specific data you need for the task at hand. You'll also find that queries are useful for providing choices for combo and list boxes, which make entering data in your database much easier.

Note The examples in this chapter are based on the tables and data from the LawTrack Contacts sample database (*Contacts.mdb*), a backup copy of the data for the LawTrack Contacts sample database (*ContactsDataCopy.mdb*), the Housing Reservations database (*Housing.mdb*), and the backup copy of the data for the Housing Reservations sample database (*HousingDataCopy.mdb*) on the companion CD included with this book. The query results you see from the sample queries you build in this chapter might not exactly match what you see in this book if you have reloaded the sample data using zfrmLoadData in either application or have changed any of the data in the tables.

Microsoft Access provides five ways to begin creating a new query.

- In the Database window, click the Queries button on the Object bar, and then click the New button on the Database window toolbar. You will see the New Query dialog box that lets you either start a new query from scratch in Design view or select one of the four query wizards. (You'll learn about query wizards in Chapter 8.)

- Click the Queries button on the Database window Object bar, and then double-click the Create query In Design view link at the top of the query list to go directly to the query designer.

- Click the Queries button on the Database window Object bar, and then double-click the Create query by using wizard link to open the Simple Query Wizard.

- Choose Query from the Insert menu. The New Query dialog box opens and lets you either start a new query from scratch in Design view or select one of the four query wizards. If you have selected either a table or a query in the Database window before you choose Query from the Insert menu, and you then choose the Design View option, the query designer opens with the table or query you selected in the top part of the Query window.

- With the focus on the Database window, choose Query from the New Object button on the toolbar. Again, you will see the New Query dialog box that allows you to choose to go directly to Design view or select one of the wizards. As with the previous method, if you have selected a table or query before you click the New Object button, and then you choose Design View, that table or query appears in the top part of the Query window.

To open an existing query in Design view, click the Queries button in the Database window, select the query you want, and click the Design button. Figure 7-1 shows the Query list for the LawTrack Contacts database.

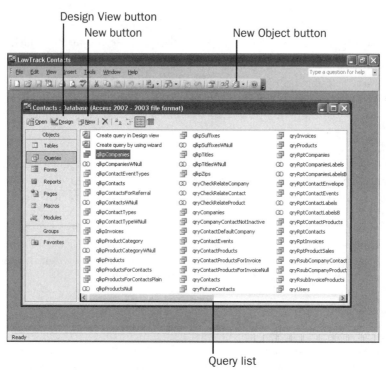

Figure 7-1. Opening a query in Design view from the Database window.

Figure 7-2 shows a query that has been opened in Design view. The upper part of the Query window contains field lists, and the lower part contains the design grid.

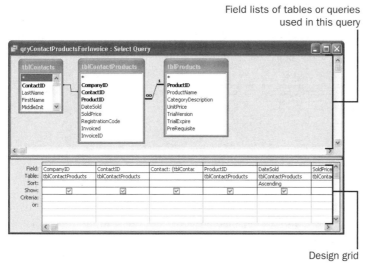

Field lists of tables or queries used in this query

Design grid

Figure 7-2. A query open in Design view.

Selecting Data from a Single Table

One advantage of using queries is that they allow you to find data easily in multiple related tables. Queries are also useful, however, for sifting through the data in a single table. All the techniques you use for working with a single table apply equally to more complex multiple-table queries. This chapter covers the basics about building queries to select data from a single table. The next chapter shows you how to build more complex queries with multiple tables, totals, parameters, and more.

The easiest way to start building a query on a single table is to open the Database window, select the table you want, and on the toolbar select Query from the New Object button's drop-down list. (See Figure 7-1.) Do this now with the tblContacts table in the LawTrack Contacts database, and then select Design View in the New Query dialog box. Click OK to open the window shown in Figure 7-3 on the next page.

> **Tip** The New Object button "remembers" the last new object type that you created. If you've created only tables up to this point, you have to use the button's drop-down list to select Query. Once you start a new query in this manner, the New Object button defaults to Query until you use the button's drop-down list to create a different type of object.

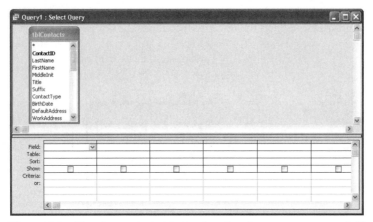

Figure 7-3. The Query window in Design view for a new query on tblContacts.

As mentioned earlier, the Query window in Design view has two main parts. In the upper part are field lists with the fields for the tables or queries you chose for this query. The lower part of the window is the design grid, in which you do all the design work. Each column in the grid represents one field that you'll work with in this query. As you'll see later, a field can be a simple field from one of the tables or a calculated field based on several fields in the tables.

You use the first row of the design grid to select fields—the fields you want in the resulting recordset, the fields you want to sort by, and the fields you want to test for values. As you'll learn later, you can also generate custom field names (for display in the resulting recordset), and you can use complex expressions or calculations to generate a calculated field.

The second row shows you the name of the table from which you selected a field. If you don't see this row, you can display it by choosing Table Names from the View menu. This isn't too important when building a query on a single table, but you'll learn later that this row provides valuable information when building a query that fetches data from more than one table or query.

In the Sort row, you can specify whether Access should sort on the selected or calculated field in ascending or in descending order. In the Show row, you can use the check boxes to indicate the fields that will be included in the recordset. By default, Access includes all the fields you place in the Design grid. Sometimes you'll want to include a field in the query to allow you to select the records you want (such as contacts born in a certain date range), but you won't need that field in the recordset. You can add that field to the design grid so that you can define criteria, but you should clear the Show check box beneath the field to exclude it from the recordset.

Finally, you can use the Criteria row and the row(s) labeled *Or* to enter the criteria you want to use as filters. Once you understand how a query is put together, you'll find it easy to specify exactly the fields and records that you want.

Specifying Fields

The first step in building a query is to select the fields you want in the recordset. You can select the fields in several ways. Using the keyboard, you can tab to a column in the design grid and press Alt+Down Arrow to open the list of available fields. (To move to the design grid, press F6.) Use the Up Arrow and Down Arrow keys to highlight the field you want, and then press Enter to select the field.

Another way to select a field is to drag it from one of the field lists in the upper part of the window to one of the columns in the design grid. In Figure 7-4, the LastName field is being dragged to the design grid. When you drag a field, the mouse pointer turns into a small rectangle.

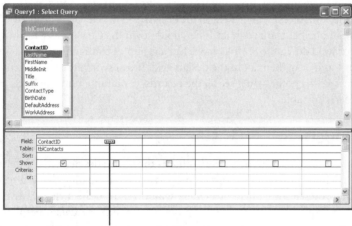

LastName field being dragged and
dropped to Design grid

Figure 7-4. Dragging a field to a column in the design grid.

At the top of each field list in the upper part of the Query window (and also next to the first entry in the Field drop-down list in the design grid) is an asterisk (*) symbol. This symbol is shorthand for selecting "all fields in the table or the query" with one entry on the Field line. When you want to include all the fields in a table or a query, you don't have to define each one individually in the design grid unless you also want to define some sorting or selection criteria for specific fields. You can simply add the asterisk to the design grid to include all the fields from a list. Note that you can add individual fields to the grid in addition to the asterisk in order to define criteria for those fields, but you should clear the Show check box for the individual fields so that they don't appear twice in the recordset.

> **Tip** **Another way to select all fields**
>
> To select all the fields in a table, double-click the title bar of the field list in the upper part of the Query window—this highlights all the fields. Then click any of the highlighted fields and drag them as a group to the Field row in the design grid. While you're dragging, the mouse pointer changes to a multiple rectangle icon, indicating that you're dragging multiple fields. When you release the mouse button, you'll see that Access has copied all the fields to the design grid for you.

For this exercise, select ContactID, LastName, FirstName, WorkStateOrProvince, and Birth-Date from the tblContacts table in the LawTrack Contacts database. You can select the fields one at a time by dragging and dropping them into the design grid. You can also double-click each field name, and Access will move it to the design grid into the next available slot. Finally, you can click on one field you want and then hold down the Ctrl key as you click on additional fields or hold down the Shift key to select a group of contiguous fields. Grab the last field you select and drag them all to the design grid. If you switch the Query window to Datasheet view at this point, you'll see all the records, containing only the fields you selected from the underlying table.

Setting Field Properties

In general, a field that is output by a query inherits the properties defined for that field in the table. You can define a different Description property (the information that is displayed on the status bar when you select that field in a Query window in Datasheet view), Format property (how the data is displayed), Decimal Places property (for numeric data other than integers), Input Mask property, Caption property (the column heading), and Smart Tags property. I'll show you the details of how to use a Smart Tag in Chapter 12, "Customizing a Form."

> For details about field properties, see Chapter 4, "Creating Your Database and Tables."

When you learn to define calculated fields later in this chapter, you'll see that it's a good idea to define the properties for these fields. If the field in the query is a foreign key linked to another table, you can also set the Lookup properties as described in Chapter 5, "Modifying Your Table Design." Access propagates Lookup properties that you have defined in your table fields; however, you can use the properties on the Lookup tab on the query's Field Properties window to override them.

> **Note** The Access query designer lets you define Lookup properties for any text or numeric field (other than AutoNumber). The field doesn't have to be a defined foreign key to another table. You might find this useful when you want the user to pick from a restricted value list—such as *M* or *F* for a Gender field.

To set the properties of a field, click any row of that field's column in the design grid, and then click the Properties button on the toolbar or choose Properties from the View menu to display the Field Properties window, shown in Figure 7-5. Even though the fields in your query inherit their properties from the underlying table, you won't see those properties displayed here. For example, the BirthDate field in tblContacts has both its Description and Caption set to Birth Date and a Format set to mm/dd/yyyy. If you click in the BirthDate field in your query and open the Properties window, you will see that none of the properties show values. Use the property settings in the Field Properties window to override any inherited properties and to customize how a field looks when viewed *for this query*. Try entering new property settings for the BirthDate field, as shown in Figure 7-5.

Tip   One of the quickest ways to see if a field in a query has the properties you want is to switch to Datasheet view. If the field doesn't display the way you want, you can switch back to Design view and override the properties in the query.

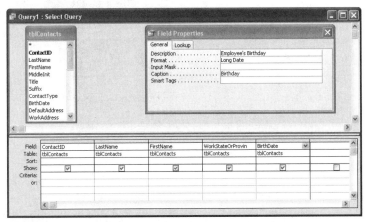

Figure 7-5.   Setting properties for the BirthDate field.

If you make these changes and switch to Datasheet view, you'll see that the BirthDate column heading is now *Birthday*; that the date displays day name, month name, day number, and year; and that the text on the status bar matches the new description, as shown in Figure 7-6 on the next page.

Field caption is changed

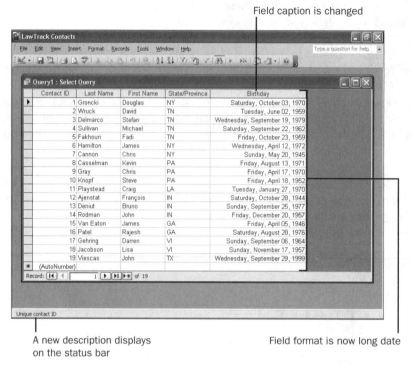

A new description displays
on the status bar

Field format is now long date

Figure 7-6. The BirthDate field displayed with new property settings.

Entering Selection Criteria

The next step is to further refine the records you want by specifying criteria on one or more fields. The example shown in Figure 7-7 selects contacts working in the state of New York.

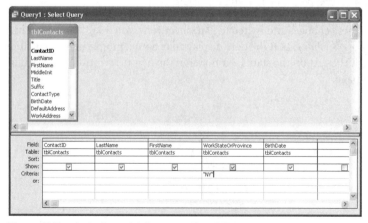

Figure 7-7. A design grid that specifies "NY" as a selection criterion.

Entering selection criteria in a query is similar to entering a validation rule for a field, which you learned about in Chapter 4. To look for a single value, simply type it in the Criteria row for the field you want to test. If the field you're testing is a text field and the value you're looking for has any blank spaces in it, you must enclose the value in quotation marks. Note that Access adds quotation marks for you around single text values. (In Figure 7-7, I typed **NY**, but Access replaced what I typed with "NY" after I pressed Enter.)

If you want to test for any of several values, enter the values in the Criteria row, separated by the word *Or*. For example, specifying *NY Or GA* searches for records for New York or Georgia. You can also test for any of several values by entering each value in a separate Criteria or Or row for the field you want to test. For example, you can enter *NY* in the Criteria row, *GA* in the next row (the first Or row), and so on—but you have to be careful if you're also specifying criteria in other fields, as explained in the section "AND vs. OR" on the following page.

Inside Out

Be careful when your criterion is also a keyword

You should be careful when entering criteria that might also be a Microsoft Access keyword. In the examples shown here, I could have chosen to use criteria for the two-character abbreviation for the state of Oregon (OR)—but *or*, as you can see in the examples, is also a keyword. In many cases, Access is smart enough to figure out what you mean from the context. You can enter:

Or Or Ny

in the criteria under State, and Access assumes that the first *Or* is criteria (by placing quotation marks around the word for you) and the second *Or* is the Boolean operator keyword. If you want to be sure that Access interprets your criteria correctly, always place double quotation marks around criteria text. If you find that Access guessed wrong, you can always correct the entry before saving the query.

In the section "AND vs. OR," you'll see that you can also include a comparison operator in the Criteria row so that, for example, you can look for values less than (<), greater than or equal to (>=), or not equal to (<>) the value that you specify.

Working with Dates and Times in Criteria

Access stores dates and times as eight-byte decimal numbers. The value to the left of the decimal point represents the day (day zero is December 30, 1899), and the fractional part of the number stores the time as a fraction of a day, accurate to seconds. Fortunately, you don't have to worry about converting internal numbers to specify a test for a particular date value because Access handles date and time entries in several formats.

You must always surround date and time values with pound signs (#) to tell Access that you're entering a date or a time. To test for a specific date, use the date notation that is most comfortable for you. For example, *#April 15, 1962#*, *#4/15/62#*, and *#15-Apr-1962#* are all the same date if you chose English (United States) in the regional settings in the Windows Control Panel. Similarly, *#5:30 PM#* and *#17:30#* both specify 5:30 in the evening.

Inside Out:

Understanding date/time criteria

You must be careful when building criteria to test a range in a date/time field. Let's say you want to look at all records between two dates in the ContactEvents table (which has a date/time field—ContactDateTime—that holds the date *and* time of the contact. For all contact events in the month of June 2003, you might be tempted to put the following in the Criteria line under ContactDateTime.

```
>=#6/1/2003# AND <=#6/30/2003#
```

When you look at the results, you might wonder why no rows show up from June 30, 2003 even when you know that you made and recorded several calls on that day. The reason is simple. Remember, a date/time contains an integer offset value for the date and a fraction for the time. Let's say you called someone at 9:00 A.M. on June 30, 2003. The internal value is actually 37,802.375—June 30, 2003 is 37,802 days later than December 30, 1899 (the zero point), and .375 is the fraction of a day that represents 9:00 A.M. When you say you want rows where ContactDateTime is less than or equal to June 30, 2003, you're comparing to the internal value 37,802—just the day value, which is midnight on that day. You won't find the 9:00 A.M. record because the value is greater than 37,802, or later in the day than midnight. To search successfully, you must enter:

```
>=#6/1/2003# AND <#7/1/2003#
```

AND vs. OR

When you enter criteria for several fields, all the tests in a single Criteria row or Or row must be true for a record to be included in the recordset. That is, Access performs a logical AND operation between multiple criteria in the same row. So if you enter *NY* in the Criteria row for WorkStateOrProvince and *<#1 JAN 1972#* in the Criteria row for BirthDate, the record must be for the state of New York *and* must be for someone born before 1972 to be selected. If you enter *NY Or GA* in the Criteria row for WorkStateOrProvince and *>=#01/01/1946# AND <#1 JAN 1972#* in the Criteria row for BirthDate, the record must be for the state of New York or Georgia, *and* the person must have been born between 1946 and 1971.

Figure 7-8 shows the result of applying a logical AND operator between any two tests. As you can see, both tests must be true for the result of the AND to be true and for the record to be selected.

AND	True	False
True	True (Selected)	False (Rejected)
False	False (Rejected)	False (Rejected)

Figure 7-8. The result of applying the logical AND operator between two tests.

When you specify multiple criteria for a field and separate the criteria by a logical OR operator, only one of the criteria must be true for the record to be selected. You can specify several OR criteria for a field, either by entering them all in a single Criteria cell separated by the logical OR operator, as shown earlier, or by entering each subsequent criterion in a separate Or row. When you use multiple Or rows, if the criteria *in any one of the Or rows* is true, the record will be selected. Figure 7-9 shows the result of applying a logical OR operator between any two tests. As you can see, only one of the tests must be true for the result of the OR to be true and for the record to be selected.

OR	True	False
True	True (Selected)	True (Selected)
False	True (Selected)	False (Rejected)

Figure 7-9. The result of applying the logical OR operator between two tests.

Inside Out:

Don't get confused by And and Or

It's a common mistake to get *Or* and *And* mixed up when typing a compound criteria for a single field. You might think to yourself, "I want all the contacts in the states of Washington *and* California," and then type: **WA And CA** in the Criteria row for the WorkStateOrProvince field. When you do this, you're asking Access to find rows where *(WorkStateOrProvince = "WA") And (WorkStateOrProvince = "CA")*. Because a field in a record can't have more than one value at a time (can't contain both the values WA and CA in the same record), there won't be any records in the output. To look for all the rows for these two states, you need to ask Access to search for *(WorkStateOrProvince = "WA") Or (WorkStateOrProvince = "CA")*. In other words, type **WA Or CA** in the Criteria row under the WorkStateOrProvince field.

Let's look at a specific example. In Figure 7-10, you specify *NY* in the first Criteria row of the WorkStateOrProvince field and *>=#01/01/1946# AND <#1 JAN 1972#* in that same Criteria row for the BirthDate field. (By the way, when you type in #1 JAN 1972# and press Enter, Access changes your entry to #1/1/1972#.) In the next row (the first Or row), you specify *GA* in the WorkStateOrProvince field. When you run this query, you get all the contacts from the state of New York who were born between 1946 and 1971. You also get any records for the state of Georgia regardless of the birth date.

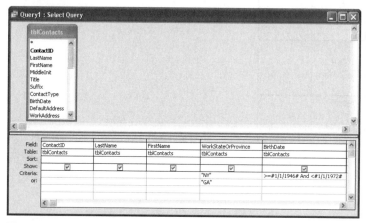

Figure 7-10. A design grid that specifies multiple AND and OR selection criteria.

In Figure 7-11, you can see the recordset (in Datasheet view) that results from running this query.

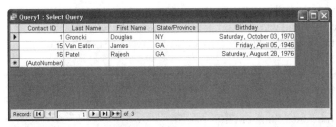

Figure 7-11. The recordset of the query shown in Figure 7-10.

If you also want to limit contacts in Georgia to those who were born between 1946 and 1971, you must specify *>=#01/01/1946# AND <#1/1/1972#* again under BirthDate in the first Or row—that is, in the same row that filters for OR under WorkStateOrProvince. Although this seems like extra work, this gives you complete flexibility to filter the data as you want. You could, for example, include people who were born before 1969 in New York and people who were born after 1970 in Georgia by placing a different criteria under BirthDate in the two rows that filter WorkStateOrProvince.

Between, In, and Like

In addition to comparison operators, Access provides three special operators that are useful for specifying the data you want in the recordset. Table 7-1 describes these operators.

Table 7-1. Criteria Operators for Queries

Predicate	Description
Between	Useful for specifying a range of values. The clause *Between 10 And 20* is the same as specifying *>=10 And <=20*.
In	Useful for specifying a list of values separated by commas, any one of which can match the field being searched. The clause *In ("NY", "GA", "TN")* is the same as *"NY" Or "GA" Or "TN"*.
Like*	Useful for searching for patterns in text fields. You can include special characters and ranges of values in the Like comparison string to define the character pattern you want. Use a question mark (?) to indicate any single character in that position. Use an asterisk (*) to indicate zero or more characters in that position. The pound-sign character (#) specifies a single numeric digit in that position. Include a range in brackets ([ ]) to test for a particular range of characters in a position, and use an exclamation point (!) to indicate exceptions. The range *[0-9]* tests for numbers, *[a-z]* tests for letters, and *[!0-9]* tests for any characters except 0 through 9. For example, the clause *Like "?[a-k]d[0-9]*"* tests for any single character in the first position, any character from *a* through *k* in the second position, the letter *d* in the third position, any character from 0 through 9 in the fourth position, and any number of characters after that.

* As you'll learn in Chapter 18, "Building Views, Functions, and Stored Procedures" and Article 1, "Understanding SQL," the pattern characters supported by SQL Server when working in a Microsoft Access Project file are different. The pattern characters discussed here work in Desktop applications (.mdb and .mde files) only.

Suppose you want to find all contacts in the state of Tennessee or New York who were born between 1955 and 1972 and whose first name begins with the letter *D*. Figure 7-12 shows how you would enter these criteria. Figure 7-13 shows the recordset of this query.

Inside Out

Choosing the correct date/time criteria

If you're really sharp you're probably looking at Figure 7-12 and wondering why I chose *Between #1/1/1955# And #12/31/1972#* instead of *>= #1/1/1955# And < #1/1/1973#* to cover the case where the BirthDate field might also include a time. In this case I know that the BirthDate field has an input mask that doesn't allow you to enter time values. So I know that using Between and the simple date values will work for this search.

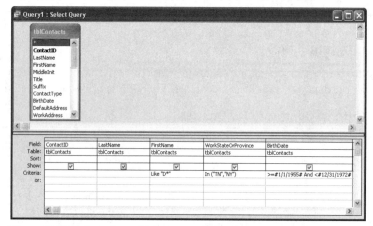

Figure 7-12. A design grid that uses Between, In, and Like.

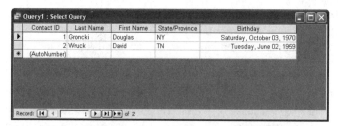

Figure 7-13. The recordset of the query shown in Figure 7-12.

For additional examples that use the Between, In, and Like comparison operators, see "Defining Simple Field Validation Rules," page 111, and the "Predicate" sections in Article 1 on the companion CD.

Using Expressions

You can use an expression to combine fields or to calculate a new value from fields in your table and make that expression a new field in the recordset. You can use any of the many built-in functions that Access provides as part of your expression. You *concatenate*, or combine, text fields by stringing them end-to-end, or you use arithmetic operators on fields in the underlying table to calculate a value. Let's switch to the *HousingDataCopy.mdb* database (*Housing.mdb*) to build some examples.

Creating Text Expressions

One common use of expressions is to create a new text (string) field by concatenating fields containing text, string constants, or numeric data. You create a string constant by enclosing the text in double or single quotation marks. Use the ampersand character (&) between fields or strings to indicate that you want to concatenate them. For example, you might want to create an output field that concatenates the LastName field, a comma, a blank space, and then the FirstName field.

Try creating a query on the tblEmployees table in the *HousingDataCopy.mdb* database that shows a field containing the employee last name, a comma and a blank, first name, a blank, and middle name. You can also create a single field containing the city, a comma and a blank space, the state or province followed by one blank space, and the postal code. Your expressions should look like this:

```
LastName & ", " & FirstName & " " & MiddleName
City & ", " & StateOrProvince & " " & PostalCode
```

You can see the Query window in Design view for this example in Figure 7-14. I clicked in the Field row of the second column and then pressed Shift+F2 to open the Zoom window, where it is easier to enter the expression. Note that you can click the Font button to select a larger font that's easier to read. Once you choose a font, Access uses it whenever you open the Zoom window again.

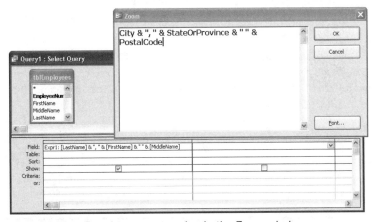

Figure 7-14. Entering an expression in the Zoom window.

Note Access requires that all fields in the Field row in a query have a name. For single fields, Access uses the name of the field. When you enter an expression, Access generates a field name in the form *ExprN:*. See "Specifying Field Names," page 245, for details about changing the name of fields or expressions.

When you look at the query result in Datasheet view, you should see something like that shown in Figure 7-15.

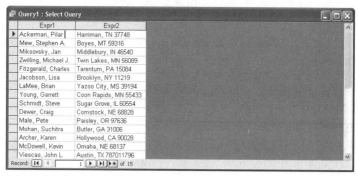

Figure 7-15. A query result with concatenated text fields.

Try typing within the Expr1 field in Datasheet view. Because this display is a result of an expression (concatenation of strings), Access won't let you update the data in this column.

Inside Out

Eliminating extra spaces when concatenating null values

If you look very closely at Figure 7-15, you can see that I captured the image with the insertion point displayed at the end of the Expr1 field in the first row. Do you notice that there's an extra space after the first name? This happened because that person has no middle name, so what we're seeing is the extra blank we inserted after the first name that is supposed to provide spacing between the first name and middle name.

This isn't too much of a problem in this particular expression because you're not going to notice the extra blank displayed at the end of the name. But if you create the expression in the form *First (blank) Middle (blank) Last* and if a record has no middle name, the extra blank will be noticeable.

When you use an ampersand, any Null field in the expression doesn't cause the entire expression to be Null. A little secret: You can also use the arithmetic plus sign (+) to concatenate strings. As you'll learn when you create arithmetic expressions, if a field in the expression is Null, the expression evaluates to Null. So, to solve the extra blank problem, you can create an expression to concatenate the parts of a name as follows:

```
FirstName & (" " + MiddleName) & " " & LastName
```

If MiddleName is a Null, the arithmetic expression inside the parentheses evaluates to Null, and the extra blank disappears!

Defining Arithmetic Expressions

In a reservations record (tblReservations in the Housing Reservations database), code in the form that confirms a reservation automatically calculates the correct TotalCharge for the reservation before Access saves a changed row. As I mentioned when discussing the field independence rule in Chapter 3, this isn't normally a good idea, but I designed it this way to demonstrate what you have to code to maintain the calculated value in your table. (Access won't automatically calculate the new value for you.) You can see how this code works in Chapter 23, "Automating Your Application with Visual Basic." This technique also saves time later calculating a total by month or total by facility in a report.

Table 7-2 shows the operators you can use in arithmetic expressions.

Table 7-2. Operators Used in Arithmetic Expressions

Operator	Description
+	Adds two numeric expressions.
-	Subtracts the second numeric expression from the first numeric expression.
*	Multiplies two numeric expressions.
/	Divides the first numeric expression by the second numeric expression.
\	Rounds both numeric expressions to integers and then divides the first integer by the second integer. The result is truncated to an integer.
^	Raises the first numeric expression to the power indicated by the second numeric expression.
Mod	Rounds both numeric expressions to integers, divides the first integer by the second integer, and returns only the remainder.

The expression to calculate the TotalCharge field is complex because it charges the lower weekly rate for portions of the stay that are full weeks and then adds the daily charge for extra days. Let's say you want to compare the straight daily rate with the discounted rate for longer stays. To begin, you need an expression that calculates the number of days. You can do this in a couple of different ways. First, you can use a handy built-in function called DateDiff to calculate the difference between two Date/Time values in seconds, minutes, hours, days, weeks, months, quarters, or years. In this case, you want the difference between the check-in date and the check-out date in days.

The syntax for calling DateDiff is as follows:

```
DateDiff(<interval>, <date1>, <date2>[, <firstdayofweek>])
```

The function calculates the difference between *<date1>* and *<date2>* using the interval you specify and returns a negative value if *<date1>* is greater than *<date2>*. You can supply a *<firstdayofweek>* value (the default is 1, Sunday) to affect how the function calculates the "ww" interval. Table 7-3 explains the values you can supply for *interval*.

> **Note** You can also use the settings you find in Table 7-3 for the *interval argument* in the DatePart function (which extracts part of a Date/Time value) and the DateAdd function (which adds or subtracts a constant to a Date/Time value).

Table 7-3. **Interval Settings for DateDiff Function**

Setting	Description
"yyyy"	Calculates the difference in years. DateDiff subtracts the year portion of the first date from the year portion of the second date, so *DateDiff*("yyyy", #31 DEC 2002#, #01 JAN 2003#) returns 1.
"q"	Calculates the difference in quarters. If the two dates are in the same calendar quarter, the result is 0.
"m"	Calculates the difference in months. DateDiff subtracts the month portion of the first date from the month portion of this second date, so *DateDiff*("m", #31 DEC 2002#, #01 JAN 2003#) returns 1.
"y"	Calculates the difference in days. DateDiff handles this option the same as "d" below. (For other functions, this extracts the day of the year.)
"d"	Calculates the difference in days.
"w"	Calculates the difference in weeks based on the day of the week of *<date1>*. If, for example, the day of the week of the first date is a Tuesday, DateDiff counts the number of Tuesdays between the first date and the second date. For example, April 30, 2003, is a Wednesday, and May 5, 2003, is a Monday, so *DateDiff*("w", #30 APR 2003#, #05 MAY 2003#) returns 0.
"ww"	Calculates the difference in weeks. When the first day of week is Sunday (the default), DateDiff counts the number of Sundays greater than the first date and less than or equal to the second date. For example, April 30, 2003, is a Wednesday, and May 5, 2003, is a Monday, so *DateDiff*("ww", #30 APR 2003#, #05 MAY 2003#) returns 1.
"h"	Calculates the difference in hours.
"n"	Calculates the difference in minutes.
"s"	Calculates the difference in seconds.

The second way to calculate the number of days is to simply subtract one date from the other. Remember that the integer portion of a Date/Time data type is number of days. If you're sure that the fields do not contain any time value, subtract the check-in date from the check-out date to find the number of days. Let's see how this works in the sample database.

Open the *HousingDataCopy.mdb* database and start a new query on tblReservations. Add EmployeeNumber, FacilityID, RoomNumber, CheckInDate, CheckOutDate, and TotalCharge to the query design grid. You need to enter your expression in a blank column on the Field row. Using DateDiff, start the expression by entering:

```
DateDiff("d", [CheckInDate], [CheckOutDate])
```

To calculate the number of days by subtracting, the expression is:

```
[CheckOutDate] - [CheckInDate]
```

To calculate the amount owed at the daily rate, multiply either of the previous expressions by the DailyRate field. With DateDiff, the final expression is:

```
DateDiff("d", [CheckInDate], [CheckOutDate]) * [DailyRate]
```

If you want to use subtraction, you must enter:

```
([CheckOutDate] - [CheckInDate]) * [DailyRate]
```

You might be wondering why the second expression includes parentheses. When evaluating an arithmetic expression, Access evaluates certain operations before others, known as *operator precedence*. Table 7-4 shows you operator precedence for arithmetic operations. In an expression with no parentheses, Access performs the operations in the order listed in the table. When operations have the same precedence (for example, multiply and divide), Access performs the operations left to right.

Table 7-4. Arithmetic Operator Precedence

Microsoft Access Evaluates Operators in the Following Order:

1	Exponentiation (^)
2	Negation—a leading minus sign (-)
3	Multiplication and division (*, /)
4	Integer division (\)
5	Modulus (Mod)
6	Addition and subtraction (+, -)

Microsoft Access evaluates expressions enclosed in parentheses first, starting with the innermost expressions. (You can enclose an expression in parentheses inside another expression in parentheses.) If you do not include the parentheses in the previous example, Access would first multiply CheckInDate times DailyRate (because multiplication and division occur before addition and subtraction) and then subtract that result from CheckOutDate. That not only gives you the wrong answer but also results in an error because you cannot subtract a Double value (the result of multiplying a date/time times a currency) from a date/time value.

After you select the fields from the table and enter the expression to calculate the total based on the daily rate, your query design grid should look something like Figure 7-16 on the next page.

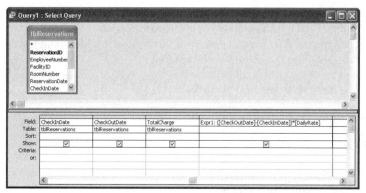

Figure 7-16. Entering an expression to calculate the amount owed based on the daily rate.

When you switch to Datasheet view, you can see the calculated amount from your expression as shown in Figure 7-17.

Employee	Facility	Room	Check-In	Check-Out	Charge	Expr1
8	Main Campus	501	5/12/2003	5/22/2003	$660.00	700
9	North Satellite	110	4/1/2003	4/8/2003	$290.00	315
14	Main Campus	302	5/5/2003	5/8/2003	$300.00	300
3	Main Campus	505	5/1/2003	5/11/2003	$750.00	800
10	North Satellite	308	4/3/2003	4/15/2003	$1,125.00	1080
9	North Satellite	610	5/22/2003	5/26/2003	$180.00	180
9	North Satellite	106	4/21/2003	5/5/2003	$855.00	910
13	South Campus	203	5/23/2003	6/10/2003	$1,180.00	1260
2	South Campus	105	5/23/2003	5/29/2003	$420.00	420
9	Main Campus	512	5/28/2003	5/30/2003	$140.00	140
12	Main Campus	503	6/18/2003	7/7/2003	$805.00	855
1	North Satellite	107	6/27/2003	7/12/2003	$625.00	675
14	Main Campus	204	7/7/2003	7/28/2003	$1,050.00	1155
7	South Campus	101	6/21/2003	6/28/2003	$415.00	455
14	Main Campus	101	7/9/2003	7/25/2003	$1,040.00	1120
3	Main Campus	406	6/26/2003	7/8/2003	$570.00	600
8	South Campus	207	7/1/2003	7/7/2003	$390.00	390

Record: of 43

Figure 7-17. Viewing the results of your calculated expression in a datasheet.

Note that not all the calculated amounts are larger than the amount already stored in the record. When the reservation is for six days or fewer, the daily rate applies, so your calculation should match the existing charge. You might want to display only the records where the new calculated amount is different than the amount already stored. For that, you can add another expression to calculate the difference and then select the row if the difference is not zero.

Switch back to design view and enter a new expression to calculate the difference in an empty column. Your expression should look like:

```
TotalCharge - ((([CheckOutDate] - [CheckInDate]) * [DailyRate])
```

In the Criteria line under this new field, enter <>0. Your query design should look like Figure 7-18, and the datasheet for the query now displays only the rows where the calculation result is different, as shown in Figure 7-19.

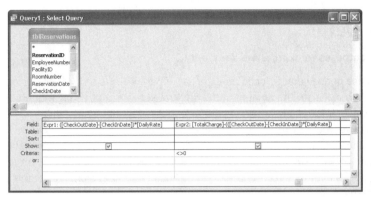

Figure 7-18. Entering an expression and a criterion to find the rows that are different.

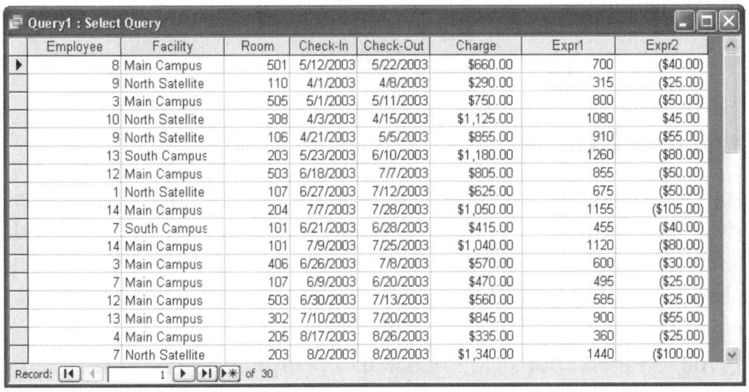

Employee	Facility	Room	Check-In	Check-Out	Charge	Expr1	Expr2
8	Main Campus	501	5/12/2003	5/22/2003	$660.00	700	($40.00)
9	North Satellite	110	4/1/2003	4/8/2003	$290.00	315	($25.00)
3	Main Campus	505	5/1/2003	5/11/2003	$750.00	800	($50.00)
10	North Satellite	308	4/3/2003	4/15/2003	$1,125.00	1080	$45.00
9	North Satellite	106	4/21/2003	5/5/2003	$855.00	910	($55.00)
13	South Campus	203	5/23/2003	6/10/2003	$1,180.00	1260	($80.00)
12	Main Campus	503	6/18/2003	7/7/2003	$805.00	855	($50.00)
1	North Satellite	107	6/27/2003	7/12/2003	$625.00	675	($50.00)
14	Main Campus	204	7/7/2003	7/28/2003	$1,050.00	1155	($105.00)
7	South Campus	101	6/21/2003	6/28/2003	$415.00	455	($40.00)
14	Main Campus	101	7/9/2003	7/25/2003	$1,040.00	1120	($80.00)
3	Main Campus	406	6/26/2003	7/8/2003	$570.00	600	($30.00)
7	Main Campus	107	6/9/2003	6/20/2003	$470.00	495	($25.00)
12	Main Campus	503	6/30/2003	7/13/2003	$560.00	585	($25.00)
13	Main Campus	302	7/10/2003	7/20/2003	$845.00	900	($55.00)
4	Main Campus	205	8/17/2003	8/26/2003	$335.00	360	($25.00)
7	North Satellite	203	8/2/2003	8/20/2003	$1,340.00	1440	($100.00)

Figure 7-19. The datasheet now shows only the rows where the calculation is different than the stored value.

Finding the rows that differ in this way has the added benefit of displaying the calculated difference. If you're only interested in finding the rows that differ but don't care about the amount of the difference, you don't need the second expression at all. You can find the rows you want by placing the expression <>*[TotalCharge]* in the Criteria line under the first expression you entered. This asks Access to compare the amount calculated at the straight daily rate with the value in the TotalCharge field stored in the record and display the row only when the two values are not equal.

You might have inferred from the earlier discussion about entering criteria that you can only use constant values in the Criteria or Or line. As you can see, you can also compare the value of one field or expression with another field or expression containing a reference to a field.

Inside Out

Adding parentheses to expressions for clarity

You might have noticed that I placed an extra set of parentheses around the original expression we built to calculate the amount at the daily rate before subtracting that amount from the stored value. If you study Table 7-4 carefully, you'll see that I really didn't have to do this because Access would perform the multiplication before doing the final subtract. However, I find it's a good practice to add parentheses to make the sequence of operations crystal clear—I don't always remember the order of precedence rules, and I don't want to have to go looking up the information in Help every time I build an expression. Adding the parentheses makes sure I get the results I want.

So far, you have built fairly simple expressions. When you want to create a more complex expression, sometimes the Expression Builder can be useful, as discussed in the next section.

Using the Expression Builder

For more complex expressions, Access provides a utility called the Expression Builder. Let's say you want to double-check the total amount owed for a reservation in the sample database. You have to work with several fields to do this—CheckInDate, CheckOutDate, DailyRate, and WeeklyRate. You need to calculate the number of weeks to charge at the WeeklyRate and then charge the remaining days at the DailyRate. To see how the Expression Builder works, start a new query on the tblReservations table. Click in an empty field in the design grid, and then click the Build button on the toolbar. Access opens the Expression Builder window shown in Figure 7-20.

Build

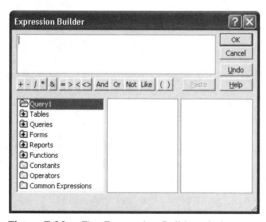

Figure 7-20. The Expression Builder window.

In the upper part of the window is a blank text box in which you can build an expression. You can type the expression yourself, but it's sometimes more accurate to find field names, operators, and function names in the three list boxes in the lower part of the window and to use the various expression operator buttons just below the text box.

The expression you need to build, which I'll walk you through in detail in the next few pages, will ultimately look like this:

```
((DateDiff("d", [tblReservations]![CheckInDate], [tblReservations]![CheckOutDate]
) \ 7) * [WeeklyRate]) + ((DateDiff("d", [tblReservations]![CheckInDate], [tblRes
ervations]![CheckOutDate]) Mod 7) * [DailyRate])
```

You can use the Expression Builder to help you correctly construct this expression. Start by double-clicking the Functions category in the left pane, then click Built-In Functions to see the list of function categories in the center pane, and the list of functions within the selected category in the right pane. Click on the Date/Time category to narrow down the choices. Here you can see the DateDiff function (that you used earlier) as well as several other built-in functions you can use. (You can find a list of the most useful functions and their descriptions in Article 3 on the companion CD.)

Double-click the DateDiff function to add it to the expression window in the top of the Expression Builder. When you add a function to your expression in this way, the Expression Builder shows you the parameters required by the function. You can click any parameter to highlight it and type in a value or select a value from one of the lists in the bottom panes. Click <<interval>> and overtype it with "d". (See Table 7-3 for a list of all the possible interval settings.) You need to insert the CheckInDate field from tblReservations for <<date1>> and the CheckOutDate field for <<date2>>. Click <<date1>> to highlight it and double-click the Tables list to open up the list of table names. Scroll down until you find tblReservations and click it to see the list of field names in the second pane. Double-click CheckInDate. Then click <<date2>>, and double-click CheckOutDate. You don't need the <<firstweekday>> or <<firstweek>> parameters, so click on them and press the Delete key to remove them. (You can also remove the extra commas if you like.) The Expression Builder should now look like Figure 7-21.

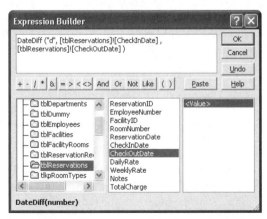

Figure 7-21. Creating a calculation using table field names in the Expression Builder window. (The remainder of the expression is hidden to the right.)

You'll notice that the Expression Builder pastes *[tblReservations]![CheckInDate]* into the expression area, not just *CheckInDate*. There are two good reasons for this. First, the Expression Builder doesn't know whether you might include other tables in this query and whether some of those tables might have field names that are identical to the ones you're selecting now. The way to avoid conflicts is to *fully qualify* the field names by preceding them with the table name. When working in queries, separate the table name from the field name with a period or an exclamation point. Second, you should enclose all names of objects in Access in brackets ([ ]). If you designed the name without any blank spaces, you can leave out the brackets, but it's always good practice to include them.

Inside Out

Understanding name separators in SQL

As you'll learn in Chapter 23, "Automating Your Application with Visual Basic," in most cases you should separate the name of an object from the name of an object within that object (for example, a field within a table) with an exclamation point. When you build an expression in the Expression Builder, you'll find that the Expression Builder separates names using exclamation points. However, as you'll learn in Article 1 on the companion CD, "Understanding SQL," the standard for the SQL database query language uses a period between the name of a table and the name of a field within the table. To be most compatible with the SQL standard when constructing a query expression, use a period between a table name and a field name. Access accepts either an exclamation point or a period in query design.

Next, you need to divide by 7 to calculate the number of weeks. You're not interested in any fractional part of a week, so you need to use the integer divide operator (\). Note there is no operator button for integer divide. The operator buttons are arranged horizontally between the upper and lower panes. So, you can either type in the operator or scroll down in the leftmost pane, click Operators to open that list, select Arithmetic in the second pane to filter the rightmost list, and double-click the integer divide operator (\) in the rightmost list to add it to your expression. Make sure the insertion point in the top pane is positioned after the integer divide operator and type the number 7.

The next operation you need is to multiply the expression you have thus far by the WeeklyRate field from tblReservations. If you like, you can add left and right parentheses around the expression before adding the multiply operator and the field. Remember from Table 7-4 that multiplication and division are of equal precedence, so Access evaluates the division before the multiplication (left to right) even if you don't add the parentheses. But, as I noted earlier, I like to make the precedence of operations crystal clear, so I recommend you add the parentheses. Press the Home key to go to the beginning of the expression, click the left parenthesis button, press the End key to go to the end, click the right parenthesis button, click the multiply operator (*) button, and finally select the WeeklyRate field from the tblReservations field list.

> **Note** WeeklyRate and DailyRate are currency fields. DateDiff returns an integer, and the result of an integer divide (\) or a modulus (Mod) operation is an integer. Whenever you ask Access to evaluate an arithmetic expression, it returns a result that has a data type sufficiently complex to contain the result. As you might expect, multiplying an integer (a simple data type) with a currency field (a more complex data type) returns a currency field.

You need to add this entire expression to the calculation for remaining days at the daily rate, so press Home again and add one more left parenthesis, and press the End key and click the right parenthesis button to complete this first part of the expression. Click the addition operator to add it to your expression. Rather than scan back and forth to add parentheses as we build the second part of the expression, click the left parenthesis button twice to start building the calculation for extra days. Add the DateDiff function again, click <<interval>>, and type "d". Click <<date1>>, find the CheckInDate field in tblReservations again and double-click it to add it to your expression. Click <<date2>> and double-click the CheckOutDate field. Remove <<firstweekday>> and <<firstweek>> from the function.

Now, you need to know how many days beyond full weeks are in the reservation. You might be tempted to divide by 7 again and try to extract the remainder, but there's a handy operator that returns only the remainder of a division for you—Mod. Scan down in the left pane and click Operators. In the middle pane, click Arithmetic to see only the arithmetic operators in the right pane. Double-click Mod to add it to your expression.

We're almost done. Type the number 7 and click the right parenthesis button to close the Mod calculation. Click the multiply operator button, then go back to tblReservations and double-click the DailyRate field. Click the right parenthesis button one last time to finish the expression.

Click OK to paste your result into the design grid. Go ahead and add ReservationID, FacilityID, RoomNumber, CheckInDate, CheckOutDate, and TotalCharge to your query grid. When you switch to Datasheet view, your result should look like Figure 7-22.

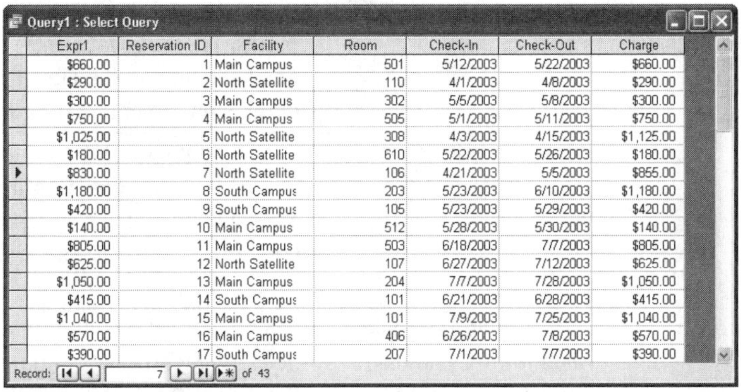

Expr1	Reservation ID	Facility	Room	Check-In	Check-Out	Charge
$660.00	1	Main Campus	501	5/12/2003	5/22/2003	$660.00
$290.00	2	North Satellite	110	4/1/2003	4/8/2003	$290.00
$300.00	3	Main Campus	302	5/5/2003	5/8/2003	$300.00
$750.00	4	Main Campus	505	5/1/2003	5/11/2003	$750.00
$1,025.00	5	North Satellite	308	4/3/2003	4/15/2003	$1,125.00
$180.00	6	North Satellite	610	5/22/2003	5/26/2003	$180.00
$830.00	7	North Satellite	106	4/21/2003	5/5/2003	$855.00
$1,180.00	8	South Campus	203	5/23/2003	6/10/2003	$1,180.00
$420.00	9	South Campus	105	5/23/2003	5/29/2003	$420.00
$140.00	10	Main Campus	512	5/28/2003	5/30/2003	$140.00
$805.00	11	Main Campus	503	6/18/2003	7/7/2003	$805.00
$625.00	12	North Satellite	107	6/27/2003	7/12/2003	$625.00
$1,050.00	13	Main Campus	204	7/7/2003	7/28/2003	$1,050.00
$415.00	14	South Campus	101	6/21/2003	6/28/2003	$415.00
$1,040.00	15	Main Campus	101	7/9/2003	7/25/2003	$1,040.00
$570.00	16	Main Campus	406	6/26/2003	7/8/2003	$570.00
$390.00	17	South Campus	207	7/1/2003	7/7/2003	$390.00

Record: 7 of 43

Figure 7-22. Viewing the result of a complex calculation expression.

Do you notice any stored values that don't match what you just calculated? (Hint: Look at the row with the selection arrow.) If you haven't changed the sample data, you'll find several rows that I purposefully updated with invalid TotalCharge values. Here's a challenge: Go back to Design view and enter the criteria you need to display only the rows where your calculated charge doesn't match the TotalCharge stored in the table. You can find the solution saved as *qxmplUnmatchedCharges* in the *HousingDataCopy.mdb* sample database.

Tip Is the Builder useful? You decide.

I personally never use the Expression Builder when I'm creating applications in Microsoft Access. I find it more cumbersome than directly typing in the expression I think I need and then trying it out. I included this discussion because some developers might find the Expression Builder helps them learn how to build correct expression and function call syntax.

We used the DateDiff function to solve this problem, but Access also has several other useful functions to help you deal with date and time values. For example, you might want to see only a part of the date or time value in your query. You might also want to use these functions to help you filter the results in your query. Table 7-5 explains each date and time function and includes filter examples that use the ContactDateTime field from the tblContactEvents table in the LawTrack Contacts sample database.

Table 7-5. Date and Time Functions

Function	Description	Example
Day(*date*)	Returns a value from 1 through 31 for the day of the month.	To select records with contact events that occurred after the 10th of any month, enter **Day([Contact-DateTime])** in an empty column in the Field line and enter **>10** as the criterion for that field.
Month(*date*)	Returns a value from 1 through 12 for the month of the year.	To find all contact events that occurred in March (of any year), enter **Month([ContactDateTime])** in an empty column in the Field line and enter **3** as the criterion for that field.
Year(*date*)	Returns a value from 100 through 9999 for the year.	To find contact events that happened in 2003, enter **Year([ContactDate-Time])** in an empty column in the Field line and enter **2003** as the criterion for that field.
Weekday(*date*)	As a default, returns a value from 1 (Sunday) through 7 (Saturday) for the day of the week.	To find contact events that occurred between Monday and Friday, enter **Weekday([ContactDateTime])** in an empty column in the Field line and enter **Between 2 And 6** as the criterion for that field.

Table 7-5. Date and Time Functions

Function	Description	Example
Hour(*date*)	Returns a value from 0 through 23 for the hour of the day.	To find contact events that happened before noon, enter **Hour([Contact-DateTime])** in an empty column in the Field line and enter **<12** as the criterion for that field.
DateAdd(*interval, amount, date*)	Adds an amount in the interval you specify to a date/time value.	To find contact events that occurred more than six months ago, enter **<DateAdd("m", -6, Date())** as the criterion under ContactDateTime. (See also the Date function below.)
DatePart(*interval, date*)	Returns a portion of the date or time, depending on the interval code you supply. Useful interval codes are "q" for quarter of the year (1 through 4) and "ww" for week of the year (1 through 53).	To find contact events in the second quarter, enter **DatePart("q", [Contact-DateTime])** in an empty column in the Field line, and enter **2** as the criterion for that field.
Date()	Returns the current system date.	To select contact events that happened more than 30 days ago, enter **<(Date() – 30)** as the criterion under ContactDateTime.

 For additional useful functions, see Article 3 on the companion CD, "Visual Basic Function Reference."

Specifying Field Names

Every field must have a name. By default, the name of a simple field in a query is the name of the field from the source table. However, when you create a new field using an expression, the expression doesn't have a name unless you or Access assign one. You have seen that when you create an expression in the Field row of the design grid, Access adds a prefix such as *Expr1* followed by a colon—that is the name that Access is assigning to your expression. Remember, the column heading for the field is, by default, the field name unless you specify a different caption property setting. As you know, you can assign or change a caption for a field in a query by using the field's property sheet.

Understanding Field Names and Captions

In the world of tables and queries, every field—even calculated ones—must have a name. When you create a field in a table, you give it a name. When you use a table in a query and include a field from the table in the query output, the name of the field output by the query is the same as the field name in the table. If you create a calculated field in a query, you must assign a name to that field. If you don't, Access assigns an ugly *ExprN* name for you. But you can override this and assign your own field name to expressions. You can also override the default field name for a simple field with another name. When you use a query in another query or a form or report, or you open a query as a recordset in Visual Basic, you use the field name to indicate which field you want to fetch from the query.

You can also define a Caption property for a field. When you do that, what you put in the caption becomes the external label for the field. You'll see the caption in column headings in Datasheet view. Later, when you begin to work with forms and reports, you'll find that the caption becomes the default label for the field. If you don't define a caption, Access shows you the field name instead.

You can change or assign field names that will appear in the recordset of a query. This feature is particularly useful when you've calculated a value in the query that you'll use in a form, a report, or another query. In the queries shown in Figures 7-14, 7-16, and 7-18, you calculated a value and Access assigned a temporary field name. You can replace this name with something more meaningful. For example, in the first query you might want to use something like FullName and CityStateZip. In the second query, RecalculatedCharge might be appropriate. To change a name generated by Access, replace *ExprN* with the name you want in the Field row in the query design grid. To assign a new name to a field, place the insertion point at the beginning of the field specification and insert the new name followed by a colon. Figure 7-23 shows the first query with the field names changed.

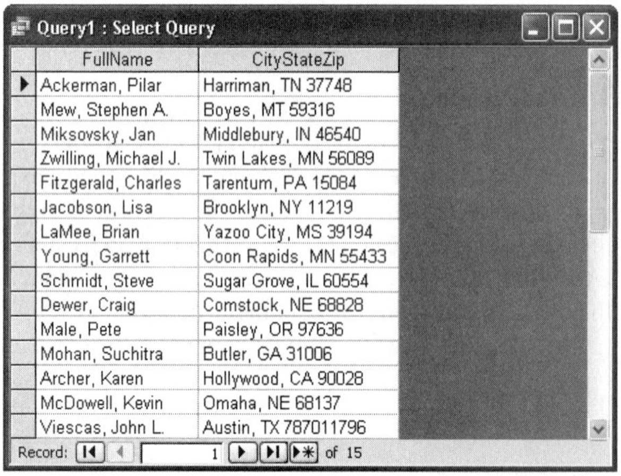

FullName	CityStateZip
Ackerman, Pilar	Harriman, TN 37748
Mew, Stephen A.	Boyes, MT 59316
Miksovsky, Jan	Middlebury, IN 46540
Zwilling, Michael J.	Twin Lakes, MN 56089
Fitzgerald, Charles	Tarentum, PA 15084
Jacobson, Lisa	Brooklyn, NY 11219
LaMee, Brian	Yazoo City, MS 39194
Young, Garrett	Coon Rapids, MN 55433
Schmidt, Steve	Sugar Grove, IL 60554
Dewer, Craig	Comstock, NE 68828
Male, Pete	Paisley, OR 97636
Mohan, Suchitra	Butler, GA 31006
Archer, Karen	Hollywood, CA 90028
McDowell, Kevin	Omaha, NE 68137
Viescas, John L.	Austin, TX 787011796

Figure 7-23. The result of changing the *Expr1* and *Expr2* field names shown in Figure 7-15.

Note that I could have made the column headings you see even more readable by also assigning a caption to these fields via the Field Properties window. I might have chosen something like Person Name for the first field and City-State-Zip for the second field. Keep in mind that setting the caption does not change the actual name of the field when you use the query in a form, report, or Visual Basic code.

Sorting Data

Normally, Access displays the rows in your recordset in the order in which they're retrieved from the database. You can add sorting information to determine the sequence of the data in a query. Click in the Sort row for the field you want to sort on, and select Ascending or Descending from the drop-down list. In the example shown in Figure 7-24, the query results are to be sorted in descending order based on the calculated NewTotalCharge field. (Note that I have given the calculated field a field name.) The recordset will list the most expensive reservations first. The resulting Datasheet view is shown in Figure 7-25 on the next page. You can find this query saved as *qryXmplChargeCalcSorted* in the *HousingDataCopy.mdb* sample database.

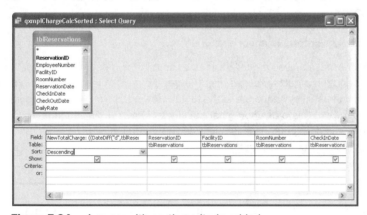

Figure 7-24. A query with sorting criteria added.

NewTotalCharge	Reservation ID	Facility	Room	Check-In	Check-Out	Charge
$1,340.00	23	North Satellit	203	8/2/2003	8/20/2003	$1,340.00
$1,240.00	31	Main Campu	502	9/8/2003	9/23/2003	$1,210.00
$1,180.00	8	South Campu	203	5/23/2003	6/10/2003	$1,180.00
$1,050.00	13	Main Campu	204	7/7/2003	7/28/2003	$1,050.00
$1,040.00	15	Main Campu	101	7/9/2003	7/25/2003	$1,040.00
$1,025.00	5	North Satellit	308	4/3/2003	4/15/2003	$1,125.00
$935.00	25	Main Campu	209	7/14/2003	7/25/2003	$990.00
$845.00	20	Main Campu	302	7/10/2003	7/20/2003	$845.00
$845.00	33	Main Campu	202	9/8/2003	9/18/2003	$845.00
$830.00	7	North Satellit	106	4/21/2003	5/5/2003	$855.00
$805.00	11	Main Campu	503	6/18/2003	7/7/2003	$805.00
$750.00	4	Main Campu	505	5/1/2003	5/11/2003	$750.00
$690.00	41	Main Campu	101	10/7/2003	10/22/2003	$690.00
$680.00	35	Main Campu	504	8/29/2003	9/11/2003	$680.00
$660.00	1	Main Campu	501	5/12/2003	5/22/2003	$660.00
$660.00	28	Main Campu	108	7/27/2003	8/6/2003	$660.00
$640.00	43	Main Campu	304	11/2/2003	11/16/2003	$640.00
$625.00	12	North Satellit	107	6/27/2003	7/12/2003	$625.00
$570.00	16	Main Campu	406	6/26/2003	7/8/2003	$570.00
$560.00	19	Main Campu	503	6/30/2003	7/13/2003	$560.00

Record: 1 of 43

Figure 7-25. The recordset of the query shown in Figure 7-24 in Datasheet view.

Inside Out

Why specifying sort criteria is important

When Microsoft Access solves a query, it tries to do it in the most efficient way. When you first construct and run a query, Access might return the rows in the sequence you expect (for example, in primary key sequence of the table). However, if you want to be sure Access always returns rows in this order, you must specify sort criteria. As you later add and remove rows in your database, Access might decide that fetching rows in a different sequence might be faster, which, in the absence of sorting criteria, might result in a different row sequence than you intended.

You can also sort on multiple fields. Access honors your sorting criteria from left to right in the design grid. If, for example, you want to sort by FacilityID ascending and then by NewTotalCharge descending, you should include the FacilityID field to the left of the New-TotalCharge field. If the additional field you want to sort is already in the design grid but in the wrong location, click the column selector box (the tinted box above the field row) to select the entire column and then click the selector box again and drag the field to its new location. If you want the field that is out of position to still appear where you originally placed it, add the field to the design grid again in the correct sorting sequence, clear the Show check box (you don't want two copies of the field displayed), and set the Sort specification. Figure 7-26 shows the query shown in Figure 7-24 modified to sort first by FacilityID and then by NewTotalCharge, but leaves FacilityID displayed after ReservationID. I saved this query in the *HousingDataCopy.mdb* sample database as *qxmplChargeCalcSortedTwo*.

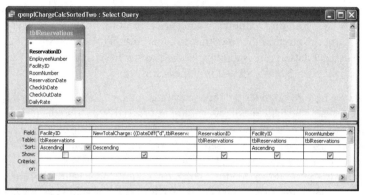

Figure 7-26. Sorting on two fields while maintaining the original field sequence in the query output.

Inside Out

A reminder why Lookup properties can be confusing

If you open the datasheet of *qxmplChargeCalcSortedTwo* and scroll down in the recordset, you'll find the Facility column sorted Main Campus Housing A, Main Campus Housing B, South Campus Housing C, and North Satellite Housing D. Why does South appear before North if the values are supposed to be sorted ascending? Remember, in Chapter 5 I warned you about Lookup properties confusing the display you see. The information you're seeing in the datasheet comes from the Lookup defined on the FacilityID column in tblReservations—you're seeing the related facility name from tblFacilities. However, the actual value of FacilityID is a number. You can click on the FacilityID column, open the Field Properties window, click the Lookup tab, and set the Display Control property to Text Box to see the actual number value. When you do this and look at the datasheet again, you'll see that the values are sorted correctly.

Testing Validation Rule Changes

You learned in Chapter 4, "Creating Your Database and Tables," how to define both field and table validation rules. You also learned in Chapter 5, "Modifying Your Table Design," that you can change these rules even after you have data in your table. Access warns you if some of the data in your table doesn't satisfy the new rule, but it doesn't tell you which rows have problems.

Checking a New Field Validation Rule

The best way to find out if any rows will fail a new field validation rule is to write a query to test your data before you make the change. The trick is you must specify criteria that are the converse of your proposed rule change to find the rows that don't match. For example, if you are planning to set the Required property to Yes or specify a Validation Rule property of

Chapter 7

Is Not Null on a field (both tests mean the same thing), you want to look for rows containing a field that Is Null. If you want to limit the daily price of a room to <= 90, then you must look for values that are > 90 to find the rows that will fail. Another way to think about asking for the converse of a validation rule is to put the word *Not* in front of the rule. If the new rule is going to be <= 90, then Not <= 90 will find the bad rows.

Let's see what we need to do to test a proposed validation rule change to tblFacilityRooms in the sample database. The daily room rate should not exceed $90.00, so the new rule in the DailyRate field will be <=90. To test for rooms that exceed this new limit, start a new query on tblFacilityRooms. Include the fields FacilityID, RoomNumber, RoomType, DailyRate, and WeeklyRate in the query's Design grid. (You need at least FacilityID and RoomNumber—the primary key fields—to be able to identify which rows fail.) Under DailyRate, enter the converse of the new rule: Enter either **>90** or **Not <=90**. Your query should look like Figure 7-27.

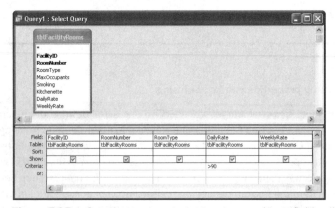

Figure 7-27. Creating a query to test a proposed new field validation rule.

If you run this query against the original data in the sample database, you'll find 31 rooms that are priced higher than the new proposed rule. As you'll learn in "Working in Query Datasheet View," page 252, you can update these rows by typing a new value directly in the query datasheet.

Let's try something. Select one of the invalid values you found in the query datasheet and try to type in the new maximum value of $90.00. If you try to save the row, you'll get an error message because there's a table validation rule that prevents you from setting a DailyRate value that when multiplied by 7 is more than the WeeklyRate value. It looks like you'll have to fix both values if you want to change your field validation rule.

Checking a New Table Validation Rule

Checking a proposed new field validation rule is simple. But what about making a change to a table validation rule? Typically, a table validation rule compares one field with another, so to check a new rule, you'll need more complex criteria in your query.

There's already a table validation rule in tblFacilityRooms in the *HousingDataCopy.mdb* sample database. The rule makes sure that the weekly rate is not more than 7 times the daily rate—it wouldn't be much of a discount if it were! Suppose you now want to be sure that the weekly rate reflects a true discount from the daily rate. Your proposed new rule might make sure that the weekly rate is no more than 6 times the daily rate—if an employee stays a full week, the last night is essentially free. Your new rule might look like the following:

```
([DailyRate]*6)>=[WeeklyRate]
```

So, you need to write a query that checks the current values in the WeeklyRate field to see if any will fail the new rule. Note that you could also create an expression to calculate DailyRate times 6 and compare that value with the WeeklyRate value. When the expression you want to test involves a calculation on one side of the comparison with a simple field value on the other side of the comparison, it's easier to compare the simple field with the expression. Remember, you need to create the converse of the expression to find rows that won't pass the new rule.

You can start with the query you built in the previous section or create a new query. You need at least the primary key fields from the table as well as the fields you need to perform the comparison. In this case, you need to compare the current value of WeeklyRate with the expression on DailyRate. Let's turn the expression around so that it's easier to see what you need to enter in the query design grid. The expression looks like this:

```
[WeeklyRate]<=([DailyRate]*6)
```

To test the converse on the WeeklyRate field's Criteria row of your query, you need either:

```
>([DailyRate]*6)
```

or:

```
Not <=([DailyRate]*6)
```

Your test query should look like Figure 7-28.

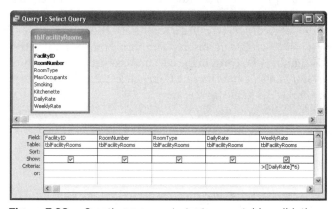

Figure 7-28. Creating a query to test a new table validation rule.

If you run this query, you'll find that all the rows in the table fail the new test. When I loaded sample data into the table, I created weekly rates that are approximately 6.4 times the daily rate—so none of the rates pass the new test. In Chapter 9 you'll learn how to create an update query to fix both the daily and weekly rates to match the new rules discussed in this section.

Working in Query Datasheet View

When you're developing an application, you might need to work in table or query Datasheet view to help you load sample data or to solve problems in the queries, forms, and reports you're creating. You might also decide to create certain forms in your application that display information in Datasheet view. Also, the techniques for updating and manipulating data in forms are very similar to doing so in datasheets—so you need to understand how datasheets work to be able to explain to your users how to use your application. If you're using Access as a personal database to analyze information, you might frequently work with information in Datasheet view. In either case, you should understand how to work with data editing, and the best way to learn how is to understand viewing and editing data in Datasheet view.

Before you get started with the remaining examples in this chapter, open *ContactsData-Copy.mdb* from your sample files folder. In that database, you'll find a query named qryContactsDatasheet that we'll use in the remainder of this chapter. I defined this query to select key fields from tblContacts and display a subdatasheet from tblContactEvents.

Moving Around and Using Keyboard Shortcuts

Open the query qryContactsDatasheet in the *ContactsDataCopy.mdb* database. You should see a result similar to Figure 7-29. Displaying different records or fields is simple. You can use the horizontal scroll bar to scroll through a table's fields, or you can use the vertical scroll bar to scroll through a table's records.

In the lower left corner of the table in Datasheet view, you can see a set of navigation buttons and the Record Number box, as shown in Figure 7-30. The Record Number box shows the *relative record number* of the current record (meaning the number of the selected record in relation to the current set of records, also called a recordset). You might not see the current record in the window if you've scrolled the display. The number to the right of the new record button shows the total number of records in the current recordset. If you've applied a filter against the table (see "Searching for and Filtering Data," page 272), this number might be less than the total number of records in the table or query.

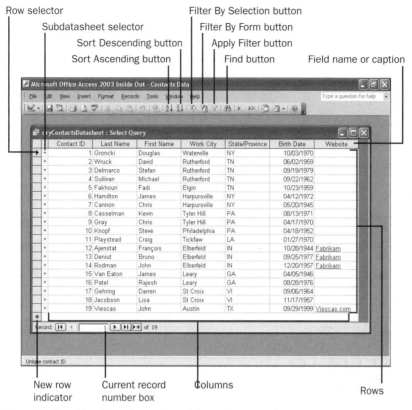

Figure 7-29. The Datasheet view of the qryContactsDatasheet query.

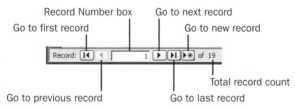

Figure 7-30. The navigation bar buttons and Record Number box.

You can quickly move to the record you want by typing a value in the record number box and pressing Enter or by using the navigation buttons. You can also choose the Go To command from the Edit menu to move to the first, last, next, or previous record, or to move to a new, empty record. You can make any record current by clicking anywhere in its row; the number in the record number box will change to indicate the row you've selected.

You might find it easier to use the keyboard rather than the mouse to move around in a datasheet, especially if you're typing in new data. Table 7-6 on the next page lists the keyboard shortcuts for scrolling in a datasheet. Table 7-7 on the next page lists the keyboard shortcuts for selecting data in a datasheet.

253

Table 7-6. Keyboard Shortcuts for Scrolling in a Datasheet

Keys	Scrolling Action
Page Up	Up one page
Page Down	Down one page
Ctrl+Page Up	Left one page
Ctrl+Page Down	Right one page

Table 7-7. Keyboard Shortcuts for Selecting Data in a Datasheet

Keys	Selecting Action
Tab	Next field
Shift+Tab	Previous field
Home	First field, current record
End	Last field, current record
Up Arrow	Current field, previous record
Down Arrow	Current field, next record
Ctrl+Up Arrow	Current field, first record
Ctrl+Down Arrow	Current field, last record
Ctrl+Home	First field, first record
Ctrl+End	Last field, last record
F5	Record Number box
Ctrl+Spacebar	The current column
Shift+Spacebar	The current record
F2	When in a field, toggles between selecting all data in the field and single-character edit mode

Working with Subdatasheets

Microsoft Access 2000 introduced a new feature that lets you display information from multiple related tables in a single datasheet. In the design we developed in Chapter 3 for the LawTrack Contacts sample database, Contacts can have multiple Contact Events and Contact Products. In some cases, it might be useful to open a query on Contacts and be able to see either related Events or Products in the same datasheet window.

You might have noticed the little plus-sign indicators in the datasheet for qryContacts-Datasheet in Figure 7-29. Click the plus sign next to the second row to open the Contact Events subdatasheet as shown in Figure 7-31.

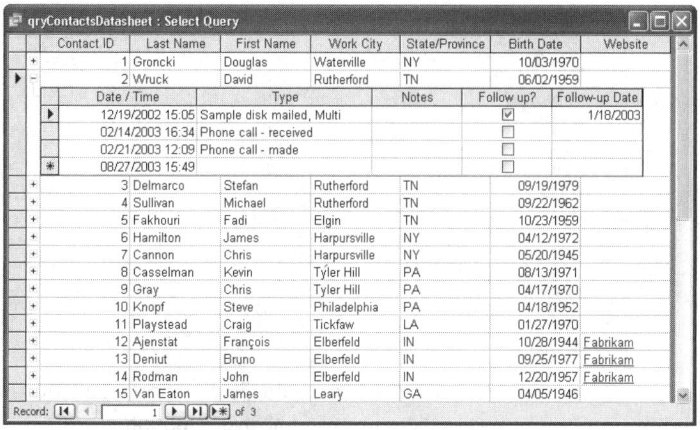

	Contact ID	Last Name	First Name	Work City	State/Province	Birth Date	Website	
+	1	Groncki	Douglas	Waterville	NY	10/03/1970		
–	2	Wruck	David	Rutherford	TN	06/02/1959		

	Date / Time	Type	Notes	Follow up?	Follow-up Date
▶	12/19/2002 15:05	Sample disk mailed, Multi		☑	1/18/2003
	02/14/2003 16:34	Phone call - received		☐	
	02/21/2003 12:09	Phone call - made		☐	
✱	08/27/2003 15:49			☐	

	Contact ID	Last Name	First Name	Work City	State/Province	Birth Date	Website
+	3	Delmarco	Stefan	Rutherford	TN	09/19/1979	
+	4	Sullivan	Michael	Rutherford	TN	09/22/1962	
+	5	Fakhouri	Fadi	Elgin	TN	10/23/1959	
+	6	Hamilton	James	Harpursville	NY	04/12/1972	
+	7	Cannon	Chris	Harpursville	NY	05/20/1945	
+	8	Casselman	Kevin	Tyler Hill	PA	08/13/1971	
+	9	Gray	Chris	Tyler Hill	PA	04/17/1970	
+	10	Knopf	Steve	Philadelphia	PA	04/18/1952	
+	11	Playstead	Craig	Tickfaw	LA	01/27/1970	
+	12	Ajenstat	François	Elberfeld	IN	10/28/1944	Fabrikam
+	13	Deniut	Bruno	Elberfeld	IN	09/25/1977	Fabrikam
+	14	Rodman	John	Elberfeld	IN	12/20/1957	Fabrikam
+	15	Van Eaton	James	Leary	GA	04/05/1946	

Record: 1 of 3

Figure 7-31. Viewing the contact event details for the second contact in a subdatasheet.

A subdatasheet doesn't appear automatically in a query, even if you've defined subdatasheet properties for your table as described in Chapter 4, "Creating Your Database and Tables." I had to open the Properties window for the query in Design view and specify the subdatasheet you see. Figure 7-32 shows you the properties I set. You can find more details about setting these properties in Chapter 4 and in Chapter 8, "Building Complex Queries."

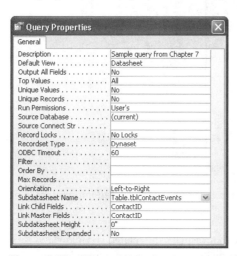

Figure 7-32. The subdatasheet properties in qryContactsDatasheet.

You can click the plus sign next to each order row to see the contact event detail information for that contact. If you want to expand or collapse all the subdatasheets, choose Subdatasheet on the Format menu, and select the option you want as shown in Figure 7-33 on the next page.

255

Figure 7-33. The Subdatasheet menu allows you to easily expand all subdatasheets, collapse all subdatasheets, or remove the currently displayed subdatasheet.

The information from the related tblContactEvents table is interesting, but what if you want to see the products the contact has purchased instead? To do this, choose Subdatasheet on the Insert menu while in Datasheet view to see the dialog shown in Figure 7-34.

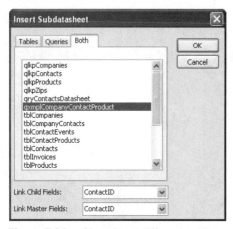

Figure 7-34. Choosing a different table to display other related information in a subdatasheet.

I built a query in the sample database that displays the related company and product information for a contact. Click the Queries or Both tab and select *qxmplCompanyContactProduct* to define the new subdatasheet.

When you return to the qryContactsDatasheet window, choose Subdatasheet from the Format menu and select the option on the submenu to Expand All. You will now see information about each product ordered as shown in Figure 7-35. Note that you can also entirely remove a subdatasheet by choosing Remove on the menu shown in Figure 7-33.

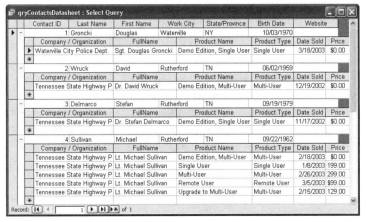

Figure 7-35. Reviewing all product information for a contact from the subdatasheet.

In the next section, you'll learn more about editing data in Datasheet view. You can use these editing techniques with the main datasheet as well as with any expanded subdatasheet.

Caution   When you close qryContactsDatasheet after modifying the subdatasheet as explained in this section, Access will prompt you to ask if you want to save your changes. You should select No to retain the original subdatasheet on tblContactEvents that I defined so that the remaining examples in this chapter make sense.

Changing Data

Not only can you view and format data in a datasheet, you can also insert new records, change data, and delete records.

Understanding Record Indicators

You might have noticed as you moved around in the datasheet that icons occasionally appeared on the row selector at the far left of each row. (See Figure 7-29.) These *record indicators* and their meanings are listed on the next page.

Indicates that this is the current row.

 Indicates that you are making or have made a change to one or more entries in this row. Microsoft Access saves the changes when you move to another row. Before moving to a new row, you can press Esc once to undo the change to the current value, or press Esc twice to undo all changes in the row. If you're updating a database that is shared with other users through a network, Access locks this record when you save the change so that no one else can update it until you're finished. If someone else has the record locked, Access shows you a warning dialog box when you try to save the row. You can wait a few seconds and try to save again.

 Indicates a blank row at the end of the table that you can use to create a new record.

Adding a New Record

As you build your application, you might find it useful to place some data in your tables so that you can test the forms and reports that you design. You might also find it faster sometimes to add data directly to your tables by using Datasheet view rather than by opening a form. If your table is empty, Access shows a single blank row when you open the table or a query on the table in Datasheet view. If you have data in your table, Access shows a blank row beneath the last record. You can jump to the blank row to begin adding a new record either by choosing the Go To command from the Edit menu and then choosing New Record from the submenu, by clicking the New Record button on the toolbar, or by pressing Ctrl+plus sign. Access places the insertion point in the first column when you start a new record. As soon as you begin typing, Access changes the record indicator to the pencil icon to show that updates are in progress. Press the Tab key to move to the next column.

If the data you enter in a column violates a field validation rule, Access notifies you as soon as you attempt to leave the column. You must provide a correct value before you can move to another column. Press Esc, choose Undo Typing from the Edit menu, or click the Undo button on the toolbar to remove your changes in the current field.

Press Shift+Enter at any place in the record or press the Tab key in the last column in the record to commit your new record to the database. You can also choose the Save Record command from the Records menu. If the changes in your record violate the validation rule for the table, Access warns you when you try to save the record. You must correct the problem before you can save your changes. If you want to cancel the record, press Esc twice or click the Undo button on the toolbar until it appears dimmed. If you want to use the Edit menu to undo the current record, you must choose Undo Current Field/Record from the Edit menu until that menu item appears dimmed and changes to Can't Undo. (The first Undo removes the edit from the current field, and choosing Undo again removes any previous edit in other fields until you have removed them all.)

Access provides several keyboard shortcuts to assist you as you enter new data, as shown in Table 7-8.

Table 7-8. Keyboard Shortcuts for Entering Data in a Datasheet

Keys	Data Action
Ctrl+semicolon (;)	Enters the current date
Ctrl+colon (:)	Enters the current time
Ctrl+Alt+Spacebar	Enters the default value for the field
Ctrl+single quotation mark (') or Ctrl+double quotation mark (")	Enters the value from the same field in the previous record
Ctrl+Enter	Inserts a carriage return in a memo or text field
Ctrl+plus sign (+)	Moves to the new record row
Ctrl+minus sign (-)	Deletes the current record

Inside Out

Setting keyboard options

You can set options that affect how you move around in datasheets and forms. Choose Options from the Tools menu and click the Keyboard tab to see the options shown here.

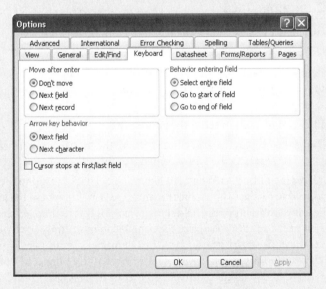

You can change the way the Enter key works by selecting an option under Move after enter. Select Don't move to stay in the current field when you press Enter. When you select Next field (the default), pressing Enter moves to the next field or the next row if you're on the last field. Select Next record to save your changes and move to the next row when you press Enter.

You can change what part of the data of the field is selected when you move into a field by setting an option under Behavior Entering Field. Choose Select Entire Field (the default), to highlight all data in the field. Choose Go To Start Of Field to place the insertion point before the first character, and choose Go To End Of Field to place the insertion point after the last character.

Under Arrow key behavior select Next field (the default) if you want to move from field to field when you press the Right Arrow or Left Arrow key. Choose Next character to change to the insertion point and move one character at a time when you press the Right Arrow or Left Arrow key. You can select Cursor stops at first/last field if you don't want pressing the arrow keys to move you off the current row.

I personally prefer to set the Move after enter option to Don't move and the Arrow key behavior option to Next character. I use the Tab key to move from field to field, and I don't want to accidentally save the record when I press Enter. I leave the Behavior entering field option at the default setting of Select entire field so that the entire text is selected, but setting Arrow key behavior to Next character allows me to press the arrow keys to shift to single-character edit mode and move in the field.

Selecting and Changing Data

When you have data in a table, you can easily change the data by editing it in Datasheet view. You must select data before you can change it, and you can do this in several ways.

- In the cell containing the data you want to change, click just to the left of the first character you want to change (or to the right of the last character), and then drag the insertion point to highlight all the characters you want to change.
- Double-click any word in a cell to select the entire word.
- Click at the left edge of a cell in the grid (that is, where the mouse pointer turns into a large white cross). Access selects the entire contents of the cell.

Any data you type replaces the old, selected data. In Figure 7-36, I have moved to the left edge of the First Name field, and Access has shown me the white cross mentioned in the last bullet. I can click to select the entire contents of the field. In Figure 7-37, I have changed the value to Mike, but haven't yet saved the row. (You can see the pencil icon indicating a change is pending.) Access also selects the entire entry if you tab to the cell in the datasheet grid (unless you have changed the keyboard options as noted earlier). If you want to change only part of the data (for example, to correct the spelling of a street name in an address field), you can shift to single-character mode by pressing F2 or by clicking the location at which you want to start your change. Use the Backspace key to erase characters to the left of the insertion point and use the Delete key to remove characters to the right of the insertion point. Hold down the Shift key and press the Right Arrow or Left Arrow key to select multiple characters to replace. You can press F2 again to select the entire cell. A useful keyboard shortcut for changing data is to press Ctrl+Alt+Spacebar to restore the data in the current field to the default value specified in the table definition.

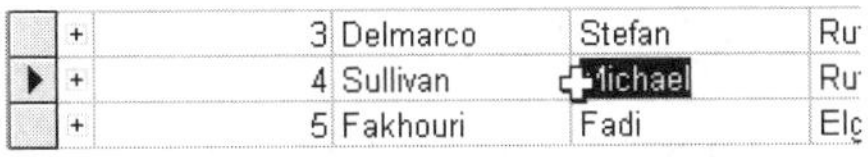

		3	Delmarco	Stefan	Ru
▶	+	4	Sullivan	Michael	Ru
	+	5	Fakhouri	Fadi	Elc

Figure 7-36. The old data is selected.

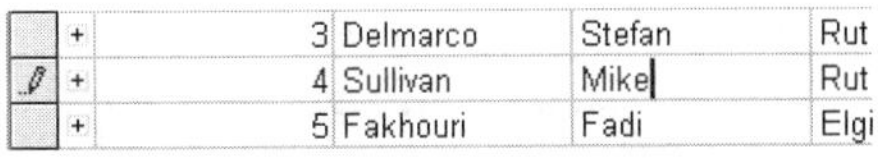

		3	Delmarco	Stefan	Rut
𝄜	+	4	Sullivan	Mike	Rut
	+	5	Fakhouri	Fadi	Elgi

Figure 7-37. The new data is typed in, replacing the old.

Replacing Data

What if you need to make the same change in more than one record? Access provides a way to do this quickly and easily. Select any cell in the column whose values you want to change (the first row if you want to start at the beginning of the table), and then choose the Replace command from the Edit menu or press Ctrl+H to see the dialog box shown in Figure 7-38. Suppose, for example, that you suspect that the city name *Elberfeld* is misspelled as *Elberfield* in multiple rows. (All the city names are spelled correctly in the sample table.) To fix this using Replace, select the Work City field in any row of qryContactsDatasheet, choose the Replace command, type **Elberfield** in the Find What text box, and then type **Elberfeld** in the Replace With text box, as shown in Figure 7-38. Click the Find Next button to search for the next occurrence of the text you've typed in the Find What text box. Click the Replace button to change data selectively, or click the Replace All button to change all the entries that match the Find What text. Note that you can choose options to look in all fields or only the current field; to select an entry only if the Find What text matches the entire entry in the field; to search All, Up, or Down; to exactly match the case for text searches (because searches in Access are normally case-insensitive); and to search based on the formatted contents (most useful when updating date/time fields).

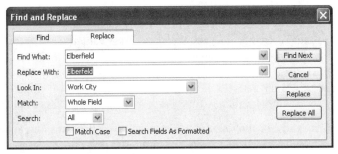

Figure 7-38. The Find And Replace dialog box.

Copying and Pasting Data

You can copy or cut any selected data to the Windows Clipboard and paste this data into another field or record. To copy data in a field, tab to the cell or click at the left edge of the cell in the datasheet grid to select the data within it. Choose the Copy command from the Edit menu or press Ctrl+C. To delete (cut) the data you have selected and place a copy on the

Clipboard, choose the Cut command from the Edit menu or press Ctrl+X. To paste the data in another location, move the insertion point to the new location, optionally select the data you want to replace, and choose the Paste command from the Edit menu or press Ctrl+V. If the insertion point is at the paste location (you haven't selected any data in the field), Access inserts the Clipboard data.

Inside Out

Using the Office Clipboard

If you select and copy to the Clipboard several items of text data, Access shows you the Office Clipboard task pane. Unlike the Windows Clipboard, this facility allows you to copy several separate items and then select any one of them later to paste into other fields or documents. You might find this feature useful when you want to copy the contents of several fields from one record to another. You can, for example, copy a City field and then copy a State field while in one record and then later individually paste the values into another row. If you don't see the Office Clipboard task pane, you can open it by choosing Office Clipboard from the Edit menu.

To select an entire record to be copied or cut, click the row selector at the far left of the row. You can drag through the row selectors or press Shift+Up Arrow or Shift+Down Arrow to extend the selection to multiple rows. Choose the Copy command from the Edit menu or press Ctrl+C to copy the contents of multiple rows to the Clipboard. You can also choose the Cut command from the Edit menu or press Ctrl+X to delete the rows and place them on the Clipboard.

You can open another table or query and paste the copied rows into that datasheet, or you can use the Paste Append command on the Edit menu to paste the rows at the end of the same datasheet. When you paste rows into another table, the rows you're adding must satisfy the validation rules of the receiving table, and the primary key values (if any) must be unique. If any validation fails, Access shows you an error message and cancels the paste. You cannot paste copies of entire records into the same table if the table has a primary key other than the AutoNumber data type. (You'll get a duplicate primary key value error if you try to do this.) When the primary key is AutoNumber, Access generates new primary key values for you.

The Cut command is handy for moving those records that you don't want in an active table to a backup table. You can have both tables open (or queries on both tables open) in Datasheet view at the same time. Simply cut the rows you want to move, switch to the backup table window, and paste the cut rows by using the Paste Append command.

When you paste one row, Access inserts the data and leaves your insertion point on the new record but doesn't save it. You can always click Undo to avoid saving the single pasted record. When you paste multiple rows, Access must save them all as a group before allowing you to edit further. Access asks you to confirm the paste operation. (See Figure 7-39.) Click Yes to proceed, or click No if you decide to cancel the operation.

Figure 7-39. This dialog box asks whether you want to proceed with a paste operation.

Note You can't change the physical sequence of rows in a relational database by cutting rows from one location and pasting them in another location. Access always pastes new rows at the end of the current display. If you close the datasheet after pasting in new rows and then open it again, Access displays the rows in sequence by the primary key you defined. If you want to see rows in some other sequence, see "Sorting and Searching for Data," later in this chapter.

Deleting Rows

To delete one or more rows, select the rows using the row selectors and then press the Delete key. For details about selecting multiple rows, see the previous discussion on copying and pasting data. You can also use the Ctrl+ minus sign to delete the current or selected row. When you delete rows, Access gives you a chance to change your mind if you made a mistake. (See Figure 7-40.) Click Yes in the dialog box to delete the rows, or click No to cancel the deletion. Because this database has referential integrity rules defined between tblContacts and several other tables, you won't be able to delete contact records using qryContactsDatasheet. (Access shows you an error message telling you that related rows exist in other tables.) You would have to remove all related records from tblContactEvents, tblContactProducts, and tblCompanyContacts first.

Warning After you click Yes in the confirmation dialog box, you cannot restore the deleted rows. You have to reenter them or copy them from a backup.

Figure 7-40. The dialog box that appears when you delete rows.

Working with Hyperlinks

Microsoft Access 97 (also known as version 8.0) introduced the Hyperlink data type. The Hyperlink data type lets you store a simple or complex link to a file or document outside your database. This link pointer can contain a Uniform Resource Locator (URL) that points to a location on the World Wide Web or on a local intranet. It can also use a Universal Naming Convention (UNC) file name to point to a file on a server on your local area network (LAN) or on your local computer drives. The link might point to a file that is a Web page or in a format that is supported by an ActiveX application on your computer.

A Hyperlink data type is actually a memo field that can contain a virtually unlimited number of characters. The link itself can have up to four parts.

- An optional descriptor that Access displays in the field when you're not editing the link. The descriptor can start with any character other than a pound sign (#) and must have a pound sign as its ending delimiter. If you do not include the descriptor, you must start the link address with a pound sign.

- The link address expressed as either a URL (beginning with a recognized Internet protocol name such as http: or ftp:) or in UNC format (a file location expressed as \\server\share\path\filename). If you do not specify the optional descriptor field, Access displays the link address in the field. Terminate the link address with a pound sign (#).

- An optional subaddress that specifies a named location (such as a cell range in a Microsoft Excel spreadsheet or a bookmark in a Microsoft Word document) within the file. Separate the subaddress from the ScreenTip with a pound sign (#). If you entered no subaddress, you still must enter the pound sign delimiter if you want to define a ScreenTip.

- An optional ScreenTip that appears when you move your mouse pointer over the hyperlink.

For example, a hyperlink containing all four items might look like the following:

```
Viescas Download Page#http://www.viescas.com/Info/
links.htm#Downloads#Click to see the files you can download from Viescas.com
```

A hyperlink that contains a ScreenTip but no bookmark might look like:

```
Viescas.com Books#http://www.viescas.com/Info/
books.htm##Click to see recommended books on Viescas.com
```

When you have a field defined using the Hyperlink data type, you work with it differently than with a standard text field. I included the Website field from tblContacts in the sample qryContactsDatasheet query (in *ContactsDataCopy.mdb*). Open the query and scroll to the right, if necessary, so that you can see the Website field, and place your mouse pointer over one of the fields that contains data, as shown in Figure 7-41.

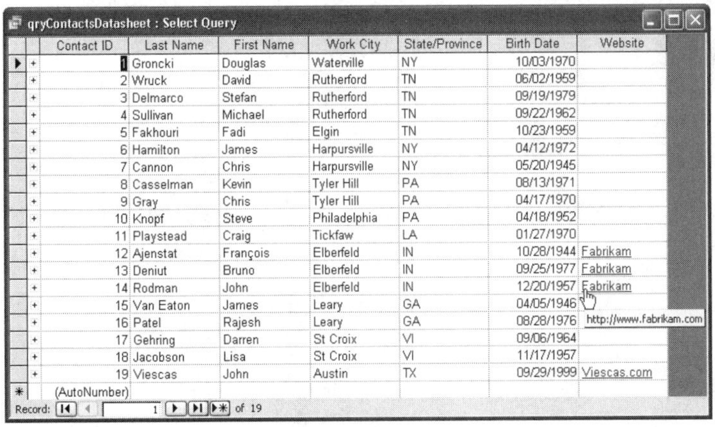

Contact ID	Last Name	First Name	Work City	State/Province	Birth Date	Website
1	Groncki	Douglas	Waterville	NY	10/03/1970	
2	Wruck	David	Rutherford	TN	06/02/1959	
3	Delmarco	Stefan	Rutherford	TN	09/19/1979	
4	Sullivan	Michael	Rutherford	TN	09/22/1962	
5	Fakhouri	Fadi	Elgin	TN	10/23/1959	
6	Hamilton	James	Harpursville	NY	04/12/1972	
7	Cannon	Chris	Harpursville	NY	05/20/1945	
8	Casselman	Kevin	Tyler Hill	PA	08/13/1971	
9	Gray	Chris	Tyler Hill	PA	04/17/1970	
10	Knopf	Steve	Philadelphia	PA	04/18/1952	
11	Playstead	Craig	Tickfaw	LA	01/27/1970	
12	Ajenstat	François	Elberfeld	IN	10/28/1944	Fabrikam
13	Deniut	Bruno	Elberfeld	IN	09/25/1977	Fabrikam
14	Rodman	John	Elberfeld	IN	12/20/1957	Fabrikam
15	Van Eaton	James	Leary	GA	04/05/1946	
16	Patel	Rajesh	Leary	GA	08/28/1976	
17	Gehring	Darren	St Croix	VI	09/06/1964	
18	Jacobson	Lisa	St Croix	VI	11/17/1957	
19	Viescas	John	Austin	TX	09/29/1999	Viescas.com
(AutoNumber)						

Figure 7-41. Placing the mouse pointer over a hyperlink field in Datasheet view shows the hyperlink or the ScreenTip.

Activating a Hyperlink

Notice that the text in a hyperlink field is underlined and that the mouse pointer becomes a hand with a pointing finger when you move the pointer over the field. If you leave the pointer floating over the field for a moment, Access displays the ScreenTip. In the tblContacts table, the entries in the Website hyperlink field for some of the contacts contain pointers to Microsoft Web sites. When you click a link field, Access starts the application that supports the link and passes the link address and subaddress to the application. If the link starts with an Internet protocol, Access starts your Web browser. In the case of the links in the tbl-Contacts table, all are links to pages on the Microsoft Office Web site. If you click one of them, your browser should start and display the related Web page, as shown in Figure 7-42 on the next page.

Figure 7-42. The result of clicking a Web site link in the tblContacts table.

Inserting a New Hyperlink

To insert a hyperlink in an empty hyperlink field, tab to the field or click in it with your mouse. If you're confident about the format of your link, you can type it in, following the rules for the four parts noted earlier. If you're not sure, choose Hyperlink from the Insert menu to see the dialog box shown in Figure 7-43. This dialog box helps you correctly construct the four parts of the hyperlink.

The dialog box opens with Existing File or Web Page selected in the Link to column and Current Folder selected in the inner window, as shown in Figure 7-43. What you see in the list in the center window depends on your current folder, the Web pages you've visited recently, and the files you've opened recently. You'll see a Look in drop-down list box where you can navigate to any drive or folder on your system. You can also click the Browse the Web button (the button with a globe and a spyglass) to open your Web browser to find a Web site you want, or the Browse for File button (with an open folder icon) to open the Link To File dialog box to find the file you want. Select Existing File or Web Page and click the Recent Files button to see a list of files that you recently opened.

Figure 7-43. The dialog box used to insert a hyperlink; it shows a list of files in the current folder.

I clicked the Browsed Pages option because I knew the hyperlink I wanted was a Web page that I had recently visited. You can enter the descriptor in the Text to display box at the top. I clicked the ScreenTip button to open the Set Hyperlink ScreenTip dialog box you see in Figure 7-44. You can type the document or Web site address directly into the Address box. (Yes, that's my real Web site address!)

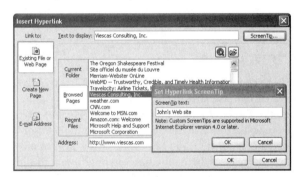

Figure 7-44. Choosing a Web site address from a list of recently visited Web sites.

Whether you are creating a link to an Internet site or to a file, after you have chosen a link address, you can use the Bookmark button (see Figure 7-44) to specify a location within the file or Internet site document. When you click the Bookmark button, Access scans the selected document or Web site and shows you a dialog box with a list of the bookmarks found. In a Microsoft Word document, bookmarks are named locations within the document. Within a Microsoft Excel document, bookmarks are named ranges or workbooks. On a Web page, bookmarks are named links within a page. For example, in *http://www.viescas.com/Info/links.htm#Downloads*, Downloads is a bookmark on the links.htm page.

In addition to linking to Web site locations, you can link to another location in the current database. On the far left of the Insert Hyperlink dialog box, you can choose Object in This Database to see a list of all the object types and objects in the current database. You can actually create a hyperlink that opens a specified table, query, form, report, data page, macro, or module.

Click the Create New Page option on the far left to enter the name of a new Web page document and specify the path. You'll also see options to edit the new document now or later. If you choose to edit now, Access creates a new data page and opens it to be edited. (See Chapter 27, "Building Data Access Pages," for details.)

The last option on the left, E-mail Address, lets you enter an e-mail address or choose from a list of recently used addresses. This generates a mailto: hyperlink that will invoke your e-mail program and start a new e-mail to the address you enter. You can also optionally specify a subject for the new e-mail by adding a question mark after the e-mail address and entering what you want to appear on the subject line.

Click OK to save your link in the field in the datasheet.

> **Note** If you decide to type a hyperlink address directly into the field, and the link is a Web address that starts with something other than http://, be sure to enter the protocol name as well. For example, to enter an e-mail address, type: **mailto:JohnV@Viescas.com**. If you only type JohnV@Viescas.com, Access will convert this to *http://JohnV@Viescas.com*, which is incorrect.

Editing an Existing Hyperlink

Getting into a hyperlink field to change the value of the link is a bit tricky. You can't simply click in a hyperlink field because that activates the link. What you can do is click in the field before the hyperlink and use the Tab key to move to the link field. Then press F2 to shift to character edit mode to edit the text string that defines the link. Figure 7-45 shows you a hyperlink field after following this procedure. You can use the arrow keys to move around in the text string to change one or more parts. In many cases, you might want to add an optional descriptor at the beginning of the link text, as shown in the figure.

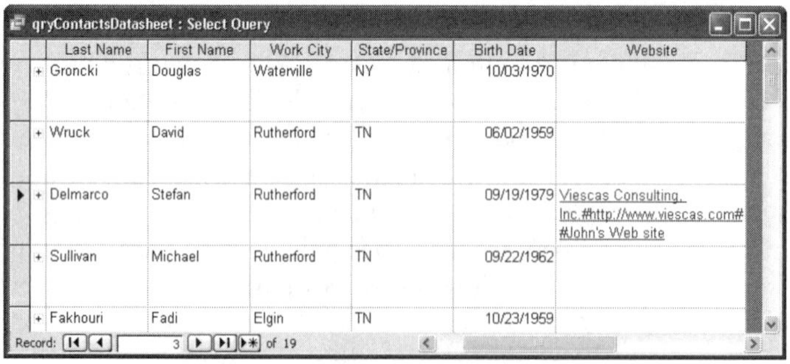

Figure 7-45. Editing the text that defines a hyperlink.

The most comprehensive way to work with a hyperlink field is to right-click a link field to open a shortcut menu. Choosing Hyperlink from this menu lets you see options. You can edit the hyperlink (which opens the dialog box shown in Figure 7-43), open the link document, copy the link to the Clipboard, add the link to your Windows list of favorites, change the text displayed in the field, or remove the hyperlink.

Sorting and Searching for Data

When you open a table in Datasheet view, Microsoft Access displays the rows sorted in sequence by the primary key you defined for the table. If you didn't define a primary key, you'll see the rows in the sequence in which you entered them in the table. If you want to see the rows in a different sequence or search for specific data, Access provides you with tools to do that. When you open a query in Datasheet view (such as the sample qryContactsDatasheet we're using in this chapter), you'll see the rows in the order specified by sort specifications in the query. If you haven't specified sorting information, you'll see the data in the same sequence as you would if you opened the table or query in Datasheet view.

Sorting Data

Access provides several ways to sort data in Datasheet view. As you might have noticed, two handy toolbar buttons allow you to quickly sort the rows in a query or table datasheet in ascending or descending order, based on the values in a single column. To see how this works, open the qryContactsDatasheet query, click anywhere in the State/Province column, and click the Sort Ascending button on the toolbar. Access sorts the display to show you the rows ordered alphabetically by state, as shown in Figure 7-46 on the next page.

Figure 7-46. Sorting contacts by state or province.

You can click the Sort Descending button to sort the rows in descending order.

If you want to sort on more than one field, you must use the filtering and sorting feature. Let's assume that you want to sort by State/Province, then by City within State/Province, and then by Last Name. Here's how to do it:

1. Choose Filter from the Records menu, and then choose Advanced Filter/Sort from the submenu. You'll see the Filter window (shown in Figure 7-47) with a list of fields in the qryContactsdatasheet query shown in the top part of the window.

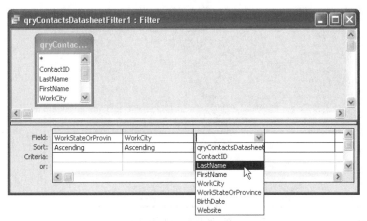

Figure 7-47. Selecting the LastName field in the Filter window.

2 Access normally places the insertion point in the first column of the Field row in the lower part of the window. If you don't see the insertion point there, click in that cell.

3 Because you recently sorted by State/Province, the Filter window will show this field already added to the filter grid. If you skipped the sort step in Figure 7-46 or closed and reopened the datasheet without saving the sort, open the field list in the first column by clicking the drop-down arrow or by pressing Alt+Down Arrow on the keyboard. Select the WorkStateOrProvince field in the list. You can also place the WorkStateOrProvince field in the first column by finding WorkStateOrProvince in the list of fields in the top pane of the window and dragging it into the Field row in the first column of the filter grid.

4 Click in the Sort row, immediately below the WorkStateOrProvince field, and select Ascending from the drop-down list.

5 Add the WorkCity and LastName fields to the next two columns, and select Ascending in the Sort row for both.

6 Click the Apply Filter toolbar button or choose Apply Filter/Sort from the Filter menu to see the result shown in Figure 7-48 on the next page.

> **Note** When you choose Advanced Filter/Sort for the first time, the Filter toolbar might not appear. If you don't see the toolbar, right-click the menu bar, and the toolbar appears.

qryContactsDatasheet : Select Query

Contact ID	Last Name	First Name	Work City	State/Province	Birth Date	Website
16	Patel	Rajesh	Leary	GA	08/28/1976	
15	Van Eaton	James	Leary	GA	04/05/1946	
12	Ajenstat	François	Elberfeld	IN	10/28/1944	Fabrikam
13	Deniut	Bruno	Elberfeld	IN	09/25/1977	Fabrikam
14	Rodman	John	Elberfeld	IN	12/20/1957	Fabrikam
11	Playstead	Craig	Tickfaw	LA	01/27/1970	
7	Cannon	Chris	Harpursville	NY	05/20/1945	
6	Hamilton	James	Harpursville	NY	04/12/1972	
1	Groncki	Douglas	Waterville	NY	10/03/1970	
10	Knopf	Steve	Philadelphia	PA	04/18/1952	
8	Casselman	Kevin	Tyler Hill	PA	08/13/1971	
9	Gray	Chris	Tyler Hill	PA	04/17/1970	
5	Fakhouri	Fadi	Elgin	TN	10/23/1959	
3	Delmarco	Stefan	Rutherford	TN	09/19/1979	
4	Sullivan	Michael	Rutherford	TN	09/22/1962	
2	Wruck	David	Rutherford	TN	06/02/1959	
19	Viescas	John	Austin	TX	09/29/1999	Viescas.com
17	Gehring	Darren	St Croix	VI	09/06/1964	
18	Jacobson	Lisa	St Croix	VI	11/17/1957	

Record: 1 of 19

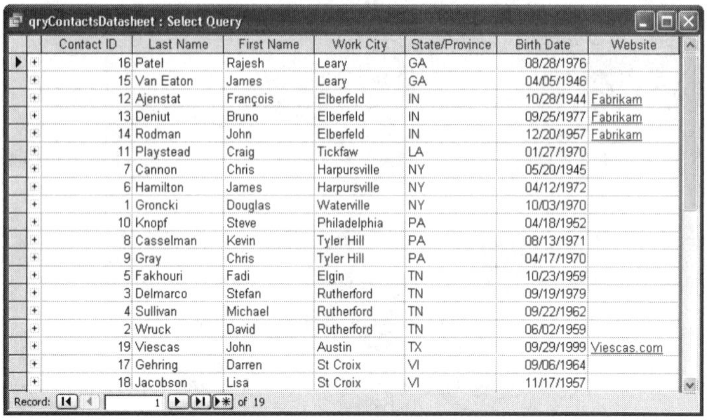

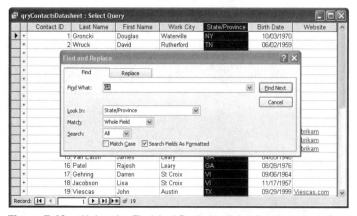

Figure 7-48. Sorting contact records by state or province, city, and then last name.

Note If you compare Figure 7-46 with Figure 7-48, it looks like the records in Figure 7-46 were already sorted by city name within state. You might be tempted to leave out the sort on city in this exercise, but if you do that, you will not see the city names maintained in the same order. Remember, if you want data presented in a certain sequence, you must ask for it that way!

Searching for and Filtering Data

If you want to look for data anywhere in your table, Access provides several powerful searching and filtering capabilities.

To perform a simple search on a single field, select that field, and then open the Find And Replace dialog box (shown in Figure 7-49) by choosing the Find command from the Edit menu, by pressing Ctrl+F, or by clicking the Find button on the toolbar.

Figure 7-49. Using the Find And Replace dialog box to search for data.

In the Find What text box, type the data that you want Access to find. You can include wild-card characters similar to that of the LIKE comparison operator. See "Defining Simple Field Validation Rules," in Chapter 4, to perform a generic search. Use an asterisk (*) to indicate a string of unknown characters of any length (zero or more characters), and use a question mark (?) to indicate exactly one unknown character or a space. For example, *AB??DE* matches *Aberdeen* and *Tab idea* but not *Lab department*.

By default, Access searches the field that your insertion point was in before you opened the Find And Replace dialog box. To search the entire table, select the table or query name from the Look In drop-down list box. By default, Access searches all records from the top of the recordset unless you change the Search drop-down list box to search down or up from the current record position. Select the Match Case check box if you want to find text that exactly matches the uppercase and lowercase letters you typed. By default, Access is case-insensitive unless you select this check box.

The Search Fields As Formatted check box appears dimmed unless you select a field that has a format or input mask applied. You can select this box if you need to search the data as it is displayed rather than as it is stored by Access. Although searching this way is slower, you probably should select this check box if you are searching a date/time field. For example, if you're searching a date field for dates in January, you can specify *-Jan-* if the field is format-ted as Medium Date and you select the Search Fields As Formatted check box. You might also want to select this check box when searching a Yes/No field for Yes because any value except 0 is a valid indicator of Yes.

Click Find Next to start searching from the current record. Each time you click Find Next again, Access moves to the next value it finds, and loops to the top of the recordset to con-tinue the search if you started in the middle. After you establish search criteria and you close the Find And Replace dialog box, you can press Shift+F4 to execute the search from the cur-rent record without having to open the dialog box again.

Using Filter By Selection   If you want to see all the rows in your table that contain a value that matches one in a row in the datasheet grid, you can use the Filter By Selection feature. Select a complete value in a field to see only rows that have data in that column that com-pletely matches. Figure 7-50 on the next page shows the value TN selected in the State/Prov-ince column and the result after clicking the Filter By Selection button. If the filtering data you need is in several contiguous columns, click the first column, hold down the Shift key and click the last column to select all the data, and then click the Filter By Selection button to see only rows that match the data in all the columns you selected.

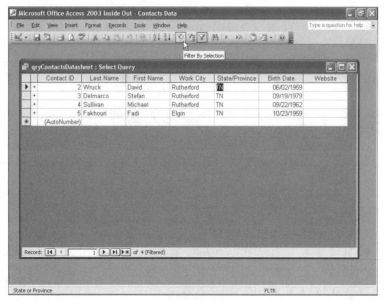

Figure 7-50. The list of contacts in Tennessee, compiled using Filter By Selection.

Alternatively, if you want to see all the rows in your table that contain a part of a value that matches one in a row in the datasheet grid, you can select the characters that you want to match and use Filter By Selection. For example, to see all contacts that have the characters erf in their work city name, find a contact that has erf in the work city name field and highlight those characters. Click the Filter By Selection button on the toolbar or choose Filter from the Records menu and then Filter By Selection from the submenu. When the search is completed you should see only the six contacts who work in the cities named Elb*erf*eld and Ruth*erf*ord. To remove a filter, click the Remove Filter button on the toolbar or choose Remove Filter/Sort from the Records menu.

> **Note** If you select characters at the beginning of a field and use them with Filter By Selection, you will see only rows whose value begins with the characters you selected. Likewise, selecting characters at the end of a field finds only rows whose column value ends in a matching value. Selecting characters in the middle of a field searches for those characters anywhere in the same column.
>
> If you apply a filter to a subdatasheet, you will filter all the subdatasheets that are open.

You can also add a filter to a filter. For example, if you want to see all contacts who live in Rutherford in Tennessee, find the value TN in the State/Province column, highlight it, and then click the Filter By Selection button. In the filtered list, find a row containing the word Rutherford in the Work City, select the word, and click the Filter By Selection button again. Click the Remove Filter button on the toolbar to remove all your filters.

274

Using Filter By Form   Filter By Selection is great for searching for rows that match *all* of several criteria (Last Name like "*van*" *and* State/Province equals "TN"), but what if you want to see rows that meet *any* of several criteria (Last Name like "*van*" and State/Province equals "TN" or State/Province equals "GA")? You can use Filter By Form to easily build the criteria for this type of search.

When you click the Filter By Form button on the table Datasheet toolbar, Access shows you a Filter By Form example that looks like your datasheet but contains no data. If you have no filtering criteria previously defined, Access shows you the Look For tab and one Or tab at the bottom of the window. Move to each column in which you want to define criteria and either select a value from the drop-down list or type in search criteria. Notice that each drop-down list shows you all the unique values available for each field, so it's easy to pick values to perform an exact comparison. You can also enter criteria, much the same way that you did to create validation rules in Chapter 4, "Creating Your Database and Tables." For example, you can enter *Like "*van*"* in the Last Name field to search for the letters *van* anywhere in the name. You can use criteria such as *>#01 JAN 1962#* in the Birth Date date/time field to find rows for contacts born after that date. You can enter multiple criteria on one line, but *all* of the criteria you enter on a single line must be true for a particular row to be selected.

> **Tip**   When your table or query returns tens of thousands of rows, fetching the values for each drop-down list in Filter By Form can take a long time. You can specify a limit by choosing Options from the Tools menu. On the Edit/Find tab, you can specify a value for Don't display lists where more than this number of records read. The default value is 1,000.

If you want to see rows that contain any of several values in a particular column (for example, rows from several states), enter the first value in the appropriate column, and then click the Or tab at the bottom of the window to enter an additional criterion. In this example, *"GA"* was entered in the State/Province column on the Look For tab and *"TN"* on the first Or tab; you can see "TN" being selected for the second Or tab in Figure 7-51.

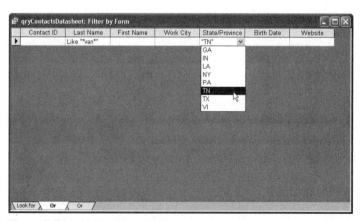

Figure 7-51.   Using Filter By Form to search for one of several states.

Each tab also specifies Like "*van*" for the last name. (As you define additional criteria, Access makes additional Or tabs available at the bottom of the window.) Figure 7-52 shows the result of applying these criteria by clicking the Apply Filter button on the toolbar.

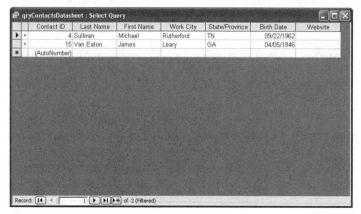

Figure 7-52. The contacts with names containing *van* in the states of TN and GA.

> **Tip** Saving and reusing your filters
>
> Access always remembers the last filtering and sorting criteria you defined for a datasheet. The next time you open the datasheet, click the Apply Filter toolbar button to apply the last filter you created (as long as you replied Yes to the prompt to save formatting changes when you last closed the datasheet). If you want to save a particular filter/sort definition, choose Filter from the Records menu, and then choose Advanced Filter/Sort from the sub-menu. Choose Save As Query from the File menu, and give your filter a name. The next time you open the table, return to Advanced Filter/Sort, and then choose Load From Query from the File menu to find the filter you previously saved.

You can actually define very complex filtering criteria using expressions and the Or tabs in the Filter By Form window. If you look at the Advanced Filter/Sort window, you can see that Access builds all your criteria in a design grid that looks similar to a Query window in Design view. In fact, filters and sorts use the query capabilities of Access to accomplish the result you want, so in Datasheet view you can use all the same filtering capabilities you'll find for queries.

In the next chapter, we'll explore creating more complex queries—including creating queries from multiple tables or queries, calculating totals, and designing PivotTable and PivotChart views.

Building Complex Queries

Creating queries on a single table as you did in the previous chapter is a good way to get acquainted with the basic mechanics of the query designer. It's also useful to work with simple queries to understand how datasheets work.

However, for many tasks you'll need to build a query on multiple tables or queries (yes, you can build a query on a query!), calculate totals, add parameters, customize query properties, or work in SQL view. In fact, there are some types of queries that you can build only in SQL view. This chapter shows you how.

Caution   When you build an application, you should *never* allow users to view or edit data directly from table or query datasheets. Although you can protect the integrity of your data somewhat with input masks, validation rules, and relationships, you cannot enforce complex business rules.

For example, in the Housing Reservations application, you need to ensure that a particular room isn't booked more than once for a given time period. In the LawTrack Contacts application, your application shouldn't allow a support contract to be sold for a product that the contact hasn't purchased. You can't run such integrity checks from tables or queries. However, you *can* enforce such complex business rules by writing Visual Basic code in the forms you design so that your users can edit data while maintaining data integrity.

The purpose of this chapter is to teach you the concepts you must learn to build the queries you'll need for your forms and reports. In Chapter 23, "Automating Your Application with Visual Basic," you'll learn how to build complex business rule validation into your forms.

Selecting Data from Multiple Tables

At this point, you've been through all the variations on a single theme—queries on a single table. It's easy to build on this knowledge to retrieve related information from many tables and to place that information in a single view. You'll find this ability to select data from multiple tables very useful in designing forms and reports.

Note The examples in this chapter are based on the tables and data in *Housing-DataCopy.mdb* and *ContactsDataCopy.mdb* on the companion CD included with this book. These databases are copies of the data from the Housing and LawTrack Contacts application samples, respectively, and they contain the sample queries used in this chapter. The query results you see from the sample queries you build in this chapter might not exactly match what you see in this book if you have changed the sample data in the files. Also, all the screen images in this chapter were taken on a Windows XP system with the display theme set to Windows XP. Your results may look different if you are using a different operating system or a different theme.

Creating Inner Joins

A *join* is the link you need to define between two related tables in a query so that the data you see makes sense. If you don't define the link, you'll see all rows from the first table combined with all rows from the second table (also called the *Cartesian product*). When you use an *inner join* (the default for joins in queries), you won't see rows from either table that don't have a matching row in the other table. This type of query is called an *equi-join query*, meaning that you'll see rows only where there are *equal* values in *both* tables. For example, in a query that joins departments and employees, you won't see any departments that have no employees or any employees that aren't assigned to a department. To see how to build a query that returns all rows from one of the tables, including rows that have no match in the related table, see "Using Outer Joins," page 287.

As you learned in Chapter 3, "Designing Your Database Application," correctly designing your tables requires you to split out (normalize) your data into separate tables to avoid redundant data and problems updating the data. For many tasks, however, you need to work with the data from multiple tables. For example, in the Housing application, to work with Employees and the Departments to which they are assigned, you can't get all the information you need from just tblEmployees. Sure, you can see the employee's DepartmentID, but what about the department name and location? If you want to sort or filter employees by department name, you need both tblDepartments and tblEmployees.

In the previous chapter, we built several queries on tblReservations. Because that table has Lookup properties defined, you can see the facility name in the reservation record, but as you discovered, that's really a numeric field. If you want to sort on the real name value or see other information about the facility, you must create a query that uses both tblFacilities and tblReservations.

Try the following example, in which you combine information about a reservation and about the facility in which the reservation was confirmed. Start by opening the *HousingData-Copy.mdb* database. Click the Queries button, and then click the New button. Select Design View in the New Query dialog box, and click OK to open a new Query window in Design view. Access immediately opens the Show Table dialog box. In this dialog box, you select tables and queries that you want in your new query. Select the tblFacilities and tblReservations tables (hold down the Ctrl key as you click each table name), click the Add button, and then close the dialog box.

Troubleshooting

How can I be sure I'm using the correct table in the query designer?

It's a good idea to select the Show Table Names option on the Tables/Queries tab of the Options dialog box (choose the Options command from the Tools menu) whenever your query is based on more than one table. Because you might have the same field name in more than one of the tables, showing table names in the design grid helps to ensure that your query refers to the field you intend it to.

Whenever you have relationships defined, the query designer automatically links (joins) multiple tables on the defined relationships. You might also want to select Enable AutoJoin on the Tables/Queries tab. When you select this option and build a query on two tables that aren't directly related, the query designer attempts to link the two tables for you. The query designer looks at the primary key of each table. If it can find a field with the same name and data type in one of the other tables you added to the query designer, the query designer builds the link for you. Some advanced users might prefer to always create these links themselves.

The two tables, tblFacilities and tblReservations, aren't directly related to each other. If you look in the Relationships window (choose Relationships from the Tools menu), you'll see a relationship defined between tblFacilities and tblFacilityRooms on the FacilityID field. There's also a relationship between tblFacilityRooms and tblReservations on the combination of the FacilityID and the RoomNumber fields. So, tblFacilities is related to tblReservations via the FacilityID field, but indirectly. In other words, the FacilityID field in tblReservations is a *foreign key* that points to the related row in tblFacilities. So, it's perfectly legitimate to build a query that links these two tables on the FacilityID field.

Inside Out

Query joins don't always need to match relationships

It's a good idea to define relationships between related tables to help ensure the integrity of your data. However, you don't need to define a relationship between the foreign key in a table and the matching primary key in every other related table. For example, if table A is related to table B, and table B is related to table C, you don't necessarily need a relationship defined between table A and table C even though table C might contain a foreign key field that relates it to table A. Even when you haven't explicitly defined a relationship between table A and table C, it is perfectly valid to join table A to table C in a query as long as there's a legitimate matching field in both tables.

The upper part of the Query window in Design view should look like that shown in Figure 8-1. Access first links multiple tables in a query based on the relationships you have defined. If no defined relationship exists, and you have Enable AutoJoin selected on the Tables/Queries tab in the Options dialog box (this option is enabled by default), then Access attempts to match the primary key from one table with a field that has the same name and data type in the other table.

Access shows the links between tables as a line drawn from the primary key in one table to its matching field in the other table. As already noted, no direct relationship exists between the two tables in this example. With Enable AutoJoin enabled, however, Access sees that the FacilityID field is the primary key in tblFacilities and finds a matching FacilityID field in tblReservations. So, it should create a join line between the two tables on the FacilityID fields. If you don't see this line, you can click FacilityID in tblFacilities and drag and drop it on FacilityID in tblReservations, just like you learned to do in "Defining Relationships" on page 123. You can also choose Join Properties from the View menu and click New in the resulting dialog box to define the two tables and the related fields.

> **Note** If you haven't defined relationships, when you create a query that uses two tables that are related by more than one field (for example, tblFacilityRooms and tblReservations in this database), the Join Properties dialog box lets you define only one of the links at a time. You must click the New button again to define the second part of the join. If you're using drag and drop, you can do this with only one field at a time even though you can select multiple fields in either table window.

In this example, you want to add to the query the FacilityID and FacilityName fields from the tblFacilities table and the ReservationID, EmployeeNumber, FacilityID, RoomNumber, CheckInDate, and CheckOutDate fields from the tblReservations table. (I resized the columns in the query grid in Figure 8-1 so you can see almost all the fields.)

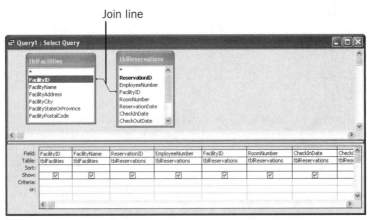

Figure 8-1. A query that selects information from the tblFacilities and tblReservations tables.

When you run the query, you see the recordset shown in Figure 8-2. The fields from the tblFacilities table appear first, left to right. I resized the columns displayed in Figure 8-2 so that you can see all the fields. You might need to scroll right in the datasheet to see them on your machine.

Inside Out

A query is really defined by its SQL

The query designer converts everything you build in a query grid into SQL—the lingua franca of database queries. Access actually stores only the SQL and rebuilds the query grid each time you open a query in Design view. Later in this chapter, we'll examine some of the actual syntax behind your queries, and you can study the full details of SQL in Article 1, "Understanding SQL," on the companion CD.

Join line   Fields from tblReservations

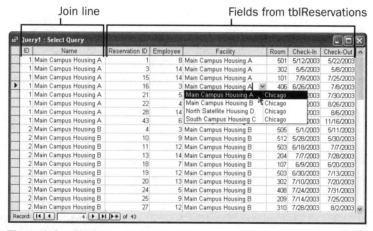

Figure 8-2. The recordset of the query shown in Figure 8-1. The facility information in the drop-down list comes from the Lookup properties defined in the tblReservations table.

Notice the facility name in the column for the FacilityID field from the tblReservations table. (The caption for the field is Facility.) If you check the definition of the FacilityID field in the tblReservations table, you'll see a Lookup combo box defined—the query has inherited those properties. Click in a field in the Facility column in this datasheet, and the combo box appears. If you choose a different Facility name from the drop-down list, you will change the FacilityID field for that reservation. But the room number already in the row might not exist in the new Facility, so you might get an error if you try to save the row. This is yet another example of a business rule that you will have to ensure is verified in a form you create for users to edit this data.

If you choose a different Facility (the FacilityID field in tblReservations), you can see the ID and Name change on the left side of the datasheet. When you change the value in a foreign key field (in this case, the FacilityID field in tblReservations) in a table on the *many* side of a one-to-many query (there are many reservations for each facility), Access performs an

AutoLookup to retrieve the related row from the *one* side (tblFacilities) to keep the data synchronized. You'll find this feature handy later when you build a form that displays and edits information from a query like this.

Try changing the Facility column (remember, this is the FacilityID field from tblReservations) in the first row from Main Campus Housing A to South Campus Housing C. When you select the new value for the FacilityID field in tblReservations, you should see the ID field from tblFacilities change to 3 and the Name entry (the FacilityName field from tblFacilities) change from Main Campus Housing A to South Campus Housing C. Note that in this case you're changing only the linking FacilityID field in tblReservations, not the name of the facility in tblFacilities. Access is retrieving the row from tblFacilities that matches the changed FacilityID value in tblReservations to show you the correct name.

Note If you change the facility in one of the rows in this query, Access won't let you save the row if the room number in the reservation doesn't exist in the new facility you picked.

One interesting aspect of queries on multiple tables is that in many cases you can update the fields from either table in the query. See "Limitations on Using Select Queries to Update Data" on page 323 for a discussion of when joined queries are not updatable. For example, you can change the facility name in the tblFacilities table by changing the data in the Name column in this query's datasheet.

Caution In most cases, Access lets you edit fields from the table on the *one* side of the join (in this case, tblFacilities). Because the facility name comes from a table on the *one* side of a one-to-many relationship (one facility has many reservations, but each reservation is for only one facility), if you change the name of the facility in any row in this query, you change the name for all reservations for the same facility.

Although the dangers to doing this are apparent, this is actually one of the benefits of designing your tables properly. If the facility is renamed (perhaps it gets renamed in honor of a beloved ex-president of the company), you need to change the name in only one place. You don't have to go find all existing reservations for the facility and update them all.

You might use a query like the one in Figure 8-1 as the basis for a report on reservations by facility. However, such a report would probably also need to include the employee name and department to be truly useful. Switch back to Design view, click the Show Table button on the toolbar (or choose Show Table from the Query menu) and add tblEmployees and tblDepartments to the query.

Tip If you have enough room on your screen to place the Database window and the Query window side by side, you can also drag and drop any table or query from the Database window to your query.

You'll run into a small problem when you add tblDepartments to your query: There are two relationships defined between tblDepartments and tblEmployees. First, each employee must have a valid department assigned, so there's a relationship on DepartmentID. Also, any manager for a department must be an employee of the department, and an employee can manage only one department, so there's a second relationship defined between EmployeeNumber in tblEmployees and ManagerNumber in tblDepartments.

The query designer doesn't know which relationship you want to use as a join in this query, so it includes them *both* in the query grid. If you leave both join lines in your query, you'll see only reservations for managers of departments because the join between EmployeeNumber in tblEmployees and ManagerNumber in tblDepartments forces the query to only include employees who are also managers. You should click on the join line between EmployeeNumber in tblEmployees and ManagerNumber in tblDepartments and press the Delete key to remove the join.

If you're going to use this query in a report, you probably don't need the EmployeeNumber and FacilityID from tblReservations, so you can delete them. Next click on RoomNumber and choose Column from the Insert menu to give you a blank column to work with. You need the employee name for your report, but you most likely don't need the separate FirstName, MiddleName, and LastName fields. Use the blank column to create an expression as follows:

```
EmpName: tblEmployees.FirstName & " " & (tblEmployees.MiddleName + " ") & LastName
```

Note that you're using the little trick, which you learned in the previous chapter: using an arithmetic operation to eliminate the potential extra blank when an employee has no middle name. Drag and drop the Department field from tblDepartments on top of RoomNumber in the Design grid—this should place it between the EmpName field you just defined and RoomNumber. Your query grid should now look like Figure 8-3.

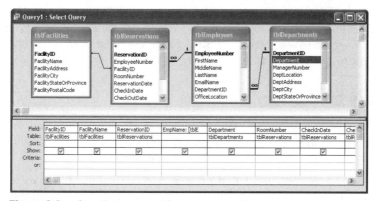

Figure 8-3. Creating a complex query using four tables.

You can switch to Datasheet view to see the results of your work as shown in Figure 8-4.

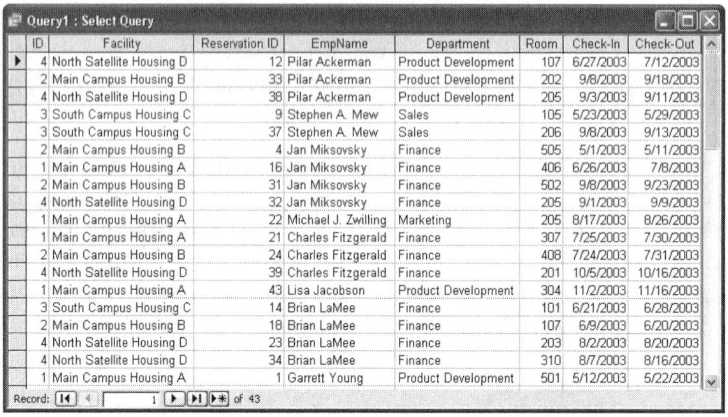

ID	Facility	Reservation ID	EmpName	Department	Room	Check-In	Check-Out
4	North Satellite Housing D	12	Pilar Ackerman	Product Development	107	6/27/2003	7/12/2003
2	Main Campus Housing B	33	Pilar Ackerman	Product Development	202	9/8/2003	9/18/2003
4	North Satellite Housing D	38	Pilar Ackerman	Product Development	205	9/3/2003	9/11/2003
3	South Campus Housing C	9	Stephen A. Mew	Sales	105	5/23/2003	5/29/2003
3	South Campus Housing C	37	Stephen A. Mew	Sales	206	9/8/2003	9/13/2003
2	Main Campus Housing B	4	Jan Miksovsky	Finance	505	5/1/2003	5/11/2003
1	Main Campus Housing A	16	Jan Miksovsky	Finance	406	6/26/2003	7/8/2003
2	Main Campus Housing B	31	Jan Miksovsky	Finance	502	9/8/2003	9/23/2003
4	North Satellite Housing D	32	Jan Miksovsky	Finance	205	9/1/2003	9/9/2003
1	Main Campus Housing A	22	Michael J. Zwilling	Marketing	205	8/17/2003	8/26/2003
1	Main Campus Housing A	21	Charles Fitzgerald	Finance	307	7/25/2003	7/30/2003
2	Main Campus Housing B	24	Charles Fitzgerald	Finance	408	7/24/2003	7/31/2003
4	North Satellite Housing D	39	Charles Fitzgerald	Finance	201	10/5/2003	10/16/2003
1	Main Campus Housing A	43	Lisa Jacobson	Product Development	304	11/2/2003	11/16/2003
3	South Campus Housing C	14	Brian LaMee	Finance	101	6/21/2003	6/28/2003
2	Main Campus Housing B	18	Brian LaMee	Finance	107	6/9/2003	6/20/2003
4	North Satellite Housing D	23	Brian LaMee	Finance	203	8/2/2003	8/20/2003
4	North Satellite Housing D	34	Brian LaMee	Finance	310	8/7/2003	8/16/2003
1	Main Campus Housing A	1	Garrett Young	Product Development	501	5/12/2003	5/22/2003

Record: [◄◄] [◄] 1 [►] [►I] [►*] of 43

Figure 8-4. The recordset of the query shown in Figure 8-3.

Do you notice anything strange about the sequence of rows? Why aren't the rows sorted by facility name and then perhaps employee name? If you were to put the EmployeeNumber back into the query grid and take a look at the data again, you would discover that Access sorted the rows by EmployeeNumber and then by ReservationID. Access looked at all the information you requested and then figured out the quickest way to give you the answer—probably by fetching rows from tblEmployee first (which are sorted on the primary key, EmployeeID) and then fetching the matching rows from tblReservations.

Remember from the previous chapter that the only way you can guarantee the sequence of rows is to specify a sort on the fields you want. In this case, you might want to sort by facility name, employee last name, employee first name, and check-in date. You buried first name and last name in the EmpName expression, so you can't use that field to sort the data by last name. You can find the correct answer saved as *qxmplSortReservations* in the sample database. (Hint: You need to add tblEmployees.LastName and tblEmployees.FirstName to the grid to be able to specify the sort.)

Building a Query on a Query

When you're building a very complex query, sometimes it's easier to visualize the solution to the problem at hand by breaking it down into smaller pieces. In some cases, building a query on a query might be the only way to correctly solve the problem.

For this set of examples, let's switch to the data in the LawTrack Contacts database. Start Access and open *ContactsDataCopy.mdb*. Customers who purchase a Single User copy of the software marketed by LawTrack can later decide to upgrade to the Multi-User edition for a reduced price. Assume you're a consultant hired by LawTrack, and the company has asked you to produce a list of all customers and their companies who purchased a Single User copy and then later purchased the upgrade.

To solve this, you might be tempted to start a new query on tblContacts and add the tblCompanies, tblContactProducts, and tblProducts tables. You would include the CompanyID and CompanyName fields from tblCompanies; the ContactID, FirstName, and LastName fields from tblContacts; and the ProductID and ProductName fields from tblProducts. Then you would place a criterion like *"Single User" And "Upgrade to Multi-User"* on the Criteria line under ProductName. However, any one row in your query will show information from only one contact and product, so one row can't contain both "Single User" and "Upgrade to Multi-User." (See the discussion in "AND vs. OR," page 228.) Your query will return no rows.

Your next attempt might be to correct the criterion to *"Single User" Or "Upgrade to Multi-User"*. That will at least return some data, but you'll get an answer similar to Figure 8-5. (You can find this query saved as *qxmplTwoProductsWrong* in the sample database.)

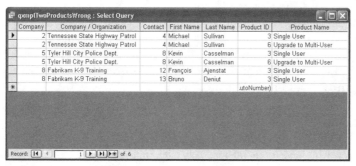

Figure 8-5. An attempt to find out which contacts have purchased both Single User and the Upgrade to Multi-User.

Because there aren't very many rows in this database, you can see that the answer is Michael Sullivan and Kevin Casselman. But if there were thousands of rows in the database, you wouldn't be able to easily find the contacts who purchased both products. And if you need the output to display in a report, you really need a single row for each contact that meets your criteria.

One way to solve this sort of problem is to build a query that finds everyone who owns Single User and save it. Then build another query that finds everyone who purchased the Multi-User upgrade and save that. Finally, build a third query that joins the first two results to get your final answer. Remember that a simple join returns only the rows that match in both tables—or queries. So, someone who appears in both queries clearly owns both products! Here's how to build the solution.

1   Build the first query to find customers who own Single User.

    a   Start a new query on tblContactProducts and add tblProducts to the query. You should see a join line between tblProducts and tblContactProducts on the ProductID field because there's a relationship defined.

    b   From tblContactProducts, include the CompanyID and the ContactID fields.

    c   Add ProductName from tblProducts, and enter **"Single User"** on the Criteria line under this field. Save this query and name it qrySingle.

2 Build the second query to find customers who bought the upgrade.

    a Start another query on tblContactProducts and add tblProducts to the query.

    b From tblContactProducts, include the CompanyID and the ContactID fields.

    c Add ProductName from tblProducts, and enter **"Upgrade to Multi-User"** on the Criteria line under this field. Save this query and name it qryMultiUpgrade.

3 Build the final solution query.

    a Start a new query on tblCompanies. Add your new qrySingle and qryMultiUpgrade queries.

    b The query designer will link tblCompanies to both queries on CompanyID, but you don't need a link to both. Click on the join line between tblCompanies and qryMultiUpgrade and delete it.

    c You do need to link qrySingle and qryMultiUpgrade. Drag and drop CompanyID from qrySingle to qryMultiUpgrade. Then, drag and drop ContactID from qrySingle to qryMultiUpgrade. Because you are defining an inner join between the two queries, the query only fetches rows from the two queries where CompanyID and ContactID match.

    d Add tblContacts to your query. Because there's a relationship defined between ContactID in tblContacts and ReferredBy in tblCompanies, the query designer adds this join line. You don't need this join (the query would return only contacts who have made referrals), so click on the line and delete it. The query designer does correctly create a join line between tblContacts and qrySingle.

    e In the query Design grid, include CompanyName from tblCompanies, and First-Name and LastName from tblContacts. Your result should look like Figure 8-6.

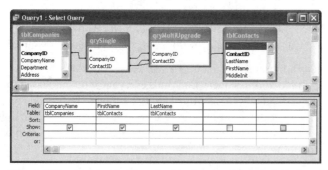

Figure 8-6. Solving the "contacts who own two products" problem the right way by building a query on queries.

Switch to Datasheet view, and, sure enough, the query gives you the right answer as shown in Figure 8-7.

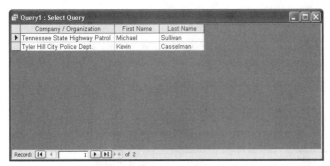

Figure 8-7. The two contacts who purchased a Single User edition and later upgraded.

This works because you're using the two queries to filter each other via the join. The qrySingle query finds contacts who own Single User. The qryMultiUpgrade query finds contacts who bought the Multi-User upgrade. The join lines between these two queries ask the final query to return rows only where CompanyID and ContactID in the first two queries match, so you won't see rows from qrySingle that don't have a matching combination of CompanyID and ContactID in qryMultiUpgrade, and vice-versa.

> For more examples of building queries on queries, see Article 1 on the companion CD, "Understanding SQL."

Using Outer Joins

Most queries that you create to request information from multiple tables will show results on the basis of matching data in one or more tables. For example, the Query window in Datasheet view shown in Figure 8-4 contains the names of facilities that have reservations in the tblReservations table—and it does not contain the names of facilities that don't have any reservations booked. As explained earlier, this type of query is called an equi-join query, meaning that you'll see rows only where there are *equal* values in *both* tables. But, what if you want to display facilities that do not have any reservations in the database? Or, how do you find employees who have no reservations? You can get the information you need by creating a query that uses an *outer join*. An outer join lets you see all rows from one of the tables even if there's no matching row in the related table. When no matching row exists, Access returns the special value Null in the columns from the related table.

Building a Simple Outer Join

To create an outer join, you must modify the join properties. Let's see if we can find any employees who don't have any reservations booked. Start a new query on tblEmployees in the HousingDataCopy database. Add tblReservations to the query. Double-click the join line between the two tables in the upper part of the Query window in Design view to see the Join Properties dialog box, shown in Figure 8-8 on the next page.

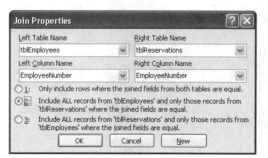

Figure 8-8. The Join Properties dialog box with the second option selected.

The default setting in the Join Properties dialog box is the first option—where the joined fields from both tables are equal. You can see that you have two additional options for this query: to see all employees and any reservations that match, or to see all reservations and any employees that match. If you entered your underlying data correctly, you shouldn't have reservations for employees who aren't defined in the database. If you asked Access to enforce referential integrity (discussed in Chapter 4, "Creating Your Database and Tables") when you defined the relationship between the tblEmployees table and the tblReservations table, Access won't let you create any reservations for nonexistent employees.

Select the second option in the dialog box. (When the link between two tables involves more than one field in each table, you can click the New button to define the additional links.) Click OK. You should now see an arrow on the join line pointing from the tblEmployees field list to the tblReservations field list, indicating that you have asked for an outer join with all records from tblEmployees regardless of match, as shown in Figure 8-9. For employees who have no reservations, Access returns the special Null value in all the columns for tblReservations. So, you can find the employees that aren't planning to stay in any facility by including the Is Null test for any of the columns from tblReservations. When you run this query, you should find exactly one employee who has no reservation, as shown in Figure 8-10. The finished query is saved as *qxmplEmployeesNoReservations* in the *HousingDataCopy.mdb* database.

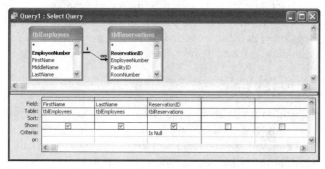

Figure 8-9. The design of a query to find employees who have no reservations.

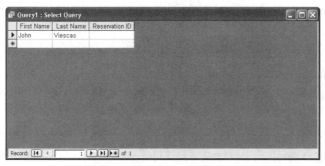

Figure 8-10. The recordset that shows employees who have no reservations.

Solving a Complex "Unmatched" Problem

As discussed earlier in this chapter, you know that to solve certain types of problems you must first build one query to define a subset of data from your tables and then use that query as input to another query to get the final answer. For example, suppose you want to find out which employees have no reservations in a certain time period. You might guess that an outer join from the tblEmployees table to the tblReservations table will do the trick. That would work fine if the tblReservations table contained reservations only for the time period in question. Remember, to find employees who haven't booked a room, you have to look for a special Null value in the columns from tblReservations. But to limit the data in tblReservations to a specific time period—let's say July and August 2003—you have to be able to test real values. In other words, you have a problem because a column from tblReservations can't be both Null and have a date value at the same time. (You can find an example of the wrong way to solve this problem saved as *qxmplEmpNotBookedJulAugWRONG* in the sample database.)

To solve this problem, you must first create a query that contains only the reservations for the months you want. As you'll see in a bit, you can then use that query with an outer join in another query to find out which employees haven't booked a room in July and August 2003. Figure 8-11 shows the query you need to start with, using tblReservations. This example includes the EmployeeNumber field as well as the FacilityID and RoomNumber fields, so you can use it to search for either employees or facilities or rooms that aren't booked in the target months.

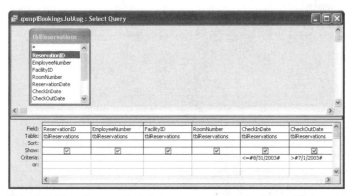

Figure 8-11. A query that lists reservation data for particular months.

Notice that if you truly want to see all reservations in these two months, you need to specify a criterion on both CheckInDate and CheckOutDate. Anyone who checked in on or before August 31, 2003—provided they didn't check out before July 1, 2003—is someone who stayed in a room between the dates of interest. You don't want anyone who checked out on July 1 (who stayed the night of June 30, but didn't stay over into July), which explains why the second criterion is >#7/1/2003# and not >=#7/1/2003#. This query is saved as *qxmplBookingsJulAug* in the *HousingDataCopy.mdb* database.

Finding Records Across Date Spans

You might be looking at the problem of finding any reservation that crosses into or is contained within a certain date span and scratching your head. You want any reservation that meets one of these criteria:

- The reservation begins before the start of the date span but extends into the date span.
- The reservation is contained wholly within the date span.
- The reservation begins before the end of the date span but extends beyond the date span.
- The reservation starts before the beginning of the date span and ends after the end of the date span.

You can see these four conditions in the following graphic.

You might be tempted to include four separate criteria in your query, but that's not necessary. As long as a reservation begins before the *end* of the span and ends after the *beginning* of the span, you've got them all! Try out the criteria shown in Figure 8-11 to see if that simple test doesn't find all of the previous cases.

After you save the first query, select it in the Database window and select Query from the New Object toolbar button's drop-down list to start a new query using the first one as input. In your new query, add tblEmployees to the Design grid by choosing Show Table from the Query menu and then selecting tblEmployees in the Show Table dialog box. Access should automatically link tblEmployees to the query on matching EmployeeNumber fields. Double-click the join line to open the Join Properties dialog box, and choose option 3 to see all rows from tblEmployees and any matching rows from the query. The join line's arrow should point from tblEmployees to the query, as shown in Figure 8-12. (When you first add tblEmployees to the query grid, it appears to the right of qxmplBookingsJulAug. I repositioned the field lists with respect to each other. You can grab either field list by its title bar with your mouse to move it.)

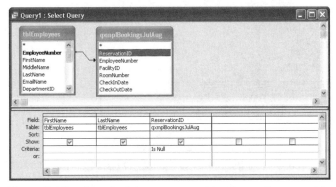

Figure 8-12. An outer join query searching for employees not booked in July and August 2003.

As you did in the previous outer join example, include some fields from the tblEmployees table and at least one field from the query that contains reservations only from July and August 2003. In the field from the query, add the special Is Null criterion. When you run this query (the results of which are shown in Figure 8-13), you should find four employees who haven't booked a room in July and August 2003—including the one employee that you found earlier who hasn't booked any room at all. This query is saved as *qxmplEmpNotBookedJulAug* in the *HousingDataCopy.mdb* database.

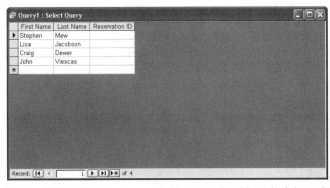

Figure 8-13. The employees without any bookings in July and August 2003.

291

Let's study another example. When you're looking at reservation requests, and each request indicates the particular type of room desired, it might be useful to know either which facilities have this type of room or which facilities do not. (Not all facilities have all the different types of rooms.) You can find a complete list of the room types in the tlkpRoomTypes table in the Housing Reservations application.

To find out which room types aren't in a facility, you might try an outer join from tlkpRoomTypes to tblFacilityRooms and look for Null again, but all you'd find is that all room types exist somewhere—you wouldn't know which room type was missing in what facility. In truth, you need to build a query first that limits room types to one facility. Your query should look something like Figure 8-14.

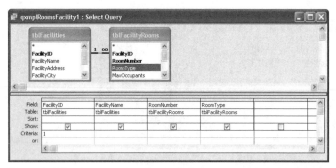

Figure 8-14. A query that lists all the rooms and their room types in Facility number 1.

Now you can build your outer join query to find out which room types aren't in the first housing facility. Start a query on tlkpRoomTypes and add the query *qxmplRoomsFacility1*. Double-click the join line and ask for all rows from tlkpRoomTypes and any matching rows from the query. Add the RoomType field from tlkpRoomTypes and the FacilityID field from the query to the grid. Under FacilityID, place a criterion of Is Null. Your query should look like Figure 8-15.

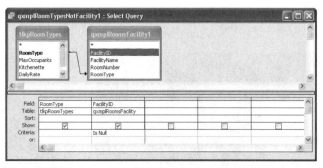

Figure 8-15. A query to find out which room types are not in Facility number 1.

If you run this query, you'll find that Facility number 1 has no one-bedroom suites with king bed and kitchenette, no one-bedroom suites with two queen beds, and no simple rooms with only a king bed. In the sample database, you'll find sample queries that return the room types for the other three facilities, so you can build queries like the one in Figure 8-15 to find out what room types are missing in those facilities.

Using a Query Wizard

Every time you have opened the New Query dialog box, you have seen the tantalizing query wizard entries. You can use query wizards to help you build certain types of "tricky" queries such as crosstab queries (discussed later in this chapter) and queries to find duplicate or unmatched rows. For example, you could have used a query wizard to build the query shown in Figure 8-9 to locate employees who have no room reservations. Let's use a query wizard to build a query to perform a similar search in the *ContactsDataCopy.mdb* sample file to find contacts who don't own any products.

To try this, click the Queries button in the Database window, and then click the New button. This time, select Find Unmatched Query Wizard in the New Query dialog box, as shown in Figure 8-16.

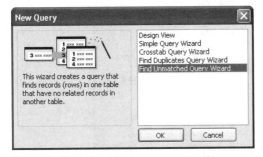

Figure 8-16. Selecting a query wizard.

The wizard opens a window with a list of tables from which you can select the initial records, as shown in Figure 8-17 on the next page. If you want to use an existing query instead of a table, select the Queries option. If you want to look at all queries and tables, select the Both option. In this case, you're looking for contacts who haven't purchased any products, so select the tblContacts table and then click the Next button.

In the next window, select the table that contains the related information you expect to be unmatched. You're looking for contacts who have purchased no products, so select the tblContactProducts table and then click the Next button to go to the next window, shown in Figure 8-18 on the next page.

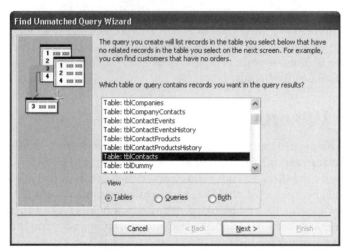

Figure 8-17. The first window of the Find Unmatched Query Wizard.

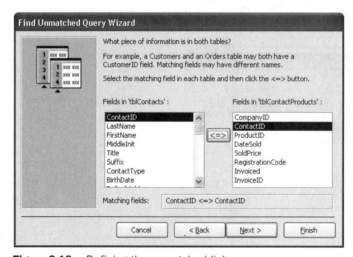

Figure 8-18. Defining the unmatched link.

Next, the wizard needs to know the linking fields between the two tables. Because no direct relationship is defined between tblContacts and tblContactProducts, the wizard won't automatically pick the matching fields for you. You should click the ContactID field in tblContacts and the ContactID field in tblContactProducts to highlight those two fields. Click the <=> button between the field lists to add those fields to the Matching fields box. Click Next to go to the window shown in Figure 8-19.

Note The Find Unmatched Query Wizard can only work with tables that have no more than one field that links the two tables. If you need to "find unmatched" records between two tables that require a join on more than one field, you'll have to build the query yourself.

Building Complex Queries

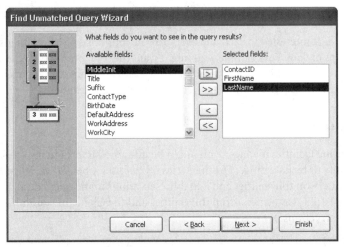

Figure 8-19. The window in which you select the fields to be displayed in a query.

This works just like the Table Wizard you learned about in Chapter 4, "Creating Your Database and Tables." Choose the fields you want to display (see Figure 8-19) by selecting a field in the left list and then clicking the > button to move the field to the right list. The query will display the fields in the order you select them. If you choose a field in error, highlight it in the right list and click the < button to move it back. You can click the >> button to select all fields or the << button to remove all fields. When you're finished selecting fields, click Next. In the final window, you can specify a different name for your query. (The wizard generates a long and ugly name.) You can choose an option to either view the results or modify the design. So that you can see the design first, select Modify the design and click Finish to open the Query window in Design view. Figure 8-20 shows the finished query to find contacts who have purchased no products.

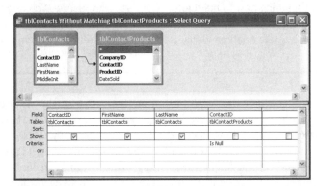

Figure 8-20. A query to find contacts who have purchased no products.

If you run this query, you'll find one contact who hasn't bought anything. Perhaps you should schedule a call to him to find out why!

Summarizing Information with Totals Queries

Sometimes you aren't interested in each and every row in your table—you'd rather see calculations across groups of data. For example, you might want the total product purchase amount for all companies in a particular state. Or you might want to know the average of all sales for each month in the last year. To get these answers, you need a *totals query*.

Totals Within Groups

If you're the housing facilities manager, you might be interested in producing sales and usage numbers by facility or by date range. For this series of exercises, open *HousingDataCopy.mdb* and start a new query on tblFacilities and add tblReservations to the query design. Include in the field grid the FacilityName field from tblFacilities and the CheckInDate and TotalCharge fields from tblReservations.

Inside Out

When totals queries are useful

I might occasionally build totals queries to display high-level summaries in a report. More often, I create a regular query that fetches all the detail I need and then use the powerful summarization facilities in reports to calculate totals. You'll learn more about summarizing data in a report in Chapter 16, "Advanced Report Design."

A totals query groups the fields you specify, and every output field must either be one of the grouping fields or the result of a calculation using one of the available aggregate functions. (See Table 8-1.) Because all fields are calculated, you cannot update any fields returned by a totals query. So, you're not likely to find totals queries useful in forms.

This does not mean that learning how to build totals queries is not useful. You need to understand the concepts of grouping and totaling to build reports. You will also find that constructing and opening a totals query in Visual Basic code is useful to perform complex validations.

Total Button

To turn this into a totals query, click the Totals button on the toolbar or choose Totals from the View menu to open the Total row in the Design grid, as shown in Figure 8-21. When you first click the Totals button on the toolbar, Access displays Group By in the Total row for any fields you already have in the Design grid. At this point the records in each field are grouped but not totaled. If you were to run the query now, you'd get one row in the recordset for each set of unique values—but no totals. You must replace Group By with an *aggregate function* in the Total row.

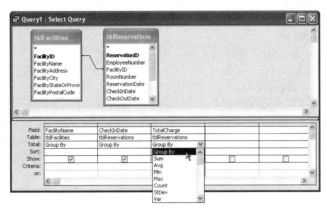

Figure 8-21. The Total row in the Design grid.

Access provides nine aggregate functions for your use. You can choose the one you want by typing its name in the Total row in the Design grid or by selecting it from the drop-down list. You can learn about the available functions in Table 8-1.

Table 8-1. Aggregate Functions

Function	Description
Sum	Calculates the sum of all the values for this field in each group. You can specify this function only with number or currency fields.
Avg	Calculates the arithmetic average of all the values for this field in each group. You can specify this function only with number or currency fields. Access does not include any Null values in the calculation.
Min	Returns the lowest value found in this field within each group. For numbers, Min returns the smallest value. For text, Min returns the lowest value in collating sequence ("dictionary"* order), without regard to case. Access ignores Null values.
Max	Returns the highest value found in this field within each group. For numbers, Max returns the largest value. For text, Max returns the highest value in collating sequence ("dictionary"* order), without regard to case. Access ignores Null values.
Count	Returns the count of the rows in which the specified field is not a Null value. You can also enter the special expression COUNT(*) in the Field row to count all rows in each group, regardless of the presence of Null values.
StDev	Calculates the statistical standard deviation of all the values for this field in each group. You can specify this function only with number or currency fields. If the group does not contain at least two rows, Access returns a Null value.

Table 8-1. Aggregate Functions

Function	Description
Var	Calculates the statistical variance of all the values for this field in each group. You can specify this function only with number or currency fields. If the group does not contain at least two rows, Access returns a Null value.
First	Returns the value for the field from the first row encountered in the group. Note that the first row might not be the one with the lowest value. It also might not be the row you think is "first" within the group. Because First depends on the actual physical sequence of stored data, it essentially returns an unpredictable value from within the group.
Last	Returns the value for the field from the last row encountered in the group. Note that the last row might not be the one with the highest value. It also might not be the row you think is "last" within the group. Because Last depends on the actual physical sequence of stored data, it essentially returns an unpredictable value from within the group.

* You can change the sort order for new databases you create by choosing Options from the Tools menu and specifying **New database sort order** on the General tab. The default value is General, which sorts your data according to the language specified for your operating system.

Let's experiment with the query you started earlier in this section to understand some of the available functions. First, you probably don't want to see information grouped by individual date. Data summarized over each month would be more informative, so create an expression to replace the CheckInDate field as follows:

```
CheckInMonth: Format([CheckInDate], "yyyy mm")
```

The Format function works similarly to the table field Format property you learned about in Chapter 4, "Creating Your Database and Tables." The first parameter is the name of the field or the expression that you want to format, and the second parameter specifies how you want the data formatted. In this case, we're asking Format to return the four-digit year and two-digit month number.

> For more information about Format settings, see "Setting Control Properties," page 451.

Change the Total row under TotalCharge to Sum. Add the TotalCharge field from tblReservations three more times, and choose Avg, Min, and Max, respectively, under each. Finally, add the ReservationID field from tblReservations and choose Count in the Total row under that field. Your query design should now look like Figure 8-22.

Switch to Datasheet view to see the result as shown in Figure 8-23. The sample data file has 180 available rooms in four different facilities. From the results of this query, you could conclude that this company has far more housing than it needs! Perhaps the most interesting row is the eighth one (where the selection arrow appears in Figure 8-23). The five reservations for Housing B in July 2003 show how the various functions might help you analyze the data further.

Chapter 8

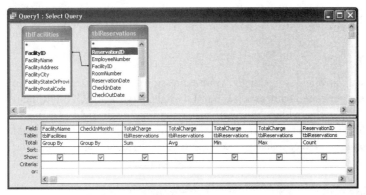

Figure 8-22. A query that explores many of the aggregate functions.

Troubleshooting

I didn't specify sorting criteria, so why is my data sorted?

A totals query has to sort your data to be able to group it, so it returns the groups sorted left to right based on the sequence of your Group By fields. If you need to sort the grouping columns in some other way, change the sequence of the Group By fields. Note that you can additionally sort any of the totals fields.

Facility	CheckInMonth	SumOfTotalCha	AvgOfTotalChar	MinOfTotalChar	MaxOfTotalChar	CountOfReserva
Main Campus Housing A	2003 05	$960.00	$480.00	$300.00	$660.00	2
Main Campus Housing A	2003 06	$570.00	$570.00	$570.00	$570.00	1
Main Campus Housing A	2003 07	$2,150.00	$716.67	$450.00	$1,040.00	3
Main Campus Housing A	2003 08	$335.00	$335.00	$335.00	$335.00	1
Main Campus Housing A	2003 11	$640.00	$640.00	$640.00	$640.00	1
Main Campus Housing B	2003 05	$890.00	$445.00	$140.00	$750.00	2
Main Campus Housing B	2003 06	$1,835.00	$611.67	$470.00	$805.00	3
Main Campus Housing B	2003 07	$3,660.00	$732.00	$325.00	$1,050.00	5
Main Campus Housing B	2003 08	$680.00	$680.00	$680.00	$680.00	1
Main Campus Housing B	2003 09	$2,055.00	$1,027.50	$845.00	$1,210.00	2
Main Campus Housing B	2003 10	$690.00	$690.00	$690.00	$690.00	1
North Satellite Housing D	2003 04	$2,270.00	$756.67	$290.00	$1,125.00	3
North Satellite Housing D	2003 05	$180.00	$180.00	$180.00	$180.00	1
North Satellite Housing D	2003 06	$625.00	$625.00	$625.00	$625.00	1
North Satellite Housing D	2003 08	$2,110.00	$703.33	$380.00	$1,340.00	3
North Satellite Housing D	2003 09	$1,475.00	$295.00	$120.00	$420.00	5
North Satellite Housing D	2003 10	$1,065.00	$532.50	$520.00	$545.00	2
South Campus Housing C	2003 05	$1,600.00	$800.00	$420.00	$1,180.00	2
South Campus Housing C	2003 06	$415.00	$415.00	$415.00	$415.00	1
South Campus Housing C	2003 07	$690.00	$345.00	$300.00	$390.00	2
South Campus Housing C	2003 09	$450.00	$450.00	$450.00	$450.00	1

Record: 8 of 21

Figure 8-23. The total revenue, average revenue, smallest revenue per reservation, largest revenue per reservation, and count of reservations by facility and month.

In the drop-down list for the Total row in the Design grid, you'll also find an Expression setting. Select this when you want to create an expression in the Total row that uses one or more of the aggregate functions listed earlier. For example, you might want to calculate a value that reflects the range of reservation charges in the group, as in the following:

```
Max([TotalCharge]) - Min([TotalCharge])
```

As you can with any field, you can give your expression a custom name. Notice in Figure 8-23 that Access has generated names such as SumOfTotalCharge or AvgOfTotalCharge. You can fix these by clicking in the field in the Design grid and prefixing the field or expression with your own name followed by a colon. In Figure 8-24, I removed the separate Min and Max fields, added the expression to calculate the range between the smallest and largest charge, and inserted custom field names. You can see the result in Datasheet view in Figure 8-25.

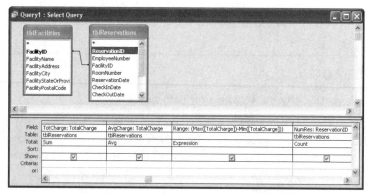

Figure 8-24. Adding an expression and defining custom field names in a totals query.

Facility	CheckInMonth	TotCharge	AvgCharge	Range	NumRes
Main Campus Housing A	2003 05	$960.00	$480.00	$360.00	2
Main Campus Housing A	2003 06	$570.00	$570.00	$0.00	1
Main Campus Housing A	2003 07	$2,150.00	$716.67	$590.00	3
Main Campus Housing A	2003 08	$335.00	$335.00	$0.00	1
Main Campus Housing A	2003 11	$640.00	$640.00	$0.00	1
Main Campus Housing B	2003 05	$890.00	$445.00	$610.00	2
Main Campus Housing B	2003 06	$1,835.00	$611.67	$335.00	3
Main Campus Housing B	2003 07	$3,660.00	$732.00	$725.00	5
Main Campus Housing B	2003 08	$680.00	$680.00	$0.00	1
Main Campus Housing B	2003 09	$2,055.00	$1,027.50	$365.00	2
Main Campus Housing B	2003 10	$690.00	$690.00	$0.00	1
North Satellite Housing D	2003 04	$2,270.00	$756.67	$835.00	3
North Satellite Housing D	2003 05	$180.00	$180.00	$0.00	1
North Satellite Housing D	2003 06	$625.00	$625.00	$0.00	1
North Satellite Housing D	2003 08	$2,110.00	$703.33	$960.00	3
North Satellite Housing D	2003 09	$1,475.00	$295.00	$300.00	5
North Satellite Housing D	2003 10	$1,065.00	$532.50	$25.00	2
South Campus Housing C	2003 05	$1,600.00	$800.00	$760.00	2
South Campus Housing C	2003 06	$415.00	$415.00	$0.00	1
South Campus Housing C	2003 07	$690.00	$345.00	$90.00	2
South Campus Housing C	2003 09	$450.00	$450.00	$0.00	1

Figure 8-25. The query shown in Figure 8-24 in Datasheet view.

Selecting Records to Form Groups

You might filter out some records before your totals query gathers the records into groups. To filter out certain records from the tables in your query, you can add to the Design grid the field or fields you want to filter. Then create the filter by selecting the Where setting in the Total row (which will clear the field's Show check box), and entering criteria that tell Access which records to exclude.

For example, the manager of the Sales department might be interested in the statistics you've produced thus far in the query in Figure 8-24, but only for the employees in the Sales department. To find this information, you need to add tblEmployees and tblDepartments to your query (and remove the extra join line between the EmployeeNumber field in tblEmployees and the ManagerNumber field in tblDepartments). Add the Department field from tblDepartments to your design, change the Total line to Where, and add the criterion **"Sales"** on the Criteria line under this field. Your query should now look like Figure 8-26.

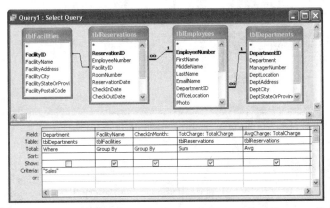

Figure 8-26. Using the Department field to select the rows that will be included in groups.

Now, when you run the query, you get totals only for the employees in the Sales department. The result is shown in Figure 8-27.

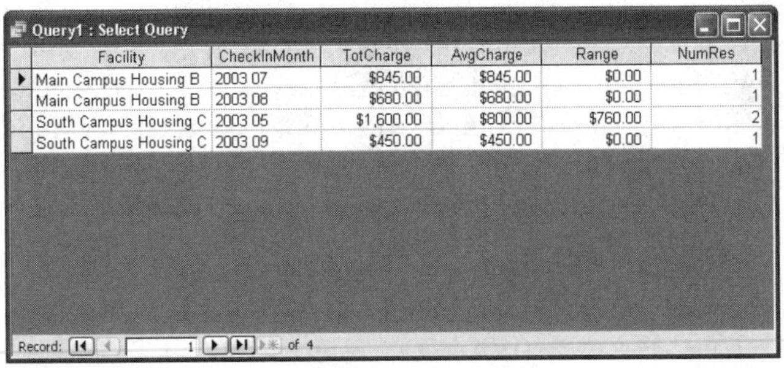

Figure 8-27. The recordset of the query shown in Figure 8-26.

Selecting Specific Groups

You can also filter groups of totals after the query has calculated the groups. To do this, enter criteria for any field that has a Group By setting, one of the aggregate functions, or an expression using the aggregate functions in its Total row. For example, you might want to know which facilities and months have more than $1,000 in total charges. To find that out, you would use the settings shown in Figure 8-26 and enter a Criteria setting of >1000 for the TotalCharge field, as shown in Figure 8-28. This query should return one row in the sample database. You can find this query saved as *qxmplSalesHousingGT1000* in the sample database.

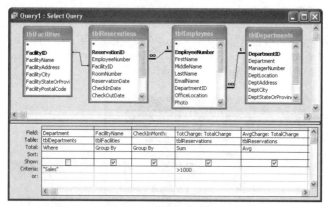

Figure 8-28.   Entering a Criteria setting for the TotCharge field.

Building Crosstab Queries

Access supports a special type of total query called a *crosstab query* that allows you to see calculated values in a spreadsheetlike format. For example, you can use this type of query to see total revenue by month for each facility in the Housing Reservations application.

Creating a Simple Crosstab Query

Open the *HousingDataCopy.mdb* database. To see revenue by facility, you'll need tblFacilities and tblReservations. Start a new query on tblFacilities and add tblReservations. Add the FacilityName field from tblFacilities to the Design grid. Revenue gets collected when the employee checks out, and you want to summarize by month. So, enter **RevMonth: Format(CheckOutDate, "yyyy mmm")** in the next empty field in the Design grid. This expression returns the year as four digits and the month as a three-character abbreviation. Finally, add the TotalCharge field from tblReservations.

Choose the Crosstab Query command from the Query menu. Access changes your query to a totals query and adds a Crosstab row to the Design grid, as shown in Figure 8-29. Each field in a crosstab query can have one of four crosstab settings: Row Heading, Column Heading, Value (displayed in the crosstab grid), or Not Shown.

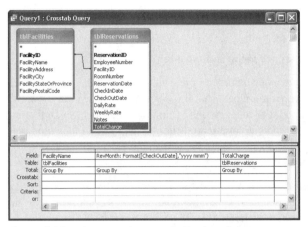

Figure 8-29. A crosstab query in Design view.

You must have at least one row heading field in a crosstab query, and you can specify more than one field as a row heading. Each row heading field must be a grouped value or expression, and the expression can include one or more of the aggregate functions—Count, Min, Max, Sum, and so on. The row heading fields form the columns on the left side of the crosstab. Think of the grouped values of the row heading fields as forming the horizontal "labels" of the rows. In this example, we'll be grouping by the FacilityName field. We'll later modify the basic query we're building here to add a second row heading using Sum—the total value of each facility's reservations.

You must also have one (and only one) field defined as a column heading, and this must also be a grouped or totaled value. These values form the headings of the columns across the crosstab datasheet. Think of a regular totals query where one of the columns "pivots," and the values in the rows become labels for additional columns in the output. These columns appear sorted in value sequence immediately following the columns you define as row headings. Because the values in the data you're selecting determine the column names when you run the query, you cannot always predict in advance the field names that the query will output.

Finally, you need one (and only one) field designated as the value. This field must be a totaled value or an expression that contains one of the aggregate functions. The value field appears in the cells that are the intersections of each of the row heading values and each of the column heading values. In the following example, the facility names will appear down the left side, the year and month values will appear as column headings across the top, and the sum of the reservation charge for each group for each month will appear in the intersection.

As in other types of totals queries, you can include other fields to filter values to obtain the result you want. For these fields, you should select the Where setting in the Total row and the Not Shown setting in the Crosstab row and then enter your criteria. You can also enter criteria for any column headings, and you can sort on any of the fields.

Troubleshooting

How do I display more than one value in a crosstab?

The fact that a crosstab query can display only one value field in the intersection of row and column headings is a severe limitation. What if you want to display both the total reservation value as well as the count of reservations? One way is to build two separate crosstab queries—one that provides the sum of the total charge as the value field, and one that provides the count of reservations as the value field—and then join the two queries on the row heading columns. That's an inelegant way to do it.

Another solution is to create a simple query that includes all the detail you need and then switch to PivotTable view to build the data display you need. You'll learn about PivotTable and PivotChart views later in this chapter.

To finish the settings for the crosstab query that you started to build in Figure 8-29, in the Crosstab row select Row Heading from the drop-down list under the FacilityName field, select Column Heading under the RevMonth expression, and select Value under the TotalCharge field. Also change the Group By setting under the TotalCharge field to Sum.

Switch to Datasheet view to see the result of your query design, as shown in Figure 8-30. (The remaining column that you can't see in the figure is 2003 Sep.)

Facility	2003 Apr	2003 Aug	2003 Jul	2003 Jun	2003 May	2003 Nov	2003 Oct	2003 S
Main Campus Housing A		$995.00	$2,060.00		$960.00	$640.00		
Main Campus Housing B		$325.00	$4,700.00	$470.00	$890.00		$690.00	$2,735.
North Satellite Housing D	$1,415.00	$2,110.00	$625.00		$1,035.00		$1,260.00	$1,280.
South Campus Housing C		$300.00	$390.00	$1,595.00	$420.00			$450.

Figure 8-30. The recordset of the crosstab query you're building.

Notice that although you didn't specify a sort sequence on the dates, Access sorted the dates left to right in ascending collating order anyway. Notice also that the month names appear in alphabetical order, not in the desired chronological order.

Access provides a solution for this: You can specifically define the order of column headings for any crosstab query by using the query's property sheet. Return to Design view and click in the upper part of the Query window, and then click the Properties button on the toolbar to see the property sheet, as shown in Figure 8-31.

To control the order of columns displayed, enter the headings exactly as they are formatted and in the order you want them in the Column Headings property, separated by commas. In this case, you are entering text values, so you must also enclose each value in double quotes. Be sure to include all the column headings that match the result of the query. (Notice that I specified all the months in 2003 even though the sample data covers only April to October.)

Chapter 8

If you omit (or misspell) a column heading, Access won't show that column at all. When you run the query with formatted column headings, you see the recordset shown in Figure 8-32.

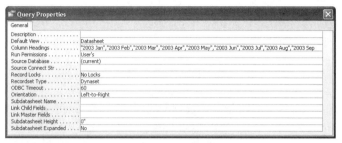

Figure 8-31. Entries in the property sheet that fix the order of column headings for the query shown in Figure 8-30.

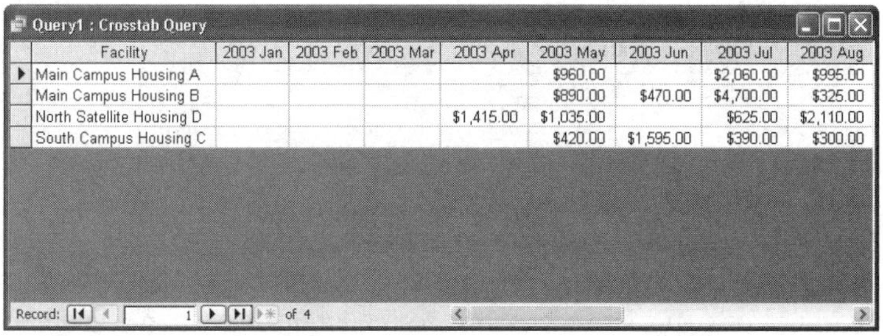

Facility	2003 Jan	2003 Feb	2003 Mar	2003 Apr	2003 May	2003 Jun	2003 Jul	2003 Aug
Main Campus Housing A					$960.00		$2,060.00	$995.00
Main Campus Housing B					$890.00	$470.00	$4,700.00	$325.00
North Satellite Housing D				$1,415.00	$1,035.00		$625.00	$2,110.00
South Campus Housing C					$420.00	$1,595.00	$390.00	$300.00

Figure 8-32. A crosstab query recordset with custom headings and custom column order, as defined in Figure 8-31.

> **Caution** Specifying correct column headings can be difficult. You must run your query first to determine what headings you'll see. You might be able to define criteria in your query that guarantee the column headings—for example, you could filter the query to return rows only from a specific year. If you misspell a column heading in the Query Properties window, the real danger is that Access gives you no warning that your query returns columns that aren't in your column heading specification. You'll see blanks in your misspelled columns, and you could mistakenly assume that no data exists for those columns.

Let's add a grand total for each row (the total per facility regardless of month) and do something about the blank cells. Wouldn't it be nice to see a zero in months when there were no reservations?

Switch back to Design view and add another TotalCharge field to the field grid. Give it a name of GrandTotal, choose Sum in the Total row, and Row Heading in the Crosstab row.

Remember the little trick we used earlier to use a plus sign (+) arithmetic operator in a concatenation to remove extra blanks? In this case, we want to do exactly the reverse—wherever there are no values, the Sum returns a Null that we want to convert to a zero. Also, remember that when you concatenate two values with the ampersand (&) operator, that operator ignores Nulls. You can force a Null to a zero by concatenating a leading zero character. If the Sum is not Null, adding a zero in front of the value won't hurt it at all.

In the TotalCharge field you chose as the value field, change Sum to Expression and change the Field line to use this expression:

```
0 & Sum(TotalCharge)
```

Any concatenation returns a string value, so you'll need to convert the value back to a currency number for display. There's a handy "convert to currency" function (CCur) that will perform this conversion for you. Further modify the expression to read:

```
CCur(0 & Sum(TotalCharge))
```

Switch back to Datasheet view, and your query result should now look like Figure 8-33.

Facility	GrandTotal	2003 Jan	2003 Feb	2003 Mar	2003 Apr	2003 May	2003 Jun	2003 Jul
Main Campus Housing A	$4,655.00	$0.00	$0.00	$0.00	$0.00	$960.00	$0.00	$2,060.00
Main Campus Housing B	$9,810.00	$0.00	$0.00	$0.00	$0.00	$890.00	$470.00	$4,700.00
North Satellite Housing D	$7,725.00	$0.00	$0.00	$0.00	$1,415.00	$1,035.00	$0.00	$625.00
South Campus Housing C	$3,155.00	$0.00	$0.00	$0.00	$0.00	$420.00	$1,595.00	$390.00

Figure 8-33. Your crosstab query now shows a grand total on each row as an additional row heading, and all empty cells are filled with zero values.

As with most tasks in Access, there's usually more than one way to solve a problem. You can also generate the missing zero values by using the Null-to-zero function (NZ) in your expression instead of using concatenation. Your expression could look like:

```
CCur(NZ(Sum(TotalCharge),0))
```

If you're not quite getting the result you expect, you can check what you have built against the *qxmplRevenueByFacilityByMonthXtab* sample query you'll find in the database.

Partitioning Data in a Crosstab Query

The total sales by month is interesting, but what can you do if you want to break the data down further? For example, you might want to know the value of sales across a range of room prices. This sort of information might be invaluable to the operator of a commercial hotel. What amount of revenue is the hotel receiving from various room prices?

You'll learn later in Chapter 16, "Advanced Report Design," that you can ask the report writer to group data by data ranges. Well, you can also do this in a totals or crosstab query. Let's continue to work in the *HousingDataCopy.mdb* database to see how this works.

Start a new query on tblFacilities and add tblReservations. Add the FacilityName field from tblFacilities, and create a CkOutMonth field by using the Format function to return a four-digit year and month abbreviation as you did earlier. Add the TotalCharge field from tblReservations to the query grid twice. Choose Crosstab Query from the Query menu to convert your query to a crosstab query.

On the Crosstab line, select Row Heading under the FacilityName field, your CkOutMonth expression, and the first TotalCharge field. Change the name of this first TotalCharge field to GrandTotal, and select Sum in the Group By row. For the second TotalCharge field, select Sum in the Group By row and Value in the Crosstab row.

You still don't have a Column Heading field or expression defined, but here's where the fun begins. In this query, your sales manager has asked you for a breakdown of amounts spent per month based on ranges of the DailyRate field. In this database, the lowest daily charge is $40 a day, and the highest is $100 a day. The manager has asked you to display ranges from $40 to $119 in increments of $20 ($40 to $59, $60 to $79, and so on). It turns out there's a handy function called Partition that will split out numbers like this for you. The syntax of the function is as follows:

```
Partition(<number>, <start>, <stop>, <interval>)
```

The *number* argument is the name of a numeric field or expression you want to split up into ranges. *Start* specifies the lowest value you want, *stop* specifies the highest value you want, and *interval* specifies the size of the ranges. The function evaluates each number it sees and returns a string containing the name of the range for that number. You can group on these named ranges to partition your data into groups for this crosstab query. So, the expression you need is as follows:

```
Partition(DailyRate, 40, 119, 20)
```

The function will return values "40: 59", "60: 79", "80: 99", and "100: 119". Add that expression to your query grid and select Column Heading in the crosstab row. Your query should now look like Figure 8-34.

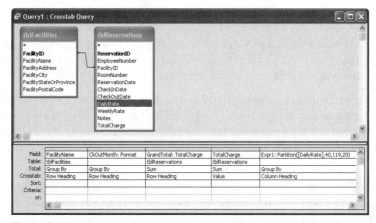

Figure 8-34. Designing a crosstab query using partitioned values.

307

Switch to Datasheet view to see the result that should satisfy your sales manager's request as shown in Figure 8-35. Note that I didn't use the trick discussed earlier to fill blank cells with zeros. In this case, the blank cells seem to visually point out the rate ranges that had no sales. You can find this query saved as *qxmplRevenueByFacilityByRateRangeXtab* in the sample database.

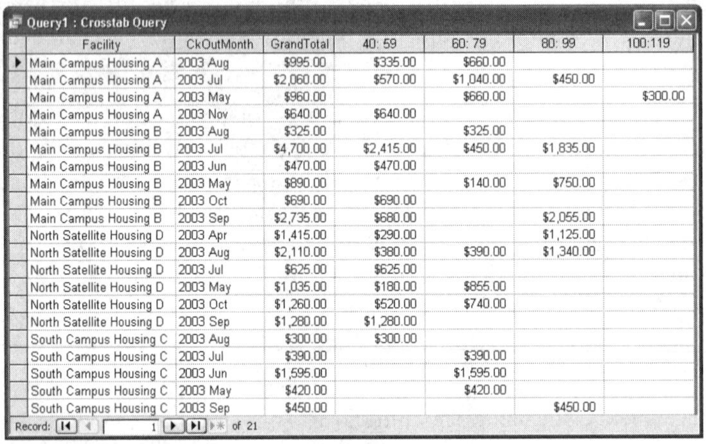

Facility	CkOutMonth	GrandTotal	40: 59	60: 79	80: 99	100:119
Main Campus Housing A	2003 Aug	$995.00	$335.00	$660.00		
Main Campus Housing A	2003 Jul	$2,060.00	$570.00	$1,040.00	$450.00	
Main Campus Housing A	2003 May	$960.00		$660.00		$300.00
Main Campus Housing A	2003 Nov	$640.00	$640.00			
Main Campus Housing B	2003 Aug	$325.00		$325.00		
Main Campus Housing B	2003 Jul	$4,700.00	$2,415.00	$450.00	$1,835.00	
Main Campus Housing B	2003 Jun	$470.00	$470.00			
Main Campus Housing B	2003 May	$890.00		$140.00	$750.00	
Main Campus Housing B	2003 Oct	$690.00	$690.00			
Main Campus Housing B	2003 Sep	$2,735.00	$680.00		$2,055.00	
North Satellite Housing D	2003 Apr	$1,415.00	$290.00		$1,125.00	
North Satellite Housing D	2003 Aug	$2,110.00	$380.00	$390.00	$1,340.00	
North Satellite Housing D	2003 Jul	$625.00	$625.00			
North Satellite Housing D	2003 May	$1,035.00	$180.00	$855.00		
North Satellite Housing D	2003 Oct	$1,260.00	$520.00	$740.00		
North Satellite Housing D	2003 Sep	$1,280.00	$1,280.00			
South Campus Housing C	2003 Aug	$300.00	$300.00			
South Campus Housing C	2003 Jul	$390.00		$390.00		
South Campus Housing C	2003 Jun	$1,595.00		$1,595.00		
South Campus Housing C	2003 May	$420.00		$420.00		
South Campus Housing C	2003 Sep	$450.00			$450.00	

Figure 8-35. The result of partitioning sales totals on ranges of room rates.

Using Query Parameters

So far you've been entering selection criteria directly in the Design grid of the Query window in Design view. However, you don't have to decide at the time you design the query exactly what value you want Access to search for. Instead, you can include a parameter in the query, and Access will prompt you for the criteria each time the query runs.

To include a parameter, you enter a name or a phrase enclosed in brackets ([ ]) in the Criteria row instead of entering a value. What you enclose in brackets becomes the name by which Access knows your parameter. Access displays this name in a dialog box when you run the query, so you should enter a phrase that accurately describes what you want. You can enter several parameters in a single query, so each parameter name must be unique as well as informative. If you want a parameter value to also display as output in the query, you can enter the parameter name in the field row of an empty column.

Let's say you're the housing manager, and you want to find out who might be staying in any facility over the next several days or weeks. You don't want to have to build or modify a query each time you want to search the database for upcoming reservations. So, you ask your database developer to provide you with a way to dynamically enter the beginning and ending dates of interest.

Let's build a query to help out the housing manager. Start a new query on tblFacilities in the *HousingDataCopy.mdb* database. Add tblReservations and tblEmployees. From tblReservations, include the ReservationID, RoomNumber, CheckInDate, CheckOutDate, and TotalCharge fields. Insert the FacilityName field from tblFacilities between ReservationID and RoomNumber. Add an expression to display the employee name in a field inserted between ReservationID and FacilityName. Your expression might look like this:

```
EmpName: tblEmployees.LastName & ", " & tblEmployees.FirstName
```

Now comes the tricky part. You want the query to ask the housing manager for the range of dates of interest. Your query needs to find the reservation rows that show who is in which rooms between a pair of dates. If you remember from the previous example in this chapter where we were looking for employees occupying rooms in July or August, you want any rows where the check-in date is less than or equal to the end date of interest, and the check-out date is greater than the start date of interest. (If they check out on the beginning date of the range, they're not staying in the room that night.) So, you can create two parameters on the Criteria line to accomplish this. Under CheckInDate, enter: <=[**Enter End Date:**], and under CheckOutDate, enter: >[**Enter Start Date:**]. Your query should look like Figure 8-36.

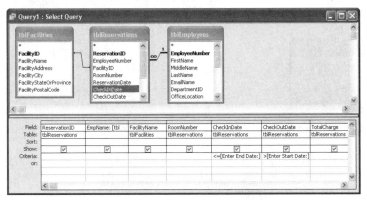

Figure 8-36. Setting query parameters to accept criteria for a range of reservation dates.

For each parameter in a query, you should tell Access what data type to expect. Access uses this information to validate the value entered. For example, if you define a parameter as a number, Access won't accept alphabetic characters in the parameter value. Likewise, if you define a parameter as a Date/Time data type, Access won't accept anything but a valid date or time value in the parameter prompt. (See Figure 8-38.) By default, Access assigns the text data type to query parameters. In general, you should always define the data type of your parameters, so choose the Parameters command from the Query menu. Access then displays the Query Parameters dialog box, as shown in Figure 8-37.

Figure 8-37. The Query Parameters dialog box.

309

In the Parameter column, enter each parameter name exactly as you entered it in the Design grid. If your parameter name includes no spaces or special characters, you can omit the brackets. (In this case, your parameters include both spaces and the colon character—either of which would require the brackets.) In the Data Type column, select the appropriate data type from the drop-down list. Click the OK button when you finish defining all your parameters.

When you run the query, Access prompts you for an appropriate value for each parameter, one at a time, with a dialog box like the one shown in Figure 8-38. Because Access displays the "name" of the parameter that you provided in the Design grid, you can see why naming the parameter with a useful phrase can help you enter the correct value later. If you enter a value that does not match the data type you specified, Access displays an error message and gives you a chance to try again. You can also click the Cancel button to abort running the query. If you click OK without typing a value, Access returns a Null value for the parameter to the query.

Figure 8-38. The Enter Parameter Value dialog box.

Notice that Access accepts any value that it can recognize as a date/time. If you respond to the query parameter prompts with May 1, 2003, for the Start Date and May 12, 2003, for the End Date, you'll see a datasheet like Figure 8-39.

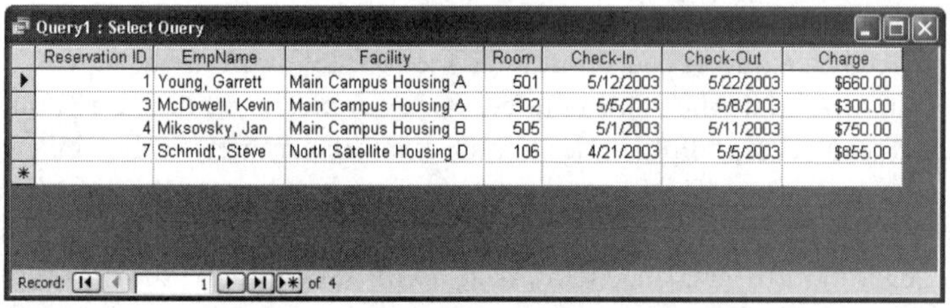

Reservation ID	EmpName	Facility	Room	Check-In	Check-Out	Charge
1	Young, Garrett	Main Campus Housing A	501	5/12/2003	5/22/2003	$660.00
3	McDowell, Kevin	Main Campus Housing A	302	5/5/2003	5/8/2003	$300.00
4	Miksovsky, Jan	Main Campus Housing B	505	5/1/2003	5/11/2003	$750.00
7	Schmidt, Steve	North Satellite Housing D	106	4/21/2003	5/5/2003	$855.00

Figure 8-39. The recordset of the query shown in Figure 8-36 when you reply with May 1, 2003, and May 12, 2003, to the parameter prompts.

You can find this query saved in the sample database as *qxmplReservationLookupParameter*.

Customizing Query Properties

Microsoft Access provides a number of properties associated with queries that you can use to control how a query runs. To open the property sheet for queries, click in the upper part of a Query window in Design view outside of the field lists and then click the Properties button. Figure 8-40 shows the property sheet Access provides for select queries.

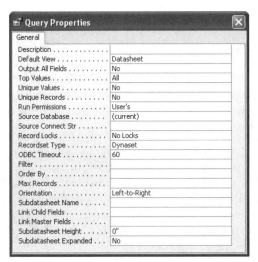

Figure 8-40. The property sheet for select queries.

Use the Description property to document what the query does. This description appears next to the query name when you view query objects in Details view in the Database window. You can also select the query in the Database window and open the Properties window to enter this property without having to open the query in Design view.

The Default View property determines how the query opens when you choose it in the Database window and click Open. Datasheet view is the default, but you might want to change this setting to PivotTable or PivotChart if you have designed either of these views for the query. See "Creating PivotTables and PivotCharts from Queries," page 324, for details.

Controlling Query Output

You normally select only specific fields that you want returned in the recordset when you run a select query. However, if you're designing the query to be used in a form and you want all fields from all tables used in the query available to the form, set the Output All Fields property to Yes. It's a good idea to keep the default setting of No and change this option only for specific queries.

Inside Out

Don't change the default setting for the Output All Fields property

You can change the default Output All Fields property for all queries on the Tables/Queries tab of the Options dialog box, but I strongly recommend that you do not do this. Queries execute most efficiently when they return only the fields that you need. Also, when your query includes more than one table and a field exists more than once in different tables, an expression you use to reference the field will fail unless you qualify the field name with the table name. You might include the field only once on the Design grid, but Output All Fields causes the query to include all copies of the field.

311

You can use the Top Values property to tell Access that you want to see the first *n* rows or the first *x*% of rows. If you enter an integer value, Access displays the number of rows specified. If you enter a decimal value between 0 and 1 or an integer less than 100 followed by a percent sign (%), Access displays that percentage of rows. For example, you might want to find the top 10 best-selling products or the top 20% of highest paid employees. Note that in most cases you'll need to specify sorting criteria—perhaps by count of products sold descending or salary descending—to place the rows you want at the "top" of the recordset. You can then ask for the top 10 or top 20% to get the answers you want.

When working in a query datasheet, you can define and apply filters and specify sorting just as you can in a table datasheet. Access stores this filtering and sorting criteria in the query's Filter and Order By properties. When you design a query, you can use the Filter and Order By properties to predefine filtering and sorting criteria. When you open the query and choose Apply Filter/Sort from the Records menu, Access applies the filter and/or sorts the data using these saved properties. If you change the filter or sorting criteria while in Datasheet view and then save the change, Access updates these properties.

You can also affect whether the fields returned by the query can be updated by changing the Recordset Type property. The default setting, Dynaset, allows you to update any fields on the *many* side of a join. It also lets you change values on the *one* side of a join if you have defined a relationship between the tables and have enabled Cascade Update Related Fields in the Edit Relationships dialog box. If you choose Dynaset (Inconsistent Updates), you can update any field that isn't a result of a calculation, but you might update data that you didn't intend to be updatable. If you want the query to be read-only (no fields can be updated), choose the Snap-shot setting.

> **Warning**   You should rarely, if at all, choose the Dynaset (Inconsistent Updates) setting for Recordset Type. This setting makes fields updatable in queries that might not otherwise allow updating. Although Access still enforces referential integrity rules, you can make changes to tables independently from each other, so you might end up reassigning relation-ships unintentionally. You can read about the details of when fields are updatable in a query later in this chapter in "Limitations on Using Select Queries to Update Data," page 323.

Working with Unique Records and Values

When you run a query, Access often returns what appear to be duplicate rows in the record-set. The default in Access 2003 is to return all records. You can also ask Access to return only unique records. (This was the default for all versions of Access prior to version 8, also called Access 97.) Unique records mean that the identifier for each row (the primary key of the table in a single-table query or the concatenated primary keys in a multiple-table query) is unique. If you ask for unique records, Access returns only rows with identifiers that are different from each other. If you want to see all possible data (including duplicate rows), set both the Unique Values property and the Unique Records property to No. (You cannot set both Unique Records and Unique Values to Yes. You can set them both to No.)

To understand how the Unique Values and Unique Records settings work, open the *Contacts-DataCopy.mdb* database and create a query that includes both the tblContacts table and the tblContactEvents table. Let's say you want to find out from which cities you've received a contact over a particular period of time. Include the WorkCity and WorkStateOrProvince fields from tblContacts. Include the ContactDateTime field from tblContactEvents, but clear the Show check box. Figure 8-41 shows a sample query with a date criterion that will show contact cities between December 2002 and March 2003. (Remember, ContactDateTime includes a time value, so you need to enter a criterion one day beyond the date range you want.) You can find this query saved as *qxmplNoUnique* in the sample database.

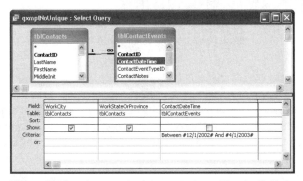

Figure 8-41.   A query to demonstrate setting both Unique Values and Unique Records to No when you're using two tables.

If you switch to Datasheet view, as shown in Figure 8-42 on the next page, you can see that the query returns 39 rows—each row from tblContacts appears once for each related contact event that has a contact date between the specified days. Some of these rows come from the same person, and some come from different people in the same city. The bottom line is there are 39 rows in tblContactEvents within the specified date range.

If you're interested only in one row per contact (per person) from tblContacts, regardless of the number of contact events, you can set the Unique Records property to Yes. The result is shown in Figure 8-43 on the next page (saved as *qxmplUniqueRecords*). This tells us that there were 17 different people who had a contact event within the date range. Again, some of these rows come from different people in the same city, which is why you see the same city listed more than once. The recordset now returns *unique records* from tblContacts (the only table providing output fields in this query).

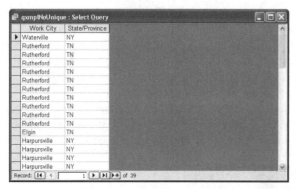

Figure 8-42. The result of retrieving all rows across a join even though the output columns are from only one of the tables.

> **Note** Setting Unique Records to Yes has no effect unless you include more than one table in your query and you include fields only from the table on the one side of a one-to-many relationship. You might have this situation when you are interested in data from one table but you want to filter it based on data in a related table without displaying the fields from the related table.

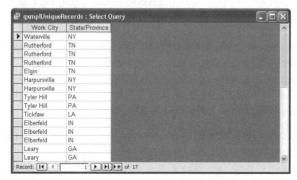

Figure 8-43. The result of retrieving unique records across a join, with output from one table.

Finally, if you're interested in only which distinct cities you received a contact from in the specified date range, and you want to see each city name only once, then set Unique Values to Yes. (Access automatically resets Unique Records to No.) The result is shown in Figure 8-44 (saved as *qxmplUniqueValues*).

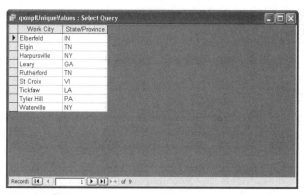

Figure 8-44. The result of setting the Unique Values property to Yes.

When you ask for unique values, you're asking Access to calculate and remove the duplicate values. As with any calculated value in a query, fields in a unique values query can't be updated.

Defining a Subdatasheet

In the previous chapter, I showed you how to work with and modify subdatasheets from query Datasheet view. Now, let's take a closer look at the properties you can set in a query to predefine a subdatasheet within the query. Let's say you want to create a query to show company information and make a subdatasheet available that displays information about the primary contact for the company. You can use the qryContactsDatasheet query that you studied in the previous chapter, but you'll need to modify that query first for this exercise.

In the *ContactsDataCopy.mdb* database, open *qryContactsDatasheet* in Design view. To link this query to another that displays company information, you'll need the CompanyID field. Click the Show Table button on the toolbar, and add the tblCompanyContacts table to the query. You should see a join line linking ContactID in the two tables. Add the CompanyID and DefaultForContact fields from tblCompanyContacts to the Design grid. It makes sense to list only the default company for each contact, so add a criterion of True on the Criteria line under the DefaultForContact field. You should clear the Show check box because you don't really need to see this field in the output. Your query design should now look like Figure 8-45. Choose Save As from the File menu, and save the query as qryContactsDatasheetCOID. You can also find this query saved in the sample database as *qryXmplContactsDatasheetCOID*.

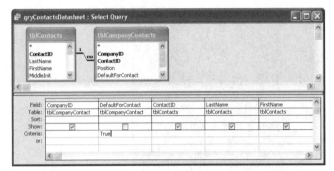

Figure 8-45. Modifying a query that displays contacts to add a linking CompanyID field.

You need the CompanyID field to provide a link to the outer datasheet that you will build shortly, but you don't necessarily need to see it in your datasheet. Switch to Datasheet view, click in the Company / Org column (this is the CompanyID field), and choose Hide Columns from the Format menu to hide the field. Note that this affects the display only. CompanyID is still a field in the query. Close the query and click Yes when Access asks you if you want to save your layout changes.

Now you're ready to build the query in which you'll use the query you just modified as a sub-datasheet. Start a new query on the tblCompanies table. Include the CompanyID, Company-Name, City, and StateOrProvince fields from tblCompanies. Click in the blank space in the top part of the query window, and click the Properties button to open the Query Properties window. Click the Subdatasheet Name property and open the drop-down list. This list shows all tables and queries saved in your database. Scroll down and choose the query that that you just saved—qryContactsDatasheetCOID—and select it as shown in Figure 8-46.

You need to tell your query which field links the query you're creating to the query in the sub-datasheet. In Link Child Fields, type the name of the field in the subdatasheet query you just selected that matches a field in the query you're designing—in this case, CompanyID. Note that when you're linking to another table or query that requires more than one field to define the relationship, you enter the field names separated by semicolons. In Link Master Fields, enter the name of the field in the query you're creating that should match the value in the field in Link Child Fields—CompanyID again. (You'll see these same properties again when inserting a subform in a form in Chapter 13, "Advanced Form Design.")

Two additional properties apply to subdatasheets—Subdatasheet Height and Subdatasheet Expanded. If you leave Subdatasheet Height at its default setting of 0, the subdatasheet area expands to show all available rows when you open it. You can limit the maximum height by entering a setting in inches (or centimeters on a machine whose regional settings are set to the metric system). If the height you specify isn't large enough to show all rows, you'll see a scroll bar to move though the rows in the subdatasheet. If you set Subdatasheet Expanded to Yes, the subdatasheet for every row opens expanded when you open the query or switch to Datasheet view. Just for fun, change this setting to Yes.

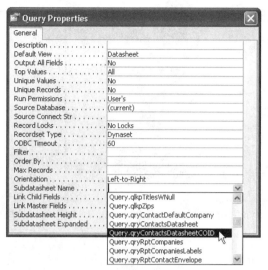

Figure 8-46. Selecting another query to provide the subdatasheet for this query.

Tip When a property box has a drop-down list of values, you can cycle through the values by double-clicking in the property value box.

Switch to Datasheet view, and your result should look like Figure 8-47.

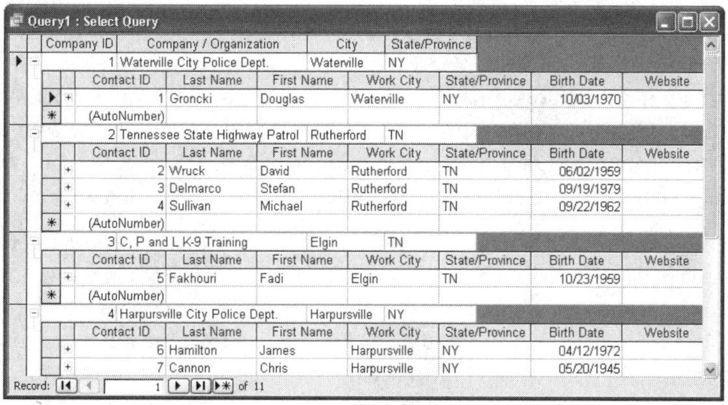

Figure 8-47. The query on company information with its contact subdatasheet information expanded.

Do you notice that there are little plus signs on the rows in the subdatasheet? Remember that original qryContactsDatasheet from which you built the new qryContactsDatasheetCOID query, also has a subdatasheet defined. If you click one of the plus signs in the subdatasheet, you'll see the related contact event subdatasheet information from qryContactsDatasheet as shown in Figure 8-48. You can actually nest subdatasheets like this up to seven levels.

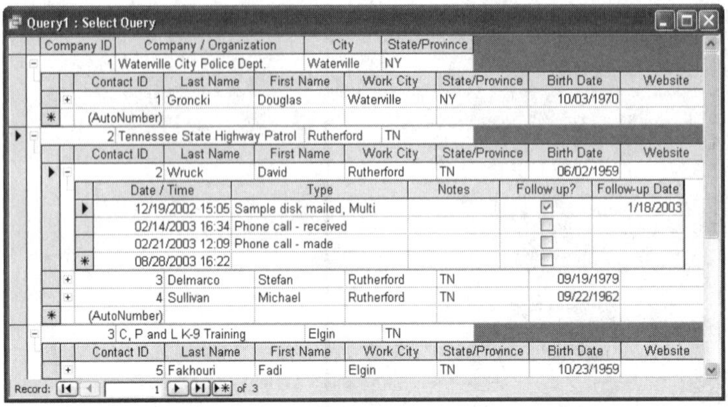

Figure 8-48. Expanding the subdatasheet of the subdatasheet to see contact event information.

You can find this query saved as *qxmplCompaniesContactsSub* in the sample database.

Other Query Properties

If you designed your database to be shared by multiple users across a network, you might want to secure the tables and grant access to other users only through queries. That way, you can give users specific permissions to tables. When you set the Run Permissions property to User's (the default), users cannot open the query unless they also have permission to access the tables included in the query. If you log on with a name that has full permissions to all tables and then create queries, you become the owner of those queries. You can set Run Permissions to Owner's to allow the person who runs your query to see the data as though they're running under your logon name. The user might not have any permission to access the data in the tables in your query, but you can grant them a filtered view with this technique. Of course, you must grant them permission to run your query. See Chapter 30, "Securing Your Database," for details about implementing security in a desktop database.

Use the Record Locks property to control the level of editing integrity for a query that is designed to access data shared across a network. The default is No Locks—to not lock any records when the user opens the query. With this setting, Access applies a lock temporarily only when it needs to write a row back to the source table. Select the Edited Record setting to lock a row as soon as a user begins entering changes in that row. The most restrictive setting, All Records, locks every record retrieved by the query as long as the user has the query open. Use this setting only when the query must perform multiple updates to a table and other users should not access any data in the table until the query is finished.

Four of the remaining properties—Source Database, Source Connect Str, ODBC Timeout, and Max Records—apply to dynamically linked tables. You can, for example, run a query against tables in another Microsoft Access database by entering the full path and file name of that database in Source Database. Access dynamically links to the database when you run the query. Use Source Connect Str when you are dynamically linking to an ODBC or non-Access database that requires connection information. ODBC Timeout specifies how long Access will wait (in seconds) for a response from the ODBC database before failing with an error. Use Max Records to limit the number of rows returned to this query from a database server. When you don't specify a number, Access fetches all rows. This might not be desirable when you're fetching data from tables that have hundreds of thousands of rows.

The last property, Orientation, specifies whether you want to see the columns in Left-to-Right or Right-to-Left order. In some languages where reading proceeds right to left, this setting is handy. You can try it out on your system. You'll find that the columns show up right to left, the caption of the query is right-aligned, the selector bar is down the right side of the datasheet, and pressing the Tab key moves through fields from right to left.

Editing and Creating Queries in SQL View

There are three types of queries that you must create in SQL view: data definition queries, pass-through queries, and union queries.

In a desktop application, Access supports a limited subset of the ANSI-Standard SQL language for data definition. You can execute basic CREATE TABLE and ALTER TABLE commands in a data definition query, but you cannot define any Access-specific properties such as the Input Mask or Validation Rule property. The syntax is so limited that I don't cover it in Article 1, "Understanding SQL," on the companion CD.

When you're using linked tables to a server database system such as Microsoft SQL Server or Oracle, you might need to execute a query on the server that takes advantage of the native SQL supported by the server. You can do most of your work in queries you build in the Access query designer, but the SQL that the query designer builds is only a subset of what your server probably supports. When you need to send a command to your database server in its native syntax, use a pass-through query. If all your data is stored in Microsoft SQL Server, you should build an Access project that links directly to the server data. You can learn about projects in Part 4, "Designing an Access Project."

So, that leaves us with union queries that you might want to build in SQL view. When you create a query that fetches data from multiple tables, you see the related fields side-by-side in the resulting datasheet. Sometimes it's useful to fetch similar data from several tables and literally stack the rows from different tables on top of one another. Think of pulling the pages containing your favorite recipes out of two different cookbooks and piling them on top of one another to make a new book. For that, you need a union query, and you must build it in SQL view.

Let's say you need to build a mailing list in the LawTrack Contacts application. You want to send a brochure to each primary contact for a company at the company's main mailing address. You also want to include any other contacts who are not the primary contact for a company, but send the mailing to their home address. Sounds easy enough to pull the primary contact mailing address from tblCompanies and the address for everyone else from tblContacts. But how do you get all this information in one set of data to make it easy to print your mailing labels in one pass?

SQL—The Basic Clauses

One way to begin learning SQL (and I strongly recommend that you do), is to take a look at any query you've built in the query designer in SQL view. You can see the SQL view of any query by opening it in Design view and then choosing SQL View from the View menu. You can learn all the details in Article 1, "Understanding SQL," but a quick overview of the main clauses will help you begin to understand what you see in SQL view.

SQL Clause	Usage
SELECT	This clause lists the fields and expressions that your query returns. It is equivalent to the Fields row in the query designer. In a totals query, aggregate functions within the SELECT clause, such as Min or Sum, come from specifications in the Totals line.
FROM	This clause specifies the tables or queries from which your query fetches data and includes JOIN clauses to define how to link your tables or queries. It is equivalent to the graphical display of table or query field lists and join lines in the top of the query designer.
WHERE	This clause specifies how to filter the rows returned by evaluating the FROM clause. It is equivalent to the Criteria and Or lines in the query designer.
GROUP BY	This clause lists the grouping fields for a totals query. Access builds this clause from the fields indicated with Group By in the Totals line of the query designer.
HAVING	This clause specifies filtering in a totals query on calculated values. This clause comes from the Criteria and Or lines under fields with one of the aggregate functions specified in the Totals line.

First, build a query to get the information you need for each company's primary contact. In the *ContactsDataCopy.mdb* database, start a new query on tblCompanies. Add tblCompany-Contacts and tblContacts and remove the extra join line between the ContactID field in tbl-Contacts and the ReferredBy field in tblCompanies. In the first column on the Field line, enter:

```
EmpName: (tblContacts.Title + " ") & tblContacts.FirstName & " " &
(tblContacts.MiddleInit + ". ") & tblContacts.LastName &
(" " + tblContacts.Suffix)
```

Add the CompanyName and Address fields from tblCompanies. In the fourth column on the Field line, enter:

```
CSZ: tblCompanies.City & ", " & tblCompanies.StateOrProvince & " " &
tblCompanies.PostalCode
```

Add the DefaultForCompany field from tblCompanyContacts, clear its Show check box, and enter True on the Criteria line. If you switch to Datasheet view, your result should look like Figure 8-49.

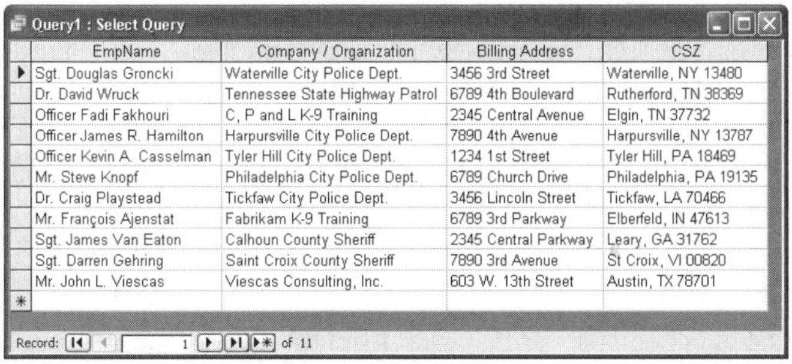

Query1 : Select Query

	EmpName	Company / Organization	Billing Address	CSZ
▶	Sgt. Douglas Groncki	Waterville City Police Dept.	3456 3rd Street	Waterville, NY 13480
	Dr. David Wruck	Tennessee State Highway Patrol	6789 4th Boulevard	Rutherford, TN 38369
	Officer Fadi Fakhouri	C, P and L K-9 Training	2345 Central Avenue	Elgin, TN 37732
	Officer James R. Hamilton	Harpursville City Police Dept.	7890 4th Avenue	Harpursville, NY 13787
	Officer Kevin A. Casselman	Tyler Hill City Police Dept.	1234 1st Street	Tyler Hill, PA 18469
	Mr. Steve Knopf	Philadelphia City Police Dept.	6789 Church Drive	Philadelphia, PA 19135
	Dr. Craig Playstead	Tickfaw City Police Dept.	3456 Lincoln Street	Tickfaw, LA 70466
	Mr. François Ajenstat	Fabrikam K-9 Training	6789 3rd Parkway	Elberfeld, IN 47613
	Sgt. James Van Eaton	Calhoun County Sheriff	2345 Central Parkway	Leary, GA 31762
	Sgt. Darren Gehring	Saint Croix County Sheriff	7890 3rd Avenue	St Croix, VI 00820
	Mr. John L. Viescas	Viescas Consulting, Inc.	603 W. 13th Street	Austin, TX 78701
*				

Record: 1 of 11

Figure 8-49. The first part of a union query to display names and addresses.

OK, that's the first part. You don't have to save this query—leave it open in Design view. Start another query on tblContacts and add tblCompanyContacts. Create an EmpName field exactly as you did in the first query. In the second column, enter:

```
CompanyName: ""
```

Say what? Well, one of the requirements to build a union query is that the two recordsets must both have the exact same number of columns and the exact same data types in the relative columns. A mailing label sent to a home address doesn't have a company name, but you need this field to line up with the ones you created in the first query. In Chapter 15, "Constructing a Report," you'll see how the Mailing Label Wizard eliminates the blank row that would otherwise be created by including this field.

Add the HomeAddress field from tblContacts in the third column and create this expression in the fourth column on the Field line:

```
CSZ: tblContacts.HomeCity & ", " & tblContacts.HomeStateOrProvince & " " &
tblContacts.HomePostalCode
```

Finally, include the DefaultForCompany field from tblCompanyContacts, clear the Show check box, but this time set a criterion of False. The Datasheet view of this query should look like Figure 8-50.

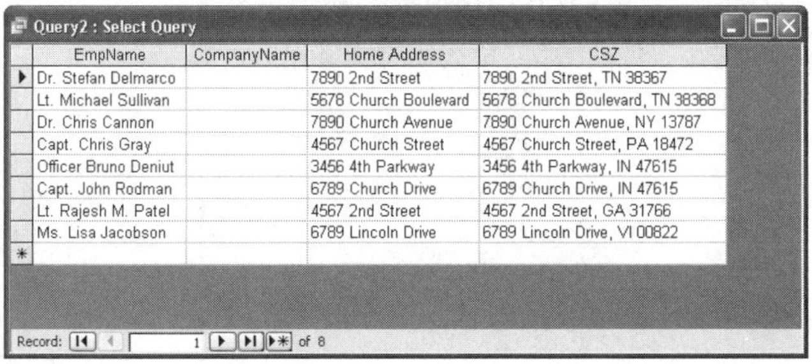

Query2 : Select Query

	EmpName	CompanyName	Home Address	CSZ
▶	Dr. Stefan Delmarco		7890 2nd Street	7890 2nd Street, TN 38367
	Lt. Michael Sullivan		5678 Church Boulevard	5678 Church Boulevard, TN 38368
	Dr. Chris Cannon		7890 Church Avenue	7890 Church Avenue, NY 13787
	Capt. Chris Gray		4567 Church Street	4567 Church Street, PA 18472
	Officer Bruno Deniut		3456 4th Parkway	3456 4th Parkway, IN 47615
	Capt. John Rodman		6789 Church Drive	6789 Church Drive, IN 47615
	Lt. Rajesh M. Patel		4567 2nd Street	4567 2nd Street, GA 31766
	Ms. Lisa Jacobson		6789 Lincoln Drive	6789 Lincoln Drive, VI 00822
*				

Record: 1 of 8

Figure 8-50. The second part of a union query to display names and addresses.

Again, you don't have to save this query. Now you're ready to assemble your union query. Go to the Database window, click Queries under Objects, and double-click the **Create query in Design view** option at the top of the list of queries. You'll see a blank third query window with the Show Table dialog box opened up in front. Click the Close button to dismiss the dialog box. When Access sees that you haven't chosen any tables or queries, it makes SQL the default option on the View button at the left end of the toolbar. Click this button to switch to SQL view on this empty query. You should see a blank window with *SELECT;* displayed in the upper left corner.

Go back to your first query and choose SQL view from the View menu (or you can open the list on the View button at the left end of the toolbar and choose SQL view there). You should see a window like Figure 8-51.

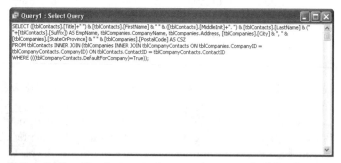

Figure 8-51. The first part of your union query in SQL view.

Select all the text you see in this window and copy it to the Clipboard. Switch to the third empty query, and replace *SELECT;* with the text you copied. Remove the ending semicolon, place the insertion point at the end of the text, press the Enter key, type the word **UNION**, and press the Enter key again.

Go to your second query, switch to SQL view, highlight all the text, and copy it to the Clipboard. Go back to the third query and paste this text at the end. Your new union query should look like Figure 8-52.

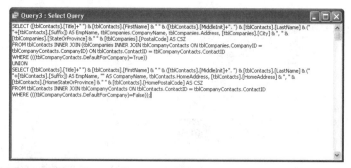

Figure 8-52. Assembling a union query using the SQL from two other queries.

Switch to Datasheet view to see the final result as shown in Figure 8-53.

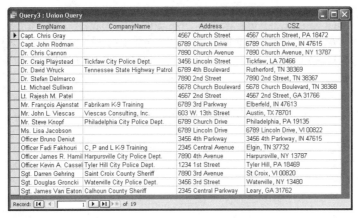

Figure 8-53. The Datasheet view of your new union query.

You should save this query, but you can close and not save the first two queries that you used to build this. You can find this query saved as qxmplAddressesUnion in the sample database. If you want to learn more about SQL, see Article 1, "Understanding SQL," on the companion CD.

Limitations on Using Select Queries to Update Data

The recordset that Access creates when you run a query looks and acts pretty much like a real table containing data. In fact, in most cases you can insert rows, delete rows, and update the information in a recordset, and Access will make the necessary changes to the underlying table or tables for you.

In some cases, however, Access won't be able to figure out what needs to be changed. Consider, for example, a calculated field named Total that is the result of multiplying two fields named Quantity and Price. If you try to increase the amount in a Total field, Access can't know whether you mean to update the Quantity field or the Price field. On the other hand, you can change either the Price field or the Quantity field and then immediately see the change reflected in the calculated Total field.

In addition, Access won't accept any change that might potentially affect many rows in the underlying table. For that reason, you can't change any of the data in a totals query or in a crosstab query. A Group By field is the result of gathering together one or more rows with the same value. Likewise, a Sum is most likely the result of adding values from potentially many rows. A Min or Max value might occur in more than one row.

When working with a recordset that is the result of a join, Access lets you update all fields from the *many* side of a join but only the non-key fields on the *one* side, unless you have specified Cascade Update Related Fields in the relationship. Also, you cannot set or change any field that has the AutoNumber data type. For example, you can't change the ContactID field values in the tblContacts table in the LawTrack Contacts sample application.

The ability to update fields on the *one* side of a query can produce unwanted results if you aren't careful. For example, you could intend to assign a contact to a different company. If

Chapter 8

you change the company name, you'll change that name for all contacts related to the current CompanyID. What you should do instead is change the CompanyID in the tblCompany-Contacts table, not the company name in the tblCompanies table. You'll learn techniques later in Chapter 13, "Advanced Form Design," to prevent inadvertent updating of fields in queries.

When you set Unique Values to Yes in the Query Properties window, Access eliminates duplicate rows. The values returned might occur in multiple rows, so Access won't know which one you mean to update. And finally, when Access combines rows from different tables in a union query, the individual rows lose their underlying table identity. Access cannot know which table you mean to update when you try to change a row in a union query, so it disallows all updates.

Query Fields That Cannot Be Updated

Some types of query fields cannot be updated:

- Any field that is the result of a calculation
- Any field in a totals or crosstab query
- Any field in a query that includes a totals or crosstab query as one of the row sources
- A primary key participating in a relationship unless Cascade Update Related Fields is specified
- AutoNumber fields
- Any field in a unique values query or a unique records query
- Any field in a union query

Creating PivotTables and PivotCharts from Queries

Microsoft Access 2002 (Office XP) introduced two very useful new features for tables, queries, and forms—PivotTables and PivotCharts. These are additional views of a table, query, or form that you can design to provide analytical views of your data. These views are built into the objects; they're not implemented via a separate ActiveX control as is the old and venerable Microsoft Graph feature.

 Inside Out

You can use PivotTables and PivotCharts on the Web, too!

PivotTables and PivotCharts are part of the Office Web Components that make data access pages work. This means you can include a PivotTable or PivotChart on data access pages you design for your Web site. You can't use the MS Graph custom control in Web pages.

You learned in this chapter that you can build a crosstab query to *pivot* the values in a column to form dynamic column headings. However, crosstab queries have a major drawback—you can include only one calculated value in the intersection of your row headings and single column heading. PivotTables in Microsoft Access are very similar to the PivotTable facility in Microsoft Excel. You can categorize rows by several values, just like you can in a crosstab query, but you can also include multiple column categories and multiple raw or calculated values in each intersection of rows and columns. As its name implies, you can also pivot the table to swap row headings with column headings.

A PivotChart is a graphical view of the data that you included in your PivotTable. You can build a PivotChart without first defining the PivotTable, and vice versa. When you design a PivotChart, you're also designing or modifying the related PivotTable to provide the data you need for your chart. When you modify a PivotTable, you'll also change (or destroy) the related PivotChart you have already designed.

As you explore the possibilities with PivotTables and PivotCharts, you'll find powerful capabilities to "slice and dice" your data or "drill down" into more detail. Unlike a crosstab query that's built on summarized data, you can begin with a table or query that contains very detailed information. The more detail you have to begin with, the more you can do with your PivotTable and PivotChart.

> **Caution** You might be tempted to design a very detailed query that returns thousands of rows for your user to work with. However, the filtering capabilities inside a PivotTable aren't nearly as efficient as defining a filter in your query to begin with. If you're loading hundreds of thousands of rows over a network, your PivotTable or PivotChart might be very, very slow. You should provide enough detail to get the job done, but no more. You should limit the fields in your query to those focused on the task at hand and include filters in your underlying query to return only the subset of the data that's needed.

Building a Query for a PivotTable

Although you can build a PivotTable directly on a table in your database, you most likely will need a query to provide the level of detail you want to pivot. Let's build a query in the *HousingDataCopy.mdb* database that provides some interesting detail.

Start a new query on tblFacilities. Add tblReservations, tblEmployees, and tblDepartments. (Be sure to remove the extra relationship between the EmployeeNumber field in tblEmployees and the ManagerNumber field in tblDepartments.) Create an expression to display the employee name in the first field:

```
EmpName: tblEmployees.LastName & ", " & tblEmployees.FirstName &
(" " + tblEmployees.MiddleName)
```

In the query grid, include the Department field from tblDepartments, the ReservationID field from tblReservations (we're going to use this field later to count the number of reservation days), the FacilityName field from tblFacilities, and the RoomNumber field from tblReservations. Add an expression in the next field to calculate the actual charge per day. You could use the DailyRate field from tblReservations, but that's not an accurate reflection of how much the room costs per day when the employee stays a week or more. Your expression should look like this:

```
DailyCharge: CCur(Round(tblReservations.TotalCharge /
(tblReservations.CheckOutDate - tblReservations.CheckInDate), 2))
```

Remember that you can calculate the number of days by subtracting the CheckInDate field from the CheckOutDate field. Divide the TotalCharge field by the number of days to obtain the actual daily rate. This division might result in a value that has more than two decimal places, so asking the Round function to round to two decimal places (the *2* parameter at the end) takes care of that. Finally, the expression uses the CCur (Convert to Currency) function to make sure the query returns a currency value.

Now comes the fun part. Each row in tblReservations represents a stay of one or more days. In this example, we ultimately want to be able to count individual days to find out the length of stay within any month. To do that, we need to "explode" each single row in tblReservations into a row per day for the duration of the reservation. In this sample database, you'll find what I call a "driver" table—ztblDates—full of dates to accomplish this feat. The table contains date values, one per day, for dates from January 1, 1992, to December 31, 2035. I created this table to "drive" the complete list of dates we need (at least, complete enough for our purposes) against the rows in tblReservations in order to provide the explosion.

Include this table in your query and notice that there's no join line to any of the tables. When you add a table with no join defined to another table or set of records, the query returns the Cartesian product of the two sets of records—every row in the first table or set of records is matched with every row in the second table or set of records. For example, if there are 90 rows in one set and 12 rows in the second set, the query returns 1080 rows (90 times 12). In this case, each reservation will now be matched with each of the separate date values in ztblDates.

As I mentioned earlier, you should try to limit the output of a query that you'll use to build a PivotTable to only the rows you need to solve the problem. Let's say the facilities manager is interested in data for July, August, and September of 2003. Add the DateValue field from ztblDates and enter **Between #7/1/2003# And #9/30/2003#** under this field on the Criteria line. You have now limited the explosion of rows to dates in the months of interest.

The final step is to further limit the rows created based on the CheckInDate and CheckOutDate fields in tblReservations. Any reservation that crosses the time span of interest is going to be for a few days or a few weeks. Add the CheckInDate and CheckOutDate fields from tblReservations and clear the Show check box under both. On the Criteria row under CheckInDate, enter:

```
<=ztblDates.DateValue
```

Under CheckOutDate, enter:

```
>ztblDates.DateValue
```

This forces the query to keep any rows where the DateValue field from ztblDates is within the time span of each reservation row. Voilà! You now have one row per date for each reservation. Your query should now look like Figure 8-54.

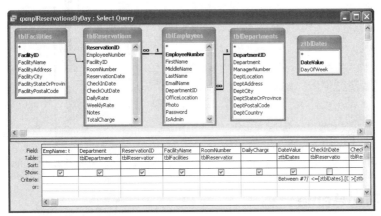

Figure 8-54. A complex query for a PivotTable.

To better understand how this query works to expand each reservation into one row per day, take a look at Table 8-2. The table represents expanded rows after applying the final two criteria on the CheckInDate and CheckOutDate fields.

Table 8-2. How ztblDates Expands Reservation Rows

ReservationID	CheckInDate	CheckOutDate	DateValue
17	July 1, 2003	July 7, 2003	July 1, 2003
17	July 1, 2003	July 7, 2003	July 2, 2003
17	July 1, 2003	July 7, 2003	July 3, 2003
17	July 1, 2003	July 7, 2003	July 4, 2003
17	July 1, 2003	July 7, 2003	July 5, 2003
17	July 1, 2003	July 7, 2003	July 6, 2003

The end result is that the query selects only the rows from ztblDates that are within the date range of the individual reservation. Because there's one (and only one) row for every date of interest coming from ztblDates, you end up with one row per day that's within the span of days in each reservation. Figure 8-55 shows you the Datasheet view of your query. You can find this query saved as *qxmplReservationsByDay* in the sample database.

Chapter 8

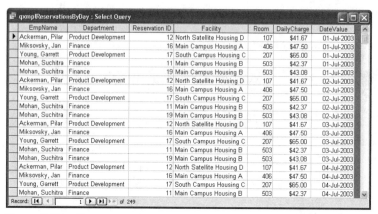

Figure 8-55. The reservations for July, August, and September expanded into one row per day.

Designing a PivotTable

Now that you have the data you need, you're ready to start building a PivotTable. From Design or Datasheet view, switch to PivotTable view by choosing PivotTable View from the View menu. You should see a blank PivotTable design area as shown in Figure 8-56. If you don't see the field list as shown in Figure 8-56, choose Field List from the View menu.

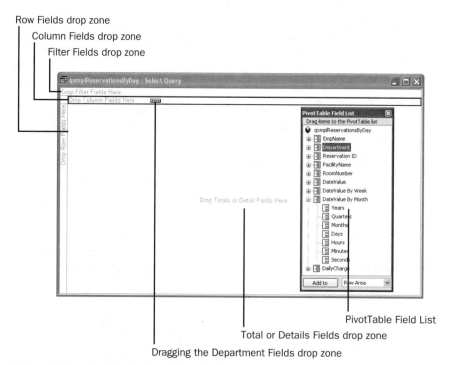

Figure 8-56. The PivotTable design window.

In general, you should use as columns those fields that have the fewest values. If you place too many values across your PivotTable, you'll find that you must scroll left a long way to see all the details. In this case, we're interested in statistics by month, and we know there are only three months of data in the underlying recordset. You'll still be able to show the details by day, if you like, because the recordset includes information by date—you can expand any Months field to show all the days in the month. We might want to see the data organized by department and facility. It might also be interesting to provide an easy way to filter on employee name, but we don't need the data from that field displayed in the table.

Open the DateValue By Month list and drag Months to the Column Fields drop zone. Drag the Department field and the FacilityName field to the Row Fields drop zone. Drag and drop the EmpName field on the Filter Fields drop zone. Finally, drag and drop the ReservationID and DailyCharge fields on the Totals or Detail Fields drop zone. Notice that fields you choose are now highlighted in bold in the PivotTable field list. Within the PivotTable, you can click any plus sign (+) to expand a category or display details, or any minus sign (–) to collapse a category or hide details. If you expand Months in the Column Fields drop zone, the PivotTable automatically adds a Days field to the Columns area. You can also expand the categories in the PivotTable Field List window by clicking the plus sign next to each category. Your PivotTable should look like Figure 8-57.

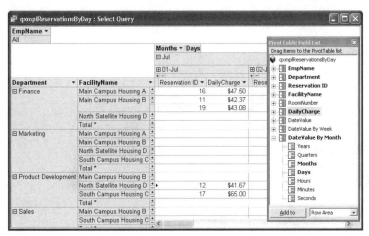

Figure 8-57. A PivotTable with fields added to all drop zones.

Now would be a good time to take a quick look at the buttons available on the toolbar that are applicable to PivotTables. Table 8-3 on the next page shows you the details.

Table 8-3. Toolbar Buttons for PivotTables

Button	Name	Usage
	AutoFilter	When highlighted, indicates automatic filtering is active for the Pivot-Table. You can click this button to remove all filters. If you define a filter, this button becomes highlighted again.
	Show Top/Bottom Items	You can select a column or row field and then click this button to define a filter to display only the first or last number or percentage of rows. This feature works similarly to the Top Values property of a query.
	AutoCalc	You can select a column, row, or detail/total field and then click this button to insert an aggregate function. The available list of functions includes those you can use in totals queries except for First and Last. (See Table 8-1, page 297.) The functions available in AutoCalc are appropriate to the field data type and location on the grid. (For example, you can't Sum a text field.)
	SubTotal	You can click on a column or row field and then click this button to insert a subtotal based on the values in that field. You must define an AutoCalc field before you add a subtotal.
	Calculated Totals And Fields	You can click this button to insert an expression in the detail/total area that calculates an additional value based on the fields in the recordset.
	Show As	After you insert AutoCalc total fields, you can click in a field and then click this button to convert the value to a percentage of the row, column, or grand totals.
	Collapse	Click on a row or column field and click this button to collapse all subcategories for this field and show summaries only.
	Expand	Performs the opposite of Collapse.
	Hide Details	Hides the details for the selected row or column and shows only totals.
	Show Details	Performs the opposite of Hide Details.
	Refresh	Refetches the underlying data. You might need to do this if others are sharing the data and updating it.
	Export to Microsoft Excel	Exports your PivotTable in XML format to an HTML (.htm, .html) file and opens it in Microsoft Excel.
	Field List	Opens or closes the PivotTable field list.
	Properties	Opens or closes the Properties window.

You're going to need some total calculations for your PivotTable. Click anywhere in the Reservation ID column, click the AutoCalc button to drop down the list of available functions, and select Count. Click anywhere in the DailyCharge column, click the AutoCalc button, and select Sum. Click the Daily Charge column heading and then click the Hide Details button to show only totals. Your PivotTable should now look like Figure 8-58. (I closed the PivotTable field list to show you more of the PivotTable.)

Chapter 8

qxmplReservationsByDay : Select Query					
EmpName ▾					
All					
			Months ▾ Days		
			⊞ Jul		⊞ Aug
			+–		+–
Department ▾	FacilityName ▾		Count of Reservation ID	Sum of DailyCharge	Count of Reservation ID	Sum of I
⊟ Finance	Main Campus Housing A		12	$782.50	
	Main Campus Housing B		29	$1,481.21	1
	North Satellite Housing D				33
	Total *		41	$2,263.71	34
⊟ Marketing	Main Campus Housing A		21	$1,370.00	14
	Main Campus Housing B		21	$1,050.00	
	North Satellite Housing D				
	South Campus Housing C		2	$100.00	4
	Total *		44	$2,520.00	18
⊟ Product Development	Main Campus Housing B		11	$990.00	
	North Satellite Housing D		11	$458.37	
	South Campus Housing C		6	$390.00	
	Total *		28	$1,838.37	
⊟ Sales	Main Campus Housing B		10	$845.00	3
	South Campus Housing C				
	Total *		10	$845.00	3
Grand Total *					

Figure 8-58. Adding two totals calculations and hiding all the details.

There are literally hundreds of properties you can set in a PivotTable. Let's change the captions of the two totals fields to something more meaningful. Click on the Count Of Reservation ID field and then click the Properties button on the toolbar to open the Properties window as shown in Figure 8-59.

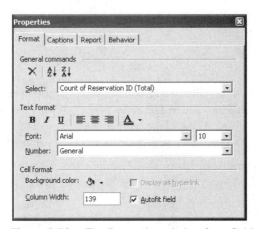

Figure 8-59. The Properties window for a field in a PivotTable.

As you can see, you can modify the text format on the first tab. You can also drop down the Select combo box to choose any other element you have defined thus far. The Properties window changes depending on the type of element you choose. Click the Captions tab and change the caption to Room Days. Go back to the Format tab, choose Sum of Daily Charge (Total) from the Select box, click the Captions tab again, and change the caption to Revenue.

You could spend a couple of days playing around in this PivotTable to see what else you can do. One last thing we might want to do before turning this into a PivotChart is to actually *pivot* the table. You do that by grabbing the fields in the column area and moving them to the row area and vice-versa. I decided I'd rather see details about departments first, then facility usage within department, so I placed Department to the left of FacilityName when I moved the fields. You can see the final result in Figure 8-60.

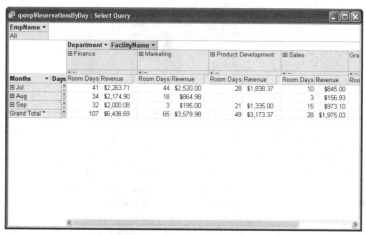

Figure 8-60. A pivoted PivotTable showing only totals.

If you switch to Design view, you can open the Properties window for the query and set the Default View property to PivotTable. I saved this query as *qxmplReservationByDayPT* in the sample database. You should save this query under a new name so that you can start fresh building a PivotChart in the next section.

Designing a PivotChart

Designing a PivotChart is almost as easy as building a PivotTable. You will most likely use Pivot-Charts in reports (as an embedded subform) and in data access pages, but you can also create a PivotChart view of a table, query, or form. As mentioned earlier when discussing PivotTables, you most often need to start with a query to pull together the information you need.

To start building a new PivotChart from scratch, open the *qxmplReservationsByDay* sample query again and switch to PivotChart view. You can see the PivotChart design window in Figure 8-61.

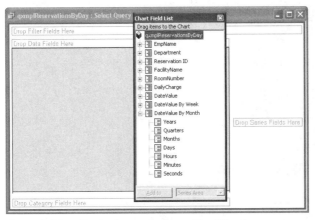

Figure 8-61. Beginning to design a PivotChart on a query.

Notice that the filter area is still near the top left corner of the window. However, the area for data fields is now along the top of the gray chart drawing area in the center. Drop fields that you want to use for data points along the bottom axis in the bottom left corner. Drop fields that you want to use for the vertical axis on the right center area. To begin designing your PivotChart, expand DateValue By Month in the field list and drag and drop Months onto the Drop Category Fields Here area. Next, drag and drop Department onto the Drop Series Fields Here area on the right.

> **Tip** You can switch directly into PivotChart view from the Design view or Datasheet view of any query. If you haven't previously defined the PivotTable, you can still create your chart by dragging and dropping fields from the field list. Keep in mind that any change you make in PivotChart view also changes what you see in PivotTable view. If you want to keep separate PivotTable and PivotChart views, you should save two versions of your query.

We don't have anything charted yet, so drag the DailyCharge field from the field list to the Data Fields area along the top of the chart. Notice that the chart assumes we want to Sum the field. If you had added the ReservationID field, you would have to click on the Sum of Reservation ID field, click the AutoCalc button, and change the calculation to Count. Your Pivot-Chart should now look like Figure 8-62 on the next page.

This doesn't look all that informative yet, but we're starting to make some progress. It would be nice to add a title, a *legend* (a description of each of the colored bars), and a vertical axis with some values. You might also want to display the actual value of each bar at the top of it. Let's get started.

First, open the Properties window (click the Properties button on the toolbar) and choose Chart Workspace in the Select box on the General tab as shown in Figure 8-63 on the next page. (Notice as you go through this exercise that the tabs available in the Properties window change as you select different objects on your PivotChart.)

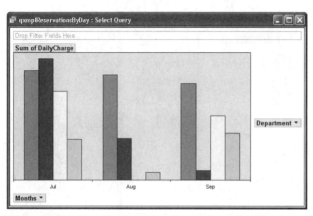

Figure 8-62. Creating totals to display in a PivotChart.

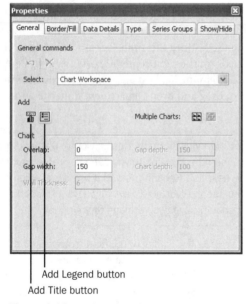

Add Legend button
Add Title button

Figure 8-63. Adding a title and legend to the PivotChart workspace.

Click the Title and Legend buttons on the left under Add to create these elements on your PivotChart. Click on Chart Workspace title that you just added (or choose Title in the Select box on the General tab), click the Format tab, and change the caption to something like Revenue by Month and Department. Notice that you can also change the font, font size, font color, and position of the title on this tab.

Go back to the General tab and select Chart Workspace again. Click the Series Groups tab to see the settings in Figure 8-64. On this tab, you can select one or more items in the Series box and create a separate set of plot bars by placing them in their own group. For each group, you can also add an axis and specify its location. Click on group 1 in the lower Add axis box, select Left in the Axis position list, and click the Add button to create the axis.

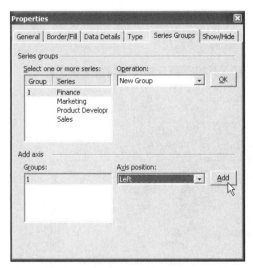

Figure 8-64. Adding an axis to your PivotChart.

Finally, go back to the General tab and select the four values in the Select box for the Department field one at a time, beginning with Finance. You'll see buttons to Add Data Label, Add Trendline, or Add Errorbar as shown in Figure 8-65. Select Add Data Label for each department name to add the total value at the top of each column.

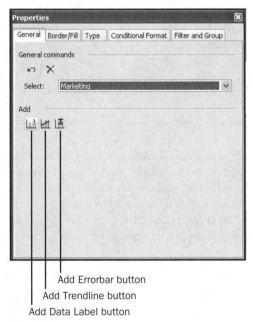

Figure 8-65. Adding labels to data points.

Your PivotChart should now look like Figure 8-66.

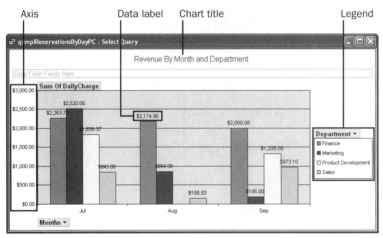

Figure 8-66. A PivotChart to show revenue totals by month and department.

Inside Out

Manipulating the caption of a data field in a PivotChart

If you think about it, you went to some trouble to assign a different caption to Sum of Daily-Charge when you built the sample PivotTable. There's actually no way to correct the caption of a data field in PivotChart view. I recommend that you save what you've done so far, and then switch to PivotTable view, hide the details, and change the caption for Sum of Daily-Charge to Revenue as you did earlier. When you switch back to PivotChart view, you'll find the new caption displayed. You can find this chart saved as *qxmplReservationByDayPC* in the sample database.

If you want to see what your PivotChart might look like plotted in a different way, you can click the Chart Type button on the toolbar to open the Properties window with the Pivot-Chart workspace selected and the focus on the Type tab. The chart we've been building thus far is a simple column chart, but you can choose from Bar, Line, Smooth Line, Pie, Scatter, and several other options. Be aware that changing the chart type often throws away some detail settings, so you might have to tweak properties again to get exactly what you want.

Now that you understand the fundamentals of building complex select queries and working with PivotTables and PivotCharts with Access, you're ready to move on to updating sets of data with action queries in the next chapter.

Modifying Data with Action Queries

In Chapter 7, "Creating and Working with Simple Queries," you learned how to insert, update, and delete single rows of data within a datasheet. In Chapter 8, "Building Complex Queries," you discovered that you can use queries to select the data you want—even from multiple tables. You also learned under what conditions you cannot update a field in a query. Now you can take the concept of queries one step further and use action queries to quickly change, insert, create, or delete sets of data in your database.

The four types of queries you'll study in this chapter are

- **Update query** Allows you to update the fields in one or more rows.
- **Make-table query** Allows you to create a new table by selecting rows from one or more existing tables.
- **Append query** Allows you to copy rows from one or more tables into another table.
- **Delete query** Allows you to remove one or more rows from a table.

Note The examples in this chapter are based on the tables and data in *HousingData-Copy.mdb* and *ContactsDataCopy.mdb* on the companion CD included with this book. These databases are copies of the data from the Housing and LawTrack Contacts application samples, respectively, and they contain the sample queries used in this chapter. The query results you see from the sample queries you build in this chapter might not exactly match what you see in this book if you have changed the sample data in the files.

Updating Groups of Rows

It's easy enough to use a table or a query in Datasheet view to find a single record in your database and change one value. But what if you want to make the same change to many records? Changing each record one at a time could be very tedious.

Remember that in Chapter 7, "Creating and Working with Simple Queries," you learned how to construct queries to test proposed new validation rules. In the *HousingDataCopy.mdb* database, there's a table-level validation rule defined in tblFacilityRooms that doesn't let you

337

enter a WeeklyRate value that is greater than 7 times the DailyRate value. If you want to change this rule to ensure that the WeeklyRate value is no more than 6 times the DailyRate value (thereby ensuring that the weekly rate is a true discount), you must first update the values in the table to comply with the new rule.

You could open tblFacilityRooms in Datasheet view and go through the individual rows one by one to set all the WeeklyRate values by hand. But why not let Microsoft Access do the work for you with a single query?

Testing with a Select Query

Before you create and run a query to update many records in your database, it's a good idea to first create a select query using criteria that select the records you want to update. You'll see in the next section that it's easy to convert this select query to an update query or other type of action query after you're sure that Access will process the right records.

You could certainly update all the rows in tblFacilityRooms, but what about rows where the WeeklyRate value is already less than or equal to 6 times the DailyRate value? You don't want to update rows that already meet the proposed validation rule change—you might actually increase the WeeklyRate value in those rows. For example, a room might exist that has a DailyRate value of $50 and a WeeklyRate value of $275. If you blanket update all rows to set the WeeklyRate field to six times the DailyRate field, you'll change the WeeklyRate value in this row to $300. So, you should first build a query on tblFacilityRooms to find only those rows that need to be changed.

Open *HousingDataCopy.mdb* and start a new query on tblFacilityRooms. Include the FacilityID, RoomNumber, DailyRate, and WeeklyRate fields. Enter the criterion >[**DailyRate**]*6 under the WeeklyRate field. Your query should look like Figure 9-1.

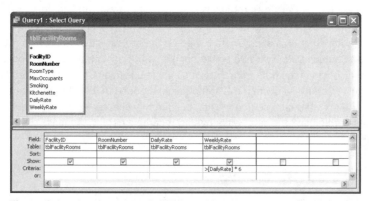

Figure 9-1. A select query to find weekly rates that will fail the new table validation rule.

When you run the query, you'll see 151 records that you want to change, as shown in Figure 9-2. (There are 180 records in the table.)

Facility	Room No.	Daily	Weekly
1	102	$100.00	$640.00
1	103	$45.00	$290.00
1	104	$50.00	$320.00
1	105	$40.00	$255.00
1	106	$50.00	$320.00
1	107	$90.00	$575.00
1	202	$100.00	$640.00
1	203	$45.00	$290.00
1	204	$50.00	$320.00
1	205	$40.00	$255.00
1	206	$50.00	$320.00
1	207	$90.00	$575.00
1	302	$100.00	$640.00
1	303	$45.00	$290.00
1	304	$50.00	$320.00
1	305	$40.00	$255.00
1	306	$50.00	$320.00

Record: 1 of 151

Figure 9-2. The recordset of the select query shown in Figure 9-1.

Converting a Select Query to an Update Query

Now you're ready to change the query so that it will update the table. When you first create a query, Access builds a select query by default. You can find commands for the four types of action queries—make-table, update, append, and delete—on the Query menu when the query is in Design view. (Switch back to Design view if you haven't already done so.) You can also select one of these options from the Query Type toolbar button's drop-down list, as shown in Figure 9-3. Select Update Query to convert the select query to an update query.

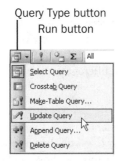

Figure 9-3. The Query Type toolbar button's drop-down list.

When you convert a select query to an update query, Access changes the title bar of the Query window in Design view and adds a row labeled Update To to the design grid, as shown in Figure 9-4 on the next page. You use this row to specify how you want your data changed. In this case, you want to change the WeeklyRate value to [**DailyRate**]* 6 for all rows where the rate is currently too high.

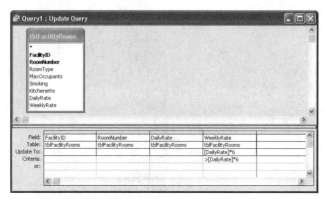

Figure 9-4. An update query with its Update To setting.

> **Tip** What can I put in Update To?
>
> You can enter any valid expression in the Update To row. You can include in the expression one or more of the fields from the source tables in the query. For example, if you want to raise the DailyRate value for a certain type of room by 10 percent, rounded to the nearest dollar (zero decimal places), you can include the DailyRate field in the design grid and enter
>
> ```
> Round( CCur( [DailyRate] * 1.1 ), 0 )
> ```
>
> in the Update To row. Note that the above formula uses the Round and CCur built-in functions discussed in the previous chapter to round the result to the nearest dollar.

Running an Update Query

If you want to be completely safe, you should make a backup copy of your table before you run an update query. To do that, go to the Database window, select the table you're about to update, and choose the Copy command from the Edit menu. Then choose the Paste command from the Edit menu, and give the copy of your table a different name when Access prompts you with a dialog box. (Be sure you select the default Structure and Data option.) Now you're ready to run the update query.

To run the query, choose the Run command from the Query menu or click the Run button on the toolbar. Access first scans your table to determine how many rows will change based on your selection criteria. It then displays a confirmation dialog box like the one shown in Figure 9-5.

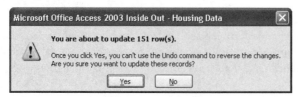

Figure 9-5. The dialog box that reports the number of rows that will be changed by an update query.

You already know that you need to update 151 records, so you can perform the update by clicking the Yes button in the dialog box. (If the number of rows indicated in the dialog box is not what you expected or if you're not sure that Access will update the right records or fields, click the No button to stop the query without updating.) After the update query runs, you can look at the table or create a new select query to confirm that Access made the changes you wanted. Figure 9-6 shows the result—no weekly rate is greater than 6 times the daily rate.

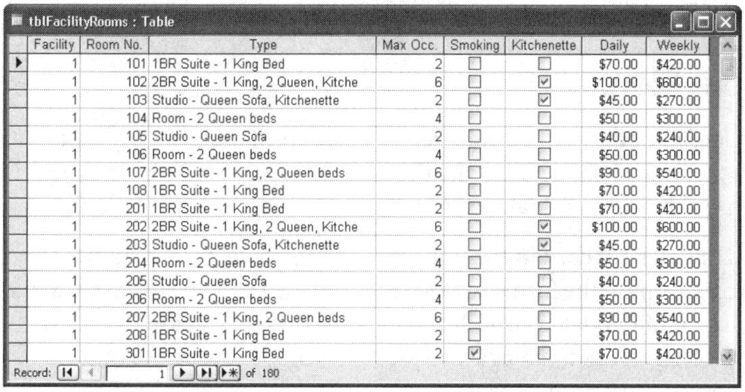
tblFacilityRooms : Table

Facility	Room No.	Type	Max Occ.	Smoking	Kitchenette	Daily	Weekly
1	101	1BR Suite - 1 King Bed	2	☐	☐	$70.00	$420.00
1	102	2BR Suite - 1 King, 2 Queen, Kitche	6	☐	☑	$100.00	$600.00
1	103	Studio - Queen Sofa, Kitchenette	2	☐	☑	$45.00	$270.00
1	104	Room - 2 Queen beds	4	☐	☐	$50.00	$300.00
1	105	Studio - Queen Sofa	2	☐	☐	$40.00	$240.00
1	106	Room - 2 Queen beds	4	☐	☐	$50.00	$300.00
1	107	2BR Suite - 1 King, 2 Queen beds	6	☐	☐	$90.00	$540.00
1	108	1BR Suite - 1 King Bed	2	☐	☐	$70.00	$420.00
1	201	1BR Suite - 1 King Bed	2	☐	☐	$70.00	$420.00
1	202	2BR Suite - 1 King, 2 Queen, Kitche	6	☐	☑	$100.00	$600.00
1	203	Studio - Queen Sofa, Kitchenette	2	☐	☑	$45.00	$270.00
1	204	Room - 2 Queen beds	4	☐	☐	$50.00	$300.00
1	205	Studio - Queen Sofa	2	☐	☐	$40.00	$240.00
1	206	Room - 2 Queen beds	4	☐	☐	$50.00	$300.00
1	207	2BR Suite - 1 King, 2 Queen beds	6	☐	☐	$90.00	$540.00
1	208	1BR Suite - 1 King Bed	2	☐	☐	$70.00	$420.00
1	301	1BR Suite - 1 King Bed	2	☑	☐	$70.00	$420.00

Record: 1 of 180

Figure 9-6. The updated data in the tblFacilityRooms table.

If you think you might want to perform this update again, you can save the query and give it a name. This sample query is saved in the sample database as *qxmplUpdateWeekly*. In the Database window, Access distinguishes action queries from select queries by displaying a special icon, followed by an exclamation point, before action query names. For example, Access displays a pencil and an exclamation point next to the new update query that you just created. You'll see later that make-table queries have a small datasheet with a starburst in one corner, append queries have a green cross, and delete queries have a red *X*. Note that if you open an action query from the Database window, you'll execute it. If you want to see the datasheet of the action query, open it in Design view first, then switch to Datasheet view.

> **Note** It's a good idea to include identifying fields (such as FacilityID and RoomNumber in the above example) when you build a test select query that you plan to convert to an action query. However, Access discards any fields that do not have criteria specified or are not being updated when you save your final action query. This is why you won't see anything but the WeeklyRate field in qxmplUpdateWeekly.

To run an action query again, select it in the Database window and click the Open button. When you run an action query from the Database window, Access displays a confirmation dialog box similar to the one shown in Figure 9-7 on the next page. Click the Yes button to complete the action query. If you want to disable this extra confirmation step (I don't recommend that you do so), choose the Options command from the Tools menu and, on the Edit/Find tab of the Options dialog box, clear the Action Queries check box under Confirm.

Chapter 9

Figure 9-7. The dialog box that asks you to confirm an action query.

Updating Multiple Fields

When you create an update query, you aren't limited to changing a single field at a time. You can ask Access to update any or all of the fields in the record by including them in the design grid and then specifying an update formula.

Before Access updates a record in the underlying table or query, it makes a copy of the original record. Access applies the formulas you specify using the values in the original record and places the result in the updated copy. It then updates your database by writing the updated copy to your table. Because updates are made to the copy before updating the table, you can, for example, swap the values in a field named A and a field named B by specifying an Update To setting of [B] for the A field and an Update To setting of [A] for the B field. If Access were making changes directly to the original record, you'd need to use a third field to swap values because the first assignment of B to A would destroy the original value of A.

If you remember from Chapter 7, we also discussed the possibility of reducing the highest daily rate charged for a room to $90. If you do that, you must also update the WeeklyRate value to make sure it doesn't exceed six times the new daily rate. First, build a query to find all rows that have a value in the DailyRate field that exceeds the new maximum. As before, start a query on tblFacilityRooms and include the FacilityID, RoomNumber, DailyRate, and WeeklyRate fields. Place the criterion >**90** under the DailyRate field. Your query should look like Figure 9-8. If you run this query, you'll find 10 rows that meet this criterion in the sample database.

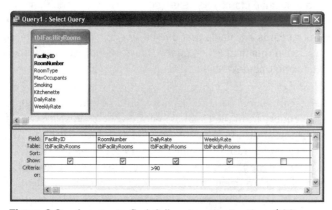

Figure 9-8. A query to find daily rates greater than $90.

Now comes the tricky part. Change your query to an update query and enter **90** on the Update To row under DailyRate. You might be tempted to set Update To under WeeklyRate to [**DailyRate**]*6 again, but you would be wrong. The reference to [DailyRate] gets you the *original* value of that field in each row—*before* it gets updated to the value 90. You know you're going to set DailyRate in rows that qualify to 90, so enter the constant **540** or the expression (**90 * 6**) in the Update To line under WeeklyRate. Your update query should now look like Figure 9-9.

Tip   Performing multiple updates with expressions that reference table fields

If you want to increase (or decrease) DailyRate by some percentage, then you should repeat the calculation for the new DailyRate value and multiply by 6 to calculate the new WeeklyRate. For example, if you want to increase the rate by 10 percent, your expression in Update To for the DailyRate field is

```
CCur(Round([DailyRate] * 1.1, 0))
```

Then your expression under WeeklyRate should be

```
CCur(Round([DailyRate] * 1.1), 0)) * 6
```

Remember, DailyRate in any expression references the *old* value in the row before it is updated.

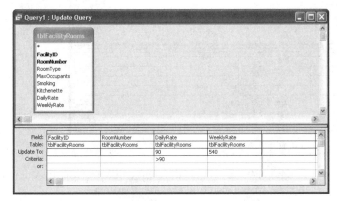

Figure 9-9.   A query to find daily rates greater than $90.

You can find this query saved as *qxmplUpdateDailyWeekly* in the sample database.

Creating an Update Query Using Multiple Tables or Queries

The target of an update query should generally be one table, but you might need to update a table based on criteria you apply to a related query or table. Consider the tblContacts table in the LawTrack Contacts sample application. The table contains an Inactive field that you can set to Yes to remove that contact from most displays without removing the row from the database. Although you can edit each contact individually and choose to mark them inactive, you occasionally might want to run an update query that automatically sets this flag when the contact hasn't had any activity for a long time.

You studied how to solve a complex unmatched problem in Chapter 8, "Building Complex Queries." You need to apply a similar concept to this problem—find the contacts who have activity since a certain date of interest and then use an outer join to identify those who have no activity so that you can mark them inactive.

The sample database contains contact events from November 2, 2002, through April 25, 2003. If you were using this data actively, you would be entering new contact events every day, but this sample data is static. Let's assume that today is October 1, 2003, and you want to flag any contact who hasn't had any event in the last six months.

First, you need to find out who hasn't contacted you since April 1, 2003. Start by opening the *ContactsDataCopy.mdb* sample database. Start a query on tblContactEvents and include the fields ContactID and ContactDateTime in the query grid. Under ContactDateTime, enter a criterion of >=#4/1/2003#. Your query should look like Figure 9-10.

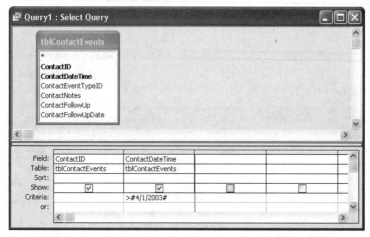

Figure 9-10. A query to find contact events since April 1, 2003.

If you run this query, you'll find 10 rows for six different contacts. Save this query as qryContactsSinceApril2003. (You can also find the query saved as *qxmplContactEventsSince01April2003* in the sample database.)

Next, you want to find who has not contacted you in this time frame. Start a new query on tblContacts and add the query you just built. You should see a join line linking the ContactID field in tblContacts and the ContactID field in your query. Remember from Chapter 8 that you need an outer join from the table to the query to fetch all rows from tblContacts and any matching rows from the query. Double-click the join line to open the Join Properties dialog box and choose the option to include all rows from tblContacts and any matching rows from qryContactsSinceApril2003. You should now have an arrow pointing from the table to the query.

Include in the query grid the ContactID, FirstName, LastName, and Inactive fields from tbl-Contacts and the ContactID field from the query. You want contacts who aren't in the list of "recent" contact events, so add the Is Null test on the Critiera line under ContactID from the query. Your query should now look like Figure 9-11.

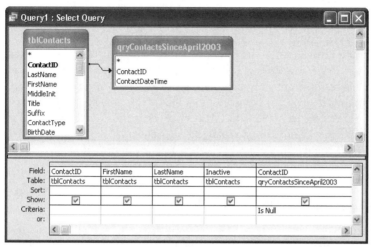

Figure 9-11. A query to find contacts with no contact events since April 1, 2003.

If you run this query, you'll find out that there are no contact events after the specified date for 12 of the 18 contacts. Remember, this is only an example.

Now you have the contacts you want to set as inactive. In Design view, turn the query into an update query. Under the Inactive field, set Update To to True. You can now run this query to verify that it does mark the 12 contacts Inactive. You can find this query saved as *qxmplUpdateInactive* in the sample database.

Inside Out

Making update queries generic with parameters

In Chapter 7, "Creating and Working with Simple Queries," you learned how to create a date/time comparison expression using the DateDiff function. In Chapter 8, "Building Complex Queries," you learned how to define parameters in your queries. In the example to update inactive status, you entered a specific comparison date in the select query you built. If you really want to save and run a query like this periodically, the select query shouldn't use a static value that you would have to change each time you wanted to perform this update. Using DateDiff, you can define a comparison with an offset relative to the current date. With a parameter, you can create a dynamic prompt for the date you want at the time you run the query.

You might also want to write a converse query that clears the Inactive field for contacts who *do* have recent contact events.

345

Creating a New Table with a Make-Table Query

Sometimes you might want to save as a new table the data that you extract with a select query. If you find that you keep executing the same query over and over against data that isn't changing, it can be faster to access the data from a table rather than from the query, particularly if the query must join several tables.

In the last chapter, you created a very complex query using a Cartesian product to drive your PivotTable and PivotChart. At the end of each month or quarter, you might want to use a query like this to create a series of reports. When you have tens of thousands of reservations in your database, this complex query might take a long time to run for each report. You will save a lot of time if you first save the result of the complex query as a temporary table and then run your reports from that table. Also, once reservations are completed for a prior period of time, they're not likely to change, so permanently saving the data selected by a query as a table could be useful for gathering summary information that you intend to keep long after you delete the detailed data on which the query is based.

Creating a Make-Table Query

In the Housing Reservations application, assume that at the end of each quarter you want to create and save a table that captures reservations detail for the quarter by facility, department, and employee. Open the *HousingDataCopy.mdb* sample database to follow along with the examples in this section. You might recall from the exercises in building the complex query to provide data for a PivotTable that you need to include tblDepartments, tblFacilities, tblEmployees, and tblReservations. You might also want to include a second copy of tblEmployees to capture the department manager and a copy of tblFacilityRooms to capture the room types. You're essentially unnormalizing the data to create a single archive table that you can also use in reports.

As with most action queries, it's a good idea to start with a select query to verify that you're working with the correct data. Start a new query on tblFacilities. Add tblFacilityRooms, tblReservations (and remove the extra join line between tblFacilities and tblReservations), tblEmployees, and tblDepartments. Be sure to also remove the extra relationship between the EmployeeNumber field in tblEmployees and the ManagerNumber field in tblDepartments. Add tblEmployees one more time—the first gets you employees who have reservations, and the second one gives you the managers for the departments. Access names this second table tblEmployees_1 to avoid a duplicate name. Create a join line from EmployeeNumber in tblEmployees_1 to ManagerNumber in tblDepartments.

To avoid confusion with the two copies of tblEmployees, click on tblEmployees_1 to select it and open the Field List Properties window as shown in Figure 9-12. You can actually assign an alias name to any field list (table or query) in your query. In this case, change the name of the second copy of tblEmployees to Managers.

Chapter 9

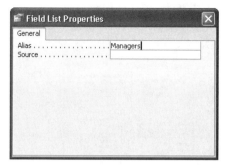

Figure 9-12. Assigning an alias name to a field list in a query.

Now you're ready to begin defining fields. Create an expression to display the employee name in the first field:

```
EmpName: tblEmployees.LastName & ", " & tblEmployees.FirstName &
 (" " + tblEmployees.MiddleName)
```

In the query grid, include the Department field from tblDepartments, and then add the manager name in the next column with an expression:

```
MgrName: Managers.LastName & ", " & Managers.FirstName &
(" " + Managers.MiddleName)
```

Notice that you're using the new alias name of the second copy of tblEmployees. On the Field line, add the ReservationID field from tblReservations, the FacilityName field from tblFacilities, the RoomNumber field from tblReservations, and the RoomType field from tblFacilityRooms. Add an expression in the next field to calculate the actual charge per day. Remember, you could use the DailyRate field from tblReservations, but that's not an accurate reflection of how much the room costs per day when the employee stays a week or more. Your expression should look like this:

```
DailyCharge: CCur(Round(tblReservations.TotalCharge /
    (tblReservations.CheckOutDate - tblReservations.CheckInDate), 2))
```

Your query design should now look something like Figure 9-13 on the next page.

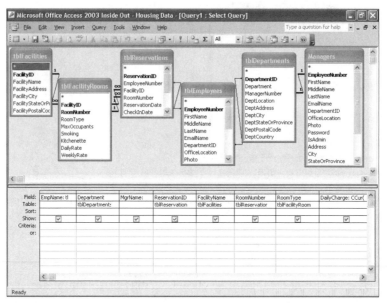

Figure 9-13. Designing a complex query to gather together many details about reservations.

Each row in tblReservations represents a stay of one or more days, but any report you create later might need to work with detail by individual day. To do that, you need to "explode" each single row in tblReservations into a row per day for the duration of the reservation. Recall from Chapter 8 that you'll find a "driver" table—ztblDates—full of dates to accomplish this task. The table contains date values, one per day, for dates from January 1, 1992, to December 31, 2035.

Include this table in your query and notice that there's no join line to any of the tables. When you add a table with no join defined to another table or set of records, the query returns the *Cartesian product* of the two sets of records—every row in the first table or set of records is matched with every row in the second table or set of records. In this case, each reservation will now be matched with each of the separate date values in ztblDates.

When you run this query later to create your working statistics table, you're not going to want to have to open up the query each time in Design view to filter the dates. A couple of parameters would be a good idea here. Add the DateValue field from ztblDates and enter **Between** [**Start Date**] **And** [**End Date**] under this field on the Criteria line. Choose Parameters from the Queries menu, enter both parameters ([**Start Date**] and [**End Date**]) and set the data type to Date/Time. You have now provided a way to limit the "explosion" of rows to the dates of interest.

The final step is to further limit the rows created based on the CheckInDate and CheckOutDate fields in tblReservations. Any reservation that crosses the time span of interest is going to be for a few days or a few weeks. Add the CheckInDate and CheckOutDate fields from tblReservations and clear the Show check box under each. In the Criteria row under Check-InDate, enter

```
<=ztblDates.DateValue
```

Under CheckOutDate, enter

```
>ztblDates.DateValue
```

This forces the query to keep any rows where DateValue from ztblDates is within the time span of each reservation row. You now have one row per date for each reservation. Your query should now look like Figure 9-14.

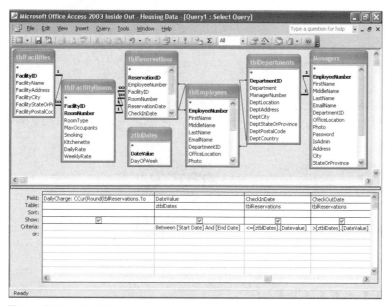

Figure 9-14. Building a complex parameter query to expand reservation details over a specified time span.

Switch to Datasheet view to verify that you'll get the rows you want. The sample data contains reservations from April 1, 2003, through November 16, 2003. To get data for the third quarter of 2003, you can reply to the two parameter prompts with July 1, 2003, and September 30, 2003. Your result should look like Figure 9-15 on the next page.

To convert this select query to a make-table query, switch back to Design view and choose Make-Table Query from the Query menu. Access displays the Make Table dialog box, shown in Figure 9-16 on the next page. Type in an appropriate name for the summary table you are creating, and click OK to close the dialog box.

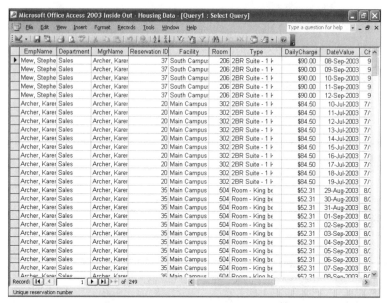

Figure 9-15. The recordset of the select query shown in Figure 9-14, for the third quarter of 2003.

Figure 9-16. The Make Table dialog box.

At any time, you can change the name of the table your query creates. Choose the Properties command from the View menu whenever the query is in Design view and change the Destination Table property. In this case, I entered a working table name. (I tend to prefix my working tables with the letter *z* to put them at the bottom of the table list.) After you run this query for a particular quarter, you're probably going to rename the table to indicate the actual quarter's worth of data that the table contains. You can find this make-table query saved in the sample database as *qxmplReservationDetailsMakeTable*.

Running a Make-Table Query

After you set up a make-table query, you can run it by choosing Run from the Query menu or by clicking the Run button on the toolbar. After you respond to the date parameter prompts, Access selects the records that will be placed in the new table and displays a confirmation dialog box, as shown in Figure 9-17, that informs you how many rows you'll be inserting into the new table.

Click the Yes button to create your new table and insert the rows. Switch to the Database window and click the Tables button to bring up the table list, which should now include the name of your new table. Open the table in Datasheet view to verify the information, as shown in Figure 9-18.

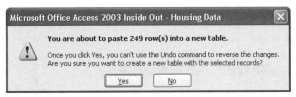

Figure 9-17. The dialog box that asks you to confirm the preliminary results of a make-table query.

Figure 9-18. The result of running the qxmplReservationDetailsMakeTable query.

Inside Out

Make-table query limitations

One of the shortcomings of a make-table query is it propagates only the field name and data type to the resulting table. Running the query does not set other property settings such as Caption or Decimal Places in the target table. This is why you see only field names instead of the original captions in Datasheet view. Notice also that the sequence of rows in the new table (Figure 9-18) does not match the sequence of rows you saw when you looked at the Datasheet view of your make-table query (Figure 9-15). Because the data in a table created with a make-table query has no primary key, Access returns the rows in the order that they're stored physically in the database.

You might want to switch to Design view, as shown in Figure 9-19, to correct field names or to define formatting information. As you can see, Access copies only basic field attributes when creating a new table.

At a minimum, you should define a primary key that contains the DateValue and ReservationID fields. You might also want to define default formats for the date/time fields. If you're planning to create reports on this data that sort or group by department or facility, you should add indexes to those fields.

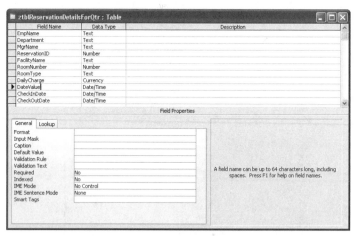

Figure 9-19. The Design view of the table created by the qxmplReservationDetails-MakeTable make-table query.

Inserting Data from Another Table

Using an append query, you can copy a selected set of information from one or more tables and insert it into another table. You can also use an append query to bring data from another source into your database—for example, a list of names and addresses purchased from a mailing list company—and then edit the data and insert it into an existing table. (You learned how to import data from external sources in Chapter 6, "Importing and Linking Data.")

An append query, like a make-table query, provides a way to collect calculated totals or unnormalized rows from several tables. The difference is that a make-table query always creates a new table from the data you select, but an append query copies the data into an existing table that might or might not already contain data. You must always modify the design of the table that a make-table query creates (if only to add efficient search indexes) to make it work optimally. Because the target table must already exist for an append query, you can explicitly define needed field properties and indexes (including a primary key) in advance. However, it's easier to run into errors because you're trying to insert data that's already there (based on the primary key you defined), because the data you're adding doesn't match the data type you defined in the table, or because the new data fails one or more validation rules.

See "Troubleshooting Action Queries," page 360, for a specific discussion of potential errors.

Creating an Append Query

In the previous example, you saw how to take one of the complex queries you learned about in Chapter 8 and turn it into a make-table query. In truth, if you plan to collect such data over several months or years, you should probably design a table to hold the results and use append queries to periodically insert new historical data.

Another good use of append queries is to copy old transaction data to an archive table—either in the current database or another database. For example, after several months or years, the contact events table in the LawTrack Contacts application might contain thousands of rows. You might want to keep all events, but copying them to an archive table and deleting them from the main table can improve application performance. (You'll learn about delete queries later in this chapter.)

Let's build an append query to select old contact events and copy them to an archive table. Open the *ContactsDataCopy.mdb* database to follow along in this exercise. You'll find an empty tblContactEventsHistory table defined in this database.

Start a new query on tblContactEvents. Because the ContactEventTypeID field is a "lookup" to tlkpContactEventTypes, it would be a good idea to preserve the original description of the event rather than the code number. If you kept the original ContactEventTypeID, any changes you made in the future to the related ContactEventDescription would also change the meaning in the archived records. So, add the tblkpContactEventTypes table so that you can store the current description rather than the ID in the history table. You should see a join line linking the ContactEventTypeID fields in the two tables.

Add the fields ContactID and ContactDateTime from tblContactEvents to the query design grid. Include in the grid the ContactEventTypeDescription field from tlkpContactEvent-Types. Finally, add to the query design grid the ContactNotes field from tblContactEvents. Because you are saving events in a history table, you don't need the ContactFollowUp and ContactFollowUpDate fields from tblContactEvents.

You want to be able to filter the records on the date and time of the event. Each time you run this query, you probably don't want to archive any recent events, so you need to create a prompt to select events that are a specified number of months old. A couple of handy date/time functions are available for you to do this: DateSerial and DateAdd. DateSerial returns a date value from a year, month, and day input. You can use it to calculate the first date of the current month like this:

```
DateSerial(Year(Date()), Month(Date()), 1)
```

Remember from Table 7-5, page 244, that the Date function returns today's date, the Year function returns the four-digit year value from a date value, and the Month function returns the month number from a date value. Supplying the value 1 for the day number gets you the date of the first day of the current month.

Chapter 9

> **Tip** You can usually think of more than one way to calculate a date value that you want. To calculate the date of the first day of the current month, you could also write the expression
>
> ```
> (Date() - Day(Date()) + 1)
> ```
>
> This subtracts the day number of the current date from the current date—resulting in the last day of the previous month—and adds one. For example, August 17, 2003, minus 17 yields July 31, 2003, plus one yields August 1, 2003.

DateAdd adds or subtracts seconds, minutes, hours, days, months, or years from a date value. You specify the interval you want by choosing a value from Table 7-3 on page 236—in this case, you want *m* to indicate that you want to add or subtract months. Finally, you can include a parameter so that you can specify the number of months you want to subtract. So, under the ContactDateTime field, include the criterion

```
<DateAdd("m", -[MonthsAgo], DateSerial(Year(Date()),Month(Date()),1))
```

Choose Parameters from the Query menu and define the parameter MonthsAgo as Integer. The DateAdd function will return the date that is the number of specified months in the past from the first date of the current month. For example, if today is August 17, 2003, when you respond **6** to MonthsAgo, the expression returns February 1, 2003 (six months prior to August 1). Making sure that the value in ContactDateTime is less than this value ensures that you archive only contacts that are at least six months old. Your query up to this point should look like Figure 9-20.

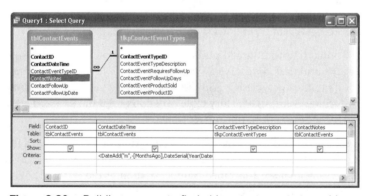

Figure 9-20. Building a query to find old contact events to archive.

The sample database contains contact events from November 2, 2002, through April 25, 2003. If you want to experiment with this query, you need to take into account the current date on your machine. For example, if you're running this query in November of 2003, you must specify a MonthsAgo value of no more than 12 to see any records. Likewise, specifying a MonthsAgo value of less than 6 shows you all the records.

Now, it's time to turn this into an append query. Choose Append Query from the Query menu or select Append Query from the drop-down list next to the Query Type button on the toolbar. You'll see the dialog box shown in Figure 9-21 asking you where you want the selected rows inserted (appended).

Figure 9-21. Specifying the target table of an append query.

Notice that the default is to append the data into a table in the current database. You can click the Another Database option and either type in the path and name of the target database or click the Browse button to find the file you want. This feature could be particularly handy if you want to archive the records to another file. In this case, choose tblContactEventsHistory in the current database and click the OK button. Your query design now looks like Figure 9-22.

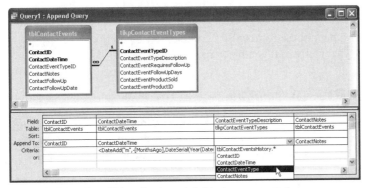

Figure 9-22. Specifying the target fields in an append query.

Notice that Access added an Append To line and automatically filled in the matching field names from the target table. Remember, you want to append the field ContactEventType-Description from tlkpContactEventTypes to the ContactEventType field in the history table, so choose that field from the drop-down list on the Append To line under ContactEvent-TypeDescription.

You're now ready to run this query in the next section. You can find the query saved as *qxmpl-ArchiveContactEvents* in the sample database. You'll also find a companion *qxmplArchiveCon-tactProducts* query.

Running an Append Query

As with other action queries, you can run an append query as a select query first to be sure that you'll be copying the right rows. You can either start out by building a select query, running it, and then converting it to an append query, or you can build the append query directly and then switch to Datasheet view from Design view to examine the data that the query will add. Although you can find and delete rows that you append in error, you can save time if you make a backup of the target table first.

After you confirm that the query will append the right rows, you can either run it directly from Design view or save it and run it from the Database window. When you run the qxmpl-ArchiveContactEvents query and respond to the MonthsAgo prompt so that Access archives events earlier than January 1, 2003, Access should tell you that 23 rows will be appended, as shown in Figure 9-23. If you want to append the rows to the tblContactEventsHistory table, click Yes in the confirmation dialog box. Note that once you click Yes, the only way to undo these changes is to go to the target table and either select and delete the rows manually or build a delete query to do it.

Figure 9-23. The dialog box that asks you to confirm the appending of rows.

Go ahead and append these 23 rows. In "Troubleshooting Action Queries," page 360, we'll take a look at what happens if you try to run this query again.

Deleting Groups of Rows

You're not likely to keep all the data in your database forever. You'll probably summarize some of your detailed information as time goes by and then delete the data you no longer need. You can remove sets of records from your database using a delete query.

Testing with a Select Query

Once you have copied all the old contact event and contact product data to the archive tables, you might want to remove this information from the active tables. This is clearly the kind of query that you will want to save so that you can use it again and again. You can design the query to automatically calculate which records to delete based on the current system date and a month parameter as you did in the append queries.

As with an update query, it's a good idea to test which rows will be affected by a delete query by first building a select query to isolate these records. Start a new query on tblContactEvents and include the asterisk (*) field in the query grid. A delete query acts on entire rows, so including the "all fields" indicator will ultimately tell the delete query from which table the rows should be deleted. Add the ContactDateTime field to the design grid, and clear the Show check box. This time, let's use a specific date value to pick rows to delete. In the Criteria line under the ContactDateTime field enter

```
<[Oldest Date to Keep:]
```

Chapter 9

Choose Parameters from the Query menu, and define your parameter as a Date/Time data type. Your query should look like Figure 9-24.

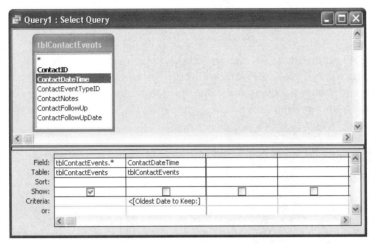

Figure 9-24. A query with a date parameter to select old contact events.

When you switch to Datasheet view for this query, Access prompts you for a date parameter, as shown in Figure 9-25. In the Enter Parameter Value dialog box, enter 1/1/2003 to see all the old contact events from 2002 or earlier. The result is shown in Figure 9-26.

Figure 9-25. Entering the query date parameter.

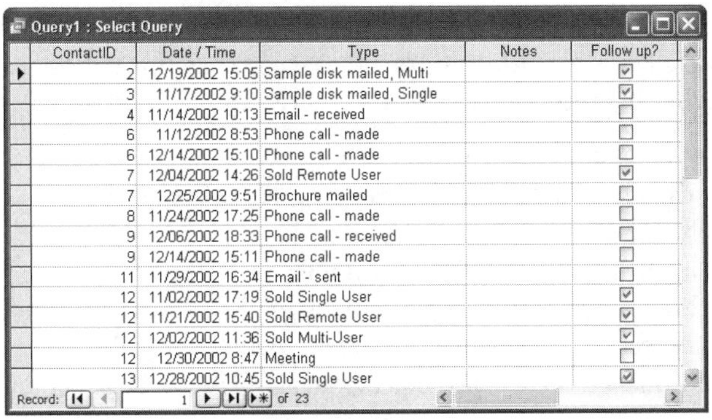

ContactID	Date / Time	Type	Notes	Follow up?
2	12/19/2002 15:05	Sample disk mailed, Multi		☑
3	11/17/2002 9:10	Sample disk mailed, Single		☑
4	11/14/2002 10:13	Email - received		☐
6	11/12/2002 8:53	Phone call - made		☐
6	12/14/2002 15:10	Phone call - made		☐
7	12/04/2002 14:26	Sold Remote User		☑
7	12/25/2002 9:51	Brochure mailed		☐
8	11/24/2002 17:25	Phone call - made		☐
9	12/06/2002 18:33	Phone call - received		☐
9	12/14/2002 15:11	Phone call - made		☐
11	11/29/2002 16:34	Email - sent		☐
12	11/02/2002 17:19	Sold Single User		☑
12	11/21/2002 15:40	Sold Remote User		☑
12	12/02/2002 11:36	Sold Multi-User		☑
12	12/30/2002 8:47	Meeting		☐
13	12/28/2002 10:45	Sold Single User		☑

Figure 9-26. Verifying the rows to delete.

Chapter 9

357

> **Tip** Access recognizes several different formats for date parameters. For example, for
> the first day in 2003, you can enter any of the following.
>
> 1/1/2003   January 1, 2003   1 JAN 2003

The append query you saw earlier that copied these rows to an archive table copied 23 rows,
which matches what you see here. After you verify that this is what you want, go back to
Design view and change the query to a delete query by choosing Delete Query from the
Query menu. Your query should look like Figure 9-27. *Do Not Run This Query!* I'll explain
why in the next section.

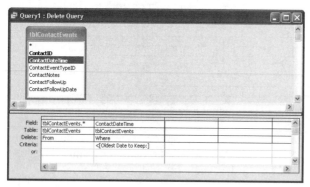

Figure 9-27.   Converting your query to a delete query.

Notice that the query has a new Delete line. In any delete query, you should select From under
the "choose all fields" (*) field for the one table from which you want to delete rows. All other
fields should indicate Where and have one or more criteria on the Criteria and Or lines.

Using a Delete Query

Because you won't be able to retrieve any deleted rows, it's a good idea to first make a backup
copy of your table, especially if this is the first time that you've run this delete query. Use the
procedure described earlier in "Running an Update Query" on page 340 to make a copy of
your table.

As you just learned, you can create a delete query from a select query by choosing the Delete
Query command from the Query Type menu when your query is in Design view. You must be
sure that at least one table includes the "all the rows" indicator (*) and has From specified on
the Delete line. Simply choose Run from the Query menu or click the Run button on the toolbar to delete the rows you specified. Because you included a parameter in this query, you'll need
to respond to the Enter Parameter Value dialog box (shown in Figure 9-25) again. Access selects
the rows to be deleted and displays the confirmation dialog box shown in Figure 9-28.

Are you *really, really* sure you want to delete these rows? Are you sure these rows are safely
tucked away in the archive table? If so, click the Yes button to proceed with the deletion. Click

the No button if you're unsure about the rows that Access will delete. (I recommend you click No for now and read on!) You can find this query saved as *qxmplDeleteOldContactEventsUnsafe* in the sample database. (Does the query name give you a clue?)

Figure 9-28. The dialog box that asks you to confirm the deletion of rows.

Deleting Inactive Data

You now know how to copy old contact event and contact product data to an archive table, and how to delete the old contact events from the main table. In some applications, you might want to delete more than just the event records. For example, in an order entry database, you might want to archive and delete old customers who haven't given you any business in more than two years.

In the LawTrack Contacts application, you can mark old contacts as inactive so that they disappear from the primary forms you use to edit the data. In an earlier section, "Updating Groups of Rows," I showed you how to identify contacts who haven't had any activity in a specified period of time and set the Inactive field so they don't show up anymore. Because of this feature, archiving and deleting old contacts isn't an issue.

However, you might still want to delete old contact events and contact products that you have archived. I just showed you how to create a delete query to remove rows, but there's a safer way to do it if you have copied the rows elsewhere. Go back to the query you have been building and add tblContactEventsHistory. Create a join line between the ContactID field in tblContactEvents and the ContactID field in tblContactEventsHistory. Create another join line between the ContactDateTime field in tblContactEvents and the same field in tblContactEventsHistory. Your query should now look like Figure 9-29.

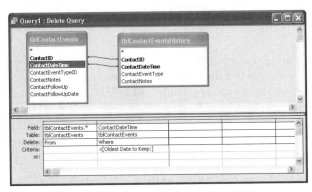

Figure 9-29. A query to safely delete archived rows.

Remember that the default for a join is to include rows only where the values in both tables match. Now your delete query won't return any rows from tblContactEvents (where you're performing the delete) unless the row already exists in tblContactEventHistory! Run this query now and reply with any date you like. The query won't delete rows from tblContactEvents unless a copy is safely ensconced in the archive table. You can find this query saved as *qxmplDeleteOldContactEventsSafe* in the sample database. There's also a companion query, *qxmplDeleteOldContactProductsSafe*, to deal with contact products.

Troubleshooting Action Queries

Access analyzes your action query request and the data you are about to change before it commits changes to your database. When it identifies errors, Access always gives you an opportunity to cancel the operation.

Solving Common Action Query Errors and Problems

Access identifies (traps) four types of errors during the execution of an action query.

- **Duplicate primary keys**   This type of error occurs if you attempt to append a record to a table or update a record in a table that would result in a duplicate primary key or a duplicate of a unique index key value. Access will not update or append any rows that would create duplicates. For example, if the primary key of a contact event archive table is ContactID and ContactDateTime, Access won't append a record that contains a ContactID and ContactDateTime already in the table. Before attempting to append such rows, you might have to modify your append query to not select the duplicate rows.

- **Data conversion errors**   This type of error occurs if you attempt to append data to an existing table and the data type of the receiving field does not match that of the sending field (and the data in the sending field cannot be converted to the appropriate data type). For example, this error will occur if you attempt to append a text field to an integer field and the text field contains either alphabetic characters or a number string that is too large for the integer field. You might also encounter a conversion error in an update query if you use a formula that attempts a calculation on a field that contains characters. For information on data conversions and potential limitations, see Table 5-3 on page 156.

- **Locked records**   This type of error can occur when you run a delete query or an update query on a table that you share with other users on a network. Access cannot update records that are in the process of being updated by some other user. You might want to wait and try again later when no one else is using the affected records to be sure that your update or deletion occurs. Even if you're not sharing the data on a network, you can encounter this error if you have a form or another query open on the data you're updating and have started to change some of the data.

- **Validation rule violations**   If any of the rows being inserted or any row being updated violates either a field validation rule or the table validation rule, Access notifies you of an error and does not insert or update any of the rows that fail the validation test.

When you have a referential integrity rule defined, you cannot update or delete a row in a way that would violate the rule.

Another problem that can occur, although it isn't an error, is that Access truncates data that is being appended to text or memo fields if the data does not fit. Access does not warn you when this happens. You must be sure (especially with append queries) that the receiving text and memo fields have been defined large enough to store the incoming data.

Looking at an Error Example

Earlier in this chapter, you learned how to create an append query to copy old contact events to an archive table. What do you suppose would happen if you copied rows through December 31, 2002, forgot to delete them from the main table, and then later asked to copy rows through April 30, 2003? If you try this starting with an empty archive table in the *ContactsDataCopy.mdb* database, run *qxmplArchiveContactEvents* once and then run it again with the same or later cut-off month, you'll get an error dialog box similar to the one shown in Figure 9-30.

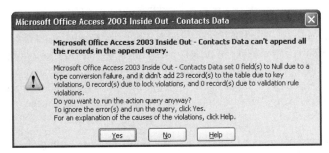

Figure 9-30. The dialog box that alerts you to action query errors.

The dialog box in Figure 9-30 declares that 23 records won't be inserted because of duplicate primary key values. Access didn't find any data conversion errors, locking problems, or validation rule errors. Note that if some fields have data conversion problems, Access might still append the row but leave the field set to Null. When you see this dialog box, you can click the Yes button to proceed with the changes that Access can make without errors. You might find it difficult later, however, to track down all the records that were not updated successfully. Click the No button to cancel the append query.

To solve this problem, you can change the "select" part of the query to choose only the rows that haven't already been inserted into the target table. Remember from the previous chapter the technique you used to find "unmatched" rows. You'll apply that same technique to solve this problem.

Open the query you built in the previous section (or *qxmplArchiveContactEvents*) in Design view. Add tblContactEventsHistory (the target table) to your query. Create join lines from the ContactID field in tblContactEvents to the same field in tblContactEventHistory. Do the same with ContactDateTime. Double-click each join line to open the Join Properties dialog box and choose the option to include all rows from tblContactEvents and the matching rows from tblContactEventsHistory. You must do this for each join line so that you end up with both lines pointing to tblContactEventsHistory. Include the ContactID field from tblContactEventsHistory in the design grid, clear the Append To box underneath it (you don't want to try to insert ContactID twice), and place the criterion Is Null on the Criteria line. Your query should now look like Figure 9-31.

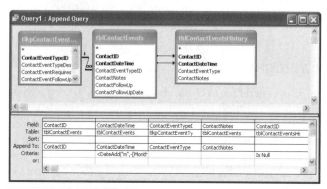

Figure 9-31. Designing an append query to avoid duplicate row errors.

The end result is that this query will select rows from tblContactEvents only if they don't already exist in the archive table. You can now run this query as many times as you like. If all the rows you choose already exist, the query simply inserts no additional rows. You can find this query saved as *qxmplArchiveContactEventsNoDuplicates* in the sample database. There's also a companion query, *qxmplArchiveContactProductsNoDuplicates*, to handle the archiving of contact product records.

 At this point, you should have a reasonable understanding of how action queries can work for you. You can find some more examples of action queries in Article 1, "Understanding SQL," on the companion CD. Now it's time to go on to building the user interface for your application with forms and reports.

Part 3

Creating Forms and Reports in a Desktop Application

Using Forms

If you've worked through this book to this point, you should understand all the mechanics of designing and building databases (and connecting to external ones), entering and viewing data in tables, and building queries. An understanding of tables and queries is important before you jump into forms because most of the forms you design will be bound to an underlying table or a query.

This chapter focuses on the external aspects of forms—why forms are useful, what they look like, and how to use them. You'll look at examples of forms from the LawTrack Contacts sample database. In Chapters 11, 12, and 13, you'll learn how to design, build, and customize your own forms by learning to build some of the forms you see in the LawTrack Contacts and Housing Reservations databases.

Uses of Forms

Forms are the primary interface between users and your Microsoft Access application. You can design forms for many different purposes.

- **Displaying and editing data** This is the most common use of forms. Forms provide a way to customize the presentation of the data in your database. You can also use forms to change or delete data in your database or add data to it. You can set options in a form to make all or part of your data read-only, to fill in related information from other tables automatically, to calculate the values to be displayed, or to show or hide data on the basis of either the values of other data in the record or the options selected by the user of the form.

- **Controlling application flow** You can design forms that work with macros or with Microsoft Visual Basic procedures to automate the display of certain data or the sequence of certain actions. You can create special controls on your form, called *command buttons*, that run a macro or a Visual Basic procedure when you click them. With macros and Visual Basic procedures, you can open other forms, run queries, restrict the data that is displayed, execute a menu command, set values in records and forms, display menus, print reports, and perform a host of other actions. You can also design a form so that macros or Visual Basic procedures run when specific events occur—for example, when someone opens the form, tabs to a specific control, clicks an option on the form, or changes data in the form. See Part 5, "Automating an Access Application," for details about using macros and Visual Basic with forms to automate your application.

- **Accepting input.** You can design forms that are used only for entering new data in your database or for providing data values to help automate your application.

- **Displaying messages** Forms can provide information about how to use your application or about upcoming actions. Access also provides a MsgBox macro action and a *MsgBox* Visual Basic function that you can use to display information, warnings, or error messages. See Chapter 23, "Automating Your Application with Visual Basic," for more detail.

- **Printing information** Although you should design and use reports to print most information, you can also print the information displayed in a form. Because you can specify one set of options when Access displays a form and another set of options when Access prints a form, a form can serve a dual role. For example, you might design a form with two sets of display headers and footers, one set for entering an order and another set for printing a customer invoice from the order.

A Tour of Forms

The LawTrack Contacts sample database is full of interesting examples of forms. The rest of this chapter takes you on a tour of some of the major features of those forms and shows you some of the basic techniques for editing data in a form. In the next chapter, you'll learn how to design and build forms for this database.

Begin by opening the LawTrack Contacts database (*Contacts.mdb*) and clicking the Forms button in the Database window to see the list of available forms. Note that when you open the database, you see a copyright notice followed by a message telling you which form to open to start the application.

Headers, Detail Sections, and Footers

You'll normally place the information that you want to display from the underlying table or query in the detail section in the center of the Form window. You can add a header at the top of the window or a footer at the bottom of the window to display information or controls that don't need to change as you move through the records.

An interesting form in the LawTrack Contacts database that includes both a header and a footer is *frmContactSummary*. The application uses this form to display the summary results of a contact search whenever the search finds more than five matching contacts. You can also open this form directly from the Database window—if you do so, it will show you all the contacts in the database. Find the *frmContactSummary* form in the forms list in the Database window, select the form, and then click the Open button to see a window similar to the one shown in Figure 10-1.

Using Forms

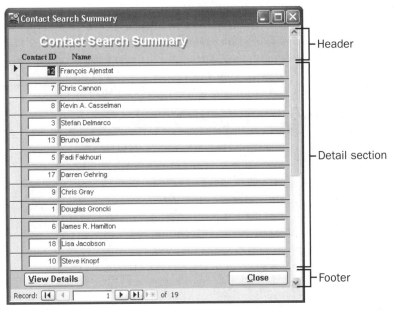

Figure 10-1. The frmContactSummary form, which has a header, a detail section, and a footer.

The area at the top of the window containing the title *Contact Search Summary* is the header for the form. The header also includes the column names. The area at the bottom of the window is the footer for the form. You can click the View Details button to see all details for the currently selected contact (the contact with the arrow on the record selector), or you can click Close to close the form. At the bottom left corner of the form is the Record Number box that you saw in tables and queries in Datasheet view. Click the arrow button immediately to the right of the record number to move the record selector arrow to the next contact record in the detail section of the form; notice that the header and footer don't change when you do this. If you move down several records, you can see the records scroll up in the detail section of the form.

If you click the View Details button in the footer, this form closes and the frmContacts form opens, showing details of the contact record that you selected before you clicked the button. The way the form is designed, the View Details button opens the frmContacts form using a filter to show you the currently selected contact. If you decide that you don't want to see details, you can click the Close button in the form footer to dismiss the form.

Multiple-Page Forms

When you have a lot of information from each record to display in a form, you can design a *multiple-page form*. Open the *frmContactsPages* form in the LawTrack Contacts database to see an example. When you open the form, you'll see the first page of contact data for the first contact. You can use the Record Number box and the buttons in the lower left corner of the form to move through the records, viewing the first page of information for each contact.

Figure 10-2 shows the first page of the 18th contact record—the records are sorted by last name. (For those of you who want to visit my Web site, that's my real Web site address in the form!) To see the second page of information for any contact, press the Page Down key. Figure 10-3 shows the second page of my contact record. (Notice that this form has a header but no footer.) As you view different pages of a multiple-page form, the header at the top of the form (with the form title and some command buttons) doesn't change.

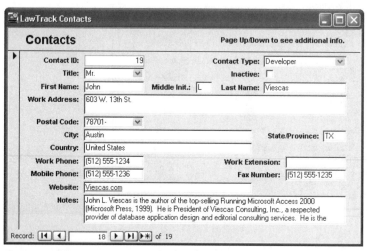

Figure 10-2. The first page of a record in the multiple-page frmContactsPages form.

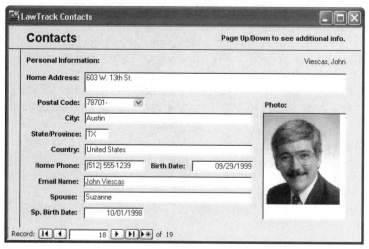

Figure 10-3. The second page of a record in the frmContactsPages form.

Continuous Forms

You can create another type of form that is useful for browsing through and editing a list of records when each record has only a few data fields. This type of form is called a *continuous form*. Rather than showing you only a single record at a time, a continuous form displays formatted records one after the other, in the manner of a datasheet.

The frmContactSummary form shown earlier in Figure 10-1 is a simple continuous form. The frmLkpContactEventTypes form, shown in Figure 10-4, is also a continuous form. You can use the vertical scroll bar to move through the record display, or you can click the buttons in the lower left corner of the form to move from record to record. Also, you can click the New Record button to move to the blank row below the last record. The application uses this form to let you view and edit the different types of contact events that you might want to log.

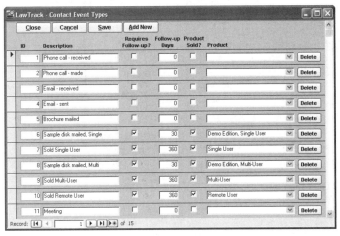

Figure 10-4. The frmLkpContactEventTypes form is a continuous form.

Subforms

Subforms are a good way to show related data from the *many* side of a one-to-many relationship. For example, the frmCompanies form, shown in Figure 10-5 on the next page, has a subform to display the related contacts. Although this form looks much like a single display panel, it has a subform (which looks more like a datasheet than a form) embedded in the main form. The main part of the frmCompanies form displays information from the tblCompanies table, while the subform in the lower part of the window shows information from the tblCompanyContacts table about the contacts related to the current company.

This form looks quite complicated, but it really isn't difficult to build. Because the LawTrack Contacts database is well designed, it doesn't take much effort to build the queries that allow the form to display information from three different tables. Most of the work of creating the form goes into selecting and placing the controls that display the data. To link a subform to a main form, you have to set only two properties that tell Access which linking fields to use. (These are actually the same Link Master Fields and Link Child Fields properties you learned about in Chapter 8, "Building Complex Queries," when you defined a subdatasheet for a query.) In Chapter 13, "Advanced Form Design," you'll build a subform and link it to a form.

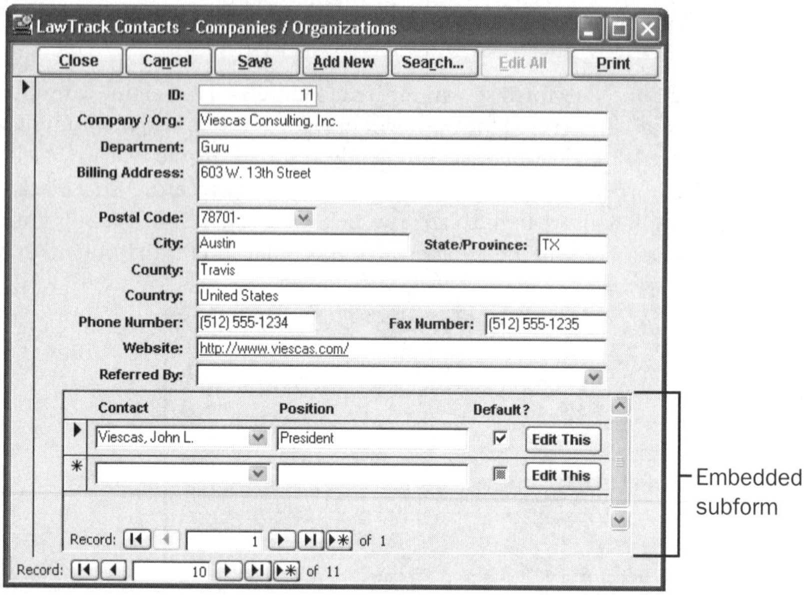

Figure 10-5. The frmCompanies form with an embedded subform that shows the related contacts.

Pop-Up Forms

Sometimes it's useful to provide information in a window that stays on top regardless of where you move the focus in your application. You've probably noticed that the default behavior for windows in Microsoft Windows is for the active window to move to the front and for all other windows to move behind the active one. One exception is the Office toolbars. If you grab a toolbar and undock it, it stays floating on top so that you can still access its commands regardless of what you are doing behind it. This sort of floating window is called a *pop-up window*.

You can create forms in Access that open in pop-up windows (called pop-up forms in Access). If you open any form in the LawTrack Contacts application and then choose About LawTrack Contacts from the Help menu, this opens the frmAbout form shown in Figure 10-6, which is designed as a pop-up form. See Chapter 24, "The Finishing Touches," for more details about how to create custom menus for forms. If you still have frmCompanies open, you can choose About LawTrack Contacts from the Help menu. Or, you can switch to the Database window and open the *frmAbout* form directly to see how it behaves. Notice that if you click in the open form or Database window behind it, the frmAbout form stays on top. Click the Close button on the pop-up form to close it.

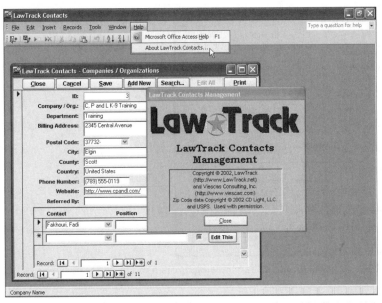

Figure 10-6. The frmAbout pop-up form "floats" on top of frmCompanies, which has the focus.

Modal Forms

As you add functionality to your application, you'll encounter situations in which you need to obtain some input from the user or convey some important information to the user before Access can proceed. Access provides a special type of form, called a *modal form*, that requires a response before the user can continue working in the application. The fdlgContactSearch dialog box in the LawTrack Contacts database, shown in Figure 10-7 on the next page, is a modal form. This dialog box normally opens when you click the Contacts button on the main switchboard form and then click the Search button on the resulting Select Contacts (frmContactList) form. This window also opens if you first open *frmContacts* and then click the Search button. You can open the form on which the dialog box is based directly from the Database window. You'll notice that as long as this dialog box is open, you can't select any other window or menu in the application. To proceed, you must either enter some search criteria and click the Search button or click the Cancel button to dismiss the form.

Chapter 10

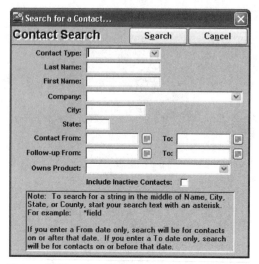

Figure 10-7. The fdlgContactSearch dialog box is a modal form.

Inside Out

Using name prefixes to organize your objects

Have you noticed the different prefixes on the form names that I designed in the LawTrack Contacts application? I like to create a prefix that helps me know more about the type of form when I look at the form list in the Database window. For example, I prefix the names of forms that are designed to open in PivotChart view with *cht*. I prefix dialog forms with *fdlg*, normal edit forms with *frm*, forms designed to edit lookup tables with *frmLkp*, and subforms with *fsub*. You might want to adopt a similar naming convention to help you keep your list of forms organized.

Special Controls

The information in a form is contained in *controls*. The most common control you'll use on a form is a simple text box. A *text box* can display data from an underlying table or query, or it can display the result of an expression calculated in the control. You've probably noticed that many controls allow you to choose from among several values or to see additional content. You can also use controls to trigger a macro or a Visual Basic procedure. These controls are discussed in the next five sections.

Option Buttons, Check Boxes, Toggle Buttons, and Option Groups

Whenever the data you're displaying can have only two or three valid values, you can use *option buttons*, *check boxes*, or *toggle buttons* to see or set the value you want in the field. For example, when there are two values, as in the case of a simple Yes/No field, you can use a check box to graphically display the value in the field. A check box that's selected means the value is Yes, and a check box that's clear means the value is No. The Inactive control on the frmContactsPages form (see Figure 10-2) and the Default? control in the subform of frm-Companies (see Figure 10-5) are good examples of the use of a check box.

Stand-alone option buttons and toggle buttons work in the same way as a check box. When the value of an option button is Yes or True, the option button has a black dot in it. When the value of an option button is No or False, the option button appears empty. Likewise a toggle button appears pressed in when True, and not pressed in when False.

To provide a graphical choice among more than two values, you can place option buttons, check boxes, or toggle buttons in an *option group*. When grouped this way, each control in the group should have a unique integer value. When the control appears selected, the value of the option group is the value of the control. Because an option group can have only one value, when you select a control within the group, all other controls in the group appear unselected because their values no longer match the value of the option group.

For example, open *frmProducts* (this form displays the different products available), and click the Print button to see the fdlgProductPrintOptions form (shown in Figure 10-8) that lists the various contact reporting options. (You cannot open fdlgProductPrintOptions directly from the Database window—it has Visual Basic code that runs when the form opens to verify that the companion frmProducts form is already open. If not, the code tells Access to not allow the form to open.) If you open this form and click the available option buttons, you can see that when you click one button, the previously selected one clears. When you click one of the sales report buttons on this form, the form reveals additional date range options for your sales report.

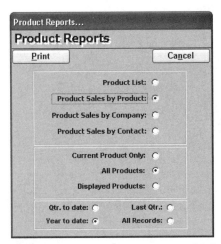

Figure 10-8. Option groups on the fdlgProductPrintOptions form.

List Boxes and Combo Boxes

When you want to display a list of data values in an open list, a *list box* is a good choice. When you view objects in the Database window in Details view, you're looking at the tables, queries, forms, reports, macros, or modules in a list box. Likewise, in Windows Explorer the list of file names and properties in the pane on the right side when you're in Details view is a list box.

A list box can show a list of values you entered when you designed the control, a list of values returned by an SQL statement, the values of one or more fields in a table or in a query, or a list of field names from a table or a query. When you select a value from the list, you set the value of the control. You can use a list box on a form that edits data to display the value of one of the fields. When you choose a new value in the list box, you update the underlying field.

You can also define a list box in which you can select multiple values. When you do this, however, the list box cannot update an underlying field. This type of list box is useful to allow a user to choose multiple items or options that your application code will use to perform some action.

In the example shown in Figure 10-9 (the frmContactList form), the list box allows multiple selections and includes the set of names from the tblContacts table. This list box lets you select one or more entries by holding down the Shift key to select a contiguous range or by holding down the Ctrl key to select several noncontiguous entries. When you click the Edit button, a Visual Basic procedure evaluates your choices and opens the frmContacts form (see Figure 10-2) to display the selected contacts.

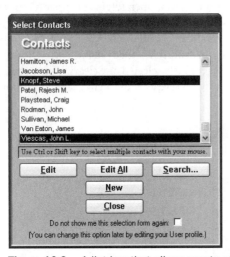

Figure 10-9. A list box that allows you to pick multiple contacts to edit.

A list box like this one can use data from more than one field. In fact, the query behind this list box returns both the ContactID field (the primary key) from tblContacts and the expression that you see containing last name, first name, and middle initial. The list box hides the ContactID, but Visual Basic code behind the form uses that hidden value to quickly find the contacts you want.

Combo boxes are similar to list boxes. The primary difference is that a *combo box* has both a text box *and* a drop-down list. One major advantage of a combo box is that it only requires space in the form for one of the values in the underlying list. However, you can choose only one value in a combo box.

The PostalCode field in the frmCompanies form (see Figure 10-5) is set using a combo box, as shown in Figure 10-10. The combo box uses four fields from the underlying query—the Zipcode, City, State, and County fields from the lookup query qlkpZips. When you select a postal code, the combo box sets the PostalCode field in the underlying record—a very useful feature. Visual Basic code attached to this control also automatically copies the related City, County, and State data from the selected row in the combo box to the fields on the form for you. As long as you know the postal code, you don't have to enter the other related information. You'll find a similar combo box used in the application wherever you need to enter a postal code on a form.

Figure 10-10. An open combo box.

> **Note** In most cases, you will choose settings that disallow choosing a value that's not in the list in your combo boxes that update fields. You can also write Visual Basic code to examine a new value that a user tries to enter and determine whether it should appear in the list. You can learn about how to create code to deal with "not in list" values in Chapter 23.

Tab Controls

Earlier in this chapter, you saw that one way to deal with the need to display lots of information on one form is to use a multiple-page form (frmContactsPages, shown in Figure 10-2 and Figure 10-3). Another way to organize the information on a single form is to use the *tab control* to provide what look like multiple folder tabs that reveal different information depending on the tab chosen—much like the Options dialog box in Microsoft Access (choose Options from the Tools menu) provides View, General, Edit/Find, Keyboard, Datasheet, Forms/Reports, Pages, Advanced, International, Error Checking, Spelling, and Tables/Queries tabs. In the LawTrack Contacts database, a contact has basic contact information and notes, as well as related companies, contact events, and products. Open the *frmContacts* form to see how the tab control displays only one of these pieces of information at a time, as shown in Figure 10-11 on the next page.

You can click the Companies tab (as shown in Figure 10-12 on the next page) or any of the other tabs to see additional information. Note that there's no programming required to implement tab selection and data display. See Chapter 13, "Advanced Form Design," for details about how to use the tab control.

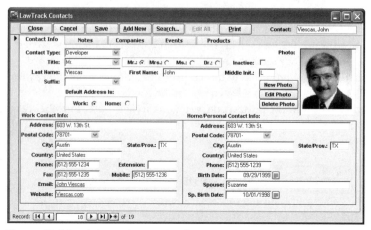

Figure 10-11. Information on the Contact Info tab in the frmContacts form.

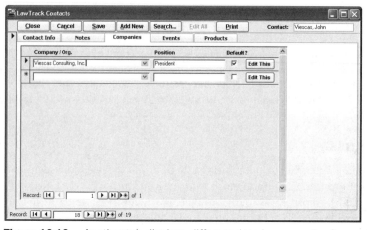

Figure 10-12. Another tab displays different data in a complex form.

ActiveX Objects

You saw the contact picture in the frmContactsPages form earlier. This picture is stored in a field in the tblContacts table using Microsoft's ActiveX technology. The logo in the top part of the main switchboard form in the LawTrack Contacts database, on the other hand, is a picture that Access has stored as part of the form. The control that you use to display a picture or any other ActiveX object is called an *object frame*. A *bound object frame* control is used to display an ActiveX object that is stored in a field in a table—such as the picture on frmContactsPages or frmContacts. When you edit the object in a bound object frame, you're updating the field in the table. An *unbound object frame* control is used to display an object that is not stored in a table. Access stores the object with the form definition, and you cannot edit it in Form view.

When you include a bound object frame control on a form and bind the control to an OLE object field in the database, you can edit that object by selecting it and then right-clicking the picture to open the shortcut menu. On the Bitmap Image Object submenu, choose Edit, as shown in Figure 10-13.

Note If you use an unbound object frame on a form, you can edit the contents of the frame only when you have the form in Design view.

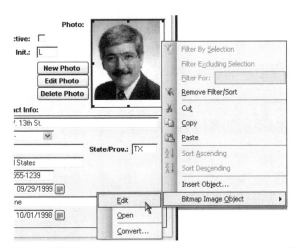

Figure 10-13. You can select a picture and then edit it by choosing the Bitmap Image Object command from the shortcut menu and then choosing Edit from the submenu.

Note The LawTrack Contacts application also provides handy New Photo, Edit Photo, and Delete Photo buttons on the frmContacts form. When the form loads, it examines your Windows registry and determines the default program on your machine to edit Bitmap (.bmp) or JPEG (.jpg) files. When you click the New or Edit button, Visual Basic code behind the form starts that program for you. You don't have to worry about navigating the complex shortcut menu.

If the object is a picture, a graph, or a spreadsheet, you can see the object in the object frame control and you can activate its application by double-clicking the object. If the object is a sound file, you can hear it by double-clicking the object frame control.

Figure 10-13 shows one of the photographs stored in the tblContacts table that is bound in an object frame control on the frmContacts form. When you double-click the picture—or select the picture and choose Bitmap Image Object from the shortcut menu and then choose Edit from the submenu—Access starts the default application on your machine to edit bitmaps. On most machines, this is the Microsoft Paint application. In Windows, Paint is an ActiveX

Chapter 10

application that can "activate in place," as shown in Figure 10-14. You can still see the Access form and menus, but Paint has added its own toolbars and menu commands. You can update the picture by using any of the Paint tools. You can paste in a different picture by copying a picture to the Clipboard and choosing the Paste command from Paint's Edit menu. After you make your changes, simply click in another area on the Access form to deactivate Paint and store the result of your edits in the object frame control. If you save the record, Access saves the changed data in your OLE object field.

Note If you have registered an application other than Microsoft Paint to handle bitmap objects, that application will be activated when you select Edit from the submenu.

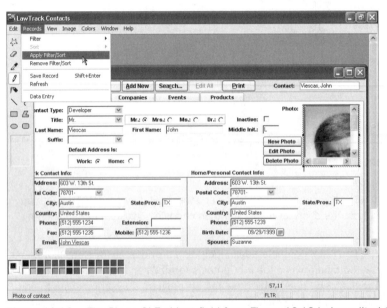

Figure 10-14. The Photo OLE object field from Figure 10-13 being edited "in place" with its host application.

Command Buttons

Another useful control is the command button, which you can use to link many forms to create a complete database application. In the LawTrack Contacts database, for example, most of the forms are linked to the main switchboard form (frmMain), shown in Figure 10-15, in which the user can click command buttons to launch various functions in the application. The advantage of command buttons is really quite simple—they offer an easy way to trigger a macro or a Visual Basic procedure. The procedure might do nothing more than open another form, print a report, or run an action query to update many records in your database. As you'll see when you get to the end of this book, you can build a fairly complex application using forms, reports, macros, and some simple Visual Basic procedures.

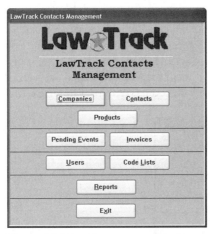

Figure 10-15. The command buttons on the frmMain switchboard form.

PivotTables and PivotCharts

In Chapter 8, "Building Complex Queries," you learned how to create the PivotTable or Pivot-Chart view of a query. You can also build a form that is connected to a table or query and switch to either PivotTable or PivotChart view to define a custom view of the underlying data. For example, take a look at the form ptContactProducts, as shown in Figure 10-16. This form is designed to open only in PivotTable view or Design view. Note that even though the query on which this form is based is updatable, you cannot update any of the field values via the PivotTable.

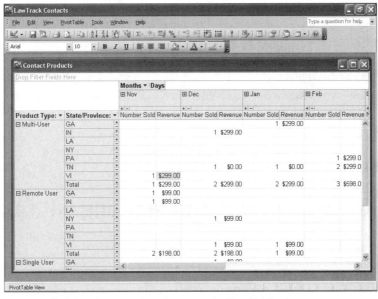

Figure 10-16. A form designed to open in PivotTable view.

Chapter 10

PivotCharts can be useful in an application to provide a related graphical representation of data displayed on a form. In the LawTrack Contacts sample database, you can find the form chtProductSales that charts sales by product and by month. This form is embedded in a report that displays product details (rptProductSalesByProductWChart) and in a sample form that lets you edit product information while viewing the related past sales data as a chart (frmProductsWithSales). You can see frmProductsWithSales in Figure 10-17.

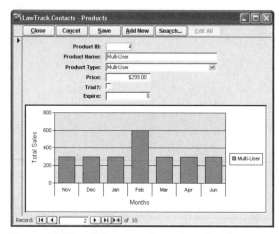

Figure 10-17. A form to edit product data with an embedded subform in PivotChart view to show related sales information.

Designing a form as a PivotTable or PivotChart has three distinct advantages over performing these functions in queries.

1   You can restrict the views of the form to display only the PivotTable or the PivotChart or both. You can set a default view for a query, but you cannot prevent the user from switching to Datasheet or Design view.

2   You can embed a form designed as a PivotTable or PivotChart in another form or in a report to display related information. You cannot embed a query in a form or report.

3   You can write Visual Basic code behind the form to dynamically modify the PivotTable or PivotChart. You can also restrict the changes a user can make to the table or chart. You cannot write code behind a query.

You'll learn more about designing forms as PivotTables or PivotCharts in Chapter 13, "Advanced Form Design."

Moving Around on Forms and Working with Data

The rest of this chapter shows you how to move around on and work with data in the various types of forms discussed earlier in the chapter.

Viewing Data

Moving around on a form is similar to moving around in a datasheet (see "Working in Query Datasheet View," page 252, but there are a few subtle differences between forms and datasheets (usually having to do with how a form was designed) that determine how a form works with data. You can use the *frmContactsPlain* form in the LawTrack Contacts database (which is a copy of frmContacts without custom menus and toolbars) to explore the ways in which forms work.

First, open the LawTrack Contacts database. Next, click the Forms button in the Database window. Select the *frmContactsPlain* form, and click the Open button to see the form shown in Figure 10-18.

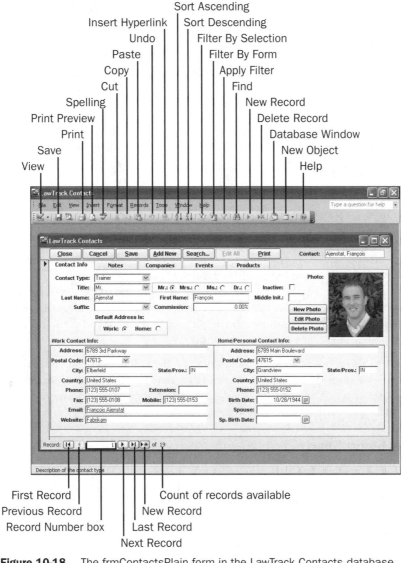

Figure 10-18. The frmContactsPlain form in the LawTrack Contacts database.

Moving Around

The way you move around on a form depends in part on the form's design. For example, the frmContactsPlain form contains three subforms embedded within the tab control—one for contact companies, another for contact events, and a third for contact products. The two boxes you see on the Contact Info tab aren't subforms—they're rectangle controls that I added to enhance the grouping of the main detail fields.

The fsubContactEventsPlain subform on the Events tab is a continuous form. You move around in it in ways similar to how you move around in a datasheet. On this subform you can use the vertical scroll bar on the right side to move the display up or down. The subform can be toggled between two different views—Form view (its current state) and Datasheet view. If you want to see the Datasheet view of the fsubContactEventsPlain subform, click in any of the fields on the subform (to ensure that the focus is on the subform) and then open the View menu. From the Subform submenu, choose the Datasheet command, and the fsubContactEvents subform will now look like Figure 10-19. (Notice that the PivotTable and PivotChart options on this submenu appear dimmed—I have disallowed those views in the design of this subform.) You can choose the Subform command from the View menu again and choose Form on the submenu to restore the continuous form display.

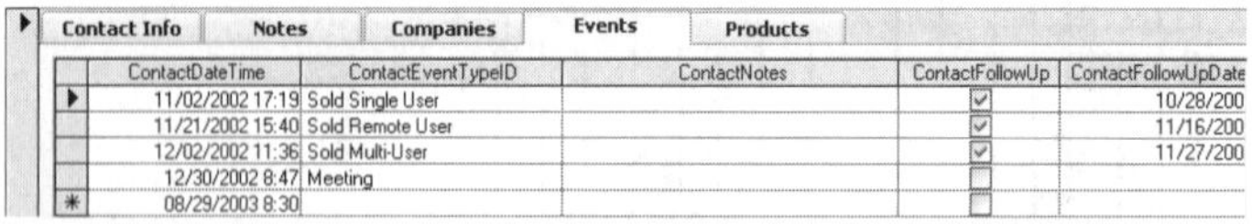

Figure 10-19. The subform fsubContactEventsPlain in Datasheet view on the Events tab of frmContactsPlain.

In the frmContactsPlain form, you view different contact records by using the navigation buttons and Record Number box at the bottom of the form. To see the next contact, use the main form's navigation buttons. To see different companies, events, or products for a particular contact, use the vertical scroll bar within the subform or the navigation buttons within the subform window. Note that you can also design a subform without its own Record Number box and navigation buttons. You might want to do this if you think the second set of navigation buttons will be confusing to your users.

You can also choose the Go To command from the Edit menu to move to the first, last, next, or previous record in the main form or in the subform. You can select any field in the form by clicking anywhere in that field. To use the Go To command you must first move to the form or the subform containing those records you want to view.

Keyboard Shortcuts

If you're typing in new data, you might find it easier to use the keyboard rather than the mouse to move around on a form. Some of the keyboard shortcuts you can use with forms are listed in Table 10-1 (for moving around in fields and records) and in Table 10-2 on page 384 (for actions in a list box or in a combo box). Note that a form that edits data can be in one of two modes: Edit mode or Navigation mode. You're in *Edit mode* on a form when you can see a flashing insertion point in the current field. To enter *Navigation mode*, tab to the next field or press the F2 key to select the current field. As you can see in the following tables, some keyboard shortcuts work differently depending on the mode. Other keyboard shortcuts work in only one mode or the other.

Table 10-1. Keyboard Shortcuts for Fields and Records

Key(s)	Movement in Fields and Records
Tab	Moves to the next field.
Shift+Tab	Moves to the previous field.
Home	In Navigation mode, moves to the first field of the current record. In Edit mode, moves to the beginning of the current field.
End	In Navigation mode, moves to the last field of the current record. In Edit mode, moves to the end of the current field.
Ctrl+Page Up	Moves to the current field of the previous record.
Ctrl+Page Down	Moves to the current field of the next record.
Ctrl+Up Arrow	In Navigation mode, moves to the current field of the first record. In Edit mode, moves to the beginning of the current field.
Ctrl+Down Arrow	In Navigation mode, moves to the current field of the last record. In Edit mode, moves to the end of the current field.
Ctrl+Home	In Navigation mode, moves to the first field of the first record. In Edit mode, moves to the beginning of the current field.
Ctrl+End	In Navigation mode, moves to the last field of the last record. In Edit mode, moves to the end of the current field.
Ctrl+Tab	If in a subform, moves to the next field in the main form. If the subform is the last field in tab sequence in the main form, moves to the first field in the next main record. If the focus is on a field on a tab, moves the focus to the first field in the tab order on the next tab. If the focus is on a subform within a tab, moves the focus to the tab. If the subform within the tab is the last control on the form, moves the focus to the tab on the next record. If the focus is on a tab (not a field within the tab), cycles forward through the tabs.
Ctrl+Shift+Tab	If in a subform, moves to the previous field in the main form. If the subform is the first field in tab sequence in the main form, moves to the last field in the next main record. If the focus is on a field on a tab, moves the focus to the first field in the tab order on the previous tab. If the focus is on a subform within a tab, moves the focus to the tab. If the subform within the tab is the first control on the form, moves the focus to the tab on the previous record. If the focus is on a tab (not a field within the tab), cycles backward through the tabs.

Chapter 10

Table 10-1. Keyboard Shortcuts for Fields and Records

Key(s)	Movement in Fields and Records
Ctrl+Shift+Home	In Navigation mode, moves to the first field in the record. When in Navigation mode in a field on a tab, moves the focus to the tab. When the focus is on a tab (not a field within the tab), moves to the first tab on the tab control. In Edit mode, selects all characters from the current cursor position to the beginning of the field.
Ctrl+Shift+End	In Navigation mode, moves to the last field in the record. When in Navigation mode in a field on a tab, moves the focus to the tab. When the focus is on a tab (not a field within the tab), moves to the last tab on the tab control. In Edit mode, selects all characters from the current cursor position to the end of the field.
F5	Moves to the Record Number box.
Enter	Depends on your settings for the Move after enter option on the Keyboard tab in the Options dialog box.
Shift+Enter	Saves the current record.

Table 10-2. Keyboard Shortcuts for a List Box or a Combo Box

Key(s)	Action in a List Box or a Combo Box
F4 or Alt+Down Arrow	Opens or closes a combo box or a drop-down list box.
Down Arrow	Moves down one line in a list box or in a combo box when the list is open.
Up Arrow	Moves up one line in a list box or in a combo box when the list is open.
Page Down	Moves down to the next group of lines.
Page Up	Moves up to the next group of lines.
Tab	Exits the box and moves to the next field.

Adding Records and Changing Data

You'll probably design most forms so that you can insert new records, change field values, or delete records in Form view or in Datasheet view. The following sections explain procedures for adding new records and changing data.

Adding a New Record

The procedure for entering a new record varies depending on the design of the form. With a form that's been designed for data entry only, you open the form and enter data in the (usually empty) data fields. Sometimes forms of this type open with default values in the fields or with data entered by a macro or a Visual Basic procedure. In the LawTrack Contacts application, frmCompanyAdd and frmContactAdd are two examples of forms that open in Data Entry mode. You can see frmContactAdd in Figure 10-20.

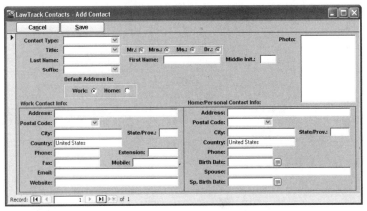

Figure 10-20.   The frmContactAdd form in Data Entry mode.

When you're editing company information in frmCompanies and need to enter a new contact that doesn't exist, the application opens this form to allow you to fill in the required information for the new contact. After you save the record, the new contact becomes available to assign to the company displayed in frmCompanies.

You'll normally create a form that allows you to display and edit data and also add new records. The frmContactsPlain form is this type of form. On this form, you can go to a new record in several ways. Open the *frmContactsPlain* form and try the following:

- Click the Last Record button on the navigation bar at the bottom of the Form window and then click the Next Record button.
- Click the New Record button on the navigation bar at the bottom of the form.
- Choose Go To from the Edit menu and choose New Record on the submenu.
- Click the New Record button on the toolbar.
- Press Ctrl+Plus Sign.
- Choose Data Entry from the Records menu.
- Click the Add New command button in the header area of the form.

The first five methods take you to the empty record at the end of the recordset being edited by this form. This is similar to going to the blank row at the end of a table or query datasheet to begin entering data for a new row. The last two methods shift the form into Data Entry mode as shown in Figure 10-21 on the next page. Notice that there now appears to be only one record—the new record you're about to enter, and that record displays the default value specified for Country even though you haven't started to enter any data yet.

Record selector

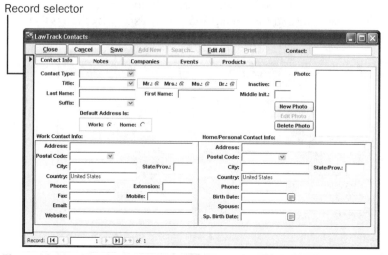

Figure 10-21. The frmContactsPlain form in Data Entry mode.

Access places the cursor in the first field when you start a new record. As soon as you begin typing, Access changes the indicator on the record selector (if your form shows the record selector) to a pencil icon to indicate that updates are in progress. Press the Tab key to move to the next field.

> **Note** If you put a normal edit form in Data Entry mode, you can choose Remove Filter/Sort from the Records menu to return to normal data display. The frmContactsPlain form also provides an Edit All button on the form to perform the same function.

If you violate a field's validation rule, Access notifies you as soon as you attempt to leave the field. You must provide a correct value before you can move to another field. Press Shift+Enter in any field in the record or press the Tab key in the last field in the record to save your new record in the database. If the data you enter violates a table validation rule, Access displays an error message and does not save the record. If you want to cancel a new record, press the Esc key twice. (There's also a Cancel button on frmContactsPlain that clears your edits and closes the form.)

If you're adding a new record in a form such as frmContactsPlain, you'll encounter a special situation. You'll notice when you tab to the picture object frame control that you can't type anything in it. This is because the field in the underlying table is an OLE Object data type, and this control is a bound object frame. To enter data in this type of field in a new record, you must create the object in an application that supports ActiveX before you can store the data in Access. To do this, select the bound object frame control and choose the Object command from the Insert menu. Access displays the Insert Object dialog box, shown in Figure 10-22. To create a new object, select the object type you want (in this case, Bitmap Image), and click OK. Access starts the application that's defined in the Windows registry as the default application for this type of data (for bitmaps, usually the Paint application).

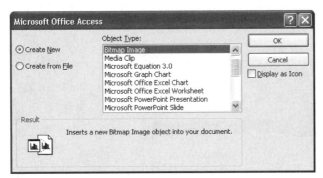

Figure 10-22. The Insert Object dialog box.

If you have an appropriate file available to copy into the ActiveX object field in Access, select the Create From File option in the dialog box. Access changes the option list to let you enter the path name and file name, as shown in Figure 10-23. You can click the Browse button to open the Browse dialog box, which lets you search for the file you want. After you select a file, you can select the Link check box to create an active link between the copy of the object in Access and the actual file. If you do so, whenever you change the file, the linked object in Access will also change. Select the Display As Icon check box to display the application icon in the bound object frame instead of the picture. Your picture will still be stored or linked in your table even when you choose to display the icon.

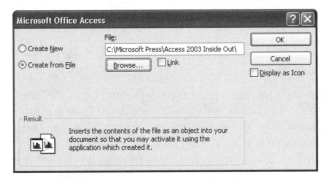

Figure 10-23. Inserting an object from a file.

The frmContactsPlain form also includes two text boxes that let you specify the e-mail address or the Web site address of the contact. To add or edit a hyperlink, you can tab to the hyperlink field (remember that if the link field contains a valid link, clicking in it activates the link!) and then choose Hyperlink from the Insert menu or click the Insert Hyperlink button on the toolbar. (You can also right-click the link field, choose Hyperlink from the shortcut menu, and then choose Edit Hyperlink from the submenu.) Access displays the dialog box shown in Figure 10-24, which lets you edit or define the link.

You can enter the descriptor in the Text To Display box at the top. I clicked the ScreenTip button to open the Set Hyperlink ScreenTip dialog box you see in Figure 10-24 on the next page.

Chapter 10

387

The ScreenTip appears when you hover over the hyperlink with your mouse pointer. You can type the document address directly into the Address box.

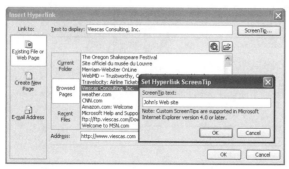

Figure 10-24. The Insert Hyperlink dialog box showing a link to the Viescas.com Web site.

Click the Create New Page option on the far left to see a pane where you can enter the name of a new Web page document and specify the path. You'll also see options to edit the new document now or later. If you choose to edit now, Access creates a new data page and opens it to be edited. (See Chapter 27, "Building Data Access Pages," for details.)

The last option on the left, E-Mail Address, lets you enter an e-mail address or choose from a list of recently used addresses. This generates a Mailto: hyperlink that will invoke your e-mail program and start a new e-mail to the address you specify here. You can also optionally enter a Subject for the new e-mail, which adds a question mark after the e-mail address followed by the subject in the stored hyperlink.

Click OK to save your link. See "Working with Hyperlinks," page 7xxx, for more details and cautions about hyperlinks.

Try adding a new record by using the frmContactsPlain form. Open the form, choose the Go To command from the Edit menu, and choose New Record from the submenu. You should see a screen similar to the one shown earlier in Figure 10-21. Select any Contact Type you like from the drop-down list. You can pick a Title from the list or click one of the option buttons provided to make it easy to pick a common title. You must enter at least a Last Name (the only required field in tblContacts). Tab to the Photo field, and follow the procedure discussed above to create a new picture. You can find several appropriately sized bitmap pictures of contacts on the companion CD in the Pictures subfolder. (You can also click the New Photo button—Visual Basic code behind the form opens your default bitmap editor program.)

Inside Out

Dealing with AutoNumber primary keys and potentially duplicate data

As discussed in Chapter 3, "Designing Your Database Application," it's usually preferable to use a combination of data fields that have a unique value in each row to create a primary key. However, choosing a combination of fields in tblContacts that would be guaranteed to be unique in all rows could prove difficult. The combination of first name and last name could easily result in a duplicate when two different people have the same name. Adding postal code might help, but you still might run into two people named *John Smith* who live in the same area.

The simple solution for tables in a Microsoft Access desktop database is to use an AutoNumber field as the primary key. In fact, in the LawTrack Contacts database, tblCompanies, tblContacts, tblInvoices, and tblProducts all use an AutoNumber field for the primary key. This guarantees that all rows will have a unique primary key, but it doesn't guard against duplicate records—entering the same person twice.

To avoid potential duplicates, you should consider writing Visual Basic code to check a new row just before Access saves it. I included some simple code to perform a Soundex check on the last name in both frmContacts and frmContactsPlain. (Soundex is an algorithm created by the United States National Archive and Records Administration to generate a code from a name to identify names that sound alike.) If you try to add a person in a new row with the last name *Canon*, you'll see a warning about a potential duplicate (*Cannon*, for example) and a list of all similar names. The warning allows you to cancel saving the new row. You can learn how this code works in Chapter 23.

One last point about using AutoNumber: As soon as you begin to enter new data in a table that has an AutoNumber field, Access assigns a new number to that field. If you decide to cancel the new record before saving it, Access won't reuse this AutoNumber value. Access does this to ensure that multiple users sharing a database don't get the same value for a new table row. So, if you expect primary key numbers to remain consecutive, you should not use AutoNumber.

Chapter 10

To begin adding some events for your new contact, click the Events tab to reveal the appropriate subform. Note that when you click in the subform, Access saves the contact data you entered in the main form. Access does this to ensure that it can create a link between the new record in the main form and any record you might create in the subform. (The new contact ID has to be saved in the main form before you can create related contact category records in a subform.)

The Date/Time field automatically fills in with the current date and time on your machine. You can correct this value or click the small calendar button to open a calendar form to set a new date and time graphically. Select an event type, as shown in Figure 10-25 on the next page, or type a new one. If you enter an event type that isn't already defined, code behind the form prompts you to ask whether you want to add a new event type. If you respond Yes, you'll see a dialog form open to allow you to enter the details for your new event type.

When you press Tab in the last field or press Shift+Enter in any field, Access adds the new event for you. Access also inserts the information required to link the record in the main form and the new record in the subform. Access fetches the ContactID from the record in the outer form and creates the new record in the tblContactEvents table with the related ContactID value. You can't see or edit the ContactID field on either the outer form or the subform. You don't need to see it in the outer form because ContactID in tblContacts is an AutoNumber field. Because Access automatically copies the value for you for new rows in the subform, you don't need to see it there either.

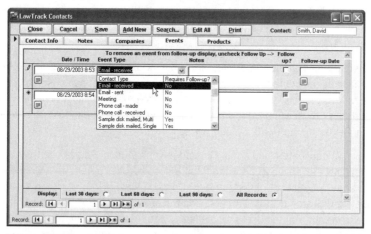

Figure 10-25. Adding a new contact event record in the frmContactsPlain form.

You can define very functional forms using combo boxes, tab controls, and subforms. To really make your application user-friendly, you need to further automate your forms with Visual Basic. For details about how many of the forms in the sample databases are automated with Visual Basic, see Chapter 23.

Changing and Deleting Data

If your form permits updates, you can easily change or delete existing data in the underlying table or query. If the form is designed to be used in Datasheet view, you can use the same techniques you learned in Chapter 7 to work with your data.

In Form view, your data might appear in one of several formats. If the form is designed to be a single form, you can see the data for only one record at a time. If the form is designed as a continuous form, you might be able to see data for more than one record at a time.

As with datasheets, you must select a field in the form in order to change the data in the field. To select a field, either tab to the field or click in the field with the mouse. (Remember, if the field contains a hyperlink, clicking in it will activate the link. To edit a hyperlink, either tab to the field or right-click the field to open the shortcut menu, from which you can choose commands to edit the hyperlink.) After you select a field, you can change the data in it by using the same techniques you used for working with data in a datasheet. You can type over individual characters, replace a sequence of characters, or copy and paste data from one field to another.

You might find that you can't tab to or select some fields in a form. When you design a form, you can set the properties of the controls on the form so that a user can't select the control. These properties prevent users from changing fields that you don't want updated, such as calculated values or fields from the *one* side of a query. You can also set the tab order to control the sequence of field selection when you use Tab or Shift+Tab to move around on the form. See Chapter 12, "Customizing a Form," for details.

Deleting a record in a single form or in a continuous form is different from deleting a record in a datasheet. First, you must select the record as you would select a record in a datasheet. If the form is designed with record selectors, simply click the record selector to select the record. If the form does not have record selectors, choose the Select Record command from the Edit menu. To delete a selected record, press the Delete key or choose the Delete command from the Edit menu. You can also choose the Delete Record command from the Edit menu to delete the current record without first having to select it.

When a record you're trying to delete contains related records in other tables, you will see an error message unless the relationship defined between the tables tells Access to cascadedelete the related fields and records. See Chapter 4 for details about defining relationships between tables. In frmContacts and frmContactsPlain in the LawTrack Contacts application, Visual Basic code behind the forms checks to see if dependent rows exist in other tables. This code issues a custom error message, shown in Figure 10-26, that gives you specific information about the problem. (The standard Access error message is not very user-friendly.) Rather than automatically delete dependent records (you might have asked to delete the contact record in error), the application requires you to specifically go to the tabs that show the related records and delete all these records first. You can see how this code works in Chapter 24.

Figure 10-26. The LawTrack Contacts application shows you a custom error message when you attempt to delete a contact that has dependent records in other tables.

Searching for and Sorting Data

When you use forms to display and edit your data, you can search for data or sort it in a new order in much the same way that you search for and sort data in datasheets. See Chapter 7, "Creating and Working with Simple Queries." The following sections show you how to use some of the form filter features to search for data in a form or use the quick sort commands to reorder your data.

Performing a Simple Search

You can use Microsoft Access's Find feature in a form just as you would in a datasheet. First select the field, and then choose the Find command from the Edit menu or click the Find button on the toolbar to open the Find And Replace dialog box that you saw in Figure 7-49 on page 272. You can enter search criteria exactly as you would for a datasheet. Note that in a form you can also perform a search on any control that you can select, including controls that display calculated values.

Performing a Quick Sort on a Form Field

As you can with a datasheet, you can select just about any control that contains data from the underlying recordset and click the Sort Ascending or Sort Descending button on the toolbar to reorder the records you see, based on the selected field. If you want to perform a quick sort, open the *frmContactsPlain* form, click in the PostalCode field in the form under Work Contact Info, and then click the Sort Descending button on the toolbar. The contact with the highest postal code is displayed first.

Adding a Filter to a Form

One of Access's most powerful features is its ability to further restrict or sort the information displayed in the form without your having to create a new query. This restriction is accomplished with a filter that you define while you're using the form. When you apply the filter, you see only the data that matches the criteria you entered.

As with datasheets, you can define a filter using Filter By Selection, Filter By Form, or the Advanced Filter definition facility. Open the *frmContactsPlain* form and click the Filter By Form button on the toolbar. Access adds features to the form to let you enter filter criteria, as shown in Figure 10-27. In this example, we're looking for all contacts who are contact type Developer, whose last name begins with *V*, and who work in the city of Austin. You'll see that for each field Access provides a drop-down list that contains all the values for that field currently in the database. If your database contains many thousands of rows, Access might not show the list if the field has more than several hundred unique values—it would take an unacceptably long time to retrieve the entire list. When the list is too long, Access gives you simple Is Null and Is Not Null choices instead. You can also type in your own criteria, as shown in the Last Name field in Figure 10-27.

As you can with datasheets, you can enter one set of criteria and then click an Or tab at the bottom of the blank form to enter additional criteria. If you don't like some of the criteria you've entered, click the Clear Grid button on the toolbar to start over. Click the Apply Filter button on the toolbar to filter your records. Click the Close button on the toolbar to exit the Filter By Form window without applying the new filter. Note that if you specify criteria on a subform, Access applies the filter only for records related to the record currently displayed on the main form. For example, you can't create a filter on the Products tab for contacts who own the Multi-User edition and then expect to see all the contacts who own that product— you'll see only products for the current contact that match the value *Multi-User*.

Load From Query   Clear Grid

   Save As Query   Apply Filter

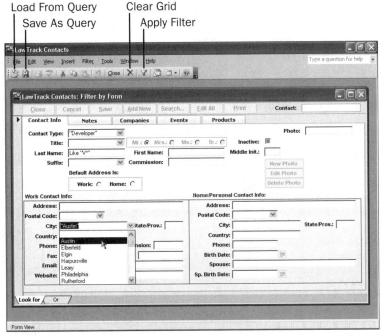

Figure 10-27. The Filter By Form window for the frmContactsPlain form.

To turn off the filter, click the Remove Filter button on the toolbar or choose the Remove Filter/Sort command from the Records menu. To see the filter definition, choose Filter from the Records menu and then choose Advanced Filter/Sort from the submenu. After you apply the filter shown in Figure 10-27 and do an ascending quick sort on the work PostalCode field, the Advanced Filter/Sort window should look something like that shown in Figure 10-28.

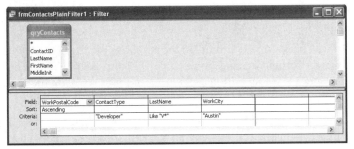

Figure 10-28. The Advanced Filter/Sort window for the frmContactsPlain form with criteria previously entered using the Filter By Form command.

Chapter 10

> **Note** If you use one of the Sort (ascending or descending) buttons, you'll discover that this "quick sort" uses the form's filter definition to create the sorting criteria. For example, if you do a quick sort to arrange contacts in descending order by last name, you'll find the LastName field in the form filter with the Sort row set to Descending when you choose Advanced Filter/Sort from the Filter submenu of the Records menu.

If you often use the same filter with your form, you can save the filter as a query and give it a name. Open the Advanced Filter/Sort window and create the filter. Choose the Save As Query command from the File menu and type in a name for the query when Access prompts you. You can also click the Save As Query button on the toolbar when you're in the Filter By Form window.

You can load an existing query definition to use as a filter. Click the Load From Query button on the toolbar when you're in Filter By Form, or open the Advanced Filter/Sort window, and choose the Load From Query command from the File menu. Access presents a list of valid select queries (those that are based on the same table or tables as the form you're using).

Printing Forms

You can use a form to print information from a table or query. When you design the form, you can specify different header and footer information for the printed version. You can also specify which controls are visible. For example, you might define some gridlines that are visible on the printed form but are not displayed on the screen.

An interesting form to print in the LawTrack Contacts database is the *frmContactSummary-Xmpl* form. Open the form, and then click the Print Preview button on the toolbar or choose the Print Preview command from the File menu. Click the Zoom button and scroll to the top of the first page. You should see a screen that looks like the one shown in Figure 10-29. Notice that the form footer that you saw earlier in Figure 10-1 does not appear in the printed version. In fact, this form has one set of headers and footers designed for printing and another set for viewing the form on the screen.

You can use the scroll bars to move around on the page. Use the Page Number box in the lower left corner of the form in the same way that you use the Record Number box on a form or in a datasheet. Click the Zoom button again to see the entire page on the screen.

Choose Page Setup from the File menu. Access displays the Page Setup dialog box, which you can use to customize the way the form prints. Click the Margins tab to set top, bottom, left, and right margins. Click the Page tab (shown in Figure 10-30) to select Portrait or Landscape print mode, the paper size and source, and the printer. Access will store these specifications with the definition of your form.

Using Forms

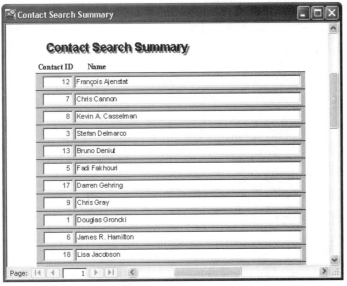

Figure 10-29. The window for the frmContactSummaryXmpl form in Print Preview.

Figure 10-30. The Page tab of the Page Setup dialog box for forms.

Click the Columns tab of the Page Setup dialog box to see additional options, as shown in Figure 10-31 on the next page. We'll explore the Columns options in detail in Chapter 14, "Using Reports."

Figure 10-31. The Columns tab of the Page Setup dialog box for forms.

You should now have a good understanding of how forms work and of many design elements that you can include when you build forms. Now, on to the fun part—building your first form in the next chapter.

Building a Form

From the perspective of daily use, forms are the most important objects you'll build in your Microsoft Office Access 2003 application because they're what users see and work with every time they run the application. This chapter shows you how to design and build forms in an Access desktop application. You'll learn how to work with a Form window in Design view to build a basic form based on a single table, and you'll learn how to use an Access form wizard to simplify the form-creation process. The last section of this chapter, "Simplifying Data Input with a Form," shows you how to use some of the special form controls to simplify data entry on your forms.

Note The examples in this chapter are based on the forms, queries, tables, and data in *ContactsDataCopy.mdb* on the companion CD included with this book. The results you see from the samples in this chapter may not exactly match what you see in this book if you have changed the sample data in the file. Also, all the screen images in this chapter were taken on a Windows XP system with the display theme set to Windows XP. Your results may look different if you are using a different operating system or a different theme.

Forms and Object-Oriented Programming

Microsoft Access was not designed to be a full object-oriented programming environment, yet it has many characteristics found in object-oriented application development systems. Before you dive into building forms, it's useful to examine how Access implements objects and actions, particularly if you come from the world of procedural application development.

In classic procedural application development, the data you need for the application is distinct from the programs you write to work with the data and from the results produced by your programs. Each program works with the data independently and generally has little structural connection with other programs in the system. For example, an order entry program accepts input from a clerk and then writes the order to data files. Later, a billing program processes the orders and prints invoices. Another characteristic of procedural systems is that events must occur in a specific order and cannot be executed out of sequence. A procedural system has difficulty looking up supplier or price information while in the middle of processing an order.

In an object-oriented system, however, an object is defined as a subject that has *properties*, and you can invoke certain actions, or *methods*, to be performed on that subject. Objects can contain other objects. When an object incorporates another object, it inherits the attributes and properties of the other object and expands on the object's definition. In Access, queries define actions on tables, and the queries then become new logical or virtual tables known as *recordsets*. That is, a query doesn't actually contain any data, but you can work with the data fetched by the query as though it were a table. You can base a query on another query with the same effect. Queries inherit the integrity and formatting rules defined for the tables. Forms further define actions on tables or queries, and the fields you include in forms initially inherit the underlying properties, such as formatting and validation rules, of the fields in the source tables or queries. You can define different formatting or more restrictive rules, but you cannot override the rules defined for the tables.

Within an Access database, you can interrelate application objects and data. For example, you can set startup properties that prepare your application to run. As part of the application startup, you will usually open a switchboard form. The switchboard form might act on some of the data in the database, or it might offer controls that open other forms, print reports, or close the application.

For more information about startup properties, see Chapter 24, "The Finishing Touches."

Figure 11-1 shows the conceptual architecture of an Access form. In addition to operating on tables or queries in a database, forms can contain other forms, called *subforms*. These subforms can, in turn, define actions on other tables, queries, or forms. Events that occur in forms and subforms (such as changing the value of a field or moving to a new record) can trigger macro actions or Visual Basic procedures. As you'll learn when you read about advanced form design, macro actions and Visual Basic procedures can be triggered in many ways. The most obvious way to trigger an action is by clicking a command button on a form. But you can also define macros or Visual Basic procedures that execute when an event occurs, such as clicking in a field, changing the data in a field, pressing a key, adding or deleting a row, or simply moving to a new row in the underlying table or query.

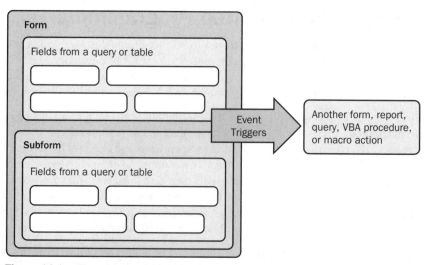

Figure 11-1. The conceptual architecture of an Access form.

Building a Form

In Chapter 23, "Automating Your Application with Visual Basic," you'll learn how several of the more complex forms in the LawTrack Contacts and Housing Reservations sample databases are automated with Visual Basic. Figure 11-2 shows a few of the automated processes for the frmContacts form in the LawTrack Contacts database. For example, printing the contract currently displayed in the form is triggered by using a command button.

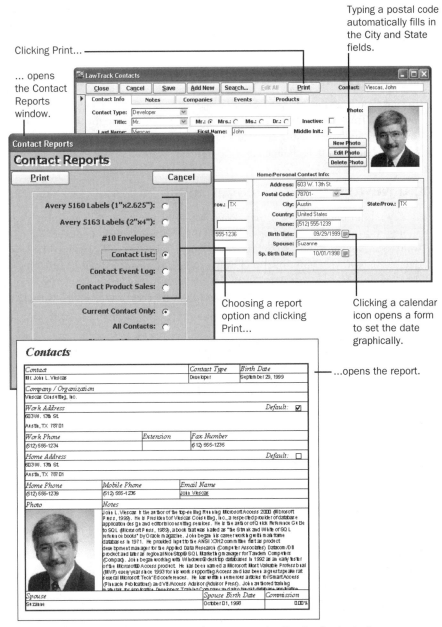

Figure 11-2. Some of the automated processes for the frmContacts form.

In addition to automating print options, code behind the frmContacts form automatically fills in the city and state when you enter a postal code and provides a graphical way to choose a date if you click the button next to a date. On the Events tab, when you enter a sale of a product to the contact, code automatically generates a product record.

Object-oriented systems are not restricted to a specific sequence of events. So a user entering a contact event in Access can minimize the window and start a search in a companies or products form window without having to first finalize or cancel work already in progress in frmContacts.

Starting from Scratch—A Simple Input Form

To start, you'll create a simple form that accepts and displays data in the tblCompanies table in the LawTrack Contacts database. Later, you'll create a form for the tblProducts table in this same database by using an Access form wizard. To follow along in this section, open the *ContactsDataCopy.mdb* database.

Building a New Form with Design Tools

To begin building a new form that allows you to display and edit data from a table, click the Tables button on the Object bar of the Database window, and then select the table that you want to use for the form. (To follow this example, select the tblCompanies table in the sample database.) Note that you can also click the Queries button and select a query to provide the data for your form. Select Form from the New Object toolbar button's drop-down list, or choose the Form command from the Insert menu. Access opens the New Form dialog box, shown in Figure 11-3.

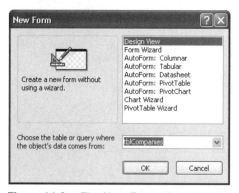

Figure 11-3. The New Form dialog box.

In the combo box in the lower part of the dialog box, Access displays the name of the table or query that you selected in the Database window. If you want to select a different table or query, you can open the combo box's drop-down list to see all the tables and queries in your database. You'll build this first form without the aid of a form wizard so that you'll understand the variety of components that go into form design.

Building a Form

Select Design View in the dialog box, and then click OK. Access opens the Form window in Design view and, with it, a toolbox that contains several design tools, as shown in Figure 11-4. (You might not see all the windows shown in Figure 11-4.) If you've already experimented with forms in Design view and have moved some of the windows around, Access opens them where you last placed them on the screen.

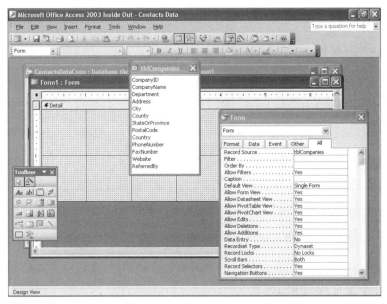

Figure 11-4. A Form window with its tools in Design view.

Access starts with a form that has only a *Detail section*. The section has a grid on a background that is the color defined for 3D Objects in your Windows Display Properties window—usually a light gray or beige. You can click an edge or corner of the Detail section and then drag to make the section larger or smaller. You can remove the grid dots from the Detail section by choosing the Grid command from the View menu. If you want to add a *Header section* or a *Footer section* to the form, choose the Form Header/Footer command from the View menu.

The Detail section starts out at 5 inches (12.7 centimeters) wide by 2 inches (5.08 centimeters) high. The measurement gradations on the rulers are relative to the size and resolution of your screen. By default, Access sets the grid at 24 dots per inch horizontally and 24 dots per inch vertically. You can change the density of the grid dots by altering the Grid X and Grid Y properties on the form's property sheet.

The Grid X and Grid Y property settings determine the intervals per unit of measurement in the grid. You can enter a number from 1 (coarsest) through 64 (finest). You set the unit of measure (U.S. or metric) by default when you select a country in the regional settings in Windows Control Panel. (You open this dialog box by double-clicking the Regional and Language Settings icon in Windows Control Panel.)

Inside Out

Choosing a form width and height

Although you can design a form that is up to 22 inches (55.87 centimeters) wide, and each form section can also be up to 22 inches high (a total of 66 inches if you include all three sections), you should design your forms to fit on your users' screens. I tend to design all my forms to comfortably fit on the lowest common screen resolution—800×600. A form to fit this size should be about 7.8 inches (19.8 centimeters) wide, and the sum of the heights of the sections should be about 4.25 inches (10.8 centimeters) to allow space for menus and toolbars and the Windows taskbar. If your user has set a higher screen resolution, extra space will be available on the Access desktop to work with multiple form windows at a time.

You can find a handy form, *zsfrm800x600*, in several of the sample databases. When you're working in a higher resolution, you can open this form and overlay it on the form you're designing. If your form fits behind the sample form, your form should display properly at the lowest common resolution.

For example, if your unit of measurement is inches and you specify a Grid X setting of 10, Access divides the grid horizontally into 0.1-inch increments. When your measurement is in inches and you set the Grid X and Grid Y values to 24 or less, Access displays the grid dots on the grid. In centimeters, you can see the grid dots when you specify a setting of 9 or less. If you set a finer grid for either Grid X or Grid Y, Access won't display the grid dots but you can still use the grid to line up controls. Access always displays grid lines at 1-inch intervals (U.S.) or 1-centimeter intervals (metric), even when you set fine Grid X or Grid Y values.

Some Key Form Design Terms

As you begin to work in form design, you need to understand a few commonly used terms.

A form that displays data from your tables must have a *record source*. A *record source* can be the name of a table, the name of a query, or an SQL statement.

When a control can display information (text boxes, option groups, toggle buttons, option buttons, check boxes, combo boxes, list boxes, bound object frames, and many ActiveX controls), its *control source* defines the name of the field from the record source or the expression that provides the data to display. A control that has an expression as its control source is not updatable.

When a form has a record source, it is *bound* to the records in that record source—the form displays records from the record source and can potentially update the fields in the records. When a control is on a bound form and its control source is the name of a field in the record source, the control is *bound* to the field—the control displays (and perhaps allows you to edit) the data from the bound field in the current row of the record source. A control cannot be bound unless the form is also bound.

A form that has no record source is *unbound*. A control that has no control source is unbound.

The following sections describe some of the tools you can use to design a form.

The Toolbox

The toolbox, shown in Figure 11-5, is the "command center" of form design. You can move the toolbox by dragging its title bar, and you can change the shape of the toolbox by dragging its sides or corners. You can even move the toolbox to the top of the workspace and dock it as a toolbar. You can close the toolbox by clicking the Close button in the upper right corner of the toolbox, by choosing the Toolbox command from the View menu, or by clicking the Toolbox button on the toolbar.

> **Tip**   If you don't see the toolbox displayed with the Form window in Design view, choose the Toolbox command from the View menu or click the Toolbox button on the toolbar.

Figure 11-5.   The form design toolbox.

The toolbox contains buttons for all the types of controls you can use when you design a form. It also contains a button (named More Controls) that gives you access to all the ActiveX controls (for example, the calendar control that comes with Access) that you have installed on your system. To select a particular control to place on a form, click the control's button in the toolbox. When you move the mouse pointer over the form, the mouse pointer turns into an icon that represents the tool you selected. Position the mouse pointer where you want to place the control, and press the left mouse button to place the control on the form. If you want to size the control as you place it, drag the mouse pointer to make the control the size you want. (You can also size a control after it's placed by dragging the sizing handles at its sides or corners.)

Left to right, top to bottom, the tools in the toolbox are described in Table 11-1 on the next page.

Chapter 11

Table 11-1. Toolbox Tools

Tool	Description
	Select Objects tool. This is the default tool. Use this tool to select, size, move, and edit existing controls.
	Control Wizards button. Click this button to activate the control wizards. Click the button again to deactivate the wizards. When this button appears pressed, a control wizard helps you enter control properties whenever you create a new option group, combo box, list box, or command button. The Combo Box and List Box Wizards also offer you an option to create Visual Basic code to move to a new record based on a selection the user makes in the combo or list box. The Command Button Wizard offers to generate Visual Basic code that performs various automated actions when the user clicks the button.
	Label tool. Use this tool to create label controls that contain fixed text. By default, controls that can display data have a label control automatically attached. You can use this tool to create stand-alone labels for headings and for instructions on your form.
	Text Box tool. Use this tool to create text box controls for displaying text, numbers, dates, times, and memo fields. You can bind a text box to one of the fields in an underlying table or query. If you allow a text box that is bound to a field to be updated, you can change the value in the field in the underlying table or query by entering a new value in the text box. You can also use a text box to display calculated values.
	Option Group tool. Use this tool to create option group controls that contain one or more toggle buttons, option buttons, or check boxes. (See the descriptions of these controls later in this table.) You can assign a separate numeric value to each button or check box that you include in the group. When you have more than one button or check box in a group, you can select only one button or check box at a time, and the value assigned to that button or check box becomes the value for the option group. If you have incorrectly assigned the same value to more than one button or check box, all buttons or check boxes that have the same value appear highlighted when you click any of them. You can select one of the buttons or check boxes in the group as the default value for the group. If you bind the option group to a field in the underlying query or table, you can set a new value in the field by selecting a button or a check box in the group.

Table 11-1. Toolbox Tools

Tool	Description
	Toggle Button tool. Use this tool to create a toggle button control that holds an on/off, a true/false, or a yes/no value. When you click a toggle button, its value becomes −1 (to represent on, true, or yes), and the button appears pressed. Click the button again, and its value becomes 0 (to represent off, false, or no). You can include a toggle button in an option group and assign the button a unique numeric value. If you create a group with multiple controls, selecting a new toggle button clears any previously selected toggle button, option button, or check box in that group (unless other buttons or check boxes in the group also have the same value). If you bind the toggle button to a field in the underlying table or query, you can toggle the field's value by clicking the toggle button.
	Option Button tool. Use this tool to create an option button control (sometimes called a radio button control) that holds an on/off, a true/false, or a yes/no value. When you click an option button, its value becomes −1 (to represent on, true, or yes), and a filled circle appears in the center of the button. Click the button again, and its value becomes 0 (to represent off, false, or no), and the filled circle clears. You can include an option button in an option group and assign the button a unique numeric value. If you create a group with multiple controls, selecting a new option button clears any previously selected toggle button, option button, or check box in that group (unless other buttons or check boxes in the group also have the same value). If you bind the option button to a field in the underlying table or query, you can toggle the field's value by clicking the option button.
	Check Box tool. Use this tool to create a check box control that holds an on/off, a true/false, or a yes/no value. When you click a check box, its value becomes −1 (to represent on, true, or yes), and a check mark appears in the box. Click the check box again, and its value becomes 0 (to represent off, false, or no), and the check mark disappears from the box. You can include a check box in an option group and assign the check box a unique numeric value. If you create a group with multiple controls, selecting a new check box clears any previously selected toggle button, option button, or check box in that group (unless other buttons or check boxes in the group also have the same value). If you bind the check box to a field in the underlying table or query, you can toggle the field's value by clicking the check box.

Chapter 11

Table 11-1. **Toolbox Tools**

Tool	Description
	Combo Box tool. Use this tool to create a combo box control that contains a list of potential values for the control and an editable text box. To create the list, you can enter values for the Row Source property of the combo box. You can also specify a table or a query as the source of the values in the list. Access displays the currently selected value in the text box. When you click the down arrow to the right of the combo box, Access displays the values in the list. Select a new value in the list to reset the value in the control. If the combo box is bound to a field in the underlying table or query, you can change the value in the field by selecting a new value in the list. You can bind multiple columns to the list, and you can hide one or more of the columns in the list by setting a column's width to 0. You can bind the actual value in the control to such a hidden column. When a multiple-column list is closed, Access displays the value in the first column whose width is greater than 0. Access displays all nonzero-width columns when you open the list.
	List Box tool. Use this tool to create a list box control that contains a list of potential values for the control. To create the list, you can enter the values in the Row Source property of the list box. You can also specify a table or a query as the source of the values in the list. List boxes are always open, and Access highlights the currently selected value in the list box. You select a new value in the list to reset the value in the control. If the list box is bound to a field in the underlying table or query, you can change the value in the field by selecting a new value in the list. You can bind multiple columns to the list, and you can hide one or more of the columns in the list by setting a column's width to 0. You can bind the actual value in the control to such a hidden column. Access displays all non-zero-width columns that fit within the defined width of the control. If the list box control is unbound, you can allow the user to select multiple values in the list (also called a multi-select list box).
	Command Button tool. Use this tool to create a command button control that can activate a macro or a Visual Basic procedure.
	Image tool. Use this tool to place a static picture on your form. You cannot edit the picture on the form, but Access stores it in a format that is very efficient for application speed and size. If you want to use a picture as the entire background of your form, you can set the form's Picture property.
	Unbound Object Frame tool. Use this tool to add an object from another application that supports object linking and embedding. The object becomes part of your form, not part of the data from the underlying table or query. You can add pictures, sounds, charts, or slides to enhance your form. When the object is a chart, you can specify a query as the source of data for the chart, and you can link the chart display to the current record in the form by one or more field values.

Table 11-1. Toolbox Tools

Tool	Description
	Bound Object Frame tool. Use this tool to display and edit an OLE Object data type field from the underlying data. Access can display most pictures and graphs directly on a form. For other objects, Access displays the icon for the application in which the object was created. For example, if the object is a sound object created in Windows Sound Recorder, you'll see a speaker icon on your form.
	Page Break tool. Use this tool to add a page break between the pages of a multiple-page form.
	Tab Control tool. Use this tool to create a series of tab pages on your form. Each page can contain a number of other controls to display information. The tab control works much like many of the option dialog boxes or property sheet windows in Access—when a user clicks a different tab, Access displays the controls contained on that tab. See Chapter 13, "Advanced Form Design," for details about using the Tab Control tool.
	Subform/Subreport tool. Use this tool to embed another form in the current form. You can use the subform to show data from a table or a query that is related to the data in the main form. Access maintains the link between the two forms for you.
	Line tool. Use this tool to add lines to a form to enhance its appearance.
	Rectangle tool. Use this tool to add filled or empty rectangles to a form to enhance its appearance.
	More Controls button. Click this button to open a dialog box showing all the ActiveX controls you have installed on your system. Not all ActiveX controls work with Microsoft Access.

For more information about using controls on forms, see Chapter 12, "Customizing a Form," and Chapter 13, "Advanced Form Design."

Tip When you select a tool that is a form control, your mouse pointer reverts to the Select Objects tool after you place the selected control on your form. If you plan to create several controls using the same tool—for example, a series of check boxes in an option group—double-click the control button in the toolbox to "lock" it. You can unlock it by clicking any other tool button (including the Select Objects tool).

Chapter 11

The Field List

Use the field list in conjunction with the toolbox to place bound controls (controls linked to fields in a table or a query) on your form. You can open the field list by clicking the Field List button on the toolbar or by choosing the Field List command from the View menu. Access displays the name of the underlying table or query in the field list title bar, as shown in Figure 11-6. You can drag the edges of the window to resize the field list so that you can see any long field names. You can drag the title bar to move the window out of the way. When the list of available field names is too long to fit in the current size of the window, use the scroll bar along the right side of the window to move through the list.

Figure 11-6. A field list showing the names of the fields in the bound table or query.

To use the field list to place a bound control on a form, first select the type of control you want in the toolbox. (If no control tool is selected, the default type is the text box control.) Then drag the field you want from the field list and drop it into position on the form. If you select a control that's inappropriate for the data type of the field, Access selects the default control for the data type. For example, if you select anything but the Bound Object Frame tool when placing an ActiveX object field (OLE Object data type) on a form, Access creates a bound object frame control for you anyway. If you try to drag any field using the subform/subreport, unbound object frame, line, rectangle, or page break control, Access creates a text box control or bound object frame control, as appropriate, instead. If you drag a field from the field list without choosing a control, Access uses either the display control you defined for the field in the table definition or a control appropriate for the field data type.

The Property Sheet

The form, each section of the form (header, detail, footer), and each control on the form has a list of properties associated with it, and you set these properties using a property sheet. Each control on a form, each section on a form, and the form itself are all *objects*. The kinds of properties you can specify vary depending on the object. To open the property sheet for an object, select the object and then click the Properties button on the toolbar or choose the Properties command from the View menu. Access opens a window similar to the one shown in Figure 11-7. If the Properties window is already open, you can view the properties specific to an object by clicking the object. You can also choose the object name from the drop-down box at the top of the Properties window.

Figure 11-7. The property sheet for a form.

You can drag the title bar to move the property sheet window around on your screen. You can also drag the edges of the window to resize it so that you can see more of the property settings. Because a form has more than 100 properties that you can set and because many controls have more than 70 properties, Access provides tabs at the top of the property sheet so that you can choose to display all properties (the default) or to display only format properties, data properties, event properties, or other properties. A form property sheet displaying only the data properties is shown in Figure 11-8.

Figure 11-8. A form property sheet displaying only the data properties.

When you click in a property box that provides a list of valid values, a down arrow button appears on the right side of the property box. Click this button to see a drop-down list of the values. For properties that can have a very long value setting, you can select the property and then press Shift+F2 to open a Zoom window. The Zoom window provides an expanded text box for entering or viewing an entry.

In many cases, a builder is available to help you create property settings for properties that can accept a complex expression, a query definition, or code (a macro or a Visual Basic procedure) to respond to an event. When a builder is available for a property setting, Access displays a small button with an ellipsis (…) next to the property box when you select the property; this is the Build button. If you click the Build button, Access responds with the appropriate builder window.

For example, suppose that you want to see the companies displayed in this form in ascending order by company name. The easiest way to accomplish this is to create a query that includes the fields from tblCompanies sorted on the CompanyName field, and then specify that query as the *Record Source* property for the form. To start, display the property sheet for the form, click the Data tab to display the form's data properties, click in the Record Source property, and then click the Build button next to Record Source to start the Query Builder. Access asks whether you want to build a new query based on the table that is currently the source for this form. If you click Yes, Access opens a new Query window in Design view with the tblCompanies field list displayed in the upper part of the window, as shown in Figure 11-9.

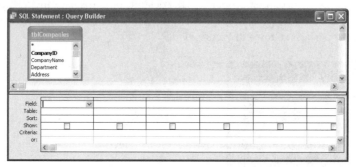

Figure 11-9. Using the Query Builder to create a query for the form's Record Source property.

You'll need all the fields in the tblCompanies table for this form, so select them and drag them to the design grid. For the CompanyName field, specify Ascending as the sorting order. Your result should look like the window shown in Figure 11-10.

Tip To easily select all the fields from a field list displayed in the upper part of the Query window, double-click the title bar of the field list. Access highlights all the fields for you. Then simply click any of them and drag the fields as a group to the design grid.

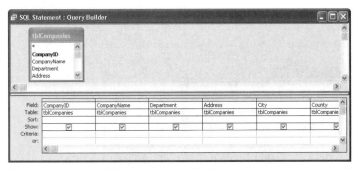

Figure 11-10. Building a query for the Record Source property of the form.

If you close the Query window at this point, Access asks whether you want to update the property. If you click Yes, Access stores the SQL text for the query in the Record Source property box. A better approach is to save the query and give it a name, such as qryCompaniesSortedByName, so do that now. Then, when you close the query, Access asks whether you want to save the query and update the property. If you click Yes, Access places the name of the query (rather than the SQL text) in the property sheet.

Building a Simple Input Form for the tblCompanies Table

Now let's create a simple input form for the tblCompanies table in the LawTrack Contacts database. If you've followed along to this point, you should have a blank form based on the qryCompaniesSortedByName query that you created using the Query Builder. If you haven't followed along, switch to the Database window, open the Tables list, select the tblCompanies table, and select Form from the New Object toolbar button's drop-down list (or choose Form from the Insert menu).

Select the Design View option in the New Form dialog box. You'll see the Form window in Design view and a set of design tools, as shown earlier in Figure 11-4. If necessary, open the toolbox, field list, and property sheet by clicking the appropriate buttons on the toolbar. Select the Record Source property, and then click the Build button and follow the procedures discussed in the previous sections, whose results are shown in Figures 11-9 and 11-10; this will create the query you need and make it the source for the form.

In the blank form for the qryCompaniesSortedByName query, drag the bottom of the Detail section downward to make some room to work. All the fields in tblCompanies are defined to be displayed with a text box, so you don't need to select a tool from the toolbox. If you'd like to practice, though, double-click the Text Box tool in the toolbox before dragging fields from the field list. In this way, you can drag fields one at a time to the Detail section of the form. Follow this procedure to drag each of the fields, except the ReferredBy field, from the field list to the Detail section. Your form should now look something like the one shown in Figure 11-11 on the next page.

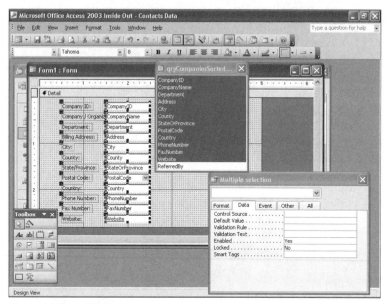

Figure 11-11. The text box controls that are created on a form when you drag fields from the qryCompaniesSortedByName field list.

> **Tip** A quick way to place several successive fields on a form is to click the first field you want in the field list, scroll down until you see the last field you want, and then hold down the Shift key while you click the last field. This procedure selects all the fields between the first and last fields you selected. You can also double-click the title bar of the field list to select all the fields in the field list. Holding down the Ctrl key and clicking several noncontiguous fields works, too. Click any of the highlighted fields and drag the fields as a group to the Detail section of the form.

When you position the field icon that you've dragged from the field list, the upper left corner of the new text box will be at the position of the mouse pointer when you release the mouse button. Note that the default text box control has a label control automatically attached to display the bound field's Caption property (or the field name if the field does not have a caption), positioned 1 inch to the left of the text box. Also, in Form Design view, the label control displays its Caption property, and the text box control displays its Control Source property (the name of the field to which it is bound).

You should drop each text box about 1.25 inches (3 centimeters) from the left edge of the Detail section to leave room to the left of the text box for Access to place the control labels. If you don't leave room, the text boxes will overlap the labels. Even if you do leave room, if a caption is too long to fit in the 1-inch space between the default label and the default text box (for example, Company / Organization in Figure 11-11), the text box will overlap the label.

Building a Form

In the example shown in Figure 11-11, the property sheet indicates that you have selected multiple controls. (In this case, I dragged all the selected fields to the Detail section at one time.) Whenever you select multiple controls on a form in Design view, Access displays the properties that are common to all the controls you selected. If you change a property in the property sheet while multiple controls are selected, Access makes the change to all the selected controls.

Moving and Sizing Controls

By default, Access creates text boxes that are 1 inch wide. For some of the fields, 1 inch is larger than necessary to display the field value—especially if you are using the default 8-point font size. For other fields, the text box isn't large enough. You probably also want to adjust the location of some of the controls.

To change a control's size or location, you usually have to select the control first. Be sure that the Select Objects tool is selected in the toolbox. Click the control you want to resize or move, and moving and sizing handles appear around the control. The handles are small boxes that appear at each corner of the control—except at the upper left corner, where the larger handle indicates that it cannot be used for sizing. In Figure 11-11, handles appear around all the text boxes because they are all selected. To select just one control, click anywhere in the design area where there is no control; this changes the selection to the Detail section. Then click the control you want. If the control is wide enough or high enough, Access provides additional handles at the midpoints of the edges of the control.

To change the size of a control, you can use the sizing handles on the edges, in either of the lower corners, or in the upper right corner of the control. When you place the mouse pointer over one of these sizing handles, the pointer turns into a double arrow, as shown in Figure 11-12. With the double-arrow pointer, drag the handle to resize the control. You can practice on the form by shortening the CompanyID text box so that it's 0.5 inch long. The name and address fields need to be stretched until they are each about 1.75 inches long. You might also want to adjust the state or province and Web site fields.

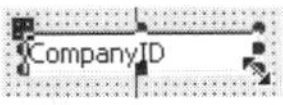

Figure 11-12. You can drag a corner handle of a selected control to change the control's width or height or both.

To move a control that is not currently selected, click the control and drag it to a new location. After you select a control, you can move it by placing your mouse pointer anywhere between the handles along the edge of the control. When you do this, the mouse pointer turns into an open hand, as shown in Figure 11-13, and you can then drag the control to a new location. Access displays an outline of the control as you move the control to help you position it correctly. When a control has an attached label, moving either the control or the label in this way moves both of them.

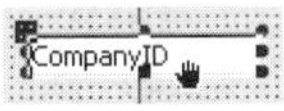

Figure 11-13. You can drag the edge of a selected control to move the control.

You can position a control and its attached label independently by dragging the larger handle in the upper left corner of the control or label. When you position the mouse pointer over this handle, the pointer turns into a hand with a pointing finger, as shown in Figure 11-14. Drag the control to a new location relative to its label.

Figure 11-14. You can drag the large handle of a selected control to move the control independently of its label.

You can delete a label from a control by selecting the label and pressing the Delete key. If you want to create a label that is independent of a control, you can use the Label tool. If you inadvertently delete a label from a control and you've made other changes so that you can no longer undo the deletion, you can attach a new label by doing the following:

1 Use the Label tool to create a new unattached label.
2 Select the label, and then choose Cut from the Edit menu to move the label to the Clipboard.
3 Select the control to which you want to attach the label, and then choose Paste from the Edit menu.

The Formatting Toolbar

The Formatting toolbar, shown in Figure 11-15, provides a quick and easy way to alter the appearance of a control by allowing you to click buttons rather than set properties. Select the object you want to format and then click the appropriate button on the toolbar. This toolbar is also handy for setting background colors for sections of the form. Table 11-2 describes each of the toolbar buttons.

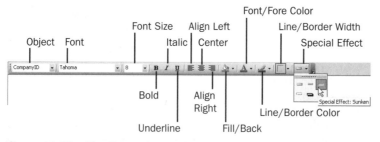

Figure 11-15. The Formatting toolbar.

> **Tip** You can select only one of the alignment buttons—Align Left, Align Right, or Center—at a time. If you do not click a button, alignment is set to General—text data aligns left and numeric data aligns right. You can also set the Text Align property in the property sheet.

Table 11-2. **Formatting Toolbar**

Button	Description
Object	Use to select a specific object on your form. This is particularly handy if you stack multiple controls on top of each other. You can also select objects from the drop-down list in the Properties window.
Font	Use to set the font for labels, text boxes, command buttons, toggle buttons, combo boxes, and list boxes.
Font Size	Use to set font size.
Bold	Click to set font style to bold.
Italic	Click to set font style to italic.
Underline	Click to underline text.
Align Left	Click to left-align text.
Center	Click to center text.
Align Right	Click to right-align text.
Fill/Back Color	Use to set the background color of the control or form area. You can also set the background color to transparent.
Font/Fore Color	Use to set the foreground color of the control.
Line/Border Color	Use to set the border color of the control. You can also set the border color to transparent.
Line/Border Width	Use to set the border width from hairline to 6 points wide.
Special Effect	(Shown with options opened.) Use to set the look of the control to flat, raised, sunken, etched, shadowed, or chiseled.

Depending on the object you select, some of the Formatting toolbar options might not be available. For example, you can't set text color on a bound object frame control, nor can you set fill or border colors on a toggle button because these areas are always set to gray for this kind of control. If you have the property sheet open and you scroll through it so that you can see the properties the Formatting toolbar sets, you can watch the settings in the property sheet change as you click different options on the toolbar.

Setting Text Box Properties

The next thing you might want to do is change some of the text box properties. Figure 11-16 shows some of the properties for the CompanyID text box control. Because the CompanyID field in the tblCompanies table is an AutoNumber field, which a user cannot change, you should change the properties of this control to prevent it from being selected on the form. Access provides two properties that you can set to control what the user can do. The *Enabled* property determines whether the control can receive the focus (the user can click in or tab to the control). The *Locked* property determines whether the user can enter data in the control. The defaults are Enabled Yes and Locked No.

You can set the Enabled property of the control to No so that the user cannot click in or tab to the control. When you do this, Access prohibits access to the field but causes the control and its label to appear dimmed because the control is not locked. (When Access sees that a control is disabled but is still potentially updatable despite being bound to an AutoNumber, it causes the control to appear dimmed.) To display the control and its label normally, just set Locked to Yes.

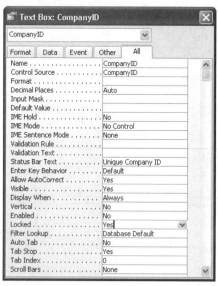

Figure 11-16.   Some of the properties for the CompanyID text box control.

If you specify a Format, Decimal Places, or Input Mask property setting when you define a field in a table, Access copies these settings to any text box that is bound to the field. Any data you enter using the form must conform to the field validation rule defined in the table; however, you can define a more restrictive rule for the form. Any new row inherits default values from the table unless you provide a different default value in the property sheet. The Status Bar Text property derives its value from the Description property setting you entered for the field in the table. You can learn more about control properties in the next chapter, "Customizing a Form," and in Part 5, "Automating an Access Application."

Setting Label Properties

You can also set separate properties for the labels attached to controls. Click the label for CompanyID to see the property sheet shown in Figure 11-17. Access copies the Caption property from the field in the underlying table to the Caption property in the associated control label. The default settings for the text box control on a form specify that all text boxes have labels and that the caption should have a trailing colon. When you added the CompanyID text box to the form, Access used the caption from the field's definition in the tblCompanies table (Company ID instead of the field name CompanyID), and added the trailing colon. Also, all controls on a form must have a name, so Access generated a name (Label0) that is the control type followed by an integer.

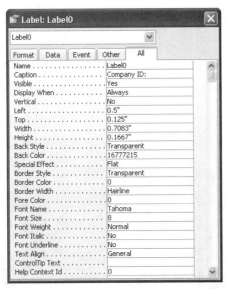

Figure 11-17. The property sheet for the CompanyID label control.

You also can correct the caption from inside a label by selecting the label, moving the mouse pointer inside the label until the pointer changes into an I-beam shape, and then clicking to set the insertion point inside the label text. You can delete unwanted characters, and you can type in new characters. When you finish correcting a label caption, you might find that the control is either too large or too small to adequately display the new name. You can change settings using the property sheet to adjust the size of a label, or you can select the control and drag the control's handles to adjust the size and alignment of the control.

> **Tip**   To quickly adjust the size of a label, select the label, choose the Size command from the Format menu, and then choose To Fit from the submenu.

Setting Form Properties

You can display the form's properties in the property sheet (as shown in Figure 11-18) by clicking anywhere outside the Detail section of the form or by choosing the Select Form command from the Edit menu. On the Format tab in Figure 11-18 on the next page, I set the caption to Companies / Organizations. This value will appear on the Form window's title bar in Form view or in Datasheet view.

Toward the bottom of the list of properties in Figure 11-18 are the Grid X and Grid Y properties that control the density of dots on the grid as discussed earlier in this chapter. The defaults are 24 dots per inch across (Grid X) and 24 dots per inch down (Grid Y), if your measurements are in U.S. units. For metric measurements, the defaults are 5 dots per centimeter in both directions. Access also draws a shaded line on the grid every inch or centimeter to help you line up controls. If you decide to turn on the Snap to Grid command on the Format menu to help you line up controls on your form, you might want to change the density of the grid dots to give you greater control over where you place objects on the form.

Chapter 11

417

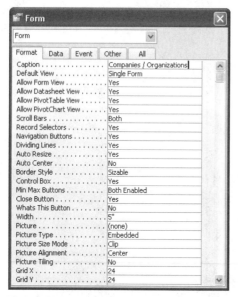

Figure 11-18. The form Format properties for the tblCompanies form.

Note You won't see the grid dots if you set either the Grid X or Grid Y property to more than 24 in U.S. measurements or more than 9 in metric measurements.

The properties beginning with On Current on the Event tab of the property sheet can be set to run macros or Visual Basic procedures. The events associated with these properties can trigger macro actions.

Customizing Colors and Checking Your Design Results

Let's explore some of the interesting effects you can design using colors. To make the fields on the form stand out, you can click in the Detail section and then set the background to dark gray using the Back Color button on the Formatting toolbar. To make the labels stand out against this dark background, drag the mouse pointer around all the label controls or click the horizontal ruler directly above all the label controls, and then set the Back Color to white. If you haven't already moved and resized the labels, you can select all the labels and then widen them all to the left by clicking the left edge sizing handle of any of the labels and dragging left. This pulls the long Company / Organization caption over so that it doesn't overlap the CompanyName field. If you also want to make the Detail section fit snugly around the controls on your form, drag the edges of the Detail section inward.

Tip To select all controls in a vertical area, click the horizontal ruler above the area containing the controls you want to select. Likewise, to select all controls in a horizontal area, click the vertical ruler.

When you finish working on this form in Design view, it might look something like the one shown in Figure 11-19. (I closed the field list and toolbox windows to get them out of the way.)

Chapter 11

Building a Form

First click here to
select all labels...

...and then choose white
as the background color.

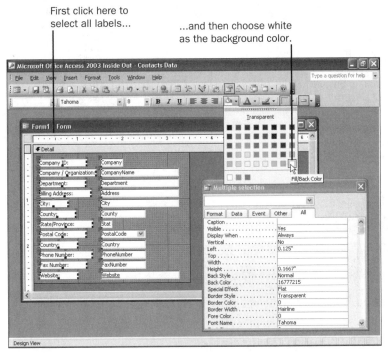

Figure 11-19. Adding contrast to the Companies / Organizations form.

Click the View button on the toolbar and select Form View to see your form. It will look similar to the form shown in Figure 11-20 on the next page. (You can find this form saved as *frmXmplCompany1* in the sample database.) Note that the labels are all different sizes and the contrast might be too distracting. You could further refine the look of this form by making all the labels the same size and perhaps aligning the captions to the right. You could also make the label background transparent or the same color as the Detail section and change the font color to white. You'll learn more about customizing your form design in the next chapter.

To size the Form window to exactly fit the boundaries of your form design, choose Size to Fit Form from the Window menu, as shown in the figure. Click the Save button on the toolbar or choose Save from the File menu to save your new form design.

Inside Out

Understanding the Allow Design Changes property

Microsoft Access 2000 introduced a feature to allow you to further modify the design of your forms even while you are in Form view. You can set the Allow Design Changes property of the form to All Views. This lets you open the property sheet while in Form view to make additional design changes, as shown in Figure 11-20. All new forms in Access have the Allow Design Changes property set to All Views by default. You should be sure to set this property to Design View Only before using any form in a finished application.

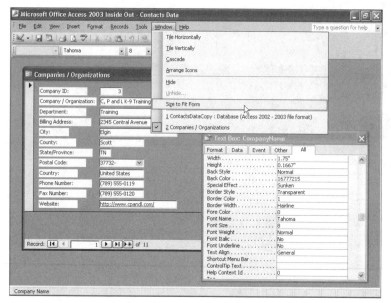

Figure 11-20. The finished Companies / Organizations form in Form view.

Working with Form Wizards

Now that you understand the basic mechanics of form design, you could continue to build all your forms from scratch in Design view. However, even the most experienced developers take advantage of the many wizards built into Microsoft Access to get a jump-start on design tasks. This section shows you how to use a form wizard to quickly build a custom form.

Creating the Basic Products Form with a Form Wizard

Begin by opening the *ContactsDataCopy.mdb* database, and then click the Tables button on the Object bar and select the tblProducts table. Next select Form from the New Object toolbar button's drop-down list or choose Form from the Insert menu. Access opens the New Form dialog box, as shown in Figure 11-21.

As you can see, you have nine choices in this dialog box: Design View (which you used in the previous section), Form Wizard, AutoForm: Columnar, AutoForm: Tabular, AutoForm: Datasheet, AutoForm: PivotTable, AutoForm: PivotChart, Chart Wizard, and PivotTable Wizard. The five AutoForm wizards quickly build a form, selecting all the defaults along the way. The Chart Wizard builds a form containing a graph object and walks you through all the steps to define the data for the graph and customize the way the graph works. The PivotTable Wizard creates a form with an embedded Microsoft Excel object and then shows you how to use Excel's PivotTable capabilities to create a data summary for display in your Access application. Note that in the New Form dialog box you can change the data source for your form by changing the table or query name displayed in the combo box.

Building a Form

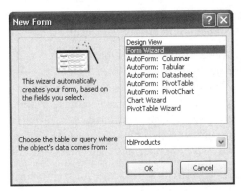

Figure 11-21. The New Form dialog box, in which you select a form wizard.

For this example, select Form Wizard and click OK. Access opens the window shown in Figure 11-22. You can select any field in the Available Fields list and click the single right arrow (>) button to copy that field to the Selected Fields list. You can also click the double right arrow (>>) button to copy all available fields to the Selected Fields list. If you copy a field in error, you can select the field in the Selected Fields list and click the single left arrow (<) button to remove the field from the list. You can remove all fields and start over by clicking the double left arrow (<<) button. For this example, click the double right arrow button to use all the fields in the tblProducts table in the new form.

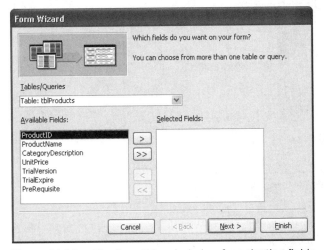

Figure 11-22. The Form Wizard window for selecting fields.

As you'll learn in Chapter 13, "Advanced Form Design," you can select fields from one table or query and then change the data source name in the Tables/Queries combo box to select a different but related table or query. If you have defined the relationships between tables in your database, the Form Wizard can determine how the data from multiple sources is related and can offer to build either a simple form to display all the data or a more complex one that shows some of the data in the main part of the form with related data displayed in an embedded subform. You'll use this technique to build a more complex form in Chapter 13.

At any time, you can click the Finish button to go directly to the last step of the wizard. You can also click the Cancel button at any time to stop creating the form.

After you select all the fields except the PreRequisite field from the tblProducts table, click Next. In the window that appears, the wizard gives you choices for the layout of your form. You can choose to display the controls on your form in columns, arrange the controls across the form in a tabular format (this creates a continuous form), create a form that opens in Datasheet view, place the fields in a block "justified" view, create a form using the data in PivotTable view, or create a form in PivotChart view. As you click on each option, the wizard shows you a graphic sample of each layout. For this example, select Columnar, and then click Next.

The wizard next displays a window in which you can select a style for your form, as shown in Figure 11-23. Note that if you choose to display the form in Datasheet view, the style won't apply to the datasheet but will appear if you shift from Datasheet view to Form view. The nice thing about this window is that the wizard shows you a sample of each selection on the left side of the window. You can look at each one and decide which you like best. In this example, the Stone style is selected. In Chapter 12, "Customizing a Form," you'll learn how to use the AutoFormat facility to create a custom look for your forms.

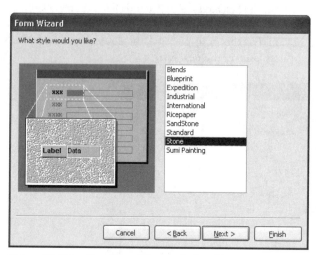

Figure 11-23. The Form Wizard window for selecting the style for your form.

Note When you select a style in the Form Wizard, the new style becomes the default for new forms you create using a wizard until you change the style setting again, either in the Form Wizard or AutoFormat wizards. See Chapter 12, "Customizing a Form."

Click Next to display the final window, where the Form Wizard asks for a title for your form. Type an appropriate title, such as *Products*. The wizard places this title in the Caption property of the form and also saves the form with this name. (If you already have a form named Products, Access appends a number to the end of the name to create a unique name.) Select the Open the form to view or enter information option, and then click the Finish button to go directly to Form view. Or you can select the Modify the form's design option, and then click Finish to open the new form in Design view. The finished form is shown in Form view in Figure 11-24.

Products
Product ID
1
Product Name
Demo Edition, Single User
Product Type
Single User
Price
$0.00
Trial?
Yes
Expire
30
Prerequisite
Record: 1 of 9

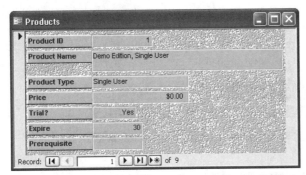

Figure 11-24. The Products form in a columnar format using the Stone style.

Notice that the Stone style uses labels sized alike with no ending colons on the captions. The TrialVersion field (labeled *Trial?*) appears right-aligned even though the form displays text because Access treats the underlying Yes/No data type as a number. You'll learn more about working with styles in the next chapter, "Customizing a Form."

If you're curious to see the tabular format, you can start a new form on the tblProducts table and use the Form Wizard again. Select all the fields except the PreRequisite field, select Tabular for the layout, and set the style back to Standard. For a title, type **Products - Tabular,** and open the new form in Form view. It should look something like the form shown in Figure 11-25. Close this form when you finish looking at it.

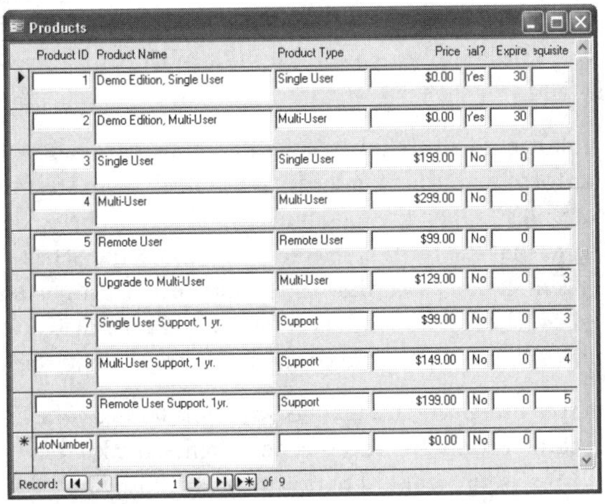

Products
Product ID Product Name Product Type Price ial? Expire equisite
1 Demo Edition, Single User Single User $0.00 Yes 30
2 Demo Edition, Multi-User Multi-User $0.00 Yes 30
3 Single User Single User $199.00 No 0
4 Multi-User Multi-User $299.00 No 0
5 Remote User Remote User $99.00 No 0
6 Upgrade to Multi-User Multi-User $129.00 No 0 3
7 Single User Support, 1 yr. Support $99.00 No 0 3
8 Multi-User Support, 1 yr. Support $149.00 No 0 4
9 Remote User Support, 1yr. Support $199.00 No 0 5
utoNumber) $0.00 No 0
Record: 1 of 9

Figure 11-25. The Products form in a tabular format.

Note I modified the form you see in Figure 11-25 to preserve the default sunken effect for text box controls in the Standard style. If you create this form on a Windows XP system, choose Use Windows Themed Controls on Forms on the Forms/Reports tab of the Options dialog box, and choose the default Windows XP theme in the Display Properties window, the text boxes appear flat on your form.

You can also investigate what a Justified form looks like by going through the exercise again and selecting Justified for the layout in the second window in the Form Wizard. If you choose the Industrial style, your result should look something like the one shown in Figure 11-26. Close this form when you finish looking at it.

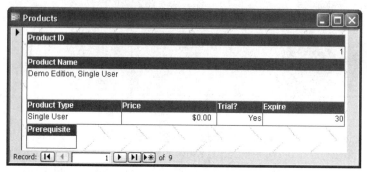

Figure 11-26. The Products form in a justified format.

Modifying the Products Form

The Form Wizard took care of some of the work, but there's still a lot you can do to improve the appearance and usability of this form. And even though the Form Wizard adjusted the display control widths, they're still not perfect. Most of the text boxes are larger than they need to be. The Form Wizard created a two-line text box for product name when one should suffice. I personally prefer to see field labels right-aligned and bold so they're easier to read. Finally, the ProductID field is an AutoNumber, so you should probably lock it and disable it so the user cannot type in the field.

You can either start with the columnar format form using the Stone style (shown in Figure 11-24) or start a new columnar form with the Standard style. (I decided to start over in Standard style for the following examples.) Open the form in Design view. To help align controls, click outside the Detail section so that the form is selected (or choose the Select Form command from the Edit menu), and make sure that the Grid X and Grid Y properties on the form's property sheet are set to 24. (Leave the settings at Grid X = 5 and Grid Y = 5 if you're working in metric measurements.) Be sure the Grid command is checked on the View menu.

Begin by shrinking the ProductID and UnitPrice text box controls to be about the same size as the TrialExpire control. Select the ProductID text box and change the Enabled property to No and the Locked property to Yes as you learned to do earlier. Choose Special Effect: Flat from the drop-down list of the Special Effect button on the toolbar to give your users a visual clue that they won't be able to type in the ProductID text box.

The ProductName text box needs to be only about two inches wide. You can set the width specifically by clicking on the control, opening the Properties window, clicking the Format tab, and typing 2" in the Width property (the tenth property down the list). Make the text box for CategoryDescription the same size as the ProductName text box to give your form a more uniform look. The Form Wizard created a text box that is two lines high for Product-Name, but it doesn't need to be bigger than one line. Select the control and then grab the bottom sizing box in the middle of the control and drag it up to make the control smaller. Choose Size on the Format menu and then To Fit on the submenu to resize the control to display one line. Click the Format tab in the Properties window and change the Scroll Bars property to None—the Form Wizard specified a vertical scroll bar in the two-line control that it designed. It doesn't make sense to show a scroll bar in a one-line control that is already wide enough to display all the data.

Now that you've made the ProductName text box smaller, you have extra space between it and the CategoryDescription text box. Select the CategoryDescription, UnitPrice, TrialVersion, and TrialExpire text boxes and move them up close to the ProductName text box. Unless you turned off Snap To Grid on the Format menu, it should be easy to line up the controls in their new positions.

Next, fix all the labels. Click in the horizontal ruler above the column of labels to select them all. Click the Right Align and Bold buttons on the toolbar to change their appearance. Grab the dividing line between the Form Header and Detail sections and drag it down to open up some space in the header. Click the Label tool in the toolbox and place it in the header. Type **Products** in the label and then set the Font Size to 14. Click the Bold and Italic buttons for emphasis. Finally, click the Format menu, choose Size, and then choose To Fit from the submenu to make the label large enough to display the characters in the larger font. After you shrink the right and bottom margins of your form, it should look similar to the one shown in Figure 11-27. Notice that none of the labels attached to the text boxes shows an ending colon. The Standard style doesn't include them.

Note If you're working in Windows XP with themed controls, you should select all the text box controls other than ProductID, set the Line/Border Color to something other than black, and then set the Special Effect property back to Sunken to see the sunken effect shown in Figure 11-27.

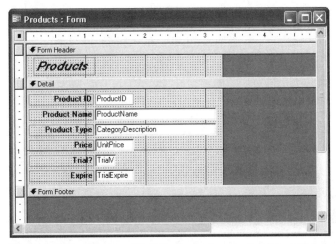

Figure 11-27. The modified Products form in Design view.

Finally, switch to Form view and choose Size to Fit Form from the Window menu. Your form should look something like the one shown in Figure 11-28. The form now looks a bit more customized—and somewhat more like the frmProducts form in the LawTrack Contacts application. You can find this form saved as *fxmplProducts1* in the sample database.

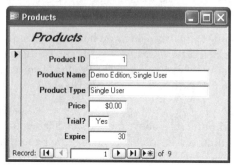

Figure 11-28. The modified Products form in Form view.

Simplifying Data Input with a Form

One drawback to working with a relational database is that often you have to deal with information stored in multiple tables. That's not a problem if you're using a query to link data, but working with multiple tables can be confusing if you're entering new data. Microsoft Access provides some great ways to show information from related tables, thus making data input much simpler.

Taking Advantage of Combo Boxes and List Boxes

In Chapter 10, "Using Forms," you saw how you can use a combo box or a list box to present a list of potential values for a control. To create the list, you can type the values in the Row Source property box of the control. You can also specify a table or a query as the source of the values in the list. Access displays the currently selected value in the text box portion of the combo box or as a highlighted selection in the list.

The CategoryDescription field in tblProducts is a simple text data type. To help ensure data consistency, there's a separate lookup table that contains a list of predefined product types. There's also a referential-integrity rule that keeps you from entering anything other than a predefined type in the CategoryDescription field. However, you can type anything you like in the CategoryDescription text box (labeled *Product Type*) that the Form Wizard designed. Go ahead and type any random string of characters in the text box and then try to save the record. You should see an unfriendly technobabble message about "related record is required in 'tlkpProductCategory'".

You can help avoid this problem by providing a combo box to edit and display the Category-Description field instead. The combo box can display the list of valid values from table tlkp-ProductCategory to make it easy for your user to choose a valid value. The combo box can also limit what the user enters to only values in the list. In Chapter 23, "Automating Your Application with Visual Basic," you'll learn how to write Visual Basic code to detect when a user tries to enter something that's not in the list so that you can provide your own, more user-friendly, message.

To see how a combo box works, you can replace the CategoryDescription text box control with a combo box on the Products form. In Design view, select the CategoryDescription text box control and then press the Delete key to remove the text box control from the form (this also removes the related label control). Be sure the Control Wizards button is selected in the toolbox, and then click the Combo Box button in the toolbox and drag the CategoryDescription field from the field list to the form. The new control appears on the form, and Access starts the Combo Box Wizard, as shown in Figure 11-29, to help you out.

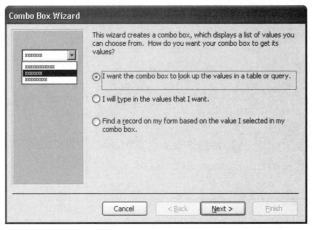

Figure 11-29. The first window of the Combo Box Wizard.

> **Tip** You can change a text box to a combo box by choosing Change To from the Format menu and then choosing Combo Box from the submenu. However, after you change a text box to a combo box in this way, you have to set the properties for the display list yourself.

Follow this procedure to build your combo box.

1 You want the combo box to display values from the tlkpProductCategory lookup table, so select the first option, and then click the Next button to go to the next window.

2 In the second window, the wizard displays a list of available tables in the database. Note that the wizard also provides an option to view queries or both tables and queries. Scroll down in the list and click Table: tlkpProductCategory to select that table, and click Next to go to the next window.

3 In the third window, the wizard shows you the single field in the table, Category-Description. Select that field and click the right arrow (>) to move it to the Selected Fields list. Click Next to go on.

4   The fourth window allows you to select up to four fields to sort either Ascending or Descending. Select the CategoryDescription field in the first box. The button next to the first box indicates *Ascending*, and you want to leave it that way. If you click the button, it changes to *Descending*, which is not what you want. (You can click the button again to set it back.) Click Next to go to the next window.

5   The wizard shows you the lookup values that your combo box will display as an embedded datasheet, as shown below. To size a column, click your mouse on the dividing line at the right edge of a column at the top, click, and drag the line. You can adjust the size of the column to be sure it displays all of the available descriptions properly. Click Next to go on.

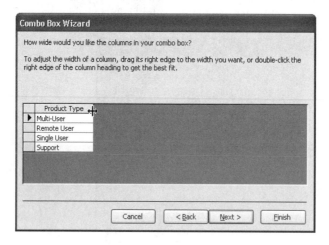

6   In the next window, the wizard asks whether you want to store the value from the combo box in a field from the table or query that you're updating with this form or simply save the value selected in an unbound control "for later use." You'll see in Part 5 of this book that unbound controls are useful for storing calculated values or for providing a way for the user to enter parameter data for use by your macros or Visual Basic procedures. In this case, you want to update the CategoryDescription field, so be sure to select the Store that value in this field option and select CategoryDescription from the drop-down list. Click Next to go to the last window of the wizard.

7   In the final window, shown on the next page, the wizard suggests a caption that you probably want to correct. In this case, enter **Product Type** in the box. Click Finish, and you're all done.

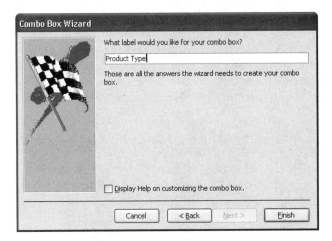

If you have the property sheet open, you can study the properties set by the Combo Box Wizard, as shown in Figure 11-30. The Control Source property shows that the combo box is bound to the CategoryDescription field. The Row Source Type property indicates that the data filling the combo box comes from the table or query entered in the Row Source property box. Notice that the wizard generated an SQL statement in the Row Source property box. You can also specify a value list as the Row Source property, or you can ask Access to create a list from the names of fields in the query or table specified in the Row Source property.

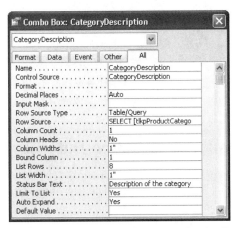

Figure 11-30. The properties set by the Combo Box Wizard.

The Column Count property is set to 1 to indicate that one column should be created from the list. You have the option of asking Access to display column headings when the combo box is open, but you don't need that for this example, so leave the Column Heads property set to No. The wizard sets the Column Widths property based on the width you set in step 5. The next property, Bound Column, indicates that the first column (the only column in this case) is the one that sets the value of the combo box and, therefore, the value of the bound field in the table.

When you open the form in Form view, it should look like the one shown in Figure 11-31. You can see that the CategoryDescription combo box now shows the list of valid values from the lookup table. Notice also that the label the wizard attached looks more like the labels that the Form Wizard originally created. You can make this label look like the others by changing it to a bold font and aligning it right. (You can find this form saved as *fxmplProducts2* in the sample database.)

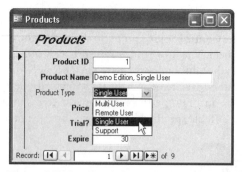

Figure 11-31. The finished CategoryDescription combo box in operation.

> **Tip** If you want Access to select the closest matching entry when you type a few leading characters in a combo box, set the control's Auto Expand property to Yes.

Using Toggle Buttons, Check Boxes, and Option Buttons

If your table contains a field that has a yes/no, a true/false, or an on/off value, you can choose from three types of controls that graphically display and set the status of this type of field: toggle buttons, check boxes, and option buttons.

The tblProducts table has a TrialVersion field that indicates whether the particular product is a free trial edition that expires in a specific number of days. As you can see in the original text box control created by the Form Wizard (see Figure 11-24), the word Yes or No appears depending on the value in the underlying field. This field might be more appealing and understandable if it were displayed in a check box control.

Inside Out

Choosing toggle buttons and check boxes and option buttons—how to decide?

Although you can certainly use any of these three controls to display an underlying Yes/No data type, you should try to use these controls in your application similarly to the way Windows uses them. Your users might be confused if you try to use them in a different way.

- Use a *toggle button* control to display an option value. A toggle button works best to display an option that is on or off.

- Use a *check box* control to display all simple yes/no or true/false values.

- Use an *option button* control when the user needs to make a choice from several options. You should not use an option button to display simple yes/no or true/false values.

I personally never use a toggle button or option button except inside an option group control. You can learn more about working with the option group control in Chapter 13, "Advanced Form Design."

To change the TrialVersion control on the Products form, first delete the TrialVersion text box control. Next select the Check Box tool, and then drag the TrialVersion field from the field list onto the form in the open space you left in the form. Your form in Design view should now look like the one shown in Figure 11-32. Notice that the default check box also includes a label, but the label is positioned to the right of the control and does not include a colon. If you want to move the label, select it, and then use the large handle shown earlier in Figure 11-14 to move the label to the left of the check box. You should also change the font to bold to match the other labels.

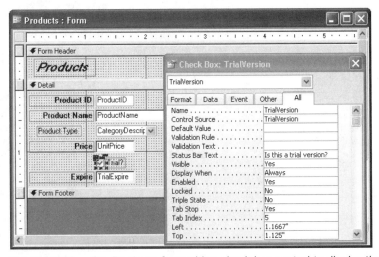

Figure 11-32. The Products form with a check box control to display the TrialVersion field.

After making final adjustments to the TrialVersion label, click the Form View button to see the result. Your form should look like the one shown in Figure 11-33. One of the interesting side effects of using a special control to display data in a form is that the control properties carry over to Datasheet view. Switch to the Datasheet view of this form. The CategoryDescription field is displayed as a drop-down list on the datasheet and the TrialVersion field still looks like a check box. You might decide to design some forms to be used in Datasheet view, but you can customize the look of the datasheet by using controls other than text boxes while in Design view. By the way, this design sample is saved as *fxmplProducts3* in the sample database.

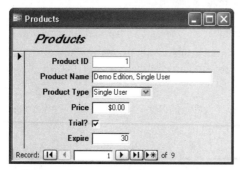

Figure 11-33.   The final Products form in Form view.

By now, you should be getting a feel for the process of building forms. In the next chapter, you'll learn how to customize the appearance of your forms.

Customizing a Form

In Chapter 11, "Building a Form," you created a form from scratch based on the tblCompanies table in the *ContactsDataCopy.mdb* sample database. You also had a chance to build a simple form on tblProducts using a wizard. These forms are functional, but they're not yet professional grade. In this chapter, you'll learn how to customize your forms to make them more attractive and useful.

 Note   The examples in this chapter are based on the forms, queries, tables, and data in *HousingDataCopy.mdb* on the companion CD included with this book. The results you see from the samples in this chapter may not exactly match what you see in this book if you have changed the sample data in the file. Also, all the screen images in this chapter were taken on a Windows XP system with the display theme set to Windows XP. Your results may look different if you are using a different operating system or a different theme.

Aligning and Sizing Controls

To learn how to customize a form, switch to the *HousingDataCopy.mdb* sample database. You need a form to edit and display employee data, and the easiest way to get started is to create a blank form based on the tblEmployees table. First, click the Tables button in the Object bar in the Database window. Select the tblEmployees table and choose Form from the New Object toolbar button. In the New Form dialog box, choose Design View, and click OK to start your new form.

Drag down the bottom margin of the Detail area to give yourself some room to work. Click the Format menu and make sure Snap to Grid is not selected. (I'm asking you to do this on purpose so that you can learn ways to line up and evenly space controls.) Open the field list, and drag and drop each field into a vertical column on your form about 1.5 inches from the left edge, beginning with the EmployeeNumber field and ending with the BirthDate field. Your starting point should look something like Figure 12-1 on the next page. (If you don't want to do the work yourself to get to this point, you can find this form saved as *frmXmplEmployee1* in the sample database.)

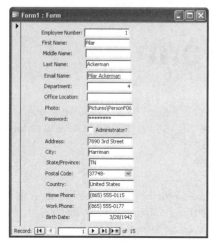

Figure 12-1. Starting to build a form to display and edit employee data.

Note The *HousingDataCopy.mdb* sample database has a special template form called Normal that has its default control properties set to preserve the sunken and etched special effects. This ensures that you'll see the default sunken text boxes when you follow the exercises in this chapter, even when you're running on a Windows XP machine with themed controls enabled. You'll learn more about creating template forms later in this chapter.

If you threw the form together quickly to help you enter some data (as you did in the previous chapter to create a simple Companies input form in the *LawTrackDataCopy.mdb* database), it probably doesn't matter if the form doesn't look perfect. But all the text boxes are the same size, which means some are too large and some are too small to display the data. Also, the labels are different sizes and not right-aligned. Finally, all the text boxes and labels are out of alignment. If you're designing the form to be used continuously in an application, it's worth the extra effort to fine-tune the design so that it will look professional and be easy to use.

Note Even if you follow along precisely with the steps described in this chapter, your results might vary slightly. All the alignment commands are sensitive to your current screen resolution. When your screen driver is set to a high resolution (for example, 1280×1024), the distance between grid points is logically smaller than it is when the screen driver is set to a low resolution (such as 800×600). You should design your forms at the same resolution as the computers that will run your application.

To examine the alignment and relative size of controls on your form, you can open the property sheet in Design view and click various controls. For example, Figure 12-2 shows the property sheets for the EmployeeNumber and the FirstName text box controls. You can see by looking at the values for the Left property (the distance from the left edge of the form) that the EmployeeNumber control is a bit closer to the left margin than is the FirstName control.

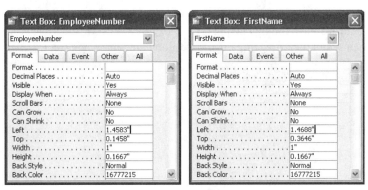

Figure 12-2. The properties that define the placement and size of the EmployeeNumber and FirstName text box controls.

You could move around the form and adjust controls so that they fit your data. You could painstakingly enter values for each control's Left property to get all controls in a column to line up exactly and then set the Top property (defining the distance from the top of the Detail section) for controls that you want to appear in a row. You could also adjust the values for the Width and Height properties so that controls and labels are the same width and height where appropriate. Fortunately, there are easier ways to make all these adjustments.

Sizing Controls to Fit Content

One adjustment you might want to make on this employees form is to boldface the font for all the labels. Remember from the previous chapter that you can click in the horizontal ruler at the top of the design area to select all controls in a column, so do this to select all the label controls on the left. You can then hold down the Shift key and click the Administrator? label that's not in the column to include it in your selection. Click the Bold button on the Formatting toolbar to change the font in all selected controls.

However, now that you have changed the font, the label controls are no longer large enough to display all the characters, as shown in Figure 12-3 on the next page. (Notice, for example, that the letter *y* in Employee Number appears clipped off at the bottom.) Also, although all the text boxes and the combo box appear high enough to adequately display the data in the default Tahoma 8-point font, they're actually too small.

Microsoft Office Access 2003 has a command called Size/To Fit that sizes label controls to fit the width of the caption text in the label. This command also ensures that text boxes and combo boxes are tall enough to display your data using the font size you've selected. You can, if you like, select all the controls so that you can resize them all at once. You can choose Select All from the Edit menu to highlight all the controls on your form. To select a specific group of controls, click the first one and then hold down the Shift key as you click each additional control that you want to select. You can also drag the mouse pointer across the form—as long as you don't start dragging while you are over a control—and the mouse pointer will delineate a selection box. (If you start by clicking on a control and then attempt to delineate other controls by dragging, you'll only move the control.) Any controls that are inside the selection box when you release the mouse button will be selected. You can also select all controls in a vertical or a horizontal band by making the rulers visible (choose the Ruler command from the View menu) and then dragging the mouse along the top or side ruler.

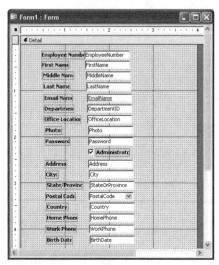

Figure 12-3. With the boldface font, the label controls are no longer large enough.

After you select the controls you want, choose the Size command from the Format menu, and then select To Fit from the submenu. The Detail section should now look something like that shown in Figure 12-4. (You cannot see the entire Employee Number label because the right end of it is hidden under the EmployeeNumber text box.)

Tip You can "size to fit" any individual control or label by clicking the control to select it and then double-clicking any of its sizing handles.

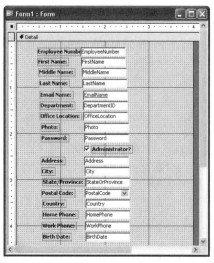

Figure 12-4. The result of sizing all controls to fit.

Tip Setting selection options

If you think you'll select multiple controls often, you might want to experiment with an option setting that governs how you can select controls with your mouse pointer. From the Tools menu, choose Options, and then click the Forms/Reports tab of the Options dialog box. When you select the Partially enclosed option, the selection box you draw with your mouse needs to touch only part of a control to select it. If you select the Fully enclosed option, the selection box must contain the entire control in order for the control to be selected. Fully enclosed is most useful for complex forms with many controls that are close to each other so that you don't have to worry about inadvertently selecting controls that you touch but don't fully enclose with the selection box.

Inside Out

Limitations in use of the Size/To Fit command

The Size/To Fit command works very well to set the height of labels, text boxes, and combo boxes based on the font you have chosen. It also does a reasonable job setting the width of labels based not only on the font but also on the characters you have specified in the Caption property. However, it's not perfect, so you should be aware of the following:

- When a label contains a long caption and has a large font that is bold or italic or both, the result of the Size/To Fit command is often not wide enough. You will have to adjust the width manually.

- The Size/To Fit command does not adjust the width of a text box or combo box because it cannot predict in advance how many characters might need to be displayed from the Control Source property. You must specifically set the width based on the data you expect the control to display.

- The Size/To Fit command does not work for list boxes. When you switch to Form view, and your list box Row Source contains enough rows to fill the list box, you might find that you see only part of a row at the bottom. (You'll see only the top part of the characters.) You must switch back and forth between Design view and Form view, adjusting the height of the control manually so that it displays complete rows.

Switch to Form view and scroll through several of the records to get an idea of which controls aren't wide enough to display the data from the table and which ones could be made narrower. You could painstakingly resize each control to exactly fit what you see in the sample data, but this is a bad idea for two reasons:

1. The data is a sample of only 15 records, so new data you enter later might be much longer in some fields. You should size the fields that aren't long enough to be 25% to 50% wider than what you think you need right now.

2. A form that has a hodgepodge of a dozen or more different control widths won't make for a very visually pleasing design. You should pick two or three standard widths to use, even if some of the controls end up being wider than necessary.

Chapter 12

You can logically group the text box controls and the combo box control in this form into three separate lengths, as follows:

- Short: EmployeeNumber, DepartmentID, and StateOrProvince
- Medium: FirstName, MiddleName, LastName, Password, PostalCode, HomePhone, WorkPhone, and BirthDate
- Long: EmailName, OfficeLocation, Photo, Address, City, and Country

> **Note** The Photo field in tblEmployees is a text field containing the name of the picture file. In Chapter 23, "Automating Your Application with Visual Basic," you'll learn how to load the file into an image control using Visual Basic code to display the picture. Also, although you can resize the check box control, the size of the graphic image inside the control doesn't change.

You can make the necessary adjustments by leaving the medium-length fields as they are and adjusting the fields in the other two groups. First, select the EmployeeNumber control and then hold down the Shift key while you select the DepartmentID and StateOrProvince controls. Next, click the sizing box in the middle of the right edge of one of the controls and drag the right edge to the left until all three controls are about half their original size. Now, click the EmailName control and hold down the Shift key while you select the OfficeLocation, Photo, Address, City, and Country controls. Click the sizing box in the middle of the right edge of one of these controls and drag the edge right until all three controls are about 50% bigger than their original size. Your layout should now look something like Figure 12-5.

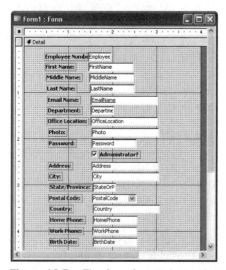

Figure 12-5. The form for employee data with the controls sized to better fit the data.

Before you go on, you might want to save the form and name it frmEmployees. You can find the form at this stage saved as *frmXmplEmployee2* in the sample database.

Adjusting Control Layout

You could have also used the AutoForm: Columnar Form Wizard to get a jump-start on your employees form. However, that wizard chooses the last AutoForm template you used (Sumi Painting in the last chapter). It also lays out controls in two columns, without any regard to clusters of fields that might work well lined up side by side. Setting up two columns to edit this data is probably a good idea to make better use of the screen space that is wider than it is tall, but by doing it yourself, you can pick which fields go in which column. For example, you might want to place the work-related fields (EmailName, Department, WorkPhone, Office-Location, Password, and IsAdmin) in one column, and personal fields (Address, City, State-OrProvince, PostalCode, Country, HomePhone, BirthDate, and Photo) in another.

To adjust your sample employees form in this way, follow these steps.

1 Stretch the Detail area to about 6 inches wide to give yourself some room to work.

2 Select as a group the Address, City, StateOrProvince, PostalCode, Country, and HomePhone controls and move them into a new column on the right. You're going to end up with two fewer controls in the right column than in the left, so line up the Address control opposite the MiddleName control.

3 Grab the Photo control and move it over under HomePhone opposite Password.

4 Select the WorkPhone control and move it into the space vacated by Photo.

5 Move the BirthDate control under Photo and across from IsAdmin (the Administrator check box).

6 Grab the bottom edge of the Detail section and shrink the section so that it's now wider than it is high.

7 Select the Employee Number label, grab the positioning handle in the upper left corner, and move the label to the left out from under the EmployeeNumber text box.

When you're done, you should have a form design that looks something like the one shown in Figure 12-6. Now you're ready to fine-tune your form using alignment and control-size adjustments.

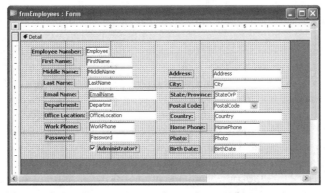

Figure 12-6.   The employees form after you arrange the controls into columns that make sense.

"Snapping" Controls to the Grid

It's a good idea to design your form so that all the controls are spaced evenly down the form and all controls in a column line up. One way that you might find convenient to do this is to take advantage of the grid. If you enable Snap to Grid on the Format menu, when you move any control, its upper left corner "snaps" to the nearest grid point. You can use this feature to help you line up controls both horizontally and vertically.

You can adjust the density of the grid by changing the Grid X and Grid Y properties in the property sheet of the form. Be sure that the property sheet is open, and then choose Select Form from the Edit menu. For this example, set the Grid X and Grid Y properties to 16 (0.0625 inch between grid points). This works well for the default 8-point Tahoma font because the "sized to fit" text boxes will be 0.17 inch high. You can place these text boxes every 0.25 inch (four grid points) down the form, which leaves adequate space between the controls. This reduced density also makes it easier to see the grid points so that you can move controls close to the point you want. You could set Grid X and Grid Y to 4, but that reduces flexibility for placing your controls.

The fastest way to snap all controls to the grid is to choose Select All from the Edit menu, choose Align from the Format menu, and then choose To Grid from the submenu. The result might look something like that shown in Figure 12-7.

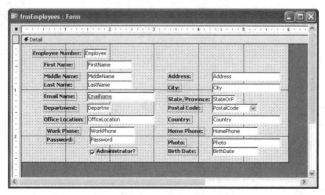

Figure 12-7. The employees form after you "snap" the controls to the grid.

If you want to position each control individually, enable Snap to Grid by making sure that it is selected on the Format menu. (You'll see a check mark in front of this command when it is active.) Click each text box, combo box, or check box control and drag it vertically to positions every 0.25 inch (every fourth grid point) down the grid. When you release the mouse button, you'll see the upper left corner of the control "snap" to the nearest grid point. As you saw in the previous chapter, when you select and move a control that has an attached label, Access moves a control and its label as a unit. If you previously moved a label up or down independent of its attached control by using the positioning handle in the upper left corner, you might need to select either the control or its label and use the positioning handle again to realign each label and associated control.

> **Note**   For a simple form with a few controls, Snap to Grid works well to help you line up controls. For more complex forms, using the Format/Align commands produces a better result. Read the next section to learn about these commands.

Snapping to the grid can help you spread the controls apart to make them easier to work with. You'll see in the next few steps that it's easy to line them all up properly.

Lining Up Controls

You now have your controls spaced down the form, but they might not be equally spaced, and they probably aren't aligned vertically and horizontally. These problems are easy to fix. First, if your form ended up looking like the sample in Figure 12-7 with one or more pairs of controls touching, you need to create some more space by moving down the bottom controls in each column. First, click on the IsAdmin check box at the bottom of the first column to select it and press the Down Arrow key once for each pair of touching controls. (I needed to move the control down two rows of dots in my sample.) Do the same, if necessary, to the BirthDate control at the bottom of the second column. Next, select all the text box controls and the check box control in the first column. You can do this by clicking the first text box control (not its associated label) and then holding down the Shift key as you click each of the remaining controls in the column. Or you can click in the ruler above the controls. Choose Vertical Spacing from the Format menu, and then select Make Equal from the submenu. Finally, choose all the text box controls and the combo box control in the second column, and execute the Make Equal command again.

Now you're ready to line up the labels. To get started, select all the labels in the left column. (You can do this the same way you selected all the data bound controls in a column.) When you have selected them, your form should look something like the one shown in Figure 12-8. Notice that Access also shows the large positioning handles in the upper left corner of all the related controls but no sizing handles.

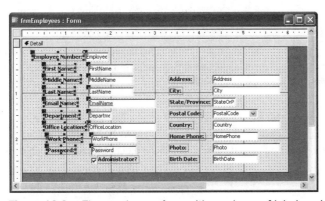

Figure 12-8.   The employees form with a column of labels selected.

The labels will look best if their right edges align. You have two choices at this point. If you turn off the Snap to Grid command, you can have Access align all the labels with the label whose right edge is farthest to the right, even if that edge is between dots on the grid. If you leave Snap to Grid on, you can have Access align the labels with the label farthest to the right and then snap the entire group to the nearest grid point.

Note For this example, I left Snap to Grid turned on, but you can try it both ways to see which gives you the best result. Try it with Snap to Grid on, and then click the Undo button on the toolbar and try it with Snap to Grid turned off.

When you're ready to align the selected labels on your form, choose the Align command from the Format menu, and then select the Right command from the submenu. While you're at it, click the Align Right button on the toolbar to align the captions to the right edge of all the label controls. Click outside the design area to select the form, which will cancel the selection of the labels. Your form should look similar to the one shown in Figure 12-9.

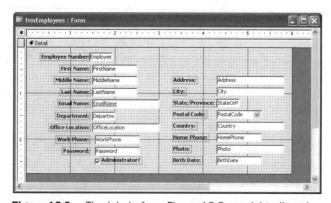

Figure 12-9. The labels from Figure 12-8 are right aligned.

To further improve the alignment of the controls on the employees form (assuming your form now looks like Figure 12-9), do the following.

1   The EmployeeNumber text box is a bit too far to the left. Click the control to select it and then click the positioning handle in the upper left corner and drag the control to the right. If you still have Snap to Grid turned on, it should line up with the FirstName control.

2   Select the EmployeeNumber, FirstName, MiddleName, LastName, EmailName, DepartmentID, OfficeLocation, WorkPhone, Password, and IsAdmin controls. Choose Align from the Format menu, and then select Left from the submenu.

3   Select the labels in the right column and right align them. Also click the Align Right button on the toolbar to align the captions to the right edge of the label controls.

4   In my sample, the labels in the right column end up a bit too close to the related data controls. Fixing this is a bit tricky. Select the longest label (State/Province), grab its positioning handle in the upper left corner, and drag it left one row of dots. Grab the

sizing handle in the middle of the right edge and expand the label size until it snaps to one row of dots away from the StateOrProvince text box. Now, select all the labels again, align them left, and then align them right. Note that by first setting the right edge of the longest label, then aligning all the labels first to the left, the longest label is now assured to protrude farthest to the right. Thus, when the labels are all aligned right again, they line up at the new right offset of the longest label.

5 I like all my labels to appear to the left of the related control, so click the Administrator? label to select it, grab its positioning handle in the upper left corner, and drag it to the left of the IsAdmin check box. If you still have Snap to Grid turned on and you do this carefully, the label should line up vertically with the other labels in the column and horizontally with the check box. While you're at it, click the Align Right button on the toolbar. If you like, click in the Administrator? label and add a colon to the end of the text.

6 Close up the bottom of the Detail area a bit so that you have the same amount of space below the bottom control as you do above the top control.

After you complete these steps, your form should look something like the one shown in Figure 12-10.

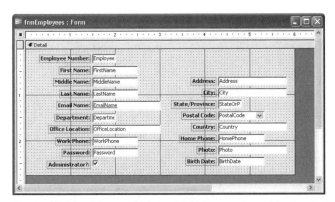

Figure 12-10. The controls and labels are aligned horizontally and vertically.

Tip Moving controls in a horizontal or vertical plane

If you want to move one or more controls only horizontally or only vertically, hold down the Shift key as you select the control (or the last control in a group) that you want to move, and then drag either horizontally or vertically. When Access detects movement either horizontally or vertically, it "locks" the movement and won't let the objects stray in the other axis. If you inadvertently start to drag horizontally when you mean to move vertically (or vice versa), click the Undo button and try again. Moving controls in this way is especially useful when you have Snap to Grid turned off.

If you switch to Form view, you can see the result of your work as shown in Figure 12-11 on the next page. You can find this form saved as *frmXmplEmployee3* in the sample database.

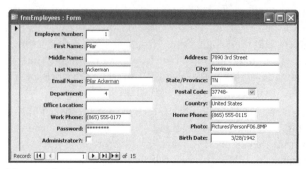

Figure 12-11. The employees form with controls aligned and sized.

> **Tip** Forms have an Auto Resize property. If you set this property to Yes, Access sizes the Form window to exactly fit the form. Note that Access won't automatically resize a form if you've switched from Design view to Form view. You can set the Auto Center property to Yes to center the Form window in the current Access workspace.

Enhancing the Look of a Form

The employees form you've built thus far looks fairly plain. It uses default fonts and a background color that's inherited from the color you have defined in Windows for 3-D objects (sometimes called the Button Face color). In this section, you'll learn about additional enhancements you can make to your form's design.

Lines and Rectangles

Microsoft Access comes with two drawing tools, the Line tool and the Rectangle tool, that you can use to enhance the appearance of your forms. You can add lines to separate parts of your form visually. Rectangles are useful for surrounding and setting off a group of controls on a form.

On your employees form, it might be helpful to add a line to separate the primary information about the employee in the first column from personal information in the second column. To make sufficient room for the line, you should move the controls in the first column to the left. The easiest way to do this is to switch to Design view, select all the affected controls and labels, and then move them as a group. Start by clicking the top ruler just above the right edge of the controls, and then drag in the ruler toward the left until the selection indicator touches all the controls in the left column. (If you can't see the rulers, be sure that the Ruler command is selected on the View menu.) Release the mouse button, and all the controls and labels in the left column will be selected. To be sure you move all these controls as a group, choose Group from the Format menu. Access shows you that the controls are now grouped by placing a rectangular line around all the controls. Place the mouse pointer over the edge of the group so that the pointer changes to a hand shape (see Figure 12-12), and slide the entire group left a bit.

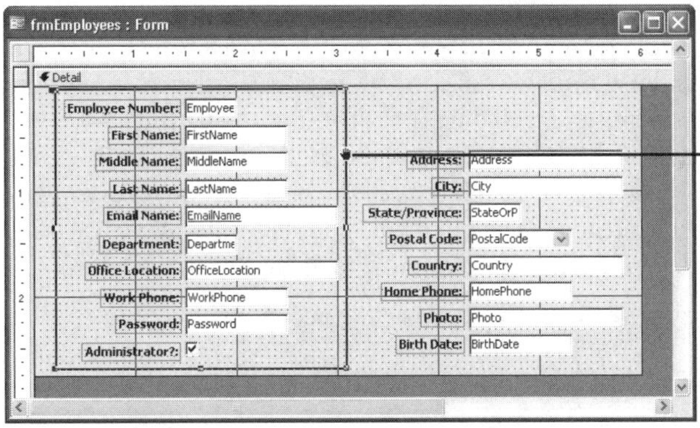

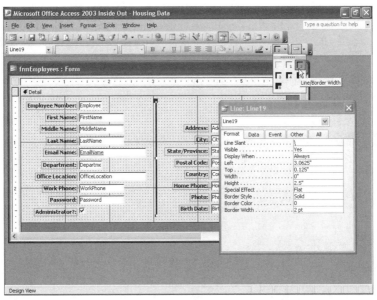

Figure 12-12. Moving a set of grouped controls.

Next select the Line tool from the toolbox. To draw your line, click near the top of the form between the two columns, about two grid rows below the top edge, and drag toward the form's bottom edge. If the line isn't exactly vertical, you can drag the bottom end left or right to adjust it. You can also set its Width property to 0 in the property sheet to make it perfectly vertical. (As you might imagine, setting the Height property to 0 makes the line horizontal.) Use the Line/Border Width button on the toolbar to make the line a little thicker if you want. (Or, change the Border Width property in the Properties window.) Click the down arrow next to the button and choose the border width you want. Your form should now look similar to the one shown in Figure 12-13.

Tip When drawing a line on your form, you can make your line exactly horizontal or exactly vertical if you hold down the Shift key as you click and draw the line.

Figure 12-13. Use the Line tool to draw a line on a form; use the Border Width button to adjust the line width.

You can add emphasis to the form by drawing a rectangle around all the controls. To do this, you might first need to move all the controls down and to the right a bit and make the Detail section slightly wider and taller. First, expand your form by about 0.5 inch across and down. Choose Select All from the Edit menu, and then drag all the controls so that you have about 0.25 inch of space around all the edges. (This might seem like too much space, but we'll use the extra space to have some fun later.) Select the Rectangle tool, click where you want to place one corner of the rectangle, and drag to the intended location of the opposite corner. When you draw a rectangle around all the controls, your form will look similar to the one shown in Figure 12-14.

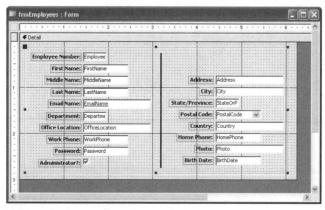

Figure 12-14. The employees form after a rectangle with a default etched look is added.

Note that the rectangle control actually covers and is on top of all the other controls. However, because the default rectangle is transparent with an etched special effect, you can see the other controls through the rectangle. If you prefer a solid rectangle, you can select the rectangle control and then use the Fill/Back Color button on the toolbar to select the color you want. (A light gray will work best.) When you add a solid control like this after you've created other controls, the solid control will cover the previous controls. You can select the control and choose Send to Back from the Format menu to reveal the covered controls and keep the solid control in the background.

Go ahead and make the rectangle a solid light gray and send it to the back. Now switch to Form view, and choose Size to Fit Form from the Window menu. Your employees form should look similar to the one shown in Figure 12-15.

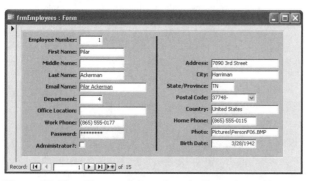

Figure 12-15. The employees form in Form view with a line and a solid rectangle added.

Colors and Special Effects

You can also use color and special effects to highlight objects on your form. For example, you can make all the controls appear to "float" on a raised surface on the form. To do so, switch to Design view and select the rectangle you just created. Use the Special Effect button on the toolbar to change the rectangle from Etched to Raised. Your form will look similar to the one shown in Figure 12-16.

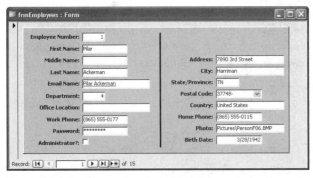

Figure 12-16. The rectangle behind the controls appears raised above the surface of the form background.

Next select the Rectangle tool again, and set Back Color to dark gray and Special Effect to Sunken using the buttons on the toolbar. Draw a second rectangle so that it forms a border about halfway between the edge of the first rectangle and the edge of the grid. Choose Send to Back from the Format menu to send this latest rectangle to the background. Switch to Form view to see the result. The first gray rectangle now appears to float on the form, surrounded by a "moat" of dark gray, as shown in Figure 12-17.

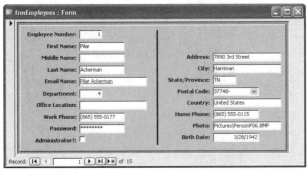

Figure 12-17. The first light gray rectangle appears to float on the form using special effects.

You can find this form saved as *frmXmplEmployee4* in the sample database.

Chapter 12

447

Inside Out

Matching color settings to system colors

Although you can certainly pick from a broad palette of colors for any design object, you might want to design your forms so that they always inherit colors from the options the user has set in the Windows Display dialog box. In fact, if you select the Detail section of the employees form you've been building, open the Properties window, and find the Back Color property, you'll find a strange negative number: -2147483633. This happens to be a special code number that means to use the color set in Windows for button faces and other 3-D objects. Following is a list of color code numbers that you can use to set colors in your forms and controls to match those set in Windows objects:

Code	Meaning
–2147483648	Scroll bar color
–2147483647	Desktop color
–2147483646	Color of the title bar for the active window
–2147483645	Color of the title bar for the inactive window
–2147483644	Menu background color
–2147483643	Window background color
–2147483642	Window frame color
–2147483641	Color of text on menus
–2147483640	Color of text in windows
–2147483639	Color of text in caption, size box, and scroll arrow
–2147483638	Border color of active window
–2147483637	Border color of inactive window
–2147483636	Background color of multiple-document interface (MDI) applications (the color of the area under the toolbars in Access)
–2147483635	Background color of items selected in a control
–2147483634	Text color of items selected in a control
–2147483633	Color of shading on the face of command buttons and other 3-D objects
–2147483632	Color of shading on the edge of command buttons
–2147483631	Grayed Text that appears dimmed (disabled) text
–2147483630	Text color on push buttons
–2147483629	Color of text in an inactive caption (a caption in a window that does not have the focus)
–2147483628	Highlight color for 3-D display elements
–2147483627	Darkest shadow color for 3-D display elements
–2147483626	Next lightest 3-D color after the highlight color
–2147483625	Color of text in ToolTips
–2147483624	Background color of ToolTips

Fonts

Another way you can enhance the appearance of your forms is by varying the fonts and font sizes you use. When you select any control that can display text or data, Access makes font, font size, and font attribute controls available on the Formatting toolbar so that you can easily change how the text in that control looks. Click the down arrow next to the Font Name combo box to open a list of all the available fonts, as shown in Figure 12-18. Select the font you want for the control.

Figure 12-18. A partial list of fonts in the Font Name combo box.

> **Note** The font list shows all fonts currently installed on your computer. Use the Fonts folder in Windows Control Panel to add or remove fonts. A double-T icon next to the font name in the list indicates a TrueType font that is suitable for both screen display and printing. A printer icon next to the font name indicates a font designed for your printer but that might not look exactly the same when displayed on your screen. A font with no icon indicates a font designed for your screen; a screen font might look different when you print it.

If you want to add some variety, you can use bold or italic type in a few key places. In this case, select all the labels on the form and select a serif font such as Times New Roman.

You can add a label to the header of the form to display a title such as Employees. To open up the header and footer of the form, choose Form Header/Footer from the View menu. Grab the bottom edge of the footer and close it up so that it has zero height. Expand the header to give yourself some room to work. Choose the Label tool from the toolbox, draw a label about 1.5 inches wide and 0.5 inches high, type the word **Employees** in the label, and press Enter. Set the label in the header to the Tahoma font (a sans serif font), bold, italic, and 18 points in size. Double-click one of the sizing boxes to size the control to fit and drag the right edge to the right if all the letters don't show in the label. You can see a portion of this work under way in Figure 12-19 on the next page.

Chapter 12

449

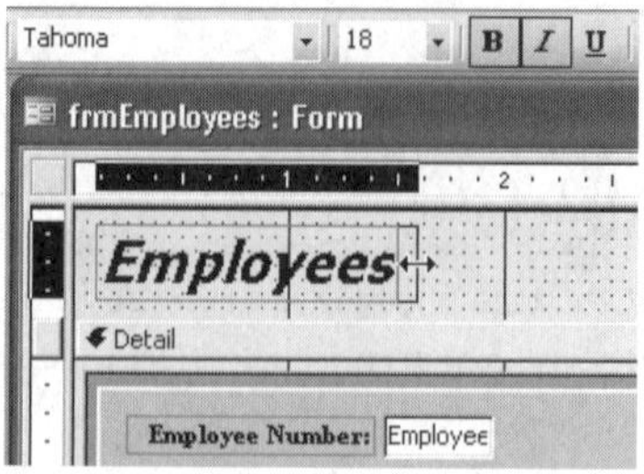

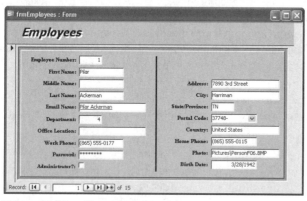

Figure 12-19. Using font settings in a form header label.

You can create a special "shadowed" effect behind this label in the header by doing the following.

1 Copy the label you just created to the Clipboard, and paste it in the header.

2 Change the foreground color of the pasted label to white, and then choose Send to Back from the Format menu.

3 Turn off the Snap to Grid command on the Format menu, and use the arrow keys to move the white label so that it is slightly lower and to the right of the first label.

4 Click the Form Header bar to select that section and set the background color to light gray to provide some contrast.

When you finish, the form should look similar to the one shown in Figure 12-20. (You can find this form saved in the sample database as frmXmplEmployee5.)

Figure 12-20. The employees form using some different fonts for variety.

> **Tip** A form with too many fonts or font sizes will look busy and jumbled. In general, you should use only two or three fonts per form. Use one font and font size for most bound data displayed in controls. Make label text bold or colored for emphasis. Select a second font for controls in the headers and perhaps a third (at most) for information in the footers.

Setting Control Properties

Microsoft Access gives you many properties for each control to allow you to customize the way your form works. These properties affect formatting, the presence or absence of scroll bars, the enabling or locking of records, the tab order, and more.

Formatting Properties

In the property sheet for each text box, combo box, and list box are three properties that you can set to determine how Access displays the data in the form. These properties are Format, Decimal Places, and Input Mask, as shown in Figure 12-21.

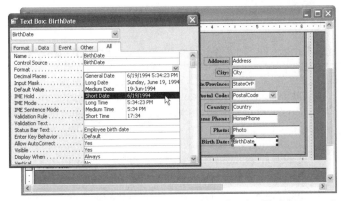

Figure 12-21. The list of format settings for the BirthDate control, which uses the Date/Time data type.

Tip **Always use four-digit year values**

I recommended earlier that you change the date display in your regional settings section of Windows Control Panel to display a four-digit year. Although Access adjusts the century digits automatically when you enter two-digit years, you will avoid confusion about the actual value stored after the year 1999 if you always display the full year. All samples you see in this book using the Short Date format show four-digit years because I changed the settings on my machine. If your machine is set to display a two-digit year, you will see a different result everywhere I used the Short Date format.

For details on the Input Mask property, see Chapter 4, "Creating Your Database and Tables." For details on dynamically changing format properties (also called conditional formatting) based on the value currently displayed, see Chapter 13, "Advanced Form Design."

Chapter 12

Access copies these properties from the definition of the fields in the underlying table. If you haven't specified a Format property in the field definition, Access sets a default Format property for the control, depending on the datatype of the field bound to the control. In the control's property sheet, you can customize the appearance of the data on your form by selecting a format setting from the Format property's drop-down list or by entering a custom set of formatting characters. The following sections present the format settings and formatting characters available for each data type.

Specifying a Format for Numbers and Currency

If you don't specify a Format property setting for a control that displays a number or a currency value, Access displays numbers in the General Number format and currency in the Currency format. You can choose from among seven Format property settings, as shown in Table 12-1.

Table 12-1. Format Property Settings for Number and Currency Data Types

Format	Description
General Number	Displays numbers as entered with up to 11 significant digits. If a number contains more than 11 significant digits or the control you are using to display the value is not wide enough to show all digits, Access first rounds the displayed number and then uses scientific (exponential) notation for very large or very small numbers (more than 10 digits to the right or to the left of the decimal point).
Currency	Displays numeric data according to the Currency setting in the regional settings section of Windows Control Panel. In the U.S. layout, Access uses a leading dollar sign, maintains two decimal places (rounded), and encloses negative numbers in parentheses.
Euro	Display numeric data according to your Currency setting, but always uses a leading Euro symbol.
Fixed	Displays numbers without thousands separators and with two decimal places. The number displayed is rounded if the underlying value contains more than two decimal places.
Standard	Displays numbers with thousands separators and with two decimal places. The number displayed is rounded if the underlying value contains more than two decimal places.
Percent	Multiplies the value by 100, displays two decimal places, and adds a trailing percent sign. The number displayed is rounded if the underlying value contains more than four decimal places.
Scientific	Displays numbers in scientific (exponential) notation.

You can also create a custom format. You can specify a different display format for Access to use (depending on whether the numeric value is positive, negative, 0, or Null) by providing up to four format specifications in the Format property. The specifications must be separated by semicolons. When you enter two specifications, Access uses the first for all nonnegative numbers and the second for negative numbers. When you provide three specifications, Access uses the third specification to display numbers with a value of 0. Use the fourth specification to indicate how you want Null values handled.

To create a custom number format, use the formatting characters shown in Table 12-2. Notice that you can include text strings in the format and specify a color to use.

Table 12-2. Formatting Characters for Number and Currency Data Types

Character	Usage
Decimal separator	Use to indicate where you want Access to place the decimal point. Use the decimal separator defined in the regional settings section of Windows Control Panel. In the English (United States) layout, the separator is a period (.).
Thousands separator	Use to indicate placement of the thousands separator character that is defined in the regional settings section of Windows Control Panel. In the English (United States) layout, the separator is a comma (,). When the position immediately to the left of the separator is a # and no digit exists in that position, the thousands separator also does not display.
0	Use this placeholder character to indicate digit display. If no digit exists in the number in this position, Access displays 0.
#	Use this placeholder character to indicate digit display. If no digit exists in the number in this position, Access displays a blank space.
– + $ ( ) or a blank space	Use these characters anywhere you want in your format string.
"text"	Use double quotation marks to embed any text you want displayed.
\	Use to always display the character immediately following (the same as including a single character in double quotation marks).
!	Use to force left alignment. You cannot use any other *digit* placeholder characters (0 or #) when you force left alignment; however, you can use character placeholders as shown in Table 12-3 on page 455.

Table 12-2. Formatting Characters for Number and Currency Data Types

Character	Usage
*	Use to designate the immediately following character as the fill character. Access normally displays formatted numeric data right aligned and filled with blank spaces to the left. You can embed the fill character anywhere in your format string. For example, you can specify a format string for a Currency value as follows: $#,##0*^.00 Using the above format, the value $1,234.57 appears as follows: $1,234^^^^^^^^^.57 Access generates fill characters so that the displayed text completely fills the display area.
%	Place as the last character in your format string to multiply the value by 100 and include a trailing percent sign.
E– or e–	Use to generate scientific (exponential) notation and to display a minus sign preceding negative exponents. It must be used with other characters, as in 0.00E–00.
E+ or e+	Use to generate scientific (exponential) notation and to display a minus sign preceding negative exponents and a plus sign preceding positive exponents. It must be used with other characters, as in 0.00E+00.
[color]	Use brackets to display the text in the color specified. Valid color names are Black, Blue, Green, Cyan, Red, Magenta, Yellow, and White. A color name must be used with other characters, as in 0.00[Red].

Inside Out

Don't get fooled by the Format property

Keep in mind that what you specify in the Format and Decimal Places properties affects only what you see on your screen—these settings do not modify the actual data in the underlying table in any way. For example, if you specify a format that displays two decimal places, but the underlying data type contains additional precision (such as a Currency data type that always contains four decimal places), you'll see a rounded value. If you later sum the values, the total might not agree with the sum of the displayed values. Likewise, if you specify a format that displays only the date portion of a Date/Time data type, you won't see any time portion unless you click in the control. If I had a penny for every time I've had to explain this concept in the support newsgroups, I would be very wealthy, indeed!

For example, to display a number with two decimal places and comma separators when positive, enclosed in parentheses and shown in red when negative, *Zero* when 0, and *Not Entered* when Null, you would specify the following:

```
#,##0.00;(#,##0.00)[Red];"Zero";"Not Entered"
```

To format a U.S. phone number and area code from a numeric field, you would specify the following:

```
(000) 000-0000
```

Specifying a Format for Text

If you don't specify a Format property setting for a control that displays a text value, Access left aligns the data in the control. You can specify a custom format with one entry, or two entries separated by semicolons. If you include a second format specification, Access uses that specification to show empty values (a zero length string). If you want to test for Null, you must use the Immediate If (IIf) and IsNull built-in functions. See the Inside Out sidebar, "Showing the Null value in text fields," on page 457 for details.

By default, Access fills text placeholder characters (@ and &) using characters from the underlying data from *right to left*. If a text field contains more characters than the number of placeholder characters you provide, Access first uses up the placeholder characters and then displays the remaining characters as though you had specified the @ placeholder character in that position. Table 12-3 lists the formatting characters that are applicable to the Text data type.

Table 12-3. Formatting Characters for the Text Data Type

Character	Usage
@	Use this placeholder character to display any available character in this position. If all available characters in the underlying text have been placed, any extra @ placeholder characters generate blanks. For example, if the text is *abc* and the format is @@@@@, the resulting display is left-aligned and has two blank spaces on the left preceding the characters.
&	Use to display any available character in this position. If all available characters in the underlying text have been placed, any extra & placeholder characters display nothing. For example, if the text is *abc* and the format is &&&&&, the resulting display shows only the three characters left-aligned.
<	Use to display all characters in lowercase. This character must appear at the beginning of the format string and can be preceded only by the ! specification.
>	Use to display all characters in uppercase. This character must appear at the beginning of the format string and can be preceded only by the ! specification.

Table 12-3. Formatting Characters for the Text Data Type

Character	Usage
– + $ ( ) or a blank space	Use these characters anywhere you want in your format string.
"text"	Use double quotation marks to embed any text you want displayed.
\	Use to always display the character immediately following (the same as including a single character in double quotation marks).
!	Use to force placeholders to fill *left to right* instead of right to left. If you use this specification, it must be the first character in the format string.
*	Use to designate the immediately following character as the fill character. Access normally displays formatted text data left-aligned and filled with blank spaces to the right. You can embed the fill character anywhere in your format string. For example, you can specify a format string as follows: >@@*!@@@@@ Using the above format, the value *abcdef* appears as follows: A!!!!!!!!!!!!!!!BCDEF (And the above string has a leading blank.) If you force the pattern to be filled from the left by adding a leading exclamation point, the data appears as follows (with a trailing blank): AB!!!!!!!!!!!!!!!CDEF (And the above string has a trailing blank.) Access generates fill characters so that the displayed text completely fills the display area.
[color]	Use brackets to display the text in the color specified. Valid color names are Black, Blue, Green, Cyan, Red, Magenta, Yellow, and White. A color name must be used with other characters, as in >[Red]. (Keep in mind that in the absence of placeholder characters, Access places the characters as though you had specified @ in all positions.)

For example, if you want to display a six-character part number with a hyphen between the second character and the third character, filled from the left, specify the following:

!@@-@@@@

To format a check amount string in the form of *Fourteen Dollars and 59 Cents* so that Access displays an asterisk (*) to fill any available space between the word *and* and the cents amount, specify the following:

**@@@@@@@@

Using this format in a text box wide enough to display 62 characters, Access displays *Fourteen Dollars and 59 Cents* as

```
Fourteen Dollars and **********************************59 Cents
```

and *One Thousand Two Hundred Dollars and 00 Cents* as

```
One Thousand Two Hundred Dollars and ******************00 Cents
```

Inside Out

Showing the Null value in text fields

As you might have noticed, there is no third optional format specification you can supply for a Null value in a text field as there is with Number, Currency, and Date/Time data types. If the field is Null, Access displays it as though it is empty. If the field can contain an empty string or a Null, you can distinguish it visibly by using the second optional format specification. Assuming your text field is five characters long, your Format specification could look like

```
@@@@@;"<empty string>"
```

If the field has a value, Access displays the value. If the field is an empty string, you will see *<empty string>* in the text box until you click in it. If the field is Null, the text box will be blank.

An alternative is to use the IIf and IsNull built-in functions in the Control Source property of the text box. Your control source could look like

```
=IIf(IsNull([FieldToDisplay]), "*Null Value*",[FieldToDisplay])
```

If you do this, however, you won't be able to update the field because the source will be an expression.

Specifying a Format for Date/Time

If you don't specify a Format property setting for a control that displays a date/time value, Access displays the date/time in the General Date format. You can also select one of the six other Format property settings shown in Table 12-4 on the next page.

You can also specify a custom format with one entry, or two entries separated by semicolons. If you include a second format specification, Access uses that specification to show Null values. Table 12-5, also on the next page, lists the formatting characters that are applicable to the Date/Time data type.

For example, to display a date as full month name, day, and year (say, *December 20, 2003*) with a color of cyan, you would specify the following:

```
mmmm dd, yyyy[Cyan]
```

Table 12-4. Format Property Settings for the Date/Time Data Type

Format	Description
General Date	Displays the date as numbers separated by the date separator character. Displays the time as hours, minutes, and seconds separated by the time separator character and followed by an AM/PM indicator. If the value has no time component, Access displays the date only. If the value has no date component, Access displays the time only. Example: 3/17/2004 06:17:55 PM.
Long Date	Displays the date according to the Long Date setting in the regional settings section of Windows Control Panel. Example: Wednesday, March 17, 2004.
Medium Date	Displays the date as dd-mmm-yyyy. Example: 17-Mar-2004.
Short Date	Displays the date according to the Short Date setting in the regional settings section of Windows Control Panel. Example: 3/17/2004. To avoid confusion for dates in the twenty-first century, I strongly recommend you take advantage of the new Use Four-Digit Year Formatting options. Choose Options from the Tools menu to set these options on the General tab.
Long Time	Displays the time according to the Time setting in the regional settings section of Windows Control Panel. Example: 6:17:12 PM.
Medium Time	Displays the time as hours and minutes separated by the time separator character and followed by an AM/PM indicator. Example: 06:17 PM.
Short Time	Displays the time as hours and minutes separated by the time separator character, using a 24-hour clock. Example: 18:17.

Table 12-5. Formatting Characters for the Date/Time Data Type

Character	Usage
Time separator	Use to show Access where to separate hours, minutes, and seconds. Use the time separator defined in the regional settings section of Windows Control Panel. In the English (United States) layout, the separator is a colon (:).
Date separator	Use to show Access where to separate days, months, and years. Use the date separator defined in the regional settings section of Windows Control Panel. In the English (United States) layout, the separator is a forward slash (/).
c	Use to display the General Date format.
d	Use to display the day of the month as one or two digits, as needed.
dd	Use to display the day of the month as two digits.

Customizing a Form

Table 12-5. Formatting Characters for the Date/Time Data Type

Character	Usage
ddd	Use to display the day of the week as a three-letter abbreviation. Example: Saturday = Sat.
dddd	Use to display the day of the week fully spelled out.
ddddd	Use to display the Short Date format.
dddddd	Use to display the Long Date format.
w	Use to display a number for the day of the week. Example: Sunday = 1.
m	Use to display the month as a one-digit or two-digit number, as needed.
mm	Use to display the month as a two-digit number.
mmm	Use to display the name of the month as a three-letter abbreviation. Example: March = Mar.
mmmm	Use to display the name of the month fully spelled out.
q	Use to display the calendar quarter number (1–4).
y	Use to display the day of the year (1–366).
yy	Use to display the last two digits of the year.
yyyy	Use to display the full year value (within the range 0100–9999).
h	Use to display the hour as one or two digits, as needed.
hh	Use to display the hour as two digits.
n	Use to display the minutes as one or two digits, as needed.
nn	Use to display the minutes as two digits.
s	Use to display the seconds as one or two digits, as needed.
ss	Use to display the seconds as two digits.
ttttt	Use to display the Long Time format.
AM/PM	Use to display 12-hour clock values with trailing AM or PM, as appropriate.
A/P or a/p	Use to display 12-hour clock values with trailing A or P, or a or p, as appropriate.
AMPM	Use to display 12-hour clock values using morning/afternoon indicators as specified in the regional settings section of Windows Control Panel.
– + $ ( ) or a blank space	Use these characters anywhere you want in your format string.
"text"	Use double quotation marks to embed any text you want displayed.
\	Use to always display the character immediately following (the same as including a single character in double quotation marks).

Chapter 12

Table 12-5. Formatting Characters for the Date/Time Data Type

Character	Usage
*	Use to designate the immediately following character as the fill character. Access normally displays formatted date/time data right aligned and filled with blank spaces to the left. You can embed the fill character anywhere in your format string. For example, you can specify a format string as follows: mm/yyyy ** hh:nn Using the above format, the value March 17, 2004 06:17:55 PM appears as follows: 03/2004 ************* 18:17 Access generates fill characters so that the displayed text completely fills the display area.
[color]	Use brackets to display the text in the color specified. Valid color names are Black, Blue, Green, Cyan, Red, Magenta, Yellow, and White. A color name must be used with other characters, as in ddddd[Red].

Specifying a Format for Yes/No Fields

You can choose from among three standard formats—Yes/No, True/False, or On/Off—to display Yes/No data type values, as shown in Table 12-6. The Yes/No format is the default. As you saw earlier, it's often more useful to display Yes/No values using a check box or an option button rather than a text box.

Table 12-6. Format Property Settings for the Yes/No Data Type

Format	Description
Yes/No (the default)	Displays 0 as No and any nonzero value as Yes.
True/False	Displays 0 as False and any nonzero value as True.
On/Off	Displays 0 as Off and any nonzero value as On.

You can also specify your own custom word or phrase for Yes and No values. Keep in mind that a Yes/No data type is actually a number internally. (-1 is Yes and 0 is No.) So, you can specify a format string containing three parts separated by semicolons just as you can for a number. Leave the first part empty (a Yes/No value is never a positive number) by starting with a semicolon, specify a string enclosed in double quotation marks (and with an optional color modifier) followed by a semicolon in the second part for the negative Yes values, and specify another string (also with an optional color modifier) in the third part for the zero No values.

To display *Invoice Sent* in red for Yes and *Not Invoiced* in blue for No, you would specify the following:

```
;"Invoice Sent"[Red];"Not Invoiced"[Blue]
```

How the Format and Input Mask properties work together

If you specify both an Input Mask property setting (see Chapter 4, "Creating Your Database and Tables") and a Format property setting, Access uses the Input Mask setting to display data when you move the focus to the control and uses the Format setting when the control does not have the focus. If you don't include a Format setting but do include an Input Mask setting, Access formats the data using the Input Mask setting. Be careful not to define a Format setting that conflicts with the Input Mask. For example, if you define an Input Mask setting for a phone number that looks like

`!\(###") "000\-0000;0;_`

(which stores the parentheses and hyphen with the data) and a Format setting that looks like

`(&&&) @@@-@@@@`

your data will be displayed as

(206() 5) 55—1212

Adding a Scroll Bar

When you have a field that can contain a long data string (for example, the Notes field in the tbReservationRequests table), it's a good idea to provide a scroll bar in the control to make it easy to scan through all the data. This scroll bar appears whenever you select the control. If you don't add a scroll bar, you must use the arrow keys to move up and down through the data.

To add a scroll bar, first open the form in Design view. Select the control, and open its property sheet. Then set the Scroll Bars property to Vertical. For example, if you open the frmXmplReservationRequests form in Form view and tab to (or click in) the Notes text box, the vertical scroll bar appears, as shown in Figure 12-22.

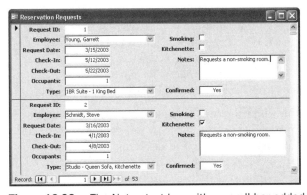

Figure 12-22. The Notes text box with a scroll bar added.

Chapter 12

461

Enabling and Locking Controls

You might not want users of your form to select or update certain controls. You can set these conditions with the control's Enabled and Locked properties. For example, if you use a control to display an AutoNumber field, you can be certain that Access will provide the field's value. So it's a good idea to set the control's Enabled property to No (so that the user can't select it) and the control's Locked property to Yes (so that the user can't update it). Table 12-7 shows the effects of the Enabled and Locked property settings. Note, however, that if you want the user to be able to use the Access built-in Find facility to search for a particular AutoNumber value, you should leave Enabled set to Yes to allow the user to select the field and find values in it.

Table 12-7. Settings for the Enabled and Locked Properties

Enabled	Locked	Description
Yes	Yes	Control can have the focus. Data is displayed normally and can be copied or searched but not changed.
No	No	Control cannot have the focus. Control and data appear dimmed.
Yes	No	Control can have the focus. Data is displayed normally and can be copied and changed.
No	Yes	Control cannot have the focus. Data is displayed normally but can't be copied or changed.

In some cases, you might want to allow a control to be selected with the mouse but to be skipped over as the user tabs through the controls on the form. You can set the control's Tab Stop property to No while leaving its Enabled property set to Yes. This might be useful for controls for which you also set the Locked property to Yes. Setting the Tab Stop property to No keeps the user from tabbing into the control, but the user can still select the control with the mouse to use the Find command or to copy the data in the control to the Clipboard.

Setting the Tab Order

As you design a form, Access sets the tab order for the controls in the order in which you place the controls on the form. When you move a control to a new location, Access doesn't automatically change the tab order. Also, when you delete a control and replace it with another, Access places the new control at the end of the tab order. If you want to change the tab order that Access created, you can set a different tab order.

You probably should do this with your sample employees form because you moved controls around after you initially placed them on the form. (If you want to test the existing order, try tabbing through the controls in one record in frmXmplEmployee5—you should see the cursor jump from OfficeLocation in the first column to Photo in the second column and then back to Password in the first column.) Open your form in Design view, select the Detail area (or any control in the Detail area), and then choose the Tab Order command from the View menu to open the Tab Order dialog box, as shown in Figure 12-23.

Figure 12-23. The Tab Order dialog box.

You can click the Auto Order button to reorder the controls so that the tab order corresponds to the arrangement of the controls on the form, from left to right and from top to bottom—but that's probably not what you want in this case. Because this form has two columns, you might want to rearrange the tab order to first move down one column and then the other. You can make custom adjustments to the list by clicking the row selector for a control to highlight it and then clicking the row selector again and dragging the control to its new location in the list. As you can see, the Photo and WorkPhone controls don't appear where they should in the Custom Order list. Click Photo and drag it down after HomePhone. Click WorkPhone and drag it up to follow OfficeLocation. Click OK to save your changes to the Custom Order list.

You can also change an individual control's place in the tab order by setting the control's Tab Index property. The Tab Index property of the first control on the form is 0, the second is 1, and so on. If you use this method to assign a new Tab Index setting to a control and some other control already has that Tab Index setting, Access resequences the Tab Index settings for controls appearing in the order after the one you changed. The result is the same as if you had dragged the control to that relative position (as indicated by the new Tab Index setting) in the Tab Order dialog box. (I personally find it easier to use the Tab Order dialog box.)

Adding a Smart Tag

Those of you who have worked with Microsoft Word 2002 or Microsoft Excel 2002 might already be familiar with *smart tags*. They're little applications that you can hook into your documents to recognize items such as names, addresses, or stock symbols and provide options, or actions, for recognized fields. For example, you might have an address smart tag in a Word document that provides an option to open a map to the location. In an Excel spreadsheet, you might define a smart tag for a stock symbol column to go look up the latest price on the Web.

If you have Microsoft Visual Studio, you can actually build your own smart tag applications with Visual Basic. You can download the Smart Tags Software Development Kit (SDK) by going to *http://www.microsoft.com/downloads/* and performing a search on the keywords "smart tags." Most Word and Excel smart tag applications have two parts: a recognizer and a set of actions. When a smart tag is active in Word or Excel, the recognizer code runs as you type in data and decides if what you typed is something for which the smart tag has an action. If the smart tag recognizes the text, it passes available actions back to the application, and you see a Smart Tag option available that you can click to invoke one of the actions.

Microsoft Office Access 2003 supports smart tags, but in a slightly different way than Word or Excel. You can define a smart tag for labels, text boxes, combo boxes, and list boxes. For text boxes, combo boxes, and list boxes, the smart tag uses the current value of the control as specified in the Control Source property. For labels, the smart tag uses the contents of the Caption property. Because data in Access not only has a specific data type but also a specific meaning, the recognizer code in a smart tag does not come into play. Access assumes that you know that the data in the label, text box, combo box, or list box is something the smart tag understands. So, you can use smart tags in Access that have only actions defined.

Microsoft Office 2003 installs a few smart tags that you can use in Access. These include:

- Date—A smart tag that uses a date/time value to schedule a meeting or show your Microsoft Outlook calendar on that date.

- Financial Symbol—A smart tag that can accept a NYSE or NASDAQ stock symbol and display the latest quote, company report, or news from the MSN Money Central Web site.

- Person Name—A smart tag that can accept a person name (first name and last name) or e-mail address and send an e-mail, schedule a meeting, open the matching contact from your contacts list, or add the name to your contacts list.

> **Caution** If you assign a smart tag to a control containing data that the smart tag cannot handle, the smart tag won't work, and it might generate an error.

In your employees form, EmailName is a hyperlink field that opens a new message to the e-mail address when you click it. However, you might also want to use the Person Name smart tag to provide additional options. To add this smart tag, open your form in Design view, click the EmailName text box, open the Properties window, and scroll down to the last property in the list—Smart Tags. Click the property and then click the Build button to open the Smart Tags dialog box as shown in Figure 12-24.

Click **Person name** and click OK to set the property. Note that you can also click the More Smart Tags button to go to the Microsoft Web site to download and install additional smart tags. One that you might find useful is the MSNBC smart tag, which can provide automatic links to news, weather, and sports based on city name. Baseball fans might want to download and install the ESPN smart tag that provides news and statistics based on team or player name.

Figure 12-24.   The Smart Tags dialog box.

After defining a smart tag, switch to Form view. Controls that have a smart tag defined display a small triangle in the lower right corner. Hover near the triangle with your mouse pointer or tab into the control, and you'll see the smart tag information box appear. Click the down arrow next to the box to see the action choices as shown in Figure 12-25. Click the action you want to activate that action.

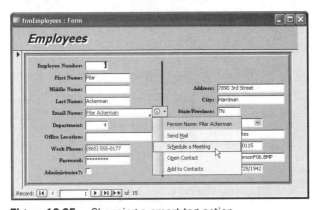

Figure 12-25.   Choosing a smart tag action.

Understanding Other Control Properties

As you've already discovered, many of the properties for controls that can be bound to fields from your form's record source are exactly the same as those you can set in table Design view on the General or Lookup tab. (See Chapter 4, "Creating Your Database and Tables," for details.) If you do not specify a different setting in the control, the form uses the properties you defined for the field in your table. In some cases, a particular field property setting migrates to a different property in the bound control on your form. For example, the Description property of a field becomes the Status Bar Text property of the bound control. The Caption property of a field moves to the Caption property of a bound control's associated label.

Table 12-8 describes control settings not yet discussed and explains their usage. The table lists the properties in the sequence you will find them on the All tab in the Properties window.

Table 12-8. Other Control Properties

Property	Description
Enter Key Behavior	Default (the default setting) specifies that pressing the Enter key in this control performs the action described in the Move after enter setting on the Keyboard tab of the Options dialog box. The New Line in Field setting specifies that pressing Enter creates a new line in the underlying text. This setting is useful for large text or memo fields, especially when the control is more than one line high and has a vertical scroll bar defined.
Allow AutoCorrect	Specify Yes (the default) to enable auto correction as you type text, similar to the AutoCorrect feature in Microsoft Word. You can customize AutoCorrect options by choosing AutoCorrect Options from the Tools menu. Specify No to turn off this feature.
Visible	Specify Yes (the default) to make the control visible in Form view. Specify No to hide the control. You will find this property useful when you begin to automate your application and write code to optionally display/hide controls depending on the contents of other fields. See Chapter 23, "Automating Your Application with Visual Basic," for details.
Display When	Choose Always (the default) to display this control in Form view, Print Preview, and when you print the form. Choose Print Only to display the control only when you view the form in Print Preview or you print the form. Choose Screen Only to display the control only when in Form view.
Vertical	You can design a control that displays text to run vertically down the form (narrow width and tall height). When you do that, you can set Vertical to Yes to turn the text display 90 degrees clockwise. The default is No.
Filter Lookup	Choose Database Default (the default setting) to honor the options you set on the Edit/Find tab of the Options dialog box. Choose Never to disable lookup of values in Filter By Form. Choose Always to enable lookup of values in Filter By Form regardless of your Options settings.

Table 12-8. Other Control Properties

Property	Description
Auto Tab	Choose Yes to cause an automatic tab to the next field when the user enters a number of characters equal to the field length. The default is No.
Can Grow, Can Shrink	These properties apply to controls on a Report or in Print Preview. See Chapter 16, "Advanced Report Design," for details.
Left, Top, Width, Height	These properties specify the location and size of the control. Access automatically adjusts these settings when you move a control to a new location or adjust its size. You can enter specific values if you want a control to be placed in a particular location or have a specific size.
Back Style	Choose Normal (the default) to be able to specify a color for the background of the control. Choose Transparent to allow the color of any control or section behind the control to show through.
Back Color, Special Effect, Border Style, Border Color, Border Width, Fore Color, Font Name, Font Size, Font Weight, Font Italic, Font Underline	Access automatically sets these properties when you choose a setting on one of the available buttons on the Formatting toolbar. You can enter a specific setting in these properties rather than choose a toolbar option. For the color options, you can click the Build button next to the property to select a custom color from the palette of available colors on your machine.
Text Align	The default setting is General, which aligns text left and numbers right. You also can choose Left, Center, and Right options (also available on the Formatting toolbar) to align the text to the left, in the center, or to the right, respectively. The final option, Distribute, spreads the characters evenly across the available display space in the control.
Shortcut Menu Bar	You can design a custom shortcut menu for your forms and reports, and you enter the name of your custom menu in this property. See Chapter 24, "The Finishing Touches," for details.
ControlTip Text	You can enter a custom message that appears as a control tip when you hover your mouse pointer near the control for a few seconds. You might find this especially useful for command buttons to further describe the action that occurs when the user clicks the button.

Chapter 12

Table 12-8. Other Control Properties

Property	Description
Help Context ID	You can create a custom Help file for your application and identify specific topics with a context ID. If you want a particular topic to appear when your user presses F1 when the focus is in this control, enter the ID of the topic in this property. See Chapter 24, "The Finishing Touches," for details.
Tag	You can use this property to store additional descriptive information about the control. You can write Visual Basic code to examine and set this property or take a specific action based on the property setting. The user cannot see the contents of the Tag property.
Before Update through On Key Press	You can set these properties to run a macro, a function, or an event procedure when the specific event described by the property occurs for this control. See Part 5 for details.
Reading Order	Choose Context (the default) to set the order the characters are displayed based on the first character entered. When the first character is from a character set that is normally read right to left (such as Arabic), the characters appear right to left. Choose Left-To-Right or Right-To-Left to override the reading order.
Keyboard Language	System (the default setting) assumes the keyboard being used is the default for your system. You can also choose from any available installed keyboard.
Scroll Bar Align	Choose System (the default) to align scroll bars based on the form's Orientation property setting. See the section "Understanding Other Form Properties" on page 474 for details. Choose Right or Left to override the form setting.
Numeral Shapes	On an Arabic or Hindi system, you can choose settings to alter the way numbers are displayed. The default setting is System, which displays numbers based on your system settings.
Left Margin, Top Margin, Right Margin, Bottom Margin, Line Spacing	In a text box control, you can specify alternative margins and line spacing for the text displayed. The default for all these properties is 0, which provides no additional margin space and spaces the lines based on the font type and size.
Is Hyperlink	Fields that are the Hyperlink data type are always displayed as a hyperlink. You can change this setting to Yes to treat non-Hyperlink data type fields as hyperlinks. The default is No.

Inside Out

Be careful when setting control validation rules

Two properties that deserve special mention are Validation Rule and Validation Text. As you know, you can specify these properties for most fields in your table. When you build a form that is bound to data from your table, the validation rules in the table always apply. However, you can also specify a validation rule for many bound controls on your form. You might want to do this if, on this particular form, you want a more restrictive rule to apply.

However, you can get in trouble if you specify a rule that conflicts with the rule in the underlying table. For example, in the *HousingDataCopy.mdb* sample database, you can find a validation rule on the BirthDate field in tblEmployees that disallows entering a birth date for someone who is less than 18 years old. The validation rule is as follows:

```
<=(Date()-(365*18))
```

What do you suppose happens if you subsequently enter a Validation Rule property for the BirthDate text box control on your form that requires the person to be 18 or younger? You can try it by opening your employees form in Design view, clicking the BirthDate text box, and entering the following in the Validation Rule property in the Properties window:

```
>(Date()-(365*18))
```

So that you can determine which validation rule is preventing you from changing the data, set the Validation Text property to something like "Violating the control validation rule." Now, switch to Form view and try to type in a value that you know violates the table rule, such as 1/1/2003. When you try to tab out of the field, you should see the message from the table: "You cannot enter an employee who is younger than 18 years old." Now, try to enter a date for an older person, such as 1/1/1955 and press Tab to move out of the control. You should see the validation text that you just entered for the control. The bottom line is you have set up the rules so that no value is valid when you try to edit with this form. (You'll have to press Esc to clear your edit to be able to close the form.)

Setting Form Properties

In addition to the controls on a form, the form itself has a number of properties that you can use to control its appearance and how it works.

Allowing Different Views

When you build a form from scratch (such as the employees form you've been working on in this chapter), the Default View property of the form is Single Form. This is the view you'll see first when you open the form. With the Single Form setting, you can see only one record at a time and you have to use the Record Number box, the Previous Record and Next Record arrow buttons to the left and right of the Record Number box, or the Go To command on the Edit menu to move to another record. If you set the Default View property of the form to Continuous Forms, you can see multiple records on a short form and you can use the scroll bar on the right side of the form to scroll through the records. Because one record's data in the tblEmployees table fills your employees form, the Single Form setting is probably the best choice.

Another set of properties lets you control whether a user can change to Form view, Datasheet view, PivotTable view, or PivotChart view. These properties are Allow Form View, Allow Datasheet View, Allow Pivot Table View, and Allow Pivot Chart View. The default setting for all these properties is Yes, meaning that a user can use the toolbar or the View menu to switch between any of the views. If you're designing a form to be used in an application, you will usually want to eliminate some of the views. For your employees form, set all but the Allow Form View property to No; the Datasheet View, PivotTable View, and PivotChart View options on the Form View toolbar button's drop-down list should become unavailable (appear dimmed).

> **Tip** Keep users out of Design view
>
> You can make it more difficult to enter Design view by designing a custom menu and toolbar for all your forms. See Chapter 24, "The Finishing Touches," for details. There are only two ways to completely prevent a user from opening a form in Design view or switching to Design view. You can secure the database (see Chapter 30, "Securing Your Database"), or you can give your users an execute-only copy of your application (see Chapter 31, "Distributing Your Application").

Setting Navigation Options

Because the employees form you've been designing displays one record at a time, it is not useful to display the row selector on the left side of the form. You've also designed the form to show all the data in a single window, so a scroll bar along the right side of the window isn't necessary. You also don't need a horizontal scroll bar. You probably should keep the Record Number box at the bottom of the form, however. To make these changes, set the form's Record Selectors property on the property sheet to No, the Scroll Bars property to Neither, and the Navigation Buttons property to Yes. Your form should look something like the one shown in Figure 12-26.

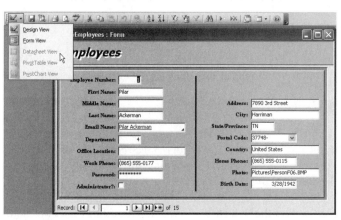

Figure 12-26. The employees form with views restricted and without a record selector or scroll bars.

Defining a Pop-Up and/or Modal Form

You might occasionally want to design a form that stays on top of all other forms even when it doesn't have the focus. Notice that the toolbox, property sheet, and field list in Design view all have this characteristic. These are called *pop-up forms*. You can make your employees form a pop-up form by setting the form's Pop Up property to Yes. Figure 12-27 shows the employees form as a pop-up form on top of the Database window, which has the focus. Note that the form can "float" on top of other forms or windows, and it can also be moved over the toolbars and menu bars. A form that isn't a pop-up form cannot leave the Access workspace below the toolbars.

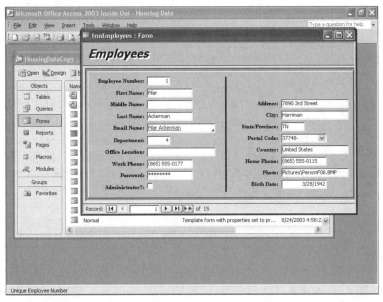

Figure 12-27. The employees form as a pop-up form on top of the Database window.

Caution   If you play with the frmXmplEmployee5 form to do this, be sure to set the form's Pop Up property back to No or don't save your design changes when you close the form.

As you'll learn in Part 5, "Automating an Access Application," it's sometimes useful to create forms that ask the user for information that's needed in order to perform the next task. Forms have a Modal property that you can set to Yes to "lock" the user into the form when it's open. The user must make a choice in the form or close the form in order to go on to other tasks. When a modal form is open, you can switch to another application but you can't select any other form, menu, or toolbar button in Access until you dismiss the modal form. You've probably noticed that most dialog boxes are modal forms. Modal isn't a good choice for your employees form, but you'll use the Modal property later to help control application flow.

Chapter 12

Controlling Edits, Deletions, Additions, and Filtering

You can set several form properties to control whether data in the form can be updated or whether data in the underlying tables can change. You can also prevent or allow user-applied filters on the form. These properties and their settings are shown in Table 12-9.

Table 12-9. Form Properties for Controlling Editing and Filtering

Property	Description
Filter	Contains the latest criteria applied as a filter on this form. Forms also have a FilterOn property that you can't see in the Form window in Design view. When FilterOn is True, the data displayed in the form is filtered by the criteria string found in the Filter property. On a new form, the Filter property is empty.
Order By	Contains the latest sorting criteria applied to this form. Forms also have an OrderByOn property that you can't see in the Form window in Design view. When OrderByOn is True, the data displayed in the form is sorted by the criteria string found in the Order By property. On a new form, the Order By property is empty.
Allow Filters	Determines whether a user can see selected records by applying filtering and sorting criteria and whether the user can see all records by choosing the Show All Records command from the Records menu. If you set the Data Entry property to Yes and set the Allow Filters property to No, the user can enter only new data and cannot change the form to view other existing records. The valid settings for the Allow Filters property are Yes and No. The default setting is Yes.
Allow Edits	Determines whether a user can change control values in this form. The valid settings are Yes and No. The default setting is Yes. Note that when you set Allow Edits to No, you cannot change the value of any control on the form, including unbound controls.
Allow Deletions	Determines whether a user can delete records in this form. The valid settings are Yes and No. The default setting is Yes.
Allow Additions	Determines whether a user can add records using this form. The valid settings are Yes and No. The default setting is Yes.
Data Entry	Determines whether the form opens a blank record in which you can insert new data. Access won't retrieve rows from the form's recordset. The valid settings are Yes and No, and the default setting is No. Setting Data Entry to Yes is effective only when Allow Additions is set to Yes.

Defining Window Controls

In some cases, you might want to prevent the user from opening the form's Control menu (clicking the Control-menu button in the upper left corner of a window displays a shortcut menu containing the Restore, Move, Size, Minimize, Maximize, Close, and Next commands) or from using the Minimize and Maximize buttons. If you want to perform special processing before a form closes (such as clearing the application status before your main switchboard closes), you might want to provide a command button to do the processing and then close the form with a Visual Basic command. (See Part 5 for details about writing a command to close a form.) You can set the form's Control Box property to No to remove the Control-menu icon from the form window and the Close button from the upper right corner. This also removes the Minimize and Maximize buttons.

You can set the form's Close Button property to No to remove the Close button but leave the Control-menu button (with Close disabled on the Control menu). You can set the form's Min Max Buttons property to Both Enabled, None, Min Enabled, or Max Enabled. If you disable a Minimize or Maximize button, the related command on the form's Control menu becomes disabled. Finally, you can set the Whats This Button property to Yes to display the Help button, but to do this you must set the Min Max Buttons property to No.

> **Caution** You can set a form's Control Box property to No to remove all control features from the form's title bar. This means that both the Control-menu button (which contains the Close command) and the form's Close button (at the right end of the title bar) will not appear. If you also set the form's Modal property to Yes, you should always provide an alternative way to close a modal form, such as a command button that executes a macro or Visual Basic command to close the form. Otherwise, the only way to close the form is to use the Windows Ctrl+F4 key combination. See Part 5 for details about writing a command to close a form.

Setting the Border Style

In most cases, you'll want to create forms with a normal border—one that allows you to size the window and move it around. Forms have a Border Style property that lets you define the look of the border and whether the window can be sized or moved. The Border Style property settings are shown in Table 12-10.

Table 12-10. Settings for the Border Style Property

Setting	Description
None	The form has no borders, Control-menu button, title bar, Close button, or Minimize and Maximize buttons. You cannot resize or move the form when it is open. You can select the form and press Ctrl+F4 to close it unless the form's Pop Up property is set to Yes. You should write Visual Basic code to provide an alternative way to close this type of form.
Thin	The form has a thin border, signifying that the form cannot be resized.
Sizeable	This is the default setting. The form can be resized.
Dialog	If the Pop Up property is set to Yes, the form's border is a thick line (like that of a true Windows dialog box), signifying that the form cannot be resized. If the Pop Up property is set to No, the Dialog setting is the same as the Thin setting.

Chapter 12

473

Understanding Other Form Properties

Table 12-11 describes form settings not yet discussed and explains their usage. The table lists the properties in the sequence you will find them on the All tab in the Properties window.

Table 12-11. Other Form Properties

Property	Description
Recordset Type	The default setting, Dynaset, specifies that all controls bound to fields in the record source will be updatable as long as the underlying field would also be updatable. If your form is bound to a query, see the section "Limitations on Using Select Queries to Update Data," page 323. Dynaset (Inconsistent Updates) specifies that all fields (other than fields resulting from expressions or AutoNumber fields) can be updated, even if the update would break a link between related tables. (I do not recommend this option because it can allow a user to attempt to make a change that would violate integrity rules.) Snapshot specifies that the data is read-only and cannot be updated.
Record Locks	No Locks (the default) specifies that Access will not lock any edited row until it needs to write the row back to the table. This is the most efficient choice for most applications. Edited Record specifies that Access apply a lock to the row the instant you begin typing in the record. This can lock out other users in a shared environment. All Records (not recommended) locks every record in the record source as soon as you open the form.
Dividing Lines	When you design your form with a Header or a Footer section, Yes (the default) specifies that you will see a horizontal line separating each section. No removes the line(s).
Auto Resize	The default Yes setting automatically resizes the form window to its design height and width when you open the form. Choose No if you want to set a specific window size.
Auto Center	Choose No (the default) to open the form on the screen wherever it was placed when you last saved its definition from Design view or Form view. Choose Yes to automatically center the form in the Access workspace when you open it.
Width	Specifies the width of the form in inches or centimeters. Access automatically updates this property when you drag the right edge of the design area wider or narrower in Design view. You cannot set this property to nothing (blank).

Table 12-11. **Other Form Properties**

Property	Description
Picture	Enter the path and file name of a graphic file to use as the background of the form. You can click the Build button next to the property to locate the picture you want. You might find this useful to display an image such as a company logo on the background of your forms.
Picture Type	Choose Embedded (the default) to store a copy of the picture in your form design. Use Linked to save space in your database, but the form must then always load the picture from the specified Picture path when it opens; if you move the picture to a different location, it might not be displayed.
Picture Size Mode	Clip (the default) specifies that the picture appear in its original resolution. If the form is larger than the picture, the picture will not cover the entire form area. If the form is smaller than the picture, you'll see only part of the picture. Use Stretch to stretch the picture to the dimensions of the form, but the picture might appear distorted. Use Zoom to stretch the picture to the dimensions of the form without distorting it; but if the aspect ratio of the picture does not match the display space of the form, the picture won't cover the entire form background.
Picture Alignment	This property applies only when Picture Size Mode is Clip or Zoom. The default setting, Center, centers the picture in the form window area. Form Center centers the picture in the form design area. You can also specify that the picture align in the top left, top right, bottom left, or bottom right corner of the form.
Picture Tiling	The default setting, No, places one copy of the picture on the form. Choose Yes if you want multiple copies "tiled" on the form. When you choose Yes, you must set Picture Alignment to Clip or Zoom, and the picture should be smaller than the form design or form window. Setting Picture Tiling to Yes is useful if your picture is a small pattern bitmap.
Cycle	Use the default setting, All Records, to tab to the next record when you press the Tab key in the last control in the tab order. Choose Current Record to disallow tabbing from one record to another. Choose Current Page on a multi-page form to disallow tabbing onto the next or previous page—you must use Page Up or Page Down to move between pages. When you set Current Record or Current Page, you must use the navigation buttons or menu commands to move to other records.

Chapter 12

Table 12-11. Other Form Properties

Property	Description
Menu Bar, Toolbar, and Shortcut Menu Bar	You can design a custom menu bar, toolbar, and shortcut menu for your forms and reports, and you enter the name of your custom menus or toolbars in these properties. See Chapter 24, "The Finishing Touches," for details.
Shortcut Menu	The default setting, Yes, indicates shortcut menus will be available for the form and all controls on the form (either the built-in ones or ones you design). Choose No to disable shortcut menus.
Layout for Print	The default setting, No, indicates that printer fonts installed on your machine will not be available in any font property settings, but screen fonts and True Type fonts will be available. Choosing Yes disables screen fonts but makes printer fonts and True Type fonts available.
Fast Laser Printing	The default setting, Yes, specifies that Access will use laser printer line fonts to draw lines and rectangles if you print the form on a printer that supports this option. Choose No to send all lines to your printer as graphics.
Help File	When you create a custom help file for your application, enter the path and file name in this property. See Chapter 24, "The Finishing Touches," for details.
Help Context ID	You can create a custom Help file for your application and identify specific topics with a context ID. If you want a particular topic to appear when your user presses F1 when using this form, enter the ID of the topic in this property. If the focus is in a control that also has a Help Context ID defined, the topic for that control is displayed. See Chapter 24, "The Finishing Touches," for details.
Subdatasheet Height and Subdatasheet Expanded	These properties are identical to those that you can define for tables and queries. Your form must be in Datasheet view and must have a subform that is also in Datasheet view. See Chapter 13, "Advanced Form Design," for details.
Palette Source	Enter the name of a graphic file or Windows palette file that provides a color palette to display this form. You might need to set this property if you have also set the Picture property so that the colors of the background picture display properly. The default setting, (Default), uses your current Windows palette.
Tag	You can use this property to store additional descriptive information about the form. You can write Visual Basic code to examine and set this property or take a specific action based on the property setting. The user cannot see the contents of the Tag property.

Table 12-11. Other Form Properties

Property	Description
On Current through After Final Render	You can set these properties to run a macro, a function, or an event procedure when the specific event described by the property occurs for this form. See Part 5 for details.
Has Module	If you create Visual Basic event procedures for this form, Access automatically sets this property to Yes. If you change this property from Yes to No, Access warns you that doing so will delete all your code and gives you a chance to cancel the change. See Part 5 for details.
Orientation	The default in most versions of Microsoft Access is Left-to-Right. In versions that support a language that is normally read right to left, the default is Right-to-Left. When you use Right-to-Left, captions appear right-justified, the order of characters in controls is right to left, and the tab sequence proceeds right to left.
Allow Design Changes	The default, All Views, allows you to continue to make design changes when in Form view. The Formatting toolbar is displayed, and you can see the Properties window if it is open. Choose Design View Only before you release your application to your users.
Moveable	The default setting, Yes, allows the user to move the form in the Access window. Set this property to No to lock the form on the screen where you last saved it.
Fetch Defaults	Choose Yes (the default) to have the form fetch the default values from the field definitions when you move to a new row. Set this property to No to use only the Default Value settings you have specified for controls.

Setting Form and Control Defaults

When you're building an application, you should establish a standard design for all your forms and the controls on your forms. Although you can use the AutoFormat templates, you might want to create a standard design that is different.

Changing Control Defaults

You can use the Set Control Defaults command on the Format menu to change the defaults for the various controls on your form. If you want to change the default property settings for all new controls of a particular type, select a control of that type, set the control's properties to the desired default values, and then choose the Set Control Defaults command from the Format menu. The settings of the currently selected control will become the default settings for any subsequent definitions of that type of control on your form.

Chapter 12

For example, you might want all new labels to show blue text on a white background. To make this change, place a label on your form and set the label's Fore Color property to blue and its Back Color property to white using the Fore Color and Back Color toolbar buttons. Choose the Set Control Defaults command from the Format menu while this label is selected. Any new labels you place on the form will have the new default settings.

Working with AutoFormat

After you define control defaults that give you the "look" you want for your application, you can also set these defaults as an *AutoFormat* that you can use in the form wizards. To create an AutoFormat definition, open the form that has the control defaults set the way you want them and then click the AutoFormat button on the toolbar or choose AutoFormat from the Format menu. Click the Customize button to open the dialog box shown in Figure 12-28. Select the Create a new AutoFormat option to save a format that matches the form you currently have open, and then click OK. In the next dialog box, type a name for your new format and then click OK. Your new format will now appear in the list of form AutoFormats. As you saw in Chapter 11, "Building a Form," you can select any of the form AutoFormats to dictate the look of a form created by the form wizards.

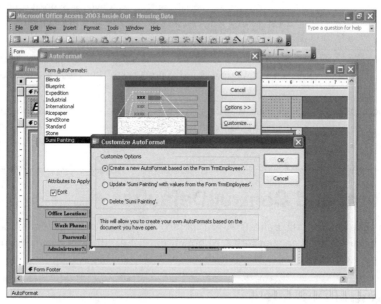

Figure 12-28. Creating a new AutoFormat definition.

If you have previously defined an AutoFormat, you can update it or delete it using the Auto-Format dialog box. You can also update or delete any of the built-in formats.

Defining a Template Form

You can also create a special form to define new default properties for all your controls. To do this, open a new blank form and place on it one of each type of control for which you want to define default properties. Modify the properties of the controls to your liking, use these controls to reset the control defaults for the form (by choosing Set Control Defaults from the Format menu for each control), and save the form with the name *Normal*. The Normal form becomes the *form template* for the current database. Any new control that you place on any new form created after you define your form template (except forms for which you've already changed the default for one or more controls) will use the default property settings you defined for that control type on the Normal form. Note that defining a form template does not affect any existing forms. Also, you can revert to the standard settings by deleting the form Normal from your database.

To define a name other than *Normal* for your default form and report templates, choose Options from the Tools menu, and then click the Forms/Reports tab. Enter the new name in the Form Template text box. Then save your template under the new name you specified on the Forms/Reports tab. Note that this new setting becomes the default for all databases on your machine, but if Access doesn't find a form in your database with the name you specified, it uses the standard default settings instead.

If you want to see how this works in the *HousingDataCopy.mdb* sample database, choose Options from the Tools menu. On the Forms/Reports tab, enter **zsfrmTemplate** in the box under Form template, and click OK. Next, click the Forms button in the Object list in the Database window, and double-click the Create form in Design view option at the top of the window. Your new form should have a header and footer and the rice paper background. Try dropping a few controls onto the form. Although I started with the Rice Paper template, I modified the look of labels, text boxes, combo boxes, list boxes, and command buttons in the template form to be different. Figure 12-29 shows you my template in Design view. Note that your new form not only inherits control properties but also the height and width of each of the sections from the template.

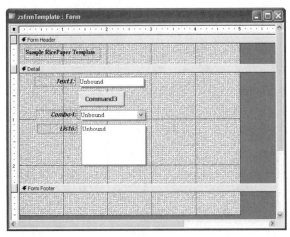

Figure 12-29. The zsfrmTemplate sample template form in the *HousingDataCopy.mdb* sample database.

Caution Be sure to change your default template name back to Normal before going on to the next chapter. This setting affects all your databases, but won't hurt anything unless you happen to have a form named zsfrmTemplate in some of your databases.

Now you should be comfortable with designing forms and adding special touches to make your forms more attractive and usable. In the next chapter, you'll learn advanced form design techniques: using multiple-table queries in forms, building forms within forms, and working with ActiveX controls, PivotTables, and PivotCharts.

Advanced Form Design

In the previous two chapters, you learned how to design and build a form that works with data from a single table, and you saw how to display data from another table by using a combo box or a list box. You also learned various techniques to enhance the appearance of your forms, and you explored control and form properties you can set to specify how a form looks and works.

In this chapter, you'll learn how to design a form that consolidates information from multiple tables. You'll find out how to

- Create a form based on a query that joins multiple tables
- Embed a subform in a main form so that you can work with related data from two tables or queries at the same time
- Use an option group to display and edit information
- Define conditional formatting of a control based on the data values in the form
- Use the tab control to handle multiple subforms within one area on a form
- Create a form that spreads many data fields across multiple pages
- Use an ActiveX control on your forms
- Design a form in PivotTable or PivotChart view and embed a linked PivotChart form in another form

Note The examples in this chapter are based on the tables and data in *HousingData-Copy.mdb* and *ContactsDataCopy.mdb* on the companion CD included with this book. These databases are copies of the data from the Housing Reservations and LawTrack Contacts application samples, respectively, and they contain the sample queries and forms used in this chapter. The results you see from the samples you build in this chapter might not exactly match what you see in this book if you have changed the sample data in the files. Also, all the screen images in this chapter were taken on a Windows XP system with the display theme set to Windows XP, and Use Windows Themed Controls on Forms has been enabled on the Forms/Reports tab of the Options dialog box for the sample databases.

Basing a Form on a Multiple-Table Query

When you bring together data from multiple tables using select queries, the result of that query is called a *recordset*. A recordset contains all the information you need, but it's in the unadorned Datasheet view format. Forms enable you to present this data in a more attractive and meaningful way. And in the same way that you can update data with queries, you can also update data using a form that is based on a query.

Creating a Many-to-One Form

It's easy to design a form that allows you to view and update the data from a single table. Although you can include selected fields from related tables using a list box or a combo box, what if you want to see more information from the related tables? The best way to do this is to design a query based on two (or more) related tables and use that query as the basis of your form.

When you create a query with two or more tables, you're usually working with one-to-many relationships among the tables. As you learned earlier, Microsoft Access lets you update any data in the table that is on the *many* side of the relationship and any nonkey fields on the *one* side of the relationship. This means that when you base a form on a query, you can update all of the fields in the form that come from the *many* table and most of the fields from the *one* side. Because the primary purpose of the form is to search and update records on the *many* side of the relationship while reviewing information on the *one* side, this is called a many-to-one form.

In Chapter 8, "Building Complex Queries," you learned how to build a multiple-table query that displays information from several tables in the *HousingDataCopy.mdb* sample database. Later, you explored the fundamentals of form construction by creating simple forms to display company and product data in the *ContactsDataCopy.mdb* sample database.

In Chapter 12, "Customizing a Form," you built and enhanced a simple form to display employee information from the housing database. (See Figure 12-20 on page 450.) You could have used a combo box to display a department name instead of a number in your employees form. But what if you want to see the additional details about the department when you view an employee record? To do this, you need to base your employee form on a query that joins multiple tables.

Designing a Many-to-One Query

To build the query you need, follow these steps:

1 Open the *HousingDataCopy.mdb* sample database, click Queries on the Object bar, and then double-click the Create query in Design view shortcut at the top of the query name list to open a new Query window in the Design view.

2 Add the tblDepartments table and two copies of the tblEmployees table from the Show Table dialog box. (You need the second copy to fetch the department manager name.)

3 Remove the extra relationship line between EmployeeNumber in the first copy of tblEmployees and ManagerNumber in the tblDepartments table.

4 Right-click the second copy of tblEmployees (the title bar of the field list displays *tblEmployees_1*), and choose Properties from the shortcut menu. In the Properties window, give the field list an alias name of Managers to make the purpose of this field list clear and then close the Properties window.

5 Click the EmployeeNumber field in the Managers field list and drag and drop it on ManagerNumber in the tblDepartments field list. This link establishes who the department manager is.

6 Drag the special "all fields" indicator (*) from the tblEmployees field list to the design grid.

7 Create an expression, **Manager: Managers.LastName & ", " & Managers.FirstName**, in the next empty column in the design grid to display the department manager name.

8 From the tblDepartments table, drag DeptLocation, DeptAddress, DeptCity, Dept-StateOrProvince, and DeptPostalCode to the query design grid. Do not include the DepartmentID field from tblDepartments; you want to be able to update the Depart-mentID field, but only in the tblEmployees table. If you include the DepartmentID field from the tblDepartments table, it might confuse you later as you design the form. You'll use a combo box on DepartmentID on the form to display the department name. Save your query as qryEmployeesDepartmentManager.

You can find a query already built for this purpose (named *qryXmplEmployeesDepartment-Manager*) in the sample database, as shown in Figure 13-1.

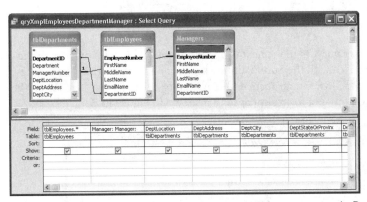

Figure 13-1. The qryXmplEmployeesDepartmentManager query in Design view.

Designing a Many-to-One Form

Now that you have the query you need, find the query definition in the Database window and open a new form based on the query. You can use the Form Wizard to quickly build a starting point for your form. Click Form Wizard in the New Form dialog box and click OK to get started.

If you choose all the fields from your query, the Form Wizard will try to cram them all in an area that is approximately 5.5 inches wide and 3 inches high. You'll end up with text boxes and combo boxes that are too narrow, and with labels overlapping all the related controls. You can get the wizard to create a better starting layout by choosing only the first 20 fields. In the Available Fields list, click the EmployeeNumber field to select it. Click the single right arrow button in the middle to move that field to the Selected Fields list. Click the arrow key again multiple times until you have moved all the fields through the DeptLocation field to the Selected Fields list. Your field selections should look like Figure 13-2. Click Next to go to the second window of the wizard.

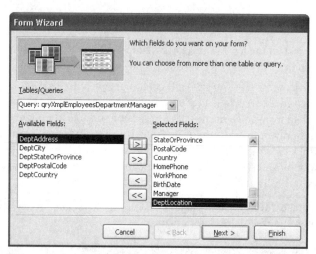

Figure 13-2. Selecting fields from a multiple-table query in the Form Wizard.

Select a columnar layout in the next window, and select the style you want in the window that follows. (I started with the Sumi Painting style for all forms in the Housing Reservations sample database.) Give your form a title of Employees in the last step. When the wizard finishes, you should see a form similar to that shown in Figure 13-3.

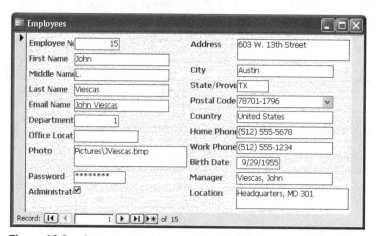

Figure 13-3. A many-to-one form to display data from multiple tables.

This form could use some polishing, but the wizard has placed the fields you chose on the form for you. To be able to see the department name, instead of Department ID, switch to Design view and perform the following steps:

1   Click the DepartmentID text box and then choose Change To on the Format menu and Combo Box on the submenu. This converts the text box to a combo box.

2   Stretch the DepartmentID combo box to the right until it is approximately the same size as the EmailName text box above it.

3   Open the Properties window and set Row Source to tblDepartments, Column Count to 2 (the first two fields of tblDepartments are DepartmentID and DepartmentName), and ColumnWidths to 0";1.5" (to hide the DepartmentID and display the department name).

Switch back to Form view, and the result should look like Figure 13-4. You can find this form saved as *frmXmplEmployee6* in the sample database.

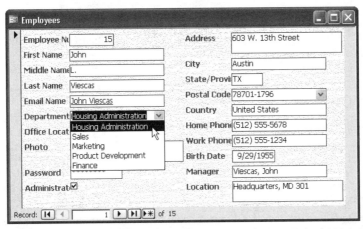

Figure 13-4. Changing the DepartmentID control to a combo box now displays the related department name.

Try changing the department on the first employee to something else and watch what happens. You should see the corresponding manager name and department location information pop into view, as shown in Figure 13-5 on the next page. Because you haven't set the Locked property for any of the fields, you can also update the location information for the displayed department. However, if you do this, the new location information appears for all employees assigned to that department.

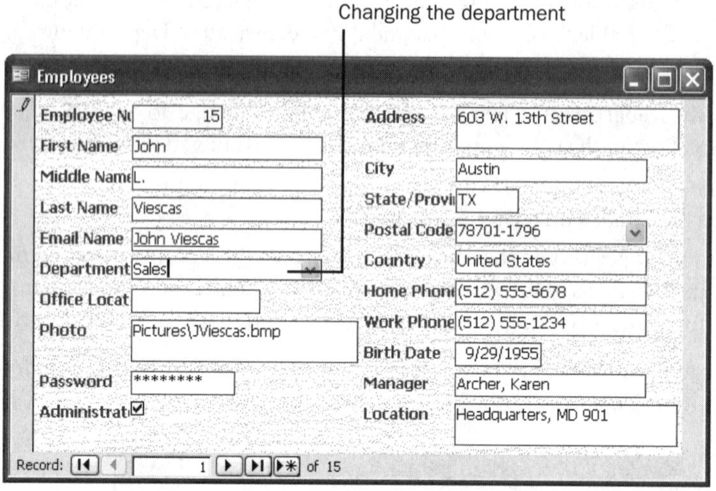

Changing the department

Figure 13-5. Changing the department displays new related information automatically on this many-to-one form.

Inside Out

Understanding Windows XP themed controls

Microsoft Access 2003 provides a new option to help your forms look more consistent with Windows XP. When you choose the Windows XP theme in Windows, you can choose Options from the Tools menu in Access and select Use Windows Themed Controls on Forms on the Forms/Reports tab. You can set this option for each individual database. When you do this, Access uses the Windows XP theme for your command buttons. It also applies the Windows XP theme for label, text box, option group, option button, check box, combo box, list box, image, unbound object frame, bound object frame, subform, and rectangle controls. All these controls appear flat when all the following conditions are true:

- Special Effect is Sunken or Etched, or Special Effect is Flat and Border Style is not Transparent.
- Border Style is Solid, or Border Style is Transparent and Special Effect is not Flat.
- Border Color is 0 or −2147483640 (the system color code for the dialog font color).
- Border Width is Hairline, 1, or 2.

Because the default settings for many controls match the above specification, a control that you expect to appear sunken or etched will look flat instead. For example, the default text box control has Special Effect set to Sunken, Border Style set to Transparent, and Border Color set to 0.

You can selectively restore the default look for controls by creating a template form in your database. (See the previous chapter for details about creating a template form.) However, the form wizards do not honor these settings unless you add your template form as a custom style and instruct the wizards to use that style. The only other solution is to selectively change one of the previously mentioned settings (for example, set Back Color to 1 instead of 0) for controls that you do not want themed.

Creating and Embedding Subforms

If you want to show data from several tables and be able to update the data in more than one of the tables, you probably need to use something more complex than a standard form. In the LawTrack Contacts database, the main contacts information is in the tblContacts table. Contacts can have multiple contact events and might be associated with more than one company or organization. The information about companies is in the tblCompanies table.

Because any one contact might belong to several companies or organizations and each company probably has many contacts, the tblContacts table is related to the tblCompanies table in a many-to-many relationship. See Chapter 4, "Creating Your Database and Tables," for a review of relationship types. The tblCompanyContacts table provides the link between companies and contacts.

Similarly, a particular contact within a company might own one or more products, and a product should be owned by multiple contacts. Because any one contact might have purchased many different products and any one product might be owned by multiple contacts, the tblCompanyContacts table is related to the tblProducts table in a many-to-many relationship. The tblContactProducts table establishes the necessary link between the contacts and the products owned. Figure 13-6 on the next page shows the relationships.

When you are viewing information about a particular contact, you also might want to see and edit the related company information and the product detail information. You could create a complex query that brings together the desired information from all five tables and use a single form to display the data, similar to the many-to-one employees form you built in the previous section. However, the focus would be on the contact products (the lowest table in the one-to-many relationship chain), so you would be able to see in a single form row only one product per row. You could design a form that has its Default View property set to Continuous Forms, but you would see the information from tblContacts and tblCompanyContacts repeated over and over.

Subforms can help solve this problem. You can create a main form that displays the contacts information and embed in it a subform that displays all the related rows from tblCompanyContacts. To see the related product information, you could then build a subform within the form that displays the tblCompanyContacts data to show the product information from tblContactProducts.

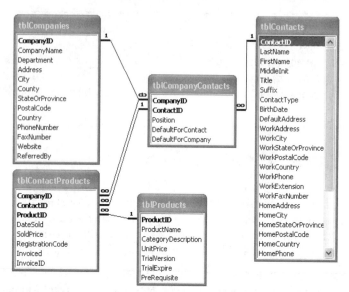

Figure 13-6. The relationships between companies, contacts, and products in the LawTrack Contacts application.

Specifying the Subform Source

You can embed up to 10 levels of subforms within another form (a form that has a subform that also has a subform, and so on). It's best to start by designing the innermost form and working outward because you must design and save an inner form before you can embed it in an outer one. In this exercise, you need to build a form on tblContactProducts, embed that in a form that shows data from tblCompanyContacts, and then finally embed that form and subform in a form to display contact information. But first, you must create the record sources for these subforms. Begin by designing the data source for the first subform.

In the example described previously, you want to create or update rows in the tblContact-Products table to create, modify, or delete links between company contact records in the tblCompanyContacts table and products in the tblProducts table. You could certainly base the subform directly on the tblContactProducts table and display the product name via a combo box on the form that looks up the name based on the value in the ProductID field. However, the user might find it useful to have the current list price for the product displayed to be sure the product isn't being sold at the wrong price. To do that, you need a query linking tblContactProducts and tblProducts.

Start by opening a new query in Design view. In the Show Table dialog box, add the field lists for the tblContactProducts and tblProducts tables to the Query window. You want to be able to update all the fields in the tblContactProducts table, so copy them to the design grid. You can do so by using the all fields indicator (*). Add the ProductName, CategoryDescription, UnitPrice, and TrialVersion fields from the tblProducts table.

Your query should look similar to the one shown in Figure 13-7. (This query is saved as *qxmplContactProducts* in the sample database.) Notice that the tblProducts table has a one-to-many relationship with the tblContactProducts table. This means that you can update any field in the tblContactProducts table (including all three primary key fields, as long as you don't create a duplicate row) because the tblContactProducts table is on the *many* side of the relationship. Save the query so that you can use it as you design the subform. You can save your query as qryContactProducts, as shown in Figure 13-7, or use the sample query.

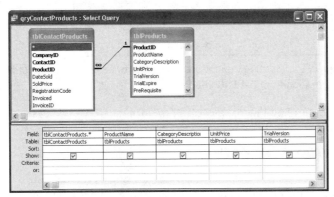

Figure 13-7. A query for updating the tblContactProducts table from a subform while displaying related information from the tblProducts table.

Next, you need a query for the form to display the information from tblCompanyContacts. You'll embed a subform to display contact products in this form and ultimately embed this form in the outermost form to display contact data. Again, you could use the tblCompany-Contacts table as the record source for this form, but you might want to display additional information such as company name and department name from the related tblCompanies table. You also want to restrict the rows displayed to the one row for each contact that defines the default company for the contact.

Start a new query on the tblCompanyContacts table. Add the tblCompanies table to the design grid. You should see a link between the two tables on the CompanyID field in each. In the design grid, include the CompanyID, ContactID, Position, and DefaultForContact fields from tblCompanyContacts. Under the DefaultForContact field, enter a criterion of True to restrict the output to the records that define the default company for each contact. Add the CompanyName and Department fields from the tblCompanies table.

Your query should look like the one shown in Figure 13-8 on the next page. (This query is saved as *qxmplContactCompaniesDefault* in the sample database.) Notice that the tblCompanies table has a one-to-many relationship with the tblCompanyContacts table. This means that you can update any field in the tblCompanyContacts table (including the primary key fields, as long as you don't create a duplicate row) because the tblCompanyContacts table is on the *many* side of the relationship. Save the query so that you can use it as you design your form. You can save your query as qryContactCompaniesDefault, as shown in Figure 13-8, or use the sample query.

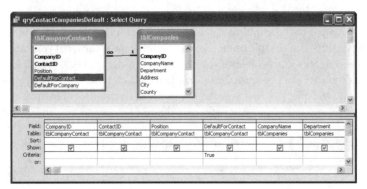

Figure 13-8. A query for updating the tblCompanyContacts table from a subform while displaying related information from the tblCompanies table.

You're now ready to start building the forms and subforms.

Designing the Innermost Subform

For the innermost subform, you'll end up displaying the single ProductID field bound to a combo box that shows the product name. After you choose a ProductID, you want to show the user the product category, name, and list price—but in controls that can't be updated. (You don't want a user to be able to accidentally change product names and list prices via this form!) Of course, you need the DateSold and SoldPrice fields from tblContactProducts so that you can update these fields.

For this purpose, you could use a form in either Datasheet or Continuous Forms view. It's simple to build a subform designed to be used in Datasheet view because you only need to include the fields you want to display in the Detail section of the form, without any regard to alignment or placement. Access takes care of ordering, sizing, and providing column headers in the datasheet. However, I like to use Continuous Forms view because that view lets you control the size of the columns—in Datasheet view, a user can resize the columns, including shrinking a column so that it's no longer visible. Furthermore, if the subform is in Single Form view or Continuous Forms view, the Size/To Fit command will make the subform control on the outer form the right size. If the subform is in Datasheet view, however, the Size/To Fit command will size the control to the size of the subform in Form view, not to an even number of datasheet rows wide or high. Also, the user is free to resize the row height and column width in Datasheet view, so how you size the subform control in Design view is only a guess.

It turns out that the Form Wizard does a good job assembling this first subform for you. Click Queries on the Object bar and select either the qryContactProducts query you built or the sample *qxmplContactProducts* query. Choose Form from the New Object button on the toolbar, select Form Wizard in the New Form dialog box, and click OK to start the wizard. You're going to ask the wizard to create a tabular form, which displays the fields you select in the order you select them in Continuous Forms view.

You don't need the CompanyID and ContactID fields—as you'll learn later, the form in which you'll embed this subform will supply these values via special properties you'll set in the subform control. First, click the ProductID field to select it, and click the single right arrow to move it to the Selected Fields list. Choose the additional fields you need in this order: CategoryDescription, ProductName, UnitPrice, DateSold, and SoldPrice. (If we had planned ahead, we could have placed the fields in this sequence in the query we're using as the record source.) Click Next to go to the next window in the wizard, as shown in Figure 13-9.

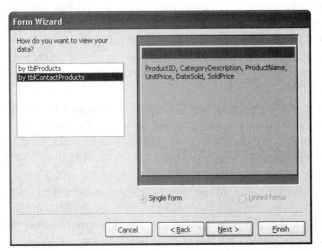

Figure 13-9. When you use the Form Wizard to build a form on a query using two tables, the wizard offers data layout choices.

Although you won't take advantage of the wizard features shown in this window this time, it's interesting to note the options if you click the **by tblProducts** option. The wizard offers to build a form on tblProducts and a subform on tblContactProducts, or two separate forms that are linked with a command button. In this case, you want to build a single continuous form, so click **by tblContactProducts**, and then click Next to go to the next window. Choose the Tabular layout and the Standard style in the next two windows. In the final window, give your new form a name such as fsubContactProducts, choose the option to modify the form's design, and click Finish. Your result should look like Figure 13-10.

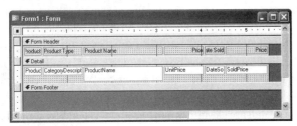

Figure 13-10. The continuous form created by the Form Wizard to edit contact product information.

> **Note** If you are not on a Windows XP system or you have Windows XP themes disabled, the text boxes in Figure 13-10 appear sunken.

You could probably use this form as is, but perform the following steps to perfect the design:

1 Select all the labels and click the Bold toolbar button to make the captions more readable.

2 The two price text box controls are wider than necessary, and the DateSold text box control isn't wide enough. Click the horizontal ruler above the UnitPrice control to select the control and its label. Hold down the Shift key and click the ruler above the SoldPrice control to add that control and its label to the selection. Open the Properties window (its title bar shows that you have multiple controls selected) and enter **0.75"** in the Width property.

3 Because you've make the SoldPrice text box and its label shorter, you can now move them over to occupy the blank space and make room for other controls to the left. Click the ruler above the SoldPrice text box control again to select it and its label, and click either control and slide them both to the right near the right edge of the form design area.

4 Click the ruler above the DateSold text box control to select it and its label. Click either control and slide them both to the left closer to UnitPrice. Grab the sizing handle in the middle of the right edge of either control and expand them both into the space you created by moving the SoldPrice text box so the right edge of the DateSold text box control is near the SoldPrice text box control.

5 The ProductName text box control does not need to be quite so wide and doesn't need to be two lines high. Click the ruler above the ProductName control to select it and its label. Type **1.6"** in the Width property to shrink both controls. Grab either control and slide them right closer to the UnitPrice control. Click the CategoryDescription text box control and hold down the Shift key and click the ProductName text box control to add it to the selection. Choose Size on the Format menu and To Shortest on the submenu to make the ProductName control the same height as CategoryDescription. Go to the Properties window and set the Scroll Bars property to None to ensure that neither control has a scroll bar.

6 The CategoryDescription text box control is wide enough, but the ProductID text box control could be wider to accommodate the combo box you're about to build. Click the ruler above the CategoryDescription text box control to select it and its label. Click either control and slide them right close to the ProductName text box control.

7 Click the ruler above the ProductID text box control to select it and its label. Grab the sizing handle in the middle of the right edge of either control and stretch them to the right close to the CategoryDescription control.

8 Click anywhere in the Detail area away from the ProductID text box control to remove the selection from the control and its label. Click the ProductID text box control to select it, and choose Change To on the Format menu and Combo Box on the submenu

to convert the text box to a combo box. In the Properties window, set Row Source to tblProducts, Column Count to 2, Column Widths to **0.25"; 1.5"**, and List Width to **2"**.

9 You need to lock the three fields from tblProducts so they cannot be updated via this form. Click the CategoryDescription text box control, and hold down the Shift key while you click the ProductName text box control and the UnitPrice text box control to add them to the selection. Change the Special Effect property to Flat to give the user a visual indication that these controls are different. In the Properties window, set Locked to Yes. (See the note later about making controls appear sunken on a Windows XP system when you're using Windows themed controls on your forms.)

10 Open up the form footer by dragging down its bottom edge. Click the Text Box tool in the toolbox and drop a text box in the Footer section under the SoldPrice text box control. Make your new control the same size as the SoldPrice control and line them up using the Align command on the Format menu that you learned about in the previous chapter. Click the attached label, set its font to Bold, and in the Properties window type **Total:** in the Caption property. Click the new text box, and in the Properties window set Control Source to **=Sum([SoldPrice])**, Format to Currency, Enabled to No, and Locked to Yes.

> **Tip** You might have noticed that when you select a combination of controls in different sections of a form, Access lets you move the controls only horizontally. This is a handy way to slide controls across your design without disturbing where they're placed vertically.

All you have left to do is to shrink the bottom of the Detail area to eliminate the extra space below the row of controls, select the form and set the form's Scroll Bars property in the Properties window to Vertical Only (your design should horizontally fit all the fields within the subform control on the main form so that the user won't need to scroll left and right), and set the Navigation Buttons property to No. (You can use the vertical scroll bar to move through the multiple rows.)

Because you didn't pick all the fields from the query, the wizard tried to help you out by creating an SQL statement to fetch only the fields you used on the form. You'll need all the fields for the subform filtering to work correctly. So, delete the SQL statement from the form's Record Source property and set the property back to the name of your query. The result of your work should look something like Figure 13-11.

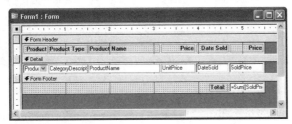

Figure 13-11. The subform to edit contact products in Design view.

> **Note** If you want the ProductID, DateSold, SoldPrice, and Total controls to appear sunken on a Windows XP system with the Windows XP theme enabled as shown in Figures 13-11 and 13-12, you must select these controls, change the Border Color property to gray, and change the Special Effect property to Sunken. If the Windows XP theme is disabled, these controls appear sunken without any modification.

You can switch to the subform's Form view to check your work. You can see the Continuous Forms view in Figure 13-12. Because this form isn't linked as a subform yet (which will limit the display to the current order), the totals displayed in the form footer are the totals for all orders. You can find this form saved as *fsubXmplContactProducts* in the sample database.

	Product	Product Type	Product Name	Price	Date Sold	Price
▶	1 ▾	Single User	Demo Edition, Single User	$0.00	3/18/2003	$0.00
	1 ▾	Single User	Demo Edition, Single User	$0.00	11/17/2002	$0.00
	1 ▾	Single User	Demo Edition, Single User	$0.00	3/16/2003	$0.00
	1 ▾	Single User	Demo Edition, Single User	$0.00	4/1/2003	$0.00
	1 ▾	Single User	Demo Edition, Single User	$0.00	2/15/2003	$0.00
	1 ▾	Single User	Demo Edition, Single User	$0.00	12/5/2002	$0.00
	2 ▾	Multi-User	Demo Edition, Multi-User	$0.00	12/19/2002	$0.00
					Total:	$4,038.00

Figure 13-12. The contact products subform in Continuous Forms view.

Inside Out

Using a subform in Datasheet view

If you'll be using a subform in Datasheet view when it's embedded in another form, you have to switch to Datasheet view to adjust how the datasheet looks and then save the subform from Datasheet view to preserve the look you want. You must also use the Datasheet view of the form to make adjustments to fonts and row height. The font in Datasheet view is independent of any font defined for the controls in Form view.

Also, if you build a tabular form such as the one shown in Figure 13-12 and then decide to use it as a subform in Datasheet view, you will see the field names as the column headings rather than the captions. In Datasheet view, columns display the defined caption for the field only when the bound control has an attached label. In a tabular form, the labels are detached from their respective controls and displayed in a separate section of the form design.

Designing the First Level Subform

You can now move on to the form to display the company contact information and act as a link between contacts and contact products. The purpose of the final form will be to view contacts and edit their contact products, so you don't need to have anything fancy in the middle or allow any updates. To begin, click Queries on the Object bar in the Database window and select either the query you built earlier (qryContactCompaniesDefault) or the sample query I provided (*qxmplContactCompaniesDefault*). Choose Form on the New Objects button on the toolbar, select Design View in the New Form dialog box, and click OK.

To make this form easy to build, set some control defaults first. Open the Properties window, click the Label tool in the toolbox, and click the Bold button on the Formatting toolbar to give all your labels a default bold font. Click the Text Box tool and change Special Effect to Flat, Label Align to Right and Label X (the offset of the label to the right) to −.05".

Open the field list, click the CompanyID field to select it, and hold down the Ctrl key while you click the CompanyName and Department fields to add them to the selection. Drag and drop these fields together onto your form about 2 inches from the left edge and near the top of the Detail design area. Drag and drop the Position field onto the form directly below Department. If you have Snap To Grid turned on, it should be easy to line up the controls. Otherwise, select all the text box controls and use the Align command on the Format menu to line them up. Set the Locked property of all text box controls to Yes. Select the label control attached to the CompanyID text box and change the caption from Company / Org.: to **Company ID:**. At this stage, your design should look like Figure 13-13.

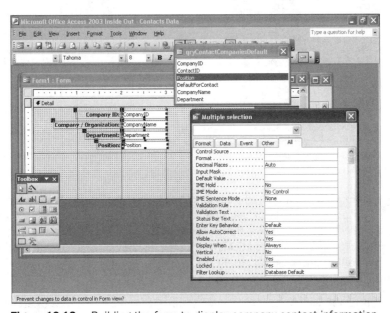

Figure 13-13. Building the form to display company contact information.

Embedding a Subform

You can use a couple of techniques to embed a subform in your outer form. First, you can cancel the selection of the Control Wizards button in the toolbox, select the Subform/Subreport tool in the toolbox, and then click the upper left corner of the outer form's empty area and drag the mouse pointer to create a subform control. (If you leave the Control Wizards button selected, Access starts a wizard to help you build the subform when you place a subform control on your outer form. Because you already built the subform, you don't need the wizard's help.) Once the subform control is in place, set its Source Object property to point to the subform you built (or use the sample *fsubXmplContactProducts*).

A better way to embed the subform (if you have a large enough screen to do this) is to place the Form window and the Database window side by side, find the form you want to embed as a subform, and then drag it from the Database window and drop it onto your form. To do this, go back to the Database window, click Forms on the Object bar, and move the window off to the right side so you can see the form you're building positioned underneath on the left. Click the subform you built in the previous section (or the *fsubXmplContactProducts* form that I supplied) and drag and drop it onto your form at the left edge below the Position label and text box. Figure 13-14 shows this action in progress.

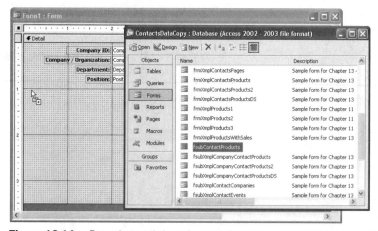

Figure 13-14. Dragging and dropping one form onto the Design view of another form to create a subform.

Adding a subform in this way has the advantages that your new subform control will be sized correctly horizontally, will have a height to display at least one row, and will have some of its other properties automatically set. If the form you are designing has a table as its record source and Access can find related fields of the same name in the record source of the subform you're adding, Access automatically defines the link properties as well. You'll have to set these properties yourself later in this exercise.

You don't need the label that Access added to your subform control, so you can select it and delete it. Click the subform control to select it (if you click more than once, you'll select an object on the form inside the subform control), drag the sizing handle in the middle of the bottom of the control so that it is about 2 inches high, and then choose Size from the Format menu and To Fit on the submenu to correctly size the control to display multiple rows. Move up the bottom of the Detail section of the outer form if necessary so that there's only a small margin below the bottom of the resized subform control. Your form should look something like Figure 13-15.

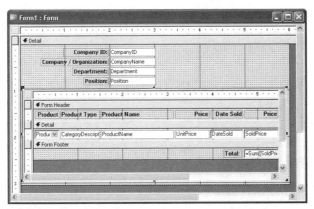

Figure 13-15. The contact products subform embedded in your form to display company contact information.

Tip Sizing a subform control

Sizing a subform that you display in Form view is quite simple. You might need to do this if you create the subform control directly on the form. Choose the subform control, choose Size from the Format menu, and then choose To Fit from the submenu. In this case, you're using a subform in Continuous Forms view, so Access will size the subform control to the correct width and to the nearest vertical height to fully display rows in the Detail section. Note that if your subform default view is Datasheet view, using the Size/To Fit command won't work unless the form's Design view is exactly the same size as the datasheet. You have to switch in and out of Form view and manually adjust the size of the subform control.

You must set a couple of key properties to finish this work. If you remember from Figure 13-6, the tblCompanyContacts table is related to the tblContactProducts table on both the CompanyID and the ContactID fields. When you view records in an outer form and you want Access to filter the rows in the subform to show only related information, you must make sure that Access knows the field(s) that link the two sets of data. With the subform control selected, go to the Properties window, and set the Link Child Fields and Link Master Fields properties as shown in Figure 13-16 on the next page.

The Link Child Fields property refers to the "child" form—the one in the subform. You must enter the names of the fields in the record source of the form inside the subform that should be filtered based on what row you have displayed in the outer form, separated by semicolons. Likewise, the Link Master Fields property should contain the name(s) of the related field(s) on the outer form. In most cases, both properties will contain only one field name, but the names might not be the same. In this case, you know it takes two fields to correctly relate the rows. Switch to Form view, and your form should look like Figure 13-17 on the next page. As you move from record to record in the outer form, Access uses the values it finds in the field(s) defined in Link Master Fields as a filter against the fields in the subform defined in Link Child Fields.

Chapter 13

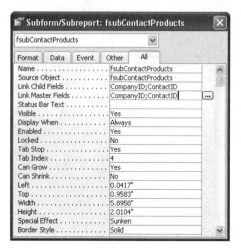

Figure 13-16. Setting the link field properties of a subform control to tell Access how the data in the outer form is related to the data in the inner form.

Figure 13-17. A form to display company contact information with a subform that displays the related products owned.

We don't know yet which contact owns these products because we haven't built the final outer form yet to display contact information. You should return to Design view and make some adjustments to the length of the CompanyName, Department, and Position text boxes. You should also set the form's Scroll Bars property to Neither and the Record Selectors property to No. You really don't want users adding and deleting records in this outer form, so set Allow Additions and Allow Deletions to No. Save your form as fsubCompanyContact-Products. (Note that if you made any changes to the form inside the subform control, Access will also ask you if you want to save that form, too.) You can also find this form saved as *fsubXmplCompanyContactProducts* in the sample database.

> **Tip** If the record source of the outer form is a single table, Access automatically sets the Link Master Fields and Link Child Fields properties for you when it can find a related field in the table or query that you define as the record source of the form within the subform control. It does this when you either drag the subform to the main form or set the Source Object property of the subform control.

Specifying the Main Form Source

Now it's time to create the main form. You need a table or a query as the source of the form. You want to be able to view (and perhaps update) the contacts who own the products shown in the form and subform you've built thus far, so your row source should include the tblContacts table. You don't need any other related tables, but you might want to use a query so that you can sort the contacts by name.

Start a new query on the tblContacts table and include all the fields in the design grid. Add criteria to sort in ascending order under LastName and FirstName. (You'll recall from Chapter 7, "Creating and Working with Simple Queries," that the sequence of fields in the design grid is important for sorting—so be sure that LastName is before FirstName in the query design grid.) Save your query as qryContactsSorted. Your query should look something like that shown in Figure 13-18. You can find this query saved as *qxmplContactsSorted* in the sample database.

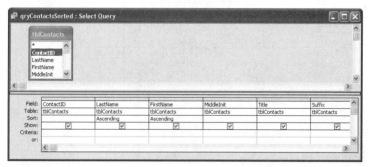

Figure 13-18. A query for sorting contact records to be used in a form.

Creating the Main Form

Building the form for the tblContacts table is fairly straightforward. In fact, you can select the query you just created and use a form wizard to build the basic form in columnar format. I recommend that you build this form from scratch as you did to build the form for company contacts because there are only a few fields you need to include, and you want to place them differently than the wizard would. To begin, click Queries on the Object bar in the Database window and select either the query you just built (qryContactSorted) or the sample query I provided (*qxmplContactsSorted*). Choose Form on the New Objects button on the toolbar, select Design View in the New Form dialog box, and click OK.

As you did with the company contacts form, set some control defaults first. Open the Properties window, click the Label tool in the toolbox, and click the Bold button on the Formatting toolbar to give all your labels a default bold font. Click the Text Box tool and change Label Align to Right and Label X (the offset of the label to the right) to −.05". (If you have Windows XP themes enabled, also change Border Color to 1 and Special Effect to Sunken.) Click the Combo Box tool and make the same adjustments to the default Label Align and Label X properties.

Open the field list, click the ContactType field, and drag and drop it about 1 inch from the left margin near the top of the design area. One at a time, add the Title, LastName, and Suffix fields in a column under ContactType. In a row aligned with the LastName text box, drag and drop the FirstName field about 3 inches out, and the MiddleInit field about 5 inches out. (Access expands the width of the design area when you do this.) You can shrink the Middle-Init text box to about a half-inch wide. When you add the fields ContactType, Title, and Suffix one at a time, Access honors the Lookup properties for the fields and creates a combo box control for each. If you select multiple fields and add them all at once, you'll get text boxes for all of them.

The sample design shown in Figure 13-19 has a space at the bottom of the Detail section where you can place the subform to display company contact and product data. You can find this main form saved as *frmXmplContacts1* in the sample database.

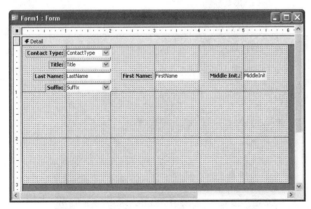

Figure 13-19. A main form to display contact data, with space for a subform.

Now you're ready to add the subform. This time, select the Subform/Subreport tool in the toolbox and draw the control starting near the left edge under the Suffix combo box and extending to fill the blank area. Select the label control that came with the subform and delete it. Select the subform control, open the Properties window, and select the fsubCompanyContactProducts form you created earlier (or my sample *fsubXmplCompanyContactProducts* form) from the drop-down list in the Source Object property box. Enter **ContactID** in the Link Child Fields and Link Master Fields properties. Finally, double-click one of the subform control sizing handles or choose Size/To Fit from the Format menu to properly size the subform control. Your result should look something like Figure 13-20. Save your form as frmContactsProducts. You can find this form saved as *frmXmplContactsProducts* in the sample database.

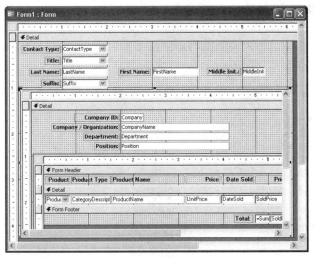

Figure 13-20. The new subform embedded in the form to edit contacts.

In this case, the ContactID field from tblContacts on the outer form is the link to the related rows on the subform. If you recall, the combination of CompanyID and ContactID forms the link between the forms on the second and third level.

Inside Out

Editing the form inside a subform control

Access 2000 introduced a feature that allows you to directly edit your subform once you have defined it as the source for your subform control. As you can see in Figure 13-20, the design of the fsubCompanyContactProducts form is visible in the subform control on the outermost form. Likewise, the design of the fsubContactProducts form is visible inside that. You can click any control in the inner forms and change its size or adjust its properties using the property sheet or the Formatting toolbar. You might need to temporarily expand the size of the subform control in order to work with the inner form easily. However, you cannot use File/Save As to save your changes to a different form definition. If you want to edit the form inside a subform control in its own window, select the subform control, and then choose Subform in New Window from the View menu.

Click the Form View button on the toolbar to see the completed form, as shown in Figure 13-21 on the next page. Because you properly set the linking field information for the subform controls, you can see the companies for each contact and the products for each company and contact in the subforms as you move from one contact to another. Note that the inner set of navigation buttons is for the first subform. Use the scroll bar in the innermost subform to move through the product detail records. Also, because you locked the controls in the first subform (the company contact information), you cannot edit the controls you see there.

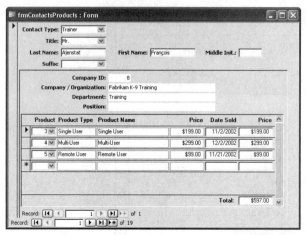

Figure 13-21. A form to edit contacts in a main form and products owned by the contact in subforms.

Note If you look at the frmContacts form in the LawTrack Contacts application, you'll see a products subform on the Products tab that has no intervening company contacts subform. This form has some Visual Basic procedures that automatically supply the default company ID for the contact and disallow adding a product if the contact doesn't have a default company defined. You can see how this code works in Chapter 23, "Automating Your Application with Visual Basic."

Creating a Subdatasheet Subform

In Chapter 7, you learned how to define a subdatasheet for a query. You can do the same thing with forms as long as the forms are saved to be displayed in Datasheet view. The best way to see how this works is to create modified versions of the three forms just built.

Start by opening your fsubContactProducts form (or the sample *fsubXmplContactProducts* form) in Design view. Change the Default View property of the form to Datasheet and save the form as fsubContactProductsDS. Switch to Datasheet view, and your form now looks like Figure 13-22.

Notice that several of the columns are much wider than they need to be. If you scroll down to the bottom, you don't see the subtotal that's in the form footer anymore. Also, because the labels for these fields are in the form header (see Figure 13-11) and not attached to their respective controls, you see the actual field names instead of the field captions. Let's not worry about the captions for now, but you should adjust the column widths to be more reasonable. You can do that by double-clicking the dividing line to the right of each column heading. This auto-sizes the columns to the widest data (or column caption) displayed. If the data you see isn't representative of the widest data you might store, you need to adjust the width by hand. You must save the form to preserve this sizing, so choose Save As from the File menu and save the form as *fsubContact-ProductsDS*. You can find this form saved as *fsubXmplContactProductsDS* in the sample database.

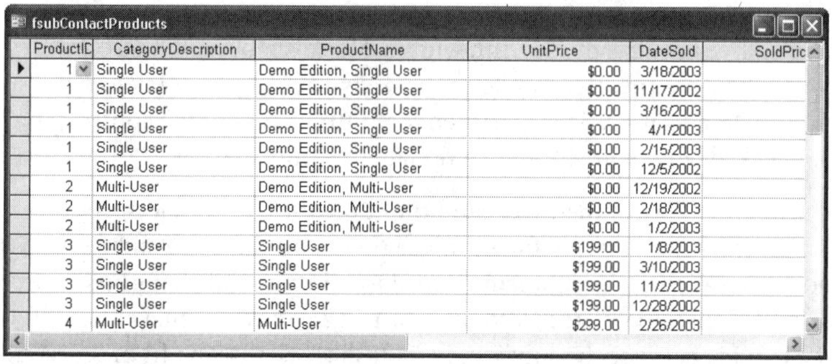

Figure 13-22. The contact products subform changed to be displayed in Datasheet view.

Next, open your fsubCompanyContactProducts form (or the *fsubXmplCompanyContact-Products* sample form) in Design view. Change the Default View property of the form to Datasheet. Click the subform control to select it and change the Source Object property to point to the new datasheet subform you just saved—fsubContactProductsDS. Save the form as fsubCompanyContactProductsDS.

If you like, you can select the form again, and change the Subdatasheet Height and Subdatasheet Expanded properties. Because both this form and the embedded subform are set to be displayed in Datasheet view, you can set these properties exactly as you would for a table or query. You can specify a specific height in inches that you want to reserve for the subdatasheet (the subform inside this form). If you leave the default value of 0", the subdatasheet opens to display all available rows when you click the plus sign on any row to expand the subdatasheet for that row. You can also change Subdatasheet Expanded to Yes to always expand all subdatasheets within the subform when you open the form (as though you clicked the plus sign on all displayed rows). For now, leave these properties as is.

Switch to Datasheet view, and your form should look like Figure 13-23.

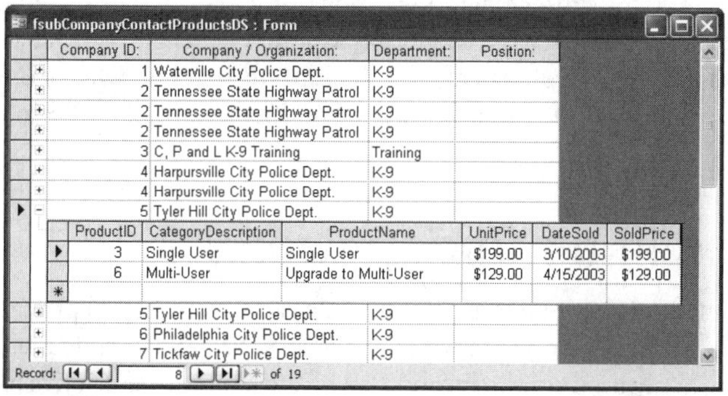

Figure 13-23. The form to display company contact information in Datasheet view with a subdatasheet to display products.

Because the controls on this form have attached labels (see Figure 13-15), the captions from those labels appear as the column headings. Notice that the subdatasheet form has its columns sized as you saved them when you designed the subform. You can resize the columns in either display and save the form to save the new column width settings. Keep in mind that your user is also free to resize the column widths. However, because these are forms, you have more control over what the user can do than you have in a query. Try to type something in the Company / Organization or Department columns. Because the controls in the underlying form are locked, you won't be able to update this information.

To finish putting this all together, you can now edit your frmContactsProducts form (or the *frmXmplContactsProducts* sample form) to use these new datasheet subforms. Open your form in Design view, click the subform control to select it, and change its Source Object property to fsubCompanyContactProductsDS. You also need to make the subform control about 7 inches wide because the subform in Datasheet view won't fit in the current window. However, you can also shorten the height of the subform control to about 1.5 inches.

Save your modified form as frmContactsProductsDS and switch to Form view. Your form should now look like Figure 13-24.

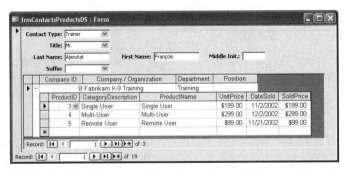

Figure 13-24. A form to edit contacts in a main form and products owned by the contact in subforms displayed in Datasheet view.

Remember that one of the shortcomings of designing your form this way is you have to make a "best guess" at the size of the subform window, and your users can modify the width of the columns in both datasheets as they wish. I personally don't like this design very much, but you might find it useful to conserve vertical space in a subform design when displaying complex data levels. You can find this form saved as *frmXmplContactsProductsDS* in the sample database.

Displaying Values in an Option Group

Whenever you have a field that contains an integer code value, you need to provide some way for the user to set the value based on what your application knows the code means, not the number. You could certainly use a combo box or a list box to supply a descriptive list. However, when the number of different values is small, an option group might be the ideal solution.

In the LawTrack Contacts application, the tblContacts table contains both a home and a work address. The DefaultAddress field contains an integer code value that is used by some reports to generate a mailing address. When DefaultAddress is 1, the application uses the work address; and when DefaultAddress is 2, the home address is the default. However, a user isn't likely to always remember that 1 means work and 2 means home. You should provide a way to make these values obvious.

In the *ContactsDataCopy.mdb* sample file, you can find a form called *frmXmplContacts* that has the basic contact information and the two sets of addresses already laid out. Figure 13-25 shows you that form in Form view.

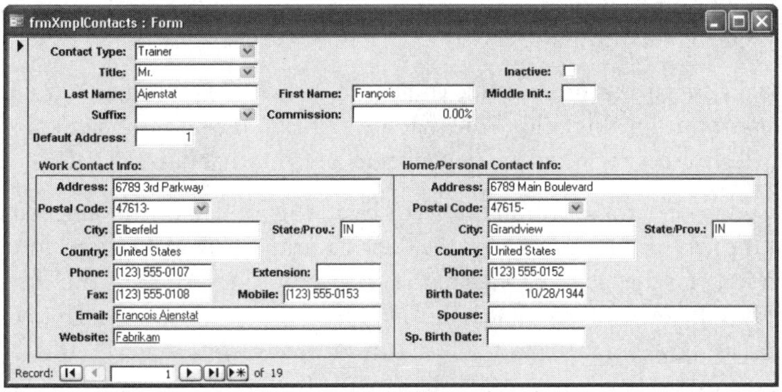

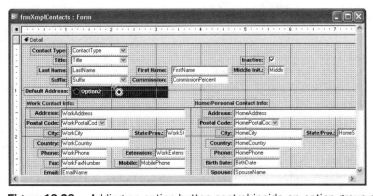

Figure 13-25. A form to edit contact name and address information.

You can see that the Default Address field could be confusing on this form. To fix this, switch to Design view and delete the DefaultAddress text box control. Click the Option Group tool in the toolbox to select it, then open the field list and drag the Default Address field onto the form under the Suffix combo box control. (I set the defaults for the option group control on this form so that it should fit nicely under the Suffix control and be wide enough to add some buttons.)

Next, double-click the Option Button tool in the toolbox to allow you to define multiple buttons without having to go back to the toolbox to select the tool again. When you move your mouse pointer inside the option group control, you'll see the control become highlighted to indicate you're placing the button inside the control. Drag one toward the left end of the control (the label will appear to the right of the button), and a second one to the middle. Figure 13-26 shows what the form looks like as you add the second button.

Figure 13-26. Adding an option button control inside an option group control.

Click the Select Objects tool in the toolbox to turn off the Option Button tool. Click the first button and open the Properties window. Near the top of the list, you can see that Access has set the Option Value property of this button to 1. If you click the other button, you'll find that its Option Value property is 2. Because the option group control is bound to the DefaultValue field, the first button will be highlighted when you're on a record that has a value of 1 (work address) in this field, and the second button will be highlighted when the value is 2. If you click a different button when editing a record, Access changes the value of the underlying field to the value of the button.

You can actually assign any integer value you like to each option button in a group, but Access has set these just fine for this field. Note that if you assign the same value to more than one button, they'll all appear selected when you're on a record that has that value.

To make the purpose of these buttons perfectly clear, you need to fix the attached labels. Click the label for the first button and change the Caption property from Option2 to Work. Set the Caption property for the label attached to the second button to Home. (You could also make the font Bold while you're at it to match the other labels on the form.) Switch to Form view to see the results as shown in Figure 13-27. Save this form as frmContacts2. You can also find this form saved as *frmXmplContacts2* in the sample database.

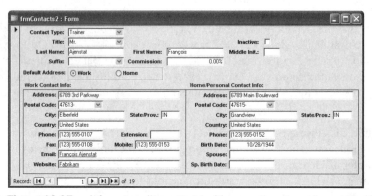

Figure 13-27. A form to edit contacts with an option group to set the default address.

Using Conditional Formatting

Access includes a feature that allows you to define dynamic modification of the formatting of text boxes and combo boxes. You can define an expression that tests the value in the text box or combo box or any other field available in the form. If the expression is true, Access will modify the Bold, Italic, Underline, Back Color, Fore Color, and Enabled properties for you based on the custom settings you associate with the expression.

This feature can be particularly useful for controlling field display in a subform in Continuous Forms view. For example, you might want to highlight the ProductName field in the innermost subform shown in Figure 13-21 when the product is a trial version. Or, you might want to change the font of the address fields in the form shown in Figure 13-27 depending on the value of the DefaultAddress field.

For the first example, you can use the fsubCompanyContactProducts subform that you built earlier (or the *fsubXmplCompanyContactProducts* sample form you'll find in the sample database). To define conditional formatting, first open the form you need to modify in Design view. Click the subform control and then click the ProductName field within the sub-form to select it. Choose Conditional Formatting from the Format menu to see the Conditional Formatting dialog box.

In the Default Formatting box, you can see the currently defined format for the control. You can use the Bold, Italic, Underline, Back Color, Fore Color, and Enabled buttons to modify the default. When you first open this dialog box, Access displays a single blank Condition 1. In the leftmost combo box, you can choose Field Value Is to test for a value in the field, Expression Is to create a logical expression that can test other fields on the form or compare another field with this one, and Field Has Focus to define settings the control will inherit when the user clicks in the control.

When you choose Field Value Is, the dialog box displays a second combo box with logical comparison options such as Less Than, Equal To, or Greater Than. Choose the logical comparison you want, and then enter in the text boxes on the right the value or values to compare the field with.

In this case, you want to set the format of ProductName based on the value of the TrialVersion field. So, choose Expression Is and in the expression box **enter:**

`[TrialVersion]=True`

Set the formatting properties you want the control to have if the test is true by using the buttons to the right. In this case, set the Fill/Back Color to a bright yellow as shown in Figure 13-28, and click OK.

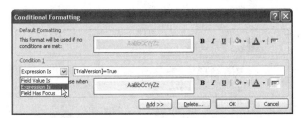

Figure 13-28. Defining conditional formatting for the ProductName field.

Switch to Form view to see the result as shown in Figure 13-29 on the next page. You can find the sample saved as *fsubXmplCompanyContactProducts2*.

You can make a similar change to frmContacts2 that you saved earlier, or you can use the sample *frmXmplContacts2* form. Open that form in Design view, click the WorkAddress text box control to select it, and hold down the Shift key as you click the WorkPostalCode, WorkCity, and WorkStateOrProvince controls to add them to the selection. (Yes, you can set conditional formatting for multiple controls at one time.) Choose Conditional Formatting from the Format menu to see the Conditional Formatting dialog box.

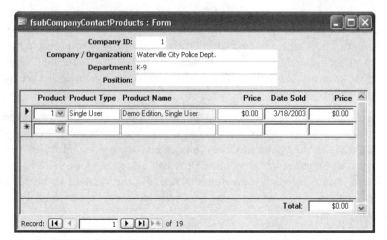

Figure 13-29. Seeing the result of conditional formatting for the ProductName field.

Choose Expression Is in the combo box, and enter [**DefaultAddress**]=1 in the Condition field to test whether the default is the work address. Underline and highlight the text as shown in Figure 13-30 and click OK to close the dialog box and set the conditional formatting for the controls you selected.

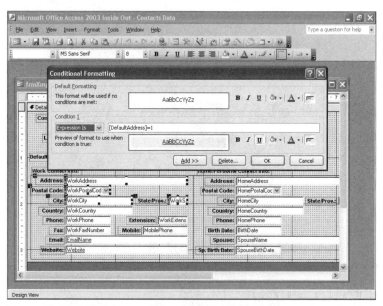

Figure 13-30. Defining conditional formatting for a group of controls.

Click the HomeAddress text box and hold down the Shift key as you click the HomePostal-Code, HomeCity, and HomeStateOrProvince controls to add them to the selection. Choose Conditional Formatting from the Format menu again, choose Expression Is in the combo box, enter [**DefaultAddress**]=2 in the condition field, and underline and highlight the text. Click OK to save the change, and save your form as frmContacts3. Switch to Form view to see the result as shown in Figure 13-31. You can also find this form saved as *frmXmplContacts3* in the sample database.

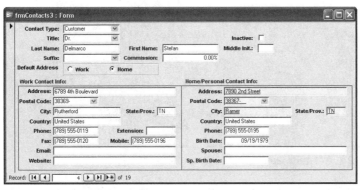

Figure 13-31. The default address fields are highlighted and underlined in the contacts form based on the value of the DefaultAddress field.

To define additional tests, click the Add button at the bottom of the Conditional Formatting dialog box. Each time you click this button, Access displays an additional Condition definition row. In the second and subsequent rows, you can choose from Field Value Is or Expression Is in the leftmost combo box. (You can check for focus only in the first test.) For example, you might want to set the background of the product name to one color if it's a trial version, and use another color for products priced greater than $200.

Working with the Tab Control

As you have just seen, a subform is an excellent way to create a form that lets you edit information from the *one* side of a relationship in the main form (contacts) while editing or viewing data from the *many* side of a relationship (contact events or contact products) in the subform window. Building a subform is very simple for a single one-to-many relationship. But what can you do when you have either multiple relationships or lots of data you need to deal with on a form and including all this information makes your form too large to fit on your screen? Access provides a tab control that lets you place multiple controls on individual tabs within a form. The controls on a tab can be as complex as subforms (in the case of the LawTrack Contacts database, to display related companies, events, and products) or as simple as text boxes (which can display the potentially lengthy information in the Notes field). You can see the frmContactsPlain form (the simple copy of the form that doesn't have all the bells and whistles of the production form) with the tab that shows contact events selected in Figure 13-32. You can click on the other available tabs to see the detail information for the contact—the companies associated with the contact (in a subform on that tab), and the products the contact has purchased (in another subform).

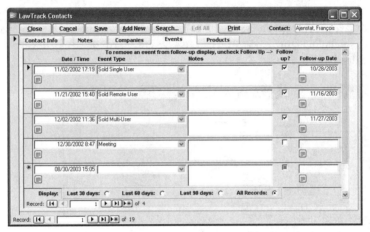

Figure 13-32. A form to edit contact events using the tab control.

Working with the tab control is quite simple. If you like, you can start with a simple columnar form built by the Form Wizard. Use qxmplContactsSorted as the record source, and include the ContactType, Title, LastName, FirstName, MiddleInit, and Suffix fields. Switch to Design view and create some space at the bottom of the form to add your tab control. You can also start with *frmXmplContacts1*, which you can find in the *ContactsDataCopy.mdb* sample database. To build a control that lets you alternately see company, contact event, or liner notes information for the current contact, perform the following steps.

1 Click the Tab Control tool in the toolbox, and drag an area on the form starting on the left side just under the Suffix combo box control and approximately 6 inches wide and 2 inches high. Access shows you a basic tab control with two tabs defined. Open the property sheet window, and set the Tab Fixed Width property to 1" so that all the tabs will be the same size and wide enough to add captions later.

2 While the tab control has the focus, choose Tab Control Page from the Insert menu, as shown here. Access will add a third tab to the control.

3 Access always inserts new tabs at the end of the tab sequence. If you want to place the new tab in the middle of the tab order, you can select the tab and set its Page Index

property. The Page Index of the first tab is 0, the second is 1, and so on. Another way to set the tab sequence is to right-click the control, and then choose Page Order from the shortcut menu to see the dialog box shown next. Select a tab, and move it up or down to get the sequence you want.

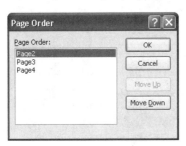

4 Click the first tab, open the Properties window (if it's not already open), and set the Caption property to Companies.

5 Click the second tab, and set the Caption property to Events.

6 Click the third tab, and set the Caption property to Notes.

7 Click the Companies tab to bring it to the front. Click the Subform/Subreport tool in the toolbox, and set the Auto Label property in the Properties window to No. Add a subform control to the Companies tab, set its Source Object property to fsubXmplContactCompanies (the sample database contains built-in subforms to make this exercise easy), and set the Link Child Fields and Link Master Fields properties to ContactID. You can also drag the subform from the Database window and drop it onto the tab if you like.

8 Click the Events tab, and add the fsubXmplContactEvents form to that tab as a subform. Be sure to set the link properties of the subform control to ContactID.

9 Click the Notes tab to bring it to the front. Open the field list, drag the Notes field onto this tab, and remove the attached label. Expand the Notes text box control to almost fill the tab.

10 Adjust the positioning and size of the controls on each tab. Place each control very near the upper left corner of each tab. The actual Top and Left settings will vary depending on where you placed the tab control. (These settings are relative to the Detail area of the form, not the tab control.) You can place one where you want it and then copy the Top and Left settings to the other two controls so that they exactly line up. It's important that you do this so that the controls don't appear to jump around on the tab control as you move from tab to tab. Select each control, choose Size from the Format menu, and then choose To Fit from the submenu.

Your result should look something like Figure 13-33 on the next page. You can find this form saved as *frmXmplContacts4* in the sample database.

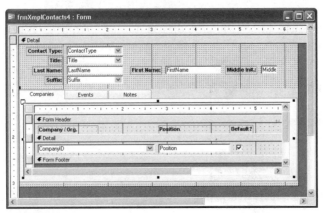

Figure 13-33. The completed tab control in Design view.

Note that clicking each tab in Design view reveals the controls you stored on that tab. Switch to Form view to see the form in action. Table 13-1 lists other useful tab control property settings.

Table 13-1. Useful Tab Control Formatting Properties

Property	Settings	Usage
Multi Row	No (default)	If the control has more tabs than will fit in a single row, the control displays horizontal scroll arrows in the upper right corner of the tab control to move through all the tabs.
	Yes	If the control has more tabs than will fit in a single row, the control displays multiple rows of tabs.
Style	Tabs (default)	The control displays tabs to select the various pages.
	Buttons	The control displays buttons (which look like command buttons but work like the buttons in an option group) to select the various pages.
	None	The control displays neither tabs nor buttons. Different pages can be displayed from a Visual Basic procedure or a macro by setting relative tab numbers in the tab control's Value property.
Tab Fixed Height	0 (default)	The tab height is based on the font properties of the tab control or the size of the bitmap you define as a picture to be displayed on the tab.
	[size in inches]	The tab height is fixed at the value entered.
Tab Fixed Width	0 (default)	The tab width is based on the font properties of the tab control and on the number of characters in the caption or the size of the picture on the tab.
	[size in inches]	The tab width is fixed at the value entered.

Creating Multiple-Page Forms

As you've seen, Microsoft Access makes it easy to display a lot of related information about one subject in a single form, either by using a query as the source of the form or by displaying the related information in a subform. As described in the previous section, if you have too much information to fit in a single, screen-sized form you can use the tab control. Another way to handle the problem is to split the form into multiple pages.

You can create a form that's up to 22 logical inches high. If you're working on a basic 800-by-600-pixel screen, you cannot see more than about 4.5 logical inches vertically at one time (if toolbars are displayed). If the information you need to make available in the form won't fit in that height, you can split the form into multiple pages by using a page break control. When you view the form, you can use the Page Up and Page Down keys to move easily through the pages.

Creating a smoothly working multiple-page form takes some planning. First, you should plan to make all pages the same height. If the pages aren't all the same size, you'll get choppy movement using the Page Up and Page Down keys. You should also design the form so that the page break control is in a horizontal area by itself. If the page break control overlaps other controls, your data might be displayed across the page boundary. You also need to be aware that when you set the form's Auto Resize property to Yes, Access sizes the form to the largest page.

The *frmXmplContactsPages* form in the *ContactsDataCopy.mdb* database is a good example of a multiple-page form. If you open the form in Design view, open the Properties window, and select the Detail section of the form, you can see that the height of this area is exactly 5.8 inches. If you click the page break control, shown at the left edge of the Detail section in Figure 13-34, you'll find that it's set at exactly 2.9 inches from the top of the page. Because this is at exactly half the height of the Detail section, the page break control splits the section into two equally-sized pages.

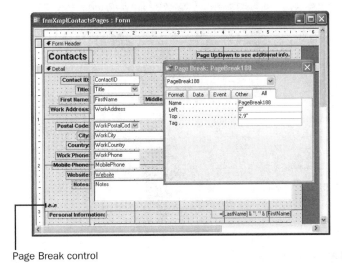

Page Break control

Figure 13-34. The frmXmplContactsPages form with a page break control added.

When you look at this form in Form view (as shown in Figures 13-35 and 13-36) and use the Page Up and Page Down keys, you'll see that the form moves smoothly from page to page. If you switched from Design view to Form view, you must first choose Size to Fit Form from the Window menu to see the form page up and down correctly. When you open this form from the Database window, it sizes correctly because the form has its Auto Resize property set to Yes.

If you're in a control on the second page of the form and you press Page Down again, you'll move smoothly to the second page of the next record. Note that certain key information (such as the contact name) is duplicated on the second page so that it's always clear which record you're editing. If you look at the second page of the form in Design view, you'll find a locked text box control at the top of the second page that displays the contact name again.

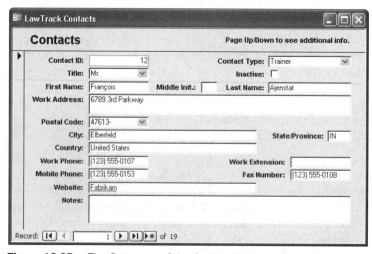

Figure 13-35. The first page of the frmXmplContactsPages form.

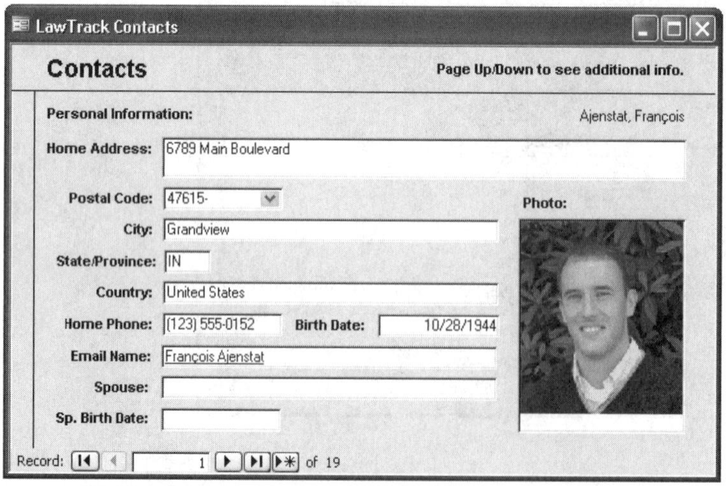

Figure 13-36. The second page of the frmXmplContactsPages form.

Advanced Form Design

A key form property that makes multiple-page forms work is the Cycle property. On this sample form, the Cycle property is set to Current Page. As you learned in Table 12-11 in Chapter 12, other options are All Records (the default) and Current Record. If you don't set the Cycle property to Current Page, you must place the first and last controls on a page that can receive the focus exactly on the page boundary. If you don't do this, you'll find that the form scrolls partially down into the subsequent page as you tab from the last control on one page to the first control on the next page. Because it's not likely that you'll design your form with controls exactly aligned on the page boundary, you must use some special techniques to properly align form pages if you want to allow tabbing between pages or records. See "Controlling Tabbing on a Multiple-Page Form," page 886, for details.

Introducing ActiveX Controls— The Calendar Control

Although Access certainly provides a useful collection of controls to help you design your forms, for some tasks you might need something more complex. Access supports many ActiveX controls that provide functionality beyond the basic control set you can find in the form design toolbox. An *ActiveX* control is a small program that supports the ActiveX interface to allow Access to see the control's properties and build a window to display the control's user interface.

Microsoft Office 2003 installs dozens of ActiveX controls on your machine. It uses many of these in other applications such as Microsoft Office Outlook 2003 or Microsoft Office Excel 2003. As you'll see later in Chapter 27, "Building Data Access Pages," Access makes some of these controls available directly in the toolbox, such as Office PivotTable, Office Chart, and Office Spreadsheet. These controls are available for forms you design, but they're not intended for that purpose. Controls that you can effectively use in your Access forms include the Calendar control (which presents a calendar to make it easy to select a date value), the ListView control (which allows you to navigate data in a tree structure), the ProgressBar control (which allows you to graphically display progress of a complex task, but you must write code to update the bar), and the Slider control (with which a user can set a value by moving a slider).

The LawTrack Contacts application contains many date/time fields, so the Calendar control might be ideal to provide a graphical way to set a date value. In the *ContactsDataCopy.mdb* sample database, open *frmXmplContactEvents* as shown in Figure 13-37 on the next page. This is a simple form to directly edit records from the tblContactEvents table. In this table, the ContactDateTime field includes both a date and a time, but the ContactFollowUpDate is a date value only. The Calendar ActiveX control, which provides a date value only, might be ideal to use to set this value.

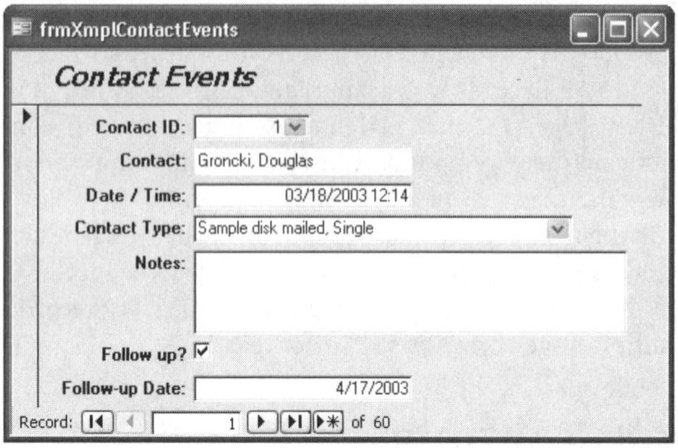

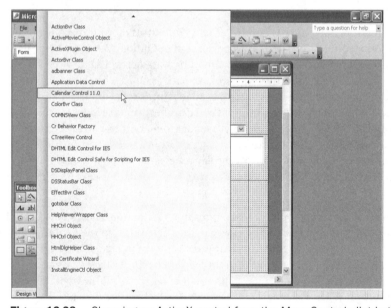

Figure 13-37. A form to edit contact events using standard controls.

Switch to the Design view of this form, delete the ContactFollowUpDate text box control, and expand the Detail area downward about 2 inches to give yourself some room to work. Open the toolbox and click the More Controls tool to open the list of all registered ActiveX controls on your machine as shown in Figure 13-38. You can hover your mouse over the small arrows at the top or bottom of the list to move up or down.

Figure 13-38. Choosing an ActiveX control from the More Controls list in the toolbox.

Click the Calendar Control 11.0 item in the list to select that control. The list closes, and your mouse pointer changes to a small cross hairs with a hammer when you hover over the form design area. Click on the design area just under the FollowUp check box control and draw the control about 3 inches wide and 2 inches high. Make sure the control is selected and open the Properties window. Most ActiveX controls have custom properties that Access recognizes and shows in the Properties window. Most controls also display these custom properties in their own dialog boxes. Click the Other tab in the Properties window to see the list of custom properties available for this control. You can click the custom property and then click the Build button next to the property box to open the Custom Properties dialog box for this control as shown in Figure 13-39. (You can't actually type anything in the custom property box—it's simply a way that Access provides to allow you to easily open the control's properties dialog box.) Another way to open the Custom Properties dialog box for the Calendar ActiveX control is to right-click the control, choose Calendar Object near the top of the shortcut menu, and choose Properties on the submenu.

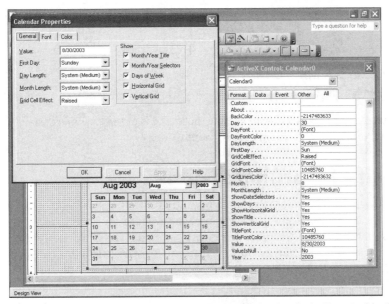

Figure 13-39. The custom properties for the Calendar ActiveX control in the Properties window and in the control's Custom Properties dialog box.

You're going to set this control bound to the ContactFollowUpDate field, so you don't need to worry about setting the Month, Day, or Year properties of the control. You might set these values if you wanted to use the control to provide a date value for some other purpose.

This control might look better with some additional contrast, so click the BackColor property and click the Build button to open the control's Custom Properties dialog box to set the color. (If you know the color code you want, you can also enter it directly in the property box.) Change the Color Set combo box to Standard Colors, scroll down the Color Palette window until you find White near the bottom of the list and click it, and then click OK to change the background color of the control. Click the All tab in the Properties window and set the Control Source property near the top of the list to the ContactFollowUpDate field. Switch to Form view, and your form should now look like Figure 13-40 on the next page. Notice that when you move through the records, the calendar changes to display the value stored in the record. You can change the calendar date by clicking one of the date boxes to update the field. You can find this form saved as *frmXmplContactEventsCalendar* in the sample database.

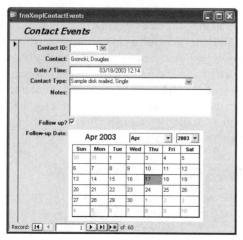

Figure 13-40. The Calendar ActiveX control in action.

In Chapter 24, you'll learn how to execute the methods of the Calendar ActiveX control to command it to move to a different year, month, or day.

Working with PivotChart Forms

Even when the main purpose of your application is to enter, store, and organize data to support an active business function, you probably want to add features that allow management to analyze the business processes. PivotTables and PivotCharts are ideal for this purpose. In Chapter 8, you learned how to create the PivotTable and PivotChart views of a query. Designing the PivotTable or PivotChart view of a form is exactly the same with some interesting twists:

- You can use any query or table as the record source of the form, but only fields bound to controls on the form are available to design the PivotTable or PivotChart.

- You can set form properties to control what the user can modify in the PivotTable or PivotChart view, including locking the form so they can't modify what you designed at all.

- Because a form has event properties, you can control what the user can modify by writing a Visual Basic procedure to respond to the event.

- You can embed a form designed in PivotTable or PivotChart view as the subform of another form and set the Link Child and Link Master properties to filter the table or chart to display information relevant to the record on the outer form.

Building a PivotChart Form

In the Housing Reservations application, you might want to track room revenue by month or quarter. In the LawTrack Contacts application, charting product sales or the number of contact events by week or month might be critical for judging how effectively the business is running.

In most cases, you should start by designing a query that fetches the fields you want to display in your PivotTable or PivotChart. In the LawTrack Contacts application, you might want to display product sales data by product or by company. The *ContactsDataCopy.mdb* sample file has a query that gathers this information, *qryXmplProductSalesForChart*, as shown in Figure 13-41.

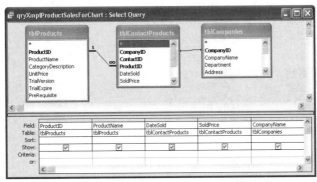

Figure 13-41. A query to select product sales data by product or by company.

Open the *ContactsDataCopy.mdb* sample database, click Queries on the Object bar, select the qryXmplProductSalesForChart query, and choose AutoForm from the New Object button on the toolbar. Switch to PivotChart view to begin designing a chart to show sales by product by month. From the chart's field list (click the Field List button on the toolbar if you don't see this window), drag and drop Product Name onto the Drop Series Fields Here area. Drag and drop SoldPrice onto the Drop Data Fields Here area—the chart automatically calculates a sum for you. Open up the Date Sold By Month list and drag and drop Months onto the Drop Category Fields Here area.

Right-click the Axis title on the left and choose Properties from the shortcut menu. Click the Format tab and enter **Total Sales** in the Caption property box. Click the General tab and choose Category Axis 1 Title from the Select list. Click the Format tab again and change the Caption property to **Months**. Go back to the General tab and choose Chart Workspace from the Select list. Click the Add Legend button in the Add area to create a legend on the right side of the chart. Click the Show/Hide tab and clear all the options in the Let users view section, and clear the Field buttons / drop zones and Field List options to remove them from the chart. Your chart should now look like Figure 13-42 on the next page.

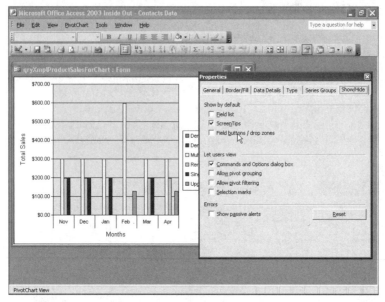

Figure 13-42. Building a chart to display product sales by product and month.

Switch to Design view and set the Default View property to PivotChart and disallow all views except PivotChart view. Also disallow Edits, Deletions, and Additions. Finally change the Shortcut Menu property to No to keep the user from getting into the chart property settings that way. (You can see how much more control you have over what the user can do in a form.) Save the form as chtProductSalesByProduct. You can also find this form saved as *chtXmpl-ProductSales* in the sample database.

Embedding a Linked PivotChart

To demonstrate how you can link the chart you just built into a form that displays product information, you can start with frmXmplProducts3 from Chapter 11. Open that form in Design view. Widen the design area to about 4.5 inches and expand the Detail area's height to about 3.75 inches to give you a space to place the chart. Drag and drop the form you just created from the Database window onto the blank area of the form and select and delete the attached label.

Notice that the subform control automatically sizes to the design height and width of the form, which is probably not big enough to show the chart very well. The subform control doesn't have a clue what height and width might work well to display the PivotChart view of the subform. (Does this remind you of the sizing problems you have with a subform in Datasheet view?) Stretch the width and height of the subform control to fill up the blank space you created. Open the Properties window, and with the subform control selected, set the Locked property to Yes. Verify that the Link Child and Link Master properties are set to ProductID. (Because the outer form is based on a table, dragging and dropping the subform should have set these properties automatically.) Switch to Form view (and choose Size to Fit Form from the Window menu to size the window correctly) to see the result of your work as shown in Figure 13-43. Note that if a particular product has no sales, the chart will be blank for that product record. You can also find this form saved as *frmXmplProductsWithSales* in the sample database.

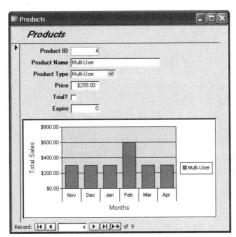

Figure 13-43. A form to display product information with a sales chart in a subform.

Note You might be wondering why the scale on the left in Figure 13-43 doesn't seem to match what you designed in Figure 13-42. The PivotChart view adjusts its horizontal and vertical scales to match the size of the display window. If you had designed the subform control taller, you might have seen the scale match.

This is the last chapter about designing forms for desktop applications. You'll learn about how form design is different for Microsoft Access projects in Chapter 19, "Designing Forms in an Access Project," and you'll learn some additional design techniques in Chapter 23, "Automating Your Application with Visual Basic."

Using Reports

You can certainly format and print tables and queries in Datasheet view, and that technique is useful for producing printed copies of simple lists of information. Although you primarily use forms to view and modify data, you can also use forms to print data—including data from several tables. However, because the primary function of forms is to allow you to view single records or small groups of related records displayed on the screen in an attractive way, forms aren't the best way to print and summarize large sets of data in your database.

This chapter explains why and when you should use a report instead of another method of printing data, and it describes the features that reports offer. The examples in this chapter are based on the LawTrack Contacts sample database. After you learn what you can do with reports, you'll look at the process of building reports in the following two chapters.

 Note The examples in this chapter are based on the reports, tables, and data in the *ContactsDataCopy.mdb* on the companion CD included with this book. You can find similar reports in the LawTrack Contacts sample application, but all the reports in that sample file have custom menus and toolbars defined, so you won't see the built-in menus and toolbars when you open those reports. The results you see from the samples in this chapter might not exactly match what you see in this book if you have changed the sample data in the files. Also, all the screen images in this chapter were taken on a Windows XP system with the display theme set to Windows XP. Your results might look different if you are using a different operating system or a different theme.

Uses of Reports

Reports are the best way to create a printed copy of information that is extracted or calculated from data in your database. Reports have two principal advantages over other methods of printing data.

- Reports can compare, summarize, subtotal, and total large sets of data.

- Reports can be created to produce attractive invoices, purchase orders, mailing labels, presentation materials, and other output you might need in order to efficiently conduct business.

Reports are designed to group data, to present each grouping separately, and to perform calculations. They work as follows:

- You can define up to 10 grouping criteria to separate the levels of detail.
- You can define separate headers and footers for each group.
- You can perform complex calculations not only within a group or a set of rows but also across groups.
- In addition to page headers and footers, you can define a header and a footer for the entire report.

As with forms, you can embed pictures or charts in any section of a report. You can also embed subreports or subforms within report sections.

A Tour of Reports

You can explore reports by examining the features of the sample reports in the *Contacts-DataCopy.mdb* sample database. A good place to start is the *rptContactProducts* report. Open the database, and go to the Database window. Click the Reports button on the Object bar, and scroll down the list of reports until you see the *rptContactProducts* report, as shown in Figure 14-1. Double-click the report name (or select it and click the Preview button) to see the report in Print Preview—a view of how the report will look when it's printed.

> **Note** All the reports in the sample databases are set to print to the system default printer. The default printer on your system is probably not the same printer that I used as a default when I designed the report. Some of the sample reports are designed with margins other than the default of 1 inch on all sides. If your default printer cannot print as close to the edge of the paper as the report is designed, Access will adjust the margins to the minimums for your printer. This means that some reports might not appear exactly as you see them in the book, and some data might appear on different pages.

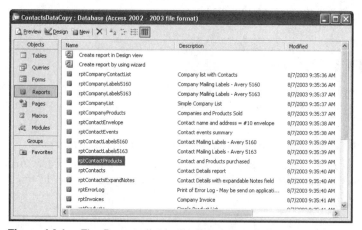

Figure 14-1. The Reports list in the Database window.

Print Preview—A First Look

The rptContactProducts report is based on the qryRptContactProducts query, which brings together information from the tblContacts, tblProducts, and tblContactProducts tables. When the report opens in Print Preview, you'll see a view of the report in the Contact Products window, as shown in Figure 14-2. When you open the report from the Database window, the report shows information for all contact product sales.

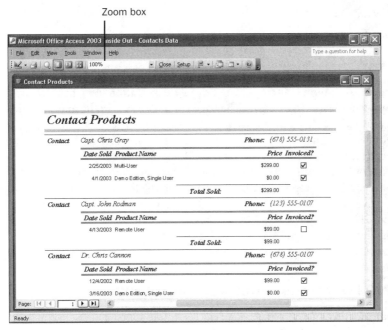

Figure 14-2. The rptContactProducts report in Print Preview.

Checking Out Reports in the Sample Application

You can see all the reports described in this chapter in the LawTrack Contacts application. Start the application by opening the database (*Contacts.mdb*), opening frmSplash, and then signing on as me—you don't need a password. To see the final version of the Contact Products report, for example, click the Products button on the main switchboard form, and then click the Print button on the LawTrack Contacts – Products form to open the Product Reports dialog box. Choose Product Sales by Contact. Also select the Current Product Only and All Records options, and then click Print. You'll see the report in Print Preview for the product that was displayed on the Products form. You can also explore the reports by clicking the Reports button on the main switchboard. All reports in the application have a custom menu and toolbar that prevent you from switching to Design view when running the application. When you're finished looking at the reports in *Contacts.mdb*, be sure to go back to the *ContactsDataCopy.mdb* file to follow the remaining examples in this chapter.

You can expand the window in Print Preview to see a large portion of the rptContactProducts report at one time. Use the vertical and horizontal scroll bars to position the report so that you can see most of the upper half of the first page, as shown in Figure 14-2. You can also turn off Num Lock and use the arrow keys to move up, down, left, and right. If you are using a standard SVGA screen (800×600 pixels), select 75% in the Zoom Control box on the toolbar to see more of the report. If your screen resolution is 1024×768 or higher, you should be able to easily view the report at 100%.

To view other pages of the report, use the navigation bar at the bottom left of the window, as shown here.

Page: |◄ ◄ 2 ► ►|

The four buttons, from left to right, are the First Page button, Previous Page button, Next Page button, and Last Page button. The Page Number box is in the middle of the navigation bar. To move forward one page at a time, click the Next Page button. You can also click the Page Number box (or press F5 to select it), change the number, and press Enter to move to the exact page you want. Press Esc to exit the Page Number box. As you might guess, the Previous Page button moves you back one page, and the two outer buttons move you to the first or the last page of the report. You can also move to the top of the page by pressing Ctrl+Up Arrow, move to the bottom of the page by pressing Ctrl+Down Arrow, move to the left edge of the page by pressing Home or Ctrl+Left Arrow, and move to the right edge of the page by pressing End or Ctrl+Right Arrow. Pressing Ctrl+Home moves you to the upper left corner of the page, and pressing Ctrl+End moves you to the lower right corner of the page.

Headers, Detail Sections, Footers, and Groups

Although the rptContactProducts report looks simple at first glance, it actually contains a lot of information. Figure 14-3 shows you the report again with the various sections of the report marked. You can see a page header that appears at the top of every page. As you'll see later when you learn to design reports, you can also define a header for the entire report and choose whether to print this report header on a page by itself or with the first page header.

The data in this report is grouped by contact name, and the detail lines are sorted within contact name by date sold. You can print a heading for each group in your report, and this report has a heading for each contact. This report could easily be modified, for example, to display the product category in a header line (to group the products by category), followed by the related detail lines.

Next Access prints the detail information, one line for each row in the recordset formed by the query. In the Detail section of a report, you can add unbound controls to calculate a result using any of the columns in the record source.

Contact Group header
Page header

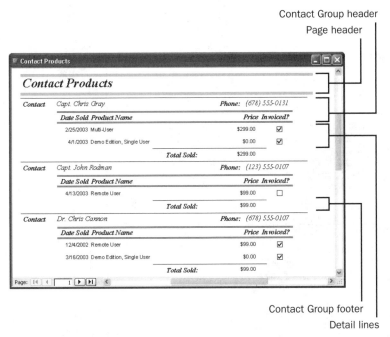

Contact Group footer
Detail lines

Figure 14-3. The rptContactProducts report has a subtotal for each contact.

Below the detail product lines for each contact, you can see the group footer for the contact. You could also calculate percentages for a detail record or for a group by including a control that provides a summary in the group footer (total for the group) or report footer (total for the report). To calculate the percentage, you would create an additional control that divides the detail or group value by the total value in an outer group or in the report footer. Access can do this because its report writer can look at the detail data twice—once to calculate any group or grand totals, and a second time to calculate expressions that reference those totals. If you scroll down to the bottom of the page, you'll see a page number, which is in the page footer.

Note If you're working with a report that has many pages, it might take a long time to move to the first or last page or to move back one page. You can press Esc to cancel your movement request. Microsoft Access then closes the report.

A slightly more complex report is *rptProductSalesByProduct*. Open that report, and go to the last page. At the end of this report, as shown in Figure 14-4 on the next page, you can see the quantity and sales totals for the last product in this report, for the last category in the report, and for all sales in the database (Grand Total). There are two products in the Single User category, but the first is a demonstration edition that has a zero price, so the total sales amount of the category matches the total sales amount of the second product. The grand total is in the report footer.

Product Group header
Page header

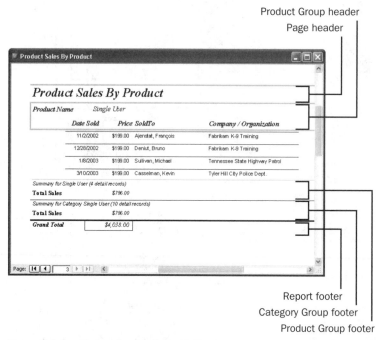

Report footer
Category Group footer
Product Group footer

Figure 14-4. The rptProductSalesByProduct report's grand total calculation is in the report footer.

Subreports

Just as you can embed subforms within forms, you can embed subreports (or subforms) within reports. Subreports are particularly useful for showing related details or totals for the records that make up the source rows of your report. In the LawTrack Contacts database, you can bring together information about contacts and products—either contacts and the products they own or products and the contacts who own them. You can place detailed data about contacts and products in a subreport and then embed that subreport in the Detail section of a report that displays company data—much as you did for the fsubContactProducts form exercise in the previous chapter.

You can see an example of this use of a subreport in the *rptCompanyProducts* report and in the *rsubCompanyProducts* subreport in the LawTrack Contacts database. Switch to the Database window, click Reports on the Object bar, and open the *rsubCompanyProducts* subreport in Design view by selecting the report in the Database window and then clicking the Design button, as shown in Figure 14-5. The Report window in Design view is shown in Figure 14-6.

Chapter 14

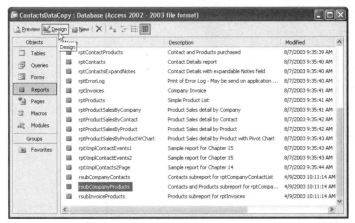

Figure 14-5. The rsubCompanyProducts report about to be opened in Design view.

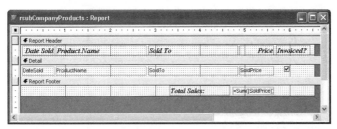

Figure 14-6. The Report window for the rsubCompanyProducts report in Design view.

You can see that this report looks very much like the continuous form you designed earlier to be a subform. If you look at the Record Source property for the subreport, you'll find that it uses the qryRsubCompanyProducts query, which isn't at all simple. The query brings together information from the tblProducts, tblContactProducts, tblContacts, and tblCompanyContacts tables. This subreport doesn't display any company information at all. Open the subreport in Print Preview. You'll see a list of various products and the contacts who own them, in date sold order, as shown in Figure 14-7 on the next page.

Close the subreport and open the *rptCompanyProducts* report in Print Preview, shown in Figure 14-8. Notice as you move from company to company that the data displayed in the subreport changes to match the company currently displayed. The data from the rsubCompanyProducts report now makes sense within the context of a particular company. Access links the data from each subreport in this example using the Link Master Fields and Link Child Fields properties of the subreport (which are set to the linking CompanyID field)—just as with the subforms you created in Chapter 13, "Advanced Form Design."

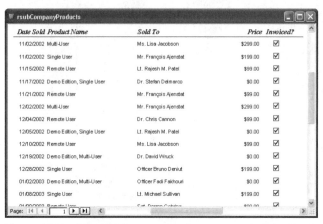

Figure 14-7. The rsubCompanyProducts report in Print Preview.

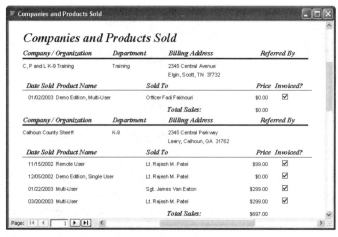

Figure 14-8. The rptCompanyProducts report with an embedded subreport.

As you'll see in the next section, when we examine some features of the rptInvoices report, that report also uses subreports to link information from three related tables to each row displayed from the tblInvoices table.

Objects in Reports

As with forms, you can embed objects in reports. The objects embedded in or linked to reports are usually pictures or charts. You can embed a picture or a chart as an unbound object in the report itself, or you can link a picture or a chart as an object bound to data in your database.

The rptInvoices report in the LawTrack Contacts database has an image object. When you open the *rptInvoices* report in Print Preview, you can see the LawTrack logo (a stylized font graphic) embedded in the report title as an unbound bitmap image object, as shown in Figure 14-9. This object is actually a part of the report design.

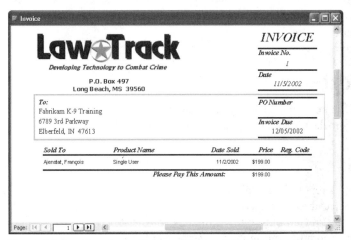

Figure 14-9. An unbound bitmap image object (the LawTrack logo) embedded in the rptInvoices report.

To see an example of a bound object, open *rptContacts* in Print Preview, as shown in Figure 14-10. This picture is a bound bitmap image object from the tblContacts table—a picture of the contact. (If you believe I was born in 1999, I have a bridge I'd like to sell you!)

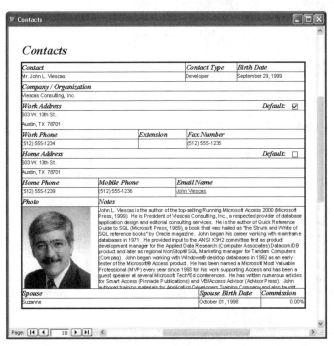

Figure 14-10. A bound bitmap image object displayed in the rptContacts report.

> **Note** You might notice that the Notes field in Figure 14-10 on the previous page doesn't show all the text. There's a special version of this report called *rptContactsExpandNotes* that fixes this problem with Visual Basic code. See Chapter 23, "Automating Your Application with Visual Basic," for details.

Printing Reports

Earlier in this chapter you learned the basics of viewing a report in Print Preview. Here are a few more tips and details about setting up reports for printing.

Print Setup

Before you print a report, you might first want to check its appearance and then change the printer setup. Select the *rptContacts* report (which you looked at earlier) in the Database window, and click the Preview button to see the report. After Microsoft Access shows you the report, click the Zoom button, and then size the window to see the full-page view. Click the Two Pages button to see two pages side by side, as shown in Figure 14-11.

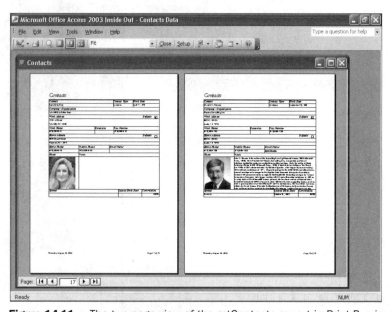

Figure 14-11.   The two-page view of the rptContacts report in Print Preview.

This report is narrow enough to print two contacts side by side in landscape mode on 14-inch-long paper. To print it that way, you need to modify some parameters in the Page Setup dialog box.

Open the Page Setup dialog box by choosing Page Setup from the File menu. (You can also define the page setup for any report without opening the report: Select the report in the

Database window, and choose Page Setup from the File menu.) Access displays a dialog box similar to the one shown in Figure 14-12.

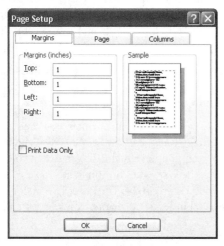

Figure 14-12. The Page Setup dialog box.

To print the rptContacts report with two logical pages per physical page, you first need to adjust the margins. You haven't changed the page orientation yet, so the settings that are currently the top and bottom will become the left and right margins, respectively, after you rotate the page. (And left and right margins become top and bottom, respectively.) The pages need to print very close to the edges of the paper, so set the top margin (this becomes the left margin in Landscape orientation) to 0.25 inch, set the bottom margin to about 0.5 inch, and set the left and right margins to 0.5 inch. Effectively, the left margin will be the smallest after you change the orientation. Click the Page tab to display the next set of available properties, as shown in Figure 14-13.

Figure 14-13. The Page tab of the Page Setup dialog box.

On the Page tab, you can select the orientation of the printed page—Portrait to print vertically down the length of the page, or Landscape to print horizontally across the width of the page. Since we're trying to print two pages across a single sheet of paper, select the Landscape option. The report is also about 6½ inches wide, so you'll need wider paper to fit two logical pages to a printed page. Select Legal (8½-by-14-inch) paper from the Size list under Paper.

In general, it's best to leave the printer set to the default printer that you specified in your Windows settings. If you move your application to a computer that's attached to a different type of printer, you won't have to change the settings. You can print any report you design in Access on any printer supported by Windows with good results.

However, if you've designed your report to print on a specific printer, you can save those settings by using the Page Setup dialog box. To do this, select the Use Specific Printer option on the Page tab and then click the Printer button to open a dialog box in which you can select any printer installed on your system. Click the Properties button to adjust settings for that printer in its properties dialog box, shown in Figure 14-14. The Properties dialog box you see might look different, depending on the capabilities of the printer you selected and how Windows supports that printer.

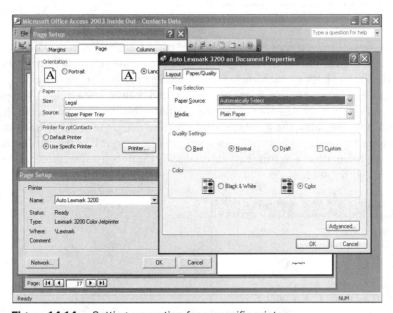

Figure 14-14. Setting properties for a specific printer.

After you finish selecting options on the Page tab, click the Columns tab, as shown in Figure 14-15, to set up a multiple-column report. In this case, you want to print two "columns" of information. After you set the Number of Columns property to a value greater than 1 (in this case, 2), you can set spacing between rows and spacing between columns. By default, this page sets the Same As Detail option and displays the design Width and Height of your report. You can also clear the Same As Detail check box and set a custom width and height that are larger or smaller than the underlying report design size. Note that if you specify a smaller size, Access crops the report. When you have detail data that fits in more than one column or row, you can also tell Access whether you want the detail produced down and then across the page or vice versa.

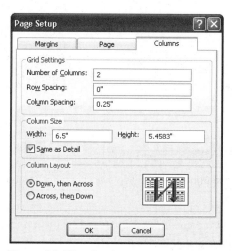

Figure 14-15. Setting report column properties.

> **Note** If you created the report or have permission to modify the design of the report, you can change the page layout settings and save them with the report. The next time you print or view the report, Access will use the last page layout settings you specified. All the reports in the sample databases were created using the default Admin user ID. If you start Access without security or sign on with the default ID, you will have full ownership of all objects in the sample databases. See Chapter 30, "Securing Your Database," for details about security and the default user ID.

After you enter the appropriate settings in the Page Setup dialog box, your report in Print Preview should look like the one shown in Figure 14-16 on the next page. You'll need to set the Force New Page property on the report's Detail section to None to allow two records to be printed on a single page. You can find this modified version of the Contacts report saved in the sample database as *rptXmplContacts2Page*.

The most common use for setting multiple columns is to print mailing labels. You can find four example reports in the sample database that do this: *rptCompanyLabels5160* and *rptContactLabels5160* that print company and contact labels 2-across in Avery 5160 format; and *rptCompanyLabels5163* and *rptContactLabels5163* that print company and contact labels 3-across in Avery 5163 format.

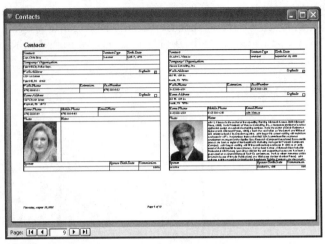

Figure 14-16. The rptContacts report in Print Preview, displayed in landscape orientation and in two columns.

That covers the fundamentals of reports and how to view them and set them up for printing. The next two chapters will show you how to design and build reports for your application.

Chapter 15

Constructing a Report

Constructing a report is very similar to building a form. In this chapter, you'll apply many of the techniques that you used in working with forms, and you'll learn about some of the unique features of reports. After a quick tour of the report design facilities, you'll build a simple report for the LawTrack Contacts database, and then you'll use a report wizard to create the same report.

Note The examples in this chapter are based on the reports, tables, and data in *ContactsDataCopy.mdb* on the companion CD included with this book. You can find similar reports in the LawTrack Contacts sample application, but all the reports in that sample file have custom menus and toolbars defined, so you won't see the built-in menus and toolbars when you open those reports. The results you see from the samples in this chapter might not exactly match what you see in this book if you have changed the sample data in the files. Also, all the screen images in this chapter were taken on a Windows XP system with the display theme set to Windows XP. Your results might look different if you are using a different operating system or a different theme.

Starting from Scratch—A Simple Report

In a contact tracking application, the user is going to want to take a look at recent events and perhaps work through a list of events that require follow-ups. Although the user could search for events in a form, the application should also provide a report that lists events by contact and shows the phone numbers the user needs. This report can be filtered by the application to print out only recent and upcoming events.

Most reports gather information from several tables, so you'll usually design a query that brings together data from related tables as the basis for the report. In this section, you'll build a relatively simple report to list contact events as you tour the report design facilities. The report you'll build uses the tblContacts, tblContactEvents, and tlkpContactEventTypes tables in the *ContactsDataCopy.mdb* sample database. The report groups contact event data by contact, prints a single line for each contact event, and calculates the number of contact events and the number of follow-ups for each contact.

Building the Report Query

To construct the underlying query for the report, you need to start with the tblContactEvents table. In the Database window, click Tables on the Object bar, select the tblContactEvents table, and choose Query on the New Object toolbar button. In the New Query dialog box, select Design View and click OK to start your query. Click the Show Table button on the toolbar and add the tblContacts and the tlkpContactEventTypes tables to your query. You should see join lines between tblContacts and tblContactEvents on ContactID, and between tlkpContactEventTypes and tblContactEvents on ContactEventTypeID.

From the tblContacts table, add ContactID to the design grid. The report needs to show the contact name, but it would be better to show the information concatenated in one field rather than separate title, first name, middle name, last name, and suffix fields. In the next column, enter this expression on the Field line:

```
Contact: ([tblContacts].[Title]+" ") & [tblContacts].[FirstName] & " " &
([tblContacts].[MiddleInit]+". ") & [tblContacts].[LastName] &
(", "+[tblContacts].[Suffix])
```

Notice that the expression uses the plus sign concatenation operator to eliminate extra blanks when one of the fields contains a Null value—a technique you learned about in Chapter 7, "Creating and Working with Simple Queries."

The query also needs to include the contact's phone number, but the tblContacts table includes both a work and a home phone number. You can create an expression to examine the DefaultAddress field to decide which one to display. Microsoft Access provides a handy function, Choose, that accepts an integer value in its first argument and then uses that value to choose one of the other arguments. For example, if the first argument is 1, the function returns the second argument; if the first argument is 2, the function returns the third argument, and so on. The DefaultAddress field contains a 1 to indicate work address and a 2 to indicate home address. In the third Field cell in the query design grid, enter the following:

```
Phone: Choose([tblContacts].[DefaultAddress], [tblContacts].[WorkPhone],
[tblContacts].[HomePhone])
```

To complete your query, include the ContactDateTime field from the tblContactEvents table and the ContactEventTypeDescription field from the tlkpContactEventTypes table. (ContactEventTypeID in tblContactEvents is a meaningless number.) Then include the ContactNotes, ContactFollowUp, and ContactFollowUpDate fields from the tblContactEvents table. Figure 15-1 shows the query you need for this first report. (You can find this query saved as *qryRptContactEvents* in the sample database.)

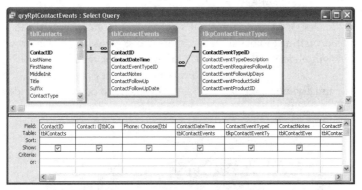

Figure 15-1. A query that selects contact and contact event data for a report.

Note that although you're designing a report that will summarize the data, you are not build-ing a totals query. If you used a totals query as the record source for the report, you would see only the summary in the report. One of the beauties of reports is that you can see the detail information and also ask the report to produce summaries. Also, you don't need to specify any sorting criteria here—you'll do that later in the report's Sorting And Grouping window.

Designing the Report

Now you're ready to start designing the report. In the Database window, select the query you just built and then select Report from the New Object toolbar button's drop-down list (or choose Report from the Insert menu). Microsoft Access displays the New Report dialog box, as shown in Figure 15-2.

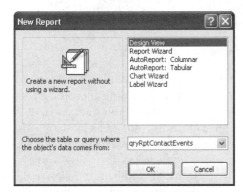

Figure 15-2. The New Report dialog box.

The field list, the property sheet, the toolbox, and the Formatting toolbar are similar to the features you used in building forms. See Chapter 11, "Building a Form," for detailed descriptions of their uses.

The name of the query you selected appears in the combo box in the lower part of the dialog box. (If you want to select a different table or query, open the drop-down list to see a list of all the tables and queries in your database and select another.) Later in this chapter, you'll use a report wizard to create a report. But for now, select Design View and click OK to open a new Report window in Design view, as shown in Figure 15-3. You can see both the Report Design toolbar and the Formatting toolbar at the top of the Access window. The Report window is in the background (but on top of the Database window), and the field list, property sheet, and toolbox are open to assist you in building your report. (If necessary, you can click the Field List, Properties, and Toolbox commands on the View menu to open these windows.)

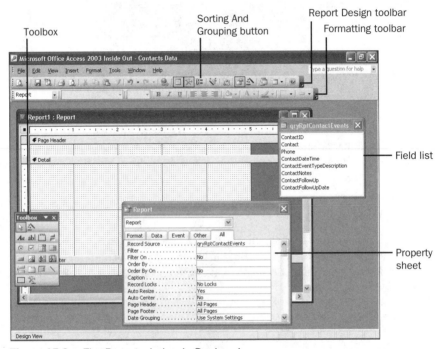

Figure 15-3.   The Report window in Design view.

The blank report has Page Header and Page Footer sections and a Detail section between them, which is 2 inches high and 5 inches wide. The rulers along the top and left edges of the Report window help you plan space on the printed page. If you want standard 1-inch side margins, the body of the report can be up to 6½ inches wide on an 8½-by-11-inch page. The available vertical space depends on how you design your headers and footers and how you define the top and bottom margins. As with forms, you can drag the edge of any report section to make the section larger or smaller. Note that the width of all sections is the same, so if you change the width of one section, Access changes the width of all other sections to match.

Within each section you can see a grid that has 24 dots per inch horizontally and 24 dots per inch vertically, with a solid gray line displayed at 1-inch intervals. If you're working in centimeters, Access divides the grid into 5 dots per centimeter both vertically and horizontally. You can change these settings using the Grid X and Grid Y properties in the report's property sheet. (If the dots are not visible in your Report window, choose the Grid command from the View menu; if the Grid command is checked and you still can't see the dots, try resetting the Grid X and Grid Y properties to lower numbers in the property sheet.)

The page header and page footer will print in your report at the top and bottom of each page. You can choose the Page Header/Footer command from the View menu to add or remove the page header and page footer. You can also add a report header that prints once at the beginning of the report and a report footer that prints once at the end of the report. To add these sections to a report, choose the Report Header/Footer command from the View menu. You'll learn how to add group headers and group footers in the next section.

Sorting and Grouping Information

A key way in which reports differ from forms is that on reports you can group information for display using the Sorting And Grouping window. Click the Sorting And Grouping button on the toolbar (shown in Figure 15-3) to open the Sorting And Grouping window, as shown in Figure 15-4. In this window you can define up to 10 fields or expressions that you will use to form groups in the report. The first item in the list determines the main group, and subsequent items define groups within groups. (You saw the nesting of groups in the previous chapter in the rptProductSalesByProduct report; each product category had a main group, and within that main group was a subgroup for each product.)

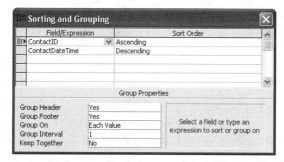

Figure 15-4. Creating groups and specifying sort order in the Sorting And Grouping window.

In the simple report you're creating for contact events, you need to group data by contact ID so that you can total the number of contact events as well as contact events that require follow-up for each contact. If you click the first row of the Field/Expression column, a down arrow button appears on the right side of the field. Click this arrow (or press Alt+Down Arrow) to open the list of fields from the underlying query or table. Select the ContactID field to place it in the Field/Expression column. You can also use the Field/Expression column to enter an expression based on any field in the underlying table or query. You let Access know you're entering an expression by first typing an equal sign (=) followed by your expression.

By default, Access sorts each field or expression in ascending order. You can change the sorting order by selecting Descending from the drop-down list that appears when you click the Sort Order column. In this case, you want to include the ContactID field so that you can form a group for each contact. The report will sort the rows in ascending numerical order by the ContactID field. If you wanted to see the contacts in alphabetical order by last name, you would need to include the LastName field in your query (even if you didn't display it on the report), and group and sort on the LastName field. You could use the Contact expression that you included in the query, but then the report would sort the rows by title and first name.

You will need a place to put a header for each group (at least for the ContactID field) and a footer for two calculated total fields (the count of contact events and the count of follow-ups). To add these sections, change the settings for the Group Header and the Group Footer properties to Yes, as shown in Figure 15-4. When you do that, Access adds those sections to the Report window in Design view for you. You'll learn how to use the Group On, Group Interval, and Keep Together properties in the next chapter. For now, leave them set to their default values.

It would also be nice to see the contact events in descending date order for each contact (most recent events first). Add the ContactDateTime field below ContactID, but leave Group Header or Group Footer set to No. Click the Sort Order box and change it to Descending. Close the Sorting And Grouping window by clicking the Close button on its title bar or by clicking the Sorting And Grouping button on the toolbar.

> **Tip**   You can specify sorting criteria in the query for a report, but after you set any criteria in the Sorting And Grouping window, the report overrides any sorting in the query. The best way to ensure that your report data sorts in the order you want is to always specify sorting criteria in the Sorting And Grouping window and not in the underlying query.

Completing the Report

Now you're ready to finish building a report based on the tblContactEvents table. Take the following steps to construct a report similar to the one shown in Figure 15-5. (You can find this report saved as *rptXmplContactEvents1* in the sample database.)

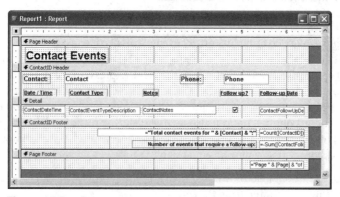

Figure 15-5.   The contact events report in the Report window in Design view.

Constructing a Report

1. Place a label control in the Page Header section, and type **Contact Events** as the label's caption. Select the label control, and then, using the Formatting toolbar, select the Arial font in 18-point bold and underlined. Choose Size from the Format menu, and then choose To Fit from the submenu to set the control size to accommodate the new font size.

2. Drag and drop the Contact field from the field list into the ContactID Header section. Use Arial 10-point bold for the label control and the text box control. Select the text box control and make it about 2 inches wide so that there's room to display all the characters in the contact name. Also drag and drop the Phone field into the header, and set the resulting text box control and the label control to Arial 10-point bold. Size all these controls to fit and line them up near the top of the section.

3. You'll need some column labels in the ContactID Header section. The easiest way to create them is to set up the text box control so that it has an attached label with no colon, set the defaults for the label control to the font you want, drag and drop the fields you need into the Detail section, and then cut the label controls from their respective text box controls and paste them into the header.

   First, widen the design area of the report to about 6.5 inches to give yourself some room to work. Next, make sure the property sheet is open, and then click the Text Box tool in the toolbox. Select the All tab in the Properties window, scroll down the property sheet, and check that the Auto Label property is set to Yes and that the Add Colon property is set to No. Click the Label tool, and set its font to Arial 8-point bold and underlined. Now lengthen the Detail section to give yourself some room, and then drag and drop the ContactDateTime, ContactEventTypeDescription, ContactNotes, ContactFollowUp, and ContactFollowUpDate fields from the field list into the Detail section one at a time.

   Select the label for ContactDateTime, and then choose the Cut command from the Edit menu (or press Ctrl+X) to separate the label from the control and place the label on the Clipboard. Click the ContactID Header bar, and then choose the Paste command from the Edit menu (or press Ctrl+V) to paste the label into the upper left corner of the ContactID Header section. Notice that you can now move the label independently in the ContactID Header section. (If you try to move the label before you separate it from the control to which it's attached, the control moves with it.) Separate the labels from the ContactEventTypeDescription, ContactNotes, Contact-FollowUp, and ContactFollowUpDate controls one at a time, and move the labels to the ContactID Header section of the report.

 Tip As you paste each label, you'll see warning smart tags appear notifying you that the labels aren't associated with any control. This is useful to know when you create labels in a detail section. But in this case, this is what you want, so click the smart tag and choose the Ignore Error option to turn it off for each label.

4   Line up the column labels in the ContactID Header section, placing the Date / Time label near the left margin, the Contact Type label about 1.1 inches from the left margin, the Notes label about 2.75 inches from the left margin, the Follow Up? label about 4.5 inches from the left margin, and the Follow-up Date label about 5.4 inches from the left margin. You can set these distances in the Left property of each label's property sheet. Line up the tops of the labels by dragging a selection box around all five labels using the Select Object tool and then choosing the Align command from the Format menu and then Top from the submenu.

5   You can enhance the appearance of the report by placing a line control across the bottom of the ContactID Header section. Click the Line tool in the toolbox, and place a line in the ContactID Header section. To position this control at the bottom of the section, you need to find out the section's height. Click the ContactID Header bar to select the section, open the Properties window, and find the Height property. Next, select the line control, and set the following properties: Left 0, Width 6.5, and Height 0. Set the Top property equal to the Height of the section. (It's difficult to see this line in Figure 15-5, because it is hidden against the bottom of the section. You'll see it when you switch to Print Preview.)

6   Align the text box controls for ContactDateTime, ContactEventTypeDescription, ContactNotes, ContactFollowUp, and ContactFollowUpDate under their respective labels. You can align each one by placing each text box control to the right of the left edge of its label, select them both, and then left align them. Align the ContactFollowUp check box control visually under the center of its label. Select all the controls in the Detail section and top align them.

7   The text box control for ContactDateTime can be made smaller, and you need to make the ContactEventTypeDescription text box control about 1.6 inches wide. Set the Text Align property for the ContactDateTime and ContactFollowUpDate text box controls to Left. Access sized the text box for the ContactNotes field several lines high because ContactNotes is a Memo data type. Select the ContactNotes and ContactDateTime text box controls together, and choose Format/Size/To Shortest to make the Contact-Notes text box the same height as the ContactDateTime text box.

8   The height of the Detail section determines the spacing between lines in the report. You don't need much space between report lines, so make the Detail section smaller, until it's only slightly higher than the row of controls for displaying your data.

9   Add a text box in the ContactID Footer section under the ContactFollowUpDate text box control and delete its attached label. To calculate the number of events, click the text box control and in the Control Source property enter:

=**Count([ContactID])**

It's a good idea to repeat the grouping information in the footer in case the detail lines span a page boundary. One way to do that is to add an expression in a text box. Add a second text box to the left of the first one (also delete its label) and stretch it to about 3.5 inches wide. Click the leftmost text box control to select it, and in the Control Source property in the Properties window, type:

=**"Total contact events for " & [Contact] & ":"**

Change the text box alignment to Right and change its font to Bold.

10 Add a second text box control in the ContactID footer under the first one. In the Control Source property in the Properties window, enter:

=-Sum([ContactFollowUp])

Keep in mind that a True value in a yes/no field is the value –1. So, summing the values and then displaying the negative should give you a count of the contact events that require a follow-up. Click the attached label control and change the Caption property in the Properties window to:

Number of events that require a follow-up:

Change Font Underline to no, align the label right, and size it to fit.

11 Add a line to the bottom of the ContactID Footer to separate the end of the information about one contact from the next one. You can click the heading bar of the ContactID Footer to select the section and then look in the Properties window to find out the section's height, which should be about 0.5 inches. Select the line again, and in the Properties window set Left to 0, Top to the height of the section, Width to 6.5, Height to 0, and Border Width (the thickness of the line) to 2 pt.

12 Finally, create an unbound text box in the lower right corner of the Page Footer section and delete its label. Enter the expression =**"Page "** & [**Page**] & **" of "** & [**Pages**] in the Control Source property of the text box. [Page] is a report property that displays the current page number. [Pages] is a report property that displays the total number of pages in the report.

After you finish, click the Print Preview button on the toolbar to see the result, shown in Figure 15-6. Notice that in this figure, the detail lines are sorted in descending order by contact date/time. You'll recall from Figure 15-4 that the sorting and grouping specifications include a request to sort within group on ContactDateTime.

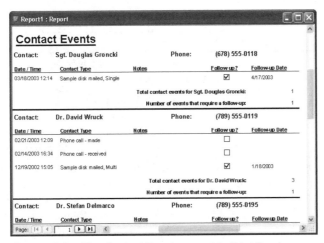

Figure 15-6. The Contact Events report in Print Preview.

Chapter 15

Using a Report Wizard

The report wizards that Microsoft Access provides to assist you in constructing reports are similar to the form wizards you used earlier to create forms. To practice using a report wizard, build the Contact Events report again. Open the Database window, click the Queries button, and select the *qryRptContactEvents* query. Select Report from the New Object toolbar button's drop-down list or choose Report from the Insert menu to open the New Report dialog box.

Selecting a Report Type

The New Report dialog box offers six options, as shown in Figure 15-7 and described in Table 15-1.

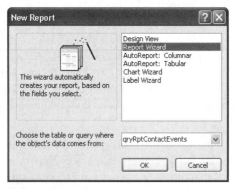

Figure 15-7. The report wizard options in the New Report dialog box.

Table 15-1. New Report Options.

Option	Description
Design View	You selected this option in the first example in this chapter to create a report from scratch.
Report Wizard	This option opens the main Report Wizard, where you can select the fields you want to include and select formatting options, grouping options, and summary options. (You'll use this wizard in this exercise to create the Contact Events report again.)
AutoReport: Columnar	Using this report wizard is the same as selecting AutoReport from the New Object toolbar button's drop-down list. This option creates a very simple columnar report that lists the fields from a table or a query in a single column down the page. It generates a report using the last style you selected either in a wizard or via AutoFormat in a Report window in Design view.

Table 15-1. **New Report Options.**

Option	Description
AutoReport: Tabular	This report wizard displays the data from fields in a query or a table in a single row across the report in the Detail section. If the wizard detects a one-to-many relationship in a query, it automatically creates a group header containing the fields from the *one* side and leaves the remaining fields in the Detail section. However, it does not generate any totals. It generates a report using the last style you selected either in a wizard or via AutoFormat in a Report window in Design view.
Chart Wizard	This report wizard helps you create an unbound OLE object containing a Microsoft Graph application object to chart data from your database. (The newer PivotChart view of a form offers more options than the Graph application.)
Label Wizard	This report wizard lets you select name and address fields and format them to print mailing labels. You can select from a number of popular label types. The Label Wizard will size the labels correctly.

Because you want to control all options, including setting a group and subtotals, select the Report Wizard option, and click OK.

Specifying Wizard Options

In the first window of the wizard, shown in Figure 15-8 on the next page, select the fields you want in your report. You can select all available fields in the order in which they appear in the underlying query or report by clicking the double right arrow (>>) button. If you want to select only some of the fields or if you want to specify the order in which the fields appear in the report, select one field at a time in the list box on the left and click the single right arrow (>) button to move the field to the list box on the right. If you make a mistake, you can select the field in the list box on the right and then click the single left arrow (<) button to move the field to the list box on the left. Click the double left arrow (<<) button to remove all selected fields from the list box on the right and start over.

To create the Contact Events report, you should select all the fields. Then, click the Next button to go to the next window.

> **Tip**   You can also select fields from one table or query and then change the table or query selection in the Tables/Queries combo box. The Report Wizard uses the relationships you defined in your database to build a new query that correctly links the tables or queries you specify. If the wizard can't determine the links between the data you select, it warns you and won't let you proceed unless you include data only from related tables.

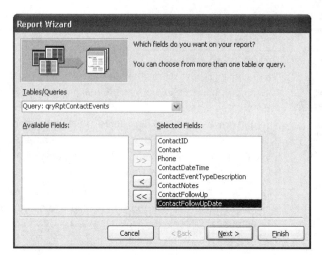

Figure 15-8. Selecting fields in the Report Wizard.

The wizard examines your data and tries to determine whether there are any natural groups in the data. Since this query includes information from the tblContacts table that has a one-to-many relationship to information from the tblContactEvents table, the wizard assumes that you might want to group the information by contacts (the ContactID, Contact, and Phone fields), as shown in Figure 15-9. If you don't want any report groups or you want to set the grouping criteria yourself, select by tblContactEvents. In this case, the wizard has guessed correctly, so click Next to go to the next step.

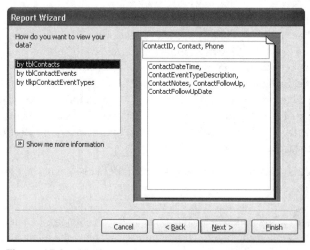

Figure 15-9. Verifying primary grouping criteria in the Report Wizard.

In the next window (shown in the background in Figure 15-10), the wizard shows you the grouping already selected for ContactID and asks whether you want to add any grouping levels below that. (If you chose to set the criteria yourself—by choosing by tblContactEvents in the previous window—you will see a similar window with no first group selected.) You can select up to four grouping levels. The wizard doesn't allow you to enter an expression as a grouping value—something you can do when you build a report from scratch. If you want to use an expression as a grouping value in a report wizard, you have to include that expression in the underlying query. For this report, you could also group within each contact by the ContactDateTime, so select that field and click the single right arrow to temporarily add it as a grouping level.

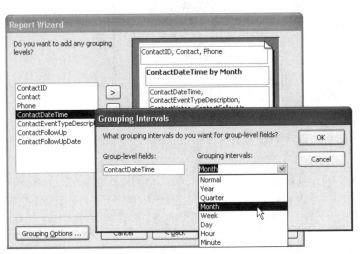

Figure 15-10. Setting the grouping interval on an additional grouping field in the Report Wizard.

When you add grouping levels, the wizard makes the Grouping Options button available for those levels. You can click the ContactDateTime by Month grouping level in the right window and then click this button to see the Grouping Intervals dialog box, shown in Figure 15-10. For a text field, you can group by the entire field or by one to five of the leading characters in the field. For a date/time field, you can group by individual values or by year, quarter, month, week, day, hour, or minute. For a numeric field, you can group by individual values or in increments of 10, 50, 100, 500, 1,000, and so on, up to 500,000. As you can see, the wizard has automatically assumed grouping by month when you added the ContactDateTime field as a grouping level. You don't need that grouping level in this sample, so cancel the Grouping Intervals dialog box, and click the single left arrow to remove it. Then click Next.

In the next window, shown in Figure 15-11 on the next page, the wizard asks you to specify any additional sorting criteria for the rows in the Detail section. (The report at this point will be sorted by the grouping level fields you specified in the previous window.) You can select up to four fields from your table or query by which to sort the data. By default, the sorting order is ascending. Click the button to the right of the field selection combo box to toggle the order to descending. You can't enter expressions as you can in the Sorting And Grouping window. In this report, choose the ContactDateTime field from the first combo box and click the button to the right once to toggle it to Descending, as shown in the figure.

Chapter 15

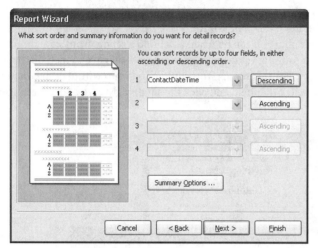

Figure 15-11. Specifying sorting criteria in the Report Wizard.

Click the Summary Options button to open the dialog box shown in Figure 15-12. Here you can ask the wizard to display in the group footers summary values for any numeric fields the wizard finds in the Detail section. In this case, the wizard sees that the ContactFollowUp field is the only one in the Detail section that is a number (a yes/no data type). As you'll see later, the wizard automatically generates a count of the rows, which explains why Count isn't offered as an option.

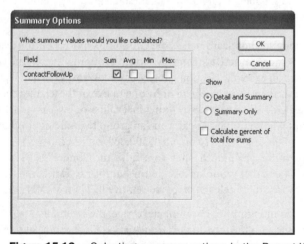

Figure 15-12. Selecting summary options in the Report Wizard.

Select Sum for this field. (You can add the minus sign after the Wizard is done to get the correct count.) Note that you also have choices to calculate the average (Avg) of values over the group or to display the smallest (Min) or largest (Max) value. You can select multiple options. You can also indicate that you don't want to see any of the detail lines by selecting the Summary Only option. (Sometimes you're interested in only the totals for the groups in a report, not all of the detail.) If you select the Calculate percent of total for sums option, the wizard will also display, for any field for which you have selected the Sum option, an additional field that shows what percent of the grand total this sum represents. When you have the settings the way you want them, click OK to close the dialog box. Click Next in the Report Wizard window to go on.

In the next window, shown in Figure 15-13, you can select a layout style and a page orientation for your report. When you select a layout option, the wizard displays a preview on the left side of the window. In this case, the Align Left 1 layout option in Portrait orientation will come closest to the hand-built report you created earlier in this chapter. You should also select the check box for adjusting the field widths so that all the fields fit on one page.

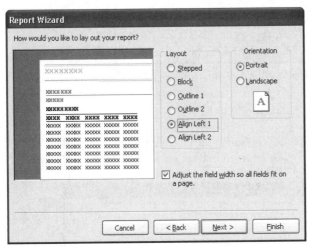

Figure 15-13.   Selecting a layout style and page orientation in the Report Wizard.

Click Next to go to the next window of the wizard. In this window you can select from several built-in report styles. If you defined your own custom report style using AutoFormat in a Report window in Design view (similar to the way you defined a format for a form in Chapter 12, "Customizing a Form"), you can also select your custom style. The built-in styles include Bold, Casual, Compact, Corporate, Formal, and Soft Gray. The Bold and Casual styles are probably better suited for informal reports in a personal database. The other formats look more professional. For this example, select the Corporate style. Click Next to go to the final window of the wizard, shown in Figure 15-14 on the next page.

Here, you can type a report title. Note that the wizard uses this title to create the report caption that appears in the title bar of the window when you open the report in Print Preview, the label that serves as the report header, and the report name. It's probably best to enter a title that's appropriate for the caption and label and not worry about the title being a suitable report name. If you're using a naming convention (such as prefixing all reports with rpt as I've done in the sample databases), it's easy to switch to the Database window after the wizard is done to rename your report. In this case, enter **Contact Events** as the title.

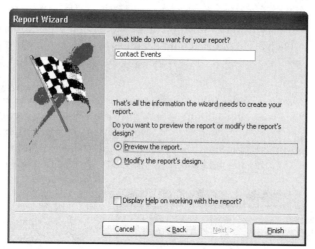

Figure 15-14. The Report Wizard window for specifying a report title.

Viewing the Result

Select the Preview the report option in the final window, and then click the Finish button to create the report and display the result in Print Preview, as shown in Figures 15-15 and 15-16.

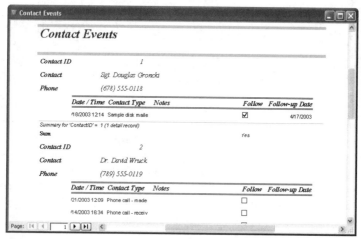

Figure 15-15. The first page of the Contact Events report created using the Report Wizard.

You can press Esc at any time to return to Design view for the report. It's easy to use Design view to modify minor items (such as adjusting the width and alignment of the Contact-DateTime and ContactEventDescription fields and resizing the labels) to obtain a result nearly identical to the report you constructed earlier. You also need to fix the expression in the text box that calculates the Sum of the ContactFollowUp field and change the format to display the number. (The wizard set the format to Yes/No.) You should also change the Sum label associated with this calculation. You can find the wizard's report saved (after I fixed a few items) as *rptXmplContactEvents2* in the sample database. As you might imagine, report wizards can help you to get a head start on more complex report designs.

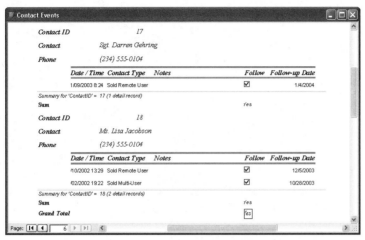

Figure 15-16. The last page of the Contact Events report showing the grand total.

You should now feel comfortable with constructing reports. In the next chapter, you'll learn how to build more complex reports that contain subreports and calculated values.

Advanced Report Design

In the previous chapter, you learned how to create a relatively simple report with a single sub-total level. You also saw how a report wizard can help you construct a new report. This chapter shows you how to

- Design a report with multiple subtotal groups
- Add complex calculations to a report
- Embed a report within another report
- Create a report with an embedded PivotChart form

To learn how to work with these features, you'll create the *Facility Occupancy by Date* report for the Housing Reservations database. In a second example, you'll learn how to use the results from two queries in an embedded subreport and an embedded PivotChart to produce a report that summarizes and graphs revenue by facility and month.

Note   The examples in this chapter are based on the reports, queries, tables, and data in *HousingDataCopy2.mdb* on the companion CD included with this book. You can find similar reports in the Housing Reservations sample application, but all the reports in that sample file have custom menus and toolbars defined, so you won't see the built-in menus and toolbars when you open those reports. The results you see from the samples in this chapter might not exactly match what you see in this book if you have changed the sample data in the files. Also, all the screen images in this chapter were taken on a Windows XP system with the display theme set to Windows XP. Your results might look different if you are using a different operating system or a different theme.

Building a Query for a Complex Report

To explore some of the advanced features you can include in a report, let's build a report in the Housing database that displays room occupancy information by facility, date, room, and employee. As noted in the previous chapter, reports tend to bring together information from many tables, so you are likely to begin constructing a report by designing a query to retrieve the data you need for the report. For this example, you need information from the tblFacilities, tblReservations, and tblEmployees tables in the *HousingDataCopy2.mdb* database. Open a new Query window in Design view, and add these tables to the query.

The tblReservations table contains one row per reservation, and the reservation could span many days. If you want to report on occupancy by day, you must use the special trick you learned in Chapter 8, "Building Complex Queries": Include a table containing all the dates you want and add special criteria to expand each row in tblReservations into one row per day. The sample database contains a handy table, ztblDates, that has rows containing all the dates from January 1, 1992, to December 31, 2035, so add that table to your query. To continue, add the fields listed in Table 16-1 to the design grid. (You can find this query saved as *qryXmplRptReservationsByDay* in the sample database.)

Table 16-1. Fields in the qryXmplRptReservationsByDay Query

Field/Expression	Source Table	Criterion
EmpName: tblEmployees.LastName & ", " & tblEmployees.FirstName & (" "+tblEmployees.MiddleName)		
ReservationID	tblReservations	
FacilityName	tblFacilities	
RoomNumber	tblReservations	
DateValue	ztblDates	Between #4/1/2003# And #6/30/2003#
CheckInDate	tblReservations	<= [ztblDates].[DateValue]
CheckOutDate	tblReservations	>[ztblDates].[DateValue]
TotalCharge	tblReservations	

Your Query window should look similar to the one shown in Figure 16-1.

You might be wondering why the query has a criterion to limit the range of dates returned from the ztblDates table. The sample database contains reservations from March 12, 2003, through October 29, 2003 (296 records). Although you could certainly create a report that includes all reservations, a user is typically going to want to look at records only for a specific date span. (For example, the housekeeping department might be interested in seeing this report only for the next few days or week.) Also, because the ztblDates table contains more than 16,000 rows, this query could take up to a minute to run—or more on a slow machine—unless you filter the rows. In Chapter 23, "Automating Your Application with Visual Basic," you'll learn how to provide the user with a custom date range dialog box to limit the records. For this example, the query includes a filter to limit the rows to the second quarter of 2003.

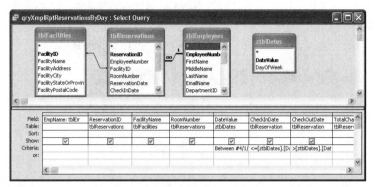

Figure 16-1. The qryXmplRptReservationsByDay query for the Facility Occupancy by Date report.

You can either save your query as qryMyRptReservationsByDay and select it in the Database window, or select the *qryXmplRptReservationsByDay* query in the Database window to follow along in the next section.

Creating the Basic Facility Occupancy by Date Report

For many reports, building the source query is the most difficult step. Once you have the data you need and understand the grouping options and properties you can set, building the report is easy. I actually like to use the Report Wizard to get a jump-start on laying out my reports. The wizard works especially well when the record source contains 10 or fewer fields.

To start designing the Facility Occupancy by Date report, select the query in the Database window, choose Report from the New Object toolbar button, click Report Wizard in the New Report dialog box, and click OK. Build the basic report by taking the following steps:

1   In the first window of the wizard, choose the FacilityName, DateValue, RoomNumber, and EmpName fields and click Next.

2   In the second window, the wizard suggests grouping the report by the RoomNumber field. However, you need to define custom sorting and grouping later, so click the left arrow to undo that selection, and then click Next.

3   In the next window, the wizard offers to sort the information for you. You can ask the wizard to establish some of the sorting and grouping settings you need by asking for an ascending sort on FacilityName, DateValue, and RoomNumber. Click Next.

4   Because you didn't ask the wizard to create any groups, the wizard suggests a Tabular layout, and this is just fine. Be sure that Orientation is set to Portrait and the Adjust the field width so all fields fit on a page option is selected. Click Next.

5 All the reports in this application use the Bold style. Choose that style and click Next.

6 In the final window of the wizard, enter **Facility Occupancy By Date – 2nd Quarter 2003** as the report title, select the Modify the report's design option, and click Finish to create your report.

The report the wizard built should look like that shown in Figure 16-2.

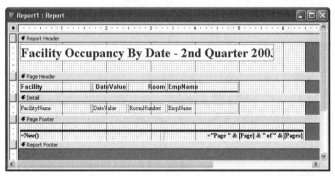

Figure 16-2. The initial Facility Occupancy By Date report created by the Report Wizard.

The wizard always places the report title label in the Report Header section, but that appears only once on the first page of the report. Especially when the report is likely to contain many pages, I like to see the report title repeated at the top of each page so that the subject of the report is clear throughout. You can move the report title from the Report Header section to the Page Header section. To do this, follow these steps:

1 Expand the bottom of the Page Header section about 0.5 inch.

2 Select all the label controls and the line control in the page header. (You can do this by clicking and dragging along the vertical ruler to the left of these controls.) Use the Down Arrow key to move the controls down to provide some space for the label from the Report Header section. If you use the Down Arrow key, you don't have to worry about the labels becoming vertically misaligned from the text box controls in the Detail section. (Caution: If you hold down the Down Arrow key, Access moves your selected controls down into the Detail section when they hit the bottom margin of the Page Header section.)

3 Click the label control in the Report Header section and drag it down into the space you created in the Page Header section. You might want to select the column heading labels and the line control again and use the Up Arrow key to close up any gap below the bottom of the report title label control. Also, move the bottom of the Page Header section up so that there's only a small space between the line and the bottom of the section.

4 Close up the bottom of the Report Header section so that it has zero height.

5 If you can't see all the characters in the report title label, click it and expand it to the right by grabbing the sizing handle in the center of the right edge.

While you're refining the look of the report, click the DateValue label control and change its caption to Date. Also click the EmpName label control and change its caption to Employee. Select all the controls in the Page Footer section and delete them. You'll learn later how to create controls to display the current date and time and page numbers.

Your report should now look like Figure 16-3. Click the Save button on the toolbar to preserve your work to this point.

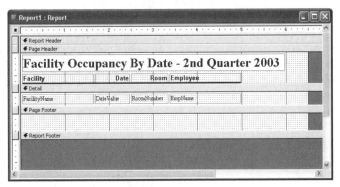

Figure 16-3. The Facility Occupancy By Date report after adjusting what the wizard built.

Defining the Sorting and Grouping Criteria

The next thing you need to do is define the sorting and grouping criteria for the report. Click the Sorting And Grouping button on the toolbar to open the Sorting And Grouping window. This report should display the daily reservation data from the query in the Detail section, with summaries of reservations by date, by month, and by facility. Note that in the Sorting And Grouping window, you specify grouping values from the outermost to the innermost (like specifying a sorting criteria left to right). So, select the FacilityName field in the first line of the Sorting And Grouping window, and then set the Group Footer property to Yes. Notice that when you set the Group Header or Group Footer property to Yes for any field or expression in the Sorting And Grouping window, Microsoft Access shows you a grouping symbol on the row selector for that row. Access also adds an appropriate section to your report. You want to make sure that a group header doesn't get "orphaned" at the bottom of a page, so set the Keep Together property to With First Detail. Note that you can also ask Access to attempt to keep all the detail for this level of grouping on one page by setting the Keep Together property to Whole Group. When you do this, Access will produce a new page if all the detail for the next group won't fit on the current page. As you'll see later, the report sections also have properties that you can set to force a new page with the start of each group.

The DateValue field from the query returns the date each room is occupied across a reservation span. When housing managers look at this report for more than one month, they might want to see subtotals by month. You can create a group on month by clicking the DateValue in the Field/Expression column and setting the Group On property to Month. See the sidebar, "Understanding Grouping Options," for details about other options you can set. Also set the Group Footer property to Yes to create a space to place monthly totals on your report. It's a good idea to set Keep Together to With First Detail for this group, too.

You can include the DateValue field in the Field/Expression column again, but set Group On to Each Value to create a subtotal by day. You can click the selection button on the left of the RoomNumber line and then drag it down to create a blank row for a second DateValue. (This window doesn't provide an Insert command.) Choose DateValue in the Field/Expression column and then set Group Footer to Yes and Keep Together to Whole Group so that a set of rows for a particular day doesn't split across a page boundary. Remember that there's no sorting specification in the query you built or in the sample *qryXmplRptReservationsByDay* query. There wouldn't be any point in defining a sort in the query because reports ignore any sorting specification from the query when you define any criteria in the Sorting And Grouping window. Your result should look something like that shown in Figure 16-4. (Note that I clicked the first DateValue selection so that you can see the Group Property settings for that field.)

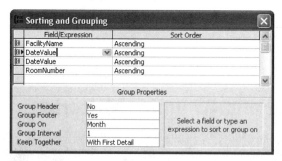

Figure 16-4. The sorting and grouping criteria for the Facility Occupancy By Date report.

Your report design should now look like Figure 16-5.

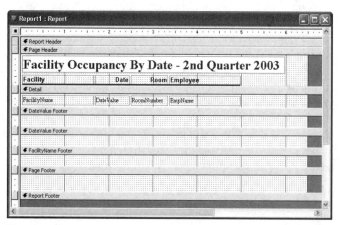

Figure 16-5. The Facility Occupancy By Date report with new footer sections after defining sorting and grouping criteria.

Click the Save button again to preserve your work to this point. You can find this stage of the report design saved as *rptXmplFacilityDateOccupancyStep1* in the sample database.

Understanding Grouping Options

For each field or expression in the upper part of the Sorting And Grouping window, you can set Group On and Group Interval properties. Normally, you'll want to start a new grouping of data whenever the value of your field or expression changes. You can, however, specify that a new grouping starts whenever a field or an expression changes from one range of values to another. The type of range you can specify varies depending on the data type of the field or the expression.

For text grouping fields, you can tell Microsoft Access to start a new group based on a change in value of one or more leading characters in the string. For example, you can create a new group based on a change in the first letter of the field (rather than on a change anywhere in the field) to create one group per letter of the alphabet—a group of items beginning with A, a group of items beginning with B, and so on. To group on such a prefix, set the Group On property to Prefix Characters and the Group Interval property to the number of leading characters that differentiates each group.

For numbers, you can set the Group On property to Interval. When you specify this setting, you can enter a setting for the Group Interval property that clusters multiple values within a range. Access calculates ranges from 0. For example, if you specify 10 as the interval value, values ranging from –20 to 29 would be grouped from –20 through –11, –10 through –1, 0 through 9, 10 through 19, and 20 through 29.

For date/time fields, you can set the Group On property to calendar or time subdivisions and multiples of those subdivisions, such as Year, Qtr, Month, Week, Day, Hour, or Minute. Include a setting for the Group Interval property if you want to group on a multiple of the subdivision—for example, set Group On to Year and Group Interval to 2 if you want groupings for every two years.

When you create groupings in which the Group Interval property is set to something other than Each Value, Access sorts only the grouping value, not the individual values within each group. If you want Access to sort the detail items within the group, you must include a separate sort specification for those items. For example, if you group on the first letter of a LastName field and also want the names within each group sorted, you must enter LastName as the field in the Sorting And Grouping window with Group Header (and possibly Group Footer) set to Yes, Sort Order set to Ascending, Group On set to Prefix Characters, and Group Interval set to 1. You must then enter LastName again as an additional sorting and grouping field with Sort Order set to Ascending and Group On set to Each Value.

Setting Section and Report Properties

You've probably noticed that Microsoft Access has a property sheet for each section in the Report window in Design view. You can set section properties not only to control how the section looks but also to control whether Access should attempt to keep a group together or start a new page before or after the group. There's also a property sheet for the report as a whole. You don't need to change any of these properties at this point, but the following sections explain the available property settings.

Section Properties

When you click in the blank area of any group section or Detail section of a report and then click the Properties button, Access displays a property sheet, such as the one shown in Figure 16-6.

Figure 16-6.   The property sheet for a report section.

The available properties and their uses are described in Table 16-2.

Table 16-2. Properties for a Section

Property	Description
Name	Access automatically generates a unique section name for you.
Force New Page	Set this property to Before Section to force the section to print at the top of a new page. Set this property to After Section to force the next section to print at the top of a new page. You can also set this property to Before & After to force the section to print on a page by itself. The default setting is None.

Table 16-2. **Properties for a Section**

Property	Description
New Row Or Col	When you use the Page Setup dialog box to format your report with more than one column (vertical) or more than one row (horizontal) of sections, you can set this property to Before Section, After Section, or Before & After to produce the section again at the top, bottom, or both top and bottom of a new column or row. This property is useful for forcing headers to print at the top of each column in a multiple-column report. The default setting is None.
Keep Together	Set this property to No to allow a section to flow across page boundaries. The default Yes setting tells Access to attempt to keep all lines within a section together on a page. (You can tell Access to attempt to keep detail lines together with group headers and footers by setting the Keep Together property to Whole Group or With First Detail for the grouping specification in the Sorting And Grouping window.)
Visible	Set this property to Yes to make the section visible or to No to make the section invisible. You can set this property from a macro or from a Visual Basic procedure while Access formats and prints your report. You can make sections disappear depending on data values in the report.
Can Grow	Setting this property to Yes allows the section to expand to accommodate controls that might expand because they display memo fields or long text strings. You can design a control to display only one line of text, but you should allow the control to expand to display more lines of text as needed. If you set the Can Grow property for any control in the section to Yes, Access automatically sets the Can Grow property of the section to Yes.
Can Shrink	This property is similar to Can Grow. You can set it to Yes to allow the section to become smaller if controls in the section become smaller to enclose less text. Unlike Can Grow, setting the Can Shrink property for any control in the section to Yes does not automatically set Can Shrink for the section to Yes. The default setting is No.
Height	This property defines the height of the section. You normally change this property by dragging the bottom edge of the section. If you want a specific height, you can enter it here, and Access changes the display to match as long as all controls fit within the defined height. If you attempt to set the height smaller than will accommodate the controls in the section, Access sets the height to the minimum that can contain the controls.

Chapter 16

Table 16-2. Properties for a Section

Property	Description
Back Color	The default back color of a section is the color value for white (16,777,215). You can choose a custom color value by clicking in the property and then clicking the Build button (...) next to the property box to open the Color dialog box. You can also choose colors from the Fill/Back Color button on the toolbar.
Special Effect	The default setting is a flat effect. You can also set a raised or sunken effect for a section on the Formatting toolbar or by choosing this effect from the drop-down list for the property.
Tag	Use this property to store additional identifying information about the section. You can use this property in macros and in Visual Basic procedures to temporarily store information that you want to pass to another routine.
On Format	Enter the name of a macro or a Visual Basic procedure that you want Access to execute when it begins formatting this section. See Chapter 21, "Understanding Event Processing," and Chapter 23, "Automating Your Application with Visual Basic," for details.
On Print	Enter the name of a macro or a Visual Basic procedure that you want Access to execute when it begins printing this section or when it displays the section in Print Preview. See Chapter 21, "Understanding Event Processing," for details.
On Retreat	Enter the name of a macro or a Visual Basic procedure that you want Access to execute when it has to "back up" over a section after it finds that the section won't fit on the current page and you've set the Keep Together property to Yes. This event happens after On Format but before On Print, so you can use it to undo settings you might have changed in your On Format routine. Access calls On Format again when it formats the section on a new page.

For page headers and footers, only the Name, Visible, Height, Back Color, Special Effect, Tag, On Format, and On Print properties are available.

Report Properties

If you choose the Select Report command from the Edit menu (or click in the Report window beyond the right edge of the Detail section) and then click the Properties button, Access displays the report's properties in the property sheet, as shown in Figure 16-7.

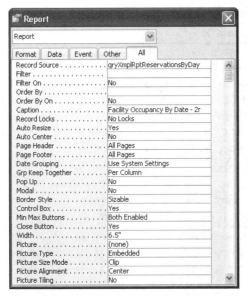

Figure 16-7. The property sheet for a report.

Some of the available properties and their uses are described in Table 16-3.

Table 16-3. Properties for a Report

Property	Description
Record Source	This property displays the name of the table or query that provides the data for your report.
Filter	This property shows any filter applied by a macro or Visual Basic procedure the last time the report was opened. You can also define a specific Filter setting that you want to save with the report definition. You cannot define a filter for a report, as you can with a form, using menu commands or toolbar buttons.
Filter On	Set this property to Yes if you want the filter defined for the report to be applied automatically each time the report opens. Note that you can set the Filter and Filter On properties from a macro or a Visual Basic procedure. The default setting is No.
Order By	This property shows any ordering criteria applied by a macro or a Visual Basic procedure the last time the report was opened. You can also define a specific Order By setting that you want to save with the report definition.

Table 16-3. Properties for a Report

Property	Description
Order By On	Set this property to Yes if you want the Order By property defined for the report to be applied automatically each time the report opens. Note that you can set the Order By and Order By On properties from a macro or a Visual Basic procedure. Remember that Order By and Order By On have no effect if you have specified any settings in the Sorting And Grouping window. The default setting is No.
Caption	Use this property to set the text that appears in the title bar when you open the report in Print Preview. If you don't specify a caption, Access displays Report: and the name of the report in the Print Preview window title bar.
Record Locks	Set this property to All Records if the data for your report is on a network shared by others and you want to be sure that no one can update the records in the report until Access creates every page in the report. You should not set this property to All Records for a report that you plan to view in Print Preview because you'll lock out other users for the entire time that you're viewing the report on your screen. The default setting is No Locks.
Auto Resize	This setting affects the size of the Report window when you open the report in Print Preview. The default setting Yes asks Access to zoom the report to show the first entire page and size the window to fit within the Access workspace on your screen. Unless you have a very high-resolution monitor, most portrait layout reports will be unreadable with this setting. When you specify No, the report opens at 100% resolution in a window sized the same as you last saved the Report window from Design view. I recommend you change this setting to No for most reports.
Auto Center	This setting affects the positioning of the Report window when you open the report in Print Preview. The default setting No leaves the upper left corner in the same location as you last saved the Report window from Design view. When you specify Yes, the Report window opens centered in the Access workspace.

Table 16-3. Properties for a Report

Property	Description
Page Header	This property controls whether the page header appears on all pages. You might choose not to print the page header on the first and last pages if these pages contain a report header or a report footer. Valid settings are All Pages (the default), Not with Rpt Hdr, Not with Rpt Ftr, and Not with Rpt Hdr/Ftr.
Page Footer	This property controls whether the page footer appears on all pages. You might choose not to print the page footer on the first and last pages if these pages contain a report header or a report footer. Valid settings are All Pages (the default), Not with Rpt Hdr, Not with Rpt Ftr, and Not with Rpt Hdr/Ftr.
Date Grouping	Use this property to determine how Access groups date and time values that you've specified in the Sorting And Grouping window. You can set this property to US Defaults or Use System Settings (the default). For US Defaults, the first day of the week is Sunday and the first week of the year starts on January 1. If you specify Use System Settings, the first day of the week and first week of the year are determined by the regional settings section in Windows Control Panel.
Grp Keep Together	Set this property to Per Page if you want Access to honor the Sorting And Grouping Keep Together property by page. Set it to Per Column (the default) for a multiple-column report if you want Access to attempt to keep a group together within a column. This property has no effect in a typical report with a single column.
Pop Up	Set this property to Yes to make the Report window in Print Preview open as a pop-up. A pop-up window stays visible on top of other windows even when another window has the focus. The default setting is No.
Modal	Set this property to Yes to disallow clicking on any other window when the Report window is open in Print Preview. The default setting is No.

Chapter 16

Table 16-3. Properties for a Report

Property	Description
Border Style	The default setting, Sizable, allows the Report window in Print Preview to be resized.
	When you choose None, the report's Print Preview window has no borders, Control menu, title bar, Close button, or Minimize and Maximize buttons. You cannot resize or move the report when it is open. You can select the report and press Ctrl+F4 to close it unless the report's Pop Up property is set to Yes. You should write Visual Basic code to provide an alternative way to close this type of report.
	When you choose Thin, the Report window in Print Preview has a thin border, signifying that the report cannot be resized.
	When you choose Dialog and the Pop Up property is set to Yes, the border of the Report window in Print Preview is a thick line (like that of a true Windows dialog box), signifying that the report cannot be resized. If the Pop Up property is set to No, the Dialog setting is the same as the Thin setting.
Control Box	You can set the Control Box property to No to remove the Control menu and the Close, Minimize, and Maximize buttons from the Report window in Print Preview. The default setting is Yes. You must use Ctrl+F4 to close the window when this property is set to No.
Min Max Buttons	You can set the Min Max Buttons property to Both Enabled, None, Min Enabled, or Max Enabled. If you disable a Minimize or Maximize button, the related command on the Control menu becomes dimmed when the Report window is in Print Preview. The default setting is Both Enabled.
Close Button	You can set the Close Button property to No to remove the Close button from the Report window in Print Preview but leave the Control menu (with Close disabled on the Control menu). The default setting is Yes.
Width	Access sets this property when you increase the width of the report in the design grid. If you want a specific width, you can enter it here, and Access changes the display to match as long as all controls fit within the defined width. If you attempt to set the width smaller than will accommodate the controls in any section, Access sets the width to the minimum that can contain the controls.

Table 16-3. **Properties for a Report**

Property	Description
Picture, Picture Type	To use a bitmap as the background of a report, you enter the full path name and file name in the Picture property. If you set the Picture Type property to Embedded, Access copies the specified bitmap to the Report object. If you set the Picture Type property to Linked, Access uses the path name stored in the Picture property to load the bitmap each time you open the report. The default setting for Picture is (none), and the default setting for Picture Type is Embedded.
Picture Size Mode	When your background picture is not the same size as your page, you can set the Picture Size Mode property so that Access adjusts the size. The Clip setting displays the picture in its original size, and if the page is smaller than the picture, Access clips the sides and top and bottom edges of the picture as necessary. The Zoom setting maintains the aspect ratio and shrinks or enlarges the picture to fit the page. If your picture doesn't have the same horizontal-to-vertical dimensions (aspect ratio) as your page, Access centers the image and shows some blank space at the sides or top and bottom of the page. The Stretch setting expands the picture to fit the page size and will distort the image if the aspect ratio of the picture does not match the aspect ratio of the page. The default setting is Clip.
Picture Alignment	When you set the Picture Size Mode property to Clip or Zoom, you can use Picture Alignment to place the picture in the center of the page or in one of the corners. The default setting is Center.
Picture Tiling	When you set the Picture Size Mode property to Clip or Zoom and your picture is smaller than the page size, you can set the Picture Tiling property to Yes so that Access will place multiple copies of the picture across and/or down the page. The default setting is No.
Picture Pages	You can set this property to show the picture on all pages, the first page, or no pages. The default setting is All Pages.
Menu Bar	Enter the name of a custom menu bar. Access displays the menu bar when you open the report in Print Preview. See Chapter 24, "The Finishing Touches," for details on creating custom menu bars and custom toolbars.
Toolbar	Enter the name of a custom toolbar. Access displays the toolbar when you open the report in Print Preview. See Chapter 24 for details.

Chapter 16

Table 16-3. Properties for a Report

Property	Description
Shortcut Menu Bar	Enter the name of a custom shortcut menu. Access displays the shortcut menu when you open the report in Print Preview and right-click in the Report window.
Grid X, Grid Y	Specify the number of horizontal (X) or vertical (Y) divisions per inch or per centimeter for the dots in the grid. When you use inches (when Measurement is set to U.S. in the regional settings section of Windows Control Panel), you can see the dots whenever you specify a value of 24 or less for both X and Y. When you use centimeters (when Measurement is set to Metric), you can see the dots when you specify values of 9 or less. The default setting is 24 for inches and 10 for metric.
Layout For Print	When this property is set to Yes, you can select from among the TrueType and printer fonts installed on your machine. When this property is set to No, only TrueType and screen fonts are available. The default setting is Yes.
Fast Laser Printing	Some laser printers support the drawing of lines (such as the edges of rectangles, the line control, or the edges of text boxes) with rules. If you set the Fast Laser Printing property to Yes, Access sends rule commands instead of graphics to your printer to print rules. Rules print faster than graphics. The default setting is Yes.
Help File, Help Context Id	You can set the Help File property to specify the location of a help file in any format supported by Windows and Microsoft Office 2003, including the HTML help format. Use the Help Context Id property to point to a specific help topic within the file. See Chapter 24, "The Finishing Touches," for details.
Palette Source	With this property, if you have a color printer, you can specify a device-independent bitmap (.dib) file, a Microsoft Windows Palette (.pal) file, a Windows icon (.ico) file, or a Windows bitmap (.bmp) file to provide a palette of colors different from those in the Access default palette. You might need to set this property if you have also set the Picture property so that the colors of the background picture display properly. The default setting, (Default), uses your current Windows palette.
Tag	Use this property to store additional identifying information about the report. You can use this property in macros and in Visual Basic procedures to temporarily store information that you want to pass to another routine.

Table 16-3. **Properties for a Report**

Property	Description
On Open	Enter the name of a macro or a Visual Basic procedure that you want Access to execute when it opens your report.
On Close	Enter the name of a macro or a Visual Basic procedure that you want Access to execute when you close the Print Preview window or when Access has finished sending the report to your printer.
On Activate	Enter the name of a macro or a Visual Basic procedure that you want Access to execute when the Report window gains the focus in Print Preview. This property provides a convenient method of opening a custom menu bar or toolbar.
On Deactivate	Enter the name of a macro or a Visual Basic procedure that you want Access to execute when the Report window loses the focus in Print Preview. This property provides a convenient method of closing a custom menu bar or toolbar.
On No Data	Enter the name of a macro or a Visual Basic procedure that you want Access to execute when the report opens but the record source contains no data. Your procedure can display an informative message and cancel opening the report.
On Page	Enter the name of a macro or a Visual Basic procedure that you want Access to execute when all the sections of a page have been formatted but have not yet been printed. In Visual Basic, you can use special commands to draw custom graphics on the page just before it prints.
On Error	Enter the name of a macro or a Visual Basic procedure that you want Access to execute when any errors occur in the report.
Has Module	This property indicates whether the report has associated Visual Basic procedures. Access automatically changes this setting to Yes when you define any Visual Basic event procedures for the report. Caution: If you change this property to No when the report has procedures, Access warns you that this deletes your code.
Orientation	The default in most versions of Microsoft Access is Left-to-Right. In versions that support a language that is normally read right to left, the default is Right-to-Left. When you use Right-to-Left, captions appear right-justified, and the order of characters in controls is right to left.
Moveable	The default setting, Yes, allows the user to move the Report window in Print Preview. Set this property to No to lock the form on the screen where you last saved it.

Chapter 16

571

See Chapter 21, "Understanding Event Processing," and Chapter 23, "Automating Your Application with Visual Basic," for details about the properties that begin with the word *On*.

Using Calculated Values

Much of the power of Microsoft Access reports comes from their ability to perform both simple and complex calculations on the data from the underlying tables or queries. Access also provides dozens of built-in functions that you can use to work with your data or to add information to a report. The following sections provide examples of the types of calculations you can perform.

Adding the Print Date and Page Numbers

One of the pieces of information you might frequently add to a report is the date on which you prepared the report. You'll probably also want to add page numbers. Access provides two built-in functions that you can use to add the current date and time to your report. The Date function returns the current system date as a date/time value with no time component. The Now function returns the current system date and time as a date/time value.

Note   When you create a report using the Report Wizard, it adds a similar control to the Page Footer section, and it uses the Now function that returns the date and the time. However, the wizard sets the Format to Long Date, which displays only the date portion. Go figure.

To add the current date to your report, create an unbound text box control (delete the label) in the Page Footer section and set its Control Source property to =**Date**(). Then, in the Format property box, specify Long Date. You can see an example of using the Date function in Figure 16-8. The result in Print Preview is shown in Figure 16-9.

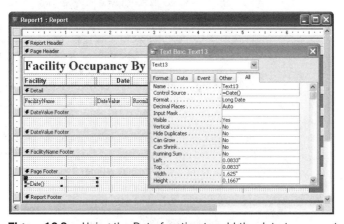

Figure 16-8.   Using the Date function to add the date to a report.

Chapter 16

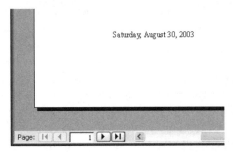

Saturday, August 30, 2003

Figure 16-9. The current date displayed in the report in Print Preview.

To add a page number, use the Page property for the report. You can't see this property in any of the property sheets because it is maintained by Access. Access also provides the Pages property, which contains a count of the total number of pages in the report. To add the current page number to a report (in this example, in the Page Footer section), create an unbound text box control (delete the label) and set its Control Source property to =**"Page "** & [**Page**] & **" of "** & [**Pages**], as shown in Figure 16-10.

Figure 16-10. Using the Page and Pages properties to add page numbers to a report.

> **Tip** **You can change the value of the Page property in code**
> You can reset the value of the Page property in a macro or a Visual Basic procedure that you activate from an appropriate report property. For example, if you're printing several multiple-page invoices for different customers in one pass, you might want to reset the page number to 1 when you start to format the page for a different customer. You can include a Group Header section for each customer and then use a macro or a Visual Basic procedure to set the Page property to 1 each time Access formats that section (indicating that you're on the first page of a new customer invoice).

Performing Calculations

Another task you might perform frequently is calculating extended values from detail values in your tables. You'll recall from Chapter 3, "Designing Your Database Application," that it's usually redundant and wasteful of storage space to define in your tables a field that you can calculate from other fields. (The only situation in which this is acceptable is when saving the calculated value will greatly improve performance in parts of your application.)

Performing a Calculation on a Detail Line

You can use arithmetic operators to create complex calculations in the Control Source property of any control that can display data. You can also use any of the many built-in functions or any of the functions you define yourself in a module. If you want, you can use the Expression Builder that you learned about in Chapter 7, "Creating and Working with Simple Queries," to build the expression for any control. You let Access know that you are using an expression in a Control Source property by starting the expression with an equal sign (=).

> **Note** To use a field in a calculation, that field must be in the table or query specified in the Record Source property of the report.

One calculated value that housing management might find useful is the daily revenue for each room. You could have calculated that value in the query that is the record source of the report, but you can also calculate it as an expression in a text box in the Detail section of the report. To add the expression you need, follow these steps:

1. Choose the Text Box tool in the toolbox and place it in the Detail section to the right of the EmpName text box. Select the attached label and delete it.

2. In the Control Source property of the new text box, enter:
   =CCur(Round([TotalCharge]/([CheckOutDate]–[CheckInDate]),2))

   Because you included the TotalCharge, CheckInDate, and CheckOutDate fields in the query, you can reference them in your expression. This expression calculates the daily revenue by dividing the total charge for the reservation by the number of days.

3. Set the Format property of the text box to Currency.

4. Set the Width property to 0.75 inches, move it close to the EmpName text box, and line up the tops of the two text boxes. Also, make the height of both text boxes the same by selecting them both and then choosing Size from the Format menu and To Tallest on the submenu.

5. Select the red line in the Page Header section and set its Width property to 5.75 inches so that it stretches over your new text box. (Hint: The line control is difficult to select by itself because of the row of closely spaced labels on top of it. You can use the Select Objects tool to draw a selection box across the Employee label control and the line, then hold down the Shift key and click the Employee label control to remove it from the selection.)

6. Click the Label tool in the toolbox and draw a label control next to the Employee label in the Page Header. Type **Charge** in the label and press Enter. (If you don't type anything, the label disappears when you select away from it.)

7. The default label control in the Bold style has a red font and is Arial 9 point, but the other labels are black and Arial 10 point. You can click one of the other labels in the page header, click the Format Painter button on the toolbar, and then click your new label to transfer the format.

8. Make the new label the same height as the other labels in the page header and give it the same width as the text box below it (0.75 inches). Align the left edge of the label with the left edge of the text box, and the top of the label with the top of the other labels in the section.

Your report in Design view should now look like Figure 16-11.

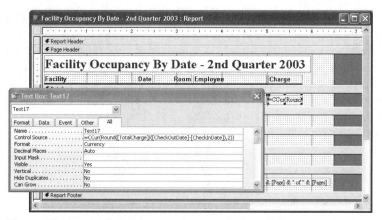

Figure 16-11. Adding an expression to calculate daily revenue.

Figure 16-12 shows the result in Print Preview. (The figure shows data from the third page of the report.) You can see that Access has performed the required calculations for each day of each reservation.

Facility Occupancy By Date - 2nd Quarter 2003

Facility	Date	Room	Employee	Charge
Main Campus Housing A	20-Apr-2003	202	Yu, Wei	$91.43
Main Campus Housing A	20-Apr-2003	302	Emory, John	$92.50
Main Campus Housing A	20-Apr-2003	505	Dickson, Holly	$40.00
Main Campus Housing A	21-Apr-2003	202	Yu, Wei	$91.43
Main Campus Housing A	21-Apr-2003	302	Emory, John	$92.50
Main Campus Housing A	21-Apr-2003	502	Sawyer, Ciam	$95.38
Main Campus Housing A	21-Apr-2003	502	Zimmerman, Marc	$95.00

Figure 16-12. The calculated detail line values within a group in Print Preview.

Inside Out

Avoiding #Error in a Calculated Control

Instead of starting with an unbound text box to perform a calculation, you might decide to drag and drop one of the fields that you'll use in the calculation from the field list onto your report. When you do that, Access gives the text box the same name as the field. If you modify the control source to an expression that uses the field, you'll see #Error in the text box when you view or print the report.

When you enter a name in an expression, Access first searches for another control that has that name. If it doesn't find the control, then it looks in the field list. So, if the name of the control is TotalCharge and you include an expression that uses [TotalCharge], the expression is referencing itself! Access can't figure out how to display the value of the TotalCharge text box, so it displays #Error instead. If you decide to drag and drop a field that you'll change to an expression, be sure to change the Name property of the control (for example, txtTotalCharge) before you enter the expression.

Of course, you'll also see #Error if your expression references a function that doesn't exist or provides invalid parameters to a function. However, using the name of the control itself inside the expression that is the control source is one of the most common sources of #Error.

Adding Values Across a Group

Another task commonly performed in reports is adding values across a group. In the previous chapter, you saw a simple example of this in a report that used the built-in Sum function. In the Facility Occupancy By Date report, you have three levels of grouping: one by facility, another by month, and another by date. When you specified sorting and grouping criteria earlier in this chapter, you asked Access to provide group footers. This gives you sections in your report in which you can add unbound controls that use any of the aggregate functions (Sum, Min, Max, Avg, Count, First, Last, StDev, or Var) in expressions to display a calculated value for all the rows in that group. In this example, you can create unbound controls in the Facility and both DateValue footers to hold the totals by facility, by month, and by date, for the daily charge for each room, as shown in Figure 16-13. In the Control Source property of each text box control, enter:

=Sum(CCur(Round([TotalCharge]/([CheckOutDate]−[CheckInDate]),2)))

Notice in this case, you must repeat the original expression inside the aggregate function. (See the tip on this page for an explanation.)

Tip How to calculate totals on expressions

An important point to remember about using an aggregate expression in a group section is that the expression cannot refer to any calculated controls in the Detail section. As you'll learn later, you can reference an outer control from an inner one (for example, a total calculation in a group from inside the Detail section), but not vice-versa. So, you cannot create a calculated field in the Detail section, for example, that multiplies two numbers and then reference that control in the summary expression. You can, however, repeat the calculation expression in the summary. If a detail control named Total has an expression such as =[Quantity] * [Price], you must use an expression such as =Sum([Quantity] * [Price]) in your grouping section, not =Sum([Total]).

You should also add a line control at the top of each footer section to provide a visual clue that the values that follow are totals. In this example, I placed lines approximately 4.5 inches in from the left and about one inch long, but they're difficult to see in Design view because they're right up against the top of the section.

Creating a Grand Total

Use the Report Footer section to create grand totals for any values across the entire set of records in a report. You can use any of the aggregate functions in the report footer just as you did in the two grouping section footers. Figure 16-13 shows you a Sum function used in a control in the report footer to produce a total for all records in the report.

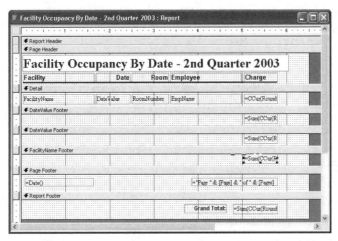

Figure 16-13. Adding summaries by facility, by month, and by date.

If you switch to Print Preview, go to the last page in the report, and scroll down, you should see a result similar to that shown in Figure 16-14. (You should set the name of this grand total field to txtSumGrand so that you can use it to calculate percentages later.) You can find this stage of the report design saved as *rptXmplFacilityDateOccupancyStep2* in the sample database.

South Campus Housing C	29-Jun-2003	107 Adams, Terry	$59.67
South Campus Housing C	29-Jun-2003	202 Huff, Arlene	$45.71
			$105.38
South Campus Housing C	30-Jun-2003	107 Adams, Terry	$59.67
South Campus Housing C	30-Jun-2003	202 Huff, Arlene	$45.71
			$105.38
			$3,579.02
			$9,148.69
		Grand Total:	$95,768.49

Saturday, August 30, 2003   Page 77 of 77

Figure 16-14. The totals displayed in the report in Print Preview.

> **Note** If you want to create percentage calculations for any of the groups over the grand total, you must create the control for the grand total in the report footer so that you can reference the total in percentage calculation expressions. See "Calculating Percentages," page 580. If you don't want the total to print, set the control's Visible property to No.

Hiding Redundant Values and Concatenating Text Strings

You probably noticed in several of the preceding examples that the FacilityName and DateValue fields print for every detail line. When a particular detail line displays or prints values that match the previous line, the report looks less readable and less professional. You can control this by using the Hide Duplicates text box property (which is available only in reports). Switch to the Design view of this report, and set the Hide Duplicates property to Yes for the FacilityName text box and the DateValue text box in the Detail section. The report will now print the facility name and the date only once per group or page, as shown in Figure 16-15. (The figure shows information from the last page of the report.) When Access moves to a new grouping level or page, it prints the facility name even if it matches the previous value displayed.

Facility Occupancy By Date - 2nd Quarter 2003

Facility	Date	Room	Employee	Charge
South Campus Housing C	23-Jun-2003	107	Adams, Terry	$59.67
		202	Huff, Arlene	$45.71
				$105.38
South Campus Housing C	24-Jun-2003	107	Adams, Terry	$59.67
		202	Huff, Arlene	$45.71
				$105.38
South Campus Housing C	25-Jun-2003	107	Adams, Terry	$59.67
		202	Huff, Arlene	$45.71
				$105.38
South Campus Housing C	26-Jun-2003	107	Adams, Terry	$59.67
		202	Huff, Arlene	$45.71
				$105.38
South Campus Housing C	27-Jun-2003	107	Adams, Terry	$59.67
		202	Huff, Arlene	$45.71
				$105.38
South Campus Housing C	28-Jun-2003	107	Adams, Terry	$59.67
		202	Huff, Arlene	$45.71
				$105.38
South Campus Housing C	29-Jun-2003	107	Adams, Terry	$59.67
		202	Huff, Arlene	$45.71
				$105.38
South Campus Housing C	30-Jun-2003	107	Adams, Terry	$59.67
		202	Huff, Arlene	$45.71
				$105.38
				$3,579.02
				$9,148.69
		Grand Total:		$95,768.49

Figure 16-15. Setting Hide Duplicates to Yes eliminates redundant values in each group.

Notice that when the report gets to the end of data for a month or a facility, it's not clear what the total lines mean. For example, on the last page of the report as shown in Figure 16-15, the $105.38 is clearly the total for the last date, but it's not obvious that $3,579.02 is the total for the month of June for the facility or that $9,148.69 is the total revenue for the facility. You can use string concatenation to display data that looks like a label but that also includes information from the record source. Sometimes it's useful to combine descriptive text with a value from a text field in the underlying query or table or to combine multiple text fields in one control. In Figure 16-16, you can see a descriptive label (created by a single text box control) on one of the subtotal lines.

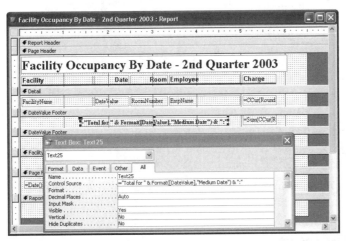

Figure 16-16. A text constant and a string derived from a field in the record source are concatenated as a "label" in a text box.

This "label" concatenates the words Total for with an expression that uses the Format function—applied here to the DateValue field to get the date in medium date format—and an ending string containing a colon. You can use the same technique in the group footer to create a "label" that reads Total for facility followed by the facility name and a trailing colon. You could certainly define a label followed by a text box followed by another label to create the same display. The advantage of using a single control is that you don't have to worry about lining up three controls or setting the font characteristics. In fact, because the string in the middle, containing the facility name, could vary significantly in length, you cannot create three separate controls that correctly line up all possible values end-to-end. Set the Text Alignment property of these controls to Right so that they line up correctly next to the summary controls, and set the font color to red so that the information stands out.

When you look at the report in Print Preview, as shown in Figure 16-17 on the next page, you can see that the duplicate values for facility name and for the date have been eliminated. You can also see the nice result from using a concatenated string in a text box to generate labels for the total lines.

Chapter 16

Facility Occupancy By Date - 2nd Quarter 2003

Facility	Date	Room	Employee	Charge
South Campus Housing C	23-Jun-2003	107	Adams, Terry	$59.67
		202	Huff, Arlene	$45.71
			Total for 23-Jun-03:	$105.38
South Campus Housing C	24-Jun-2003	107	Adams, Terry	$59.67
		202	Huff, Arlene	$45.71
			Total for 24-Jun-03:	$105.38
South Campus Housing C	25-Jun-2003	107	Adams, Terry	$59.67
		202	Huff, Arlene	$45.71
			Total for 25-Jun-03:	$105.38
South Campus Housing C	26-Jun-2003	107	Adams, Terry	$59.67
		202	Huff, Arlene	$45.71
			Total for 26-Jun-03:	$105.38
South Campus Housing C	27-Jun-2003	107	Adams, Terry	$59.67
		202	Huff, Arlene	$45.71
			Total for 27-Jun-03:	$105.38
South Campus Housing C	28-Jun-2003	107	Adams, Terry	$59.67
		202	Huff, Arlene	$45.71
			Total for 28-Jun-03:	$105.38
South Campus Housing C	29-Jun-2003	107	Adams, Terry	$59.67
		202	Huff, Arlene	$45.71
			Total for 29-Jun-03:	$105.38
South Campus Housing C	30-Jun-2003	107	Adams, Terry	$59.67
		202	Huff, Arlene	$45.71
			Total for 30-Jun-03:	$105.38
			Total for June 2003:	$3,579.02
			Total for facility South Campus Housing C:	$9,148.69

Figure 16-17. The total lines now have descriptive captions using data from the record source.

Calculating Percentages

In any report that groups and summarizes data, you might want to determine what percentage of an outer group total or the grand total is represented in a particular sum. You can do this in a report because Access makes two passes through the data. On the first pass, it calculates simple expressions in detail lines, sums across groups, sums across the entire report, and calculates the length of the report. On the second pass, it resolves any expressions that reference totals that were calculated in the first pass. Consequently, you can create an expression in a detail or group summary section that divides by a sum in an outer group or the grand total to calculate percentages.

Figure 16-18 shows an example of a percentage calculation in the FacilityName Footer section. The expression divides the sum of the calculated charge for this facility by the value in a field called txtSumGrand—the name of the grand total control in the report footer. (Remember when you created the grand total, I instructed you to give it this name.)

Set the Format property of the text box to Percent, and switch to Print Preview. Scroll down to find a total by month or by facility, and you'll also see the percent of the grand total, as shown in Figure 16-19. You can find this stage of the report design saved as *rptXmplFacilityDateOccupancyStep3* in the sample database.

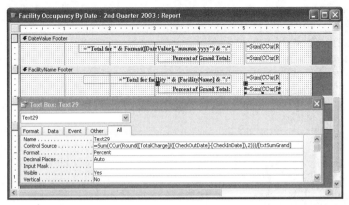

Figure 16-18. Adding a calculation for a percentage of a grand total.

Main Campus Housing A	30-Jun-2003	101 Sutton, Brad	$61.25
		204 Yu, Wei	$50.00
		207 Reiter, Tsvi Michael	$85.77
		402 Lugo, Jose	$100.00
		403 Watters, Jason M.	$42.22
		502 Yu, Wei	$100.00
		Total for 30-Jun-03:	$439.24
		Total for June 2003:	$8,361.01
		Percent of Grand Total:	8.73%
		Total for facility Main Campus Housing A:	$23,518.33
		Percent of Grand Total:	24.56%

Figure 16-19. A percentage calculation for two groups in Print Preview.

Using Running Sum

In addition to producing totals for any group you define, Access lets you create running totals within the Detail section or any group header or footer. For any text box that displays a numeric value, you can set the Running Sum property to produce a total that is reset at the start of each group or that continues totaling through the entire report. Let's further refine *rptXmplFacilityDateOccupancyStep3* to see how this works.

First, you need to adjust the sizes of some of the controls to provide more horizontal space within the design width of the report. Click the Date label control in the page header and hold down the Shift key while you click the DateValue text box in the Detail section to select them both. In the Properties window, shorten the width to 0.7 inches. Likewise, select the Room label control and the RoomNumber text box control and change the width to 0.5 inches. Click either control and slide them both to the left to close up the gap you created when you shortened the date controls.

Chapter 16

Click the Employee label control and the EmpName text box control and set the width for both to 1.3 inches. Slide both those controls to the left to close up the gap. Select both the Charge label control and the calculated text box control below it and slide them both to the left, close to the employee controls. Click the line control in the page header that runs beneath all the labels and set its width to 6.45 inches. Select all the controls in both DateValue footers, the FacilityName footer, and the report footer, and slide them to the left so that they now line up with the new position of the charge calculation text box in the Detail section.

Now you have some horizontal room to add another label control and companion text box control. Start by selecting the Charge label control, copy it to the Clipboard, and paste it back into the page header. Move it just to the right of the existing Charge label control and line it up vertically with all the other labels. Change its caption to **Cum. Charge** and stretch it to the right so you can see all the characters in the new caption.

Tip If you select the Page Header section before you perform the paste, Access places the control in the upper left corner of the section and doesn't change the size of the section. If you leave the original control selected when you perform the paste, Access places the new copy below the original and expands the section, which you might not want it to do.

Likewise, select the text box control below the original Charge label control, copy it to the Clipboard, and paste it back into the Detail section. Move it to the left of the existing charge calculation text box and line it up horizontally with all the other text boxes. Line up the new text box control with the label control above it and make it the same width as the label control. Finally, select the new text box control and set its Running Sum property in the Properties window to Over Group. Your report should now look like Figure 16-20.

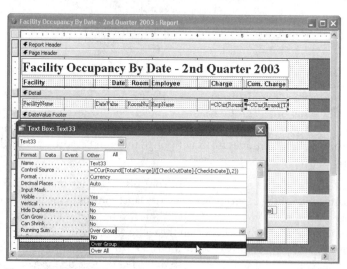

Figure 16-20. Adding a running sum calculation on the charge.

No, this isn't a second copy of the charge calculation. As you'll see when you look at the report in Print Preview, this produces (as the name of the property implies) a running sum of the charge calculation within the Detail section. As Access encounters each new row in the Detail section, it adds the current value of calculation to the previous accumulation and displays the result. Because you asked for the sum Over Group, Access resets the accumulating total each time it encounters a new group.

Next, let's use a little trick to generate a line number for each line in the Detail section. To make room for this line number, select all the column labels in the page header (but not the line underneath them), and all the controls in the Detail section, both DateValue footers, the Facility Name footer, and the report footer. Slide them all to the right about one-half inch (but not beyond the right edge of the report). Insert a small text box in the space you just created in the Detail section. Above this text box, create a label that displays # as its caption. (You can use the Format Painter button again to copy the format from one of the existing label controls to the new one.)

Remember that as Access formats each detail line, it takes the current value of the field (actually, the current value of the text box), adds it to the previous total, and displays the result. If you set the text box equal to any constant numeric value, Access uses that value for each detail line it produces. So, the trick is to set this text box equal to 1 (=1 in the Control Source property) and then set the Running Sum property. If you choose Over All for Running Sum, Access will number the first line 1, add 1 for the second line and display 2, add 1 for the third line and display 3, and so on throughout the report. Note from the settings in Figure 16-21 that I set a format that places a period after each displayed value.

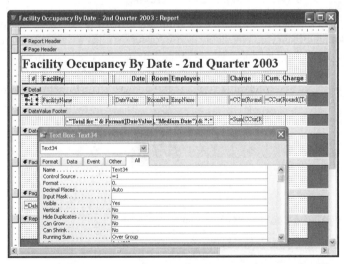

Figure 16-21. Using the Running Sum property to generate a line number.

If you switch to Print Preview, you can see the result of using Running Sum, as shown in Figure 16-22. The charge accumulates over each group, and then resets for the next group. The line numbers start at 1 and also reset for each group. You can find this report saved as *rptXmplFacilityDateOccupancyStep4* in the sample database.

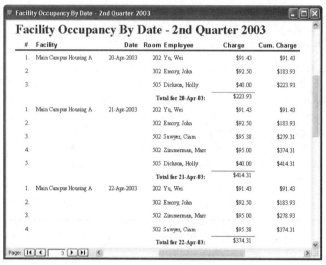

Figure 16-22. The result of using Running Sum to produce a cumulative total for each group and a line number for each detail line.

Taking Advantage of Conditional Formatting

In Chapter 13, you learned how to define conditional formatting for a text box control. Access makes an identical facility available to you for reports. Let's say, for example, that you want to highlight any daily total that is more than $400 or any monthly total that is greater than $10,000. To do this, open the report from the previous example in Design view, select the Sum text box in the first DateValue Footer section that displays the sum of the charge, and choose Conditional Formatting from the Format menu. Access displays the Conditional Formatting dialog box, as shown in Figure 16-23.

Figure 16-23. Setting conditional formatting for a text box.

Just as you can in a text box control on a form, you can define a test against the current value in the control or enter an expression. In this case, choose Field Value Is in the first drop-down list box, Greater Than in the second box, and enter the value **400** in the third box. Under Condition 1, set the Back Color to some dark color and the Fore Color to white. Click OK to save the conditional format. You can specify a similar condition for the Sum text box in the second DateValue footer (by month) to test for a monthly total greater than 10,000.

> **Note** In the Detail section, you can reference any other field in the current row to create an expression. But, when you create a conditional formatting expression in a grouping section, any field reference you use in an expression uses the value of the current row. In a group footer, for example, the current row is the last row displayed in the previous Detail section.

When you switch to Print Preview, you can see the result, as shown in Figure 16-24. You can find this sample saved as *rptXmplFacilityDateOccupancyStep5*. (Page 42 in the sample shows both conditional formats in action.)

7.			505 Smith, Samantha	$73.33	$482.17
8.			505 Evans, John	$74.74	$556.91
9.			506 Pellow, Frank	$60.00	$616.91
10.			512 Zimmerman, Marc	$63.00	$679.91
			Total for 29-Jun-03:	**$679.91**	
1.	Main Campus Housing B	30-Jun-2003	205 Osada, Michiko	$75.45	$75.45
2.			209 Oveson, Scott	$84.50	$159.95
3.			304 Adams, Terry	$50.62	$210.57
4.			305 Gode, Scott	$75.45	$286.02
5.			309 Yu, Wei	$90.00	$376.02
6.			401 Delaney, Aidan	$46.67	$422.69
7.			405 Sutton, Brad	$76.15	$498.84
8.			505 Smith, Samantha	$73.33	$572.17
9.			505 Evans, John	$74.74	$646.91
			Total for 30-Jun-03:	**$646.91**	
			Total for June 2003:	**$15,115.65**	
			Percent of Grand Total:	15.78%	
		Total for facility Main Campus Housing B:		$32,748.66	
			Percent of Grand Total:	34.20%	

Figure 16-24. The result of setting conditional formatting.

> To see a more complex example of conditional formatting in action, open *rptEmployeeRes* in the sample database. That report uses conditional formatting to check for overlapping reservation requests, highlight them, and reveal a warning label in the section header.

Creating and Embedding a Subreport

In many of your reports, you will probably design the Detail section to display a single line of information from the underlying record source. As you learned earlier in this chapter, it's fairly easy to link several tables to get lots of detail across several *one-to-many* relationships in your database. You also saw how to use the Hide Duplicates property to display a hierarchy across several rows of detail.

However, as with forms and subforms, which you learned about in Chapter 13, "Advanced Form Design," you can embed subreports (or subforms) in the Detail section of your report to display multiple detail lines from a table or query that has a *many* relationship to the *one* current line printed in the Detail section. You must use this technique when you want to display information from more than one *many* relationship on a single page. In the LawTrack Contacts database, for example, if you want to provide details about contact events and products owned by a contact, you must use subreports. You could create a very complex query that joins all the information, but you'd get one row for each unique combination of contact event and product. If a contact has 100 events and owns six products, each of the six product rows is matched with each of the 100 contact event rows. You'll get 600 rows for that contact in a query that joins the tblContacts, tblContactEvents, and tblContactProducts tables—each product record appears 100 times, and each contact event record appears six times.

Understanding Subreport Challenges

Subreports present a unique challenge. Unlike a subform where you can scroll through all available related rows in one window, a subreport has no scroll bar. The subreport expands to list all the related rows. If the rows won't fit on one page, it can be difficult to repeat the header information at the top of the subsequent pages. Although you can define a report header in a report that you use as a subreport, that header prints only once at the top of the subreport space on the page where the subreport starts.

To understand how this works, let's examine two approaches to listing department information in a report with related employee information in a subreport. In the *HousingDataCopy2.mdb* sample database, open *rptDepartmentsWSubBad* in Design view as shown in Figure 16-25. When you drop a report onto the design of another report to create a subreport, Access sizes the subreport control to the height of one line from the report inside the control. The figure shows the subreport control expanded so that you can see the subreport inside it. I selected the control and dragged down the bottom edge, but you might find it easier to change the Height property in the properties window because the bottom sizing box is difficult to grab with your mouse.

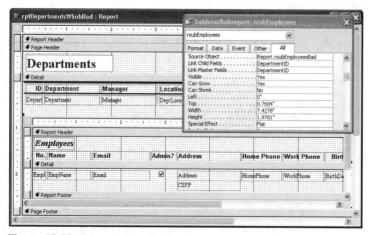

Figure 16-25. A report to display departments with related employees in a subreport.

The outer report, Departments, uses a query based on the tblDepartments and the tbl-Employees tables to provide information about each department and the department's manager. The report inside the subreport control, Employees, has another query on the tblEmployees table. The report looks simple enough—a heading for each department row and a heading inside the subreport to provide column headings for the employee information. You can also see that a subreport works just like a subform—you define the Link Master Fields and Link Child Fields properties of the subreport control to link the information from the two reports.

Now switch to Print Preview and go to the second and third pages of the report as shown in Figures 16-26 and 16-27 to see what really happens when a department has more employees than will fit on one page.

Departments

ID	Department	Manager	Location	Address		
3	Marketing	Osada, Michiko	Headquarters, MD 915	1234 Main Street Chicago, IL 60601		

Employees

No.	Name	Email	Admin?	Address	Home Phone	Work Phone	Birth Date
15	Alexander, Sean	SAlexander	☐	6789 Willow Avenue Eagle River, AK 99577	(907) 555-0140	(907) 555-0163	10/18/1954
21	Bueno, Janaina B	JBueno	☐	5678 Willow Street Uniontown, PA 15401	(724) 555-0114	(724) 555-0190	2/6/1968
11	Carroll, Matthew	MCarroll	☐	4567 1st Boulevard Dallas, TX 75248	(972) 555-0102	(972) 555-0173	12/18/1966
26	Delaney, Aidan	ADelaney	☐	1234 Lincoln Boulevard Parade, SD 57625	(605) 555-0114	(605) 555-0192	11/6/1972
3	Dievendorff, Dick	DDievendorff	☐	5678 4th Avenue Ware, MA 01082	(413) 555-0107	(413) 555-0163	12/31/1946
22	Emanuel, Michael	MEmanuel	☐	3456 Church Street HickoryCorners, MI 4906	(269) 555-0145	(269) 555-0168	3/29/1964
49	Emory, John	JEmory	☐	7890 2nd Street Albion, PA 16401	(814) 555-0132	(814) 555-0184	6/2/1950

Figure 16-26. The top of the second page of the departments and employees report.

Departments

45	Smith, Samantha	SSmith	☐	7890 Lincoln Avenue Keller, TX 76248	(817) 555-0106	(817) 555-0158	3/6/1948
9	Verhoff, Rob	RVerhoff	☐	7890 Willow Avenue Greenwood, ME 04255	(207) 555-0116	(207) 555-0176	8/11/1945
50	Zimmerman, Mar	MZimmerman	☐	2345 3rd Drive Touchet, WA 99360	(509) 555-0143	(509) 555-0171	9/9/1948

Figure 16-27. The top of the third page of the departments and employees report with missing headers.

As you can see, the third page has nothing more than the page header to help identify the information being printed. The department information from the Detail section printed once on the second page, as did the report header from the subreport. When the subreport overflowed onto a second page, the column heading information from the report header defined for the subreport didn't print again.

To see how to solve this problem, open *rptDepartmentsWSub* in Design view, as shown in Figure 16-28. Again, the figure shows the subreport control expanded so that you can see the subreport inside it.

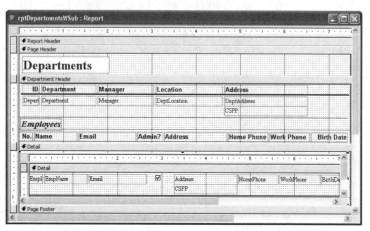

Figure 16-28. The design of a report and subreport that handles the page overflow problem.

Can you figure out the difference? The secret is the outer report has a group defined on department, even though there is only one detail row per department. All the department information and the headers for the columns in the subreport appear in this group header. Remember that you set the Repeat Section property of a group header to Yes to force it to appear again at the top of a page if the information in the Detail section overflows the page. The Detail section contains only the subreport, and the subreport has no headers. If you switch to Print Preview and go to the third page in this report, as shown in Figure 16-29, you can see that the appropriate headers appear again when the Marketing department overflows onto another page.

Departments

ID	Department	Manager	Location	Address
3	Marketing	Osada, Michiko	Headquarters, MD 915	1234 Main Street
				Chicago, IL 60601

Employees

No.	Name	Email	Admin?	Address	Home Phone	Work Phone	Birth Date
27	Petculescu, Cristi	CPetculescu	☐	6789 Main Street	(814) 555-0113	(814) 555-0187	3/18/1946
				Mill Creek, PA 17060			
45	Smith, Samantha	SSmith	☐	7890 Lincoln Avenue	(817) 555-0106	(817) 555-0158	3/6/1948
				Keller, TX 76248			
9	Verhoff, Rob	RVerhoff	☐	7890 Willow Avenue	(207) 555-0116	(207) 555-0176	8/11/1945
				Greenwood, ME 04255			
50	Zimmerman, Mar	MZimmerman	☐	2345 3rd Drive	(509) 555-0143	(509) 555-0171	9/9/1948
				Touchet, WA 99360			

Figure 16-29. The top of the third page of the departments and employees report with headers correctly repeated.

Chapter 16

Building a Report with a Subreport

The manager of Housing Administration has just asked you to produce a report that summarizes for each facility the revenue by month. You know the manager is someone who likes to see a visual representation as well as the data, so you need to design a report that will ultimately display a revenue chart as well. You'll learn how to add the PivotChart in the last section of this chapter.

Building the Subreport Query

If all you needed to do was display total revenue by facility and by month, you could build one totals query that joins the tblFacilities table with the tblReservations table and group by facility. However, the need to add the chart means you'll need a subreport to calculate the monthly totals so that you can display the chart that graphically shows all the month values immediately below the numerical data. If you try to add a chart to the Detail area of a report that displays totals by month, the chart will show one graph point for the current month, not all months.

In the previous examples, you have been using a complex query to calculate revenue by day—an accounts receivable perspective. But guests in a hotel usually don't pay for their stay until the day they check out. So, to calculate actual revenue received for a month, you should use the check-out date and the total amount owed.

Start a new query on the tblReservations table. In the query design grid, include the FacilityID (you'll need this field to provide the link between the subreport and the main report), CheckOutDate, and TotalCharge fields. You could turn this into a totals query to sum the total charge by month, but it's just as easy to do that in the report. Your query should look like Figure 16-30. You can find this query saved in the sample database as *qryXmplFacilityRevenue*.

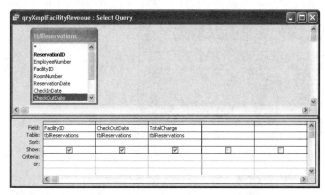

Figure 16-30. A query for a subreport to calculate revenue by facility and month.

Designing the Subreport

The report you need for the subreport is very simple. Select your query and choose Report from the New Object toolbar button. In the New Report dialog box, select Design View and

Chapter 16

click OK to start designing your report. If you want your report to look like the others in the application, choose AutoFormat from the Format menu and select the Bold format. Remember from the discussion in the previous section that you'll see what's in the report header and report footer of a report that you use as a subreport, but Access never displays the page header or page footer. On the View menu, clear Page Header/Footer. Open the View menu again and select Report Header/Footer.

Open the Sorting And Grouping window, add the CheckOutDate field in the Field/Expression column, set the Group Header property to Yes, Group On to Month, and then close the window. Because you want the report to calculate and display totals by month only, close up the Detail section to zero height. Widen the report design area to about 5.5 inches. Close up the Report Header section to zero height because you'll add the column labels to the outer report.

Draw a line across the top of the CheckOutDate Header section starting near the left edge and extending to about 5.1 inches wide. Underneath this line about 1.5 inches from the left, drag and drop the CheckOutDate field from the field list and delete the attached label. In the Properties window, set the Format property to **mmmm yyyy** to display the month name and four-digit year. Drag and drop the TotalCharge field from the field list into the CheckOut-Date Header section about 3.75 inches from the left. In the Properties window, change the Name property of the control to **TotalChargeSum** and change the Control Source to =**Sum**([**TotalCharge**]). (Remember, you must change the name of the control to avoid a circular reference in the expression!) Line up the two text boxes in the CheckOutDate Header section horizontally.

Finally, select the Text Box tool in the toolbox and add a text box to the Report Footer section lined up under the TotalChargeSum text box. Set its Control Source property to =**Sum**([**Total-Charge**]), set the Format property to Currency, and change the font to Bold. Change the caption of the attached label to **Grand Total**. Your report should look something like Figure 16-31. You can find this report saved as *rsubXmplFacilityRevenueByMonth* in the sample database.

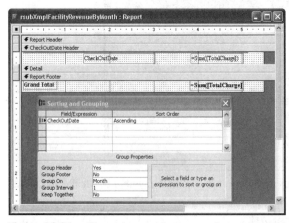

Figure 16-31. The subreport to summarize revenue by month.

Embedding a Subreport

You can find the query you need for the outer report saved as *qryRptFacilities* in the sample database. This query includes the FacilityID, FacilityName, and FacilityAddress fields. It also includes an expression (named FacilityCSPP) that concatenates the FacilityCity, FacilityState-OrProvince, and FaciltyPostalCode fields so that they display nicely on one line in the report.

Click Queries on the Object bar in the Database window, select *qryRptFacilities*, and choose Report from the New Object button on the toolbar. In the New Report dialog box, select Design View and click OK to start your report design. Choose AutoFormat from the Format menu and select the Bold format. Expand the report to 6.5 inches wide. Add a label control to the Page Header section and type **Facility Revenue** in the label. Change the Font to Times New Roman, the Font Size to 20, and size the label to fit.

Open the Sorting And Grouping window. Select the FacilityName field on the first line in the Field/Expression column. Change Group Header to Yes, and Keep Together to With First Detail, and close the window. Expand the FacilityName Header section to about 1.25 inches high to give yourself some room to work. Select the FacilityName Header section and, in the Properties window, set the Force New Page property to Before Section.

Drag and drop all four fields from the field list onto the FacilityName Header section of the report one at a time, as shown in Figure 16-32. Select the Label tool in the toolbox and place a label control under the FacilityCSPP text box control about 2.5 inches in from the left. Type **Month** in the label and press Enter. (You can ignore the smart tag warning about an unattached label.) Add a second label control about 4.5 inches in from the left, type **Revenue** in the label, and press Enter. Line up the two labels horizontally.

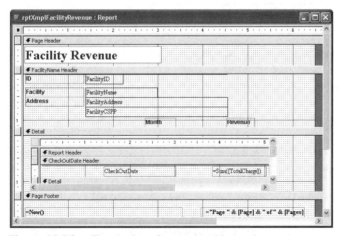

Figure 16-32. The design of a report with a subreport.

Press F11 to go to the Database window, select Reports on the Object bar, and position the window to the right so that you can see your report design behind the window. Drag and drop the report you created in the previous section from the Database window onto the Detail section of the report into the upper right corner about 0.25 inch in from the left edge.

In the Properties window, set the Link Child Fields and Link Master Fields properties to **FacilityID**. Delete the label that Access attached to the subreport control.

As a finishing touch, you can add a date text box control and a page number text box control to the Page Footer section as you learned to do earlier in this chapter. Your report should look something like Figure 16-32. You can find this report saved as *rptXmplFacilityRevenue* in the sample database.

Switch to Print Preview to see the result as shown in Figure 16-33. Note that you might need to switch back and forth between Design view and Print Preview to adjust the position of the Month and Revenue labels over the columns from the subreport.

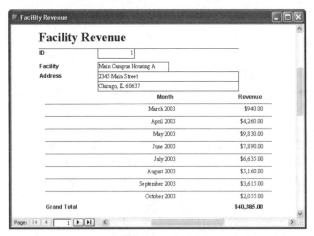

Figure 16-33. The report to display facility information with monthly revenue in a subreport.

Adding a PivotChart to a Report

You can now design a form in PivotChart view to graphically display monthly revenue data. Note that a report doesn't have a PivotChart or PivotTable view, but it is perfectly legal to embed a form into a report as a subreport. (But you cannot embed a report in a form as a subform.)

Designing the PivotChart Form

When you built the subreport for the Facility Revenue report, you used a simple query on the tblReservations table. For the chart, you need to include the name of the facility—the ID won't make much sense in the legend for the chart. In the sample database, you can find a query named *qryXmplChtFacilityRevenue* that includes both the tblFacilities and the tblReservations tables. The fields in the query are FacilityID and FacilityName from the tblFacilities table and CheckOutDate and TotalCharge from the tblReservations table.

To build the chart you need, select the query in the Database window and then choose Auto-Form from the New Object button on the toolbar. This quickly builds a simple form that includes all the fields from the query. You won't need FacilityID in the final chart, so delete it. Switch to PivotChart view to begin designing the chart.

Open the chart field list and drag and drop the FacilityName field onto the Drop Series Fields Here area of the chart. Click the plus sign next to the Check-Out By Month field to expand its list and drag and drop Months onto the Drop Category Fields Here area. Drag and drop the Total Charge field onto the Drop Data Fields Here area—the chart calculates a Sum of this field for you. Open the Properties window and select Chart Workspace on the General tab. Click both the Add Title and Add Legend buttons to add these elements to your chart.

Click the Chart Workspace Title element to select it. In the Properties window, click the Format tab and enter **Facility Revenue** in the Caption box. In the PivotChart, click the vertical Axis Title and in the Properties window enter **Revenue** in the Caption box. In the PivotChart, click the horizontal Axis Title and change its Caption to **Months**. Go back to the General tab and select Chart Workspace. On the Show/Hide tab, clear all the options under Show by default and Let users view so that users cannot modify the chart. Your chart should now look like Figure 16-34. Switch back to Design view and set the Default View property to PivotChart. Be sure to save the form and give it a name such as chtFacilityRevenue.

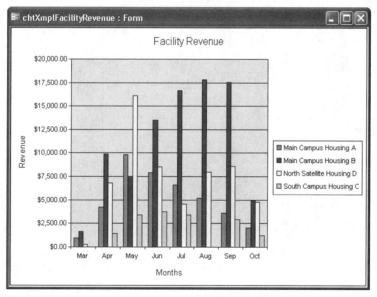

Figure 16-34. A PivotChart form to display facility revenue by month.

Embedding a PivotChart in a Report

The rest is easy. Go to the Database window and select the report you created in the previous section to display facilities with revenue by month in a subreport. Open that report in Design view. (You can also open the sample *rptXmplFacilityRevenue* report.) Select the subreport control and choose Size from the Format menu and To Fit from the submenu to resize the subreport exactly one line high to give yourself some room to work. Don't worry about displaying all the lines in the subreport—when you dragged and dropped it onto the report,

Chapter 16

Access set its Can Grow property to Yes. When you view the report, Access will expand the subreport control to display all the lines.

Expand the Detail section to about 5.5 inches high. Select the Subform/Subreport tool in the toolbox and draw the control in the Detail section under the previous subreport approximately 5.5 inches wide and 4 inches high. The size of the subreport control affects the resolution of the chart you're going to put inside it, so you want it big enough to be easily readable. Delete the label from the control. Move the subreport control up near the previous subreport control.

With the new subreport control selected, open the Properties window and set the Source Object property to the PivotChart form you created earlier. (Or, you can use the example chtXmplFacilityRevenue form in the sample database.) Set both the Link Child Fields and Link Master Fields properties to FacilityID. Your report design should now look like Figure 16-35. Notice that the subreport window shows you the Form view design of the form, not the chart.

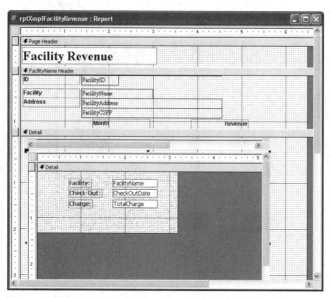

Figure 16-35. A report with an embedded PivotChart form as a subreport.

Switch to Print Preview to see the result as shown in Figure 16-36. Now that layout should make the facilities manager happy! You can find the report saved as *rptXmplFacilityRevenue-Chart* in the sample database.

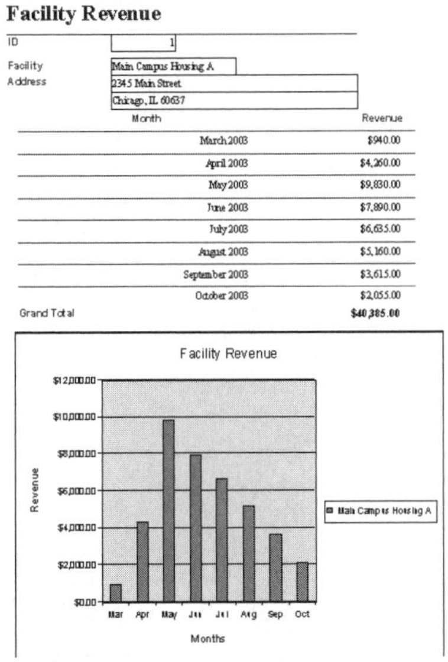

Facility Revenue
ID
1
Facility
Main Campus Housing A
Address
2345 Main Street
Chicago, IL 60637
Month
Revenue
March 2003
$940.00
April 2003
$4,260.00
May 2003
$9,830.00
June 2003
$7,890.00
July 2003
$6,635.00
August 2003
$5,160.00
September 2003
$3,615.00
October 2003
$2,055.00
Grand Total
$40,385.00
Facility Revenue
$12,000.00
$10,000.00
$8,000.00
$6,000.00
$4,000.00
$2,000.00
$0.00
Revenue
Mar Apr May Jun Jul Aug Sep Oct
Months
Main Campus Housing A

Figure 16-36. The report with an embedded subreport and PivotChart in Print Preview.

At this point, you should thoroughly understand the mechanics of constructing reports and working with complex formulas. The next part of the book explores how to apply all you've learned to this point to building an Access Project that uses Microsoft SQL Server to store your tables and queries (views, stored procedures, and functions).

Part 4

Designing an Access Project

Building Tables in an Access Project

If you worked through the previous chapters in this book, you created all the components and have all the knowledge necessary to produce a fully functioning desktop application in Microsoft Office Access 2003. If you built an application only for your personal use, you might never need to learn more about advanced Access features. But if you plan to share your application with multiple users and/or work with large amounts of data, it might be time to consider building an Access project.

Unlike an Access desktop database (.mdb), an Access project does not contain any tables or queries. When you define a project, you must specify a connection to a Microsoft SQL Server database. The database server provides the tables and queries—views, functions, and stored procedures—that your application will use.

As with any database design, the first step in creating an Access project is building the tables. In this chapter, you will learn how to

- Create a new project file by building a new database on the server.
- Create a new project file by connecting to an existing database on the server.
- Create a new table in Design view.
- Select the best data type for each column.
- Create check constraints to validate the data in your tables.
- Define a primary key for your tables.
- Add indexes to your tables.
- Learn how to create relationships for your tables.
- Learn how to manage your relationships and tables using database diagrams.
- Set options that affect how you work in table design.

Creating a New Project File

Before you can get started building a new project file, you need to make sure that you can interface with an SQL Server database that can support your Access project. The file extension that Access uses to store your project files is .adp. You must either

- Have access to SQL Server version 2000 or later and also have full Create Database and Modify Database permissions, or
- Have installed the Microsoft SQL Server Desktop Engine (MSDE) that comes with Microsoft Office 2003. See the Appendix for more information on installing MSDE.

> **Note** Although it is possible to use SQL Server 6.5 or later when creating an Access project (.adp), many of the tools discussed in this chapter are supported only by SQL Server 2000 or later. If you do not have access to SQL Server 2000, try installing the MSDE instead so that you can become familiar with all the design options supported by project files (.adp) in Access 2003.

Building a New SQL Server Database

Any Access project file (.adp) must be connected to an SQL Server database to store its tables, views, functions, and stored procedures. When you create a new project file, you can also create a new database. If you don't already have a database to connect to on the server, you need to create one. Click the Project using new data selection in the New section of the New File task pane, as shown in Figure 17-1.

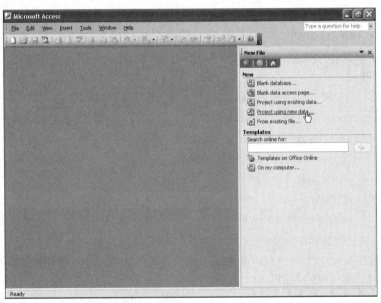

Figure 17-1. Choosing the option to create a new Access project using new data.

> **Tip** If the New File task pane isn't visible, you can choose New from the File menu to display it.

In the dialog box that appears, as shown in Figure 17-2, select the drive and folder you want from the Save in drop-down list. In this example, I selected the My Documents folder on my computer. Next, go to the File name text box and type the name of your new Access project. Access appends an .adp extension to the file name for you. Name the new project file ContactTracking and click the Create button to create your project file.

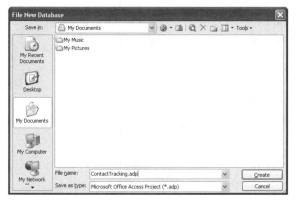

Figure 17-2. Naming the new project file in the File New Database dialog box.

Access creates the project for you and opens it. Because this is a new project, the Microsoft SQL Database Wizard opens and asks you what SQL Server you want to connect to and what you want to name your new database. If you are connected to a large network, it might take a while for the wizard to appear because it has to search the entire network to compile a list of all available SQL Servers.

Inside Out

An Access project is not a database

When you were working with .mdb files, you had all the elements of a database in one convenient file. Because an .mdb file can stand on its own, it's logical to refer to it as a database. Project files are different. In an Access project, the actual database is composed of all the tables, functions, views, and stored procedures that are kept on the server. Your Access project file merely connects to the database to make available these objects that are on the server, and you build the forms, reports, data access pages, macros, and modules that define your application in the project file. SQL Server (or the MSDE) has its own database name, which can be different from the project file you create in Access. It is important to keep this difference in mind, because when you talk about the database in an Access project, you are actually talking about the database stored on the server.

601

Figure 17-3 shows the first window of the Microsoft SQL Server Database Wizard. The first field shows the name of the server to which you want to connect. Click the drop-down list to display all the servers that the wizard found. If the name of the server you want to connect to is not listed, you can type the full name in the box instead. If you are using a copy of MSDE installed on your desktop computer, select the (local) option from the drop-down list.

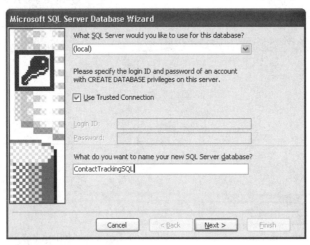

Figure 17-3. Choosing the server connection and database name.

In most cases, you want to place a check mark in the Use Trusted Connection check box. This tells Access that you want to connect to the server using the established Windows security protocols (the default for MSDE). If you or an administrator has decided to enforce SQL Server security using a database server login, you need to complete the Login ID and Password fields using an account with valid Create Database permissions on the server. You must clear the Used Trusted Connection check box to enable the Login ID and Password boxes.

Access automatically generates a database name by appending SQL to the end of the project file name you entered in the File New Database dialog box. If you want to use a different name, you can type it in. For this exercise, we will use the provided Contact-TrackingSQL name.

Click Next to proceed. If Access discovers that the name you chose conflicts with an existing database on the server, it suggests a new one (the same name with a number appended to the end—such as ContactTrackingSQL2). If the wizard can establish a connection to your server, you will see the screen displayed in Figure 17-4. Click Finish to close the wizard, and you are now ready to begin building your new Access project.

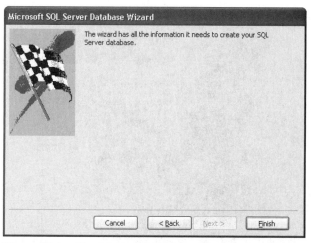

Figure 17-4. The Wizard is ready to create the new database on the server.

Troubleshooting

I keep getting errors when I try to create a new database. What am I doing wrong?

In order for Access to be able to create a new database, the following must be true:

- Access must detect a valid server on the local desktop computer or on the network. If you are attempting to connect to SQL Server, check with your administrator and make sure that the server is properly registered and that your computer can link over your network to the computer on which the server resides. If you are using MSDE, make sure it is fully installed and configured and that you have started it. (See the Appendix for more information.)

- You must have Create Database permissions that can be verified through a trusted connection or by using SQL Server security. If you are connecting to SQL Server, check with the administrator to make sure these permissions have been created for you. On MSDE, these permissions should exist by default. If you are still having trouble, try using **sa** as the login ID with no password (the default System Administrator login).

Connecting to an Existing SQL Server Database

If the database has already been created for you, or if you want to build a project that connects to an existing database, choose Project using existing data from the New File task pane, as shown in Figure 17-5 on the next page.

Tip If the New File task pane isn't visible, you can choose New from the File menu to display the New File task pane.

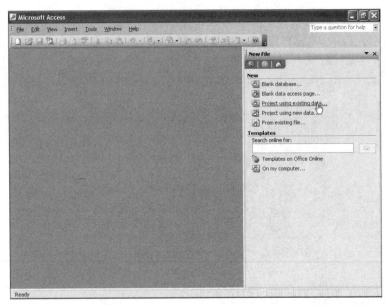

Figure 17-5. Choosing the option to create a new Access project using existing data.

In the dialog box that appears, as shown in Figure 17-6, select the drive and folder you want from the Save in drop-down list. Then go to the File name text box and type the name of your new Access project. Access appends an .adp extension to the file name for you. For this example, name the new project file ContactTracking2. Click the Create button to create your project file.

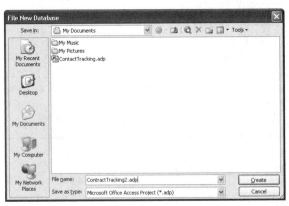

Figure 17-6. Naming the new project file in the File New Database dialog box.

Next, Access displays the Data Link Properties dialog box, as shown in Figure 17-7. If you are connected to a large network, it might take a while for the screen to appear because the wizard has to search the entire network for all valid servers. After the screen appears, select the server to which you want to connect from the drop-down list in the first box. If the name of the server you want to connect to is not listed, you can type the full name in the box instead. If you are using a copy of MSDE installed on your desktop computer, select the (local) option from the drop-down list.

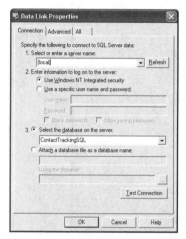

Figure 17-7. Specifying how to connect to an existing database using the Data Link Properties dialog box.

Select Use Windows NT Integrated security if you want to allow SQL Server to verify your permissions through the Windows NT settings. (In this context, Windows NT means Windows NT 4.0, Windows 2000, Windows XP, and Windows Server 2003 with SQL Server version 7 or later.) If you have a specific SQL Server login ID and password assigned to you, click the Use a specific user name and password option instead and enter them. When the server requires an SQL Server login, you can also specify that the password is blank (which is not the same as leaving the Password field blank), and you can ask Access to remember the login ID and password you enter.

If the database you want to connect to is already on the server, you can select the database from the second drop-down list. If the database you want is not listed, it might not exist on the server to which you have chosen to connect. Try connecting to a different server, or check with your administrator to make sure the database you want has been created.

Note If you followed the previous instructions to create a new project with a new database, you can use the ContactTrackingSQL database that you created earlier.

You can also choose to attach a database file to the server by selecting the Attach a database file as a database name option. This allows you to connect a pre-existing SQL Server master data file (.mdf) to the server and use it to build your project on. You can also use this option to attach Microsoft Access desktop database tables (.mdb) to your server, but the tables will be read-only. When you choose to attach a database, you must enter the database name you want for the attached file and specify the location of the file you want to attach. If you don't know the exact location of the database file, you can browse for it by clicking on the browse (...) button. This will display the dialog box shown in Figure 17-8 on the next page.

Chapter 17

605

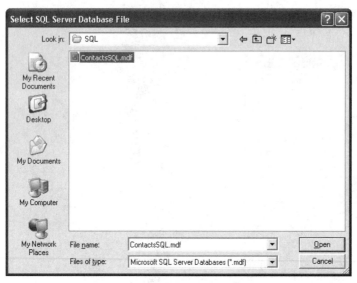

Figure 17-8. Locating a master data file to attach to SQL Server.

Use the dialog box to locate the .mdf file you want to attach and then click the Open button. Access displays the path to the database file in the Data Link Properties dialog box as shown in Figure 17-9. Make sure you type a unique name for your database in the box above where the path name is listed. For example, if you are attaching the ContactsSQL.mdf file, enter **ContactsSQL** as the database name.

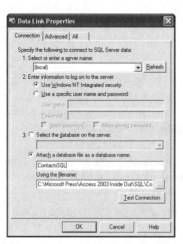

Figure 17-9. Attaching a database file as a database name.

> **Tip** If you want to work with the tables, functions, views, and stored procedures in the sample project files included on the companion disk, you will need to attach the ContactsSQL.mdf file provided on the disk to SQL Server or the MSDE using the preceding instructions.

When you are ready, click the Test Connection button. If Access is able to connect, it will display a Test Connection Succeeded message. If it fails, a problem might exist with the server connections. Contact your network administrator or consult your SQL Server documentation for more assistance.

> If you are having errors connecting to the server, see the Troubleshooting sidebar on page 603. If Access informs you the server is running but it can't connect to your database, see the Inside Out tip on page 638 for more help.

Click OK in the Data Link Properties dialog box, and the new Access project using existing data is created, as shown in Figure 17-10. You are now ready to edit the existing database.

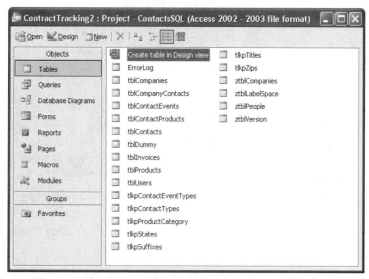

Figure 17-10. The database window of a new project connected to an existing database.

Creating a Table in Design View

Now that you have created a project file, let's take a look at creating a table. The features that allow you to create tables by using wizards or by entering data in a desktop application (.mdb) do not exist in an Access project (.adp). The only method for creating tables (other than importing them from another source or using specific code to create them) is to create them in Design view.

Creating a new table is easy. Open the project file (*ContactTracking.adp*) connected to the new database (ContactTrackingSQL) that you created earlier. Make sure the Database window is visible, and select Tables on the Object bar. Click the New button on the Database window toolbar, and a blank table opens in Design view, as shown in Figure 17-11 on the next page.

> **Note** You can also create a new table in Design view by selecting Table from the Insert menu.

Chapter 17

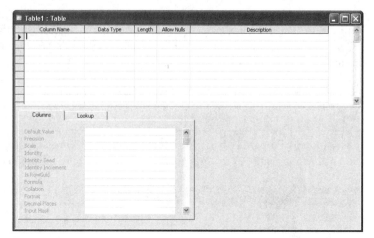

Figure 17-11. Creating a new table in Design view in an Access project.

Because the tables of an Access project are stored in SQL Server, the table design inherits some of the new properties and definitions supported by SQL Server. You might notice that fields are now called columns, and instead of records you have rows. This naming convention is similar to the design elements discussed in Chapter 3, "Designing Your Database Application." Functionally, columns are the same as fields, and rows are the same as records.

Listed horizontally are some additional properties that SQL Server uses to define the columns in your table. You can also see properties listed on the tab control in the bottom section of the window. Some of the listed properties are unavailable (they appear dimmed) depending on the data types that you select for your columns.

For details about column properties, see Table 17-3, "SQL Server Table Column Properties," page 616.

In Chapter 4, "Creating Your Database and Tables," you learned how to create tables for an Access desktop database (.mdb) by building some of the tables in the ContactTracking database. Now let's learn how to build those same tables in an Access project (.adp).

Defining Columns

First, let's build the Companies table that we designed in Chapter 3. With the table in Design view, click in the first row under Column Name, type the name of the first column, **CompanyID**, and press Tab. Notice that Access fills in a default data type and length. You'll learn how to change this default later in this chapter. Click the down arrow in the Data Type cell or press Alt+Down Arrow to open the list of data type options, as shown in Figure 17-12.

Chapter 17

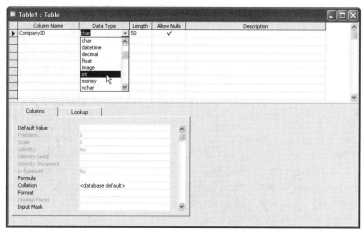

Figure 17-12. Selecting from the drop-down list of data type options.

Inside Out

Rules for identifiers and column names

As you learned in Chapter 4, it is a good idea to follow a sensible naming convention when defining fields in your Access .mdb tables. One of the primary reasons for this was so that it would be easier to interface with SQL Server later on. As you'll learn in Chapter 29, "Upsizing a Desktop Application to a Project," it's possible to convert an existing desktop database (.mdb) to a project with connected tables, views, functions, and stored procedures in SQL Server. If you plan your field (column) names carefully, this process happens much more smoothly.

All objects in an SQL Server database, including tables, views, functions, and stored procedures, must have names that follow a set of naming conventions called the *Rules for Identifiers*. These rules also apply to naming your columns in a table in an Access project. (Remember, the table is actually stored in SQL Server.)

A column name can be up to 128 characters long and can include any combination of letters, numbers, and the symbol characters @, _, #, or $. The column name must begin with a letter, _, @, or #. The name also must not contain spaces and cannot be a Transact SQL reserved word (such as Select, Alter, or Create).

Microsoft *SQL Server Books Online* provides an invaluable reference to all the features of Microsoft SQL Server 2000. You can download a free online copy (a set of help files) from *http://www.microsoft.com/sql/techinfo/productdoc/2000/books.asp*. In *SQL Server Books Online*, you can find a list of all the reserved words in Transact SQL.

Chapter 17

You should give your columns meaningful names and should use the same name throughout for a column that occurs in more than one table. You should avoid using column names that might also match any name internal to Microsoft Access, Visual Basic, or SQL Server. For example, all objects have a Name property, so it's a good idea to qualify a column containing a name. For example, use CustomerName, CompanyName, VendorName, or something similar. You should also avoid names that are the same as built-in functions, such as Date, Time, Now, or Space.

You will see that if you type a column name that doesn't meet the Rules for Identifiers criteria, the name appears in delimited brackets ([ ]). **Delimited** means that the object name does not meet the criteria of the Rules for Identifiers naming convention. Delimited object names must always be encased in brackets ([ ]) or double quotes (" "). When names are delimited, SQL Server can still recognize and use them, but it must spend extra processing time converting those delimited names to **limited** names that meet the criteria for the Rules for Identifiers naming convention. Also, whenever you refer to objects with delimited names in forms, queries, or other procedures, you must continue to enclose them in brackets or double quotes. As you can see, you will have an easier time building your database and it will run more efficiently if you name all your objects using the Rules for Identifiers.

Column Data Types

Before you define all the columns for the Companies table, you need to understand the data types available in SQL Server. Table 17-1 describes all the data types supported by the Access project table design facility. For the most part, the listed data types are similar to the ones supported by an Access desktop database (.mdb). A table stored in SQL Server provides a much wider selection of data types than does an Access desktop database (.mdb). This allows you to be more exact in the amount of space that each column must consume, and thus gives you the opportunity to save space and processing time for your database.

Table 17-1. SQL Server Data Types

Data Type	Length (Bytes)	Description	Equivalent Desktop Database Data Type
bigint	8	Fixed-point integer from -2^{63} to $+2^{63} - 1$	(None)
binary	Fixed, up to 8000	Fixed-length binary data	(None)
bit	1	True/false values. SQL Server can store up to eight columns of the bit data type in one byte.	Yes/No
char	Fixed length, up to 8000	Non-Unicode (single-byte character set) fixed-length character values	(None)

Table 17-1. **SQL Server Data Types**

Data Type	Length (Bytes)	Description	Equivalent Desktop Database Data Type
datetime	8	Date/time value from January 1, 1753, to December 31, 9999, precise to 0.03 seconds	Date/Time
decimal	5, 9, 13, or 17, depending on precision	An alias for numeric. Fixed-precision numeric data from -10^{38} to $+10^{38}$. Precision (the number of digits) can be up to 38, and Scale (the number of digits to the right of the decimal point) can be as large as the specified precision.	Number (Decimal)
float	8	Floating-precision numeric data from -1.79×10^{308} to $+1.79 \times 10^{308}$. Although you can define any precision from 1 to 53 bits in SQL Server, the table design facility in a project automatically sets precision to 53 (8 bytes) when you select float.	Number (Double)
image	16 plus length of the image	OLE Object data	OLE Object
int	4	Fixed-point integer from −2,147,483,648 to +2,147,483,647	Number (Long Integer)
money	8	Currency data from -2^{63} to $+2^{63} - 1$, with four decimal places	Currency
nchar	Fixed, up to 8000 (4000 characters)	Unicode (double-byte character set) fixed-length character values	(None)
ntext	16 plus length of the text (maximum 1 billion characters)	Varying length Unicode character values	Memo

Chapter 17

Table 17-1. SQL Server Data Types

Data Type	Length (Bytes)	Description	Equivalent Desktop Database Data Type
numeric	9	An alias for decimal. Fixed-precision numeric data from -10^{38} to $+10^{38}$. Precision (the number of digits) can be up to 38, and Scale (the number of digits to the right of the decimal point) can be as large as the specified precision.	Number (Decimal)
nvarchar	Varying, up to 8000 (4000 characters)	Varying length Unicode character values	Text
real	4	Floating-precision numeric data from -3.4×10^{38} to $+3.4 \times 10^{38}$. Although you can define any precision from 1 to 53 bits in SQL Server, the table design facility in a project automatically sets precision to 24 (4 bytes) when you select real.	Number (Single)
small-datetime	4	Date/time value from January 1, 1900, through June 6, 2079, precise to one minute	(None)
smallint	2	Fixed-point integer from $-32,768$ to $+32,767$	Number, Integer
smallmoney	4	Currency data from $-214,748.3648$ to $+214,748.3647$, with four decimal places	(None)
sql_variant	8016	Data type that can store values of different data types, except for text, ntext, image, and timestamp types. When you define a column using the sql_variant data type, each row in your table can have a different type of data in that column.	(None)

612

Table 17-1. **SQL Server Data Types**

Data Type	Length (Bytes)	Description	Equivalent Desktop Database Data Type
text	16 plus length of the text (maximum 2 billion characters)	Varying length non-Unicode character values	Memo
timestamp	8	Database-wide unique number that changes each time a row is updated. SQL Server uses timestamp values to identify when the data was last affected and in what order the rows were affected. You can define only one timestamp column per table, and you should not define an index for a timestamp column because the values are always changing.	(None)
tinyint	1	Fixed-point Integer from 0 to 255	Number, Byte
unique-identifier	16	Globally unique identifier (GUID). Declaring the uniqueidentifier data type is useful if the data in your table needs to be uniquely identified apart from all the other data in all the other tables in all the other databases that are networked with your database. You can specify only one column per table as the uniqueidentifier data type.	Number, GUID
varbinary	Varying, up to 8000	Varying length binary data	(None)
varchar	Varying, up to 8000	Varying length non-Unicode character values	Text

Chapter 17

> **Note** You can also create user-defined data types in Microsoft SQL Server 2000. For example, you might want to define a data type named StateProvince that is always two characters and must not be null. If you or your administrator have created user-defined data types in your database, Access displays them in the list of available data types in a table's Design view.

Inside Out

Understanding sql_variant

An sql_variant is a special data type that can store a variety of other data types. To do this, SQL Server stores an additional piece of information with the column called *metadata* (information that describes other data). Each row in an sql_variant column can store different data types except for text, ntext, timestamp, image, and another sql_variant. Because sql_variant can hold a variety of data types, it can also behave differently than you might expect when comparing and converting the values it contains. It will also take SQL Server longer to work with sql_variant data types because it has to interpret the metadata in each row to learn what type of data is stored there. If you know that the data in your column will always be the same type, you should use the specific data type declaration for that column instead of sql_variant.

Completing the Columns in the Companies Table

You now know enough about column data types to finish the basic design of the Companies table. Earlier, you entered CompanyID as the first column in the table. Now, select int as the data type—equivalent to a long integer in a desktop database—for this column. You can see that Access sets the length property for you. For some of the remaining columns that are character data types (including char, nchar, ntext, nvarchar, text, and varchar), you will be able to set the data length you want.

The property in the table's Design window, Allow Nulls, specifies whether Null values can be entered in this column. This is similar to the Required property in Access .mdb files, but works in the opposite fashion. By default, Allow Nulls is always selected (true). If you want to require data in this column, you should click the Allow Nulls property to remove the check mark. (If you are tabbing from one column to the next, you can also press the Spacebar to toggle the Allow Nulls property.) Because CompanyID needs to be a unique identifier with a value in every row, remove the check mark from Allow Nulls.

The Description property for each column allows you to enter a descriptive phrase. Access displays this description in the status bar (at the bottom of the Access window) whenever you select this column in a view query or a function query in Datasheet view or in a form in Form view or Datasheet view. For this example, enter **Unique Company ID** in the Description property for the CompanyID column. You don't need to worry about setting any of the custom properties on the Columns or Lookup tabs in the lower part of the window for now.

Tab down to the next line, enter **CompanyName** for the Column Name property, and then choose nvarchar as the data type. Enter **50** in the length property to restrict the length of data entered to no more than 50 characters. Every row should have a value in the CompanyName column, so clear Allow Nulls for this column. In Description, enter **Company Name**.

Use the information listed in Table 17-2 list to complete the design of the table shown in Figure 17-13.

Table 17-2. **Column Definitions for the Companies Table**

Column Name	Data Type	Length	Allow Nulls	Description
CompanyID	int	4	No	Unique Company ID
CompanyName	nvarchar	50	No	Company Name
Department	nvarchar	50	Yes	Department
Address	nvarchar	255	Yes	Address
City	nvarchar	50	Yes	City
County	nvarchar	50	Yes	County
StateOrProvince	nvarchar	20	Yes	State or Province
PostalCode	nvarchar	20	Yes	Postal/Zip Code
PhoneNumber	nvarchar	30	Yes	Phone Number
FaxNumber	nvarchar	30	Yes	Fax Number
Website	ntext	16	Yes	Web site address
ReferredBy	int	4	Yes	Contact who referred this company

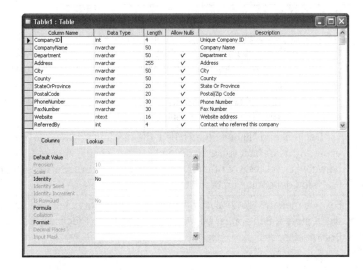

Figure 17-13. The column definitions for the Companies table.

When you are finished entering all the column definitions, click the Save button on the toolbar to save the table. Access displays the Choose Name dialog box as shown in Figure 17-14. Name the table **Companies** and click OK.

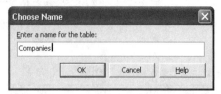

Figure 17-14. Entering a name for a new table in an Access project.

You haven't defined a primary key for this new Companies table, so Access displays a warning and asks you if you want to add a primary key now. You'll return to this table later to define the primary key, so click No to finish saving the table and then close the table definition window.

Understanding Column Properties

You can further define how your database will store and handle your data by specifying additional column properties. Table 17-3 displays a complete listing of the properties you might need when creating columns. Depending on which data type you select, certain properties become available in the lower half of the table's Design window to customize your column definition. All the properties are displayed, but only some of them are relevant depending on the data type you choose. (For example, it doesn't make much sense to specify the number of decimal places for the text nvarchar data type.) Unavailable properties appear dimmed.

Table 17-3. SQL Server Table Column Properties

Property	Description
Default Value	The default value entered in the column if no other value is entered. You can type in a default value directly or select from a drop-down list of global default values. SQL Server enters the Default Value property for a column when it saves the row, not when you first begin to enter data in the row. If you want to display a default value for data entry in a column, create a form and bind it to the table, and then set the default value of the control in the form.
Precision	For Decimal and Numeric data types, the maximum number of digits allowed. The default value is 18, and you can specify an integer value between 1 and 38. For other numeric data types, SQL Server sets the Precision depending on the data type.
Scale	For Decimal and Numeric data types, the maximum number of decimal digits stored. Scale must be less than or equal to Precision. See also Decimal Places.

Table 17-3. SQL Server Table Column Properties

Property	Description
Identity	For fixed-point data types (integer and decimal), this converts the column to a system-generated number that functions much like AutoNumber in Access desktop databases. An identity column cannot be null and cannot have a default value. In addition, you can specify the starting value (Seed) and Increment value for Identity. The default value is No. Set Identity to Yes to create an identity column or Yes (Not For Replication) to create an identity column that maintains its value when the data is replicated.
Identity Seed	The starting value for an identity column. The default value is 1.
Identity Increment	The amount that each value in the Identity is incremented for new rows. You can enter an integer between 1 and 2,147,483,647. The default value is 1.
Is RowGuid	If the data type of the column is uniqueidentifier, setting this to Yes tells SQL Server to use it as a globally unique identifier for replication. The default setting is No.
Formula	The formula for a computed column.
Collation	The collating (sorting) sequence that SQL Server applies by default to a text column when its values are returned as rows in the results of a query. Click in the property and then click the Build (...) button to open a dialog box to choose from other collation sequences available on your machine or on the server. The default is the collation sequence defined for your database.
Format	The display format for the column. For details about custom formats, see "Setting Control Properties," page 451.
Decimal Places	The number of decimal places *displayed*. (This is not the same as Scale, which controls the decimal places *stored*.) The default value is [Auto], which indicates that the number of decimal places displayed automatically adjusts depending on the precision of the number stored in the column. See also Scale.
Input Mask	An input mask that controls and formats how data is entered. For details about input masks, see "Defining Input Masks," page 114.
Caption	You can enter a fully descriptive column name that Access displays in form labels and in report headings. Because you should create column names with no embedded spaces, you can use the Caption property to specify a name that includes spaces for Access to use in labels and headers associated with this column in queries, forms, and reports.
Indexed	Identifies whether the column is indexed. The default is No. You can specify Yes (duplicates OK) to create a nonunique index or Yes (no duplicates) to create a unique index. See also "Adding Indexes" on page 619.
Hyperlink	The text column value can be displayed as a hyperlink. The default is No.

Chapter 17

Table 17-3. SQL Server Table Column Properties

Property	Description
IME Mode and IME Sentence Mode	On machines with an Asian version of Windows and an appropriate Input Method Editor (IME) installed, these properties control the conversion of characters in kanji, hiragana, katakana, and hangul character sets.
Furigana	You can specify an alternate column name for this property and SQL Server copies the Furigana (Japanese Text) equivalent of the typed text into the named column.
Postal Address	On a Japanese language system, this property allows you to specify a control or a column that displays an address based on an entered postal code. You can also use this feature to display a bar code based on an entered address.

The table design facility also lets you define Lookup properties for columns identical to those available in an Access desktop database. You can define Lookup properties for bigint, bit, char, decimal, float, int, nchar, ntext, numeric, nvarchar, real, smallint, text, tinyint, and varchar data types. You can specify a Display Control for each of the columns as a text box, list box, or combo box. For the bit data type, you can also specify a check box as the Display Control. This allows you to display related information instead of the actual data when you view a table, form, view, or function in Datasheet view. When you create new forms, the controls on the form bound to columns inherit the lookup from the table design. The same suggestions I made about lookups in Chapter 5 also apply here. For more information, see "Taking a look at Lookup Properties" on page 171.

Troubleshooting

I'm using SQL Server 7, so why can't I see all the column properties or create lookups?

This book assumes that you are working with SQL Server 2000 or later in these chapters on Access projects. It is possible to build projects in earlier versions of SQL Server, but not all the features discussed here are supported, including many column properties and the ability to specify lookups at the table level.

Defining a Primary Key

As you learned in Chapter 3, it is important to define a primary key to uniquely identify each row in a table. Doing so allows you to define relationships with other tables and reduces redundant data. Also, you cannot update a table that does not have a primary key. Defining a primary key for a table in an Access project is very similar to defining a primary key in an Access desktop database (.mdb).

Remember, you didn't define a primary key for the Companies table. Open that table again in Design view. To define a primary key, select the column that you want to make into a primary key—in this case, the CompanyID column. Then click the Primary Key button on the Table Design toolbar or choose the Primary Key command from the Edit menu. Access automatically creates a UNIQUE index on the selected column and creates a primary key named *PK_Companies*. Access displays a key symbol to the left of the selected column to acknowledge your definition of the primary key, as shown in Figure 17-15. Be sure to save your changes. Note that when you need to define multiple columns as the primary key, you can select a group of columns by holding down Ctrl and clicking on each one.

Figure 17-15.   Defining the primary key for the Companies table.

Because an index is created when you define the primary key, you also have the ability to modify the properties of the primary key as an index. To modify the primary key, you need to access the Indexes/Keys tab of the table properties by right clicking on any column in Design view and selecting Indexes/Keys from the shortcut menu, or by clicking the Properties button on the toolbar and then choosing the Indexes/Keys tab. To learn more about modifying the index properties of the primary key, see the next section.

Adding Indexes

Creating indexes in a table allows for faster access to the information in the table when it is being queried, much the same way that you use the index in this book—you find the term you want and jump directly to the pages containing that term. You don't have to leaf through all the pages to find the information you are looking for.

Similar to an Access desktop database, SQL Server implements the primary key by creating an index on it. As noted earlier, you must define a primary key to be able to update an SQL Server table from your Access project. You must also define primary keys for your tables to be able to create relationships between tables.

Chapter 17

619

However, you might often use criteria on other columns in a table to select data using a query (view, function, or stored procedure), and you can increase the efficiency of these queries by adding one or more additional indexes to those columns. Access projects support two basic types of indexes: clustered and nonclustered. When you define a clustered index on a table, SQL Server physically sequences the rows in the table based on the values in the index. This, in effect, becomes the default ordering for rows that you fetch from the table. As you can imagine, you can create only one clustered index on a table. If a clustered index doesn't already exist, SQL Server makes the primary key a clustered index when you define it. You can define up to 249 nonclustered indexes to help make fetching your data using criteria faster.

> **Tip**   Indexes don't always speed up the performance of your database. They occupy extra disk space and can also slow down INSERT, UPDATE, and DELETE actions on the table because the index has to be updated each time such an action occurs. A good rule of thumb is to create indexes only on columns in the table that you know you will use often in criteria.

Assume that your users will often query the Companies table using criteria on the City column. To speed up this search, let's create an index on the City column. Open the Companies table in Design view and then open the Properties window on the Indexes/Keys tab by right-clicking on any column in Design view and selecting Indexes/Keys on the shortcut menu. This opens the Properties window and selects the Indexes/Keys tab as shown in Figure 17-16.

Figure 17-16.   Viewing the Indexes/Keys tab of the table's Properties window.

The Indexes/Keys tab always shows you the first index created on the table—usually the primary key. If there were more than one index on this table, you could view each of them by selecting them from the drop-down list labeled Selected index. Right now, the only index on the Companies table is the primary key. To begin defining a new index, click the New button. By default, Access starts a new index called IX_Companies on the first column of the table (the CompanyID column in this case).

To create the index on the City column, start by typing in a more descriptive name for the index in the Index name field. Click in the name field and change the name to IX_Companies_City by adding _**City** to the end of the index name. When you look up the index in the future, it will be easier to identify what it is for.

Below the Index name field is a box with two headings labeled Column name and Order. Here you specify which columns you want to be a part of the index and the order in which each column should be sorted. You can include up to 16 columns in an index. You can specify Ascending or Descending order for each column in the index. If the index contains multiple columns, each column will be sorted in the order it was added to the index. Right now, CompanyID is the only member of the index. Click on the CompanyID name to display a drop-down list and replace CompanyID by selecting City from the list. Leave the sort order as Ascending. Because the City column is the only member of this index, you don't need to specify any other columns under Column name.

The Index Filegroup is the filegroup in which SQL Server saves the index information. SQL Server manages indexes using filegroups, and by default, stores them in the PRIMARY filegroup. If a large quantity of indexes needs to be defined in the database, you or an administrator might decide to create additional filegroups to better organize your indexes. If additional filegroups are available, you will be able to select them from the drop-down list. For the ContactTracking database, the PRIMARY filegroup should be sufficient for storing all your indexes.

If you place a check mark in the Create UNIQUE check box, each value entered in the index or key must be unique. You then have the option to specify whether you are creating a unique index or a unique constraint. If you select Constraint, SQL Server creates an index along with a constraint that checks to make sure the value is unique before adding or updating a row in the table. The benefit of the constraint is that you can supply validation text that is more descriptive than the generic message SQL Server generates for the unique index. However, creating a unique index offers some extra features not available when creating a unique constraint. For example, because a unique index is a physical index, SQL Server sorts the key values in the order specified with the column name, which might enhance the performance of some queries. A unique index also allows you to choose the Ignore duplicate key option. If you select Ignore duplicate key, during a transaction to update or add rows, SQL Server discards any rows that would create duplicates. Because it is possible for the City column to contain duplicate values, you do not want to create a unique index on the City column. For this index, leave the Create UNIQUE check box blank.

Caution When you choose the Ignore duplicate key option for a unique index, an Update operation that would create a duplicate value will instead delete the row to be updated. This happens because an Update operation is actually a Delete of the affected rows followed by an Insert of the changed rows. The Delete will succeed, but the Insert will be discarded because it is a duplicate.

The Fill factor and Pad Index options allow you to specify additional information to fine-tune the index performance in the database. The Fill factor percent indicates what percent of each index page the database should leave empty when building and updating the index. If

Chapter 17

space is left on each index page, it is possible for SQL Server to add new entries to the middle of the index when data is inserted without having to build new pages for the index. Specifying a Fill factor greater than the default 0% (no room left on each page) is useful only for tables with large indexes that are updated often. If you specify a Fill factor greater than 0%, then you also have the option to check the Pad Index box. Pad Index uses the Fill factor percent to pad the interior of each index node—each node (group of index pages with similar key values) in the index will have additional space to grow. Like Fill factor, Pad Index is useful only for tables with large indexes that are updated often. The index on the City column does not need to take advantage of Fill factor or Pad Index, so leave Fill factor at the default of 0%.

Selecting the Create as CLUSTERED box creates the index as a clustered index. Remember, only one index per table can be created as a clustered index because a clustered index dictates the physical order of the rows in the table. The primary key (CompanyID) is already defined as clustered, so leave the Create as CLUSTERED check box blank.

The next option is Do not automatically recompute statistics. To enhance performance, SQL Server creates and maintains statistics on the distribution of data values in your tables. If you select this option, and the server already has computed statistics for this index on the table, the existing statistics will be reused instead of being re-created. Using this option might speed the creation of an index on a very large table, but the statistics might not be as accurate because of the changes in the index. As a result, the index might not be as efficient as it could be. Because this is the first time you have created an index on the City column, no existing statistics are available to be recomputed. Selecting this option won't do anything, so leave it blank.

If you create a unique constraint, it is important to enter a descriptive message in the Validation Text box. If the validation of the unique constraint fails, then the message in the Validation Text box will be displayed instead of the cryptic message that SQL Server displays by default. Be sure to state the names of the columns in the index. For example, instead of entering a message such as **Duplicate value in Companies table**, be more specific by entering **A duplicate value for City was entered in the Companies table**. This lets users know how to correct the data input. The City index is not a unique constraint, so you do not need to enter any validation text.

When you have completed the index on the City column, the information on the Indexes/Keys tab should look like Figure 17-17. You can close the Properties window or click New to add more indexes. If you create an index by mistake, select it from the Selected index drop-down list and click the Delete button to remove it. Be sure to save the table so that the index will be created on the table.

> **Tip**   You can also create single column indexes by selecting Yes (duplicates OK) or Yes (no duplicates) on the Indexed property in the table's Design view. Selecting Yes (duplicates OK) will create an index similar to the one you just created. Selecting Yes (no duplicates) will create a unique constraint index on that column. Be careful, though: If you set the Indexed property to No, SQL Server deletes any associated single column indexes on that column.

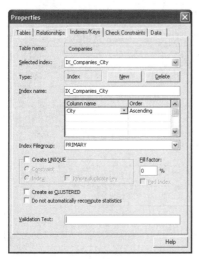

Figure 17-17.   Creating the IX_Companies_City index.

Creating Additional Tables in Contact Tracking

So far, we've discussed how to build the Companies table in an Access project. Before you can define constraints and relationships, you'll need to build several more tables. Let's start by building the Contacts table and the CompanyContacts table. Table 17-4 shows you the columns you need for the Contacts table.

Table 17-4. Column Definitions for the Contacts Table

Column Name	Data Type	Length	Allow Nulls	Description
ContactID	int	4	No	Unique contact ID
LastName	nvarchar	50	No	Last name
FirstName	nvarchar	50	Yes	First name
MiddleInit	nvarchar	1	Yes	Middle initial
Title	nvarchar	10	Yes	Person title
Suffix	nvarchar	10	Yes	Person suffix (Jr., Sr., II, etc.)
ContactType	nvarchar	50	Yes	Description of the contact type
BirthDate	datetime	8	Yes	Birth date
DefaultAddress	smallint	2	Yes	Specify Work or Home as the default address
WorkAddress	nvarchar	255	Yes	Address
WorkCity	nvarchar	50	Yes	City

Chapter 17

623

Table 17-4. Column Definitions for the Contacts Table

Column Name	Data Type	Length	Allow Nulls	Description
WorkStateOrProvince	nvarchar	20	Yes	State or Province
WorkPostalCode	nvarchar	20	Yes	Postal/Zip code
WorkCountry	nvarchar	50	Yes	Country
WorkPhone	nvarchar	30	Yes	Work phone
WorkExtension	nvarchar	20	Yes	Phone extension
WorkFaxNumber	nvarchar	30	Yes	Fax number
HomeAddress	nvarchar	255	Yes	Address
HomeCity	nvarchar	50	Yes	City
HomeStateOrProvince	nvarchar	20	Yes	State or Province
HomePostalCode	nvarchar	20	Yes	Postal/Zip code
HomeCountry	nvarchar	50	Yes	Country
HomePhone	nvarchar	30	Yes	Home phone
MobilePhone	nvarchar	30	Yes	Mobile phone
EmailName	ntext	16	Yes	E-mail name
Website	ntext	16	Yes	Web site address
Photo	image	16	Yes	Photo of contact
SpouseName	nvarchar	75	Yes	Spouse name
SpouseBirthDate	datetime	8	Yes	Spouse birth date
Notes	ntext	16	Yes	Notes
CommissionPercent	float	8	Yes	Commission when referencing a sale
Inactive	bit	1	No	Contact is inactive

Define ContactID as your primary key for this table by clicking the ContactID column name and then clicking the Primary Key button on the toolbar to define the key. Save the table and name it Contacts.

Next you need to build the linking table that will act as the "glue" between the Companies table and the Contacts table—CompanyContacts. Table 17-5 shows the columns you need to define to create the CompanyContacts table.

Table 17-5. Column Definitions for the Company Contacts Table

Column Name	Data Type	Length	Allow Nulls	Description
CompanyID	int	4	No	Company/Organization
ContactID	int	4	No	Person within Company

Table 17-5. Column Definitions for the Company Contacts Table

Column Name	Data Type	Length	Allow Nulls	Description
Position	nvarchar	50	Yes	Person's position within the Company
DefaultFor-Contact	bit	1	No	Is this the default Company for this Contact?
DefaultFor-Company	bit	1	No	Is this the default Contact for this Company?

Define the combination of CompanyID and ContactID as the primary key for this table by clicking the selection button next to CompanyID and then holding down the Ctrl key and clicking the button next to ContactID. Click the Primary Key button on the toolbar to define the key and save the table as CompanyContacts. Now that we have three different tables created in the project, let's learn how to define some constraints that will control how users can enter data into them.

Defining Check Constraints

Constraints are a way of limiting the values that can be entered in a column or group of columns. Constraints are handy because you can use them to enforce data consistency from your users and ensure the relational integrity of your database. You might already be familiar with some of these constraints. Access projects use a group of constraints to create elements in the table design interface that are familiar to Access desktop database (.mdb) users. These elements include the ability to specify a default value in a column, declaring primary and foreign keys, and creating a table index as a unique index.

Access projects also include the ability to create additional custom constraints called **check constraints** for the columns you create in your tables. Check constraints are similar to Access desktop database table and field validation rules. You can define constraints to ask the database to check the values of a column (or a group of columns) before the database saves a row to make sure they meet the criteria you specified. Check constraints differ from validation rules because they are applied to the whole row when the row is added or updated. If you enter a value that fails a check constraint criterion, you won't see the validation message until you try to save the row. SQL Server evaluates check constraints in the order that you created them on the table. Let's take a look at how to create a check constraint.

Open the Contacts table in Design view, and then right-click any column to display the shortcut menu and select Constraints. This opens the Properties window with the Check Constraints tab selected. Because you haven't created any check constraints yet, the options in the window will be dimmed and empty. To begin creating a new check constraint, click the New button. This starts a definition for a new check constraint as shown in Figure 17-18 on the next page.

The Constraint name is the name of the current constraint. By default, Access has created a constraint named CK_Contacts. This isn't a very descriptive name for the constraint. Unfortunately, you cannot rename the constraint until you enter a valid expression in the Constraint expression box, so start by typing in a valid expression.

625

Chapter 17

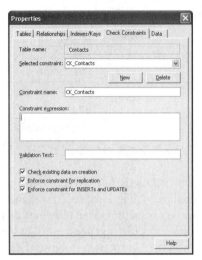

Figure 17-18. Creating a new check constraint on the Contacts table.

A constraint expression can be any valid SQL expression that evaluates to true or false. One of the rules you need to enforce for the Contacts table is that no contact can have a commission percent greater than 90%. To define this rule, you must enter an expression in the Constraint expression box that evaluates to false if anyone enters a commission percent greater than 90% for a contact. To create the commission percent expression, type the following in the Constraint expression box: **CommissionPercent <= 0.9.**

When you attempt to save a value in CommissionPercent and this expression evaluates to false (you entered a commission percent greater than 90%), Access displays the validation message, and the row will not be saved. You can use many other types of expressions to validate the data that is being added or updated. For now, let's finish creating the commission percent check constraint and make sure it works.

Now that you have a valid expression in the Constraint expression box, you can change the name of the check constraint to something more meaningful. Click in the Constraint name field and enter **CK_Contacts_CommissionPercent** as the constraint name. This is a useful name because when you look at objects in the database, CK tells you that this object is a check constraint, Contacts tells you that it is applied to the Contacts table, and CommissionPercent tells you which column is being validated.

> **Note** You might notice that if you try to move the focus out of the Constraint expression box while it contains a partially complete or incorrect expression, Access immediately generates an error stating that the expression could not be validated. You can click Yes to keep working on the expression or you can click No to move the focus away from the Constraint expression box. If the Constraint expression box is blank, Access offers you the option to delete the constraint. In this case, click No to continue working on the constraint. Be careful: Access cannot save the constraint unless the expression is valid.

Because all check constraints are evaluated only when the entire row is updated, it is important to make sure that the validation text is descriptive enough to tell the user where the problem is so that it can be fixed. In the Validation Text box, type **You cannot specify a commission greater than 90%**. This will alert the user that the commission percent value is too great if the validation of the constraint fails.

If you want to make sure that all existing contacts meet the commission percent constraint, leave the Check existing data on creation option selected. When you select this option, SQL Server will not save the constraint if any existing rows fail. The Enforce constraint for replication option allows you to apply the constraint to any copies of the database that you distribute for replication. This option is useful if you ever plan to replicate your database. For now, you can leave this option blank. In order for the constraint to be applied whenever data is inserted or updated, you must leave the Enforce constraint for INSERTs and UPDATEs option selected. When you are done creating the commission percent check constraint, it should look like Figure 17-19. If you need to add additional check constraints, click the New button. You can also delete a check constraint by choosing it from the Selected constraint drop-down list and then clicking the Delete button.

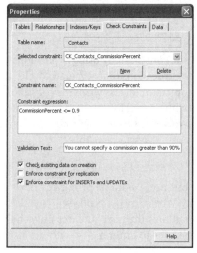

Figure 17-19. Completing the commission percent check constraint on the Contacts table.

When you are finished creating check constraints, close the Properties window and save the table. When you save the table, the check constraints are saved as well. Now open the table in Datasheet view and see if the check constraint is working correctly. Tab to the Commission-Percent column in an existing row and try entering a commission percent of 100%. Press the Down Arrow key to move to a different record, and you should see the error message in Figure 17-20 on the next page.

Chapter 17

627

Figure 17-20. The message that is displayed when validation fails on the check constraint for commission percent.

Creating Additional Constraint Expressions

Now that you know how to create a check constraint, let's take a look at some other types of expressions that you can use to validate your data.

- The IN keyword allows you to specify a list of values that the data must match. For example, if you want to make sure the suffix values in the Contacts table are limited to Jr., Sr., PhD., or II, use an expression like this:

  ```
  [Suffix] IN ('Jr.', 'Sr.', 'PhD.', or 'II')
  ```

- You can use the LIKE keyword to specify the formatting of data. If you want to make sure the WorkPostalCode column in Contacts is five numeric digits, use an expression like this:

  ```
  [WorkPostalCode] LIKE '[0-9][0-9][0-9][0-9][0-9]'
  ```

- You can also check multiple columns in one constraint by using expressions joined with the AND and OR operators. All constraint expressions must evaluate to TRUE or the database won't save the row. If you want the constraint to pass when the constraint expression evaluates to FALSE, prefix the expression with the NOT operator. For example, in the Contacts table, if you want to make sure that WorkStateOrProvince information is always supplied whenever WorkCity is supplied, use an expression like this:

  ```
  (NOT ([WorkStateOrProvince] Is Null)) OR ([WorkCity] Is Null)
  ```

When the user supplies a city (Springfield) but not a state or province (IL or MA), both NOT ([WorkStateOrProvince] Is Null) and ([WorkCity] Is Null) will be false, and the constraint will fail. Note that this constraint allows the user to enter only the state or province without a city, but doesn't allow the user to enter a city without also specifying a state or province.

> **Tip** Although you can join multiple constraint expressions together with AND and OR operators, it is generally a good idea to keep the expressions separate unless one column value relies on another column value for validation. Use parentheses around multiple comparison expressions and Boolean operators to ensure that your expression evaluates as you expect.

Another good use of check constraints is to purposefully take advantage of the ability to provide validation text. The current design of the Companies table requires the input of a company name in every row by setting the Allow Nulls property for CompanyName to False (no check mark). When you enter a row without a company name, you get a message from SQL Server similar to the one shown in Figure 17-21.

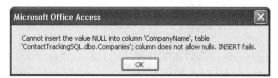

Figure 17-21. The message SQL Server returns when validation for the Allow Nulls property fails.

Instead of using the Allow Nulls property to require data entry, you could create a check constraint that uses an expression like this:

```
Not [CompanyName] Is Null
```

Then you can include the validation text: **You must supply a Company / Organization name.** Now your users see a much easier to understand message when they forget to enter a company name, and you will still be requiring an entry in the CompanyName column for every row added.

> **Note** If you decide to use a check constraint to require data entry in certain columns, be sure to set the Allow Nulls property for those columns to True. SQL Server always checks the Allow Nulls setting first. If that fails, SQL Server never checks any constraints. So, if a user attempts to save a row that incorrectly contains a Null, the user sees the cryptic SQL Server message instead of the one you specified. However, you cannot use this technique for a primary key column because SQL Server requires that all columns in a primary key must not have the Allow Nulls property unchecked.

Defining Relationships

Now that you have learned how to build tables in an Access project, you can start defining relationships between them. As you learned in Chapters 3 and 4, defining relationships is valuable because it enforces referential integrity between the tables. It also makes building queries and forms on those tables easier. The same is true in an Access project linked to SQL Server.

Defining Relationships in Table Design View

After you've built the tables, you're ready to start defining relationships. In an Access project, you can define a relationship in Design view. All you need are two tables—one that has a primary key and another that contains a related foreign key. Open the CompanyContacts table in Design view, right-click on any column, and select Relationships. This opens the Properties window with the Relationships tab selected. Because you haven't created any relationships yet, options in the window will be dimmed and empty. To create a new relationship, click the New button and a new relationship will be displayed as shown in Figure 17-22 on the next page.

Relationship name displays the name of the relationship that you are currently editing. By default, Access has named the new relationship FK_CompanyContacts_Companies. Fortunately, this is a good name for the relationship you are about to create. FK identifies this as a foreign key constraint (or relationship). The two table names identify the members of the relationship. The infinity symbol preceding the name in the Selected relationship box indicates that you are editing or creating this relationship from the table on the many side of the relationship. If you had opened the Contacts table first before beginning to define this relationship, the relationship design window would show you a primary key symbol instead. Because you are actually defining a constraint on the table on the many side of the relationship, that table name appears first in the name.

Figure 17-22. Creating a new relationship in the CompanyContacts table.

Underneath Relationship name are two drop-down lists that allow you to specify which tables are members of the relationship. By default, Access will specify the current table as the Foreign key table and the first table listed alphabetically in the table list as the Primary key table. Because you have only created three tables so far, the Companies table will be listed as the Primary key table. These are the two tables you want to use in the relationship, so you don't have to change the selected tables. If you have already created some other tables in your project, then the Companies table might not be listed as the Primary key table. If it isn't, simply select it from the drop-down list.

Below the table listings are two drop-down lists that you can use to specify which columns will be members of this relationship. You want to create a one-to-many relationship between Companies and CompanyContacts. The column that they share in the relationship is the CompanyID column. To create the relationship, select CompanyID from the first drop-down list under both the Primary key table and the Foreign key table.

After you have selected the columns you want for this relationship, you need to specify a few more options before you save the table and this new relationship. When you select Check existing data on creation, SQL Server will examine the data in the existing tables and make sure that none of it violates the constraints of the relationship. If SQL Server finds any problems, it displays an error when you try to save the table, and the save operation will fail. Choosing this option is a good idea for any relationship you create, because it ensures that no integrity problems exist with the current data in the tables. If you already have any data in your tables, make sure you select the Check existing data on creation option.

Selecting Enforce relationship for replication makes sure that the foreign key constraint (the relationship) is copied to any replicated databases. For now, you can leave the Enforce relationship for replication option unselected.

The next option, Enforce relationship for INSERTs and UPDATEs, allows you to enforce referential integrity for this relationship, ensuring that any added or updated data does not violate the constraint of the relationship. If you select Enforce relationship for INSERTs and UPDATEs, you also have the option of choosing Cascade Update Related Fields and/or Cascade Delete Related Records. These two options allow you to control what happens to data in related rows when data in the table containing the primary key changes. If you choose Cascade Update Related Fields, whenever data in the primary key columns is updated, any related data in the foreign key of the related table is also updated. If you choose Cascade Delete Related Records, whenever a row in the table containing the primary key is deleted, all related rows in the table containing the foreign key are also deleted. You should carefully consider selecting Cascade Delete Related Records because choosing this option will always delete foreign rows when you delete any rows in your primary key table. For this relationship, make sure that you leave Enforce relationship for INSERTs and UPDATEs selected. Also, place a check mark in Cascade Update Related Fields so that any changes to the primary key will be propagated to the related tables. Leave the option for Cascade Delete Related records blank.

When you are done creating the relationship between the Company table and the Company Contacts table, your Properties window should look like the one shown in Figure 17-23 on the next page. If you need to add additional relationships, click the New button. You can also delete a relationship by choosing it from the Selected relationship drop-down list and then clicking the Delete button. Be sure to save your table to save the changes you made to relationships.

Figure 17-23. A relationship defined between the Companies table and the CompanyContacts table.

Chapter 17

Defining Relationships Using Database Diagrams

Database diagrams are similar to the Relationships window in an Access desktop database (.mdb), but diagrams are more versatile. You can create multiple database diagrams to organize your table relationships into different visual groups. You can also edit any portion of your table(s) directly from the Diagram window.

To demonstrate how database diagrams work, let's create a new one and use it to define the relationship between the CompanyContacts table and the Contacts table. To create a new database diagram, make sure the Database window is active and click Database Diagrams on the Object bar. Then double-click on **Create database diagram in designer** to open a new diagram in Design view. (You can also select Diagram from the Insert menu.) Access opens a blank Diagram window and displays the Add Table dialog box as shown in Figure 17-24.

Figure 17-24. Adding tables to the Diagram window.

To add a table to the Diagram window, select it from the list and then click Add (or double-click on the table name). Add Companies, CompanyContacts, and Contacts to the Diagram window. When you are finished, click the Close button.

Because you have already defined the relationship between the Companies table and the CompanyContacts table, you'll see the relationship represented in the Diagram window as a line drawn from one table to the other, as shown in Figure 17-25. Note that you might need to click the header of each table and drag it within the Diagram window to position the tables as shown. The key represents the one side (or primary key side) and the infinity symbol represents the many side (or foreign key side). A one-to-one relationship would be represented with keys on each end of the line.

You can right-click on any of the tables shown in the Diagram window to see a list of options that you can use to control how the table is displayed or to edit its properties. For example, you can select Column Properties, Column Names (the default), Keys (show only columns that are keys), Name Only (just the table names), or Custom View. You should already be familiar with what many of these options do because they have the same functionality as the options you saw in a table's Design view. If you want to add any more tables, right-click on the diagram and select Add Table. You can remove tables from the diagram by right-clicking on the table header and selecting Hide Table. (Hiding the table does not delete it.)

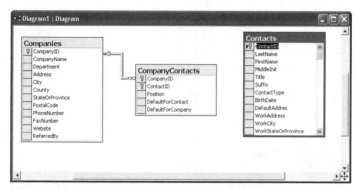

Figure 17-25.   The Diagram window after adding three tables.

If you open a table's properties (by selecting Properties from the shortcut menu or by double-clicking on any of the table headers), you will notice the addition of the Tables, Columns, and Lookup tabs. You can select the table you want to edit on the Tables tab and set certain table properties. After you select a table, you can choose a column to edit on the Columns tab. The options you see on the Lookup tab are the same as on the Lookup tab you see in the bottom half of a table's Design view. By using these tabs and manipulating how much of the table is displayed in the diagram, you can easily design or redesign any part of your tables directly from the Diagram window.

Now let's define the relationship between CompanyContacts and Contacts. In the Diagram window, you can do this simply by dragging the primary key from one table and dropping it into another. To do this, click on the selector for the ContactID column name in Contacts and drag and drop the column onto the CompanyContacts table. When you release the mouse button, Access displays the dialog box shown in Figure 17-26 on the next page, so that you can define the relationship.

This window is very similar to what you see on the Relationships tab of a table's properties. Relationship name displays the default name for this relationship. If you want, you can type in a different name. If the keys in each table share the same name, Access automatically picks them out for you. Otherwise, you can choose the primary and foreign keys from the drop-down lists under each table name. You can also specify the relationship criteria as described earlier. For this relationship, make sure that the ContactID column is the only column specified for both tables. Leave check marks in Check existing data on creation and Enforce relationship for INSERTs and UPDATEs. Also place a check mark in Cascade Update Related Fields. Make sure all other options are left blank. When you are done, click the OK button to create the relationship. The Diagram window will now show the relationship between the CompanyContacts table and the Contacts table as shown in Figure 17-27. Note that the asterisk on Contacts and CompanyContacts indicates that an update is pending for both tables.

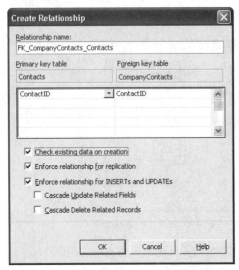

Figure 17-26. Using the Create Relationship dialog box to define a relationship from the Diagram window.

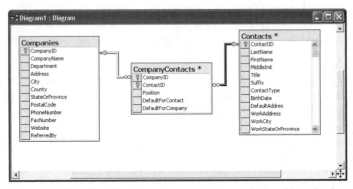

Figure 17-27. The Diagram window with two relationships displayed.

You have now created two relationships that represent the many-to-many relationship between the Companies table and the Contacts table. The relationships you create in a Diagram window won't be saved until you save the diagram itself. When you close the Diagram window or click the Save button on the toolbar, Access prompts you to provide a name for the diagram. (If you close the Diagram window without first saving your changes, Access asks you if you want to save the diagram.) Go ahead and name this diagram **dgmContactTracking**. Access also prompts you to save the pending changes to the two tables. Click Yes to save the new relationship.

Setting Table Design Options

Now that you understand the basic mechanics of defining tables and relationships in your Access project, let's take a look at several options that allow you to customize how you design your tables. To view the database options, choose Options from the Tools menu.

You can find the first options that affect table design on the General tab, as shown in Figure 17-28. As I mentioned in Chapter 4, I highly recommend that you select All databases under Use four-digit year formatting. When you select this option, Access displays all year values in date/time formats with four digits instead of two. This is important because when you see a value in two-digit date format, such as 15 MAR 12, you won't be able to easily tell whether this is March 15, 1912, or March 15, 2012. Although you can affect the display of some formats in your Windows Regional Settings in Control Panel, you won't affect them all unless you set four-digit formatting in Access.

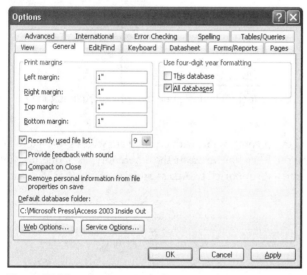

Figure 17-28. Settings that affect table design on the General tab of the Options dialog box.

Under **Use four-digit year formatting**, you have two options. If you choose **This database**, the setting creates a property in the database you currently have open and affects only that database. If you choose **All databases**, the setting creates an entry in your Windows registry that affects all databases that you open on your machine. I recommend that you choose the **All databases** setting.

The next tab that contains useful settings that affect table design is the Tables/Queries tab. Click that tab to see the settings shown in Figure 17-29 on the next page.

In the upper left corner of this tab, you can set the default field sizes for text fields. When you choose a data type that supports text (char, nchar, varchar, nvarchar), Access automatically fills in the length you choose. Under Default field type in the upper right corner, you can

Chapter 17

choose the field type that Access selects when you type in a new column name in a table's Design view and then tab to the Data Type column.

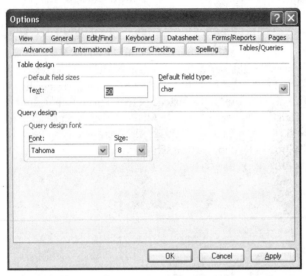

Figure 17-29. Settings that affect table design on the Tables/Queries tab of the Options dialog box.

Now that you've started to get comfortable with creating an Access project and tables, you can read the next chapter to learn how to create the different types of queries (functions, stored procedures, and views) supported by Access projects.

Building Queries in an Access Project

As you already know from Chapters 7, 8, and 9, you can quickly build nearly all the queries that you need in an Access desktop database (.mdb) using the query designer. The query designer in an Access project file (.adp) offers an interface that is similar to the one you use in an Access desktop database (.mdb). So, with only a small learning curve, you can soon be building queries in your Access projects.

Remember that your Access project file doesn't store your data or your queries. You must connect your project to the Microsoft SQL Server Data Engine (MSDE) or Microsoft SQL Server, and it's the server that contains your data and queries. SQL Server offers query capabilities that go far beyond the already robust features of an Access desktop database (.mdb). SQL Server offers several different types of queries that allow you to tap into the power potential of SQL Server. You can build many of the queries you need for your application using the query designer. However, to use the full potential of SQL Server, you'll need to learn its programming language, Transact-SQL, and build queries in the text editor. Transact-SQL not only includes SQL statements that are compliant with the ANSI SQL-92 intermediate standard but also offers extended capabilities that make it more like a programming language wrapped around the existing query language.

Note   You can find a reference guide to the SQL supported by Microsoft Access and Microsoft SQL Server in Article 1, "Understanding SQL," on the companion CD. To obtain a complete reference to Transact-SQL, download a free copy of the *Microsoft SQL Server 2000 Books Online* (a set of help files) from *http://www.microsoft.com/sql/techinfo/productdoc/2000/books.asp*.

When you open a project file that is properly connected to an SQL Server or MSDE database, you can view the queries in the database by clicking the Queries button on the Object bar, as shown in Figure 18-1 on the next page. Although the queries appear to be stored directly in your project file, they're actually in the database.

Note   To follow along with the examples in this chapter, you can open the *Contacts.adp* sample project file, or you can create a new project file and connect it to the *ContactsSQL.mdf* sample database. You can find both files on your companion CD. See Chapter 17, "Building Tables in an Access Project," for details about how to create a new project file and connect it to an existing database.

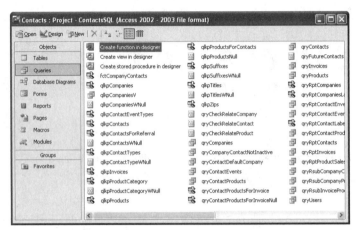

Figure 18-1.   The queries in the *ContactsSQL.mdf* sample database as seen from the *Contacts.adp* sample project file.

Inside Out

Additional steps you must take to be able to work with the sample project file

To be able to use the LawTrack Contacts sample project file (Contacts.adp) and its associated SQL Server database (*ContactsSQL.mdf*), you must first either install the Microsoft SQL Server Data Engine (MSDE) or have permission to create databases on a Microsoft Access SQL Server version 2000 on your network. You can install MSDE from your Microsoft Office 2003 installation disks—see the Appendix, "Installing Microsoft Office," for details.

The simplest method is to install and start MSDE on your computer. When you first open the *Contacts.adp* sample project file, Visual Basic code executes and attempts to connect to your local server and find the ContactsSQL database used by the project. If it can't find the database on your local server, the code gives you the option to open the Data Link Properties dialog box to connect the database files to your server from the default sample file installation location. See the topic "Connecting to an Existing SQL Server Database" on page 603 for details. If you have installed the sample files in a different location or have moved the sample database files, this method might not work reliably.

Another method is to use the sample command files provided on the companion CD to connect the database to your local server before you open the sample project for the first time. You'll find four small files in the \Microsoft Press\Access 2003 Inside Out\SQL folder to help you attach the sample database files to and detach the sample database files from your local server. Two of the files are .bat batch files that you can run by double-clicking them in Windows Explorer or by typing them at a command prompt. The *Attach Contacts.bat* file connects the *ContactsSQL.mdf* and *ContactsSQL.ldf* files to your server, and the *Detach Contacts.bat* file disconnects them (a good precaution to follow before moving or updating the database files from outside Access). But you might have to do a little preparatory work before you use either of these files.

If you view the *Attach Contacts.bat* file, you'll see it contains only two lines:

```
OSQL -E -i "C:\Microsoft Press\Access 2003 Inside Out\SQL\Attach Contacts.SQL"
Pause
```

The batch file invokes OSQL, a command-line program that lets you run SQL commands, which then calls an SQL script file, *Attach Contacts.SQL*. The second line pauses the execution so that you can see any return messages from the server. The SQL script also consists of only one line, this time an SQL command:

```
sp_attach_db "ContactsSQL", "C:\Microsoft Press\Access 2003 Inside Out
\SQL\ContactsSQL.mdf", "C:\Microsoft Press\Access 2003 Inside Out\SQL
\Contacts SQL.ldf"
```

The Detach Contacts.bat file also runs the OSQL program, but it points to the Detach Contacts.SQL file that contains an sp_detach_db command.

In order to work correctly as written, all four files must be located in your Access 2003 Inside Out\SQL folder (installed under C:\Microsoft Press), and your database files must be located in the same subfolder and be named *ContactsSQL.mdf* and *ContactsSQL.ldf*. You can easily adapt these files, however, by opening each file in a plain text editor such as Notepad and carefully adjusting the database names and/or paths as necessary. After adjusting the files as necessary, run the *Attach Contacts.bat* file by locating it in Windows Explorer and double-clicking it. You should now be able to open the *Contacts.adp* sample project file with no problems.

View

In an Access project file, you can work with three different types of objects in SQL Server as queries. A **view** most closely resembles select queries that you can create in an Access desktop database—a logical table that returns one or more columns from one or more tables. The major differences between a view in an Access project (.adp) and a select statement in an Access desktop database (.mdb) are that views cannot accept parameters, and you can include a sorting specification (ORDER BY) only when you also include the TOP keyword in the SELECT clause.

Function

A *function* can return a table (an *in-line function*), a set of columns from multiple tables (a *table-valued function*), or a single calculated value (a *scalar function*). You can call functions from other functions, from views, or from stored procedures (described next). You can use an in-line function as the record source for a form or report or the row source for a combo box or a list box, but not as the record source for a data access page. The one major restriction in a function is it cannot call any non-deterministic function—a function that subsequently returns a different value even when passed the same set of parameters. For example, the GETDATE built-in function is non-deterministic because it always returns a different value depending on the setting of your system clock. Of course, a function can accept parameters.

Stored Procedure

A *stored procedure* is arguably the most powerful programming object that you can create in SQL Server. With a stored procedure, you can define the equivalent of a desktop select query, a select query with parameters, or an action (UPDATE, INSERT, DELETE, or SELECT INTO)

Chapter 18

639

query. You can also use the full capabilities of the Transact-SQL language to define complex sets of actions to perform when your code executes the stored procedure. When a stored procedure returns a logical table, you can use it as the record source in a form or report or the row source in a combo box or list box. If the stored procedure returns a logical table as the result of executing multiple select statements, the table is "read-only." When your stored procedure returns a logical table from a single select statement, you can use it as the record source in an updatable form.

The object of this chapter is to familiarize you with the query design facilities in an Access project file. The chapter is not intended to teach you everything there is to know about Transact-SQL—that would require another entire book. However, you should be able to take what you learn in this chapter and apply the design techniques that you learned in the three query design chapters for desktop databases and build most of the queries that you need for an application built with a project file.

The first section of this chapter, "Building Queries Using the Query Designer," explains step by step how to build the types of queries you are already familiar with. You can use the query designer to create views, in-line functions, and stored procedures that return a logical table. The second section, "Building Queries Using a Text Editor," shows you how to get started building more complex queries using Transact-SQL. In the text editor, you can create complex stored procedures, scalar functions, and table-valued functions.

Building Queries Using the Query Designer

Particularly if you are already familiar with building queries in a desktop database, using the query designer in an Access project is the best way to get started designing queries for SQL Server.

Understanding the Query Designer

As noted earlier, you can use the query designer to create three different types of queries—views, in-line functions, and stored procedures that return a result from a single select statement. Although these queries have different purposes, most of the tools you use to create them in Design view are the same. Let's start by looking at the common elements in the query designer for all query types. Later sections of this chapter cover the differences for each query type.

Adding Tables, Views, and Functions

Let's start by creating a new view. Start Access and open the *Contacts.adp* sample project file or a project file that you have connected to the *ContactsSQL.mdf* sample database. Click the Queries button on the Object bar in the Database window and then double-click Create view in designer. Access opens a blank view in the query designer window and displays the Add Table dialog box shown in Figure 18-2.

The Add Table dialog box allows you to specify which tables, views, and functions you can use as a record source for your new query. You can switch between the different types of record sources by clicking the tabs at the top of the window. Double-click a record source name to add that record source to the design grid. You can also click a name to select it, hold down the Ctrl key and click multiple noncontiguous names to select them, or hold down the Shift key and select a range of names. After you have selected all the record sources you want, click the Add button to add them to your new query.

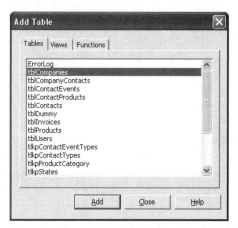

Figure 18-2. Adding tables, views, and functions to a new query.

Go ahead and add the tblCompanies table to this view and click Close.

The Panes in the Query Designer

After you add the tblCompanies table and close the Add Table dialog box, you see a query design window as shown in Figure 18-3. By default, the query design window shows two panes: the diagram pane at the top of the window and the grid pane below it.

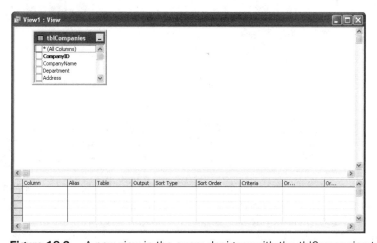

Figure 18-3. A new view in the query designer with the tblCompanies table added.

Chapter 18

The diagram pane shows a graphical representation of the tables, functions, and views that you are using to create the query and the relationships between them. The grid pane shows you information about the columns you are using in the query, similar to the design grid for a query in a desktop database. However, the query designer in a project lists the columns down instead of across. For each column, you can see the column name, any alias you assign to the column, the source table of the column, an indication that the column will be output by the query (similar to the Show check box in a desktop database query design grid), and the sorting and filtering criteria for the column.

When you're working in a desktop database, you must switch to SQL view to see the SQL that defines the query. However, in a project file, you can view and edit the SQL by opening the SQL pane. Click the SQL button on the toolbar or choose Show Panes on the View menu and then choose SQL on the submenu to open the SQL pane as shown in Figure 18-4.

> **Tip** One way to learn more about building queries using SQL is to always display the SQL pane when you're building a query. Each time you add or delete a record source, add or delete a relationship in the diagram pane, or change specifications in the design grid, Access updates the SQL pane to reflect your changes.

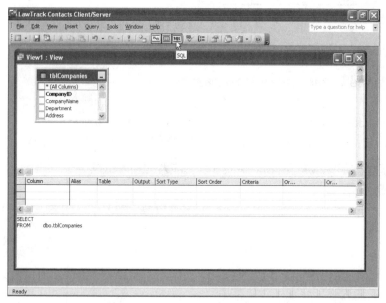

Figure 18-4. A new view in the query designer with the SQL pane displayed.

You can enter an SQL statement directly in the SQL pane, and the query designer updates the display as soon as you move the focus away from the SQL pane (by clicking in the grid pane or the diagram pane). However, the query designer can graphically represent only a small subset of the possible SQL statements you might use. If you enter SQL code that the designer cannot display, you receive a warning message stating that the code cannot be represented graphically. The next time you open the query in Design view, you will see the SQL-only text version.

Selecting Columns

You can add columns to your query in several ways. You can drag a column name from the diagram pane and drop it on the grid pane. You can also add a column by clicking the box to the left of the column name in the diagram pane. When you do this, a check mark appears next to the column name, and Access adds the column to the grid pane as shown in Figure 18-5.

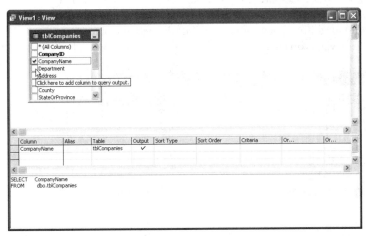

Figure 18-5. Adding a column to the view by placing a check mark next to the column name in the diagram pane.

You can also select a column from the Column drop-down list in the grid pane as shown in Figure 18-6. If you have specified multiple record sources in the diagram pane, you can filter the list of available column names in the Column drop-down list by first choosing the record source from the Table drop-down list. Add the CompanyName and the Department columns to the view by clicking next to the column listings in the diagram pane.

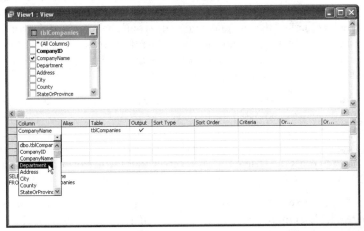

Figure 18-6. Adding a column to a view by selecting the column name from the drop-down list in the grid pane.

Chapter 18

643

Working in the Diagram Pane

After you have started working on the query, you can add other record sources by right-clicking in the blank area of the diagram pane and selecting Add Table from the shortcut menu. You can also click the Add Table button on the toolbar or choose Add Table from the Query menu. Access displays the Add Table dialog box so that you can select additional record sources (Figure 18-2). You can remove any record source from the diagram pane by right-clicking on the record source and selecting Remove, or by clicking the title bar of the record source to select it and pressing the Delete key. Add the tblCompanyContacts and the tblContacts tables using the Add Table dialog box. Click Close when you are done. Your design grid should now look like Figure 18-7.

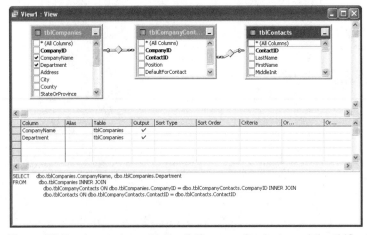

Figure 18-7. A new view with the tblCompanyContacts and the tblContacts tables added.

If a relationship exists between two tables in the diagram pane, Access automatically creates an inner join and displays a line connecting the primary key of one table (the key symbol) to the foreign key of the related table (the infinity symbol), similar to the way such a relationship is represented in a desktop database diagram (as discussed in Chapter 17). Remember from Chapter 8, "Building Complex Queries," that an inner join returns only the rows from the two tables that have matching values in both tables. Note in Figure 18-7 the two INNER JOIN clauses that Access created (in the SQL pane) and the lines connecting the three tables (in the diagram pane) that represent the defined relationships.

When you include views or functions in your query, Access creates a join for you if it can find fields with the same name and data type in two of the record sources. You can create additional joins by clicking on one column name in a record source and dragging and dropping it onto the related column name in a separate record source. To remove a join, click on it once to select it and then press the Delete key on your keyboard. You can also remove a join by right-clicking on it and selecting Remove from the shortcut menu.

You can specify the type of join you want by right-clicking on the line representing the join between the two tables. On the shortcut menu, you can select an option to select all rows from either table in the join. This is the same as specifying a left or a right join when writing the query in SQL. (Notice that Access updates the syntax in the SQL pane to say LEFT JOIN or RIGHT JOIN if you select one of these two options.) You can specify additional options for the join by viewing the join properties. Right-click on the join between the tblCompanies and tblCompanyContacts tables and select Properties. Access displays the Properties window as shown in Figure 18-8.

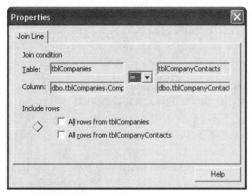

Figure 18-8. Specifying the join line properties between the tblCompanies table and the tblCompanyContacts table.

Inside Out

Left, right, and full outer join—what's the difference?

When you specify an outer join in the FROM clause of an SQL statement, you're asking the database to return all the rows from one or both record sources that participate in the join, regardless of whether the rows in one record source have matching rows in the other record source. A left or right outer join returns all the rows from only one of the two record sources. *Left* or *right* specifies whether the record source on the *left* (the first one in the join statement when reading left to right) or the one on the *right* is the one that returns all its rows. Access adds record source names to the FROM clause in the sequence that you add the record sources to the diagram pane. You can later move record sources around in the diagram pane, but the first one you added still remains the one on the left in the SQL statement.

As you learned in Chapter 8, you can modify the join properties in a query in a desktop database to return all the rows from one table or the other. When you do this, Access modifies the SQL code behind the scenes to use a left or right join, as appropriate. You cannot create a query in an Access desktop database that returns all rows from both tables.

However, SQL Server supports returning all rows from both record sources, and when you modify the join properties to ask for this, Access changes the SQL to specify a full outer join. When you run a full outer join query, you might see some rows that contain column values from the first record source and null values in the columns from the second record source, some rows that contain column values from both record sources, and some rows that contain null values in the columns from the first record source and column values from the second record source.

The top section of the Properties window allows you to specify an operator for the join condition. The default operator, an equal sign, asks the database to return rows only where the values in the column on one side of the join exactly match the values in the joined column of the other table. However, you can use a different operator if you want the query to return rows that are unmatched (<>), greater than (>), greater than or equal to (>=), less than (<), or less than or equal to (<=) the corresponding rows in the joined table. If you specify anything other than an equal join (also known as an equi-join) between the two tables, the diamond-shaped symbol on the join line in the diagram pane displays that operator within the diamond symbol. The diamond symbol in the diagram pane remains blank for an equal join.

The bottom section of the Properties window allows you to specify whether you want all rows returned from one or both of the tables. Doing so is the same as right-clicking on the join line in the diagram pane and choosing one of the Select All Rows from... options. Click the check box to the left of the All rows from tblCompanies option. Notice that the diamond-shaped symbol on the left side of the window changes, as shown in Figure 18-9. One side of it is now box-shaped (similar to the shape of home plate on a baseball field). The diamond on the join line in the diagram pane also changes with the box side of the shape facing toward the tblCompanies table. This graphical representation means that all records are being selected from the tblCompanies table (an outer join).

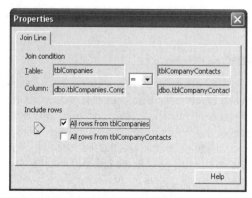

Figure 18-9. Specifying the join line properties between the tblCompanies and the tblCompanyContacts tables with All rows from tblCompanies selected.

If you modify the SQL to specify a left or a right join between the two tables, the diamond symbol changes to a box shape on the side of the join line that connects to the table returning all rows. If you ask for a full outer join in the SQL, the entire diamond symbol becomes a box. Clear the All rows from tblCompanies check box and close the Properties window.

Working in the Grid Pane

You can specify a number of options for each column in the grid pane. In the Alias field, you can assign a different name to the column when it is output by the query. If you specified a Caption property for the column in the table when you created it, the query displays the caption as the heading of the column when you open the query in Datasheet view. However, the column name or the alias you specify is still the correct name to use when referring to the query column from other queries and in forms and reports.

In addition to selecting a column name from one of the record sources, you can enter an expression for a column. The expression can be as simple as a literal value or can be a complex mathematical or concatenation expression using columns from the record sources. When you enter an expression for a column, you must also enter an alias name to assign a name to the output column. If you do not enter an alias, Access generates an alias name as Expr$N$, where N is an integer value starting with 1 for the first generated alias, 2 for the second, and so on.

The Sort Type option allows you to specify how you want a column to be sorted in the query results. If you request a sort on multiple columns, you can indicate the Sort Order for each column to rank the order in which the database performs the sort. For example, assume you want to sort this view by department and then by company name. In the grid pane, select Ascending for both the Department and CompanyName columns from the Sort Type drop-down list. Because you want Department sorted first, be sure to choose a value of 1 in the Sort Order drop-down list. Your view design should now look like Figure 18-10. Also note that when you specify a sort on a column, an A-Z sort icon appears next to the column name in the diagram pane with an arrow indicating in which direction the sort is being applied.

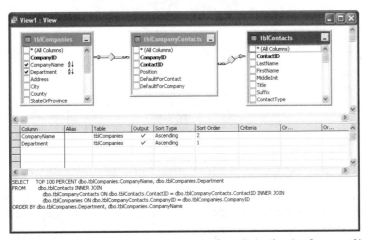

Figure 18-10. Specifying Sort Type and Sort Order for the CompanyName and Department columns.

If you want to change the order in which the columns appear in the query results, in the grid pane click the selection button to the left of the column name you want to move and drag it up or down the grid pane to move it to the desired location.

> **Note** Remember, changing the order in which the columns are displayed in a result set does not change the order in which they are sorted (unlike in an Access desktop database).

Chapter 18

Use the Criteria field to enter criteria you want to apply to the column in the query. You can enter criteria exactly as you would in a query in an Access desktop database, except you must use single quotes to surround character and date/time literals, and you must use % and _ wildcards in LIKE criteria instead of * and ?, respectively. (See Chapters 7 and 8 for details about specifying criteria in a query.) You can use the Or fields to specify additional criteria. Entering criteria in separate Or fields is the same as using the OR Boolean operator between two criteria statements.

You can convert any query in the query designer into an aggregate query (one that groups, totals, and otherwise performs math on the results) by clicking the Group By button on the toolbar or choosing Group By from the Query menu. This is identical to clicking the Totals button on the toolbar or choosing Totals from the View menu when working with queries in an Access desktop database, but you have many more aggregate function options in an Access project.

After you select the Group By option, Access displays an additional column in the grid pane that lets you choose the different aggregate functions that you can apply to your columns, as shown in Figure 8-11.

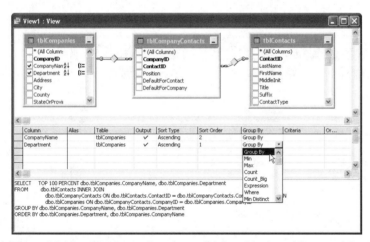

Figure 18-11. The Group By column displayed in the grid pane of the query designer.

Table 18-1 lists the different options and functions that you can select in the query designer in the Group By column. Note that some of these functions can be used only on columns containing a numeric data type. As you can see, SQL Server supports many more functions than are available in a desktop database.

Table 18-1. SQL Server Query Designer Group By Options

Option	Description
Avg Avg Distinct	Returns the average of all non-null values in the column. Avg Distinct averages only the unique values. (Duplicates are ignored.) You can specify an average only on a numeric column.
Checksum_Agg Checksum_Agg Distinct	Returns the checksum value of an integer column, ignoring null values. Checksum_Agg Distinct calculates the checksum using only the unique values. (Duplicates are ignored.) You can specify a checksum only on a column or expression that is the int data type.
Count Count Distinct Count_Big Count_Big Distinct	Returns the count of all non-null items in the column. Count_Big is the same as Count except it always returns a bigint data type, whereas Count always returns an int data type. Count Distinct and Count_Big Distinct count only unique values. (Duplicates are ignored.)
Expression	Indicates that the column contains an expression using one or more aggregate functions.
Group By	Groups the aggregate calculations on the values in this column. You can specify Group By for more than one column.
Max Max Distinct	Returns the highest value in the column (the last value alphabetically for text data types). Max Distinct, included for compatibility with the ANSI SQL-92 standard, considers only the unique values in the column, but does not return a result different from Max. All null values are ignored.
Min Min Distinct	Returns the lowest value in the column (the first value alphabetically for text data types). Min Distinct, included for compatibility with the ANSI SQL-92 standard, considers only the unique values in the column, but does not return a result different from Min. All null values are ignored.
StDev StDevP	Returns the standard deviation for all values in the column. StDevP returns the standard deviation for the population of all values in the column. The column can contain only numeric values.
Sum Sum Distinct	Returns the total of all values in the column. Sum Distinct totals only the unique values. (Duplicates are ignored.) The column can contain only numeric values.
Var VarP	Returns the statistical variance for all values in the column. VarP returns the statistical variance for the population of all values in the column.
Where	Specifies that this column or expression is not included in an aggregate expression in the SELECT list or in the GROUP BY clause, but is available to filter the rows before the query forms the groups. Access generates a WHERE clause immediately following the FROM clause in the SQL that defines your query.

Chapter 18

A useful tool when you're building queries in the query designer is the Verify SQL Syntax button. You can find this button between the SQL button and the Group By button on the toolbar. When you click the button, Access calls SQL Server to verify that the SQL syntax of your query is correct. If SQL Server finds any errors, Access returns a message stating the nature of the syntax error. This tool is especially helpful if you are writing SQL directly into the SQL pane or if you are evaluating an SQL statement from the text editor. (See "Building Queries Using a Text Editor" later in this chapter for more information.)

Viewing Other Properties

You can specify a variety of additional properties for a query, such as the number of rows you want returned, lookups for the columns returned, and information about any input parameters you might use. To view the properties for any query type in Design view, right-click anywhere in the diagram pane or grid pane and select Properties from the shortcut menu, or click the Properties button on the toolbar. You can also view the properties for a query by selecting the query designer window and then choosing Properties from the View menu. The properties for each query type are different because each query type supports different features. You will learn more about the properties for each type of query later in this chapter.

Working with Views

Views are the simplest type of query that SQL Server supports. Views offer a way for you to control what data is displayed and the order in which it is displayed. Views are great tools for the SQL Server developer because they allow the developer to control access to the data in the tables. Instead of assigning individual user permissions to certain parts of a table, you can create a view and give the user permissions to see and change data only through the view.

Below are some reasons you might use a view:

- You want a secure and updatable replacement for a table. With a properly designed view, your users can still add, delete, and update rows, but they don't need permission to access the underlying tables directly. You can give users permission to use the view, and, if you want, you can restrict access to specific columns simply by removing them from the view.

- You want to organize the recordsets that you use for your forms and reports. You can use a view as the record source for any form or report or as the row source for any combo box or list box. If you carefully plan a naming convention, you can create one view for each form or report to make it easy to know which object uses the recordset. For example, vwFrmCompanies might be the view that supplies the recordset for the frmCompanies form.

- You want to add querying power to your recordsets. Unlike a table, views can automatically sort or filter information based on fixed date ranges or predetermined values. For example, if you have users that need to work only with the invoices for the current month, you can build a view as a recordset that displays invoices only for the current month.

- You can use views as a record source anywhere that you can use a table as a record source. You can also use functions and stored procedures as record sources in your views.

> **Note** Views are usually meant to provide updatable recordsets, but this isn't always the case. Views are not updatable when you include an aggregate function that summarizes the data or when you group the data. Views are also partially updatable if you are building a recordset from multiple tables because only the many side of the recordset provided by a view is updatable. Keep this in mind as you construct your views.

Now that you know about some of the uses for views, finish building the view that you started building previously. To keep the first example fairly simple, start by removing some elements from the existing view. First, remove the tblCompanyContacts and tblContacts tables by right-clicking on them and selecting Remove from the shortcut menu. Also, if you turned on the Group By option, turn it off by clicking the Group By button on the toolbar. When you are done, your view should look like Figure 18-12.

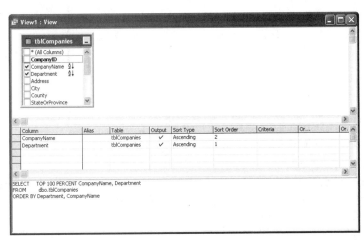

Figure 18-12. A view in the query designer with only the Companies table included.

Design this view so that it would be a suitable record source for the Companies form. Include all the columns from the tblCompanies table in the result set by placing a check mark next to the name of each column in the diagram pane. You do not need to include the upsize_ts field because that is a nonupdatable system field that Access uses to help make update commands more efficient. You can also select all columns by placing a check mark next to the *(All Columns) option, but because you want to specify a sort on one of the output columns, add each of the columns individually. (There is a way to specify a sort when using the *(All Columns) option as you will see in the next section, "Working with In-Line Functions.")

Because you previously added the CompanyName and Department fields to the view, Access adds the CompanyID field below the Department field when you select it. Click the selection button next to the CompanyID field in the grid pane and drag it to the top of the list.

This view will be used as the record source for the Companies form, so it will be easier to browse through the records of the Companies form if they are sorted by company name. You also want the company name to be the only column that the result set is sorted on, so remove the Sort Type from the Department column by changing the value in the drop-down list to Unsorted. Notice that when you do so, Access automatically adjusts the Sort Order for the CompanyName column to 1. Click the Save button on the toolbar to save the view. In the Save As dialog box, type **vwCompanies** as the name of the view and click OK. The completed view should look like Figure 18-13. You can find this view saved as *vwXmplCompanies* in the sample database.

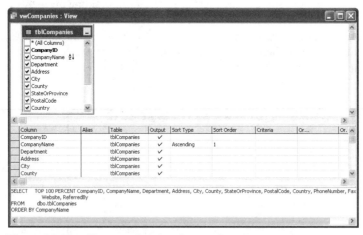

Figure 18-13. The completed vwCompanies view.

> **Note** You'll notice throughout this chapter that you are instructed to save a query each time you modify it before you switch to Datasheet view. Unlike a query in a desktop database, an Access project must save your query in SQL Server before it can run it for you. If you attempt to switch to Datasheet view before you have saved your changes, Access displays a warning dialog box informing you that you must first save your changes. You can click Yes to save your changes and run the query or click No to return to Design view.

After you save the view, take a look at the result set by clicking the View button on the toolbar. (Datasheet view is the default for this button when you have a view open in Design view.) Notice that all the columns for the tblCompanies table are displayed, and they are sorted alphabetically by company name.

> **Note** You can update columns and delete or insert rows in your vwCompanies view. As with any Datasheet view in Access, you add new rows by entering data in the new row at the end of the datasheet, so new rows won't necessarily be in alphabetical order by company name. You will see the rows in the correct order the next time you open the view.

Inside Out

SELECT TOP 100 PERCENT

You might have noticed that when you specify the Sort Type property for any column, Access automatically adds a TOP 100 PERCENT clause to the SQL statement for the view. This clause returns all (100 percent) of the records returned by the SELECT statement starting from the beginning (top) of the recordset. The clause might seem redundant, but it is required in order for the results to be sortable. In the current ANSI SQL standard, views return unordered recordsets, and the standard does not allow the ORDER BY clause in a view. The standard also does not define the TOP clause. SQL Server 2000 and later, however, define an extension to the standard that allows you to include an ORDER BY clause in a view, but only when you also include the nonstandard TOP clause. SQL Server also allows you to specify a TOP clause without also including an ORDER BY clause.

You might remember from Chapter 8 that queries in an Access desktop database also support a TOP and ORDER BY clause; however, you can include an ORDER BY clause without also specifying TOP. If you think about it, using TOP without an ORDER BY specification doesn't make sense unless you want a specific number of arbitrary rows returned by the query. When you include TOP and ORDER BY, the query returns the top rows based on the sort sequence specified.

You should remember the requirement in SQL Server to add the TOP clause to any SELECT statement that includes an ORDER BY clause, especially when working in the text editor to create views, functions, and stored procedures.

Before moving on to create more complex queries using in-line functions, take a look at the different properties you can specify for a view. Right-click anywhere in the design area and select Properties from the shortcut menu or click the Properties button on the toolbar. Figure 18-14 on the next page shows the Properties window for the vwCompanies view.

You can see four tabs in the Properties window for a view. The Columns, Lookup, and Data tabs contain properties similar to those that you can specify for a table. The Columns tab lets you override the extended properties for each individual column in the view such as Description, Caption, Format, and Decimal Places. The Lookup tab allows you to define lookups for each column. The Data tab allows you to specify filters and subdatasheet information. For more information on these properties, refer to the table properties section "Understanding Column Properties" on page 616. The tab you might not be familiar with is the View tab. The properties that you can set on the View tab are listed in Table 18-2 on the next page.

Chapter 18

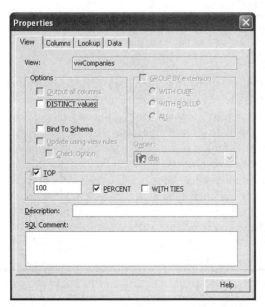

Figure 18-14.   The View tab of the Properties window for views.

Table 18-2. Options on the Properties window View tab

Feature	Description
View	The currently assigned name for this view. You cannot change this value in the Properties window, but it is updated if you save the view under a different name.
Output all columns	Choosing this option is the same as selecting the *(All Columns) option in the diagram pane. All columns in the table(s) are returned.
DISTINCT values	The view displays only distinct values and filters out all duplicate rows.
Bind To Schema	Selecting this option prevents all users from modifying the design of any underlying record sources for this view (tables, functions, and stored procedures). This is a useful option because if anyone changes the underlying record sources, this view (and any other view, function, or stored procedure based on the same record sources) could become invalidated and no longer function properly.
Update using view rules	When you construct a view using multiple record sources and then you perform updates via the view, Access often sends update commands to the server using the base table that was changed, not the view. When you select this option, Access always performs update commands using the view.

Table 18-2. **Options on the Properties window View tab**

Feature	Description
Check Option	If you select the Update using view rules option, you can select this option to ensure that any row modified in the view also satisfies any conditions in the WHERE clause of the view. This prevents users from inserting or changing a row that would be eliminated by the criteria in the WHERE clause.
GROUP BY extension	These additional options are available if you specified Group By in the view:
	WITH CUBE specifies that the view should return a multidimensional result set for the columns specified in the GROUP BY clause that summarizes all combinations of aggregate functions and columns in the view.
	WITH ROLLUP specifies that the view should return a multidimensional result set for the columns specified in the GROUP BY clause that provides a singular summary for each combination of aggregate functions and columns in the view.
	ALL includes all duplicates in the result set. (By default, the GROUP BY clause eliminates duplicates.)
Owner	The SQL Server owner of the view. The default owner is dbo.
TOP	Specify this option so that the view results can be sorted and only the top percentage or number of rows are returned. PERCENT specifies a percentage of rows to return instead of a number.
	WITH TIES returns all tied rows when more than one row qualifies for the cutoff of the TOP limit because they contain duplicate values on the sorting criteria. For example, if you request TOP 10 WITH TIES and the sorted column contains five rows with the value 1 and eight rows with the value 2, the view returns 13 rows because multiple rows contain the same value as the 10th row.
Description	Stores a description of the view in the view definition.
SQL Comment	Allows you to add a comment about the view. This comment can be seen by anyone who can view the SQL syntax for the view.

Working with In-Line Functions

When working with in-line functions in the query designer, you can think of them as a balance between the simplicity of views and the power of stored procedures. Like views, in-line functions have the ability to return recordsets that can be edited and updated. Like stored procedures, in-line functions can use parameters. Parameters are variables that are passed to the function that can control the way it behaves. For example, you can create a function that retrieves records that were created within a certain date range and use parameters to specify the beginning and end dates of the date range when the function is executed.

Chapter 18

Following are some reasons you might use an in-line function:

- You need an updatable recordset that can be built based on conditional parameters. For example, you might need to edit the contact information for every contact at a certain company. You can build an in-line function that fetches the contacts only for the company you specify and edit their information directly in the query results.

- In-line functions are great for returning aggregate data, such as a count of records or an average retail price. Views can return this information as well, but the requirements for fetching this data often rely on user-provided information, which you can easily ask for using an in-line function with parameters.

- On a similar note, in-line functions are a good record source for reports. Reports are often produced using a specific date range or a particular person. In-line functions give you the ability to build the record source based on the specific needs of the person retrieving the report.

- You can use an in-line function as a record source anywhere that you can use a table or view as a record source. You can also use views, other functions, and stored procedures as record sources in your in-line functions.

> **Note** When working with in-line functions, you will find it easier to create a function that returns a recordset that is not updatable. The same design considerations that cause view recordsets to be nonupdatable also apply to in-line functions. However, because in-line functions are often used to aggregate data, they will frequently return recordsets that can't be updated. Keep this difference in mind when deciding which type of query to build. If you need a recordset that is updatable but doesn't require parameters, use a view. If you need to aggregate data or accept parameters, use an in-line function. If you need to build a function that is updatable, pay close attention to how you build an in-line function and always test it to make sure that you can update the recordset it returns.

Now that you know more about some of the uses of in-line functions, let's build one in the query designer. For this example, you'll build a function that returns the contact information for every contact associated with a specific company. You'll use multiple joins to associate the contact information with the company information, and you'll sort the results by each contact's last name and first name. To select the rows, you'll use a parameter to specify the company for which you want to return the contact information.

Open the *Contacts.adp* sample database, select Queries on the Object bar in the Database window, and double-click Create function in designer to start a new in-line function. From the Add Table dialog box, add the tblCompanies, tblCompanyContacts, and tblContacts tables, and then close the dialog box. Notice that when you add the tables to the diagram pane, Access automatically displays the two joins that represent the relationships between these tables. If you open the SQL pane, you can see that Access has also created the appropriate INNER JOIN clauses in the FROM clause. These are the exact joins that you need to use for this query to fetch related rows from the three tables. Next, specify which columns you want to return in the query. Select the CompanyName column from the tblCompanies table and the *(All Columns) option from the tblContacts table. Because you want to sort by the contact's last name and first name, also add the LastName and FirstName columns to your query.

When you are done, the query designer window should look like Figure 18-15 (with the SQL pane displayed).

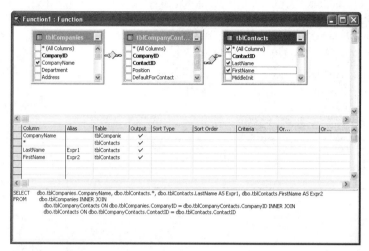

Figure 18-15. A new in-line function in the query designer with three tables added.

Click the Save button on the toolbar and name the function fctCompanyContacts in the Save As dialog box. Next, click the View button on the toolbar to view the in-line function results. Notice that all contact information is returned unsorted and the contact LastName and First-Name columns are repeated in the result set. You still have more work to do before this function will work the way you want.

First, return to Design view, and specify the sorting criteria and prevent the LastName and FirstName columns from repeating in the result set. Select Ascending from the drop-down list under Sort Type for the LastName column. Access automatically gives it a Sort Order of 1. Next, select Ascending for the FirstName column and note the Sort Order of 2. To prevent the columns from appearing twice, remove the check marks under Output next to the LastName and FirstName columns. This ensures that the last name and first name information is displayed only once when returned by the *(All Columns) column.

Now you need to specify the parameter that filters the company for which you want the contact information. As with queries in a desktop database, you can use a parameter anywhere that you could otherwise specify a literal. So, you can use a parameter in a criteria expression for the CompanyName column. In a query in an Access project, you declare a parameter by using the @ symbol followed by the name of your parameter. Unlike parameters in an Access desktop database, you cannot use blanks or other special characters in a parameter name, but you can use the underscore character to provide spacing in the name. To allow the user to enter all or part of a company name, in the criteria for the CompanyName column enter the following:

```
LIKE @Enter_Company_Name + N'%'
```

The capital letter *N* preceding the '%' indicates that you want a National Language literal to be used in the concatenation. A National Language (or Unicode) literal uses two bytes for each character and supports a more extensive range of characters. Because the CompanyName column is a Unicode field (data type nvarchar), if you type a simple string literal, Access inserts the capital letter *N* for you to ensure that the characters in your string can be compared with the full range of characters that might be stored in the column. Note that a filter icon now appears next to the CompanyName column in the diagram pane to indicate that you have defined a criteria for this column.

Now the function is complete. Click the Save button on the toolbar to save your changes. The finished function should look like Figure 18-16.

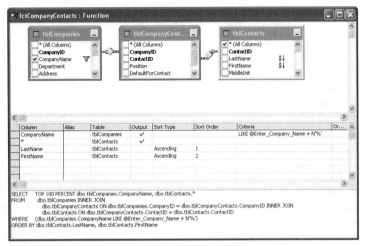

Figure 18-16. An in-line function with a parameter used as criteria to filter the CompanyName column.

Now you're ready to test your new function. Switch to Datasheet view, and Access displays an Enter Parameter Value dialog box as shown in Figure 18-17.

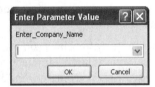

Figure 18-17. Access displays the Enter Parameter Value dialog box when you run a query that uses parameters.

The sample database contains several company names that begin with the letter *T*, so type that letter in response to the parameter prompt and click OK. Access displays the result as shown in Figure 18-18.

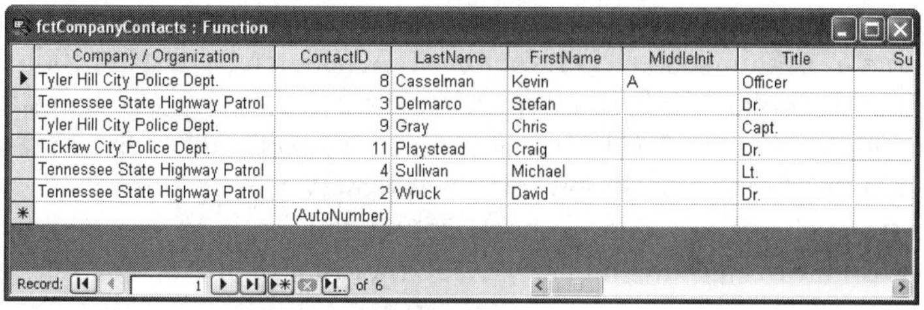

Company / Organization	ContactID	LastName	FirstName	MiddleInit	Title	Su
▶ Tyler Hill City Police Dept.	8	Casselman	Kevin	A	Officer	
Tennessee State Highway Patrol	3	Delmarco	Stefan		Dr.	
Tyler Hill City Police Dept.	9	Gray	Chris		Capt.	
Tickfaw City Police Dept.	11	Playstead	Craig		Dr.	
Tennessee State Highway Patrol	4	Sullivan	Michael		Lt.	
Tennessee State Highway Patrol	2	Wruck	David		Dr.	
*	(AutoNumber)					

Record: 14 ◀ 1 ▶ ▶I ▶* ⊗ ▶I. of 6

Figure 18-18. The result of searching for contacts associated with companies that have a name beginning with the letter *T*.

Notice that the query found three companies having names that begin with the letter *T*, but the results are sorted by the contacts' last names and first names as designed in the query.

> **Tip** It is always a good idea to use descriptive names for the parameters you use in functions and stored procedures, even if you plan to hide them from the user with a code or a form interface. First, a descriptive name helps you remember how the query uses the parameter. Second, if a user runs the query from the Database window, the name of the parameter should explain what you want the user to enter.

Before moving on to stored procedures, take a quick look at the different properties you can specify for a function. Return to Design view, right-click anywhere in the design area and select Properties from the shortcut menu. Access displays the Properties window for the in-line function, as shown in Figure 18-19.

Figure 18-19. The In-line Function tab of the Properties window for an in-line function.

The tabs available in the Properties window for in-line functions are similar to those for views, except an in-line function includes an In-line Function tab and a Function Parameters tab. The Columns, Lookup, and Data tabs are the same as the corresponding tabs in the Properties window for views. The In-line Function tab offers many of the same options as the View tab in the Properties window for views. However, an in-line function does not offer the Update using view rules or Check Option options. For more information on the other options on the In-line Function tab, refer back to Table 18-2 on page 654.

Click the Function Parameters tab to view the list of parameters specified for this in-line function, as shown in Figure 18-20. This is a good way to verify all the parameters you specified for an in-line function (or a stored procedure). You can't add additional parameters in this window because Access wouldn't know where the parameters should be used in the query. However, you can specify a data type and a default value for parameters that you have already created. Keep in mind that you're entering a literal value in the Default column, so you must enclose character literals and date/time literals in single quotes.

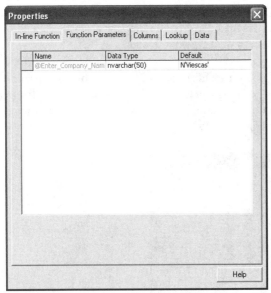

Figure 18-20.   The Function Parameters tab of the Properties window for an in-line function.

The figure shows that I've entered a default value of N'Viescas'. You can find this query saved as *fctXmplCompanyContacts* in the sample database. When you run this query, you can choose <DEFAULT> in the drop-down list in the Enter Parameter Value dialog box, and the query will return the records for companies that have a name beginning with that character string.

Working with Stored Procedures

Stored procedures are the most powerful type of query you can build in the query designer. These queries have most of the capabilities of views and in-line stored procedures, plus the added ability to perform action queries (updating, deleting, and adding data). The real power and potential of stored procedures is considerably beyond what the query designer is capable of building. As the name implies, stored procedures allow you to write complex procedures that include logic testing (If…Else), looping (While), creating temporary tables, and error trapping using Transact-SQL. However, you will find plenty of situations where building a stored procedure in the query designer comes in handy.

The primary use of stored procedures that you build in the query designer is to perform action queries. Like functions, stored procedures can accept parameters and can return updatable recordsets. So, you can use a stored procedure as the record source of a form or report. However, you cannot use stored procedures as the record source of other views or in-line functions.

Because the best use for a stored procedure built in the query designer is to perform an action query, let's build a stored procedure that inserts (*appends* in Access terminology) a record into the tblCompanies table. To perform this task, you have two options. You can use an append query (an INSERT statement that uses a query to fetch one or more rows to be inserted), or you can use an append values query (an INSERT statement that uses a VALUES clause to specify the column values for one new row).

Both methods work fine for adding a record to the tblCompanies table, but the append values syntax is more straightforward, especially when you need to insert only one row. It also has the added benefit of being easier to convert to a text stored procedure, which you will do later in this chapter.

Begin by opening the *Contact.adp* project, selecting Queries on the Object bar, and double-clicking the Create stored procedure in designer shortcut. Add the tblCompanies table to the new stored procedure from the Add Table dialog box and then close the dialog box. Be sure the SQL pane is visible by clicking the SQL button on the toolbar so that you can watch Access build this query in SQL. This will be helpful information to know when you build one yourself later on in the text editor.

Next, specify that this is an append values query. To do this, locate the Query Type drop-down list on the toolbar, as shown in Figure 18-21, and select the Append Values Query option. The query designer window changes and shows only two options in the grid pane: Column and New Value.

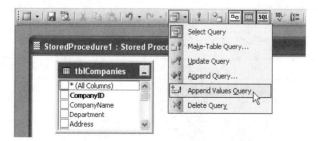

Figure 18-21. Selecting Append Values Query from the Query Type drop-down list.

Chapter 18

Use Column to specify which columns you want to append to the Companies table, and use New Value to indicate the values you want to add for each column. Notice that you can select which columns you want to append by clicking the box to the left of each column name in the diagram pane. When you select a column, Access displays a plus sign (rather than a check mark) in the box. Because you want to add an entire row to the tblCompanies table, go ahead and click next to each column name except the CompanyID and upsize_ts columns. (The CompanyID column is the Autonumber data type, so SQL Server automatically generates the next value when you insert a row, and the upsize_ts column is a system-maintained timestamp value that helps Access improve the performance of updates.) When you are done, the query designer should look like Figure 18-22.

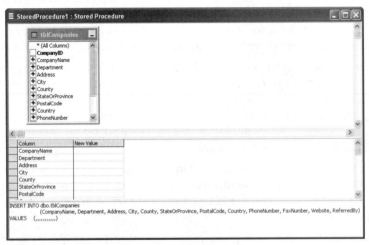

Figure 18-22. Selecting the columns to which the stored procedure will append values.

Now you need to specify the values that you want to append to the tblCompanies table. You could simply enter values in the New Value field for each column and execute the stored procedure. However, the next time you wanted to add a row to the Companies table, you would have to build the procedure all over again.

Instead, you can use parameters for each value. When you do this, Access prompts you for the values you want to insert into a new row each time you run the stored procedure. You can also execute the stored procedure from Visual Basic code and supply the column values by setting the parameters. To make each new value a parameter, you need to enter a valid parameter name next to each column name. Remember, a parameter name must begin with the @ character and cannot contain blanks or special characters other than the underscore character. Refer to the list below for suggested parameter names for each column name.

Column Name	Parameter Name
CompanyName	@CompanyName
Department	@Department
Address	@Address

Column Name	Parameter Name
City	@City
County	@County
StateOrProvince	@StateOrProvince
PostalCode	@PostalCode
Country	@Country
PhoneNumber	@PhoneNumber
FaxNumber	@FaxNumber
Website	CAST(@Website AS nvarchar(50))
ReferredBy	@ReferredBy

Notice that you must convert (CAST) the @Website parameter to an nvarchar data type because the data type of the Website column is ntext, and the query designer doesn't accept a parameter for an ntext data type column. Converting the parameter to an nvarchar data type allows the parameter to be used to append data to the Website column. Interestingly, when you enter this parameter, Access displays a dialog box telling you that the conversion might be unnecessary. However, if you attempt to enter a simple parameter name, Access tells you that this produces a data type conversion error and won't let you leave the New Value box until you correct it.

After you enter all the parameter names, the stored procedure is complete. Click the Save button on the toolbar and name the procedure spAddOneCompany. Your finished stored procedure should look like Figure 18-23. You can also find this query saved as *spXmplAddOneCompany* in the sample database.

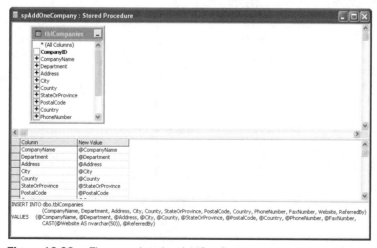

Figure 18-23. The completed spAddOneCompany stored procedure.

Chapter 18

You can see the stored procedure in action by clicking the View button or the Run button on the toolbar. Access prompts you for each of the parameter values in succession. Input a value for each parameter and click OK, but only the CompanyName field is required to successfully save a new row. (The ReferredBy parameter is an integer value that identifies the ContactID of the person who referred this company. Enter a valid ContactID or leave the value blank.) When the procedure is complete, you receive a message stating that the procedure completed successfully but didn't return any records. Now open the tblCompanies table in Datasheet view. Notice that the information you provided appears as a new row in the table.

> **Caution**   When working with action queries in an Access desktop database (.mdb), you can switch to Datasheet view and see a recordset that represents the potential changes to the data. The desktop database action query doesn't actually execute until you click the Run button. This is not the case with stored procedures in the query designer in a project file (.adp). Viewing a stored procedure is the same as executing it. Be careful how you build your action queries and always test them on a backup copy of your tables before executing them against your production tables.

Before moving on to text queries, let's take a look at the properties for a stored procedure. Because the stored procedure you've been building is an append query, you won't be able to see all the available properties for a stored procedure in the Properties window for your query. Open the sample *spXmplCompanyParameter* query in Design view—this is a simple stored procedure on the tblCompanies table that uses a parameter to filter the CompanyName column. As before, you can view the properties for a stored procedure by right-clicking anywhere in the design area and selecting Properties from the shortcut menu. Access displays the Properties window for the stored procedure, as shown in Figure 18-24.

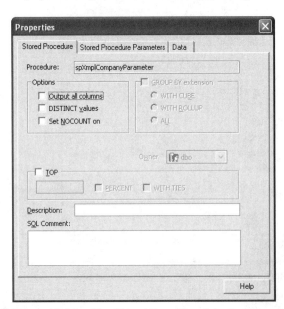

Figure 18-24.   The Stored Procedure tab of a stored procedure Properties window.

Notice that, unlike a function or view, you cannot define extended properties for columns (such as Caption or Format properties), and you cannot define a lookup field for any output column. You can, however, define filters and subdatasheet information on the Data tab just like you can for views and functions. The information and options on the Stored Procedure Parameters tab are identical to those that you can find on the Function Parameters tab for a function, as you saw earlier in Figure 18-20.

On the Stored Procedure tab, you can see many options that are similar to those available for views and functions. The one option unique to stored procedures is Set NOCOUNT on. Normally when you execute a stored procedure, the procedure returns a count of the rows affected. When you execute the procedure from another procedure, you can query the number of rows affected by referencing the built-in @@ROWCOUNT function. When you select the Set NOCOUNT on option, the stored procedure won't return the record count. For some complex procedures that you use in an Access project, you should select this option. When the procedure includes multiple SELECT statements, and one or more statements early in the procedure return a row count of 0, Access assumes that the output from the procedure will be zero rows. If the final SELECT returns a recordset, Access won't display it if NOCOUNT is set to off (the default). By setting NOCOUNT to on, the procedure doesn't return any row count, so Access displays the final recordset correctly.

For more information on the remaining properties, refer back to Table 18-1 on page 649.

Building Queries Using a Text Editor

Thus far you have learned how to build queries using the query designer. You have already discovered that you can duplicate the functionality of Access desktop database (.mdb) queries by using the similar interface provided by the Access project query designer. However, SQL Server offers substantially more querying power than can be harnessed by using only the graphical query designer. To get the most out of SQL Server's querying power, you must create queries using Transact-SQL in the text editor.

You won't find any shortcuts to build a query in the text editor in the queries list in the Database window. To begin building a query using the text editor, you can select Queries on the Object bar in the Database window and click the New button on the Database window toolbar, or you can choose Query from the Insert menu. When you do this, Access displays the New Query dialog box, as shown in Figure 18-25.

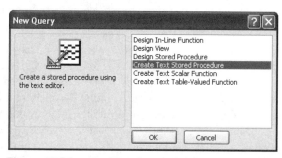

Figure 18-25. The New Query dialog box in an Access project file.

You can see that this dialog box gives you options to begin designing in-line functions, views, and stored procedures in the query designer. The remaining three types of queries are the ones that you can build in the text editor—text stored procedures, text scalar functions, and text table-valued functions.

> **Note** SQL Server actually supports only three types of queries: views, functions, and stored procedures. To make designing the common select and action queries easier, Access projects offer the query designer versions of these query types. Because functions and stored procedures can be so much more robust than the query designer can visually display, Access projects also offer the option to design these query types using a text editor to take better advantage of their available features.

To create a text query, you must use Transact-SQL. Transact-SQL (or T-SQL) is a special form of SQL used by SQL Server that includes extra commands and features to extend its capabilities. Think of Transact-SQL as "Basic for SQL Server." It extends the capabilities of SQL by introducing control-of-flow statements (such as IF...ELSE and WHILE), parameter inspection during execution, error trapping, complex mathematical calculations, and transaction batching. Transact-SQL is robust enough to perform many of the actions for which you would normally use Visual Basic or another programming language. But the real beauty of Transact-SQL is that the queries are compiled and run from SQL Server, thus increasing the speed and performance of your database.

Because Transact-SQL is such a powerful and complex language, this chapter only scratches the surface when describing its features. The next section, "Building a Text Stored Procedure," shows you step by step how to build a fairly complex stored procedure in the Contacts database using Transact-SQL. The remaining two sections provide brief descriptions of how to use text scalar functions and text table-valued functions along with examples to get you started building some of your own.

The text editor itself is a relatively simple tool that offers some features that can make the job of writing text-based queries a little easier. When you open a new query in the text editor, some of the syntax is already provided for you. The provided syntax lays the groundwork for the type of query you want to create and also includes some of the default commands that you might need to use in most text queries of that type. In fact, the provided syntax is the only difference between creating one type of query (such as a stored procedure) over another (such as a table-valued function). If you want, you can change one query type into another (as long as you haven't yet saved the query) simply by changing the provided syntax in the text editor.

If you want to add SQL statements to the editor, you can type them in yourself or you can use the query designer to build one. To use the query designer to build an SQL statement, you can right-click in the text editor and select Insert SQL from the shortcut menu or click the Insert SQL button on the toolbar. When you are done creating the query in the query designer (which Access opens as a dialog box), close the query designer. Access asks you if you want to insert the SQL you created into the text editor. If you click Yes, Access copies the SQL you created to the text editor window at the location where you last placed the cursor.

You can also use the query designer to edit an existing SQL statement. To do this, highlight the SQL statement, right-click on the highlighted selection, and choose Edit SQL from the shortcut menu. You can also click the Edit SQL button on the toolbar. Either method displays the highlighted text in a query designer dialog box where you can modify the text or check the SQL syntax using the syntax checker.

> **Caution** Save your work often and keep backup copies of your text queries. (Notepad works great for this purpose.) The text editor does not have any undo features and can be very unforgiving if you make a mistake.

Building a Text Stored Procedure

The most powerful query type that you can create in an Access project is the stored procedure. Thus far, you've had a glimpse of what stored procedures can do by designing one using the query designer. To take full advantage of the capabilities of stored procedures, you must create them using the text editor. Here are some of the abilities that you have with a text stored procedure:

- Use just about any SQL statement including SELECT, DELETE, UPDATE, and INSERT.
- Modify or create other database objects. You can create tables and views as well as modify their properties and contents.
- Execute other stored procedures and functions. You can make use of any available stored procedure, function, or system variable by calling it or executing it from a stored procedure.
- Declare parameters and variables. You can input and output specific data as well as declare variables that are referenced and changed within the stored procedure.
- Use control-of-flow statements. Much like the statements available in Visual Basic procedures, control-of-flow statements in stored procedures allow you to check for conditions, loop through statements multiple times, and trap errors.
- Group multiple statements using transactions. You can make sure an entire group of operations completes successfully by batching them inside a transaction and monitoring any errors. If any operation fails, you can ask SQL Server to roll back all changes made to the database within the transaction.

Let's take the stored procedure you created in the query designer and rebuild it in the text editor. Along the way, you'll improve it by declaring variables, adding control-of-flow statements, including error trapping, and calling another stored procedure.

Beginning a New Stored Procedure in the Text Editor

Open the *Contacts.adp* sample project file. Select Queries on the Object bar of the Database window, click the New button on the Database window toolbar, and select Create Text Stored Procedure in the New Query dialog box (Figure 18-25). Click OK, and Access opens the text editor with some Transact-SQL code and comments already inserted, as shown in Figure 18-26 on the next page.

Chapter 18

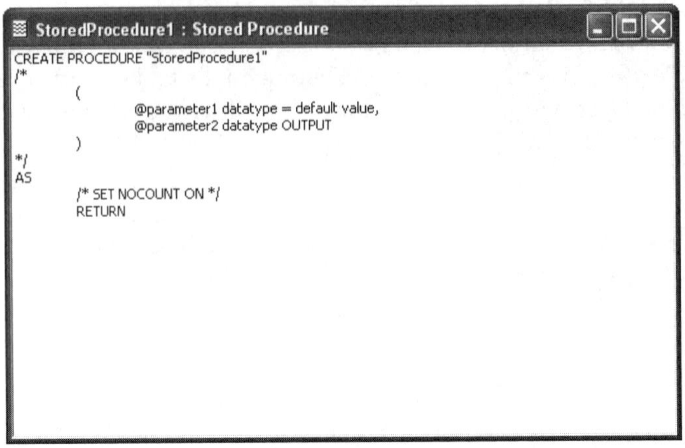

Figure 18-26. A new stored procedure in the text editor.

You can create a stored procedure using any text editing tool and import it into the Query Analyzer of SQL Server. In order for SQL Server to recognize that you are trying to create a stored procedure, you need to use the CREATE PROCEDURE statement followed by the name of the procedure in double quotes. Similarly, if you want to change an existing stored procedure, you use the ALTER PROCEDURE statement followed by the name of the procedure you want to alter. (You don't need to use quotes when referring to an existing procedure unless the procedure name contains blanks or special characters.) If you were to save this procedure, close it, and reopen it in Access, you would see the ALTER statement instead of the CREATE statement, because you would be altering an existing procedure.

The /* and */ symbols mark the beginning and end of a block of comments. Anything written within those symbols is designated as a comment and is there only to provide information about the purpose of the stored procedure. You can also enter a single-line comment by typing two hyphens (--) at its beginning. Here are a couple of examples:

```
/* This is a multiple-line block of text
that describes a section of the stored procedure */

-- This is a single-line comment
```

Note You can see that the only keywords in the skeleton stored procedure shown in Figure 18-26 that aren't within comment blocks are CREATE, AS, and RETURN. Access includes the parameter declaration section and the SET NOCOUNT ON statement encased in block comments because it assumes that you won't always want to use these sections. However, the syntax of these sections is correct, so it's a simple matter to remove the comment symbols to make them a part of your procedure.

If your procedure requires parameters, you must declare them enclosed in parentheses immediately following the procedure name. Declare parameters for each item of data that you need to input into the procedure or that you will output from the procedure. To declare a parameter, enter the name of the parameter (the first character must be @), one or more spaces, and the data type of the parameter. When the data type is one of the text data types, you can also specify the maximum length in parentheses following the data type name. For some numeric data types, you can optionally specify the precision and scale in parentheses following the data type name. See Table 17-1 on page 610 for a list of data types supported by SQL Server.

You can optionally specify a default value by following the data type specification with an equal sign and the value that you want to assign as the default. Remember to enclose character and date/time literals in single quotes. By default, all parameters are input parameters. If you want to use a parameter for output, use the OUTPUT keyword at the end of the parameter declaration. If you want to declare multiple parameters, separate them with commas. You will learn more about parameters as you work with them in the example in this section. Here is an example that creates a single input parameter called @City that is the data type nvarchar, has a size of (30), and has a default value of Null:

```
(
@City nvarchar(30) = NULL
)
```

By default, SQL Server returns a row count message (the number of rows returned/affected) to Access after every SQL statement it executes. This is a useful feature if you are monitoring the row count for each SQL statement internally in the procedure. However, as stated earlier, if you are using multiple SQL statements in your procedure and the first one returns no rows, Access assumes that the entire procedure doesn't return any rows. If you execute a statement afterwards that *does* return rows (in Datasheet view, for example), Access will not display them. To avoid this, use the SET NOCOUNT statement followed by the ON keyword (this tells Access not to read the row count after each SQL statement). Because this statement is already included in the skeleton stored procedure, simply remove the beginning and end comment markers to enable it.

You enter the body of your stored procedure after the SET NOCOUNT statement and before the RETURN statement. This includes all SQL statements, control-of-flow statements, and output information. When you re-create the spAddOneCompany stored procedure, you will place the INSERT statement here.

The RETURN statement tells the stored procedure to exit the procedure unconditionally. If you are evaluating conditions in the middle of the procedure and need to stop execution for any reason, you can use the RETURN statement to do so.

Re-creating the Stored Procedure from the Query Designer Example

Based on the information covered so far, you might have already guessed what you need to do to re-create the spAddOneCompany stored procedure. You must declare an input parameter for each value you need to add to the tblCompanies table. Then add the INSERT statement after the AS statement to add the record to the table. In this example, you don't need SET NOCOUNT ON because the procedure contains only one SQL statement. The code to accomplish this is as follows:

```
CREATE PROCEDURE sptAddOneCompany
-- This procedure creates a new record in the Companies table
        (
        @Company_Name nvarchar(50),
        @Department nvarchar(50) = Null,
        @Address nvarchar(255) = Null,
        @City nvarchar(50) = Null,
        @County nvarchar(50) = Null,
        @State_Or_Province nvarchar(20) = Null,
        @PostalCode nvarchar(20) = Null,
        @Country nvarchar(50) = N'United States',
        @Phone_Number nvarchar(30) = Null,
        @Fax_Number nvarchar(30) = Null,
        @Website ntext = Null,
        @Referred_By int = Null
                                    )
AS
INSERT INTO dbo.tblCompanies
    (CompanyName, Department, Address, City, County, StateOrProvince,
    PostalCode, Country, PhoneNumber, FaxNumber, Website, ReferredBy)
VALUES
    (@Company_Name, @Department, @Address, @City, @County,
    @State_Or_Province, @PostalCode, @Country, @Phone_Number, @Fax_Number,
    @Website, @Referred_By)
RETURN
```

> **Tip** You can easily build this code in the skeleton procedure by inserting a blank line after the AS keyword and then starting the SQL designer by clicking the Insert SQL button on the toolbar. Follow the steps from earlier in this chapter to create the INSERT statement that you need, and then close the designer. Click Yes when Access offers to paste the SQL into your procedure. You can also open the *spAddOneCompany* procedure that you created earlier (or the sample *spXmplAddOneCompany* query), copy the SQL to the Clipboard, and paste it into your new procedure.

You can find this procedure saved as *sptXmplAddOneCompany* in the sample database. When you save and execute this stored procedure, you are prompted for each input parameter. You can enter a value for each input, or select <DEFAULT> or <NULL> from the drop-down list. (In most cases, the default is null.) Be sure to enter a value for the company name. When you are done, you will receive a message as shown in Figure 18-27.

There were no records returned because you didn't specify any in the stored procedure. If you open the tblCompanies table, you will see that the record was added successfully. If you don't enter a company name, you receive a cryptic message like the one shown in Figure 18-28 because the company name is a required column in the Companies table, and you won't find a new row in the tblCompanies table.

Figure 18-27. A message stating the stored procedure executed successfully.

Figure 18-28. A message stating the stored procedure failed.

As the stored procedure is written, there is no way to prevent this message from occurring if the user doesn't provide a company name. However, there are several options you could use to control the input in the stored procedure. You could use a form with ADO code in a Visual Basic module that controls the input, requires the user to enter a company name, and then passes it to the stored procedure. You can also modify the stored procedure itself to check for the correct values and return more descriptive information if it fails, as you'll do next. You'll learn about using ADO later in Chapter 29, "Upsizing a Desktop Application to a Project."

Note If you remove the RETURN statement in the example text stored procedure, save it, and open it again in Design view, Access displays it using the query designer because you haven't added any SQL commands that cannot be represented in the designer. As long as the stored procedure is only a single SQL statement with no other clauses, Access prefers to show it to you in the designer. The rest of the examples in this chapter can be edited only by using the text editor.

Adding Control-of-Flow Statements to Your Stored Procedure

Before you modify the stored procedure, you need to learn about some new statements you can use to check the company name. In this section, you will learn how to

- Declare variables, assign values to them, and test them
- Include IF/ELSE statements that test variables and execute an alternate set of statements
- Include BEGIN/END statements to define a block of statements that SQL Server should execute after an IF or ELSE statement
- Use the @@ROWCOUNT and @@IDENTITY system variables

Chapter 18

You have already learned how to create and use parameters in your procedures. You can also declare variables that store data that you can work with internally while the procedure is executing. Declaring variables is similar to declaring parameters, except you must use the DECLARE statement, which must follow the AS statement. You can declare multiple variables in one DECLARE statement, separated by commas. For example, the following code creates two variables called @CompanyID and @retMsg:

```
DECLARE @CompanyID int,
        @retMsg varchar(150)
```

The default value for all variables is Null. If you want to assign a value to a variable, you can use either the SELECT statement or the special SET statement. Both statements have similar syntaxes. The following are examples:

```
-- Assign a value to the @retMsg variable using SELECT
SELECT @retMsg = 'This message value was created using the SELECT statement.'
--Assign a value to the @retMsg variable using SET
SET @retMsg = 'This message value was created using the SET statement.'
```

With the SELECT statement, you can assign values to multiple variables by separating the assignments with commas. For example, the following SELECT statement assigns values to two variables:

```
SELECT @retMsg = 'Assign two values.', @CompanyID = 0
```

With the SET statement, you can assign only one value per statement. After you have declared a variable, you can use it anywhere in your procedure that you would normally be able to use a value of the same data type.

IF/ELSE statements allow you to test a condition and execute alternate tasks. When you use an IF statement, you can include any valid expression that can evaluate to true or false. You can also use a SELECT statement that evaluates to true or false, but you must encase it in parentheses. If SQL Server evaluates the IF statement as true, it executes the next line of code following the IF statement. If SQL Server evaluates the IF statement to false, it looks for an ELSE statement. If there is an ELSE statement, SQL Server executes the code immediately following the ELSE statement. If there is no ELSE statement, SQL Server continues executing the rest of the procedure after the IF statement. An example of an IF statement with an ELSE statement follows:

```
IF @Company_Name is Null
RETURN

ELSE
SET @retMsg = 'The company name was provided.'
```

When the condition in the IF statement evaluates as true, SQL Server executes only the next statement immediately following the IF statement. So what do you do if you want to execute multiple statements based on the evaluation of a single IF statement? One option is to include the IF statement again, with a new line of code after the second and subsequent IF statements. Another option is to create a batch of code using the BEGIN/END statements. SQL Server treats all lines of code between a BEGIN and an END statement as a single batch or line of code. If you want to execute multiple statements based on an IF condition, use the BEGIN and END statements to batch them. For example:

```
If @Company_Name is Null
  BEGIN
    SET @retMsg = 'You must supply a company name.'
    SELECT @retMsg AS "Status"
    RETURN
  END
```

In this example, if the @Company_Name variable is Null, then the procedure assigns an informative message to a character variable, returns that variable in a column named Status, and exits using a RETURN statement. Notice the use of the AS statement. This keyword specifies that the value of @retMsg should be returned as a recordset with the column heading *Status*. If the IF statement evaluates to true, you see a result similar to Figure 18-29. You can find an example procedure that includes this test saved in the sample database as *sptXmplAddOneCompanyTest*.

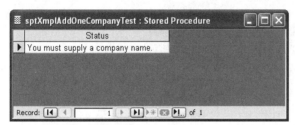

Figure 18-29. The procedure returns an error message as a recordset when you do not supply a company name.

SQL Server provides a variety of default system stored procedures and variables that you can use to improve the performance of your procedures. One useful variable that SQL Server provides is the @@ROWCOUNT variable. (The names of system variables always begin with two @ symbols.) @@ROWCOUNT stores the number of rows that were returned by the last SQL statement that was executed, useful for determining whether any records were returned. Another useful variable is the @@IDENTITY variable. After executing an SQL statement that updates, adds, or deletes a row that contains an identity column (equivalent to an AutoNumber in a desktop database), the @@IDENTITY variable contains the identity value of the last updated row.

Tip To learn more about the system variables, functions, and stored procedures that are available to improve the performance of your own user-defined stored procedures, refer to *Microsoft SQL Server Books Online*. Remember that you can download a free copy of the Books Online (a comprehensive set of help files) from *http://www.microsoft.com /sql/techinfo/productdoc/2000/books.asp*.

Chapter 18

673

Now that you've learned about some more of the available features in a stored procedure, you can solve the problem that occurs if a user fails to supply a company name. As you probably guessed, you need to use an IF/ELSE statement to evaluate the input of the @Company_Name parameter. Modify your sptAddOneCompany procedure to look like the following:

```
ALTER PROCEDURE sptAddOneCompany
-- This procedure creates a new record in the Companies table
        (
        @Company_Name nvarchar(50),
        @Department nvarchar(50) = Null,
        @Address nvarchar(255) = Null,
        @City nvarchar(50) = Null,
        @County nvarchar(50) = Null,
        @State_Or_Province nvarchar(20) = Null,
        @PostalCode nvarchar(20) = Null,
        @Country nvarchar(50) = N'United States',
        @Phone_Number nvarchar(30) = Null,
        @Fax_Number nvarchar(30) = Null,
        @Website ntext = Null,
        @Referred_By int = Null
                                )
AS

SET NOCOUNT ON

-- Declare a variable to return the new company ID
--   and a status message
DECLARE @CompanyID int,
        @retMsg varchar(150)

-- Make sure there's a company name
If @Company_Name is Null
  BEGIN
    -- Nope.  Set and return an error message and exit.
    SET @CompanyID = 0
    SET @retMsg = 'You must supply a company name.'
    SELECT @retMsg AS "Status", @CompanyID AS "CompanyID"
    RETURN
  END

-- Company name supplied, so attempt the insert
INSERT INTO dbo.tblCompanies
    (CompanyName, Department, Address, City, County, StateOrProvince,
    PostalCode, Country, PhoneNumber, FaxNumber, Website, ReferredBy)
VALUES
    (@Company_Name, @Department, @Address, @City, @County,
    @State_Or_Province, @PostalCode, @Country, @Phone_Number, @Fax_Number,
    @Website, @Referred_By)

-- If rowcount is not zero
If @@ROWCOUNT > 0
  -- Row inserted successfully
  BEGIN
```

```
    SET @CompanyID = @@IDENTITY
    SET @retMsg = 'New Company Added Successfully'
  END

ELSE
  -- Insert failed, return a zero company ID and an error message
  BEGIN
    SET @CompanyID = 0
    SET @retMsg = 'There was an Error. No Company was added.'
  END

-- Return the status of the insert and the new ID, if any
SELECT @retMsg AS "Status", @CompanyID AS "CompanyID"
RETURN
```

Not only does this improved procedure check the value of the @Company_Name parameter, but it also returns a recordset at the end of the procedure to let you know if it succeeded. To do this, it uses another set of IF/ELSE statements to evaluate the @@ROWCOUNT variable and assign values to the @retMsg and @CompanyID variables. When the insert is successful, the procedure uses the @@IDENTITY variable to find out the ID of the new company row so that it can return the value as part of the successful insert message. The SELECT statement at the end of the procedure returns the message and the company ID. You can find this query saved in the sample database as *sptXmplAddOneCompanyTest*.

Grouping Multiple Statements with Transactions

One of the great features of stored procedures and Transact-SQL is that you can control multiple SQL statements in one stored procedure. So far you've learned how to add a new record to the tblCompanies table and check for required values before executing the INSERT command. What if the business rules for this database specifically state that you cannot add a company without adding at least one valid contact? You could create two separate procedures—one to add a company and another to add the contact—but that won't guarantee that the rows in each table are related. Creating separate procedures also means that your users might execute one procedure and not the other and the job ends up only half done.

The solution is to use an SQL Server transaction. When you use a transaction, you can batch all your SQL statements into one procedure and commit the changes to the tables only if all the SQL statements succeed. If any errors occur or any constraints are violated, you can roll back the entire transaction and avoid having only a part of your procedure succeed. Creating a transaction in a procedure involves using three Transact-SQL statements: BEGIN TRANSACTION, COMMIT TRANSACTION, and ROLLBACK TRANSACTION. Using these statements is fairly simple. You indicate the beginning of a transaction batch by using the BEGIN TRANSACTION keywords. Then you include all the SQL statements that you want to be a part of the transaction. If all the statements succeed, you use the COMMIT TRANSACTION statement to commit the changes to the database. If your conditional statements within the transaction identify that an error or a failure occurred, you use the ROLLBACK TRANSACTION statement to undo all the changes made by any SQL statements in the transaction batch.

Chapter 18

The basic syntax for a transaction batch is simple. The difficult part is using effective conditional statements to evaluate if there is a problem that requires you to roll back the transaction. One particularly useful system variable for doing this is the @@Error variable. You can check the @@Error variable after the execution of each SQL statement. If @@Error is nonzero, you know that you must roll back the transaction.

You can use a transaction to execute multiple SQL statements in a single procedure, but that doesn't mean that all the SQL statements should be a part of the procedure. Each procedure should be straightforward and have a unique purpose. When you create the stored procedure that adds the company row and the contact row, you will create a separate procedure to add the contact. This way, you will have one procedure with the singular purpose of creating a complete company and another with the purpose of adding a contact.

After you have created a procedure that adds the contact information to the contact table, you can execute it from your sptAddOneCompany procedure. In order for the contact procedure to tell the company procedure that it succeeded, you need to use output parameters that it can pass back to the company procedure. Let's take a look at the procedure that adds the contact information (sptAddContact).

```
CREATE PROCEDURE sptAddContact
-- This procedure creates a new record in the Contacts table
    (
        @Last_Name nvarchar(50),
        @First_Name nvarchar(50) = Null,
        @Middle_Init nvarchar(1) = Null,
        @Title nvarchar(10) = Null,
        @Suffix nvarchar(10) = Null,
        @Contact_Type nvarchar(50) = Null,
        @Birth_Date datetime = Null,
        @Default_Address smallint = 1,
        @Work_Address nvarchar(255) = Null,
        @Work_City nvarchar(50) = Null,
        @Work_State_Or_Province nvarchar(20) = Null,
        @Work_Postal_Code nvarchar(20) = Null,
        @Work_Country nvarchar(50) = 'United States',
        @Work_Phone nvarchar(30) = Null,
        @Work_Extension nvarchar(20) = Null,
        @Work_Fax_Number nvarchar(30) = Null,
        @Home_Address nvarchar(255) = Null,
        @Home_City nvarchar(20) = Null,
        @Home_State_Or_Province nvarchar(20) = Null,
        @Home_Postal_Code nvarchar(20) = Null,
        @Home_Country nvarchar(50) = 'United States',
        @Home_Phone nvarchar(30) = Null,
        @Mobile_Phone nvarchar(30) = Null,
        @Email_Name ntext = Null,
        @Website ntext = Null,
        @Photo image = Null,
        @Spouse_Name nvarchar(75) = Null,
        @Spouse_Birth_Date datetime = Null,
        @Notes ntext = Null,
```

```
            @Commission_Percent float = 0,
            @ContactID int OUTPUT
                            )

AS
SET NOCOUNT ON

-- Exit procedure if @Last_Name is null
IF @Last_Name IS NULL
BEGIN
    SET @ContactID = 0
    RETURN
END

-- Otherwise, perform the insert
    INSERT INTO tblContacts
        (LastName, FirstName, MiddleInit, Title, Suffix, ContactType,
        BirthDate, DefaultAddress, WorkAddress, WorkCity,
        WorkStateOrProvince, WorkPostalCode, WorkCountry, WorkPhone,
        WorkExtension, WorkFaxNumber, HomeAddress, HomeCity,
        HomeStateOrProvince, HomePostalCode, HomeCountry, HomePhone,
        MobilePhone, EmailName, Website, Photo, SpouseName, SpouseBirthDate,
        Notes, CommissionPercent)

    VALUES
        (@Last_Name, @First_Name, @Middle_Init, @Title, @Suffix,
        @Contact_Type, @Birth_Date, @Default_Address, @Work_Address,
        @Work_City, @Work_State_Or_Province, @Work_Postal_Code,
        @Work_Country, @Work_Phone, @Work_Extension,
        @Work_Fax_Number, @Home_Address, @Home_City,
        @Home_State_Or_Province, @Home_Postal_Code, @Home_Country,
        @Home_Phone, @Mobile_Phone, @Email_Name, @Website, @Photo,
        @Spouse_Name, @Spouse_Birth_Date, @Notes, @Commission_Percent)

If @@ROWCOUNT > 0
    SET @ContactID = @@IDENTITY
ELSE
    SET @ContactID = 0

RETURN
```

If you like, you can open the example sptXmplAddContact procedure and then choose Save As from the File menu to save a new copy with a new name. As you can see, the sptAddContact procedure is fully capable of adding a complete contact record to the tblContacts table. It also includes @ContactID as an output parameter. If sptAddContact is called from any other procedure, it returns the @ContactID to let the calling procedure know if the insert succeeded. If @ContactID is 0, no record was added. Otherwise, @ContactID is equal to the identity value of the newly added row.

Now that you've built the sptAddContact stored procedure, you're ready to update the *sptAddOneCompany* stored procedure. (You might want to open that query in Design view, choose Save As from the File menu, save a copy as sptAddCompanyAndContact, and then modify the new copy.) Not only do you need to populate the tblContacts and tblCompanies tables, you also need to add a record to the tblCompanyContacts linking table to create the relationship between the rows. As you might have guessed, you'll use a transaction to monitor these three INSERT actions and make sure they all complete successfully.

In order to execute the sptAddContact stored procedure, you need to use the EXECUTE command. To do so, you type the command followed by the name of the procedure you want to execute and any required parameters that you need to supply. You can provide the parameters in the order they are specified in the called procedure, or you can identify them specifically by name. The following is an example that identifies them specifically by name:

```
EXECUTE sptAddContact
          @Last_Name = @Contact_Last_Name,
          @ContactID = @intContactID OUTPUT
```

You must declare both @Contact_Last_Name and @intContactID as local variables. Adding the OUTPUT keyword to the @ContactID assignment in the procedure call indicates that you expect the called procedure to return a value @intContactID. After the called procedure completes, you can use the local variable (@intContactID) to evaluate what was returned from the procedure—for example, check it to make sure a ContactID was returned.

Now that you have learned about the various features and abilities of a stored procedure, it's time to put together a more complex procedure that uses everything covered so far. Your procedure after you have updated it to use transactions to monitor multiple SQL statements should be as follows:

```
ALTER PROCEDURE sptAddCompanyAndContact
/* This procedure creates a new record in the Companies table.
It also adds a corresponding record to the Contacts table and
completes the relation by adding a linking record to the
CompanyContacts table */
        (
                @Company_Name nvarchar(50),
                @Contact_Last_Name nvarchar(50),
                @Contact_First_Name nvarchar(50) = Null,
                @Contact_Extension nvarchar(20) = Null,
                @Department nvarchar(50) = Null,
                @Address nvarchar(255) = Null,
                @City nvarchar(50) = Null,
                @County nvarchar(50) = Null,
                @State_Or_Province nvarchar(20) = Null,
                @Postal_Code nvarchar(20) = Null,
                @Country nvarchar(50) = 'United States',
                @Phone_Number nvarchar(30) = Null,
                @Fax_Number nvarchar(30) = Null,
                @Website ntext = Null,
                @Referred_By int = Null,
    --Identifies whether the procedure succeeded:
                @retSuccess bit = 1 OUTPUT,
                @retMsg varchar(150) = Null OUTPUT
        )
```

```
AS
SET NOCOUNT ON

    DECLARE
        @intCompanyID int,
        @intContactID int,
        @retErr int            --Will capture any error messages

--Make sure all the variables and output parameters are set to the defaults
    SELECT @intCompanyID = 0, @intContactID = 0, @retSuccess = 1, @retErr = 0

-- Exit procedure if @Company_Name is null
IF @Company_Name IS NULL
BEGIN
    SELECT @intCompanyID = 0, @retMsg = 'You must supply a company name. '
    SELECT @intCompanyID AS 'New CompanyID', @intContactID AS 'New ContactID',
        @retMsg AS 'Last Status Message'
    RETURN
END

-- Exit procedure if @Contact_Last_Name is null
IF @Contact_Last_Name IS NULL
BEGIN
  SELECT @intContactID = 0, @retMsg = 'You must supply a contact last name. '
  SELECT @intCompanyID AS 'New CompanyID', @intContactID AS 'New ContactID',
        @retMsg AS 'Last Status Message'
    RETURN
END

/* We have values for @Company_Name and @Contact_Last_Name
    So let's begin the TRANSACTION and add the rows */
BEGIN TRANSACTION

-- First, add the company row
INSERT INTO dbo.tblCompanies
    (CompanyName, Department, Address, City, County,
    StateOrProvince, PostalCode,
    Country, PhoneNumber, FaxNumber, Website, ReferredBy)

VALUES
    (@Company_Name, @Department, @Address, @City, @County,
    @State_Or_Province, @Postal_Code,
    @Country, @Phone_Number, @Fax_Number, @Website, @Referred_By)

SET @retErr = @@Error   --Check for any errors
IF @retErr <> 0
    SELECT @retSuccess = 0, @intCompanyID = 0,
        @retMsg = 'Insert failed. No company was added. '

ELSE
    SELECT @retSuccess = 1, @intCompanyID = @@IDENTITY,
        @retMsg = 'New company added successfully '

--Next, add the contact row by Executing sptAddContact
--But don't do it if Company insert already failed
```

679

```
IF @retSuccess = 1
BEGIN
        EXECUTE sptXmplAddContact
                @Last_Name = @Contact_Last_Name,
                @First_Name = @Contact_First_Name,
                @Work_Address = @Address,
                @Work_City = @City,
                @Work_State_Or_Province = @State_Or_Province,
                @Work_Postal_Code = @Postal_Code,
                @Work_Country = @Country,
                @Work_Phone = @Phone_Number,
                @Work_Extension = @Contact_Extension,
                @Work_Fax_Number = @Fax_Number,
                @Website = @Website,
                @ContactID = @intContactID OUTPUT

        SET @retErr = @@Error   --Check for any errors
        -- Also test @intContactID returned by the procedure
        IF @retErr <> 0 Or @intContactID = 0
            SELECT @retSuccess = 0,
                    @retMsg = 'Insert failed. No contact was added. '
        ELSE
            SELECT @retSuccess = 1, @intContactID = @@IDENTITY,
                    @retMsg = 'New contact added successfully '
END

--Finally, add the row to the CompanyContacts table
--But don't do it if either previous insert failed
IF @retSuccess = 1
BEGIN
    INSERT INTO dbo.tblCompanyContacts
        (CompanyID, ContactID, DefaultForContact, DefaultForCompany)
    VALUES
        (@intCompanyID, @intContactID,1,1)


    SET @retErr = @@Error   --Check for any errors
    IF @retErr <> 0
        SELECT @retSuccess = 0,
          @retMsg = 'Insert failed. No company-contact was added.'
    ELSE
        SELECT @retMsg = 'New company-contact added successfully.'
END

If @retSuccess = 1
BEGIN
    COMMIT TRANSACTION
END

ELSE
BEGIN
    ROLLBACK TRANSACTION
END
```

```
-- Return the new company ID, contact ID, and status message.
-- The IDs will be zero if the procedure failed.
SELECT @intCompanyID AS 'New CompanyID', @intContactID AS 'New ContactID',
       @retMsg AS 'Last Status Message'

RETURN
```

The procedure uses a local bit variable, @retSuccess, to track the success or failure of the INSERT statements. When any statement fails, the procedure does not attempt to execute subsequent INSERT statements. At the end of the procedure, the code checks the value of @retSuccess and commits all updates if the value is true (1) or rolls back all updates if the value is false (0).

Also note that the company address and phone information is used for the work address and phone information for the contact. Because this is a company contact that you're creating, you can assume that they will be the same. You can leave out the contact's home address and other information that is not relevant to creating a useful company contact record.

You can find this procedure saved as *sptXmplAddCompanyAndContact* in the sample database. To test this procedure, you can open the tblContacts table in Design view and clear the Allow Nulls property for the FirstName column. Run the procedure and supply a company name and contact last name, but do not supply a contact first name. You should see the procedure fail, and you won't find a new company record saved in the database even though the INSERT to the tblCompanies table succeeded.

> **Note**   When you run the sptXmplAddCompanyAndContact stored procedure, Access prompts you for the two output parameters, @retSuccess and @retMsg. You should not enter values for these two parameters. You would normally execute this stored procedure from another query or a Visual Basic procedure. Because the two output parameters have default values declared, you do not need to supply these parameters when you execute this procedure from another procedure.

So far, we have covered many commands that are commonly used in stored procedures, but we have only scratched the surface. If you want to learn more about creating stored procedures and Transact-SQL in general, *SQL Server Books Online* is an excellent place to start.

> **Tip**   You can also look up some of the SQL Server system functions in Article 3, "Function Reference," on the book's companion CD. They are organized by type of function (Arithmetic, Conversion, Date/Time, etc.) and are listed in order of their Visual Basic equivalents.

Building a Text Scalar Function

Another type of query that you can build in the text editor is a text scalar function. Scalar functions are very similar in concept to the system functions that SQL Server provides. They are usually defined to serve a singular purpose and return a single value. For example, you can build a scalar function if you repeatedly need to compute a single aggregate value when working with recordsets in your database. You can build the scalar function and then execute it whenever you need to compute the value. For example, if you often need to know the average price of products sold in a given time range, you can build a scalar function to compute that value for you. Then you only have to execute the scalar function instead of computing the value in the query every time you need to use it.

Like stored procedures, scalar functions can make use of the many features of Transact-SQL. They can accept parameters, execute multiple SQL statements, and use variables. The key point to keep in mind with scalar functions is that they always return a single value.

Because scalar functions always return a single value, they can be used just about anywhere you can use a single value, variable, or parameter in other views, functions, and stored procedures. The flexibility of scalar functions makes them very useful as you design and implement the other queries in your database.

> **Note** When you refer to scalar functions or any other type of functions that you have built, you must always include the parentheses () after the name of the function in your EXECUTE statement. This is the standard syntax for calling a function and must be used even if the function does not accept any parameters.

Take a look at the syntax for creating a scalar function in the text editor. First, create a new scalar function by selecting **Create Text Scalar Function** from the New Query dialog box (Figure 18-25). Access creates a new scalar function as shown in Figure 18-30.

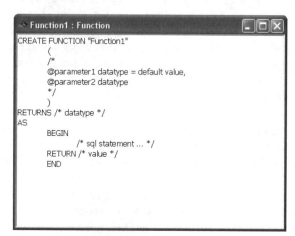

Figure 18-30. A new scalar function in the text editor.

The first half of the function should look familiar to you. The section in parentheses is where you declare any parameters that you will use in the scalar function. Remember to separate the parameters you declare with commas, and remember to remove the comment symbols (/* and */). Also note that you cannot declare OUTPUT parameters because scalar functions have only one output: the return value.

The RETURNS statement allows you to identify the data type of the value the scalar function is returning. The body of the scalar function must be entirely contained within one BEGIN/END statement block that follows the AS keyword. If you need to declare any local variables, define them within the BEGIN/END statement block. The last statement you use before the END keyword is the RETURN statement followed by the parameter or variable that contains the information the scalar function will return.

Building a Text Table-Valued Function

The last type of query that you can build using the text editor is a text table-valued function. In execution, the table-valued function is similar to a select query. It returns an entire recordset (or table) when it executes. The major difference is that table-valued functions can contain multiple SQL statements that are used to produce the final recordset that they return. As a result, table-valued functions can return tables that are the result set of several complex queries. The recordsets that table-valued functions return are read-only.

In a table-valued function, you can use the same Transact-SQL syntax as with scalar functions. The difference is a table-valued function returns a logical table instead of a single value, and it uses one or more INSERT statements to create the logical table that it returns. If you need to build a recordset that is based on multiple queries on other tables that might require parameters to determine the outcome, a table-valued function is very handy because it can perform this entire process in one function. Because table-valued functions return recordsets, you can use them anywhere you can use a single SQL statement in other views, functions, and stored procedures. Just remember that you can't alter the result set of a table-valued function.

Take a look at the syntax for creating a table-valued function in the text editor. First, create a new table-valued function by selecting **Create Text Table-Valued Function** from the New Query dialog box (Figure 18-25). Access creates a new table-valued function as shown in Figure 18-31 on the next page.

Chapter 18

```
Function1 : Function                                    _ □ X
CREATE FUNCTION "Function1"
        (
        /*
        @parameter1 datatype = default value,
        @parameter2 datatype
        */
        )
RETURNS /* @table_variable TABLE (column1 datatype, column2 datatype) */
AS
        BEGIN
                /* INSERT INTO @table_variable
                                sql select statement  */
                /* alternative sql statement or statements */
        RETURN
        END
```

Figure 18-31.   A new table-valued function in the text editor.

The syntax for a table-valued function is very similar to the syntax for a scalar function. The first section in parentheses is where you declare any parameters you might need. Again, you can only declare input parameters because the only output of a table-valued function is a single table recordset. The RETURNS statement identifies the value that the function will return (in this case, a table variable). You must also specify the column names and data types for the table variable in the parentheses following the table variable name. Be sure to separate column declarations with commas. Of course, you should also remove the comment symbols (/* and */) that surround the required table declaration.

Similar to scalar functions, table-valued functions must contain the full body of the function within a BEGIN/END statement block that follows the AS keyword. You can use any number of SQL statements within the statement block, and you can also perform inserts, updates, and deletes on your declared table variable. If you need to use any local variables, be sure to declare them within the block. The last statement in the BEGIN/END block must be a RETURN statement. SQL Server returns all rows that your code has inserted into the RETURNS table.

In this chapter you learned about the different types of queries that you can build in an Access project. You can see that in a project, you have more query options available than you do in an Access desktop database (.mdb) and that the queries also offer powerful features that aren't available in a desktop database. Even though we only took a brief look at each type of query, you should have a good idea of the different features of each query type and how to best use them to accomplish your query tasks in an Access project. Combined with the knowledge you gained in the previous query chapters, you should be ready to tackle creating views, functions, and stored procedures of your own. The next chapter will cover creating forms in an Access project.

Designing Forms in an Access Project

The most noticeable differences between Access desktop databases (.mdb) and Access project files (.adp) are in the tables and queries (views, functions, and stored procedures). Because Access projects store all their tables and queries in SQL Server, project tables and queries have many new design elements that you must understand to effectively use them. However, you won't notice many differences when building forms.

For the most part, forms in an Access project are identical to forms in an Access desktop database. In fact, you can successfully begin building forms that edit data from tables and views without knowing any details about the differences. However, to create a form that uses an in-line function or a stored procedure as its record source, especially if the function or procedure requires parameters, you must understand how forms in an Access project are different. The same is true if you want to create a combo box or a list box that uses a parameter query as its row source.

 Note This chapter assumes that you have already read the earlier chapters on form design (Chapters 11, 12, and 13) and have a good grasp of the basic form design concepts. You should be familiar with the form designer and know how to create forms that allow you to add and update data in tables. You can find the examples discussed in this chapter in the project file version of the LawTrack Contacts sample application, *Contacts.adp*, on the companion CD.

Understanding Form Differences in an Access Project

When you first open a form in a project file, you might not notice some of the subtle differences immediately. Figure 19-1 on the next page shows you the *frmContactsSimple* form open in the LawTrack Contacts project file.

Take a close look at the navigation bar at the bottom of the form and notice that the bar has two new buttons. The first, an X inside an oval, is the Cancel Query button. To its right is the Maximum Record Limit button with an exclamation point on it.

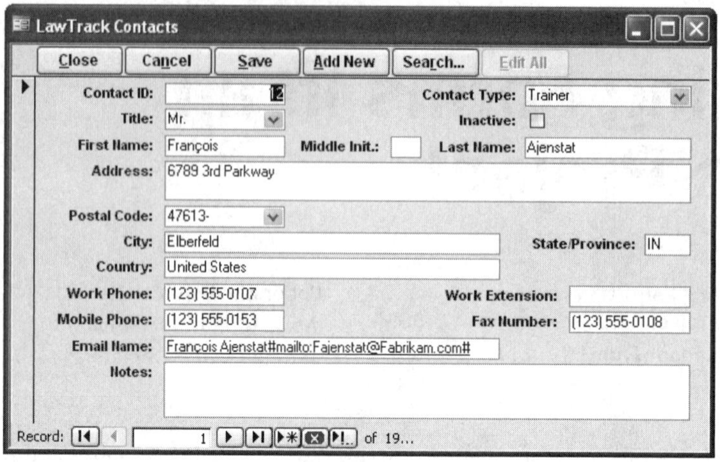

Figure 19-1. A sample form open in a project file.

When the user first opens a form in a project, Access begins fetching the rows to display in the form and displays the first row immediately. When the recordset for the form has many rows, Access continues to fetch the data as the user begins to work with the form. Access enables the Cancel Query button while it is still fetching rows. If the user needs only the first few rows fetched by the form, the user can click the button to ask Access to stop fetching rows, thereby freeing up resources on the server. This is a useful option when the user already has enough rows to work with and the server is taking too long to download the remaining records. If the user later decides to see all the rows, choosing Refresh from the Records menu asks Access to re-fetch the rows. The user can click the Cancel Query button again during the process or allow Access to fetch all the rows.

Access fetches all recordsets bound to a form in a project file as snapshots—literally copies of the data from the server. This method takes fewer resources from the server and places less strain on the network connection because Access uses the local copy of the data to display the information in the form instead of fetching data from the server whenever the user moves to different rows. When Access has enough information about the structure and relationships of the tables in the recordset, it allows the user to update the data in the form. When the user changes data and saves it, Access sends a specific Update command to the server to keep the data on the server synchronized with the data displayed in the form. Access does not write back the entire recordset or even the entire updated row.

To improve overall performance of your project, you can set properties to limit the number of rows fetched for all forms or datasheets in the project. You can also set a limit on a form-by-form basis. (You'll learn the details about these property settings later in this chapter.) When you set a limit for a form, that limit overrides any limit set for the project, but only for the record source of the form. If SQL Server has more rows to return than the limit allows, it returns as many rows as it can until it reaches the maximum limit. The rows that are actually returned are determined by the sort order of the recordset (the ORDER BY clause of the SQL statement). If there is no sort order in the recordset, the row order of the primary table takes precedence. If you have set the limit too low, the user can click the Maximum Record Limit button, and Access displays the dialog box shown in Figure 19-2.

Figure 19-2. Changing the maximum record count for the current form.

The user can change the Maximum Record Count value, click OK, and then choose Refresh from the Records menu to make more rows available in the form. However, if the user changes this value and then closes the form, Access asks if the changes to the form design should be saved. The good news is you can set a form property to hide this button from your users.

Choosing Option Settings

In the Options dialog box, you can find settings that affect how all forms work in your Access project. With the *Contacts.adp* sample project file open, select the Database window, and then choose Options from the Tools menu. Click the Edit/Find tab to see some of the options that apply to your forms, as shown in Figure 19-3.

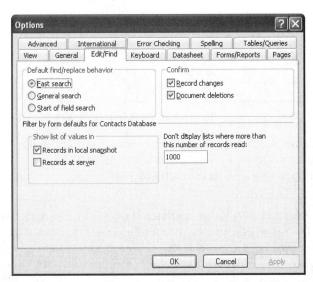

Figure 19-3. The Edit/Find options in the Options dialog box in an Access project file.

Even when you have disabled Server Filter By Form, users can still use the standard Filter By Form feature that you learned about in Chapter 10, "Using Forms." As you might recall, the Filter By Form feature provides drop-down lists to help the user select filter values.

By default, Access displays only those values it finds in the local snapshot copy of the form's recordset. You can select the Records at server option in the Show list of values in category to ask Access to fetch a complete list of values (for example, all the contact LastName values) from the server. You can also limit the number of values that Access fetches either from the local snapshot or the server by setting the Don't display lists when more than this number of records read option. When the number of values exceeds the number you set in the option, Access offers only Is Null and Is Not Null values in the drop-down list. The default value of 1000 should be sufficient for most purposes without causing performance problems.

Click the Advanced tab to see the other option you can set to affect how forms work in your Access project file, as shown in Figure 19-4.

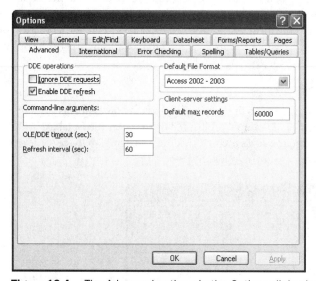

Figure 19-4. The Advanced options in the Options dialog box in an Access project file.

In the Client-server settings section, you can enter a new value for Default max records. If you have a slow connection with the server, it is a good idea to lower the value of the default maximum records to decrease the amount of time the user has to wait for a recordset to finish downloading.

When you create a new form in an Access project, Access sets the Max Records property of the form equal to the Default max records setting for the project. You can always override this setting by changing the Max Records property of a form, setting the value for an individual form either higher or lower. However, the Max Records property of a form applies only to the form's record source—it does not apply to the recordsets in the row sources of any combo boxes or list boxes on the form. The default value for Default max records in an Access project is 10,000, but I set the value in the LawTrack Contacts project file to 60,000 because several of the forms have a ZIP code combo box that returns more than 50,000 rows.

You'll find that the Max Records property for all forms in the sample project file are set to the lower 10,000 value.

> **Tip**   Normally, a user is looking for only one or two records to view or edit at any given time. If the user is browsing forms or opening reports that download the full recordset of a table, the server is wasting a lot of resources delivering records that aren't really needed. Instead, try to create recordsets that only return the amount of data that the user needs to work with. You can do this by using a variety of methods, such as building queries as record sources that limit the size of the recordset, using server filters, or using code to build or filter the recordset based on the choices of the user (searching for a record). Using methods like these makes the database easier to use and also lowers the strain you place on the server.

Setting Project Form Properties

Let's take a look at some of the new properties you can set for an individual form in an Access project. In the *Contacts.adp* project file, open the *frmContactsSimple* form in Design view. Open the Properties window by choosing Properties from the View menu. Select the Data tab to see the data properties for the form, as shown in Figure 19-5.

Figure 19-5.   The data properties of a form in an Access project file.

The Record Source Qualifier property and the properties beginning with Recordset Type and ending with Input Parameters are properties that you'll find in forms in an Access project (.adp) but not in forms in an Access desktop database (.mdb). You can click the Other tab in the Properties window to find the one other property that is unique to forms in an Access project, Max Rec Button.

Table 19-1 on the next page shows all the properties that are different for a form in an Access project. You can refer to this table for a brief definition of how each property is used.

Table 19-1. **Additional Form Properties in an Access Project**

Property	Tab	Description
Record Source Qualifier	Data	Identifies the SQL Server owner of the record source for this form. Unless a different owner has been specified by an administrator on SQL Server, this value is normally dbo. (short for database owner).
Recordset Type	Data	Identifies the type of recordset. When the record source for the form is a recordset that Access considers updatable, set this property to Updatable Snapshot (the default) to be able to update data via the form. When you want the data in the form to be read-only, choose Snapshot. An updatable snapshot requires more resources because Access must fetch additional information from the server about how to update the record source.
Max Records	Data	Sets the maximum number of records that SQL Server returns from the form's record source. The value in this property can be higher or lower than the Default max records setting for the project, and it overrides that setting. This property does not limit the rows returned by the row source of a combo box or a list box. The record limit for the row source of a combo box or list box is determined by the Default max records setting for the project.
Server Filter	Data	Specifies a filter that Access sends to the server to limit the rows in the recordset when the user opens the form. You must set Server Filter By Form to Yes (see below) if you want the user to be able to change this filter.
Server Filter By Form	Data	The default setting, No, disables Server Filter By Form mode. Server Filter By Form mode is similar to Filter By Form that you learned about in Chapter 10, "Using Forms," except that Access sends the filter to the server rather than filtering the records after fetching them. When you set this property to Yes, Access opens the form's Server Filter By Form window when the user opens the form. The user can edit any server filter saved with the form or specify a different filter. The user must click the Apply Server Filter button on the toolbar to apply the filter and see the result.

Table 19-1. **Additional Form Properties in an Access Project**

Property	Tab	Description
Unique Table	Data	When you connect your project to an SQL Server version 6.5 or 7.0 database, and the form uses as its record source a view or stored procedure that contains two or more related tables, Access sometimes cannot determine the information it needs to update the data displayed by the form. You can set the Unique Table property to the table that provides the unique rows in the recordset—the table on the many side of a one-to-many relationship—so that Access knows how to update the data. You do not need to set this property when your project is connected to an SQL Server 2000 or later database. (The version of MSDE that ships with Office 2003 is SQL Server 2000.)
Resync Command	Data	When you connect your project to an SQL Server version 6.5 or 7.0 database, when the form uses as its record source a view or stored procedure that contains two or more related tables, and when you had to specify the Unique Table property to enable updates, you must specify a special Transact-SQL statement to inform Access how to resynchronize the data after an update. Access uses the Resync Command to re-fetch related rows on the one side of a relationship when you change the foreign key on the many side of a relationship. Resync Command is typically a copy of the SQL from the view or stored procedure in the record source with parameters added to the WHERE clause to specify the key values of the many table in the relationship. You do not need to set this property when your project is connected to an SQL Server 2000 or later database. (The version of MSDE that ships with Office 2003 is SQL Server 2000.)
Input Parameters	Data	Allows you to specify the values of any input parameters that are used in the SQL record source of the form.
Max Rec Button	Other	Specifies whether or not the Max Records button is visible on the form.

The remaining sections of this chapter provide more detailed explanations and examples of how these properties work in your project forms.

Setting Recordset Type

In Chapter 12, "Customizing a Form," you learned how to set the Allow Edits, Allow Deletions, and Allow Additions properties of a form to restrict what data the user can update via the form. When you want to disallow all edits, deletions, and additions in a form in an Access project, you can also change the Recordset Type property. By default, the Recordset Type property of a form in a project is Updatable Snapshot. As long as Access determines that the record source of the form is updatable, the user is able to edit, delete, and add records using the form. However, when you change the Recordset Type to Snapshot, the form becomes read-only.

To see an example, open the *frmXmplZIPReadOnly* form in the LawTrack Contacts project file. Figure 19-6 shows you the form open in Form view.

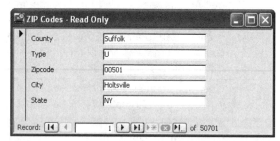

Figure 19-6. A sample form whose Recordset Type property is set to Snapshot.

Notice that the New Record button on the navigation bar is disabled. Although this might indicate that the Allow Additions property is set to No, this is usually a good indication that the recordset in the form is not updatable. Try typing in any of the fields on the form, and Access plays an alert sound and displays the message "Field '<field name>' is based on an expression and can't be edited" on the status bar. (The message doesn't make sense in this context, but that's what Access displays.)

Switch to Design view, open the Properties window, and change Allow Edits, Allow Deletions, and Allow Additions to No and Recordset Type to Updatable Snapshot. Switch back to Form view and try it out. You won't be able to type in any of the fields, but Access no longer plays a sound or displays a message on the status bar. As you can see, knowing about the Recordset Type property adds one more tool to your bag of tricks. (Be sure to not save the form design changes when you close the form.)

Understanding Max Records

You learned earlier that you can set Default max records (in the Options dialog box) for the entire project and the Max Records property for individual forms. You already know that Default max records for the Contacts project is set to a very high number—60,000 records. To see the interaction of these two settings in action, open the *frmXmplContacts10* sample form and drop down the Postal Code combo box list, as shown in Figure 19-7.

Notice that the form's navigation bar indicates only 10 records in the recordset, but the Postal Code combo box shows a matching value in the list from the row source. ZIP code 47613 is far beyond the 10-row limit in the form, so the combo box must be working from the default maximum records limit set for the project.

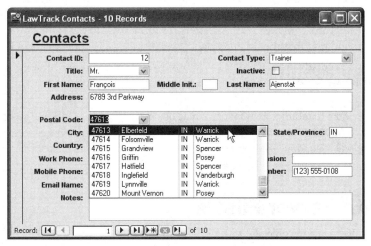

Figure 19-7. A form that has a Max Records setting of 10.

To see what happens when you change the Default max records setting for the project, try this little exercise:

1. Switch to Design view.
2. Choose Options from the Tools menu and click the Advanced tab.
3. Set the Default max records option for the entire project to 100 and click OK.
4. Switch back to Form view and drop down the list in the Postal Code combo box.

   Your result should now look like Figure 19-8.

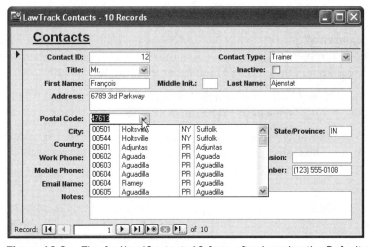

Figure 19-8. The frmXmplContacts10 form after lowering the Default max records setting for the project.

Notice that the value for Postal Code in the current record no longer matches a value in the list. The combo box list does not have a match for the current value of the field because the list is now limited to 100 rows, the default maximum records value for the entire project. But the form is still limited to 10 records—the overriding limit set for the form recordset in the form's Max Records property. You can scroll down the combo box list and find that the list ends at ZIP code 00771—the 100th value in the list.

5 Return to the Advanced tab of the Options dialog box and reset Default max records to **60000**. Click OK and then close the form *without* saving it.

> **Caution** Be sure to return to the Options dialog box and change the Default max records setting back to **60000**. If you don't do this, none of the ZIP code combo boxes in the project will work properly. Also, don't save any changes when you close the sample form.

Working with Server Filters

You should already be familiar with using filters in forms from working through the earlier forms chapters in this book. In addition to regular filters, Access projects also include the ability to apply server filters. Server filters function similarly to regular filters except they are applied before the recordset is retrieved from the server and sent to the form. When you apply regular filters in forms, Access first fetches the recordset from the server and then applies the filter on your client machine to limit the rows actually displayed in the form. Applying filters on the server side is advantageous because it reduces the load on the server and it cuts down on network traffic.

Although server filters are very advantageous, you can use them only when your form has a table or a view as its record source. You can define a server filter for a form that is bound to an in-line function, but Access ignores it. If you try to define a server filter for a form bound to a stored procedure, Access displays a warning message when you try to open the form: "A Server Filter cannot be applied to a stored procedure Record Source. Filter not applied." Tables and views do not support parameters, so you cannot design a form that uses both parameters and server filters. As you'll learn later in this chapter, parameters can be just as effective as server filters when you bind your form to a function or stored procedure.

To see how server filters work, open the LawTrack Contacts project file (*Contacts.adp*) and then open the *frmXmplContactsServFilter* form. Access displays a result as shown in Figure 19-9.

Notice that the form displays only two of the 19 contacts in the database. If you change to Design view and look at the Server Filter property, you'll find the following:

```
LastName LIKE 'V%'
```

The Server Filter property contains criteria that you might find in a WHERE clause, but without the WHERE keyword. Remember that Access sends this filter to the server, so you must use SQL Server syntax: single quotes surrounding date/time and string literals, and % and _ wildcard characters in a LIKE comparison instead of * and ?. If you need to specify multiple criteria, you can do so by joining them with multiple AND or OR Boolean operators. Here is an example:

```
ContactType = 'Customer' AND ((WorkPostalCode BETWEEN '10000' AND
    '15999') OR (WorkStateOrProvince = 'PA'))
```

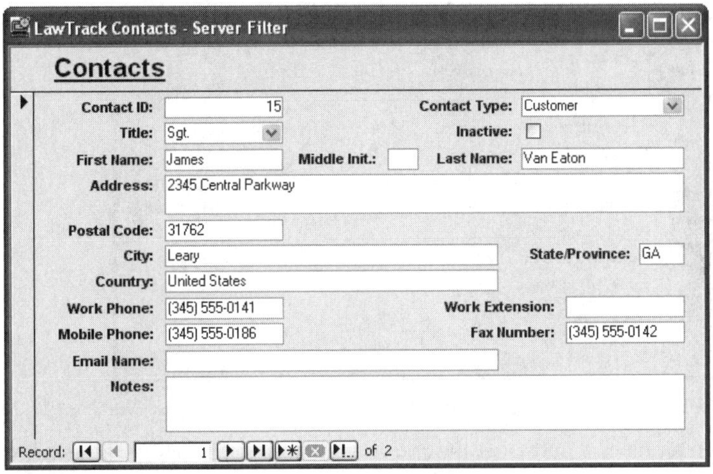

Figure 19-9. A form based on a view that has a server filter defined.

You can change the Server Filter property to the criteria shown above and then change to Form view. Notice that the form now displays six records instead of two. Notice also that the Server Filter by Form button is not available on the toolbar, and you cannot choose Filter on the Records menu and then click Server Filter by Form on the submenu—the form's Server Filter By Form property is set to No. If you close the form and save your changes, the form will be permanently filtered using your new criteria, and the user won't be able to change it.

> **Tip** If you are unsure how to write the server filter, try setting the form's Server Filter By Form property to Yes, changing to Form view, and then applying the filter you want using the filter by form interface. When you change back to Design view, you'll find the filter you defined entered in the Server Filter property of the form with correct syntax. Set the form's Server Filter By Form property to No and save your changes. Access uses the filter you created automatically every time the form is opened.

If you want to allow users to set the Server Filter property, you can set the form's Server Filter By Form property to Yes. To see how this works, open the *frmXmplContactsServFilterByForm* form. Rather than display records, Access shows you the Server Filter by Form interface with the currently defined filter, as shown in Figure 19-10 on the next page.

The filter options in the Server Filter by Form window are similar to the options you have when performing a normal filter by form. You can enter filter criteria in each of the boxes and also add multiple criteria for a single column by adding additional criteria on the successive Or tabs. By default, the drop-down lists offer only the Is Null and Is Not Null options. If you want, you can display a full list of values for a particular text box by changing the Filter Lookup

695

property of the text box to Always in Design view. You can also select the Records at server option on the Edit/Find tab of the Options dialog box, as shown earlier in Figure 19-3.

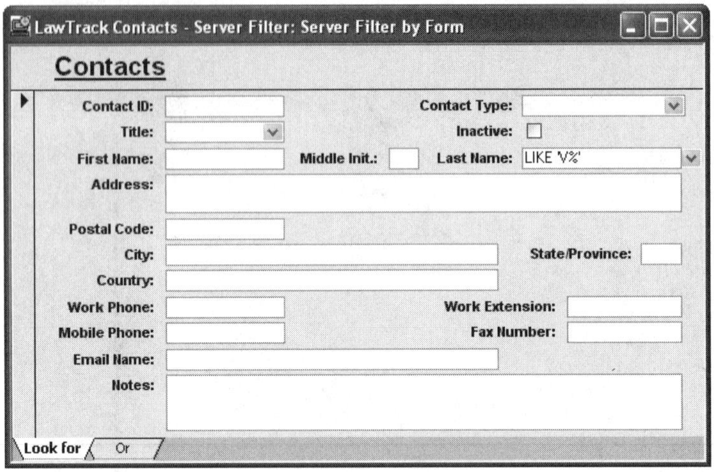

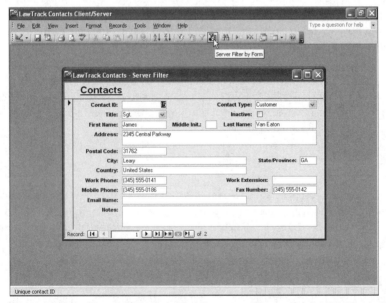

Figure 19-10. A form with a predefined server filter that allows server filter by form.

To apply a server filter, simply enter the criteria you want in the appropriate text boxes and then click the Apply Server Filter button on the toolbar to apply the filter. If you click the button without changing the filter on the sample form, your result should look like Figure 19-11. Notice that the Server Filter by Form button is available on the toolbar to return to Server Filter by Form mode. For more information on filtering by forms, refer to Chapter 10.

Figure 19-11. The results of applying the server filter on the frmXmplContactsServFilterByForm form.

Setting Input Parameters

Server filters are great if you need to filter the data from a table or view. However, they don't work if your recordset is an in-line function or a stored procedure. Fortunately, in-line functions and stored procedures can use input parameters to control the data they return.

When you use a parameter query as the record source for a form, you can let Access prompt the user for the parameters when the user opens the form. However, forms in an Access project also have an input parameter that allows you to specify an alternative way to resolve parameters that are required for the in-line function or stored procedure that serves as the form's record source.

In the sample database, you can find a simple stored procedure, *spXmplCompanyParameter*, that returns rows from the tblCompanies table and includes a parameter to filter the company name. To demonstrate the various techniques that you can use to resolve the parameter when you use this query in a form, I built three forms. The first, *frmXmplCompaniesParmFromSP*, doesn't have any special property settings to help resolve the parameter. When you open the form, Access prompts you for the input parameter, as shown in Figure 19-12.

Figure 19-12. When you open a simple form bound to a parameter query, Access prompts you for the parameter values.

Although the parameter name is relatively self-explanatory, it doesn't really give you any clue that you can enter all or part of a company name. For example, if you type the letter *T* and click OK, Access displays a result as shown in Figure 19-13.

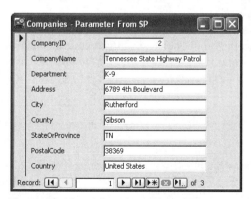

Figure 19-13. A form based on a parameter query displaying all companies that have a name beginning with the letter *T*.

If you don't want the user to see the parameter prompt at all, you can set the Input Parameters property of the form. Open the *frmXmplCompaniesParmFromSP* form in Design view. In the Properties window, click the Data tab and locate the Input Parameters property. When a form is bound to a record source that accepts input parameters, you can enter a value for each of the parameters in this property. (Separate the parameter declarations with commas.) To specify a parameter, you need to supply the parameter name, the data type of the parameter, and a value for the parameter. As you have already seen, the name of the parameter for the stored procedure used by this form is @Enter_Company_Name. If you want this form to always display only companies that have names beginning with the letter *T*, enter the following in the Input Parameters property:

```
@Enter_Company_Name nvarchar(50) = 'T'
```

The form should now look like Figure 19-14.

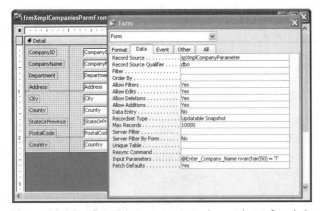

Figure 19-14. Resolving a parameter by setting a form's Input Parameters property.

Switch to Form view by clicking the View button on the toolbar. Notice that the form automatically displays the rows for companies that have a name beginning with the letter *T*. If you think about it, this is similar to specifying a server filter for a form that uses a table or view as its record source. The form sends a filter to the server, and the user cannot change the filter. When you close the form, Access prompts you to ask if you want to save the change you just made. Keep in mind that if you save this change, Access no longer prompts you for the parameter when you open the form.

Inside Out

Why not create a query that includes the filter I want instead of hard-coding a server filter or input parameter in my form?

Instead of creating a form that defines a fixed filter or parameter value, you could certainly create a separate query that includes the filter as part of its WHERE clause and use that query for your form. However, you might want to create your application so that it opens different forms depending on the user's authority. Some users might be allowed to view all rows. For others, you might want to always provide a filtered view of the data. You can design two forms, one that allows the user to view all rows or specify a parameter to view any rows and another that lets a more restricted user view only specific rows. You can use the same query as the record source for both forms. In the form that you open for the restricted user, create a static server filter or provide a fixed input parameter value that the user cannot change. By using the same query for both forms, you simplify the number of queries that you must define to support your application.

What if you wanted to allow the user to specify a different company every time the form opens? You could certainly leave the Input Parameters property blank and let Access prompt the user for the parameter. However, if the variable name is too cryptic or you want something that would be easier for your users to understand, you can enter a more descriptive term in the Input Parameters property as follows:

```
@Enter_Company_Name nvarchar(50) = [Enter all or part of a company name:]
```

Wait a minute! What's going on here? What the above setting accomplishes is a substitution of the parameter name in the query with a parameter value that provides more information. I created a sample form in the database that includes this parameter substitution in the Input Parameters property. When the user opens this form, Access prompts for the substituted parameter name, not the original name, as shown in Figure 19-15. Now your users might get a better idea of what information is being requested.

Figure 19-15. A more descriptive request for a parameter value.

But what if they don't know the name of the company? What if a company name begins with an article, such as The Microsoft Corporation, and the user gets frustrated when entering the letter *M* produces an incorrect result? One solution is to create a separate form with a combo box or list box that provides a list containing all the company names. Then the user could select a value from the list, and you can specify an Input Parameters setting that resolves the query parameter by referencing the value that the user selects.

In the sample database, you can find a form, *fdlgXmplCompanyParm*, that provides a list of company names in a combo box called cmbCompany. You can open the form and select a company name from the list, as shown in Figure 19-16 on the next page.

Click OK, and a form opens to display the company you selected, as shown in Figure 19-17 on the next page. This form, *frmXmplCompanesParmFromForm*, uses the same parameter stored procedure as its record source. But notice that Access didn't prompt for the parameter.

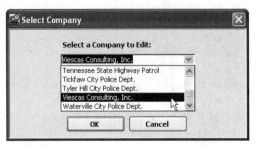

Figure 19-16. Choosing a value from a combo box on a form that resolves a stored procedure parameter.

Figure 19-17. A form using a parameter query, and the parameter is resolved from a value chosen from a list in another form.

The secret is that the form's Input Parameters property has a special setting, as follows:

```
@Enter_Company_Name nvarchar(50) = [Forms]![fdlgXmplCompanyParm]![cmbCompany]
```

The interesting value assigned to the parameter is a reference to the combo box on the fdlgXmplCompanyParm form. This special syntax asks Access to look at all the open forms ([Forms]!), find the form named fdlgXmplCompanyParm, and then find the control on the form named cmbCompany. In truth, the fdlgXmplCompanyParm form has a little bit of Visual Basic code behind the two command buttons to make the example run smoothly. But the critical lesson is the special syntax that you can use in input parameters to redirect resolution of the parameter value to the value in a control on another form. For more details about Visual Basic and the rules for referencing objects in Access, see Chapter 22, "Understanding Visual Basic Fundamentals."

You should now have a good understanding of the differences between forms in an Access project file (.adp) and those in a desktop database (.mdb). In the next chapter, you'll learn about the differences for reports.

Building Reports in an Access Project

As you learned in the previous chapters on Access projects, the most noticeable differences between Access desktop databases (.mdb) and Access project files (.adp) are in the tables and queries (views, functions, and stored procedures). You need to consider only a few differences when working with forms—and even fewer when working with reports.

As with forms, reports in an Access project are nearly identical to reports in an Access desktop database. You can get started building most reports without knowing any details about the differences. In the last chapter, you learned about how different types of queries used as record sources can affect the way you build your forms. The same is true for reports. Because you are working with data from SQL Server, it is important to understand the key differences of each query type and how to maximize their efficiency when using them as record sources in your reports.

 Note This chapter assumes that you have already read the earlier chapters on report design (Chapters 14, 15, and 16) and have a good grasp of the basic report design concepts. You should be familiar with the report designer and know how to create reports that allow you to view grouped and/or aggregate data. You can find the examples discussed in this chapter in the project file version of the LawTrack Contacts sample application, *Contacts.adp*, on the companion CD.

Understanding Report Differences in an Access Project

To understand the report differences in an Access project, open the LawTrack Contacts project file (*Contacts.adp*), and then open the *rptProductsPlain* report in Print Preview. Figure 20-1 on the next page shows the report in Print Preview. (This is one of the few reports in the sample project file that does not have a custom menu or a custom toolbar.)

Notice that the navigation bar at the bottom of the report includes the Cancel Query and Max Records buttons that you can see on forms in a project, but they are disabled. When you're viewing reports in a project file, these buttons are always disabled. Unlike forms, Access project reports always fetch all records before displaying any data. Keep in mind that a report represents a complete summary of information that is meant to be displayed or printed, not updated. A report might include grouping or totals that requires the entire recordset in order to be calculated correctly. If a report only returned a partial recordset, totals and averages included in the report would be inaccurate.

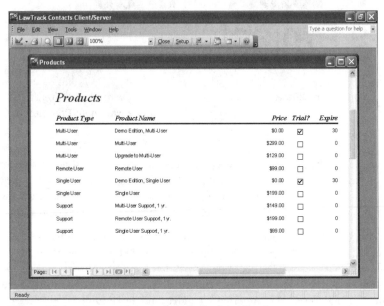

Figure 20-1.   A report in a project file in Print Preview.

Because reports always return all the rows in the record source, it is important to limit the record source to only the rows that the user needs to see. If a large report returns mostly unnecessary information, a lot of time and server resources will be wasted. Instead, try to create recordsets that return only the data that the user needs to view. For example, you might want to print a report about companies that have a training department or the invoices for a specific company and date. You can do this by using a variety of methods, such as building queries as record sources that limit the size of the recordset, using server filters, or using code to build or filter the recordset based on the choices of the user (searching for a record) in a form before opening the report. Using methods like these make the database easier to use and also lower the strain you place on the server.

Setting Project Report Properties

Let's take a look at some of the new properties you can set for a report in an Access project. Click the View button on the toolbar to switch the *rptProductsPlain* report to Design view. (If you didn't open the report previously, then select it in the Database window and click the Design button on the Database window toolbar.) Open the Properties window by choosing Properties from the View menu. Select the Data tab to see the data properties for the report, as shown in Figure 20-2.

Record Source Qualifier, Server Filter, and Input Parameters are properties that you'll find in reports in an Access project (.adp) but not in reports in an Access desktop database (.mdb).

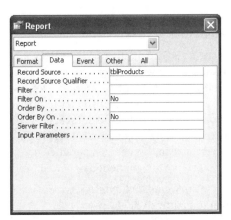

Figure 20-2. The data properties of a report in an Access project file.

If you have read through Chapter 19, "Designing Forms in an Access Project," these properties should already be familiar to you. Table 20-1 shows all the properties that are different for a report in an Access project. You can refer to this table for a brief definition of how each property is used.

Table 20-1. Additional Report Properties in an Access Project

Property	Tab	Description
Record Source Qualifier	Data	Identifies the SQL Server owner of the record source for this report. Unless a different owner has been specified by an administrator on SQL Server, this value is normally *dbo* (short for database owner).
Server Filter	Data	Specifies a filter that Access sends to the server to limit the rows fetched from the server when the user opens the report.
Input Parameters	Data	Allows you to specify the values of any input parameters that are used in the SQL record source of the report.

Working with Server Filters

As you learned in Chapter 19, when you specify a server filter, Access includes the filter in the request it sends to the server. The server selects the rows that meet the criteria in the server filter and sends only the requested data back to Access. Server filters are advantageous because they reduce the size of the recordset, fetching only the data the user needs to see. You can also set the Filter property on a report, but Access doesn't apply that filter until it has fetched all the unfiltered data from the server. Using a server filter cuts down on the time a server must spend processing the recordset and eliminates the time that Access would otherwise spend applying the filter on your client machine. You can imagine that using a server filter can have a significant impact on the efficiency of your reports, particularly when the underlying tables needed for a report contain hundreds of thousands of rows.

Although server filters are very advantageous, you can use them only when your report has a table or a view as its record source. You can define a server filter for a report that is bound to an in-line function, but Access ignores it. If you try to define a server filter for a report bound to a stored procedure, Access displays a warning message when you try to open the report: "A Server Filter cannot be applied to a stored procedure Record Source. Filter not applied." Tables and views do not support parameters, so you cannot design a report that uses both parameters and server filters. As you'll learn later in this chapter, parameters can be just as effective as server filters when you bind your report to a function or stored procedure.

To see how server filters work, open the *rptXmplCompanyContactsServerFilter* report in Print Preview. Access displays a result as shown in Figure 20-3.

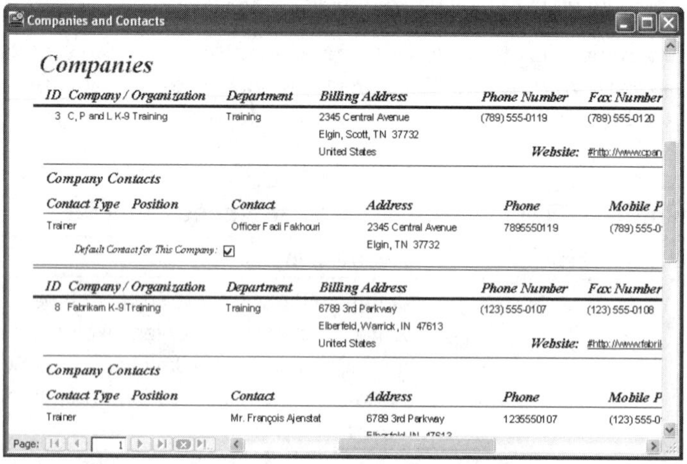

Figure 20-3. A report based on a view that has a server filter defined.

Notice that the report displays only two of the 11 companies in the database. If you switch to Design view and look at the Server Filter property, you'll find the following:

```
Department = 'Training'
```

This example is similar to the server filter example shown in Chapter 19 and illustrates how the server filter can be used effectively in both forms and reports. The Server Filter property contains criteria that you might find in a WHERE clause, but without the WHERE keyword. Remember that Access sends this filter to the server, so you must use SQL Server syntax: single quotes surrounding date/time and string literals, and % and _ wildcard characters in a LIKE comparison instead of * and ?. If you need to specify multiple criteria, you can do so by joining them with multiple AND or OR Boolean operators. Here is an example of a simple criterion:

```
StateOrProvince LIKE 'T%'
```

You can change the Server Filter property to the criteria shown above and then change to the Report window. Notice that the report now displays three companies instead of two. You can also specify criteria as complex as necessary to get the job done. This report uses a subreport to display the contact information for each company. If you want to filter on the contact information, you must use a subquery. (See Article 1, "Understanding SQL," on the companion CD for details about using subqueries to filter data.) For example, if you want to list all companies that have a contact who is contact type 'Customer' in the state of Pennsylvania, you could specify the following filter:

```
CompanyID IN (SELECT CompanyID FROM tblCompanyContacts
INNER JOIN tblContacts
ON tblCompanyContacts.ContactID = tblContacts.ContactID
WHERE tblContacts.ContactType = 'Customer'
AND tblContacts.WorkStateOrProvince = 'PA')
```

Using the above filter returns the two companies in Pennsylvania that have one or more contacts categorized as customers.

> **Tip**   Access provides the option to specify both server filters and regular filters in your reports. Remember that server filters are always more efficient because the server applies the filter before returning the data. Unless you have a very compelling reason to filter the data after it is returned to the report, always use server filters instead.

Working with Input Parameters

Server filters are great if you need to filter the data from a table or view. However, they don't work if your recordset is an in-line function or a stored procedure. Fortunately, in-line functions and stored procedures can use input parameters to control the data they return.

When you use a parameter query as the record source for a report, you can let Access prompt the user for the parameters when the user opens the report. However, reports in an Access project also have an input parameter that allows you to specify an alternative way to resolve parameters that are required in the in-line function or stored procedure that serves as the report's record source.

Inside Out

What type of query should I use as the record source of a report?

When considering what type of query to use as the record source of a report, the question really boils down to using server filters versus using input parameters. You can use either method to return the data you want to display, but each method has its own advantages.

Server filters are easy to define and are best used when you know you are going to be filtering the data the same way every time you view the report. Examples include filtering products by a particular category, displaying a list of active employees, or showing the current sales tax rate for the 50 states. Use a view or a table whenever you use server filters.

Input parameters are versatile and are best used when you need to allow your users to specify criteria to limit the recordset of the report. Examples include showing all the employees for a selected company, displaying a list of all sales within a specified date range, or looking up the detailed information for a particular contact. Use an in-line function or a stored procedure whenever you use input parameters.

If you don't intend to use either server filters or input parameters, use a view as your record source because it is simple and efficient.

In the sample database, you can find a simple stored procedure, *spXmplInvoiceParm*, that returns rows from the tblCompanies and tblInvoices tables and includes parameters to filter the company name and the date of the invoice. In Chapter 19, you learned the various techniques that you can use to resolve the parameter when you use this query in a form using three sample forms. In the sample *Contacts.adp* project file, you can find three sample reports that illustrate these same techniques when working with reports in an Access project. The first report, *rptXmplInvoicesParmFromSP*, doesn't have any special property settings to help resolve the parameters. When you open the report, Access prompts you for the input parameters, one at a time, as shown in Figure 20-4.

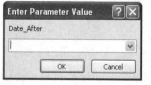 

Figure 20-4. When you open a simple report bound to a parameter query, Access prompts you for the parameter values.

Although the parameter names are relatively self-explanatory, the Date_After parameter doesn't tell you that you'll see invoices produced on or after the date you enter. Also, the Enter_Company_Name parameter doesn't give you any clue that you can enter all or part of a company name. For example, if you type 1/15/2003 for the date and the letter *T* for the company name and click OK, Access displays a result as shown in Figure 20-5. (You should see four invoices.)

If you don't want the user to see the parameter prompt at all, you can set the Input Parameters property of the report. Open the *rptXmplInvoicesParmFromSP* report in Design view. In the Properties window, click the Data tab and locate the Input Parameters property. When a report is bound to a record source that accepts input parameters, you can enter a value for each of the parameters in this property. (Separate the parameter declarations with commas.) To specify a parameter, you need to supply the parameter name, the data type of the parameter, and a value for the parameter. As you have already seen, the name of the parameter for the stored procedure used by this report is @Enter_Company_Name. If you want this report to always display invoices created within the last 90 days and only for companies that have names beginning with the letter *T*, enter the following in the Input Parameters property:

```
@Enter_Company_Name nvarchar(50) = 'T',@Date_After datetime = (Date()-90)
```

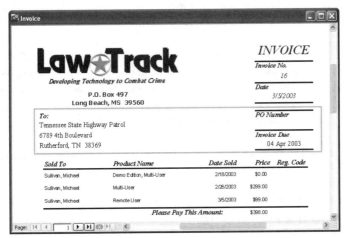

Figure 20-5. A report based on a parameter query displaying all invoices created on or after January 15, 2003, for companies that have a name beginning with the letter *T*.

Notice that you're taking advantage of the Access built-in Date function to fetch the current date and then subtract 90 days to provide one of the parameter values. The report should now look like Figure 20-6.

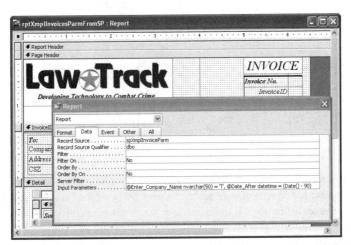

Figure 20-6. Resolving a parameter by setting a report's Input Parameters property.

The sample database contains records only up through April 8, 2003, so to get any results, you'll have to temporarily set your system clock back. Set your system date to March 15, 2003, and then switch to Print Preview by clicking the View button on the toolbar. Access shouldn't prompt you for any parameters, and you should see six invoices.

Chapter 20

Notice that the report automatically displays the rows for companies that have a name beginning with the letter *T*. If you think about it, this is similar to specifying a server filter for a report that uses a table or view as its record source. The report sends a filter to the server, and the user cannot change the filter. When you close the report, Access asks if you want to save the change you just made. Keep in mind that if you save this change, Access no longer prompts for the parameters when you open the report.

> **Note** You might notice that the examples and the steps for applying server filters and using input parameters are very similar in both forms and reports. Keep in mind that both server filters and input parameters are properties that modify the result returned by the record source. After you understand the principles behind server filters and input parameters, you can use them effectively in both your forms and your reports.

What if you want to allow the user to specify a different company every time the report opens? You could certainly leave the Input Parameters property blank and let Access prompt the user for the parameters. However, if the variable names are too cryptic or you want something that would be easier for your users to understand, you can enter more descriptive terms in the Input Parameters property as follows:

```
@Date_After datetime = [Invoices on or after date:],
@Enter_Company_Name nvarchar(50) = [Enter all or part of a company name:]
```

As you learned in the previous chapter, the above settings accomplish a substitution of each parameter name in the query with a parameter value that provides more information. I created a sample report in the database that includes this parameter substitution in the Input Parameters property, *rptXmplInvoicesCustomParameter*. When the user opens this report, Access prompts with the substituted parameter names, not the original names, as shown in Figure 20-7. Now your users might have a better idea of what information is being requested.

 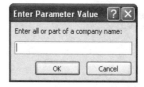

Figure 20-7. More descriptive requests for parameter values.

If you have read the previous chapter and followed the examples on input parameters, everything discussed so far for reports should seem familiar. You can use input parameters to control the data the server returns. If the parameter name is too cryptic, you can substitute a more descriptive request for information. However, you can still run into problems if your users don't know what company they are looking for or can't remember how to spell the company name.

Chapter 19 proposed using a form with a combo box to select the name of the company you want to view. This solution also works great for reports. You can build a form similar to the one shown in Chapter 19, except now you're using it to open a report instead of a form, and the form needs to prompt for two parameter values. This method is especially useful if you want to limit the data in the report to a specific date range by using a form to supply the beginning and end date parameters to your report. Now let's take a look at an example of a form that can be used to select a starting date and a company name to view in a report.

In the sample database, you can find a form, *fdlgXmplInvoiceParm*, that provides a box to enter a date (called txtDate) and a list of company names in a combo box (called cmbCompany). You can open the form, enter a date, and select a company name from the list, as shown in Figure 20-8.

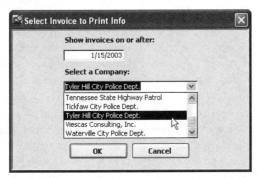

Figure 20-8. Entering a date and choosing a value from a combo box on a form that resolves stored procedure parameters.

Click OK, and a report opens to display the invoices after the date you entered for the company you selected, as shown in Figure 20-9. This report, *rptXmplInvoicesParmFromForm*, uses the same parameter stored procedure (*spXmplInvoiceParm*) as its record source. However, now Access doesn't need to prompt the user for the report parameters.

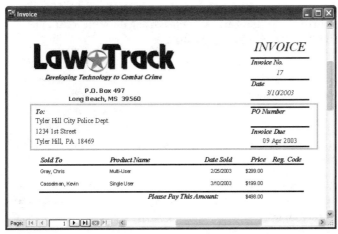

Figure 20-9. A report using a parameter query, and the parameter is resolved from a value chosen from a list in another form.

As you learned in the previous chapter, the secret is that the report's Input Parameters property has a special setting as follows:

```
@Date_After datetime = [Forms]![fdlgXmplInvoiceParm]![txtDate],
@Enter_Company_Name nvarchar(50) = [Forms]![fdlgXmplInvoiceParm]![cmbCompany]
```

The interesting values assigned to the parameters are references to the two controls on the fdlgXmplInvoiceParm form. The special syntax *[Forms]!* asks Access to look at all the open forms, find the form named fdlgXmplInvoiceParm, and then find the control on the form named txtDate and the control named cmbCompany. The report doesn't open on its own, however. Special code attached to the buttons on the fdlgXmplInvoiceParm form opens the report when the user clicks the OK button. For now, you only need to understand that once the report is opened, the input parameter of the report knows to look at the fdlgXmplInvoiceParm form for the needed input parameter information. For more details about Visual Basic, see Chapter 22, "Understanding Visual Basic Fundamentals."

> **Tip** **Make sure that any subreports or subforms that you use in a report are also efficient**
> As you begin to work with more advanced report designs in your Access project, you might want to start using embedded subforms and subreports to display more complex information. Remember that you need to keep server efficiency in mind when designing your subforms and subreports as well. Use parameters and server filters where appropriate to restrict the data to only what the user needs to see. If you are using a subform in your report (for example, to display a PivotChart), be sure to set the Recordset Type property to Snapshot (instead of Updatable Snapshot) because this requires fewer server resources.

The properties for reports that are unique to an Access project have a lot in common with those for forms. The key point to keep in mind is that forms and reports are different in an Access project only because of the way they need to interact with SQL Server. The major design elements are the same, so once you understand how forms and reports interact with SQL Server, you can design your forms and reports using the same techniques you used when building these objects in Access desktop databases.

This concludes the part of the book dedicated to Access projects. You should now have a good understanding of how an Access project is different from an Access desktop database and you should also understand the power and versatility that SQL Server can offer to your application design. If you are thinking about converting an existing Access desktop database to an Access project, Microsoft Access provides an upsizing wizard to help with this task. For more information on the upsizing wizard and converting a desktop database to a project, see Chapter 29, "Upsizing a Desktop Application to a Project."

Now the fun begins. The next part of this book, "Automating an Access Application," discusses how to capture events on your forms and reports and how to make your application come alive with Visual Basic.

Part 5

Automating an Access Application

Understanding Event Processing

Although you can make Microsoft Access do a lot for you by setting properties when you design forms and reports, you really can't make your application "come alive" until you build macros or Visual Basic procedures that respond to *events*. An event can be as simple as the user clicking a button—and your code responds by opening a related form or report. An event can also trigger complex actions, such as creating a booking record when the user selects an available room.

In this chapter, you'll first learn what event processing is all about—both in Windows and specifically within Access. The middle part of the chapter contains a comprehensive reference for all the events available within Access, a discussion of event sequence, and a list of the specific macro actions you can use to respond to events. The final part of the chapter gives you an overview of the macro design facility and shows you a few examples of an application automated with macros.

Note The examples in this chapter are based on the *WeddingMC.mdb* sample database on the companion CD included with this book. The results you see from the samples in this chapter might not exactly match what you see in this book if you have changed the sample data in the files. Also, all the screen images in this chapter were taken on a Windows XP system with the display theme set to Windows XP. Your results might look different if you are using a different operating system or a different theme.

Access as a Windows Event-Driven Application

If you're reading this book, you're using Microsoft Office and Microsoft Windows. You probably use Windows every day and don't give a second thought to how it actually works. Understanding Windows is essential to programming events in Microsoft Access.

Understanding Events in Windows

Microsoft Windows is an event-driven and message-based operating system. When you start an application on your system, that application sends messages to Windows to tell Windows that it wants to respond to certain events. When an event occurs (such as moving your mouse over the application window or clicking somewhere), Windows sends a message to the application to notify it that the event happened. The message usually includes critical information, such as the location of the mouse pointer when the event occurred. The application then responds to the event—usually by sending a message back to Windows to act upon the event. Figure 21-1 shows you a conceptual view of this process.

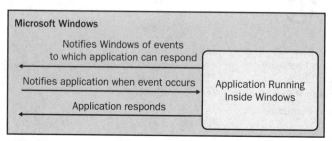

Figure 21-1. A conceptual view of messages and events in Microsoft Windows.

For example, when you have Windows Explorer open and click on a file name, Windows sends a message to Explorer to tell it where you clicked. Explorer sends a message back to Windows to tell it to highlight what you selected. Another example is the clock utility that runs on your taskbar. Windows starts this utility when Windows initializes unless you've set a taskbar option to not display the clock. When the utility starts, it asks Windows to notify it when the system clock time changes. When the clock utility receives a message from Windows that the system clock time has changed to a different minute, it sends a message back to Windows to tell it to change the characters displayed on the taskbar.

The most important aspect of this entire process is that the user is in control of the applications that are running. As the user of your personal computer, you decide what you want the applications to do next. And because Windows can handle multiple messages at a time, you can start a process in an application (perhaps a search in Windows Explorer for a file) and then switch to or start another application to do something else (such as playing a game of solitaire while you wait for the search to finish).

Leveraging Access Events to Build an Application

If you think of forms and reports in your Access application as little applications running under Access, you have the right idea. When you set an event property (one of the properties on the Event tab in the Properties window) in a report, a form, or a control on a form that points to a macro or a Visual Basic procedure, you're notifying Access that you want to respond to that event. The code you write in your macro or Visual Basic procedure provides the response to the occurrence of the event.

Access passes on to forms and controls on forms some typical Windows events such as mouse clicks (the Click and DblClick events) or characters entered from the keyboard (the Change, KeyDown, and KeyPress events). Access also defines a wide range of events that are specific to the objects it supports. For example, the BeforeUpdate event signals that the value in a control is about to change or a record being edited in the form is about to be saved. You can perform data validation in your macro or Visual Basic code that responds to BeforeUpdate and have your macro or code send a message back to Access to cancel the save if some business rule is about to be violated.

Although events in Access occur in a specific sequence, you should keep in mind that other events can occur while any code you've written to respond to an event is running. Also, some events signal that an action is about to happen, but might not have completed yet. For example, the form Open event signals that a command has been issued to open the form, but the form isn't displayed on the screen yet.

The next section gives you a comprehensive overview of all events in Access and describes how you can use them.

Summary of Form and Report Events

Microsoft Access provides 60 different events on forms, form controls, and reports that can trigger macros or Visual Basic procedures. You indicate that you want to respond to an event by providing the name of a macro, a Visual Basic function (preceded by an equal sign), or the special setting [Event Procedure] as the setting of the event property in the Properties window. When you specify [Event Procedure], Access looks for a Visual Basic procedure in the module stored with the form or report that has the name of the event. For details about Visual Basic procedures, see Chapter 22, "Understanding Visual Basic Fundamentals."

This section summarizes those events and organizes them in the following functional categories:

- Opening and closing forms and reports
- Changing data
- Detecting focus changes
- Detecting filters applied to forms
- Trapping keyboard and mouse events
- Detecting changes in PivotTables and PivotCharts
- Printing
- Trapping errors
- Detecting timer expiration

> **Note** The event property names listed on the following pages are the names you will see in the property sheet in form or report Design view. To reference an event property from a macro or a Visual Basic procedure, do not include the blanks in the name. For example, the On Load event property in a form property sheet is the OnLoad property of the form. The exceptions to this rule are the 18 events associated with PivotTables and PivotCharts. For those event properties, the name of the event property is the same as the name of the event, which might not match the property name you see in the Properties window.

Opening and Closing Forms and Reports

Event Property (Event Name)	Description
On Close (Close)	Runs the specified macro, Visual Basic function, or Visual Basic event procedure when the user or a close command in your code requests to close the form or the report but before Access clears the screen. Your code that responds to the event cannot cancel the Close event. For forms, the Close event occurs after the Unload event.
On Load (Load)	Runs the specified macro, Visual Basic function, or Visual Basic event procedure when Access loads a form and then displays the form's records. Your code that responds to the event can set values in controls or set form or control properties. The Load event occurs after the Open event and before the Resize event. Your code cannot cancel a Load event.
On Open (Open)	Runs the specified macro, Visual Basic function, or Visual Basic event procedure when the user or an open command in your code requests to open the form or the report but before Access displays the first record. To gain access to a control on the form or report, your code must specify a GoToControl action or SetFocus method to set the focus on the control. The Open event occurs before Access loads the form or report record-set, so your code that responds to the event can prompt the user for parameters and apply filters. Your code can also change the form or report record source in this event.
On Resize (Resize)	Runs the specified macro, Visual Basic function, or Visual Basic event procedure when a form changes size. This event also occurs when a form opens, after the Load event but before the Activate event. Your code can use this event to force immediate repainting of the resized form or to recalculate variables that are dependent on the size of the form.
On Unload (Unload)	Runs the specified macro, Visual Basic function, or Visual Basic event procedure when the user or your code requests that the form be closed but before Access removes the form from the screen. Your code can cancel an Unload event if it determines that a form should not be closed.

Changing Data

Event Property (Event Name)	Description
After Del Confirm (AfterDelConfirm)	Runs the specified macro, Visual Basic function, or Visual Basic event procedure after the user has requested that one or more rows on the form be deleted and after the user has confirmed the deletion. The AfterDelConfirm event also occurs if your code that responds to the BeforeDelConfirm event cancels the deletion. In a Visual Basic procedure, you can test a status parameter to determine whether the deletion was completed, was canceled by your code in the BeforeDelConfirm event, or was canceled by the user. If the deletion was successful, you can use the Requery action within your code that responds to the AfterDelConfirm event to refresh the contents of the form or combo boxes. Your code cannot cancel this event. In an Access project (.adp), this event occurs before the Delete event.
After Insert (AfterInsert)	Runs the specified macro, Visual Basic function, or Visual Basic event procedure after the user has saved a new record. Your code can use this event to requery a recordset after Access has inserted a new row. Your code cannot cancel this event.
After Update (AfterUpdate)	Runs the specified macro, Visual Basic function, or Visual Basic event procedure after the data in the specified form or form control has been updated. See the following section, "Understanding Event Sequence and Form Editing," for details. Your code that responds to this event cannot cancel it. In the AfterUpdate event of a control, you can, however, use a RunCommand action to choose the Undo command from the Edit menu, or execute the Undo method of the control. This event applies to all forms and to combo boxes, list boxes, option groups, text boxes, and bound object frames as well as to check boxes, option buttons, and toggle buttons that are not part of an option group.
Before Del Confirm (BeforeDelConfirm)	Runs the specified macro, Visual Basic function, or Visual Basic event procedure after Access has deleted one or more rows on the form, but before Access displays the standard confirmation dialog box. If your code cancels this event, Access replaces the deleted rows and does not display the confirmation dialog box. In a Visual Basic procedure, you can display a custom confirmation dialog box and then set a return parameter to suppress the standard confirmation dialog box. In an Access project (.adp), this event occurs before the Delete event.

Event Property (Event Name)	Description
Before Insert (BeforeInsert)	Runs the specified macro, Visual Basic function, or Visual Basic event procedure when the user types the first character in a new record. This event is useful in providing additional information to a user who is about to add records. If your code cancels this event, Access erases any new data on the form. This event occurs prior to the BeforeUpdate event.
Before Update (BeforeUpdate)	Runs the specified macro, Visual Basic function, or Visual Basic event procedure before Access saves changed data in a control to the form's record buffer or saves the changed record to the database. See the following section, "Understanding Event Sequence and Form Editing," for details. Your code that responds to this event can examine both the current and previous values of a control. Your code can cancel this event to stop the update and place the focus on the changed control or record. This event is most useful for performing complex validations of data on forms or in controls. This event applies to the same controls as the After-Update event.
On Change (Change)	Runs the specified macro, Visual Basic function, or Visual Basic event procedure whenever the user changes any portion of the contents of a combo box control or a text box control. Your code cannot cancel this event. See also the KeyDown and KeyPress keyboard events.
On Delete (Delete)	Runs the specified macro, Visual Basic function, or Visual Basic event procedure just before Access deletes one or more rows. This event occurs once per row being deleted, and your code that responds to the event can examine the data in each row to be deleted. Your code can provide a customized warning message. Your code can also provide automatic deletion of dependent rows in another table (for example, of all the orders for the customer about to be deleted) by executing a delete query. Your code can cancel this event to prevent individual rows from being deleted. (Cancel the BeforeDelConfirm event to cancel deletion of all rows.)

Event Property (Event Name)	Description
On Dirty (Dirty)	Runs the specified macro, Visual Basic function, or Visual Basic event procedure whenever the user first changes the contents of a bound control on a bound form (a form that has a record source). This event also occurs if your code changes the value of a bound control from a macro (SetValue) or a Visual Basic procedure. Your code that responds to this event can verify that the current record can be updated. Your code can cancel this event to prevent the update. After this event occurs, the Dirty property of the form is True until the record is saved.
On Not In List (NotInList)	Runs the specified macro, Visual Basic function, or Visual Basic event procedure when the user types an entry in a combo box that does not exist in the current recordset defined by the Row Source property for the combo box. Your code cannot cancel this event. Your code can allow the user to create a new entry for the combo box (perhaps by adding a record to the table on which the Row Source property is based). In a Visual Basic procedure, you can examine a parameter passed to the event procedure that contains the unmatched text. Your code can also set a return value to cause Access to display the standard error message, display no error message (after your code has issued a custom message), or requery the list after your code has added data to the Row Source property.
On Undo (Undo)	Runs the specified macro, Visual Basic function, or Visual Basic event procedure when the user undoes a change in a form or a text box or combo box control that has been committed to the form's record buffer. See the following section, "Understanding Event Sequence and Form Editing," for details. The Undo event does not occur when the user chooses the Undo Typing command. Your code that responds to the event can examine both the current and previous values of the control and cancel the event if the change should not be undone.
On Updated (Updated)	Runs the specified macro, Visual Basic function, or Visual Basic event procedure after the data in a form's object frame control changes. Your code cannot cancel this event. In a Visual Basic procedure, your code can examine a status parameter to determine how the change occurred.

Caution You can cause an endless loop if your code changes the contents of a control within the event procedure for the control's Change event.

Detecting Focus Changes

Event Property (Event Name)	Description
On Activate (Activate)	Runs the specified macro, Visual Basic function, or Visual Basic event procedure in a form or a report when the Form or Report window receives the focus and becomes the active window. This event does not occur for pop-up or modal forms. This event also does not occur when a normal Form or Report window regains the focus from a pop-up or modal form unless the focus moves to another form or report. This event is most useful for displaying custom toolbars when a form or a report receives the focus. Your code cannot cancel this event.
On Current (Current)	Runs the specified macro, Visual Basic function, or Visual Basic event procedure in a bound form when the focus moves from one record to another but before Access displays the new record. Access also triggers the Current event when the focus moves to the first record as a form opens. This event is most useful for keeping two open and related forms synchronized. Your code cannot cancel this event. Your code can, however, use GoToRecord or similar action to move to another record if it decides that the form display should not move to the new record.
On Deactivate (Deactivate)	Runs the specified macro, Visual Basic function, or Visual Basic event procedure when a form or a report loses the focus to a window within the Access application that is not a pop-up or modal window. This event is useful for closing custom toolbars. Your code cannot cancel this event.
On Enter (Enter)	Runs the specified macro, Visual Basic function, or Visual Basic event procedure when the focus moves to a bound object frame, a combo box, a command button, a list box, an option group, or a text box, as well as when the focus moves to a check box, an option button, or a toggle button that is not part of an option group. Your code cannot cancel this event. This event occurs only when the focus moves from another control on the same form. If the user changes the focus to another control with the mouse, this event occurs after LostFocus in the current control and before the GotFocus, MouseDown, MouseUp, and Click events for the new control. If the user changes the focus to a control using the keyboard, this event occurs after the KeyDown, Exit, and LostFocus events in the control that previously had the focus but before the GotFocus, KeyPress, and KeyUp events in the control that is receiving the focus.

Event Property (Event Name)	Description
On Exit (Exit)	Runs the specified macro, Visual Basic function, or Visual Basic event procedure when the focus moves from a bound object frame, a combo box, a command button, a list box, an option group, or a text box, as well as when the focus moves from a check box, an option button, or a toggle button that is not part of an option group to another control on the same form. Your code cannot cancel this event. This event does not occur when the focus moves to another window. If the user leaves a control using the mouse, this event occurs before the Enter, GotFocus, MouseDown, MouseUp, and Click events in the new control. If the user leaves a control using the keyboard, the KeyDown and Exit events in this control occur, and then the Enter, KeyPress, and KeyUp events occur in the new control.
On Got Focus (GotFocus)	Runs the specified macro, Visual Basic function, or Visual Basic event procedure when an enabled form control receives the focus. If a form receives the focus but has no enabled controls, the GotFocus event occurs for the form. Your code cannot cancel this event. The GotFocus event occurs after the Enter event. Unlike the Enter event, which occurs only when the focus moves from another control on the same form, the GotFocus event occurs every time a control receives the focus, including from other windows.
On Lost Focus (LostFocus)	Runs the specified macro, Visual Basic function, or Visual Basic event procedure when an enabled form control loses the focus. The LostFocus event for the form occurs whenever a form that has no enabled controls loses the focus. Your code cannot cancel this event. This event occurs after the Exit event. Unlike the Exit event, which occurs only when the focus moves to another control on the same form, the LostFocus event occurs every time a control loses the focus, including to other windows.

Detecting Filters Applied to Forms

Event Property (Event Name)	Description
On Apply Filter (ApplyFilter)	Runs the specified macro, Visual Basic function, or Visual Basic event procedure when a user applies a filter on a form from the user interface or via the ApplyFilter command. Setting the form's Filter, OrderBy, FilterOn, or OrderByOn properties from code does not trigger this event. Your code can examine and modify the form's Filter and OrderBy properties or cancel the event. Within a Visual Basic procedure, you can examine a parameter that indicates how the filter is being applied.
On Filter (Filter)	Runs the specified macro, Visual Basic function, or Visual Basic event procedure when the user opens the Filter By Form or the Advanced Filter/Sort window. Your code can use this event to clear any previous Filter or Order By setting, set a default Filter or Order By criterion, or cancel the event to prevent the window from opening and provide your own custom filter form. Within a Visual Basic procedure, you can examine a parameter that indicates whether a user has asked to open the Filter By Form or the Advanced Filter/Sort window.

Trapping Keyboard and Mouse Events

Event Property (Event Name)	Description
On Click (Click)	Runs the specified macro, Visual Basic function, or Visual Basic event procedure when the user clicks a command button or clicks an enabled form or control. Your code cannot cancel this event. The Click event occurs for a form only if no control on the form can receive the focus.
On Dbl Click (DblClick)	Runs the specified macro, Visual Basic function, or Visual Basic event procedure when the user double-clicks a bound object frame, a combo box, a command button, a list box, an option group, or a text box, as well as when the user double-clicks a check box, an option button, or a toggle button that is not part of an option group. The Click event always occurs before DblClick. That is, when the user clicks the mouse button twice rapidly, the Click event occurs for the first click followed by DblClick for the second click. Access runs the macro or Visual Basic procedure before showing the user the normal result of the double-click. Your code can cancel the event to prevent the normal response to a double-click of a control, such as activating the application for an ActiveX object in a bound control or highlighting a word in a text box. The DblClick event occurs for a form only if no control on that form can receive the focus.

Event Property (Event Name)	Description
On Key Down (KeyDown)	Runs the specified macro, Visual Basic function, or Visual Basic event procedure when the user presses a key or a combination of keys. Your code cannot cancel this event. In a Visual Basic procedure, you can examine parameters to determine the key code (the numeric code that represents the key pressed) and whether the Shift, Ctrl, or Alt key was also pressed. You can also set the key code to 0 in Visual Basic to prevent the control from receiving keystrokes. If the form has a command button whose Default property is set to Yes (this indicates that the command button responds to Enter as though the button had been clicked), KeyDown events do not occur when the Enter key is pressed. If the form has a command button whose Cancel property is set to Yes (this indicates that the command button responds to the Esc key as though the button had been clicked), KeyDown events do not occur when the Esc key is pressed. See also the Change event. The KeyDown event occurs before KeyPress and KeyUp. If the key the user presses (such as the Tab key) causes the focus to move to another control, the control that has the focus when the user presses the key signals a KeyDown event, but the control that receives the focus signals the KeyPress and KeyUp events. If you set the form's KeyPreview property to Yes, this event also occurs for the form.
On Key Press (KeyPress)	Runs the specified macro, Visual Basic function, or Visual Basic event procedure when the user presses a key or a combination of keys that would result in a character being delivered to the control that has the focus. (For example, KeyPress does not occur for the arrow keys.) Your code cannot cancel this event. In a Visual Basic procedure, you can examine the ANSI key value and set the value to 0 to cancel the keystroke. The KeyPress event occurs after KeyDown and before KeyUp. If the form has a command button whose Default property is set to Yes, the KeyPress event occurs for the form and the command button when the Enter key is pressed. If the form has a command button whose Cancel property is set to Yes, the KeyPress event occurs for the form and the command button when the Esc key is pressed. See also the Change event. If you set the form's KeyPreview property to Yes, this event also occurs for the form.

Chapter 21

723

Event Property (Event Name)	Description
On Key Up (KeyUp)	Runs the specified macro, Visual Basic function, or Visual Basic event procedure when the user releases a key or a combination of keys. Your code cannot cancel this event. In a Visual Basic procedure, you can examine parameters to determine the key code and whether the Shift, Ctrl, or Alt key was also pressed. If you set the form's KeyPreview property to Yes, this event also occurs for the form. If the form has a command button whose Default property is set to Yes, the KeyUp event occurs for the form and the command button when the Enter key is released. If the form has a command button whose Cancel property is set to Yes, the KeyUp event occurs for the form and the command button when the Esc key is released.
On Mouse Down (MouseDown)	Runs the specified macro, Visual Basic function, or Visual Basic event procedure when the user presses any mouse button. Your code cannot cancel this event. In a Visual Basic procedure, you can determine which mouse button was pressed (left, right, or middle); whether the Shift, Ctrl, or Alt key was also pressed; and the X and Y coordinates of the mouse pointer (in twips) when the button was pressed. (Note: There are 1440 *twips* in an inch.)
On Mouse Move (MouseMove)	Runs the specified macro, Visual Basic function, or Visual Basic event procedure when the user moves the mouse over a form or a control. Your code cannot cancel this event. In a Visual Basic procedure, you can determine which mouse button was pressed (left, right, or middle) and whether the Shift, Ctrl, or Alt key was also pressed. You can also determine the X and Y coordinates of the mouse pointer (in twips).
On Mouse Up (MouseUp)	Runs the specified macro, Visual Basic function, or Visual Basic event procedure when the user releases any mouse button. Your code cannot cancel this event. In a Visual Basic procedure, you can determine which mouse button was released (left, right, or middle); whether the Shift, Ctrl, or Alt key was also pressed; and the X and Y coordinates of the mouse pointer (in twips) when the button was released.
On Mouse Wheel (MouseWheel)	Runs the specified macro, Visual Basic function, or Visual Basic event procedure when the user rolls the mouse wheel while the focus is on a form. In a Visual Basic procedure, you can determine whether rolling the wheel caused the form to display a new page and the count of rows that the view was scrolled. (When the user rolls the mouse wheel, the form scrolls up or down through the records in the form.)

Detecting Changes in PivotTables and PivotCharts

Event Property (Event Name)	Description
After Final Render (AfterFinalRender)	In PivotChart view, runs the specified macro, Visual Basic function, or Visual Basic event procedure after all elements in the chart have been rendered (drawn on the screen). Your code cannot cancel this event.
After Layout (AfterLayout)	In PivotChart view, runs the specified macro, Visual Basic function, or Visual Basic event procedure after all charts have been laid out but before they have been rendered. In a Visual Basic procedure, you can reposition the title, legend, chart, and axis objects during this event. Your code can also reposition and resize the chart plot area. Your code cannot cancel this event.
After Render (AfterRender)	In PivotChart view, runs the specified macro, Visual Basic function, or Visual Basic event procedure when a particular chart object has been rendered. In a Visual Basic procedure, you can examine the drawing object and the chart objects and use methods of the drawing object to draw additional objects. Your code cannot cancel this event. This event occurs before the AfterFinalRender event.
Before Query (BeforeQuery)	In PivotTable view, runs the specified macro, Visual Basic function, or Visual Basic event procedure when the PivotTable queries its data source. Your code cannot cancel this event.
Before Render (BeforeRender)	In PivotChart view, runs the specified macro, Visual Basic function, or Visual Basic event procedure before an object is rendered. In a Visual Basic procedure, you can determine the type of rendering and the type of object that is about to be rendered. Your code can cancel this event if it determines that the object should not be rendered. This event occurs before the AfterRender and AfterFinalRender events.
Before Screen Tip (BeforeScreenTip)	In PivotTable or PivotChart view, runs the specified macro, Visual Basic function, or Visual Basic event procedure before a ScreenTip is displayed. In a Visual Basic procedure, you can examine and change the text of the tip or hide the tip by setting the text to an empty string. Your code cannot cancel this event.
On Cmd Before Execute (Command-BeforeExecute)	In PivotTable or PivotChart view, runs the specified macro, Visual Basic function, or Visual Basic event procedure before a command is executed. In a Visual Basic procedure, you can determine the command to be executed and cancel the event if you want to disallow the command. This event occurs before the CommandExecute event.

Event Property (Event Name)	Description
On Cmd Checked (Command-Checked)	In PivotTable and PivotChart view, runs the specified macro, Visual Basic function, or Visual Basic event procedure when the user has selected (checked) a command. In a Visual Basic procedure, you can determine the command selected and disallow the command by setting the value of the Checked parameter to False. Your code cannot cancel this event.
On Cmd Enabled (Command-Enabled)	In PivotTable and PivotChart view, runs the specified macro, Visual Basic function, or Visual Basic event procedure when a command has been enabled. In a Visual Basic procedure, you can determine the type of command and disable it. Your code cannot cancel this event.
On Cmd Execute (CommandExecute)	In PivotTable and PivotChart view, runs the specified macro, Visual Basic function, or Visual Basic event procedure after a command has executed. In a Visual Basic procedure, you can determine the type of command and issue additional commands if desired. Your code cannot cancel this event.
On Data Change (DataChange)	In PivotTable view, runs the specified macro, Visual Basic function, or Visual Basic event procedure when the data fetched or calculated by the PivotTable has changed. In a Visual Basic procedure, you can examine the reason for the change, which could include changing the sort, adding a total, or defining a filter. Your code cannot cancel this event. This event often precedes the DataSetChange event.
On Data Set Change (DataSetChange)	In PivotTable view, runs the specified macro, Visual Basic function, or Visual Basic event procedure when the data source has changed. Your code cannot cancel this event.
On Connect (OnConnect)	In PivotTable view, runs the specified macro, Visual Basic function, or Visual Basic event procedure when the PivotTable connects to its data source. Your code cannot cancel this event.
On Disconnect (OnDisconnect)	In PivotTable view, runs the specified macro, Visual Basic function, or Visual Basic event procedure when the PivotTable disconnects from its data source. Your code cannot cancel this event.
On PivotTable Change (Pivot-TableChange)	In PivotTable view, runs the specified macro, Visual Basic function, or Visual Basic event procedure when a field, field set, or total is added or deleted. In a Visual Basic procedure, you can examine the reason for the change. Your code cannot cancel this event.
On Query (Query)	In PivotTable view, runs the specified macro, Visual Basic function, or Visual Basic event procedure when the PivotTable must requery its data source. Your code cannot cancel this event.

Event Property (Event Name)	Description
On Selection Change (Selection-Change)	In PivotTable or PivotChart view, runs the specified macro, Visual Basic function, or Visual Basic event procedure when the user makes a new selection. Your code cannot cancel this event.
On View Change (ViewChange)	In PivotTable or PivotChart view, runs the specified macro, Visual Basic function, or Visual Basic event procedure when the table or chart is redrawn. In a Visual Basic procedure, you can determine the reason for a PivotTable view change. When the form is in PivotChart view, the reason code is always -1. Your code cannot cancel this event.

Printing

Event Property (Event Name)	Description
On Format (Format)	Runs the specified macro, Visual Basic function, or Visual Basic event procedure just before Access formats a report section to print. This event is useful for hiding or displaying controls in the report section based on data values. If Access is formatting a group header, your code has access to the data in the first row of the Detail section. Similarly, if Access is formatting a group footer, your code has access to the data in the last row of the Detail section. Your code can test the value of the Format Count property to determine whether the Format event has occurred more than once for a section (due to page overflow). Your code can cancel this event to keep a section from appearing on the report.
On No Data (NoData)	Runs the specified macro, Visual Basic function, or Visual Basic event procedure after Access formats a report that has no data for printing and just before the reports prints. Your code can cancel this event to keep a blank report from printing.
On Page (Page)	Runs the specified macro, Visual Basic function, or Visual Basic event procedure after Access formats a page for printing and just before the page prints. In Visual Basic, you can use this event to draw custom borders around a page or add other graphics to enhance the look of the report.
On Print (Print)	Runs the specified macro, Visual Basic function, or Visual Basic event procedure just before Access prints a formatted section of a report. If your code cancels this event, Access leaves a blank space on the report where the section would have printed.

Chapter 21

Event Property (Event Name)	Description
On Retreat (Retreat)	Runs the specified macro, Visual Basic function, or Visual Basic event procedure when Access has to retreat past already formatted sections when it discovers that it cannot fit a "keep together" section on a page. Your code cannot cancel this event.

Trapping Errors

Event Property (Event Name)	Description
On Error (Error)	Runs the specified macro, Visual Basic function, or Visual Basic event procedure whenever a run-time error occurs while the form or report is active. This event does not trap errors in Visual Basic code; use the On Error statement in the Visual Basic procedure instead. Your code cannot cancel this event. If you use a Visual Basic procedure to trap this event, you can examine the error code to determine an appropriate action.

Detecting Timer Expiration

Event Property (Event Name)	Description
On Timer (Timer)	Runs the specified macro, Visual Basic function, or Visual Basic event procedure when the timer interval defined for the form elapses. The form's Timer Interval property defines how frequently this event occurs in milliseconds. If the Timer Interval property is set to 0, no Timer events occur. Your code cannot cancel this event. However, your code can set the Timer Interval property for the form to 0 to stop further Timer events from occurring.

You should now have a basic understanding of events and how you might use them. In the next section, you'll see some of these events in action.

Understanding Event Sequence and Form Editing

One of the best ways to learn event sequence is to see events in action. In the *WeddingMC.mdb* sample database, you can find a special form that you can use to study events. Open the sample database and then open the WeddingEvents form as shown in Figure 21-2. (The form's Caption property is set to Wedding List.)

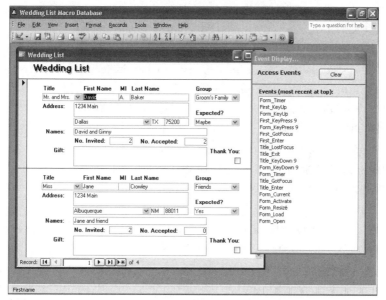

Figure 21-2. A form to study event sequence.

When you open the form, it also opens an event display pop-up form that shows the events that have occurred. All the events (except the Mouse events, which fire so frequently that they would make it hard to study other events) are set to write the event name to the pop-up window. The pop-up window shows the most recent events at the top. When you open the form, the initial events are as follows:

1. **Form Open.** This signals that the form is about to open.

2. **Form Load.** This signals that the form is now open and the record source for the form is about to be loaded.

3. **Form Resize.** The form's Auto Resize property is set to Yes, so this indicates that Access is resizing the window to show an exact multiple of rows. (The form's Default View property is set to Continuous Forms.)

4. **Form Activate.** The form has now received the focus.

5. **Form Current.** The form has now moved to the first row in the record source.

6. **Title Enter.** The first control in the tab order has been entered.

7. **Title GotFocus.** The first control in the tab order now has the focus.

After the form opened, I pressed the Tab key to move from the Title field to the First Name field. (The name of the control is First.) The form has its Key Preview property set to Yes, so you can see the keyboard events for both the form and the controls. The events occurred in the following sequence:

1. **Form KeyDown.** The form detected that the Tab key (key code 9) was pressed.

2. **Title KeyDown.** The Title combo box control detected that the Tab key was pressed.

3. **Title Exit.** Pressing the Tab key caused an exit from the Title combo box control.

4. **Title LostFocus.** The Title combo box control lost the focus as a result of pressing Tab.

5. **First Enter.** The First text box control (First Name) was entered.

6. **First GotFocus.** The First text box control received the focus.

7. **Form KeyPress.** The form received the Tab key.

8. **First KeyPress.** The First text box control received the Tab key.

9. **Form KeyUp.** The form detected that the Tab key was released.

10. **First KeyUp.** The First text box detected that the Tab key was released.

In Figure 21-2, you can also see a Form Timer event listed. The Timer Interval property for this form is set to 20,000 (the value is milliseconds), so you should see the timer event occur every 20 seconds as long as you have the form open.

You can have fun with this form moving around and typing in new data. You'll be able to see each character that you enter. You'll also see the control and form BeforeUpdate and After-Update events when you commit changed values.

Figure 21-3 shows you a conceptual diagram of how editing data in a form works and when the critical Current, BeforeUpdate, and AfterUpdate events occur.

Of course, the ultimate goal is to update data in your database table. When Access opens a form, it builds a special buffer to contain the contents of the current record displayed on the form. As you move from control to control on the form, Access pulls the field bound to each control from this record buffer and puts it into a special control buffer. As you type in the control, you're changing the control buffer and not the record buffer or the actual record in the database.

If you have changed the data in a control and then you move to another control, Access signals the BeforeUpdate event for the control. If you do not cancel the event, Access then copies the updated contents of the control buffer into the record buffer and signals the control's AfterUpdate event. Access then fetches into the control buffer the contents of the field bound to the control to which you moved from the record buffer and displays it in the control.

If you undo any edit, Access signals the appropriate Undo event, and either refreshes the control buffer from the record buffer (if you undo a control) or the original record from the database into the record buffer (if you undo all edits). When you save a changed record, either by choosing Save Record from the Records menu, moving to another record, or closing the form, Access first signals the BeforeUpdate event of the form. If you do not cancel this event, Access writes the changed record to your table and signals the AfterUpdate event of the form.

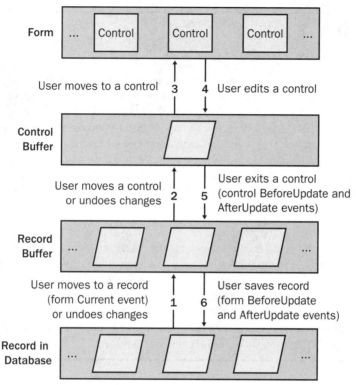

Figure 21-3.   Behind the scenes of editing on a bound form.

Summary of Macro Actions

Now that you understand events, it's useful to study the macro actions available to respond to events. Microsoft Access provides 56 macro actions. You can find these actions organized in the following functional categories:

- Opening and closing Access objects—tables, queries, forms, reports, data access pages, and objects in an Access project file (.adp extension)
- Printing data
- Executing a query
- Testing conditions and controlling action flow
- Setting values
- Searching for data
- Building a custom menu and executing menu commands
- Controlling display and focus
- Informing the user of actions
- Renaming, copying, deleting, saving, importing, and exporting objects
- Running another application

Inside Out

Do I really recommend macros?

No, I don't! Although macros are a good way to learn to build simple automation in an Access application, they don't work well for a production application. First, as you'll see later in this chapter, the debugging facilities are very limited. If you run into any problem in your macro code, it can be very difficult to figure out the solution. Second, you cannot trap any errors in macros. In many cases, you cannot avoid errors. For example, if you attempt to GoToRecord Previous when you're on the first record, you'll get an error. Writing a test to detect that the form is already displaying the first record is difficult in a macro. If you use Visual Basic, you can trap the error and respond appropriately (ignore it!) without the user ever seeing the error.

So, why am I teaching you macro actions? In truth, the best (and perhaps only) way to perform certain actions in Visual Basic is to execute the equivalent macro action. For example, the only way to open a form that does not have any Visual Basic code is to execute the OpenForm action from within your Visual Basic procedure. (When a form has a module, an advanced way to open one or more copies of a form is to set a module object to the form's module.) As you'll learn in the next chapter, you execute macro actions in Visual Basic as methods of a special object called DoCmd. (In the following tables, I'll note the macro actions that have a better native equivalent in Visual Basic.)

Opening and Closing Access Objects

Macro Action	Purpose
Close	Closes either the specified window or, if no window is specified, the active window for a table, query, form, or report. If the Database window has the focus when you execute a Close action with no window specified, Access closes the database. You can also indicate whether to save the object when Access closes it.
OpenData-AccessPage	Opens a data access page in Browse (Page) or Design view.
OpenDiagram	In an Access project file (.adp) connected to an SQL Server database, opens a table relationship diagram in the server database in Design view. You cannot execute this action in an Access desktop database (.mdb).

Macro Action	Purpose
OpenForm	Opens a form in Form, Design, Datasheet, PivotTable, or PivotForm view or in Print Preview. You can also apply a filter or a Where condition in Form, Datasheet, PivotTable, or PivotForm view or in Print Preview. Access ignores any filter or Where condition when you open the object in Design view. If the form is already open, the OpenForm action puts the focus on the form and applies any new filter or Where condition you specify. From a Visual Basic procedure, you normally execute the macro action to open a form. However, you can also open a form that has a module by setting a form object equal to a new instance of the form's class module. See Chapter 22, "Understanding Visual Basic Fundamentals," for details.
OpenFunction	In an Access project file (.adp) connected to an SQL Server database, opens a function in the server database in Datasheet, Design, Pivot-Table, or PivotChart view or in Print Preview. If the function is a data definition command or the equivalent of an Access action query, executes the function without returning data. If the function returns data that is editable, you can specify whether the function datasheet should be opened to add new records only; to add, edit, and delete records; or to provide a read-only view of the data.
	In Visual Basic, you can also use the Open or Execute method to open the function and return any results to a recordset. You must use the OpenFunction macro action within a Visual Basic procedure if you want the function to open in the user interface.
	You cannot execute this action in an Access desktop database (.mdb).
OpenModule	Opens a module or procedure in Design view. If you specify a module name and no procedure name, Access opens the module to the Declarations section. You can also specify only a procedure name as long as the procedure is a public procedure in a standard module.
	In a Visual Basic procedure, you should open a module by setting a module object equal to the name of the module in the Modules collection.
	To open the module of a form or report, the form or report itself must be open.

Chapter 21

Macro Action	Purpose
OpenQuery	In an Access desktop database (.mdb), opens a query in Datasheet, Design, PivotTable, or PivotChart view or in Print Preview. If you specify an action query, Access performs the updates specified by the query. If the query returns data that is editable, you can specify whether the query datasheet should be opened to add new records only; to add, edit, and delete records; or to provide a read-only view of the data.

In Visual Basic, you can use the OpenRecordset method to create a recordset from a query that returns records, or use the Execute method to run an action query.

You cannot execute this action in an Access project file (.adp). |
| OpenReport | Prints a report (the default), opens a report in Print Preview, or opens the report in Design view. For printing and Print Preview, you can also specify a filter or a Where condition. |
| OpenStored-Procedure | In an Access project file (.adp) connected to an SQL Server database, opens a stored procedure in the server database in Datasheet, Design, PivotTable, or PivotChart view or in Print Preview. If the stored procedure returns data that is editable, you can specify whether the stored procedure datasheet should be opened to add new records only; to add, edit, and delete records; or to provide a read-only view of the data.

In Visual Basic, you can also use the Open or Execute method to open the stored procedure and return any results to a recordset.

You cannot execute this action in an Access desktop database (.mdb). |
| OpenTable | Opens a table in Datasheet, Design, PivotTable, or PivotChart view or in Print Preview. You can specify whether the table datasheet should be opened to add new records only; to add, edit, and delete records; or to provide a read-only view of the data.

In Visual Basic, you can also use the OpenRecordset method to create a recordset from a table. |
| OpenView | In an Access project file (.adp) connected to an SQL Server database, opens a view in the server database in Datasheet, Design, PivotTable, or PivotChart view or in Print Preview. If the view returns data that is editable, you can specify whether the view datasheet should be opened to add new records only; to add, edit, and delete records; or to provide a read-only view of the data.

In Visual Basic, you can also use the Open or Execute method to open the view and return the results to a recordset.

You cannot execute this action in an Access desktop database (.mdb). |

Printing Data

Macro Action	Purpose
OpenForm	Optionally opens a form in Print Preview. You can specify a filter or a Where condition.
OpenFunction	In an Access project file (.adp) connected to an SQL Server database, optionally opens a function in Print Preview. You cannot execute this action in an Access desktop database (.mdb).
OpenQuery	In an Access desktop database (.mdb), optionally opens a query in Print Preview. You cannot execute this action in an Access project file (.adp).
OpenReport	Optionally prints a report or opens a report in Print Preview. You can specify a filter or a Where condition.
OpenStored-Procedure	In an Access project file (.adp) connected to an SQL Server database, optionally opens a stored procedure in the server database in Print Preview. You cannot execute this action in an Access desktop database (.mdb).
OpenTable	Optionally opens a table in Print Preview.
OpenView	In an Access project file (.adp) connected to an SQL Server database, optionally opens a view in the server database in Print Preview. You cannot execute this action in an Access desktop database (.mdb).
OutputTo	Outputs the named table, query, form, report, module, data access page, view, stored procedure, or function to another file format. The formats include HTML (.htm, .html), Data Access Page (.htm, .html), Microsoft Excel (.xls), Microsoft Internet Information Server (.htx, .idc), text files (.txt), Rich Text Format (.rtf), Microsoft Access report Snapshot Format (.snp), or Microsoft Active Server Page (.asp). You can also optionally start the application to edit the file. For forms, the data output is from the form's Datasheet view. For reports in formats other than Snapshot Format, Access outputs all controls containing data (including calculated controls) except ActiveX controls. When you output a report in Snapshot Format, Access creates an image of the report that can be opened with the license-free snapshot reader.
PrintOut	Prints the active datasheet, form, data access page, module, or report. You can specify a range of pages, the print quality, the number of copies, and collation. Use an Open action first if you want to apply a filter or a Where condition.

Chapter 21

Executing a Query

Macro Action	Purpose
OpenFunction	In an Access project file (.adp) connected to an SQL Server database, opens a function in the server database in Datasheet view or in Print Preview. If the function is a data definition command or the equivalent of an Access action query, executes the function without returning data. If the function returns data that is editable, you can specify whether the function datasheet should be opened to add new records only; to add, edit, and delete records; or to provide a read-only view of the data.
	You cannot execute this action in an Access desktop database (.mdb).
OpenQuery	In an Access desktop database (.mdb), runs a select query and displays the recordset in Datasheet view or in Print Preview. Executes an action query. If the query returns data that is editable, you can specify whether the query datasheet should be opened to add new records only; to add, edit, and delete records; or to provide a read-only view of the data.
	You cannot execute this action in an Access project file (.adp).
OpenStored-Procedure	In an Access project file (.adp) connected to an SQL Server database, opens a stored procedure in the server database in Datasheet view or in Print Preview. If the stored procedure is a data definition command or the equivalent of an Access action query, executes the procedure without returning data. If the stored procedure returns data that is editable, you can specify whether the stored procedure datasheet should be opened to add new records only; to add, edit, and delete records; or to provide a read-only view of the data.
	You cannot execute this action in an Access desktop database (.mdb).
OpenView	In an Access project file (.adp) connected to an SQL Server database, opens a view in the server database in Datasheet view or in Print Preview. If the view returns data that is editable, you can specify whether the view datasheet should be opened to add new records only; to add, edit, and delete records; or to provide a read-only view of the data.
	You cannot execute this action in an Access desktop database (.mdb).

Macro Action	Purpose
RunSQL	Executes the specified action query statement (INSERT INTO, DELETE, SELECT...INTO, UPDATE) or data definition query statement (CREATE TABLE, ALTER TABLE, DROP TABLE, CREATE INDEX, DROP INDEX). (Note: You can't enter more than 255 characters in the SQL Statement argument. If you need to run a more complex query, define a query object and use the OpenQuery action.)
	In Visual Basic, you should use the Execute method to run an action or data definition query contained in a string argument of any length. Also, the RunSQL command executed from Visual Basic accepts an SQL statement up to 32,767 characters.

Testing Conditions and Controlling Action Flow

Macro Action	Purpose
CancelEvent	Cancels the event that caused this macro to run. You can't use a CancelEvent action in a macro that defines menu commands or in response to an event that cannot be canceled.
	In Visual Basic, you should set the Cancel parameter of the event procedure to True to cancel the event.
Quit	Closes all Access windows and exits Access. You can set options to save all changes (the default), prompt the user to save, or exit without saving.
	In Visual Basic, you should use the Quit method of the Application object, which has the same options.
RunCode	Executes a Visual Basic function procedure. Other actions following this action execute after the function completes. You cannot call a Visual Basic subprocedure from this action. (Note: If the function returns values, you cannot inspect them in the macro.)
	In Visual Basic, you should call the subprocedure or assign the function call to a return variable.
RunCommand	Executes an Access built-in command. The list of available commands includes all commands you can execute from any of the built-in menus.

Chapter 21

Macro Action	Purpose
RunMacro	Runs a macro. Actions following this action run after the other macro completes. You can specify a number of times for the macro to execute or a condition that when true halts the macro execution. Caution: A macro can run itself, but you should provide conditional testing that exits the macro so that you don't create an unending loop.
	In Visual Basic, use the Do and For statements to create iterative or conditional code loops. Although it is possible to execute RunMacro in a Visual Basic procedure, you should write the equivalent Visual Basic statements within your procedure instead.
StopAllMacros	Stops all macros, including any macros that called this macro.
	You cannot execute this action from Visual Basic.
StopMacro	Stops the current macro.
	You cannot execute this action from Visual Basic.

Setting Values

Macro Action	Purpose
Requery	Refreshes the data in a control that is bound to a query (such as a list box, a combo box, a subform, or a control based on an aggregate function such as DSum). When other actions (such as inserting or deleting a record in the underlying query) might affect the contents of a control that is bound to a query, use the Requery action to update the control values. Use Requery without an argument to refresh the data in the active object (form or datasheet).
	In Visual Basic, you should use the Requery method of the object you want to requery.
SendKeys	Stores keystrokes in the keyboard buffer. If you intend to send keystrokes to a modal form or a dialog box, you must execute the SendKeys action before opening the modal form or the dialog box.
	In Visual Basic, you should use the SendKeys statement.
SetValue	Changes the value of any control or property that you can update. For example, you can use the SetValue action to calculate a new total in an unbound control or to affect the Visible property of a control (which determines whether you can see that control).
	In Visual Basic, you should use a Let or Set statement.

Inside Out

Avoid SendKeys if at all possible

Although you can set an optional parameter to wait until Windows processes the keystrokes, you have only limited control over where Windows actually delivers the keys. For example, if the user clicks on another window at the moment you issue the SendKeys action, Windows delivers the keystrokes to that window. If you want to deliver the keystrokes to a dialog box, you must issue the SendKeys action with no wait, immediately open the dialog box, and keep your fingers crossed that Windows will send the keystrokes there. For example, if you want to open the Find dialog box to perform a search on the LastName control and set the default Match to Any Part of Field, you need to execute the following commands:

```
GoToControl Control Name: LastName
SendKeys Keystrokes: %HA%N
Wait: No
RunCommand Command: Find
```

The SendKeys command queues up Alt+H A Alt+N, which is the key combination you could use to move to the Match option (letter H is the hotkey), type the letter A to select the entry beginning with that letter (Any Part of Field), and then use Alt+N to get back to the Find What (letter N is the hotkey) box. This works a vast majority of the time, but if some other application pops forward a dialog box right after the SendKeys and before the RunCommand, the keystrokes won't go where you intended.

The bottom line is always work hard to figure out an alternative way to accomplish a task that you might be tempted to do with SendKeys. In the example above, a custom search form would work much better. See Chapter 23, "Automating Your Application with Visual Basic," for details about how to build a custom search form (also known as custom Query by Form).

Searching for Data

Macro Action	Purpose
ApplyFilter	Restricts the information displayed in a table, form, or report by applying a named filter, a query, or an SQL WHERE clause to the records in the table or to the records in the underlying table or query of the form or report. ApplyFilter always operates on the currently active window and does not work for subforms.
	In Visual Basic, you should set the form or report Filter or OrderBy property and set FilterOn or OrderByOn to True.

Macro Action	Purpose
FindNext	Finds the next record that meets the criteria previously set by a Find-Record macro action or in the Find And Replace dialog box. In Visual Basic, you should provide your own custom search form and perform the search by using the Find, FindFirst, or FindNext methods of the form's recordset.
FindRecord	Finds a record that meets the search criteria. You can specify in the macro action all the parameters available in the Find And Replace dialog box. In Visual Basic, you should provide your own custom search form and perform the search by using the Find, FindFirst, or FindNext methods of the form's recordset.
GoToRecord	Moves to a different record and makes it current in the specified table, query, or form. You can move to the first, last, next, or previous record. When you specify the next or the previous record, you can also specify a parameter to move by more than one record. You can also go to a specific record number or to the new-record placeholder at the end of the set. In Visual Basic, you can also use RunCommand RecordsGoToFirst, Records-GoToLast, RecordsGoToNew, RecordsGoToNext, or RecordsGoToPrevious. A more efficient technique is to search in the form's recordset and move the form to the desired record by setting the form's Bookmark property.

Building a Custom Menu and Executing Menu Commands

Macro Action	Purpose
AddMenu	Adds a drop-down menu to a custom menu bar or to a custom shortcut menu for a form or a report. This is the only action allowed in a macro referenced by a Menu Bar property or Shortcut Menu Bar property. The arguments to AddMenu specify the name of this menu bar and the name of another macro that contains all the named commands for the menu and the actions that correspond to those commands. An AddMenu action can also build submenus by referring to another macro that uses an AddMenu action. The recommended method for constructing custom menus is to use the Toolbar Customize facility. For details, see Chapter 24, "The Finishing Touches."

Macro Action	Purpose
RunCommand	Executes an Access built-in command. The list of available commands includes all commands you can execute from any of the built-in menus. If you use macros to define a custom menu, you can use a RunCommand action to make selected Access menu commands available on your custom menu.
	The recommended method to create custom menus and toolbars is to use the Customize command on the Tools menu. See Chapter 24 for details.
SetMenuItem	Sets the enabled or checked status of a menu item on a custom menu bar or a custom shortcut menu. Menu items can be enabled or disabled, checked or unchecked.
	In Visual Basic, you should set the Enabled property of a custom CommandBar control to enable or disable it. Set the State property of a custom CommandBar control to check or uncheck it.

Controlling Display and Focus

Macro Action	Purpose
Echo	Controls the display of intermediate actions while a macro runs.
	In Visual Basic, you should set the Echo property of the Application object to True or False.
GoToControl	Sets the focus to the specified control.
	In Visual Basic, you should use the SetFocus method of the control to move the focus.
GoToPage	Moves to the specified page in a form.
	In Visual Basic, you should use the GoToPage method of the form object.
Hourglass	Changes the mouse pointer to an hourglass icon while a macro runs.
	In Visual Basic, you can also set the MousePointer property of the Screen object.
Maximize	Maximizes the active window.
Minimize	Minimizes the active window.
MoveSize	Moves and sizes the active window.
RepaintObject	Forces the repainting of the window for the specified object. Forces recalculation of any formulas in controls on that object. If you do not specify an object type and name, repaints the active window.
	In Visual Basic, you should use the Repaint method of a form.

Macro Action	Purpose
Requery	Refreshes the data in a control that is bound to a query (such as a list box, a combo box, a subform, or a control based on an aggregate function such as DSum). When other actions (such as inserting or deleting a record in the underlying query) might affect the contents of a control that is bound to a query, use the Requery action to update the control values. Use Requery without an argument to refresh the data in the active object (form or datasheet). In Visual Basic, you should use the Requery method of the object.
Restore	Restores a maximized or minimized window to its previous size.
SelectObject	Selects the specified object. Restores the object's window if it was minimized. If the object is in the process of opening (for example, a form referenced in a previous OpenForm action), SelectObject forces the object to finish opening before performing the next action. Use this action after OpenForm when you need to immediately reference the form, a property of a control on the form, or data in a control on the form. In Visual Basic, you should use the SetFocus method of the form to force it to finish opening or to move the focus to the form window.
SetWarnings	When enabled, causes an automatic Enter key response to all system warning or informational messages while a macro runs. For warning messages displayed in a dialog box, pressing the Enter key selects the default button (usually OK or Yes). Run this action when your code is about to execute action queries, and you do not want the user to see the update warnings. SetWarnings No does not halt the display of error messages. Use the Echo macro action with the Echo On argument set to No to avoid displaying the error messages. In Visual Basic, you should set the SetWarnings property of the Application object to True or False.
ShowAllRecords	Removes any filters previously applied to the active table, query, or form. You can also use the macro action RunCommand with the Command argument set to RemoveFilterSort to achieve the same result.
ShowToolbar	Shows or hides any of the standard toolbars or any custom toolbars. In Visual Basic, you can also set the Visible property of a Command-Bar object.

Informing the User of Actions

Macro Action	Purpose
Beep	Produces a sound.
MsgBox	Displays a warning or an informational message in a dialog box and optionally produces a sound. The user must click OK to dismiss the dialog box and proceed.
	In Visual Basic, you should use the MsgBox function. When you use the function, your code can also specify optional buttons and test the return value to determine which button the user clicked.
SetWarnings	When enabled, causes an automatic Enter key response to all system warning or informational messages while a macro runs. For warning messages displayed in a dialog box, pressing the Enter key selects the default button (usually OK or Yes). Run this action when your code is about to execute action queries, and you do not want the user to see the update warnings. SetWarnings No does not halt the display of error messages. Use the Echo macro action with the Echo On argument set to No to avoid displaying the error messages.
	In Visual Basic, you should set the SetWarnings property of the Application object to True or False.

Renaming, Copying, Deleting, Saving, Importing, and Exporting Objects

Macro Action	Purpose
CopyDatabaseFile	In an Access project file (.adp) connected to an SQL Server database, copies the currently connected database to a new file. The user must have system administrator privileges on the server to perform this action.
	You cannot execute this action in an Access desktop database (.mdb).
CopyObject	Copies any database object to the current database using a new name, or copies any database object to another Access database using any specified name.
DeleteObject	Deletes any table, query, form, report, macro, module, data access page, view, stored procedure, function, or diagram. If you do not specify an object, the action deletes the object currently selected in the Database window.
	In Visual Basic, you should use the Delete method of the object collection to delete an object.

Macro Action	Purpose
OutputTo	Outputs the named table, query, form, report, module, data access page, view, stored procedure, or function to another file format. The formats include HTML (.htm, .html), Data Access Page (.htm, .html), Microsoft Excel (.xls), Microsoft Internet Information Server (.htx, .idc), text files (.txt), Rich Text Format (.rtf), Microsoft Access report Snapshot Format (.snp), or Microsoft Active Server Page (.asp). You can also optionally start the application to edit the file. For forms, the data output is from the form's Datasheet view. For reports in formats other than Snapshot Format, Access outputs all controls containing data (including calculated controls) except ActiveX controls. When you output a report in Snapshot Format, Access creates an image of the report that can be opened with the license-free snapshot reader.
Rename	Renames the specified object in the current database.
Save	Saves any table, query, form, report, macro, module, data access page, view, stored procedure, function, or diagram. If you do not specify an Object Type and Object Name, the definition of the currently active object is saved. If you provide only an Object Name, the active object is saved with the new name you specify (a Save As operation).
SendObject	Outputs a table, query, view, stored procedure, or function datasheet, or a form datasheet to an HTML (.htm, .html), an Excel (.xls), a Rich Text Format (.rtf), or a text (.txt) file and embeds the data in an electronic mail message. You can output a report in any of the above formats, but the data includes only the contents of text boxes for the Excel file format, or the contents of text boxes and attached labels for any other format. You can also output the image of a report in Snapshot (.snp) format. You can output a module as plain text or a data access page as HTML (.htm, .html). You can specify to whom the message is to be sent, the message subject, additional message text, and whether the message can be edited before it is sent. You must have e-mail software installed that conforms to the Messaging Application Programming Interface (MAPI) standard.
TransferDatabase	Exports data to or imports data from another Access, dBASE, Paradox, Microsoft FoxPro, or SQL database. You can also use this action to attach tables or files from other Access, dBASE, Paradox, FoxPro, or SQL databases, or from text or spreadsheet files. You can also import or export the definition of queries, views, stored procedures, functions, diagrams, forms, reports, macros, or modules to or from another Access desktop database (.mdb) or project file (.adp).
Transfer-Spreadsheet	Exports data to, or links or imports data from, Excel or Lotus 1-2-3 spreadsheet files.

Macro Action	Purpose
TransferSQL-Database	In an Access project file (.adp) connected to an SQL Server database, transfers the currently connected database to another server and database name. You can optionally transfer only the table structure. The user must have system administrator privileges on the target server to perform this action.
	You cannot execute this action in an Access desktop database (.mdb).
TransferText	Exports data to, or links or imports data from, text files. You can also link or import tables embedded within HTML (.htm, .html) files.

Running Another Application

Macro Action	Purpose
RunApp	Starts another Windows-based or MS-DOS–based application.
	In Visual Basic, use the Shell function or ActiveX application automation to open and control another application.

The Macro Design Facility—An Overview

This section explains how to work with the macro design facility in Microsoft Access.

Working with the Macro Design Window

Open the Wedding List Macro sample database (*WeddingMC.mdb*). Click the Macros button in the Database window, and then click the New button to open a new Macro window similar to the one shown in Figure 21-4 on the next page. In the upper part of the Macro window you define your new macro, and in the lower part you enter settings, called *arguments*, for the actions you've selected for your macro. The upper part shows at least two columns, Action and Comment. You can view all four columns shown in Figure 21-4 by clicking the Macro Names and Conditions buttons on the toolbar. You can also display these two optional columns in all new macros by choosing Options from the Tools menu and setting the Names column and Conditions column options under Show in Macro Design on the View tab.

Notice that the area at the lower right displays a brief help message. The message changes depending on where the insertion point is located in the upper part of the window. (Remember: you can always press F1 to open a context-sensitive Help topic.)

In the Action column, you can specify any one of the 56 macro actions provided by Access. If you click in any box in the Action column, a down arrow button appears at the right side of the box. Click this button to open a drop-down list of the macro actions, as shown in Figure 21-5 on the next page.

Macro Names button Conditions button

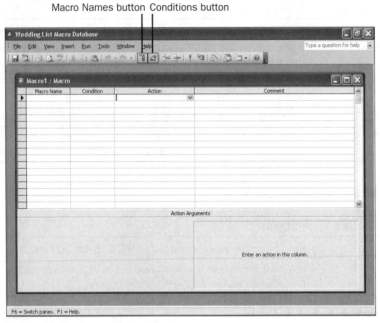

Figure 21-4. A new Macro window.

Figure 21-5. The drop-down list of macro actions.

To see how the Macro window works, select the MsgBox action now. (Scroll down the list to find MsgBox.) You can use the MsgBox action to open a pop-up modal dialog box with a message in it. This is a great way to display a warning or an informative message in your database without defining a separate form.

Assume that this message will be a greeting, and type **Greeting message** in the corresponding box in the Comment column. You'll find the Comment column especially useful for documenting large macros that contain many actions. You can enter additional comments in any blank box in the Comment column (that is, any box without an action next to it).

After you select an action such as MsgBox, Access displays the appropriate argument boxes in the lower part of the window, as shown in Figure 21-6, in which you enter the arguments for the action.

	Action Arguments	
Message	Welcome to the Wedding List Datab.	
Beep	Yes	
Type	Information	
Title	Greetings	Enter the text to display in the message box title bar. For example, 'Customer ID Validation.' Press F1 for help on this argument.

Figure 21-6. Arguments for a MsgBox action that displays a greeting message.

> **Tip** As you can in the Table and Query windows in Design view, you can use the F6 key to move between the upper and lower parts of the Macro window.

You use the Message argument box to set the message that you want Access to display in the dialog box you're creating. The setting in the Beep argument box tells Access whether to sound a beep when the message is displayed. In the Type argument box, you can choose a graphic indicator, such as a red critical icon, that will appear with your message in the dialog box. In the Title argument box, you can type the contents of your message box's title bar. Use the settings shown in Figure 21-6 in your macro. (The entire message should read, "Welcome to the Wedding List Database.")

Saving Your Macro

You must save a macro before you can run it. Choose the Save (or Save As) command from the File menu. When you choose Save, Access opens the dialog box shown in Figure 21-7. Enter the name **TestGreeting**, and click OK to save your macro.

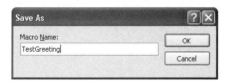

Figure 21-7. The Save As dialog box for saving a macro.

Testing Your Macro

You can run some macros (such as the simple one you just created) directly from the Database window or from the Macro window because they don't depend on controls on an open form or report. If your macro does depend on a form or a report, you must link the macro to the appropriate event and run it that way. (You'll learn how to do this later in this chapter.)

However you run your macro, Access provides a way to test it by allowing you to single step through the macro actions.

To activate single stepping, switch to the Database window, click the Macros tab, select the macro you want to test, and click the Design button. This opens the macro in the Macro window. Either click the Single Step button on the Macro toolbar or choose the Single Step command from the Run menu. Now when you run your macro, Access opens the Macro Single Step dialog box before executing each action in your macro. In this dialog box, you'll see the macro name, the action, and the action arguments.

Try this procedure with the TestGreeting macro you just created. Open the Macro window, click the Single Step button, and then click the Run button. The Macro Single Step dialog box opens, as shown in Figure 21-8. (Later in this section, you'll learn how to code a condition in a macro. The Macro Single Step dialog box also shows you the result of testing your condition.)

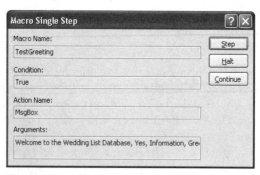

Figure 21-8.   The Macro Single Step dialog box.

If you click the Step button in the dialog box, the action you see in the dialog box will run and you'll see the dialog box opened by your MsgBox action with the message you created, as shown in Figure 21-9. Click the OK button in the message box to dismiss it. If your macro had more than one action defined, you would have returned to the Macro Single Step dialog box, which would have shown you the next action. In this case, your macro has only one action, so Access returns you to the Macro window.

Figure 21-9.   The dialog box created by the MsgBox action in the TestGreeting macro.

If Access encounters an error in any macro during normal execution of your application, Access first displays a dialog box explaining the error it found. You then see an Action Failed dialog box, which is similar to the Macro Single Step dialog box, containing information about the action that caused the problem. At this point, you can click only the Halt button. You can then edit your macro to fix the problem.

Before you read on in this chapter, you might want to return to the Macro window and click the Single Step button again so that it's no longer selected. Otherwise you'll continue to single step through every macro you run until you exit and restart Access or click Continue in one of the Single Step dialog boxes.

Defining Multiple Actions

In Microsoft Access, you can define more than one action within a macro, and you can specify the sequence in which you want the actions performed. The Wedding List Macro database contains several examples of macros that have more than one action. Open the database if it is not open already. Click the Macros button, and select the macro named AutoexecXmpl. Click the Design button to open the Macro window. The macro is shown in Figure 21-10.

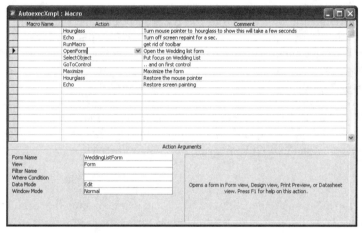

Figure 21-10. The AutoexecXmpl macro, which defines multiple actions that Access executes when you run the macro.

> **Tip** If you create a macro and name it Autoexec, Access runs the macro each time you open the database in which it is stored. The preferred method to run startup code is to define a startup form by choosing Startup from the Tools menu. For details, see Chapter 24, "The Finishing Touches."

If this macro were named AutoExec, Access would execute each action automatically whenever you open the database. This sample macro is an example of a macro you might design to start the application when the user opens your database.

Nine actions are defined in this macro. First, the Hourglass action displays an hourglass mouse pointer to give the user a visual clue that the next several steps might take a second or two. It's always a good idea to turn on this visual cue, even if you think the next several actions won't take very long. Next, the Echo command executes (its Echo On argument is set to No) to ask Access not to repaint the screen after any of the succeeding actions. When you plan to execute several actions in a row that can each potentially cause changes to the display, you can turn repainting off to minimize annoying screen flashing. A similar command is available in Visual Basic (the Echo method of the Application object).

The next action, RunMacro, runs another macro, Offbars, that hides the standard Form View toolbar. You'll find RunMacro handy if you use any short series of actions again and again in macros. You can create a macro with the repeated commands and then call that macro from another macro whenever you need to execute those common actions. If you open the Offbars macro that's called from this RunMacro action, you can see that it contains a ShowToolbar action to hide the Form View toolbar.

The next action, OpenForm, opens WeddingListForm. As you can see in Figure 21-10, the OpenForm action uses four arguments to define how it should work. The Form Name argument indicates the form you want to open. The View argument tells Access what view you want. (The six choices for the View argument are Form, Design, Print Preview, Datasheet, PivotTable, and PivotChart.) Edit is the default for the Data Mode argument, which allows the user to add, edit, or delete records while using this form. The other choices for this argument are Add—to open the form in data entry mode, and Read Only—to open the form but not allow any changes to the data. The default setting for the Window Mode argument is Normal, which opens the form in the mode set by its design properties. You can override the design property settings to open the form in Hidden mode, as an icon in the Icon mode, or in the special Dialog mode. When you open a form hidden, the user can reveal it by choosing Unhide from the Window menu. When you open a form in Dialog mode, Access does not run further actions or Visual Basic statements until you close that form.

Access doesn't always wait for one action to complete before going on to the next one. For example, an OpenForm action merely starts a task to begin opening the form. Particularly if the form displays a lot of data, Access might take several seconds to load all the data and finish displaying the form. Because you're running Microsoft Windows, your personal computer can handle many tasks at once. Access takes advantage of this by going to the next task without waiting for the form to completely open. However, because this macro is designed to maximize WeddingListForm, the form must be completely open in order for this to work.

You can force a form to finish opening by telling Access to put the focus on the form. This macro does so by using the SelectObject action to identify the object to receive the focus (in this case, WeddingListForm), followed by the GoToControl action to put the focus on a specific control on the form. Once the GoToControl action puts the focus on the control, the Maximize action sizes the active window (the window containing the object that currently has the focus) to fit the entire screen. The final two actions in the macro (the Hourglass and Echo actions again) restore the mouse pointer to let the user know that the macro is finished and turn screen painting back on.

> **Note** Because macros might be used by inexperienced programmers, Access automatically restores Hourglass and Echo when it finishes running a macro. If it didn't do this, the screen would never repaint and the mouse would continue to show an hourglass. The user would think that Access is broken. However, it's good practice to always restore what you turn off, which is why the sample AutoExecXmpl macro includes both Hourglass and Echo even though they aren't required. As you'll learn in the next chapter, Visual Basic isn't quite so forgiving. If you turn Echo off in a Visual Basic procedure and forget to turn it back on before your code exits, your screen will appear frozen!

Learning to define multiple actions within a macro is very useful when you want to automate the tasks you perform on a day-to-day basis. Now that you've learned how to do this, the next step is to learn how to group actions by tasks.

Grouping Macros

You'll find that most of the forms you design for an application require multiple macros to respond to events—some to edit fields, some to open reports, and still others to respond to command buttons. You could design a separate macro saved with its own unique name in the Database window to respond to each event, but you'll soon have hundreds of macros in your application.

You can create a simpler set of more manageable objects by defining *macro objects* that contain several named macros within each object. (This sort of macro object is called a *macro group* within Microsoft Access Help.) One approach is to create one saved macro object per form or report. Another technique is to categorize macros by type of action—for example, one macro containing all the OpenForm actions and another containing all the OpenReport actions.

Let's take a look at a form that depends on a macro group. Figure 21-11 shows the Print-Options form from the Wedding List Macro database in Form view. This form contains two command buttons, Print and Cancel, each of which triggers a different macro. The two macros are contained within a macro object called DoReport.

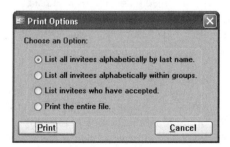

Figure 21-11. The Wedding List Print Options form.

To look at the macro object, switch to the Database window, click the Macros button, and then select DoReport from the list of macro objects in the Database window. Click the

Design button to open this macro object in the Macro window. The macro group is shown in Figure 21-12.

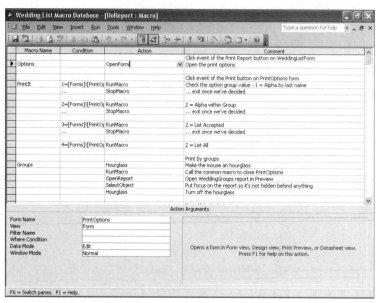

Figure 21-12. The DoReport macro group.

To create a group of named macro procedures within a macro object, you must open the Macro Name column in the Macro window. (If you don't see the Macro Name column, click the Macro Names button on the toolbar.) You can create a series of actions at the beginning of the macro definition, without a name, that you can reference from an event property or a RunMacro action by using only the name of the macro object. As you saw earlier in the AutoexecXmpl macro, naming a macro object in a RunMacro action (without any qualifier) asks Access to run the unnamed actions it finds in that macro object.

To create a set of named actions within a macro object, place a name on the first action within the set in the Macro Name column. To execute a named set of actions within a macro object from an event property or a RunMacro action, enter the name of the macro object, a period, and then the name from the Macro Name column. For example, to execute the PrintIt set of actions in the DoReport macro, enter DoReport.PrintIt in the event property or the Macro Name parameter.

In the sample DoReport macro group, each of the seven names in this column represents an individual macro within the object. (You must scroll down to see the other names.) The first macro, Options (triggered by the Print Report button on WeddingListForm), opens the Print Options form, and the second macro, PrintIt, determines which report was selected. The next four macros, Groups, Alpha, Accepted, and PrintF, display the appropriate report in Print Preview mode, based on the result of the second macro. The last macro, Cancel, merely closes the Print Options form if the user clicks the Cancel button. As you might have guessed, Access runs a macro starting with the first action of the macro name specified and executes each action in sequence until it encounters a StopMacro action, another macro name, or no further actions. As you'll see later, you can control whether some actions execute by adding tests in the Condition column of the macro.

If you open the PrintOptions form in Design view (see Figure 21-13) and look at the properties for each of the command buttons, you'll see that the On Click property contains the name of the macro that executes when the user clicks the command button. If you open the drop-down list for any event property, you can see that Access lists all macro objects and the named macros within them to make it easy to select the one you want.

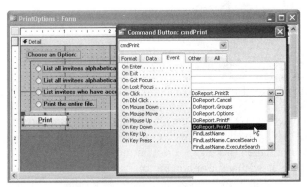

Figure 21-13. The On Click property of a command button set to execute a macro.

Remember, the macro name is divided into two parts. The part before the period is the name of the macro object, and the part after the period is the name of a specific macro within the object. So, for the first command button control, the On Click property is set to DoReport.PrintIt. When the user clicks this button, Access runs the PrintIt macro in the DoReport macro object. After you specify a macro name in an event property, you can click the Build button next to the property and Access opens that macro in a Macro window.

Conditional Expressions

In some macros, you might want to execute some actions only under certain conditions. For example, you might want to update a record, but only if new values in the controls on a form pass validation tests. Or you might want to display or hide certain controls based on the value of other controls.

The PrintIt macro in the DoReport macro group is a good example of a macro that uses conditions to determine which action should proceed. Select DoReport from the list of macros in the Wedding List Macro database, and click the Design button to see the Macro window. Click in the Condition column of the first line of the PrintIt macro, and press Shift+F2 to open the Zoom window, shown in Figure 21-14. (If you can't see the Condition column, click the Conditions button on the toolbar.)

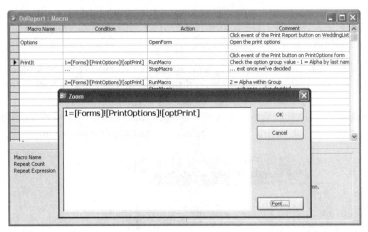

Figure 21-14. A condition in the DoReport macro group shown in the Zoom window.

As you saw earlier, this macro is triggered by the On Click property of the Print button on the PrintOptions form. This form allows the user to print a specific report by selecting the appropriate option button and then clicking the Print button. If you look at the form in Design view (see Figure 21-13), you'll see that the option buttons are located within an option group control on the form. Each option button sets a specific numeric value (in this case, 1 for the first button, 2 for the second button, 3 for the third button, and 4 for the fourth button) in the option group, which you can test in the Condition column of a macro.

When you include a condition in a macro, Access won't run the action on that line unless the condition evaluates to True. If you want to run a series of actions on the basis of the outcome of a test, you can enter the test in the Condition column on the first action line and enter an ellipsis (…) in the Condition column for the other actions in the series. This causes Access to evaluate the condition only once and execute additional actions (those with an ellipsis in the Condition column) if the original test evaluated to True.

In this particular example, the condition tests the value of the option group control on the form. You can reference any control on an open form by using the syntax

`FORMS!formname!controlname`

where *formname* is the name of an open form and *controlname* is the name of a control on that form. In this case, the direct reference is *[FORMS]![PrintOptions]![optPrint]*. (*optPrint* is the name of the option group control. You can see this in the Name property on the Other tab of the property sheet for this control.) For more details about the rules for referencing objects in Access, see Chapter 22, "Understanding Visual Basic Fundamentals."

> **Tip** If your object names do not contain any embedded blanks or other special characters, you don't need to surround *formname* or *controlname* with brackets when you use this syntax to reference a control on a form; Access inserts the brackets as needed.

Once you understand how to refer to the value of a control on a form, you can see that the PrintIt macro tests for each of the possible values of the option group control. When it finds a match, PrintIt runs the appropriately named macro within the macro object to open the requested report and then stops. If you look at the individual report macros, you'll see that they each run a common macro, DoReport.Cancel, to close the PrintOptions form (which isn't needed after the user chooses a report), and then open the requested report in Print Preview and put the focus on the window that displays the report.

Converting Your Macros to Visual Basic

As you'll learn in the rest of this book, Visual Basic, rather than macros, is what you should use to automate any serious applications. If you've spent some time getting familiar with programming in Access using macros but would now like to move to Visual Basic, you're in luck! Access provides a handy tool to convert the actions in macros called from events on your forms and reports to the equivalent Visual Basic statements.

To see how this works, open WeddingListForm in Design view. Choose Macro from the Tools menu, and then click Convert Form's Macros To Visual Basic on the submenu, as shown in Figure 21-15.

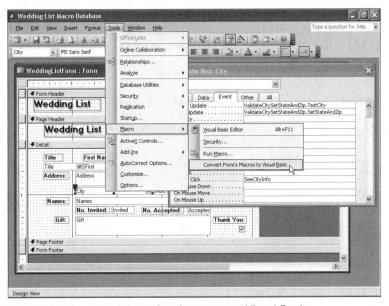

Figure 21-15. Converting a form's macros to Visual Basic.

In the next dialog box, the Convert Wizard offers you the option to insert error-handling code and to copy the comments from your macros into the new code. You should leave both options selected, and then click Convert to change your macros to Visual Basic. After the wizard is finished, you should see all macro references in event properties changed to [Event Procedure]. Click the On Current event property for WeddingListForm, and then click the

Build button (...) to the right of the property. You'll see the converted code displayed as shown in Figure 21-16.

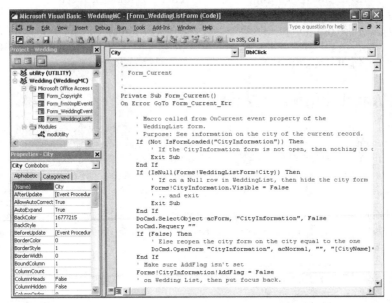

Figure 21-16. The macro from the Current event of WeddingListForm converted to Visual Basic.

Note Converting your macros to Visual Basic does not delete any of your original macros. Also, the wizard doesn't convert any macros referenced by a RunMacro command—you'll have to do that yourself.

Note In Chapter 23, "Automating Your Application with Visual Basic," I'll introduce you to some enhancements I made to the Wedding List sample database after I converted all the macros to Visual Basic using this wizard. You can find this version of the database saved as *WeddingList.mdb* on the companion CD.

Understanding Visual Basic Fundamentals

In this chapter, you'll learn how to create, edit, and test Visual Basic code in your Access applications. The chapter covers the following major topics:

- The Microsoft Visual Basic Editor (VBE) and its debugging tools

- Variables and constants and how to declare them

- The primary object models defined in access—the Access model, the Data Access Objects (DAO) model, and the ActiveX Data Objects (ADO) model

  You'll need to understand these models to be able to manipulate objects such as forms, form controls, and recordsets in your code.

- Visual Basic procedural statements

  - Function and Sub statements

  - Property Get, Property Let, and Property Set (for use in class modules) statements

  - Flow-control statements, including Call, Do, For, If, and Select Case

  - DoCmd and RunCommand statements

  - On Error statement

- A walk-through of some example code you'll find in the sample databases

If you're new to Visual Basic, you might want to read through the chapter from beginning to end, but keep in mind that the large section in the middle of the chapter on procedural statements is designed to be used primarily as a reference. If you're already familiar with Visual Basic, you might want to review the sections on the Visual Basic Editor and the object models, and then use the rest of the chapter as reference material.

 Note You can find many of the code examples from this chapter in the modExamples module in the *Contacts.mdb* and *Housing.mdb* sample databases on the companion CD.

The Visual Basic Development Environment

In Access for Windows 95 (version 7.0), Visual Basic replaced the Access Basic programming language included with versions 1 and 2 of Access. The two languages are very similar because both Visual Basic and Access Basic evolved from a common design created before either product existed. (It's called *Visual* Basic because it was the first version of Basic designed specifically for the Windows graphical environment.) In recent years, Visual Basic has become the common programming language for Microsoft Office applications, including Access, Microsoft Excel, Microsoft Word, and Microsoft PowerPoint.

Having a common programming language across applications provides several advantages. You have to learn only one programming language, and you can easily share objects across applications by using Visual Basic with ActiveX object automation. Microsoft Office Access 2003 uses the Visual Basic Editor common to all Office applications and to the Visual Basic programming product. The Visual Basic Editor provides color-coded syntax, an Object Browser, and other features. It also provides excellent tools for testing and confirming the proper execution of the code you write.

Modules

You save all Visual Basic code in your database in modules. Access provides two ways to create a module: as a module object or as part of a form or report object.

Module Objects

You can view the module objects in your database by clicking the Modules button on the Object bar in the Database window. Figure 22-1 shows the standard and class modules in the LawTrack Contacts sample database. You should use module objects to define procedures that you need to call from queries or from several forms or reports in your application. You can call a public procedure defined in a module from anywhere in your application.

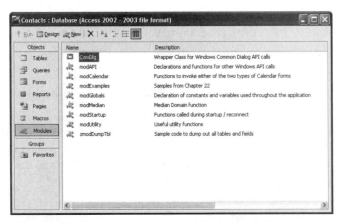

Figure 22-1. The module objects in the LawTrack Contacts database.

When you click the New button above the modules list, Access creates a new *standard module*. You use a standard module to define procedures that you can call from anywhere in your application. It's a good idea to name modules based on their purpose. For example, a module that contains procedures to perform custom calculations for queries might be named modQueryFunctions, and a module containing procedures to work directly with Windows functions might be named modWindowsAPIFunctions.

Advanced developers might want to create a special type of module object called a *class module*. A class module is a specification for a user-defined object in your application, and the Visual Basic procedures you create in a class module define the properties and methods that your object supports. You create a new class module by selecting the Database window and then choosing Class Module from the Insert menu. You'll learn more about objects, methods, properties, and class modules later in this chapter.

Form and Report Modules

To make it easy to create Visual Basic procedures that respond to events on forms or reports, Access supports a module associated with each form or report. (You can design forms and reports that do not have a related module.) A module associated with a form or report is also a class module that allows you to respond to events defined for the form or report as well as define extended properties and methods of the form or report. Within a form or report class module, you can create specially named event procedures to respond to Access-defined events, private procedures that you can call only from within the scope of the class module, and public procedures that you can call as methods of the class. See "Collections, Objects, Properties, and Methods" on page 791 for more information about objects and methods. You can edit the module for a form or a report by opening the form or report in Design view and then clicking the Code button on the toolbar or choosing Code from the View menu. As you'll learn later, you can also open a form or a report by setting an object equal to a new instance of the form or report's class module.

Using form and report modules offers three main advantages over standard modules.

- All the code you need to automate a form or a report resides with that form or report. You don't have to remember the name of a separate form-related or report-related module object.

- Access loads module objects into memory when you first reference any procedure or variable in the module and leaves them loaded as long as the database is open. Access loads the code for a form or a report only when the form or the report is opened. Access unloads a form or a report class module when the object is closed; therefore, form and report modules consume memory only when you're using the form or the report to which they are attached.

- If you export a form or report, all the code in the form or report module is exported with it.

However, form and report modules have one disadvantage: Because the code must be loaded each time you open the form or report, a form or report with a large supporting module opens notice-ably more slowly than one that has little or no code. In addition, saving a form or report design can take longer if you have also opened the associated module and changed any of the code.

One enhancement that first appeared in Access 97 (version 8.0)—the addition of the HasModule property—helps Access load forms and reports that have no code more rapidly. Access automatically sets this property to True if you try to view the code for a form or report, even if you don't define any event procedures. If HasModule is False, Access doesn't bother to look for an associated Visual Basic module, so the form or report loads very quickly.

> **Caution** If you set the HasModule property to False (No) in the Properties window, Access deletes any code module associated with the form or report. However, Access warns you and gives you a chance to change your mind if you set the HasModule property to No in error.

The Visual Basic Editor Window

When you open a module in Design view, Access opens the Visual Basic Editor and asks the editor to display your code. Open the LawTrack Contacts (*Contacts.mdb*) sample database, click the Modules button in the Database window, select the modExamples module, and then click the Design button to see the code for the modExamples module opened in the Visual Basic Editor, as shown in Figure 22-2.

What you see on your screen might differ from Figure 22-2, particularly if you have opened the Visual Basic Editor previously and moved some windows around. In the upper left corner of the figure, you can see the Visual Basic Project Explorer window docked in the workspace. (Choose Project Explorer from the View menu or press Ctrl+R to see this window if it's not visible.) In this window, you can discover all module objects and form and report class modules saved in the database. You can double-click any module to open it in the Code window, which you can see maximized in the upper right corner.

Docked in the lower left corner is the Properties window. (Choose Properties Window from the View menu or press F4 to see this window if it's not visible.) When you have a form or report that has a Visual Basic module open in Design view in Access, you can click that object in the Project Explorer to see all its properties. If you modify a property in the Properties window, you're changing it in Access. To open a form or report that is not open, you can select it in the Project Explorer and then choose Object from the View menu.

In the lower right corner you can see the Locals window docked. (Choose Locals Window from the View menu to see this window if it's not visible.) As you will see later, this window allows you to instantly see the values of any active variables or objects when you pause execution in a procedure. In the lower center you can see the Immediate window docked. (Choose Immediate Window from the View menu or press Ctrl+G to see this window if it's not visible.) It's called the Immediate Window because you can type any valid Visual Basic statement in this window and press Enter to execute the statement immediately. You can also use a special "what is" command character (?) to find out the value of an expression or variable. For example, you can type ?5*20 and press Enter, and Visual Basic responds with the answer on the following line: *100*.

Return to Microsoft Access window

Insert a new module or procedure

Design mode

Halt execution and reset   Open Project Explorer window

Pause execution   Open Project Properties window

Run procedure   Open Object Browser

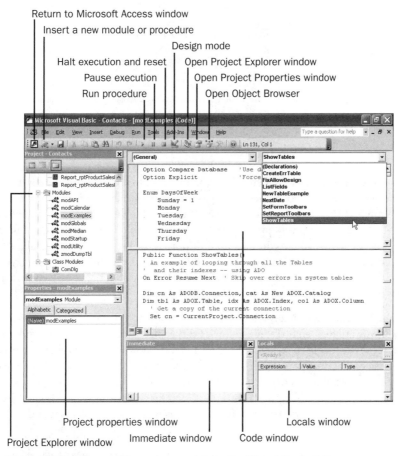

Figure 22-2.   The modExamples module in the Visual Basic Editor.

Project Explorer window

Project properties window

Immediate window

Code window

Locals window

Chapter 22

You can undock any window by grabbing its title bar and dragging it away from its docked position on the edge toward the center of the screen. You can also undock a window by right-clicking anywhere in the window and clearing the Dockable property. As you will see later, you can set the Dockable property of any window by choosing Options from the Tools menu. When a window is set as Dockable but not docked along an edge, it becomes a pop-up window that floats on top of other windows—similar to the way an Access form works when its PopUp property is set to Yes, as you learned in Chapter 12, "Customizing a Form." When you make any window not Dockable, it shares the space occupied by the Code window.

You cannot set the Code window as Dockable. The Code window always appears in the part of the workspace that is not occupied by docked windows. You can maximize the Code window to fill this remaining space, as shown in Figure 22-2. You can also click the Restore button for this window and open multiple overlaid code windows for different modules within the Code window space.

At the top of the Code window, just below the toolbar, you can see two drop-down list boxes.

- **Object list box** When you're editing a form or report class module, open this list on the left to select the form or the report, a section on the form or the report, or any control on the form or the report that can generate an event. The Procedure list box then shows the available event procedures for the selected object. Select General to view the Declarations section of the module, where you can set options or declare variables shared by multiple procedures. In a form or a report class module, General is also where you'll see any procedures you have coded that do not respond to events. When you're editing a standard module object, this list displays only the General option. In a class module object, you can choose General or Class.

- **Procedure list box** Open this list on the right to select a procedure in the module and display that procedure in the Code window. When you're editing a form or report module, this list shows the available event procedures for the selected object and displays in bold type the event procedures that you have coded and attached to the form or the report. When you're editing a module object, the list displays in alphabetic order all the procedures you coded in the module. In a class module when you have selected Class in the Object list box, you can choose the special Initialize or Terminate procedures for the class.

In Figure 22-2, I dragged the divider bar at the top of the scroll bar on the right of the Code window downward to open two edit windows. I clicked in the lower window and chose ShowTables from the Procedure list box. You might find a split window very handy when you're tracing calls from one procedure to another. The Procedure list box always shows you the name of the procedure that currently has the focus. In the Code window, you can use the arrow keys to move horizontally and vertically. When you enter a new line of code and press Enter, Visual Basic optionally verifies the syntax of the line and warns you of any problems it finds.

If you want to create a new procedure in a module, you can type either a *Function* statement, a *Sub* statement, or a *Property* statement on any blank line above or below an existing procedure and then press Enter, or click anywhere in the module and choose Procedure from the drop-down list of the Insert button on the toolbar, or choose Procedure from the Insert menu. (For details about the Function and Sub statements, see the section "Functions and Subroutines" on page 812. For details about the Property statement, see the section "Understanding Class Modules," page 815) Visual Basic creates a new procedure for you (it does not embed the new procedure in the procedure you were editing) and inserts an *End Function*, *End Sub*, or *End Property* statement. When you create a new procedure using the Insert button or the Insert menu, Visual Basic opens a dialog box where you can enter the name of the new procedure, select the type of the procedure (Sub, Function, or Property), and select the scope of the procedure (Public or Private). To help you organize your procedures, Visual Basic inserts the new procedure in alphabetical sequence within the existing procedures.

Caution If you type a Function, Sub, or Property statement in the middle of an existing procedure, Visual Basic accepts the statement if it's syntactically correct, but your project won't compile because you cannot place a Function, Sub, or Property procedure inside another Function, Sub, or Property procedure.

If you're working in a form or report module, you can select an object in the Object list box and then open the Procedure list box to see all the available events for that object. An event name displayed in bold type means you have created a procedure to handle that event. Select an event whose name isn't displayed in bold type to create a procedure to handle that event.

Visual Basic provides many options that you can set to customize how you work with modules. Choose Options from the Tools menu, and then select the Editor tab to see the settings for these options, as shown in Figure 22-3.

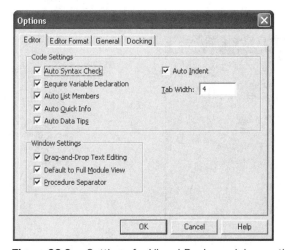

Figure 22-3.   Settings for Visual Basic modules on the Editor tab in the Options dialog box.

On the Editor tab, some important options to consider are Auto Syntax Check, to check the syntax of lines of code as you enter them; and Require Variable Declaration, which forces you to declare all your variables. (You'll see later why that's important.) If you want to see required and optional parameters as you type complex function calls, choose the Auto List Members option. Auto Quick Info provides drop-down lists where appropriate built-in constants are available to complete parameters in function or subroutine calls. When you're debugging code, Auto Data Tips lets you discover the current value of a variable by hovering your mouse pointer over any usage of the variable in your code.

Drag-and-Drop Text Editing allows you to highlight code and drag it to a new location. Default to Full Module View shows all your code for multiple procedures in a module in a single scrollable view. If you clear that option, you will see only one procedure at a time and must page up or down or select a different procedure in the Procedure list box to move to a different part of the module. When you're in full module view, selecting Procedure Separator asks Visual Basic to draw a line between procedures to make it easy to see where one procedure ends and another begins.

Selecting Auto Indent asks Visual Basic to leave you at the same indent as the previous line of code when you press the Enter key to insert a new line. I wrote all of the sample code you'll see in this book and in the sample databases with indents to make it easy to see related lines of code within a loop or an If…Then…Else construct. You can set the Tab Width to any value

Chapter 22

from 1 through 32. This setting tells Visual Basic how many spaces you want to indent when you press the Tab key while writing code.

On the Editor Format tab of the Options dialog box, you can set custom colors for various types of code elements and also choose a display font. I recommend using a monospaced font such as Courier New for all code editing.

On the General tab, shown in Figure 22-4, you can set some important options that dictate how Visual Basic acts as you enter new code and as you debug your code. You can ignore all the settings under Form Grid Settings because they apply to forms designed in Visual Basic, not Microsoft Access.

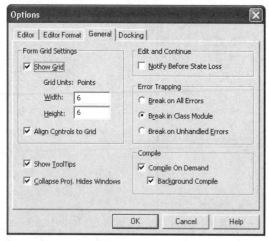

Figure 22-4. Settings for Visual Basic modules on the General tab in the Options dialog box.

If your code has halted, in many cases you can enter new code or correct problems in code before continuing to test. Some changes you make, however, will force Visual Basic to reset rather than let you continue to run from the halted point. If you select the Notify Before State Loss option, Visual Basic will warn you before allowing you to make code changes that would cause it to reset.

In the Error Trapping section, you can select one of three ways to tell Visual Basic how to deal with errors. As you'll discover later in this chapter, you can write statements in your code to attempt to catch errors. If you think you have a problem in your error-trapping code, you can select Break on All Errors. With this setting, Visual Basic ignores all error trapping and halts execution on any error. If you have written class modules that can be called from other modules, to catch an untrapped error that occurs within a class module, choose Break in Class Module to halt on the statement within the class module that failed. (I recommend this setting for most testing.) If you choose Break on Unhandled Errors, and an untrapped error occurs within a class module, Visual Basic halts on the statement that invoked the class module.

The last two important options on this tab are Compile On Demand and Background Compile. With Compile On Demand set, Visual Basic compiles any previously uncompiled new code whenever you run that code directly or run a procedure that calls that code. Background

Compile lets Visual Basic use spare CPU cycles to compile new code as you are working in other areas.

Finally, on the Docking tab you can specify whether the Immediate window, Locals window, Watch window, Project Explorer, Properties window, or Object Browser can be docked. We will take a look at the Immediate window and Watch window in the next section. You can use the Object Browser to discover all the supported properties and methods of any object or function defined in Microsoft Access, Visual Basic, or your database application.

Inside Out

Understanding the relationship between Access and Visual Basic

Microsoft Access and Visual Basic work as two separate but interlinked products in your Access application. Access handles the storage of the Visual Basic project (both the source code and the compiled code) in your desktop database (.mdb) or project (.adp) file, and it calls Visual Basic to manage the editing and execution of your code.

Because Access tightly links your forms and reports with class modules stored in the Visual Basic project, some complex synchronization must happen between the two products. For example, when you open a form module and enter a new event procedure in the Visual Basic Code window, Access must set the appropriate event property to [Event Procedure] so that both the form and the code are correctly linked. Likewise, when you delete all the code in an event procedure, Access must clear the related form or control property. So, when you open a form or report module from the Visual Basic Editor window, you'll notice that Access also opens the related form or report object in the Access window.

When Access first began using Visual Basic (instead of Access Basic) in version 7 (Microsoft Access for Windows 95), it was possible to end up with a corrupted Visual Basic project or corrupted form or report object if you weren't careful to always compile and save both the code and the form or report definition at the same time when you made changes to either. It was particularly easy to encounter corruption if multiple developers had the database open at the same time. This corruption most often occurred when Access failed to merge a changed module back into the Visual Basic project when the developer saved changes.

Microsoft greatly improved the reliability of this process when it switched in version 9 (Microsoft Access 2000) to saving the entire Visual Basic project whenever you save a change. However, this change means that two developers can no longer have the same database open and be working in the code at the same time. This also means that your Access file can grow rapidly if you're making frequent changes to the code and saving your changes.

When you're making multiple changes in an Access application, I recommend that you always compile your project when you have finished changing a section of code. (Choose Compile from the Debug menu in the Visual Basic Editor.) You should also save all at once multiple objects that you have changed by clicking the Save button in the VBE window and always responding Yes to the Save dialog box that Access shows you when you have multiple changed objects open.

Chapter 22

Working with Visual Basic Debugging Tools

You might have noticed that the debugging tools for macros are very primitive. You can't do much more than run macros in single-step mode to try to find the source of an error. The debugging tools for Visual Basic are significantly more extensive. The following sections describe many of the tools available in Visual Basic. You might want to scan these sections first and then return after you have learned more about the Visual Basic language and have begun writing procedures that you need to debug.

Setting Breakpoints

If you still have the modExamples module open, scroll down until you can see all of the ShowTables function, as shown in Figure 22-5. (I closed the Immediate and Locals windows to make it possible to see all the code.) This sample function examines all the table definitions in the current database and displays the table name, the names of any indexes defined for the table, and the names of columns in each index by printing to a special object called *Debug* (another name for the Immediate Window).

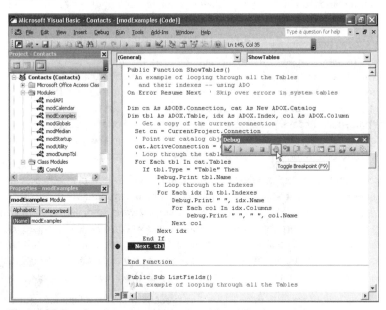

Figure 22-5.   Setting a breakpoint in a Visual Basic module.

One of the most common ways to test particularly complex code is to open the module you want to examine, set a stopping point in the code (called a breakpoint), and then run the code. Visual Basic halts before executing the statement on the line where you set the breakpoint. As you'll soon see, when Visual Basic stops at a breakpoint, you can examine all sorts of information to help you clean up potential problems. While a procedure is stopped, you can look at the values in variables—including all object variables you might have defined. In addition, you can also change the value of variables, single-step through the code, reset the code, or restart at a different statement.

To set a breakpoint, click anywhere on the line of code where you want Visual Basic execution to halt and either click the Toggle Breakpoint button on the Debug toolbar (open this toolbar by right-clicking any toolbar and choosing Debug on the shortcut menu), choose Toggle Breakpoint from the Debug menu, or press F9 to set or clear a breakpoint. When a breakpoint is active, Access highlights the line of code (in red by default) where the breakpoint is established and displays a dot on the selection bar to the left of the line of code. Note that you can set as many breakpoints as you like, anywhere in any module. After you set a breakpoint, the breakpoint stays active until you close the current database, specifically clear the breakpoint, or choose Clear All Breakpoints from the Debug menu (or press Ctrl+Shift+F9). In the example shown in Figure 22-5, I set a breakpoint to halt the procedure at the bottom of the loop that examines each table. When you run the procedure later, you'll see that Visual Basic will halt on this statement just before it executes the statement.

Using the Immediate Window

"Action central" for all troubleshooting in Visual Basic is a special edit window called the Immediate window. You can open the Immediate window while editing a module by clicking the Immediate Window button on the Debug toolbar or choosing Immediate Window from the View menu. Even when you do not have a Visual Basic module open, you can open the Immediate window from anywhere in Access by pressing Ctrl+G.

Executing Visual Basic Commands in the Immediate Window   In the Immediate window (shown earlier in Figure 22-2), you can type any valid Visual Basic command and press Enter to have it executed immediately. You can also execute a procedure by typing in the procedure name followed by any parameter values required by the procedure. You can ask Visual Basic to evaluate any expression by typing a question mark character (sometimes called the "what is" character) followed by the expression. Access displays the result of the evaluation on the line below. You might want to experiment by typing ?(5 * 4) / 10. You will see the answer *2* on the line below.

Because you can type in any valid Visual Basic statement, you can enter an *assignment statement* (the name of a variable, an equals sign, and the value you want to assign to the variable) to set a variable that you might have forgotten to set correctly in your code. For example, there's a public variable (you'll learn more about variables later in this chapter) called gintDontShow-CompanyList that the LawTrack Contacts sample application uses to save whether the current user wants to see the Select Companies pop-up window when clicking Companies on the main switchboard. Some users might prefer to go directly to the Companies/Organizations form that edits all companies rather than select or filter the list. If you have been running the LawTrack Contacts application, you can find out the current value of the string by typing

```
?gintDontShowCompanyList
```

Visual basic displays the value of this variable, which should be either 0 or −1. You can set the value of this string to False (0) by typing

```
gintDontShowCompanyList = 0
```

You can verify the value of the variable you just set by typing

```
?gintDontShowCompanyList
```

Chapter 22

If you assigned 0 to the variable, you should see that value echoed in the Immediate window.

To have a sense of the power of what you're doing, go to the Database window in Access by clicking the View Microsoft Access button on the left end of the toolbar in the Visual Basic Editor window. Open the *frmMain* form in Form view. Click the Companies button to find out whether the Select Companies form or the Companies/Organizations form opens. If you go directly to the Select Companies form, then gintDontShowCompanyList must be False (0). Close the form that opens.

Now, go back to the Visual Basic Editor window, either by using the Windows Alt+Tab feature or by clicking the Visual Basic button on your Windows taskbar. In the Visual Basic Immediate window, set the value to True by entering in the Immediate window

```
gintDontShowCompanyList = -1
```

Go back to the main switchboard and try the Companies button again. Because you set the public variable to True, you should go directly to the Companies/Organizations form. Now that you have the form open to edit companies, you can set a filter directly from the Immediate window. Leave the form open and go back to that window and enter the expression

```
Forms!frmCompanies.Filter = "[StateOrProvince] = 'PA'"
```

If you want, you can ask what the filter property is to see if it is set correctly. Note that nothing has happened yet to the form. Next, turn on the form's FilterOn property by entering

```
Forms!frmCompanies.FilterOn = True
```

Return to the form, and you should now see from the navigation bar that the form is filtered down to two rows—all the companies in the state of Pennsylvania. If you want to try another example, return to the Immediate window and enter

```
Forms!frmCompanies.Section(0).Backcolor = 255
```

The background of Section(0), the detail area of the form, should now appear red! Note that none of these changes affect the design of the form. You can close the form, and the next time you open it, the form will have a normal background color, and the records won't be filtered.

Using Breakpoints   You saw earlier how to set a breakpoint within a module procedure. To see how a breakpoint works, open the *modExamples* module in the VBE window, find the ShowTables function, and be sure you have set a breakpoint on the Next tbl statement as shown in Figure 22-6.

Because the ShowTables procedure is a function that might return a value, you have to ask Visual Basic to evaluate the function in order to run it. The function doesn't require any parameters, so you don't need to supply any. To run the function, type **?ShowTables()** in the Immediate window, as shown in Figure 22-6, and press Enter. (I undocked the Immediate window to make it easier to see in the figure.)

> **Note** You can also ask Visual Basic to run any public procedure by clicking in the procedure and clicking the Run button on either the Standard or Debug toolbar.

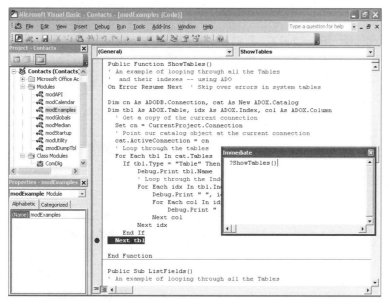

Figure 22-6. Running a module function from the Immediate window.

Visual Basic runs the function you requested. Because you set a breakpoint, the code stops on the statement with the breakpoint, as shown in Figure 22-7. The first table in the database is actually a linked table (a Microsoft Excel spreadsheet), so you won't see any output. Click the Continue button on the toolbar to run through the loop a second time to display the first table.

Note that I chose Locals Window from the View menu to reveal the Locals window you can see across the bottom of Figure 22-7. In the Locals window, Visual Basic shows you all the active variables. You can, for example, click the plus sign next to the word cat (a variable set to the currently opened database catalog) to browse through all the property settings for the database and all the objects within the database. You can click on the tbl variable to explore the columns and properties in the table. See the section titled "Collections, Objects, Properties, and Methods" on page 791 for details about all the objects you see in the "tree" under the database catalog.

The Immediate window displays the output of three Debug.Print statements within the function you're running, as also shown in Figure 22-7 on the next page.

The first line shows the name of the first table (Errorlog) that the function found in the database. The second (indented) line shows the name of the index for that table. The third line shows the name of the one column in the index.

If you want to see the results of executing the next loop in the code (examining the next table object in the catalog), click the Continue button on the toolbar. If you want to run the code a single statement at a time, choose Step Into or Step Over from the Debug menu or open the

Chapter 22

Debug toolbar and click the Step Into or Step Over button. Step Into and Step Over work the same unless you're about to execute a statement that calls another procedure. If the next statement calls another procedure, Step Into literally steps into the called procedure so that you can step through the code in the called procedure one line at a time. Step Over calls the procedure without halting and stops on the next statement in the current procedure.

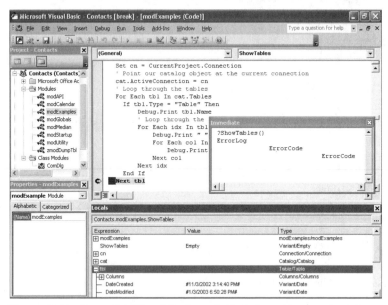

Figure 22-7. Executing Visual Basic code that stops at a breakpoint.

When you are finished studying the loop in the ShowTables function, be sure to click the Reset button on the toolbar to halt code execution.

> **Note** The Tables collection in the catalog includes tables, linked tables, system tables, and queries. Because the ShowTables procedure only looks for tables, you will need to loop through the code several times until the procedure finds the next object that defines a table. You should quickly find the ErrorLog, ErrTable, and ErrTableSample tables, but the code must then loop through all the queries and linked tables (more than 40 of them) before finding the SwitchboardDriver table.

Working with the Watch Window

Sometimes setting a breakpoint isn't enough to catch an error. You might have a variable that you know is being changed somewhere by your code (perhaps incorrectly). By using the Watch window, you can examine a variable as your code runs, ask Visual Basic to halt when an expression that uses the variable becomes true, or ask Visual Basic to halt when the variable changes.

An interesting set of variables in the LawTrack Contacts sample database are gintDontShow-CompanyList, gintDontShowContactList, and gintDontShowInvoiceList (all defined in the modGlobals module). When any of these variables are set to True, the main switchboard bypasses the intermediate list/search form for companies, contacts, and invoices, respectively. You played with one of these variables earlier, but it would be interesting to trap when these are set or reset.

> **Caution** There are a couple of known issues with setting breakpoints in Access 2003. First, code will not halt if you have cleared the Use Special Access Keys option in the Startup dialog window (choose Startup from the Tools menu). Second, the Break When Value Is True and Break When Value Changes options in the Add Watch dialog box will not work if the value or expression you're watching is changed in a form or report module that is not already open in the Visual Basic Editor. For this example to work, the form modules for *frmMain*, *frmSignon*, and *frmUsers* must be open. You can verify that these modules are open by opening the Windows menu in the VBE window. The *Contacts.mdbd* sample file should have modules open, but these modules might not be open in your copy if you have closed them and compiled and saved the project. You can find these modules in the Project Explorer window. Open the list of objects in the Microsoft Class Objects category and then double-click the form modules that you need to open them.

To set a watch for when the value changes, open the Watch window by choosing it in the View menu, right-click in the Watch window, and choose Add Watch from the shortcut menu. You can also choose Add Watch from the Debug menu. You should see the Add Watch dialog box, as shown in Figure 22-8.

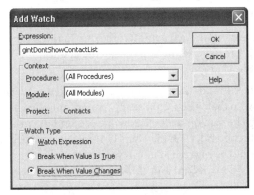

Figure 22-8. Setting a watch for when a variable's value changes.

In the Expression text box, enter the name of the variable you want the code to watch. In this case, you want to watch when the variable gintDontShowContactList changes. You don't know where the variable is set, so set the Procedure and Module selections to (All Procedures) and (All Modules), respectively. Select the Watch Type option to Break When Value Changes, and click OK to set the watch. Go to the Immediate window and set gintDontShowContactList to True by entering **gintDontShowContactList** = –1 and pressing Enter. Now return to the Database window and start the application by opening the *frmSplash* form. (Code in the Load event of this form hides the Database window and then opens the LawTrack Contacts Sign On form.)

Because you set a watch to halt when gintDontShowContactList changes, the code execution should halt in the module for the frmSignOn form as shown in Figure 22-9. (I closed the Project Explorer and Properties window so that I could see the Code window without these windows in the way.)

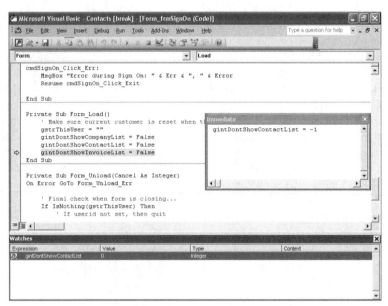

Figure 22-9. Visual Basic code halted immediately after a watch variable has changed.

Note that the code halts on the statement immediately after the one that reset the watched variable. If you didn't set the variable to True before you started the application, Visual Basic won't halt because the value won't be changing.

Click the Continue button to let the code continue executing. Return to the Access window, and in the LawTrack Contacts Sign On dialog box, choose my name (John Viescas) and press Enter or click the Sign On button. The sign on dialog box will close, and the main switchboard form opens. In the main switchboard, click the Users button to open the user edit form. The first and only record should be my record unless you've created other users. Select the Don't Show Contact List option in my record and click the Save button. The procedure halts again, as shown in Figure 22-10.

It appears that this code is setting the gintDontShowContactList variable to some value on the user edit form. (As you'll learn later, Me is a shorthand way to reference the form object where your code is running, so *Me.DontShowContactList* references a control on the form.) Click the Continue button again to let the code finish execution. Return to the Microsoft Access window and click the Close button on the Users form to return to the main switchboard.

If you open *frmUsers* in Design view (you can't do this while the procedure is still halted) and examine the names of the check box controls on the form, you'll find that the check box you selected is named DontShowContactList. When the code behind frmUsers detects a change to the options for the currently signed-on user, it makes sure the option variables in modGlobals get changed as well. Be sure to close the *frmUsers* form when you're finished looking at it.

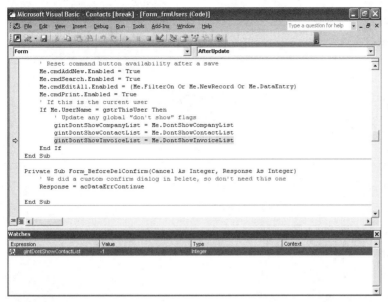

Figure 22-10. The gintDontShowContactList variable is set to the value of a form control.

Examining the Procedure Call Sequence (Call Stack)

After stopping code that you're trying to debug, it's useful sometimes to find out what started the current sequence of code execution and what procedures have been called by Visual Basic. For this example, you can continue with the watch on the variable gintDontShowContactList.

You should now be at the main switchboard form (frmMain) in the application. Click the Exit button to close the application and return to the Database window. (You'll see a prompt asking you if you're sure you want to exit—click Yes. You might also see a prompt offering to back up the data file—click No.) The code should halt again in the Close event of the frm-Main form. Click the Call Stack button on the Debug toolbar or choose Call Stack from the View menu to see the call sequence shown in Figure 22-11 on the next page.

The Call Stack dialog box shows the procedures that have executed, with the most recent procedure at the top of the list, and the first procedure at the bottom. You can see that the code started executing in the cmdExit_Click procedure of the frmMain form. This happens to be the Visual Basic event procedure that runs when you click the Exit button. If you click that line and then click the Show button, you should see the cmdExit_Click procedure in the module for the frmMain form (the switchboard) with the cursor on the line that executes the DoCmd.Close command to close the form. This line calls the Access built-in Close command (the <Non-Basic Code> you see in the call stack list), which in turn triggered the Close event procedure for the form. It's the Close event procedure code that sets the gintDontShow-ContactList variable back to False (0). Be sure that the Call Stack window is closed and click Continue on the toolbar to let the code finish.

Chapter 22

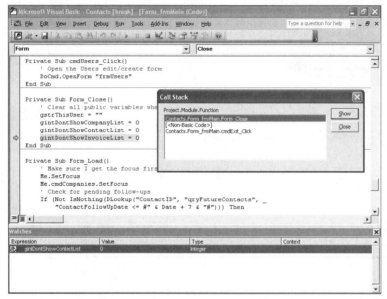

Figure 22-11. The call sequence is shown in the Call Stack dialog box.

> **Note** Be sure to delete the watch after you are finished seeing how it works by right-clicking it in the Watch window and choosing Delete Watch from the shortcut menu.

Variables and Constants

In addition to using Visual Basic code to work with the controls on any open forms or reports (as you can with macros), you can declare and use named variables in Visual Basic code for storing values temporarily, calculating a result, or manipulating any of the objects in your database. To create a value available anywhere in your code, you can define a global variable, as you can find in the modGlobals module in the LawTrack Contacts sample database.

Another way to store data in Visual Basic is with a constant. A *constant* is a data object with a fixed value that you cannot change while your application is running. You've already encountered some of the built-in constants in Microsoft Access—Null, True, and False. Visual Basic also has a large number of intrinsic constants—built-in constants that have meaningful names—that you can use to test for data types and other attributes or that you can use as fixed arguments in functions and expressions. You can view the list of intrinsic constants by searching for the Visual Basic Constants topic in Help. You can also declare your own constant values to use in code that you write.

In the following sections, you'll learn about using variables to store and calculate data and to work with database objects.

Data Types

Visual Basic supports data types for variables and constants that are similar to the data types you use to define fields in tables. It also allows you to define a variable that is a pointer to an object (such as a form or a recordset). The data types are described in Table 22-1.

Table 22-1. Visual Basic Data Types

Data Type	Size	Data-Typing Character	Can Contain
Boolean	2 bytes	(none)	True (−1) or False (0)
Byte	1 byte	(none)	Binary data ranging in value from 0 through 255
Integer	2 bytes	%	Integers from −32,768 through 32,767
Long	4 bytes	&	Integers from −2,147,483,648 through 2,147,483,647
Single	4 bytes	!	Floating-point (imprecise) numbers from approximately -3.4×10^{38} through 3.4×10^{38}
Double	8 bytes	#	Floating-point (imprecise) numbers from approximately -1.79×10^{308} through 1.79×10^{308}
Currency	8 bytes	@	A scaled integer with four decimal places from −922,337,203,685,477.5808 through 922,337,203,685,477.5807
Decimal	14 bytes	(none)	A precise number with up to 29 digits and up to 28 decimal places from -79.228×10^{27} to 79.228×10^{27} (Visual Basic in Access supports the Decimal data type only as a type within the Variant data type.)
String	10 bytes plus 2 bytes per character	$	Any text or binary string up to approximately 2 billion bytes in length, including text, hyperlinks, memo data, and "chunks" from an ActiveX object; a fixed-length string can be up to 65,400 characters long
Date	8 bytes	(none)	Date/time values ranging from January 1, 100, to December 31, 9999
Object	4 bytes	(none)	A pointer to an object—you can also define a variable that contains a specific type of object, such as the Database object

Chapter 22

Table 22-1. Visual Basic Data Types

Data Type	Size	Data-Typing Character	Can Contain
Variant	16 bytes through approximately 2 billion bytes	(none)	Any data, including Empty, Null, and date/time data (Use the VarType function to determine the current data type of the data in the variable. A Variant can also contain an array of Variants. Use the IsArray function to determine whether a Variant is an array.)
User-defined	Depends on elements defined	(none)	Any number of variables of any of the previous data types

You can implicitly define the data type of a variable by appending a data-typing character, as noted in the table above, the first time you use the variable. For example, a variable named *MyInt%* is an integer variable. If you do not explicitly declare a data variable that you reference in your code and do not supply a data-typing character, Visual Basic assigns the Variant data type to the variable. (See "Declaring Constants and Variables" on page 778 to learn how to explicitly declare data variables.) Note that although the Variant data type is the most flexible (and, in fact, is the data type for all controls on forms and reports), it is also the least efficient because Visual Basic must do extra work to determine the current data type of the data in the variable before working with it in your code. Variant is also the only data type that can contain the Null value.

The Object data type lets you define variables that can contain a pointer to an object. See "Collections, Objects, Properties, and Methods" on page 791 for details about objects that you can work with in Visual Basic. You can declare a variable as the generic Object data type, or you can specify that a variable contains a specific type of object. The major object types are AccessObject, Application, Catalog, Column, Command, Connection, Container, Control, Database, Document, Error, Field, Form, Group, Index, Key, Parameter, Procedure, Property, QueryDef, Recordset, Relation, Report, Table, TableDef, User, View, and Workspace.

Tip Using Option Explicit is a good idea

You can request that Visual Basic generate all new modules with an Option Explicit statement by selecting the Require Variable Declaration check box on the Editor tab of the Options dialog box, as shown in Figure 22-3. If you set this option, Visual Basic includes an Option Explicit statement in the Declarations section of every new module. This helps you avoid errors that can occur when you use a variable in your code that you haven't properly declared in a Dim, Public, Static, or Type statement or as part of the parameter list in a Function statement or a Sub statement. (See "Functions and Subroutines" on page 812.) When you specify this option in a module, Visual Basic flags any undeclared variables it finds when you ask it to compile your code. Using an Option Explicit statement also helps you find variables that you might have misspelled when you entered your code.

Variable and Constant Scope

The scope of a variable or a constant determines whether the variable or the constant is known to only one procedure, all procedures in a module, or all procedures in your database. You can create variables or constants that can be used by any procedure in your database (public scope). You can also create variables or constants that apply only to the procedures in a module or only to a single procedure (private scope). A variable declared inside a procedure is always private to that procedure (available only within the procedure). A variable declared in the Declarations section of a module can be private (available only to the procedures in the module) or public. You can pass values from one procedure to another using a parameter list, but the values might be held in variables having different names in the two procedures. See the sections on the Function, Sub, and Call statements later in this chapter.

To declare a public *variable*, use the *Public* statement in the Declarations section of a standard module or a class module. Remember that all modules attached to forms or reports are class modules. To declare a public *constant*, use the Public keyword with a *Const* statement in the Declarations section of a standard module. You cannot declare a public constant in a class module. To declare a variable or a constant that all procedures in a module can reference, define that variable or constant in the Declarations section of the module. (A variable defined in a Declarations section is private to the module unless you use the Public statement.) To declare a variable or a constant used only in a particular procedure, define that variable or constant as part of the procedure.

Unlike the first two versions of Access, Access for Windows 95, Access 97, and Visual Basic in Access 2000 and later allow you to use the same name for variables or constants in different module objects or at different levels of scope. In addition, you can declare public variables in form and report modules as well as public variables and constants in standard modules.

To use the same name for public variables and constants in different module objects or form or report modules, specify the name of the module to which it belongs when you refer to it. For example, you can declare a public variable named intX in a module object with the name modMyModule and then declare another public variable named intX in a second module object, named modMyOtherModule. If you want to reference the intX variable in modMyModule from a procedure in modMyOtherModule (or any module other than modMyModule), you must use

```
modMyModule.intX
```

You can also declare variables or constants with the same name at different levels of scope within a module object or a form or report module. For example, you can declare a public variable named intX and then declare a local variable named intX within a procedure. (You can't declare a public variable within a procedure.) References to intX within the procedure refer to the local variable, while references to intX outside the procedure refer to the public variable. To refer to the public variable from within the procedure, qualify it with the name of the module, just as you would refer to a public variable from within a different module.

Declaring a public variable in a form or report module can be useful for variables that are logically associated with a particular form or report but that you might also want to use elsewhere. Like the looser naming restrictions, however, this feature can sometimes create confusion. In general, it's still a good idea to keep common public variables and constants in standard modules and to give public variables and constants names that are unique across all variable names in your application.

> **Note** For information on the syntax conventions used in the remainder of this chapter, refer to "Syntax Conventions" in the Conventions Used In This Book section of the front matter.

Declaring Constants and Variables

The following sections show the syntax of the statements you can use to define constants and variables in your modules and procedures.

Const Statement

Use a Const statement to define a constant.

Syntax

```
[Public | Private] Const {constantname [As datatype]
  = <const expression>},...
```

Notes

Include the Public keyword in the Declarations section of a standard module to define a constant that is available to all procedures in all modules in your database. Include the Private keyword to declare constants that are available only within the module where the declaration is made. Constants are private by default, and a constant defined within a procedure is always private. You cannot define a Public constant in a class module. (All constants in a class module are private.)

The *datatype* entry can be Byte, Boolean, Integer, Long, Currency, Single, Double, Date, String, or Variant. You cannot declare a constant as an object. Use a separate As type clause for each constant being declared. If you don't declare a type, Visual Basic assigns the data type that is most appropriate for the expression provided. (You should always explicitly declare the data type of your constants.)

The *<const expression>* entry cannot include variables, user-defined functions, or Visual Basic built-in functions (such as Chr). You can include simple literals and other previously defined constants.

Example

To define the constant PI to be available to all procedures in all modules, enter the following in the Declarations section of any standard module.

```
Public Const PI As Double = 3.14159
```

Inside Out

Use variable naming conventions

It's a good idea to prefix all variable names you create with a notation that indicates the data type of the variable, particularly if you create complex procedures. This helps ensure that you aren't attempting to assign or calculate incompatible data types. (For example, the names will make it obvious that you're creating a potential error if you try to assign the contents of a long integer variable to an integer variable.) It also helps ensure that you pass variables of the correct data type to procedures. Finally, including a prefix helps ensure that you do not create a variable name that is the same as an Access or Visual Basic reserved word. The following table suggests data type prefixes that you can use for many of the most common data types.

Data Type	Prefix	Data Type	Prefix
Boolean	bol	Document	doc
Byte	byt	Field	fld
Currency	cur	Form	frm
Double	dbl	Index	idx
Integer	int	Key	key
Long	lng	Parameter	prm
Single	sgl	Procedure	prc
String	str	Property	prp
User-defined (using the Type statement)	usr	QueryDef	qdf
Variant	var	Recordset	rst
Catalog	cat	Report	rpt
Column	col	Table	tbl
Command	cmd	TableDef	tbl
Connection	cn	View	vew
Control	ctl	Workspace	wks
Database	db		

Dim Statement

Use a Dim statement in the Declarations section of a module to declare a variable or a variable array that can be used in all procedures in the module. Use a Dim statement within a procedure to declare a variable used only in that procedure.

Syntax

```
Dim {[WithEvents] variablename
  [([<array dimension>],... )] [As [New]
  datatype]},...
```

where *<array dimension>* is

```
[lowerbound To ] upperbound
```

Notes

If you do not include an *<array dimension>* specification but you do include the parentheses, you must include a ReDim statement in each procedure that uses the array to dynamically allocate the array at run time. You can define an array with as many as 60 dimensions. If you do not include a *lowerbound* value in an *<array dimension>* specification, the default lower bound is 0. You can reset the default lower bound to 1 by including an *Option Base 1* statement in the module Declarations section. The *lowerbound* and *upperbound* values must be integers, and *upperbound* must be greater than or equal to *lowerbound*. The number of members of an array is limited only by the amount of memory on your machine.

Valid *datatype* entries are Byte, Boolean, Integer, Long, Currency, Single, Double, Date, String (for variable-length strings), String * *length* (for fixed-length strings), Object, Variant, or one of the object types described earlier in this chapter. You can also declare a user-defined variable structure using the Type statement and then use the user type name as a data type. You should always explicitly declare the data type of your variables. If you do not include the As *datatype* clause, Visual Basic assigns the Variant data type.

Use the New keyword to indicate that a declared object variable is a new instance of an object that doesn't have to be set before you use it. You can use the New keyword only with object variables to create a new instance of that class of object without requiring a Set statement. You can't use New to declare dependent objects. If you do not use the New keyword, you cannot reference the object or any of its properties or methods until you set the variable to an object using a Set statement.

Use the WithEvents keyword to indicate an object variable within a class module that responds to events triggered by an ActiveX object. Form and report modules that respond to events on the related form and report objects are class modules. You can also define custom class modules to create custom objects. If you use the WithEvents keyword, you cannot use the New keyword.

Visual Basic initializes declared variables at compile time. Numeric variables are initialized to zero (0), variant variables are initialized to empty, variable-length string variables are initialized as zero-length strings, and fixed-length string variables are filled with ANSI zeros (Chr(0)). If you use a Dim statement within a procedure to declare variables, Visual Basic reinitializes the variables each time you run the procedure.

Examples

To declare a variable named intMyInteger as an integer, enter the following:

```
Dim intMyInteger As Integer
```

To declare a variable named dbMyDatabase as a database object, enter the following:

```
Dim dbMyDatabase As Database
```

To declare an array named strMyString that contains fixed-length strings that are 20 characters long and contains 50 entries from 51 through 100, enter the following:

```
Dim strMyString(51 To 100) As String * 20
```

To declare a database variable, a new table variable, and two new field variables for the table; set up the objects; and append the new table to the Tabledefs collection, enter the following:

```
Public Sub NewTableExample()
    Dim db As DAO.Database
    Dim tdf As New DAO.TableDef, _
        fld1 As New DAO.Field, _
        fld2 As New DAO.Field
    ' Initialize the table name
    tdf.Name = "MyTable"
    ' Set the name of the first field
    fld1.Name = "MyField1"
    ' Set its data type
    fld1.Type = dbLong
    ' Append the first field to the Fields
    ' collection of the table
    tdf.Fields.Append fld1
    ' Set up the second field
    fld2.Name = "MyField2"
    fld2.Type = dbText
    fld2.Size = 20
    ' Append the second field to the table
    tdf.Fields.Append fld2
    ' Establish an object on the current database
    Set db = CurrentDb
    ' Create a new table by appending tdf to
    ' the Tabledefs collection of the database
    db.TableDefs.Append tdf
End Sub
```

Chapter 22

> See "Collections, Objects, Properties, and Methods" on page 791 for details about working with DAO objects. See "Functions and Subroutines" on page 812 for details about the Sub statement.

To declare an object variable to respond to events in another class module, enter the following:

```
Option Explicit
Dim WithEvents objOtherClass As MyClass

Sub LoadClass ()
    Set objOtherClass = New MyClass
End Sub
```

```
Sub objOtherClass_Signal(ByVal strMsg As string)
    MsgBox "MyClass Signal event sent this " & _
      "message: " & strMsg
End Sub
```

In class module MyClass, code the following:

```
Option Explicit
Public Event Signal(ByVal strMsg As String)

Public Sub RaiseSignal(ByVal strText As String)
    RaiseEvent Signal(strText)
End Sub
```

In any other module, execute the following statement:

```
MyClass.RaiseSignal "Hello"
```

Enum Statement

Use an Enum statement in a module Declarations section to assign long integer values to named members of an enumeration. You can use an enumeration name as a restricted Long data type.

Syntax

```
[Public | Private] Enum enumerationname
    <member> [= <long integer expression>]
    ...
End Enum
```

Notes

Enumerations are constant values that you cannot change when your code is running. Include the Public keyword to define an enumeration that is available to all procedures in all modules in your database. Include the Private keyword to declare an enumeration that is available only within the module where the declaration is made. Enumerations are public by default.

You must declare at least one *member* within an enumeration. If you do not provide a *<long integer expression>* assignment, Visual Basic adds 1 to the previous value or assigns 0 if the *member* is the first member of the enumeration. The *<long integer expression>* cannot include variables, user-defined functions, or Visual Basic built-in functions (such as CLng). You can include simple literals and other previously defined constants or enumerations.

Enumerations are most useful as a replacement for the Long data type in a Function or Sub statement. When you call the function or sub procedure in code, you can use one of the enumeration names in place of a variable, constant, or literal. If you select the Auto List Members option (see Figure 22-3), Visual Basic displays the available names in a drop-down list as you type the sub or function call in your code.

Example

To declare a public enumeration for days of the week and use the enumeration in a procedure, enter the following:

```
Option Explicit
Public Enum DaysOfWeek
    Sunday = 1
    Monday
    Tuesday
    Wednesday
    Thursday
    Friday
    Saturday
End Enum

Public Function NextDate(lngDay As DaysOfWeek) As Date
' This function returns the next date
' that matches the day of week requested
Dim intThisDay As Integer, datDate As Date
    ' Get today
    datDate = Date
    ' Figure out today's day of week
    intThisDay = WeekDay(datDate)
    ' Calculate next day depending on
    ' whether date requested is higher or lower
    If intThisDay < lngDay Then
        NextDate = datDate + (lngDay - intThisDay)
    Else
        NextDate = datDate + (lngDay + 7) - intThisDay
    End If
End Function
```

You can test the function from the Immediate window by entering the following:

```
?NextDate(Monday)
```

Event Statement

Use the Event statement in the Declarations section of a class module to declare an event that can be raised within the module. In another module, you can define an object variable using the WithEvents keyword, set the variable to an instance of this class module, and then code procedures that respond to the events declared and triggered within this class module.

Syntax

```
[Public] Event eventname ([<arguments>])
```

where *<arguments>* is

```
{[ByVal | ByRef] argumentname [As datatype]},...
```

Chapter 22

Notes

An Event must be public, which makes the event available to all other procedures in all modules. You can optionally include the Public keyword when coding this statement.

You should declare the data type of any arguments in the event's argument list. Note that the names of the variables passed by the triggering procedure can be different from the names of the variables known by this event. If you use the ByVal keyword to declare an argument, Visual Basic passes a copy of the argument to your event. Any change you make to a ByVal argument does not change the original variable in the triggering procedure. If you use the ByRef keyword, Visual Basic passes the actual memory address of the variable, allowing the event to change the variable's value in the triggering procedure. (If the argument passed by the triggering procedure is an expression, Visual Basic treats it as if you had declared it by using ByVal.) Visual Basic always passes arrays by reference (ByRef).

Example

To declare an event that can be triggered from other modules, enter the following in the class module MyClass:

```
Option Explicit
Public Event Signal(ByVal strMsg As String)

Public Sub RaiseSignal(ByVal strText As String)
    RaiseEvent Signal(strText)
End Sub
```

To respond to the event from another module, enter the following:

```
Option Explicit
Dim WithEvents objOtherClass As MyClass

Sub LoadClass ()
    Set objOtherClass = New MyClass
End Sub

Sub objOtherClass_Signal(ByVal strMsg As string)
    MsgBox "MyClass Signal event sent this " & _
      "message: " & strMsg
End Sub
```

To trigger the event in any other module, execute the following:

```
MyClass.RaiseSignal "Hello"
```

Private Statement

Use a Private statement in the Declarations section of a standard module or a class module to declare variables that you can use in any procedure within the module. Procedures in other modules cannot reference theses variables.

Syntax

```
Private {[WithEvents] variablename
  [([<array dimension>],... )]
  [As [New] datatype]},...
```

where *<array dimension>* is

```
[lowerbound To ] upperbound
```

Notes

If you do not include an *<array dimension>* specification but you do include the parentheses, you must include a ReDim statement in each procedure that uses the array to dynamically allocate the array at run time. You can define an array with up to 60 dimensions. If you do not include a *lowerbound* value in an *<array dimension>* specification, the default lower bound is 0. You can reset the default lower bound to 1 by including an *Option Base 1* statement in the module Declarations section. The *lowerbound* and *upperbound* values must be integers, and *upperbound* must be greater than or equal to *lowerbound*. The number of members of an array is limited only by the amount of memory on your machine.

Valid *datatype* entries are Byte, Boolean, Integer, Long, Currency, Single, Double, Date, String (for variable-length strings), String * *length* (for fixed-length strings), Object, Variant, or one of the object types described earlier in this chapter. You can also declare a user-defined variable structure using the Type statement and then use the user type name as a data type. You should always explicitly declare the data type of your variables. If you do not include the As *datatype* clause, Visual Basic assigns the Variant data type.

Use the New keyword to indicate that a declared object variable is a new instance of an object that doesn't have to be set before you use it. You can use the New keyword only with object variables to create a new instance of that class of object without requiring a Set statement. You can't use New to declare dependent objects. If you do not use the New keyword, you cannot reference the object or any of its properties or methods until you set the variable to an object using a Set statement.

Use the WithEvents keyword to indicate an object variable within a class module that responds to events triggered by an ActiveX object. Form and report modules that respond to events on the related form and report objects are class modules. You can also define custom class modules to create custom objects. If you use the WithEvents keyword, you cannot use the New keyword.

Visual Basic initializes declared variables at compile time. Numeric variables are initialized to zero (0), variant variables are initialized to empty, variable-length string variables are initialized as zero-length strings, and fixed-length string variables are filled with ANSI zeros (Chr(0)).

Chapter 22

Example

To declare a long variable named lngMyNumber that can be used in any procedure within this module, enter the following:

```
Private lngMyNumber As Long
```

Public Statement

Use a Public statement in the Declarations section of a standard module or a class module to declare variables that you can use in any procedure anywhere in your database.

Syntax

```
Public {[WithEvents]variablename
  [([<array dimension>],... )]
  [As [New] datatype]},...
```

where *<array dimension>* is

```
[lowerbound To ] upperbound
```

Notes

If you do not include an *<array dimension>* specification but you do include the parentheses, you must include a ReDim statement in each procedure that uses the array to dynamically allocate the array at run time. You can define an array with up to 60 dimensions. If you do not include a *lowerbound* value in an *<array dimension>* specification, the default lower bound is 0. You can reset the default lower bound to 1 by including an *Option Base 1* statement in the module Declarations section. The *lowerbound* and *upperbound* values must be integers, and *upperbound* must be greater than or equal to *lowerbound*. The number of members of an array is limited only by the amount of memory on your machine.

Valid *datatype* entries are Byte, Boolean, Integer, Long, Currency, Single, Double, Date, String (for variable-length strings), String * *length* (for fixed-length strings), Object, Variant, or one of the object types described earlier in this chapter. Note, however, that you cannot declare a Public fixed-length string within a class module. You can also declare a user-defined variable structure using the Type statement and then use the user type name as a data type. You should always explicitly declare the data type of your variables. If you do not include the As *datatype* clause, Visual Basic assigns the Variant data type.

Use the New keyword to indicate that a declared object variable is a new instance of an object that doesn't have to be set before you use it. You can use the New keyword only with object variables to create a new instance of that class of object without requiring a Set statement. You can't use New to declare dependent objects. If you do not use the New keyword, you cannot reference the object or any of its properties or methods until you set the variable to an object using a Set statement.

Use the WithEvents keyword to indicate an object variable within a class module that responds to events triggered by an ActiveX object. Form and report modules that respond to events on the related form and report objects are class modules. You can also define custom class modules to create custom objects. If you use the WithEvents keyword, you cannot use the New keyword.

Visual Basic initializes declared variables at compile time. Numeric variables are initialized to zero (0), variant variables are initialized to empty, variable-length string variables are initialized as zero-length strings, and fixed-length string variables are filled with ANSI zeros (Chr(0)).

Example

To declare a long variable named lngMyNumber that can be used in any procedure in the database, enter the following:

```
Public lngMyNumber As Long
```

ReDim Statement

Use a ReDim statement to dynamically declare an array within a procedure or to redimension a declared array within a procedure at run time.

Syntax

```
ReDim [Preserve] {variablename
  (<array dimension>,...) [As datatype]},...
```

where <*array dimension*> is

```
[lowerbound To ] upperbound
```

Notes

If you're dynamically allocating an array that you previously defined with no <*array dimension*> specification in a *Dim*, *Public*, or *Private* statement, your array can have up to 60 dimensions. You cannot dynamically reallocate an array that you previously defined with an <*array dimension*> specification in a *Dim*, *Public*, or *Private* statement. If you declare the array only within a procedure, your array can have up to 60 dimensions. If you do not include a *lowerbound* value in an <*array dimension*> specification, the default lower bound is 0. You can reset the default lower bound to 1 by including an *Option Base 1* statement in the module Declarations section. The *lowerbound* and *upperbound* values must be integers, and *upperbound* must be greater than or equal to *lowerbound*. The number of members of an array is limited only by the amount of memory on your machine. If you previously specified dimensions in a Public, Private, or Dim statement or in another ReDim statement within the same procedure, you cannot change the number of dimensions.

Include the Preserve keyword to ask Visual Basic not to reinitialize existing values in the array. When you use Preserve, you can change the bounds of only the last dimension in the array.

Valid *datatype* entries are Byte, Boolean, Integer, Long, Currency, Single, Double, Date, String (for variable-length strings), String * *length* (for fixed-length strings), Object, Variant, or one of the object types described earlier in this chapter. You can also declare a user-defined variable structure using the Type statement and then use the user type name as a data type.

Chapter 22

787

You should always explicitly declare the data type of your variables. If you do not include the As *datatype* clause, Visual Basic assigns the Variant data type. You cannot change the data type of an array that you previously declared with a Dim, Public, or Private statement. After you establish the number of dimensions for an array that has module or global scope, you cannot change the number of its dimensions using a ReDim statement.

Visual Basic initializes declared variables at compile time. Numeric variables are initialized to zero (0), variant variables are initialized to empty, variable-length string variables are initialized as zero-length strings, and fixed-length string variables are filled with ANSI zeros (Chr(0)). When you use the Preserve keyword, Visual Basic initializes only additional variables in the array. If you use a ReDim statement within a procedure to both declare and allocate an array (and you have not previously defined the array with a Dim, Public, or Private statement), Visual Basic reinitializes the array each time you run the procedure.

Example

To dynamically allocate an array named strProductNames that contains 20 strings, each with a fixed length of 25, enter the following:

```
ReDim strProductNames(20) As String * 25
```

Static Statement

Use a Static statement within a procedure to declare a variable used only in that procedure and that Visual Basic does not reinitialize while the module containing the procedure is open. Visual Basic opens all standard and class modules (objects you can see in the Modules list in the Database window) when you open the database containing those objects. Visual Basic keeps form or report class modules open only while the form or the report is open.

Syntax

```
Static {variablename [({<array dimension>},...)]
  [As [New] datatype]},...
```

where *<array dimension>* is

```
[lowerbound To ] upperbound
```

Notes

If you do not include an *<array dimension>* specification but you do include the parentheses, you must include a ReDim statement in each procedure that uses the array to dynamically allocate the array at run time. You can define an array with up to 60 dimensions. If you do not include a *lowerbound* value in an *<array dimension>* specification, the default lower bound is 0. You can reset the default lower bound to 1 by including an *Option Base 1* statement in the module Declarations section. The *lowerbound* and *upperbound* values must be integers, and *upperbound* must be greater than or equal to *lowerbound*. The number of members of an array is limited only by the amount of memory on your machine.

Valid *datatype* entries are Byte, Boolean, Integer, Long, Currency, Single, Double, Date, String (for variable-length strings), String * *length* (for fixed-length strings), Object, Variant, or one of the object types described in this chapter. You can also declare a user-defined variable structure using the Type statement and then use the user type name as a data type. You should always explicitly declare the data type of your variables. If you do not include the As *datatype* clause, Visual Basic assigns the Variant data type.

Use the New keyword to indicate that a declared object variable is a new instance of an object that doesn't have to be set before you use it. You can use the New keyword only with object variables to create a new instance of that class of object without requiring a Set statement. You can't use New to declare dependent objects. If you do not use the New keyword, you cannot reference the object or any of its properties or methods until you set the variable to an object using a Set statement.

Visual Basic initializes declared variables at compile time. Numeric variables are initialized to zero (0), variant variables are initialized to empty, variable-length string variables are initialized as zero-length strings, and fixed-length string variables are filled with ANSI zeros (Chr(0)).

Examples

To declare a static variable named intMyInteger as an integer, enter the following:

```
Static intMyInteger As Integer
```

To declare a static array named strMyString that contains fixed-length strings that are 20 characters long and contains 50 entries from 51 through 100, enter the following:

```
Static strMyString(51 To 100) As String * 20
```

Type Statement

Use a Type statement in a Declarations section to create a user-defined data structure containing one or more variables.

Syntax

```
[Public | Private] Type typename
    {variablename [({<array dimension>},...)]
      As datatype}
    ...
End Type
```

where *<array dimension>* is

```
[lowerbound To ] upperbound
```

Notes

A Type statement is most useful for declaring sets of variables that can be passed to procedures (including Windows API functions) as a single variable. You can also use the Type statement to declare a record structure. After you declare a user-defined data structure, you can use *typename* in any subsequent Dim, Public, Private, or Static statement to create a variable of that type. You can reference variables in a user-defined data structure variable by entering the variable name, a period, and the name of the variable within the structure. (See the second part of the example that follows.)

Include the Public keyword to declare a user-defined type that is available to all procedures in all modules in your database. Include the Private keyword to declare a user-defined type that is available only within the module in which the declaration is made. You must enter each *variablename* entry on a new line. You must indicate the end of your user-defined data structure using an End Type statement.

Valid *datatype* entries are Byte, Boolean, Integer, Long, Currency, Single, Double, Date, String (for variable-length strings), String * *length* (for fixed-length strings), Object, Variant, or one of the object types described earlier in this chapter. You can also declare a user-defined variable structure using the Type statement and then use the user type name as a data type. You should always explicitly declare the data type of your variables. If you do not include the As *datatype* clause, Visual Basic assigns the Variant data type.

If you do not include an *<array dimension>* specification but you do include the parentheses, you must include a ReDim statement in each procedure that uses the array to dynamically allocate the array at run time in any variable that you declare as this Type. You can define an array with as many as 60 dimensions. If you do not include a *lowerbound* value in an *<array dimension>* specification, the default lower bound is 0. You can reset the default lower bound to 1 by including an *Option Base 1* statement in the module Declarations section. The *lowerbound* and *upperbound* values must be integers, and *upperbound* must be greater than or equal to *lowerbound*. The number of members of an array is limited only by the amount of memory on your machine.

Note that a Type declaration does not reserve any memory. Visual Basic allocates the memory required by the Type when you use *typename* as a data type in a Dim, Public, Private, or Static statement.

Example

To define a user type structure named MyRecord containing a long integer and three string fields, declare a variable named usrContacts using that user type, and then set the first string to "Jones", first enter the following:

```
Type MyRecord
    lngID As Long
    strLast As String
    strFirst As String
    strMid As String
End Type
```

Within a procedure, enter the following:

```
Dim usrContacts As MyRecord
usrContacts.strLast = "Jones"
```

Collections, Objects, Properties, and Methods

You've already dealt with two of the main collections supported by Microsoft Access—Forms and Reports. The Forms collection contains all the form objects that are open in your application, and the Reports collection contains all the open report objects.

As you'll learn in more detail later in this section, collections, objects, properties, and methods are organized in several object model hierarchies. An object has *properties* that describe the object and *methods* that are actions you can ask the object to execute. For example, a Form object has a Name property (the name of the form) and a Requery method (to ask the form to requery its record source). Many objects also have *collections* that define sets of other objects within the object. For example, a Form object has a Controls collection that is the set of all control objects (text boxes, labels, and so on) defined on the form.

You don't need a thorough understanding of collections, objects, properties, and methods to perform most application tasks. It's useful, however, for you to know how Access and Visual Basic organize these items so that you can better understand how Access works. If you want to study advanced code examples available in the many sample databases that you can download from public forums, you'll need to understand collections, objects, properties, and methods and how to correctly reference them.

The Access Application Architecture

An Access desktop application (.mdb) has two major components—the application engine, which controls the programming and the user interface, and the JET DBEngine, which controls the storage of data and the definition of all the objects in your database. An Access project (.adp) also uses the application engine, but it depends on its Connection object to define a link to the SQL Server database that contains the tables, views, functions, and stored procedures used by the application.

As you'll see later, Visual Basic supports two distinct object models (Data Access Objects—DAO, and ActiveX Data Objects—ADO) for manipulating objects stored by the database engine. Figure 22-12 on the next page shows the application architecture of Access.

When you open a database, the application engine loads the appropriate object collections from the database and application files to enable it to list the names of all the tables, queries, views, database diagrams, stored procedures, forms, reports, data access pages, macros, and modules to display in the Database window. The application engine establishes the top-level Application object, which contains a Forms collection (all the open forms), a Reports collection (all the open reports), a Modules collection (all the open modules, including form and report modules), a References collection (all Visual Basic library references), and a CommandBars collection (all the built-in menus and toolbars as well as custom ones). Each form, report, and command bar, in turn, contains a Controls collection (all of the controls on the form, report, or command bar). Among some of the more interesting properties of the Application object is the ADOConnectString property that contains the information you can use to connect to this database from another database.

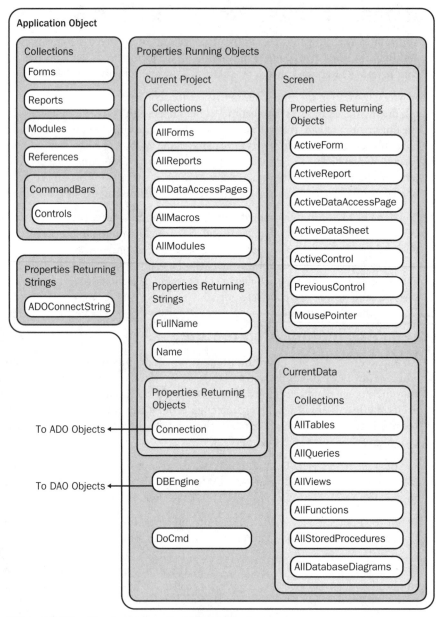

Figure 22-12. The Access application architecture.

The Application object also contains two special objects, the Screen object and the DoCmd object. The Screen object has seven very useful properties: ActiveForm, ActiveReport, Active-DataAccessPage, ActiveDatasheet, ActiveControl, PreviousControl, and MousePointer. Without knowing the actual names, you can reference the control (if any) that currently has the focus, the data access page (if any) that has the focus, the datasheet (if any) that has the focus, the form (if any) that has the focus, the report (if any) that has the focus, or the name of the control that previously had the focus. You can use the MousePointer property to examine the current status of the mouse pointer (arrow, I-beam, hourglass, and so on) and set the pointer. (Additional details about referencing properties of objects appear later in this chapter.) The DoCmd object lets you execute most macro actions within Visual Basic. See "Running Macro Actions and Menu Commands" on page 832. If your application is an Access desktop database (.mdb), the DBEngine object under the Application object connects you to the JET desktop database engine to manipulate its objects using the Data Access Objects (DAO) model.

Two properties allow you to directly find out the names of all objects stored in your database without having to call the database engine. In an Access desktop database (.mdb), you can find out the names of all your tables and queries via the CurrentData property. In an Access project file (.adp) that is connected to SQL Server, you can additionally find out the names of database diagrams, stored procedures, functions, and views via this same property. In either type of Access file, you can discover the names of all your forms, reports, data access pages, macros, and modules via the CurrentProject property. Finally, the FullName property of the CurrentProject object tells you the full path and file name of your application file, and the Name property tells you the file name only.

The Data Access Objects (DAO) Architecture

The first (and oldest) of the two models you can use to fetch data and examine or create new data objects is the Data Access Objects (DAO) model. This model is best suited for use within Access desktop applications (.mdb) because it provides objects, methods, and properties specifically tailored to the way Access and the JET DBEngine work together. To use this model, you must instruct Visual Basic to load a reference to the Microsoft DAO 3.6 Object Library. To verify that your project includes this reference, open any module in Design view and choose References from the Tools menu. If you don't see this library in the checked list at the top of the References dialog box, scroll down the alphabetical list until you find the library, select it, and click OK to add the reference. Access 2003 creates this reference for you in any new database that you create.

The Application object's DBEngine property serves as a bridge between the application engine and the JET DBEngine. The DBEngine property represents the DBEngine object, which is the top-level object in the Data Access Objects (DAO) hierarchy. Figure 22-13 on the next page shows you a diagram of the hierarchy of collections defined in the DAO model.

The DBEngine object controls all the database objects in your database through a hierarchy of collections, objects, and properties. When you open an Access database, the DBEngine object first establishes a Workspaces collection and a default Workspace object (the first object in the Workspaces collection). If your workgroup is secured, Access prompts you for a password and a user ID so that the DBEngine can create a User object in the Users collection and a Group object in the Groups collection within the default workspace. If your workgroup is not secured, the DBEngine signs you on as a default user called Admin.

Finally, the DBEngine creates a Database object within the Databases collection of the default Workspace object. The DBEngine uses the current User and/or Group object information to determine whether you're authorized to access any of the objects within the database.

Chapter 22

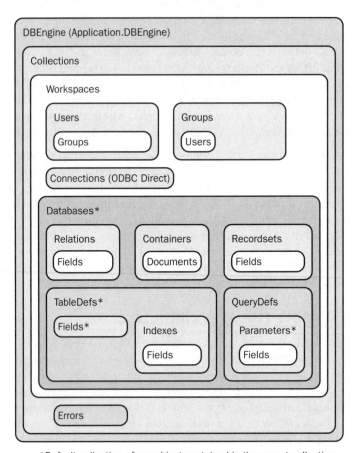

*Default collection of any object contained in the parent collection

Figure 22-13. The Data Access Objects (DAO) model.

After the DBEngine creates a Database object, the application engine checks the database's startup options to find out whether to display a startup form, menu bar, and title or to use one or more of the other startup options. You can set these options by choosing the Startup command from the Tools menu. After checking the startup options, the application engine checks to see whether a macro group named Autoexec exists in the database. If it finds Autoexec, the application engine runs this macro group. In versions 1 and 2 of Access, you'd often use the Autoexec macro group to open a startup form and run startup routines. In Access 2003, however, you should use the startup options to specify a startup form, and then use the event procedures of the startup form to run your startup routines.

> See Chapter 30, "Securing Your Database," for details about security in Microsoft Access. See Chapter 24, "The Finishing Touches," for details on creating startup properties and custom command bars.

You can code Visual Basic procedures that can create additional Database objects in the Databases collection by opening additional .mdb files. Each open Database object has a Containers collection that the Jet DBEngine uses to store the definition (using the Documents collection) of all your tables, queries, forms, reports, data access pages, macros, and modules.

You can use the TableDefs collection to examine and modify existing tables. You can also create new TableDef objects within this collection. Each TableDef object within the TableDefs collection has a Fields collection that describes all the fields in the table, and an Indexes collection (with a Fields collection for each Index object) that describes any indexes that you created on the table. Likewise, the Relations collection contains Relation objects that describe how tables are related and what integrity rules apply between tables, and each Relation object has a Fields collection that describes the Fields that participate in the Relation.

The QueryDefs collection contains QueryDef objects that describe all the queries in your database. You can modify existing queries or create new ones. Each QueryDef object has a Parameters collection for any parameters required to run the query and a Fields collection that describes the Fields returned by the query. Finally, the Recordsets collection contains a Recordset object for each open recordset in your database, and the Fields collection of each Recordset object tells you the Fields in the Recordset.

To reference any object within the DAO model, you can always start with the DBEngine object. If you want to work in the current database, that Database object is always the first database in the Databases collection of the first Workspace object. For example:

```
Dim dbMyDB As DAO.Database
Set dbMyDB = DBEngine.Workspaces(0).Databases(0)
```

Access also provides a handy shortcut object to the current database called CurrentDb. So, you can also establish a pointer to the current database as follows:

```
Set dbMyDB = CurrentDb
```

> **Note** In one of the examples at the end of this chapter, you'll learn how to create a new TableDef object and then open a Recordset object on the new table to insert rows. You can find code examples in the LawTrack Contacts application that manipulate objects using both DAO and ADO.

The ActiveX Data Objects (ADO) Architecture

With Access 2000, Microsoft introduced a more generic set of data engine object models to provide references not only to objects stored by the JET DBEngine but also to data objects stored in other database products such as Microsoft SQL Server. These models are called the ActiveX Data Objects (ADO) architecture. With Microsoft Access 97 (version 8.0), you could download the Microsoft Data Access Components from the Microsoft Web site to be able to use the ADO model. Access 2000 and later provide direct support for ADO with built-in libraries and direct references to key objects in the model from the Access Application object.

Because these models are designed to provide a common set of objects across any data engine that supports the ActiveX Data Objects, they do not necessarily support all the features you can find in the DAO architecture that was specifically designed for the Microsoft JET DBEngine. For this reason, if you are designing an application that will always run with the JET DBEngine, you are better off using the DAO model. If, however, you expect that your application might one day "upsize" to an ActiveX data engine such as SQL Server, you should consider using the ADO architecture as much as possible. If you create your Access application as an Access project (.adp) linked to SQL Server, you should use only the ADO models.

Figure 22-14 shows you the two major models available under the ADO architecture. The basic ADODB model lets you open and manipulate recordsets via the Recordset object and execute action or parameter queries via the Command object. The ADO Extensions for DDL and Security model (ADOX) allows you to create, open, and manipulate tables, views (non-parameter unordered queries), and procedures (action queries, parameter queries, ordered queries, functions, triggers, or procedures) within the data engine Catalog object (the object that describes the definition of objects in your database). You can also examine and define Users and Groups defined in the Catalog object with ADOX.

To use the ADODB model, you must instruct Visual Basic to load a reference to the Microsoft ActiveX Data Objects Library. For objects in the ADOX model, you need the Microsoft ADO Extensions for DDL and Security library. (You should normally find only one version on your machine. If you find multiple versions in the list, choose the latest one.) To verify that your project includes these references, open any module in Design view and choose References from the Tools menu. If you don't see these libraries in the checked list at the top of the References dialog box, scroll down the alphabetical list until you find the library you need, select it, and click OK to add the reference. Access 2003 creates a reference to the ADODB library for you in any new database that you create.

Note that there are some objects in common between DAO, ADODB, and ADOX. If you use multiple models in an application, you must be careful to qualify object declarations. For example, a Recordset object type in the DAO model is a DAO.Recordset, whereas a Recordset in the ADODB model is an ADODB.Recordset.

The link to ADODB and ADOX is via the CurrentProject.Connection property. Once you open an ADODB.Connection object, you can work with other collections, objects, and properties within the ADODB model. Likewise, by establishing an ADOX.Catalog object and setting its Connection property, you can work with any collection, object, or property within the ADOX model.

For all objects within either ADODB or ADOX, you must first establish a base object (connection or catalog, respectively). For example:

```
Dim cn As ADODB.Connection, rst As New ADODB.Recordset
Set cn = CurrentProject.Connection
rst.Open = "tblContacts", cn
```

Or

```
Dim catThisDB As New ADOX.Catalog, tbl As ADOX.Table
Set catThisDB.ActiveConnection = CurrentProject.Connection
Set tbl = catThisDB.Tables("tblContacts")
```

Chapter 22

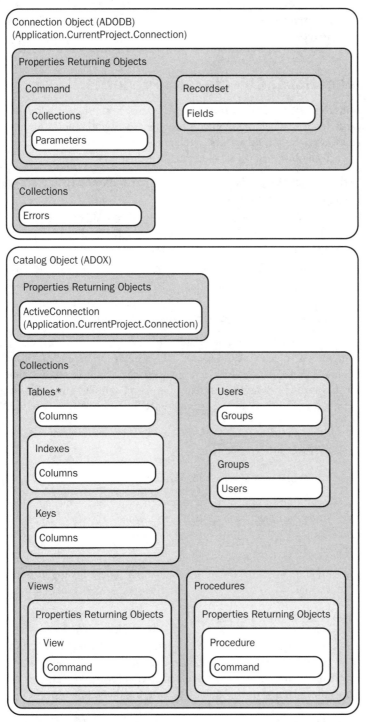

*Default collection of any object contained in the parent collection

Figure 22-14. The ActiveX Data Objects (ADODB) and ActiveX Data Objects Extensions for DDL and Security (ADOX) models.

> **Note**   One of the extensive examples at the end of this chapter uses ADO exclusively to manipulate recordsets in the LawTrack Contacts sample database.

Referencing Collections, Objects, and Properties

In the previous chapter, you were introduced to the most common way to reference objects in the Forms and Reports collections, controls on open forms and reports, and properties of controls. There are two alternative ways to reference an object within a collection. The three ways to reference an object within a collection are as follows:

- **CollectionName![Object Name]**   This is the method you used in the previous chapter. For example: *Forms![frmContacts]*.
- **CollectionName("Object Name")**   This method is similar to the first method but uses a string constant (or a string variable) to supply the object name, as in *Forms("frmContacts")* or *Forms(strFormName)*.
- **CollectionName(RelativeObjectNumber)**   Visual Basic numbers objects within most collections from zero (0) to CollectionName.*Count minus 1*. You can determine the number of open forms by referring to the Count property of the Forms collection: *Forms.Count*. You can refer to the second open form in the Forms collection as *Forms(1)*.

Forms and reports are relatively simple because they are top-level collections within the application engine. As you can see in Figure 22-13, when you reference a collection or an object maintained by the DBEngine object, the hierarchy of collections and objects is quite complex. If you want to find out the number of Workspace objects that exist in the Workspaces collection, for example, you need to reference the Count property of the Workspaces collection like this:

```
DBEngine.Workspaces.Count
```

(You can create additional workspaces from Visual Basic code.)

Using the third technique described above to reference an object, you can reference the default (first) Workspace object by entering the following:

```
DBEngine.Workspaces(0)
```

Likewise, you can refer to the currently open database in a desktop application (.mdb) by entering the following:

```
DBEngine.Workspaces(0).Databases(0)
```

When you want to refer to an object that exists in an object's default (or only) collection (see Figures 22-13 and 22-14), you do not need to include the collection name. Therefore, because the Databases collection is the default collection for the Workspaces collection, you can also refer to the currently open database by entering the following:

```
DBEngine.Workspaces(0)(0)
```

As you can see, even with this shorthand syntax, object names can become quite cumbersome if you want to refer, for example, to a particular field within an index definition for a table within the current database in the default Workspace object—or a column within an index definition for a table within the current catalog. For example, using this full syntax, you can reference the name of the first field in the tblContacts table in *Contacts.mdb* like this:

```
DBEngine(0)(0).TableDefs("tblContacts").Fields(0).Name
```

(Whew!) If for no other reason, object variables are quite handy to help minimize name complexity.

In particular, you can reduce name complexity by using an object variable to represent the current database. When you set the variable to the current database, you can call the CurrentDb function rather than use the database's full qualifier. For example, you can declare a Database object variable, set it to the current database by using the CurrentDb function, and then use the Database object variable name as a starting point to reference the TableDefs, QueryDefs, and Recordsets collections that it contains. (See "Assigning an Object Variable—Set Statement" on page 801 for the syntax of the Set statement.) Likewise, if you are going to work extensively with fields in a TableDef or columns in a Table object, you are better off establishing an object variable that points directly to the TableDef or Table object. For example, you can simplify the complex expression to reference the name of the first field in the tblContacts table in *Contacts.mdb* like this:

```
Dim db As DAO.Database, tdf As DAO.TableDef
Set db = CurrentDb
Set tdf = db.Tabledefs![tblContacts]
Debug.Print tdf.Fields(0).Name
```

> **Note** When you use *DBEngine.Workspaces(0).Databases(0)* to set a database object, Visual Basic establishes a pointer to the current database. You can have only one object variable set to the actual copy of the current database, and you must never close this copy. A safer technique is to set your database variable using the CurrentDb function. Using this technique opens a new database object that is based on the same database as the current one. You can have as many copies of the current database as you like, and you can close them when you finish using them.

When to Use "!" and "."

You've probably noticed that a complex, fully qualified name of an object or a property in Access or Visual Basic contains exclamation points (!) and periods (.) that separate the parts of the name.

Use an exclamation point preceding a name when the name refers to an object that is *in* the preceding object or collection of objects. A name following an exclamation point is generally the name of an object you created (such as a form or a table). Names following an exclamation point must be enclosed in brackets ([ ]) if they contain embedded blank spaces or a special character, such as an underscore (_). You must also enclose the name of an object you created in brackets if the name is the same as an Access or SQL reserved word. For example, most objects have a Name property—if you name a control or field "Name," you must use brackets when you reference your object.

To make this distinction clear, you might want to get into the habit of always enclosing in brackets names that follow an exclamation point, even though brackets are not required for names that don't use blank spaces or special characters. Access automatically inserts brackets around names in property sheets, design grids, and action arguments.

Use a period preceding a name that refers to a collection name, a property name, or the name of a method that you can perform against the preceding object. (Names following a period should never contain blank spaces.) In other words, use a period when the following name is *of* the preceding name (as in the TableDefs collection *of* the Databases(0) object, the Count property *of* the TableDefs collection, or the MoveLast method *of* the DAO Recordset object). This distinction is particularly important when referencing something that has the same name as the name of a property. For example, the reference

```
DBEngine.Workspaces(0).Databases(0).TableDefs(13).Name
```

refers to the name of the fourteenth TableDef object in the current database. In the *Contacts .mdb* database, if you use **Debug.Print** to display this reference, Visual Basic returns the value *tblCompanyContacts*. However, the reference

```
DBEngine.Workspaces(0).Databases(0).TableDefs(13)![Name]
```

refers to the contents of a field called Name (if one exists) in the fourteenth TableDef object in the current database. In the LawTrack Contacts database, this reference returns an error because there is no Name field in the tblCompanyContacts table.

Inside Out

What about Me?

If you spend some time looking at any of the code behind forms and reports in the sample databases, you'll notice many references such as *Me.Name* or *Me.ProductName*. Whenever you write code in a form or report module, you'll likely need to reference some of the controls on the form or report or some of the properties of the form or report. You already know that you can reference an open form by using, for example

```
Forms![frmProducts]
```

And to reference a control on the open frmProducts form, you could use

```
Forms![frmProducts]![ProductName]
```

Rather than type the collection name (Forms) and the form name (frmProducts) each time, you can use a shortcut—*Me*. This special keyword is a reference to the object where your code is running. Also, when Access opens a form, it loads the names of all controls you defined on the form as properties of the form—which are also properties of the Me object. (It also does the same for controls on open reports.) So, you can reference the Product-Name control in code behind the frmProducts form by entering

```
Me.ProductName
```

This can certainly make entering code faster. Also, because Me is an object, your code executes more quickly.

Assigning an Object Variable—Set Statement

Use the Set statement to assign an object or object reference to an object variable.

Syntax

```
Set objectvariablename = [New] objectreference
```

Notes

As noted earlier, you can use object variables to simplify name references. Also, using an object variable is less time-consuming than using a fully qualified name. At run time, Visual Basic must always parse a qualified name to first determine the type of object and then determine which object or property you want. If you use an object variable, you have already defined the type of object and established a direct pointer to it, so Visual Basic can quickly go to that object. This is especially important if you plan to reference, for example, many controls on a form. If you create a form variable first and then assign the variable to point to the form, referencing controls on the form via the form variable is much simpler and faster than using a fully qualified name for each control.

You must first declare *objectvariablename* using a Dim, Private, Public, or Static statement. The object types you can declare include AccessObject, Application, ADOX.Catalog, ADOX.Column, ADODB.Command, ADOX.Command, ADODB.Connection, DAO.Connection, DAO.Container, Control, DAO.Database, DAO.Document, ADODB.Error, DAO.Error, ADODB.Field, DAO.Field, Form, ADOX.Group, DAO.Group, ADOX.Index, DAO.Index, ADOX.Key, ADODB.Parameter, DAO.Parameter, ADOX.Procedure, ADODB.Property, ADOX.Property, DAO.Property, DAO.QueryDef, ADODB.Recordset, DAO.Recordset, DAO.Relation, Report, ADOX.Table, DAO.TableDef, ADOX.User, DAO.User, ADOX.View, and DAO.Workspace object. You can also declare a variable as the generic Object data type and set it to any object (similar to the Variant data type). In addition, you can declare a variable as an instance of the class defined by a class module. The object type must be compatible with the object type of *objectreference*. You can use another object variable in an *objectreference* statement to qualify an object at a lower level. (See the examples next.) You can also use an object *method* to create a new object in a collection and assign that object to an object variable. For example, it's common to use the OpenRecordset method of a QueryDef or TableDef object to create a new Recordset object. See the example in the next section, "Object Methods."

An object variable is a reference to an object, not a copy of the object. You can assign more than one object variable to point to the same object and change a property of the object. When you do that, all variables referencing the object will reflect the change as well. The one exception is that several Recordset variables can refer to the same recordset, but each can have its own Bookmark property pointing to different rows in the recordset. If you want to create a new instance of an object, include the New keyword.

Examples

To create a variable reference to the current database, enter the following:

```
Dim dbMyDB As DAO.Database
Set dbMyDB = CurrentDb
```

To create a variable reference to the tblContacts table in the current database using the dbMyDB variable defined above, enter the following:

```
Dim tblMyTable As DAO.TableDef
Set tblMyTable = dbMyDB![tblContacts]
```

Notice that you do not need to explicitly reference the TableDefs collection of the database, as in dbMyDB.TableDefs![tblContacts] or dbMyDB.TableDefs("tblContacts"), because Table-Defs is the default collection of the database. Visual Basic assumes that [tblContacts] refers to the name of an object in the default collection of the database.

To create a variable reference to the Notes field in the tblContacts table using the tblMyTable variable defined above, enter the following:

```
Dim fldMyField As DAO.Field
Set fldMyField = tblMyTable![Notes]
```

To create a variable reference to the catalog for the current database, enter the following:

```
Dim catThisDB As New ADOX.Catalog
catThisDB.ActiveConnection = CurrentProject.Connection
```

Note that you must use the New keyword because there's no way to open an existing catalog without first establishing a connection to it. You open a catalog by declaring it as a new object and assigning a Connection object to its ActiveConnection property. The above example takes advantage of the existence of the Application.CurrentProject.Connection property rather than first setting a Connection object. If you already have another Catalog object open, you can create a copy of it by using

```
Dim catCopy As ADOX.Catalog
Set catCopy = catThisDB
```

To create a variable reference to the tblContacts table in the current database using the catThisDB variable defined on the previous page, enter the following:

```
Dim tblMyTable As ADOX.Table
Set tblMytable = catThisDB![tblContacts]
```

Notice that you do not need to explicitly reference the Tables collection of the database, as in catThisDB.Tables![tblContacts] or catThisDB.Tables("tblContacts"), because Tables is the default collection of the catalog. Visual Basic assumes that [tblContacts] refers to the name of an object in the default collection of the catalog.

To create a variable reference to the Notes column in the tblContacts table using the tblMytable variable defined above, enter the following:

```
Dim colMyColumn As ADOX.Column
Set colMyColumn = tblMyTable![Notes]
```

Again, you do not need to explicitly reference the Columns collection of the Table object, as in tblMyTable.Columns![Notes] because the Columns collection is the default collection of a Table object.

Object Methods

When you want to apply an action to an object in your database (such as open a query as a recordset or go to the next row in a recordset), you apply a *method* of either the object or an object variable that you have assigned to point to the object. In some cases, you'll use a method to create a new object. Many methods accept parameters that you can use to further refine how the method acts on the object. For example, you can tell the DAO OpenRecordset method whether you're opening a recordset on a local table, a dynaset (a query-based recordset), or a read-only snapshot.

Visual Basic supports many different object methods—far more than there's room to properly document in this book. Perhaps one of the most useful groups of methods is the group you can use to create a recordset and then read, update, insert, and delete rows in the recordset.

Working with DAO Recordsets

To create a recordset, you must first declare a Recordset object variable. Then open the recordset using the DAO OpenRecordset method of the current database (specifying a table name, a query name, or an SQL statement to create the recordset) or the OpenRecordset method of a DAO.QueryDef, DAO.TableDef, or other DAO.Recordset object. (As you'll learn in the section "Working with ADO Recordsets," if you're working in ADO, you use the Open method of a New ADODB.Recordset object.)

In DAO, you can specify options to indicate whether you're opening the recordset as a local table (which means you can use the Seek method to quickly locate rows based on a match with an available index), as a dynaset, or as a read-only snapshot. For updatable recordsets, you can also specify that you want to deny other updates, deny other reads, open a read-only recordset, open the recordset for append only, or open a read-only forward scroll recordset (which allows you to move only forward through the records and only once).

Chapter 22

The syntax to use the OpenRecordset method of a Database object is as follows:

```
Set RecordSetObject = DatabaseObject.OpenRecordset(source,
    [type], [options], [lockoptions])
```

RecordSetObject is a variable you have declared as DAO.Recordset, and *DatabaseObject* is a variable you have declared as DAO.Database. *Source* is a string variable or literal containing the name of a table, the name of a query, or a valid SQL statement. Table 22-2 describes the most common settings you can supply for *type*, *options*, and *lockoptions*.

Table 22-2. OpenRecordset Parameter Settings

Setting	Description
Type (Select one.)	
dbOpenTable	Returns a table recordset. You can use this option only when *source* is a table local to the database described by the Database object. *Source* cannot be a linked table. You can establish a current index in a table recordset and use the Seek method to find rows using the index. If you do not specify a *type*, OpenRecordset returns a table if *source* is a local table name.
dbOpenDynaset	Returns a dynaset recordset. *Source* can be a local table, a linked table, a query, or an SQL statement. You can use the Find methods to search for rows in a dynaset recordset. If you do not specify a *type*, OpenRecordset returns a dynaset if *source* is a linked table, a query, or an SQL statement.
dbOpenSnapshot	Returns a read-only snapshot recordset. You won't see any changes made by other users after you open the recordset. You can use the Find methods to search for rows in a snapshot recordset.
dbOpenForwardOnly	Returns a read-only snapshot recordset that you can move forward through only once. You can use the MoveNext method to access successive rows.
Options (You can select multiple options, placing a plus sign between option names to add them together.)	
dbAppendOnly	Returns a table or dynaset recordset that allows inserting new rows only. You can use this option only with the dbOpenTable and dbOpenDynaset types.
dbSeeChanges	Asks Access to generate a run-time error in your code if another user changes data while you are editing it in the recordset.
dbDenyWrite	Prevents other users from modifying or inserting records while your recordset is open.
dbDenyRead	Prevents other users from reading records in your open recordset.

Table 22-2. OpenRecordset Parameter Settings

Setting	Description
dbInconsistent	Allows you to make changes to all fields in a multiple table recordset (based on a query or an SQL statement), including changes that would be inconsistent with any join defined in the query. For example, you could change the customer identifier field (foreign key) of an orders table so that it no longer matches the primary key in an included customers table—unless referential integrity constraints otherwise prevent you from doing so. You cannot include both dbInconsistent and dbConsistent.
dbConsistent	Allows you to only make changes in a multiple table recordset (based on a query or an SQL statement) that are consistent with the join definitions in the query. For example, you cannot change the customer identifier field (foreign key) of an orders table so that its value does not match the value of any customer row in the query. You cannot include both dbInconsistent and dbConsistent.
Lockoptions (Select one.)	
dbPessimistic	Asks Access to lock a row as soon as you place the row in an editable state by executing an Edit method. This is the default if you do not specify a lock option.
dbOptimistic	Asks Access to not attempt to lock a row until you try to write it to the database with an Update method. This generates a run-time error if another user has changed the row after you executed the Edit method.

For example, to declare a recordset for the tblFacilities table in the Housing Reservations (*Housing.mdb*) database and open the recordset as a table so that you can use its indexes, enter the following:

```
Dim dbHousing As DAO.Database
Dim rcdFacilities As DAO.RecordSet
Set dbHousing = CurrentDb
Set rcdFacilities = dbHousing.OpenRecordSet("tblFacilities", dbOpenTable)
```

To open the *qryContactProducts* query in the LawTrack Contacts database (*Contacts.mdb*) as a dynaset, enter the following:

```
Dim dbLawTrack As DAO.Database
Dim rcdContactProducts As DAO.RecordSet
Set dbLawTrack = CurrentDb
Set rcdContactProducts = _
  dbLawTrack.OpenRecordSet("qryContactProducts")
```

(Note that opening a recordset as a dynaset is the default when the source is a query.)

Chapter 22

> **Note** Any table recordset or dynaset recordset based on a table is updatable. When you ask Access to open a dynaset on a table, Access internally builds a query that selects all columns from the table. A dynaset recordset based on a query will be updatable if the query is updatable. See "Limitations on Using Select Queries to Update Data" on page 323 for details.

After you open a recordset, you can use one of the Move methods to move to a specific record. Use *recordset*.MoveFirst to move to the first row in the recordset. Other Move methods include MoveLast, MoveNext, and MovePrevious. If you want to move to a specific row in the recordset, use one of the Find methods. You must supply a string variable containing the criteria for finding the records you want. The criteria string looks exactly like an SQL WHERE clause but without the WHERE keyword. (See Article 1, "Understanding SQL," on the companion CD) For example, to find the first row in the qryContactProducts query's recordset whose SoldPrice field is greater than $200, enter the following:

```
rcdContactProducts.FindFirst "SoldPrice > 200"
```

To delete a row in an updatable recordset, move to the row you want to delete and then use the Delete method. For example, to delete the first row in the qryContactProducts query's recordset that hasn't been invoiced yet (the Invoiced field is false), enter the following:

```
Dim dbLawTrack As DAO.Database
Dim rcdContactProducts As DAO.RecordSet
Set dbLawTrack = CurrentDb
Set rcdContactProducts = _
  dbLawTrack.OpenRecordSet("qryContactProducts")
rcdContactProducts.FindFirst "Invoiced = 0"
' Test the recordset NoMatch property for "not found"
If Not rcdContactProducts.NoMatch Then
    rcdContactProducts.Delete
End If
```

If you want to update rows in a recordset, move to the first row you want to update and then use the Edit method to lock the row and make it updatable. You can then refer to any of the fields in the row by name to change their values. Use the Update method on the recordset to save your changes before moving to another row. If you do not use the Update method before you move to a new row or close the recordset, the database discards your changes.

For example, to increase by 10 percent the SoldPrice entry of the first row in the rcdContact-Products query's recordset whose SoldPrice value is greater than $200, enter the following:

```
Dim dbLawTrack As DAO.Database
Dim rcdContactProducts As DAO.RecordSet
Set dbLawTrack = CurrentDb
Set rcdContactProducts = _
  dbLawTrack.OpenRecordSet("qryContactProducts")
rcdContactProducts.FindFirst "SoldPrice > 200"
 ' Test the recordset NoMatch property for "not found"
If Not rcdContactProducts.NoMatch Then
```

Chapter 22

```
  rcdContactProducts.Edit
  rcdContactProducts![SoldPrice] = _
    rcdContactProducts![SoldPrice] * 1.1
  rcdContactProducts.Update
End If
```

To insert a new row in a recordset, use the AddNew method to start a new row. Set the values of all required fields in the row, and then use the Update method to save the new row. For example, to insert a new company in the LawTrack Contacts tblCompanies table, enter the following:

```
Dim dbLawTrack As DAO.Database
Dim rcdCompanies As DAO.RecordSet
Set dbLawTrack = CurrentDb
Set rcdCompanies = _
  dbLawTrack.OpenRecordSet("tblCompanies")
rcdCompanies.AddNew
rcdCompanies![CompanyName] = "Winthrop Brewing Co."
rcdCompanies![Address] = "155 Riverside Ave."
rcdCompanies![City] = "Winthrop"
rcdCompanies![StateOrProvince] = "WA"
rcdCompanies![PostalCode] = "98862"
rcdCompanies![PhoneNumber] = "(509) 555-8100"
rcdCompanies.Update
```

Note that because all the main data tables in *Contacts.mdb* are linked tables, rcdCompanies is a dynaset recordset, not a table recordset.

Working with ADO Recordsets

Recordsets in ADO offer many of the same capabilities and options as recordsets in DAO, but the terminology is somewhat different. Because you will most often use ADO with data stored in a server database such as SQL Server, the options for an ADO recordset are geared toward server-based data. For example, ADO uses the term *cursor* to refer to the set of rows returned by the server. Fundamentally, a cursor is a pointer to each row you need to work with in code. Depending on the options you choose (and the options supported by the particular database server), a cursor might also be read-only, updatable, or forward-only. A cursor might also be able to reflect changes made by other users of the database (a keyset or dynamic cursor), or it might present only a snapshot of the data (a static cursor).

To open an ADO recordset, you must use the Open method of a new ADO Recordset object. The syntax to use the Open method of a Recordset object is as follows:

```
RecordSetObject.Open [source], [connection],
  [cursortype], [locktype], [options]
```

RecordSetObject is a variable you have declared as a New ADO.Recordset. *Source* is a Command object, a string variable, or string literal containing the name of a table, the name of a view (the SQL Server term for a query), the name of a stored procedure, the name of a function that returns a table, or a valid SQL statement. A stored procedure might be a parameter query or a query that specifies the sorting of rows from a table or view. A function might also accept parameters. If you supply a Command object as the source, you do not need to supply a *connection* (you define the connection in the Command object). Otherwise, *connection* must be the name of a Connection object that points to the target database.

Table 22-3 describes the settings you can supply for *cursortype*, *locktype*, and *options*.

Table 22-3. Open Method Parameter Settings

Setting	Description
CursorType (Select one.)	
adOpenForwardOnly	Returns a read-only snapshot cursor (recordset) that you can move forward through only once. You can use the MoveNext method to access successive rows. If you do not supply a CursorType setting, adOpenForwardOnly is the default.
adOpenKeyset	Returns a Keyset cursor. This is roughly analogous to a DAO dynaset. If you are using ADO to open a recordset against a source in an Access .mdb file, you should use this option to obtain a recordset that behaves most like a DAO recordset. In this type of cursor, you will see changes to rows made by other users, but you will not see new rows added by other users after you have opened the cursor.
adOpenDynamic	Returns a dynamic cursor. This type of cursor lets you see not only changes made by other users but also added rows. Note, however, that certain key properties you might depend on in a DAO recordset such as RecordCount might not exist or might always be zero.
adOpenStatic	Returns a read-only snapshot cursor. You won't be able to see changes made by other users after you've opened the cursor.
LockType (Select one.)	
adLockReadOnly	Provides no locks. The cursor is read-only. If you do not provide a lock setting, this is the default.
adLockPessimistic	Asks the target database to lock a row as soon as you place the row in an editable state by executing an Edit method.
adLockOptimistic	Asks the target database to not attempt to lock a row until you try to write it to the database with an Update method. This generates a run-time error in your code if another user has changed the row after you executed the Edit method. You should use this option when accessing rows in an Access .mdb file.

Table 22-3. Open Method Parameter Settings

Setting	Description
Options (You can combine one Cmd setting with one Async setting with a plus sign.)	
adCmdText	Indicates that *source* is an SQL statement.
adCmdTable	Indicates that *source* is a table name (or a query name in a desktop database). In DAO, this is analogous to opening a dynaset recordset on a table.
adCmdTableDirect	Indicates that *source* is a table name. This is analogous to a DAO dbOpenTable.
adCmdStoredProc	Indicates that *source* is a stored procedure. In DAO, this is analogous to opening a dynaset on a sorted query.
adAsyncFetch	After fetching the initial rows to populate the cursor, additional fetching occurs in the background. If you try to access a row that has not been fetched yet, your code will wait until the row is fetched.
adAsyncFetch-NonBlocking	After fetching the initial rows to populate the cursor, additional fetching occurs in the background. If you try to access a row that has not been fetched yet, your code will receive an end of file indication.

For example, to declare a recordset for the tblFacilities table in the Housing Reservation database (*Housing.mdb*) and open the recordset as a table so you can use its indexes, enter the following:

```
Dim cnThisConnect As ADODB.Connection
Dim rcdFacilities As New ADODB.RecordSet
Set cnThisConnect = CurrentProject.Connection
rcdFacilities.Index = "PrimaryKey"
rcdFacilities.Open "tblFacilities", cnThisConnect, adOpenKeyset, _
    adLockOptimistic, adCmdTableDirect
```

Note that you must establish the index you want to use before you open the recordset.

To open the qryContactProducts query in the LawTrack Contacts database as a keyset, enter the following:

```
Dim cnThisConnect As ADODB.Connection
Dim rcdContactProducts As New ADODB.RecordSet
Set cnThisConnect = CurrentProject.Connection
rcdContactProducts.Open "qryContactProducts", _
  cnThisConnect, adOpenKeyset, adLockOptimistic, adCmdTable
```

After you open a recordset, you can use one of the Move methods to move to a specific record. Use *recordset*.MoveFirst to move to the first row in the recordset. Other Move methods include MoveLast, MoveNext, and MovePrevious. If you want to search for a specific row in the recordset, use the Find method or set the recordset's Filter property. Unlike the Find methods

Chapter 22

in DAO, the Find method in ADO is limited to a single simple test on a column in the form *"<column-name> <comparison> <comparison-value>"*. Note that to search for a Null value, you must say: "[SomeColumn] = Null", not "[SomeColumn] Is Null" as you would in DAO. Also, *<comparison>* can be only <, >, <=, >=, <>, =, or LIKE. Note that if you want to use the LIKE keyword, you can use either the ANSI wildcards "%" and "_" or the Access JET wildcards "*" and "?", but the wildcard can appear only at the end of the *<comparison-value>* string.

If you want to search for rows using a more complex filter, you must assign a string variable or an expression containing the criteria for finding the records you want to the Filter property of the recordset. This limits the rows in the recordset to only those that meet the filter criteria. The criteria string must be made up of the simple comparisons that you can use with Find, but you can include multiple comparisons with the AND or OR Boolean operators.

For example, to find the first row in the qryContactProducts query's recordset whose Sold-Price field is greater than $200, enter the following:

```
rcdContactProducts.MoveFirst
rcdContactProducts.Find "SoldPrice > 200"
' EOF property will be true if nothing found
If Not rcdContactProducts.EOF Then
' Found a record!
```

To find all rows in qryContactProducts where the product was sold after February 1, 2003, and SoldPrice is greater than $200, enter the following:

```
rcdContactProducts.Filter = &
  "DateSold > #2/1/2003# AND SoldPrice > 200"
' EOF property will be true if filter produces no rows
If Not rcdODetails.EOF Then
' Found some rows!
```

To delete a row in a keyset, simply move to the row you want to delete and then use the Delete method. For example, to delete the first row in the qryContactProducts query's recordset that hasn't been invoiced yet (the Invoiced field is false), enter the following:

```
Dim cnThisConnect As ADODB.Connection
Dim rcdContactProducts As New ADODB.RecordSet
Set cnThisConnect = CurrentProject.Connection
rcdContactProducts.Open "qryContactProducts", _
  cnThisConnect, adOpenKeyset, adLockOptimistic, adCmdTable
rcdContactProducts.MoveFirst
rcdContactProducts.Find "Invoiced = 0"
' Test the recordset EOF property for "not found"
If Not rcdContactProducts.EOF Then
    rcdContactProducts.Delete
End If
```

If you want to update rows in a recordset, move to the first row you want to update. Although ADO does not require you to use the Edit method to lock the row and make it updatable you can optionally use the Edit method to signal your intention to the database engine. You can refer to any of the updatable fields in the row by name to change their values. You can use the Update method on the recordset to explicitly save your changes before moving to another row. ADO automatically saves your changed row when you move to a new row. If you need to discard an update, you must use the CancelUpdate method of the recordset object.

For example, to increase by 10 percent the SoldPrice entry of the first row in the rcdContact-Products query's recordset whose SoldPrice value is greater than $200, enter the following:

```
Dim cnThisConnect As ADODB.Connection
Dim rcdContactProducts As New ADODB.RecordSet
Set cnThisConnect = CurrentProject.Connection
rcdContactProducts.Open "qryContactProducts", _
  cnThisConnect, adOpenKeyset, adLockOptimistic, adCmdTable
rcdContactProducts.Filter "SoldPrice > 200"
' Test the recordset EOF property for "not found"
If Not rcdContactProducts.EOF Then
  rcdContactProducts![SoldPrice] = _
    rcdContactProducts![SoldPrice] * 1.1
  rcdContactProducts.MoveNext
End If
```

To insert a new row in a recordset, use the AddNew method to start a new row. Set the values of all required fields in the row, and then use the Update method to save the new row. For example, to insert a new company in the LawTrack Contacts tblCompanies table, enter the following:

```
Dim cnThisConnect As ADODB.Connection
Dim rcdCompanies As New ADODB.RecordSet
Set cnThisConnect = CurrentProject.Connection
rcdCompanies.Open "tblCompanies", cnThisConnect, _
  adOpenKeyset, adLockOptimistic, adCmdTable
rcdCompanies.AddNew
rcdCompanies![CompanyName] = "Winthrop Brewing Co."
rcdCompanies![Address] = "155 Riverside Ave."
rcdCompanies![City] = "Winthrop"
rcdCompanies![StateOrProvince] = "WA"
rcdCompanies![PostalCode] = "98862"
rcdCompanies![PhoneNumber] = "(509) 555-8100"
rcdCompanies.Update
```

Other Uses for Object Methods

As you'll learn later in this chapter in more detail, you must use a method of the DoCmd object to execute the equivalent of most macro actions within Visual Basic. You must use the RunCommand method of either the Application or DoCmd object to execute commands you can find on any of the Access menus.

You can also define a public function or subroutine (see the next section) within the module associated with a Form or Report object and execute that procedure as a method of the form or report. If your public procedure is a function, you must assign the result of the execution of the method to a variable of the appropriate type. If the public procedure is a subroutine, you can execute the form or report object method as a Visual Basic statement. For more information about object methods, find the topic about the object of interest in Help, and then click the Methods hyperlink.

Functions and Subroutines

You can create two types of procedures in Visual Basic—*functions* and *subroutines*—also known as Function procedures and Sub procedures. (As you'll learn later in the section "Understanding Class Modules," class modules also support a special type of function—Property Get, and special subroutines—Property Let and Property Set, that let you manage properties of the class.) Each type of procedure can accept *parameters*—data variables that you pass to the procedure that can determine how the procedure operates. Functions can return a single data value, but subroutines cannot. In addition, you can execute a public function from anywhere in Microsoft Access, including from expressions in queries and from macros. You can execute a subroutine only from a function, from another subroutine, or as an event procedure in a form or a report.

Function Statement

Use a Function statement to declare a new function, the parameters it accepts, the variable type it returns, and the code that performs the function procedure.

Syntax

```
[Public | Private | Friend] [Static] Function functionname
  ([<arguments>]) [As datatype]
    [<function statements>]
    [functionname = <expression>]
    [Exit Function]
    [<function statements>]
    [functionname = <expression>]
End Function
```

where *<arguments>* is

```
{[Optional][ByVal | ByRef][ParamArray] argumentname[()]
  [As datatype][= default]},...
```

Notes

Use the Public keyword to make this function available to all other procedures in all modules. Use the Private keyword to make this function available only to other procedures in the same module. When you declare a function as private in a module, you cannot call that function from a query or a macro or from a function in another module. Use the Friend keyword in a class module to declare a function that is public to all other code in your application but is not visible to outside code that activates your project via automation.

Include the Static keyword to preserve the value of all variables declared within the procedure, whether explicitly or implicitly, as long as the module containing the procedure is open. This is the same as using the Static statement (discussed earlier in this chapter) to explicitly declare all variables created in this function.

You can use a type declaration character at the end of the *functionname* entry or use the As *datatype* clause to declare the data type returned by this function. Valid *datatype* entries are Byte, Boolean, Integer, Long, Currency, Single, Double, Date, String (for variable-length strings), String * *length* (for fixed-length strings), Object, Variant, or one of the object types described earlier in this chapter. If you do not declare a data type, Visual Basic assumes that the function returns a variant result. You can set the return value in code by assigning an expression of a compatible data type to the function name.

You should declare the data type of any arguments in the function's parameter list. Note that the names of the variables passed by the calling procedure can be different from the names of the variables known by this procedure. If you use the ByVal keyword to declare an argument, Visual Basic passes a copy of the argument to your function. Any change you make to a ByVal argument does not change the original variable in the calling procedure. If you use the ByRef keyword, Visual Basic passes the actual memory address of the variable, allowing the procedure to change the variable's value in the calling procedure. (If the argument passed by the calling procedure is an expression, Visual Basic treats it as if you had declared it by using ByVal.) Visual Basic always passes arrays by reference (ByRef).

Use the Optional keyword to declare an argument that isn't required. All optional arguments must be the Variant data type. If you declare an optional argument, all arguments that follow in the argument list must also be declared as optional. You can specify a *default* value only for optional parameters. Use the IsMissing built-in function to test for the absence of optional parameters. You can also use the ParamArray argument to declare an array of optional elements of the Variant data type. When you call the function, you can then pass it an arbitrary number of arguments. The ParamArray argument must be the last argument in the argument list.

Use the Exit Function statement anywhere in your function to clear any error conditions and exit your function normally, returning to the calling procedure. If Visual Basic runs your code until it encounters the End Function statement, control is passed to the calling procedure but any errors are not cleared. If this function causes an error and terminates with the End Function statement, Visual Basic passes the error to the calling procedure. See "Trapping Errors" on page 834 for details.

Example

To create a function named MyFunction that accepts an integer argument and a string argument and returns a double value, enter the following:

```
Function MyFunction (intArg1 As Integer, strArg2 As _
   String) As Double
     If strArg2 = "Square" Then
```

```
    MyFunction = intArg1 * intArg1
  Else
    MyFunction = Sqr(intArg1)
  End If
End Function
```

Sub Statement

Use a Sub statement to declare a new subroutine, the parameters it accepts, and the code in the subroutine.

Syntax

```
[Public | Private | Friend] [Static] Sub subroutinename
  ([<arguments>])
    [ <subroutine statements> ]
    [Exit Sub]
    [ <subroutine statements> ]
End Sub
```

where *<arguments>* is

```
{[Optional][ByVal | ByRef][ParamArray]
  argumentname[()] [As datatype][ = default]},...
```

Notes

Use the Public keyword to make this subroutine available to all other procedures in all modules. Use the Private keyword to make this procedure available only to other procedures in the same module. When you declare a sub as private in a module, you cannot call that sub from a function or sub in another module. Use the Friend keyword in a class module to declare a sub that is public to all other code in your application but is not visible to outside code that activates your project via automation.

Include the Static keyword to preserve the value of all variables declared within the procedure, whether explicitly or implicitly, as long as the module containing the procedure is open. This is the same as using the Static statement (discussed earlier in this chapter) to explicitly declare all variables created in this subroutine.

You should declare the data type of all arguments that the subroutine accepts in its argument list. Valid *datatype* entries are Byte, Boolean, Integer, Long, Currency, Single, Double, Date, String (for variable-length strings), String * *length* (for fixed-length strings), Object, Variant, or one of the object types described earlier in this chapter. Note that the names of the variables passed by the calling procedure can be different from the names of the variables as known by this procedure. If you use the ByVal keyword to declare an argument, Visual Basic passes a copy of the argument to your subroutine. Any change you make to a ByVal argument does not change the original variable in the calling procedure. If you use the ByRef keyword,

Visual Basic passes the actual memory address of the variable, allowing the procedure to change the variable's value in the calling procedure. (If the argument passed by the calling procedure is an expression, Visual Basic treats it as if you had declared it by using ByVal.) Visual Basic always passes arrays by reference (ByRef).

Use the Optional keyword to declare an argument that isn't required. All optional arguments must be the Variant data type. If you declare an optional argument, all arguments that follow in the argument list must also be declared as optional. You can specify a *default* value only for optional parameters. Use the IsMissing built-in function to test for the absence of optional parameters. You can also use the ParamArray argument to declare an array of optional elements of the Variant data type. When you call the subroutine, you can then pass it an arbitrary number of arguments. The ParamArray argument must be the last argument in the argument list.

Use the Exit Sub statement anywhere in your subroutine to clear any error conditions and exit your subroutine normally, returning to the calling procedure. If Visual Basic runs your code until it encounters the End Sub statement, control is passed to the calling procedure but any errors are not cleared. If this subroutine causes an error and terminates with the End Sub statement, Visual Basic passes the error to the calling procedure. See "Trapping Errors" on page 834 for details.

Example

To create a subroutine named MySub that accepts two string arguments but can modify only the second argument, enter the following:

```
Sub MySub (ByVal strArg1 As String, ByRef strArg2 As String)
    <subroutine statements>
End Sub
```

Understanding Class Modules

Whenever you create event procedures behind a form or report, you're creating a *class module*. A class module is the specification for a user-defined object in your database, and the code you write in the module defines the methods and properties of the object. Of course, forms and reports already have dozens of methods and properties already defined by Access, but you can create extended properties and methods when you write code in the class module attached to a form or report.

You can also create a class module as an independent object by selecting the Database window and choosing Class Module from the Insert menu. In the LawTrack Contacts sample database (*Contacts.mdb*), you can find a class module called ComDlg that provides a simple way to call the Windows open file dialog box from your Visual Basic code.

As previously discussed, you define a method in a class module by declaring a procedure (either a function or a sub) public. When you create an active instance of the object defined by the class module, either by opening it or by setting it to an object variable, you can execute the public function or sub procedures you have defined by referencing the function or sub name as a method of the object. For example, when the form frmCustomers is open, you can execute the cmdCancel_Click sub by referencing it as a method of the form's class. (The cmdCancel_Click sub is public in all forms in the sample database so that the Exit button on the main switchboard can use it to command the form to clear edits and close itself.) The name of any form's class is in the form *Form_formname*, so you execute this method in your code like this:

```
Form_frmCustomers.cmdCancel_Click
```

When you create a class module that you see in the Modules list in the Database window, you can create a special sub that Visual Basic runs whenever code in your application creates a new instance of the object defined by your class. For example, you can create a private Class_Initialize sub to run code that sets up your object whenever other code in your application creates a new instance of your class object. You might use this event to open recordsets or initialize variables required by the object. You can also create a private Class_Terminate sub to run code that cleans up any variables or objects (perhaps closing open recordsets) when your object goes out of scope or the code that created an instance of your object sets it to Nothing. (Your object goes out of scope if a procedure activates your class by setting it to a non-static local object variable and then the procedure exits.)

Although you can define properties of a class by declaring public variables in the Declarations section of the class module, you can also define specific procedures to handle fetching and setting properties. When you do this, you can write special processing code that runs whenever a caller fetches or sets one of the properties defined by these procedures. To create special property processing procedures in a class module, you need to write Property Get, Property Let, and Property Set procedures as described in the following sections.

Property Get

Use a Property Get procedure to return a property value for the object defined by your class module. When other code in your application attempts to fetch the value of this property of your object, Visual Basic executes your Property Get procedure to return the value. Your code can return a data value or an object.

Syntax

```
[Public | Private | Friend] [Static] Property Get propertyname
  ([<arguments>]) [As datatype]
    [<property statements>]
    [propertyname = <expression>]
    [Exit Property]
    [<property statements>]
    [propertyname = <expression>]
End Property
```

where *<arguments>* is

```
{[Optional][ByVal | ByRef][ParamArray] argumentname[()]
  [As datatype][= default]},...
```

Notes

Use the Public keyword to make this property available to all other procedures in all modules. Use the Private keyword to make this property available only to other procedures in the same module. When you declare a property as private in a class module, you cannot reference that property from another module. Use the Friend keyword to declare a property that is public to all other code in your application but is not visible to outside code that activates your project via automation.

Include the Static keyword to preserve the value of all variables declared within the property procedure, whether explicitly or implicitly, as long as the module containing the procedure is open. This is the same as using the Static statement (discussed earlier in this chapter) to explicitly declare all variables created in this property procedure.

You can use a type declaration character at the end of the *propertyname* entry or use the As *datatype* clause to declare the data type returned by this property. Valid *datatype* entries are Byte, Boolean, Integer, Long, Currency, Single, Double, Date, String (for variable-length strings), String * *length* (for fixed-length strings), Object, Variant, or one of the object types described earlier in this chapter. If you do not declare a data type, Visual Basic assumes that the property returns a variant result. The data type of the returned value must match the data type of the *propvalue* variable you declare in any companion Property Let or Property Set procedure. You can set the return value in code by assigning an expression of a compatible data type to the property name.

You should declare the data type of all arguments in the property procedure's parameter list. Note that the names of the variables passed by the calling procedure can be different from the names of the variables known by this procedure. If you use the ByVal keyword to declare an argument, Visual Basic passes a copy of the argument to your procedure. Any change you make to a ByVal argument does not change the original variable in the calling procedure. If you use the ByRef keyword, Visual Basic passes the actual memory address of the variable, allowing the procedure to change the variable's value in the calling procedure. (If the argument passed by the calling procedure is an expression, Visual Basic treats it as if you had declared it by using ByVal.) Visual Basic always passes arrays by reference (ByRef).

Use the Optional keyword to declare an argument that isn't required. All optional arguments must be the Variant data type. If you declare an optional argument, all arguments that follow in the argument list must also be declared as optional. You can specify a *default* value only for optional parameters. Use the IsMissing built-in function to test for the absence of optional parameters. You can also use the ParamArray argument to declare an array of optional elements of the Variant data type. When you attempt to access this property in an object set to the class, you can then pass it an arbitrary number of arguments. The ParamArray argument must be the last argument in the argument list.

Use the Exit Property statement anywhere in your property procedure to clear any error conditions and exit your procedure normally, returning to the calling procedure. If Visual Basic runs your code until it encounters the End Property statement, control is passed to the calling procedure but any errors are not cleared. If this procedure causes an error and terminates with the End Property statement, Visual Basic passes the error to the calling procedure. See "Trapping Errors" on page 834 for details.

Examples

To declare a Filename property as a string and return it from a variable defined in the Declarations section of your class module, enter the following:

```
Option Explicit
Dim strFileName As String
Property Get Filename() As String
    ' Return the saved file name as a property
    Filename = strFilename
End Property
```

To establish a new instance of the object defined by the ComDlg class module and then fetch its Filename property, enter the following in a function or sub:

```
Dim clsDialog As New ComDlg, strFile As String
  With clsDialog
    ' Set the title of the dialog box
    .DialogTitle = "Locate LawTrack Contacts Data File"
    ' Set the default file name
    .FileName = "ContactsData.mdb"
    ' .. and start directory
    .Directory = CurrentProject.Path
    ' .. and file extension
    .Extension = "mdb"
    ' .. but show all mdb files just in case
    .Filter = "LawTrack File (*.mdb)|*.mdb"
    ' Default directory is where this file is located
    .Directory = CurrentProject.Path
    ' Tell the common dialog that the file and path must exist
    .ExistFlags = FileMustExist + PathMustExist
    ' If the ShowOpen method returns True
    If .ShowOpen Then
      ' Then fetch the Filename property
      strFile = .FileName
    Else
      Err.Raise 3999
    End If
  End With
```

Property Let

Use a Property Let procedure to define code that executes when the calling code attempts to assign a value to a data property of the object defined by your class module. You cannot define both a Property Let and a Property Set procedure for the same property.

Syntax

```
[Public | Private | Friend] [Static] Property Let propertyname
  ([<arguments>,] propvalue [AS datatype])
    [ <property statements> ]
    [Exit Property]
    [ <property statements> ]
End Property
```

where *<arguments>* is

```
{[Optional][ByVal | ByRef][ParamArray]
  argumentname[()] [As datatype][ = default]},...
```

Notes

Use the Public keyword to make this property available to all other procedures in all modules. Use the Private keyword to make this property available only to other procedures in the same module. When you declare a property as private in a class module, you cannot reference the property from another module. Use the Friend keyword to declare a property that is public to all other code in your application but is not visible to outside code that activates your project via automation.

Include the Static keyword to preserve the value of all variables declared within the property procedure, whether explicitly or implicitly, as long as the module containing the procedure is open. This is the same as using the Static statement (discussed earlier in this chapter) to explicitly declare all variables created in this property procedure.

You should declare the data type of all arguments in the property procedure's parameter list. Valid *datatype* entries are Byte, Boolean, Integer, Long, Currency, Single, Double, Date, String (for variable-length strings), String * *length* (for fixed-length strings), Object, Variant, or one of the object types described earlier in this chapter. Note that the names of the variables passed by the calling procedure can be different from the names of the variables as known by this procedure. Also, the names and data types of the arguments must exactly match the arguments declared for the companion Property Get procedure. If you use the ByVal keyword to declare an argument, Visual Basic passes a copy of the argument to your property procedure. Any change you make to a ByVal argument does not change the original variable in the calling procedure. If you use the ByRef keyword, Visual Basic passes the actual memory address of the variable, allowing the procedure to change the variable's value in the calling procedure. (If the argument passed by the calling procedure is an expression, Visual Basic treats it as if you had declared it by using ByVal.) Visual Basic always passes arrays by reference (ByRef).

Use the Optional keyword to declare an argument that isn't required. All optional arguments must be the Variant data type. If you declare an optional argument, all arguments that follow in the argument list must also be declared as optional. You can specify a *default* value only for optional parameters. Use the IsMissing built-in function to test for the absence of optional parameters. You can also use the ParamArray argument to declare an array of optional elements of the Variant data type. When you attempt to assign a value to this property in an object set to the class, you can then pass it an arbitrary number of arguments. The ParamArray argument must be the last argument in the argument list.

You must always declare at least one parameter, *propvalue*, that is the variable to contain the value that the calling code wants to assign to your property. This is the value or expression that appears on the right side of the assignment statement executed in the calling code. If you declare a data type, it must match the data type declared by the companion Property Get procedure. Also, when you declare a data type, the caller receives a data type mismatch error if the assignment statement attempts to pass an incorrect data type. You cannot modify this value, but you can evaluate it and save it as a value to be returned later by your Property Get procedure.

Use the Exit Property statement anywhere in your property procedure to clear any error conditions and exit your procedure normally, returning to the calling procedure. If Visual Basic runs your code until it encounters the End Property statement, control is passed to the calling procedure but any errors are not cleared. If this procedure causes an error and terminates with the End Property statement, Visual Basic passes the error to the calling procedure. See "Trapping Errors" on page 834 for details.

Examples

To declare a Filename property, accept a value from a caller, and save the value in a variable defined in the Declarations section of your class module, enter the following:

```
Option Explicit
Dim strFileName As String
Property Let FileName(strFile)
  If Len(strFile) <= 64 Then _
    strFileName = strFile
End Property
```

To establish a new instance of the object defined by the ComDlg class module and then set its Filename property, enter the following:

```
Dim clsDialog As New ComDlg, strFile As String
  With clsDialog
    ' Set the title of the dialog
    .DialogTitle = "Locate LawTrack Contacts Data File"
    ' Set the default file name
    .FileName = "ContactsData.mdb"
  End With
```

Property Set

Use a Property Set procedure to define code that executes when the calling code attempts to assign an object to an object property of the object defined by your class module. You cannot define both a Property Let and a Property Set for the same property.

Syntax

```
[Public | Private | Friend] [Static] Property Set propertyname
  ([<arguments>,] object [As objecttype])
    [ <property statements> ]
    [Exit Property]
    [ <property statements> ]
End Property
```

where *<arguments>* is

```
{[Optional][ByVal | ByRef][ParamArray]
    argumentname[()] [As datatype][ = default]},...
```

Notes

Use the Public keyword to make this property available to all other procedures in all modules. Use the Private keyword to make this property available only to other procedures in the same module. When you declare a property as private in a class module, you cannot reference the property from another module. Use the Friend keyword to declare a property that is public to all other code in your application but is not visible to outside code that activates your project via automation.

Include the Static keyword to preserve the value of all variables declared within the property procedure, whether explicitly or implicitly, as long as the module containing the procedure is open. This is the same as using the Static statement (discussed earlier in this chapter) to explicitly declare all variables created in this property procedure.

You should declare the data type of all arguments in the property procedure's parameter list. Valid *datatype* entries are Byte, Boolean, Integer, Long, Currency, Single, Double, Date, String (for variable-length strings), String * *length* (for fixed-length strings), Object, Variant, or one of the object types described earlier in this chapter. Note that the names of the variables passed by the calling procedure can be different from the names of the variables as known by this procedure. Also, the names and data types of the arguments must exactly match the arguments declared for the companion Property Get procedure. If you use the ByVal keyword to declare an argument, Visual Basic passes a copy of the argument to your property procedure. Any change you make to a ByVal argument does not change the original variable in the calling procedure. If you use the ByRef keyword, Visual Basic passes the actual memory address of the variable, allowing the procedure to change the variable's value in the calling procedure. (If the argument passed by the calling procedure is an expression, Visual Basic treats it as if you had declared it by using ByVal.) Visual Basic always passes arrays by reference (ByRef).

Use the Optional keyword to declare an argument that isn't required. All optional arguments must be the Variant data type. If you declare an optional argument, all arguments that follow in the argument list must also be declared as optional. You can specify a *default* value only for

Chapter 22

optional parameters. Use the IsMissing built-in function to test for the absence of optional parameters. You can also use the ParamArray argument to declare an array of optional elements of the Variant data type. When you attempt to assign a value to this property in an object set to the class, you can then pass it an arbitrary number of arguments. The ParamArray argument must be the last argument in the argument list.

You must always declare at least one parameter, *object*, that is the variable to contain the object that the calling code wants to assign to your property. This is the object reference that appears on the right side of the assignment statement executed in the calling code. If you include an *objecttype* entry, it must match the object type declared by the companion Property Get procedure. Also, when you declare an object type, the caller receives a data type mismatch error if the assignment statement attempts to pass an incorrect object type. You can evaluate the properties of this object, set its properties, execute its methods, and save the object pointer in another variable that your Property Get procedure can later return.

Use the Exit Property statement anywhere in your property procedure to clear any error conditions and exit your procedure normally, returning to the calling procedure. If Visual Basic runs your code until it encounters the End Property statement, control is passed to the calling procedure but any errors are not cleared. If this procedure causes an error and terminates with the End Property statement, Visual Basic passes the error to the calling procedure. See Trapping Errors on page 834 for details.

Examples

To declare a ControlToUpdate property, accept a value from a caller, and save the value in an object variable defined in the Declarations section of your class module, enter the following:

```
Option Explicit
Dim ctlToUpdate As Control
Property Set ControlToUpdate(ctl As Control)
   ' Verify we have the right type of control
  Select Case ctl.ControlType
     ' Text box, combo box, and list box are OK
    Case acTextBox, acListBox, acComboBox
       ' Save the control object
       Set ctlToUpdate = ctl
    Case Else
       Err.Raise 3999
  End Select
End Property
```

To establish a new instance of the object defined by the ComDlg class module and then set its Filename property, enter the following in a function or sub:

```
Dim clsDialog As New ComDlg, strFile As String
   With clsDialog
     ' Set the title of the dialog
     .DialogTitle = "Locate LawTrack Contacts Data File"
     ' Set the default file name
     .FileName = "ContactsData.mdb"
   End With
```

Controlling the Flow of Statements

Visual Basic provides many ways for you to control the flow of statements in procedures. You can call other procedures, loop through a set of statements either a calculated number of times or based on a condition, or test values and conditionally execute sets of statements based on the result of the condition test. You can also go directly to a set of statements or exit a procedure at any time. The following sections demonstrate some (but not all) of the ways you can control flow in your procedures.

Call Statement

Use a Call statement to transfer control to a subroutine.

Syntax

```
Call subroutinename [(<arguments>)]
```

or

```
subroutinename [<arguments>]
```

where *<arguments>* is

```
{[ByVal | ByRef] <expression> },...
```

Notes

The Call keyword is optional, but if you omit it, you must also omit the parentheses surrounding the parameter list. If the subroutine accepts arguments, the names of the variables passed by the calling procedure can be different from the names of the variables as known by the subroutine. You can use the ByVal and ByRef keywords in a Call statement only when you're making a call to a dynamic link library (DLL) procedure. Use ByVal for string arguments to indicate that you need to pass a pointer to the string rather than pass the string directly. Use ByRef for nonstring arguments to pass the value directly. If you use the ByVal keyword to declare an argument, Visual Basic passes a copy of the argument to the subroutine. The subroutine cannot change the original variable in the calling procedure. If you use the ByRef keyword, Visual Basic passes the actual memory address of the variable, allowing the procedure to change the variable's value in the calling procedure. (If the argument passed by the calling procedure is an expression, Visual Basic treats it as if you had declared it by using ByVal.)

Examples

To call a subroutine named MySub and pass it an integer variable and an expression, enter the following:

```
Call MySub (intMyInteger, curPrice * intQty)
```

An alternative syntax is

```
MySub intMyInteger, curPrice * intQty
```

Do...Loop Statement

Use a Do...Loop statement to define a block of statements that you want executed multiple times. You can also define a condition that terminates the loop when the condition is false.

Syntax

```
Do [{While | Until} <condition>]
    [<procedure statements>]
    [Exit Do]
    [<procedure statements>]
Loop
```

or

```
Do
    [<procedure statements>]
    [Exit Do]
    [<procedure statements>]
Loop [{While | Until} <condition>]
```

Notes

The <condition> is a comparison predicate or expression that Visual Basic can evaluate to True (nonzero) or False (zero or Null). The While clause is the opposite of the Until clause. If you specify a While clause, execution continues as long as the <condition> is true. If you specify an Until clause, execution of the loop stops when <condition> becomes true. If you place a While or an Until clause in the Do clause, the condition must be met for the statements in the loop to execute at all. A While condition must be true, and an Until condition must be false for the code following the Do to execute. If you place a While or an Until clause in the Loop clause, Visual Basic executes the statements within the loop before testing the condition.

You can place one or more Exit Do statements anywhere within the loop to exit the loop before reaching the Loop statement. Generally you'll use the Exit Do statement as part of some other evaluation statement structure, such as an If...Then...Else statement.

Example

To read all the rows in the tblCompanies table until you reach the end of the recordset (the EOF property is true), enter the following:

```
Dim dbLawTrack As DAO.Database
Dim rcdCompanies As DAO.RecordSet
Set dbLawTrack = CurrentDb
```

```
Set rcdCompanies = dbLawTrack.OpenRecordSet("tblCompanies")
Do Until rcdCompanies.EOF
    <procedure statements>
    rcdClubs.MoveNext
Loop
```

For...Next Statement

Use a For...Next statement to execute a series of statements a specific number
of times.

Syntax

```
For counter = first To last [Step stepamount]
    [<procedure statements>]
    [Exit For]
    [<procedure statements>]
Next [counter]
```

Notes

The *counter* must be a numeric variable that is not an array or a record element. Visual Basic
initially sets the value of *counter* to *first*. If you do not specify a *stepamount*, the default
stepamount value is +1. If the *stepamount* value is positive or 0, Visual Basic executes the loop
as long as *counter* is less than or equal to *last*. If the *stepamount* value is negative, Visual Basic
executes the loop as long as *counter* is greater than or equal to *last*. Visual Basic adds *stepamount*
to *counter* when it encounters the corresponding Next statement. You can change the value
of *counter* within the For loop, but this might make your procedure more difficult to test
and debug. Changing the value of *last* within the loop does not affect execution of the loop.
You can place one or more Exit For statements anywhere within the loop to exit the loop
before reaching the Next statement. Generally you'll use the Exit For statement as part of
some other evaluation statement structure, such as an If...Then...Else statement.

You can nest one For loop inside another. When you do, you must choose a different *counter*
name for each loop.

Example

To list in the Immediate window the names of the first five queries in the LawTrack Contacts
database, enter the following in a function or sub:

```
Dim dbLawTrack As DAO.Database
Dim intI As Integer
Set dbLawTrack = CurrentDb
For intI = 0 To 4
    Debug.Print dbLawTrack.QueryDefs(intI).Name
Next intI
```

Chapter 22

For Each...Next Statement

Use a For Each...Next statement to execute a series of statements for each item in a collection or an array.

Syntax

```
For Each item In group
    [<procedure statements>]
    [Exit For]
    [<procedure statements>]
Next [item]
```

Notes

The *item* must be a variable that represents an object in a collection or an element of an array. The *group* must be the name of a collection or an array. Visual Basic executes the loop as long as at least one item remains in the collection or the array. All the statements in the loop are executed for each item in the collection or the array. You can place one or more Exit For statements anywhere within the loop to exit the loop before reaching the Next statement. Generally you'll use the Exit For statement as part of some other evaluation statement structure, such as an If...Then...Else statement.

You can nest one For Each loop inside another. When you do, you must choose a different *item* name for each loop.

Example

To list in the Immediate window the names of all the queries in the LawTrack Contacts database, enter the following in a function or sub:

```
Dim dbLawTrack As DAO.Database
Dim qdf As DAO.QueryDef
Set dbLawTrack = CurrentDb
For Each qdf In dbLawTrack.QueryDefs
    Debug.Print qdf.Name
Next qdf
```

GoTo Statement

Use a GoTo statement to jump unconditionally to another statement in your procedure.

Syntax

```
GoTo {label | linenumber}
```

Notes

You can label a statement line by starting the line with a string of no more than 40 characters that starts with an alphabetic character and ends with a colon (:). A line label cannot be a Visual Basic or Access reserved word. You can also optionally number the statement lines in your procedure. Each line number must contain only numbers, must be different from all other line numbers in the procedure, must be the first nonblank characters in a line, and must contain 40 characters or less. To jump to a line number or a labeled line, use the GoTo statement and the appropriate *label* or *linenumber*.

Example

To jump to the statement line labeled SkipOver, enter the following:

```
GoTo SkipOver
```

If...Then...Else Statement

Use an If...Then...Else statement to conditionally execute statements based on the evaluation of a condition.

Syntax

```
If <condition1> Then
    [<procedure statements 1>]
[ElseIf <condition2> Then
    [<procedure statements 2>]]...
[Else
    [<procedure statements n>]]
End If
```

or

```
If <condition> Then <thenstmt> [Else <elsestmt>]
```

Notes

Each condition is a numeric or string expression that Visual Basic can evaluate to True (non-zero) or False (0 or Null). A condition can also consist of multiple comparison expressions and Boolean operators. In addition, a condition can also be the special TypeOf...Is test to evaluate a control variable. The syntax for this test is

```
TypeOf <ControlObject> Is <ControlType>
```

where <*ControlObject*> is the name of a control variable and <*ControlType*> is one of the following: BoundObjectFrame, CheckBox, ComboBox, CommandButton, Chart, Custom-Control, Image, Label, Line, ListBox, OptionButton, OptionGroup, PageBreak, Rectangle, Subform, Subreport, TextBox, ToggleButton, or UnboundObjectFrame.

If the condition is true, Visual Basic executes the statement or statements immediately following the Then keyword. If the condition is false, Visual Basic evaluates the next ElseIf condition or executes the statements following the Else keyword, whichever occurs next.

The alternative syntax does not need an End If statement, but you must enter the entire If…Then statement on a single line. Both *<thenstmt>* and *<elsestmt>* can be either a single Visual Basic statement or multiple statements separated by colons (:).

Example

To set an integer value depending on whether a string begins with a letter from *A* through *F*, from *G* through *N*, or from *O* through *Z*, enter the following:

```
Dim strMyString As String, strFirst As String, _
  intVal As Integer
' Grab the first letter and make it upper case
strFirst = UCase(Left(strMyString, 1))
If strFirst >= "A" And strFirst <= "F" Then
    intVal = 1
ElseIf strFirst >= "G" And strFirst <= "N" Then
    intVal = 2
ElseIf strFirst >= "O" And strFirst <= "Z" Then
    intVal = 3
Else
    intVal = 0
End If
```

RaiseEvent Statement

Use the RaiseEvent statement to signal a declared event in a class module.

Syntax

```
RaiseEvent eventname [(<arguments>)]
```

where *<arguments>* is

```
{ <expression> },...
```

Notes

You must always declare an event in the class module that raises the event. You cannot use Raise-Event to signal a built-in event (such as Current) of a form or report class module. If an event passes no arguments, you must not include an empty pair of parentheses when you code the Raise-Event statement. An event can only be received by another module that has declared an object variable using WithEvents that has been set to the class module or object containing this class.

See the *WeddingList.mdb* sample database—described in Chapter 23, "Automating Your Application with Visual Basic"—for an example using RaiseEvent to synchronize two forms.

Chapter 22

Example

To define an event named Signal that returns a text string and then to signal that event in a class module, enter the following:

```
Option Explicit
Public Event Signal(ByVal strMsg As String)

Public Sub RaiseSignal(ByVal strText As String)
    RaiseEvent Signal(strText)
End Sub
```

Select Case Statement

Use a Select Case statement to execute statements conditionally based on the evaluation of an expression that is compared to a list or range of values.

Syntax

```
Select Case <test expression>
    [Case <comparison list 1>
        [<procedure statements 1>]]
    ...
    [Case Else
        [<procedure statements n>]]
End Select
```

where *<test expression>* is any numeric or string expression; where *<comparison list>* is

```
{<comparison element>,...}
```

where *<comparison element>* is

```
{expression | expression To expression |
  Is <comparison operator> expression}
```

and where *<comparison operator>* is

```
{= | <> | < | > | <= | >=}
```

Notes

If the *<test expression>* matches a *<comparison element>* in a Case clause, Visual Basic executes the statements that follow that clause. If the *<comparison element>* is a single expression, the *<test expression>* must equal the *<comparison element>* for the statements following that clause to execute. If the *<comparison element>* contains a To keyword, the first expression must be less than the second expression (either in numeric value if the expressions are numbers or in collating sequence if the expressions are strings) and the *<test expression>* must be between the first expression and the second expression. If the *<comparison element>* contains the Is keyword, the evaluation of *<comparison operator> expression* must be true.

If more than one Case clause matches the <*test expression*>, Visual Basic executes only the set of statements following the first Case clause that matches. You can include a block of statements following a Case Else clause that Visual Basic executes if none of the previous Case clauses matches the <*test expression*>. You can nest another Select Case statement within the statements following a Case clause.

Example

To assign an integer value to a variable, depending on whether a string begins with a letter from *A* through *F*, from *G* through *N*, or from *O* through *Z*, enter the following in a function or sub:

```
Dim strMyString As String, intVal As Integer
Select Case UCase$(Mid$(strMyString, 1, 1))
    Case "A" To "F"
        intVal = 1
    Case "G" To "N"
        intVal = 2
    Case "O" To "Z"
        intVal = 3
    Case Else
        intVal = 0
End Select
```

Stop Statement

Use a Stop statement to suspend execution of your procedure.

Syntax

```
Stop
```

Notes

A Stop statement has the same effect as setting a breakpoint on a statement. You can use the Visual Basic debugging tools, such as the Step Into and the Step Over buttons and the Debug window, to evaluate the status of your procedure after Visual Basic halts on a Stop statement. You should not use the Stop statement in a production application.

While...Wend Statement

Use a While...Wend statement to continuously execute a block of statements as long as a condition is true.

Syntax

```
While <condition>
    [<procedure statements>]
Wend
```

Notes

A While…Wend statement is similar to a Do…Loop statement with a While clause, except that you can use an Exit Do statement to exit from a Do loop. Visual Basic provides no similar Exit clause for a While loop. The *<condition>* is an expression that Visual Basic can evaluate to True (nonzero) or False (0 or Null). Execution continues as long as the *<condition>* is true.

Example

To read all the rows in the tblCompanies table until you reach the end of the recordset, enter the following in a function or sub:

```
Dim dbLawTrack As DAO.Database
Dim rcdCompanies As DAO.RecordSet
Set dbLawTrack = CurrentDb
Set rcdCompanies = dbLawTrack.OpenRecordSet("tblCompanies")
While Not rcdCompanies.EOF
    <procedure statements>
    rcdCompanies.MoveNext
Wend
```

With…End With Statement

Use a With statement to simplify references to complex objects in code. You can establish a base object using a With statement and then use a shorthand notation to refer to objects, collections, properties, or methods on that object until you terminate the With statement. When you plan to reference an object many times within a block of code, using With also improves execution speed.

Syntax

```
With <object reference>
    [<procedure statements>]
End With
```

Example

To use shorthand notation on a recordset object to add a new row to a table, enter the following:

```
Dim rcd As DAO.Recordset, db As DAO.Database
Set db = CurrentDb
Set rcd = db.OpenRecordset("MyTable", _
  dbOpenDynaset, dbAppendOnly)
With rcd
    ' Start a new record
    .Addnew
    ' Set the field values
    ![FieldOne] = "1"
    ![FieldTwo] = "John"
```

```
        ![FieldThree] = "Viescas"
        .Update
        .Close
End With
```

To write the same code without the With statement, you would have to say:

```
Dim rcd As DAO.Recordset, db As DAO.Database
Set db = CurrentDb
Set rcd = db.OpenRecordset("MyTable", dbOpenDynaset, dbAppendOnly)
        ' Start a new record
        rcd.Addnew
        ' Set the field values
        rcd![FieldOne] = "1"
        rcd![FieldTwo] = "John"
        rcd![FieldThree] = "Viescas"
        rcd.Update
        rcd.Close
```

Running Macro Actions and Menu Commands

From within Visual Basic, you can execute most of the macro actions that Access provides and any of the built-in menu commands. Only a few of the macro actions have direct Visual Basic equivalents. To execute a macro action or menu command, use the methods of the DoCmd object, described below.

DoCmd Object

Use the methods of the DoCmd object to execute a macro action or menu command from within a Visual Basic procedure.

Syntax

DoCmd.*actionmethod* [*actionargument*],...

Notes

Some of the macro actions you'll commonly execute from Visual Basic include ApplyFilter, Close, DoMenuItem, FindNext and FindRecord (for searching the recordset of the current form and immediately displaying the result), Hourglass, Maximize, Minimize, MoveSize, OpenForm, OpenQuery (to run a query that you don't need to modify), OpenReport, and ShowToolBar. Although you can run the Echo, GoToControl, GoToPage, RepaintObject, and Requery actions from Visual Basic using a method of the DoCmd object, it's more efficient to use the Echo, SetFocus, GoToPage, Repaint, and Requery methods of the object to which the method applies.

Examples

To open a form named frmCompanies in Form view for data entry, enter the following:

```
DoCmd.OpenForm "frmCompanies", acNormal, , , acAdd
```

To close a form named frmContacts, enter the following:

```
DoCmd.Close acForm, "frmContacts"
```

Executing a Menu Command

To execute a menu command, use the RunCommand method of either the DoCmd or Application object and supply a single action argument that is the numeric code for the command.

Syntax

```
[DoCmd.]RunCommand [actionargument],...
```

Notes

You can also use one of many built-in constants for *actionargument* to reference the command you want. When you use RunCommand, you can optionally leave out the DoCmd or Application object.

Examples

To execute the Save Record command from the Records menu, enter the following:

```
RunCommand acCmdSaveRecord
```

To switch an open form to PivotChart view (execute the PivotChart View command on the View menu), enter the following:

```
RunCommand acCmdPivotChartView
```

To open the Find window while the focus is on a form (choose the Find command from the Edit menu), enter the following:

```
RunCommand acCmdFind
```

> **Note** Visual Basic provides built-in constants for many of the macro action and RunCommand parameters. For more information, search on "Microsoft Access Constants" and "RunCommand Method" in Help.

Chapter 22

Actions with Visual Basic Equivalents

A few macro actions cannot be executed from a Visual Basic procedure. All but one of these actions, however, have equivalent statements in Visual Basic, as shown in Table 22-4.

Table 22-4. Visual Basic Equivalents for Macro Actions

Macro Action	Visual Basic Equivalent
AddMenu	No equivalent
MsgBox	MsgBox statement or function
RunApp	Shell function
RunCode	Call subroutine
SendKeys	SendKeys statement
SetValue	Variable assignment (=)
StopAllMacros	Stop or End statement
StopMacro	Exit Sub or Exit Function statement

Trapping Errors

One of the most powerful features of Visual Basic is its ability to trap all errors, analyze them, and take corrective action. In a well-designed production application, the user should never see any of the default error messages or encounter a code halt when an error occurs. Also, setting an error trap is often the best way to test certain conditions. For example, to find out if a query exists, your code can set an error trap and then attempt to reference the query object. In an application with hundreds of queries, using an error trap can also be faster than looping through all QueryDef objects. To enable error trapping, you use an On Error statement.

On Error Statement

Use an On Error statement to enable error trapping, establish the procedure to handle error trapping (the error handler), skip past any errors, or turn off error trapping.

Syntax

```
On Error {GoTo lineID | Resume Next | GoTo 0}
```

Notes

Use a GoTo *lineID* clause to establish a code block in your procedure that handles any error. The *lineID* can be a line number or a label.

Use a Resume Next clause to trap errors but skip over any statement that causes an error. You can call the Err function in a statement immediately following the statement that you suspect might have caused an error to see whether an error occurred. Err returns 0 if no error has occurred.

Use a GoTo 0 statement to turn off error trapping for the current procedure. If an error occurs, Visual Basic passes the error to the error routine in the calling procedure or opens an error dialog box if there is no previous error routine.

In your error handling statements, you can examine the built-in Err variable (the error number associated with the error) to determine the exact nature of the error. You can use the Error function to examine the text of the error message associated with the error. If you use line numbers with your statements, you can use the built-in Erl function to determine the line number of the statement that caused the error. After taking corrective action, use a Resume statement to retry execution of the statement that caused the error. Use a Resume Next statement to continue execution at the statement immediately following the statement that caused the error. Use a Resume statement with a statement label to restart execution at the indicated label name or number. You can also use an Exit Function or Exit Sub statement to reset the error condition and return to the calling procedure.

Examples

To trap errors but continue execution with the next statement, enter the following:

```
On Error Resume Next
```

To trap errors and execute the statements that follow the MyError: label when an error occurs, enter the following:

```
On Error GoTo MyError
```

To turn off error trapping in the current procedure, enter the following:

```
On Error GoTo 0
```

If you create and run the following function with zero as the second argument, such as MyErrExample(3,0), the function will trigger an error by attempting to divide by zero, trap the error, display the error in an error handling section, and then exit gracefully.

```
Public Function MyErrExample(intA As Integer, intB As Integer) As Integer
' Set an error trap
On Error GoTo Trap_Error
  ' The following causes an error if intB is zero
  MyErrExample = intA / intB
ExitNice:
  Exit Function
Trap_Error:
  MsgBox "Something bad happened: " & Err & ", " & Error
  Resume ExitNice
End Function
```

Some Complex Visual Basic Examples

A good way to learn Visual Basic techniques is to study complex code that has been developed and tested by someone else. In the LawTrack Contacts and Housing Reservations sample databases, you can find dozens of examples of complex Visual Basic code that perform various tasks. The following sections describe two of the more interesting ones in detail.

A Procedure to Randomly Load Data

You've probably noticed a lot of sample data in both the LawTrack Contacts and Housing Reservations databases. No, I didn't sit at my keyboard for hours entering sample data! Instead, I built a Visual Basic procedure that accepts some parameters entered on a form. In both databases, the form to load sample data is saved as *zfrmLoadData*. If you open this form in *Contacts.mdb* from the Database window, you'll see that you use it to enter a beginning date, a number of days (max 365), a number of companies to load (max 50), a maximum number of contacts per company (max 10), and a maximum number of events per contact (max 25). You can also select an option to delete all existing data before randomly loading new data. (The zfrmLoadData form in the Housing Reservations database offers some slightly different options.) Figure 22-15 shows this form with the values I used to load the LawTrack Contacts database.

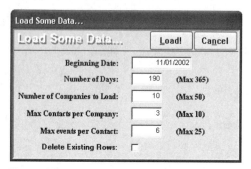

Figure 22-15. The zfrmLoadData form in the LawTrack Contacts sample database in Form view.

As you might expect, when you click the Load button, my procedure examines the values entered and loads some sample data into tblCompanies, tblContacts, tblCompanyContacts, tblContactEvents, and tblContactProducts. The code picks random company names from ztblCompanies (a table containing a list of fictitious company names) and random person names from ztblPeople (a table containing names of Microsoft employees who have agreed to allow their names to be used in sample data). It also chooses random ZIP codes (and cities, counties, and states) from tlkpZips (a table containing U.S. postal ZIP code, city name, state name, county name, and telephone area codes as of December 2002 that I licensed from CD Light, LLC—*http://www.zipinfo.com*). Figure 22-16 shows you the design of the query used in the code to pick random company names.

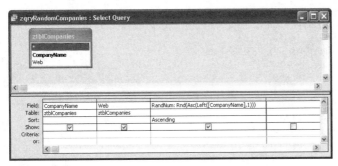

Figure 22-16. A query to pick random company names.

The query creates a numeric value to pass to the Rnd (random) function by grabbing the first character of the CompanyName field and then calculating the ASCII code value. The Rnd function returns some floating-point random value less than 1 but greater than or equal to zero. Asking the query to sort on this random number results in a random list of values each time you run the query.

> **Note** If you open *zqryRandomCompanies* in Datasheet view, the RandNum column won't appear to be sorted correctly. In fact, the values change as you scroll through the data or resize the datasheet window. The database engine actually calls the Rnd function on a first pass through the data to perform the sort. Because the function depends on a value of one of the columns (LastName), Access assumes that other users might be changing this column—and therefore, the calculated result—as you view the data. Access calls the Rnd function again each time it refreshes the data display, so the actual values you see aren't the ones that the query originally used to sort the data.

If you want to run this code and load sample data, open *zfrmLoadData* and either pick a date starting after April 25, 2003, or select the Delete Existing Rows option before clicking Load.

You can find the code in the cmdLoad_Click event procedure that runs when you click the Load button on the zfrmLoadData form. I've added line numbers to some of the lines in this code listing in the book so that you can follow along with the line-by-line explanations in Table 22-5, which follows the listing. This procedure primarily uses the ADO object model, and the similar code behind the zfrmLoadData form in the Housing Reservations database uses the DAO object model.

```
1 Private Sub cmdLoad_Click()
2 ' Code to load a random set of companies,
  '   contacts, events, and products
  ' Connection variable
3 Dim cn As ADODB.Connection
  ' Database variable
  Dim db As DAO.Database
  ' Table delete list (if starting over)
  Dim rstDel As New ADODB.Recordset
  ' Company recordset; Contact recordset (insert only)
  Dim rstCo As New ADODB.Recordset, rstCn As New ADODB.Recordset
```

```
    ' CompanyContact recordset, ContactEvent recordset (insert only)
    Dim rstCoCn As New ADODB.Recordset, rstCnEv As New ADODB.Recordset
    ' A random selection of zips
    Dim rstZipRandom As New ADODB.Recordset
    ' ..and company names
    Dim rstCoRandom As New ADODB.Recordset
    ' .. and people names
    Dim rstPRandom As New ADODB.Recordset
    ' A recordset to pick "close" zip codes for contacts
    Dim rstZipClose As New ADODB.Recordset
    ' A recordset to pick contact events
    Dim rstEvents As New ADODB.Recordset
    ' Place to generate Picture Path
4   Dim strPicPath As String
    ' Places for path to backend database and folder
    Dim strBackEndPath As String, strBackEndFolder As String
    ' Place to generate a safe "compact to" name
    Dim strNewDb As String
    ' Places to save values from the form controls
    Dim datBeginDate As Date, intNumDays As Integer
    Dim intNumCompanies As Integer, intNumContacts As Integer
    Dim intNumEvents As Integer
    ' Lists of street names and types
5   Dim strStreetNames(1 To 9) As String, strStreetTypes(1 To 5) As String
    ' As string of digits for street addresses and area codes
    Const strDigits As String = "1234567890"
    ' List of Person Titles by gender
    Dim strMTitles(1 To 6) As String, strFTitles(1 To 7) As String
    ' Place to put male and female picture file names
    Dim strMPicture() As String, intMPicCount As Integer
    Dim strFPicture() As String, intFPicCount As Integer
    ' Some working variables
    Dim intI As Integer, intJ As Integer, intK As Integer
    Dim intL As Integer, intM As Integer, intR As Integer
    Dim varRtn As Variant, intDefault As Integer
    Dim datCurrentDate As Date, datCurrentTime As Date
    ' Variables to assemble Company and Contact records
    Dim strCompanyName As String, strCoAddress As String
    Dim strAreaCode As String, strPAddress As String
    Dim strThisPhone As String, strThisFax As String
    Dim strWebsite As String
    Dim lngThisCompany As Long, intCoType As Integer
    Dim lngThisContact As Long, strProducts As String
    ' Set up to bail if something funny happens (it shouldn't)
6     On Error GoTo BailOut
      ' Initialize Streets
7     strStreetNames(1) = "Main"
      strStreetNames(2) = "Central"
      strStreetNames(3) = "Willow"
      strStreetNames(4) = "Church"
      strStreetNames(5) = "Lincoln"
      strStreetNames(6) = "1st"
      strStreetNames(7) = "2nd"
      strStreetNames(8) = "3rd"
```

```
      strStreetNames(9) = "4th"
      strStreetTypes(1) = "Street"
      strStreetTypes(2) = "Avenue"
      strStreetTypes(3) = "Drive"
      strStreetTypes(4) = "Parkway"
      strStreetTypes(5) = "Boulevard"
      ' Initialize person titles
      strMTitles(1) = "Capt."
      strMTitles(2) = "Dr."
      strMTitles(3) = "Lt."
      strMTitles(4) = "Mr."
      strMTitles(5) = "Officer"
      strMTitles(6) = "Sgt."
      strFTitles(1) = "Capt."
      strFTitles(2) = "Dr."
      strFTitles(3) = "Lt."
      strFTitles(4) = "Mrs."
      strFTitles(5) = "Ms."
      strFTitles(6) = "Officer"
      strFTitles(7) = "Sgt."
      ' Search for male picture names (should be in Current Path\Pictures)
   8  strPicPath = Dir(CurrentProject.Path & "\Pictures\PersonM*.bmp")
      ' Loop until Dir returns nothing (end of list or not found)
   9  Do Until (strPicPath = "")
        ' Add 1 to the count
        intMPicCount = intMPicCount + 1
        ' Extend the file name array
  10    ReDim Preserve strMPicture(1 To intMPicCount)
        ' Add the file name to the array
        strMPicture(intMPicCount) = strPicPath
        ' Get next one
        strPicPath = Dir
  11  Loop
      ' Search for female picture names (should be in Current Path\Pictures)
      strPicPath = Dir(CurrentProject.Path & "\Pictures\PersonF*.bmp")
      ' Loop until Dir returns nothing (end of list or not found)
  12  Do Until (strPicPath = "")
        ' Add 1 to the count
        intFPicCount = intFPicCount + 1
        ' Extend the file name array
        ReDim Preserve strFPicture(1 To intFPicCount)
        ' Add the file name to the array
        strFPicture(intFPicCount) = strPicPath
        ' Get next one
        strPicPath = Dir
  13  Loop
      ' Capture values from the form
  14  datBeginDate = CDate(Me.BeginDate)
      intNumDays = Me.NumDays
      intNumCompanies = Me.NumCompanies
      intNumContacts = Me.NumContacts
      intNumEvents = Me.NumEvents
      ' Open the current database
  15  Set db = CurrentDb
```

Chapter 22

839

```
       ' Grab the current connection
       Set cn = CurrentProject.Connection
       ' Do they want to delete old rows?
16     If (Me.chkDelete = -1) Then
         ' Verify it
17       If vbYes = MsgBox("Are you SURE you want to delete " & _
           "all existing rows? " & vbCrLf & vbCrLf & _
           "(This will also compact the data file.)", _
           vbQuestion + vbYesNo + vbDefaultButton2, gstrAppTitle) Then
           ' Open the table that tells us the safe delete sequence
18         rstDel.Open "SELECT * FROM ztblDeleteSeq ORDER BY Sequence", cn, _
             adOpenForwardOnly, adLockReadOnly
           ' Loop through them all
19         Do Until rstDel.EOF
             ' Execute a delete
20           cn.Execute "DELETE * FROM " & rstDel!TableName, _
               adCmdText + adExecuteNoRecords
             ' Go to the next row
             rstDel.MoveNext
           Loop
           ' Figure out the path to the backend data
           ' Could open the ADOX Catalog to do this, but DAO database is easier
21         strBackEndPath = Mid(db.TableDefs("tblContacts").Connect, 11)
           ' Figure out the backend folder
22         strBackEndFolder = Left(strBackEndPath, _
             InStrRev(strBackEndPath, "\"))
           ' Calculate a "compact to" database name
           strNewDb = "TempContact" & Format(Now, "hhnnss") & ".mdb"
           ' Compact the database into a new name
23         DBEngine.CompactDatabase strBackEndPath, _
             strBackEndFolder & strNewDb
           ' Delete the old one
24         Kill strBackEndPath
           ' Rename the new
           Name strBackEndFolder & strNewDb As strBackEndPath
25       End If
26     End If
       ' Initialize the randomizer on system clock
27     Randomize
       ' Open all output recordsets
28     rstCo.Open "tblCompanies", cn, adOpenKeyset, adLockOptimistic
       rstCn.Open "tblContacts", cn, adOpenKeyset, adLockOptimistic
       rstCoCn.Open "tblCompanyContacts", cn, adOpenKeyset, adLockOptimistic
       rstCnEv.Open "tblContactEvents", cn, adOpenKeyset, adLockOptimistic
       ' Open the random recordsets
       rstZipRandom.Open "zqryRandomZips", cn, adOpenKeyset, adLockOptimistic
       rstCoRandom.Open "zqryRandomCompanies", cn, _
         adOpenKeyset, adLockOptimistic
       rstPRandom.Open "zqryRandomNames", cn, adOpenKeyset, adLockOptimistic
       ' Open the Events/products list
       rstEvents.Open "zqryEventsProducts", cn, adOpenKeyset, adLockOptimistic
       ' Move to the end to get full recordcount
       rstEvents.MoveLast
       ' Turn on the hourglass
```

```
29    DoCmd.Hourglass True
      ' Initialize the status bar
30    varRtn = SysCmd(acSysCmdInitMeter, "Creating Companies...", _
      intNumCompanies)
      ' Outer loop to add Companies
31    For intI = 1 To intNumCompanies
      ' Start a new company record
      rstCo.AddNew
      ' First, get a random company type
32    intCoType = Int((4 * Rnd) + 1)
      ' Clear the saved website
      strWebsite = ""
      ' Generate a name based on type
33    Select Case intCoType
        ' City
        Case 1
          strCompanyName = rstZipRandom!City & " City Police Dept."
        ' County
        Case 2
          strCompanyName = rstZipRandom!County & " County Sheriff"
        ' State
        Case 3
          strCompanyName = rstZipRandom!StateName & " State Highway Patrol"
        Case 4
          ' Grab the next random "company" name
          strCompanyName = rstCoRandom!CompanyName & " K-9 Training"
          ' .. and the website
          rstCo!Website = rstCoRandom!CompanyName & "#" & _
              rstCoRandom!Web & "##" & rstCoRandom!CompanyName & " Website"
          strWebsite = rstCo!Website
          ' .. and move to the next row
          rstCoRandom.MoveNext
      End Select
34    rstCo!CompanyName = strCompanyName
      ' Generate a random street number
35    intR = Int((7 * Rnd) + 1)
      strCoAddress = Mid(strDigits, intR, 4)
      ' Now pick a random street name
      intR = Int((9 * Rnd) + 1)
      strCoAddress = strCoAddress & " " & strStreetNames(intR)
      ' and street type
      intR = Int((5 * Rnd) + 1)
      strCoAddress = strCoAddress & " " & strStreetTypes(intR)
      rstCo!Address = strCoAddress
      ' Fill in random values from the zip code table
36    rstCo!City = rstZipRandom!City
      rstCo!County = rstZipRandom!County
      rstCo!StateOrProvince = rstZipRandom!State
      rstCo!PostalCode = rstZipRandom!ZipCode
      ' Generate a random Area Code
37    intR = Int((8 * Rnd) + 1)
      strAreaCode = Mid(strDigits, intR, 3)
      ' Generate a random phone number (0100 - 0148)
      intR = Int((48 * Rnd) + 1) + 100
```

Chapter 22

841

```
        strThisPhone = strAreaCode & "555" & Format(intR, "0000")
        rstCo!PhoneNumber = strThisPhone
        ' Add 1 for the fax number
        strThisFax = strAreaCode & "555" & Format(intR + 1, "0000")
        rstCo!FaxNumber = strThisFax
        ' Save the new Company ID
38      lngThisCompany = rstCo!CompanyID
        ' .. and save the new Company
        rstCo.Update
        ' Now, do some contacts for this company
        '  - calc a random number of contacts
39      intJ = Int((intNumContacts * Rnd) + 1)
        ' Set up the recordset of Zips "close" to the Work Zip
40      rstZipClose.Open "SELECT * FROM tlkpZips " & _
          "WHERE ZipCode BETWEEN '" & _
          Format(CLng(rstZipRandom!ZipCode) - 5, "00000") & _
          "' AND '" & Format(CLng(rstZipRandom!ZipCode) + 5, "00000") & _
          "'", cn, adOpenKeyset, adLockOptimistic
        ' Move to last row to get accurate count
        rstZipClose.MoveLast
        ' Make the first contact the company default
        intDefault = True
        ' Loop to add contacts
41      For intK = 1 To intJ
          ' Start a new record
          rstCn.AddNew
          ' Put in the name info from the random people record
42        rstCn!LastName = rstPRandom!LastName
          rstCn!FirstName = rstPRandom!FirstName
          rstCn!MiddleInit = rstPRandom!MiddleInit
          rstCn!Suffix = rstPRandom!Suffix
          ' Select title  and picture based on gender of person
43        If rstPRandom!Sex = "f" Then
            ' Pick a random female title and picture
            intR = Int((7 * Rnd) + 1)
            rstCn!Title = strFTitles(intR)
            ' Make sure we have some picture file names
            If intFPicCount <> 0 Then
              ' Pick a random file name
              intR = Int((intFPicCount * Rnd) + 1)
              strPicPath = strFPicture(intR)
            Else
              ' Set empty picture name
              strPicPath = ""
            End If
44        Else
            ' Pick a random male title and picture
            intR = Int((6 * Rnd) + 1)
            rstCn!Title = strMTitles(intR)
            ' Make sure we have some picture file names
            If intMPicCount <> 0 Then
              ' Pick a random file name
              intR = Int((intMPicCount * Rnd) + 1)
              strPicPath = strMPicture(intR)
```

```
            Else
              ' Set empty picture name
              strPicPath = ""
            End If
45          End If
            ' If company type is training
46          If intCoType = 4 Then
              ' Set contact type to Trainer
              rstCn!ContactType = "Trainer"
              ' Copy the company website
              rstCn!Website = strWebsite
              ' Set up a dummy email
              rstCn!EmailName = rstPRandom!FirstName & _
                " " & rstPRandom!LastName & "#mailto:" & _
                Left(rstPRandom!FirstName, 1) & rstPRandom!LastName & _
                "@" & Mid(strWebsite, InStr(strWebsite, "http://www.") + 11)
              ' strip off the trailing "/"
              rstCn!EmailName = Left(rstCn!EmailName, Len(rstCn!EmailName) - 1)
            Else
              ' Otherwise use generic "Customer"
              rstCn!ContactType = "Customer"
            End If
            ' Pick a random birth date between Jan 1, 1940 and Dec 31, 1979
            ' There are 14,610 days between these dates
            intR = Int((14610 * Rnd) + 1)
            rstCn!BirthDate = #12/31/1939# + intR
            ' Set Default Address to 'work'
            rstCn!DefaultAddress = 1
            ' Copy work address from Company
            rstCn!WorkAddress = strCoAddress
            rstCn!WorkCity = rstZipRandom!City
            rstCn!WorkStateOrProvince = rstZipRandom!State
            rstCn!WorkPostalCode = rstZipRandom!ZipCode
            rstCn!WorkPhone = strThisPhone
            rstCn!WorkFaxNumber = strThisFax
            ' Generate a random street number for home address
            intR = Int((7 * Rnd) + 1)
            strPAddress = Mid(strDigits, intR, 4)
            ' Now pick a random street name
            intR = Int((9 * Rnd) + 1)
            strPAddress = strPAddress & " " & strStreetNames(intR)
            ' and street type
            intR = Int((5 * Rnd) + 1)
            strPAddress = strPAddress & " " & strStreetTypes(intR)
            rstCn!HomeAddress = strPAddress
            ' Position to a "close" random zip
48          intR = rstZipClose.RecordCount
            intR = Int(intR * Rnd)
            rstZipClose.MoveFirst
            If intR > 0 Then rstZipClose.Move intR
            rstCn!HomeCity = rstZipClose!City
            rstCn!HomeStateOrProvince = rstZipClose!State
            rstCn!HomePostalCode = rstZipClose!ZipCode
            ' Generate a random phone number (0150 - 0198)
```

Chapter 22

```
                          intR = Int((48 * Rnd) + 1) + 149
                          rstCn!HomePhone = strAreaCode & "555" & Format(intR, "0000")
                          ' Add 1 for the fax number
                          rstCn!MobilePhone = strAreaCode & "555" & Format(intR + 1, "0000")
                          ' Save the new contact ID
                  49      lngThisContact = rstCn!ContactID
                          ' Finally, save the row
                          rstCn.Update
                          ' If got a random photo name, load it
                  50      If strPicPath <> "" Then
                            ' Open the special photo editing form on the new row
                  51        DoCmd.OpenForm "zfrmLoadPhoto", _
                              WhereCondition:="ContactID = " & lngThisContact, _
                              WindowMode:=acHidden
                            ' Set the picture path in SourceDoc property
                            Forms!zfrmLoadPhoto!Photo.SourceDoc = CurrentProject.Path & _
                              "\Pictures\" & strPicPath
                            ' Set type to embedded
                            Forms!zfrmLoadPhoto!Photo.OLETypeAllowed = acOLEEmbedded
                            ' Get it added to row by setting Action
                            Forms!zfrmLoadPhoto!Photo.Action = acOLECreateEmbed
                            ' Close the form (which will save the picture)
                            DoCmd.Close acForm, "zfrmLoadPhoto"
                          End If
                          ' Insert linking CompanyContact record
                  52      rstCoCn.AddNew
                          ' Set the Company ID
                          rstCoCn!CompanyID = lngThisCompany
                          ' Set the Contact ID
                          rstCoCn!ContactID = lngThisContact
                          ' Make this the default company for the contact
                          rstCoCn!DefaultForContact = True
                          ' Set default for company - 1st contact will be the default
                          rstCoCn!DefaultForCompany = intDefault
                          ' Reset intDefault after first time through
                          intDefault = False
                          ' Save the linking row
                          rstCoCn.Update
                          ' Now, do some contacts events for this contact
                          '  - calc a random number of events
                  53      intM = Int((intNumEvents * Rnd) + 1)
                          ' Clear the Products sold string
                          strProducts = ""
                          ' Loop to add some events
                  54      For intL = 1 To intM
                            ' Start a new row
                            rstCnEv.AddNew
                            ' Set the Contact ID
                            rstCnEv!ContactID = lngThisContact
                            ' Calculate a random number of days
                            intR = Int(intNumDays * Rnd)
                            datCurrentDate = datBeginDate + intR
                            ' Calculate a random time between 8am and 8pm (no seconds)
                            datCurrentTime = CDate(Format(((0.5 * Rnd) + 0.3333), "hh:nn"))
```

Chapter 22

```
              ' Set the contact date/time
              rstCnEv!ContactDateTime = datCurrentDate + datCurrentTime
55 TryAgain:
              ' Position to a random event
56            intR = rstEvents.RecordCount
              intR = Int(intR * Rnd)
              rstEvents.MoveFirst
              If intR > 0 Then rstEvents.Move intR
              ' If a product sale event,
57            If (rstEvents!ContactEventProductSold = True) Then
                  ' Can't sell the same product twice to the same contact
                  If InStr(strProducts, _
                    Format(rstEvents!ContactEventProductID, "00")) <> 0 Then
                    ' ooops.  Loop back to pick a different event
58                  GoTo TryAgain
                  End If
              End If
              ' Set the Event Type
59            rstCnEv!ContactEventTypeID = rstEvents!ContactEventTypeID
              ' Set the follow-up
              rstCnEv!ContactFollowUp = rstEvents!ContactEventRequiresFollowUp
              ' Set the follow-up date
              If (rstEvents!ContactEventRequiresFollowUp = True) Then
                  rstCnEv!ContactFollowUpDate = datCurrentDate + _
                    rstEvents!ContactEventFollowUpDays
              End If
              ' Save the record
60            rstCnEv.Update
              ' If this event is a product sale,
61            If (rstEvents!ContactEventProductSold = True) Then
                  ' Call the routine to also add a product record!
                  varRtn = Add_Product(lngThisCompany, lngThisContact, _
                    rstEvents!ContactEventProductID, datCurrentDate)
                  ' Add the product to the products sold string
                  strProducts = strProducts & " " & _
                    Format(rstEvents!ContactEventProductID, "00")
              End If
              ' Loop to do more events
62            Next intL
          ' Move to the next random person record
63        rstPRandom.MoveNext
          ' and loop to do more contacts
64        Next intK
65        rstZipClose.Close
          Set rstZipClose = Nothing
          ' Move to the next random zip record
66        rstZipRandom.MoveNext
          ' Update the status bar
67        varRtn = SysCmd(acSysCmdUpdateMeter, intI)
      ' Loop until done
68    Next intI
      ' Clear the status bar
69    varRtn = SysCmd(acSysCmdClearStatus)
      ' Done with error trapping, too
```

Chapter 22

845

```
       On Error GoTo 0
       ' Be nice and close everything up
       rstCo.Close
       Set rstCo = Nothing
       rstCn.Close
       Set rstCn = Nothing
       rstCoCn.Close
       Set rstCoCn = Nothing
       rstCnEv.Close
       Set rstCnEv = Nothing
       rstZipRandom.Close
       Set rstZipRandom = Nothing
       rstCoRandom.Close
       Set rstCoRandom = Nothing
       ' Turn off the hourglass
70     DoCmd.Hourglass False
       MsgBox "Done!", vbExclamation, gstrAppTitle
       DoCmd.Close acForm, Me.Name
       Exit Sub
71 BailOut:
       MsgBox "Unexpected error: " & Err & ", " & Error
       ' Turn off the hourglass
       DoCmd.Hourglass False
       varRtn = SysCmd(acSysCmdClearStatus)
       Exit Sub
72 End Sub
```

Table 22-5 lists the statement line numbers and explains the code on key lines in the preceding Visual Basic code example.

Table 22-5. Explanation of Code in Example to Load Random Data

Line	Explanation
1	Declare the beginning of the subroutine. The subroutine has no arguments.
2	You can begin a comment anywhere on a statement line by preceding the comment with a single quotation mark. You can also create a comment statement using the Rem statement.
3	Declare local variables for an ADO Connection object, a DAO Database object, and all the ADO Recordset objects used in this code.
4	Beginning of the declarations of all local variables. You should always explicitly define variables in your code.
5	This procedure uses several arrays in which it stores street names, street types, male person titles, female person titles, and the paths to male and female pictures. Code later in the procedure randomly chooses values from these arrays.
6	Set an error trap; the BailOut label is at line 71.
7	Code to initialize the arrays begins here. Note that separate arrays handle male and female titles.

Table 22-5. Explanation of Code in Example to Load Random Data

Line	Explanation
8	Use the Dir function to find available male picture names in the Pictures sub-folder under the location of the current database. Note that if you move the sample database, this code won't find any pictures to load. When Dir finds a matching file, it returns the file name as a string. The code subsequently calls Dir with no arguments inside the following loop to ask for the next picture.
9	Begin a loop to load male pictures, and keep looping until the picture file name is an empty string (Dir found no more files).
10	Note the use of ReDim Preserve to dynamically expand the existing file name array for male pictures without losing any entries already stored.
11	End of the loop started at statement number 9.
12	This loop finds all the female pictures available and loads them into the array that holds picture file names for females.
13	End of the loop started at statement number 12.
14	The next several lines of code capture the values from the form. Validation rules in the form controls make sure that the data is valid.
15	Initialize the database and connection objects.
16	Check to see if you selected the option to delete all existing rows.
17	Use the MsgBox function to verify that you really want to delete existing data.
18	Table ztblDeleteSeq contains the table names in a correct sequence for deletes from the bottom up so that this code doesn't violate any referential integrity rules.
19	Start a loop to process all the table names in ztblDeleteSeq.
20	Use the Execute method of the Connection object to run the DELETE SQL commands.
21	Figure out the path to the linked data file by examining the Connect property of one of the linked tables.
22	Extract the folder name of the data file using the Left and InStrRev functions.
23	Use the CompactDatabase method of the DBEngine object to compact the data file into a new one—TempContact*hhmmss*.mdb—where *hhmmss* is the current time to avoid conflicts.
24	Use the Kill command to delete the old file and the Name command to rename the compacted temp copy.
25	Terminate the If statement on line 17.
26	Terminate the If statement on line 16.
27	Initialize the randomizer so that all random recordsets are always different.
28	Open all the recordsets needed in this code.
29	Turn the mouse pointer into an hourglass to let you know the transaction is under way and might take a while. You could also set the Screen.MousePointer property to 11 (busy).

Chapter 22

Table 22-5. **Explanation of Code in Example to Load Random Data**

Line	Explanation
30	The SysCmd utility function provides various useful options such as finding out the current directory for msaccess.exe (the Microsoft Access main program), and the current version of Access. It also has options to display messages and a progress meter on the status bar. This code calls SysCmd to initialize the progress meter you see as the code loads the data.
31	Start the main loop to load company data.
32	Use the Rnd function to calculate an index into the array containing the four possible company types—a city, county, or state police department, or a canine training company. Remember, LawTrack sells software to help police agencies track the activities of their canine patrol teams or to help canine trainers keep training and medical records for dogs.
33	Use a Select Case statement to evaluate the company type and create the company name. When the company type is a city, county, or state police department, the code chooses the next row from the query that returns random ZIP code data. When the company type is a training facility, the code chooses the next random company name and also generates a fake Web site address.
34	Set the generated company name in the new company record.
35	The next several lines of code use the Rnd function to randomly generate a four-digit street address and randomly choose a street name and street type from the arrays loaded earlier.
36	Grab the city, county, state, and ZIP code from the current row in the random ZIP code query.
37	Use Rnd again to generate a phone area code and phone and fax numbers.
38	The primary key of tblCompanies is an AutoNumber field. Access automatically generates the next number as soon as you update any field in a new record. This code saves the new company ID to use in related records and writes the company record with the Update method.
39	Calculate a random number of contacts to load for the new company based on the maximum you specified in the form.
40	Open a recordset that chooses the ZIP codes that are 5 higher or lower than the random ZIP code for the company. (It makes sense that the employees of the company live nearby.)
41	Start the loop to add contacts for this company.
42	Update the new contacts record with a random name plucked from the random person names query.
43	The records in the ztblPeople table have a gender field to help choose an appropriate title and picture for the contact. The statements following this If statement load female data, and the statements following the Else statement on line 44 load male data.

Table 22-5. Explanation of Code in Example to Load Random Data

Line	Explanation
44	This Else statement matches the If on line 43. Statements following this choose male data.
45	This End If closes the If on line 43.
46	If the company type is training, then also generate a special contact type and a dummy e-mail name.
47	Finish generating fields for the contacts record, including a random birth date and addresses.
48	Choose a random ZIP code for the contact near the company ZIP code from the recordset opened on line 40. Also generate phone and fax numbers.
49	The primary key for tblContacts is also an AutoNumber field, so save the new value to use to generate related records and save the new contact.
50	If the code found a good picture file name earlier (male or female), then the following code adds that picture to the record.
51	There's no good way to load an OLE Object data type field using recordsets. The following code opens a special form in hidden mode to save the picture. The code opens the form to edit the contacts record just saved and uses a Bound Object Frame control on the form to get the job done. After setting the control's SourceDoc property and specifiying that the picture is to be embedded, the code asks the control to store the picture by setting its Action property.
52	Create the linking record in tblCompanyContacts from the saved CompanyID and ContactID. The first contact created is always the default contact for the company.
53	Calculate a random number of events to load for this contact.
54	Start the loop to add contact events. The following several lines calculate a random contact date and time within the range you specified on the form.
55	Code at line 58 goes here if the random product picked was already sold to this contact.
56	Choose a random event.
57	If the random event is a product sale, verify that this product isn't already sold to this contact. A product can be sold to a contact only once.
58	The code loops back up to line 55 to choose another event if this is a duplicate product.
59	Finish updating the fields in the new contact event record.
60	Save the new contact event.
61	If the event was a product sale, call the Add_Product function that's also in this form module to add a row to tblContactProducts. This code passes the company ID, contact ID, product ID, and the date of the event to the function. It also saves the product ID to be sure it isn't sold again to this contact.
62	This Next statement closes the loop started on line 54.

Table 22-5. Explanation of Code in Example to Load Random Data

Line	Explanation
63	Move to the next random person record.
64	Loop back up to line 41.
65	Close the recordset of ZIP codes close to the company ZIP code.
66	Get the next random ZIP code for the next company.
67	Update the status bar to indicate your're done with another company.
68	Loop back up to line 31.
69	Clear the status bar and close up shop.
70	Clear the hourglass set on line 29. Also issue the final MsgBox confirming that all data is now loaded. Finally, close this form and exit.
71	Any trapped error comes here. This code simply displays the error, clears the mouse pointer and the status bar, and exits. If you don't reset the mouse pointer and clear the status bar, Access won't do it for you!
72	End of the subroutine.

A Procedure to Examine All Error Codes

In the Housing Reservations database (*Housing.mdb*), I created a function that dynamically creates a new table and then inserts into the table (using DAO) a complete list of all the error codes used by Microsoft Access and the text of the error message associated with each error code. You can find a partial list of the error codes in Help, but the table in the Housing Reservations sample database provides the best way to see a list of all the error codes. You might find this table useful as you begin to create your own Visual Basic procedures and set error trapping in them.

The name of the function is CreateErrTable, and you can find it in the modExamples module. The function statements are listed next. You can execute this function by entering the following in the Immediate window:

```
?CreateErrTable
```

The sample database contains the ErrTable table, so the code will ask you if you want to delete and rebuild the table. You should click Yes to run the code. Again, I've added line numbers to some of the lines in this code listing so that you can follow along with the line-by-line explanations in Table 22-6, which follows the listing.

```
1 Function CreateErrTable ()
    ' This function creates a table containing a list of
    '  all the valid Access application error codes
2   ' Declare variables used in this function
3   Dim dbMyDatabase As DAO.Database, tblErrTable As DAO.TableDef, _
        fldMyField As DAO.Field, idxPKey As DAO.Index
4   Dim rcdErrRecSet As DAO.Recordset, lngErrCode As Long, _
        intMsgRtn As Integer
```

```
5    Dim varReturnVal As Variant, varErrString As Variant, _
     ws As DAO.Workspace
     ' Create Errors table with Error Code and Error
     ' String fields
     ' Initialize the MyDatabase database variable
     ' to the current database
6    Set dbMyDatabase = CurrentDb
7    Set ws = DBEngine.Workspaces(0)
     ' Trap error if table doesn't exist
     ' Skip to next statement if an error occurs
8    On Error Resume Next
9    Set rcdErrRecSet = _
     dbMyDatabase.OpenRecordset("ErrTable")
10   Select Case Err  ' See whether error was raised
11     Case 0  ' No error-table must exist
12       On Error GoTo 0  ' Turn off error trapping
13       intMsgRtn = MsgBox("ErrTable already " & _
          "exists. Do you want to delete and " & _
          "rebuild all rows?", vbQuestion + vbYesNo)
14       If intMsgRtn = vbYes Then
            ' Reply was YES-delete rows and rebuild
            ' Run quick SQL to delete rows
15         dbMyDatabase.Execute_
            "DELETE * FROM ErrTable;", dbFailOnError
16       Else                  ' Reply was NO-done
17         rcdErrRecSet.Close  ' Close the table
18         Exit Function       ' And exit
19       End If
20     Case 3011, 3078          ' Couldn't find table,
                                ' so build it
21       On Error GoTo 0    ' Turn off error trapping
         ' Create a new table to contain error rows
22       Set tblErrTable = _
         dbMyDatabase.CreateTableDef("ErrTable")
         ' Create a field in ErrTable to contain the
         ' error code
23       Set fldMyField = tblErrTable.CreateField( _
          "ErrorCode", dbLong)
         ' Append "ErrorCode" field to the fields
         ' collection in the new table definition
24       tblErrTable.Fields.Append fldMyField
         ' Create a field in ErrTable for the error
         ' description
25       Set fldMyField = _
         tblErrTable.CreateField("ErrorString", dbText)
         ' Append "ErrorString" field to the fields
         ' collection in the new table definition
26       tblErrTable.Fields.Append fldMyField
         ' Append the new table to the TableDefs
         ' collection in the current database
27       dbMyDatabase.TableDefs.Append tblErrTable
         ' Set text field width to 5" (7200 twips)
         ' (calls sub procedure)
```

Chapter 22

```
28        SetFieldProperty tblErrTable![ErrorString], _
            "ColumnWidth", dbInteger, 7200
          ' Create a Primary Key
29        Set idxPKey = tblErrTable.CreateIndex("PrimaryKey")
          ' Create and append the field to the index fields collection
30        idxPKey.Fields.Append idxPKey.CreateField("ErrorCode")
          ' Make it the Primary Key
          idxPKey.Primary = True
          ' Create the index
31        tblErrTable.Indexes.Append idxPKey
          ' Set recordset to Errors Table recordset
32        Set rcdErrRecSet = _
            dbMyDatabase.OpenRecordset("ErrTable")
33    Case Else
          ' Can't identify the error-write message
          ' and bail out
34        MsgBox "Unknown error in CreateErrTable " & _
            Err & ", " & Error$(Err), 16
35        Exit Function
36    End Select
      ' Initialize progress meter on the status bar
37    varReturnVal = SysCmd(acSysCmdInitMeter, _
        "Building Error Table", 32767)
      ' Turn on hourglass to show this might take a while
38    DoCmd.Hourglass True
      ' Start a transaction to make it go fast
39    ws.BeginTrans
      ' Loop through Microsoft Access error codes,
      ' skipping codes that generate
      ' "Application-defined or object-define error"
      ' message
40    For lngErrCode = 1 To 32767
41      varErrString = AccessError(lngErrCode)
42      If Not IsNothing(varErrString) Then
43        If varErrString <> "Application-" & _
            "defined or object-defined error" Then
              ' Add each error code and string to
              ' Errors table
44          rcdErrRecSet.AddNew
45          rcdErrRecSet("ErrorCode") = lngErrCode
              ' Some error messages are longer
              ' than 255-truncate
46          rcdErrRecSet("ErrorString") = _
              Left(varErrString, 255)
47          rcdErrRecSet.Update
48        End If
49      End If
        ' Update the status meter
50      varReturnVal = SysCmd(acSysCmdUpdateMeter, _
          lngErrCode)
        ' Process next error code
51    Next lngErrCode
52    ws.CommitTrans
      ' Close recordset
```

```
53    rcdErrRecSet.Close
      ' Turn off the hourglass-you're done
54    DoCmd.Hourglass False
      ' And reset the status bar
55    varReturnVal = SysCmd(acSysCmdClearStatus)
      ' Select new table in the Database window
      ' to refresh the list
56    DoCmd.SelectObject acTable, "ErrTable", True
      ' Open a confirmation dialog box
57    MsgBox "Errors table created."
58 End Function
```

Table 22-6 lists the statement line numbers and explains the code on each line in the preceding Visual Basic code example.

Table 22-6. Explanation of Code in Example to Examine Error Codes

Line	Explanation
1	Declare the beginning of the function. The function has no arguments.
2	You can begin a comment anywhere on a statement line by preceding the comment with a single quotation mark. You can also create a comment statement using the Rem statement.
3	Declare local variables for a Database object, a TableDef object, a Field object, and an Index object.
4	Declare local variables for a Recordset object, a Long Integer, and an Integer.
5	Declare local variables for a Variant that is used to accept the return value from the SysCmd function, a Variant that is used to accept the error string returned by the AccessError function, and a Workspace object.
6	Initialize the Database object variable by setting it to the current database.
7	Initialize the Workspace object by setting it to the current workspace.
8	Enable error trapping but execute the next statement if an error occurs.
9	Initialize the Recordset object variable by attempting to open the ErrTable table. If the table does not exist, this generates an error.
10	Call the Err function to see whether an error occurred. The following Case statements check the particular error values that interest you.
11	The first Case statement tests for an Err value of 0, indicating no error occurred. If no error occurred, the table already existed and opened successfully.
12	Turn off error trapping because you don't expect any more errors.
13	Use the MsgBox function to ask whether you want to clear and rebuild all rows in the existing table. The vbQuestion intrinsic constant asks MsgBox to display the question icon, and the vbYesNo intrinsic constant requests Yes and No buttons (instead of the default OK button). The statement assigns the value returned by MsgBox so that you can test it on the next line.

Chapter 22

Table 22-6. Explanation of Code in Example to Examine Error Codes

Line	Explanation
14	If you click Yes, MsgBox returns the value of the intrinsic constant vbYes. (vbYes happens to be the integer value 6, but the constant name is easier to remember than the number.)
15	Run a simple SQL statement to delete all the rows in the error table.
16	Else clause that goes with the If statement on line 14.
17	Close the table if the table exists and you clicked the No button on line 13.
18	Exit the function.
19	End If statement that goes with the If statement on line 14.
20	Second Case statement. Error codes 3011 and 3078 are both "object not found."
21	Turn off error trapping because you don't expect any more errors.
22	Use the CreateTableDef method on the database to start a new table definition. This is the same as clicking the Tables button in the Database window and then clicking the New button.
23	Use the CreateField method on the new table to create the first field object—a long integer (the intrinsic constant dbLong) named ErrorCode.
24	Append the first new field to the Fields collection of the new Table object.
25	Uses the CreateField method to create the second field—a text field named Error-String.
26	Append the second new field to the Fields collection of the new Table object.
27	Save the new table definition by appending it to the TableDefs collection of the Database object. If you were to halt the code at this point and repaint the Database window, you would find the new ErrTable listed.
28	Call the SetFieldProperty subroutine in this module to set the column width of the ErrorString field to 7200 twips (5 inches). This ensures that you can see most of the error text when you open the table in Datasheet view.
29	Use the CreateIndex method of the TableDef to begin building an index.
30	Create a single field and append it to the Fields collection of the index. The following statement sets the Primary property of the index to True to indicate that this will be the primary key.
31	Save the new primary key index by appending it to the Indexes collection of the TableDef.
32	Open a recordset by using the OpenRecordset method on the table.
33	This Case statement traps all other errors.
34	Show a message box with the error number and the error message.
35	Exit the function after an unknown error.
36	End Select statement that completes the Select Case statement on line 10.

Table 22-6. Explanation of Code in Example to Examine Error Codes

Line	Explanation
37	Call the SysCmd function to place a "building table" message on the status bar, and initialize a progress meter. The CreateErrTable function will look at 32,767 different error codes.
38	Turn the mouse pointer into an hourglass to indicate that this procedure will take a few seconds.
39	Use the BeginTrans method of the Workspace object to start a transaction. Statements within a transaction are treated as a single unit. Changes to data are saved only if the transaction completes successfully with a CommitTrans method. Using transactions when you're updating records can speed performance by reducing disk access.
40	Start a For loop to check each error code from 1 through 32,767.
41	Assign the error text returned by the AccessError function to the variable varErrString.
42	Call the IsNothing function in the modUtility module of the sample database to test whether the text returned is blank. You don't want blank rows, so don't add a row if the AccessError function for the current error code returns a blank string.
43	Lots of error codes are defined as "Application-defined or object-defined error." You don't want any of these, so this statement adds a row only if the AccessError function for the current error code doesn't return this string.
44	Use the AddNew method to start a new row in the table.
45	Set the ErrorCode field equal to the current error code.
46	Some error messages are very long. You want to save only the first 255 characters, so set the ErrorString field equal to the first 255 characters of error text. The text is stored in the varErrString variable.
47	Use the Update method to save the new row.
48	End If statement that completes the If statement on line 43.
49	End If statement that completes the If statement on line 42.
50	After handling each error code, update the progress meter on the status bar to show how far you've gotten.
51	Next statement that completes the For loop begun on line 40. Visual Basic increments lngErrCode by 1 and executes the For loop again until lngErrCode is greater than 32,767.
52	CommitTrans method that completes the transaction begun on line 39.
53	After looping through all possible error codes, close the recordset.
54	Change the mouse pointer back to normal.
55	Clear the status bar.
56	Put the focus on the ErrTable table in the Database window.
57	Display a message box confirming that the function has completed.
58	End of the function.

Chapter 22

> **Note** You can find the ADO equivalent of the previous example in the modExamples module in the LawTrack Contacts sample database.

You should now have a basic understanding of how to create functions and subroutines using Visual Basic. In the next chapter, you'll enhance what you've learned as you study major parts of the LawTrack Contacts, Housing Reservations, and Wedding List applications.

Automating Your Application with Visual Basic

Now that you've learned the fundamentals of using Microsoft Visual Basic, it's time to put this knowledge into practice. In this chapter, you'll learn how to create the Visual Basic code you need to automate many common tasks.

You can find dozens of examples of automation in the LawTrack Contacts, Housing Reservations, and Wedding List sample databases. As you explore the databases, whenever you see something interesting, open the form or report in Design view and take a look at the Visual Basic code behind the form or report. This chapter walks you through a few of the more interesting examples in these databases.

 Note You can find the code explained in this chapter in the LawTrack Contacts (*Contacts.mdb*) and Housing Reservations (*Housing.mdb*) sample applications on the companion CD.

Why Aren't We Using Macros?

Although you can certainly use macros to automate simple applications, macros have certain limitations. For example, as you might have noticed when examining the list of available events in Chapter 21, "Understanding Event Processing," many events require or return parameters that can be passed to or read from a Visual Basic procedure but not a macro. Also, even though you can write a macro to handle general errors in forms and reports, you can't really analyze errors effectively within a macro nor do much to recover from an error. And as you saw in Chapter 21, the debugging facilities for macros are very simplistic.

When to Use Macros

Use macros in your application in any of the following circumstances:

- Your application consists of only a few forms and reports.

- Your application might be used by users unfamiliar with Visual Basic who will want to understand how your application is constructed and possibly modify or enhance it.

- You're developing an application prototype, and you want to rapidly automate a few features to demonstrate your design. However, once you understand Visual Basic, automating a demonstration application is just as easy using event procedures.

- You don't need to trap errors. Keep in mind, though, that any professional-grade Access application should always trap and handle errors and hide most errors from the user.

- You don't need to evaluate or set parameters passed by certain events, such as AfterDel-Confirm, ApplyFilter, BeforeDelConfirm, Error, Filter, KeyDown, KeyPress, KeyUp, MouseDown, MouseMove, MouseUp, NotInList, and Updated.

- You don't need to open and work with recordsets or other objects.

In fact, I can think of only one reason you'll ever need to use a macro: You must write an AutoKeys macro to define any keystrokes that you want to intercept globally in your application. In many cases, you'll find that using Visual Basic code in the KeyPress event of your forms works just as well. In Chapter 24, "The Finishing Touches," you'll learn how to create an AutoKeys macro.

When to Use Visual Basic

Although macros can be useful, a number of tasks cannot be carried out with macros, and there are others that are better implemented using a Visual Basic procedure. Use a Visual Basic procedure instead of a macro in any of the following circumstances:

- You need discrete error handling in your application.

- You want to define a new function.

- You need to handle events that pass parameters or accept return values (other than Cancel).

- You need to create new objects (tables, queries, forms, or reports) in your database from application code.

- Your application needs to interact with another Windows-based program via ActiveX automation or Dynamic Data Exchange (DDE).

- You want to be able to directly call Windows API functions.

- You want to define application code that is common across several applications in a library.

- You want to be able to open and work with data in a recordset on a record-by-record basis.

- You need to use some of the native facilities of the relational database management system that handles your attached tables (such as SQL Server procedures or data definition facilities).

- You want maximum performance in your application. Because modules are compiled, they execute slightly faster than macros. You'll probably notice a difference only on slower processors.

- You are writing a complicated application that will be difficult to debug.

Quite frankly, the ability to trap errors in Visual Basic should be reason enough to use Visual Basic instead of macros. For example, the only way to test some conditions is to set an error trap and then attempt to execute the statement that depends on the condition you want to test. If you trap an error, then you know that the condition failed, and you can write code to deal with the problem.

Assisting Data Entry

You can do a lot to help make sure the user of your application enters correct data by defining default values, input masks, and validation rules. But what can you do if the default values come from a related table? How can you assist a user who needs to enter a value that's not in the row source of a combo box? How do you ensure that the user enters a hyperlink in the correct format? Is there a way you can make it easier for your user to pick dates and times? And how do you show and help the user edit linked picture files? You can find the answers to these questions in the following sections.

Filling In Related Data

If you remember from Chapter 3, "Designing Your Database Application," the tblContact-Products table in the LawTrack Contacts database has a SoldPrice field that reflects the actual sales price at the time of a sale. The tblProducts table has a UnitPrice field that contains the normal selling price of the product. When the user is working in the Contacts form (frm-Contacts) and wants to sell a new product, you don't want the user to have to go look up the current product price before entering it into the record.

You also learned in Chapter 13, "Advanced Form Design," how to build a form with subforms nested two levels to edit contacts, the default company for each contact, and the products sold to that company and registered to the current contact. However, if you open *frmContacts* and click the Products tab, as shown in Figure 23-1 on the next page, you'll notice that there doesn't appear to be any linking company data between contacts and the products sold. (The subform to display contact products isn't nested inside another subform to show the companies for the current contact.) Again, the user shouldn't have to look up the default company ID for the current contact before selling a product.

Chapter 23

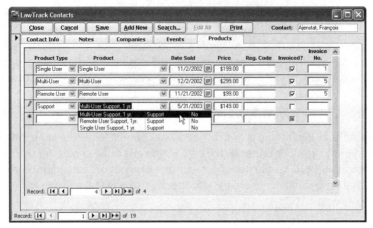

Figure 23-1. Selling a product to a contact involves filling in the price and the default company.

As you can see, a combo box on the subform (fsubContactProducts) helps the user choose the product to sell. Part of the secret to setting the price (the SoldPrice field in tblContact-Products) automatically is in the row source query for the combo box, qlkpProductsFor-Contacts, as shown in Figure 23-2.

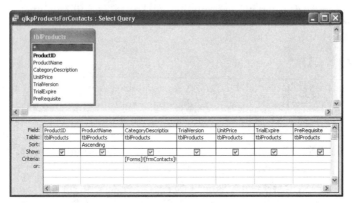

Figure 23-2. The row source for the Product combo box on fsubContactProducts.

You certainly need the ProductID field for the new record in tblContactProducts. Displaying the ProductName field in the combo box is more meaningful than showing the ProductID number, and, as you can see in Figure 23-1, the list in the combo box also shows you the Cat-egoryDescription and whether the product is a trial version. But why did I include the Unit-Price, TrialExpire, and PreRequisite columns in the query's design grid?

As it turns out, you can retrieve any of these fields from the current row in the combo box by referencing the combo box Column property. (You'll see later in this chapter, in "Validating Complex Data," page 878, how other code behind the form uses the additional fields to make sure the contact already owns any prerequisite product.) You can see the simple line of code that copies the UnitPrice field by opening the Visual Basic module behind the fsub-ContactProducts form. Go to the Database window, click Forms on the Object bar, scroll down the list of forms and select the *fsubContactProducts* form, and then click the Code button on the toolbar or choose Code from the View menu. In the Visual Basic Editor (VBE) Code window, scroll down until you find the cmbProductID_AfterUpdate procedure. The code is as follows:

```
Private Sub cmbProductID_AfterUpdate()
  ' Grab the default price from the hidden 5th column
  Me.SoldPrice = Me.cmbProductID.Column(4)
End Sub
```

Notice that you use an index number to fetch the column you want and that the index starts at zero. You can reference the fifth column in the query (UnitPrice) by asking for the Column(4) property of the combo box. Notice also that the code uses the Me shortcut object to reference the form object where this code is running. So, every time you pick a different product, the AfterUpdate event occurs for the ProductID combo box, and this code fills in the related price automatically.

If you open the *frmContacts* form in Design view, select the *fsubContactProducts* form on the Products tab, and examine the Link Child and Link Master properties, you'll find that the two forms are linked on ContactID. However, the tblContactProducts table also needs a CompanyID field in its primary key. Code in the module for the fsubContactProducts form handles fetching the default CompanyID for the current contact, so you don't need an intermediary subform that would clutter the form design. If you still have the module for the *fsubContactProducts* form open in the VBE window, you can find the code in the Form_BeforeInsert procedure. The code is as follows:

```
Private Sub Form_BeforeInsert(Cancel As Integer)
Dim varCompanyID As Variant
  ' First, disallow insert if nothing in outer form
  If IsNothing(Me.Parent.ContactID) Then
    MsgBox "You must define the contact information on a new row before " & _
      "attempting to sell a product", vbCritical, gstrAppTitle
    Cancel = True
    Exit Sub
  End If
  ' Try to lookup this contact's Company ID
  varCompanyID = DLookup("CompanyID", "qryContactDefaultCompany", _
    "(ContactID = " & Me.Parent.ContactID.Value & ")")
  If IsNothing(varCompanyID) Then
    ' If not found, then disallow product sale
    MsgBox "You cannot sell a product to a Contact that does not have a " & _
      "related Company that is marked as the default for this Contact." & _
      "  Press Esc to clear your edits and click on the Companies tab " & _
      "to define the default Company for this Contact.", vbCritical, _
      gstrAppTitle
      Cancel = True
  Else
      ' Assign the company ID behind the scenes
      Me.CompanyID = varCompanyID
  End If
End Sub
```

This procedure executes whenever the user sets any value on a new row in the subform. First, it makes sure that the outer form has a valid ContactID. Next, the code uses the DLookup domain function to attempt to fetch the default company ID for the current contact. The query includes a filter to return only the rows from tblCompanyContacts where the Default-ForContact field is True. If the function returns a valid value, the code sets the required CompanyID field automatically. If it can't find a CompanyID, the code uses the MsgBox statement to tell the user about the error.

> **Note** The IsNothing function that you see used in code throughout all the sample applications is not a built-in Visual Basic function. This function tests the value you pass to it for "nothing"—Null, zero, or a zero-length string. You can find this function in the modUtility standard module in all the sample databases.

Inside Out

Understanding the useful domain functions

Quite frequently in code, in a query, or in the control source of a control on a form or report, you might need to look up a single value from one of the tables or queries in your database. Although you can certainly go to the trouble of defining and opening a recordset in code, Microsoft Access provides a set of functions, called domain functions, that can provide the value you need with a single function call. The available functions are as follows:

Function Name	Description
DFirst, DLast	Return a random value from the specified domain (the table or query that's the record source)
DLookup	Looks up a value in the specified domain
DMax	Returns the highest (Max) value in the specified domain
DMin	Returns the lowest (Min) value in the specified domain
DStDev, DstDevP	Return the standard deviation of a population sample or a population of the specified domain
DSum	Returns the sum of an expression from a domain
DVar, DVarP	Return the variance of a population sample or a population of the specified domain

The syntax to call a domain function is as follows:

```
<function name>(<field expression>, <domain name> [, <criteria> ])
```

where

function name is the name of one of the functions listed above

field expression is a string literal or name of a string variable containing the name of a field or an expression using fields from the specified domain

domain name is a string literal or name of a string variable containing the name of a table or query in your database

criteria is a string literal or name of a string variable containing a Boolean comparison expression to filter the records in the domain

Note that when a domain function finds no records, the returned value is a Null, so you should always assign the result to a Variant data type variable. When you construct a criteria expression, you must enclose string literals in quotes and date/time literals in the # character. (If you use double quotes to delimit the criteria string literal, then use single quotes around literals inside the string, and vice versa.) For example, to find the lowest work postal code value for all contacts where contact type is customer and the birth date is before January 1, 1970, enter:

```
DMin("WorkPostalCode", "tblContacts", "[ContactType] = 'customer' And
[BirthDate] < #01/01/1970#")
```

Handling the NotInList Event

In almost every data entry form you'll ever build, you'll need to provide a way for the user to set the foreign key of the edited record on the *many* side of a relationship to point back to the correct *one* side record—for example, to set the ProductID field in the tblContactProducts table when selling a product on the Products tab of the frmContacts form. But what if the user needs to create a new product? Should the user have to open the form to edit products first to create the new product before selling it? The answer is a resounding no, but you must write code in the NotInList event of the combo box to handle new values and provide a way to create new rows in the tblProducts table.

Figure 23-3 on the next page shows you what happens when the user tries to type a product name that's not already in the tblProducts table. In this case, the customer wants to purchase a two-year support contract instead of the already available one-year product. You can see that something has intercepted the new product name to confirm that the user wants to add the new product.

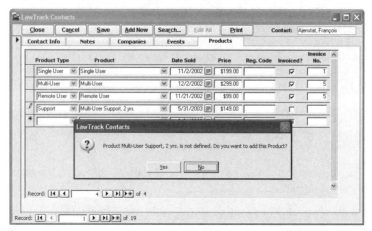

Figure 23-3. Entering a product that isn't defined in the database.

First, the combo box has been defined with its Limit To List property set to Yes. Second, there's an event procedure defined to handle the NotInList event of the combo box, and it is this code that's asking whether the user wants to add a product. If the user clicks Yes to confirm adding this product, the event procedure opens the frmProductAdd form in Dialog mode to let the user enter the new data, as shown in Figure 23-4. Opening a form in Dialog mode forces the user to respond before the application resumes execution. The code that opens this form passes the product name entered and the product type that the user selected before entering a new product name. The user can fill in the price and other details. The user can also click Cancel to avoid saving the record and close the form. If the user clicks Save, the form saves the new product record and closes to allow the code in the NotInList event procedure to continue.

Figure 23-4. The frmProductAdd form open and ready to define the new product.

To see how this works, open the *fsubContactProducts* form in Design view, click the cmb-ProductID combo box, find the NotInList event in the Properties window, and click the Build button to open the code. The code for the procedure is shown below.

```
Private Sub cmbProductID_NotInList(NewData As String, Response As Integer)
Dim strType As String, strWhere As String
    ' User has typed in a product name that doesn't exist
```

```
    strType = NewData
    ' Set up the test predicate
    strWhere = "[ProductName] = """ & strType & """"
    ' Ask if they want to add this product
    If vbYes = MsgBox("Product " & NewData & " is not defined. " & _
      "Do you want to add this Product?", vbYesNo + vbQuestion + _
      vbDefaultButton2, gstrAppTitle) Then
      ' Yup.  Open the product add form and pass it the new name
      ' - and the pre-selected Category
      DoCmd.OpenForm "frmProductAdd", DataMode:=acFormAdd, _
        WindowMode:=acDialog, _
        OpenArgs:=strType & ";" & Me.cmbCategoryDescription
      ' Verify that the product really got added
      If IsNull(DLookup("ProductID", "tblProducts", strWhere)) Then
        ' Nope.
        MsgBox "You failed to add a Product that matched what you entered." & _
          "  Please try again.", vbInformation, gstrAppTitle
        ' Tell Access to continue - we trapped the error
        Response = acDataErrContinue
      Else
        ' Product added OK - tell Access so that combo gets requeried
        Response = acDataErrAdded
      End If
    Else
      ' Don't want to add - let Access display normal error
      Response = acDataErrDisplay
    End If
End Sub
```

As you can see, Access passes two parameters to the NotInList event. The first parameter (NewData) contains the string you typed in the combo box. You can set the value of the second parameter (Response) before you exit the sub to tell Access what you want to do. You wouldn't have access to these parameters in a macro, so you can see that this event requires a Visual Basic procedure to handle it properly.

The procedure first creates the criteria string that it uses later to verify that the user saved the product. Next the procedure uses the MsgBox function to ask whether the user wants to add this product to the database (the result shown in Figure 23-3 on the previous page). If you've ever looked at the MsgBox function Help topic, you know that the second parameter is a number that's the sum of all the options you want. Fortunately, Visual Basic provides named constants for these options, so you don't have to remember the number codes. In this case, the procedure asks for a question mark icon (vbQuestion) and for the Yes and No buttons (vbYesNo) to be displayed. It also specifies that the default button is the second button (vbDefaultButton2)—the No button—just in case the user quickly presses Enter upon seeing the message.

If the user clicks Yes in the message box, the procedure uses DoCmd.OpenForm to open the frmProductAdd form in Dialog mode and passes it the product name entered and the product type selected by setting the form's OpenArgs property. Note the use of the named parameter syntax in the call to DoCmd.OpenForm to make it easy to set the parameters you want. You *must* open the form in Dialog mode. If you don't, your code continues to run while the form opens. Whenever a dialog box form is open, Visual Basic code execution stops until the dialog box closes, which is critical in this case because you need the record to be saved or canceled before you can continue with other tests.

After the frmProductAdd form closes, the next statement calls the DLookup function to verify that the product really was added to the database. If the code can't find a new matching product name (the user either changed the product name in the add form or clicked Cancel), it uses the MsgBox statement to inform the user of the problem and sets a return value in the Response parameter to tell Access that the value hasn't been added but that Access can continue without issuing its own error message (acDataErrContinue).

If the matching product name now exists (indicating the user clicked Save on the frmProduct-Add form), the code tells Access that the new product now exists (acDataErrAdded). Access requeries the combo box and attempts a new match. Finally, if the user replies No in the message box shown in Figure 23-3, the procedure sets Response to acDataErrDisplay to tell Access to display its normal error message.

The other critical piece of code is in the Load event for the frmProductAdd form. The code is as follows:

```
Private Sub Form_Load()
Dim intI As Integer
  If Not IsNothing(Me.OpenArgs) Then
    ' If called from "not in list", Openargs should have
    '    Product Name; Category Description
    ' Look for the semi-colon separating the two
    intI = InStr(Me.OpenArgs, ";")
    ' If not found, then all we have is a product name
    If intI = 0 Then
      Me.ProductName = Me.OpenArgs
    Else
      Me.ProductName = Left(Me.OpenArgs, intI - 1)
      Me.CategoryDescription = Mid(Me.OpenArgs, intI + 1)
      ' lock the category
      Me.CategoryDescription.Locked = True
      Me.CategoryDescription.Enabled = False
      ' .. and clear the tool tip
      Me.CategoryDescription.ControlTipText = ""
    End If
  End If
End Sub
```

If you remember, the cmbProductID NotInList event procedure passes the original string the user entered and selected the product type (the CategoryDescription field) as the OpenArgs parameter to the OpenForm method. This sets the OpenArgs property of the form being opened. The OpenArgs property should contain the new product name, a semicolon, and the selected product type, so the Form_Load procedure parses the product name and product type by using the InStr function to look for the semicolon. (The InStr function returns the offset into the string in the first parameter where it finds the string specified in the second parameter, and it returns 0 if it doesn't find the search string.) The code then uses the two values it finds to set the ProductName and CategoryDescription fields. Also, when the code finds a category description, it locks that combo box so that the user can't change it to something other than what was selected on the new product row in the original form.

Fixing an E-Mail Hyperlink

As you learned in Chapter 7, "Creating and Working with Simple Queries," you should either use the Insert Hyperlink feature or be sure to type a correct protocol when you enter something other than an *http://* address. Your users might not know to type a *mailto:* protocol prefix when entering an e-mail address into a Hyperlink field on one of your forms. However, you can write code to examine the address and fix it before the user saves the record.

One of the forms that has an e-mail address is the frmContacts form in the LawTrack Contacts application. You can find the code that examines and attempts to fix the address in the After Update event procedure for the EmailName text box. (If the user enters some valid protocol other than http:// or mailto:, this code won't alter it.) The code is as follows:

```
Private Sub EmailName_AfterUpdate()
' If you just type in an email name: Somebody@hotmail.com
' Access changes it to: Somebody@hotmail.com#http://somebody@hotmail.com# !!
' This code tries to fix it
Dim intI As Integer
    ' Don't do anything if email is empty
    If IsNothing(Me.EmailName) Then Exit Sub
    ' Fix up http:// if it's there
    Me.EmailName = Replace(Me.EmailName, "http://", "mailto:")
    ' Now look for the first "#" that delimits the hyperlink display name
    intI = InStr(Me.EmailName, "#")
    ' And put the person name there instead if found
    If intI > 0 Then
      Me.EmailName = (Me.FirstName + " ") & Me.LastName & _
        Mid(Me.EmailName, intI)
    End If
End Sub
```

If the user clears the EmailName text box, the code doesn't do anything. If there's something in the text box, the code uses the Replace function to search for an incorrect *http://* and replace it with the correct *mailto:* protocol identifier. As you know, a Hyperlink field can optionally display text instead of the hyperlink, followed by a # character delimiter, and then the actual hyperlink address. The code uses the InStr function to check for the presence of the delimiter. (The InStr function returns the offset into the string in the first parameter where it finds the string specified in the second parameter.) If the code finds the delimiter, it replaces the contents of the field with the person's first and last name as display text followed by the text starting with the # delimiter. (The Mid function called with no length specification—the optional third parameter—returns all characters starting at the specified offset.)

Providing a Graphical Calendar

You can always provide an input mask to help a user enter a date and time value correctly, but it's much more helpful if the user can choose the date using a graphical calendar. Both the

LawTrack Contacts and the Housing Reservations sample applications provide this enhancement. The two applications actually have two different versions of a calendar form—one that employs the Calendar ActiveX control (frmCalendarOCX), and a second (frmCalendar) that uses Visual Basic code to "draw" the calendar on a form using an option group and toggle button controls.

This graphical facility is available in the sample applications wherever you see a small command button next to a date or date/time field on a form. Click the button to open the calendar and set the value. One date field that uses the ActiveX version of the calendar is the Birth Date field on the frmContacts form. You can see the open calendar in Figure 23-5.

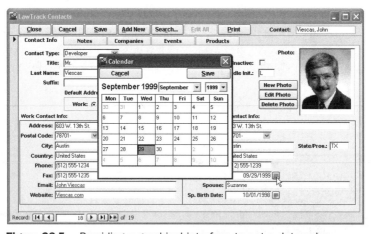

Figure 23-5. Providing a graphical interface to set a date value.

The code in the Click event of this command button calls a public function to open the form and pass it the related control that should receive the resulting date value. You can find this code in the module for the frmContacts form as shown below.

```
Private Sub cmdContactBirthCal_Click()
Dim varReturn As Variant
  ' Clicked the calendar icon asking for graphical help
  ' Put the focus on the control to be updated
  Me.BirthDate.SetFocus
  ' Call the get a date function
  varReturn = GetDateOCX(Me.BirthDate, True)
End Sub
```

When the user clicks the command button, Access moves the focus to it. The code moves the focus back to the date field to be edited and calls the public function where the real action happens. You can find the code for the function GetDateOCX in the modCalendar module, and the code is also listed below.

```
Option Compare Database
Option Explicit
' Place holder for the form class
Dim frmCalOCX As Form_frmCalendarOCX
```

```
' End Declarations Section
Function GetDateOCX(ctlToUpdate As Control, _
  Optional intDateOnly As Integer = 0)
'-----------------------------------------------------------
' Inputs: A Control object containing a date/time value
'         Optional "date only" (no time value) flag
' Outputs: Sets the Control to the value returned by frmCalendar
' Created By: JLV 11/15/02
' Last Revised: JLV 11/15/02
'-----------------------------------------------------------
' Set an error trap
On Error GoTo ProcErr
  ' Open the OCX calendar form by setting a new object
  ' NOTE: Uses a module variable in the Declarations section
  '       so that the form doesn't go away when this code exits
  Set frmCalOCX = New Form_frmCalendarOCX
  ' Call the calendar form's public method to
  ' pass it the control to update and the "date only" flag
  Set frmCalOCX.ctlToUpdate(intDateOnly) = ctlToUpdate
  ' Put the focus on the OCX calendar form
  frmCalOCX.SetFocus
ProcExit:
  ' Done
  Exit Function
ProcErr:
  MsgBox "An error has occurred in GetDateOCX.  " _
    & "Error number " & Err.Number & ": " & Err.Description _
    & vbCrLf & vbCrLf & _
    "If this problem persists, note the error message and " _
    & "call your programmer.", , "Oops . . .      (unexpected error)"
  Resume ProcExit
End Function
```

The function begins by setting an error trap that executes the code at the ProcErr label if anything goes wrong. You might remember from the previous chapter that you can open a form that has code behind it by setting an object to a new instance of the form's class module. This is exactly what this function does to get the form open. In addition, it calls the Property Set procedure for the form's ctlToUpdate property to pass it the control object that should be updated after the user picks a date value. The function also passes along an optional variable to indicate whether the control needs a date and time or a date only (intDateOnly). Once the calendar form is open and has the control it needs to update, this function is finished. Notice that the object variable used to open the form is declared in this module's Declarations section. It cannot be declared inside the function because the variable would go out of scope (and the form would close) when the GetDateOCX function exits.

The final pieces of code that make this all work are in the module behind the frmCalendar-OCX form. You see the portion of the code that initializes the form listed below.

```
Option Compare Database
Option Explicit
' This form demonstrates both using a custom control (MSCal.OCX)
' and manipulating a Class via Property Set
```

Chapter 23

869

```
' See also the GetDateOCX function that activates this form/module.
' Place to save the "date only" indicator
Dim intDateOnly As Integer
' Variable for the Property Set
Dim ctlThisControl As Control
' Optional variable for the Property Set
Dim intSet As Integer
' Place to save the date value
Dim varDate As Variant
' End Declarations Section

Private Sub Form_Load()
  ' Hide myself until properties are set
  Me.Visible = False
End Sub

Public Property Set ctlToUpdate(Optional intD As Integer = 0, ctl As Control)
' This procedure is called as a property of the Class Module
' GetDateOCX opens this form by creating a new instance of the class
'  and then sets the required properties via a SET statement.
' First, validate the kind of control passed
  Select Case ctl.ControlType
    ' Text box, combo box, and list box are OK
    Case acTextBox, acListBox, acComboBox
    Case Else
      MsgBox "Invalid control passed to the Calendar."
      DoCmd.Close acForm, Me.Name
  End Select
  ' Save the pointer to the control to update
  Set ctlThisControl = ctl
  ' Save the date only value
  intDateOnly = intD
  ' If "date only"
  If (intDateOnly = -1) Then
    ' Resize my window
    DoCmd.MoveSize , , , 3935
    ' Hide some stuff just to be sure
    Me.txtHour.Visible = False
    Me.txtMinute.Visible = False
    Me.lblColon.Visible = False
    Me.lblTimeInstruct.Visible = False
    Me.SetFocus
  End If
  ' Set the flag to indicate we got the pointer
  intSet = True
  ' Save the "current" value of the control
  varDate = ctlThisControl.Value
  ' Make sure we got a valid date value
  If Not IsDate(varDate) Then
    ' If not, set the default to today
    varDate = Now
    Me.Calendar1.Value = Date
    Me.txtHour = Format(Hour(varDate), "00")
    Me.txtMinute = Format(Minute(varDate), "00")
```

Chapter 23

```
    Else
        ' Otherwise, set the date/time to the one in the control
        ' Make sure we have a Date data type, not just text
        varDate = CDate(varDate)
        Me.Calendar1.Value = varDate
        Me.txtHour = Format(Hour(varDate), "00")
        Me.txtMinute = Format(Minute(varDate), "00")
    End If
End Property
```

I know it looks complicated, but it really isn't. The first event that happens is the Load event
for the form, and code in that event procedure hides the form until the GetDateOCX function uses the Property Set statement to pass the control to update to the form. The ctlTo-
Update Property Set procedure saves the control object (the control next to the button the
user clicked on the form) in a variable in the Declarations section. If the optional int-
DateOnly variable is True (the control needs only a date value, not a date and time value), the
form shrinks to hide those text boxes. (You can see these controls if you open *frmCalendar-
OCX* in Design view.) Next, it checks to see if the control already has a value, and initializes
the calendar value and two text boxes to display an optional hour and minute using either the
value already in the control or the system date and time.

After the initialization code finishes, the form waits until the user enters a value and clicks
Save or decides not to change the value by clicking Cancel. The code for the two procedures
that respond to the command buttons is as follows:

```
Public Sub cmdCancel_Click()
    ' Close without saving
    DoCmd.Close acForm, Me.Name
End Sub

Private Sub cmdSave_Click()
' Saves the changed value back in the calling control
' Do some error trapping here in case the calling control can't
' accept a date/time value.
    On Error GoTo Save_Error
    ' Make sure we got a valid control to point to
    If intSet Then
        ' OK - save the value
        If (intDateOnly = -1) Then
            ' Passing back date only
            ctlThisControl.Value = Me.Calendar1.Value
        Else
            ' Do date and time
            ctlThisControl.Value = Me.Calendar1.Value + _
                TimeValue(Me.txtHour & ":" & Me.txtMinute)
        End If
    End If
Save_Exit:
    DoCmd.Close acForm, Me.Name
    Exit Sub
Save_Error:
    MsgBox "An error occurred attempting to save the date value.", _
```

```
    vbCritical, gstrAppTitle
    ErrorLog "frmCalendarOCX_Save", Err, Error
    Resume Save_Exit
End Sub
```

Clicking the Cancel button (cmdCancel_Click) simply closes the form without changing any value in the control passed to the form. The code that saves the value the user selects on the graphical calendar is in the Click event for the cmdSave command button. This code verifies that the Property Set procedure executed correctly and then saves the selected value back into the control object—which happens to point to the control on the form that should be updated.

Inside Out

ActiveX or not ActiveX, that is the question!

If you look behind all the little calendar buttons that activate a graphical way to set a date or date/time value, you'll find that only the button next to the Birth Date field on the frm-Contacts form uses the ActiveX version of the calendar discussed in this chapter. All the others use the custom form I designed with some complex code to actually build and manipulate a calendar created with an option group control. So why did I do that?

As you learned in Chapter 13, "Advanced Form Design," you can probably find dozens of ActiveX controls registered on your machine, but only some of them work in Access. To complicate matters, Microsoft has issued different versions of some of these controls with each new version of Microsoft Access. You can use these controls with confidence if you're installing your application on a machine that has the same version and service pack level of Access that you used to create the application. However, if you install your application in Runtime mode on a machine that has a different version of Access installed, your ActiveX control might not work at all. (See Chapter 31, "Distributing Your Application," for details about creating a distributable installation of your application.) The user sees a "Can't create object" error message when opening a form that uses the ActiveX control.

I discovered that even the simple Calendar ActiveX control was giving me problems when I tried to distribute applications that used it. So, I came up with a way to provide a very similar interface using standard Access controls and Visual Basic. This is why most of the calendar buttons use my custom form (frmCalendar) instead of the form that depends on the ActiveX control. I recommend that you try the ActiveX control first. If you find that your application has problems on some machines on which you attempt to install your application, you might need to get creative and build your own solution using native Access tools.

Working with Linked Photos

Although you can certainly store and display photos in an Access application using the OLE Object data type, if your application might need to interact with a Web application, you cannot use this feature. Web applications, including data access pages, cannot handle the internal format of a stored OLE Object data type. Also, if your application needs to handle hundreds or thousands of photos, you could easily exceed the two gigabyte file size limit for an mdb file. The alternative method is to store the pictures as files and save the picture path as a text field in your tables. However, you'll need to write code in your desktop or project application to display the pictures.

The Housing Reservations database (*Housing.mdb*) is designed to work on the Web. Open the *Housing.mdb* sample database and then open the *frmEmployees* form, as shown in Figure 23-6. The employee picture you see is fetched from the path stored in the Photo field of the table.

Figure 23-6. The picture on the Employees form is loaded from a picture path.

Displaying a Linked Photo

To display an image from a path, you can use the image control. When you first add the control to your form, a wizard asks you for the image you want to display. You can choose any image file on your hard drive just to keep the wizard happy. After the wizard finishes, clear the Picture property of the image control, and reply Yes to the "Do you want to remove this picture from the form?" warning message.

Now, you're ready to write some code to pick up the path and dynamically load the picture into the image control each time the user moves to a new record. You need code similar to the following in the form's Current event procedure:

```
Private Sub Form_Current()
' Load the current image, if any, when moving to new row
Dim strPath As String
  ' If on new record,
  If Me.NewRecord Then
    ' ... then set the message
    Me.lblMsg.Caption = "Click Add to create a photo for this employee."
    ' Make it visible
    Me.lblMsg.Visible = True
```

```
          ' .. and hide the image frame
          Me.imgEmployee.Visible = False
          Exit Sub
      End If
      ' Try to load image - set error trap
      On Error Resume Next
      ' If nothing in the photo text,
      If IsNothing(Me.Photo) Then
          ' ... then set the message
          Me.lblMsg.Caption = "Click Add to create a photo for this employee."
          ' Make it visible
          Me.lblMsg.Visible = True
          ' .. and hide the image frame
          Me.imgEmployee.Visible = False
      Else
          strPath = Me.Photo
          ' Check for characters that indicate a full path
          If (InStr(strPath, ":") = 0) And (InStr(strPath, "\\") = 0) Then
              ' Just a file name, so add the current path
              strPath = CurrentProject.Path & "\" & strPath
          End If
          ' Attempt to assign the file name
          Me.imgEmployee.Picture = UCase(strPath)
          ' If got an error,
          If Err <> 0 Then
              ' ... then set the message
              Me.lblMsg.Caption = "Photo not found.  Click Add to correct."
              ' Make it visible
              Me.lblMsg.Visible = True
              ' .. and hide the image frame
              Me.imgEmployee.Visible = False
          Else
              ' Reveal the picture
              Me.imgEmployee.Visible = True
              ' And set the form palette so the picture displays correctly
              Me.PaintPalette = Me.imgEmployee.ObjectPalette
          End If
      End If
      End Sub
```

> **Note**   You can find the sample code to load a picture in the Form Current event procedure of the *frmEmployees* form. The sample printed here includes only the code to load the picture. The actual procedure includes additional code that tests the authority of the logged-in user and enables or disables editing accordingly.

The code first checks the form's NewRecord property to see if the user has moved to a new row that won't have a picture path stored yet. If so, the code hides the image control, sets the caption of an informative label (the lblMsg control) behind the image and makes the label visible, and then exits the procedure. When not on a new row, the code checks to see if the Photo field that contains the picture path is empty. If so, it hides the image control and displays the message as though the form is on a new record. If there's something in the path, the code checks to see if a full path and file name are stored (a value containing a colon to indicate a drive letter, or a path containing the characters \\ that indicate a Universal Naming Convention path). If the Photo field does not contain what appears to be a full path, the code inserts the path of the current database in front of the file name.

Finally, the code sets an error trap and then attempts to set the Picture property of the image control to the full path to load the picture into the control. If that fails, the code displays a warning message in the label behind the image and hides the image. If the picture load is successful, the code helps ensure that the colors in the picture are true by setting the form's PaintPalette property equal to the color palette used in the image.

Deleting and Updating an Image Path

Clearing the file name saved in the record is the easy part, so let's take a look at that first. Behind the Delete button that you can see on the frmEmployees form, you can find the following code:

```
Private Sub cmdDelete_Click()
' User asked to remove the picture
  ' Clear photo
  Me.txtPhoto = Null
  ' Hide the frame
  Me.imgEmployee.Visible = False
  ' Clear the image
  Me.imgEmployee.Picture = ""
  ' Set the message
  Me.lblMsg.Caption = "Click Add to create a photo for this employee."
  ' Make it visible
  Me.lblMsg.Visible = True
  ' Put focus in a safe place
  Me.FirstName.SetFocus
End Sub
```

When the user clicks the command button asking to delete the photo, the code sets the photo path to Null, hides the image, and displays the informative label. But what if the user deletes the picture and then decides to clear pending edits by pressing the Esc key or by choosing Undo from the Edit menu? You need some code in the form's Undo event to put the picture back. The code you can find in the module for *frmEmployees* is as follows:

```
Private Sub Form_Undo(Cancel As Integer)
Dim strPath As String
' User trying to undo changes.  See if we need to reload the picture
  ' See if Photo has changed
  If Me.txtPhoto = Me.txtPhoto.OldValue Then
    ' Nope - nothing to do
    Exit Sub
  End If
  ' Try to load image - set error trap
  On Error Resume Next
  ' If nothing in the photo text,
  If IsNothing(Me.txtPhoto.OldValue) Then
```

```
          ' ... then set the message
          Me.lblMsg.Caption = "Click Add to create a photo for this employee."
          ' Make it visible
          Me.lblMsg.Visible = True
          ' .. and hide the image frame
          Me.imgEmployee.Visible = False
      Else
          strPath = Me.txtPhoto.OldValue
          ' Check for characters that indicate a full path
          If (InStr(strPath, ":") = 0) And (InStr(strPath, "\\") = 0) Then
              ' Just a file name, so add the current path
              strPath = CurrentProject.Path & "\" & strPath
          End If
          ' Attempt to assign the file name
          Me.imgEmployee.Picture = strPath
          ' If got an error,
          If Err <> 0 Then
              ' ... then set the message
              Me.lblMsg.Caption = "Photo not found.  Click Add to correct."
              ' Make it visible
              Me.lblMsg.Visible = True
              ' .. and hide the image frame
              Me.imgEmployee.Visible = False
          Else
              ' Reveal the picture
              Me.imgEmployee.Visible = True
              ' And set the form palette so the picture displays correctly
              Me.PaintPalette = Me.imgEmployee.ObjectPalette
          End If
      End If
  End Sub
```

Every editable bound control on a form has an OldValue property that tells you the value of the control before the user changed it. When the user hasn't changed the value, the OldValue of the control equals the current value. So, this code checks to see if there's a picture path in the OldValue property of the Photo field that's different from the current value. If so, the code uses the OldValue to reload the picture.

The last tricky part is to provide the user with a way to enter the picture path to add or update a picture in a record. Although you could certainly use the InputBox function to ask the user for the path, it's much more professional to call the Windows Open File dialog box so that the user can navigate to the desired picture using familiar tools. The bad news is that calling any procedure in Windows is complex and usually involves setting up parameter structures and a special declaration of the external function. The good news is Microsoft Office includes a special FileDialog object that greatly simplifies this process. You need to add a reference to the Microsoft Office library to make it easy to use this object—from the VBE window, choose References from the Tools menu and be sure the Microsoft Office 11.0 Object Library is selected. Once you do this, you can include code using the FileDialog object to load a picture path. You can find the following code behind the Click event of the Add button (cmdAdd) in the *frmEmployees* form:

```
Private Sub cmdAdd_Click()
' User asked to add a new photo
Dim strPath As String
  ' Grab a copy of the Office file dialog
  With Application.FileDialog(msoFileDialogFilePicker)
    ' Select only one file
    .AllowMultiSelect = False
    ' Set the dialog title
    .Title = "Locate the Employee picture file"
    ' Set the button caption
    .ButtonName = "Choose"
    ' Make sure the filter list is clear
    .Filters.Clear
    ' Add two filters
    .Filters.Add "JPEGs", "*.jpg"
    .Filters.Add "Bitmaps", "*.bmp"
    ' Set the filter index to 2
    .FilterIndex = 2
    ' Set the initial path name
    .InitialFileName = CurrentProject.Path & "\Pictures"
    ' Show files as thumbnails
    .InitialView = msoFileDialogViewThumbnail
    ' Show the dialog and test the return
    If .Show = 0 Then
      ' Didn't pick a file - bail
      Exit Sub
    End If
    ' Should be only one filename - grab it
    strPath = Trim(.SelectedItems(1))
    ' Set an error trap
    On Error Resume Next
    ' Set the image
    Me.imgEmployee.Picture = strPath
    ' Make sure that "took" OK
    If Err = 0 Then
      ' Got a good file selection ...
      ' See if the photo is in a subpath of this project
      If Left(strPath, Len(CurrentProject.Path)) = CurrentProject.Path Then
        ' Strip it off and store a relative path
        strPath = Mid(strPath, Len(CurrentProject.Path) + 2)
      End If
      ' Set the path in the record
      Me.txtPhoto = strPath
      ' Hide the message
      Me.lblMsg.Visible = False
      ' and reveal the new photo
      Me.imgEmployee.Visible = True
    Else
      ' Oops.
      ' Clear photo
      Me.txtPhoto = Null
      ' Hide the frame
      Me.imgEmployee.Visible = False
      ' Clear the image
```

```
        Me.imgEmployee.Picture = ""
        ' Set the message
        Me.lblMsg.Caption = "Failed to load the picture you selected." & _
           " Click Add to try again."
        ' Make it visible
        Me.lblMsg.Visible = True
      End If
    End With
    ' Put focus in a safe place
    Me.FirstName.SetFocus
End Sub
```

The code establishes a pointer to the FileDialog object using a With statement, sets the various properties of the object including the allowed file extensions and the initial path, and then uses the Show method to display the Windows Open File dialog box. If the file path returned is a subfolder of the current location of the database file, the code stores a relative path and then loads the picture using code similar to that in the form's Current event.

Validating Complex Data

Although you can certainly take advantage of the Input Mask property and the field and table Validation Rule properties, your application often has additional business rules that you can enforce only by adding code behind the forms you provide to edit the data. The following examples show you how several of the business rules in the LawTrack Contacts and Housing Reservations applications are enforced with Visual Basic code.

Checking for Possible Duplicate Names

When you design a table, you should attempt to identify some combination of fields that will be unique across all records to use as your primary key. However, when you create a table to store information about people, you usually create an artificial number as the primary key of the table because you would need to combine many fields to ensure a unique value. Even when you attempt to construct a primary key from first name, last name, address, postal code, and phone number, you still can't guarantee a unique value across all rows.

Using an artificial primary key doesn't mean you should abandon all efforts to identify potentially duplicate rows. Code in the frmContacts form in the LawTrack Contacts application checks the last name the user enters for a new record and issues a warning message if it finds any close names. For example, if the user creates a new record and enters a last name like "Viscas" (assuming my record is still in the table), code behind the form detects the similar name and issues the warning shown in Figure 23-7.

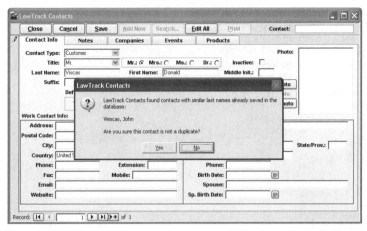

Figure 23-7. Warning you about a potentially duplicate name in the LawTrack Contacts application.

The code searches for potential duplicates by comparing the Soundex codes of the last names. The formula for generating a Soundex code for a name was created by the U.S. National Archives and Records Administration (NARA). Soundex examines the letters by sound and produces a four-character code. When the code for two names match, it's likely that the names are very similar and sound alike. So, by using Soundex, the error-checking code not only finds existing contacts with exactly the same last name but also other contacts whose name might be the same but one or both might be slightly misspelled.

Microsoft Access doesn't provide a built-in Soundex function (SQL Server does), but it's easy to create a simple Visual Basic procedure to generate the code for a name. You can find a Soundex function in the modUtility module in both the LawTrack Contacts and Housing Reservations sample databases. You can find the code that checks for a potentially duplicate name in the Before Update event procedure of the *frmContacts* form. The code is as follows:

```
Private Sub Form_BeforeUpdate(Cancel As Integer)
Dim rst As DAO.Recordset, strNames As String
  ' If on a new row,
  If (Me.NewRecord = True) Then
    ' ... check for similar name
    If Not IsNothing(Me.LastName) Then
      ' Open a recordset to look for similar names
      Set rst = CurrentDb.OpenRecordset("SELECT LastName, FirstName FROM " & _
        "tblContacts WHERE Soundex([LastName]) = '" & _
        Soundex(Me.LastName) & "'")
      ' If got some similar names, collect them for the message
      Do Until rst.EOF
        strNames = strNames & rst!LastName & ", " & rst!FirstName & vbCrLf
        rst.MoveNext
      Loop
      ' Done with the recordset
      rst.Close
      Set rst = Nothing
```

```
            ' See if we got some similar names
            If Len(strNames) > 0 Then
              ' Yup, issue warning
              If vbNo = MsgBox("LawTrack Contacts found contacts with similar " & _
                "last names already saved in the database: " & vbCrLf & vbCrLf & _
                strNames & vbCrLf & _
                "Are you sure this contact is not a duplicate?", _
                vbQuestion + vbYesNo + vbDefaultButton2, gstrAppTitle) Then
                  ' Cancel the save
                  Cancel = True
              End If
            End If
          End If
        End If
End Sub
```

The code checks only when the user is about to save a new row. It opens a recordset to fetch any other contact records where the Soundex code of the last name matches the last name about to be saved. It includes all names it finds in the warning message so that the user can verify that the new contact is not a duplicate. If the user decides not to save the record, the code sets the Cancel parameter to True to tell Access not to save the new contact.

Testing for Related Records When Deleting a Record

You certainly can and should define relationships between your tables and ask Access to enforce referential integrity to prevent saving unrelated records or deleting a record that still has related records in other tables. In most cases, you do not want to activate the cascade delete feature to automatically delete related records. However, Access displays a message "the record cannot be deleted or changed because 'tblXYZ' contains related records" whenever the user tries to delete a record that has dependent records in other tables.

You can do your own testing in code behind your forms in the Delete event and give the user a message that more clearly identifies the problem. For example, here's the code in the Delete event procedure of the *frmContacts* form in the LawTrack Contacts application:

```
Private Sub Form_Delete(Cancel As Integer)
Dim db As DAO.Database, qd As DAO.QueryDef, rst As DAO.Recordset
Dim varRelate As Variant
  ' Check for related child rows
  ' Get a pointer to this database
  Set db = CurrentDb
  ' Open the test query
  Set qd = db.QueryDefs("qryCheckRelateContact")
  ' Set the contact parameter
  qd!ContactNo = Me.ContactID
  ' Open a recordset on the related rows
  Set rst = qd.OpenRecordset()
  ' If we got rows, then can't delete
  If Not rst.EOF Then
    varRelate = Null
    ' Loop to build the informative error message
```

```
   rst.MoveFirst
   Do Until rst.EOF
     ' Grab all the table names
     varRelate = (varRelate + ", ") & rst!TableName
     rst.MoveNext
   Loop
   MsgBox "You cannot delete this Contact because you have " & _
     "related rows in " & _
     varRelate & _
     ". Delete these records first, and then delete the Contact.", _
     vbOKOnly + vbCritical, gstrAppTitle
   ' close all objects
   rst.Close
   qd.Close
   Set rst = Nothing
   Set qd = Nothing
   Set db = Nothing
   ' Cancel the delete
   Cancel = True
   Exit Sub
 End If
 ' No related rows - clean up objects
 rst.Close
 qd.Close
 Set rst = Nothing
 Set qd = Nothing
 Set db = Nothing
 ' No related rows, so OK to ask if they want to delete!
 If vbNo = MsgBox("Are you sure you want to delete Contact " & _
   Me.txtFullName & "?", _
   vbQuestion + vbYesNo + vbDefaultButton2, gstrAppTitle) Then
   Cancel = True
 End If
End Sub
```

The code uses a special UNION parameter query, qryCheckRelateContact, that attempts to fetch related rows from tblCompanyContacts, tblCompanies (the ReferredBy field), tblContactEvents, and tblContactProducts, and returns the name(s) of the table(s) that have any related rows. When the code finds rows returned by the query, it formats a message containing names more meaningful to the user, and it includes all the tables that the user must clear to be able to delete the contact. The standard Access error message lists only the first related table that Access finds. Even when the check for related records finds no problems, the code also gives the user a chance to decide not to delete the contact after all.

Verifying a Prerequisite

In some applications, it makes sense to save a certain type of record only if prerequisite records exist. For example, in a school or seminar registration application, the user might need to verify that the person enrolling has successfully completed prerequisite courses. In the LawTrack Contacts application, it doesn't make sense to sell support for a product that the contact doesn't own. It's not possible to ask Access to perform this sort of test in a validation rule, so you must write code to enforce this business rule.

Figure 23-8 shows you the message the user sees when trying to sell support for a product that the contact doesn't own. This message also appears if the user attempts to sell the special upgrade to the multi-user product, and the contact doesn't already own the prerequisite single-user product.

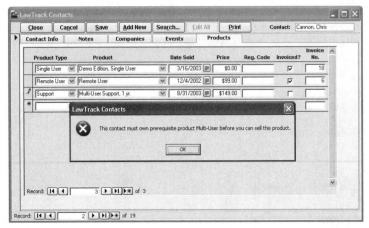

Figure 23-8. Special business rule code won't let you sell a product with a missing prerequisite.

The code that enforces this business rule is in the Before Update event procedure of the fsub-ContactProducts form. The code is as follows:

```
Private Sub Form_BeforeUpdate(Cancel As Integer)
Dim lngPreReq As Long, strPreReqName As String
  ' Check for prerequisite
  If Not IsNothing(Me.cmbProductID.Column(6)) Then
    ' Try to lookup the prerequisite for the contact
    lngPreReq = CLng(Me.cmbProductID.Column(6))
    If IsNull(DLookup("ProductID", "tblContactProducts", _
      "ProductID = " & lngPreReq & " And ContactID = " & _
      Me.Parent.ContactID)) Then
      ' Get the name of the prerequisite
      strPreReqName = DLookup("ProductName", "tblProducts", _
        "ProductID = " & lngPreReq)
      ' Display error
      MsgBox "This contact must own prerequisite product " & strPreReqName & _
        " before you can sell this product.", vbCritical, gstrAppTitle
      ' Cancel the edit
      Cancel = True
    End If
  End If
End Sub
```

Remember from Figure 23-2 that the query providing the row source for the cmbProductID combo box includes any prerequisite product ID in its seventh column. When the code finds a prerequisite, it uses the DLookup function to verify that the current contact already owns the required product. If not, then the code looks up the name of the product, includes it in an error message displayed to the user, and disallows saving the product by setting the Cancel parameter to True. This enforces the business rule and makes it crystal clear to the user what corrective action is necessary.

Maintaining a Special Unique Value

As you learned in Chapter 3, when two subjects are related many-to-many in your database, you must define a linking table to create the relationship. You will often add fields in the linking table to further clarify the relationship between a row in one of the related tables and the matching row in another. Figure 23-9 shows you the table in the LawTrack Contacts application that defines the link between companies and contacts.

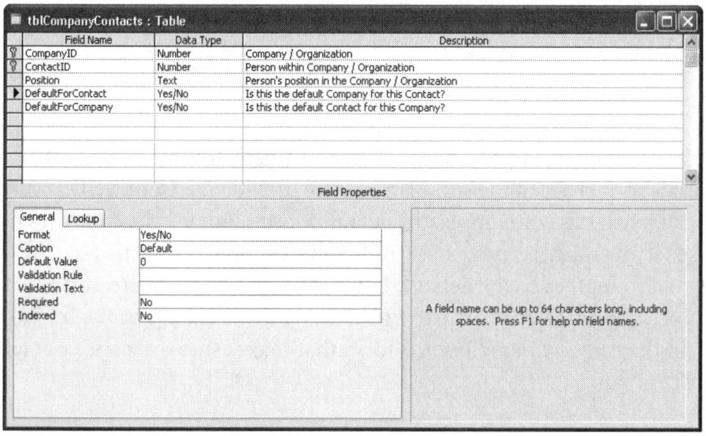

Figure 23-9. The table defining the many-to-many relationship between companies and contacts.

Two special yes/no fields in this table identify which company is the default for a contact and which contact is the default for a company. However, a contact can't have two or more default companies. Likewise, it doesn't make sense for a company to have more than one default contact. To verify this type of special unique value constraint you must add business rules in code behind the forms you provide the user to edit this data.

You can find the code that ensures that there is only one default company for each contact in code behind the fsubContactCompanies form in the LawTrack Contacts sample application (*Contacts.mdb*). The code is in the Before Update event procedure for the DefaultForContact control on the form. The code is as follows:

```
Private Sub DefaultForContact_BeforeUpdate(Cancel As Integer)
    ' Disallow update if there's no Company ID yet
    If IsNothing(Me.CompanyID) Then
        MsgBox "You must select a Company / Organization before" & _
            " you can set Default.", vbCritical, gstrAppTitle
```

```
        Cancel = True
        Exit Sub
    End If
    ' Make sure there's only one default
    ' Check only if setting Default = True
    If (Me.DefaultForContact = True) Then
        ' Try to lookup another contact set Default
        If Not IsNothing(DLookup("ContactID", "tblCompanyContacts", _
            "ContactID = " & Me.Parent.ContactID & _
            " AND CompanyID <> " & Me.CompanyID & _
            " AND DefaultForContact = True")) Then
            ' oops...
            MsgBox "You have designated another Company as the" & _
                " Default for this Contact." & _
                "  You must remove that designation before you" & _
                " can mark this Company as the Default.", _
                vbCritical, gstrAppTitle
            Cancel = True
        End If
    End If
End Sub
```

First, the code verifies that the user has chosen a company for this record. (The Link Child and Link Master properties of the subform control provide the ContactID.) Next, if the user is attempting to mark this company as the default for the contact, the code uses the DLookup function to see if any other record exists (in the tblCompanyContacts table for the current contact) that is also marked as the default. If it finds such a duplicate record, it warns the user and sets the Cancel parameter to True to prevent saving the change to the control. You'll find similar code in the *fsubCompanyContacts* form that makes sure only one contact is the primary for any company.

Checking for Overlapping Data

When you build an application that tracks the scheduling of events or reservations that can span a period of time, you most likely need to make sure that a new event or reservation doesn't overlap with an existing one. This can be a bit tricky, especially when the records you're checking have start and end dates or times.

Of course, the Housing Reservations application (*Housing.mdb*) must make sure that an employee doesn't enter an overlapping reservation request. To see how this works, open the sample database and then open the *frmSplash* form to start the application. Choose any employee name you like from the combo box in the sign-on dialog box (Kevin McDowell is a good choice), type **password** as the password, and click the Sign On button. On the main switchboard, click the Reservation Requests button, and then click Edit All in the Edit Reservation Requests dialog box.

The Reservation Requests form won't let you enter a reservation start date in the past. Click in the blank new row in the list of reservation requests, enter a reservation request for next week for a span of several days, and save the row. (Remember, you can click the Calendar buttons next to the dates to help you choose dates.) Enter another request that overlaps the reservation you just created either at the beginning, the end, or across the middle of the reservation you just entered. Try to save the row, and you should see a warning message similar to the one in Figure 23-10.

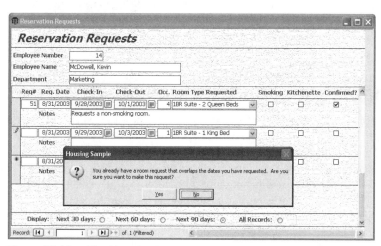

Figure 23-10. The Housing Reservations application displays a warning when you attempt to save an overlapping reservation request.

If you click No, the code cancels your save and returns you to the record to fix it. Notice that you can click Yes to save the duplicate—the application allows this because an employee might want to intentionally reserve two or more rooms on the same or overlapping dates. The code that performs this check in the Before Update event of the fsubReservationRequests form is as follows:

```
Dim varNum As Variant
  ' Check for overlap with existing request
  ' Try to grab RequestID - will be Null on unsaved row
  varNum = Me.RequestID
  If IsNull(varNum) Then varNum = 0 ' Set dummy value
  If Not IsNull(DLookup("RequestID", "tblReservationRequests", _
    "(EmployeeNumber = " & _
    Me.Parent.EmployeeNumber & ") AND (CheckInDate < #" & Me.CheckOutDate & _
    "#) AND (CheckOutDate > #" & Me.CheckInDate & "#) AND (RequestID <> " & _
    varNum & ")")) Then
    If vbNo = MsgBox("You already have a room request " & _
      "that overlaps the dates you have " & _
      "requested.  Are you sure you want to make this request?", _
      vbQuestion + vbYesNo + vbDefaultButton2, gstrAppTitle) Then
      Cancel = True
      Exit Sub
    End If
  End If
```

The code uses the DLookup function to see if another reservation exists (but a different request ID) for the same employee with dates that overlap. The criteria asks for any record that has a check-in date less than the requested check-out date (an employee can legitimately check out and then check back in on the same date) and a check-out date that is greater than the requested check-in date. You might be tempted to build more complex criteria that checks all combinations of reservations that overlap into the start of the requested period, overlap into the end of the requested period, span the entire requested period, or are contained wholly within the requested period, but the two simple tests are all you need. (Draw it out on a sheet of paper if you don't believe me!)

Controlling Tabbing on a Multiple-Page Form

In Chapter 13, "Advanced Form Design," you learned how to create a multiple-page form as one way to handle displaying more data than will fit on one page of a form on your computer screen. You also learned how to control simple tabbing on the form by setting the form's Cycle property to Current Page. One disadvantage of this approach is you can no longer use Tab or Shift+Tab to move to other pages or other records. You must use the Page Up and Page Down keys or the record selector buttons to do that. You can set Cycle to All Records to restore this capability, but some strange things happen if you don't add code to handle page alignment.

To see what happens, open the *frmXmplContactsPages* form in the LawTrack Contacts sample database (*Contacts.mdb*) from the Database window. Move to the last record using the record selector buttons, and press Page Down to move to the Home Address field for the last contact. Next press Shift+Tab once (back tab). Your screen should look something like Figure 23-11.

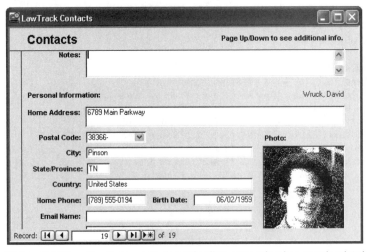

Figure 23-11. The form page doesn't align correctly when you back-tab from the Home Address field in frmXmplContactsPages.

If you leave the Cycle property set to All Records or Current Record, tabbing across page boundaries causes misalignment unless you add some code to fix it. What happens is that Access moves the form display only far enough to show the control you just tabbed to. (In this example, you're tabbing to the Notes text box control.) Open the sample *frmContactsPages* form that has the code to fix this problem and try the same exercise. You should discover that Shift+Tab places you in the Notes field, but the form scrolls up to show you the entire first page.

To allow tabbing across a page boundary while providing correct page alignment, you need event procedures in the Enter event for the first and last controls that can receive the focus on each page. If you examine the code behind the *frmContactsPages* form, you'll find these four procedures:

```
Private Sub ContactID_Enter()
    ' If tabbing forward into this field from previous record
    '  align page 1
    Me.GoToPage 1
End Sub

Private Sub HomeAddress_Enter()
    ' If tabbing forward into this field, align page 2
    Me.GoToPage 2
End Sub

Private Sub Notes_Enter()
    On Error Resume Next
    ' If tabbing backward into the last control on page 1, align it
    Me.GoToPage 1
End Sub

Private Sub Photo_Enter()
    On Error Resume Next
    ' If tabbing backward into the last control on page 2, align it
    Me.GoToPage 2
End Sub
```

This is arguably some of the simplest example code in any of the sample databases, but this attention to detail will make the users of your application very happy.

> **Note** The code also executes when you tab backward into the ContactID and Home-Address controls or forward into the Notes or Photo controls, or you click in any of the controls. Access realizes that the form is already on the page requested in each case, so it does nothing.

Automating Data Selection

One of the most common tasks to automate in a database application is filtering data. Particularly when a database contains thousands of records, users will rarely need to work with more than a few records at a time. If your edit forms always display all the records, performance can suffer greatly. So it's a good idea to enable the user to easily specify a subset of records. This section examines four ways to do this.

Working with a Multiple-Selection List Box

You work with list boxes all the time in Microsoft Windows and in Microsoft Access. For example, the file list in Windows Explorer is a list box, and the List view in the Access Database window is a list box. In the Database window, you can select only one object from the list at a time. If you click a different object, the previous object is no longer selected—this is a simple list box. In Windows Explorer, you can select one file, select multiple noncontiguous files by holding down the Ctrl key and clicking, or select a range of files by holding down the Shift key and clicking—this is a multiple-selection list box.

Suppose you're using the LawTrack Contacts application (*Contacts.mdb*) and you're interested in looking at the details for several contacts at one time but will rarely want to look at the entire list. Start the application by opening the *frmSplash* form, select John Viescas as the User Name, and click Sign On (no password required). Click the Contacts button on the main switchboard form, and the application opens the Select Contacts form (frmContactList). As shown in Figure 23-12, the frmContactList form contains a multiple-selection list box.

> **Note** You won't see the Select Contacts dialog box if the Don't Show Contact List option is selected in my user profile. If the Contacts form opens when you click the Contacts button on the main switchboard, close the form and click the Users button. Clear the Don't Show Contact List option in my profile, save the record, and close the form. You should now see the Select Contacts dialog box when you click the Contacts button on the main switchboard.

Figure 23-12. Selecting multiple contact records to edit.

Chapter 23

In this list box, the contacts are shown in alphabetic order by last name, and the list is bound to the ContactID field in the underlying table. You can edit any single contact by simply double-clicking the person's name. You can move the highlight up or down by using the arrow keys. You can also type the first letter of a contact last name to jump to the next contact whose last name begins with that letter. You can hold down the Shift key and use the arrow keys to extend the selection to multiple names. Finally, you can hold down either the Shift key or the Ctrl key and use the mouse to select multiple names.

Figure 23-12 shows three contacts selected using the Ctrl key and the mouse. When you click the Edit button, the application opens the frmContacts form with only the records you selected. As shown in Figure 23-13, the caption to the right of the Record Number box indicates three available records and that the recordset is filtered.

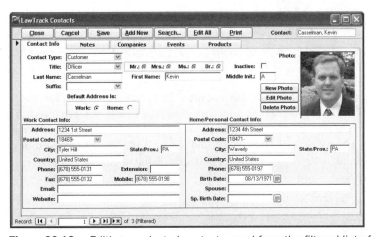

Figure 23-13. Editing a selected contact record from the filtered list of contacts.

To see how this works, you need to go behind the scenes of the frmContactList form. Click Exit on the main switchboard form to return to the Database window. (Click Yes in the "Are you sure you want to exit" dialog box, and click No if the application offers to create a backup for you.) Select *frmContactList*, and open the form in Design view, as shown in Figure 23-14. Click the list box control, and open its property sheet to see how the list box is defined. The list box uses two columns from the qlkpContacts query, hiding the ContactID (the primary key that will provide a fast lookup) in the first column and displaying the contact name in the second column. The key to this list box is that its MultiSelect property is set to Extended. Using the Extended setting gives you the full Ctrl+click or Shift+click features that you see in most list boxes in Windows. The default for this property is None, which lets you select only one value at a time. You can set it to Simple if you want to select or clear multiple values using the mouse or the Spacebar.

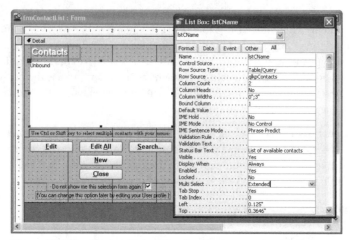

Figure 23-14. The multiple-selection list box on the frmContactList form and its property sheet.

If you scroll down to the Event properties, you'll find an event procedure defined for On Dbl Click. The code for this event procedure (which is called when you double-click an item in the list box) runs only the cmdSome_Click procedure. Right-click the cmdSome command button (the one whose caption says *Edit*), and choose Build Event from the shortcut menu to jump to the cmdSome_Click procedure that does all the work, as shown below.

```
Private Sub cmdSome_Click()
Dim strWhere As String, varItem As Variant
  ' Request to edit items selected in the list box
  ' If no items selected, then nothing to do
  If Me!lstCName.ItemsSelected.Count = 0 Then Exit Sub
  ' Loop through the items selected collection
  For Each varItem In Me!lstCName.ItemsSelected
    ' Grab the ContactID column for each selected item
    strWhere = strWhere & Me!lstCName.Column(0, varItem) & ","
  Next varItem
  ' Throw away the extra comma on the "IN" string
  strWhere = Left$(strWhere, Len(strWhere) - 1)
  ' Open the contacts form filtered on the selected contacts
  strWhere = "[ContactID] IN (" & strWhere & ") And (Inactive = False)"
  DoCmd.OpenForm FormName:="frmContacts", WhereCondition:=strWhere
  DoCmd.Close acForm, Me.Name
End Sub
```

When you set the MultiSelect property of a list box to something other than None, you can examine the control's ItemsSelected collection to determine what (if anything) is selected. In the cmdSome_Click procedure, the Visual Basic code first checks the Count property of the control's ItemsSelected collection to determine whether anything is selected. If the Count is 0, there's nothing to do, so the procedure exits.

The ItemsSelected collection is composed of variant values, each of which provides an index to a highlighted item in the list box. The For Each loop asks Visual Basic to loop through all the available variant values in the collection, one at a time. Within the loop, the code uses the value of the variant to retrieve the Contact ID from the list. List boxes also have a Column property, and you can reference all the values in the list by using a statement such as

```
Me.ListBoxName.Column(ColumnNum, RowNum)
```

where *ListBoxName* is the name of your list box control, *ColumnNum* is the relative column number (the first column is 0, the second is 1, and so on), and *RowNum* is the relative row number (also starting at 0). The variant values in the ItemsSelected collection return the relative row number. This Visual Basic code uses column 0 and the values in the ItemsSelected collection to append each selected ContactID to a string variable, separated by commas. You'll recall from studying the IN predicate in Chapter 7, "Creating and Working with Simple Queries," that a list of values separated by commas is ideal for an IN clause.

After retrieving all the ContactID numbers, the next statement removes the trailing comma from the string. The final Where clause includes an additional criterion to display only active contacts. The DoCmd.OpenForm command uses the resulting string to create a filter clause as it opens the form. Finally, the code closes the frmContactList form. (Me.Name is the name of the current form.)

Providing a Custom Query By Form

Suppose you want to do a more complex search on the frmContacts form—using criteria such as contact type, company, or products owned rather than simply using contact name. You could teach your users how to use the Filter By Form features to build the search, or you could use Filter By Form to easily construct multiple OR criteria on simple tests. But if you want to find, for example, all contacts who own the Single User edition or whom you contacted between certain dates, there's no way to construct this request using standard filtering features. The reason for this is that when you define a filter for a subform (such as the Events subform in frmContacts) using Filter By Form, you're filtering only the subform rows. You're not finding contacts who have only a matching subform row.

The only solution, then, is to provide a custom Query By Form that provides options to search on all the important fields and then build the Where clause to solve the search problem using Visual Basic code. To start, open the LawTrack Contacts application. (If you have exited to the Database window, you can start the application by opening *frmSplash*.) Sign on, click the Contacts button on the main switchboard form, and then click the Search button in the Select Contacts dialog box. You should see the fdlgContactSearch form, as shown in Figure 23-15 on the next page.

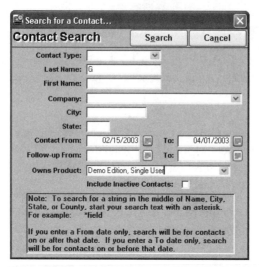

Figure 23-15. Using a custom Query By Form to perform a complex search.

Try selecting contacts whose last name begins with the letter *G*, whom you contacted between February 15, 2003, and April 1, 2003, and who own the Demo Edition Single User product (from the Owns Product drop-down list). When you click the Search button, you should see the frmContacts form open and display two contacts.

To see how this works, you need to explore the design of the fdlgContactSearch form. Switch to the Database window (press F11), and open the form in Design view. You should see a window like that shown in Figure 23-16. Notice that the form is not bound to any record source. The controls must be unbound so they can accept any criteria values that a user might enter.

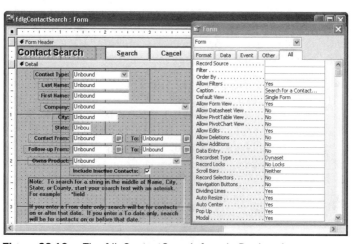

Figure 23-16. The fdlgContactSearch form in Design view.

The bulk of the work happens when you click the Search button. The code for the event procedure for the Click event of the Search button is shown below.

```
Private Sub cmdSearch_Click()
Dim varWhere As Variant, varDateSearch As Variant
Dim rst As DAO.Recordset
  ' Initialize to Null
  varWhere = Null
  varDateSearch = Null
  ' First, validate the dates
  ' If there's something in Contact Date From
  If Not IsNothing(Me.txtContactFrom) Then
    ' First, make sure it's a valid date
    If Not IsDate(Me.txtContactFrom) Then
      ' Nope, warn them and bail
      MsgBox "The value in Contact From is not a valid date.", _
        vbCritical, gstrAppTitle
      Exit Sub
    End If
    ' Now see if they specified a "to" date
    If Not IsNothing(Me.txtContactTo) Then
      ' First, make sure it's a valid date
      If Not IsDate(Me.txtContactTo) Then
        ' Nope, warn them and bail
        MsgBox "The value in Contact To is not a valid date.", _
          vbCritical, gstrAppTitle
        Exit Sub
      End If
      ' Got two dates, now make sure "to" is >= "from"
      If Me.txtContactTo < Me.txtContactFrom Then
        MsgBox "Contact To date must be greater than " & _
          "or equal to Contact From date.", _
          vbCritical, gstrAppTitle
        Exit Sub
      End If
    End If
  Else
    ' No "from" but did they specify a "to"?
    If Not IsNothing(Me.txtContactTo) Then
      ' Make sure it's a valid date
      If Not IsDate(Me.txtContactTo) Then
        ' Nope, warn them and bail
        MsgBox "The value in Contact To is not a valid date.", _
          vbCritical, gstrAppTitle
        Exit Sub
      End If
    End If
  End If
  ' If there's something in Follow-up Date From
  If Not IsNothing(Me.txtFollowUpFrom) Then
    ' First, make sure it's a valid date
    If Not IsDate(Me.txtFollowUpFrom) Then
      ' Nope, warn them and bail
```

Chapter 23

```
        MsgBox "The value in Follow-up From is not a valid date.", _
          vbCritical, gstrAppTitle
        Exit Sub
      End If
      ' Now see if they specified a "to" date
      If Not IsNothing(Me.txtFollowUpTo) Then
        ' First, make sure it's a valid date
        If Not IsDate(Me.txtFollowUpTo) Then
          ' Nope, warn them and bail
          MsgBox "The value in Follow-up To is not a valid date.", _
            vbCritical, gstrAppTitle
          Exit Sub
        End If
        ' Got two dates, now make sure "to" is >= "from"
        If Me.txtFollowUpTo < Me.txtFollowUpFrom Then
          MsgBox "Follow-up To date must be greater than " & _
            "or equal to Follow-up From date.", _
            vbCritical, gstrAppTitle
          Exit Sub
        End If
      End If
    Else
      ' No "from" but did they specify a "to"?
      If Not IsNothing(Me.txtFollowUpTo) Then
        ' Make sure it's a valid date
        If Not IsDate(Me.txtFollowUpTo) Then
          ' Nope, warn them and bail
          MsgBox "The value in Follow-up To is not a valid date.", _
            vbCritical, gstrAppTitle
          Exit Sub
        End If
      End If
    End If
    ' OK, start building the filter
    ' If specified a contact type value
    If Not IsNothing(Me.cmbContactType) Then
      ' .. build the predicate
      varWhere = "[ContactType] = '" & Me.cmbContactType & "'"
    End If
    ' Do Last Name next
    If Not IsNothing(Me.txtLastName) Then
      ' .. build the predicate
      ' Note: taking advantage of Null propagation
      '  so we don't have to test for any previous predicate
      varWhere = (varWhere + " AND ") & "[LastName] LIKE '" & _
        Me.txtLastName & "*'"
    End If
    ' Do First Name next
    If Not IsNothing(Me.txtFirstName) Then
      ' .. build the predicate
      varWhere = (varWhere + " AND ") & "[FirstName] LIKE '" & _
        Me.txtFirstName & "*'"
    End If
    ' Do Company next
    If Not IsNothing(Me.cmbCompanyID) Then
```

Chapter 23

```
' .. build the predicate
' Must use a subquery here because the value is in a linking table...
varWhere = (varWhere + " AND ") & _
  "[ContactID] IN (SELECT ContactID FROM tblCompanyContacts " & _
  "WHERE tblCompanyContacts.CompanyID = " & Me.cmbCompanyID & ")"
End If
' Do City next
If Not IsNothing(Me.txtCity) Then
  ' .. build the predicate
  ' Test for both Work and Home city
  varWhere = (varWhere + " AND ") & "(([WorkCity] LIKE '" & _
    Me.txtCity & "*')" & _
    " OR ([HomeCity] LIKE '" & Me.txtCity & "*'))"
End If
' Do State next
If Not IsNothing(Me.txtState) Then
  ' .. build the predicate
  ' Test for both Work and Home state
  varWhere = (varWhere + " AND ") & "(([WorkStateOrProvince] LIKE '" & _
    Me.txtState & "*')" & _
    " OR ([HomeStateOrProvince] LIKE '" & Me.txtState & "*'))"
End If
' Do Contact date(s) next -- this is a toughie
'   because we want to end up with one filter on the subquery table
'   for both Contact Date range and FollowUp Date range
' Check Contact From first
If Not IsNothing(Me.txtContactFrom) Then
  ' .. build the predicate
  varDateSearch = "tblContactEvents.ContactDateTime >= #" & _
    Me.txtContactFrom & "#"
End If
' Now do Contact To
If Not IsNothing(Me.txtContactTo) Then
  ' .. add to the predicate, but add one because ContactDateTime includes
  '  a date AND a time
  varDateSearch = (varDateSearch + " AND ") & _
    "tblContactEvents.ContactDateTime < #" & _
    CDate(Me.txtContactTo) + 1 & "#"
End If
' Now do Follow-up From
If Not IsNothing(Me.txtFollowUpFrom) Then
  ' .. add to the predicate
  varDateSearch = (varDateSearch + " AND ") & _
    "tblContactEvents.ContactFollowUpDate >= #" & Me.txtFollowUpFrom & "#"
End If
' Finally, do Follow-up To
If Not IsNothing(Me.txtFollowUpTo) Then
  ' .. add to the predicate
  varDateSearch = (varDateSearch + " AND ") & _
    "tblContactEvents.ContactFollowUpDate <= #" & Me.txtFollowUpTo & "#"
End If
' Did we build any date filter?
If Not IsNothing(varDateSearch) Then
  ' OK, add to the overall filter
```

```
' Must use a subquery here because the value is in a linking table...
varWhere = (varWhere + " AND ") & _
  "[ContactID] IN (SELECT ContactID FROM tblContactEvents " & _
  "WHERE " & varDateSearch & ")"
End If
' Do Product
If Not IsNothing(Me.cmbProductID) Then
  ' .. build the predicate
  ' Must use a subquery here because the value is in a linking table...
  varWhere = (varWhere + " AND ") & _
    "[ContactID] IN (SELECT ContactID FROM tblContactProducts " & _
    "WHERE tblContactProducts.ProductID = " & Me.cmbProductID & ")"
End If
' Finally, do the Inactive check box
If (Me.chkInactive = False) Then
  ' Build a filter to exclude inactive contacts
  varWhere = (varWhere + " AND ") & "(Inactive = False)"
End If
' Check to see that we built a filter
If IsNothing(varWhere) Then
  MsgBox "You must enter at least one search criteria.", _
    vbInformation, gstrAppTitle
  Exit Sub
End If
' Open a recordset to see if any rows returned with this filter
Set rst = DBEngine(0)(0).OpenRecordset("SELECT * FROM tblContacts " & _
  "WHERE " & varWhere)
' See if found none
If rst.RecordCount = 0 Then
  MsgBox "No Contacts meet your criteria.", vbInformation, gstrAppTitle
  ' Clean up recordset
  rst.Close
  Set rst = Nothing
  Exit Sub
End If
' Hide me to fix later focus problems
Me.Visible = False
' Move to last to find out how many
rst.MoveLast
' If 5 or less or frmContacts already open,
If (rst.RecordCount < 6) Or IsFormLoaded("frmContacts") Then
  ' Open Contacts filtered
  ' Note: if form already open, this just applies the filter
  DoCmd.OpenForm "frmContacts", WhereCondition:=varWhere
  ' Make sure focus is on contacts
  Forms!frmContacts.SetFocus
Else
  ' Ask if they want to see a summary list first
  If vbYes = MsgBox("Your search found " & rst.RecordCount & _
    " contacts.  " & _
    "Do you want to see a summary list first?", _
    vbQuestion + vbYesNo, gstrAppTitle) Then
    ' Show the summary
    DoCmd.OpenForm "frmContactSummary", WhereCondition:=varWhere
```

Chapter 23

```
      ' Make sure focus is on contact summary
      Forms!frmContactSummary.SetFocus
    Else
      ' Show the full contacts info filtered
      DoCmd.OpenForm "frmContacts", WhereCondition:=varWhere
      ' Make sure focus is on contacts
      Forms!frmContacts.SetFocus
    End If
  End If
  ' Done
  DoCmd.Close acForm, Me.Name
  ' Clean up recordset
  rst.Close
  Set rst = Nothing
End Sub
```

The first part of the procedure validates the contact date from and to values and the follow-up date from and to values. If any are not valid dates or the from date is later than the to date, the code issues an appropriate warning message and exits.

The next several segments of code build up a WHERE string by looking at the unbound controls one at a time. If the corresponding field is a string, the code builds a test using the LIKE predicate so that whatever the user enters can match any part of the field in the underlying table, but not all the fields are strings. When the function adds a clause as it builds the WHERE string, it inserts the AND keyword between clauses if other clauses already exist. Because the variable containing the WHERE clause is a Variant data type initialized to Null, the code can use a + concatenation to optionally add the AND keyword.

The underlying record source for the frmContacts form does not include either contact event or product information directly, so the procedure has to build a predicate using a subquery if you ask for a search by contact date, follow-up date, or product. In the case of contact date or follow-up date, the code builds a separate filter string (varDateSearch) because both fields are in the same table (tblContactEvents). If you ask for any date range check, the code builds criteria using a subquery that finds the ContactID from records in the tblContactEvent table that fall within the date range. For a search by product, the code builds criteria using a subquery that finds the ContactID from records in the tblContactProducts table that match the product you selected. Finally, if you leave the Include Inactive Contacts check box unchecked, the code adds a test to include only records that are active.

After examining all the possible filter values the user could have entered, the code checks to see if there's anything in the filter string (varWhere). There's no point in opening the form without a filter, so the code displays a message and exits, leaving the form open to allow the user to try again.

The final part of the procedure builds a simple recordset on the tblContacts table used in both the frmContacts and frmContactSummary forms, applying the WHERE clause built by the code in the first part of the procedure. If it finds no records, it uses the MsgBox function to inform the user and then gives the user a chance to try again.

Chapter 23

When you first open a Recordset object in code, its RecordCount property is 0 if the recordset is empty and is some value greater than 0 if the recordset contains some records. The Record-Count property of a Recordset object contains only a count of the number of rows visited and not the number of rows in the recordset. So if it finds some rows, the procedure moves to the last row in the temporary recordset to get an accurate count. When the record count is greater than 5 and the frmContacts form is not already open, the procedure uses the MsgBox function to give the user the option to view a summary of the records found in the frmContactSummary form or to display the records found directly in the frmContacts form. (As noted earlier, both forms use the same record source, so the code can apply the filter it built as it opens either form.) We'll examine how the frmContactSummary form works in the next section.

Selecting from a Summary List

As you saw in the cmdSearch_Click procedure in the previous section, the user gets to make a choice if more than five rows meet the entered criteria. To examine this feature in more detail, make sure the frmContacts form is not open, and ask for a search of contacts with a Contact Type of Customer in the fdlgContactSearch form. The result should look like that shown in Figure 23-17, in which 13 contacts are categorized as customers.

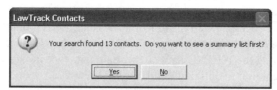

Figure 23-17. The message box that appears when the cmdSearch_Click procedure returns more than five rows.

When you click Yes, the cmdSearch_Click procedure opens the Contact Search Summary form (frmContactSummary), as shown in Figure 23-18. You can scroll down to any row, put the focus on that row (be sure the row selector indicator is pointing to that row), and then click the View Details button to open the *frmContacts* form and view the details for the one contact you selected. You can see that this is a very efficient way to help the user narrow a search down to one particular contact.

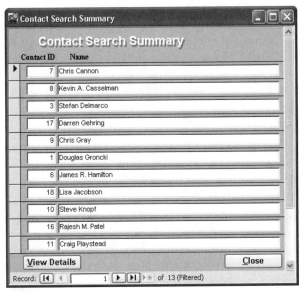

Figure 23-18. Selecting a specific contact from a search summary.

You can also double-click either the Contact ID or the Name field to see the details for that contact. Because this list is already filtered using the criteria you specified in the fdlgContact-Search form, the code that responds to your request builds a simple filter on the one Contact ID to make opening the frmContacts form most efficient. The code behind this form that responds to your request is as follows:

```
' Set up the filter
strFilter = "(ContactID = " & Me.ContactID & ")"
' Open contacts filtered on the current row
DoCmd.OpenForm FormName:="frmContacts", WhereCondition:=strFilter
' Close me
DoCmd.Close acForm, Me.Name
' Put focus on contacts
Forms!frmContacts.SetFocus
```

Filtering One List with Another

You might have noticed when editing products on the Products tab in the frmContacts form (see Figure 23-1) that you can first choose a product type to narrow down the list of products and then choose the product you want. There are only nine products in the sample application, so being able to narrow down the product selection first isn't all that useful, but you can imagine how a feature like this would be absolutely necessary in an application that had thousands of products available for sale.

The first secret is that the row source for the Product combo box is a parameter query that filters the products based on the product type you chose. When you use this technique in a form in single form view, all you need to do is requery the filtered combo box (in this case, the Product combo box) when the user moves to a new record (in the Current event of the form) and requery when the user chooses a different value in the combo box that provides the filter value (in the After Update event of the combo box providing the filter value).

However, using this technique on a form in continuous form view is considerably more complex. Even though you can see multiple rows in a continuous form, there is actually only one copy of each control on the form. If you always requery the Product combo box each time you move to a new row, the product name displayed in other rows that have a different product type will appear blank! When the value in a row doesn't match a value in the list, you get a blank result, not the actual value of the field.

The way to solve this is to include the display name in the recordset for the form and carefully overlay each combo box with a text box that always displays the correct value regardless of the filter. You can open the *fsubContactProducts* form in Design view to see how I did this. Figure 23-19 shows you the form with the two overlay text boxes (CategoryDescription and ProductName) pulled down from the underlying combo boxes (Unbound and ProductID).

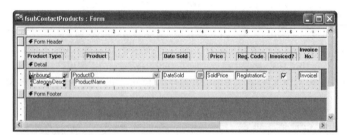

Figure 23-19. Solving a filtered combo box display problem by overlaying text boxes.

Notice that the control source of the Product combo box is actually the ProductID field, but the combo box displays the ProductName field. Also, the Product Type combo box isn't bound to any field at all—there is no CategoryDescription field in tblContactProducts—but it does display the CategoryDescription field from the lookup table. To make this work, you need to include the ProductName and CategoryDescription fields in the record source for this form. You don't want the user to update these values, but you need them to provide the overlay display. These two text boxes have their Locked property set to Yes to prevent updating and their Tab Stop property set to No so that the user will tab into the underlying combo boxes and not these text boxes. Figure 23-20 shows you the qryContactProducts query that's the row source for this form.

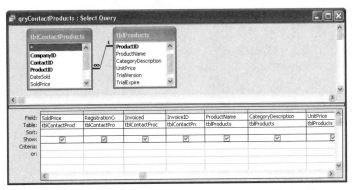

Figure 23-20. A query that provides the necessary ProductName and CategoryDescription fields from a related table so that you can display the values.

To make it all work correctly, several event procedures make sure the focus goes where necessary and that the filtered Product combo box gets requeried correctly. The code behind the fsubContactProducts form that does this is as follows:

```
Private Sub CategoryDescription_GotFocus()
   ' We have some tricky "overlay" text boxes here that
   ' shouldn't get the focus.  Move focus to the underlying
   ' combo box if that happens.
   Me.cmbCategoryDescription.SetFocus
End Sub

Private Sub cmbCategoryDescription_AfterUpdate()
   ' If they pick a new Category, then requery the
   '  product list that's filtered on category
   Me.cmbProductID.Requery
   ' Set the Product to the first row in the new list
   Me.cmbProductID = Me.cmbProductID.ItemData(0)
   ' .. and signal Product after update.
   cmbProductID_AfterUpdate
End Sub

Private Sub Form_Current()
   ' If we have a valid Category Description on this row...
   If Not IsNothing(Me.CategoryDescription) Then
      ' Then make sure the unbound combo is in sync.
      Me.cmbCategoryDescription = Me.CategoryDescription
   End If
   ' Requery the product list to match the current category
   Me.cmbProductID.Requery
End Sub
```

Chapter 23

901

```
Private Sub ProductName_GotFocus()
    ' We have some tricky "overlay" text boxes here that
    ' shouldn't get the focus.  Move focus to the underlying
    ' combo box if that happens.
    Me.cmbProductID.SetFocus
End Sub
```

As expected, the code requeries the Product combo box whenever you pick a new category (cmbCategoryDescription_AfterUpdate) or when you move to a new row (Form_Current). It also keeps the unbound combo box in sync as you move from row to row as long as the underlying record has a valid category. (A new record won't have a related CategoryDescription until you choose a Product ID, so the code doesn't update the unbound combo box on a new record.) Finally, if you try to click in CategoryDescription or ProductName, the Got-Focus code moves you to the underlying combo box where you belong. Why didn't I simply set the Enabled property for CategoryDescription and ProductName to Yes? If you do that, then you can't ever click into the category or product combo boxes because the disabled text box overlaid on top would block you.

> **Note** If you want to see what the filtered combo box looks like without the overlay, make a backup copy of *Contacts.mdb*, open the *fsubContactProducts* form in Design view, move the Category Description and Product Name text boxes down similar to Figure 23-19, and save the form. Now open the *frmContacts* form and click on the Products tab.

Linking to Related Data in Another Form or Report

Now that you know how to build a filter to limit what the user sees, you can probably surmise that using a filter is a good way to open another form or report that displays information related to the current record or set of filtered records in the current form. This section shows you how to do this for both forms and reports. Later in this section, you will learn how to use events in class modules to build sophisticated links.

Linking Forms Using a Filter

You've already seen the frmContactSummary form (Figure 23-18) that uses a simple filter to link from the record selected in that form to full details in the frmContacts form. You can find similar code behind the *fsubCompanyContacts* form used as a subform in the *frmCompanies* form. Figure 23-21 shows you the frmCompanies form and the Edit This buttons I provided on the subform.

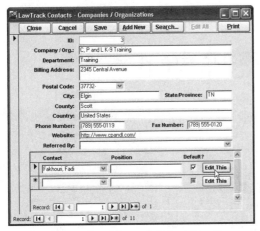

Figure 23-21. Providing a link from the Companies/Organizations form to details about a particular contact.

To see the details for a particular contact, the user clicks the Edit This button on the chosen contact record, and code opens the frmContacts form with that contact displayed. The code behind the button is as follows:

```
Private Sub cmdEdit_Click()
    ' Open Contacts on the related record
    DoCmd.OpenForm "frmContacts", WhereCondition:="ContactID = " & Me.ContactID
End Sub
```

And code in the form's Current event prevents the user from clicking on the button when on a new record that doesn't have a contact ID, as shown below.

```
Private Sub Form_Current()
    ' Disable "edit this" if on a new row
    Me.cmdEdit.Enabled = Not (Me.NewRecord)
End Sub
```

Setting the button's Enabled property to False causes it to appear dimmed, and the user cannot click the button.

Linking to a Report Using a Filter

Now let's take a look at using the Filter technique to link to related information in a report. Open the *frmInvoices* form in the LawTrack Contacts application (*Contacts.mdb*) and move to an invoice that looks interesting. Click the Print button to open the Print Invoices form (fdlgInvoicePrintOptions) that gives you the option to see the current invoice formatted in a report, display all unprinted invoices in a report, display only unprinted invoices for the current customer, or print all invoices currently shown in the frmInvoices form. (You can use Search to filter the displayed invoices to the ones you want.) Choose the Current Invoice Only option and click Print again to see the invoice in a report, as shown in Figure 23-22 on the next page.

Chapter 23

903

(The figure shows you the sequence you see after clicking the Print button on the frmInvoices form. The Print Invoices dialog box closes after opening the report.)

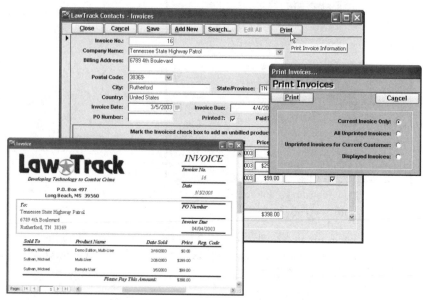

Figure 23-22. The result of asking to print the current invoice in the LawTrack Contacts database.

The code from the Click event of the Print button in the fdlgInvoicePrintOptions form is as follows:

```
Private Sub cmdPrint_Click()
Dim strFilter As String, frm As Form
  ' Set an error trap
  On Error GoTo cmdPrint_Error
  ' Get a pointer to the Invoices form
  Set frm = Forms!frmInvoices
  Select Case Me.optFilterType.Value
    ' Current Invoice
    Case 1
      ' Set filter to open Invoice report for current invoice only
      strFilter = "[InvoiceID] = " & frm!InvoiceID
    ' All unprinted invoices
    Case 2
      ' Set filter to open all unprinted invoices
      strFilter = "[InvoicePrinted] = 0"
    ' Unprinted invoices for current company
    Case 3
      ' Set filter to open unprinted invoices for current company
      strFilter = "[CompanyID] = " & frm!cmbCompanyID & _
        " AND [InvoicePrinted] = 0"
    ' Displayed invoices (if filter set on form)
    Case 4
```

```
        ' Check for a filter on the form
        If IsNothing(frm.Filter) Then
          ' Make sure they want to print all!
          If vbNo = MsgBox("Your selection will print all " & _
            "Invoices currently in the " & _
            "database.  Are you sure you want to do this?", _
            vbQuestion + vbYesNo + vbDefaultButton2, _
            gstrAppTitle) Then
            Exit Sub
          End If
          ' Set "do them all" filter
          strFilter = "1 = 1"
        Else
          strFilter = frm.Filter
        End If
    End Select
    ' Hide me
    Me.Visible = False
    ' Have a filter now.  Open the report on that filter
    DoCmd.OpenReport "rptInvoices", acViewPreview, , strFilter
    ' Update the Print flag for selected invoices
    CurrentDb.Execute "UPDATE tblInvoices SET InvoicePrinted = -1 WHERE " & _
      strFilter
    ' Refresh the form to show updated Printed status
    frm.Refresh
    ' Execute the Current event on the form to make sure it is locked correctly
    frm.Form_Current
cmdPrint_Exit:
    ' Clear the form object
    Set frm = Nothing
    ' Done
    DoCmd.Close acForm, Me.Name
    Exit Sub
cmdPrint_Error:
    ' Got an error
    ' If Cancel, that means the filter produced no Invoices
    If Err = errCancel Then
      ' Exit - report will display "no records" message
      Resume cmdPrint_Exit
    End If
    ' Got unknown error - display and log
    MsgBox "Unexpected error while printing and updating print flags: " & _
      Err & ", " & _
      Error, vbCritical, gstrAppTitle
    ErrorLog Me.Name & "_Print", Err, Error
    Resume cmdPrint_Exit
End Sub
```

The first part of this procedure sets an object reference to the frmInvoices form to make it easy to grab either the InvoiceID or the CompanyID and to reference properties and methods of the form's object. The Select Case statement examines which option button the user selected on fdlgInvoicePrintOption and builds the appropriate filter for the report. Notice that if the user asks to print all the invoices currently displayed on the form, the code first looks for a user-applied filter on the frmInvoices form. If the code finds no filter, it asks if the user wants to print all invoices. The code uses the filter it built (or the current filter on the frmInvoices form) to open the rptInvoices report in Print Preview. It also executes an SQL Update statement to flag all the invoices the user printed. If you look at code in the Current event of the *frmInvoices* form, you'll find that it locks all controls so that the user can't update an invoice that has been printed.

Synchronizing Two Forms Using a Class Event

Sometimes it's useful to give the user an option to open a pop-up form that displays additional details about some information displayed on another form. As you move from one row to another in the main form, it would be nice if the form that displayed the additional information stayed in sync.

Of course, the Current event of a form lets you know when you move to a new record. In the Wedding List sample database built with macros (*WeddingListMC.mdb*), the macros do some elaborate filtering to keep a pop-up form with additional city information in sync with the main form. However, doing it with macros is the hard way!

The primary Wedding List sample application is in *WeddingList.mdb*, and it uses Visual Basic to provide all the automation. With Visual Basic, I was able to declare and use a custom event in the *WeddingListForm* form to signal the *CityInformation* form if it's open and responding to the events. In the Current event of WeddingListForm, I don't have to worry about whether the companion form is open. The code simply signals the event and lets the City Information form worry about keeping in sync with the main form. (The user can open the City Information form at any time by clicking the City Info button on the Wedding List form.) You can see these two forms in action in Figure 23-23.

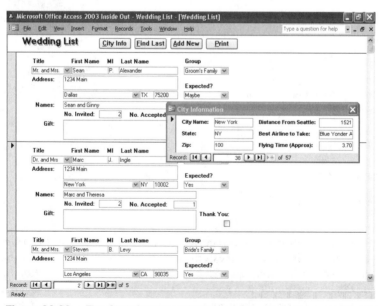

Figure 23-23. The CityInformation form popped up over the main WeddingListForm to display additional information about the invitee's home city.

Here's the code from the WeddingListForm class module that makes an event available to signal the CityInformation form:

```
Option Compare Database
Option Explicit
' Event to signal we've moved to a new city
Public Event NewCity(varCityName As Variant)
' End of Declarations Section

Private Sub Form_Current()
On Error GoTo Form_Current_Err
  ' Signal the city form to move to this city
  ' and pass the city name to the event
  RaiseEvent NewCity(Me!City)
Form_Current_Exit:
  Exit Sub
Form_Current_Err:
  MsgBox Error$
  Resume Form_Current_Exit
End Sub

Private Sub cmdCity_Click()
On Error GoTo cmdCity_Click_Err
  ' If the city form not open, do it
  If Not IsFormLoaded("CityInformation") Then
    DoCmd.OpenForm "CityInformation", acNormal, , , acFormReadOnly, acHidden
    ' Give the other form a chance to "hook" our event
    DoEvents
  End If
  ' Signal the form we just opened
  RaiseEvent NewCity(Me!City)
cmdCity_Click_Exit:
  Exit Sub
cmdCity_Click_Err:
  MsgBox Error$
  Resume cmdCity_Click_Exit
End Sub
```

In the Declarations section of the module, I declared an event variable and indicated that I'm going to pass a parameter (the city name) in the event. In the Form_Current event procedure, the code uses RaiseEvent to pass the current city name to any other module that's listening. The code doesn't have to worry about whether any other module is interested in this event—it just signals the event when appropriate and then ends. (This is not unlike how Access works. When a form moves to a new record, Access signals the Form_Current event, but nothing happens unless you have written code to respond to the event.) Note that the variable passed is declared as a Variant to handle the case when the user moves to the new row at the end—the City control will be Null in that case. A command button (cmdCity) on the WeddingListForm allows the user to open the CityInformation form. The Click event of that button opens the form hidden and uses the DoEvents function to give the CityInformation form a chance to open and indicate that it wants to listen to the NewCity event on the

WeddingListForm. After waiting for the CityInformation form to finish processing, the code raises the event to notify that form about the city in the current row.

The CityInformation form does all the work (when it's open) to respond to the event signaled by WeddingListForm and move to the correct row. The code is shown below.

```
Option Compare Database
Option Explicit
Dim WithEvents frmWedding As Form_WeddingListForm
' End of the Declarations Section

Private Sub Form_Load()
On Error GoTo Form_Load_Err
  ' If the wedding list form is open
  If IsLoaded("WeddingListForm") Then
    ' Then set to respond to the NewCity event
    Set frmWedding = Forms!WeddingListForm
  End If
Form_Load_Exit:
  Exit Sub
Form_Load_Err:
  MsgBox Error$
  Resume Form_Load_Exit
End Sub

Private Sub frmWedding_NewCity(varCityName As Variant)
  ' The Wedding List form has asked us to move to a
  ' new city via the NewCity event
  On Error Resume Next
  If IsNothing(varCityName) Then
    ' Hide me if city name is empty
    Me.Visible = False
  Else
    ' Reveal me if there's a city name, and go
    ' find it
    Me.Visible = True
    Me.Recordset.FindFirst "[CityName] = """ & _
      varCityName & """"
  End If
End Sub
```

In the Declarations section, you can find an object variable called frmWedding that has a data type equal to the class module name of WeddingListForm. The WithEvents keyword indicates that code in this class module will respond to events signaled by any object assigned to this variable. When the form opens, the Form_Load procedure checks to see that Wedding-ListForm is open (just in case you opened this form by itself from the Database window). If WeddingListForm is open, it "hooks" the NewCity event in that form by assigning it to the frmWedding variable.

The frmWedding_NewCity procedure responds to the NewCity event of the frmWedding object. Once the Load event code establishes frmWedding as a pointer to WeddingListForm, this procedure runs whenever code in the class module for that form signals the NewCity event with RaiseEvent.

The code in the event procedure is pretty simple. If the CityName parameter passed by the event is "nothing" (Null or a zero-length string), the procedure hides the form because there's nothing to display. If the event passes a valid city name, the procedure uses the Find-First method of the Recordset object of this form to move to the correct city.

> **Note** The Recordset property of a form in an Access database (.mdb file) returns a DAO recordset in Access 2003. For this reason, you should use a DAO FindFirst method, not an ADO Find method, to locate rows in a form recordset.

Automating Complex Tasks

The most complex Visual Basic code we've examined thus far in this chapter is the procedure to build a search clause from the data you enter in the fdlgContactSearch form. Trust me, we've only started to scratch the surface!

Triggering a Data Task from a Related Form

One of the more complex pieces of code in the LawTrack Contacts sample database is triggered from the fsubContactEvents form that's part of the frmContacts form. After signing on correctly to the application, the user can open the *frmContacts* form, click on the Events tab, and add an event indicating the sale of a product. As soon as the user saves the record, code behind the subform automatically adds the product to the contact, as shown in Figure 23-24.

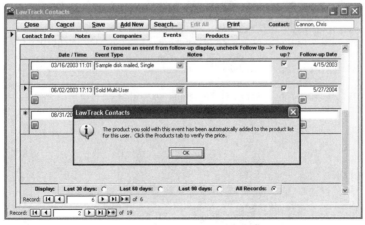

Figure 23-24. Logging a product sale event on the Events tab automatically sells the product to the contact.

If you look behind the *fsubContactEvents* form, you'll find event procedures that detect when the user has created a sale event and that execute an SQL Insert command to create the related product row. The code is as follows:

```
Option Compare Database
Option Explicit
' Flag to indicate auto-add of a product if new event requires it
Dim intProductAdd As Integer
' Place to store Company Name on a product add
Dim varCoName As Variant
' End of the Declarations Section

Private Sub ContactEventTypeID_BeforeUpdate(Cancel As Integer)
  ' Did they pick an event that involves a software sale?
  ' NOTE: All columns in a combo box are TEXT
  If Me.ContactEventTypeID.Column(4) = "-1" Then
    ' Try to lookup this contact's Company Name
    varCoName = DLookup("CompanyName", "qryContactDefaultCompany", _
      "ContactID = " & Me.Parent.ContactID.Value)
    ' If not found, then disallow product sale
    If IsNothing(varCoName) Then
      MsgBox "You cannot sell a product to a Contact " & _
        "that does not have a " & _
        "related Company that is marked as the default for this Contact." & _
        "  Press Esc to clear your edits and click on the Companies tab " & _
        "to define the default Company for this Contact.", _
        vbCritical, gstrAppTitle
      Cancel = True
    End If
  End If
End Sub

Private Sub Form_BeforeUpdate(Cancel As Integer)
  ' Did they pick an event that involves a software sale?
  ' NOTE: All columns in a combo box are TEXT
  If Me.ContactEventTypeID.Column(4) = "-1" Then
    ' Do this only if on a new record or they changed the EventID value
    If (Me.NewRecord) Or (Me.ContactEventTypeID <> _
      Me.ContactEventTypeID.OldValue) Then
      ' Set the add product flag
      '- product added by AfterUpdate code for safety
      intProductAdd = True
    End If
  End If
End Sub

Private Sub Form_AfterUpdate()
Dim strSQL As String, curPrice As Currency, _
Dim lngProduct As Long, varCoID As Variant
Dim rst As DAO.Recordset, strPreReqName As String
  ' See if we need to auto-add a product
  If (intProductAdd = True) Then
    ' Reset so we only do this once
    intProductAdd = False
```

```
' Set an error trap
On Error GoTo Insert_Err
' Save the Product ID
lngProduct = Me.ContactEventTypeID.Column(5)
' Fetch the product record
Set rst = CurrentDb.OpenRecordset("SELECT * FROM tblProducts " & _
  "WHERE ProductID = " & lngProduct)
' Make sure we got a record
If rst.EOF Then
  MsgBox "Could not find the product record for this sales event." & _
    "  Auto-create of " & _
    "product record for this contact has failed.", _
    vbCritical, gstrAppTitle
  rst.Close
  Set rst = Nothing
  GoTo Insert_Exit
End If
' Check for prerequisite product
If Not IsNull(rst!PreRequisite) Then
  ' Make sure contact owns the prerequisite product
  If IsNull(DLookup("ProductID", "tblContactProducts", _
    "ProductID = " & rst!PreRequisite & " And ContactID = " & _
    Me.Parent.ContactID)) Then
    ' Get the name of the prerequisite
    strPreReqName = DLookup("ProductName", "tblProducts", _
      "ProductID = " & rst!PreRequisite)
    ' Display error
    MsgBox "This contact must own prerequisite product " & _
      strPreReqName & " before you can sell this product." & _
      vbCrLf & vbCrLf & _
      "Auto-create of product record for this contact has failed", _
      vbCritical, gstrAppTitle
    ' Bail
    rst.Close
    Set rst = Nothing
    GoTo Insert_Exit
  End If
End If
' Save the price
curPrice = rst!UnitPrice
' Done with the record - close it
rst.Close
Set rst = Nothing
' Now, find the default company for this contact
varCoID = DLookup("CompanyID", "qryContactDefaultCompany", _
  "ContactID = " & Me.Parent.ContactID.Value)
' If not found, then disallow product sale
If IsNothing(varCoID) Then
  MsgBox "You cannot sell a product to a Contact who does not have a " & _
    "related Company that is marked as the default for this Contact.", _
    vbCritical, gstrAppTitle
  GoTo Insert_Exit
End If
' Set up the INSERT command
```

```
    strSQL = "INSERT INTO tblContactProducts " & _
      "(CompanyID, ContactID, ProductID, DateSold, SoldPrice) " & _
      "VALUES(" & varCoID & ", " & Me.Parent.ContactID & ", " & _
      lngProduct & ", #" & _
      DateValue(Me.ContactDateTime) & "#, " & curPrice & ")"
    ' Attempt to insert the Product row
    CurrentDb.Execute strSQL, dbFailOnError
    ' Got a good add - inform the user
    MsgBox "The product you sold with this event " & _
      "has been automatically added " & _
      "to the product list for this user.  " & _
      "Click the Products tab to verify the price.", _
      vbInformation, gstrAppTitle
    ' Requery the other subform to get the new row there
    Me.Parent.fsubContactProducts.Requery
  End If
Insert_Exit:
  Exit Sub
Insert_Err:
  ' Was error a duplicate row?
  If Err = errDuplicate Then
    MsgBox "LawTrack Contacts attempted to auto-add " & _
      "the product that you just indicated " & _
      "that you sold, but the Contact appears " & _
      "to already own this product.  Be sure " & _
      "to verify that you haven't tried to sell the same product twice.", _
      vbCritical, gstrAppTitle
  Else
    MsgBox "There was an error attempting to auto-add " & _
      "the product you just sold: " & _
      Err & ", " & Error, vbCritical, gstrAppTitle
    ' Log the error
    ErrorLog Me.Name & "_FormAfterUpdate", Err, Error
  End If
  Resume Insert_Exit
End Sub
```

In the Declarations section of the module, you can find two variables that the event procedures use to pass information between events. (If you declare the variables inside one of the procedures, only that procedure can use the variables.) The Before Update event procedure for the contact event type checks to see if the event is a product sale (by examining one of the hidden columns in the combo box row source). If the user is trying to log a product sale and this particular contact doesn't have a default company defined, the code displays an error message and won't let the user save that event type. Remember, a record in the tblContact-Products table must have a CompanyID as well as a ContactID.

When the user attempts to save a new or changed event record, Access runs the form's Before Update event procedure. This code again checks to see if the record about to be saved is for a product sale. However, if this isn't a new record or the user is saving an old event record but didn't change the event type, the code exits because it doesn't want to add a product record twice. (If this is an existing record and the event type didn't change, this code probably created the companion contact product record the first time the user saved the record.) The code could insert the record into tblContactProducts at this point, but, as you learned in Chapter 21, the record isn't really saved until after the Before Update event finishes. So, this code sets the module variable to tell the form's After Update event procedure to perform that task after Access has saved the changed record.

After Access saves the new or changed event record, it runs the form's After Update event procedure. If the code in the Before Update event procedure indicated that a product insert is required by setting the module intProductAdd variable to True, this code sets up to add the new record. It opens a recordset on the tblProducts table for the product that was just sold so that it can get the product price and check for any prerequisite product. If the product has a prerequisite but this contact doesn't own the prerequisite, the code displays an error message and exits.

Although previous code checked to see that this contact has a default CompanyID, this code checks again and exits if it can't find one. After the code has completed all checks and has the price and company ID information it needs, it inserts the new record into the tblContact-Products table using SQL. Notice at the bottom of the procedure you can find error-trapping code that tests to see if the insert caused a duplicate record error.

Linking to a Related Task

Let's switch to the Housing Reservations application (*Housing.mdb*) and take a look at the process for confirming a room for a reservation request. To see this in action, you must start the application by opening the *frmSplash* form, and then sign on as an administrator (Viescas, John L., or LaMee, Brian) using **password** as the password. From the main switchboard, click Reservation Requests, and then click View Unbooked in the Edit Reservation Requests dialog box. You'll see the Unbooked Requests form (*frmUnbookedRequests*) as shown in Figure 23-25 on the next page.

> **Note** The query that provides the records displayed in the *frmUnbookedRequests* form includes crieteria to exclude any requests that have a check-in date earlier than today's date. (It doesn't make sense to confirm a reservation request for a date in the past.) The latest requested check-in date in the original sample database is October 3, 2003, so you probably will see an error message when you attempt to look at unbooked requests. You can use the *zfrmLoadData* form to load new reservations and requests that are more current into the *qryUnbookedRequests* query to not eliminate old requests to be able to see how the *frmUnbookedRequests* form works.

Earlier, in "Linking to Related Data in Another Form or Report" on page 902, you learned one technique for using a command button to link to a related task. The key task in the Housing Reservations application for the housing manager (or any administrator) is to assign a room and book a reservation for pending requests. When you click one of the Book buttons on the Unbooked Requests form, code behind the form opens a form to show the manager the rooms that match the request and aren't booked for the time span requested. If you click the request from Pilar Ackerman for a one-bedroom suite with two queen beds from July 25, 2003, to August 5, 2003, you'll see the list of available rooms in the fdlgAvailable-Rooms form as shown in Figure 23-26 on the next page.

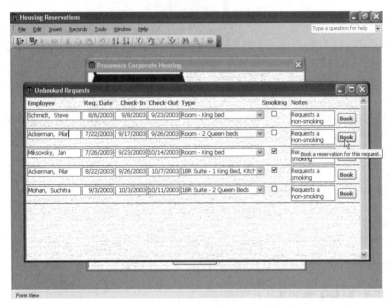

Figure 23-25. The Unbooked Requests form lets administrators view pending requests and start the booking process.

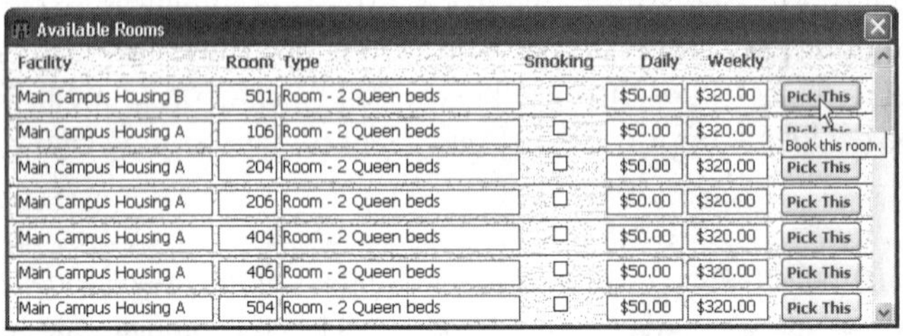

Figure 23-26. The list of available rooms matching the selected reservation request.

The code behind the Book button on the frmUnbookedRequests form is as follows:

```
Private Sub cmdBook_Click()
  ' Make sure no changes are pending
  If Me.Dirty Then Me.Dirty = False
  ' Open the available rooms form - hidden, dialog
  '   and check if any available
  DoCmd.OpenForm "fdlgAvailableRooms", _
    WhereCondition:="Smoking = " & Me.Smoking, _
    WindowMode:=acHidden
  If Forms!fdlgAvailableRooms.RecordsetClone.RecordCount = 0 Then
    MsgBox "There are no available rooms of this " & _
      "type for the dates requested." & _
      vbCrLf & vbCrLf & _
      "You can change the Room Type or dates and try again.", _
      vbInformation, gstrAppTitle
    DoCmd.Close acForm, "fdlgAvailableRooms"
```

```
    Exit Sub
  End If
  ' Show the available rooms
  ' - form will call our public sub to create the res.
  Forms!fdlgAvailableRooms.Visible = True
End Sub
```

The record source of the fdlgAvailableRooms form is a parameter query that filters out rooms already booked for the specified dates and includes the remaining rooms that match the requested room type. The code behind the Book button adds a filter for the smoking or non-smoking request because the room type doesn't include this information but each specific available room does. Behind the Pick This button on the fdlgAvailableRooms form, you can find the following code:

```
Private Sub cmdPick_Click()
Dim intReturn As Integer
  ' Call the build a reservation proc in the calling form
  intReturn = Form_frmUnbookedRequests.Bookit(Me.FacilityID, Me.RoomNumber, _
    Me.DailyRate, Me.WeeklyRate)
  If (intReturn = True) Then
    MsgBox "Booked!", vbExclamation, gstrAppTitle
  Else
    MsgBox "Room booking failed.  Please try again.", _
      vbCritical, gstrAppTitle
  End If
  DoCmd.Close acForm, Me.Name
End Sub
```

Can you figure out what's happening? Back in frmUnbookedRequests, there's a public function called Bookit that this code calls as a method of that form. It passes the critical FacilityID, RoomNumber, DailyRate, and WeeklyRate fields to complete the booking. Back in frmUnbookedRequests, the code in the public function is as follows:

```
Public Function Bookit(lngFacility As Long, lngRoom As Long, _
  curDaily As Currency, curWeekly As Currency) As Integer
' Sub called as a method by fdlgAvailableRooms to book the selected room
' Caller passes in selected Facility, Room number, and rates
Dim db As DAO.Database, rstRes As DAO.Recordset
Dim varResNum As Variant, strSQL As String, intTrans As Integer
  ' Set error trap
  On Error GoTo BookIt_Err
  ' Get a pointer to this database
  Set db = CurrentDb
  ' Open the reservations table for insert
  Set rstRes = db.OpenRecordset("tblReservations", _
    dbOpenDynaset, dbAppendOnly)
  ' Start a transaction
  BeginTrans
  intTrans = True
  ' Get the next available reservation number
  varResNum = DMax("ReservationID", "tblReservations")
  If IsNull(varResNum) Then varResNum = 0
```

```
varResNum = varResNum + 1
' Update the current row
strSQL = "UPDATE tblReservationRequests SET ReservationID = " & _
  varResNum & " WHERE RequestID = " & Me.RequestID
db.Execute strSQL, dbFailOnError
' Book it!
rstRes.AddNew
' Copy reservation ID
rstRes!ReservationID = varResNum
' Copy employee number
rstRes!EmployeeNumber = Me.EmployeeNumber
' Copy facility ID from the room we picked
rstRes!FacilityID = lngFacility
' .. and room number
rstRes!RoomNumber = lngRoom
' Set reservation date = today
rstRes!ReservationDate = Date
' Copy check-in, check-out, and notes
rstRes!CheckInDate = Me.CheckInDate
rstRes!CheckOutDate = Me.CheckOutDate
rstRes!Notes = Me.Notes
' Copy daily and weekly rates
rstRes!DailyRate = curDaily
rstRes!WeeklyRate = curWeekly
' Calculate the total charge
rstRes!TotalCharge = ((Int(Me.CheckOutDate - Me.CheckInDate) \ 7) * _
  curWeekly) + _
  ((Int(Me.CheckOutDate - Me.CheckInDate) Mod 7) * _
  curDaily)
' Save the Reservation Row
rstRes.Update
' Commit the transaction
CommitTrans
intTrans = False
' Clean up
rstRes.Close
Set rstRes = Nothing
Set db = Nothing
' Requery this form to remove the booked row
Me.Requery
' Return success
Bookit = True
BookIt_Exit:
  Exit Function
BookIt_Err:
  MsgBox "Unexpected Error: " & Err & ", " & Error, vbCritical, gstrAppTitle
  ErrorLog Me.Name & "_Bookit", Err, Error
  Bookit = False
  If (intTrans = True) Then Rollback
  Resume BookIt_Exit
End Function
```

It makes sense to have the actual booking code back in the frmUnbookedRequests form because the row the code needs to insert into tblReservations needs several fields from the current request record (EmployeeNumber, CheckInDate, CheckOutDate, and Notes). The code starts a transaction because it must simultaneously enter a ReservationID in both the tblReservationRequests table and the tblReservations table. If either fails, the error-trapping code rolls back both updates. Notice that the code opens the tblReservations table for append only to make the insert of the new reservation more efficient.

Calculating a Stored Value

As you learned in Chapter 3, "Designing Your Database Application," storing a calculated value in a table isn't usually a good idea because you must write code to maintain the value. But sometimes, in a very large database, you need to calculate and save a value to improve performance for searching and reporting. The Housing Reservations application isn't all that large—but it could be in real life. I chose to store the calculated total charge for each reservation to show you some of the steps you must take to maintain a value like this.

Users can create and edit reservation requests, but the creation of the reservation records that contain the calculated value is controlled entirely by code, so maintaining the calculated TotalCharge value in this application is simple. You've already seen the one place where a new reservation record is created—in the public Bookit function in the frmUnbookedRequests form. The little piece of code that calculates the value is as follows:

```
' Calculate the total charge
rstRes!TotalCharge = ((Int(Me.CheckOutDate - Me.CheckInDate) \ 7) * _
    curWeekly) + _
    ((Int(Me.CheckOutDate - Me.CheckInDate) Mod 7) * _
    curDaily)
```

However, in many applications, you might not be able to control the editing of a calculated value this closely. You need to carefully consider the ramifications of saving a calculated value in your table and perhaps write code that an administrator can run to periodically verify that any saved calculated value hasn't become out of sync with the other fields used to perform the calculation.

Automating Reports

In a typical application, you'll probably spend 80 to 90 percent of your coding effort in event procedures for your *forms*. That doesn't mean that there aren't many tasks that you can automate on *reports*. This last section shows you just a few of the possibilities.

Allowing for Used Mailing Labels

Have you ever wanted to create a mailing label report and come up with a way to use up the remaining labels on a partially used page? You can find the answer in the LawTrack Contacts sample application (*Contacts.mdb*). Let's say you want to send a promotional mailing to all contacts who own the Single User product offering them an upgrade to Multi-User. Open the main switchboard form (*frmMain*), click Contacts, and then click Search in the Select Contacts pop-up window. Perform a search for all contacts who own the Single User product—you should find four records in the original sample data. Click the Print button on the *frmContacts* form, select Avery 5163 Labels (2" x 4"), ask for the report to include the Displayed Contacts, and specify that your first page of labels is missing three used ones. Your screen should look like Figure 23-27 at this point.

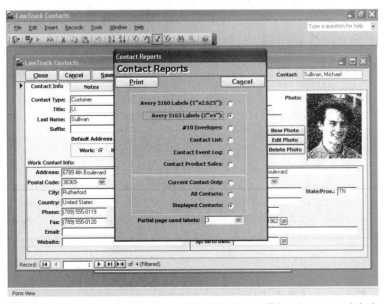

Figure 23-27. Requesting mailing labels and specifying that some labels have already been used on the first page.

Click the Print button in the dialog box, and you should see the labels print—but with three blank spaces first to avoid the used ones—as shown in Figure 23-28.

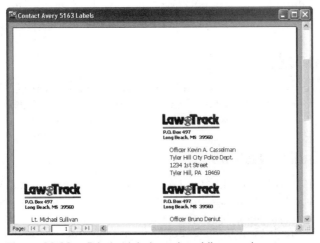

Figure 23-28. Printing labels and avoiding used ones.

You can find some interesting code in the After Update event of the option group to choose the report type in the fdlgContactPrintOptions form. The code is as follows:

```
Private Sub optReportType_AfterUpdate()
  ' Figure out whether to show the "used labels" combo
  Select Case Me.optReportType
    Case 1
      ' Show the used labels combo
      Me.cmbUsedLabels.Visible = True
      ' Hide the number of days option group
      Me.optDisplay.Visible = False
      ' up to 29 used labels on 5160
      Me.cmbUsedLabels.RowSource = "0;1;2;3;4;5;6;7;8;9;10;11;12;13;" & _
        "14;15;16;17;18;19;20;21;22;23;24;25;26;27;28;29"
    Case 2
      ' Show the used labels combo
      Me.cmbUsedLabels.Visible = True
      ' Hide the number of days option group
      Me.optDisplay.Visible = False
      ' up to 9 used labels on 5163
      Me.cmbUsedLabels.RowSource = "0;1;2;3;4;5;6;7;8;9"
    Case 3, 4
      ' Don't need the combo for Envelopes and contact list
      Me.cmbUsedLabels.Visible = False
      ' .. or the number of days filter
      Me.optDisplay.Visible = False
    Case 5, 6
      ' Don't need the used labels combo for contact events or products
      Me.cmbUsedLabels.Visible = False
      ' Do need the day filter
      Me.optDisplay.Visible = True
  End Select
End Sub
```

You can have up to 29 used labels when printing on Avery 5160 (1" x 2.625") label paper. You can have up to 9 used labels when printing on Avery 5163 (2" x 4") label paper. The combo box that you can use to indicate the number of used labels has a Value List as its row source type, so the code sets up the appropriate list based on the label type you choose.

However, the real trick to leaving blank spaces on the report is in the query that is the record source for the rptContactLabels5163 report. In the sample database, you can find a table, ztblLabelSpace, that has 30 records, and each record has one field containing the values 1 through 30. The SQL for the query is as follows:

```
PARAMETERS [Forms]![fdlgContactPrintOptions]![cmbUsedLabels] Long;
SELECT "" As Contact, "" As CompanyName, "" As Address, "" As CSZ,
Null As ContactID, "" As Zip, "" As LastName, "" As FirstName,
"" As ContactType, "" As WorkCity, "" As WorkStateOrProvince,
"" As HomeCity, "" As HomeStateOrProvince, 0 As Inactive
FROM ztblLabelSpace
WHERE ID <= [Forms]![fdlgContactPrintOptions]![cmbUsedLabels]
UNION ALL
SELECT ([tblContacts].[Title]+" ") & [tblContacts].[FirstName] & " " &
```

```
([tblContacts].[MiddleInit]+". ") & [tblContacts].[LastName] &
(", "+[tblContacts].[Suffix]) AS Contact,
Choose([tblContacts].[DefaultAddress], qryContactDefaultCompany.CompanyName,
Null) As CompanyName,
Choose([tblContacts].[DefaultAddress],[tblContacts].[WorkAddress],
[tblContacts].[HomeAddress]) AS Address,
Choose([tblContacts].[DefaultAddress],[tblContacts].[WorkCity] & ", " &
[tblContacts].[WorkStateOrProvince] & "   " & [tblContacts].[WorkPostalCode],
[tblContacts].[HomeCity] & ", " & [tblContacts].[HomeStateOrProvince]
& "   " & [tblContacts].[HomePostalCode]) AS CSZ,
tblContacts.ContactID,
Choose([tblContacts].[DefaultAddress],[tblContacts].[WorkPostalCode],
[tblContacts].[HomePostalCode]) AS Zip,
tblContacts.LastName, tblContacts.FirstName, tblContacts.ContactType,
tblContacts.WorkCity, tblContacts.WorkStateOrProvince, tblContacts.HomeCity,
tblContacts.HomeStateOrProvince, tblContacts.Inactive
FROM tblContacts
LEFT JOIN qryContactDefaultCompany
ON tblContacts.ContactID = qryContactDefaultCompany.ContactID;
```

The first SELECT statement (up to the UNION ALL) creates dummy blank columns for each field used by the report and uses the ztblLabelSpace table and a filter on the combo box in the fdlgContactPrintOptions form (Figure 23-27) to return the correct number of blank rows. The query uses a UNION with the actual query that returns contact data to display information on the report.

Because this label report prints a logo and a label control containing the return address, there's one final bit of code that keeps these from appearing on the blank labels in the rptContactLabels5163 report. The code is as follows:

```
Private Sub Detail_Format(Cancel As Integer, FormatCount As Integer)
  ' Don't print the return logo and address if this is a "spacer" record
  If IsNull(Me.ContactID) Then
    Me.imgLawTrack.Visible = False
    Me.lblRtnAddr.Visible = False
  Else
    Me.imgLawTrack.Visible = True
    Me.lblRtnAddr.Visible = True
  End If
End Sub
```

The Format event of the Detail section depends on the fact that the ContactID in the "spacer" rows is Null. When printing a blank row for spacing, the code hides the logo and the return address label.

Drawing on a Report

When you want to draw a border around a report print area, sometimes you'll need to write some code to ask Access to draw lines or a border after placing the data on the page. This is especially true if one or more controls on the report can grow to accommodate a large amount of data.

I used the Report Wizard to create the basic rptContacts report using the Justified format. (I customized the report after the wizard finished.) The wizard created a fairly decent layout with a border around all the fields, but it didn't make the text box to display notes large enough to display the text for all contacts. Figure 23-29 shows you the report displaying my contact record from the database. You can see that the notes about me are cut off at the bottom.

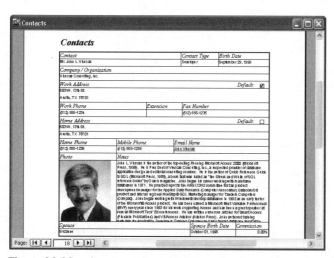

Figure 23-29. A report using a border around the data, but one of the text boxes isn't large enough to display all the text.

It's simple enough to change the Can Grow property of the text box to Yes to allow it to expand, but the rectangle control used to draw the border around all the text doesn't also have a Can Grow property. The solution is to remove the rectangle and use the Line method of the report object in the report's Format event of the Detail section to get the job done. Below is the code you can find in this event procedure in the *rptContactsExpandNotes* report.

```
Private Sub Detail_Print(Cancel As Integer, PrintCount As Integer)
Dim sngX1 As Single, sngY1 As Single
Dim sngX2 As Single, sngY2 As Single, lngColor As Long
  ' Set coordinates
  sngX1 = 120
  sngY1 = 120
  sngX2 = 9120
  ' Adjust the height if Notes has expanded
  sngY2 = 7680 + (Me.Notes.Height - 2565)
  ' Draw the big box around the data
  ' Set width of the line
  Me.DrawWidth = 8
  ' Draw the rectangle around the expanded fields
  Me.Line Step(sngX1, sngY1)-Step(sngX2, sngY2), RGB(0, 0, 197), B
End Sub
```

The Line method accepts three parameters:

1. The upper left and lower right corners of the line or box you want to draw, expressed in *twips*. (There are 1440 twips per inch.) Include the Step keyword to indicate that the coordinates are relative to the current graphics position, which always starts at 0, 0. When you use Step for the second coordinate, you provide values relative to those you specified in the first set of coordinates.

2. The color you want to draw the line or box, expressed as a red-green-blue (RGB) value. (The RGB function is handy for this.)

3. An indicator to ask for a line, a rectangle, or a filled rectangle. No indicator draws a line. Include the letter B to ask for a rectangle. Add the letter F to ask for a filled rectangle.

Before you call the Line method, you can set the DrawWidth property of the report to set the width of the line. (The default width is in pixels.)

The only tricky part is figuring out the coordinates. On the original report, the rectangle starts at 0.0833 inches in from the left and down from the top, so multiplying that value by 1440 twips per inch gave me the starting values of 120 down from the top and 120 in from the left edge. The width of the rectangle needs to be about 6.3333 inches, so the relative coordinate for the upper right corner is 6.3333 × 1440, or about 9,120 twips. The height of the rectangle needs to be at least 5.3333 inches, or about 7,680 twips, and the height needs to be adjusted for the amount that the Notes text box expands. The Notes text box is designed to be a minimum of 1.7813 inches high, or 2,565 twips, so subtracting 2,565 from the actual height of the Notes text box when it's formatted (the Height property is also in twips) gives you the amount you need to add to the original height of the rectangle. Trust me, I didn't get it right on the first try!

If you open the *rptContactsExpandNotes* report and move to my record on page 18, you'll see that the rectangle now expands nicely to fit around the Notes text box that grew to display all the text in my record. Figure 23-30 shows you the report with the rectangle drawn by the code behind the report.

> **Caution** You can find the Line method documented in Access 2003 Help, but the syntax shown is completely wrong. Interestingly, the example provided with the Help topic uses the correct syntax that I've just shown you.

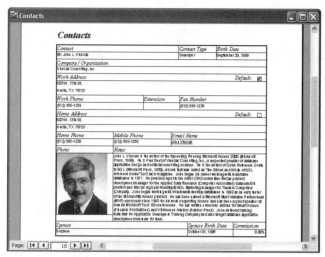

Figure 23-30. A report with a custom rectangle drawn around expanded text.

Dynamically Filtering a Report When It Opens

The two most common ways to open a report filtered to print specific records are

- Use the WhereCondition parameter with the DoCmd.OpenReport method (usually in code in an event procedure behind a form) to specify a filter.

- Base the report on a parameter query that prompts the user for the filter values or that references control values on an open form.

In some cases, you might design a report that you intend to open from several locations in your application, and you can't guarantee that the form to provide filter values will always be open. Or, you might have multiple reports that need the same filter criteria, and you don't want to have to design a separate filter form for each report. To solve these problems, you can add code to the report to have it open its own filter dialog box from the report's Open event procedure. Let's go back to the Housing Reservations application (*Housing.mdb*) to take a look at a report that uses this technique.

In the Housing Reservations application, both the rptFacilityOccupancy report and the rpt-FacilityRevenueChart report depend on a single form, fdlgReportDateRange, to provide a starting and ending date for the report. To see the *rptFacilityOccupancy* report, you can start the application by opening the *frmSplash* form, sign on as an administrator (Viescas, John L. or LaMee, Brian), click the Reports button on the main switchboard, and then click the Reservations button in the Facilities category on the Reports switchboard. (You can also simply open the report directly from the Database window.) When you open the report, you'll see a dialog box prompting you for the dates you want as shown in Figure 23-31 on the next page.

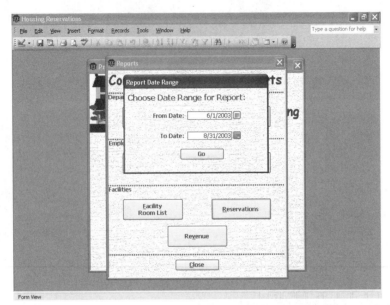

Figure 23-31. A parameter dialog box opened from the report that you asked to view.

Unless you've reloaded the sample data, the database contains reservations from April 1, 2003, through November 1, 2003, so asking for a report for June, July, and August should work nicely. Enter the dates you want and click Go to see the report, as shown in Figure 23-32.

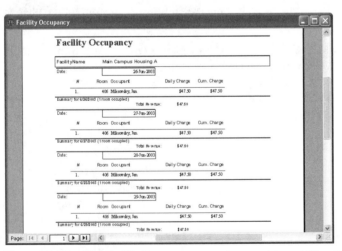

Figure 23-32. The Facility Occupancy report uses a shared filter dialog box to let you specify a date range.

The report has a parameter query in its record source, and the parameters point to the from and to dates on the fdlgReportDateRange form that you see in Figure 23-31. However, the code behind the Reservations button on the Reports switchboard opens the report unfiltered.

It's the code in the report's Open event procedure that opens the dialog box so that the query in the record source can find the parameters it needs. The code is as follows:

```
Private Sub Report_Open(Cancel As Integer)
  ' Open the date range dialog
  ' .. report record source is filtered on this!
  DoCmd.OpenForm "fdlgReportDateRange", WindowMode:=acDialog
End Sub
```

This works because a report object doesn't attempt to open the record source for the report until after the code in the Open event finishes. So, you can place code in the Open event to dynamically change the record source of the report or, as in this example, open a form in Dialog mode to wait until that form closes or hides itself. The code behind the dialog form, fdlgReportDateRange, is as follows:

```
Private Sub Form_Load()
  ' If passed a parameter, reset defaults to last quarter
  If Not IsNothing(Me.OpenArgs) Then
    ' Set the start default to first day of previous quarter
    Me.txtFromDate.DefaultValue = "#" & _
      DateSerial(Year(Date), ((Month(Date) - 1) \ 3) * 3 - 2, 1) & "#"
    ' Set the end default to last day of previous quarter
    Me.txtToDate.DefaultValue = "#" & _
      DateSerial(Year(Date), ((Month(Date) - 1) \ 3) * 3 + 1, 1) & "#"
  End If
End Sub

Private Sub cmdGo_Click()
  ' Hide me so report can continue
  Me.Visible = False
End Sub
```

The code in the form's Load event checks to see if the report that is opening the form has passed a parameter in the OpenArgs property. If so, the code resets the default values for the two date text boxes to the start and end dates of the previous quarter. If you look at the code behind the *rptFacilityRevenueChart* report, you'll find that this report asks for the different default values. But it's the code in the Click event of the Go command button that gets things rolling. The code behind the form responds to your clicking the Go button to hide itself so that the report can continue. It can't close because the record source of the report depends on the two date parameters. As noted earlier, hiding this form opened in Dialog mode allows the code in the Open event of the report to finish, which lets the report finally load its record source. As you might suspect, there's code in the Close event of the report to close the parameter form when you close the report or the report finishes printing.

As you've seen in this chapter, Visual Basic is an incredibly powerful language, and the tasks you can accomplish with it are limited only by your imagination. In the next chapter of this book, you'll learn how to set startup properties, create custom menus, and build a main switchboard form for your application.

The Finishing Touches

You're in the home stretch. You have almost all the forms and reports required for the tasks you want to implement in your application, but you need some additional forms to make it easier to navigate to different tasks. To add a professional touch, you should design a custom menu bar and a custom toolbar for most forms (and perhaps for some reports) and custom shortcut menus for forms, form controls, and reports. You should take advantage of built-in tools to check the efficiency of your design, and you should make sure that none of your forms allow design changes when in Form view. Finally, you need to set the startup properties of your database to let Microsoft Access know how to get your application rolling, and you need to perform a final compile of your Visual Basic code to achieve maximum performance.

Creating Custom Menus and Toolbars

When your application is running, the user probably won't want or need some of the Access design features. However, you might want to provide some additional toolbar buttons on your form toolbar and menu bar so that the user has direct access to commands such as Save Record and Find Next. For example, open the LawTrack Contacts sample database (*Contacts.mdb*), open the *frmContactsPlain* form in Form view (which uses the standard Form View toolbar), right-click the toolbar, and select Custom Form Toolbar. You can see some useful differences between the two toolbars, as shown in Figure 24-1. Buttons the user won't need (such as Form View, Save, Print, Print Preview, Format Painter, and New Object) aren't available on the custom toolbar. (None of the forms in the LawTrack Contacts database are designed to be printed.) However, the Custom Form Toolbar does have Close and Save Record buttons added at the left end, and the New Record and Delete Record buttons are clustered with the new Save Record button. In the LawTrack Contacts application, all forms (except *frmContactsPlain* and a few other example forms) have their Toolbar property set to use the custom toolbar.

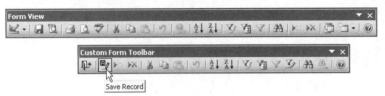

Figure 24-1. Comparing the standard Form View toolbar (top) and the Custom Form Toolbar (bottom) from the LawTrack Contacts sample database.

The same is true of the built-in menu bars and shortcut menus. For example, you don't want your users to be able to select Design view from any of the built-in menus. For most forms, you also don't want the user to be able to switch to PivotTable or PivotChart view. The following sections show you how to build custom menus and toolbars.

Understanding the Customize Toolbar Facility

To create a new toolbar or modify an existing one, you must enter toolbar customize mode. Open the Customize dialog box by choosing Toolbars from the View menu and then choosing Customize from the submenu. (You can also right-click on any open toolbar to open the toolbar shortcut menu and then choose Customize from that menu.) The Customize dialog box with the Toolbars tab selected is shown in Figure 24-2.

Figure 24-2. The Toolbars tab of the Customize dialog box.

When you open the Customize dialog box, all toolbar buttons become editable. You can

- Remove any button from any open toolbar (including any built-in toolbar) by clicking the button and dragging it off its toolbar.
- Move any button by clicking it and dragging it to a new location on its toolbar or another toolbar.

- Copy a button from one toolbar to another by holding down the Ctrl key while you drag.
- Add a button by dragging it from the Commands list to any toolbar.
- Right-click a button to open a shortcut list of properties that you can modify to change the look of the toolbar button.
- Right-click a button and choose Properties from the shortcut list to view all the properties for a button and define a custom action for a toolbar button.
- Click a button and then click Modify Selection on the Commands tab of the Customize dialog box to open the properties for the selected button.
- Click the Rearrange Commands button in the Customize dialog box to select any menu or toolbar and add a new command, delete a command, or move commands.

On the left side of the Customize dialog box, you can see the names of all the built-in toolbars in Access. A check mark next to a toolbar name in this list indicates that the toolbar is currently open. You can open any of the toolbars by selecting the check box next to the toolbar name.

> **Note** The term toolbar refers generically to toolbars, menu bars, and shortcut menus. As you'll learn later, you can set the Type property of a custom toolbar to define whether it appears as a toolbar, menu bar, or shortcut menu.

Near the end of the list, you'll see three special built-in toolbars that Access displays only if you select them in this dialog box: Shortcut Menus, Utility 1, and Utility 2. The two utility toolbars are empty, so you can add buttons of your choice to them to create custom toolbars that are available in all the databases you open on your machine. The Shortcut Menus toolbar is a "placeholder" for all shortcut menus, including custom ones that you have defined for your application. You'll learn how to create a custom shortcut menu later in this chapter. In the LawTrack Contacts sample database, you can see a Custom Form Menu Bar, a Custom Form Toolbar, a Custom Print Menu, and a Custom Report Toolbar already defined at the bottom of the list.

> **Caution** If you open one of the built-in toolbars in a context in which the toolbar would not normally be open, the toolbar remains open until you close it. For example, if you open the Customize dialog box while the focus is on the Database window and then open the Form Design toolbar, the toolbar remains open no matter what you are doing in Access. Likewise, if you close a toolbar in a context in which that toolbar is normally open (for example, if you close the Formatting toolbar in a Form window in Design view), that toolbar remains closed until you open it again within the usual context or from the Customize dialog box.

Inside Out

Setting options that affect all Office applications

In the Customize dialog box, you can click the Options tab to see options you can set that affect all Microsoft Office applications. By default, none of the Office applications show you all the commands available when you first click a menu. Instead, Office keeps track of which menu commands you use most frequently (known as adaptive menus) and shows you those first. When you leave the Show full menus after a short delay option set (the default), Office applications reveal the hidden menu items if you leave the menu open for a second or two. If you clear the option to reveal all commands after a short delay, you can still click the arrow at the bottom of the menu command list to show all commands. If you leave the shortened menu feature enabled, you can select Reset menu and toolbar usage data if you think the menus aren't showing your most frequently used commands when you first open them.

You can select the Always show full menus option to disable these features. As an application developer, I like to see all the menu commands whenever I open a menu, so this is always the first option I reset after installing a new version of Microsoft Office.

Also on the Options tab are check boxes that you can select to display large icons in buttons on toolbars, to list font names in their font, to display ScreenTips, and to display shortcut keys in ScreenTips. If you're working on a large monitor at a high resolution (1024×768 or 1280×1024), you might find the larger toolbar icons easier to see. The buttons with large icons are approximately 50 percent wider and taller than the standard buttons. There's also an option on this tab to animate your menus in various ways when you open them—interesting effects if you have a fast graphics card on your PC.

Any new toolbar that you define is available only in the database that you had open at the time you created the toolbar. If you want to define a custom toolbar that is available in all the databases that you work with on your computer, you must modify one of the built-in toolbars. You can also use the two blank toolbars—Utility 1 and Utility 2—to create a custom set of toolbar buttons that are available in any database on your machine. One drawback to these two toolbars is that you cannot give them custom names. Also, any changes that you make to these toolbars on your machine won't move with your database to another machine. Any change you make to any built-in toolbar (including Utility 1 and Utility 2) is effective only for your computer. If you have made changes to one of the built-in toolbars or menu bars, you can select it in the Customize dialog box and click the Reset button to return the toolbar to its default. Access prompts you to confirm this action so that you don't inadvertently erase any custom changes you've made.

Creating a Custom Form Toolbar

You can create a custom toolbar for your forms to remove some of the built-in features and add other commands that your user might find useful. You can also create a custom toolbar for reports, and the design process for either is the same. The following sections show you how to create a custom form toolbar.

Defining a New Toolbar

Click the New button on the Toolbars tab in the Customize dialog box to begin defining a new toolbar, and Access prompts you for a name for your new toolbar. If you want to follow the example in this section to create a new toolbar in the LawTrack Contacts sample database, provide a name like **Sample Custom Toolbar** in the New Toolbar dialog box and click OK. You'll see the name appear at the bottom of the Toolbars list, and an empty toolbar in the form of a small, gray window will open in the Access workspace. Select your new toolbar in the Toolbars list, and click the Properties button to open the dialog box shown in Figure 24-3.

Figure 24-3. The Toolbar Properties dialog box.

> **Note** If you want to build a custom toolbar to use with one or more of your forms, it's a good idea to first open one of the target forms in Form view because this makes the built-in form menu and toolbar available. As you'll see below, it's often easiest to copy the commands or toolbar buttons you want from built-in menus or toolbars rather than build them from scratch. In all of the examples in this section, I have the frmContactsPlain form in the LawTrack Contacts database open in Form view.

In the Toolbar Properties dialog box, you can select any toolbar from the Selected Toolbar drop-down list. If you select a custom toolbar (not a built-in one), you can rename it and set its type—Menu Bar to define a custom menu, Toolbar to define a custom toolbar, and Popup to define a custom shortcut menu. Because we're building a toolbar, be sure Type is set to Toolbar. If you want to, you can position your toolbar (you'll have to click Close in the Toolbar Properties dialog box, position the toolbar, and then choose Properties again in the Customize dialog box) and then restrict where the user can move it. For example, you can dock the toolbar at the bottom of your screen and then set Docking to either Can't Change or No Vertical. You can also dock the toolbar on either side and choose No Horizontal.

For custom toolbars, you can select Show on Toolbars Menu to make the toolbar available in the list of toolbars displayed from the View menu's Toolbars command or when the user right-clicks any toolbar or menu bar. You can't change this option for built-in toolbars. You can choose from additional options that determine whether this toolbar can be customized, resized, moved, or hidden. Finally, for built-in toolbars, you can click the Restore Defaults button to undo any changes you made. (This button appears dimmed in Figure 24-3 because a custom toolbar is selected.) Close this dialog box to go to the next step.

Click the Commands tab in the Customize dialog box to display the list of available commands, shown in Figure 24-4. The custom toolbar in the LawTrack Contacts sample database starts with a Close button and a Save Record button at the left end of the toolbar. You can find the Close command partway down the Commands list in the File category. As you can see, the Save Record command is located two down from Close. When you find the command you want in the Commands list, drag it onto your new toolbar. Notice that the icon for the custom Close command doesn't match the one on the Custom Form Toolbar in the LawTrack Contacts application. You'll learn how to change the icon later.

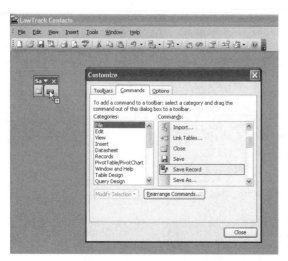

Figure 24-4. The Customize dialog box and command category buttons; the custom toolbar under construction is open at the left.

The next several buttons for the LawTrack Contacts custom toolbar are all available on the built-in Form View toolbar. You can copy them from this toolbar rather than hunt for them in the Commands list. You can drag buttons from one toolbar to another, but when you do that, you're *moving* the button. In other words, you're deleting the button from the built-in toolbar and adding it to your custom toolbar. To copy a button from an existing toolbar, press the Ctrl key and hold it down while you drag the button. When you're copying a button, Access displays a small plus sign in a white box next to your mouse cursor, as shown in Figure 24-4. A large I-beam appears on the receiving toolbar to indicate where you're dropping the new command.

> **Note** If you didn't open a form before starting to build your toolbar, you can also force open the built-in Form View toolbar by selecting it in the Toolbars list on the Toolbars tab of the Customize dialog box. Unless you're building the toolbar while a form is open in Form view, some buttons appear dimmed (disabled) and some buttons are not visible. As soon as you open a form in Form view, the appropriate buttons become available. If you force the Form View toolbar open, remember to close it before exiting the customize facility or it will stay open all the time.

If you want to duplicate the Custom Form Toolbar in the LawTrack Contacts database, copy the following buttons from the built-in Form View toolbar or the Commands tab of the Customize dialog box in this order (starting to the right of the Close and Save Record buttons): New Record, Delete Record, Cut, Copy, Paste, Undo, Sort Ascending, Sort Descending, Filter By Selection, Filter By Form, Apply/Remove Filter (labeled Toggle Filter in the Records category), Advanced Filter/Sort, Find, Find Next, and Help. (You won't see these buttons on the Form View toolbar unless you also have a form open.) You can find the Advanced Filter/Sort command in the Records category and the Find Next command in the Edit category.

Customizing Your New Toolbar

After you build a toolbar, you can rearrange the buttons and add dividing lines between them. You can also change the button image, the label in the ScreenTip, and the button style. Finally, and perhaps most importantly, you can define a custom macro or function that you want Access to execute when the user clicks the toolbar button. If you're not still in toolbar customize mode, choose Toolbars from the View menu and then choose Customize from the submenu to open the Customize dialog box, shown in Figure 24-2. (Access opens the dialog box and displays the last tab you selected, so you might see the Commands or Options tab instead.)

Creating Button Images To make your custom toolbar look just like the Custom Form Toolbar in the LawTrack Contacts database, you first need to change the Close button to show a different image. If there's another button that has an image you want to use, you can right-click that button to open the shortcut menu and choose Copy Button Image to place that button's bitmap on the Clipboard. Move to the button you want to change, right-click, and choose Paste Button Image. (See Figure 24-5 on the next page.)

If you're good at visualizing button images by setting individual pixel colors on a 16-by-16-pixel square, choose Edit Button Image from the shortcut menu to open a simple design window for the bitmap image. Finally, if you have a 16-by-16-pixel bitmap or icon file that you want to use as a button image, open that file in an image-editing program (for example, Microsoft Paint on the Windows Accessories menu of the Start button), copy the bitmap to the Clipboard, and then choose Paste Button Image from the shortcut menu. In this case, I used an arrow pointing to an open door. You can find this image on the companion CD, saved as *CloseArrow.bmp*.

Figure 24-5. Pasting a custom button image onto a toolbar button.

Arranging Buttons To make buttons easier to use, it's often useful to cluster buttons that perform similar functions by adding a dividing line between those clusters. To create a dividing line to the left of any button, right-click the button and turn on the Begin A Group property near the bottom of the shortcut menu. (Access makes this property unavailable for the first button or menu on a toolbar.) On the Custom Form Toolbar in the LawTrack Contacts application, you can find a dividing line before the Save Record, Cut, Undo, Sort Ascending, Filter By Selection, Find, and Help buttons.

Assigning Custom Actions Last, but not least, you can define a custom macro or function that you want Access to run instead of the built-in action whenever the user clicks the button. In the LawTrack Contacts application, every form that edits data has a Save command button (cmdSave), and code in the Click event of this button calls a save routine specific to the form. The cmdSave_Click event in each form is public so that it can be called as a method of the form. In the modUtility module, you can find a public function called SaveRecord that finds the currently active form (if any) and then calls that form's cmdSave_Click event. The code is as follows:

```
Function SaveRecord() As Variant
'------------------------------------------------------------
' Called from a custom menu or toolbar Save Record
' Attempts to find the public cmdSave_Click
' procedure in the currently active form and
' execute the save by calling that form's procedure.
' If there is no active form the function exits.
' Created By: JLV 06/09/03
' Last Revised: JLV 06/09/03
'------------------------------------------------------------
' Place to save the currently active form
Dim frm As Form
    ' Skip any error
```

```
On Error Resume Next
' Attempt to get the active form
Set frm = Screen.ActiveForm
' If error, bail
If Err <> 0 Then Exit Function
' Now try to call the form's save procedure
frm.cmdSave_Click
' Done
Err.Clear
End Function
```

The Save Record button (and the Save Record command on the custom form menu) calls this function so that the custom record save code for each form executes instead of the standard Access command. The code uses the ActiveForm property of the Screen object to find the form that currently has the focus, and then it calls the cmdSave_Click method of the form. So, instead of simply executing the standard Access save record, this causes a custom save procedure for the form to execute instead—which allows you to code additional tests specific to each form before finally saving the record.

To define a custom action for a toolbar button, open the Customize dialog box, right-click that button to open the shortcut menu, and choose Properties. You'll see the Control Properties window, as shown in Figure 24-6. (Access uses the name of the toolbar as the first part of the window name.)

Figure 24-6. The Control Properties window, where you can define a custom action for the control.

In the Control Properties window, you can choose any control on the toolbar from the Selected Control list at the top of the window. As you can see, you can redefine the caption for controls that display text and change the ScreenTip text if you have ScreenTips enabled. When the command is on a menu, adding an ampersand (&) before one of the letters in the Caption box establishes the access key for that menu item (the letter appears underlined); however, commands on toolbars do not have an access key. When you copy a command from the Commands list, Access includes both a Caption and a ScreenTip in case you place the command on a menu bar. The Shortcut Text property also applies only to controls you define on menus.

You can change the style of the control—Default Style (an icon only on a toolbar or an icon and text on a menu), Text Only (Always), Text Only (in Menus), or Image and Text. In addition, you can define a help file and help context for the command. (If you've copied a built-in command as shown in Figure 24-6, you probably want to leave the original help pointers set for the built-in help topic.) The Parameter and Tag properties are advanced settings for programmers who build their own command bars and commands using Visual Basic.

The critical setting in this window is the On Action property. You can set this property to a macro name or specify a public function by entering an equals sign (=) followed by the name of the function. This works exactly like the event properties in forms and controls. In this case, you want to call the SaveRecord function, and the function requires no parameters, as shown in Figure 24-6.

After you finish building your toolbar, you can use it with any form by opening that form in Design view and setting the Toolbar property to point to this custom toolbar. You can also open any report in Design view and set the Toolbar property to specify the toolbar you want displayed when the report is opened in Print Preview. I like to design my application with one custom toolbar for all forms and another for all reports. However, you can define a different custom toolbar for each form and report if you like.

Creating a Custom Form Menu Bar

After you build a custom form (or report) toolbar, it would be helpful (and consistent) to replace the built-in menu bar with a custom menu bar. You can then set the Menu Bar property of your forms (or reports) to point to the custom menu bar. For example, the Custom Form Menu Bar in the LawTrack Contacts sample database, as shown in Figure 24-7, has a limited set of commands that matches the functionality of the custom toolbar described in the previous section. When you open the File menu, you can see that the commands a user shouldn't need, such as New Database, aren't available on the custom menu.

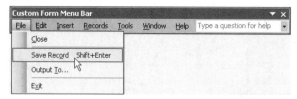

Figure 24-7. The custom File menu on the Custom Form Menu Bar eliminates unneeded commands, such as Open Database, New Database, Save, Export, and Database Properties.

> **Note** If you or your user chooses to leave adaptive menus turned on (by entering customize mode and leaving Always show full menus turned off on the Options tab), this won't affect the design of your custom menus. You can still design full menus for your application. With this option turned on, Access shows only the most recently used options first on your custom menus.

Prior to Microsoft Access 97 (version 8), the only way you could define a custom menu bar was to construct a complex series of macros. You needed one macro consisting of AddMenu actions to define the basic menu bar. You also needed an additional macro for each drop-down menu or submenu in that menu bar. You might have used as many as a dozen macros just to define one custom menu bar.

Access 2003 still supports AddMenu macros for backward compatibility, but it's much easier and more flexible to define a menu using the customize facility. For several of the standard menus, such as Edit, Insert, Records, and Window, you can copy the built-in menu "as is."

One of the advantages of copying built-in menus is that you automatically get any additional commands that appear on these menus in particular situations. For example, if you copy the built-in Edit menu, when the focus is on an OLE object, you will see OLE object editing commands at the bottom of the Edit menu on your custom menu bar. If you were to build these menus on your own, you would first have to place the focus on a control that activates these commands before opening the Customize dialog box and then copy the commands from the built-in Access menus. (No, you can't find these commands in the Edit category on the Commands tab.) If you build a custom menu on your own and copy selected focus-sensitive commands from the built-in menu, you still get the desired effect of having the commands appear only when the focus is on an appropriate object. As another example, if you copy the built-in Window menu, you get the built-in list of open windows at the bottom of your custom Window menu.

To start building a custom menu, be sure you have the frmContactsPlain form open in Form view. (This reveals all the built-in commands on the built-in menu bar.) Right-click any menu bar or toolbar, and select Customize from the shortcut menu. Click the New button on the Toolbars tab, name the menu bar **Sample Custom Menu Bar** in the New Toolbar dialog box, and click OK. Click the Properties button, and in the Toolbar Properties dialog box, set the Type to Menu Bar. Close the dialog box to go to the next step.

Next, click the Commands tab in the Customize dialog box, and scroll to the bottom of the Categories list. The custom menu bar in the LawTrack Contacts database (Custom Form Menu Bar) uses the original Edit, Insert, Records, and Window menus, but it has customized File, Tools, and Help menus, and it doesn't include the View or Format menus at all. To make your new menu match, select the New Menu category, which provides one special entry that allows you to start a new menu on the menu bar. Drag the New Menu command from the Commands list to your menu bar three times, once for each of the custom menus you need to build. Right-click each New Menu item, and change its name to reflect the menu name you want, as shown in Figure 24-8 on the next page. Adding an ampersand (&) before one of the letters in the menu name establishes the access key for that menu item, much like using an ampersand in the Caption property of a form label or command button.

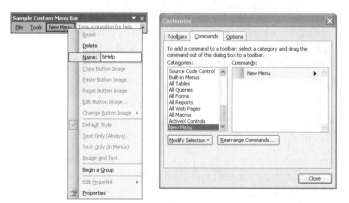

Figure 24-8. Using the New Menu command to set up custom menus on your custom menu bar.

You don't want to customize the built-in Edit, Insert, Records, or Window menus in this exercise. You can copy them either from the built-in menu bar named Menu Bar (probably docked right above the built-in toolbar) or from the Built-In Menus category on the Commands tab of the Customize dialog box. Be sure you place the menus in the same order as the standard Access menu bar (File, Edit, Insert, Records, Tools, Window, Help) so that your application is consistent with what a user is familiar with seeing in other applications. If you copy the menus from the built-in menu bar, be sure to hold down the Ctrl key! If you don't hold down the Ctrl key, you will remove them from the built-in menu bar and place them only on your custom menu bar.

Caution When you copy a built-in menu (either from an available menu bar or from the Built-In Menus category), Access does *not* make an independent copy of the original. So, if you copy a menu and then change some of its properties (for example, you delete one of the commands from the menu), you're also affecting the built-in menu. This is why you must use the New Menu command to build the custom File, View, Tools, and Help menus in this example. If you were to copy the originals and delete unwanted commands from the copies, you'd be deleting them from the built-in menus as well.

Now you can add the commands you want to your three custom menus. You can copy commands either from the Commands list or from another menu bar. Remember to hold down the Ctrl key when you copy a command from another menu bar so that you *copy* the command, not *move* it. When you drag a command to a menu bar and hover over one of the menu commands, Access drops down the current list of commands. You can then move the cursor down the list. Access shows you a horizontal bar on the drop-down menu where it will place your command if you release the mouse button at that point. It takes a bit of hand-eye coordination, but it's not too difficult. You can always grab a command and move it if you drop it in the wrong place. Figure 24-9 shows adding the Office Links command to the Tools menu just below the Spelling command.

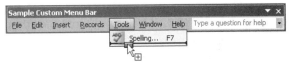

Figure 24-9. Adding the Office Links command to a custom Tools menu.

> **Tip** When you copy a command from one menu to another, Access resets the command's Begin A Group property to off. You might want to turn this property back on for commands that normally begin a group, such as the AutoCorrect Options command on the Tools menu that you'll find on the Custom Form Menu Bar in the sample databases.

To create the custom menu bar in the LawTrack Contacts sample database, you'll need to place the Close, Save Record, Output To, and Exit commands on the File menu and the Spelling, Office Links, and AutoCorrect Options commands on the Tools menu. To further customize the Save Record command, right-click it and choose Properties from the bottom of the shortcut menu to display the Control Properties dialog box, as shown in Figure 24-10. Set the On Action property to point to the SaveRecord function so that the menu command works just like the custom toolbar button you created earlier.

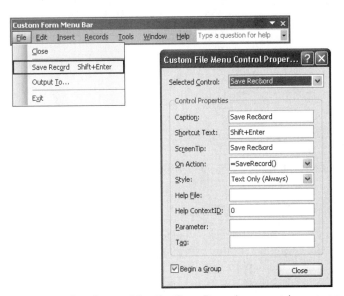

Figure 24-10. Customizing the Save Record command on your custom menu bar.

On the custom Help menu on the Custom Form Menu Bar, you can find commands for Microsoft Access Help and About LawTrack Contacts (which opens the frmAbout form). To make your new menu match, copy the Microsoft Access Help command from the built-in menu bar or from the Window and Help category on the Commands tab of the Customize dialog box. Next, go to the All Forms category on the Commands tab of the Customize dialog box, and drag the frmAbout form onto the drop-down portion of your Help menu. Open the properties of the frmAbout command, change its Caption to **About LawTrack Contacts...**, and change its Style to Text Only (Always) to remove the form icon.

When you're finished, you can place the name of your custom menu bar in the Menu Bar property of each form that you want to open with your custom menu bar displayed instead of the built-in menu bar. As with custom toolbars, you can design different custom menu bars for each form or report if you like. Open a form in Form view, and you can see both the custom menu bar and custom toolbar, as shown in Figure 24-11.

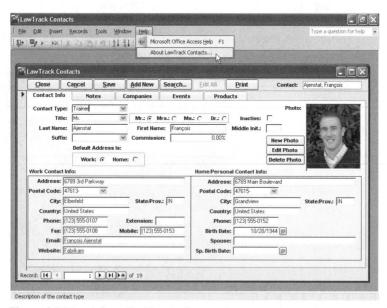

Figure 24-11. A form that has both a custom menu bar and a custom toolbar.

Creating Custom Shortcut Menus

Don't forget that your users can right-click on the forms and reports in your application to open a shortcut menu. Forms have a ShortcutMenu property that you can set to No (false) to disable all shortcut menus. But Reports don't have this property, so unless you define a custom ShortcutMenuBar for reports, users will see the built-in menu. Figure 24-12 shows you the three built-in shortcut menus—for a form, a control on a form, and a report. You can see that they provide some options that you probably don't want your users to be able to choose—such as switching to Design view or opening the Properties window for a form control.

If you specify a custom shortcut menu for a form, that custom menu also becomes the shortcut menu for all the controls on the form. You might want to allow the user access to some of the shortcut menu features for controls, such as the filter or sort options. So if you define a shortcut menu for your forms, you should also create one for the controls on your forms.

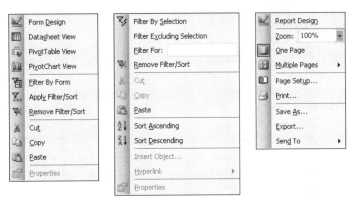

Figure 24-12. The built-in form, form control, and report shortcut menus.

Building a shortcut menu is very similar to building a custom menu bar—with a twist. Access anchors all shortcut menus on the Shortcut Menus toolbar, and it provides a special Custom entry at the right end of the toolbar where you can create your custom shortcut menus, as shown in Figure 24-13. You can open the Shortcut Menus toolbar only when you're in toolbar customize mode.

Figure 24-13. The custom shortcut menu anchored on the Shortcut Menus toolbar.

To begin defining a custom shortcut menu, enter customize mode by right-clicking any toolbar and choosing Customize from the shortcut menu or by choosing Customize from the Tools menu. Begin a new toolbar by choosing the Toolbars tab in the Customize dialog box and then clicking the New button. Give your new toolbar a name in the New Toolbar dialog box and click OK. Immediately click Properties on the Toolbars tab and change the Type to Popup. Your new toolbar disappears, and Access shows you the warning dialog box shown in Figure 24-14 that informs you that you can find your new toolbar on the Custom list of the special Shortcut Menus toolbar. Click OK to close the dialog box and then click Close in the Toolbar Properties window.

Figure 24-14. Access tells you that you can find your new shortcuts menu bar on the Shortcut Menus toolbar.

Tip   Deleting a custom shortcut menu

You cannot delete a custom shortcut menu by opening the Shortcut Menus toolbar, finding your toolbar on the Custom list, and dragging the toolbar off the list. The only way to delete a custom shortcut menu is to click Properties on the Toolbars tab of the Customize dialog box, change the Selected Toolbar to the name of your custom shortcut menu, and change Type to either Menu Bar or Toolbar. You can then select the toolbar in the Toolbars list of the Customize dialog box and click the Delete button to remove it.

Now that you have a new custom shortcut menu, you must open the Shortcut Menus toolbar by selecting it in the Toolbars list on the Toolbars tab in the Customize dialog box. You can customize the shortcut menu by dragging commands from the Commands tab or from another menu bar. Figure 24-15 shows adding the Apply Filter/Sort command to a custom form shortcut menu bar by dragging the command from the Records category on the Commands tab of the Customize dialog box.

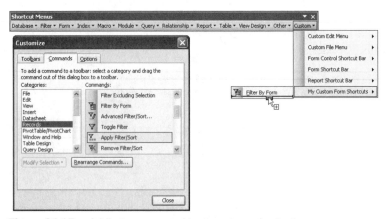

Figure 24-15.   Adding a command to a custom shortcut menu.

Setting Form, Form Control, and Report Menu and Toolbar Properties

After you create the custom menus and toolbars you need, you can set the Menu Bar and Toolbar properties for your forms and reports and the Shortcut Menu Bar property for your forms, form controls, and reports. Doing this one form, form control, or report at a time is a tedious task. However, if you have defined menu bars and toolbars and shortcut menu bars that work for all your forms, form controls, and reports, you can run some Visual Basic code to set all the properties at once.

For the sample applications, I created one custom menu bar, one custom toolbar, and one custom shortcut menu for all forms, and I created one custom shortcut menu that would work for all form controls. I also created one custom menu bar, one custom toolbar, and one custom shortcut menu for all reports. I then wrote some Visual Basic procedures to set the appropriate properties for all forms, form controls, and reports. You can find these procedures in the *modExamples* module in both the LawTrack Contacts and Housing Reservations sample databases—SetFormToolbars for forms and SetReportToolbars for reports—and you can adapt these procedures for your own use. Here's the code for SetFormToolbars:

```
Public Sub SetFormToolbars()
Dim objFrm As AccessObject, frm As Form, ctl As Control
  ' Go through every form in the database
  For Each objFrm In CurrentProject.AllForms
    ' Skip fixing any "plain" examples
    If Right(objFrm.Name, 5) <> "plain" Then
      DoCmd.OpenForm FormName:=objFrm.Name, View:=acDesign, _
        WindowMode:=acHidden
      ' Set a pointer to the form just opened
      Set frm = Forms(objFrm.Name)
      ' Set custom menu and toolbars for the form object
      ' .. only for primary forms
      If Left(frm.Name, 3) = "frm" Then
        ' Clear any saved filter while we're at it
        Forms(frm.Name).Filter = ""
        ' Set the custom menu bar
        Forms(frm.Name).MenuBar = "Custom Form Menu Bar"
        ' Set the custom toolbar
        Forms(frm.Name).Toolbar = "Custom Form Toolbar"
        ' Set the custom shortcut menu bar
        Forms(frm.Name).ShortcutMenuBar = "Form Shortcut Bar"
      End If
      ' Loop through all controls
      For Each ctl In frm.Controls
        ' Skip control types that don't have a ShortcutMenuBar property
        If (ctl.ControlType <> acCustomControl) And _
          (ctl.ControlType <> acSubform) And _
          (ctl.ControlType <> acRectangle) And _
          (ctl.ControlType <> acLabel) And _
          (ctl.ControlType <> acLine) And _
          (ctl.ControlType <> acPageBreak) Then
          ' Set the custom control shortcut menu
          ctl.ShortcutMenuBar = "Form Control Shortcut Bar"
        End If
      ' Loop through all controls on the form
      Next ctl
      ' Fix AllowDesignChanges while we're at it
      frm.AllowDesignChanges = False
      ' Close and save the result
      DoCmd.Close acForm, objFrm.Name, acSaveYes
    End If
  ' Loop to get the next form
  Next objFrm
  ' Clean up
  Set ctl = Nothing
  Set frm = Nothing
  Set objFrm = Nothing
End Sub
```

This code takes advantage of the AllForms collection that you learned about in Chapter 22 to open each form in Design view, and set the form's MenuBar, ToolBar, and ShortcutMenuBar properties to the custom form toolbars that I created. The code also examines each control on each form and sets the ShortcutMenuBar property for selected control types. (Some control types, such as lines and rectangles, do not have a ShortcutMenuBar property.) The code also resets the AllowDesignChanges property that you'll learn about later in this chapter and then saves the changes. This code takes a few seconds to run from the Visual Basic Immediate window, and it is much easier than opening each form individually to set the properties.

Fine-Tuning with the Performance Analyzer Wizard

Even the most experienced database designers (including me) don't always take advantage of all the techniques available to improve performance in an Access application. Fortunately, Access provides a Performance Analyzer Wizard to help you do a final analysis after you build most of your application. In this section, we'll let the wizard analyze the Housing Reservations sample database (*Housing.mdb*). To start the wizard, switch to the Database window, choose Analyze from the Tools menu, and then choose Performance from the submenu. Access opens the window shown in Figure 24-16.

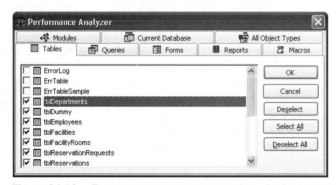

Figure 24-16. The main selection window of the Performance Analyzer Wizard.

You can select a specific category of objects to analyze—Current Database (which lets you analyze table relationships), Tables, Queries, Forms, Reports, Macros, Modules, or All Object Types. Within a category, you can click the check box next to an object name to select it for analysis. You can click the Select All button to ask the wizard to examine all objects or click Deselect All if you made a mistake and want to start over. In this example, I chose the All Object Types tab, clicked Select All, and then clicked on sample tables, queries, forms, and reports that aren't part of the actual application (all the extra examples I built for the book) to deselect them. (In the Housing Reservations database, select all tables that have names beginning with "tbl" or "tlkp," and select all queries, forms, and reports except those that have names beginning with the letter z or that have "Example" or "Xmpl" as part of the object name.)

Click OK to run the wizard. The wizard opens a window that shows you its progress as it analyzes the objects you selected. When it is finished, the wizard displays the results of its analysis, similar to those shown in Figure 24-17.

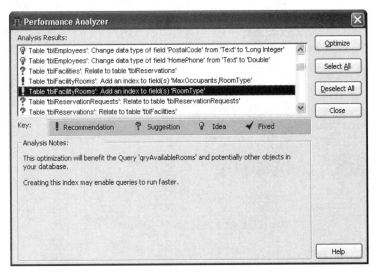

Figure 24-17. Analysis results from the Performance Analyzer Wizard.

You can scan the list of recommendations, suggestions, and ideas displayed by the wizard. (Notice the key below the Analysis Results list.) Click any *recommendation* or *suggestion* that you like, and then click the Optimize button to have the wizard implement the change on the spot. After the wizard implements a change, you'll see a check mark next to the item. If you like, you can click the Select All button to highlight all the recommendations and suggestions and then click Optimize to implement the fixes.

Personally, I'd rather choose the ones I want one at a time. For example, the idea to change the PostalCode field from text to long integer won't work if you're storing Canadian or European postal codes in your database. Also, I know that tblReservations is already related to tblFacilities through the tblFacilityRooms table, so adding a direct relationship between tblFacilties and tblReservations would be redundant.

Although you can implement recommendations and suggestions directly from the wizard, you can't do so with *ideas*. Most ideas are changes that could potentially cause a lot of additional work. For example, changing a data type of a field in a table might improve performance slightly, but it might also cause problems in dozens of queries, forms, and reports that you've already built using that table field. Other ideas are fixes that the wizard isn't certain will help; they depend on how you designed your application. I recommend that you look at the recommendations and suggestions and implement the ones that make the most sense for your application.

Disabling Form Design View

You might have noticed as you built new forms in your Access 2003 databases that Access sets the new Allow Design Changes property to All Views by default. This is a handy feature while you build forms because it allows you to change any form or control property directly from Form view and see the results immediately. Figure 24-18 shows you one of the sample forms from the *ContactsDataCopy.mdb* database opened in Form view. You can see that Access shows you the Form Design toolbars and menus and lets you open the property sheet to make changes.

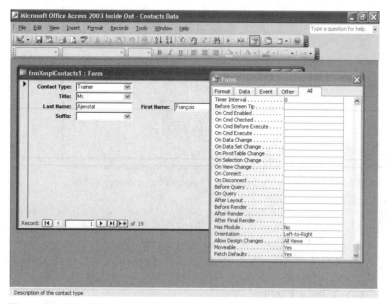

Figure 24-18. The sample frmXmplContacts1 form from Chapter 13 opened in Form view.

When you're ready to put your application in production, however, you need to reset this new property to Design View Only for all your forms so the users see your forms as you intended. (The actual property value stored with the form is True if you select All Views and False if you select Design View Only.) You could open every form in Design view, change the property, and save the form. But why do it the hard way? You can also code a simple Visual Basic procedure to open all your forms and reset the property for you.

To help you out, I included a sample procedure in the modExamples module in both the Law-Track Contacts and Housing Reservations sample databases. You can copy the FixAllowDesign procedure into your database to take care of this tedious process. Here's the procedure:

```
Sub FixAllowDesign()
Dim objFrm As AccessObject, frm As Form
    ' Go through every form in the database
    For Each objFrm In CurrentProject.AllForms
        ' Open the form in Design view
        DoCmd.OpenForm FormName:=objFrm.Name, _
```

```
    View:=acDesign
    ' Set the form object for efficiency
    Set frm = Forms(objFrm.Name)
    ' Check and reset the AllowDesignChanges property
    If frm.AllowDesignChanges = True Then
      frm.AllowDesignChanges = False
      ' Save the change
      DoCmd.RunCommand acCmdSave
    End If
    ' Close the form
    DoCmd.Close acForm, objFrm.Name
  ' Loop to the next form
  Next objFrm
End Sub
```

This procedure takes advantage of the AllForms collection to find the names of all your forms. To examine a form property or modify a property, you have to open the form in Design view. Although the Allow Design Changes property setting in the form design Properties window shows All Views and Design View Only, these actually correspond to True and False internal property values, respectively. So, if AllowDesignChanges is True, the procedure sets the value to False and saves the result. The code closes the current form before moving on to the next one.

Defining Switchboard Forms

Usually the last forms that you build are the switchboard forms that give the user direct access to the major tasks in your application.

Designing a Switchboard Form from Scratch

Your main switchboard form should be a simple form with a logo, a title, and perhaps as many as eight command buttons. The command buttons can be used to open the forms that you defined in the application. Figure 24-19 on the next page shows the main switchboard form for the LawTrack Contacts database in Design view.

One feature worth mentioning here is the use of the ampersand (&) character when setting each control's Caption property. You can use the ampersand character to define a shortcut key for the control. In the Caption property for the Companies command button, for example, the ampersand precedes the letter C. The letter C becomes the shortcut key, which means that you can choose the Companies button by pressing Alt+C as well as by more traditional methods such as clicking the button with the mouse or tabbing to the button and pressing the Spacebar or the Enter key. You must be careful, however, not to duplicate another shortcut key letter. For example, the shortcut key for the Contacts command button in this example is O, to avoid conflict with the C access key for the Companies command button.

Chapter 24

947

Figure 24-19. The main switchboard form for the LawTrack Contacts database.

 Tip If you choose Options from the Tools menu and select the Keyboard shortcut errors option on the Error Checking tab, Access displays a smart tag next to any command button or label that has a duplicate shortcut key defined.

You can use a shortcut key to make it easier to select any control that has a caption. For command buttons, the caption is part of the control itself. For most other controls, the caption is in the attached label. For example, you can define shortcut keys to select option buttons or toggle buttons in an option group by including an ampersand in the caption for each button in the group.

For each command button, you need a simple event procedure to handle the Click event and to open the appropriate form. Here is the procedure for the Products button.

```
Private Sub cmdProducts_Click()
  ' Open the Product edit/create form
  DoCmd.OpenForm "frmProducts"
End Sub
```

If you have a custom form menu bar, you should set the Menu Bar property of your switchboard form to point to the name of the custom menu bar. If you also have a custom form toolbar, you should set the form's Toolbar property to it. In the LawTrack Contacts and Housing Reservations applications, a single custom form toolbar is used for all forms.

Using the Switchboard Manager to Design Switchboard Forms

If your application is reasonably complex, building all the individual switchboard forms you need to provide the user with navigation through your application could take a while. Access has a Switchboard Manager utility that helps you get a jump on building your switchboard forms. This utility uses a creative technique to handle all switchboard forms by dynamically modifying a single form. It uses a driver table named Switchboard Items to allow you to define any number of switchboard forms with up to eight command buttons each. Information in the table tells the code behind the switchboard form how to modify the buttons displayed and what to do when the user clicks each of the buttons.

> **Note** The LawTrack Contacts application (*Contacts.mdb*) has a SwitchboardSample form that I created with the Switchboard Manager. Because I renamed the objects and fixed the code behind the SwitchboardSample form to use the SwitchboardDriver table, you can't use the Switchboard Manager to modify this form. You can open the SwitchboardSample form to see how a form built by the Switchboard Manager works, and you can follow along with the steps in this chapter to build your own switchboard.

To start the Switchboard Manager, choose Database Utilities from the Tools menu and then choose Switchboard Manager from the submenu. The utility checks to see if you already have a switchboard form and a Switchboard Items table in your database. If you don't have these, the Switchboard Manager displays the message box shown in Figure 24-20, which asks you if you want to build them.

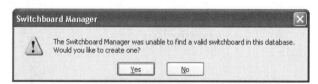

Figure 24-20. The message box that appears if the Switchboard Manager does not find a valid Switchboard form and Switchboard Items table in your database.

Click Yes to allow the Switchboard Manager to continue. After it builds a skeleton switchboard form and a Switchboard Items table (or after it establishes that you already have these objects in your database), it displays the main Switchboard Manager window. Unless your application is very simple, you won't be able to provide all the navigation your users need on one switchboard with eight options—especially considering that you should use one of the options to provide a way for the user to exit the application. So, you should plan additional switchboards that the user can navigate to from the main switchboard. One way to lay out the additional switchboards is to plan one switchboard for each major subject or group of similar features in your database.

You should first define all the switchboards that you need (called *pages* in the wizard) because a page must be defined before you can create a button to navigate to or from the page. To build an additional switchboard page, click the New button and enter a name for the new switchboard in the Create New dialog box, as shown in Figure 24-21 on the next page. Click OK to create the page.

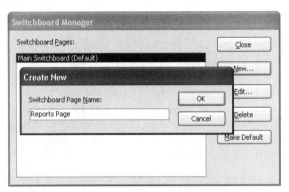

Figure 24-21. Adding an additional switchboard page to the main switchboard form.

After you create the additional switchboard pages that you need, you can select one in the main Switchboard Manager window and click the Edit button to begin defining actions on the page. You'll see a window similar to the one shown in the background in Figure 24-22. Use this window to create a new action, edit an existing action, or change the order of actions. Figure 24-22 shows a new action being created. When you create a new action, the Switchboard Manager places a button on the switchboard page to execute that action. In the Text box, enter the caption that you want displayed next to the button. Note that you can enter an ampersand (&) before one of the letters in the caption to make that letter the access key for the button. Choose the action you want from the Command drop-down list. The Switchboard Manager can create actions such as moving to another switchboard page, opening a form in add or edit mode, opening a report, switching to Design view, exiting the application, or running a macro or a Visual Basic procedure. If you choose an action such as opening a form or report, the Edit Switchboard Item dialog box shows you a list of appropriate objects in the second drop-down list.

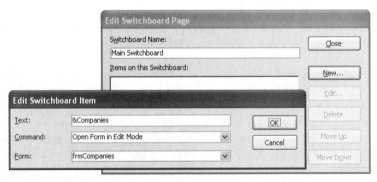

Figure 24-22. Creating a new action on a switchboard page.

On the main switchboard page, you should create actions to open other pages and an action to exit the application. On each subsequent page, you should always provide at least one action to move back through the switchboard-page tree or to go back to the main switchboard page, as shown in Figure 24-23.

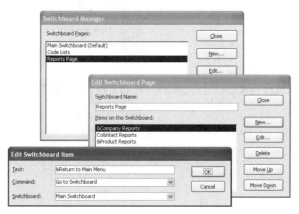

Figure 24-23. Creating an action to return to the main switchboard form from another switchboard form.

On the SwitchboardSample form, I created buttons to open Companies, Contacts, Products, Pending Events, and Invoices. I also created buttons to open pages to show code lists that can be edited and the available reports. On the Code Lists page, I added entries to open Contact Types, Event Types, Product Categories, Person Titles, Person Suffixes, and Users. I also added a button to return to the main menu. On the Reports Page, I added entries to open Company Reports, Contact Reports, and Product Reports as well as a button to return to the main menu.

After you finish, the Switchboard Manager saves the main switchboard form with the name *Switchboard*. You can rename this form if you want to. If you want to rename the Switchboard Items table, be sure to edit the Visual Basic procedures stored with the Switchboard form so that they refer to the new name. You'll also need to change the record source of the form.

Figure 24-24 shows an example Switchboard form for the LawTrack Contacts database (the SwitchboardSample form). I edited the form design to add the LawTrack logo. You can further customize the look of this form as long as you don't remove any of the option buttons or attached labels or change the names of these controls.

Figure 24-24. The resulting main switchboard form.

I personally prefer to design my own switchboard forms so that I can add specialized code behind some of the command buttons. But you can see that this wizard is a handy way to quickly design a complex set of switchboard pages without a lot of work.

Controlling How Your Application Starts and Runs

Especially if you're distributing your application for others to use, you probably want your application to automatically start when the user opens your database. As noted in the previous section, you should design switchboard forms to help the user navigate to the various parts of your application. You should also set properties and write code to ensure that your user can cleanly exit your application.

Setting Startup Properties for Your Database

At this point, you know how to build all the pieces you need to fully implement your database application. But what if you want your application to start automatically when you open your database? One way to do that is to create a macro named *Autoexec*—Microsoft Access always runs this macro if it exists when you open the database (unless you hold down the Shift key when you open the database). However, a better way to start your application is to specify an opening form in the startup properties for the database. You can set these properties by switching to the Database window and then choosing Startup from the Tools menu. Access opens the Startup dialog box, as shown in Figure 24-25.

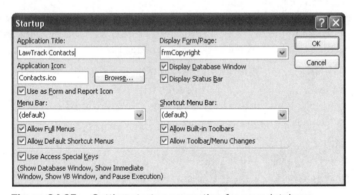

Figure 24-25. Setting startup properties for your database.

You can specify which form or data access page opens your database by selecting a form from the Display Form/Page drop-down list. You can also specify a custom title for the application, an icon for the application, a default menu bar, and a default shortcut menu bar to override the standard menus for all forms. (I prefer to set the individual form and report menu bar, toolbar, and shortcut menu properties.) If you always open the database with its folder set to the current directory, you can simply enter the icon file name, as shown in the figure. If you're not sure what folder will be current when the application opens, you should enter a fully qualified file name location. Note that you can also ask that Access display the icon you specify as the form and report icon instead of the standard Access icons.

If you clear the Display Database Window check box, Access hides the Database window when your application starts. (As you'll learn later, you can also write code that executes in your startup form to ensure that the Database window is hidden.) You can also hide the status bar if you want to by clearing the Display Status Bar check box. I like to use the SysCmd function to display information on the status bar, so I usually leave the Display Status Bar option selected. Access has a set of condensed built-in menus that don't provide, for example, access to design commands. If you clear the Allow Full Menus check box, Access provides these shortened menus as the default. You can also hide all the built-in toolbars (you should provide your own custom toolbars in this case), disallow toolbar changes, and disallow the default shortcut menus.

Finally, you can disable special keys—such as F11 to reveal the Database window, Ctrl+G to open the Debug window, or Ctrl+Break to halt code execution—by clearing the Use Access Special Keys check box. As you can see, you have many powerful options for customizing how your application starts and how it operates.

Starting and Stopping Your Application

Although you can set startup properties asking Access to hide the Database window, you might want to include code in the Load event of your startup form to make sure the window is hidden. All the sample databases provided with this book open the frmCopyright form as the startup form. This form displays information about the database, and code behind the form checks connections to linked tables or data access pages. In both the LawTrack Contacts and Housing Reservations sample applications, the code behind the frmCopyright form tells you to open the frmSplash form to actually start the application.

When the frmSplash form opens, code in the Load event uses the following procedure to make sure the Database window is hidden:

```
' Select the database window
DoCmd.SelectObject acForm, "frmSplash", True
' .. and hide it
RunCommand acCmdWindowHide
```

The procedure hides the Database window by selecting a known object in the Database window to give the Database window the focus and then executing the WindowHide command. The splash form waits for a timer to expire (the Timer event procedure) and then opens a form to sign on to the application. When you sign on successfully, the frmMain form finally opens.

The frmMain form in the LawTrack Contacts application has no Close button and no Control-menu button. The database also has an AutoKeys macro defined that intercepts any attempt to close a window using the Ctrl+F4 keys. (You'll learn about creating an AutoKeys macro in the next section.) So, you must click the Exit button on the frmMain form to close the application. On the other hand, the frmMain form in the Housing Reservations application does allow you to press Ctrl+F4 or click the Close button to close the form and exit the application.

You should always write code to clean up any open forms, reset variables, and close any open recordsets when the user asks to exit your application. Because the user can't close the frmMain form in the LawTrack Contacts application except by clicking the Exit button, you'll find such clean-up code in the command button's Click event. In the frmMain form in the Housing Reservations database, the clean-up code is in the form's Close event procedure. The code in both forms is similar, so here's the exit code in the LawTrack Contacts sample application:

```
Private Sub cmdExit_Click()
Dim intErr As Integer, frm As Form, intI As Integer
Dim strData As String, strDir As String
Dim lngOpen As Long, datBackup As Date
Dim strLowBkp As String, strBkp As String, intBkp As Integer
Dim db As DAO.Database, rst As DAO.Recordset
  If vbNo = MsgBox("Are you sure you want to exit?", _
    vbYesNo + vbQuestion + vbDefaultButton2, _
      gstrAppTitle) Then
      Exit Sub
  End If
  ' Trap any errors
  On Error Resume Next
  ' Make sure all forms are closed
  For intI = (Forms.Count - 1) To 0 Step -1
    Set frm = Forms(intI)
    ' Don't close myself!
    If frm.Name <> "frmMain" Then
      ' Use the form's "Cancel" routine
      frm.cmdCancel_Click
      DoEvents
    End If
    ' Note any error that occurred
    If Err <> 0 Then intErr = -1
  Next intI
  ' Log any error beyond here
  On Error GoTo frmMain_Error
  ' Skip backup check if there were errors
  If intErr = 0 Then
    Set db = CurrentDb
    ' Open ztblVersion to see if we need to do a backup
    Set rst = db.OpenRecordset("ztblVersion", dbOpenDynaset)
    rst.MoveFirst
    lngOpen = rst!OpenCount
    datBackup = rst!LastBackup
    rst.Close
    Set rst = Nothing
    ' If the user has opened 10 times
    ' or last backup was more than 2 weeks ago...
    If (lngOpen Mod 10 = 0) Or ((Date - datBackup) > 14) Then
      ' Ask if they want to backup...
      If vbYes = MsgBox("LawTrack highly recommends backing up " & _
        "your data to avoid " & _
        "any accidental data loss.  Would you like to backup now?", _
        vbYesNo + vbQuestion, gstrAppTitle) Then
        ' Get the name of the data file
```

```
        strData = Mid(db.TableDefs("ztblVersion").Connect, 11)
        ' Get the name of its folder
        strDir = Left(strData, InStrRev(strData, "\"))
        ' See if the "BackupData" folder exists
        If Len(Dir(strDir & "BackupData", vbDirectory)) = 0 Then
            ' Nope, build it!
            MkDir strDir & "BackupData"
        End If
        ' Now find any existing backups - keep only three
        strBkp = Dir(strDir & "BackupData\LawTrackBkp*.mdb")
        Do While Len(strBkp) > 0
            intBkp = intBkp + 1
            If (strBkp < strLowBkp) Or (Len(strLowBkp) = 0) Then
                ' Save the name of the oldest backup found
                strLowBkp = strBkp
            End If
            ' Get the next file
            strBkp = Dir
        Loop
        ' If more than two backup files
        If intBkp > 2 Then
            ' Delete the oldest one
            Kill strDir & "BackupData\" & strLowBkp
        End If
        ' Now, setup new backup name based on today's date
        strBkp = strDir & "BackupData\LawTrackBkp" & _
            Format(Date, "yymmdd") & ".mdb"
        ' Make sure the target file doesn't exist
        If Len(Dir(strBkp)) > 0 Then Kill strBkp
        ' Create the backup file using Compact
        DBEngine.CompactDatabase strData, strBkp
        ' Now update the backup date
        db.Execute "UPDATE ztblVersion SET LastBackup = #" & _
            Date & "#", dbFailOnError
        MsgBox "Backup created successfully!", vbInformation, gstrAppTitle
    End If
    ' See if error log has 20 or more entries
    If db.TableDefs("ErrorLog").RecordCount > 20 Then
        ' Don't ask if they've said not to...
        If Not (DLookup("DontSendError", "tblUsers", _
            "UserName = '" & gstrThisUser & "'")) Then
            DoCmd.OpenForm "fdlgErrorSend", WindowMode:=acDialog
        Else
            db.Execute "DELETE * FROM ErrorLog", dbFailOnError
        End If
    End If
  End If
  Set db = Nothing
End If
' Restore original keyboard behavior
' Disabled in this sample
'  Application.SetOption "Behavior Entering Field", gintEnterField
'  Application.SetOption "Move After Enter", gintMoveEnter
'    Application.SetOption "Arrow Key Behavior", gintArrowKey
```

955

```
' We're outta here!
frmMain_Exit:
  On Error GoTo 0
  DoCmd.Close acForm, Me.Name
  ' In a production application, would quit here
  DoCmd.SelectObject acForm, "frmMain", True
  Exit Sub
frmMain_Error:
  ErrorLog "frmMain", Err, Error
  Resume frmMain_Exit
End Sub
```

After confirming that the user really wants to exit, the code looks at every open form. All forms have a public cmdCancel_Click event procedure that this code can call to ask the form to clear any pending edits and close itself. The DoEvents statement gives that code a chance to complete before going on to the next form. Notice that the code skips the form named frm-Main (the form where this code is running).

If there were no errors closing all the forms, then the code opens a table that contains a count of how many times this application has run and the date of the last backup. Every tenth time the application has run or every two weeks since the last backup, the code offers to create a backup of the application data. If the user confirms creating a backup, the code creates a Backup subfolder if it does not exist, deletes the oldest backup if there are three or more in the folder, and then backs up the data using the CompactDatabase method of the DBEngine.

Next, the code checks to see if more than 20 errors have been logged by code running in the application. If so, it opens a dialog box that gives the user the option to e-mail the error log, print out the error log, skip printing the error log this time, or turn off the option to print the log. Because the error log option form opens in Dialog mode, this code waits until that form closes. Finally, the code closes this form and selects an object in the Database window to reveal that window. If this weren't a demonstration application, the code would use the Quit method of the Application object to close and exit Access.

This might seem like a lot of extra work, but taking care of details like this really gives your application a professional polish.

Creating an AutoKeys Macro

As noted earlier, the LawTrack Contacts sample application (*Contacts.mdb*) has an AutoKeys macro defined to intercept pressing Ctrl+F4. You can normally press this key combination to close any window that has the focus, but the application is designed so that you must close the frmMain form using the Exit button, not Ctrl+F4. You can create an AutoKeys macro to define most keystrokes that you want to intercept and handle in some other way. You can define something as simple as a StopMacro action to effectively disable the keystroke, create a series of macro actions that respond to the keystrokes, or use the RunCode action to call complex Visual Basic code. Figure 24-26 shows you the AutoKeys macro in the LawTrack Contacts database open in Design view.

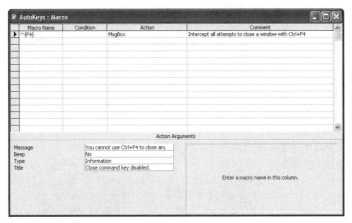

Figure 24-26. The design of an AutoKeys macro.

The critical part of a macro defined in an AutoKeys macro group is the macro name. When the name is a special combination of characters that match a key name, the macro executes whenever you press those keys. Table 24-1 shows you how to construct macro names in an AutoKeys macro group to respond to specific keys.

Table 24-1. AutoKeys Macro Key Codes

AutoKeys Macro Name	Key Intercepted
^letter or ^number	Ctrl+[the named letter or number key]
{Fn}	The named function key (F1–F12)
^{Fn}	Ctrl+[the named function key]
+{Fn}	Shift+[the named function key]
{Insert}	Insert
^{Insert}	Ctrl+Insert
+{Insert}	Shift+Insert
{Delete} or {Del}	Delete
^{Delete} or ^{Del}	Ctrl+Delete
+{Delete} or +{Del}	Shift+Delete

Keep in mind that you can also intercept any keystroke on a form in the KeyDown and KeyPress events when you want to trap a particular key on only one form or control.

Performing a Final Visual Basic Compile

The very last task you should perform before placing your application in production is to compile and save all your Visual Basic procedures. When you do this, Access stores a compiled version of the code in your database. Access uses the compiled code when it needs to execute a procedure you have written. If you don't do this, Access has to load and interpret your procedures the first time you reference them, each time you start your application. For example, if you have several procedures in a form module, the form will open more slowly the first time because Access has to also load and compile the code.

To compile and save all the Visual Basic procedures in your application, open any module—either a module object or a module associated with a form or report. Choose Compile from the Debug menu, as shown in Figure 24-27. If your code compiles successfully, be sure to save the result by choosing Save from the File menu or by clicking the Save button on the toolbar. (If you have errors in any of your code, the compiler halts on the first error it finds, displays the line of code, and displays an error message dialog box.) After successfully compiling and saving your Visual Basic project, close your database and compact it as described in Chapter 5, "Modifying Your Table Design." In Access for Windows 95, renaming your database always "decompiled" your code. This meant that if you changed the database name, you would have to compile your code again. With Access 97 and later, you don't have to recompile the code after renaming the database file.

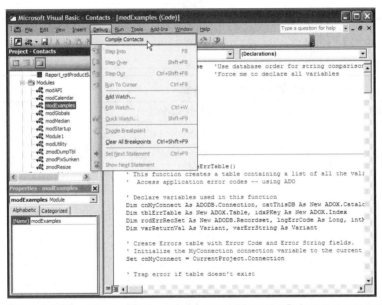

Figure 24-27. Choose the Compile command from the Debug menu to compile all the Visual Basic procedures in your database.

As you've seen in this book, you can quickly learn to build complex applications. You can use the relational database management system in Access to store and manage your data locally or on a network, and you can access information in other popular database formats or in any server-hosted or mainframe-hosted database that supports the Open Database Connectivity (ODBC) standard. You can get started with macros to become familiar with event-oriented programming and to prototype your application. With a little practice, you'll soon find yourself writing Visual Basic event procedures like a pro. In the next part of this book, you can learn about working with your Access applications on the Web. In the final part, you can learn how to implement your Access application in a client/server environment, secure your database, and prepare your database for distribution.

Part 6

Linking Access and the Web

Publishing Data on the Web

The World Wide Web, built from simple low-cost servers and universal clients, has revolutionized computing. Not so long ago, the very concept of a common global information network was unthinkable. In fact, even Microsoft was unconvinced that Web technology would ever mature successfully. Originally, The Microsoft Network (MSN) was constructed with proprietary technology, modeled after similar networks such as CompuServe and Prodigy. To connect to these networks, you had to install proprietary software on your machine.

Today, the concept of living *without* the Web is just as unthinkable, and all the formerly proprietary networks (including MSN) have spent millions of dollars to convert their networks to the universal access offered by the Web. Although MSN, CompuServe, and Prodigy all still offer specialized programs that you can install to enhance your experience as a member of any of the networks, all these programs are merely customized versions of your Web browser. You can also log on to these networks with a standard Web browser.

Database applications were among the last to appear on the Web, but today they are arguably the fastest growing type of Web application. The prospect of distributing data to or collecting it from literally a world of clients, working on disparate computers and operating systems, and not requiring software distribution other than the ubiquitous browser, is simply too compelling to resist for long.

Microsoft Access doesn't provide a complete Web development environment. However, it does provide useful tools for developing a variety of Web database applications. This chapter explores the Web, explains how the Web capabilities of Access work, and provides pointers to other tools in case Access doesn't satisfy all your needs. This chapter serves as an introduction to topics that will be covered in detail in the next few chapters.

Working with the Web

Designing and developing Web applications requires a different set of tools, a different approach, and a different mindset than performing the same tasks solely in Access. A properly designed Web application can offer significant improvements over typical desktop applications—in timeliness (frequency of update and reporting), interactivity (degree of user control), and partitioning (distributed location of application components).

With each new version of development environments, software companies provide improved tools that allow developers to more easily deliver desktop and Web solutions. Some of these tools allow developers to create desktop and Web applications that work with each other. However, there is quite a leap between desktop application development, such as Access, and Web application development. Before you begin to explore ways to create Web applications, you first need to become familiar with a couple of key underlying technologies—HTML (Hypertext Markup Language) and XML (Extensible Markup Language).

Understanding HTML

Web pages are simple text files containing a mix of textual content and codes that your browser interprets when it loads the Web page. The codes (called *tags*) that your browser understands are part of an international language specification called Hypertext Markup Language (HTML). The basic specification is documented by ISO (short for International Organization for Standardization) standard ISO/IEC 15445:2000. However, the standard that most software vendors implement is an enhanced version created and published by the World Wide Web Consortium (W3C), which is made up of representatives from major software vendors around the world. (You can visit the W3C Web site at *http://www.w3.org.*)

Actually, HTML isn't a programming language—it's a descriptive language that defines objects on your Web page. These objects can have properties, methods, and events similar to many of the objects you find in Microsoft Access. You can include procedural code (known as a script) in your Web page definition that responds to events. The two most common scripting languages are VBScript—a second cousin to the Visual Basic you use in Access—and JavaScript, a language invented by Sun Microsystems.

Most Web page developers use an HTML editor (such as Microsoft FrontPage) to create Web pages. A good editor hides the actual coding and allows the developer to create pages—in much the same way that you create Access forms or reports—by providing a what-you-see-is-what-you-get (WYSIWYG) interface. However, most developers at one time or another must dig into the HTML to do some custom work. In Chapter 27, "Building Data Access Pages," you'll go into the coding behind an Access data access page to enhance the page with VBScript, so learning the basics about HTML now will be useful to you later.

> **Tip** Most browsers can display the HTML that the browser used to create a Web page that you're viewing. In Internet Explorer, choose Source from the View menu to see the code behind any Web page. Once you understand the basics of HTML, this can be a fun way to discover advanced techniques.

Introducing HTML Coding

As noted earlier, the codes in HTML that tell your browser how to format your Web page are in the form of tags. A tag begins with the < character and ends with the > character. The characters immediately following the < character identify the type of tag, and you can usually follow this tag identifier with attributes that further qualify how the tag behaves. For example, a particular type of tag might accept attributes that tell your browser what font to use or how to align the text that follows the tag.

All tags define objects on your Web page, and all Web pages begin with the <html> tag that defines the page object. Most Web page objects can contain other object definitions (for example, a table is an object, and the rows within the table are objects), and such objects require an end tag to define the end of the object. An end tag is in the form </*tagname*>, so, for example, every page ends with a </html> tag. Tags that define objects that cannot contain other objects include
 (line break) and <img> (image), and you cannot define an end tag for these objects. Table 25-1 shows you a small subset of the HTML tags that you can use.

Table 25-1. Common HTML Tags

HTML Tags	Description
<html></html>	Designate the beginning and ending of your Web page.
<head></head>	Specify an optional heading section at the beginning of your Web page. Any text that you include in this section (with the exception of the text in a <title> tag that appears in the browser title bar—see below) does not appear on the page. In the heading section, you can define keywords for search engines and default fonts and styles to be used in the body of the page.
<title></title>	Placed in the heading section. Define text that the browser displays in its title bar.
<body></body>	Designate the body section of the page. You code the majority of other tags inside the body section.
<script></script>	Surround script language that responds to events on your page. Script languages include VBScript and JavaScript.
<div></div>	Split the page into divisions (similar to a section break in a Microsoft Word document) that can have different style attributes. You can optionally provide text between the begin and end tags to create a heading for the division.
<h1></h1>	Surround a first-level heading. You can define the default attributes of headings in your heading section, or you can specify attributes for this heading following the tag name in the begin tag.
<h2></h2>	Surround a second-level heading.
<p></p>	Define a paragraph.
 	Adds a line break. This tag doesn't have an end tag because you cannot define other objects inside a line break object.
<STRONG></STRONG>	Format the text between the tags with a larger font.
<ul></ul>	Create a bulleted list. Code the lines of text between these two tags.

Table 25-1. Common HTML Tags

HTML Tags	Description
<li></li>	Define a list item within a bulleted list. Insert the text for the line between these tags.
<a></a>	Designate a hyperlink. You code the hyperlink address following the tag name inside the begin tag. Your browser displays any text or any image object you include between the begin and end tags as a hyperlink, and your browser follows the defined hyperlink when you click on the text or image. You can use these tags between other tags, such as between <p> </p> to have only a portion of the paragraph text display as a hyperlink.
<img>	Specifies an image object that your browser displays. You define the location of the image following the tag name inside the tag. You can surround this tag with <a></a> to create a graphic hyperlink. Note that this tag does not have an end tag because you cannot define other objects inside an image object.
<table></table>	Define a table. Between these begin and end tags you use other tags such as <tr></tr> (table row) to define the format of a row and <td></td> (table data) to define the data displayed in a row. Following the tag name inside the begin tag, you can define attributes such as the width of the table, the border style, and the spacing between cells in the table.

Below is an HTML example for a very simple Web page:

```
<html>
    <head>
        <title>My Simple HTML</title>
    </head>
    <body>
        <STRONG>This is my simple page showing some simple HTML commands</STRONG>
    </body>
</html>
```

The above HTML creates the Web page displayed in Figure 25-1.

You can find this file, called *Simple.htm*, on the companion CD in the WebChapters\Simple-HTML folder. You can also type the above HTML commands in Notepad and save the text with the extension of .htm or .html. When you double-click on the file you saved, it opens in your default browser.

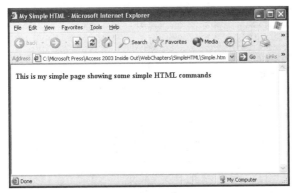

Figure 25-1. A simple Web page.

 Inside Out

Not all browsers support all tags

The rendering of the tags, members, and other features you code into your Web pages depends on which browser, such as Internet Explorer or Netscape, you are using to display the pages. In addition, different versions of the same browser might support different features. These limitations are known as cross-browser issues and can be difficult to deal with when writing advanced HTML. Writing HTML code that can be displayed on multiple browsers and platforms can be very important if you want your pages to be accessed by users all over the world. When you are creating a Web site for an intranet inside a corporation, you can usually identify which browser is the company's standard.

If you are working with an HTML editor such as VS.NET, you can look up the various tags, and in the description you can find something like the following: "This object is defined in HTML 3.2 and is defined in World Wide Web Consortium (W3C) Document Object Model (DOM) Level 1." This tells you that as long as your browser supports this version of HTML, using this tag should work. In some editors, such as Microsoft FrontPage, you can specify the browser, browser version, and server type for which the editor should generate the HTML. However, when working with the simple tags mentioned here, you shouldn't have any problems with any of the browsers.

Tag Members

As noted earlier, tags define objects on your Web page. As part of the begin tag, you can create members—also called elements (properties, methods, or events)—that let you control or further refine the object defined by the tag. Script that you write to respond to events for an object can reference members that you have defined. Table 25-2 on the next page shows you some of the member types you can define for your Web page objects.

Table 25-2. Common HTML Object Members

Member	Description
Attribute/Property	Like Access properties, these members describe something about the object defined by the tag. For example, a table object has *width* and *height* properties. This is the member type you are likely to use most often.
Behavior	These members let you specify various behaviors for the tag object. For example, in a table object, *rowover* enables alternate shading and row highlighting for table elements.
Collection	Every tag has at least one collection, called the *attributes* collection, which is a collection of all the members for the object defined by the tag. Additional collections depend on the object type. For example, the table object has a collection called *rows*, which is made up of the *tr* objects included in the table.
Event	You can include events that you want the browser to recognize, and you can write script to handle various tasks for you in response to these events. For example, the table object supports more than fifty events, including *onmouseover* and *ondblclick*.
Filters	Filters affect visual aspects of the object. For example, you can define a *glow* filter for the table object that sets a glow around the table.
Method	A method is an action that an object can perform, and you can write script to execute the method of the object. An example for the table object is the *focus* method, which just like an Access control's Set-Focus method, causes the focus to move to the object.
Object	Objects can contain other objects. When an object can contain multiple instances of another object (for example, rows in a table object), those subordinate objects are in a *collection*. When an object can have only one instance of a subordinate object, that subordinate object is an *object* member. For example, most objects, including the table object, have a single *Styles* object.
Styles	The Styles object in HTML contains a collection of attributes that are similar to the properties you can find on the Format tab of an Access object's property sheet. For example, the table object has a Styles object that has a collection of attributes that includes *bordercolor* and *borderstyle*. You can set the style attributes either by defining them directly as attributes of the object, or by setting them in the attributes collection of the Styles object. If you use the Styles object, you put a dash between the words that make up the attribute. For example, use *border-color* and *border-style* inside a Styles object.

Now that you have a basic understanding of tags and members, let's look at some specific members of commonly used tags and then study a more complex Web page design. Table 25-3 shows you some of the members of the <a> (hyperlink), <table> (table), and <img> (image) tags.

Table 25-3. Some Members of Commonly Used Tags

Tag	Member	Member Type	Description
<a>	href	Property	URL that you want to link to.
	title	Property	The title of the hyperlink. Some browsers display the title as a ToolTip for the link.
<table>	frame	Object	The frame around the table.
	border	Property	The width of the border in pixels.
	width	Property	The width of the table in pixels or as a percentage of the available browser window.
	Rows	Collection	The rows that make up the table.
	cellspacing	Property	The spacing between the cells in pixels.
	cellpadding	Property	The spacing within the cells in pixels.
<img>	alt	Property	A short description of the image. Most browsers display this property as a ToolTip.
	src	Property	The URL of the image to display.
	height	Property	Overrides the defined height of the image file.
	width	Property	Overrides the defined width of the image file.

You can now apply what you've learned to understanding a more complex page. Below is HTML for a page that contains a page title, two sections (<div>) with individual titles, a table in the first section that includes an image and a hyperlink, and a bulleted list in the second section.

```
<html>
    <head>
        <title>My More Complex Page</title>
    </head>
    <body>
        <div>My Favorite Types of Hotels</div>
        <table cellSpacing="1" cellPadding="1" width="300" border="1">
            <tr>
                <td width="127">Bed and Breakfasts</td>
                <td></td>
            </tr>
            <tr>
                <td width="127">Ski Lodges</td>
```

```
            <td><a href="http://www.whistlerblackcomb.com/">
            <img alt="Whistler, Canada" src=".\Images\Ski.jpg">
                </a>
            </td>
        </tr>
        <tr>
            <td width="127">Fishing Cabins</td>
            <td></td>
        </tr>
    </table>
    <br>
    <div>Features I Look For:</div>
    <ul>
        <li>
            Quiet</li>
        <li>
            Good Food</li>
        <li>
            Good Jazz Music Nearby</li>
    </ul>
</body>
</html>
```

The above HTML gives you the Web page displayed in Figure 25-2.

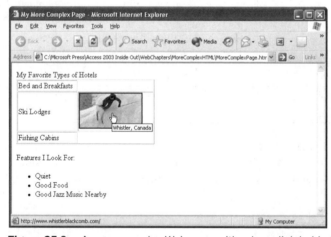

Figure 25-2. A more complex Web page with a hyperlink behind the graphic image.

 You can find this file, called *MoreComplexPage.htm*, on the companion CD in the WebChapters\MoreComplexHTML folder.

Editing HTML

For the two simple examples shown thus far, I typed the HTML directly into Notepad to create the page. As you can imagine, this can be a slow and tedious process for a complex Web page, especially if you are not an HTML guru. The good news: Many editors are available that create the HTML code for you. The not-so-good news: If much of your work involves creating more advanced Web pages, you are still going to have to learn HTML coding.

When you first start creating Web pages, you might dread having to work in HTML. But as you become more proficient at it, you'll enjoy seeing your browser convert your code into a Web page. However, if you can use an editor such as Microsoft Office FrontPage 2003 to create the HTML for you, all the better. You can see an example of working with HTML using FrontPage in Figure 25-3. FrontPage 2003 lets you see both the HTML and the graphical Design view of the page at the same time. Notice that FrontPage highlights the HTML code that generates the object selected in the Design window.

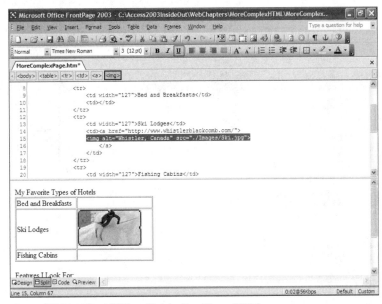

Figure 25-3. The HTML editor in FrontPage 2003.

For details about creating a simple HTML page from Microsoft Access, see Chapter 26, "Creating Static and Dynamic Web Pages."

Introducing XML

With all the businesses that are accessing the Web and using software to connect to each other and exchange data, a standard way of describing the data and its structure is necessary to allow these systems to understand the data. That standard is XML (eXtensible Markup Language). As with HTML, the current XML standard is based on an ISO standard, but the most commonly used version is the one maintained and published by W3C. Where HTML deals with presentation, XML deals with data. Because a file in XML format contains not only the data but also a description of the structure of the data, receiving systems know exactly how to process the data from the information included in the file.

For example, an insurance company might receive data from an outside company that manages some of its insurance claims. The insurance company needs to know which fields the file includes, the data type of the fields, and the order in which the fields occur in the data file. If the file is coded in XML, the company can easily import this file into Access or any other program that understands XML, even if the sending company changes the format or content of the file. With other file types, such as fixed-width text files, you must know the file format so that you can define the import/export specification for Access before you attempt to import the file.

 One of the major new features in Microsoft Office Access 2003 is an enhanced ability to work with data published using the latest XML standards. Access 2003 can now easily import and export XML files and related style sheets. (A very limited ability to work with certain XML files was implemented in Microsoft Access 2002.) You can see an example of a file imported as XML and displayed in a datasheet subform in Figure 25-4.

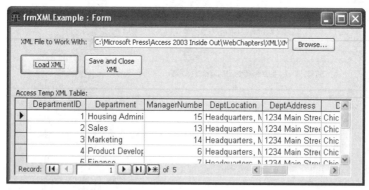

Figure 25-4. You can load, edit, and save XML files using Access.

 You can find this form saved as *frmXMLExample* in the *Housing.mdb* sample database. When you first open the form, the subform window is blank. You can enter the location of any XML file in the XML File to Work With box or click the Browse button (...) to locate an XML file on your machine. You can also use the *XMLDepartments.xml* file that you'll find in the Web-Chapters\XML folder on the companion CD. (You cannot import this file into Access 2002.) Click the Load XML button to import the file into a local table and display it in the subform window. You can actually change any of the data that you see in the subform window and then click the Save and Close XML button to write the changes back to the XML file that you imported.

When Access imports the XML file, it builds the definition of the table fields from the information in the file and then loads the data. Code behind the form then loads the table into the subform control so you can edit it. No fancy code is required to decipher what's in the file.

Microsoft has enhanced the XML capabilities in all components of Office 2003. Microsoft's new Internet development architecture, Microsoft .NET (pronounced *dot net*), depends heavily on XML. The new Internet development platform, Visual Studio .NET, makes extensive use of XML in its ADO.NET data model and manages some of its system features using XML.

With XML growing in use, does this mean you have to become an XML guru? The answer is no, but it's a good idea to know how and where you can use it. You'll learn additional details about working with XML in Chapter 28, "Working with XML and SharePoint."

Maintaining Static Web Pages

The Web pages you've seen thus far in this chapter are static—once you publish a page like these to a Web server, the information doesn't change until you replace or edit the text. Actually, static Web pages are the most common type of page you'll find on any noncommercial site on the Web. All the pages at the W3C Web site (*http://www.w3.org*) and all the pages on my Web site (*http://www.viescas.com*) are static. So, you won't see any new information on my Web site unless I edit and update the pages.

To understand how static Web pages work (and the way the Web works in general), you need to know a bit about the architecture of the Web. Like all network applications, the World Wide Web defines two roles computers can play: client or server. (Sometimes, a single computer can serve both roles.) The client software, called a browser, requests files from the server and displays them on the client computer. The server software, called a Web server, accepts requests from browsers and transmits the requested files to the browser. Figure 25-5 provides a highly simplified diagram of these components.

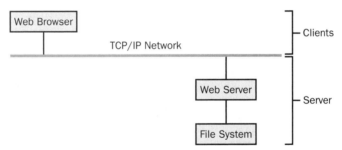

Figure 25-5. A high-level World Wide Web schematic.

> **Note** TCP/IP stands for Transmission Control Protocol/Internet Protocol. TCP describes the way computers on Internet-style networks can exchange data without loss. IP describes the identification scheme for computers on Internet-style networks.

When you publish a static page on a Web server, that server stores your text in its file system. When a browser on a client sends a request for the page to the server, the server reads the file from its file system and sends it unmodified to the client browser. To change what the server sends, you must change the text file stored in the server's file system. If the static page contains hyperlinks or script that responds to events defined on the page, it's the browser on the requesting client machine that interprets what should happen next, and it executes any script on the client computer.

What Is a Protocol?

When you connect your computer to a network, the communications software on each computer must send and receive information in a format that all the computers understand. Think of a computer network as a railway system. If one station can handle boxcars but not hopper cars, any other station that sends cargo to that station must send boxcars only. Similarly, a network protocol defines a specific type of data packaging that can be sent over your network "rails."

In early Microsoft Windows–based systems, Microsoft packaged the data using a protocol called NetBEUI. Systems networked using Novell Netware used a protocol called IPX/SPX. The World Wide Web standardized on the TCP/IP protocol. Today, most computers include software to support multiple protocols so that you can be connected to a local network using IPX/SPX or NetBEUI and also to the World Wide Web using TCP/IP.

TCP/IP is a transport protocol that defines the general packaging of the messages sent over the network. What your computer sends within the packaging parameters of a protocol depends on the applications sending and receiving the information—the application protocol. (To continue our train analogy, what kind of boxes inside the boxcar is the stationmaster on the other end prepared to unlock?) When you copy a file to a local server using Windows Explorer, Explorer packages your file information in a format the receiving file system understands. Windows then wraps these packages in an available transport protocol for sending over the network.

When you work on a Web-based network (such as the World Wide Web), your browser uses standardized application protocols to send and receive information. Two of the most common Web protocols are Hypertext Transport Protocol (HTTP) for transmitting information like Web pages and pictures, and File Transfer Protocol (FTP) for uploading and downloading files.

The key to the explosive success of the World Wide Web is the broad acceptance and adoption of the transport protocol, application protocols, and page definition standard (HTML) by virtually every computer and software manufacturer. These common standards let you point your Web browser at a Web server halfway around the world to send and receive information. You don't have to worry or care about what kind of computer or operating system is installed for the Web server. For the most part, the folks who program the Web server don't have to worry about what kind of computer you're using or what Web browser you have installed.

What can you do if your static Web page contains a table with data generated from a database? If the data in the database is reasonably static (for example, a membership name and address list that you update once a month), it doesn't really matter that your Web page displays a static copy of data from the table. Microsoft Access can make the periodic update of your Web page easy because it provides an export facility that allows you to save the data from a table, query, form, or report as an HTML table.

You can find additional information for creating static Web pages from data in an Access database in Chapter 26, "Creating Static and Dynamic Web Pages."

Of course, if you need your Web pages to display up-to-the-minute information from active database tables, static Web pages won't do at all. To solve this problem, you need to define a Web page that can dynamically fetch the latest information, format it as HTML, and send it to the requesting browser.

Creating Dynamic Web Pages

To create Web pages that display (and perhaps allow the user to update) data from a database, you must create a special type of Web page containing script that can fetch and update the data. The most common way to do this is to create an Active Server Page (ASP) that runs on the Web server to fetch requested information from a database, format it as HTML, and send it to the client browser. An alternative method is to use HTML forms that contain an ActiveX control and script to perform the same tasks. When you create an HTML form, you can design it to run the database code on the server or on the client.

With Microsoft's introduction of the .NET architecture and ASP.NET, creating dynamic Web pages is almost as easy as creating desktop database applications. These tools help you create Active Server Pages or HTML forms to handle the database processing. You can also use Microsoft FrontPage or data access pages in Microsoft Access to build HTML forms that deliver dynamic information from your database. Let's take a brief look at these technologies.

Delivering Dynamic Query Results

If, whenever a Web visitor requests a page, you want your Web page to query the database and return the result to the visitor, you must create a dynamic Web page. Figure 25-6 on the next page shows the most common network architecture you can build using Access as the database file server to report up-to-the-minute, live database contents. The browser requests a special kind of Web page—an Active Server Page—that contains a mixture of HTML and script code. The script code, running on the server and working through several layers of software, opens the database, runs the query, and formats the results. The Web server then transmits the results to the Web visitor's browser as pure HTML.

Note The script code generated by Microsoft products in Active Server Pages is Microsoft Visual Basic Scripting Edition (VBScript).

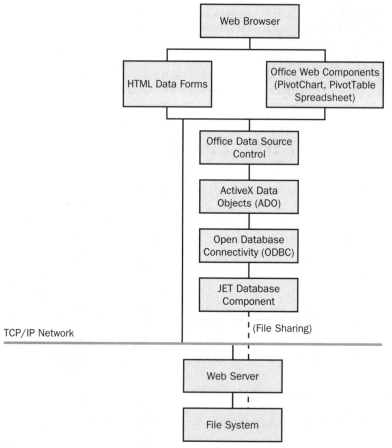

Figure 25-6. A high-level schematic for delivering database queries dynamically.

Inside Out

Installing Microsoft Internet Information Server and FrontPage

Active Server Pages that you create with Microsoft products are designed to work on Microsoft Internet Information Server (IIS). You can install IIS on Microsoft Windows NT 4.0 with Service Pack 3 or later, or on Windows 2000 Professional, Windows 2000 Server, Windows XP Professional, or Windows 2003 Server. If you have Windows XP Professional on your desktop machine, you can install a local IIS to test your work. If you didn't choose to install IIS when you installed Windows XP Professional, you can add it later by starting the Add Or Remove Programs application in Control Panel and choosing Add/Remove Windows Components.

If you plan to use Microsoft FrontPage, you must also install the FrontPage Server Extensions on your Web server. (FrontPage is included with Microsoft Office 2000 and 2002 Premium and Office XP Developer. FrontPage 2003 is not included in any of the Microsoft Office 2003 Editions and must be purchased separately.) If you installed FrontPage 2003 before installing IIS, you can enable the required Web extensions by rerunning Office 2003 Setup and choosing the option to repair your installation.

Note that you can publish Web pages that you create with Microsoft FrontPage on any Web server that has the FrontPage Server Extensions installed. Other popular Web servers running an operating system such as Apache or Linux can be configured to support FrontPage extensions.

Figure 25-6 shows the following additional components. Even if you never work with these directly, it's good to know what they are so you can decipher documentation and error messages.

- ActiveX Objects are prewritten software modules that provide commonly used functions. Most VBScript code in Active Server Pages works by loading and controlling ActiveX Objects that run on the Web server. The ActiveX objects you need to build most Active Server Pages are included with Microsoft Office and Microsoft FrontPage.

- ActiveX Data Objects (ADO) are a collection of ActiveX objects specifically designed to process databases. As you learned in Chapter 22, "Understanding Visual Basic Fundamentals," the ADO libraries are a standard part of Microsoft Access.

- Open Database Connectivity (ODBC) provides a standard interface to many different types of database systems. You configure ODBC through Windows Control Panel. See the Appendix for details about managing ODBC connections.

- The Database Management System (DBMS) organizes data into databases, tables, and fields. It also accepts commands (usually coded in SQL) that update or query the database. Microsoft Access and Microsoft SQL Server are typical Database Management Systems you can use to support Active Server Pages.

As you'll learn in Chapter 26, "Creating Static and Dynamic Web Pages," Access can export any table, query, or form (actually, the data bound to the form, not the form itself) as an Active Server Page. Creating an ASP in this way gives you a Web page that always retrieves the latest information from the database for display in a browser. Using tools in Microsoft FrontPage, you can enhance an ASP with themes, and you can create additional HTML components to provide navigation to other pages on your Web site.

Processing Live Data with HTML Forms

Among the many objects Web pages can contain are various form elements: text boxes, dropdown lists (similar to combo boxes in Access forms), check boxes, option buttons, push buttons (similar to command buttons in Access forms), and ActiveX controls. Web visitors can use these to enter data and submit it to an Active Server Page or other server-based program for processing. Typical database processing includes running customized queries and adding, changing, or deleting records in tables. Processing follows the schematic previously shown in

Figure 25-6, except that the server receives form field data from the Web page, and the Active Server Page programming is more complex.

HTML forms can't provide nearly as rich nor as helpful an interface as Access forms, but using HTML forms means authorized users anywhere can run your Web application without loading any additional software and regardless of the type of computer the user has. These are important considerations when you need to support many users, many environments, or both. The following sections discuss various ways that you can create HTML forms to process your data.

Microsoft Office FrontPage 2003

Although it doesn't provide a complete development environment, FrontPage 2003 includes components that connect HTML forms on the browser to Access databases on the server. The FrontPage Database Interface Wizard allows you to either create a new Access database for your Web site or connect to an existing database on your server. FrontPage 2003 also includes a powerful WYSIWYG editor for Web pages, additional active components, and a wealth of Web site management features.

The Database Interface Wizard in FrontPage generates HTML forms and Active Server Page code to query a database. Using HTML forms has two advantages over using Access to save a query as an Active Server Page:

1 The Database Interface Wizard can limit the number of records transmitted to the Web visitor and can then transmit additional or previous records only if the visitor requests them. A query saved from an Access database as an ASP always returns all the records defined by the query.

2 The Database Interface Wizard can accept lookup keys from the Web visitor so that a visitor could, for example, enter an order ID and receive a list of items in that order. An ASP saved from Access does not include any ability to select specific records.

Visual Studio.NET and ASP.NET

Microsoft's latest answer to software development, Visual Studio .NET, is an editor and project manager that lets you create both Windows desktop applications using one of several languages and Web applications using ASP.NET. .NET allows you to create applications using the programming language of your choice, including Visual Basic .NET, Visual C++ .NET, Visual C# .NET, or Visual J# .NET. No matter which programming language you choose, the compiled version of your program shares the same runtime library with all other languages. When you build a Web application, ASP.NET lets you use any of the available programming languages to generate HTML forms and ASP pages to implement your application.

Visual Studio uses essentially the same user interface as the Visual Basic editor supplied with Access 2003. In addition, Visual Studio provides a WYSIWYG HTML editor, ActiveX controls that generate HTML whenever you save a page that contains them, an assortment of database wizards and design tools, and an interactive debugger for both ASP.NET and scripts that run on the browser. ASP.NET also lets you choose the language that you want to use behind your Web forms, including Visual Basic. Yet, despite all these aids, Visual Studio remains at heart a programmer's environment. If you're not comfortable working directly with HTML code, Visual Basic programming, and ActiveX interfaces, this probably isn't the program for you. Otherwise, rest assured that anything you can do in code, you can do in Visual Studio .NET.

Data Access Pages in Access 2003

Access 2000 introduced a new feature, data access pages, that lets you design a special type of HTML form page that can navigate, filter, and update data in your database. The architecture to support data access pages has many components that are similar to those for Active Server Pages shown previously in Figure 25-6, but with one major difference. All the database requests originate on the client side of the Web connection, as shown in Figure 25-7. If you're using Microsoft SQL Server to store the data, the Database Management System component can execute on the server side of the network.

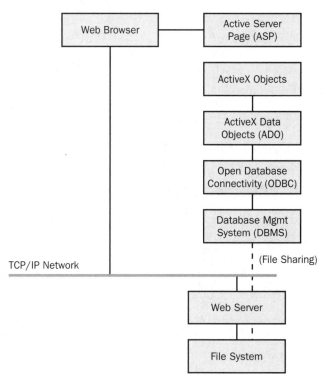

Figure 25-7. The component architecture for a Microsoft Access data access page.

The HTML pages that support data access pages must run on the client, not the server, so each user must also have installed Office ActiveX controls and ADO components. Because many World Wide Web users don't have these components, this solution works well only for local corporate intranets where all users have Office installed. Even so, you can use additional tools like FrontPage to define navigation and enhance the look of these pages. You'll learn more about the details of creating data access pages in Chapter 27, "Building Data Access Pages."

> For more information about FrontPage 2003, consult *Microsoft Office FrontPage 2003 Inside Out* from Microsoft Press. For more information about ASP.NET, consult *Microsoft ASP.NET Programming with Microsoft Visual Basic .NET Version 2003 Step by Step* from Microsoft Press. For more information about .NET, consult *Introducing Microsoft .NET* from Microsoft Press.

Sharing Your Data with SharePoint

It seems that every couple of years something new occurs in technology that causes a stir. For Microsoft, the latest hot buttons are .NET, XML, and now SharePoint. In all three cases, the technologies (.NET and XML) and product (SharePoint) have increased productivity and made life simpler for developers and users alike.

Introducing SharePoint

Microsoft SharePoint consists of two components: Microsoft SharePoint Team Services (STS) and Microsoft SharePoint Portal Server (SPS). STS allows teams of people to collaborate and share documents, tasks, and schedules. SPS is a Web portal that lets you set up your server to handle the searching and storing of documents. You can think of STS as a front end to SPS, where multiple but separate team services might use the same portal service. You can see an example of a SharePoint Team Services Web site in Figure 25-8.

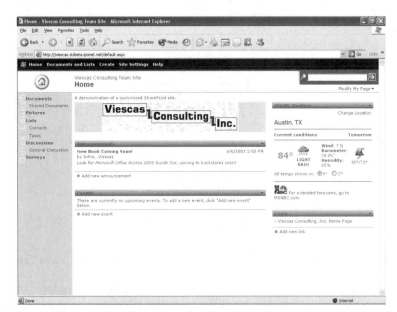

Figure 25-8.   A SharePoint Team Services Web site.

STS uses ASP.NET to create Web sites that take advantage of a technology called *Web parts*. Web parts are custom forms that you can ask STS to dynamically include on your team site pages. These Web parts allow you to customize your STS site with items such as announce-ments, contact lists, task lists, interactive discussion areas, and links to other pages relevant to the team tasks. You will learn more about Web parts and how they work in Chapter 28, "Working with XML and SharePoint."

Office and SharePoint

The Office development team has gone to great efforts to integrate all the Office products with STS so that you can share on your site documents of various types, including data from Access. In addition to being able to import data from and export data to a SharePoint site, you can create Access reports from the various lists within your site. Some of the other tasks you can perform with Office and SharePoint are

- Import data to and export data from Access.
- Link to SharePoint documents from Access to allow you to work with the data stored in SharePoint from your Access application.
- Attach local working documents to events on a SharePoint Team Services site.
- Import events into Microsoft Outlook to allow users to have a local copy of an event or reminder.
- Store on the SharePoint site Excel worksheets and Word documents for sharing.
- Use Office Web Components such as the PivotTable and PivotChart as Web parts to enhance your STS site.

Additional Office and SharePoint features will be discussed in Chapter 28, "Working with XML and SharePoint."

Discovering the Possibilities

This section gives you an overview of just a few examples of the abilities you have, using Access, to create various types of Web pages. These examples and more will be detailed in the next few chapters. In the WebChapters folder of the sample files included on the companion CD, you can find the files that demonstrate the types of pages you can generate using data from Microsoft Access. These examples includes the simple static HTML pages you can gen-erate directly from Access, complex forms and Active Server Pages you can build with FrontPage's Database Interface Wizard, and data access pages from Access.

Viewing Static HTML Pages

Figure 25-9 shows a simple HTML Web page created as a menu to allow you to link to other pages on the Web site to view reservations and requests. I used FrontPage to create the page and then added two push buttons to go to the related pages. I also applied one of the simple FrontPage themes to the page. I asked FrontPage to create the hyperlinks behind the two but-tons as relative links to files in the same folder, so the three pages should work together no mat-ter where you publish them as long as all three are in the same folder. (You can find this example page saved as *index.htm* in the WebChapters\StaticHTML folder on the companion CD.)

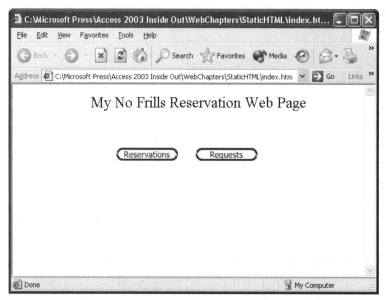

Figure 25-9. Simple HTML menu page.

If you open the simple menu page in your browser and click the Reservations button, you'll see the data from the tblReservations table in the Housing Reservations database as shown in Figure 25-10. I created this page by exporting the tblReservations table from Access as an HTML file. To move back to the menu Web page, click the Back button of your browser. You can learn more about exporting data from Access to static HTML in Chapter 26, "Creating Static and Dynamic Web Pages."

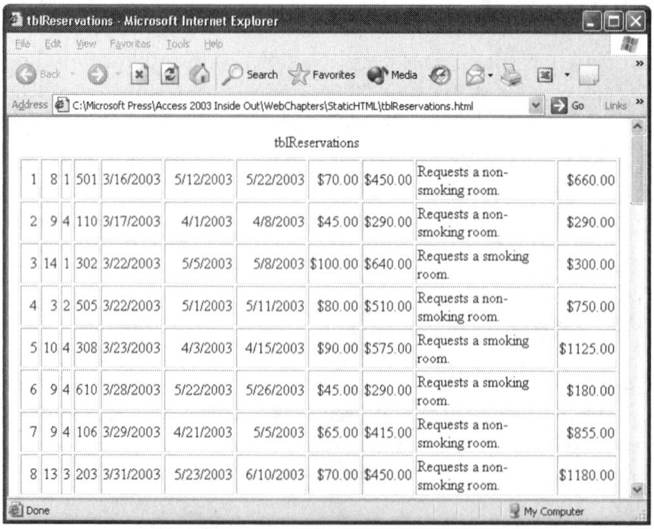

Figure 25-10. Data from a table exported from Access and used within a simple Web site.

Exploring Active Server Pages

When you want your users to be able to view the most current data from your database on a Web site, you can create an Active Server Page (.asp) that fetches the data when the user opens the page. You can also create code in the page that evaluates parameters that the user can supply in the URL or that you can pass from another Web page to filter the displayed results. An Active Server Page fetches the data on the server, so the server must be able to connect to your database. However, an Active Server Page is very efficient because the server performs all the database processing and returns to the user only the data requested.

In the \WebChapters\ActiveServerPages folder on the companion CD, you can find several Active Server Page examples. To be able to see how these pages work in a Web browser, you must publish them to a Web server and then fetch the page results using the server's Web address. You cannot open these files directly in Windows Explorer. If you are running Windows XP Professional and have installed and started Internet Information Services (IIS), you can copy the sample pages to your server's root folder to test them. You can find explicit instructions on how to do this in "Defining a System Data Source," page 1001.

You can see an interesting example of how to filter the results from an Active Server Page by opening the *ResSearch.htm* page from your server. This is a standard HTML page that includes a form to accept search criteria, as shown in Figure 25-11. If you have copied the pages to your local server, you can open this page by entering the address **http://localhost/ResSearch.htm** in your browser's address box.

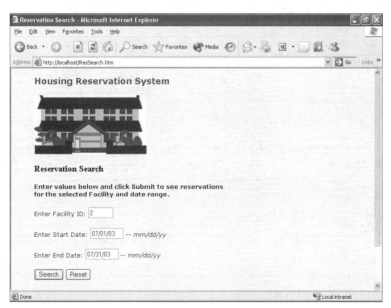

Figure 25-11. An HTML form page that provides search parameters to an active server page.

When you enter a facility ID, start date, and end date, and then click the Search button, the page passes parameters to the *Reservations.asp* Active Server Page. The page searches the Housing Reservations database and returns a result as shown in Figure 25-12.

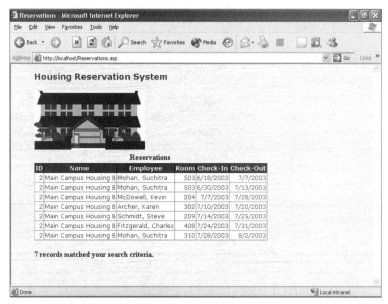

Figure 25-12. An Active Server Page that returns only the requested data.

When you know the parameters that an Active Server Page accepts, you can also enter the parameters as part of the URL. For example, if you want to see all the reservations for facility ID number 3 in the month of July 2003, you can enter the following in your Web browser's address field:

```
http://localhost/Reservations.asp?ID=3&StartDate=07/01/03&EndDate=07/31/03
```

You might have noticed the question mark at the end of an Active Server Page name followed by a long string of data in the URL of many Web pages that you visit. Now you know that the string specifies parameters that tell the Active Server Page what you want returned to your browser.

Looking at Data Access Pages

You can use data access pages to present data on the Web in a very attractive way. You can actually convert most forms and reports that you have created into data access pages and use the pages for your Web sites instead of just exporting your data as static HTML or creating an ASP page. In Figure 25-13 you see the rptFacilities report from the Housing database.

 Note After you install the files from the sample CD, be sure to open the Housing Reservations database (*Housing.mdb*) before you attempt to open any of the Web pages you find in the WebChapters\DataAccessPages folder. Code in the startup form makes sure the connections in these pages point to the location where you installed the database file.

982

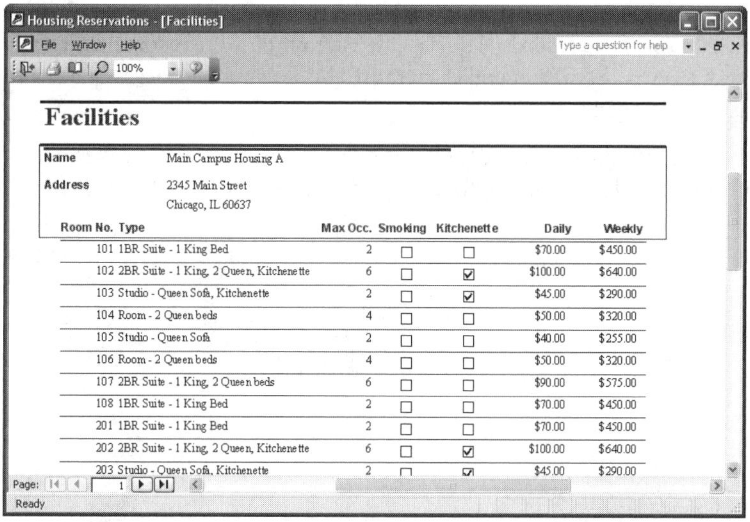

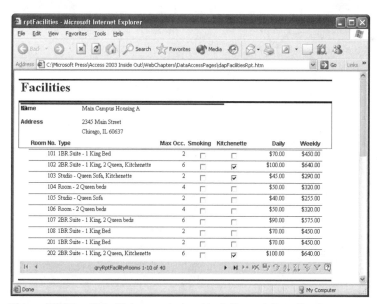

Figure 25-13. The rptFacilities report in the Housing database.

I opened this report in Design view in the Housing Reservations database and asked Access to save the report as a data access page. You can see the result in Figure 25-14.

Figure 25-14. This Web page is hard to tell apart from the Access report.

The resulting page looks nearly identical to the report. If you look closely, you can see a small minus sign next to the Name caption near the top of the page. You can click the minus sign to shrink the detail display. Initially the page opens in its collapsed format and you must click the plus sign to see the expanded format shown in the figure. Notice that the page shows you the detail for rooms only 10 records at a time. You can click on the navigation bar below the detail listing to see more records. The page doesn't request the records from the database until you ask to view them. You will learn more about using data access pages in Chapter 27, "Building Data Access Pages."

You are now ready to dig in and see how to use Access for some of your Web needs. In the next few chapters we will delve deeper into the topics that were discussed in this chapter and see additional examples.

Chapter 26

Creating Static and Dynamic Web Pages

As you learned in the previous chapter, you have many options when you want to make data that you have stored in an Access application available on the Web. In this chapter, you'll learn about two of those options, *static* and *dynamic* Web pages.

When you want to make relatively static data available in a Web page, you can export your data in HTML format. The Web page that you create in this way won't allow users to update the data, and your users will have limited search capabilities. However, you can create automated procedures in your application that make it easy to periodically update the Web page to ensure that it is current.

If your data is more dynamic, you can create an Active Server Page (.asp). When you do this, the Web server queries your database each time a user visits the page, so the data displayed is always current. As you'll learn in this chapter, you can create a page that accepts input parameters and then opens your Active Server Page to present a filtered view of your data—a custom query by form for the Web.

 Note The examples in this chapter are based on the tables and data in the Housing Reservations database (*Housing.mdb*). You can find the sample Web pages in the \WebChapters\StaticHTML and \WebChapters\ActiveServerPages folders on your companion CD.

Creating a Static HTML Document

The simplest way to publish data from your database to a Web page is to export the data as a simple, *static* HTML file. This type of file presents a snapshot of your data at the time you create the HTML file. To refresh the data on your Web page, you'll have to repeat the export process each time you want to present fresh data. You can use the export tools in Access to export data from a table, query, form, or report, but with some limitations. Table 26-1 on the next page lists these objects and the options you have when you export them to HTML.

Table 26-1. Export to HTML for Access Objects

Object	Data Exported	Comments
Table	Table datasheet	Access attempts to duplicate any formatting that you have applied to the datasheet (font, gridlines). You can also specify a template file to enhance the final output. The table name appears as a caption in the exported HTML table.
Query	Query datasheet	Same as a table. When you export a parameter query, Access prompts you for the parameters and exports the result of fetching the data after resolving the parameter values.
Form	The recordset for the outer form	Same as a table except you control formatting by setting the format of the form's Datasheet view. Access will not export data in any subform.
Report	The data displayed in the report	Access attempts to duplicate the format of the report, but does not output any line or rectangle controls. Access also exports any data in any subreport. Access exports the report one page at a time. It assigns the file name you specify for the first page and appends *PageN* (where *N* is the subsequent page number) for the second through last pages. You can specify a template file to enhance the overall appearance of the exported pages. You can include information in the template to ask Access to generate links to the various pages of the report.

The procedure to export to HTML is very similar for all object types. In the Database window, select the object you want to export, and then choose Export from the File menu. You can also right-click the object and choose Export from the shortcut menu. For this example, open the Housing Reservations database (*Housing.mdb*), click Tables on the Object bar in the Database window, select tblDepartments, and choose Export from the File menu. Access displays the Export Table 'tblDepartments' To dialog box. In the Save as type drop-down list, choose HTML Documents (*.html;*.htm). You can find the sample static HTML files installed from the companion CD in the \WebChapters\StaticHTML subfolder, as shown in Figure 26-1.

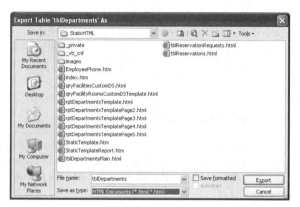

Figure 26-1. Exporting the data in an Access table as simple HTML.

Be sure to leave the Save formatted check box cleared. The object is to discover the simple format that Access uses to export to HTML. Click Export to complete the creation of your Web page. Open Windows Explorer, find the page you just created, and double-click the file to open it in your Web browser. Your result should look like Figure 26-2.

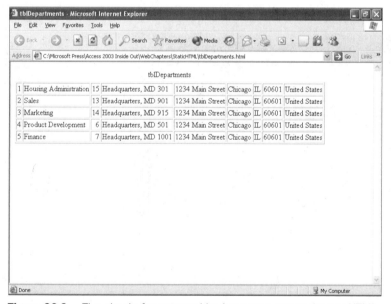

Figure 26-2. The simple format used by Access to export data to HTML.

Not very attractive, is it? Access doesn't even provide column headings. You could certainly open this page in a Web page editor and improve it, but you have additional options in Access to minimize the work needed to make this Web page more attractive. (You can find this page saved as *tblDepartmentsPlain.htm* in the \WebChapters\StaticHTML folder on your companion CD.)

Improving the Look of Exported Data in HTML

Creating more attractive HTML output from Access isn't difficult. You can customize the Datasheet view of your output source to specify a font and the appearance of the gridlines in the resulting HTML table. You can also create a template file that Access can use to make the resulting HTML more appealing.

Customizing Datasheet View

You can change the default settings for all datasheets in the Options dialog box. You can also customize the Datasheet view of any individual table, query, or form. To change settings for all datasheets, start by opening the Housing Reservations sample database, choose Options from the Tools menu, and click the Datasheet tab. You can see that you have several formatting options for datasheets, as shown in Figure 26-3.

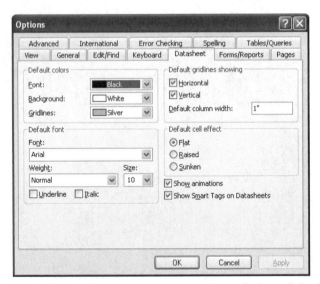

Figure 26-3. Settings for datasheets in the Options dialog box.

Caution Keep in mind that any setting that you change in the Options dialog box affects the look of all datasheets in any database on your machine. However, temporarily choosing custom settings in this dialog box might be a good option when you want to export several datasheets and do not want to change the settings for the individual objects.

Under Default colors, you can choose from a limited palette of 16 colors for Font, Background, and Gridlines. Be careful to not choose the same color for the font as for the background—the data won't be visible in the output table. Under Default font, you can choose the font name, the Weight (Thin, Extra Light, Light, Normal, Medium, Semi-bold, Bold, Extra Bold, and Heavy), the Size, and whether you want the font underlined or italic or both. The choices for Weight vary depending on the particular font you select. Keep in mind that the font you choose must also be available on the user's machine. Typical fonts on most Windows systems include Arial, Courier New, Tahoma, Times New Roman, and Verdana.

In the Default gridlines showing category, you can specify whether you want Horizontal or Vertical or both gridlines displayed. Although you can specify a Default column width, changing this setting does not affect the column widths in the HTML output. (Changing this setting does affect all datasheets that you open within Access.) Access creates the HTML table so that the column widths and heights adjust to display all the data within the width of the browser window.

Finally, setting the Default cell effect changes the look of the cells in the HTML table. When you choose Raised or Sunken, Access ignores the settings for Background and Gridlines under Default colors and the Horizontal and Vertical settings under Default gridlines showing. When you choose Raised, Access uses Silver as the background color and Gray as the gridline color. For Sunken, Access also uses Silver as the background color and uses White for the gridlines. When you choose Raised or Sunken, be careful not to choose Silver as the color for the Font because Silver is the background color.

If you want to set the format of the datasheet for an individual table, query, or form, you must first open the object in Datasheet view. Open the *qryFacilities* query in the Housing Reservations database in Datasheet view, as shown in Figure 26-4. (The query sorts by facility name.) You can see that I changed the font, font color, and gridlines.

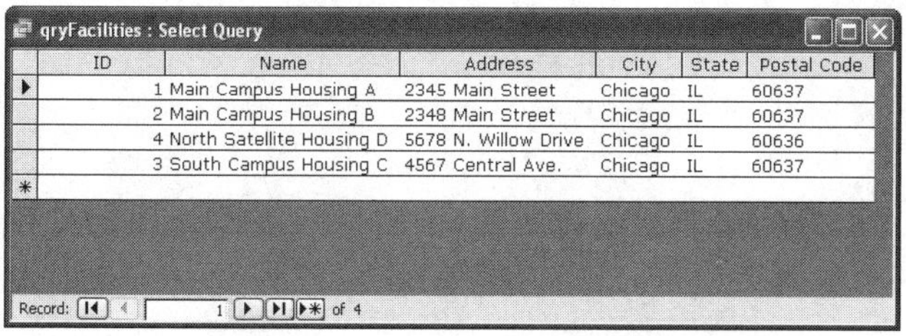

Figure 26-4. The Datasheet view of a query that has a customized format.

To see the font settings for this query's datasheet, choose Font from the Format menu. Access displays the Font dialog box, as shown in Figure 26-5 on the next page.

You can enter the name of the Font and Font style that you want or choose a setting from the list boxes. You can also enter a font Size or choose a size from the list box. For an OpenType font, you can enter fractions of points, such as 10.5. Select Underline to draw a line under all characters in both the column headings and the data. Choose a color for the font from one of 16 available on the drop-down list, but be sure that you do not select a color that is the same as the background of the grid.

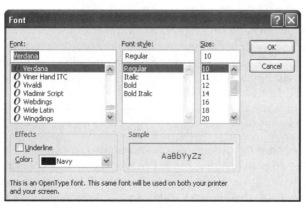

Figure 26-5. The font settings for a datasheet.

To see the other settings that affect the format of the datasheet, choose Datasheet from the Format menu. Access displays the Datasheet Formatting dialog box, as shown in Figure 26-6.

Figure 26-6. Formatting settings for a datasheet.

You can choose a Cell Effect exactly as you can in the Options dialog box. However, in this dialog box when you choose Raised or Sunken, Access disables the choices for Gridlines Shown, Background Color, and Gridline Color. Access does change the background color and gridline color to reflect the colors that it uses when you choose one of the two special effects. Although you can change settings under Border and Line Styles to affect the look of the datasheet in Access, you'll see only solid lines in the resulting HTML. If you want to see how these settings affect the datasheet in Access, select Flat under Cell Effect, then select Datasheet Border, Horizontal Gridline, Vertical Gridline, or Column Header Underline in the left combo box, and then choose a setting in the right combo box. Choices in the right combo box include Transparent, Solid, Dashes, Dots, and Double Solid.

Chapter 26

When you have finished changing font and formatting settings, click OK and then choose Save from the File menu or click the Save button on the toolbar, and then close the query. If you don't want to save your changes, close the Datasheet view and reply No when Access asks you if you want to save the layout changes.

After you set the options you want (either in the Options dialog box for all datasheets or in the Font and Datasheet Formatting dialog boxes for an individual datasheet), you're ready to export the results with formatting applied. For this example, select the *qryFacilities* query in the Database window and then choose Export from the File menu. In the Save as type drop-down list, choose HTML Documents (*.html, *.htm) as shown in Figure 26-7.

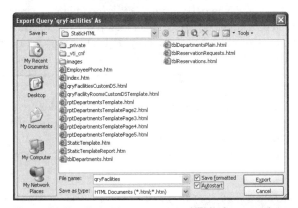

Figure 26-7. Exporting a query to HTML formatted.

Be sure to click the Save formatted check box so that Access knows to honor the formatting of the query's datasheet. When you click Save formatted, the dialog box also lets you click the Autostart option—Access will open the HTML file in your browser as soon as it completes the export. Click the Export button, and Access displays the HTML Output Options dialog box, as shown in Figure 26-8.

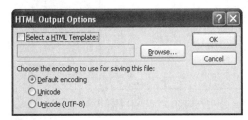

Figure 26-8. The HTML Output Options dialog box.

In this dialog box, you can also select an HTML template file to further customize the output. You'll learn how to create and use a template file that includes special embedded codes that Access understands in the next section. For now, leave the Select a HTML Template box clear. You can also select the character encoding that you want Access to use for the file. In most cases, the Default encoding option (Windows) works just fine. If your data contains unusual characters (for example, the Swedish character å) and your Web page might be viewed on non-Windows machines, you should choose Unicode or Unicode (UTF-8).

What Is Unicode?

The two Unicode options are a result of international standards established by the Unicode Consortium (*http://www.unicode.org*) to avoid problems with the internal numeric code used by different platforms to represent special characters. For example, the character å is the value 229 on a Windows machine but the value 140 on a Macintosh.

Unicode, however, presents two problems. First, not all systems support the standard. Second, Unicode can double the size or your HTML file, resulting in performance problems over slow networks. Unicode (which is UTF-16) is a 2-byte character set that is recognized by all browsers that support the Unicode standard. Unicode (UTF-8) supports most common characters in a single byte that can be understood by most platforms and uses two bytes to store special characters. If your data does contain special characters, UTF-8 provides the best compromise of speed and support for extended character sets across multiple platforms.

Click OK to complete the export of the query. When the export is finished, Access starts your browser and shows you the result that you can see in Figure 26-9. You can see that because you asked Access to export formatted, the table now has column headings and is using the font and gridlines specified for the query datasheet. You can find this sample page saved as *qryFacilitiesCustomDS*.

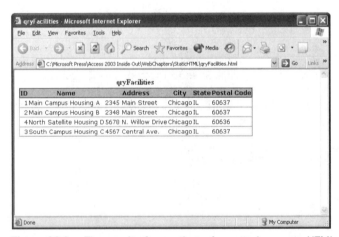

Figure 26-9. The result of exporting a formatted query to HTML.

Designing and Using HTML Output Templates

When you take the time to format a table, query, or form datasheet before you export it to HTML, you can see that the result is superior to the default export format. You can take this one step further by defining a template HTML file and asking Access to apply the template when it exports your data. In fact, creating a template is a good way to establish a common design for all your Web pages. Not only can you use a template to improve the appearance of data you export from Access, you can also use the same template to apply a common design to Web pages that you create from many HTML editors.

You can embed special comments in your template file (called tokens) that Access uses to place certain key elements in the final page. Table 26-2 lists the tokens and how Access uses them.

Table 26-2. **HTML Template Tokens Recognized by Access**

Token	Meaning
<!–AccessTemplate_Title–>	Inserts the name of the table, query, or form, or the contents of the Caption property of the report in place of this token.
<!–AccessTemplate_Body–>	Inserts the exported data as an HTML table at this location.
<!–AccessTemplate_FirstPage–>	When you are exporting a report, places a hyperlink to the first page of the report at this location.
<!–AccessTemplate_PreviousPage–>	When you are exporting a report, places a hyperlink to the previous page of the report at this location.
<!–AccessTemplate_NextPage–>	When you are exporting a report, places a hyperlink to the next page of the report at this location.
<!–AccessTemplate_LastPage–>	When you are exporting a report, places a hyperlink to the last page of the report at this location.
<!–AccessTemplate_PageNumber–>	When you are exporting a report, places the page number at this location.

In the \WebChapters\StaticHTML folder on your companion CD, you can find two template files. The first one, *StaticTemplate.htm*, does not include any of the special report tokens, so it is more suitable for exporting the datasheet of a table, query, or form. The contents of the template are as follows:

```
<html>
<head>
<title><!--ACCESSTEMPLATE_TITLE--></title>
</head>
<body leftmargin="50" background="sumiback.jpg">
<font face="Verdana" size="4" color="#333399"> <STRONG>Housing Reservation System
</STRONG></font><p>
<img src="housing.jpg" width="241" height="124">
<!--ACCESSTEMPLATE_BODY--><br>
</p>
</body>
</html>
```

The template isn't very complex, but it does specify a background graphic for the page, a heading, and an embedded JPEG file. You can see that the template places the name of the output object in the browser title bar and asks Access to insert the table results following the graphic image.

To see how this works, you can export the *qryFacilityRooms* query from the Housing Reservations database. I saved the query datasheet using a purple Verdana font and vertical gridlines only. Select this query in the Database window, choose Export from the File menu, navigate to the WebChapters\StaticHTML folder, choose HTML in the **Save as type** dropdown list, click **Save formatted** and **Autostart**, and click the Export button. In the HTML Output Options dialog box, click the **Select a HTML Template** option. Click the Browse button and find the *StaticTemplate.htm* file in the \WebChapters\StaticHTML folder. The dialog box should look like Figure 26-10. Notice that the dialog box disables the encoding options when you choose the option to use a template—the encoding for your final page will be inherited from the template.

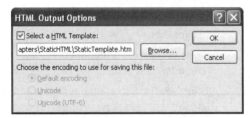

Figure 26-10. Specifying a template for data exported to HTML.

Click OK to finish the export. Access displays the result in your browser window, as shown in Figure 26-11. You can find this Web page saved as *qryFacilityRoomsCustomDSTemplate* on the companion CD.

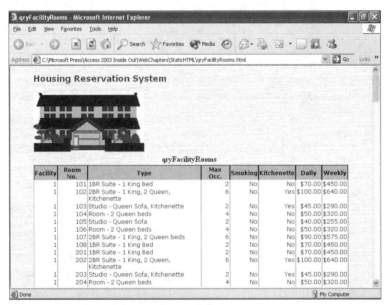

Figure 26-11. The result of exporting a formatted query using a template.

Troubleshooting

I don't see the graphic or the background on my sample page. What am I doing wrong?

Take another look at the HTML for the template file. The file specifies a background using the *sumiback.jpg* file. It also references the *housing.jpg* file to display as an image. When you include file references like these in your HTML and you do not include a relative path from the current location of the Web page, your browser expects to find the files in the same folder as the Web page. If you saved your sample file to a folder other than the \WebPages\StaticHTML folder, you won't see the graphics unless you copy the two files to the folder where you saved the sample file. Copy the two files and try opening the Web page again.

As you can see, the HTML page is vastly improved over the simple results that you get when you export data without formatting and a template. It's a simple matter to edit the final HTML to replace the query name in the title bar and the table caption with something more meaningful.

Generating an HTML Page from an Access Report

Access does a much better job of exporting reports to HTML. It attempts to mimic the layout and fonts that you designed into your original report. It also places the Caption property defined for the report in the title bar of your Web browser. The two limitations are that Access cannot export bound OLE or other graphic objects (such as check boxes) and it cannot duplicate lines and rectangles that you include in the report design. When your report contains more than one page, Access creates one HTML file per page and includes hyperlinks in the pages to make it easy to navigate from one page to another.

Creating a Template for a Report

Although Access does format reports nicely when you output them to HTML, you can further enhance the result by designing a template file. On the companion CD, you can find a template that you can use with reports, *StaticTemplateReport.htm*. The code in the template file is as follows:

```
<html>
<head>
<title><!--ACCESSTEMPLATE_TITLE--></title>
</head>
<body leftmargin="50" background="sumiback.jpg">
<font face="Verdana" size="4" color="#333399">
<STRONG>Housing Reservation System</STRONG></font><p>
<img src="housing.jpg" width="241" height="124">
<!--ACCESSTEMPLATE_BODY--><br>
<a href="<!--AccessTemplate_FirstPage-->">
<img border="0" id="img1" src="buttonA.jpg" height="30" width="100" alt="First">
</a>
<a href="<!--AccessTemplate_PreviousPage-->">
```

```
<img border="0" id="img1" src="buttonB.jpg" height="30" width="100"
alt="Previous"></a>
<a href="<!--AccessTemplate_NextPage-->">
<img border="0" id="img1" src="buttonC.jpg" height="30" width="100"
alt="Next"></a>
<a href="<!--AccessTemplate_LastPage-->">
<img border="0" id="img1" src="buttonD.jpg" height="30" width="100"
alt="Last"></a><b><font face="Verdana"><br>
Page <!--AccessTemplate_PageNumber-->.</font></b>
</p>
</body>
</html>
```

As noted earlier, when your report contains multiple pages, Access exports each page as a separate file and inserts hyperlinks to navigate through the pages. However, the default hyperlinks are simple text links that aren't very attractive. The sample template replaces the four links (First, Previous, Next, Last) with graphic button images. The template also inserts a page number at the bottom of each page. You can see that this template also specifies a background image and an embedded graphic and heading.

Exporting a Report with a Template

You can use the sample template to export any of the reports in the sample Housing Reservations database. To try it out, select the *rptDepartments* report in the Database window and choose Export from the File menu. Navigate to the WebChapters\StaticHTML subfolder. Select HTML Documents (*.html; *.htm) in the Save as type drop-down list and click Autostart as shown in Figure 26-12. Notice that Access has disabled the Save formatted option—Access always exports reports to HTML formatted.

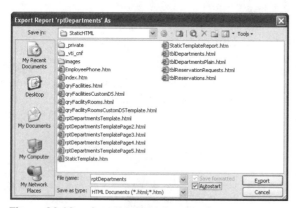

Figure 26-12. Specifying the location and options to export a report to HTML.

Click the Export button, and Access displays the HTML Output Options dialog box that you saw earlier in Figure 26-10. Be sure to select the Select a HTML Template option and then choose the *StaticTemplateReport.htm* file from the \WebChapters\StaticHTML folder as the template file, and click OK. Click OK again to export the report, and you should see a result in your browser as shown in Figure 26-13. (I moved to the second page of the report so that you can see all the design elements.)

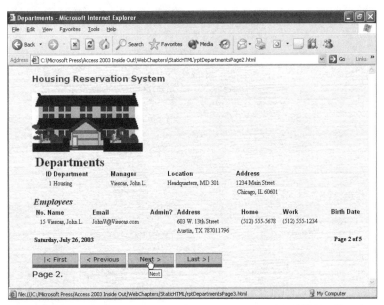

Figure 26-13. The second page of a report exported to HTML with a template applied.

Notice that the check box control used to display the Admin? column on the report is missing. (You would need to change the check box on the report to a text box before exporting to fix this.) Also, the report already includes page numbers, so the page number added by the template is redundant. (I included the page number token in the template so you can see how it works.) However, the Web page does include nice graphic hyperlinks to make it easy to move from page to page in the report.

Writing HTML from Visual Basic

Remember that HTML files are actually text files containing tags and perhaps script that your browser can interpret. After you become familiar with HTML coding, you might find it easiest to create a Visual Basic procedure to rewrite static Web pages that need to be updated periodically.

Unless you have a lot of turnover in your organization, the work phone numbers for employees probably don't change very often. So, to make this information available in a Web page, a static HTML page probably works just fine. However, you need an easy way to update the information in the Web page periodically—perhaps once a month—to make sure the information is current.

In the Housing Reservations sample database (*Housing.mdb*), you can find a procedure in the modHTML module that does just that. Following is the Visual Basic code for the Write-HTML function that you can find in the module on the next page:

```
Public Function WriteHTML() As Integer
' Function demonstrates how to format and write a
' static Web page with embedded data
' Declare some variables
Dim db As DAO.Database, rstDept As DAO.Recordset, rstEmp As DAO.Recordset
Dim strWebPath As String, strPagePath As String
  ' Trap all errors
  On Error GoTo Err_HTML
  ' Set up the location to put the page
  strWebPath = CurrentProject.Path & "\WebChapters\StaticHTML\"
  strPagePath = strWebPath & "EmployeePhone.htm"
  ' Delete the old page, if it's there
  If Len(Dir(strPagePath)) > 0 Then
    Kill strPagePath
  End If
  ' Open a new output file
  Open strPagePath For Output As #1
  ' Write the HTML headings
  ' Using Print to avoid quotes in the output
  Print #1, "<HTML>"
  Print #1, "<head><title>Employee Phone List</title></head>"
  Print #1, ""
  Print #1, "<body leftmargin=""50"" background=""sumiback.jpg"">"
  Print #1, "<p align=""left""><font size=""6"" face=""Times New Roman""" & _
    " color=darkblue>Employee Phone List</font></p>"
  Print #1, ""
  ' Point to the current database
  Set db = CurrentDb
  ' Open departments sorted by name
  Set rstDept = db.OpenRecordset("SELECT DepartmentID, Department " & _
    "FROM tblDepartments ORDER BY Department")
  ' Loop through all departments
  Do Until rstDept.EOF
    ' Write the table description, caption, and headings
    Print #1, "<table border=""3"" style=""border-collapse: collapse""" & _
      " bordercolor=steelblue width=""400"" cellpadding=""5"">"
    Print #1, "<caption><p align=""left"">" & _
      "<b><font face=""Verdana""" & _
      " color=""darkblue"">Department: " & rstDept!Department & _
      "</font></b></p></caption>"
    Print #1, ""
    Print #1, "<THEAD>"
    Print #1, "<TR>"
    Print #1, "<TH BGCOLOR=whitesmoke BORDERCOLOR=#000000 " & _
      "style=""border-style: double; border-width: 3"" >"
    Print #1, "<FONT style=FONT-SIZE:10pt FACE=""Verdana"" " & _
      "COLOR=darkblue>Employee Name</FONT></TH>"
    Print #1, "<TH BGCOLOR=whitesmoke BORDERCOLOR=#000000 " & _
      "style=""border-style: double; border-width: 3"" >"
    Print #1, "<FONT style=FONT-SIZE:10pt FACE=""Verdana"" " & _
      "COLOR=darkblue>Phone Number</FONT></TH>"
    Print #1, "</TR></THEAD>"
    Print #1, ""
    Print #1, "<TBODY>"
    ' Now open a recordset on the employees in this department
```

```
          ' sorted by last name, first name
          Set rstEmp = db.OpenRecordset("SELECT FirstName, MiddleName, " & _
            LastName, WorkPhone FROM tblEmployees " & _
            "WHERE DepartmentID = " & rstDept!DepartmentID & _
            " ORDER BY LastName, FirstName")
          ' Loop through all employees in this department
          Do Until rstEmp.EOF
            ' Write a table row for each employee
            Print #1, "  <tr>"
            Print #1, "    <td width=""65%"" style=""border-style: double; " & _
              "border-width: 3"">"
            Print #1, "    <font color=""darkblue"">" & _
              rstEmp!LastName & ", " & rstEmp!FirstName & _
              (" " + rstEmp!MiddleName) & _
              "</font></td>"
            Print #1, "    <td width=""35%"" style=""border-style: double; " & _
              "border-width: 3"">"
            Print #1, "    <font color=""darkblue"">" & _
              Format(rstEmp!WorkPhone, "(@@@) @@@-@@@@") & "</font></td>"
            Print #1, "  </tr>"
            ' Get next employee
            rstEmp.MoveNext
          Loop
          ' Close off the table
          Print #1, "</table>"
          Print #1, ""
          ' Create a space between tables
          Print #1, "</table>"
          Print #1, "<p> </p>"
          Print #1, ""
          ' Get the next department
          rstDept.MoveNext
        Loop
        ' Close off the Web page
        Print #1, "</Body>"
        Print #1, "</HTML>"
        ' Done - close up shop
        Close #1
        rstDept.Close
        Set rstDept = Nothing
        rstEmp.Close
        Set rstEmp = Nothing
        Set db = Nothing
        WriteHTML = True
    Exit_HTML:
        Exit Function
    Err_HTML:
        ' Display the error
        MsgBox "Error writing HTML: " & Err & ", " & Error
        ' Log the error
        ErrorLog "WriteHTML", Err, Error
        ' Bail
        Resume Exit_HTML
    End Function
```

The procedure begins by checking to see if the old Web page file exists using the Dir function. If it finds the file, it deletes it using the Visual Basic Kill statement. Next, the procedure takes advantage of the ability to read and write files that's built into Visual Basic. The code uses the Open statement to create a new .htm file, followed by a series of Print statements to write the heading tags to the file. You can also use a Write statement to write to a file opened this way, but Write includes double quotes around string variables or literals that you write to the file. Print writes only the text you specify.

The code opens a recordset on the tblDepartments table, sorted by department name. It creates an HTML table with a caption and a heading for each department. It opens a second recordset for all the employees in the department and loads the HTML table rows using information from the employee recordset. After writing out all the employees for the current department, the code writes tags to close off the table and create a space between tables. The code moves to the next department and loops back to start a new HTML table for the next department. When it has finished with the last department, it closes off the Web page with </Body> and </HTML> tags.

You can open the modHTML module, click anywhere in the function, and click the Run button on the toolbar to run the code. After the code completes, you can open the *Employee-Phone.htm* file that you can find in the \WebChapters\StaticHTML folder. Figure 26-14 shows you the result.

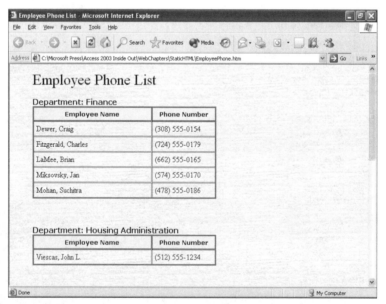

Figure 26-14. A Web page created by a Visual Basic procedure.

When you combine your Visual Basic skills with your knowledge about writing HTML, the options are limitless.

Creating a Dynamic Active Server Page

When your application contains frequently updated information and you want to make that information available to users on the Web, one of the best ways to publish current data is to use a dynamic Active Server Page. Access provides tools to export data to an Active Server Page, and you can use the same formatting tools that you learned about previously in this chapter.

However, setting up an Active Server Page to work correctly isn't simply a matter of copying the page to your Web server. Remember from Figure 25-6 on page 974 that an Active Server Page runs on the Web server and fetches the current data from your database on the server. Your Web server must be able to connect to your database, so the Active Server Page must have the correct connection information to enable the server to find your database. Additional requirements to run an Active Server Page are as follows:

- The Web server must be Microsoft Internet Information Server (IIS), version 3.0 or later. If you are running Microsoft Windows 2000 or Windows XP Professional on your desktop machine, you can install and start a local copy of IIS to test your Active Server Pages.

- The Web page must have a file name extension of .asp—this notifies the Web server that the page contains code that must execute on the server.

- The Web page must reside in a folder identified to the Web server as executable. The root folder of an IIS Web (usually C:\InetPub\wwwroot) on your local machine is marked executable when you install IIS. When you publish a Web page from Microsoft FrontPage, FrontPage marks the folder executable.

- The Web server must have Microsoft Access Open Database Connectivity (ODBC) drivers that correspond to the version of Access used to create the database, or the drivers for the correct version of SQL Server if you're publishing data from an Access project file. If you're using the Web server on a machine where you have Office 2003 installed (your machine is both the Web client *and* server), you have the correct drivers installed.

Defining a System Data Source

The export to Active Server Page feature in Access requires that you create a data source name (DSN) definition on the server that points to your database. To work properly, the DSN must be a system DSN—one that can be used by operating system services. If you plan to publish your Active Server Page on a Web server running on another machine, you must create a system DSN on that machine that connects to your database.

> **Note** A system DSN is an entry in your computer's registry, so you won't find a sample file that you can install to create the DSN. You must follow the steps shown here to create the system DSN in order to perform the exercises in this section and open the sample Active Server Pages.

To create a system DSN, you must open the ODBC Data Source Administrator. Open Windows Control Panel, double-click Administrative Tools, and then double-click Data

Sources (ODBC). Click the System DSN tab, as shown in Figure 26-15, to begin defining your data source.

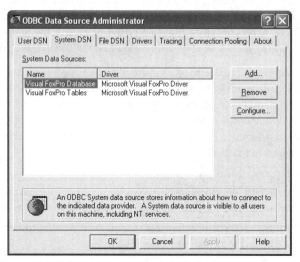

Figure 26-15. Defining a system data source in the ODBC Data Source Administrator.

Click the Add button to open the Create New Data Source dialog box, as shown in Figure 26-16.

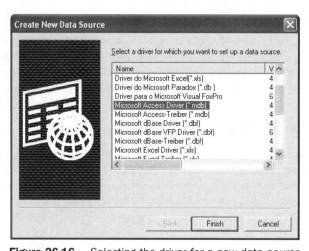

Figure 26-16. Selecting the driver for a new data source.

In the list of drivers, find either the Microsoft Access Driver (for a desktop database) or the SQL Server driver (for a project file) in the list, click it to select it, and click Finish. (Can you tell that I have foreign language support installed on my machine?) When you choose Microsoft Access Driver, the Data Source Administrator shows you the ODBC Microsoft Access Setup dialog box.

The sample Active Server Pages for the Housing Reservations database use a data source name called Housing. Type **Housing** in the Data Source Name box, and then type something to help you identify the purpose of the DSN in the Description box. Then click the Select button and find the *Housing.mdb* sample database in the Select Database dialog box that appears. After you point to the database and click OK, you return to the ODBC Microsoft Access Setup dialog box, which should now look like Figure 26-17.

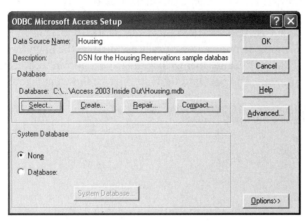

Figure 26-17. The ODBC Microsoft Access Setup dialog box ready to define a connection to the Housing Reservations sample database.

When your database is secured, you should click Database in the System Database box and then click the System Database button to point to your workgroup file. You can also click the Advanced button to define the login name and password of a user authorized to open the database. However, when you supply the login name and password in a DSN, anyone authorized to access the Web page will automatically be logged in to the database. When you don't supply a login name and password, the browser prompts the user for this information.

> For information about how to secure an Access desktop database, see Chapter 30, "Securing Your Database."

Notice that the location specified for the database is a physical drive, path, and file name. You should be sure that the location is one that is accessible to your Web server. Because you're defining this DSN for the Web server on your machine, the physical path should work fine. Be aware that you might need to use a network path or UNC (Universal Naming Convention, in the form *webservername**networkshare**filename*) to a network share when you define a DSN on your actual Web server. Click OK in the dialog box to complete the definition of your new system DSN. You can now use *Housing* as the data source name when you export Active Server Pages that use data from the Housing Reservations sample database (*Housing.mdb*).

Exporting Access Data to an Active Server Page

You can export tables, queries, and the recordset for forms to an Active Server Page with the same limitations explained earlier in Table 26-1. You cannot export a report to an Active Server Page. Now that you have your system DSN defined, exporting data and applying a template is very similar to exporting to HTML.

For this example, select the qryFacilities query again in the Database window and then choose Export from the File menu. Access displays the Export Table 'qryFacilities' As dialog box. In the Save as type drop-down list, choose Microsoft Active Server Pages (*.asp). Note that Access selects the Save formatted option automatically but disables the Save formatted and Autostart options so that you can't change them. Click the Export button, and Access displays the Microsoft Active Server Pages Output Options dialog box, as shown in Figure 26-18.

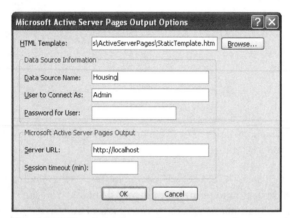

Figure 26-18. Selecting options to export data from Access as an Active Server Page.

If you leave HTML Template blank, Access sets up the Active Server Page to use the formatting specified in the table, query, or form datasheet. You can also apply a template that includes Access-specific tokens that you learned about in Table 26-2. In this case, click the Browse button and locate the StaticTemplate.htm file that you used earlier.

In the Data Source Name box, enter the name of the system data source that you created earlier—Housing. If your database isn't secured, you should not change the User to Connect As setting. The login ID of Admin is the default ID for all unsecured databases. When your database is secured, you can supply the login ID and password for a user authorized to read the database; however anyone authorized to access the Web page will then have access to your data. Remember that you can also specify this information in the system DSN. When your database is secured, I recommend that you place the security information in the system DSN. (Specify only the name of the workgroup file to ensure a secure login.) In contrast, if you enter it in this dialog box, Access stores the information with the Active Server Page, which any user authorized to access the Web site can read.

In the Server URL box, you should enter the HTTP address of the Web site where you plan to publish this Active Server Page. Because you're creating this page to execute on your local server, enter **http://localhost** as your Web server address. Click OK to export your data to an Active Server Page.

If you try to open your new Active Server Page as a file from Windows Explorer, you'll either receive an error message or the page will open in your default Web page editor. Because an Active Server Page includes script that must execute on the Web server to fetch the data and format the HTML to display in the client browser, you can open the page successfully only if you copy it to your Web server and then open it in your browser by entering the Web server URL and the address of the page.

If you are running Windows XP Professional and have installed and started Internet Information Services, you can see what your new page looks like by copying the files to your local server root Web folder. In most cases, this will be the C:\InetPub\wwwroot folder on your hard drive. Copy the qryFacilities.asp file (that you just created), and the graphics file *SumiBack.jpg* to this folder. You can then view the page by opening your Web browser, entering the following in the Address box, and pressing Enter:

```
http://localhost/qryFacilities.asp
```

Your result should look like Figure 26-19. You can also find this sample file saved as *qryFacilitiesTemplate.asp* on the companion CD.

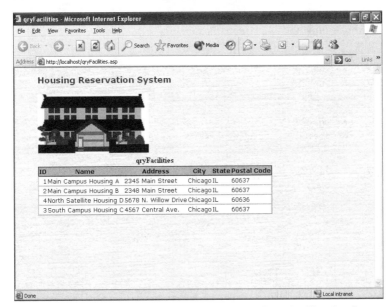

Figure 26-19. The qryFacilities query published from the Housing Reservations database using a template.

Note In some cases, you might receive an error from the server indicating that it could not open the connection. You can usually solve this problem by closing the Housing Reservations database and then trying the Active Server Page again. After your Web server successfully connects to your database, you should be able to open the Housing Reservations database, change some of the data (open the qryFacilities query and edit one or more rows), and refresh the page to see the changes appear instantly in the Active Server Page.

Programming Active Server Pages

The Active Server Pages created by the export facility in Access are very simple—they do nothing more than fetch and display the data from the original table, query, or form. To make Active Server Pages really useful, you need to dig into the code in the page, understand what it does, and then modify it to become more efficient by accepting input parameters to fetch only the data that the user needs.

Programming an Active Server Page to Use Parameters

To do its work, an Active Server Page must execute script code to open a recordset on the data to be displayed and then write the data inside HTML tags to send back to the client browser. The code in an Active Server Page generated by Access is very simple and straightforward. You can examine the code in any Active Server Page by opening it in Notepad or in your favorite Web page editor. For example, here's the HTML and VBScript code in the qry-FacilitiesTemplate.asp page:

```
<html>
<head>
<title>Facilities</title>
</head>
<body leftmargin="50" background="sumiback.jpg">
<font face="Verdana" size="4" color="#333399"> <STRONG>Housing Reservation System
</STRONG></font><p>
<img src="housing.jpg" width="241" height="124">
<%
If IsObject(Session("Housing_conn")) Then
    Set conn = Session("Housing_conn")
Else
    Set conn = Server.CreateObject("ADODB.Connection")
    conn.open "Housing","Admin",""
    Set Session("Housing_conn") = conn
End If
%>
<%
If IsObject(Session("qryFacilities_rs")) Then
    Set rs = Session("qryFacilities_rs")
Else
    sql = "SELECT tblFacilities.FacilityID, tblFacilities.FacilityName,
tblFacilities.FacilityAddress, tblFacilities.FacilityCity,
tblFacilities.FacilityStateOrProvince, tblFacilities.FacilityPostalCode
FROM tblFacilities  ORDER BY tblFacilities.FacilityName   "
    Set rs = Server.CreateObject("ADODB.Recordset")
    rs.Open sql, conn, 3, 3
    If rs.eof Then
        rs.AddNew
    End If
    Set Session("qryFacilities_rs") = rs
End If
%>
```

```
<TABLE BORDER=1 BGCOLOR=#ffffff CELLSPACING=0 RULES=rows><FONT FACE="Verdana"
COLOR=#000080><CAPTION>
    <B>Facilities</B></CAPTION></FONT>

<THEAD>
<TR>
<TH BGCOLOR=#c0c0c0 BORDERCOLOR=#000000 ><FONT style=FONT-
SIZE:10pt FACE="Verdana" COLOR=#000000>ID</FONT></TH>
<TH BGCOLOR=#c0c0c0 BORDERCOLOR=#000000 ><FONT style=FONT-
SIZE:10pt FACE="Verdana" COLOR=#000000>Name</FONT></TH>
<TH BGCOLOR=#c0c0c0 BORDERCOLOR=#000000 ><FONT style=FONT-
SIZE:10pt FACE="Verdana" COLOR=#000000>Address</FONT></TH>
<TH BGCOLOR=#c0c0c0 BORDERCOLOR=#000000 ><FONT style=FONT-
SIZE:10pt FACE="Verdana" COLOR=#000000>City</FONT></TH>
<TH BGCOLOR=#c0c0c0 BORDERCOLOR=#000000 ><FONT style=FONT-
SIZE:10pt FACE="Verdana" COLOR=#000000>State</FONT></TH>
<TH BGCOLOR=#c0c0c0 BORDERCOLOR=#000000 ><FONT style=FONT-
SIZE:10pt FACE="Verdana" COLOR=#000000>Postal Code</FONT></TH>

</TR>
</THEAD>
<TBODY>
<%
On Error Resume Next
rs.MoveFirst
do while Not rs.eof
 %>
<TR VALIGN=TOP>
<TD BORDERCOLOR=#c0c0c0  ALIGN=RIGHT><FONT style=FONT-
SIZE:10pt FACE="Verdana" COLOR=#000080><%=Server.HTMLEncode
(rs.Fields("FacilityID").Value)%><BR></FONT></TD>
<TD BORDERCOLOR=#c0c0c0 ><FONT style=FONT-
SIZE:10pt FACE="Verdana" COLOR=#000080><%=Server.HTMLEncode
(rs.Fields("FacilityName").Value)%><BR></FONT></TD>
<TD BORDERCOLOR=#c0c0c0 ><FONT style=FONT-
SIZE:10pt FACE="Verdana" COLOR=#000080><%=Server.HTMLEncode
(rs.Fields("FacilityAddress").Value)%><BR></FONT></TD>
<TD BORDERCOLOR=#c0c0c0 ><FONT style=FONT-
SIZE:10pt FACE="Verdana" COLOR=#000080><%=Server.HTMLEncode
(rs.Fields("FacilityCity").Value)%><BR></FONT></TD>
<TD BORDERCOLOR=#c0c0c0 ><FONT style=FONT-
SIZE:10pt FACE="Verdana" COLOR=#000080><%=Server.HTMLEncode
(rs.Fields("FacilityStateOrProvince").Value)%><BR></FONT></TD>
<TD BORDERCOLOR=#c0c0c0 ><FONT style=FONT-
SIZE:10pt FACE="Verdana" COLOR=#000080><%=Server.HTMLEncode
(rs.Fields("FacilityPostalCode").Value)%><BR></FONT></TD>

</TR>
<%
rs.MoveNext
loop%>
</TBODY>
```

```
<TFOOT></TFOOT>
</TABLE><br>
</body>
</html>
```

Any code included in an Active Server Page must appear between <% and %> tags. Near the beginning of the page, you can see code that Access generated that tests to see if a session variable has been saved that defines the connection that the page needs. If not, the code creates a new ADODB.Connection object and then opens it using the Housing data source name that you defined earlier. The code next checks to see if the recordset needed for the page is still open and saved as a session object. If not, the code opens a new recordset using the SQL from the object that you asked Access to export.

The VBScript code (a close second cousin to Visual Basic) then starts a Do While Not rs.eof loop to read all the records. Inside the loop, the page writes normal table HTML tags, but the code interrupts the tag to fetch the fields from the recordset and insert them into the HTML that the page returns. For example, the following code inserts the FacilityName field into the output using <TD> and </TD> (table data) tags:

```
<TD BORDERCOLOR=#c0c0c0 ><FONT style=FONT-
SIZE:10pt FACE="Verdana" COLOR=#000080><%=Server.HTMLEncode
(rs.Fields("FacilityName").Value)%><BR></FONT></TD>
```

Notice that there is a pair of code tags embedded in the middle. The code calls the server's HTMLEncode function to make sure that the characters returned use the correct coding scheme. (See the sidebar on page 992, "What Is Unicode?") The code passes the value of the FacilityName field in the current record of the recordset to the encoding function. Later in the code, you can find a MoveNext command to the recordset followed by a Loop. The VBScript code loops through all the records and causes the page to output one row per record until it is finished.

> All the VBScript code in this chapter is identical to what you might code in a Visual Basic module. However, there are some key differences between VBScript and Visual Basic. You'll learn more about coding in VBScript in the next chapter, "Building Data Access Pages."

To make an Active Server Page really useful and efficient, the page needs to be able to accept parameters either in the URL or from a calling page and filter the recordset it returns. Code in an Active Server Page can fetch parameters supplied after the question mark as part of the URL string (such as passing an "ID" value of 3 by specifying *http://localhost/ mypage.asp?ID=3*), from cookies written by the sending page, or from values sent to the page from another page that uses the POST method from an HTML form. You're probably most familiar with parameters in a URL string—you see them all the time in the Address box when you visit Active Server Pages on the World Wide Web. You'll learn more about cookies in the next chapter on data access pages.

When an Active Server Page receives parameters, the code in the page can access the parameters as members of the Request object. For example, to find out if a value has been supplied for an ID parameter, the code can test Request("ID"). When you know how to test for parameter values, it's easy to modify the code that builds the recordset for the Active Server Page to open a filtered view of the data. In the \WebChapters\ActiveServerPages folder, you can find the Active Server Page, *Reservations.asp*, that accepts three different parameters to filter the list of reservations saved in the database. Below is the VBScript code that examines the parameters and builds a filtered query to fetch the data for the page:

```
Dim lngID, strWhere, strErr, intCount
Dim datStart, datEnd
intCount = 0
strWhere = ""
On Error Resume Next
' Comment out recordset re-use - filtering every time page opens
' If IsObject(Session("qryXmplFacilityReservationsForASP_rs")) Then
'   Set rs = Session("qryXmplFacilityReservationsForASP_rs")
' Else
  lngID = Request("ID")
  If Not IsNull(lngID) And Len(lngID) > 0 Then
    strWhere = " WHERE tblFacilities.FacilityID = " & lngID
  End If
  datStart = Request("StartDate")
  datEnd = Request("EndDate")
  ' Check for date search and add/build predicate
  If IsNull(datStart) Or Len(datStart) = 0 Then
    ' No start date, check for end
    If Not IsNull(datEnd) And Len(datEnd) > 0 Then
      ' Got an end date only - create predicate
      If Len(strWhere) > 0 Then
        strWhere = strWhere & " AND tblReservations.CheckInDate <= #" & _
          datEnd & "# AND tblReservations.CheckOutDate > #" & datEnd & "#"
      Else
        strWhere = " WHERE tblReservations.CheckInDate <= #" & datEnd & _
          "# AND tblReservations.CheckOutDate > #" & datEnd & "#"
      End If
    End If
  Else
    ' Got a start, now check for end
    If IsNull(datEnd) Or Len(datEnd) = 0 Then
      ' Got a start date only - create predicate
      If Len(strWhere) > 0 Then
        strWhere = strWhere & " AND tblReservations.CheckInDate <= #" & _
          datStart & "# AND tblReservations.CheckOutDate > #" & datStart & "#"
      Else
        strWhere = " WHERE tblReservations.CheckInDate <= #" & datStart & _
          "# AND tblReservations.CheckOutDate > #" & datStart & "#"
      End If
```

```
      Else
        ' Got both dates, do range check
        If Len(strWhere) > 0 Then
          strWhere = strWhere & " AND tblReservations.CheckInDate <= #" & _
            datEnd & "# AND tblReservations.CheckOutDate > #" & datStart & "#"
        Else
          strWhere = " WHERE tblReservations.CheckInDate <= #" & datEnd & _
            "# AND tblReservations.CheckOutDate > #" & datStart & "#"
        End If
      End If
    End If
    ' Now, build the SQL for the query
    sql = "SELECT tblFacilities.FacilityID, tblFacilities.FacilityName, " & _
      "tblEmployees.LastName & ', ' & tblEmployees.FirstName & " & _
      "(' ' + tblEmployees.MiddleName) AS EmpName, " & _
      "tblReservations.RoomNumber, tblReservations.CheckInDate, " & _
      "tblReservations.CheckOutDate  FROM tblEmployees INNER JOIN " & _
      "(tblFacilities INNER JOIN tblReservations ON " & _
      "tblFacilities.FacilityID=tblReservations.FacilityID) " & _
      "ON tblEmployees.EmployeeNumber=tblReservations.EmployeeNumber " & _
      strWhere & " ORDER BY CheckInDate"
    Set rs = Server.CreateObject("ADODB.Recordset")
    rs.Open sql, conn, 3, 3
    strErr = Err.Description
    If rs.eof Then
      rs.AddNew
    End If
```

I created this Web page by exporting the *qryXmplFacilityReservationsForASP* sample query to an Active Server Page. Because this page should requery the database each time it opens, I commented out the standard code in an Access-generated Active Server Page that reuses the previous recordset. The code attempts to fetch ID, StartDate, and EndDate parameters, and then it builds a filter using these parameters to find current reservations for the requested facility and date range.

You can test this Active Server Page by copying it to your local Web server root folder and then entering the parameters as part of the URL. For example, if you want to display the reservations for facility number 3 for the month of August 2003, type the following in your browser's Address box and press Enter:

```
http://localhost/Reservations.asp?ID=3&StartDate=08/01/03&EndDate=08/31/03
```

Provided you haven't modified the data in the original sample database, the Active Server Page should return one record, as shown in Figure 26-20.

Chapter 26

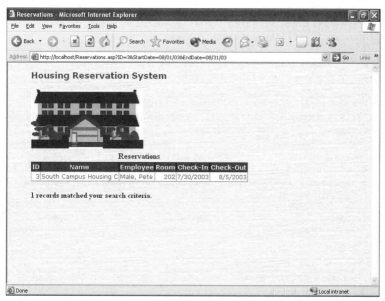

Figure 26-20. Displaying a result in an Active Server Page using parameters in the URL.

Creating a Page to Filter an Active Server Page

To make an Active Server Page that accepts parameters really useful, you need to create a page using HTML forms that can accept the parameters and pass them to your Active Server Page. The HTML to create a form is fairly straightforward. You need a <FORM> tag that includes the action to take when a POST method is requested by a SUBMIT action from one of the controls on the form. You also need INPUT tags to define the names of the parameters and the type of data that the parameters can accept. You can find a sample Web page saved as *Res-Search.htm* in the \WebChapters\ActiveServerPages folder on your companion CD. The HTML code that defines the Web page is as follows:

```
<HTML>
<HEAD>
<meta HTTP-EQUIV="Content-Type" CONTENT="text/html; charset=windows-1252">
<meta http-equiv="Content-Language" content="en-us">
<TITLE>Reservation Search</TITLE>
</HEAD>
<BODY leftmargin="50" background="sumiback.jpg">
<font face="Verdana" size="4" color="#333399"> <STRONG>Housing Reservation System
</STRONG></font><p>
<img src="housing.jpg" width="241" height="124"><h3>Reservation Search</h3>
<P>
```

```
<b><font face="Verdana" size="2">Enter values below and click Submit to see
reservations <br>for the selected Facility and date range.</font></b></P>
<FORM METHOD="POST" ACTION="Reservations.asp">
<P>
<font face="Verdana"><font size="2">Enter Facility ID: </font>
<INPUT TYPE=TEXT NAME="ID" SIZE=5 MAXLENGTH=5></font></P>
<P>
<font face="Verdana"><font size="2">Enter Start Date: </font>
<INPUT TYPE=TEXT NAME="StartDate" SIZE=8 MAXLENGTH=8><font size="2"> </font>
<EM> <font size="2">-- mm/dd/yy</font></EM></font></P>
<P>
<font face="Verdana" size="2">Enter End Date: </font>
<INPUT TYPE=TEXT NAME="EndDate" SIZE=8 MAXLENGTH=8><font size="2"> </font>
<EM> <font size="2" face="Verdana">-- mm/dd/yy</font></EM></P>
<INPUT TYPE=SUBMIT VALUE="Search">
<INPUT TYPE=RESET VALUE="Reset">
</FORM>
<HR>
<H5>
Author: John L Viescas.<br>
Copyright © 2003 Viescas Consulting, Inc. All rights reserved. <BR>
Revised:
<!--WEBBOT BOT=TimeStamp
    S-Type="EDITED"
    S-Format="%m/%d/%y" startspan
-->07/25/03<!--WEBBOT BOT=TimeStamp endspan i-checksum="12698"
--></H5>
</BODY>
</HTML>
```

I used Microsoft FrontPage to create the basic form page, and then I modified it for this example. The key parts of the page are the <FORM> tag that identifies the Web page to call when the user clicks the Search button (*Reservations.asp*), and the <INPUT> tags that define the three parameters. You can copy this file to your local Web server root folder and then open it by entering the following in your browser Address box and pressing Enter:

```
http://localhost/ResSearch.htm
```

You should see the page open and offer input boxes for the three parameters as shown in Figure 26-21.

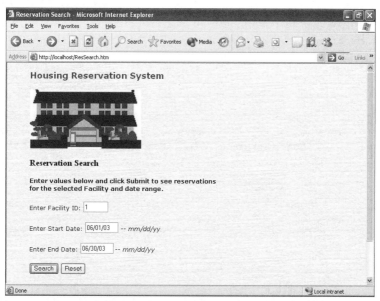

Figure 26-21. Entering parameters in a Web page that calls an Active Server Page.

If you enter the parameters shown in Figure 26-21 and click the Search button, you should see one row returned by the *Reservations.asp* Active Server Page. This is a very simple example, but you can see how using form-based Web pages linked to Active Server Pages can present a very efficient solution for your users.

You have seen what it takes to create simple static and dynamic Web pages directly from Access and customize the pages to produce the results you need for your application. In the next chapter, you'll learn how to create data access pages—an interesting alternative to Active Server Pages, particularly when used in an intranet environment.

Building Data Access Pages

As you learned in Chapter 2, "The Many Faces of Microsoft Access," Access was originally designed to be the premier desktop database application development tool for Microsoft Windows. As companies have discovered the universal appeal of writing Web-enabled applications, either for the World Wide Web or a local intranet, Microsoft has responded by adding features to Access that make the data you store in an Access application database available to Web pages.

Data access pages, introduced in Access 2000, are just one of the tools you can use to work with your Access data in a Web page. As you'll discover in this chapter, the tools that you use to design a data access page are similar in many ways to those that you use to design native Access forms and reports. So, you can leverage some of the skills you already have when you begin creating data access pages. But data access pages are also very different because you're actually designing an HTML page that isn't stored in your database, and you use VBScript instead of Visual Basic to automate how the page works.

In this chapter you'll learn

- The uses of data access pages and their underlying architecture
- How to create a data access page using a wizard
- Ways to enhance a wizard-created data access page
- How to save a form or report as a data access page
- Techniques for creating a data access page from scratch and designing a page with a PivotChart
- Basic methods to automate a data access page with VBScript
- Techniques you can use to keep the links in your data access pages current
- How to publish your completed data access pages

Note The samples in this chapter are based on the Housing Reservations application (*Housing.mdb*) and the sample data access page files that are in the WebChapters\ DataAccessPages folder that you can find on the companion CD. When you open *Housing.mdb* for the first time on your machine, code in the frmCopyright form attempts to correct the links to the sample data access pages and update the Connection property for each page. If this code fails, see the section "Updating Data Access Page Links and Connections" on page 1081.

Introducing Data Access Pages

Data access pages are completely different from any of the other objects in Access. As with linked tables, data access pages (DAPs for short) are not physically stored inside the Access database like forms and reports, but are actually HTML files with a link to an object in your Access desktop database or project file. When you open a DAP in Page view, Access starts a copy of your Web browser inside its workspace and asks it to display the .htm page linked into your DAP object definition. You can also directly open the .htm file that is your DAP outside Access using a Web browser.

Underlying Structure of a Data Access Page

Access data access pages are a combination of various technologies, which include HTML data forms (also called databound HTML controls), Office Web Components, and the Microsoft Office Data Source ActiveX control, all activated from within the dynamic HTML that defines the page. Figure 27-1 shows you an overview of the data access page architecture.

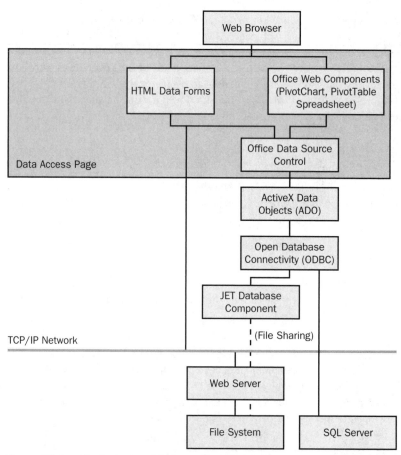

Figure 27-1. The logical architecture of a data access page.

Introduced in Internet Explorer 4.0, dynamic HTML (or DHTML) allows the Web page designer to include instructions that let the Web page modify itself while running in the browser on your client machine. Data access pages utilize this technology to dynamically load data into data-bound controls or provide data to an Office Web Component included in the page by calling the Office Data Source ActiveX control. The data source control uses ActiveX Data Objects (ADO) to fetch the requested data from your database—either from tables in an Access desktop database (.mdb) using the JET database engine or from tables stored in SQL Server by sending SQL commands to the server.

Inside Out

Understanding the difference between dynamic HTML and Active Server Pages (ASP)

Don't confuse dynamic HTML with Active Server Pages. Active Server Pages always execute on the Web server and send the result to be displayed as simple HTML to your Web browser. Dynamic HTML pages always execute in your Web browser, which can mean that your Web browser sends many commands to your database server over the network to fetch the data it needs to display the information in your Web page.

Think of it this way: An Active Server Page assembles the major parts of your house on the server and sends the prefabricated rooms to your browser to assemble them into a home. A dynamic HTML page requests the bricks, pieces of wood, and nails from the server and assembles the home from the pieces on your client machine. So, an Active Server Page fetches the individual parts on the server and sends the results that your browser can quickly put together to show you the result. An Active Server Page uses more resources on the server, but uses fewer network resources because it sends only assembled parts. A dynamic HTML page fetches the individual bits and pieces and does all the assembly at the final destination. A dynamic HTML page uses more resources on your client machine and can require more network resources to fetch the individual parts than it uses to assemble the final result.

You might begin to get nervous as you read about how a data access page works. Relax! The data access page designer in Access 2003 hides all this complexity and makes it easy to create complex Web pages that fetch data from your Access database. The data access page designer lets you design your page using an interface that's very similar to the one you use to create forms and reports.

Usefulness and Limitations

Unlike traditional HTML forms and server-based processing, data access pages don't provide a general-purpose way to extend applications all across the World Wide Web. The technical requirements (a Windows-based computer, and installation of Office 2003 or the Office Web Components) make sure of that. Put more simply, a user on a Macintosh in Paris or a user on a UNIX system in Sydney won't be able to sign on to your Web site over the Internet and open your data access page. However, data access pages do provide an efficient method of distributing applications and data to groups of users who you know have the correct environment—groups of employees on an intranet, for example, or limited Internet groups such as field service representatives, sales forces, and customers who have licensed and installed the required Office Web Components.

Consider carefully before you make data access page applications available to users connected by a dial-up link. Remember, these users will be reading your Access or SQL Server database directly from their Web browsers using file sharing, which might consume a lot of bandwidth even for well-optimized databases and queries.

Types of Pages You Can Create

Data access pages are a programmable HTML environment, so in one sense you can create any type of page you care to program in HTML. You can open any data access page (.htm) file in Notepad or any Web page editor such as Microsoft FrontPage and change the HTML code to make the page work or look differently. From within Access, however, you design data access pages in a very similar way to how you design Access forms or reports. The critical component that Access always adds to every data access page is the Microsoft Office Data Source Control (MSODSC) that greatly simplifies fetching, displaying, and updating data from your tables. When you open a data access page, the data source control opens one or more recordsets on your local machine over a network link, displays the result, and provides navigation controls to allow you to move around in the recordset just like you do on a form or report.

Data access pages typically feature groups of form fields associated with a record navigation bar. The simplest data access pages display the records from one table and provide a simple navigation bar, as shown in Figure 27-2.

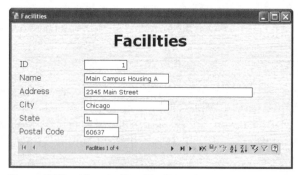

Figure 27-2. The *dapXmplFacilities* data access page displays data from one table.

When you want to edit a table that has many records, you can create a data access page that allows the user to selectively filter the records using values in a related table. Figure 27-3 shows you the *dapXmplDeptEmployees* data access page that allows you to display and edit employees filtered by department.

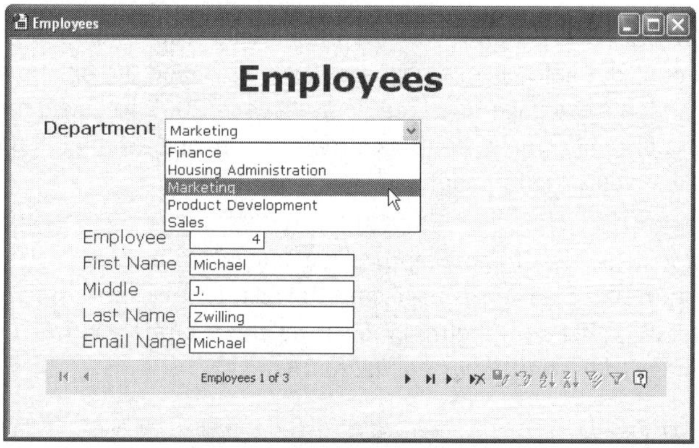

Figure 27-3. A data access page that lets you view and edit a subset of records.

When you first open this page, you'll see a blank Department drop-down list. When you choose a department from the list, the page displays the employees for the department you selected. This design is particularly efficient because it fetches only the records you want to see from the database.

You can also create a data access page that displays data from one table in a header area and shows you records from a related table in a detail area—similar to a form with an embedded subform. This type of data access page is called a *banded* page. Figure 27-4 shows you the *dapXmplFacilitiesAndRooms* data access page that is designed in this way.

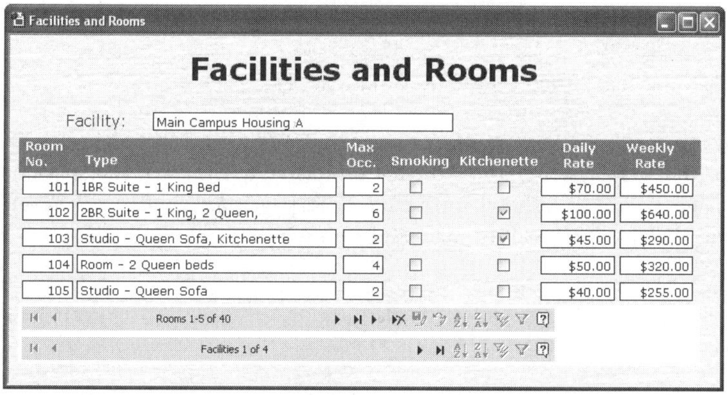

Figure 27-4. A data access page that works like a form with a subform.

Notice that this data access page has two navigation bars. You can use the outer bar to move from one housing facility to another. The inner bar shows you the different rooms defined for the facility in groups of five at a time. As you'll learn later, you can set properties to control how many records a data access page fetches to display in any area. Whether your data access page uses a single table as its source, or multiple tables, you can create a set of form fields to add, change, or display records. Of course, once you've located a record on an updatable data access page, you can update or delete it.

> **Note** Originally, in Access 2000, when you displayed multiple records on a page, had multiple tables included in your data access pages, or even specified any kind of grouping or sorting, Access would force the page to be read-only. Access 2002 removed this restriction, and you can now define this type of page as updatable as long as you tell the data source control which table you want to update.

You can also copy the look and feel of many reports in a data access page. As you'll learn later, you can often save a report as a data access page, and the result looks very similar to the original report in your Access application. Figure 27-5 shows you the *rptDepartments* report saved as a data access page (*dapXmplDepartmentsFromReport*).

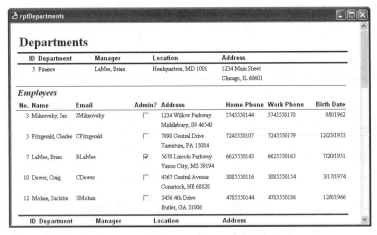

Figure 27-5. An Access report saved as a data access page.

Finally, you can create a data access page that includes an Office spreadsheet, a PivotTable, or a PivotChart that displays or charts information related to the records displayed in the main part of the page. Figure 27-6 shows you a data access page (*dapXmplFacilityRevenue*) that displays data for each housing facility and a chart showing the sales by month.

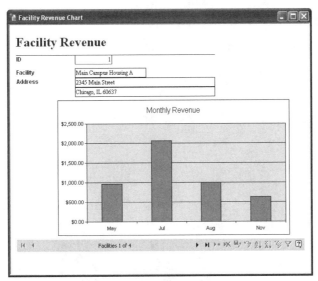

Figure 27-6.   A data access page with an embedded PivotChart.

In the remainder of this chapter, you'll learn how to build each of these types of data access pages. You'll also learn some of the basics of VBScript that you can use to automate your pages.

Designing Data Access Pages

When you first begin designing data access pages, you'll notice many similarities with designing Access forms and reports. In some ways, data access pages are a cross between forms and reports—you can create data access pages to display and edit data similar to forms, and you can create data access pages that display and total groups of information similar to a report.

Setting Options for Data Access Pages

Before jumping in and creating data access pages, let's look at some of the option settings that you can customize. To set the options for your data access pages, choose Options from the Tools menu and then click the Pages tab. The Options dialog box displays the settings you can customize as shown in Figure 27-7 on the next page.

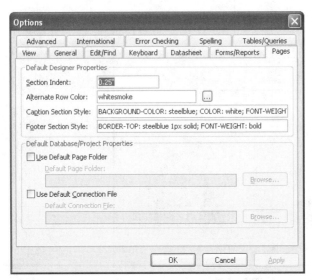

Figure 27-7. The page settings that you can customize in the Options dialog box.

In the Default Designer Properties section, you can set options to specify the default indent for each section, an alternate color for rows displayed as a table, and style keywords that the page designer sets for captions (headers) and footers. In the two style specifications, you can use any valid HTML style keyword followed by a colon and the value that you want to assign to the keyword.

For colors, you can specify the hexadecimal equivalent of the red-green-blue (RGB) value that you want, but you can also specify simple color names. For example, #FF0000 is red, #008000 is green, #00FF00 is lime, #0000FF is blue, #FFFF00 is yellow, #00FFFF is cyan, #FF00FF is magenta, #FFFFFF is white, and #000000 is black. Notice that the default settings use some interesting color names—whitesmoke and steelblue. These are special color names that Internet Explorer understands, and you can find a complete list of the names in Article 4, "Internet Explorer Web Page Color Names," on the companion CD.

You can select the Use Default Page Folder option, and Access lets you specify (or browse to find) a folder where you want to save all your data access pages. Access stores this property with each database, so you can define a separate default page folder for each database you're developing. It's a good idea to define a default folder so that it's easy later to copy all the files to a Web server.

You can select the Use Default Connection File option to specify a connection file to use to point to the data displayed by your data access pages. When a user opens your published data access page, the page must have a connection defined that points to the location of the database. As you are developing and testing your data access pages, you can save them on your local hard drive, but you must change the connection properties to publish the pages to a Web server. You can create an Office Data Connection file (.odc) or a Microsoft Data Link file (.udl) that defines a shared network path to your database and use that file in your option settings. Any new page that you create will use the path to your database defined in the connection file. See "Updating Data Access Page Links and Connections" on page 1081 for details about defining and updating connection information.

Creating Pages Using the Wizards

Access provides three shortcuts to help you create and maintain data access pages. You can see these shortcuts when you select Pages on the Object bar in the Database window.

- **Create data access page in Design view** This shortcut initializes the data access page development environment and displays a blank page.
- **Create data access page by using wizard** This option runs a wizard that prompts for specifications and then creates a data access page automatically.
- **Edit Web page that already exists** This shortcut lets you open an existing data access page not linked into your database's Pages list.

To start, let's look at how to create a simple data access page using the wizard. You will create a page similar to the page shown in Figure 27-3 (employees filtered by departments).

Click Pages on the Object bar in the Database window, and then double-click the Create data access page by using wizard shortcut. In the first Page Wizard window, shown in Figure 27-8, use the Tables/Queries drop-down list to select the table or query that contains the fields you want displayed. For this example, choose tblDepartments.

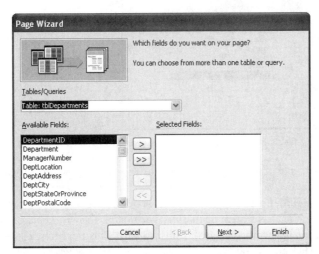

Figure 27-8.   Choosing tables and fields in the first window of the Page Wizard.

You can select any field you want from the Available Fields list and click the single-right-arrow button to move it to the Selected Fields list. To add all available fields, click the double-right-arrow button. To remove a field from the Selected Fields list, click the field to select it and then click the single-left-arrow button. To remove all fields, click the double-left-arrow button.

Note You can select fields from any number of tables, but unless those tables have relationships defined, the wizard won't be able to create the data access page correctly. If the tables you want to include do not have a defined relationship between them, it's best to quit the wizard, create and save a query, and then rebuild the data access page using the new query.

Select the Department field from the tblDepartments table. Next, select the tblEmployees table from the Tables/Queries drop-down list and select the fields EmployeeNumber, First-Name, MiddleName, LastName, EmailName, and Photo using the single-right-arrow button. (The sample *dapXmplDeptEmployees* page doesn't include the Photo field, but you'll need it later when you follow the exercises to modify the page. Adding a field to a wizard-generated grouped page is tricky, so it's best to include it now.) The wizard displays all chosen fields as shown in Figure 27-9.

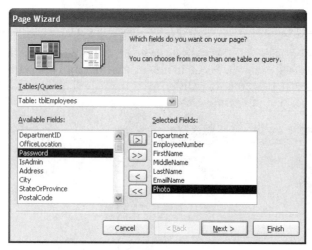

Figure 27-9. Selecting fields from two related tables to create a data access page.

Click the Next button to go to the second window of the wizard. Here you can designate one or more fields as a *grouping level*. This is useful when a table can be filtered on multiple fields and you want to allow the user to move through the values in one field at a time. You can, for example, specify grouping on the Department field. When you do this, the wizard places the Department field into a separate navigation bar on the finished page. The user can select the desired department and then click an expand button to see the details of employees in the department.

Note When data access pages were first introduced in Access 2000, you could not update the data in any page that included grouping levels. As you'll learn later in this chapter, you can now set properties in a grouped data access page to allow the tables to be updated.

In the list on the left side of the window, click the Department field to select it and then click the right arrow to create a grouping level on this field. The wizard window should now look like Figure 27-10. Click Next to go to the next window.

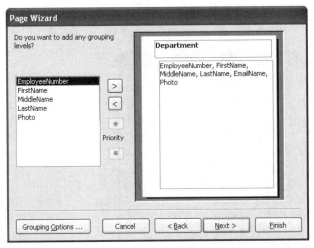

Figure 27-10. Specifying a grouping level for a data access page.

In the next window of the wizard, you can specify sorting on one or more fields. Because you have defined the Department field as a grouping level, the records at that level in the page will automatically be sorted. However, you can choose one or more of the remaining fields to sort the records displayed. Because the EmployeeNumber field is the primary key of the tbl-Employees table, the records will appear sorted by EmployeeNumber unless you specify a different sequence. In this case, choose the LastName field from the first drop-down list. Your wizard window should now look like Figure 27-11. Notice that when you choose a field in the first drop-down list, the wizard makes the second one available. The default sort sequence is Ascending, but you can click the button to the right of each field to toggle the sequence to Descending. The LastName field should be set to the Ascending sort order.

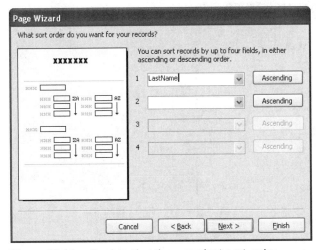

Figure 27-11. Designating the recordset sort order.

Click Next to display the wizard's final window, shown in Figure 27-12, where you can specify several options to control the appearance of the page.

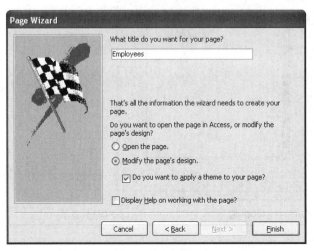

Figure 27-12.   Choosing the final options in the Page Wizard.

In the box at the top of the window, you can enter a name for your new data access page. Type **Employees** for the name of this page. You can choose to open your new page in Page view (Open the page) or in Design view (Modify the page's design). If you choose to open the page in Design view, you can also choose the Do you want to apply a theme to your page option, and the wizard opens the Theme dialog box, as shown in Figure 27-13, after creating your new data access page. Select the options to open your page in Design view and to apply a theme, and click Finish to create the page and see the Theme dialog box.

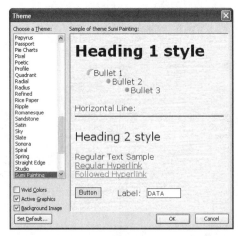

Figure 27-13.   Applying a theme to the data access page.

In the Theme dialog box, you can select from a variety of themes installed on your machine. (For instance, you can install all the available themes from Microsoft Office FrontPage and Microsoft Office Tools.) These themes make it easy to apply a predesigned set of colors, fonts, and graphics to your page. When you click a theme name in the list on the left side of the window, you can see a sample of how the theme will look on the right.

You can select the Vivid Colors option to apply brighter highlights and colors to some objects in the theme. Select Active Graphics to see animation in some themes (for example, a highlight when you hover over a button) when you view the page in a browser. If you clear the Background Image option, the background graphic for the theme disappears, which allows you to later define a solid color as the background.

If you want to set a theme as the default for all future pages, you can choose the theme you want from the list on the left, and then click the Set Default button. Because all the forms in the original application use the Sumi Painting theme, I selected that theme for the sample data access page. After you choose a theme, click OK to apply that theme to your new page and see the result in Design view as shown in Figure 27-14.

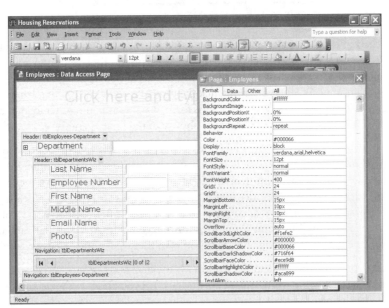

Figure 27-14. The Design view of the data access page created by the wizard.

Although you might expect the wizard to place the title you entered as a heading on the page, it doesn't do so. This is one of several changes that you'll need to make to this page before you're ready to publish it. You can see that the wizard has laid out the fields similarly to the sample *dapXmplDeptEmployees* page that you saw in Figure 27-3.

Now switch to Page view, and you'll see the name of the first department and the tblEmployees-Department navigation bar. You can click the navigation buttons to move to different departments. Click the small plus sign next to the department name to reveal the information

1027

for the first employee and a second navigation bar to move through the employees for the selected department. I moved to the third department record, clicked the plus sign, and then moved to the second employee in that department in the page, as shown in Figure 27-15.

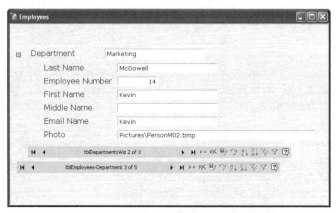

Figure 27-15. The departments and employees data access page in Page view.

You can click any field and then click the Sort Ascending or Sort Descending button to sort the rows based on the values in the field you selected. You can also apply a filter to the rows similar to the way you can in an Access form. When you move to another department, the employee information disappears, and you must click the plus sign again to see the related employee information. If you compare this to an Access form, it's not unlike an outer form that displays department information with a subform to show you the related employee records.

Later in this chapter, in "Modifying a Wizard-Generated Data Access Page" on page 1038, you'll learn how to modify this page to work and look like the sample *dapXmplDeptEmployees* page. For now, click the Save button on the toolbar (or press Ctrl+S) to open the Save As Data Access Page dialog box. You'll notice that the dialog box asks you to select a location on your hard drive to save the .htm file that contains your new page. After you choose a location, enter or change the file name (the name Employees.htm suggested by Access is fine), and click Save, you'll find a new data access page link that points to the page in the Database window.

If you didn't previously set a default location for the data access pages you design for this database, Access asks you if you want to set the location you chose as the default. And finally, if you haven't defined a default connection file that specifies a logical network path to your database, Access warns you that the connection defined in your new data access page uses an absolute path. As you'll learn later in "Updating Connections" on page 1082, you'll most likely need to change the connection for all your data access pages to a relative path before you can publish them to a Web server.

Understanding the Data Access Page Design Facility

The development environment for data access pages borrows heavily from the rest of Access and from other Microsoft development tools, but this can be both good and bad. It's good because many tools and features work in familiar ways. It's bad because just when everything starts to seem familiar, the data access page environment does something different.

Chapter 27

Figure 27-16 shows the Design view of the data access page that you created using the wizard. The largest window is the data access page design window, where you can insert, modify, or delete page elements. Within this window, the banded areas are part of the data source control that fetches and displays the data from your database. The shaded bar named Header: tblEmployees-Departments marks the start of a database processing area—the grouping on the Department field. A similar bar named Navigation: tblEmployees-Department located just above the second navigation bar marks the end of this outer grouping. Within these bars is another set of bars that delimit the detail display area for the employee fields. Any form fields bound to a database field must reside within these banded areas.

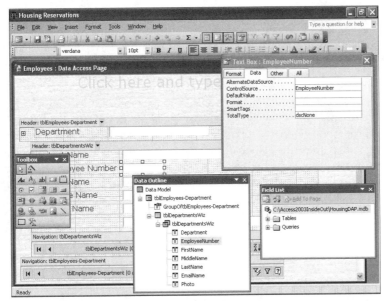

Figure 27-16. A data access page in Design view.

Note that other than the main design window, other windows you see depend on which options you choose from the View menu or the toolbar. Near the upper right corner of the design window in the figure, you can see the Properties window. Just like the Properties window in form or report design, this window shows you the available properties for the item you have currently selected.

Below the Properties window, in the lower right corner of the figure, you can see the Field List window. Unlike the field list for form or report design that shows the fields from the defined record source, this window in a data access page shows you the connected database for the page and all the available tables and queries in that database. When you create a brand new page in Design view, you can expand the lists by clicking the plus signs. You can then select fields from tables or queries and drag and drop them into the data source control.

You can see that the Housing Reservations database (*Housing.mdb*) is the top-level item in the field list. You can right-click this object and choose Connection from the shortcut menu to display the Data Link Properties dialog box. In this dialog box, you can change the database to another source or change connection properties. For more information on changing connection properties, see "Updating Data Access Page Links and Connections" on page 1081.

Just to the left of the Field List window, you can see the Data Outline window. This window shows you the tables, queries, and fields that the data source control is prepared to display. It also shows you any grouping levels that you have defined for the page. In some ways, the Data Outline window is more similar to the field list in form and report design because it lists the actual fields available for display on the page. However, you cannot add fields from this list to the data access page. Remember, I warned you earlier that some design elements will seem very familiar, but others are very different from what you've learned for forms and reports.

Finally, near the left edge of the figure, you can see the toolbox that shows you all the controls that you can add to your page design. As you'll learn later, some controls—such as the label and text box controls—are equivalent to those you'll find in form and report design. But others such as the Bound Span, Scrolling Text, and Expand buttons are unique to data access pages.

To view the properties for any element on the page, open the Properties window (if it isn't open already) by clicking the Properties button on the toolbar and then click the element. When the element is one that displays data (such as a text box), select the Data tab or the All tab in the Properties window to verify the field that the element displays. Like controls in forms and reports, the ControlSource property defines the bound field or other data (such as an expression) to be displayed in the selected design element. In Figure 27-16, for example, you can see that the EmployeeNumber field provides the data for the selected Employee-Number text box.

If you want to see the properties for the page itself, open the Properties window, and click the data access page window's title bar. You can also choose Select Page from the Edit menu. Figure 27-17 shows the page properties for the Employees sample page that you created with the wizard.

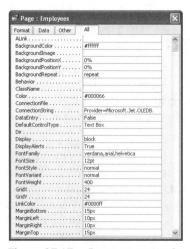

Figure 27-17. Page properties for a data access page.

If the properties seem completely unlike the properties for a form or report, remember that you're now in a design environment for Web pages. One of the major differences is that most positioning is expressed in pixels or a relative percentage from the left or top of the design area. The reason for this is that you have no control over the size of the Web visitor's browser window. The user's browser will make automatic adjustments based on the size of the user's window. You can, for example, design a data access page to look best in a browser window that's 800 by 600 pixels, but you can't control the window size absolutely like you can in an Access form.

Tip Until you've gained experience designing for a Web environment, I recommend you adjust all design elements by moving and sizing them in the design area. Also use the Align and Size commands on the Format menu (see the discussion later in this section) to make adjustments rather than trying to wrestle with the property sheet. The design engine will make appropriate adjustments to the properties for you.

Elements You Can Add to a Data Access Page

To place elements on a data access page, you can use the toolbox, which is shown near the left edge of Figure 27-16. All the controls you can use as design elements in a data access page are implemented as ActiveX objects. Many of these objects are very similar to the controls you use to design forms and reports. Table 27-1 lists the built-in objects, their Access form and report equivalents, and their specific uses.

Table 27-1. Data Access Page Tools

Toolbox Button	Tool Name (Form/Report Equivalent)	Usage
	Select Objects (Select Objects)	This is the default tool. Use this tool to select, size, move, and edit existing controls.
	Control Wizards (Control Wizards)	Click this button to activate the control wizards. Click the button again to deactivate the wizards. When this button appears pressed in, a control wizard helps you enter control properties whenever you create a new combo box, list box, or command button. The Command Button Wizard offers to generate VBScript code that performs various automated record actions when the user clicks the button. In addition, activating this wizard for a new data access page invokes the Layout Wizard when you first select one or more fields in the Field List window and click the Add To Page button at the top of the window.

Table 27-1. Data Access Page Tools

Toolbox Button	Tool Name (Form/Report Equivalent)	Usage
Aα	*Label* (Label)	Use this tool to create label controls that contain fixed text. By default, controls that can display data have a label control automatically attached. You can use this tool to create stand-alone labels for headings and for instructions on your data access page.
A	*Bound Span* (None)	Use this tool to display data that is read-only. This control works like a label, but the text displayed can be from a field in the data model of the data access page.
ab|	*Text Box* (Text Box)	Use this tool to create text box controls for displaying text, numbers, dates, times, and memo fields. You can bind a text box to one of the fields in an underlying table or query. If you allow a text box that is bound to a field to be updated, the user can change the value in the field in the underlying table or query by entering a new value in the text box. You can also use a text box to display calculated values.
▤	*Scrolling Text* (None)	Use this control to display text from a field or expression and scroll the information at a specified rate across the object. The user cannot update the data displayed by this control.
⌐xyz⌐	*Option Group* (Option Group)	Use this tool to create option group controls that contain one or more option buttons. (See the description of the Option Button tool below.) You can assign a separate numeric value to each button that you include in the group. When you have more than one button in a group, the user can select only one button at a time, and the value assigned to that button becomes the value for the option group. If you have incorrectly assigned the same value to more than one button, all buttons that have the same value appear highlighted when the user clicks any of them. You can select one of the buttons in the group as the default value for the group. If you bind the option group to a field in the underlying data, the user can set a new value in the field by selecting a button in the group.

Table 27-1. **Data Access Page Tools**

Toolbox Button	Tool Name (Form/Report Equivalent)	Usage
⦿	*Option Button* (Option Button)	Use this tool to create an option button control (sometimes called a radio button control) that holds an on/off, true/false, or yes/no value. When the user clicks an option button, its value becomes -1 (to represent on, true, or yes), and a filled circle appears in the center of the button. The user can click the button again, and its value becomes 0 (to represent off, false, or no), and the filled circle clears. You can include an option button in an option group and assign the button a unique numeric value. If you create a group with multiple controls, selecting a new option button clears any previously selected option button or check box in that group (unless other buttons or check boxes in the group also have the same value). If you bind the option button to a field in the underlying table or query, the user can toggle the field's value by clicking the option button.
☑	*Check Box* (Check Box)	Use this tool to create a check box control that holds an on/off, true/false, or yes/no value. When the user clicks a check box, its value becomes -1 (to represent on, true, or yes), and a check mark appears in the box. The user can click the check box again, and its value becomes 0 (to represent off, false, or no), and the check mark disappears from the box. If you bind the check box to a field in the underlying data, the user can toggle the field's value by clicking the check box. Unlike Access forms and reports, you cannot place a check box inside an option group.

Chapter 27

Table 27-1. Data Access Page Tools

Toolbox Button	Tool Name (Form/Report Equivalent)	Usage
	Dropdown List (Combo Box)	Use this tool to create a drop-down list control that contains a list of potential values for the control and an editable text box. You can define a specific list of values by coding Option tags in the VBScript that defines the control. (If you activate the Control Wizards button, the wizard generates this code for you when you add the drop-down list control to your page.) You can also specify a table or a query as the source of the values in the list. You can define up to two columns for the list, and you can specify one of the columns as the display value and the other as the bound value. The page displays the currently selected value in the text box. When the user clicks the down arrow to the right of the drop-down list, the page displays the values in the list. The user can select a new value in the list to reset the value in the control. If the drop-down list is bound to a field in the underlying data, the user can change the value in the field by selecting a new value in the list.
	List Box (List Box)	Use this tool to create a list box control that contains a list of potential values for the control. You can define a specific list of values by coding Option tags in the VBScript that defines the control. (If you activate the Control Wizards button, the wizard generates this code for you when you add the list box control to your page.) You can also specify a table or a query as the source of the values in the list. You can define up to two columns for the list, and you can specify one of the columns as the display value and the other as the bound value. List boxes are always open, and the page highlights the currently selected value in the list box. You select a new value in the list to reset the value in the control. If the list box is bound to a field in the underlying data, you can change the value in the field by selecting a new value in the list.

Table 27-1. **Data Access Page Tools**

Toolbox Button	Tool Name (Form/Report Equivalent)	Usage
	Command Button (Command Button)	Use this tool to create a control that can respond to a user click to activate a VBScript action. When you activate the Control Wizards button, a wizard starts that helps you add common navigation actions when you add this control to your page.
	Expand (None)	Use this tool to display an object that can respond to a user click to expand or contract a grouped display. If you click a bound data field and then click the Promote button on the toolbar, the design engine creates a grouping level for the field you chose and adds an expand control to facilitate navigation. You won't normally need to use an expand control independently. You can change the Src property of an expand control to display a plus/minus, left/right or up/down arrow, or closed/open folder.
	Record Navigation (None)	Use this tool to display an object that can respond to user clicks to navigate from record to record, sort data, apply filters, and delete rows in an updatable data access page. The design engine adds this control when you first add a field from a table or query to a blank page. You won't normally need to use the record navigation control independently.
	Office PivotTable (Subform control containing a form designed to be displayed as a PivotTable)	Use this tool to add an Office PivotTable to your page. You can bind the PivotTable to data in your database.
	Office Chart (Subform control containing a form designed to be displayed as a PivotChart)	Use this tool to add an Office PivotChart to your page. You can bind the chart to data in your database.
	Office Spreadsheet (Object Frame, Bound Object Frame)	Use this tool to add an Excel spreadsheet to your page. You can bind the spreadsheet to data in your database.

Chapter 27

Table 27-1. Data Access Page Tools

Toolbox Button	Tool Name (Form/Report Equivalent)	Usage
	Hyperlink (Text Box bound to a hyperlink field or label with a hyperlink defined in the caption)	Use this tool to display and edit data from a Hyperlink data type field in your database or provide a static link on your page. The user can click the hyperlink to activate it. When the hyperlink is not bound to a field, you can set it to open another document or go to another page on your Web site when the user clicks the link.
	Image Hyperlink (None)	Use this tool to define a picture on your page containing a hyperlink. You can set the hyperlink to open another document or go to another page on your Web site when the user clicks the hyperlink.
	Movie (Object Frame)	Use this tool to display and play a movie file (.avi, .mov, .mpg, or .asf file) from your Web page.
	Image (Image)	Use this tool to display a picture (.gif, .jpg, .bmp, .xmp, or .png file) from your Web page.
	Line (Line)	Use this tool to add lines to a page to enhance its appearance. Unlike the Line tool in form or report design, you cannot draw a line on a data access page at an angle.
	Rectangle (Rectangle)	Use this tool to add filled or empty rectangles to a page to enhance its appearance.
	More Controls (More Controls)	Click this button to open a list showing all the ActiveX controls you have installed on your system. Not all ActiveX controls work with data access pages.

Note The ClassName property for each control defines how the control operates, and you can change this property to change the look and functionality of a control. You can set the ClassName property to one of a special set of navigation classes to convert the control to a navigation button that controls the records displayed. For example, setting the ClassName property to MsoNavNext changes the control to respond to a click and move the data display to the next record. As you might guess, the other navigation class names are MsoNavFirst, MsoNavPrevious, and MsoNavLast.

Moving, Sizing, and Aligning Data Access Page Elements

To move an element, click on it and drag it to a new location. You can also hold down the Shift key and click several elements or encircle several controls with your mouse pointer to select multiple elements together and drag them to a new location. To resize an element, first select it, and then drag an edge or stretch a corner. You can select multiple elements and then resize them together. To delete an element, first select it, and then press the Delete key. To add an element, first select it in the toolbox and then, in the data access page window, click the spot where you want that element to appear. As with the toolbox in form and report design, you can double-click a tool to lock the selection so that you can add several elements of the same type without having to go back to the toolbox.

You can align and size multiple elements similarly to the process you use for controls in forms and reports—but with a significant difference. When you select multiple elements, the last element you select becomes the controlling element. So, when you select multiple elements and then choose Align from the Format menu and then Left from the submenu, the elements line up with the left edge of the last element you selected, not to the leftmost edge of all the selected elements.

Figure 27-18 shows you a data access page with multiple elements selected. You can identify the controlling element when you select multiple elements because the sizing boxes around it appear white. The sizing boxes around other elements appear black.

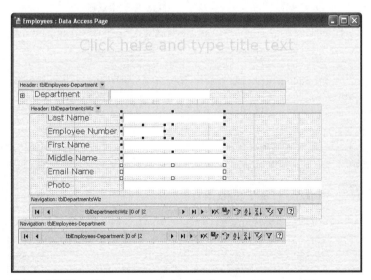

Figure 27-18.   When you select multiple elements on a data access page, the sizing boxes around the controlling element appear white.

In addition to aligning left, right, top, or bottom, you can also choose Align Middle or Align Center. For example, if you select multiple elements that are arranged horizontally across the page (such as a row of text boxes) and choose Align Middle, all the elements will shift up or down so that they center vertically on the controlling element. Applying Align Center to multiple elements that are arranged in a vertical column (such as a column of text boxes) moves the noncontrolling elements left and right so that they center horizontally on the controlling element.

As with forms and reports, you can select multiple elements and choose Horizontal Spacing or Vertical Spacing from the Format menu to adjust the spacing between the elements. Like forms and reports, you can choose Make Equal, Increase, or Decrease on the submenus of these commands. In addition, you can choose Remove to eliminate all space between the elements. This is the command to use with data access pages if you want a vertical stack or horizontal row of elements to touch each other with no space between them. If you remember from form design, you use the Align Top command to remove the space between multiple controls in a vertical column; but if you try that command on a data access page, all the controls will end up on top of each other, probably not the result you want. With data access pages you'll probably use the Align Top command to top align a horizontal "row" of elements; avoid applying it to a vertical stack of elements.

> **Tip** The original data access page editor introduced in Access 2000 did not provide any undo capability. Fortunately, Access 2002 added Undo and Redo that let you remove or reapply up to the last 20 changes.

Modifying a Wizard-Generated Data Access Page

The Employees data access page that you created with the wizard doesn't quite look like or work like the sample *dapXmplDeptEmployees* that you saw in Figure 27-3. The sample DAP uses a drop-down list box to choose the department and doesn't have a department navigation bar. Also, the caption on the navigation bar for moving to different employee records is different. Finally, the sample DAP has a page heading and doesn't require you to click an expand control after you choose a department in order to see and edit the employee information. Let's take a look at the changes you need to apply to make the wizard page work like the sample page, and while we're at it, let's improve on the original by adding the employee photo to the page. Open your wizard-generated Employees DAP in Design view to follow along in this section.

Adding a Heading to the Page

Fixing the heading is easy. Although the last window of the wizard implies that you'll see the text that you enter as the title, the wizard applies this text as the title of the window but does not create title text on the page. If you look closely at the top of the page, you can see large pale letters that tell you to Click Here and Type Title Text. Click anywhere in this area and type **Employees** to create the title for the page. When you have selected this area, you can also change settings on the Formatting toolbar or in the Properties window to change the font, font size, and font color if you want.

The wizard creates extra blank space below this title that you don't need. You can click in this blank area below the title and press the Delete key to remove this extra space and move the data display area up closer to the title. Your page should now look like Figure 27-19.

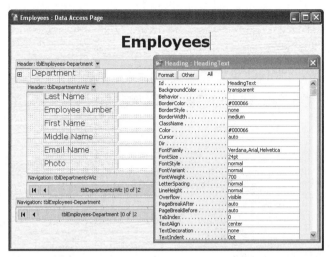

Figure 27-19. Adding a title to a wizard-generated data access page and closing up the space between the title and the data display area.

Changing the Group Filter Control

When you asked the wizard to group on the Department field, it created a special data section—tblEmployees-Department—to display the department name and filter the detail employee records. The wizard also added a second navigation bar so that you can move to different department records. Finally, the wizard added an expand control in the group heading area to provide a way for the user to expand the detail employee display after choosing a department. The wizard-generated page also automatically contracts the detail employee display when the user moves to a new department.

On the other hand, the sample *dapXmplDeptEmployees* page provides a combo box to choose a department, and the user doesn't have to click an expand control to see the details for the employees. Because the drop-down list allows the user to choose any department, you don't need a navigation bar to move through the department records.

To modify the page created by the wizard to work like the sample page, perform the following steps:

1. Open the Employees page that the wizard created in Design view.

2. Right-click on the Department text box and choose Group Filter Control from the shortcut menu. This converts the text box into a drop-down list box, and the data access page uses the contents chosen in the drop-down list box to filter the contents displayed on the rest of the page.

3. Click the expand control (the small plus sign to the left of the Department label) and press Delete to remove it.

4 Click the down arrow on the tblEmployees-Department header and clear the Record Navigation check box as shown in Figure 27-20—this removes the department navigation bar.

Your data access page should now look like Figure 27-20.

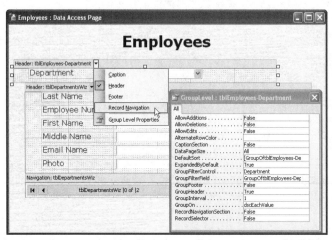

Figure 27-20. Modifying a wizard-generated data access page to use a group filter control.

You could have also deleted the Department text box and added a drop-down list, but you would have had to set the properties of the new control yourself. Taking advantage of the command on the shortcut menu in the second step is much simpler and avoids errors.

Modifying Record Navigation Controls

One of the most powerful controls you have on your pages is the record navigation control. The default navigation control provides buttons to go to the first, last, next, or previous record, just like the navigation bar on an Access form. The control also displays the current record and the total number of records available. In addition, the control includes many of the buttons that you would normally find on the Form view toolbar—go to new record, delete the current record, save changes, undo changes, quick sort ascending or descending, filter, and help buttons. You can see the list of controls in Table 27-2.

Table 27-2. Buttons on the Record Navigation Control

Button	Name	Description
	First	Moves to the first record
	Previous	Moves to the previous record

Table 27-2. Buttons on the Record Navigation Control

Button	Name	Description
tblDepartmentsWiz 2 of 4	Recordset Label	Displays the information specified in the RecordsetLabel property, which can include a title, the current record number, the number of records in the current group, and the total number of records
▶	Next	Moves to the next record
▶ǀ	Last	Moves to the last record
▶	New	Moves to a new record
▶✕	Delete	Deletes the current record
🖫	Save	Saves changes to the current record
↺	Undo	Undoes changes to the current record
A↓Z	Sort Ascending	Sorts the records in ascending order on the values in the currently selected field
Z↓A	Sort Descending	Sorts the records in descending order on the values in the currently selected field
▽	Filter By Selection	Filters for those records that match the selected field
▽	Filter Toggle	Applies or removes any filter created by choosing Filter By Selection
?	Help	Displays Help

Chapter 27

Unlike the navigation bar on a form, you can hide buttons that you don't want to make available to the user. For example, if you have a read-only page, you can hide the Delete, Save, Undo, and New buttons. You should hide these buttons on a read-only page, because Access displays them disabled on a read-only page, which could confuse your users.

Displaying and hiding the built-in buttons is simple. Right-click the record navigation control and then choose Navigation Buttons from the shortcut menu as shown in Figure 27-21. To remove a button, clear the check box next to the button name. You can also click the record navigation control to select it, click the button you want to remove inside the navigation control to select that button, and press Delete to remove the button. To restore a removed button, right-click the record navigation control, choose Navigation Buttons on the shortcut menu, and click the button name.

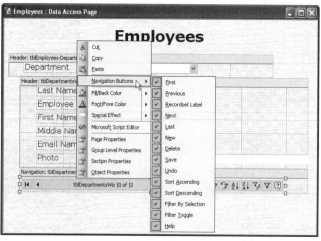

Figure 27-21. Choosing buttons to display on a record navigation control.

You don't need to remove any buttons for this page because you're going to modify the page to allow updating in the next section.

Whether you use the wizard to create your page or you design the page yourself, the default record navigation control displays the name of the recordset and built-in record location variables in the recordset label. As you can see in Figure 27-21, the wizard has created a recordset and named it "tblDepartmentsWiz." This record navigation control lets the user move through the employee records for the selected department, so it's a good idea to change this label to something more meaningful. You can also remove or change the following built-in record location variables:

- |0 displays the current record number.
- |1 displays the last record number in the current set when you design the page to display a list of records in sets. (See Figure 27-4 on page 1019.)
- |2 displays the total number of records available to display.

To change the recordset label, click the record navigation control, click the recordset label inside the control to select it, and then click the Data tab in the Properties window as shown in Figure 27-22 to see the RecordsetLabel property.

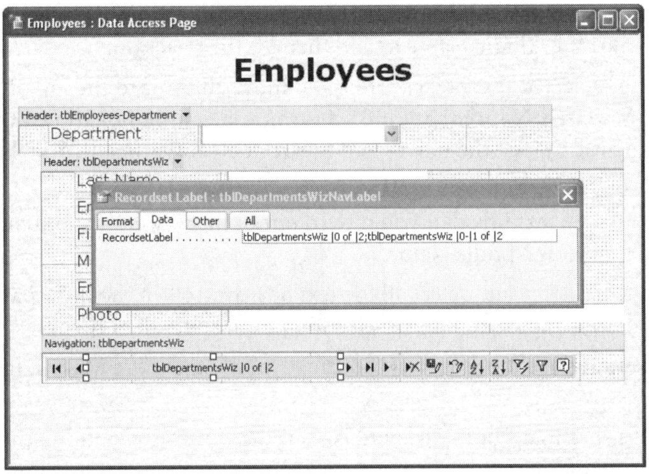

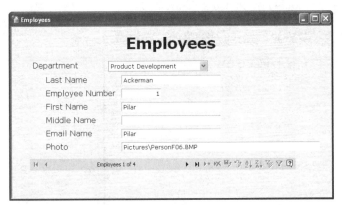

Figure 27-22. Updating the recordset label.

As you can see, the recordset label actually has two parts, separated by a semicolon. The record navigation control uses the first part when you have set the section to display one record at a time. It uses the second part when you set the group-level properties to display more than one or all records. In this case, you should change tblDepartmentsWiz in both parts to **Employees**. When you switch to Page view, your page should now look like Figure 27-23.

Figure 27-23. A wizard-generated data access page with a group filter drop-down list and a customized record-navigation control.

Rearranging Controls

Because you asked the wizard to sort by the LastName field, it placed that field first on the data access page. It makes more sense to display the fields in the sequence Employee Number,

First Name, Middle Name, and Last Name. To rearrange the controls, switch back to Design view and follow these steps:

1   Click the Last Name text box and drag it to the right to move it out of the way.

2   Click the Employee Number text box to select it and then hold down the Shift key and click First Name and Middle Name to add them to the selection.

3   Click one of the selected text box controls and move all three to the top of the tbl-DepartmentsWiz area. Notice that unlike a form, you cannot hold down the Shift key as you start to drag to lock the movement horizontally or vertically. You'll fix the alignment in a later step.

4   Click the Last Name text box that you moved out of the way earlier and move it into the empty space below Middle Name.

5   Hold down the Shift key and select all the text box controls in the tblDepartmentsWiz section, or use your mouse to draw a selection box around all of them.

6   On the Format menu, choose Vertical Spacing, and then choose Make Equal on the submenu.

7   Check to make sure that Photo or Email Name (the controls you didn't move) is the controlling element—the sizing boxes around one of them are white. If not, click either Photo or Email Name to make it the controlling element.

8   Choose Align on the Format menu and then choose Left on the submenu. Remember that unlike forms, it's the white-highlighted element that controls the alignment. So, even if Employee Number, First Name, Middle Name, and Last Name are to the left of Email Name or Photo, aligning left on Email Name or Photo moves the out-of-line controls to the right.

Your data access page should now look like Figure 27-24.

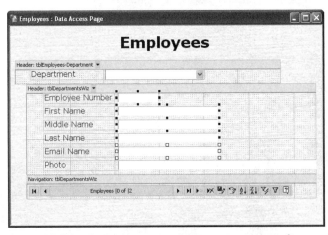

Figure 27-24.   A wizard-generated data access page after moving and realigning controls.

Now that you've moved the controls, the tab sequence won't be correct, so you should fix the TabIndex property of each text box control. The bad news is data access pages don't have a

Tab Order command on the View menu to fix the problem graphically. You know you moved Last Name after Middle Name, so you need to fix Employee Number, First Name, Middle Name, and Last Name one at a time.

Click away from the multiple selected controls to cancel the selection, then click on the Employee Number text box and choose the Other tab in the Properties window. If you followed the previous steps exactly, the TabIndex value for this control should be 31. Change the value to 30 and then click the First Name text box. Change the TabIndex property for the First Name text box to 31, for the Middle Name text box to 32, and finally for the Last Name text box to 33. Be sure to save your work before going on to the next section.

Making Read-Only Sections Updatable

When you asked the wizard to group your records, the page it created isn't updatable. However, you can change some properties to allow the user to update the employee information. In order to make the employees section updatable, you need to perform the following steps:

1 In Design view, open the property sheet.

2 Click on the Data tab in the property sheet.

3 Click on the tblDepartmentWiz section header bar.

4 In the UniqueTable property, choose tblEmployees from the drop-down list.

The Properties window should now look like Figure 27-25.

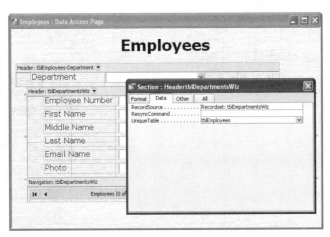

Figure 27-25. Setting the UniqueTable property.

The data access page now knows which of the two tables that you want to update, but you're not quite done.

5 Click the down arrow on the tblDepartmentsWiz header and choose Group Level Properties from the list.

6 In the Properties window, make sure that AllowAdditions, AllowDeletions, and AllowEdits are set to True. Note that these three properties work exactly as they do on Access forms.

Save the result and switch to Page view. You should now be able to click in any of the fields and change the data. You should also be able to click the New button on the navigation bar and create a new employee record. After you create a new employee record, you should also be able to delete that record. (You can't delete any of the existing records because they all have related records in other tables, and the referential integrity rules disallow the deletion.)

Displaying a Bound Image

When I designed this database, I knew I wanted to create data access pages to display and edit the data. A data access page cannot display information from an OLE Object data type field, but it can display pictures in an image control if the data contains a path to the picture. So, I designed the tblEmployees table to use a file path in the Photo field that would also work in a data access page.

I also designed the frmEmployees form to store the file path relative to the current database location instead of a full path that depends on a drive letter. This technique also works well for the published data access pages as long as copies of the picture files are on the Web server in the same relative location (in this case, in the Pictures subfolder).

Open the Employees DAP that you've been modifying in Design view, and perform the following steps to add an image box to display the employee picture:

1 Select the Photo text box control and shrink its length.

2 Select all the text box controls in the tblDepartmentsWiz section and move them to the left to give yourself some room to work.

3 Click the background of the tblDepartmentsWiz section to select it, and drag the bottom sizing handle down about 0.25 inches.

4 Open the toolbox, select the Image tool, and draw a rectangle approximately 1.25 inches wide and 2 inches high to the right of the text boxes. As soon as you add the control, Access opens an Insert Picture dialog box in case you want to point to a static picture file. Click Cancel to close the dialog box.

5 With the new image control selected, open the Properties window and click the Data tab. You can use the shorthand ".\" prefix on the path and file name to indicate the picture is in a subfolder of the current path. In the ControlSource property, enter:

EmpPix: ".\" & [Photo]

Switch to Page view, choose a department, and your result should look like Figure 27-26.

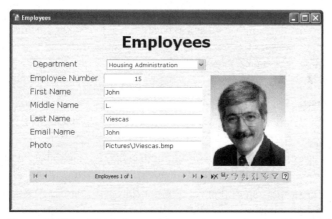

Figure 27-26. Displaying a picture using a path saved in a table field.

You can now remove the Photo text box control from the page.

Generating Data Access Pages from Forms and Reports

One simple way to create data access pages is to save an existing form or report as a data access page. Access does a fairly good job of converting simple forms or reports into data access pages, but cannot correctly or completely convert more complex ones, including

- Forms with subforms
- Reports with subreports
- Forms with tab controls
- Forms or reports that display bound OLE object controls
- Forms or reports that have ambiguous field names in the record source (for example, two fields named Address from different tables in the underlying query)

In addition, the conversion process from a report does create group subtotals correctly, but it does not properly convert grand totals, and it cannot duplicate percentages, controls that reference Access functions (such as Now()), or *Page x of y* calculations. Also, if you attempt to convert a simple form that contains a combo box or list box that has a query or table name as its Row Source property, you must first change the Row Source specification to use a select statement. If a combo box or list box on a form has more than two columns, you must fix the properties of the resulting control on the data access page to use only two columns. Finally, you cannot convert a combo box or list box that has a parameter query as its Row Source property.

The procedure for creating a data access page from an existing form or report is very simple. In fact, I created many of the sample data access pages that you find in the Housing Reservations application (*Housing.mdb*) by converting an existing form or report. You can convert a form or report to a data access page in two steps:

1. Use one of the following three methods to select the form or report you want to save as a data access page:

   - Select the form or report you want to convert in the Database window and choose Save As from the File menu.

   - Right-click the form or report you want to convert in the Database window and choose Save As from the shortcut menu.

   - Open the form or report that you want to convert in Design view and choose Save As from the File menu.

2. In the Save As dialog box that Access displays for any of the three methods, enter a name for the new data access page, change the As box to Data Access Page, and click OK.

One of the simple forms that you can convert to a data access page in the Housing Reservations application is *frmDepartments*, as shown in Figure 27-27.

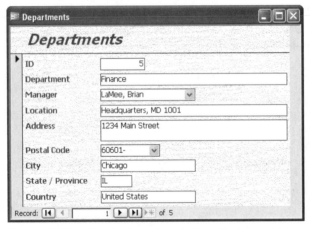

Figure 27-27. The frmDepartments form that you can convert to a data access page.

You need to fix the two combo boxes before you can successfully convert the form. The Manager combo box is based on a parameter query. Also, the Postal Code combo box uses a query that returns more than 50,000 rows—this won't perform well in a data access page. Open the *frmDepartments* form in Design view and make the following changes:

1 Select the ManagerNumber combo box and in the Row Source property box convert the original query name to a Select statement on the same query: **Select** * **From qlkp-Managers**.

2 Select the DeptPostalCode combo box, choose Change To from the Format menu, and then choose Text Box on the submenu.

3 Select the lblNewMsg label control (the Note with a light blue background that you can see in Design view and that is displayed when you're on a new row in the form) and delete it.

Now, choose Save As from the File menu, change the name to Departments, and select Data Access Page in the As drop-down list. Click OK to create the new data access page. Access shows you a New Data Access Page dialog box where you can choose the folder where you want to save the HTML file for your new data access page. Navigate to the folder you want and click OK. Access opens the resulting page in Page view, as shown in Figure 27-28. You can find this converted form saved as *dapXmplDepartments* in the sample database.

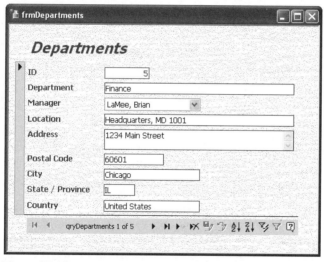

Figure 27-28. A simple Access form converted to a data access page.

Caution Be sure that you do not save the changes you made to frmDepartments when you close it.

When you have created Visual Basic code behind your form or report, converting to a data access page does not convert the code to VBScript. However, Access does save all your Visual

Basic code in a comment section at the end of the HTML file to assist you in creating similar functionality in VBScript. To see the code, switch the new page to Design view, and then click the Microsoft Script Editor button on the toolbar or press Alt+Shift+F11 to open the VBScript editor window. You can scroll down toward the bottom of the HTML to find your Visual Basic code saved as a comment, as shown in Figure 27-29. You'll learn more about working in the VBScript editor later in this chapter.

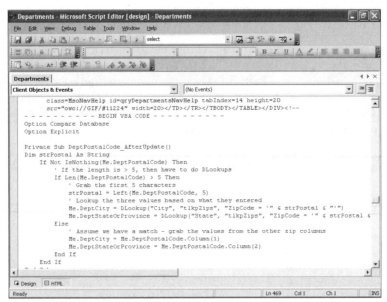

Figure 27-29. The Visual Basic code saved as a comment in a data access page saved from a form.

Converting a report to a data access page is also simple. As long as the report does not have any subreports or bound OLE objects, the data access page should look nearly identical to the report. The conversion process also handles grouping levels nicely, so your data access page ends up grouped in the same way as your report. To try this out, open rptFacilities in Design view as shown in Figure 27-30.

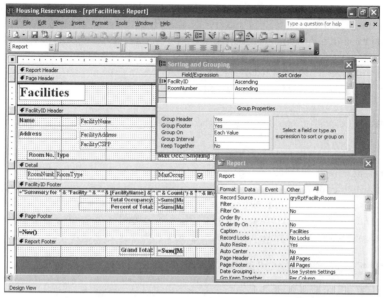

Figure 27-30. An Access report that converts easily to a data access page.

This report is reasonably simple, but it does include one group and a sort within the detail list of rooms. Because the data access page conversion cannot handle percentages, you should delete the percentage calculation text box and label in the FacilityID Footer section. You should also delete the text box that displays the current date and time (=Now()) and the text box that displays *Page x of y* in the Page Footer section and close up that section to zero height. Choose Save As from the File menu, change the name to Facilities, and choose Data Access Page in the As drop-down list. Click OK in the Save As dialog box, choose a location for the new data access page HTML file, and click OK in the New Data Access Page dialog box to convert the report. Your result should look like Figure 27-31.

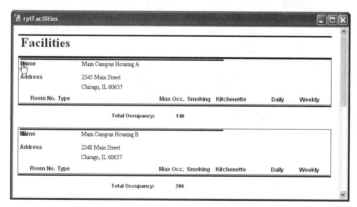

Figure 27-31. The rptFacilities report converted to a data access page.

Wait a minute! What happened to the detail rows for the rooms in each facility? Notice that there's a small plus sign hidden next to the Name label for each facility—an expand control. Click that expand control to reveal the rooms for that facility in groups of 10. Keep in mind that a data access page is designed to be displayed in a Web browser window. The user doesn't have the ability to scroll forward or backward one report page at a time, so the data access page needs to provide a way to display only the details desired.

> **Caution** Be sure that you do not save the changes you made to rptFacilities when you close it.

A better design for this data access page would be to display the facilities one at a time along with a reasonable subset of the rooms in each facility and provide navigation controls to allow the user to scroll to the next facility or the next group of room details. Also, although the total occupancy for each facility converts correctly, the grand total at the end of the report doesn't. To make the data access page more usable, switch to Design view as shown in Figure 37-32.

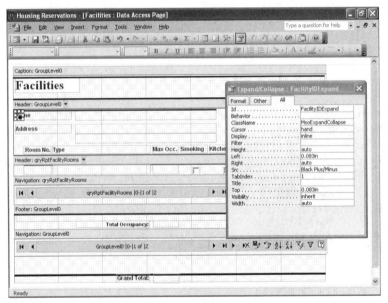

Figure 27-32. A report converted to a data access page in Design view.

Make the following changes:

1 When a page design includes an expand control in a group header or footer, the page by default does not display any of the detail records until the user clicks the expand control. To display the room detail records when the page opens, select the expand control as shown in Figure 27-32 and press the Delete key to remove it.

2 The converted page displays the facilities in groups of 10, so the user must scroll down the page a significant distance to move from one facility to the next. It makes more sense to display the facilities one at a time and let the user use the navigation bar to move from one facility to the next. To limit the display to one facility at a time, click the drop-down arrow next to Header: GroupLevel0, and select Group Level Properties. Change the DataPageSize property to 1.

3 The converted page does display a total occupancy by facility correctly, but the Grand Total at the bottom displays nothing. To correct this, you need to rebuild both the facility total and the grand total. Select the text box next to the Total Occupancy label in the GroupLevel0 Footer and delete it. Select the MaxOccupants text box in the qryRptFacilityRooms Header. Click the AutoSum button on the toolbar to create a new SumOfMaxOccupants bound span in the GroupLevel0 Footer—a new total for each facility. With the new SumOfMaxOccupants control selected, click the AutoSum button again to create a grand total in the qryRptFacilityRooms-SumOfMaxOccupants Footer at the end of the page.

4 Now, you need to get rid of the generated labels for the two new total calculation controls and line the controls up with the original labels that the conversion provided. Delete the label attached to the first SumOfMaxOccupants bound span in the GroupLevel0 Footer. Line up the bound span with the Total Occupancy label. In the qryRptFacilityRooms-SumOfMaxOccupants Footer, delete the label attached to the SumOfSumOfMaxOccupants bound span. Select the Grand Total label that came from the original report and cut it to the Clipboard. Select the new qryRptFacility-Rooms-SumOfMaxOccupants Footer, paste the Grand Total label into it, and line up the label with the SumOfSumOfMaxOccupants control.

5 Delete the Grand Total text box created by the conversion at the bottom of the page, and resize the footer sections to eliminate any extra blank space and line up the sections to the left.

Your converted report should now look something like Figure 27-33 on the next page.

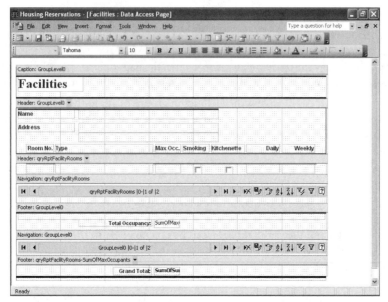

Figure 27-33. A report converted to a data access page and then modified to make it more usable.

Switch to Page view, and your result should look similar to Figure 27-34. The user can now see all pertinent information in one window and can easily navigate to different sets of rooms or different facilities.

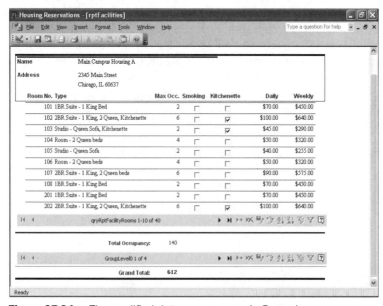

Figure 27-34. The modified data access page in Page view.

To further customize the page, you should correct the captions in the two navigation bars as you learned to do earlier. If you want to allow the user to update the data, you must set the AllowAdditions, AllowDeletions, and AllowEdits properties of each group level to True and define the Unique Table for the *qryRptFacilityRooms* section. If you don't allow edits, then you should remove the New, Delete, Save, and Undo buttons from the navigation bars. You can find this converted and modified report saved as *dapXmplFacilitiesAndRoomsRpt* in the sample database.

Creating a Data Access Page in Design View

Although you can certainly create many of your data access pages by using a wizard or by converting existing forms and reports, you'll need to create some data access pages from scratch using the design facility. For example, the Housing Reservations application has a form that lets you edit records from tblFacilities and related records in tblFacilityRooms, as shown in Figure 27-35.

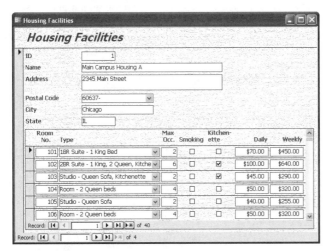

Figure 27-35. A form to edit facilities and related rooms.

However, because this form has a subform, you cannot convert it directly into a data access page. (The Save As conversion facility converts the outer part of the form to edit facilities but doesn't convert the subform.) You could use the wizard to create a data access page that groups on data from tblFacilities and displays related data from tblFacilityRooms, but the wizard doesn't have the ability to display the room information in a tabular format. The only solution is to build what you need yourself.

Selecting a Data Source

You can certainly select the Pages button on the Object bar in the Database window and double-click the Create data access page in Design view link to get started, but it's useful to first pick at least one of the tables you want to use as a data source. When you do this, the data access page designer opens the field list with the data source you selected already expanded.

To start this exercise, go to the Database window, select Tables on the Object bar, select the tblFacilities table, and choose Page from the Insert menu. Access displays the New Data Access Page dialog box as shown in Figure 27-36.

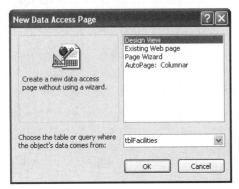

Figure 27-36. Starting a new data access page and selecting an initial data source.

Make sure you select the Design View option and click OK. Access starts a new data access page with the field list open to the data source you chose, as shown in Figure 27-37.

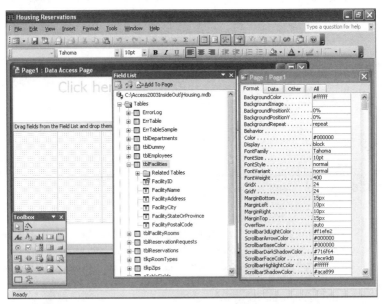

Figure 27-37. Starting a new data access page with a data source selected in the field list.

Adding Fields to Display

You can select the data source control, set its RecordSource property, add text boxes one at a time, and set the ControlSource property for each, but that's a lot of unnecessary work. The simplest way to add bound controls is to select the fields you want in the field list and drag and drop them onto the data source control. When you do this, Access automatically sets the RecordSource property for you.

Start by holding down the Ctrl key and selecting the FacilityID, FacilityName, FacilityAddress, FacilityCity, and FacilityStateOrProvince fields in the tblFacilities table. Drag and drop those fields onto the data source control about 0.25 inches down from the top. (As you'll see later, you're leaving this space at the top to add related fields from the tblFacilityRooms table.)

Don't drag and drop the FacilityPostalCode field—the field has a lookup defined on the tlkpZips table, but that table supplies more than 50,000 rows. The default limit for a data access page is 10,000 rows, so the combo box that Access would create when you drag and drop the FacilityPostalCode field won't show all the available records from tlkpZips. You could change the default data limit, but your data access page will be very slow to open. You can use this lookup on a form because Access optimizes fetching rows and doesn't actually load the records until you drop down the combo box list. A data access page, however, always loads the entire row source when you open the page. This not only might be very slow over a Web network, but it also might cause your Web browser to run out of memory as it attempts to load all 50,000 rows.

To add the FacilityPostalCode field, click away from the group of controls you just added to cancel the selection, select the Text Box tool in the toolbox, and add one text box to your page. On the Data tab of the Properties window, set the ControlSource property of this new text box to the FacilityPostalCode field. Select the attached label, and on the Other tab in the Properties window, enter **ZIP Code:** in the InnerText property. You might need to resize the label to display the entire caption. Your data access page should now look like Figure 27-38.

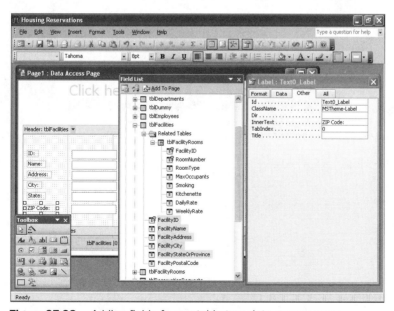

Figure 27-38. Adding fields from a table to a data access page.

Next, you need to add the fields you want from the tblFacilityRooms table. You might be tempted to open the field list for the tblFacilityRooms table that you can see by itself in the Field List window. However, to make sure that the data access page knows how to link the two tables, you should open the Related Tables list below tblFacilities and then open the field list for tblFacilityRooms below that as shown in Figure 27-38. When you choose fields from the Related Tables list, Access correctly links the two tables in the record source for the page.

In the toolbox, click the Control Wizards tool to enable the wizards. When you do this, the wizard helps you lay out the fields from the related table when you add them to the page. In the field list for the tblFacilityRooms table under Related Tables, hold down the Ctrl key and click the RoomNumber, RoomType, MaxOccupants, Smoking, Kitchenette, DailyRate, and WeeklyRate fields to select them. At the top of the Field List window, click the Add To Page button, and Access displays the Layout Wizard dialog box as shown in Figure 27-39.

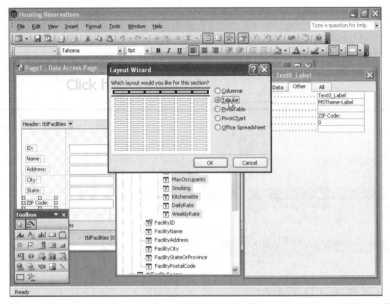

Figure 27-39. Taking advantage of the Layout Wizard to create a tabular field layout.

Select the Tabular layout and click OK. Your data access page should now look like Figure 27-40.

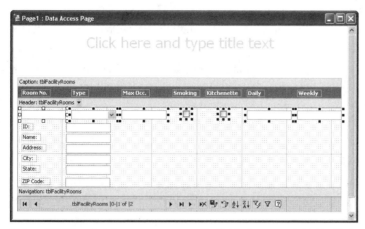

Figure 27-40. A data access page with fields from a related table inserted in tabular format.

Creating a Grouping Level

Now you're ready to make your data access page look and work like a form with a subform. To do that, you need to group the fields from the tblFacilities table, which moves them up one level. Use your mouse pointer to select all the fields from the tblFacilities table—ID, Name, Address, City, State, and ZIP Code. You can also select these fields by first clicking in the blank area of the data control to cancel the selection of the fields from the tblFacilitiesRooms table, and then hold down the Shift key as you click on the six fields from the tblFacilities table. Click the Group By Table button on the toolbar to move these fields into a new Header section. Your result should look like Figure 27-41.

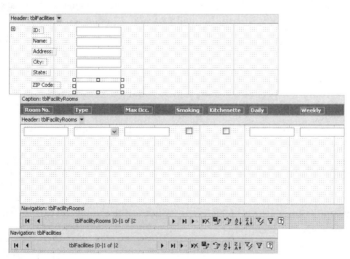

Figure 27-41. Grouping fields from the tblFacilities table into a new header to create a data access page that works like a form with a subform.

Chapter 27

Notice that Access automatically added a second navigation bar so that you can move to different records in the tblFacilities table or through the related records in the tblFacilityRooms table. To refine this data access page, perform the following steps:

1. Click the tblFacilityRooms Header to select that section and drag the bottom of the section up so that the space below the row of controls is about the same as the space above.

2. Select the RoomNumber text box and shrink its width to about .6 inches. (You can set the width specifically on the Format tab in the Properties window.)

3. Shrink the width of the MaxOccupants text box to about .5 inches.

4. Set the width of the DailyRate and WeeklyRate text boxes to about .6 inches.

5. Select the WeeklyRate text box and slide it to the right near the right edge of the tblFacilityRooms Header section. (The attached label in the Caption section should move with it.)

6. Select the DailyRate text box and then hold down the Shift key to also select the Kitchenette and Smoking check boxes. Slide all three to the right near the WeeklyRate text box.

7. Select the MaxOccupants text box and slide it to the right near the Smoking check box and label.

8. Select the RoomType drop-down list box and slide it left near the RoomNumber text box. Expand the RoomType control to the right to fill the space you cleared by moving the other controls. (Some of the room type descriptions are long.)

9. Select all the controls in the tblFacilityRooms Header section, making sure that the RoomNumber text box is the last one you add to the selection. (This is the one control that you didn't move.) On the Format menu, choose the Align command, and then choose Top from the submenu.

10. In the tblFacilities Header section, select the FacilityName, FacilityAddress, and FacilityCity controls and expand them all to about 2 inches wide.

11. Select the expand control in the tblFacilities Header section and press the Delete key to remove it.

12. Click the drop-down arrow on the tblFacilities Header bar and choose Group Level Properties. In the Properties window, set the DataPageSize property to 1.

13. Click the drop-down arrow on the tblFaciltyRooms Header bar, choose Group Level Properties, and set the DataPageSize property to 5 in the Properties window. To provide some contrast on alternating rows, in the AlternateRowColor property box, type **gainsboro**. (You can find a complete list of color names in Article 4 on the companion CD.)

14. At the top of the page where you can see *Click here and type title text*, click and type **Facilities and Rooms**. Press the Delete key once at the end of the text to remove the extra space below the heading.

15. Finally, click the title bar of the design window to select the page (or choose Select Page from the Edit menu) and set the Title property to Facilities and Rooms.

When you switch to Page view, your new data access page should look something like Figure 27-42.

Chapter 27

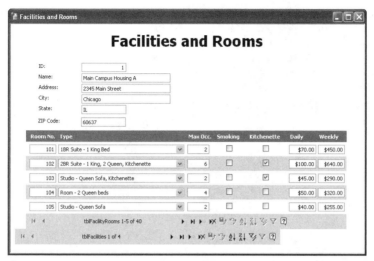

Figure 27-42. A data access page that works exactly like the frmFacilities form.

You can further enhance the page by turning on record selectors (set the RecordSelector property to True in the Group Level Properties) or by adding a theme. You should also fix the captions on the navigation bars. You can find an example page similar to this one saved as *dapXmplFacilitiesAndRooms* in the sample database.

Designing a Data Access Page with a PivotChart

In Chapter 16, "Advanced Report Design," you learned how to create a report with an embedded subform in PivotChart view to add a graphical display of your data to a report. You might be tempted to convert the sample report, rptFacilityRevenueChart, directly to a data access page, but remember that you can't do that with a report that has an embedded subreport or subform. You must build a data access page that includes a PivotChart directly in the data access page designer.

Start by selecting *qryRptFacilities* in the Database window and then choose Page on the Insert menu. In the New Data Access Page dialog box, select Design View and click OK. In the Field List window, hold down the Ctrl key and click the FacilityID, FacilityName, FacilityAddress, and FacilityCSPP (City, State, Postal) fields to select them. Click the Add To Page button at the top of the Field List window to add the fields to your new page. If you left the Control Wizards active in the toolbox, choose Columnar in the Layout Wizard dialog box and click OK. (Columnar is the default layout if you don't have the wizard turned on.) Select the FacilityName, FacilityAddress, and FacilityCSPP text boxes and expand them to about 2 inches wide. Click the FacilityCSPP label control and press Delete to remove it. You don't want users to be able to edit this data, so click the drop-down arrow on the qryRptFacilities Header, choose Group Level Properties, and set the AllowAdditions, AllowDeletions, and AllowEdits properties to False.

Scroll down in the Field List window and expand the qryRprtFacilityRevenueForDAP query. This is a special version of the qryRptFacilityRevenue query that includes data for all of 2003 and does not use parameters to prompt you for the date range. Be sure you have the Control Wizards active in the toolbox. Select the FacilityID, FacilityName, CheckOutDate, and

TotalCharge fields and click Add To Page at the top of the Field List window. Select Pivot-Chart in the Layout Wizard dialog box, as shown in Figure 27-43, and then click OK.

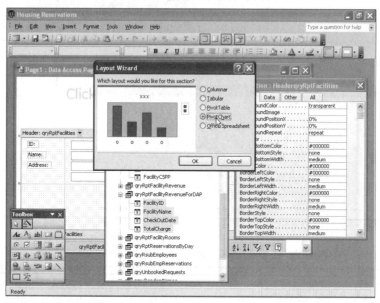

Figure 27-43. Inserting a PivotChart into a data access page.

Access displays the Relationship Wizard dialog box as shown in Figure 27-44. You must tell the wizard how to link the data in the PivotChart to the data already displayed on your data access page. In this case, choose the FacilityID field in both lists and click OK to finish adding the PivotChart to your data access page.

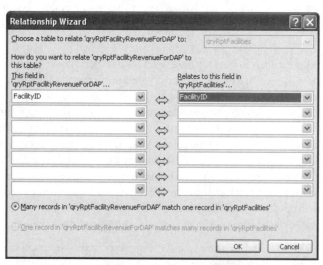

Figure 27-44. Defining the relationship between the fields displayed on the data access page and the fields bound to the PivotChart that you're adding.

> **Note** Although you can select the Office Chart control to add a PivotChart to your data access page, you won't be able to set the filter relationship to the data already on your page without editing the HTML of the page. Using the Layout Wizard ensures that the Pivot-Chart links correctly to the facility data that you have on the page.

The Layout Wizard places a small Office Chart control on your page near the top. You should select the data area and expand it so that you have room to move and enlarge the chart. Move the chart below the last text box and make it big enough to give yourself some room to work. Your page should now look like Figure 27-45.

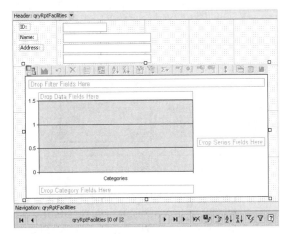

Figure 27-45. A data access page with an Office Chart added.

Building the PivotChart is identical to creating a form in PivotChart view, except the Pivot-Chart toolbar appears across the top of the control, and you must first click inside the control to activate the design facility. When you click in the control again, the control displays the Chart Field List window where you can select the fields you need and drag and drop them onto the chart. From the Chart Field List window, drag and drop the TotalCharge field onto the Drop Data Fields Here area. (The chart automatically calculates a sum for you.) Expand the CheckOutDate By Month list, and drag and drop the Months entry onto the Drop Category Fields Here area. Your data access page should now look like Figure 27-46 on the next page.

Chapter 27

Commands and Options   Chart Field List

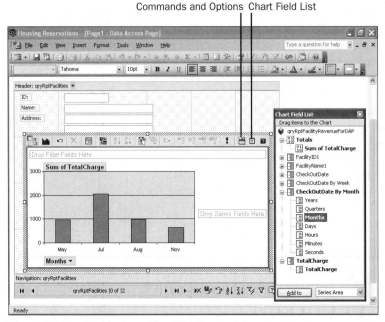

Figure 27-46. Designing a PivotChart on a data access page.

To lock down the chart so that users can't modify it, click the Commands and Options button on the Chart toolbar, as shown in Figure 27-46, select the Show/Hide tab, and clear the Field list, ScreenTips, Field buttons / drop zones, and Toolbar options under Show by default. Also clear the Allow pivot grouping and Allow pivot filtering options under Let users view. Switch to Page view, and your data access page should look something like Figure 27-47.

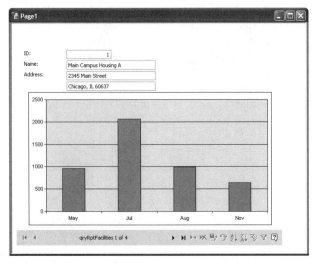

Figure 27-47. A data access page with an embedded and linked Office Chart.

You can switch back to Design view to spruce up your page by adding a heading, fixing the caption on the navigation bar, removing unneeded buttons from the navigation bar, and applying a theme. You can find an example of the data access page saved as *dapXmplFacility-Revenue* in the sample database.

Automating Data Access Pages

Although data access pages run in Internet Explorer when you publish them to a Web site, you can add code to your pages to automate them similarly in forms and reports in your Access application. The programming language you'll most commonly use is Microsoft Visual Basic Scripting (VBScript), a second cousin to the Visual Basic you use within Access.

Remember that data access pages are Web pages that use the Microsoft Office Data Source Control (MSODSC) to fetch data from your database. You can program these pages just like any other Web page, but you must create your code in a scripting language that your browser understands and embed that code within the HTML that defines the page.

For pages designed to run in Microsoft Internet Explorer, you can use one of several scripting languages, including JavaScript, JScript, and VBScript. You could certainly open your data access page HTML file in a text editor and insert the code into the file yourself. The good news is Access opens a copy of the Microsoft Script Editor to help you create the code you need. As you'll see when you create procedures to respond to events on a data access page, the script editor creates a VBScript skeleton by default for each procedure.

If you're familiar with programming in Visual Basic, then you'll feel right at home coding in VBScript. The following sections introduce you to the script editor and show you how to create simple script procedures for your data access pages.

 You can find a complete reference to the VBScript language online at *http://msdn.microsoft.com /library/default.asp?url=/library/en-us/script56/html/vbscripttoc.asp.*

Using the Microsoft Script Editor with Data Access Pages

To allow you to edit the code in your data access pages, Access has borrowed the script editor from Microsoft Visual Studio. You can open the editor to view the code behind any of your data access pages by selecting the page you want in the Database window or opening it in Design view, and then clicking the Microsoft Script Editor button on the toolbar or pressing Alt+Shift+F11. Figure 27-48 shows you the editor open and displaying the code from the sample *dapXmplEmpResRequests* data access page.

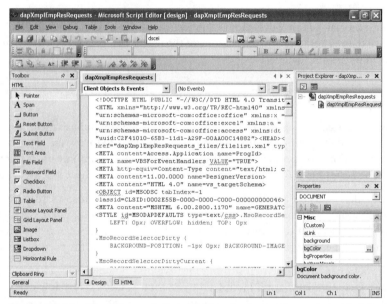

Figure 27-48. The Microsoft Script Editor displaying the code behind the dapXmplEmpRes-Requests sample data access page.

The editor as implemented in Visual Studio includes many features that you don't need or can't use when editing a data access page. When you first open the editor, you most likely will see the toolbox on the left, and the Project Explorer and Properties windows on the right. In Visual Studio, you can select one of the tools in the toolbox and use it to graphically design the object on a Web page that you're editing, but you use the Access tools to do that for a data access page. The editor also displays Design and Formatting toolbars that have no use in editing a data access page. To give yourself more room to work, you can right-click any toolbar and close the Design and Formatting toolbars by clearing the check mark next to each toolbar name on the shortcut menu. You can also close the toolbox, and the Project Explorer and Properties windows. Your screen should look like Figure 27-49.

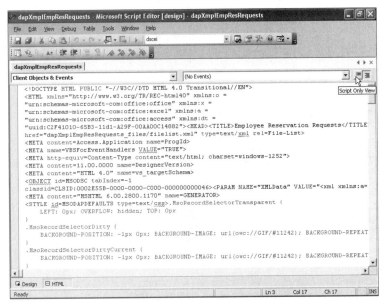

Figure 27-49. The script editor window with items closed that you don't need.

You're now looking at all the HTML code that defines your data access page. Be careful when working in this window. Because there's nothing to stop you from typing text anywhere in the window, you can easily corrupt the tags that define your data access page. Unless you're an HTML expert, I recommend that you always click the Script Only View button at the right end of the bar above the text (see Figure 27-49) to filter the text you see so that only the script code is displayed on the page.

Similar to the Visual Basic Editor (VBE), the script editor shows you two drop-down lists at the top of the text editing window. In the left list, you can find all the objects defined on the page. When you select an object on the left, you can see a list of events defined for that object in the list on the right. As with VBE, event procedures currently defined for the page are displayed in bold in the list. Figure 27-50 on the next page shows you the object list open and revealing some of the objects you can find in the sample data access page. In Figure 27-51 on the next page you can see a partial list of the events for the MSODSC object—the data source control. Notice that the sample data access page has event procedures defined for the BeforeInitialBind, BeforeInsert, and BeforeUpdate events.

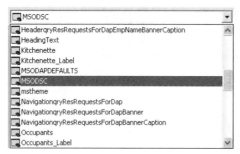

Figure 27-50. Some of the objects in the dapXmplEmpResRequests data access page.

Figure 27-51. Some of the events for the data source control object (MSODSC).

Unlike VBE, the script editor doesn't automatically change these two drop-down lists when you click inside the script for an event procedure. However, you can select an object in the left list and then select a boldfaced event in the right list, and the editor takes you to the code that handles the selected event. As you might guess, you can also select an event name in regular font, and the script editor creates a skeleton script entry for the procedure.

> **Tip** One script editor window that you might find occasionally useful is the Document Outline window. This window displays all objects defined on the data access page, the events for those objects, and a list of all scripts currently coded within the page. You can open this window by choosing Other Windows on the View menu and then selecting Document Outline on the submenu.

Creating Scripts for Data Access Pages

You can write code for a data access page to perform virtually any task you can imagine. You can respond to user input, validate data before the data source control saves it, perform actions after data changes, open and examine recordsets, execute action queries, or navigate to other Web pages. As noted earlier, VBScript is very similar to Visual Basic. You can create Function or Sub procedures, declare variables (Dim, ReDim), define loops (Do, While, For Each), perform conditional testing and branching (If, Select Case), trap errors (On Error), and open and manipulate objects. Some of the key differences are

Chapter 27

- You cannot define a specific data type for a variable in VBScript, but you can assign a data value (including Null) or an object to a declared variable.

- The script editor has no compiler. The only way to find syntax errors is to run the code.

- You must use the ActiveX Data Objects (ADO) model for all recordsets that you open. You can use the Connection property of the MSODSC object to open any table or query in the connected database.

- You must use the CreateObject function to create any object that doesn't already exist. For example, you must use CreateObject("ADODB.Recordset") to establish a new ADO recordset object.

- The set of functions available in VBScript is very extensive, but does not include all the functions available in Visual Basic. For example, you can't use any of the domain functions (DLookup, DMin, DMax, DAvg, DSum) in VBScript. Also, VBScript does not offer a Format function but does have separate FormatCurrency, FormatDateTime, FormatNumber, and FormatPercent functions that are somewhat more limited than the Visual Basic function.

- You can use most common intrinsic constants that you find in Visual Basic that begin with *vb* (vbBlack, vbOK, vbSunday, vbCrLf), but you cannot use any database or Access constants.

Understanding the Data Source Control Events

The most common events you'll want to handle in code behind a data access page are the ones generated by the data source control (the MSODSC object). It is this control that binds the data to the Web page via dynamic HTML and handles the editing of the data. As you might expect, many of the events are similar to those you already use for Access forms. Table 27-3 lists all the events for the data source control. All these events pass the dscEventInfo object to your code that you can examine and modify. Table 27-4 on page 1072 lists the properties of the dscEventInfo object.

Table 27-3. Events for the Data Source Control

Event	Description
AfterDelete	Occurs when a record has been deleted or a record deletion has been canceled. Your code can examine the Status property of the dscEventInfo object to determine whether the delete succeeded.
AfterInsert	Occurs after a new record has been successfully inserted.
AfterUpdate	Occurs after a record has been updated.
BeforeCollapse	Occurs when the user has clicked a collapse button to collapse a section. Your code can set the ReturnValue property of the dscEventInfo object to False to cancel the collapse.

Table 27-3. **Events for the Data Source Control**

Event	Description
BeforeDelete	Occurs when the user has asked to delete a record. Your code can set the ReturnValue property of the dscEventInfo object to False to cancel the delete. Your code can use the MsgBox function to display a custom message or ask the user to confirm the delete. Setting the DisplayAlert property of the dscEventInfo object to DscDataAlertContinue cancels the display of the standard confirmation dialog box.
BeforeExpand	Occurs when the user has clicked an expand button to expand a section. Your code can set the ReturnValue property of the dscEventInfo object to False to cancel the expand.
BeforeFirstPage	Occurs before the first page (record) has been displayed. This event also occurs when the user clicks the First button on a navigation bar. Your code can set the ReturnValue property of the dscEventInfo object to False to cancel the display.
BeforeInitialBind	Occurs before the data source control loads and binds to the data to be displayed on the page. Your code cannot cancel this event, but it can apply a filter to the recordset.
BeforeInsert	Occurs when the user has clicked the New Record button on a navigation bar. Your code can set the ReturnValue property of the dscEventInfo object to False to cancel the insert.
BeforeLastPage	Occurs before the last page (record) has been displayed. This event occurs when the user clicks the Last button on a navigation bar or clicks the Next button to move to the last page. Your code can set the ReturnValue property of the dscEventInfo object to False to cancel the display.
BeforeNextPage	Occurs before the next page (record) has been displayed. This event occurs when the user clicks the Next button on a navigation bar. Your code can set the ReturnValue property of the dscEventInfo object to False to cancel the display.
BeforeOverwrite	Occurs before an XML or schema file is overwritten when executing an ExportXML method. This event occurs only when the data source control is running in a Visual Basic or HTML application, not in a data access page.
BeforePreviousPage	Occurs before the previous page (record) has been displayed. This event occurs when the user clicks the Previous button on a navigation bar. Your code can set the ReturnValue property of the dscEventInfo object to False to cancel the display.
BeforeUpdate	Occurs when the data source control is about to save changed data to the record source. Your code can set the ReturnValue property of the dscEventInfo object to False to cancel the update.

Table 27-3. **Events for the Data Source Control**

Event	Description
Current	Occurs when the focus moves to a new record. Your code cannot cancel this event.
DataError	Occurs when the data source control encounters a database error. Your code can examine the Error property of the dscEventInfo object to determine the cause of the error.
DataPageComplete	Occurs when the data access page has finished loading. Your code cannot cancel this event.
Dirty	Occurs when the user has changed a bound control on the data access page. Your code can set the ReturnValue property of the dscEventInfo object to False to cancel the change.
Focus	Occurs when a new section of the data access page has received the focus. Your code cannot cancel this event.
RecordExit	Occurs when the user has navigated to a new set of records, has navigated to another Web page, or has closed the Web page. Your code can set the ReturnValue property of the dscEventInfo object to False to attempt to cancel the navigation. *Caution*: Your code cannot cancel RecordExit when the user navigates to a different Web page or closes the browser window. You can create an OnBeforeUnload event procedure for the DHTML page to warn the user to not perform these actions.
RecordsetSave-Progress	Occurs continually during the execution of an ExportXML method. Your code can examine the PercentComplete property of the dscEventInfo object to determine the progress. Your code can set the ReturnValue property of the dscEventInfo object to False to cancel the export.
Undo	Occurs when the user clicks the Undo button on a navigation bar or presses the Esc key to undo a change. This event also occurs when your code cancels the Dirty event. Your code can set the ReturnValue property of the dscEventInfo object to False to cancel the undo.

Chapter 27

Table 27-4. dscEventInfo Object Properties

Property	Description
DataPage	The DataPage object for the section that triggered the event. Your code can use the Recordset property of this object to examine the recordset open in the section. Your code can use the Fields collection of the Recordset object to examine and update the fields in the current record.
DisplayAlert	In the BeforeDelete event, indicates whether the standard delete confirmation message is displayed. Your code can set this property to DscDataAlertContinue to cancel the message display or DscDataAlertDisplay to allow the message to be displayed.
Error	In the DataError event, returns an ADO error object that your code can examine to determine the cause of the error.
PercentComplete	In the RecordSaveProgress event, returns a long integer value indicating the progress. A value of 100 indicates the process is complete.
ReturnValue	In events that can be cancelled, your code can set this property to False to cancel the event.
Section	Returns a Section object indicating the section that triggered the event.
Status	In the AfterDelete event, returns a value indicating the status of the delete. The value dscDeleteOK indicates that the delete completed successfully. The value dscDeleteCancel indicates that your code cancelled the delete. The value dscDeleteUserCancel indicates that the user cancelled the delete in response to the standard system prompt.

All event procedure code must appear between <SCRIPT> and </SCRIPT> tags. Inside the <SCRIPT> tag, you must always indicate the language that you used for the script code. You can also optionally define the event and the object that you expect to signal the event, and when you do that, you do not need Sub and End Sub statements. For example, you can write a BeforeDelete event for the MSODSC object as

```
<SCRIPT language=vbscript>
Sub MSODSC_BeforeDelete(dscEventInfo)
    MsgBox "Before delete event fired."
    dscEventInfo.DisplayAlert = DscDataAlertContinue
End Sub
</SCRIPT>
```

or

```
<SCRIPT language=vbscript for=MSODSC event=BeforeDelete(dscEventInfo)>
    MsgBox "Before delete event fired."
    dscEventInfo.DisplayAlert = DscDataAlertContinue
</SCRIPT>
```

Chapter 27

The advantage to the first method is that you can write as many procedures as you like between the <SCRIPT> and </SCRIPT> tags, including custom functions that you might need in your event procedures. Make sure that you don't embed your tags within other tags that define objects or scripts in your page. If you're not sure about the object or event name, you can ask the script editor to generate the second syntax for you by selecting the object you want in the Object drop-down list and then selecting the event from the Event drop-down list. The one drawback to asking the script editor to create the event skeleton is that it doesn't know what parameters might be passed by the event. For all events on the MSODSC object, you must add the dscEventInfo parameter after the script editor generates the skeleton for you.

Checking for Valid Data

One of the most common tasks you'll want to perform in a data access page is to validate data before the page saves it to the database. In the *Housing.mdb* sample database, you can find a data access page called *dapXmplEmpResRequests*. This page is designed to allow employees to enter new reservation requests via a data access page on the company intranet. Of course, the request should contain valid dates and be a request for a reservation in the future, and the check-out date should be later than the check-in date.

To see the code that validates any new request, select the sample data access page in the Database window and click the Microsoft Script Editor button on the toolbar. Switch to Script Only View, and you can easily find the following code excerpted from the BeforeUpdate event of the MSODSC object:

```
Dim ChkInDte, ChkOutDte
Dim rs

' Now check the dates
' Get the check in and check out dates from the recordset
ChkInDte = dscEventInfo.DataPage.Recordset.Fields("CheckInDate")
ChkOutDte = dscEventInfo.DataPage.Recordset.Fields("CheckOutDate")

' If either date is null, warn and cancel
If IsNull(ChkInDte) Or IsNull(ChkOutDte) Then
    MsgBox "Both Check In and Out Dates must be supplied!"
    dscEventInfo.returnValue = False
    Exit Sub
' Make sure the check in date is after the current date.
ElseIf datediff("d",ChkInDte,Date())>0  Then
    MsgBox "Check In Date must be later than today!"
    dscEventInfo.returnValue = False
    Exit Sub
' Finally, make sure the check out date is later than check in.
ElseIf datediff("d",ChkOutDte, ChkInDte)>0 Then
    Msgbox "Check Out Date must be later than Check In Date!"
    dscEventInfo.returnValue = False
    Exit Sub
End If
```

> **Note** Keep in mind that even though you don't have to code the Sub and End Sub statements when you include the object and event information inside the <SCRIPT> tag, your code is still running in the equivalent of a Sub procedure. Therefore, use Exit Sub to exit the procedure.

The trick to validating values about to be saved is that your code must fetch the values from the Fields collection of the Recordset object in the current DataPage object. In other ways, the code looks very similar to what you might write in Visual Basic. The code uses the MsgBox function to tell the user about any problems. Rather than set a Cancel variable, the code sets the ReturnValue property of the dscEventInfo object to False to cancel the update when there's a problem.

Creating a Primary Key Value for a New Record

None of the tables in the Housing Reservations sample application uses an AutoNumber data type to ensure a unique value in the primary key of a new record. In all the forms that allow adding new rows, you can find Visual Basic code that generates the next number for a new record. So, any data access pages that allow creation of new rows must also generate a unique number, and you can do that with VBScript.

For example, you can find the following code in the BeforeUpdate event of the MSODSC object in the example *dapXmplDepartments* data access page that allows you to edit and insert department information:

```
<SCRIPT language=vbscript event=BeforeUpdate(dscEventInfo) for=MSODSC>
Dim ThisID
Dim rs
    ' Check to see if we need to supply a Department ID
    ' This application does not use AutoNumber
    ThisID = dscEventInfo.DataPage.Recordset.Fields("DepartmentID")
    If IsNull(ThisID) Then
        ' Fetch the previous high Department ID
        Set rs = CreateObject("ADODB.Recordset")
        rs.Open "Select Max(DepartmentID) As MD From tblDepartments", _
            MSODSC.Connection
        If (rs.EOF) Then
            ThisID = 0
        Else
            ThisID = rs.Fields("MD")
        End If
        rs.Close
        dscEventInfo.DataPage.Recordset.Fields("DepartmentID") = ThisID + 1
    End If
</SCRIPT>
```

The original Visual Basic code in the frmDepartments form uses the DMax domain function to look up the highest previous value, but you can't use domain functions in VBScript. If the DepartmentID field has no value, the code opens a recordset on a query to fetch the Max

Chapter 27

current value of the DepartmentID field. The code then adds 1 to the value and stores it back in the DepartmentID field before the MSODSC saves the record.

Setting a Cookie and Opening a Related Web Page

One of the most common tasks you're likely to automate in an Access application is to open a related form based on the value in a field of the record currently displayed. For example, you might want to review employee data in the Housing Reservations database and then open related reservation requests in another window for the current employee.

The best way to accomplish this same task in a data access page is to write a cookie from one page containing the linking information and then use that information when a second page opens to filter or navigate to the related information. A *cookie* is a small file that your Web browser can write to memory or to the user's hard drive to pass information from one page to another. In the Housing Reservations sample database (*Housing.mdb*), you can find several sample data access pages that use this technique to pass filtering information.

The bad news is cookies don't work when you open a data access page from within Access. To test the sample pages, you must open them in Internet Explorer. To see these techniques in action, go to the WebChapters\DataAccessPages subfolder in the sample files and open the file *default.htm* in your browser. This page lets you choose an employee name, enter a password, and click the Sign On button, as shown in Figure 27-52.

Chapter 27

Figure 27-52. A root page for a Web site that lets employees sign on and view information.

This page is intended to be the root sign-on page for a Web site that lets employees view their own employee record, review confirmed reservations, and enter new reservation requests. When you enter a correct password for an employee and click Sign On, code in the control's

Click event writes a cookie and opens the dapXmplEmployees data access page. The code is as follows:

```
<SCRIPT language=vbscript event=onclick for=cmdSignOn>
Dim lngEmpnum
Dim rs
Dim strPswd
' Make sure they picked an employee
If len(ddlEmployees.value) = 0 Then
    MsgBox "You must select an employee!"
    Exit Sub
End If
' Test if no password is entered
If Len(txtPassword.value) = 0 then
    MsgBox "Please enter a password!"
    Exit Sub
End If
' Grab the employee number
    lngEmpNum = ddlEmployees.value
' Get a copy of the bound recordset (qryEmployeeSignon)
    Set rs = MSODSC.DataPages(0).Recordset.Clone
    rs.Find "EmployeeNumber = " & lngEmpNum
    If Not ((rs.EOF) or (rs.BOF)) Then
        strPswd = rs("Password")
    Else
        msgbox "Unable to locate the employee record you selected."
        Exit Sub
    End If
' If passwords don't match
    If Lcase(txtPassword.value) <> Lcase(strPswd) then
        MsgBox "Incorrect Password!"
        If Len(txtCount.value) = 0 Then
            txtCount.value = 1
        Else
            txtCount.value = txtCount.value + 1
        End If
        If txtCount.value > 2 Then
            MsgBox "You have entered an incorrect password " & _
                "three times.  Goodbye."
            window.close
        End If
```

Chapter 27

```
    Else
        ' Cookies don't work inside Access
        If window.location.protocol = "accdp:" Then
            MsgBox "Password is valid, but you cannot sign on " & _
                "from within Access." & _
                "  Run this page in a Web browser instead."
            Exit Sub
        End If
        ' Open the new page in the current window
        Document.cookie = "Logon=True"
        Document.cookie = "EmpNum=" & lngEmpNum
        window.open "dapXmplEmployees.htm","_self"
  ' Alternate method:  window.navigate("dapXmplEmployees.htm")
    End If
</SCRIPT>
```

The first part of the code makes sure the user has selected an employee name and entered a password. The data access page uses qryEmployeeSignon as its record source, so the code borrows that to find the employee and compare the password. If the password is incorrect, the code uses a hidden text box on the page to count the number of attempts and closes the window after the third failed attempt.

The last part of the code assigns two keyword values (called *crumbs*) to the current document cookie. Any page can reference the cookie property that contains a string of keywords and assigned values, separated by semicolons. So, a page can search the cookie string to verify that the Logon crumb is true and then fetch the value assigned to the EmpNum crumb to use in filtering. When you set a cookie value, you can also set an expiration date and time by adding the expires keyword. If this were a production application, this code should probably set an expiration time of 20 or 30 minutes so that the user must log on again after the cookie expires. It should also check to see if the user is an application administrator or department manager and set additional crumbs that subsequent pages can examine to restrict what the user can do.

> **Note** To clear a crumb, set its value to Null with an expiration date in the past, like this:
> `Document.cookie = "Logon=NULL;expires=Saturday, 01-Jan-00 00:00:00 GMT"`

Finally, the code uses the open method of the window object to open the employees data access page in the same window (_self). As noted in the commented code, an alternative method is to use the navigate method of the window object. When this code executes, the dapXmplEmployees data access page opens and displays the record for the user who signed on, as shown in Figure 27-53 on the next page.

Figure 27-53. The employees data access page uses the value saved in a cookie to display the correct employee.

As you might guess, code in this data access page looks for the cookie set by the default.htm page and moves to the correct employee record. The code is as follows:

```
<SCRIPT language=vbscript event=DataPageComplete(dscei) for=MSODSC>
Dim rs
Dim EmpNum
Dim intLoc
Dim strCookie
' Won't find any cookie if running in Access
If window.location.protocol = "accdp:" Then
    Exit Sub
End If
' Fetch the cookie, if any
strCookie = Document.cookie
' Find the EmpNum parameter
intLoc = Instr(strCookie, "EmpNum=")
' Use it as filter if found
If intLoc > 0 Then
    EmpNum = Mid(strCookie, intLoc + 7)
    ' Look for ending semicolon
    intLoc = Instr(EmpNum, ";")
    If intLoc > 0 Then
        EmpNum = Left(EmpNum, intLoc -1)
    End If
```

```
    Set rs = MSODSC.DataPages(0).Recordset.Clone
    rs.Find "EmployeeNumber = " & EmpNum
    If Not ((rs.EOF) or (rs.BOF)) Then
        msodsc.DataPages(0).Recordset.Bookmark = rs.bookmark
    End If
End If
</SCRIPT>
```

Notice that this code runs in the DataPageComplete event to be sure that the page has loaded all the data. The code first checks the window.location.protocol property to find out if the page is opened inside Access (from the Database window) instead of in a Web browser. If so, the code exits because Access doesn't support cookies. When you open the page in a browser, the code fetches the cookie string and looks for the EmpNum crumb. When it finds the crumb, it strips out the value and uses it to perform a Find on a copy of the bound recordset. When it finds the record, it assigns the bookmark property of the recordset copy to the recordset of the page—which causes the page to move to the selected record.

Of course, in a production application, this code should probably run in the BeforeInitial-Bind event and apply a filter if the user is not an administrator so that the user can view and edit only his or her own record. As you can see in Figure 27-53, the data access page has loaded all the employee records, and the user is free to use the navigation buttons to move to other records.

At the bottom of the employee page, you can see buttons to open Reservations or Reservation Requests. These buttons update the EmpNum crumb and navigate to the appropriate data access page. The code behind the Reservation Requests button is as follows:

```
<SCRIPT language=vbscript event=onclick for=cmdResRequests>
Dim EmpNum
' Cookies don't work inside Access
If window.location.protocol = "accdp:" Then
    MsgBox "You must run this page in a Web browser to use this button."
    Exit Sub
End If
' Get the EmpNum for the current record
EmpNum = EmployeeNumber.value
' Do nothing if empty
If Len(EmpNum) > 0 Then
    Document.cookie = "EmpNum=" & EmpNum
    window.navigate("dapXmplEmpResRequests.htm")
End If
</SCRIPT>
```

The code updates the EmpNum crumb because the user might have navigated to a different employee record. It uses the navigate method of the window object to open the *dap-XmplEmpResRequests* data access page, and the page displays requests for the current employee as shown in Figure 27-54 on the next page.

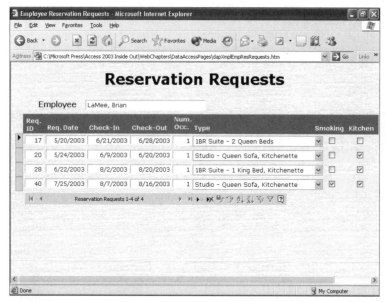

Figure 27-54. A data access page displaying reservation requests for the current employee.

Notice that in this case the user can't navigate to requests for other employees. Code in the BeforeInitialBind event of the page applies a filter to the recordset as follows:

```
<SCRIPT language=vbscript event=BeforeInitialBind(dscEventInfo) for=MSODSC>
Dim EmpNum
Dim intLoc
Dim strCookie
' Cookies don't work inside Access
If window.location.protocol = "accdp:" Then
    Exit Sub
End If
' Fetch the cookie, if any
strCookie = Document.cookie
' Find the EmpNum parameter
intLoc = Instr(strCookie, "EmpNum=")
' Use it as filter if found
If intLoc > 0 Then
    EmpNum = Mid(strCookie, intLoc + 7)
    ' Look for ending semicolon
    intLoc = Instr(EmpNum, ";")
    If intLoc > 0 Then
        EmpNum = Left(EmpNum, intLoc -1)
    End If
    ' Apply the filter
    MSODSC.RecordsetDefs("qryResRequestsForDap").ServerFilter = _
        "EmployeeNumber = " & Empnum
End If
</SCRIPT>
```

Chapter 27

Unlike searching and setting the bookmark property, applying a server filter before the page loads any data restricts the records available. In a production application, this code should apply a filter to return no rows (and perhaps display an error message) if it can't find the EmpNum crumb.

Updating Data Access Page Links and Connections

As you know, a data access page is actually an .htm file, and Access stores a link to the page in your database. If you move the page to a new location, you won't be able to open the page from the object link in your database. For example, you might not install the sample files in the same location that I used when I created the data access page samples. Or, if you copy your pages to a Web server, you'll need to update the links from your database if you want to be able to edit the pages on the server.

The MSODSC object in each page has connection properties that tell it where to find your database. If you move your database, the page won't work anymore. When you publish your pages on a Web server, you must set the connection properties so that the client Web browser or the server can find your database.

In summary, you have an object *link* in your database that tells Access where to find the HTML file that defines the data access page. In the other direction, the page has a *connection* so that it can find your database and the tables and queries that supply the data for the page. This section discusses how to deal with maintaining both links from your database to the pages and connections from the pages to your database.

Updating Links from Access to Data Access Pages

If you move or delete a data access page file and you try to open that data access page from your Access database, a dialog box appears, as shown in Figure 27-55, telling you that the HTML file associated with the link has been moved, renamed, or deleted.

Figure 27-55. Access displays a warning dialog box when you attempt to open a link to a data access page that you have moved or deleted.

You can click Update Link to open a Locate Data Access Page dialog box where you can navigate to the new location of your data access page. When you find the HTML file, click OK to update the link properties of the object in your database. You can also update the link by right-clicking the data access page object in your Database window and choosing Properties on the shortcut menu. Access displays the Properties window for the object as shown in

Figure 27-56. (Another way to open the Properties window is to select the object in the Database window and then click the Properties button on the toolbar.)

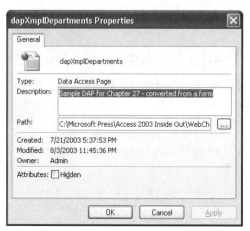

Figure 27-56. The Properties window for a data access page.

You can type a new file location in the Path box or click the Build button to open the Locate Data Access Page dialog box. See the section "Updating Links and Connections from Within Visual Basic" on page 1088 for details about how to update this property using Visual Basic.

Updating Connections

When you create a new data access page, Access assumes that you want to bind the page to the current database. Access sets the ConnectionString property of the page to a value similar to the one you'll find in the CurrentProject.Connection.ConnectionString property in your database. The connection string includes information about the database provider that the data access page must use to connect to the database, the location of the database file or server, and other properties relevant to the type of provider such as user ID and locking options. Providers supported by the Microsoft Office Data Source Control (MSODSC) are Microsoft JET 4.0 (the database engine for Access desktop databases) and Microsoft SQL Server (the database engine for Access project files).

You might have noticed that Access displays a warning message the first time you save a data access page to let you know that the connection string points to a physical drive, path, and file name. Remember from Figure 27-1 that all requests for data from a data access page originate on the client machine, so the ConnectionString property must point to a location known to all clients. Before you publish your data access page on an intranet server, you'll probably need to correct the location to point to a share on a file server to which all clients on your network have access.

A second way to specify the connection from your data access page to your database is to set the ConnectionFile property to point to a Microsoft Office Data Connection (*.odc) or Microsoft Data Link (*.udl) file that contains the connection information. The primary advantage to using a connection file instead of a connection string is that you can use the same file for all the data access pages in your database. The one disadvantage is that you must also place this connection file on a network share accessible to all users, and the ConnectionFile property must specify a network share path rather than a physical drive, path, and file name.

You can edit and update either the ConnectionString or the ConnectionFile property using the properties page of the data access page. Open any data access page in Design view, open the Properties window, and choose Select Page on the Edit menu. You can find the ConnectionFile and ConnectionString properties on the Data tab, as shown in Figure 27-57.

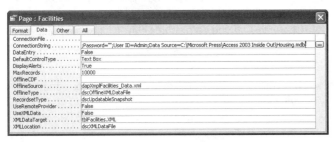

Figure 27-57. The data properties of a data access page.

Notice that the ConnectionString property points to a data source on a physical hard drive. If you move the database on your machine, you'll need to update the location. If you want to publish this page to an intranet server, you must place the database on a network share and change the data source to point to that share.

Specifying a ConnectionString Property

Although you can certainly type changes directly into the ConnectionString property box, Access provides a link to a builder to help you construct the string correctly. Open any data access page in Design view, open the Properties window, select the page, and click the ConnectionString property on the Data tab. Click the Build button at the end of the property to open the Data Link Properties dialog box as shown in Figure 27-58.

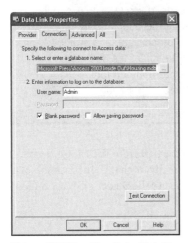

Figure 27-58. The Data Link Properties dialog box.

Inside Out

Using XML data with data access pages

By default, Access sets the data properties of data access pages to use "live" data from your database. As you learned in Chapter 25, "Publishing Data on the Web," Access can export the data from tables or queries in XML format—a standard for exchanging data between applications. Notice that the list of properties shown in Figure 27-57 contains three properties you can set to cause your data access page to work with XML. When you set the UseXMLData property to True, the data source control uses the XMLDataTarget and XMLLocation properties to locate a set of XML data to use as the source data rather than fetch the data from your database.

When the XMLLocation property is dscXMLEmbedded, the data source control looks for an XML specification within your data access page that has the name you specify in the XML-DataTarget property. To embed XML data in your data access page, you must first export the data source to XML and then copy and paste the XML into the source code for your page using the script editor. A simpler way to bind your page to XML is to set the XMLLocation property to dscXMLDataFile and set the XMLDataTarget property to the location of the XML file.

However, creating the XML for a data access page isn't always straightforward. The tables and field names in the file must exactly match the list shown in the Data Outline window. If your data access page has a drop-down list control or a list box control that uses an additional record source, that record source appears as an additional entry in the Data Outline window, so you might have to include more than one recordset in your file. You must export each recordset separately and then use a text editor to merge the several XML specifications into one file.

One simple data access page that uses a single table in its data outline is *dapXMPLFacilities*. In the WebChapters\DataAccessPages folder, you can find a tblFacilities.xml file that contains the data required by the data access page. If you want to experiment, you can open the data access page in Design view, change the UseXMLData property to True (I've already set the XMLDataTarget and XMLLocation properties), and switch to Page view. Notice that when you use XML as the source of the page, the data is read-only. However, using this technique might be useful for infrequently updated tables that you want to display in a data access page even when the database isn't available. You'll learn more about using XML in Chapter 28, "Working with XML and SharePoint."

You can click the Provider tab to change the database type from JET to SQL Server, or vice versa. You most often will use the Connection tab to specify or change the location of the database file. Notice that you can click the Build button next to the Select or enter a database name box to open the Select Access Database dialog box that you can use to find the file, as shown in Figure 27-59.

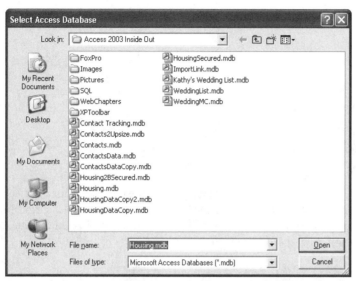

Figure 27-59. Locating a database to specify in the ConnectString property.

If you have copied your database to a network share, you can click the My Network Places link to navigate through your network to find the share and the file. When you use My Network Places, the builder stores the file location in Universal Naming Convention (UNC) format, as in *MyServer*\DAPDatabases\Housing.mdb. When you store the location in this way, any user can open this data access page as long as they have access to the share name. After you locate the database, click Open to pass the location back to the Data Link Properties dialog box. Click OK in the dialog box to save the changed connection string.

Notice that the Connection tab allows you to enter a user name and password if your Access desktop database file is secured. For unsecured desktop databases, use the Admin user name and leave the Blank password option selected. You can learn more about securing desktop databases in Chapter 30, "Securing Your Database." On the Advanced tab, you can find options to set the locking options for the recordsets opened by the page. You should normally leave these options at their default settings.

Specifying a ConnectionFile Property

The easiest way to create a connection file is to click the ConnectionFile property field in any data access page and then click the Build button that appears at the end of the property. Access displays the Select Data Source dialog box shown in Figure 27-60 on the next page.

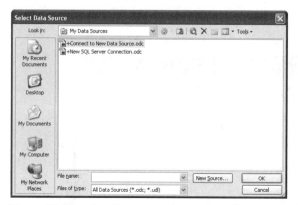

Figure 27-60. Creating a new data source file.

If you already have a data source file defined, you can use this dialog box to navigate to it and select the file, and then click OK to save the file location in the ConnectionFile property. To create a new data source file, click the New Source button. Clicking either button opens the Data Connection Wizard shown in Figure 27-61.

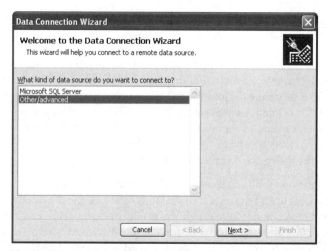

Figure 27-61. Using the Data Connection Wizard to create a new data source file.

If you're creating a data source for a data access page in an Access project file (.adp), select Microsoft SQL Server in the list. To create a data source file to an Access desktop database (.mdb), select Other/advanced and click Next. The wizard shows you the Data Link Properties dialog box, as shown in Figure 27-62.

Figure 27-62. Specifying a database provider in the Data Link Properties dialog box.

Notice that you can still create a link to SQL Server if you didn't choose that option in the Data Connection Wizard. For an Access desktop database (.mdb), select Microsoft Jet 4.0 OLE DB Provider and click the Next button to move to the Connection tab. (You can also click the Connection tab directly.) You'll see the same options that you examined previously in Figure 27-58. Specify your database location, or click the Build button to open the Select Access Database dialog box if you want to navigate to the file location.

After you specify the file and click OK in the Data Link Properties dialog box, the Data Connection Wizard shows you a confirmation page that lists the queries and tables in the database you selected. When you choose SQL Server as the data source, you use this page to navigate to the specific database on the server that you want. When you use an Access desktop database file (.mdb) as the source, you'll see a list of the first seven queries in the database, but you won't be able to modify or select anything in the list. Click Next to go to the last page of the wizard as shown in Figure 27-63.

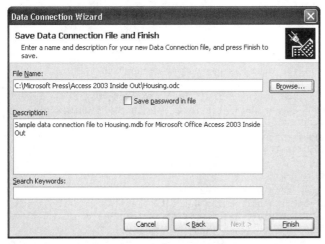

Figure 27-63. The last page of the Data Connection Wizard.

By default, the wizard stores the new data connection file in My Documents\My Data Sources. You can specify a different location by entering a full path name or by clicking the Browse button and navigating to a new location. You can type a description to help identify the purpose of the file. Notice that you can select an option to Save password in file if your database is secured. You should choose this option only when you place the data connection file on a network share that can be accessed only by authorized users.

Click Finish to save the new data connection file. You'll see the Select Data Source dialog box again where you can confirm the file name that you want to use. When you return to the Properties window, you'll see the location of the data connection file entered in the ConnectionFile property of your page. Keep in mind that this must be a location on a network share if you want to publish your pages on an intranet.

Updating Links and Connections from Within Visual Basic

As I wrote this book, I saved all the sample files in the Microsoft Press\Access 2003 Inside Out folder on my C drive. I also saved all the data access pages in the WebChapters\DataAccessPages subfolder. I knew that the installation procedure for the companion CD would allow you to specify a different location for the sample files. So, the data access page links from the *Housing .mdb* sample database to the sample data access pages might be incorrect. Also, the Connection-String property in the data access pages might point to the wrong location.

To solve this problem, I wrote some Visual Basic code that runs in the frmCopyright form that opens each time you open the database. The Load event procedure calls a function included in the form module to check and fix both the links and the ConnectionString property. If the function fails, the code displays a message to let you know that you might need to fix the problems yourself in order to work with the examples. The function is as follows:

```
Function DAPLinksUpdate(Optional varNewPath As Variant) As Integer
' Create a reference to an Access Object
Dim aoCurrDAP As AccessObject
' Create a reference to a DAP type object
Dim dapCurr As DataAccessPage
' Flag for testing the link
Dim blnAlreadyGood As Boolean
    ' Turn the error handling on
    On Error GoTo DAPLinkUpdate_Err
    ' Check to see if a value was passed for strNewPath
    If IsMissing(varNewPath) Then
        ' If not, assign it the default path under the database
        varNewPath = CurrentProject.Path & "\WebChapters\DataAccessPages\"
    End If
    ' Turn warnings off for any messages when saving
    DoCmd.SetWarnings False
    ' Set flag that links are good if no DAP
    blnAlreadyGood = True
    ' Iterate through each page in the database
    For Each aoCurrDAP In Application.CurrentProject.AllDataAccessPages
        ' Test the first page, and see if it is good
        If (blnAlreadyGood = True) Then
```

```
        If Dir(aoCurrDAP.FullName) = aoCurrDAP.Name & ".htm" Then
            ' If so, exit the loop
            Exit For
        End If
    End If
    ' Make sure to display the warning label
    Me.lblLinkUpdate.Visible = True
    ' Set flag to indicate we had to test and reset
    blnAlreadyGood = False
    ' Select the DAP.
    DoCmd.SelectObject acDataAccessPage, aoCurrDAP.Name, True
    ' Check to see that the file we're going to point to exists
    If Len(Dir(varNewPath & aoCurrDAP.Name & ".htm")) = 0 Then
        MsgBox "Data Access Page links are incorrect, and the files " & _
            "are not in the expected location. " & _
            "The Data Access Page .htm files " & _
            "must be in the " & varNewPath & " folder."
        GoTo DAPLinkBail
    End If
    ' Update the page link by updating the name of the DAP
    aoCurrDAP.FullName = varNewPath & aoCurrDAP.Name & ".htm"


    ' Now for redoing the connections
    ' Open the DAP in Design view
    DoCmd.OpenDataAccessPage aoCurrDAP.Name, acDataAccessPageDesign
    ' Assign the DAP to a DAP object
    Set dapCurr = DataAccessPages(aoCurrDAP.Name)
    ' Update the ConnectionString property
    ' Current MDB
    dapCurr.MSODSC.ConnectionString = _
            "Provider=Microsoft.Jet.OLEDB.4.0;" & _
            "Data Source=" & CurrentProject.FullName
    ' For ADP using Integrated Security
    'dapCurr.MSODSC.ConnectionString = _
            CurrentProject.BaseConnectionString
    'Close the DAP, saving the changes
    DoCmd.Close acDataAccessPage, dapCurr.Name, acSaveYes
Next aoCurrDAP
' If not ok, display the message that the DAPs were relinked
If Not blnAlreadyGood Then
    ' Let the user know.
    MsgBox "DAP Links Updated."
End If
' Return link test successful
DAPLinksUpdate = True
DAPLinkBail:
' Turn warnings back on
DoCmd.SetWarnings True

Exit Function
' Error handling
DAPLinkUpdate_Err:
    ' Let user know about the error and display the message
    MsgBox "Error relinking DAPs: " & Err.Description
```

```
        DAPLinksUpdate = False
        Resume DAPLinkBail
End Function
```

You can move this function to a public module, if you want, and call it with a specific path you want to use for your data access pages. If the function detects that a path parameter has not been supplied, it uses the current location of the database and assumes the data access page .htm file is in the \WebChapters\DataAccessPages subfolder.

The code looks at each data access page object in the database. It uses the Dir function to see if the path and file specified in the FullName property of the first data access page exist. If it finds that the first one is good, it assumes all are fine. When the code finds that the path to the first data access page is bad, it loops through all pages to update both the link and the connection. For each page, the code first verifies that it can find the HTML file in the expected location. If any fail, the code displays an error message and exits. Note that if the object name and the file name are different, this technique won't work. If the code finds the file in the expected location, it updates the FullName property of the page to correct the link. The code then opens the DAP in Design view and changes the ConnectionString property of the MSODSC object on the page.

If the function causes any errors, the error trapping code at the end of the function executes. The error trap notifies you of the error and doesn't attempt to fix any additional pages.

Uploading Your Pages to a Web Server

After you have finished developing your data access pages and have corrected the connection properties so that all clients can access your database, you need to upload or "publish" your files to your Web server. If your Web server is available via a network share, you can simply copy the files using Windows Explorer. Be sure to also copy any supporting folders and files. For example, if you have applied a theme to any of your pages, you'll find the files needed to apply the theme in a subfolder that has the same name as the data access page with _Files appended to the name.

> **Note** If you used FrontPage to incorporate your pages into a FrontPage Web, you should use FrontPage to publish your pages. This ensures that all supporting files needed by FrontPage are copied to the server. See *Microsoft Office FrontPage 2003 Inside Out* for details.

Locating the correct path name on your Web server can be somewhat tricky. In most cases, the path and file name portions of a Universal Resource Locator (URL) correspond directly to a portion of the Web server's file system, starting at a spot called the HTTP root. For example, if the server's HTTP root is F:\InetPub\wwwroot\ and the F: drive on that server has a share name of \\WebServer\FDrive, then the URL http://www.proseware.com/default.htm corresponds to \\WebServer\FDrive\InetPub\wwwroot\default.htm on the Web server. Similarly, http://www.proseware.com/housing/default.htm points to \\WebServer\FDrive\InetPub\wwwroot\housing\default.htm on the Web server.

> **Note** Occasionally, an administrator will break the pattern of defining all subdirectories under the root of the Web by defining a *virtual directory*. Web visitors normally specify the virtual directory in a URL, but the Web server translates the URL to some location outside the normal HTTP root. If, in the second example above, *housing* is a virtual directory assigned to G:\HousingApp\Res, the file name corresponding to http://www.proseware.com/housing /default.htm would be G:\HousingApp\Res\default.htm. You must know the share name to this drive or folder to be able to copy your files to the correct location.

Copying Pages Using the Windows XP My Web Sites

If you do not have a direct network share to the correct Web server path, Windows XP makes it easy to copy your Web pages to a Web server. You can create an Internet connection to a Web server (provided you know the user ID and password required to authenticate you for update on the server) by following this procedure:

1. Open My Network Places from the Windows Start menu.

2. In the Network Tasks list, click Add a network place to start the Add Network Place Wizard.

3. On the introductory page of the wizard, click Next to begin a search for Web servers on your network. If you have a slow connection, the search might take several minutes. In most cases, the search result shows you options to connect to MSN Communities or Choose another network location. Select the Choose another network location option and click Next.

4. In the Internet or network address box, type the location http, ftp, or share address that you want to open. In this example, I entered the address of my Web server: http://www.viescas.com/. (You won't be able to connect to this server because it is protected.) Click Next, and the wizard attempts to connect to the server with update authority. If the server is protected, you'll see a Connect dialog box where you must enter a user name and a password.

5. If the wizard can successfully connect, it asks you to supply a name for the network connection. Enter a name, and click Next.

6. The wizard shows you a final option to Open this network place when I click Finish. Leave this option selected and click Finish to open the Web location as shown in Figure 27-64 on the next page.

Publishing data access pages on the Internet

As you already know, the connection properties of your data access pages must be defined so that your users can access your database from their client machines—usually via a network share that's independent of your intranet Web server. If you want to publish data access pages on a Web site that's available on the World Wide Web, you obviously cannot provide a network share for every user in the world.

What you must do is change one key data property for all data access pages that you want to publish on a Web site that's available over the Internet. Take another look at the properties shown in Figure 27-57. If you change the UseRemoteProvider property to True, this instructs the data source control to send requests via http to the Web server to open a remote connection to your database. As long as your Web server is running Microsoft Internet Information Server and has Remote Data Services enabled, the server will execute the database requests on behalf of the client. Of course, the Web server must be able to connect to the database using the connection properties you provide.

For more details about publishing data access pages on the Internet, see the article at: *http://msdn.microsoft.com/library/default.asp?url=/library/en-us/dnacc2k2/html /deploydap.asp*.

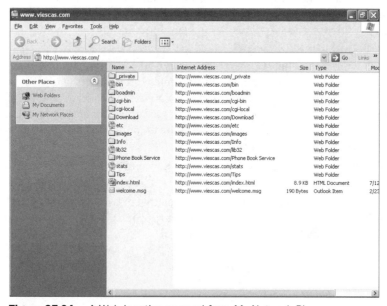

Figure 27-64. A Web location opened from My Network Places.

Click the Folders button to open the list of folders on the left. You can navigate to any folder on your hard drive or any folder on a network share and drag and drop files to copy them to the Web server folders. If you're not the manager of the Web server, be sure to check with your administrator to verify the correct location for your files.

Publishing Pages Using FTP

You might find that using a File Transfer Protocol (FTP) utility is simpler and faster than establishing a My Network Places connection to the Web server where you want to publish your data access pages. This is particularly true if you have many data access pages that you update frequently. Many of the commercially available utilities provide you with tools to automate updating of your Web site. Although I built my Web site using Microsoft FrontPage, I often update the site using an FTP utility. The utility that I use is WS_FTP Pro from Ipswitch, Inc. (*http://www.ipswitch.com*).

To use an FTP utility, you'll need the following information:

- The name of the FTP server
- A user ID that has update authority
- The password that authenticates the user ID
- The directory (folder) to use

Although completely text-based and not as user-friendly as many third-party FTP utilities, you can actually execute an ftp transfer using the Command Prompt window in Microsoft Windows. Open the Command Prompt window, and execute the following commands. The text you are to enter is shown in bold and italics indicate responses from the utility. You must substitute actual data for the placeholder names displayed in angle brackets (< >) below. Do not type the brackets.

```
ftp <FTP server name>
Connected to <server name>
220 Serv-U FTP Server v4.0 for WinSock ready...
User (<server name>): (none)): <user name>
331 User name okay, need password
password: <password>
230 User logged in, proceed
ftp> cd <directory>
250 Directory changed to <directory>
put <local file name> <server file name>
200 PORT Command successful.
150 Opening ASCII mode data connection for <server file name>
226 Transfer complete.
ftp: <xxx> bytes sent in <x.xx>Seconds <xxx.xx>Kbytes/sec.
ftp>bye
221 Goodbye!
```

You can *put* any number of files before you quit with the *bye* or *quit* command. If you need to transfer images or other binary files, execute a *binary* command before executing the *put* command. You can get a list of commands by typing **Help** and pressing Enter at the ftp prompt, and you can get a brief description of any command by typing **Help** <**command**> at the prompt.

You can also use the FTP protocol directly in Internet Explorer. To access the FTP service on my Web site, in the Address box you can type ftp://ftp.viescas.com/ and press Enter. However, Internet Explorer performs an anonymous login when you do this. An anonymous user name typically doesn't have write authority to the FTP site, so you won't be able to copy files to the site. However, this is a good way to access an FTP site to download files to your computer, if the site supports downloads using an anonymous logon. If the site requires a user name and password (and you've been granted these), you can select Login As from the File menu and then enter the user name and password to gain access.

You should now have a good understanding of how to create and publish data access pages. In the next chapter, you'll learn more about working with XML and the new Microsoft Share-Point Products and Technologies.

Chapter 28

Working with XML and SharePoint

Today's modern companies are increasing productivity and cutting costs by finding ways to share more and more information online. When data can be shared in a universal format, it doesn't matter whether an employee is down the hall, across the street, or thousands of miles away. Online sharing of information also makes it easier for companies to expand into global markets. Customers half a world away can explore a company's products and services and place orders online. Companies can tap into vendors worldwide to find the best products at the best price.

The World Wide Web has certainly been an enabling technology for increasing productivity and expanding markets. As explained in Chapter 25, "Publishing Data on the Web," the Web works because of the universal acceptance of protocol and language standards. Hypertext Markup Language (HTML) enables a Web page to be displayed on any computer and in any browser anywhere in the world. As an adjunct to HTML, Extensible Markup Language (XML) defines a standard and universal way to share data files or documents. And the new Microsoft SharePoint Products and Technologies from Microsoft leverages both these technologies to provide an enhanced Web-based data and information sharing mechanism to help companies increase productivity.

This chapter explores XML and SharePoint in more detail and shows you how you can take advantage of these technologies to share information more readily from your Microsoft Access applications.

Note The samples in this chapter are based on the Housing Reservations sample database (*Housing.mdb*) on the companion CD. You can find the XML examples in the WebChapters\XML subfolder.

Exploring XML

The current XML standard is based on an ISO standard, but the most commonly used version is the one maintained and published by W3C (World Wide Web Consortium). Because a file in XML format contains not only the data but also a description of the structure of the data, XML-enabled receiving systems know exactly how to process the data from the information included in the file.

An XML document can contain data from a single table or from an entire database. An XML document can also have supporting files that describe details about the table schema (for example, field properties and indexes) or that describe how the recipient should lay out (format) the data for display (for example, fonts and column sizes).

 Note The XML examples in this chapter are based on the tables and data in the Housing Reservations application (*Housing.mdb*) and on various XML documents (files) located in the WebChapters\XML folder on the companion CD.

Like HTML, XML uses tags to identify descriptive elements. Examples include the name of a table or the name of a field in an XML data file, the names of table properties or index properties in an XML schema file, and the size and color of a border or the name of a style sheet template in an XML layout file. However, where most browsers are forgiving of errors in HTML, such as a missing end tag in a table row, most software that can process XML insists that the tags in an XML file be very precise and follow strict rules. An XML document or set of documents that contain precise XML are said to be "well formed."

Well-Formed XML

Although you will create most XML documents using a program such as Microsoft Access that always creates well-formed XML, you might occasionally need to view and edit XML files that you receive from outside sources. You should understand the following rules that apply to well-formed XML:

- Each XML document must have a unique root element that surrounds the entire document.

- Any start tag must have an end tag. Unlike HTML that supports standalone tags (such as <br>), XML requires all tags to have explicit ends. However, some tags within XML are self-contained. For example, you code an object definition tag within a schema file like this (the /> characters at the end of the string define the end of the tag):

    `<od:object-type attributes />`

- Tags cannot overlap. For example, you cannot start the definition of one table field and then start the definition of a second table field without ending the first one.

- When you need to include certain characters that are reserved for XML syntax (such as <, &, >, ", ') within the data portion of an element, you must use a substitute character sequence. For example, you indicate a single quote within data using the special sequence *&apos*.

- All tags in XML are case-sensitive. For example, </tblfacilities> is an invalid end tag for the begin tag <TBLFacilities>.

As you examine the XML examples in this chapter, you should not encounter any XML that is not well formed.

Chapter 28

Understanding XML File Types

XML documents can be made up of a single file if necessary. However, when you want to send more than the table name, field names, and data content, you can generate additional files that help the recipient understand data properties and format the data as you intended. The four types of files that can make up a set of XML documents about one table or group of tables are as follows:

- Data document (.xml) contains the names of tables and fields and the data in the fields.
- Schema document (.xsd) contains additional information about the properties of the tables (such as indexes defined on the table) and properties of the fields (such as data type or length).
- Presentation (layout) document (.xsl) specifies the layout of the data, including fonts and column and row spacing.
- Web package (.htm) is a version of the information contained in the data, schema, and presentation documents compiled into HTML format ready for display in a browser.

When you create XML documents to display on your own Web site, you most likely will use all four file types to completely describe the data and format it for presentation. When you are sending a data file to another organization or business application, you usually send only the data and schema documents—the essential information that the recipient needs to understand your data.

> **Note** Although you can embed schema and presentation information inside a data document, you should normally send the information as separate files. Not all applications that can process XML can handle a combined file that contains the data and the schema or the data and the schema and the presentation specification. In general, it's a good idea to keep the data values, the data definition, and the layout specifications separate.

One of the best ways to understand XML files is to study some examples. So, let's look at the files Access creates when you ask it to export a small table such as the tblFacilities table in the Housing Reservations application as XML. You can learn how to create these documents from Access in "Exporting Access Tables and Queries" on page 1106.

The XML Data Document (.xml)

The data document contains very basic information about your table and the fields within the table as well as the data from the table. The data document for the tblFacilities table (*tblFacilities.xml*) is as follows:

```
<?xml version="1.0" encoding="UTF-8"?>
<dataroot xmlns:od="urn:schemas-microsoft-com:officedata"
  xmlns:xsi="http://www.w3.org/2001/XMLSchema-instance"
  xsi:noNamespaceSchemaLocation="tblFacilities.xsd"
  generated="2003-06-03T14:58:40">
<tblFacilities>
```

```
<FacilityID>1</FacilityID>
<FacilityName>Main Campus Housing A</FacilityName>
<FacilityAddress>2345 Main Street</FacilityAddress>
<FacilityCity>Chicago</FacilityCity>
<FacilityStateOrProvince>IL</FacilityStateOrProvince>
<FacilityPostalCode>60637</FacilityPostalCode>
</tblFacilities>
<tblFacilities>
<FacilityID>2</FacilityID>
<FacilityName>Main Campus Housing B</FacilityName>
<FacilityAddress>2348 Main Street</FacilityAddress>
<FacilityCity>Chicago</FacilityCity>
<FacilityStateOrProvince>IL</FacilityStateOrProvince>
<FacilityPostalCode>60637</FacilityPostalCode>
</tblFacilities>
<tblFacilities>
<FacilityID>3</FacilityID>
<FacilityName>South Campus Housing C</FacilityName>
<FacilityAddress>4567 Central Ave.</FacilityAddress>
<FacilityCity>Chicago</FacilityCity>
<FacilityStateOrProvince>IL</FacilityStateOrProvince>
<FacilityPostalCode>60637</FacilityPostalCode>
</tblFacilities>
<tblFacilities>
<FacilityID>4</FacilityID>
<FacilityName>North Satellite Housing D</FacilityName>
<FacilityAddress>5678 N. Willow Drive</FacilityAddress>
<FacilityCity>Chicago</FacilityCity>
<FacilityStateOrProvince>IL</FacilityStateOrProvince>
<FacilityPostalCode>60636</FacilityPostalCode>
</tblFacilities>
</dataroot>
```

The first line is a comment tag that notes the version of the XML standard that Access used to generate this file and states that the characters in the file comply with an 8-bit character-set standard. The next line starts the required root element of the document and identifies that the schema definition can be found in the file *tblFacilities.xsd*. The remaining lines, up to the </dataroot> end tag, identify the four rows in the table and the six fields within each row, including the data content of each field. Note that each row starts with a <tblFacilities> tag and ends with a </tblFacilities> tag. Likewise, each field begins and ends with a tag that names the field, and the data contents of each field appears between the begin and end field tags.

You can see that this file primarily contains information about the data contents. Except for the implied sequence of fields in each row and the sequence of rows within the table, no information about the definition of the table or the fields is in this file. Although this example file contains the data from only one table, it is possible to include the data from multiple tables in one XML file.

The Schema File (.xsd)

To find the structural definition of the table and fields, you must look in the companion schema file. Understanding how to read a schema file can be useful if you attempt to import an XML file sent to you, but you don't seem to be getting the results you expect. The schema file for the tblFacilities table (*tblFacilites.xsd*) is as follows:

```
<?xml version="1.0" encoding="UTF-8"?>
<xsd:schema xmlns:xsd="http://www.w3.org/2001/XMLSchema" xmlns:od="urn:schemas-
  microsoft-com:officedata">
<xsd:element name="dataroot">
<xsd:complexType>
<xsd:sequence>
<xsd:element ref="tblFacilities" minOccurs="0" maxOccurs="unbounded"/>
</xsd:sequence>
<xsd:attribute name="generated" type="xsd:dateTime"/>
</xsd:complexType>
</xsd:element>
<xsd:element name="tblFacilities">
<xsd:annotation>
<xsd:appinfo>
<od:index index-name="PrimaryKey" index-key="FacilityID " primary="yes"
  unique="yes" clustered="no"/>
<od:index index-name="FacilityPostalCode" index-key="FacilityPostalCode "
  primary="no" unique="no" clustered="no"/>
</xsd:appinfo>
</xsd:annotation>
<xsd:complexType>
<xsd:sequence>
<xsd:element name="FacilityID" minOccurs="0" od:jetType="longinteger"
  od:sqlSType="int" type="xsd:int"/>
<xsd:element name="FacilityName" minOccurs="0" od:jetType="text"
  od:sqlSType="nvarchar">
<xsd:simpleType>
<xsd:restriction base="xsd:string">
<xsd:maxLength value="50"/>
</xsd:restriction>
</xsd:simpleType>
</xsd:element>
<xsd:element name="FacilityAddress" minOccurs="0" od:jetType="text"
  od:sqlSType="nvarchar">
<xsd:simpleType>
<xsd:restriction base="xsd:string">
<xsd:maxLength value="255"/>
</xsd:restriction>
</xsd:simpleType>
</xsd:element>
<xsd:element name="FacilityCity" minOccurs="0" od:jetType="text"
  od:sqlSType="nvarchar">
<xsd:simpleType>
<xsd:restriction base="xsd:string">
<xsd:maxLength value="50"/>
</xsd:restriction>
```

```
</xsd:simpleType>
</xsd:element>
<xsd:element name="FacilityStateOrProvince" minOccurs="0" od:jetType="text"
  od:sqlSType="nvarchar">
<xsd:simpleType>
<xsd:restriction base="xsd:string">
<xsd:maxLength value="2"/>
</xsd:restriction>
</xsd:simpleType>
</xsd:element>
<xsd:element name="FacilityPostalCode" minOccurs="0" od:jetType="text"
  od:sqlSType="nvarchar">
<xsd:simpleType>
<xsd:restriction base="xsd:string">
<xsd:maxLength value="12"/>
</xsd:restriction>
</xsd:simpleType>
</xsd:element>
</xsd:sequence>
</xsd:complexType>
</xsd:element>
</xsd:schema>
```

The first line is a comment like the one found in the companion XML data file. The second line defines the beginning of the root element—the schema. The next eight lines, beginning with <xsd:element name="dataroot"> and ending with </xsd:element>, link this schema to the dataroot object defined in the tblFacilities XML file.

The tag <xsd:element name="tblFacilities"> begins the definition of the table. The information following the <xsd:appinfo> tag defines application-specific information about the structure of the table—in this case, the two indexes defined on the table. Notice that even though a desktop database (.mdb) doesn't use a clustered property, the schema definition includes this property for compatibility with SQL Server.

The tag beginning with <xsd:element name="FacilityID" contains the definition of the first field, FacilityID, and the tag specifies a data type for both the Access desktop database engine (the Microsoft JET database engine) as well as for SQL Server.

The remaining five fields are all text fields. The start tag for each field defines the JET data type (text) and the SQL Server data type (nvarchar) inside the tag. Each field start tag is then followed by tags that define the simple data type as a string as well as restrictions on the maximum length of each field. The last several lines in the schema definition are end tags that close up the last field, the sequence of fields started just before the first field definition, the complex type tag just before that, the element tag that started the table definition, and finally the end tag for the entire schema.

You can see that it's not too difficult to figure out what the schema is describing as long as you can sort out the pairs of begin and end tags. However, you probably wouldn't want to attempt to build such a schema file from scratch.

The Presentation (Layout) Document (.xsl)

As noted earlier, you can optionally include a presentation document (also called a style sheet) to describe how the table defined by the .xsd file and the data within the file included in the .xml file should be displayed. If you ask Access to also create a presentation document (*tblFacilities.xsl*) for the tblFacilities table, its contents will be as follows:

```
<?xml version="1.0"?>
<xsl:stylesheet version="1.0"
  xmlns:xsl=http://www.w3.org/1999/XSL/Transform
  xmlns:msxsl="urn:schemas-microsoft-com:xslt"
  xmlns:fx="#fx-functions" exclude-result-prefixes="msxsl fx">
<xsl:output method="html" version="4.0" indent="yes"
  xmlns:xsl="http://www.w3.org/1999/XSL/Transform"/>
<xsl:template match="//dataroot"
  xmlns:xsl="http://www.w3.org/1999/XSL/Transform">
    <html>
      <head>
        <META HTTP-EQUIV="Content-Type"
          CONTENT="text/html;charset=UTF-8"/>
        <title>tblFacilities</title>
        <style type="text/css">
        </style>
      </head>
      <body link="#0000ff" vlink="#800080">
        <table border="1" bgcolor="#ffffff" cellspacing="0"
          cellpadding="0" id="CTRL1">
        <colgroup>
          <col style="WIDTH: 0.9375in"/>
          <col style="WIDTH: 0.9375in"/>
          <col style="WIDTH: 0.9375in"/>
          <col style="WIDTH: 0.9375in"/>
          <col style="WIDTH: 0.6979in"/>
          <col style="WIDTH: 0.9375in"/>
        </colgroup>
        <tbody>
          <tr>
            <td>
              <div align="center">
                <strong>ID</strong>
              </div>
            </td>
            <td>
              <div align="center">
                <strong>Name</strong>
              </div>
            </td>
            <td>
              <div align="center">
                <strong>Address</strong>
              </div>
            </td>
            <td>
```

Chapter 28

```
    <div align="center">
      <strong>City</strong>
    </div>
  </td>
  <td>
    <div align="center">
      <strong>State</strong>
    </div>
  </td>
  <td>
    <div align="center">
      <strong>Postal Code</strong>
    </div>
  </td>
</tr>
</tbody>
<tbody id="CTRL2">
  <xsl:for-each select="tblFacilities">
    <tr>
      <td style="VERTICAL-ALIGN: top">
        <span class="" style="WIDTH: 100%;
          HEIGHT: auto; WIDTH: 100%;
          WHITE-SPACE: nowrap; TEXT-ALIGN: left">
          <xsl:value-of select="FacilityID"/>
        </span>
      </td>
      <td style="VERTICAL-ALIGN: top">
        <span class="" style="WIDTH: 100%;
          HEIGHT: auto; WIDTH: 100%;
          WHITE-SPACE: nowrap; TEXT-ALIGN: left">
          <xsl:value-of select="FacilityName"/>
        </span>
      </td>
      <td style="VERTICAL-ALIGN: top">
        <span class="" style="WIDTH: 100%;
          HEIGHT: auto; WIDTH: 100%;
          WHITE-SPACE: nowrap; TEXT-ALIGN: left">
          <xsl:value-of select="FacilityAddress"/>
        </span>
      </td>
      <td style="VERTICAL-ALIGN: top">
        <span class="" style="WIDTH: 100%;
          HEIGHT: auto; WIDTH: 100%;
          WHITE-SPACE: nowrap; TEXT-ALIGN: left">
          <xsl:value-of select="FacilityCity"/>
        </span>
      </td>
      <td style="VERTICAL-ALIGN: top">
        <span class="" style="WIDTH: 100%;
          HEIGHT: auto; WIDTH: 100%;
          WHITE-SPACE: nowrap; TEXT-ALIGN: left">
          <xsl:value-of
            select="FacilityStateOrProvince"/>
```

```
            </span>
          </td>
          <td style="VERTICAL-ALIGN: top">
            <span class="" style="WIDTH: 100%;
              HEIGHT: auto; WIDTH: 100%;
              WHITE-SPACE: nowrap; TEXT-ALIGN: left">
              <xsl:value-of select="FacilityPostalCode"/>
            </span>
          </td>
        </tr>
      </xsl:for-each>
    </tbody>
  </table>
  </body>
  </html>
  </xsl:template>
  <msxsl:script language="VBScript" implements-prefix="fx"
    xmlns:msxsl="urn:schemas-microsoft-com:xslt">
<![CDATA[
...
Standard data conversion VBScript functions included by Access
removed for brevity.
...
]]></msxsl:script>
</xsl:stylesheet>
```

Notice that the file begins with a comment and the required root element tag. The tag following the root tag specifies that the output format is HTML—ideal for a Web page. The next tag (<xsl:template) identifies the start of the template.

What follows is pure HTML—the tags you would expect to see in an HTML page to define a table layout and its headings. About two-thirds of the way into the listing, following the tags that define the column headings (ID, Name, Address, City, State, and Postal Code), you can find an <xsl:for-each tag that identifies the XML table that provides the data. This directive is followed by six blocks of <xsl:value-of directives and formatting instructions, one for each field in the table.

Following the end of the template (</xsl:template> tag), Microsoft Access includes a large amount of code written in VBScript that defines a series of data transformation functions and the VBScript equivalent of many Access built-in functions. The style sheet doesn't need most of these functions for a simple table like tblFacilities, but it might need them if you have exported the result of a query to XML and that query uses functions in expressions. As Access developers, we become spoiled by the broad range of Visual Basic functions that we can use in queries, but many simply don't exist in VBScript. So, Access must include script that emulates these functions.

The script ends, as you would expect, with an </xsl:stylesheet> end tag to terminate the stylesheet object.

The Web Package (.htm)

The final file that you can optionally create when you export to XML is an HTML (.htm) file containing the commands necessary to bring together the other three files and output standard HTML that your browser can display. This file contains VBScript that executes in the ONLOAD event of the Web page, and the script uses the Document Object Model (DOM) to convert the XML information to HTML descriptive tags. The Web package file (*tblFacilities.htm*) for the tblFacilities table is as follows:

```
<HTML xmlns:signature="urn:schemas-microsoft-com:office:access">
<HEAD>
<META HTTP-EQUIV="Content-Type" CONTENT="text/html;charset=UTF-8"/>
</HEAD>
<BODY ONLOAD="ApplyTransform()">
</BODY>
<SCRIPT LANGUAGE="VBScript">
  Option Explicit
  Function ApplyTransform()
    Dim objData, objStyle
    Set objData = CreateDOM
    LoadDOM objData, "tblFacilities.xml"
    Set objStyle = CreateDOM
    LoadDOM objStyle, "tblFacilities.xsl"
    Document.Open "text/html","replace"
    Document.Write objData.TransformNode(objStyle)
  End Function
  Function CreateDOM()
    On Error Resume Next
    Dim tmpDOM
    Set tmpDOM = Nothing
    Set tmpDOM = CreateObject("MSXML2.DOMDocument.5.0")
    If tmpDOM Is Nothing Then
      Set tmpDOM = CreateObject("MSXML2.DOMDocument.4.0")
    End If
    If tmpDOM Is Nothing Then
      Set tmpDOM = CreateObject("MSXML.DOMDocument")
    End If
    Set CreateDOM = tmpDOM
  End Function
  Function LoadDOM(objDOM, strXMLFile)
    objDOM.Async = False
    objDOM.Load strXMLFile
    If (objDOM.ParseError.ErrorCode <> 0) Then
      MsgBox objDOM.ParseError.Reason
    End If
  End Function
</SCRIPT>
</HTML>
```

Notice that the script code doesn't use the XSD file at all! It doesn't need this file because the data file (.xml) and the presentation file (.xsl) contain all the information necessary to create the Web page. The Document.Write statement is the command that actually writes the final HTML to your browser to display the table. If you open the *tblFacilities.htm* file in your browser, you'll see the result shown in Figure 28-1.

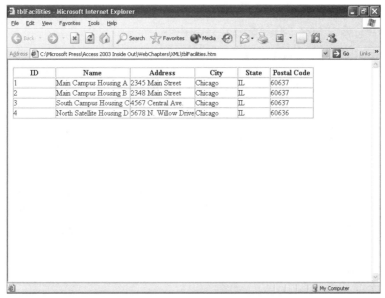

Figure 28-1. The tblFacilities.htm file displayed in Internet Explorer.

If you're using Internet Explorer, you can choose Source from the View menu to open in Notepad the final HTML generated by the script. The final HTML the browser uses looks like the HTML you found in the presentation file (.xsl) with the data merged from the data file (.xml).

For more information on the HTML and XML standards, you can visit the Web site of the World Wide Web Consortium (W3C) at *http://www.w3.org/*.

Using XML in Microsoft Access

Although Microsoft Access 2002 introduced the ability to export and import XML files, it could handle only limited XML features and could not import or export a multiple-table schema. Access 2003 not only allows you to import and export data from multiple, related tables, it also supports the exporting of forms and reports that look similar to the original object in your Access application. The new smart tag feature that you see sprinkled throughout Access 2003 also depends on XML technology.

Exporting and Importing XML from the User Interface

From the Database window of any Access desktop database (.mdb) or project file (.adp), you can export any table, query (view, function, or stored procedure in a project file), form, or report by selecting the object in the Database window and then choosing Export from the File menu. You can also import any XML file as a table by choosing Get External Data on the

Chapter 28

File menu and then choosing Import on the submenu. The following sections show you how to perform these actions.

Exporting Access Tables and Queries

You can export an entire table and any related tables; the data extracted by a query and any related data; or you can open a table or query datasheet, select several rows, and export only the selected data. If you have previously applied a filter to your table or query datasheet, you can also ask the XML export facility to apply that filter to select the data to be exported.

Let's take a look at exporting the tblFacilities table and one of its related tables in the Housing Reservations database (*Housing.mdb*). Open the database and select the tblFacilities table in the Database window. From the File menu, choose Export, and Access shows you an Export Table 'tblFacilities' To dialog box. In the Save as type drop-down list at the bottom of the window, choose XML. In this exercise, you'll export both the four records from the tblFacilities table as well as the related records from the tblFacilityRooms table, so change the file name to **tblFacilityAndRooms**. Click the Export button, and Access shows you the Export XML dialog box as shown in Figure 28-2.

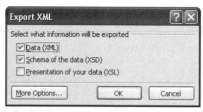

Figure 28-2. The Export XML dialog box when exporting a table.

Notice that the export XML facility assumes that you want to export both the data file (.xml) and the schema file (.xsd). If you also want to export the presentation file (.xsl) and create an HTML file that loads the data using the style sheet, check the Presentation of your data (XSL) option. If you want to quickly export your data with the default options, you can click OK to complete the export process. However, let's take a look at some of the options you can choose. Click the More Options button, and Access shows you the expanded Export XML dialog box shown in Figure 28-3.

In the expanded dialog box, you can see three tabs corresponding to the three major types of files you can choose to export. (The Presentation tab includes both the presentation file and the companion HTML file.) If you left the Data (XML) option selected in the original dialog box, you'll see the Export Data option selected on the Data tab. Notice that Access shows you the first table that it finds related to the tblFacilities table—tblFacilityRooms. Go ahead and select the box next to that table to include the related information in your XML files. You can also click the plus sign next to the table name to see other related tables that you might want to include—in this case you could expand the tree of relationships and choose tblReservations, tblReservationRequests, and even tblEmployees and tblDepartments.

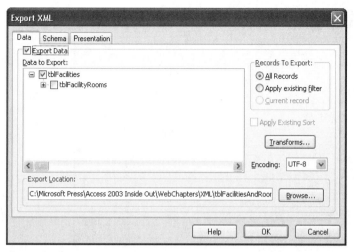

Figure 28-3. Customizing XML export options after clicking the More Options button.

In the upper right of the dialog box, you can select which records to export under Records To Export. The default is to export all records in all tables that you select. Because I previously applied a filter to tblFacilities in Datasheet view and then saved the filter, you can also see an Apply existing filter option offered. Unfortunately, Access doesn't give you any clues about the saved filter, so you would need to remember the last filter that you applied and saved with the table to take advantage of this option. There's also a dimmed option to export the current record, but you'll see that option available only when you have opened the table in Datasheet view, selected a record, and then started an export to an XML file. (You can try this on your own by opening tblFacilities in Datasheet view, selecting one record, and then choosing Export from the File menu.)

Directly under the Records To Export section, you can see a dimmed box labeled Apply Existing Sort. As you might surmise, Access would show you this option if you had previously sorted the data in the table in Datasheet view and saved the sort. Directly under the sort option is a Transforms button. If you previously saved a presentation file (.xsl) or created a presentation transform file (.xslt), you can click this button to specify the file. (Creating XSLT transformation files is beyond the scope of this book.) The export facility applies the transformation to your XML file after it completes the export.

In the Encoding box, you can choose options to export the text in UTF-8 (single-byte character set) or UTF-16 (extended character set). You should choose UTF-16 only if your data contains non-Latin characters. (English and most European languages use a Latin character set.) Finally, you can change your mind about where you want to store the resulting file and what name you want to give to the file by typing in the Export Location box or by clicking the Browse button to navigate to a new location. Click the Schema tab to see the options that you can specify for the schema file, as shown in Figure 28-4 on the next page.

Chapter 28

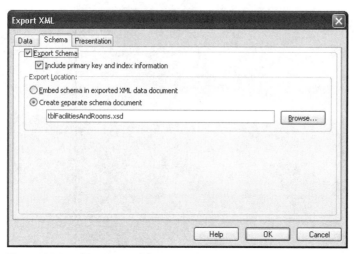

Figure 28-4. The Schema options in the Export XML dialog box.

If you selected the Schema of the data (XSD) option in the initial Export XML dialog box (Figure 28-2), you'll see the Export Schema option selected here. As you can see, you have the option to include the primary key and index definitions in your schema file. You can also choose to embed the schema inside the XML data document file, but choosing Create separate schema document (the default) gives you more flexibility. Finally, you can specify an alternate location for the schema file, but you should normally store it in the same location as the data document. On the last tab, Presentation, you can specify options for your presentation file (.xsl) as shown in Figure 28-5. (I have selected the Export Presentation option on this tab.)

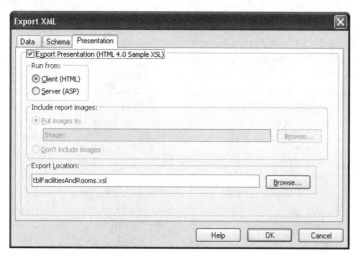

Figure 28-5. Options on the Presentation tab of the Export XML dialog box.

Notice that you have the option to create a standard HTML file (.htm) by selecting Client (HTML) or an Active Server Page file (.asp) by selecting Server (ASP). You can open an HTML file directly in your browser, but you must publish an Active Server Page to a Web server that supports dynamic pages and then request it from the server to be able to open it. Remember, however, that you're publishing your data as static XML, so neither the HTML nor the Active Server Page will fetch current data from your database or allow you to update the data in the XML file. Also, even though you have selected multiple tables on the Data tab, the Web pages will display data only from the first table. (This is a limitation of the export XML facility in Access 2003.)

As you'll see later when you ask to export a form or report to XML, Access makes the Include report images options available to allow you to include any graphics that you have used in the design of your form or report in the resulting Web page. (Yes, this option applies to forms, too!)

Click OK to complete the export. When you open the resulting *tblFacilitiesAndRooms.htm* file in your browser, it should look exactly like Figure 28-1, but if you open the XML file, you'll see that Access has included the data for both tables. You can find the sample files saved on the companion CD as *tblFacilitiesAndRoomsXmpl.htm, .xml, .xsd, and .xsl*.

> **Tip** If you're running Windows XP Professional and have installed and started Internet Information Services, you can export your data as an Active Server Page to your server folders (usually C:\Inetpub\wwwroot) by choosing Server in the Run from option on the Presentation tab. Be sure to export the XML, XSD, and XSL files to the same Web folder as the Active Server Page. You can then view the resulting Active Server Page by opening your browser and asking it to display the address:
>
> *http://localhost/tblFacilitiesAndRooms.asp*

Exporting Access Forms and Reports

A useful feature in Access is the ability to create Web pages from your Access forms and reports. Unlike when you export the data from a table or query to create a simple formatted Web page, you can export the data behind a form or report and create a special presentation file that emulates the look of the original object in Access. To do this, Access creates a special version of the XSL file using an extension to the language called ReportML. This language extension includes special tags to support form and report formatting, and you can open these files only in a browser that supports the version of VBScript and the Document Object Model (DOM) that understands them (such as Internet Explorer version 6 and later).

You might find this feature useful to produce Web reports that look similar to the design of the original object. To update the data periodically, all you need do is replace the XML file containing the data used by the Web page. The one drawback to this process is you can only export forms and reports that do not include subforms or subreports. Although Access will let you export a form that has one or more subforms, it will export and format only the data shown in the outer form.

Let's take a look at a simple form in the Housing Reservations application (*Housing.mdb*) that exports nicely as XML. Open the database and select the *frmDepartments* form in the Database window. Choose Export from the File menu, and choose XML in the Save as type drop-down list. Click Export to start the process.

In the initial Export XML dialog box (shown in Figure 28-2 previously), you'll see the option to export the data selected. Because you want to see the data formatted similar to the form, also make sure that Schema of the data (XSD) and Presentation of your data (XSL) are selected and then click the More Options button to look at the options you can customize. Figure 28-6 shows you the options on the Data tab.

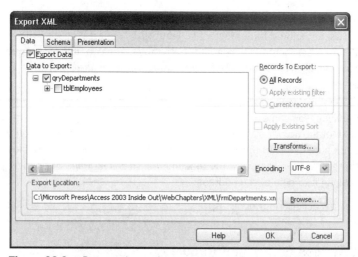

Figure 28-6. Data options when exporting a form as XML.

Notice that Access gives you the option to include additional related tables, but keep in mind that you'll see only the first table in the resulting Web page. If you opened the form in Form view first, Access would also offer you the option to export the current record only.

The options on the Schema tab are exactly as you saw earlier when exporting a table (Figure 28-4). Click the Presentation tab to see additional options related to exporting a form, as shown in Figure 28-7.

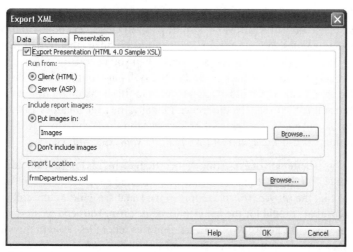

Figure 28-7. The options on the Presentation tab when exporting a form as XML.

Notice that Access now gives you the option to export any images. I created the original form using the Form Wizard and chose the Sumi Painting format, which applies a gray pattern bitmap to the form background. If you want the resulting Web page to include the background, you should leave the Put images in option selected. Click OK to export the form and its data. When you open the HTML file, it should look like Figure 28-8.

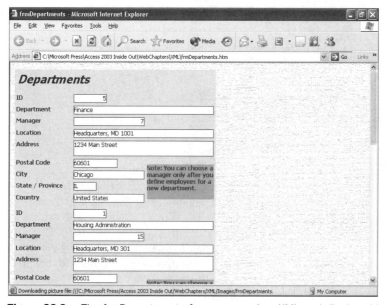

Figure 28-8. The frmDepartments form exported as XML and displayed in a Web page.

Notice that the ReportML style specification does a fairly good job of copying the fonts and styles from the original form. However, it also displays all labels, text boxes, combo boxes, and list boxes that you designed on the form, including a hidden label. When you open the form in the application, that label is revealed only when you're creating a new department. Also, the form background is the background of the Web page, but it doesn't display behind the actual form area. (The screen illustration printed in this book might not make that obvious—open the sample file to see the difference.) Finally, the page includes all the records strung back-to-back. You can find this set of files saved in the WebChapters\XML subfolder on the companion CD as *frmDepartmentsXmpl.htm, .xml, .xsd, and .xsl.*

I think Access does a better job of exporting reports than forms (as long as they don't have subreports) into an HTML/XML result that looks very much like the original. You can try this yourself by selecting the *rptDepartments* report in the Database window and following the same export steps that you did for the frmDepartments form. Your end result displayed in a Web page should look like Figure 28-9. You can find this set of files saved in the WebChapters\XML subfolder on the companion CD as *rptDepartmentsXmpl.htm, .xml, .xsd, and .xsl.*

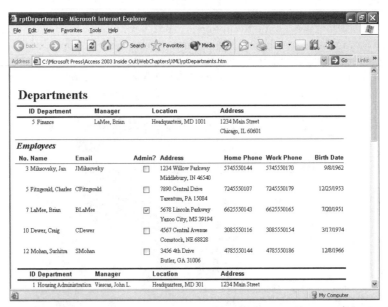

Figure 28-9. The rptDepartments report in the Housing Reservations database exported as XML and displayed in a Web page.

The result looks remarkably like the original. To make it look perfectly the same, you would need to dig into the presentation file and fix the display specifications for the phone numbers and the birth date.

For more information about working with XML and XSL files, see *Microsoft Office FrontPage 2003 Inside Out* (Microsoft Press, 2003).

Importing XML Files

As you learned in Chapter 6, "Importing and Linking Data," you can import or link many types of database files and text and spreadsheet files into your Access database. In Access 2003, you can also import XML files, but you cannot link to them. Access 2003 also supports XML files that contain multiple tables. When you import XML that includes multiple tables, Access creates one table in your database for each table it finds in the file.

To begin importing an XML file, select the Database window and then choose Get External Data on the File menu. Select Import on the submenu to see the Import dialog box shown in Figure 28-10.

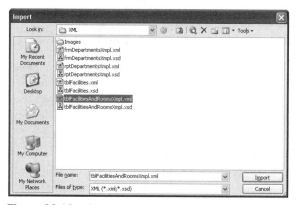

Figure 28-10. Importing an XML file into Microsoft Access.

Choose XML (*.xml, *.xsd) in the Files of type drop-down list and select the file that you want to import. In this case, let's pick the sample XML file that includes data from both the tblFacilities table and the tblRooms table (*tblFacilitiesAndRoomsXmpl.xml*). Click Import to start the process, and Access displays the Import XML dialog box as shown in Figure 28-11 on the next page. (I clicked the Options button to show you the Import Options section at the bottom of the dialog box.)

Note If you ask Access to import an XSD file, Access creates a table with the specified data structure but does not import the data. Remember, the data is in the XML file; the XSD file contains only the schema definition.

Chapter 28

Figure 28-11. Selecting options in the Import XML dialog box.

When you first see this dialog box, Access shows you the tables it found in the XML file. You can click the plus sign next to any table name to verify the field names. You can click the Transform button to specify any XSLT file that you need in order to convert the data into a format that Access can use. This file originally came from Access, so you don't need to apply any transformation.

You can also click the Options button (as shown in Figure 28-11) to select options to import the structure only (from the XSD file or embedded schema in the XML file) or the structure and the data (the default), or append the data to existing tables of the same name. In this case, you know that the Housing Reservations database already contains these tables, so attempting to append the data will result in duplicate primary key value errors. So, leave the default Structure and Data option selected and click OK to import the data.

Because the two tables already exist in the database, Access appends a number to the name of the tables it is importing from the XML file to avoid duplicate names. You can see the two new tables (tblFacilities1 and tblFacilityRooms1) in the Database window and one of them (tblFacilities1) opened in Design view in Figure 28-12. Notice that the new table correctly includes the primary key definition, but other properties such as Caption aren't preserved in the XML file.

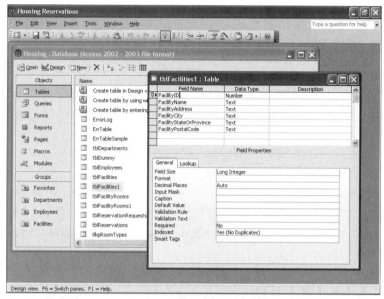

Figure 28-12. Two tables imported into Access from an XML file.

Importing and Exporting XML in Visual Basic

Importing and exporting XML from the user interface works well for simple one-time tasks, but what if you need to automate the process to make it easy for users of your application to work with XML data? You took a brief look at the example frmXMLExample form in Chapter 25, "Publishing Data on the Web." Now let's look behind the form to understand the code that automates importing and exporting XML data.

Access 2003 provides two methods of the Application object—ImportXML and ExportXML—that enable you to deal with XML files in Visual Basic code. The syntax for the ImportXML command is as follows:

```
[Application.]ImportXML <data source file> [, <import option> ]
```

where *<data source file>* is the path and file name of the file you want to import and *<import option>* is acAppendData, acStructureAndData (the default), or acStructureOnly. Notice that the three options match the options you saw in the Import XML dialog box in Figure 28-11. If the table(s) in the file you want to import already exist, Access appends a numeric digit to the table name(s).

The syntax for the ExportXML command is as follows:

```
[Application.]ExportXML <object type>, <object name>, [ <data file> ],
  [ <schema file> ], [ <presentation file> ], [ <image path> ], [ <encoding> ],
  [ <options> ], [ <filter> ], [ <additional data object> ]
```

<object type> is acExportForm, acExportFunction, acExportQuery, acExportReport, acExportServerView, acExportStoredProcedure, or acExportTable.

<object name> is the name of the object that you want to export.

<data file> is the path and file name of the XML file you want to create. If the file already exists, ExportXML overwrites it.

<schema file> is the path and file name of the XSD file you want to create. If the file already exists, ExportXML overwrites it.

<presentation file> is the path and file name of the XSL file you want to create. If the file already exists, ExportXML overwrites it.

Note that although all the export file names (data, schema, and presentation) are optional, you must specify at least one of them.

<image path> is the folder path where you want to store any images when exporting a form or report.

<encoding> is acUTF16 or acUTF8 (the default).

<options> are one or more options that you can add together using a plus sign operator (+). The options are as follows:

Option Intrinsic Constant	Description
acEmbedSchema	Embeds the schema within the XML data file. When you include the option, ExportXML ignores any <schema file> specification.
acExcludePrimaryKeyAndIndexes	Does not include the primary key or index definitions in the schema data.
acLiveReportSource	When <object type> is acExportFunction, acExportServerView, or acExportStoredProcedure, creates a link to your SQL Server 2000 database.
acPersistReportML	When the <object type> is acExportForm or acExportReport, includes ReportML code in the presentation file.
acRunFromServer	Creates an Active Server Page file instead of an HTML file when you ask for a <data file> and <presentation file>.

<filter> is a criteria string to filter the records to be exported.

<additional data object> is an object of the AdditionalData data type that you can create by executing the CreateAdditionalData method of the Application object. You specify an additional table name by executing the Add method of the object and supplying the table name as a string.

In the Housing Reservations database (*Housing.mdb*), the frmXMLExample form demonstrates how you might import an XML file and load it into a form for editing, and then export the file when you have finished making changes. Figure 28-13 shows you the form opened in Form view.

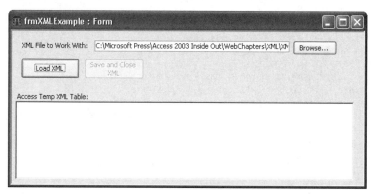

Figure 28-13. A sample form that imports XML data, lets you edit the data, and then exports the data when you have finished making your changes.

The form is designed to initially point to a sample XML file that you can find on the companion CD in the WebChapters\XML subfolder—*xmlDepartments.xml*. You can click the Browse button to point to any XML file, but you should not use any of the other sample XML files that you find in the subfolder because these are all named the same as objects that already exist in the database. Also, the code depends on the name of the file matching the name of the table defined inside the file. Click the Load XML button to import the file and display the data in the Access Temp XML Table window as shown in Figure 28-14.

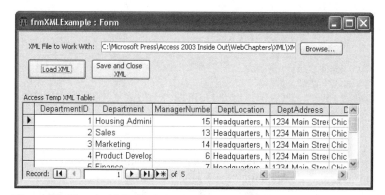

Figure 28-14. An XML file is loaded into a window in the form so that you can edit the data.

The data is actually a copy of the data you can find in the tblDepartments table. You can type in any field to change the values, just like you can in a subform datasheet that's bound to a live table in your database. To save your changes, click the Save and Close XML button to export the changed data back to the original XML file. When you load the XML file again, you should see your changes.

To understand how this works, you need to examine the code behind the Load and Save command buttons. Here's the code from the Load procedure:

```
Private Sub cmdLoadXML_Click()
' New table name created from imported XML document
Dim strTableName As String
  ' Turn off screen updates
  Application.Echo False, "Importing XML..."
  ' Turn on error handling
  On Error GoTo cmdLoadXML_Err
  ' Get the table name to be from the XML document name
  ' Note, this will only work if you name the file
  ' the same name as the table inside the XML file.
  strTableName = Mid(Me.txtXMLDocument, InStrRev(Me.txtXMLDocument, "\") + 1)
  strTableName = Left(strTableName, Len(strTableName) - 4)
  ' Change Error Handling to skip if the next gets an error
  On Error Resume Next
  ' Delete the old XML table, if it exists
  DoCmd.DeleteObject acTable, strTableName
  ' Turn error handling back on
  On Error GoTo cmdLoadXML_Err
  ' Import the XML document
  Application.ImportXML Me.txtXMLDocument, acStructureAndData
  ' Set the subform source object property to the table just imported.
  Me.subXML.SourceObject = "Table." & strTableName
  ' Enable the SaveXML button to let them save the XML
  Me.cmdSaveXML.Enabled = True
  ' Indicate XML is loaded
  intXMLLoaded = True
  ' Turn screen updating back on.
  Application.Echo True
  ' Exit the routine
  Exit Sub
' Error handling routine
cmdLoadXML_Err:
  ' Turn screen updating back on.
  Application.Echo True
  ' Tell the user the problem
  MsgBox "An error has occurred importing the XML: " & Err.Description
  ' Exit the routine
  Exit Sub
End Sub
```

As noted earlier, this code depends on the table name inside the XML file to match the name of the file. (You could also open the XML file or the XSD file as text and scan for the table name tag.) The ImportXML command is very straightforward. The code takes advantage of the fact that you can specify a table in the SourceObject property of a subform control to display the imported table.

The code behind the Save button is as follows:

```
Private Sub cmdSaveXML_Click()
Dim strTableName As String
```

```
' Get the table name to be from the XML document name
' Note, this will only work if you name the file
' the same name as the table inside
strTableName = Mid(Me.txtXMLDocument, InStrRev(Me.txtXMLDocument, "\") + 1)
strTableName = Left(strTableName, Len(strTableName) - 4)
' Export the table back out to the XML document
Application.ExportXML acExportTable, strTableName, _
  Me.txtXMLDocument, _
  Left(Me.txtXMLDocument, Len(Me.txtXMLDocument) - 4) & ".xsd"
' Clean up by resetting the sourceobject of the subform to "".
Me.subXML.SourceObject = ""
' Delete the XML table
DoCmd.DeleteObject acTable, strTableName
' Point the focus off the cmdSaveXML button
Me.cmdLoadXML.SetFocus
' Disable the cmdSaveXML button
Me.cmdSaveXML.Enabled = False
' Turn of XML Loaded flag
intXMLLoaded = False
End Sub
```

Notice that the ExportXML command also rewrites the schema file, but that's probably not necessary. The code also clears the subform by setting its SourceObject property to an empty string. It must do this so that it can delete the temporary table object—if the object were still open in the subform control, Access wouldn't allow the DeleteObject command.

As you can see, Access 2003 provides extensive features to work with XML files in your database applications. You not only can import and export XML files and export some forms and reports from the user interface but also can import and export XML from Visual Basic procedures.

Working with SharePoint

SharePoint is a new set of Web-based technologies from Microsoft that enables companies to create a central repository of many types of information that can be viewed and updated by authorized users. SharePoint Team Services runs on a Windows 2003 server and uses Microsoft SQL Server to store and manage the shared data. You can often tell how good a product is by looking at whether the company that built it actually uses it. Microsoft currently has more than 80,000 SharePoint sites set up for its own product teams, so SharePoint is an excellent product indeed.

Any company that needs a way to improve team collaboration should find SharePoint very useful. With a SharePoint Web site, you can

- Provide a central location for collaborating on documents created using Microsoft Office applications.
- Create separate workspaces for different teams.
- Assign users to different groups, allowing some to only view shared data, permitting others to modify and contribute shared data, and allowing a few to customize the design of their own or shared sites.

Chapter 28

● Customize a shared site using off-the-shelf *Web Parts* included as part of the SharePoint product. These Web Parts include:

- Announcements that can be posted by the team leaders
- Contact lists
- Content from another Web page or file embedded within the main page
- Event and issue tracking and task assignment
- Online discussion board
- Links to other pages or Web sites
- Team membership list
- Shared document sublibrary
- Online survey

Web Parts are a particularly powerful feature in SharePoint. If you are a member of a group that has design permission on the team site, you can customize the Web pages presented by SharePoint by choosing the components you want, telling SharePoint where you want the component to appear on the page, and customizing the component by setting its properties. You can also apply one of dozens of themes to the team site to give it a customized look. These features are not unlike designing a form or a data access page within Access, but you perform your design work directly within your browser.

In the process of writing this book, Microsoft allowed me to access a test SharePoint site so that I could test and demonstrate how Access and SharePoint can work together. Figure 28-15 shows the home page of my team site before I modified it.

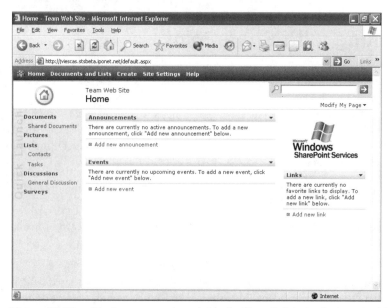

Figure 28-15. The home page template of a SharePoint site before applying any customization.

To give you a sense of the power and ease of using Web Parts, I took about five minutes to customize my test site, including adding a logo, applying a theme, inserting a live weather report on my home town, creating a link to my company home page, and posting an announcement about the publication of this book. You can see the result in Figure 28-16.

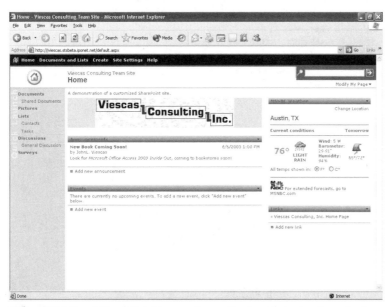

Figure 28-16. A SharePoint team site customized in just a few minutes.

I certainly could have had a lot more fun clicking the Create, Site Settings, and Modify My Page links to customize my test SharePoint site, but my focus was on discovering the ways to use SharePoint with Microsoft Access. The remainder of this chapter shows you how you can store some of your application tables on a SharePoint server and import or link to tables (called lists in SharePoint) managed by SharePoint.

Using SharePoint from Access

As noted earlier in the sections discussing XML, you can import and export XML files from Access, but you cannot link to them. Although SharePoint uses XML technology to store its lists, you can, in fact, link a SharePoint list into Access as a table that you can use in your Access desktop application. The following sections show you how to perform all three tasks from an Access desktop database—import, export, and link.

Exporting Data to SharePoint

You can actually store your Access data on a SharePoint server and then link it back into your desktop application. Before you can do that, you must export the table to SharePoint. Open the database containing the table you want to export (for this example, the Housing Reservations database—*Housing.mdb*), and select in the Database window the table you want to export. In this case, I selected the tblDepartments table. Select Export from the File menu. In the Export Table dialog box, choose SharePoint Team Services in the Save as type drop-down list. Access displays the Export SharePoint Team Services Wizard, as shown in Figure 28-17.

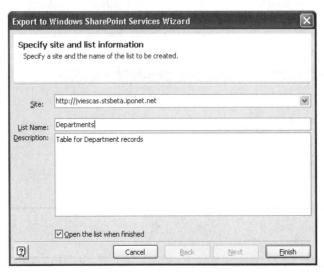

Figure 28-17. The Export SharePoint Team Services Wizard.

In the Site box, you must enter the Web address of your SharePoint team site. You can change the name of the list to be stored on your SharePoint server (the default is the name of the table), and you can enter a description (the wizard fetches the Description property of the table for you). You can also ask the wizard to go to your SharePoint team site and open the list after the export completes. In this example, I changed the list name to Departments and clicked Finish to export the table.

Note If you point to a Web address that isn't a SharePoint team site, you'll receive an error when you click Finish.

If you're not currently logged on to your SharePoint team site, you'll see a standard Web site login dialog box where you must enter your user name and password and click OK. When the export wizard finishes, it opens a dialog box to let you know it's done—click OK to dismiss the dialog box. If you selected the Open the list when finished option, you'll see your exported list on your team site as shown in Figure 28-18.

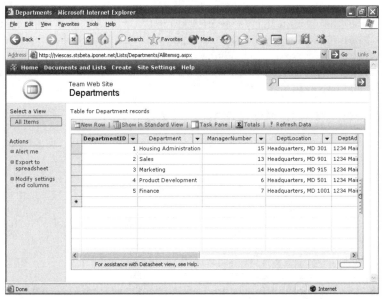

Figure 28-18. An Access table exported as a list to a SharePoint site.

You now have a copy of the data from your table available on your team site that you can share with other users. You can click the Modify settings and columns link on the left to perform tasks such as customizing the list, creating views of the list (a subset of rows or columns), setting permissions indicating which groups or members of your team can access the list, and deleting the list.

Importing a List from SharePoint

To import a SharePoint list as a table from within Access, open the database to which you want to import the list, and from the Database window, choose Get External Data from the File menu and then choose Import on the submenu. In the Import dialog box, choose Share-Point Team Services in the Files of type drop-down list, and Access displays the Import SharePoint Team Services Wizard as shown in Figure 28-19.

Figure 28-19. The first screen in the Import SharePoint Team Services Wizard.

Access remembers the team sites that you have previously used to import, export, or link data. If you see the team site that you want, select it. If you need to go to a different site, enter its Web address in the Site box. Click Next to go to the next screen where you can select the list you want to import, as shown in Figure 28-20. Note that if you're not currently logged on to the team site, you'll see a standard Web site login dialog box where you must enter your user name and password and click OK.

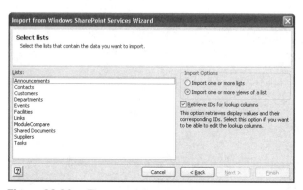

Figure 28-20. The second screen in the Import SharePoint Team Services Wizard.

Under Lists, the wizard shows you all the lists on your team site that you have permission to access. Click the list name you want to import to select it. If you want to see all the available views of a list, leave the Import one or more views of a list option selected. If you want to import an entire list and any related lists, select the Import one or more lists option. If you think a list has one or more related lookup lists, leave the Retrieve IDs for lookup columns option selected so that you fetch the actual ID value instead of the lookup value. For example, if an Orders list is related to a Customers list, selecting this option fetches the Customer ID instead of the customer name that might be defined in a lookup.

In this case, I know that a view of the Suppliers list is available (actually the Suppliers table from the Northwind sample database that comes with Access) that shows only the suppliers in the United States. Perhaps the housing manager wants a list of food suppliers to provide items for a happy hour in each of the facilities. I can select the Suppliers table and click Next to see the screen shown in Figure 28-21.

Figure 28-21. The list of available views on the Suppliers list.

Sure enough, there's the view that shows suppliers in the USA. After I select it and click Next, the import wizard shows me a final confirmation screen with the lists or views I'm importing and links to any related lists. When I click Finish, the wizard imports the view that I selected. You can see the imported table in Datasheet view in Figure 28-22. Notice that the import preserved the primary key as an AutoNumber, just like the original table. Looks like the housing manager will be serving crawdads and beer for happy hour!

ID	SupplierID	CompanyName	ContactName	ContactTitle	Address	City	Regi
2	2	New Orleans Cajun Delights	Shelley Burke	Order Administrator	P.O. Box 78934	New Orleans	LA
3	3	Grandma Kelly's	Regina Murphy	Sales Representative	707 Oxford Rd.	Ann Arbor	MI
16	16	Bigfoot Breweries	Cheryl Saylor	Regional Account Rep.	3400 - 8th Avenue	Bend	OR
19	19	New England Seafood	Robb Merchant	Wholesale Account Agent	Order Processing	Boston	MA
(AutoNumber)							

Figure 28-22. A view of a SharePoint list imported as an Access table.

Linking a SharePoint List into Access

From an Access desktop database (.mdb), you can also link to a list managed by SharePoint. When you do this, any change you make to the table in your Access application is also saved in the SharePoint list. If you have exported an Access table to SharePoint and then linked it back, this allows both your desktop application users and authorized members of your SharePoint team to work with and update the same data.

Linking a SharePoint list is similar to importing a list. From the Database window in the database where you want to link the list, choose Get External Data from the File menu. Choose Link Tables on the submenu and then choose SharePoint Team Services in the Files of type drop-down list in the Link dialog box. Access displays the Link SharePoint Team Services Wizard as shown in Figure 28-23.

Figure 28-23. Linking a SharePoint list as an Access table.

Chapter 28

Select or enter the server address you want and click Next. The wizard shows you a screen where you can select the list you want to link, with the same options as shown earlier in Figure 28-20. Choose the list you want to link and click Next to see options similar to Figure 28-21. If you asked to see any views of the list, the wizard shows you the available views. All lists have an All Items view, so that's usually the one you want to select. After choosing the view, click Next, and the wizard shows you a confirmation screen. Click Finish to link the list as a table in Access. In this case, I decided to link the Departments list that I exported earlier. You can see the table in the Database window, as shown in Figure 28-24.

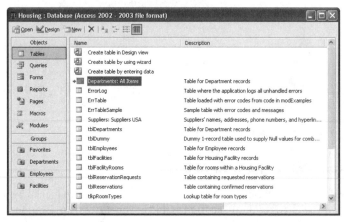

Figure 28-24. A SharePoint list linked as a table in Access.

I can use this list just like the original table in my application. Note, however, that SharePoint doesn't enforce referential integrity. If you use SharePoint lists as the tables in your application, your application must perform additional checks to ensure, for example, that an employee isn't assigned to a nonexistent department. Also, using data from a SharePoint list as a linked table in Access requires a high-speed Internet connection or local area connection to your intranet server. Performance will be poor over a dial-up connection.

Using Access from SharePoint

From your SharePoint team site, you can also export or link a list to an Access database. Interestingly, you cannot import an Access table—you must export the table from your Access database.

Exporting a List to an Access Database

When you want to export a list to an Access database, you must first open the list on your team site. If you modified the settings of your list so that it appears on the Quick Launch bar of your team home page (the list on the left in Figure 28-15), you can open it from there. Otherwise, click the lists link to see all your available lists. When you have the list open, click the Task Pane link to open the task pane on the right, as shown in Figure 28-25. Scroll down in the pane to see the Office links area, which shows you the options you have in various Office products.

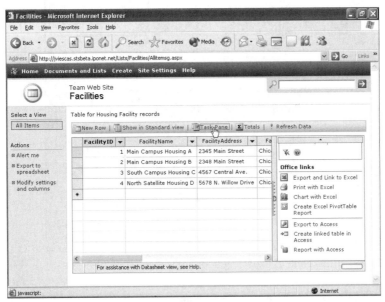

Figure 28-25. Displaying options to work with Office products in the task pane of a SharePoint list.

Notice that SharePoint shows you three options for Microsoft Access. If you click the Export to Access option, SharePoint changes the task pane to show you options to export the list to an existing database or to a new database. Pick the option you want, and click OK to continue. If you choose to export to a new database, SharePoint starts a copy of Microsoft Access on your machine and opens the New File dialog box in which you can select the location of your database and give it a name. If you choose an existing database, SharePoint starts Access and shows you an Open dialog box in which you can select the database you want to receive the list. In both cases, after the database is open, you'll see a Connect To dialog box in which you should enter your user name and password so that this copy of Access can link back to your SharePoint team site. After you log in, Access completes the export. (SharePoint actually sends a command to Access to *import* the list as a table.) I chose to export the Facilities list to a new database, and you can see the result in Figure 28-26 on the next page.

Chapter 28

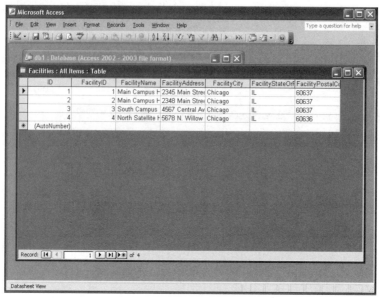

Figure 28-26. The result of exporting a list from SharePoint to Access.

Link a List into an Access Database

You can also initiate linking a list as a table into an Access desktop database from your Share-Point team site. (You cannot link a list into an Access project file.) The process is similar to exporting a list. Open the list and then open the task pane. Click the Create linked table in Access option, and then choose to link to an existing database or a new one. After you choose the database, SharePoint opens a copy of Access on your machine, and then Access asks you for your user name and password to link back to your team site. As with exporting a list, SharePoint actually sends a command to Access to link the list. When the link is complete, you should see the linked table in your Access database.

Create an Access Report on a SharePoint List

The last option, Report with Access, links the list into the Access database you choose and then commands Access to create an AutoReport on the new linked table. You follow the same steps as for exporting or linking a list, but you end up with a report. You can see the result in Figure 28-27.

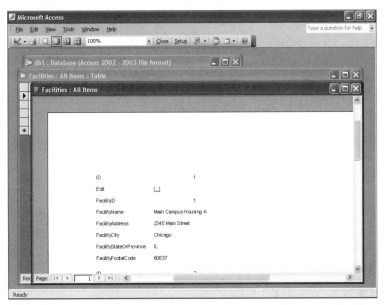

Figure 28-27. The result of choosing the Report with Access option from your SharePoint team site.

> **Caution** You cannot use any of the Access options in SharePoint with a database that has startup properties defined that open a form when you open the database. (Both the Contact Tracking and Housing Reservations sample applications have a startup form.) The startup form interferes with the commands that the SharePoint site sends to Access to export or link a list and to create a report.

Access doesn't save the report until you close the Report window and give the report a name. I recommend that you export or link the list on which you want to create a report as an Access table and then use the standard Access report design features to produce something more useful.

You should now have a good grasp of the technologies included in Microsoft Office Access 2003 to integrate with the Web. In the last part of this book, you'll learn about additional features you can use after you've finished designing your database application.

Chapter 28

1129

Part 7

After Completing Your Application

Upsizing a Desktop Application to a Project

"Some are born great, some achieve greatness, and some have greatness thrust upon 'em."[1]

You might decide from the very beginning that your application needs to be shared by many users and needs the resources of SQL Server to run correctly, so you plan to design your application using an Access .adp project file linked to an SQL Server database. If that's the case, then you don't need to read this chapter. You can read about creating an Access project file in Part 4, "Designing an Access Project."

It's more likely, however, that you built an application in an Access .mdb desktop database, perhaps even designed with client/server in mind, and now for performance or other reasons you have decided that it's time to convert it to a project file. Or, perhaps you built a great little application in a desktop database, discovered that others want to use your application, and now are looking for somewhere to turn because your application has become so popular that a desktop database structure can no longer support it.

In this chapter, you'll learn

- The benefits of using the client/server architecture.
- When you should consider upsizing to an Access project file linked to an SQL Server database.
- Strategies for upsizing an Access desktop database (.mdb).
- Changes you must or should make to your desktop database before attempting to upsize.
- How to use the Upsizing Wizard.
- How to fix your new upsized project file and the queries created by the wizard so that your application will compile and run properly.

---

1. Shakespeare, William. *Twelfth Night*, Act II, Scene V. circa 1601.

Note This chapter assumes that you have installed the Microsoft SQL Server Data Engine (MSDE) on your local machine or have access to an SQL Server 2000 or later server with permission to create databases. See the Appendix, "Installing Microsoft Office," for information on installing MSDE. This chapter uses the *Contacts.mdb*, *Contacts2Upsize.mdb*, and *Contacts.adp* sample files that you can find on your companion CD. You must also install the *Contacts.mdf* SQL Server database file on your server. See the Inside Out tip, "Additional steps you must take to be able to work with the sample project file," on page 638.

Benefits of the Client/Server Architecture

Most large-scale databases are built as client/server applications. They might be deployed over the Internet using a Web interface, or they might be deployed over a business intranet using a Visual Studio or Access Project interface. The key is that they rely on a robust database server as their backbone. Database servers (such as Microsoft SQL Server) are designed to handle many information requests at a time and also include many features to protect the data as well as to enforce strict security.

As your user base and your database size continue to grow, a client/server application that uses SQL Server will be able to scale and continue to effectively serve your users' needs. Because your application uses SQL Server, it will be able to take advantage of a number of features to reliably ensure the safety and security of your data. Let's take a look at some of the key advantages that SQL Server and the client/server architecture have over a desktop or file-server application:

- **It's always on.** SQL Server has the ability to update and run backups dynamically. You never need to have users exit the application for maintenance.

- **It's upgradeable.** Because SQL Server usually resides on its own server computer, you can upgrade and improve the server hardware to improve your database size and speed without having to make any changes to your client machines.

- **It's more secure.** SQL Server has the ability to integrate directly with a Windows NT–based platform. This makes it easier for you because you can use Windows security to control permissions in your database. It makes it harder for would-be hackers to attack it because they have to break into the entire Windows network instead of just a single database file.

- **It's faster.** Shared Access desktop databases deliver only data. The query processing is still done locally in each user's application. This can create a lot of unnecessary network traffic. SQL Server stores and processes all queries on the server and returns only the requested result information. With multiple users, this method is much faster.

- **It's more stable.** SQL Server logs transactions for all updates that it makes. This way, if one portion of an update fails, SQL Server can roll back the transaction and return the data to its original state. Data corruption or loss is much more unlikely.

- **It's more powerful.** SQL Server features a very rich dialect of SQL called Transact-SQL. Along with using other SQL features, you can use Transact-SQL to create powerful queries, functions, and rules that will ensure a consistent environment and secure access for each of your users.

Chapter 29

> **Note** You can use Access 2003 to upsize to any version of SQL Server 6.5 or later. However, you will get the best results if you upsize to SQL Server 2000 or later. This chapter assumes that you are upsizing to SQL Server 2000 or later. If you do not have access to a recent version of SQL Server, consider installing the Microsoft SQL Server Desktop Engine (MSDE) that is included with Microsoft Office 2003 on your desktop machine. See the Appendix for details about installing MSDE.

If you have decided to upsize your database to an Access project, you can do so "by hand" or by using a wizard, but in either case you first need to prepare your existing database for upsizing. You must consider the numerous differences between a desktop database and an Access project, especially in tables and queries.

> **Note** The sections in this chapter assume you are already familiar with database design in an Access desktop database as well as in an Access project. Refer to the previous chapters in this book for further information on designing and building the components discussed in this chapter.

Deciding When to Upsize

If only one person is using your desktop database, you typically won't need to upsize the database unless it's getting very large (greater than 500 MB). You're more likely to need to upsize when you have multiple users sharing the application. If you originally placed the entire database (tables, queries, forms, reports, macros, and modules) on a network share for two or three users, and you now have additional users that need to run the application, or you're experiencing performance or corruption problems, you should first consider splitting the database. You can greatly improve performance and reduce corruption problems by placing all the tables in one desktop database file on a file server share and giving each user a copy of a desktop database that uses linked tables to the shared file and that contains all your queries, forms, reports, macros, and modules. You can read more about how to split a desktop database in Chapter 31, "Distributing Your Application."

If you have already split your database, you should consider upsizing if any of the following become true:

- You need to make the application available to more users soon, and the number of simultaneous users will exceed 20.
- The amount of data is growing and has or will soon exceed 100 MB.
- Users are complaining about slow performance that you can't fix by adjusting the application design.
- You begin experiencing frequent corruptions in the shared data file that force you to take the application offline and repair the file.
- You need to add data and functionality to the application that need to be secured. (Although you can secure a desktop database, you can't achieve truly reliable security unless you're using SQL Server. See Chapter 30, "Securing Your Database," for details.)

- You have added (or are considering adding) mission-critical tasks to the application, and consequently the application cannot be unavailable for more than very short periods of time.

- Although you are backing up the shared data file every night, the volume of work that it supports has risen to the point that your organization cannot afford to re-input an entire day's work if the data file becomes hopelessly corrupted.

Of course, you should consider the items in the preceding list based on your own experience with how well the application runs and the requirements of your users. Some shared desktop database applications run just fine with 50 or more users. Others continue to work well even when the amount of data exceeds 100 MB. The real secret is making the decision while you can still "achieve greatness" rather than waiting until the situation is so bad that you have "greatness thrust upon you."

 Inside Out

Is your desktop application designed for a client/server architecture?

When you build a desktop database application, it's all too easy to design forms and reports that always display all records from your tables when the user opens them. It's also tempting to create combo boxes or list boxes that display all available values from a lookup table. These issues have little to no impact when you're the only user of the application or you share your application with only a few other users. However, fetching all rows by default can have serious performance implications when you have multiple users that need to share a large amount of data over a network.

A successful client/server application fetches only the records required for the task at hand. You can design an application so that it never (or almost never) opens a form to edit data or a report to display data without first asking the user to specify the records needed for the task at hand. For example, the LawTrack Contacts application opens a list of available companies, contacts, or invoices from which the user can choose only the desired records. This application also offers a custom query-by-form search to filter specific records based on the criteria the user enters.

You can also design the application so that it uses information about the current user to filter records. For example, the Housing Reservations database always filters employee and reservations data to display information only for the currently signed-on employee. When a department manager is signed on, the application shows data only for the current manager's department.

Even so, the two main sample applications aren't perfect examples. Both applications use a ZIP code table that contains more than 50,000 records to help users enter valid address data, and this huge table is the row source for several combo boxes. In the desktop database version, each user has a local copy of the ZIP code table, so the performance impact is minimal. When I upsized the application to a project file (.adp) and SQL Server tables, I should have changed this design to use a text box for the postal code and then written additional code behind the form to perform a single-row lookup into this table on the server to fetch the related city, county, and state information. You'll learn later in this chapter how to do that.

> The bottom line is you should take a look at the way your desktop application fetches data for the user. If it fetches all records all the time, it's probably not a good candidate for upsizing to a client/server application until you redesign it.

Deciding on a Strategy

Of course, the most work-intensive strategy is to simply start over and design your application from scratch using an Access project file connected to a new SQL Server database. Even if you choose this strategy, you still might want to start with the original table design from your desktop database, particularly if the design is sound.

You can also choose to create a new project file and SQL Server database, and then import all the tables, forms, reports, macros, and modules from your desktop application. Notice that I didn't include queries in the list of objects—you'll have to build those "by hand" because you cannot import queries from a desktop database into an Access project file.

Finally, you can elect to use the Upsizing Wizard to create a new project file and a new SQL Server database. This process isn't perfect, but it does have the advantage of preserving as much as possible of your table indexes, validation rules, and relationships. It also gives you a jump-start on converting all the queries from your old desktop application.

Upsizing Using the Import Facility

If you want to start from scratch but preserve your existing desktop database table design, you can follow the instructions in Chapter 17, "Building Tables in an Access Project," to create your new project file and SQL Server database. You can then choose Get External Data from the File menu and then choose Import on the submenu to locate your desktop database to import the tables. You can choose to import only the table structure or the structure and the data. However, the import process won't bring across any indexes, validation rules, or relationships. You also cannot import any of the queries from your old application. Note that you're actually importing the tables into the SQL Server database to which your project file is connected.

You can use this same Import facility to copy your forms, reports, macros, and modules into a new project file. (See Chapter 6, "Importing and Linking Data," for details about importing Access objects from another database.) The import process doesn't make any attempt, however, to identify and validate the record source of your forms and reports or the row source of your combo boxes and list boxes.

Before you can work with your forms and reports that use queries, you'll have to rebuild the queries one at a time using the query design facility in your project file—you cannot import queries into a project file from a desktop database. If your original desktop database had hundreds of queries, this could be a slow and tedious process. If you understand SQL, you can simplify the process by copying the underlying SQL that defines the queries in your desktop database to your project file. You do this by opening the original query in your desktop database in SQL Design view, copying the SQL text to the Clipboard, pasting it into the SQL pane of a new view, function, or stored procedure in your project file, and then modifying the text so that it will work in SQL Server. When your old application has queries that depend on other queries, you must build the base queries first.

Chapter 29

Using the Upsizing Wizard

Even if you want to save nothing more than the structure of your tables, the Upsizing Wizard is a good choice because, unlike the Import facility, the wizard attempts to preserve all the table indexes, validation rules, and relationships. If your desktop database application is already designed to work well in a client/server environment, you can also use the wizard to convert your queries, forms, reports, macros, and modules.

So, why wouldn't you want to use the wizard in all scenarios? Well, the wizard can't handle certain types of validation rules and relationships, and it does only a modestly good job upsizing your queries (but something might be better than nothing). In fact, the wizard will fail or crash if you haven't made some preparatory changes in your desktop database (or a copy of it). You'll be able to upsize only the simplest desktop databases without modifying them—and if they're simple, then they're probably not candidates to upsize. You might find that the work you have to do outweighs starting from scratch with imported tables, forms, reports, modules, and macros. The following sections describe the changes you might need to make to each object type.

Preparing Your Desktop Database

In this section, you'll learn about the various types of changes you'll need to make to successfully convert your application from a desktop database (.mdb) to a project file (.adp) connected to SQL Server. If you plan to use the Upsizing Wizard, you must make some of the changes before you attempt to run the wizard. You can delay other changes until after you've imported or upsized all your objects.

General Upsizing Considerations

By default, the Upsizing Wizard ignores any hidden objects in your database when it upsizes your database. If you're using Import, you won't see any hidden objects in the list of objects to import. If you want all your objects to be upsized, make sure they are not marked as hidden in your desktop database. To see all your hidden objects, you can choose Options from the Tools menu and select **Hidden objects** on the View tab.

SQL Server has a naming convention for objects called Rules for Identifiers that it uses to ensure that objects in the database don't have names that conflict with SQL Server reserved words, properties, or functions. Properly named objects have no spaces and do not use apostrophes ('). They also do not contain the names of any SQL Server reserved words. To ensure the smoothest upsize possible, make sure that all objects in your database conform to the SQL Server Rules for Identifiers. This is particularly important for any object name that contains an apostrophe. The Upsizing Wizard does not upsize any tables or queries that have names with apostrophes in them. You also won't be able to import any tables that have an apostrophe in the name if you choose to upsize by hand.

Security settings in an Access project are different from the security settings you might have created in your desktop database. Therefore, neither Access nor the Upsizing Wizard copy any of the existing security settings for objects that you import or upsize. Also, if your desktop database is secured, you must be logged on to Access with a user name that has at least Read Definition permission for all objects. After you upsize, you need to create new security settings in Windows for your newly created Access project as well as for the tables and queries that reside on SQL Server. See Chapter 30, "Securing Your Database," for details.

Preparing Your Tables

If you plan to import your tables rather than use the Upsizing Wizard, you don't need to make any changes to your table design in advance. However, if you plan to use the wizard, you must examine your tables and correct or remove validation rules and relationships before you attempt to run the wizard. Because the wizard attempts to upsize most properties and all rules and relationships, it will fail to convert any tables that contain settings that it can't handle. In some cases, the wizard will crash, and it might corrupt your database when it does so! Clearly, the first task you need to perform is to back up your database.

> **Caution** Always back up your desktop database before you run the Upsize Wizard, in case your database becomes corrupted during the upsizing process.

When the tables are upsized, the wizard tries to convert any Visual Basic functions in your validation rules and default value definitions to the corresponding SQL Server functions. However, not all functions in Visual Basic have corresponding functions in SQL Server. If Access cannot convert the function for a validation rule, it will skip upsizing the validation rule. If it cannot convert the function for a default value definition, it will skip upsizing the table entirely. In general, the wizard can convert the functions listed in Table 29-1.

Table 29-1. Visual Basic Functions That the Upsizing Wizard Can Convert

Asc	CVDate	Mid	Sgn
CCur	Date	Minute	Space
CDbl	Day	Mod	Str
Chr	Hour	Month	Time
CInt	Int	Now	Trim
CLng	LCase	Right	Ucase
CSng	Left	RTrim	Weekday
CStr	LTrim	Second	Year

If a Default Value or a Validation Rule property uses a function that isn't in the list, you should either delete the property setting or change it to use only functions that the wizard can convert. However, there is no guarantee that your functions will be upsized correctly, even if you are using Visual Basic functions that have Transact-SQL Server equivalents. If in doubt, remove the functions altogether and add them again after the tables have been upsized.

For example, the ContactDateTime field in the tblContactEvents table uses the Format function in the Default Value property. I cleared this property in the table field and made sure that the Default Value for the control in the form that edits this table was set correctly.

Chapter 29

Also, the tblContacts table in the LawTrack Contacts desktop database contains the following table validation rule:

```
IIf(Not ((([ContactType]="Distributor") Or ([ContactType]
    ="Developer") Or ([ContactType]="Trainer")),
    [CommissionPercent]=0,True)
```

In the *Contacts2Upsize.mdb* sample file, I eliminated the IIF function that won't convert and changed the Validation Rule property to a complex Boolean expression that the wizard is more likely to handle and that performs the same test. The Upsizing Wizard attempts to upsize all field and table validation rules to SQL Server CHECK constraints, but it cannot do so when a validation rule references Access functions. The new rule that you can find in the tblContacts table in the database to be upsized is as follows:

```
((Not ((([ContactType]='Trainer') Or ([ContactType]='Developer')
    Or ([ContactType]='Distributor'))) And ([CommissionPercent]=0))
    Or ((([ContactType]='Trainer') Or ([ContactType]='Developer')
    Or ([ContactType]='Distributor'))
```

The upsizing wizard also cannot handle relationships that loop back on themselves, either as a string of relationships (tblA → tblB → tblC → tblA) or as a relationship from a table to itself. (In fact, this is one condition that causes the wizard to crash.) Two relationships defined in the desktop database version of LawTrack Contacts do just that, as pointed out by the arrows in Figure 29-1.

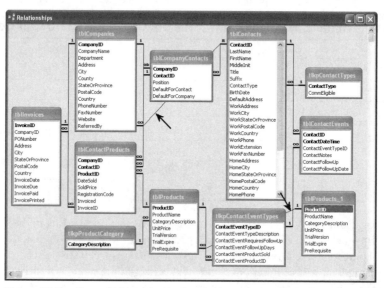

Figure 29-1. Two relationships in the desktop version of LawTrack Contacts define a relationship loop.

The first set of relationships that will cause a problem is the loop formed by the relationship from the tblCompanies table to the tblCompanyContacts table on CompanyID, the relationship between the tblCompanyContacts table and the tblContacts table on ContactID, and the relationship back from ContactID in the tblContacts table to the ReferredBy field in the tblCompanies table. You can actually remove any one of the relationships in the loop to solve the problem, but I chose to delete the one from tblContacts to tblCompanies. You won't find this relationship defined in the *Contacts2Upsize.mdb* sample database. The second relationship is the one from the ProductID field in tblProducts back to the same table using the PreRequisite field. I also removed this relationship from the sample *Contacts2Upsize.mdb* database to be upsized.

The wizard upsizes Lookup properties as extended properties in the new SQL Server tables. However, using lookups in SQL Server is inefficient and consumes valuable resources when executing queries against the server tables. I recommend removing all lookups from your tables before upsizing and using an alternative method to reference the data in your tables on SQL Server (such as using combo boxes on a form). (See "Taking a Look at Lookup Properties" on page 171 for a discussion of why you shouldn't use Lookup properties at all.)

Modifying Queries

When the Upsizing Wizard upsizes your queries, it attempts to convert each query to the most nearly equivalent SQL Server query type. As much as possible, the wizard converts SELECT queries to SQL Server functions and all action queries to SQL Server stored procedures.

When the wizard upsizes your queries, it examines each query to identify which ones use only tables in the FROM clause (base queries) and which are nested queries. (*Nested* queries use other queries as their record source.) The wizard upsizes the base queries first, followed by the nested queries.

> **Important** Some nested queries might be too complicated to upsize correctly. If you have a complex nested query, you might want to consider revising it into a simpler form before upsizing. Also, if a base query that is used in a nested query contains elements that the wizard cannot upsize, it won't upsize the nested query either.

Access supports many query types and query properties that have no equivalent or are unnecessary in SQL Server. The following types of Access queries cannot be successfully upsized to SQL Server:

- **Multiple-table queries that contain the DISTINCTROW keyword.** (The Unique Records property of the query is set to Yes.) You should consider rewriting these queries using a subquery. For example, the wizard will not upsize the following query:

```
SELECT DISTINCTROW tblContacts.FirstName, tblContacts.LastName
FROM tblContacts
INNER JOIN tblContactProducts
ON tblContacts.ContactID = tblContactProducts.ContactID
WHERE tblContactProducts.DateSold > #03/15/2003#
```

Chapter 29

The wizard can upsize the following equivalent query:

```
SELECT tblContacts.FirstName, tblContacts.LastName
FROM tblContacts
WHERE tblContacts.ContactID IN
(SELECT ContactID
FROM tblContactProducts
WHERE  tblContactProducts.DateSold > #03/15/2003#)
```

- **Crosstab queries.**   These queries have no SQL Server equivalent. The only way to duplicate the functionality of a crosstab query is to write a complicated stored procedure. Unfortunately, the Upsizing Wizard does not do this for you.

- **SQL pass-through queries.**   These queries are only used in Access desktop databases (.mdb) to interface directly with SQL Server tables. They are unnecessary in an Access project, and you should delete these queries before you run the wizard.

- **SQL Data Definition Language (DDL) queries.**   The wizard can upsize INSERT INTO (make table) queries. You should delete all other DDL queries.

- **Parameter queries that reference form controls.**   The wizard attempts to upsize all parameter queries. When the parameter is a reference to a control on a form (as in [Forms]![frmFilterChoicesForCustomer]![DateTextBox]), the wizard changes the parameter name to one that is compatible with SQL Server, but the server won't be able to resolve the parameter name to an open form in your project file. Also, SQL Server uses only the first 30 characters to identify unique parameter names, so references to forms or controls that have long names might be converted to a name that is not unique.

- **Queries that use a built-in function in the WHERE clause.**   You should consider removing any reference to a built-in function on the Criteria or Or lines in a query design so that the wizard will upsize the query. You can replace the function call with an equivalent SQL Server function after you upsize.

- **Queries that use a function that cannot be converted.**   The wizard attempts to convert queries that reference functions in the SELECT clause (the field list). However, it will not convert queries that use functions that are not in the list shown earlier in Table 29-1 on page 1139. If you want the wizard to convert queries that use functions that cannot be converted, you should remove the function reference from the query before running the wizard. You can replace the function call with an equivalent SQL Server function after you upsize. If your query calls a custom Visual Basic function that you created, you can replace the function with a custom stored procedure after you upsize.

Changing Forms and Reports

When you upsize to an Access project, the wizard copies your existing forms and reports directly into your project file. The wizard examines the Record Source property of forms and reports and the Row Source property of combo boxes and list boxes and changes some of them in an attempt to make the upsize process more successful. Forms and reports in an Access project support all the same features as forms and reports in an Access desktop database. The most likely cause of problems in using upsized forms and reports is in the record source of a form or report or the row source of a combo box or list box.

To make the upsizing process smoother, set the record source of your forms and reports and the row source of your combo boxes and list boxes to saved queries whenever possible instead of using an SQL statement. This practice makes it easier to track down problems after the upsize. When all your forms, reports, combo boxes, and list boxes reference saved queries, fixing any upsize problems with the queries will most likely fix problems with all your forms and reports. When you use SQL statements in Record Source or Row Source properties, the Upsizing Wizard won't report any problems with these queries. Be aware of any SQL statement or query in your forms and reports that uses parameters because you'll need to modify the form or report or the upsized query after the wizard finishes.

Modifying Your Code

When you upsize your database to an Access project, copies of the macros and modules are converted directly. The problems that can arise from moving your macros and modules to an Access project come from incompatibilities with the portions of your code that work with data.

If you have any macros in your existing desktop database, I strongly recommend that you convert them to modules before upsizing. Macros work in an Access project, but they can often cause a serious bottleneck in your database efficiency. If the macro fetches data, the macro will force the local client to download the full recordset of the queried tables before working with the data. You can easily rewrite macros in more efficient Visual Basic code.

All recordset manipulation in Access projects must use ActiveX Data Objects (ADO), so you must convert any existing code that uses Data Access Objects (DAO). Also, if you use Visual Basic code to build queries or filters, your code must comply with SQL Server syntax. String literals must be enclosed in single, not double, quotation marks. Date literals must be enclosed in single quotation marks, not pound signs (#). In a LIKE predicate, you must use a percent sign (%) instead of an asterisk (*) and an underscore (_) instead of a question mark (?). Also, SQL Server does not recognize the True and False keywords in a predicate that tests a Yes/No value. SQL Server uses 0 for False, but uses 1 for True instead of –1. You must change all False keywords in SQL that you build in code to the number 0. If you want your code to work in both a desktop database (before you upsize) and the converted project file, you must change any test for = True to an inverse test for <> 0. For example, change a test such as

```
Set rst = CurrentDb.OpenRecordset("SELECT * FROM tblProducts " & _
    "WHERE TrialVersion = True
```

to

```
rst.Open "SELECT * FROM tblProducts WHERE TrialVersion <> 0", _
    CurrentProject.Connection
```

If you took a close look at the code behind the forms in the LawTrack Contacts sample database, you noticed that there is a lot of code that builds and manipulates recordsets. It makes sense to use DAO in a desktop database because DAO is specifically designed to work with the Microsoft JET database engine used for .mdb files. For example, you can find the following code excerpts in the cmdSearch_Click procedure in the fdlgContactSearch form in the *Contacts.mdb* sample database:

```
Private Sub cmdSearch_Click()
Dim varWhere As Variant, varDateSearch As Variant
Dim rst As DAO.Recordset

' < code to perform initial validation removed >

    ' OK, start building the filter
    ' If specified a contact type value
    If Not IsNothing(Me.cmbContactType) Then
        ' .. build the predicate
        varWhere = "[ContactType] = '" & Me.cmbContactType & "'"
    End If
    ' Do Last Name next
    If Not IsNothing(Me.txtLastName) Then
        ' .. build the predicate
        ' Note: taking advantage of Null propogation
        '  so we don't have to test for any previous predicate
        varWhere = (varWhere + " AND ") & "[LastName] LIKE '" & _
            Me.txtLastName & "*'"
    End If
' < code to build some parts of the predicate removed>

    ' Do Contact date(s) next -- this is a toughie
    '   because we want to end up with one filter on the subquery table
    '   for both Contact Date range and FollowUp Date range
    ' Check Contact From first
    If Not IsNothing(Me.txtContactFrom) Then
        ' .. build the predicate
        varDateSearch = "tblContactEvents.ContactDateTime >= #" & _
            Me.txtContactFrom & "#"
    End If

' <code to build remaining date/time predicates removed>

    ' Finally, do the Inactive check box
    If (Me.chkInactive = False) Then
        ' Build a filter to exclude inactive contacts
        varWhere = (varWhere + " AND ") & _
            "(Inactive = False)"
    End If

    ' Check to see that we built a filter
    If IsNothing(varWhere) Then
        MsgBox "You must enter at least one search criteria.", _
            vbInformation, gstrAppTitle
        Exit Sub
    End If
```

```
' Open a recordset to see if any rows returned with this filter
Set rst = DBEngine(0)(0).OpenRecordset("SELECT * " & _
    "FROM tblContacts WHERE " & varWhere)
' See if found none
If rst.RecordCount = 0 Then
    MsgBox "No Contacts meet your criteria.", vbInformation, gstrAppTitle
    ' Clean up recordset
    rst.Close
    Set rst = Nothing
    Exit Sub
End If


' < code to open the filtered form removed >


End Sub
```

Now, here's the same code in *Contacts2Upsize.mdb* that I modified to use an ADO recordset and detect the application type to build a correct filter:

```
Private Sub cmdSearch_Click()
Dim varWhere As Variant, varDateSearch As Variant
Dim strWild As String, strDateDelim As String, intMDB As Integer
Dim frm As Form
' Use ADO recordset for upsizing
Dim rst As New ADODB.Recordset

    ' Initialize to Null
    varWhere = Null
    varDateSearch = Null

    ' Find out the project type and set the wildcard
    '  and date delimiter
    If CurrentProject.ProjectType = acMDB Then
        strWild = "*"
        strDateDelim = "#"
        intMDB = True
    Else
        strWild = "%"
        strDateDelim = "'"
    End If

' < code to perform initial validation removed >

    ' OK, start building the filter
    ' If specified a contact type value
    If Not IsNothing(Me.cmbContactType) Then
        ' .. build the predicate
        varWhere = "[ContactType] = '" & Me.cmbContactType & "'"
    End If
    ' Do Last Name next
    If Not IsNothing(Me.txtLastName) Then
        ' .. build the predicate
```

```
        ' Note: taking advantage of Null propogation
        '   so we don't have to test for any previous predicate
        varWhere = (varWhere + " AND ") & "[LastName] LIKE '" & _
            Me.txtLastName & strWild & "'"
    End If
' < code to build some parts of the predicate removed>

    ' Do Contact date(s) next -- this is a toughie
    '   because we want to end up with one filter on the subquery table
    '   for both Contact Date range and FollowUp Date range
    ' Check Contact From first
    If Not IsNothing(Me.txtContactFrom) Then
        ' .. build the predicate
        varDateSearch = "tblContactEvents.ContactDateTime >= " & _
            strDateDelim & _
            Format(CDate(Me.txtContactFrom), "dd mmm yyyy") & strDateDelim
    End If

' <code to build remaining date/time predicates removed>

    ' Finally, do the Inactive check box
    If (Me.chkInactive = False) Then
        ' Build a filter to exclude inactive contacts
        varWhere = (varWhere + " AND ") & _
            "(Inactive = 0)"
    End If

    ' Check to see that we built a filter
    If IsNothing(varWhere) Then
        MsgBox "You must enter at least one search criteria.", _
            vbInformation, gstrAppTitle
        Exit Sub
    End If

    ' Open a recordset to see if any rows returned with this filter
    ' Must always use "%" wildcard in ADO recordset - even in an MDB
    rst.Open "SELECT * FROM tblContacts WHERE " & _
        Replace(varWhere, "*", "%"), CurrentProject.Connection, _
        adOpenKeyset, adLockOptimistic
    ' See if found none
    If rst.RecordCount = 0 Then
        MsgBox "No Contacts meet your criteria.", vbInformation, gstrAppTitle
        ' Clean up recordset
        rst.Close
        Set rst = Nothing
        Exit Sub
    End If

' < code to open the filtered form removed >

End Sub
```

> **Note** When you're certain that your desktop database will always be a desktop database, you gain no advantage by using ADO to manipulate recordsets or objects. ADO has more overhead than DAO in a desktop database, and it supports only a subset of the functionality of DAO for JET databases.

The modified code tests the ProjectType property of the CurrentProject object to find out whether it is running in a desktop database (acMDB) or in a converted project file. It sets the LIKE predicate wildcard and the date delimiter character accordingly. Note that the code in both procedures already uses single quotes to delimit string literals, so I didn't have to make any changes. When building a date/time predicate, the code uses the correct delimiter determined earlier and formats the date value in the universal dd mmm yyyy format (two-digit day, three-character month name abbreviation and four-digit year). Using this technique to format the date is also a good idea in any application that might run in a non-U.S. locale. Although JET SQL expects dates in the U.S. mm/dd/yyyy format, it also understands this universal format. If you insert a date directly from a control, an international user probably has used a dd/mm/yyyy format, which JET might misinterpret.

Further down in the procedure, the code builds a predicate to test a yes/no value. The modified code uses the number 0 instead of the keyword False. Finally, the modified code opens an ADO recordset instead of a DAO recordset. It uses the Replace function to change any LIKE wildcards because ADO always expects % and _ instead of * and ?. The recordset object in both DAO and ADO supports the RecordCount property, so I didn't have to change the code to test for any records found.

Note that you don't have to change any of your DAO code before you run the Upsizing Wizard. However, the new project file will not contain a reference to the DAO library, so your code won't compile in the converted database. One good way to locate all your DAO code is to remove the DAO library from the desktop database that you plan to convert. (Remember, you should be working in a backup copy of your original database!) Open any module in Design view and choose References from the Tools menu in the Visual Basic Editor (VBE) window. Clear the check box next to Microsoft DAO 3.x Object Library and click OK. Choose Compile from the Debug menu, and the compiler halts on any reference to a DAO object in your code.

Using the Upsizing Wizard

After you have prepared your desktop database for upsizing, you're ready to run the Upsizing Wizard. Let's take a look at upsizing the *Contacts2Upsize.mdb* sample database. The upsize process does not permanently alter the original database, but the wizard does create temporary objects in this database as it upsizes it. It creates a new project file that contains the converted forms, reports, macros, and modules; converts the tables and queries to an SQL Server database; and connects the new project to that database.

Chapter 29

Ensuring That Your Server Is Started

Before you begin, you must be sure you can connect to an SQL Server database system that lets you create a new database and tables, views, and stored procedures in that database. If you installed the Microsoft SQL Server Desktop Engine (MSDE) on your desktop machine, you should make sure the server service is running. (See the Appendix for instructions to install MSDE.) With MSDE, you can double-click the SQL Server Service Manager icon in the notification area of your Windows taskbar (the group of icons at the right end of the taskbar) to open the manager, shown in Figure 29-2. (If you can't find the Service Manager on your taskbar, you can start it by clicking the Service Manager icon in the Startup group on your Start menu.)

Figure 29-2. SQL Server Service Manager.

The Server drop-down list should show the name of your current machine. The Service Manager also scans your network for other SQL Servers. If you have administrative authority on other servers, you can select one from the drop-down list and control the services running on that machine. The Services drop-down list should display the SQL Server service. You can also find entries that allow you to start and stop the Distributed Transaction Coordinator (DTC) and SQL Server Agent. You need DTC only if you execute stored procedures that need to protect updates to databases on multiple servers within a transaction. The SQL Server Agent allows you to schedule automatic execution of tasks such as backing up or compacting your databases.

Select your server, the SQL Server service, and click the Start/Continue button to start your server. (You should see a small server icon with a green arrow inside a circle on your taskbar when your server is running.) You can click the Pause button to pause your server (still running but not accepting any new connections) or the Stop button to stop it. The icon on your taskbar changes to indicate the current status of your server. You should normally leave your server running, especially when you're developing project file applications in Access. You should leave the Auto-start service when OS starts option (SQL Server Service Manager) selected to restart your server each time you start Windows.

You can close the Service Manager program window, but the service continues to run. You can right-click the server icon on your taskbar to display a shortcut menu. From this menu, you can open the Service Manager window again, start or stop services on your machine, set options, or exit the Service Manager program.

Running the Wizard

Next, start Access and open the Contacts2Upsize sample database. Choose Database Utilities from the Tools menu, and then choose Upsizing Wizard from the submenu. The wizard displays the opening window shown in Figure 29-3.

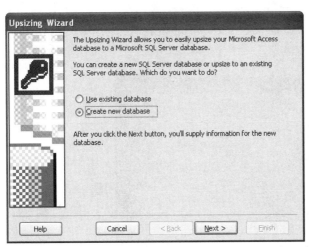

Figure 29-3. The options in the opening window of the Upsizing Wizard.

Your first choice is to upsize your tables and queries to an existing SQL Server database or to create a new database. Unless you are upsizing a database application that's part of a larger application system, I recommend that you select **Create new database** to create a new database for the exclusive use of this application. Click Next to display the second window, shown in Figure 29-4. (The wizard searches for all available SQL Servers on your network at this point, so it might take a few seconds before the window opens.)

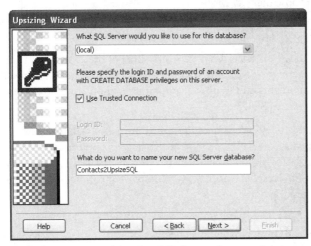

Figure 29-4. Specifying the SQL Server for your database and the name of the database to create on the server.

Chapter 29

The wizard asks you for the information it needs to connect to the SQL Server where it will create your new tables, views, functions, and stored procedures. If you are using MSDE, enter the name of your computer in the top box (or type (**local**)), and leave the check mark in the Use Trusted Connection check box. If you are connecting to SQL Server on a network, ask your server administrator whether you should clear the check box and supply a login ID and password.

In the last box, enter the name of the database you want to create. You can use the default chosen by the wizard, Contacts2UpsizeSQL, for this example. Click Next to display the next window, shown in Figure 29-5.

Figure 29-5. Choosing the tables to define on the server.

The wizard now asks you to choose the tables you want to upsize. The wizard also upsizes any queries that reference these tables. In most cases, you should click the double right arrow to select all the tables. (Choose them all for this example.) After you choose the tables you need by moving them to the list on the right, click Next to go on. The wizard displays the window shown in Figure 29-6.

In this window, you can tell the wizard not to upsize some of the attributes of your Access tables. For example, you might have defined a large number of indexes on some tables to aid searching in Access. You might want to upsize your tables without any indexes and then later define appropriate indexes in SQL Server.

In most cases, however, you will want to let the wizard upsize all your indexes, validation rules, default values, and table relationships. You also have the option to upsize your table relationships using declarative referential integrity (DRI) or triggers. Either method of upsizing your relationships results in SQL Server enforcing the same referential integrity rules defined in your desktop database.

A trigger is Transact-SQL code that the server executes whenever table data is updated, added, or deleted. You can think of triggers as being similar to Visual Basic code that you might write in a form's Before Update, Before Insert, or Delete events. A trigger can examine the data about to be changed and the new data that will be saved or inserted, and it can select data from other tables. So, a trigger can verify that related rows don't exist in a child table when an SQL command asks to delete rows in a parent table. Or, it can verify that a matching parent row exists when an SQL command attempts to insert a row in a child table. In many ways, triggers are more powerful than DRI because they can perform any integrity check that you can imagine. For example, you could write an INSERT trigger that won't allow any more students to register for a class when the class is full. You can't do that with DRI.

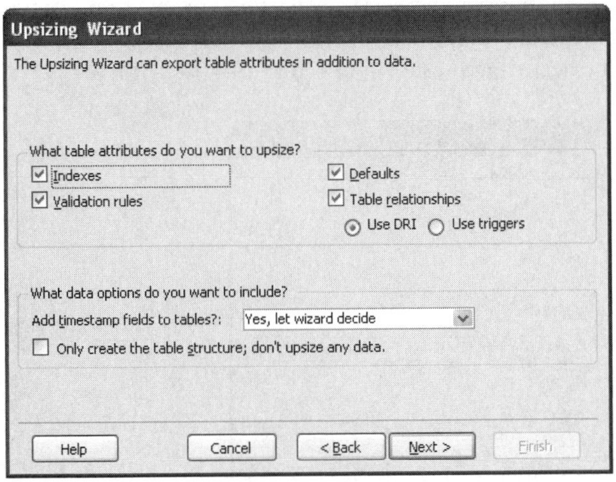

Figure 29-6. Choosing the table options for upsizing.

In SQL Server 2000 and later, DRI offers all the same relationship properties you can use in an Access desktop database, so the function and interface will seem more familiar to you. The wizard includes additional FOREIGN KEY REFERENCES check constraints when it defines your tables to activate DRI. I recommend that you let the wizard use DRI to define your relationships because DRI is simpler to understand and more similar to what you are used to working with in a desktop database. You can still define additional triggers if necessary after you upsize your database.

> **Caution** If you weren't careful to remove circular or self-referencing relationships before you started the wizard, it will fail and might crash. You should clear the Table Relationships check box if you're not sure. You can easily redefine the relationships after the wizard finishes. See Chapter 17, "Building Tables in an Access Project," for details about defining relationships.

Under **What data options do you want to include?** you can ask the wizard to add a timestamp field to all tables, no tables, or to let the wizard decide. When a table includes a timestamp field, SQL Server updates this field whenever any user makes a change to any other field in the table. Without the timestamp field, when your application needs to update a row, Access has to re-fetch the row you are about to update and compare the value of each field to the value that existed before your application requested the update. When the table contains only text and simple numeric values, this task is quick and efficient. If your table contains memo, OLE Object, or floating-point data (single or double), the comparison can take a long time and might incorrectly assume that someone else has updated the row. If you let the wizard decide, it adds a timestamp field to any table that contains a memo, OLE Object, or floating-point numeric field. In most cases, you should either let the wizard decide or add a timestamp field to all tables.

You also have an option to upsize only the table structures but not export the existing data to SQL Server. If you are upsizing a prototype application that doesn't really contain any live data, upsizing only the table structure should work just fine. In the case of *Contacts2Upsize.mdb*, I let the wizard decide about timestamp fields (by selecting **Yes, let wizard decide**) and instructed it to upsize the structure and the data (by not selecting the bottom check box). Click Next to display the next window, shown in Figure 29-7.

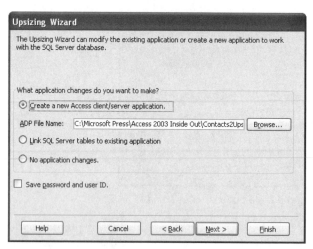

Figure 29-7. Asking the Upsizing Wizard to convert the application to an Access project file (.adp).

In this window, you have three main options:

- Build a new Access project file containing your forms, reports, data access pages, macros, and modules, and connect it to the tables, views, and stored procedures upsized in SQL Server (**Create a new Access client/server application.**).

- Upsize your tables, remove them from the existing application, and create links to the new SQL Server tables (**Link SQL Server tables to existing application.**). The wizard does not upsize your queries, forms, reports, data access pages, macros, or modules when you select this option.

- Only upsize your tables and do not change your application (**No application changes.**). The wizard upsizes only your tables when you select this option.

In this example, you are trying to completely upsize an existing desktop database to an Access project, so choose the first option. The default file name chosen by the wizard, *Contacts2UpsizeCS.adp*, is fine for this example. The third option is useful if you want to do an upsize "by hand" and have more control over the process. Unlike importing tables into a new SQL Server database, when you select this option the wizard will attempt to upsize all your table validation rules, properties, and relationships.

Note that in all three cases, you can ask the wizard to save the connection user ID and password with the connection or table link information. This option is meaningless if your server uses a trusted connection but is important if your server uses SQL Server logins and passwords. If you ask the wizard to save the password and login ID and this information is critical to maintaining security in SQL Server, you should also be sure to secure and encrypt your Access project file to prevent unauthorized access. See Chapter 30, "Securing Your Database," for details about ways to encrypt and secure an Access project file. If your server uses SQL Server logins, I recommend that you leave this option cleared. When you do this, Access prompts the user for a user ID and password when the user opens the application.

When you click Next, the wizard displays a window informing you that it has all the information it needs to proceed, shown in Figure 29-8. In this final window, you can select the first option to open the new project (ADP) file or the second option to keep your current desktop database (MDB) open. Select the first option and click the Finish button to let the wizard upsize your database. Depending on the speed of your machine, the speed of your connection to the server, and the complexity of your database, the upsizing process could take as little as several minutes to as much as half an hour or more.

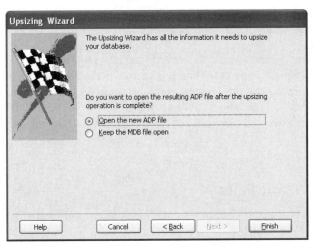

Figure 29-8. The Upsizing Wizard has all the information it needs to upsize your database.

When the wizard is done, it displays a report of what it upsized and any problems it encountered, as shown in Figure 29-9 on the next page. It's a good idea to print the report for later reference, especially if any errors occurred during the upsizing process. (The wizard also offers to save a copy of this report as a snapshot file in the folder where your original desktop database resides when you close the report.) You can use the report to pinpoint where the problem occurred and fix the issue before attempting to upsize again. You can find a copy of this file saved as *ContactsUpsizeSample.snp* with the sample files you installed from your companion CD.

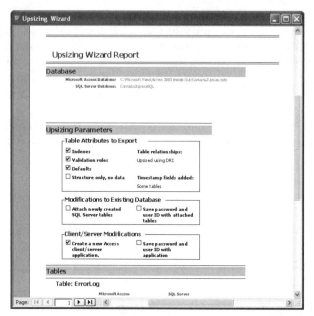

Figure 29-9. The report created by the Upsizing Wizard.

When you close this report, the wizard either opens your new project file or leaves you in your desktop database, depending on the option you selected in the final window of the wizard. If you selected the option to open the new project file, you can begin fixing any problems reported by the wizard. You might also want to open your existing desktop database file in another Access session so that you can open any queries that the wizard failed to upsize and copy and modify the SQL into new views, functions, or stored procedures that you create in you new SQL Server database.

Starting Over If the Wizard Fails

The wizard won't ever do a perfect job, but it should finish successfully and produce a report that lists only minor problems that you can correct in the new project file. You should go back and try again if any of the following is true:

- **The wizard crashes.**   This can happen when you fail to fix circular references between tables or leave validation rules in your tables that use unsupported functions. The wizard won't create a report, so you might need to run the wizard again and watch the progress dialog box that it displays closely to find out which table or relationship it was working on when it crashed.

- **The wizard fails to upsize some or all of your tables.**   This can happen if the database you asked to create already exists on the server (but is empty) or you asked the wizard to upsize into an existing SQL Server database. The wizard won't upsize tables that already exist in the server database.

- **The wizard reports excessive errors when trying to upsize your queries.**   Although you can certainly rebuild the queries in your new project file, it might be faster to fix your queries in the original desktop database so that the wizard can handle them and run the wizard again.

In most cases, the wizard will create a project file and the SQL Server database, and you must delete both of these before you can try to run the wizard again. You can open the project file, choose Database Utilities on the Tools menu, and choose Drop SQL Database on the submenu to delete the SQL Server database. If the project file doesn't exist, you can create a new one and attempt to connect to the database on the server. See "Creating a New Project File" on page 17xxx for instructions on how to do this. If you successfully connect to the database from a new project file, use the Tools menu to drop the SQL Server database. You can now close the project file and delete it. After correcting any problems in your original desktop database, you can rerun the Upsizing Wizard.

Note that getting the best result from the Upsizing Wizard is often a trial-and-error process. You might need to run the wizard several times before you obtain a satisfactory result. If you're still having problems after several tries, you can always resort to the "by hand" process—create a new project and database file, import all your tables, forms, reports, macros, and modules from your old desktop database, and build the queries you need in the Access project query designer.

Correcting the Upsize Result

Unless you're upsizing an extremely simple application (but then if you are, why are you upsizing?), you'll have some work to do after the Upsizing Wizard finishes. You'll also need to consider many of the corrections listed in this section if you're upsizing your desktop database by hand.

Adding Relationships and Constraints and Fixing Indexes

You might have had to remove some relationships so that the wizard will run. The wizard might also have reported that it could not define some of the relationships that it found in your desktop database. The same is true for validation rules. Also, the wizard does not define your primary key indexes in the most optimal way, and it often creates multiple indexes on the same column in the upsized table. The multiple indexes occur because Access actually defines additional hidden indexes when you define referential integrity between two tables. In a desktop database, these additional indexes are actually aliases of the original index, so they don't take up any additional resources. In a database upsized to SQL Server, these additional indexes use additional resources and are unnecessary.

Whether you use the Upsizing Wizard or upsize the tables by importing them, you must examine and correct the following problems:

- **Define any relationships required between your tables.**   You can do this in the Properties window in Design view or by creating a database diagram.
- **Specify required validation rules (check constraints) on your tables and columns.**   You can do this in the Properties window in Design view. Note that the wizard sometimes reports that it failed to convert a table validation rule to a constraint, but you can

find the constraint properly defined. When you need to define a complex validation rule that you cannot express as a Boolean test, you'll need to define a trigger on your table using Transact-SQL. The table designer in an Access project does not support defining triggers.

- **Make sure that the primary key in each table is defined as clustered.** A clustered index defines the physical sequence of rows in the database. Defining the primary key as a clustered index can significantly improve join performance. You can define and modify indexes for a table in Design view.

- **Define additional indexes to improve performance.** Particularly when you import your desktop database tables to SQL Server, you should be sure to define the indexes that will improve performance. Keep in mind that each additional index consumes additional resources in your database and slows down the performance of update, insert, and delete operations.

- **Remove unnecessary duplicate indexes.** When you use the Upsizing Wizard, it copies all indexes from your desktop database, including duplicate ones defined by Access to support referential integrity. You should examine the indexes defined by the wizard on each table and remove all duplicates.

For more information about how to perform these tasks, see Chapter 17, "Building Tables in an Access Project."

Correcting Query Problems

Particularly if you use the Upsizing Wizard, you'll need to create any queries that the wizard didn't convert and fix problems with ones that it did convert.

Creating Missing Queries

If you're upsizing "by hand," you must define anew all the queries required by your application. If you used the Upsizing Wizard, you need to examine the Upsizing Wizard Report, locate any that it failed to upsize, and create them in your new SQL Server database.

In the *Contacts2Upsize.mdb* sample database, the Upsizing Wizard failed to upsize a dozen queries for the following reasons:

- The wizard was unable to handle UNION queries that also include a parameter (such as qryCheckRelateCompany).

- The wizard failed to upsize some queries that reference the current date using the Date function in the WHERE clause (such as qryFutureContacts). The wizard did correctly convert the function to the equivalent SQL Server GetDate function, but it also tried to convert these queries into functions. A function cannot include a reference to a non-deterministic function (a function that returns different values when called repeatedly with the same parameters). GetDate is a nondeterministic function.

- The wizard attempted but failed to upsize queries containing references to Visual Basic functions that have no direct equivalent in SQL Server (such as the Choose function in qryRptContactEnvelope).

You might discover other types of queries (such as queries that call user-defined functions) that did not upsize from your desktop database. If you have spent some effort to prepare your queries, you shouldn't find more than a handful of queries that you'll need to create on your own in SQL Server.

Inside Out

Concatenation expressions work differently in SQL Server

When you want to concatenate fields or string expressions in a desktop database, you use the & concatenation operator. You might remember from Chapter 7, "Creating and Working with Simple Queries," that you can also use + as a concatenation operator, but when you do so, any field containing a Null value causes the entire expression to be Null. You also learned that you can make judicious use of the + concatenation operator to eliminate unwanted blanks or punctuation when one of the fields might be Null.

The bad news is SQL Server supports only the + concatenation operator, and if any column used in a concatenation expression is Null, the entire expression is Null. In several queries in the desktop database version of the LawTrack Contacts application, you can find expressions that yield a Null for many rows in the query converted to SQL Server. For example, in the qryRptContacts query, you can find the following expression:

```
([tblContacts].[Title]+" ") & [tblContacts].[FirstName] & " " &
([tblContacts].[MiddleInit]+". ") & [tblContacts].[LastName] &
(", "+[tblContacts].[Suffix]) AS Contact
```

When the Upsizing Wizard converts this query to SQL Server, it only replaces all the & operators with + and all the double quotes with single quotes. If you open this query without fixing it, you'll see a Null returned for any contact that doesn't have a Title, MiddleInit, or Suffix. To fix this problem you must use the SQL Server ISNULL function wherever you think a text field might be Null. You can give the ISNULL function an expression in the first parameter, and when the expression is Null, the function returns the second parameter. When the expression is not Null, you see the result of the original expression. Here's the corrected expression that you'll find in this query in the *ContactsSQL.mdf* database:

```
ISNULL(tblContacts.Title + ' ', '') + ISNULL(tblContacts.FirstName + ' ', '')
+ ISNULL(tblContacts.MiddleInit + ' ', '') + tblContacts.LastName +
ISNULL(', ' + tblContacts.Suffix) AS Contact
```

One of the easiest ways to copy the queries you need is to open two copies of Microsoft Access. In one, open your original desktop database. In the other, open your new project file. Choose a query that you need to copy from your desktop database, open it in Design view, and switch to SQL view by choosing SQL from the View menu. Select the SQL text (do not select any PARAMETERS clause) and copy it to the Clipboard.

In your project file, decide what type of query you need to create to support the query you are copying from your desktop database—a view, function, or stored procedure. Remember from

Chapter 18, "Building Queries in an Access Project," that a view cannot process parameters. You can use a function for most parameter queries except those that need to call nondeterministic functions. You can use a stored procedure for all other types of queries, including action queries (update, insert, delete).

Open a new query of the correct type in your project file and paste the SQL from your desktop database into the SQL pane. Correct any function calls in the text. If your old query called a Visual Basic function that you defined, you might first need to create an SQL Server function that performs the same calculation.

Also keep in mind that you must declare that any parameters and parameter names must begin with the @ character and follow the rules for names in SQL Server. In general, you should keep parameter names short and simple, and the first 30 characters must uniquely define the parameter within a function or stored procedure. Remember from Chapter 19, "Designing Forms in an Access Project," and Chapter 20, "Building Reports in an Access Project," that it's a simple matter to use the Input Parameters property of a form or report to supply parameter values to SQL Server functions and stored procedures.

Changing Functions to Views

Because functions can handle a wider range of queries than can views, the Upsizing Wizard attempts to upsize most SELECT queries as functions. As noted earlier, the best-designed client/server applications open all forms and reports that display data with a filter to fetch only the data needed. In an Access application, the most common way to do this is to use the WhereCondition parameter with an OpenForm or OpenReport command to supply a filter.

When the form or report you are opening is based on a view in a project file, Access can send the filter directly to the server, and it sets the form or report Server Filter property to indicate that it has done so. However, when a form or report uses a function or a stored procedure as its record source, the only way to ask the server to filter the rows before it sends them back to the client machine is by using a parameter. When your code uses the more common WhereCondition technique, Access must send a command to the server to execute the function or stored procedure, and the server returns *all* the rows to the client. Access then applies the filter specified in the WhereCondition on the client machine and sets the form or report Filter and FilterOn properties. Filtering the rows after they have all been fetched from the server doesn't save any resources at all!

So, you should convert to a view most non-parameter queries that the wizard upsized as functions. For example, the Upsizing Wizard converted qryCompanies and qryContacts—both of which are used in forms that are opened with WhereCondition filters—to functions. To convert a simple function back to a view, perform the following steps:

1   Rename the function to something else—for example, append *old* to the name. (SQL Server won't let you save a function and a view with the same name.)

2   Open the function in Design view and open the SQL pane. Copy the SQL to the Clipboard.

3 Start a new view, close the Add Table dialog box, and open the SQL pane.

4 Paste the SQL from the function into the view and then move the focus away from the SQL pane into one of the other panes. If the SQL designer accepts the SQL as a view, you'll see it translate the SQL into the diagram and grid panes with no errors. If you get an error, you might not be able to convert the function to a view.

5 If the query designer displayed no error, save the new view using the previous query name. Run the view to verify that it returns the result you expect.

Fixing Parameter Names in Functions and Stored Procedures

When the Upsizing Wizard successfully converts parameter queries, it changes the parameter names to follow SQL Server naming conventions. When the parameter is a reference to a control on a form, it removes the brackets around the parts of the parameter name and inserts underscore characters. It also truncates the name to 30 characters if the resulting name is longer. For example, the wizard converts the original parameter in the qryContactProductsForInvoice query from [Forms]![frmInvoices]![InvoiceID] to @Forms__frmInvoices__InvoiceI. Of course, SQL Server doesn't have a clue that this parameter is originally a reference to a form control in Access, so Access prompts you for this parameter value if you try to open the query, even if frmInvoices is open.

You'll see in the next section that you'll resolve most parameters by supplying the parameter value in the Input Parameters property of the form or report that uses a parameter query or by supplying the parameter value in additional Visual Basic code that you write. An unwieldy name like this makes little sense, so you should fix names like this in parameter queries to something more reasonable. In the final query in the sample *ContactsSQL.mdf* database, you'll find that I changed the parameter name to @InvoiceNum. Note that I could not use @InvoiceID because InvoiceID is also the name of one of the columns in the tblContactProducts table used in the query.

When you use a function that includes a parameter as the row source of a combo box or a list box, Access can resolve the parameter for you as long as the parameter name matches the name of another control on the form. One such query in the sample database is the qlkp-ProductsForContacts function. However, the Upsizing Wizard changes the complex parameter name [Forms]![frmContacts]![fsubContactProducts].[Form]![cmbCategoryDescription] to @Forms__frmContacts__fsubCont. If you change the parameter name to simply @cmb-CategoryDescription and make a minor change on the form, the new parameter function works just fine.

Fixing Parameters in Forms and Reports

You already know that you can fix the parameter name in a function or stored procedure that you use as the row source of a combo box or list box so that it matches the name of a control on the form. When the Upsizing Wizard converts a form that has a combo box or list box that references a parameter query, it changes the Row Source property from the simple name of the query to a SELECT statement. For example, it changed the Row Source property of the cmbProductID combo box to SELECT * FROM qlkpProductsForContacts. You must change this property back to just the function name if you want Access to automatically resolve the parameter for you.

You can also write additional code that changes the row source that points to a parameter function to supply the parameter value in a SELECT statement. You'll have to make this change if the parameter references a control on some other open form. For example, the ReferredBy combo box on the frmCompanies form uses a parameter to filter the list to contacts who are from a company other than the one displayed in the current company row. The function requires a company ID value to return the correct list. Although I could have used the technique to resolve the parameter by making sure that the parameter name is the same as one of the controls on the form, I chose to resolve the parameter in code instead. I set the row source to a SELECT statement, as follows:

```
SELECT * FROM qlkpContactsForReferral(0)
```

Notice that zero is not a valid company ID, so the function returns no rows when the form first opens. However, in the form's Current event procedure, I added the following line of code to send the correct parameter to the function each time the user moves to a new row:

```
Me.ReferredBy.RowSource = "Select * From qlkpContactsForReferral(" & _
    Me.CompanyID & ")"
```

In Chapters 19 and 20, you learned how to specify the Input Parameters property for a form or report to automatically resolve any parameter required by the query in the record source. You can also dynamically set the record source in a report's Open event. For example, the four reports that produce mailing labels in the LawTrack Contacts application (rptCompanyLabels5160, rptCompanyLabels5163, rptContactLabels5160, and rptContactLabels5163) all use this technique. The reports must do this because one of two different forms might be supplying the parameter that indicates how many blank labels to skip, depending on how the user navigated through the application to these reports. For example, you can find the following code in the Open event procedure of the rptContactLabels5160 report:

```
' Set my record source based on which report options form is open
If IsFormLoaded("frmContactReports") Then
    ' Change my record source
    strSQL = "SELECT * FROM qryRptContactLabels(" & _
        Forms!frmContactReports!cmbUsedLabels & ")"
Else
    strSQL = "SELECT * FROM qryRptContactLabels(" & _
        Forms!fdlgContactPrintOptions!cmbUsedLabels & ")"
Me.RecordSource = strSQL
```

Another way to resolve a parameter automatically for a record source for a form that is not a subform is to change the record source to include a reference to the form and control that contain the parameter value. I didn't use this technique in any of the forms in the LawTrack Contacts application. Let's assume you have a form called frmProducts that uses a function named qryProducts. This function requires a product ID parameter value to filter the row returned. Your application opens another form called frmProductSearch that has a combo

Chapter 29

box called cmbProductID where the user can select the product ID that he or she wants to edit. You can set the record source of the frmProducts to:

```
Select * From qryProducts(@Forms!frmProductSearch!cmbProductID)
```

When you enter this in the Record Source property, Access sets the Input Parameters property to:

```
? = Forms!frmProductSearch!cmbProductID
```

As long as the frmProductSearch form is open when you open frmProducts, Access successfully resolves the parameter to pass to the function. Note that this technique won't work for a form that you use as a subform, particularly if the reference is to a parameter value on the outer form. The sequence in which the forms load prevents Access from resolving the parameter correctly.

Fixing Combo Boxes and List Boxes That Use a Large Row Source

One last item that you should fix when upsizing to a client/server architecture is to eliminate combo boxes and list boxes that use a very large row source (more than 1,000 rows). You probably shouldn't do this in a desktop application either, but you can get away with it if the table providing the rows is on the local machine. Performance suffers when you convert the application to a client/server architecture because all tables are now on the server.

As you learned in Chapter 19, the *Contacts.adp* sample project file has an unusually high Max Records setting because several of the forms use a combo box that has a row source that returns more than 50,000 rows. I fixed this in one of the forms so that you can learn a technique to deal with this problem. If you open the frmCompanies form, you'll see that the Postal Code combo box on the form is now a simple text box, as shown in Figure 29-10.

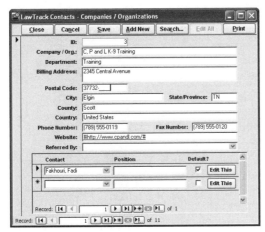

Figure 29-10. The Postal Code combo box on the frmCompanies form is replaced with a text box in the client/server version.

Chapter 29

The code in this control's After Update event procedure already had code to look up the matching city, county, and state values because the lookup table has only five-digit ZIP codes, but the user could enter a full nine-digit code. It was a simple matter to change this code to use an ADO recordset to quickly fetch the one row from the server. The new code is as follows:

```
Private Sub PostalCode_AfterUpdate()
Dim strPostal As String, rst As New ADODB.Recordset
    ' Grab the first 5 characters
    strPostal = Left(Me.PostalCode, 5)
    ' Open a recordset on tlkpZips to try to find the ZIP code
    rst.Open "SELECT City, State, County " & _
        "FROM tlkpZips WHERE ZipCode = '" & _
        strPostal & "'", CurrentProject.Connection, _
        adOpenForwardOnly, adLockReadOnly
    ' If got a record, then set the values of the related form fields
    If Not rst.EOF Then
        Me.City = rst!City
        Me.StateOrProvince = rst!State
        Me.County = rst!County
    End If
    ' Clean up
    rst.Close
    Set rst = Nothing
End Sub
```

Notice that the code uses a very efficient read-only recordset to fetch the single row from the server. This is a very efficient solution to the problem of using very large lookup tables.

You should now understand most of the issues you'll need to resolve to successfully upsize a desktop database application to a client/server architecture using a project file connected to an SQL Server database. In the next chapter, you'll learn about implementing security for your Access applications.

Chapter 30

Securing Your Database

When you're developing applications for your own use, you probably don't need to worry much about securing your database. But when you develop applications for others to use, particularly if the application manages sensitive information, you need to understand the steps you can take to make your data and application more secure.

This chapter discusses how to secure both the data and all objects (queries, forms, reports, macros, and modules) in a Microsoft Access desktop database. You can also find a discussion of the considerations for securing an application that you create with an Access project file and Microsoft SQL Server. Finally, you'll find a detailed explanation of the new macro security features implemented in Access 2003.

Securing a Desktop Database

If you explore any of the main editing forms in the Housing Reservations (*Housing.mdb*) database (for example, *frmEmployees*, *frmDepartments*, and *frmFacilities*), you'll discover code in each form's Load and Current event procedures that enables and disables various controls and features on the form depending on the sign-on status of the user. Also, when you start the application by opening the *frmSplash* form, a sign-on form opens and asks you to identify yourself and enter a password. Users of the application can be application administrators, department managers, or employees, and the code controls the actions that each different type of user can perform.

These measures might keep the casual user locked out of features they shouldn't be allowed to use, but they don't prevent anyone who has a retail copy of Access from opening the database and then rummaging around in the code to figure out how to break through this security. If you really want to prevent unauthorized access to the objects in this database, you must implement the security features built into Access.

> **Note** Few, if any, computer security systems are completely impenetrable. Although the security facilities in Access are state-of-the-art for personal computer desktop systems, a very knowledgeable person, given enough time, could probably break into your properly secured Access database. If you require utmost security for your data, you should consider moving it to a database system such as SQL Server.

Access Security Architecture

If you have had any experience with security on server or mainframe systems, the security architecture in Access will seem familiar to you. You can set up individual users who can be authorized or denied permission to various objects in your database. You can also define groups of users and assign permissions at the group level to make it easy to set up security for a large number of users. A user must be a member of the group to acquire the permissions of the group.

Access stores its security information in two separate locations. When you install Access, the setup program creates a default workgroup file (*System.mdw*) in a subfolder of your Documents and Settings folder that contains the definition of all users and groups. Access opens this file each time you open a desktop database. When you create a database, Access stores the permissions granted to individual users or groups of users within the .mdb desktop database file. You can see this architecture depicted in Figure 30-1.

> **Note** You might also find the *System.mdw* file in another location, such as in a subfolder of your Program Files folder or in the C:\Windows\System32 folder. When you install a new version of Microsoft Access on a machine that has a previous version installed, the installation program leaves the file in its original location if it is compatible with the new version you are installing.

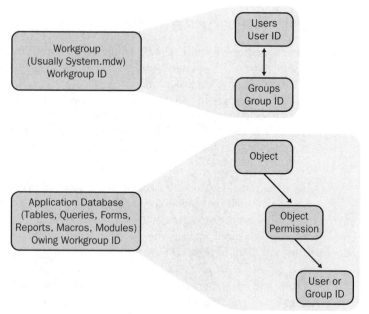

Figure 30-1. The general architecture of the Access security system. User and group profiles are stored in a workgroup file. Individual object permissions are stored in each database file.

The location of your current workgroup file is stored in your Windows registry. As you'll learn later, you can use a special utility program, the Workgroup Administrator, to change your current workgroup or to define a new workgroup file. You can also specify a different workgroup file at run time by adding a parameter on the command line of a startup shortcut. See "Creating an Application Shortcut" on page 1215 for details about runtime options. If you frequently run a shared, secured application over a network, your system administrator might set up your default workgroup as a shared file in a network folder.

Each workgroup has a unique internal identifier (Workgroup ID) that the Workgroup Administrator creates when you define a new workgroup file. Any database created under the workgroup is owned by the workgroup as well as by the user who created the database. Each user and group also has a unique internal identifier (User ID and Group ID), and, as you'll learn later, you can duplicate the same user and group ID in several different workgroups. When you assign permission to an object in your database, Access stores in the database the internal ID of the user or group along with the permission. In this way, the permissions that you grant move with the database file if you move the file to another folder or computer.

Users, Groups, and Permissions

In general, a computer security system is either *open* or *closed*. In an open security model, access is granted to all users (even users not identified to the system) unless specifically denied. In a closed model, no access is granted to anyone unless specifically defined.

At first blush, the Access security model seems open because you can start Access without logging on, create databases, and give them to other users who have Access to run or modify them as they please. You don't have to interact with security at all. In truth, the security model in Access is closed, but it appears open because all workgroup files include a default user ID that has no password and that has default ownership of, and default permission to, all objects. Whenever you open a desktop database while joined to a default workgroup file, Access silently signs you on using this default user ID.

Built-In Users and Groups

All Access workgroup files installed anywhere in the world contain one built-in user ID and two built-in groups. The user ID is called *Admin*, and, as noted earlier, if there's no password defined for this user, Access automatically logs you on as *Admin* and grants you all the rights and privileges of this user ID. A key fact is the internal identifier of the Admin user ID is identical in all workgroups anywhere in the world. This makes the Admin user ID universal.

Whenever you create a new database or an object within a database, your current user ID becomes the owner of the object and is granted full permissions to the object by default. Because most users of Access never change their default security settings, they always log on to Access as *Admin*, so anything they create is owned by the universal Admin user ID. If someone else who hasn't changed the default security settings sends you a database he or she creates, every object in the database is owned by *Admin*, and *Admin* has full permission to all

Chapter 30

objects. Your default user ID is also *Admin*, so Access considers you the owner of the database with full rights when you open the database. Clearly, you have to figure out how to make some user ID other than *Admin* the owner of your database and all the objects in it if you want to secure it.

But wait, there's more! The first built-in group is Users. Every user ID must belong to at least one group. By default, all users (even new ones you create) become permanent members of the Users group. As you'll learn later, you cannot remove a user ID from the Users group. In addition, the internal ID for the Users group is universal and identical in every workgroup. Access by default grants the Users group full permissions to any new database or object you create. Unless you explicitly remove permissions from the Users group in your database, even if a user is logged on with a user ID other than *Admin*, he or she still has full access to your databases and the objects within them because the user is always a member of the universal Users group!

The second built-in group is Admins. The internal ID of the Admins group is unique for each workgroup file, depending on the information supplied to the Workgroup Administrator program when you or the setup program created the workgroup file. Only the universal *Admin* user ID is, by default, a member of the Admins group. At least one user ID must be defined as a member of the Admins group, so you can't remove the default *Admin* user ID from the Admins group until you define another user ID and add it to that group. After you do this, you can remove the default *Admin* user ID.

The Admins group has a couple of key properties. First, only members of the Admins group may define or modify user and group profiles and reset passwords. (You can always reset your own password.) Second, the internal ID of the Admins group is the same as the internal ID for the workgroup. When you create a database, Access stores the internal workgroup ID of the workgroup to which you are joined in the database. Members of the Admins group in the workgroup you used to create the database have full authority to grant permissions to objects in the database, even if the user ID or the Admins group has no permission to any object. This means that members of Admins in the original workgroup can grant themselves permission to secured objects, even if they initially have no permission. The key fact to understand is that any database you create while connected to a particular workgroup file inherits the ID of that workgroup. Someone can be a member of Admins in another workgroup, but unless the workgroup IDs match, that person won't have security permissions to your database.

Object Permissions

Table 30-1 lists the various permissions you can assign to a database or to the objects within a database. Note that the owner of an object might not have any specific permissions, but because of the owner status he or she can grant any or all of the permissions to any user or group, including to his or her own user ID. By default, the user ID that is logged on when a new object is created automatically becomes the owner of the object. Also by default, the creator of an object automatically has all permissions to the object. As you'll learn later, as the owner of an object, you can give away ownership to another user or group ID.

Table 30-1. Permissions You Can Grant Using Access Security

Permission	Applies To	Meaning
Open/Run	Database, Form, Report, Macro	Grants permission to open or run the object. (All users have permission to run procedures in modules.)
Open Exclusive	Database	Grants permission to open the database and lock out other users.
Read Design	Table, Query, Form, Report, Macro, Module	Grants permission to open the object in Design view. For tables and queries, granting any access to the data also implies Read Design permission because the design must be available in order to correctly access the data.
Modify Design	Table, Query, Form, Report, Macro, Module	Grants permission to change the design of an object. If your application has Visual Basic code that changes the definition of queries while executing, you must grant Modify Design permission to all users for those queries.
Administer	Database, Table, Query, Form, Report, Macro, Module	Grants permission to assign permissions to the object, even though the user or group might not own the object.
Read Data	Table, Query	Allows the user or group to read the data in the table or query. Also implies Read Design permission. For a query, the user must have Read Data permissions on all tables or queries used in the query.
Update Data	Table, Query	Grants permission to update data in the table or query. Also implies Read Data and Read Design permissions. For a query, the user must have Update Data permissions on the tables or queries being updated through the query.
Insert Data	Table, Query	Grants permission to insert data in the table or query. Also implies Read Data and Read Design permissions. For a query, the user must have Insert Data permissions on the tables or queries being updated through the query.
Delete Data	Table, Query	Grants permission to delete data in the table or query. Also implies Read Data and Read Design permissions. For a query, the user must have Delete Data permissions on the tables or queries being updated through the query.

Chapter 30

Note Because data access pages are stored outside your desktop database (.mdb) file, Access cannot secure them.

Explicit and Implicit Permissions

As stated earlier, you can gain access to an object either by permissions assigned to your user ID or through permissions granted to any group to which you belong. Access uses a least restrictive permissions model, which means you have the highest permissions granted either to your user ID or to any group of which you are a member. Figure 30-2 shows a hypothetical set of users and groups and the permissions granted explicitly to each user or group for a table object. Note that individual users implicitly inherit additional permissions or ownership rights because of their membership in one or more groups. David has at least Read Data, Update Data, Insert Data, and Delete Data permissions because of his membership in the SalesMgmt group. In this example, David is the owner of the table because the original owner assigned ownership to him, not because he originally created the object. David doesn't have explicit permission to administer or modify the design of the object, but he can grant himself any missing permissions because he is the owner.

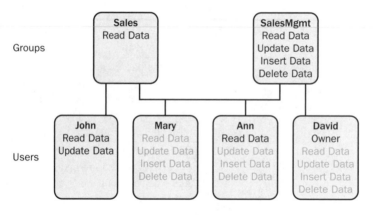

Key: Explicit permissions   Inherited permissions

Explicit Permissions:
- Sales has Read permission.
- SalesMgmt has Read, Update, Insert, and Delete permissions.
- John has Read and Update permissions.
- Mary has no explicit permissions.
- Ann has Read permission.
- David owns the object (but isn't the original creator of the object).

Actual Permissions:
- John has Read and Update permissions (even though Sales can only Read).
- Mary has Read, Update, Insert, and Delete permissions (through SalesMgmt).
- Ann has Read permission, and Update, Insert and Delete permissions (through SalesMgmt).
- David can assign permissions, including to himself (because he owns the object). He also inherits Read, Update, Insert, and Delete permissions from SalesMgmt.

Figure 30-2. An example showing explicitly assigned permissions and the permissions implicit for each user through group membership.

You can see why a user other than *Admin* might still have full permissions to all your objects—all users are always members of the Users group, which is, by default, granted full permissions to any new object. To check the permissions for any user or group, first open the database in which you want to review permissions. (You can do this for all the sample databases you've installed on your hard disk except *HousingSecured.mdb*.) You must either be the owner of the database and of all the objects you want to check or have Administer permission on the database and objects. For this example, open the unsecured *Housing.mdb* database. Choose Security from the Tools menu, and then choose User and Group Permissions from the submenu. Access opens the dialog box shown in Figure 30-3. (The dialog box initially shows the permissions for the object you selected in the Database window.)

Figure 30-3. Some of the permissions for the Admin user in the Housing Reservations sample database.

In the upper portion of the window, in the User/Group Name list, you can see the list either of users or of groups defined in the database. Choose either the List Users or the List Groups option to switch from one list to the other. In the Object Name list, you can see a list of objects. Use the Object Type drop-down list below the list to select the type of objects you want to review. Click the object of interest to see the explicitly defined permissions in the Permissions section in the lower half of the window. If you select Groups and then select the Users group, you can wander around all the objects and see that this group has full permissions for all objects. As you'll learn later, you can select one or more objects to which you have Administer permission and change the permissions for any user or group.

Caution Do not attempt to change permissions or ownership of any object until you fully understand all the implications of doing so. As you first start to learn about security facilities in Access, it's a good idea to always work in a backup copy of your database. You might end up denying yourself permission and not be able to recover!

If you click the Change Owner tab, you can peruse lists of the various objects and see what ID (either a user or a group) currently owns the object. In an unsecured database, the Admin user owns all the objects. You can select one or more objects, choose a different user or group, and click the Change Owner button to assign a new owner. Never give away ownership of an object unless you fully understand the implications of doing so. You might first want to be sure that you know how to log on as the potential new owner before assigning ownership to that new owner so that you can still control ownership of the object. If you own an object, you can always give ownership away (or back) to another user or group ID.

Using the Security Wizard

Now that you understand how Access security works, it should be obvious to you that because Access security is transparently open, you have a lot of work to do to actually secure a database. When you install Microsoft Office, the setup program builds your default workgroup from your Windows user and company name information—something that anyone who has access to your computer can figure out and duplicate. So, for starters you need a unique workgroup so that it's difficult to reproduce the workgroup ID that gives all members of the Admins group authority to change permissions. Next you need a user ID other than *Admin* to own your database and all the objects in it. You also need to remove all permissions from the Users group for all objects. To make sure no one can peruse your data and code with a disk-editing utility, you should also encode your database. (You can find the Encode/Decode Database command by choosing Security on the Tools menu.)

You could perform all these steps by hand, but fortunately Microsoft has provided a User-Level Security Wizard to help you out. The Security Wizard performs all the repetitious work involved in the previous steps.

Preliminary Preparations

Before the wizard can successfully perform its task, you must be logged on as the owner of the database that you want to secure, or you must be logged on to the same workgroup file you used when you created the database and you must be a member of the Admins group in that workgroup. Remember that one of the key steps is creating a new workgroup with a unique workgroup ID; this should not match the workgroup you used to create the database. Also, you were probably logged on as *Admin* when you created the database. You can't make a database owned by *Admin* secure, so you need to assign a new owner as well.

The Security Wizard in Access 2003 lets you secure your database even when you're logged on as any user in the Admins group in the original workgroup that was used when the database was created. You can also use the Security Wizard when you're logged on as *Admin* in any workgroup as long as *Admin* owns all the objects. When you try to use the wizard in the latter situation, the wizard forces you to create a new workgroup. The wizard transfers ownership of your database to a new user ID in the new workgroup.

> **Note**   You can also create a new workgroup and a new non-*Admin* user ID in the Admins group of that workgroup before you start the wizard, but your new user ID must own the database, or the wizard will fail when it tries to reassign ownership.

It helps you understand Access security better if you first create a new workgroup, define at least one new user ID, and remove the Admin user from the Admins group. To create a new workgroup, you need to run the Workgroup Administrator. Start Access, choose Security on the Tools menu, and then choose Workgroup Administrator on the submenu. The Workgroup Administrator starts, as shown in Figure 30-4.

Figure 30-4.   The opening dialog box in the Workgroup Administrator.

Notice that the Workgroup Administrator displays your name and company information in its opening dialog box. This is the same information that the installation program used to create your default workgroup file, so it wouldn't be difficult for anyone who has access to your machine to duplicate your original file. You can also see the full path name of the workgroup file to which you are currently joined. (Unless you have used the Workgroup Administrator since you installed Office, this is the workgroup file that the setup program created.) As shown in Figure 30-4, your default file is called System.mdw, which can be found in a subfolder of your Documents and Settings folder. If you have a different workgroup file already built, you can click the Join button to open a dialog box in which you can specify the location of that file. A Browse button in the resulting dialog box makes it easy to locate the file.

> **Caution**   Be sure to note the location of your default System.mdw file when you run the Workgroup Administrator for the first time. You'll need to run the Workgroup Administrator again after you have finished working through the examples in this chapter and locate this file to rejoin your original workgroup. Also, the default location for System.mdw (when you had no previous version of Access on your machine when you installed Office 2003) is C:\Documents and Settings\<*your Windows logon ID*>\Application Data\Microsoft\Access, but Application Data is a hidden folder. You might need to open Windows Explorer, choose Folder Options from the Tools menu, and select the **Show hidden files and folders** option on the View tab of the Folder Options dialog box.

To create and join a new workgroup, click the Create button. The Workgroup Administrator displays a second dialog box, as shown in Figure 30-5 on the next page. Enter a name, an

Chapter 30

organization name, and a pattern of case-sensitive letters and numbers up to 20 characters long as the Workgroup ID. The Workgroup Administrator uses the information in these three fields to generate a unique 64-bit internal ID. To create another workgroup file with an identical ID, you must enter the information in these three fields in *exactly* the same manner, including the same pattern of uppercase and lowercase letters. You should record this information and keep it in a safe place so that you can rebuild your workgroup file should it ever be deleted or become unusable. The information you can see in Figure 30-5 is the exact data I used to create the *Secured.mdw* workgroup file that you can find on the companion CD.

Figure 30-5. Entering the information that the Workgroup Administrator uses to create a unique ID in your new workgroup file.

Note You'll need either the sample *Secured.mdw* file or one created with the same parameters to open the *HousingSecured.mdb* sample database successfully. You can either create your own workgroup file with the settings shown in Figure 30-5 or use the Workgroup Administrator to join the *Secured.mdw* workgroup you'll find in the sample files.

Click OK to go to a dialog box where you can specify the location and name of your new workgroup file. If you're creating the file in the same folder as the existing workgroup file, be sure to give the new file a different name—something like *secured.mdw*. Click OK in that dialog box to see a confirmation dialog box as shown in Figure 30-6.

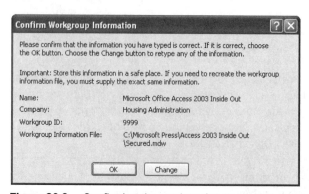

Figure 30-6. Confirming the settings for a new workgroup file.

In this dialog box, you can verify the key values that you want the Workgroup Administrator to use for your new workgroup file. (The settings in Figure 30-6 are what I used to create the *Secured.mdw* sample file.) You can click Change to return to the dialog box shown in Figure 30-5. Click OK to create the new workgroup file. The Workgroup Administrator also changes your registry settings to join you to the newly created workgroup. Click OK in the Confirm Workgroup Information dialog box, and the Workgroup Administrator returns you to its original dialog box, shown in Figure 30-4. When you return to this dialog box, you'll see the name of your new file to confirm that you have not only created a new workgroup file but also joined that file. Click OK to close the Workgroup Administrator. If you have a database open when you use the Workgroup Administrator to create or join another workgroup, Access automatically closes and reopens the database using the new workgroup as soon as you exit the Workgroup Administrator.

After you join the new workgroup, you need to add a new user, add that user to the Admins group, define a password for *Admin* (so that Access will prompt for a user name and password), and remove the *Admin* user from the Admins group. You don't need to open a database to do any of this. With Access open, choose Security from the Tools menu and then select User and Group Accounts from the submenu. (Because you don't yet have a password defined for *Admin*, Access silently logs you on as *Admin*, the only member of the Admins group in your new workgroup.) Access shows you the User and Group Accounts dialog box that you can see in Figure 30-7.

Figure 30-7. The User and Group Accounts dialog box.

If you use the Name drop-down list in the User area of the Users tab, you'll see there's only one user defined in this workgroup—*Admin*. In the lower part of the window, the two available groups appear on the left.

Under Member Of on the right side you can see that *Admin* belongs to both groups. The User area of the Users tab contains the buttons you use to define a new user, to delete the user currently selected in the Name list (but Access won't ever let you delete the *Admin* user), and to clear the password for the currently selected user. In this case, you need a new user who will

Microsoft Office Access 2003 Inside Out

both own all the objects and be a member of the Admins group. Click the New button to display the New User/Group dialog box. For the *Secured.mdw* sample file, I created a new user called HousingAdmin and assigned a Personal ID of 9999, as shown in Figure 30-8.

Figure 30-8. Defining a new user in the workgroup file to which you are currently joined.

> **Caution** The examples in this book use a simple sequence of digits to make it easy for you to duplicate the sample workgroup file and user and group IDs. When you create your own security system, you should use far more complex ID values to make it more difficult to break into your secured databases.

The Personal ID (this is *not* the user's password) must contain at least 4 and no more than 20 characters and numbers. Access uses the Name and Personal ID you enter to create the internal user identifier for this user. If you enter this exact information in another workgroup file, you will have a HousingAdmin user ID identical to this one. Note that the combination of uppercase and lowercase letters is important. In other words, entering HOUSINGADMIN and 9999 creates a user ID that has an entirely different internal identification code. As you'll discover later, the name is not case sensitive in the Logon dialog box, so you can't create a HousingAdmin and a HOUSINGADMIN user in the same workgroup.

Click OK to add the user. You should see the new user selected in the Name drop-down list. In the Available Groups list, select the Admins group and click the Add button to make the new user a member of the Admins group. You can see that the new user is already a member of the Users group, which gives it full permissions to all objects in any unsecured database. You cannot remove any user from the Users group. (You can, however, completely delete any user other than the *Admin* user.)

Next, select your current ID (Admin) in the Name drop-down list. Select the Admins group in the Member Of list, and click Remove to remove Admin from the Admins group. Note that if you try to do this before you create the new user ID and add it to Admins, Access won't let you because at least one user must be a member of the Admins group. Finally, click the

Change Logon Password tab, and enter a password in both the New Password and Verify boxes. In the *Secured.mdw* file, I set a password of *housing* for *Admin*. Click Apply to set the password. Setting a password for *Admin* forces Access to ask you for a name and password the next time you start Access in this workgroup.

After you create the new user ID, you need to quit and then restart Access. As soon as you try to open any database, Access prompts you for a user name and password because the default user ID, *Admin*, now is secured with a password. Because you haven't logged on as Housing-Admin yet and assigned a password to that account, you can enter HousingAdmin and no password in the Logon dialog box. Now that you are signed on as the HousingAdmin user, you can return to the User and Group Accounts dialog box and assign a password as you did for *Admin*. This is a good idea because this user will ultimately be the owner of the new secured database. (I did not assign a password to the HousingAdmin user in the sample *Secured.mdw* workgroup file.)

Now, you must also create a new copy of your database that is owned by the new user ID. To do that, follow these steps:

1 Log on as the new user.

2 Create a new blank database. See "Creating a New Empty Database" on page 90 for details. For this example, create a new database named *HousingCopy.mdb*.

3 Import all the objects from the database you want to secure by choosing Get External Data from the File menu, and then choosing Import from the submenu. Point to the original database (*Housing2BSecured.mdb*) and click Import, and then be sure to select all objects on all the tabs (except data access pages on the Pages tab) in the Import Objects dialog box.

If your old database contains any custom menus, toolbars, or import/export specifications, be sure to click the Options tab and select the options to import these objects. See "Importing Access Objects" on page 191 for details. In this case, select Relationships and Menus and Toolbars under Import, Definition and Data under Import Tables, and As Queries under Import Queries, and then click OK.

4 After the import completes, you should compile and save the Visual Basic project and compact the database. (See Chapter 24, "The Finishing Touches," for details.)

To compile the project, open any module in Design view. If the code you imported from the old database used either Data Access or Office objects, you should choose References from the Tools menu and include those libraries. (The Housing2BSecured database requires the Microsoft Office 11.0 Object Library.) Choose Compile Housing-Copy from the Debug menu, and if the project compiles successfully, choose Save from the File menu.

To compact the database, choose Database Utilities from the Tools menu, and then choose Compact and Repair Database from the submenu.

You should now have a new copy of your database that is owned by the new user ID you created in a new workgroup.

Chapter 30

Running the Wizard

Now you're ready to run the User-Level Security Wizard. Be sure you're logged on as the owner of the database that you want to secure. If you have followed along with the steps thus far, you can open the *HousingCopy.mdb* database that you created. If you didn't follow along and create a new workgroup and copy of the database, you can open the Housing2BSecured database using your default workgroup and the Admin user ID. This second choice involves less preparatory work, but you'll see that the wizard gives you fewer options and forces you to create a new workgroup anyway. The Security Wizard will secure the open database, so it's a good idea to have a backup copy (although the wizard will create a backup copy for you).

The following procedure assumes that you signed on as the HousingAdmin user in a new workgroup (or the supplied *Secured.mdw* workgroup file) and created a *HousingCopy.mdb* file that is owned by the HousingAdmin user. Quit and restart Access and then reopen your new database—this ensures that Access does not have the database open exclusively. To start the Security Wizard, choose Security from the Tools menu and then choose User-Level Security Wizard from the submenu. The wizard starts and displays the dialog box shown in Figure 30-9.

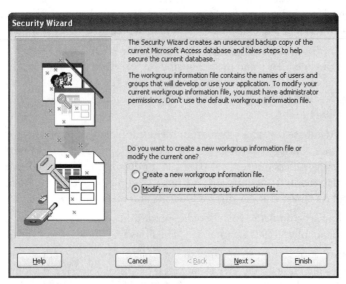

Figure 30-9. The opening window in the User-Level Security Wizard.

The first window explains what the wizard does and gives you two options. If you choose the first option, the wizard will create a new workgroup file, create a new (not Admin) user ID in that workgroup, and then secure the database using that workgroup and user ID. If you choose the second option, the wizard will secure the database using your current workgroup file and user ID. If you have been following along and you built a new workgroup and user ID and created a new copy of the database owned by that user, you should choose the second option, and then click Next to display the window shown in Figure 30-10.

> **Note** If you are logged on as Admin in your default workgroup and are securing the *Housing2BSecured.mdb* sample database, the wizard won't offer the second option at all. See the sidebar, "Exploring the Wizard's First Option," to see what you must do in this case.

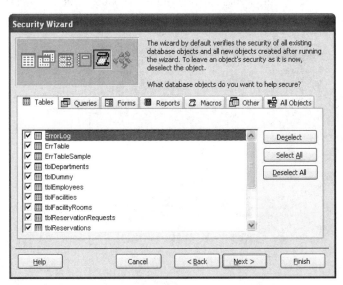

Figure 30-10. Choosing the objects that you want the wizard to secure.

In the window shown in Figure 30-10, the wizard gives you the option to secure only selected objects. By default, the wizard selects all objects. Note that you cannot secure data access pages with Access security because these objects are stored in files external to Access. If you secure the tables needed by the data access page, your browser prompts the user for a user name and password as long as the connection properties of the data access page specify an appropriate workgroup.

If you don't want to secure an object, you can click the check box next to an object name to clear it. For example, perhaps you don't need to secure certain forms and reports, but you do want to assign permissions to tables and queries. Click Next to continue.

In the screen shown in Figure 30-11 on page 1179, the wizard offers to set up one or more optional groups for you. You can click the name of each group in the box on the left to display a description of the permissions that the wizard will set up for the group in the Group Permissions box. If, for example, you want to set up a group of users who have only read and execute permissions to all objects, select the Read-Only Users check box to ask the wizard to create this group.

Exploring the Wizard's First Option

If you're curious about how the first option in the Security Wizard's opening window works, select it and click Next. (If you are logged on as the Admin user ID and are securing the *Housing2BSecured.mdb* file, the wizard offers only the first option.) The wizard displays a workgroup setup window as shown here.

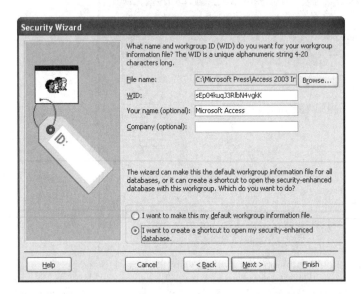

Note that the wizard asks you for the same bits of information as the Workgroup Administrator, which you used earlier, but in a different sequence. Unlike the Workgroup Administrator, this wizard requires you to enter a Workgroup ID (WID), but allows you to optionally fill in the Your Name and Company fields (the Organization field in the Workgroup Administrator). You must also specify the location and name of your new workgroup file. You can click an option to make this new workgroup the default after the wizard has finished—I don't recommend this option because it's too easy to forget that the wizard has switched workgroups on you if you want to work with or secure other databases. The best option is to let the wizard create a shortcut on your desktop that will specify the new workgroup to be used when you open the secured database.

When you choose or are forced to use this option, you'll find that the wizard later insists on creating a new user ID that is the same as your Windows logon ID. The wizard makes this ID the owner of the database and completely ignores any other users defined in your current workgroup file.

You can accept the randomly generated Group ID that the wizard displays or type in your own ID. In either case, I recommend that you write down the exact Group name and Group ID information, because you will need this information if you ever need to rebuild the group. (Like the Workgroup ID and the Personal ID, the Group ID is case sensitive.) Later, the wizard gives you the option to also define users and assign them to the groups you choose. Because you don't need any of the groups that the wizard offers, you can leave them all unselected. (You will create custom groups for this application later.) Click Next to go to the next window, shown in Figure 30-12.

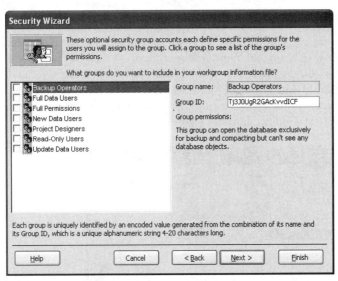

Figure 30-11. Choosing additional optional groups in the Security Wizard.

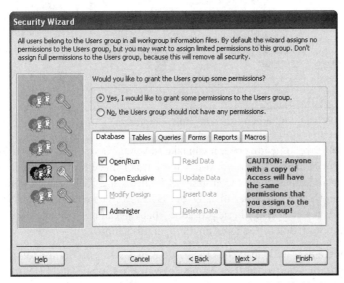

Figure 30-12. Allowing some permissions to the default Users group.

In this window, the wizard offers to leave some permissions intact for the Users group. Normally, you will want to let the wizard remove all permissions from this group (the default) to fully secure your database. (Remember, every workgroup file in the world has the same Users group, and this group has full permission to all objects by default.) If you have tried to open the *HousingSecured.mdb* database—a database that is a copy of the result you should obtain if you complete all the steps in this section—you probably discovered that you can look at all the data and the design of all objects, but you can't change anything. I accomplished this by granting to the Users group Open/Run permission on the database, and either Read Design or Read Data permission on all other objects.

You can duplicate this by first selecting Yes, I would like to grant some permissions to the Users group, and then setting the appropriate permissions for each of the object types. Select Open/Run for the database, Read Data (which also selects Read Design) for tables and queries, and Open/Run and Read Design for forms, reports, and macros. Note that the wizard cautions you about granting access when you grant permissions to the Users group. Click Next to go to the next window, shown in Figure 30-13.

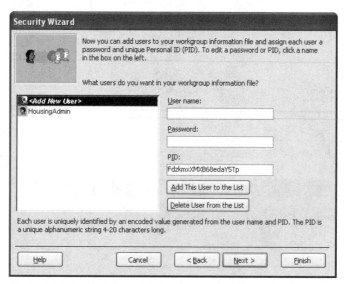

Figure 30-13. Defining additional users in your workgroup.

You can potentially save some time later if you take advantage of the wizard's offer to create new users now. For Housing2BSecured, you will eventually need one user ID for each employee. (The sample database has 15 employees defined.) You could use this panel to define all 15 employees and assign a PID (personal ID) of 9999. However, in the *Housing2BSecured.mdb* sample database, I created a Visual Basic procedure that you can use to create the users and groups you need, so you don't need to do anything in this window.

If you want to add a user to the list, click the <Add New User> entry at the top of the list, enter the information required for User Name, Password (optional), and PID, and then click Add This User to the List to move the information to the list on the left. If you don't assign passwords now, you'll have to later sign on as each user individually and use the User and Group Accounts dialog box to set the passwords.

Note that the wizard also displays existing users in the list (HousingAdmin in this case), but you can't delete or change them. The wizard indicates new users you have defined in this window by displaying an asterisk next to the person icon. If you think you made a mistake, you can select any of the new users in the list to see the data you specified. You can click Delete User from the List to remove one you added by mistake.

> **Note** If you're working in the *HousingCopy.mdb* that you created earlier, the wizard won't change the owner of the database—it already has an owner that isn't *Admin*. If you're using your default workgroup (signed on as *Admin*) and securing the *Housing2BSecured.mdb* sample database, you'll see your Windows login ID. The wizard makes this ID the new owner of the secured database. As you can see, going to the trouble of creating a new workgroup and owner of the database first allows you to control the ID of the owner of the secured database.

Click Next to go to the next window, in which the wizard allows you to assign users to groups. Because you didn't select any additional groups (in the window shown earlier in Figure 30-11), click Next to go to the wizard's final window, shown in Figure 30-14.

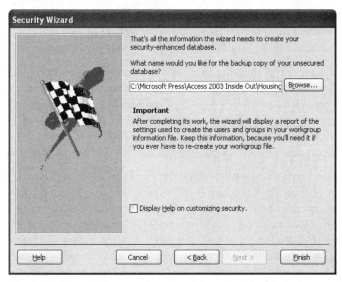

Figure 30-14. Telling the User-Level Security Wizard where to make a backup copy of your database.

In the last window, you can specify the name of the backup copy of your database file. Note that the wizard suggests using the original name of the database with a .bak extension. Click Finish to let the wizard do its work.

When the wizard is done securing your objects, it produces a report that lists the workgroup parameters it used if you asked it to create a new workgroup, and the information you'll need to re-create any users and groups the wizard built for you. When you close the Report window, the wizard offers to save the report as a Snapshot file (.snp extension) for later reference. (You can find a sample security report in the file *HousingSecureSample.snp* in the Access 2003 Inside Out folder.) You should accept the wizard's offer so that you don't lose this critical information. The wizard then closes your newly secured database, encodes it, and then reopens it.

If you didn't get the result you wanted, you can always delete the newly secured database and rename the backup file that the wizard created back to its original name. In your sample files, you'll find *HousingSecured.mdb* that is the result of running the wizard following the preceding steps on a copy of the *Housing2BSecured.mdb* database. After creating a secured copy of your database, you should save the original unsecured version in a safe place—perhaps a secured folder to which only you have access.

As long as you are signed on as the HousingAdmin user, you should be able to open any of the objects in the *HousingSecured.mdb* database in Design view and change and save the design. You still won't be able to run the application (by opening the frmSplash form) because your workgroup does not contain the group and user IDs that the application requires to run.

Setting Up Your Secured Database

After you have a secured database, you need to formulate a plan to set up users and groups and grant specific permissions. Remember, the database modified by the Security Wizard won't let users who are joined to a default workgroup into the database at all. Although I suggested that you grant some limited permissions to the Users group in the previous section, you probably won't do this in a database that you intend to fully secure.

It's easier to design a security plan if your application is already "security aware." Although you can certainly secure the objects in your database to restrict what a user can do, your application should be aware of the permission restrictions enforced by security and not let users get to parts of the application that will generate security error messages. If, for example, a user isn't allowed to view the data in a table, your application code should not provide a switchboard that allows the user to attempt to open a form or report that uses the secured table.

As you might have noticed when you try to run the unsecured Housing database application (*Housing.mdb*) by opening the frmSplash form, it forces you to sign on and then uses information from the employee and department tables to restrict access to certain features in the application. When you sign on as an employee who is not an administrator and not the manager of a department, code in the forms restricts you to viewing and editing your own record, viewing information from the tblDepartments table only for your own department, and entering new reservation requests only for yourself. An employee can't confirm a reservation but can cancel (delete) his or her own reservations and requests.

A department manager can view and edit information for all the employees in the department, can enter new reservation requests for employees in the department, and can cancel reservation requests or confirmed reservations for employees in the department. A department manager cannot view records for employees from other departments. Finally, an administrator has full access to all parts of the application and has the authority to confirm reservation requests.

So, this application is already security aware. Code in the sign-on form validates the user and sets public variables to indicate what the current user can do. For example, here's the code in the frmEmployee form (the form that displays information from the tblEmployees table) Load event:

```
' If an administrator, allowed to do anything
If (gintIsAdmin = True) Then Exit Sub
```

```
' Hide the Admin checkbox
Me.IsAdmin.Visible = False
' If a department manager, allow full edit of department employees
If (gintIsManager = True) Then
    ' Set the default department for new employees
    Me.DepartmentID.DefaultValue = glngThisDeptID
    ' Other restrictions set in current event
    Exit Sub
End If
' Just a plain vanilla user - lock it up
' Disallow new rows
Me.AllowAdditions = False
' Disallow filters
Me.AllowFilters = False
' Disallow deletions
Me.AllowDeletions = False
' User restricted to edit personal info only in Current event
```

The gintIsAdmin public variable is True if an administrator is signed on. The gintIsManager public variable is True if the user is a department manager. You can see that the code does not restrict the form for an administrator. For a department manager, the form sets the default department ID for any new employee that the manager wants to add and hides the IsAdmin field that would allow the user to change administrator status. For regular employees, the code disables adding new records, deleting records, and applying filters. You'll find code similar to this in every form that edits data. You can also look at the code in the Current event of these forms and find that additional restrictions are applied as the user moves to different records. Finally, code in some of the switchboard forms disallows access to parts of the application entirely, depending on the user's authority.

So, you can see that adding Access security to this application is going to be relatively simple. Clearly, you need three groups: application administrators, department managers, and employees. You can assign employees to these groups and then assign permissions to the groups based on the security rules already established within the application code. You could certainly define these groups and users using the User and Group Accounts and User and Group Permissions dialog boxes. However, because this database already contains employee records, you can write some Visual Basic code to do the hard work. All that's missing from the tblEmployees table is a field for the Access user name. I've already added that column (UserID) to the table in the *Housing2BSecured.mdb* database and supplied the values. You can open the modSecurity module (it should also be in your *HousingCopy.mdb* file if you imported all the objects correctly) and run the SetupUsers sub. To run this code, press Ctrl+G to open the Immediate window in the Visual Basic Editor, type **SetupUsers**, and press Enter. The code is as follows:

```
Public Sub SetupUsers()
Dim db As DAO.Database, rst As DAO.Recordset
Dim ws As DAO.Workspace, usr As DAO.User, grp As DAO.Group
    ' Use this sub to set up users and groups in the current workgroup
    ' Code reads through tblEmployees and creates users specified
    '  in the UserID field.
    ' Also creates the AppAdmin, DeptMgrs, and Employees groups.
```

```
' Open a recordset on qryEmployeeSignon that contains all the data we need
Set db = CurrentDb
Set rst = db.OpenRecordset("qryEmployeeSignon")
' Set a local error trap in case you've already run this
On Error Resume Next
' Call the undo procedure first to be sure we're starting clean
Call UndoUsersAndGroups
' Now, create the new groups
Set ws = DBEngine(0)
Set grp = ws.CreateGroup("AppAdmin", "9999")
ws.Groups.Append grp
Set grp = ws.CreateGroup("DeptMgrs", "9999")
ws.Groups.Append grp
Set grp = ws.CreateGroup("Employees", "9999")
ws.Groups.Append grp
ws.Groups.Refresh
' Now read all employee records, build users, and set groups
Do Until rst.EOF
    ' Create user
    Set usr = ws.CreateUser(rst!UserID, "9999", rst!Password)
    ws.Users.Append usr
    ' Add to Users and Employees groups
    Set grp = usr.CreateGroup("Users")
    usr.Groups.Append grp
    Set grp = usr.CreateGroup("Employees")
    usr.Groups.Append grp
    ' Check for IsAdmin
    If (rst!IsAdmin = True) Then
        ' Add to AppAdmin
        Set grp = usr.CreateGroup("AppAdmin")
        usr.Groups.Append grp
        ' And Admins
        Set grp = usr.CreateGroup("Admins")
        usr.Groups.Append grp
        ' If also dept manager,
        If rst!EmployeeNumber = rst!ManagerNumber Then
            ' Add to that group, too
            Set grp = usr.CreateGroup("DeptMgrs")
            usr.Groups.Append grp
        End If
    ' Not admin - is department manager?
    ElseIf rst!EmployeeNumber = rst!ManagerNumber Then
        ' Add to Admins and DeptMgrs
        Set grp = usr.CreateGroup("Admins")
        usr.Groups.Append grp
        Set grp = usr.CreateGroup("DeptMgrs")
        usr.Groups.Append grp
    End If
    rst.MoveNext
Loop
ws.Users.Refresh
ws.Groups.Refresh
rst.Close
Set rst = Nothing
```

```
      Set grp = Nothing
      Set usr = Nothing
      Set ws = Nothing
      Set db = Nothing
End Sub
```

As long as you're signed on as a member of the Admins group or the owner of the database, you should be able to run this code successfully. The code opens a recordset on a query that provides the necessary information from the tblEmployees and tblDepartments tables. It then calls another sub procedure to remove any previously defined users and groups (UndoUsersAndGroups). It next creates the three special groups that represent the three levels of authority in the application: AppAdmins, DeptMgrs, and Employees. Finally, it loops through all the employee records, creates a new user ID for each, and adds each user to the appropriate groups.

After you run this procedure, you can return to the Database window, choose Security on the Tools menu, choose User and Group Accounts on the submenu, and select the user BLaMee (Brian LaMee) from the Name drop-down list. Brian is both a department manager and an application administrator. You should see him assigned to the correct groups as shown in Figure 30-15.

Figure 30-15. Verifying group membership after running the procedure to create groups and users.

Next you need to set up permissions for the groups. Close the User and Group Accounts dialog box. Open the Tools menu again, choose Security, choose User and Group Permissions on the submenu, and then Click Groups in the List option to see the list of groups, as shown in Figure 30-16 on the next page.

Table 30-2 on the next page shows you the permissions that you need to assign in the Housing Reservations application. You can start by removing all permissions from the Admins group. Select that group in the User/Group Name list, and then select each type of object in the Object Type drop-down list. Start with the database itself, and clear all permissions. Click

Chapter 30

Apply before selecting a new object type. (In many cases, you can clear the Read Design permission to clear all permissions.)

Figure 30-16. Assigning permissions to groups.

You can work through the remaining entries in Table 30-2 to finish granting permissions in your *HousingCopy.mdb* database. I have already assigned these permissions in the *Housing-Secured.mdb* sample database. You can see that creating a worksheet similar to Table 30-2 can be an invaluable tool to help you think through your security design and assign the correct permissions.

Table 30-2. Group Permissions for the Housing Reservations Application

Group	Object	Permissions/Explanation
Admins	All objects	No permission.
		Remember, though, that any member of the Admins group in the workgroup that owns this database can assign themselves permissions.
AppAdmin	Database	Open/Run.
	All tables and queries	All permissions except Administer and Modify Design.
		Note that if your application code uses advanced techniques to modify queries (by opening the Querydef object and changing the SQL property), you might need to assign Modify Design permission to some queries.
	All forms and reports	Open/Run.

Table 30-2. Group Permissions for the Housing Reservations Application

Group	Object	Permissions/Explanation
DeptMgrs	Database	Open/Run.
	Table: ErrorLog	Read Design, Read Data, Insert Data.
		All forms have error trapping code that needs to insert new records into this table. Because the code has only the permissions of the signed-on user, all users must be allowed to insert data into this table.
	Table: tblDepartments	Read Design, Read Data, Update Data.
		Department managers can update information for their own department. Code in frmDepartments prevents managers from updating other departments.
	Table: tblDummy	Read Design, Read Data.
		This table supplies a Null row for some combo boxes.
	Table: tblEmployees	Read Design, Read Data, Update Data, Insert Data, Delete Data.
		Department managers have authority to add employees to their department, change information for existing employees in their department, and delete employees in their department. Code in frmEmployees prevents managers from changing employees in other departments.
	Table: tblFacilities	Read Design, Read Data.
		Managers can view facility information but cannot change it.
	Table: tblFacilityRooms	Read Design, Read Data.
		Managers can view room information but cannot change it.
	Table: tblReservation-Requests	All permissions except Modify Design and Administer.
		All employees can create, change, and delete reservation requests. Code in frmReservationRequests restricts managers to employees in their department.
	Table: tblReservations	All permissions except Modify Design, Administer, Insert Data.
		Only application administrators can confirm new reservations. Code in frmReservations restricts managers to employees in their own department and employees to their own records.

Chapter 30

Table 30-2. Group Permissions for the Housing Reservations Application

Group	Object	Permissions/Explanation
DeptMgrs	Tables: tlkpRoomTypes, tlkpZips, ztblDates, and ztblYears	Read Design, Read Data. These are read-only lookup tables.
	Table: ztblLocalValues	Read Design, Read Data, Update Data. The frmSignon form uses this table to track the last signed-on user and updates the one record in this table each time a new user signs on.
	All queries	All permissions except Administer and Modify Design. Note that if your application code uses advanced techniques to modify queries (by opening the Querydef object and changing the SQL property), you might need to assign Modify Design permission to some queries.
	All forms and reports	Open/Run.
Employees	Database	Open/Run.
	Table: ErrorLog	Read Design, Read Data, Insert Data. All forms have error trapping code that needs to insert new records into this table. Because the code has only the permissions of the signed-on user, all users must be allowed to insert data to this table.
	Table: tblDepartments	Read Design and Read Data. Code in frmDepartments restricts employees to viewing only the information about their own department.
	Table: tblDummy	Read Design, Read Data. This table supplies a Null row for some combo boxes.
	Table: tblEmployees	Read Design, Read Data, Update Data. Code in frmEmployees allows employees to view and update only their own records.
	Table: tblFacilities	Read Design, Read Data. Employees can view facility information but cannot change it.
	Table: tblFacilityRooms	Read Design, Read Data. Employees can view room information but cannot change it.

Table 30-2. Group Permissions for the Housing Reservations Application

Group	Object	Permissions/Explanation
Employees	Table: tblReservation-Requests	All permissions except Modify Design and Administer. All employees can create, change, and delete reservation requests. Code in frmReservationRequests restricts employees to their own records.
	Table: tblReservations	All permissions except Modify Design, Administer, Insert Data. Only application administrators can confirm new reservations. Code in frmReservations restricts employees to their own records.
	Tables: tlkpRoomTypes, tlkpZips, ztblDates, and ztblYears	Read Design, Read Data. These are read-only lookup tables.
	Table: ztblLocalValues	Read Design, Read Data, Update Data. The frmSignon form uses this table to track the last signed-on user and updates the one record in this table each time a new user signs on.
	All queries	All permissions except Administer and Modify Design. Note that if your application code uses advanced techniques to modify queries (by opening the Querydef object and changing the SQL property), you might need to assign Modify Design permission to some queries.
	All forms and reports	Open/Run.
Users	All objects	Permissions as assigned by the User-Level Security Wizard. The wizard normally removes all permissions from the Users group. In this example, you granted very limited permissions to the Users group so that you can open the secured database even when you're not joined to the secured workgroup.

As mentioned earlier, the Housing Reservations application is already security aware. To make it work completely as a secured database, it was a simple matter to change the code in the frmSignon form to use the information about the currently signed-on user to set the public data variables correctly. Here's the code:

```
Private Sub Form_Open(Cancel As Integer)
Dim db As DAO.Database, rst As DAO.Recordset
Dim strUser As String, intRtn As Integer
```

Chapter 30

```
Dim ws As DAO.Workspace, usr As DAO.User, grpA As DAO.Group
Dim grpD As DAO.Group, grpE As DAO.Group
    ' Make sure current data is reset when this form loads
    gstrThisEmployee = ""
    glngThisEmployeeID = 0
    glngThisDeptID = 0
    gintIsAdmin = 0
    gintIsManager = 0
    ' Get the Access User ID
    strUser = CurrentUser()
    ' Point to the current database
    Set db = CurrentDb
    Set ws = DBEngine.Workspaces(0)
    ' Be sure to refresh the workspace Users and Groups
    ws.Users.Refresh
    ws.Groups.Refresh
    ' Trap local errors
    On Error Resume Next
    ' Make sure groups are OK
    Set grpA = ws.Groups("AppAdmin")
    Set grpD = ws.Groups("DeptMgrs")
    If Err <> 0 Then
        MsgBox "Access security groups required to run this application " & _
        "are not defined." & vbCrLf & vbCrLf & _
        "You must start Access using the Secured.MDW file and logon as " & _
        "one of the valid employees in this database.  " & _
        "Logon as user 'HousingAdmin' (no password) " & _
        "to acquire Admin status so you can add other users." & _
        vbCrLf & vbCrLf & "See Chapter 30 of Microsoft Office " & _
        "Access 2003 Inside Out for details.", vbOKOnly, _
        "Housing Reservations Secured mdb"
        ' Cancel the open
        Cancel = True
        ' Go back to db window
        DoCmd.SelectObject acForm, "frmSplash", True
        Set db = Nothing
        Set ws = Nothing
        Exit Sub
    End If
    ' Set a generic error trap
    On Error GoTo Err_Load
    ' Open the Employees / Departments signon query
    Set rst = db.OpenRecordset("qryEmployeeSignon", dbOpenDynaset)
    ' Find the employee that matches the Access ID
    rst.FindFirst "[UserID] = '" & strUser & "'"
    ' Not found - bail
    If rst.NoMatch Then
        intRtn = MsgBox("Your Access userid is unknown in this database." & _
            vbCrLf & vbCrLf & _
            "You must start Access using the Secure.MDW file and logon as " & _
            "one of the valid employees in this database.  " & _
            "Logon as user 'HousingAdmin' (no password) " & _
            "to acquire Admin status so you can add other users." & _
            vbCrLf & vbCrLf & "See Chapter 30 of Microsoft Office " & _
            "Access 2003 Inside Out for details.", vbOKOnly, _
```

```
        "Housing Reservations Secured mdb")
    Cancel = True
    rst.Close
    Set rst = Nothing
    Set db = Nothing
    ' Cancel the open
    Cancel = True
    ' Go back to db window
    DoCmd.SelectObject acForm, "frmSplash", True
    Exit Sub
End If
' Got a good ID - put the focus on this form to finish loading it
Me.SetFocus
' Move focus to the password text box
Me.txtPassword.SetFocus
' Copy selected User to Public variable
gstrThisEmployee = rst!EmpName
' Save the employee and department IDs
glngThisEmployeeID = rst!EmployeeNumber
' Watch out for null dept
If IsNothing(rst!DepartmentID) Then
    glngThisDeptID = 0
Else
    glngThisDeptID = rst!DepartmentID
End If
' See if this person is the manager
If glngThisEmployeeID = rst!ManagerNumber Then
    ' Double-check to see if DeptMgrs group
    For Each usr In grpD.Users
        ' Set Is Manager only if a member of DeptMgrs group
        If usr.Name = strUser Then gintIsManager = True
    Next usr
    ' Issue warning if not a manager
    If (gintIsManager = 0) Then
        MsgBox "Warning: The data in this application indicates that " & _
            "you are a department manager, but your Access security " & _
            "profile does not. You are not logged on with Department " & _
            "Manager authority." & _
            vbCrLf & vbCrLf & _
            "Contact an application administrator to correct this " & _
            "problem.", vbExclamation, gstrAppTitle
    End If
End If
' And finally set Admin
If (rst!IsAdmin = True) Then
    ' Double-check to see if in AppAdmins group
    For Each usr In grpA.Users
        ' Set Admin only if a member of AppAdmins group
        If usr.Name = strUser Then gintIsAdmin = True
    Next usr
    ' Issue warning if not an administrator
    If (gintIsAdmin = 0) Then
        MsgBox "Warning: The data in this application indicates that " & _
            "you are an application administrator, but your Access " & _
```

Chapter 30

```
                        "security profile does not. You are not logged on with " & _
                        "Administrator authority." & _
                        vbCrLf & vbCrLf & _
                        "Contact another application administrator to correct " & _
                        "this problem.", vbExclamation, gstrAppTitle
            End If
        End If
        ' Set the combo box value
        Me.cmbUserID = rst!EmpName
        ' And then lock it so they can't change it
        Me.cmbUserID.Locked = True
        ' Close the recordset
        rst.Close
        Set rst = Nothing
        Set ws = Nothing
        Set db = Nothing
Load_Exit:
    Exit Sub
Err_Load:
    MsgBox "Unexpected error: " & Err & ", " & Error, vbCritical, gstrAppTitle
    ErrorLog Me.Name & "_Open", Err, Error
    Resume Load_Exit
End Sub
```

First, the code makes sure all the public security information used by the application is reset. Next, the code looks for two of the special groups that should be defined—AppAdmin and DeptMgrs. If either group is missing, the application assumes you're not joined to the correct secured workgroup, displays an error message, and cancels opening the form. If the groups are defined, the code opens a recordset on a query that provides employee and department information and attempts to find the current Access user name in the UserID field. If the search isn't successful, the code displays an error message and exits.

If the data in the application indicates that the user signing on is a department manager, the code verifies that the user is a member of the DeptMgrs group. If not, then the code displays a warning that manager permissions have been denied. The code performs a similar check if the employee record indicates that the user is an administrator. Finally, the code sets the value of the cmbUserID combo box on the form to the current Access user and locks it so the user can't change it. The code that verifies the user password in the cmdSignon_Click event verifies the password against what is stored in the database. It's not possible to read a user's current password from the user object.

In the Housing Reservations application, administrators and department managers can create new employee records. In the secured version, the frmEmployees form (and the frmEmployeesAdd form) needs additional code to also create the companion Access user name and group memberships. You can find the code in the form's Before Update event procedure, as follows:

```
Private Sub Form_BeforeUpdate(Cancel As Integer)
Dim varID As Variant, ws As DAO.Workspace, usr As DAO.User, grpU As DAO.Group
    ' Do some validation checks...
```

```
If IsNothing(Me.Password) Then
    MsgBox "You must enter a Password!", vbCritical, gstrAppTitle
    Cancel = True
    Me.Password.SetFocus
    Exit Sub
End If
' Verify UserID
If IsNothing(Me.UserID) Then
    MsgBox "You must enter a User ID!", vbCritical, gstrAppTitle
    Cancel = True
    Me.UserID.SetFocus
    Exit Sub
End If
' Now validate the User ID
Set ws = DBEngine(0)
' Local error trap
On Error Resume Next
' See if the user exists
ws.Users.Refresh
Set usr = ws.Users(Me.UserID)
' If got an error, must add the user
If Err <> 0 Then
    Err = 0
    ' Create a new user
    Set usr = ws.CreateUser(Me.UserID, "9999", Me.Password)
    ws.Users.Append usr
    ' Make sure new user is at least a member of Employees
    Set grpU = usr.CreateGroup("Employees")
    usr.Groups.Append grpU
    ' .. and Users
    Set grpU = usr.CreateGroup("Users")
    usr.Groups.Append grpU
    ' If IsAdmin, then also add to AppAdmin and Admins group
    If (Me.IsAdmin = True) Then
        Set grpU = usr.CreateGroup("AppAdmin")
        usr.Groups.Append grpU
        Set grpU = usr.CreateGroup("Admins")
        usr.Groups.Append grpU
    End If
    ' Now see if department manager - but not on new record
    If Not IsNothing(Me.EmployeeNumber) Then
        varID = Null
        varID = DLookup("ManagerNumber", "tblDepartments", _
            "ManagerNumber = " & Me.EmployeeNumber)
        If Not IsNull(varID) Then
            ' Found this ID as a manager - add to managers group
            Set grpU = usr.CreateGroup("DeptMgrs")
            usr.Groups.Append grpU
            Set grpU = usr.CreateGroup("Admins")
            usr.Groups.Append grpU
        End If
    End If
Else
```

```
            ' Got a good hit on user - did IsAdmin change?
            If Me.IsAdmin = Me.IsAdmin.DefaultValue Then
            ' Reverse test in case of Null
            Else
                ' Admin changed - change the group membership
                If Me.IsAdmin Then
                    ' Add Admin authority
                    Set grpU = usr.CreateGroup("AppAdmin")
                    usr.Groups.Append grpU
                    Set grpU = usr.CreateGroup("Admins")
                    usr.Groups.Append grpU
                Else
                    ' Remove Admin authority
                    usr.Groups.Delete "AppAdmin"
                    ' Check if department manager
                    varID = Null
                    varID = DLookup("ManagerNumber", "tblDepartments", _
                        "ManagerNumber = " & Me.EmployeeNumber)
                    If IsNull(varID) Then
                        ' Not a department manager - also remove Admins
                        usr.Groups.Delete "Admins"
                    End If
                End If
            End If
        End If
        ws.Users.Refresh
        ws.Groups.Refresh
        Set grpU = Nothing
        Set usr = Nothing
        Set ws = Nothing
        ' Check to see if we need to supply an Employee Number
        ' This application does not use AutoNumber
        If IsNothing(Me.EmployeeNumber) Then
            ' Get the previous high number and add 1
            varID = DMax("EmployeeNumber", "tblEmployees") + 1
            ' If this is first one, then value will be null
            If IsNull(varID) Then varID = 1
            Me.EmployeeNumber = varID
        End If
End Sub
```

The code uses the CreateUser and CreateGroup methods to accomplish the necessary changes in the workgroup file. Note that this code can run only when a user that is a member of the Admins group is signed on. This is why the code adds application administrators to the Admins group as well as one or both of the special application groups. The code uses the initial password defined for the new employee as the password for the new Access user name. However, there is no provision anywhere in the code to attempt to keep the password synchronized if someone changes the password in the employee record. You need to know the old password for a user to be able to change it, and only the user can change his or her own password. Also, a member of the Admins group could use the User and Group Accounts dialog box to reset the user's password, so any code that attempted to change the password later would break.

> **Note** Before you distribute this application to users, you should create another workgroup file that has the HousingAdmin user (password secured), a user ID for each employee, and the three special groups. Be sure that the workgroup ID of this workgroup file does not match the one that you used to create the secured database. Application administrators and department managers will be members of the Admins group in this workgroup, so the code that adds new users will work properly. However, because the workgroup ID won't match the original owning workgroup ID, members of the Admins group won't be able to change user permissions.

If you have been following along to this point, you can now return to the Database window, choose Startup from the Tools menu, and change the Display Form/Page setting to frmSplash. Close the database and quit Access. Restart Access and open the secured copy of the Housing Administration database. In the Logon dialog box that Access displays, enter **KArcher** in the Name box and **password** in the Password box and click OK.

The application should start, and you should see the application's Housing Sample Sign On dialog box open with Karen Archer's name already chosen in the User Name combo box. The application won't let you change the User Name because it matches the Access user name that you used to open the database. Type **password** in the Password box and click Sign On. The application should display its main switchboard form. If you click Departments, you should see the record for the Sales department, and you can't move to any of the other department records. Because Karen is the manager of this department, you can change information about the department. Return to the main switchboard and click Employees. The form should open and display Karen's record. You can also use the navigation buttons to move to Stephen Mew's record—the other employee in Karen's department—but you can't see information about employees from any other department.

As you can see, the desktop database security system is neither simple nor easy to implement. When you need to secure a desktop application, you should now know the steps you need to take to successfully secure a database and modify the code to work with security.

> **Caution** Before leaving this section, be sure you rejoin your standard workgroup file using the Workgroup Administrator program.

Security Considerations in a Project File

When you open an Access project file (.adp), Access does not reference a workgroup file at all. Consequently, you cannot individually secure the forms, reports, macros, and modules in your project file. Remember that tables and queries are stored in an SQL Server database, so SQL Server security applies to those objects.

You can, however, take some steps to protect your project file. First, you can convert your project file to an execute-only file (.ade). An execute-only file is a special version of your project file that contains no source code. Access compiles your project before creating the file, saves the information that Visual Basic needs to run, and then removes all your code. A user might be able to open your project file, but won't be able to open the design of any of the forms, reports, or modules. There's no source code to examine, so a user won't be able to view the code to figure out how it works or discover any techniques that you don't want divulged. You can learn more about how to create an execute-only file in Chapter 31, "Distributing Your Application."

The second step you can take is to put your execute-only file in a folder that uses Windows security to restrict access. Users authorized to run the application must have full read and write permission to the folder, but unauthorized users won't be able to open your application.

The core of any database security implementation is protecting the data itself. Because the data for your project file is stored in SQL Server, you have the full capabilities of that security system at your disposal. The security system for SQL Server is similar to that for Access desktop databases, but there are some key differences. As with desktop databases, SQL Server security is a closed system. You must be specifically granted permission to access the server, open a database, open the tables, or run queries.

Unlike a desktop database, SQL Server has no default user or group (called a *role* in SQL Server) that lets users in by default. The only reason you can gain full access to anything in the Microsoft SQL Sever Desktop Engine (MSDE) that you can install on your machine is that the installation program automatically permits any member of your Windows Administrator group to have full authority to the server and anything stored on the server. You must have Administrator authority on your machine to install the software, so you automatically get full access if you can install the software. If you're a member of a Windows domain and are an Administrator on that domain, anyone else in the domain with Administrator status can also connect to your server.

In addition, SQL Server provides more discrete levels of security than does a desktop database. For example, you can specify permissions for each column in a table. You can grant permission to a user or role, revoke permission, or deny permission—denying permission revokes the permission for the user even if the permission is granted by way of membership in a role.

Unfortunately, MSDE doesn't provide many administrative tools. If you download *Microsoft SQL Server Books Online* from the Microsoft Web site, you can find the information you need to construct commands using the OSQL command-line utility to set up additional users and grant them permissions to use your server and your databases. You can download a copy by going to *http://www.microsoft.com/sql/techinfo/productdoc/2000/books.asp*. Table 30-3 lists some of the key system stored procedures and Transact-SQL commands that you'll need to use.

Table 30-3. **Security-Related System Procedures and Commands in SQL Server**

Procedure or Command	Usage
sp_grantlogin	Grants login privileges to your server. You specify the user's domain name and Windows login ID.
sp_grantdbaccess	Grants access to a particular database on your server. You specify the user's domain name and Windows login ID and optionally provide an SQL Server identity for use in granting permission to database objects.
sp_addrole	Defines a new role (group) to which you can add users. You can grant permissions to a user or a role.
sp_addrolemember	Adds a user or role to a role. Because you can define a role as a member of another role, you can create a hierarchy of permissions.
GRANT	Grants one or more specific permissions to an object in your database or to the database itself. For the database, you can grant permission to create objects in the database. For tables, you can grant Select (read), Update, Insert, and Delete permissions. You can grant Select and Update permissions for individual columns within a table. For views, you can grant the same permissions as for tables. For functions and stored procedures, you can grant permission to execute the function or procedure. You can also grant the right to the user to grant the permission to others.
REVOKE	Removes a previously granted permission from a user or role.
DENY	Denies a permission to a user or role even if the user or role might inherit the permission through membership in a role.

The security environment is much more straightforward because you don't have to go to extraordinary lengths to secure your database or your server—they're secured by default. But the SQL Server security model is much more complex than that for a desktop database. To manage security adequately, you need the SQL Server Enterprise Manager program, but this isn't included with MSDE. If you plan to develop one or more applications using project files and SQL Server, you need the SQL Server Developer Edition. This gives you a full server and all the tools you need that you can run on your desktop system at a very reasonable cost. You can find out more about how to acquire the Developer Edition at *http://www.microsoft.com /sql/howtobuy/development.asp*.

Understanding Macro Security

As explained in Chapter 2, "The Many Faces of Microsoft Access," Microsoft has established making its products safer to use as a top priority. Prior to Microsoft Access 2003, it was quite possible for a malicious person to send you a database file that contained code that could damage your system. As soon as you opened the database, the harmful code would run—perhaps without your knowledge. Or, the programmer could embed dangerous code in a query, form, or report, and your computer would be damaged as soon as you opened that object.

Access 2003 provides enhanced security by offering you three levels of macro security on your system. You can set your security level by choosing Macro from the Tools menu and then Security on the submenu. The three levels are as follows:

- **Low.**   With this setting, you are running with the same level of security as was available in Access 2002. Access will not prompt you to verify whether you want to open and run potentially unsafe code.

- **Medium.**   This is the default setting. Access prompts you to verify that you want to open an Access database that is not signed by a trusted source. If you have installed JET 4.0 Service Pack 8, you can enable "sandbox" mode to prevent most harmful Visual Basic functions from being executed from queries or table validation rules. You can download the service pack by selecting Windows Update from the Start menu or from *http://windowsupdate.microsoft.com*. To read more about what the service pack does, go to *http://support.microsoft.com/?kbid=282010*.

- **High.**   When you choose this setting, Access lets you open only Access databases that have been digitally signed by the author, and you or your system administrator have registered the author as a trusted source.

You can change your macro security settings without opening a database. Open Access, choose Macro on the Tools menu, and choose Security on the submenu. Access displays a Security dialog box, as shown in Figure 30-17.

Figure 30-17.   Setting your macro security level in the Security dialog box.

The descriptions on the Security Level tab are misleading for Access. When you select High, Access won't let you open any database file that contains macros if the database is not signed by a trusted source. An Access desktop database or project file contains "macros" everywhere—in the validation rules in tables, in function calls included in queries, in macro objects, and in Visual Basic code. So, unless a database contains no objects or contains only tables with no validation rules defined (the *Kathy's Wedding List.mdb* sample database is an example), your database contains "macros." It's impossible to open an Access desktop database or project file with macros disabled, so the second sentence next to the High option in the dialog box is meaningless. Likewise, when you select the Medium option, choosing to not run "potentially unsafe macros" means you won't be able to open the database.

You can click the Trusted Publishers tab in this dialog box to see the signatures that you've registered on your machine or that your administrators have registered on a Windows 2000 server that is your domain controller. On this tab, you can also select the Trust all installed add-ins and templates option (selected by default). If you clear this option, none of the wizards in Access will run when you have security set to High.

When you select the Medium setting (the default) and open an existing unsigned database in Access 2003, Access displays a warning dialog box, as shown in Figure 30-18. This dialog box makes it clear that you can either open the database or cancel the open.

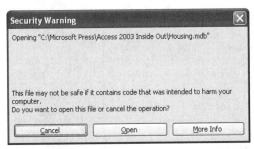

Figure 30-18.   With macro security set to Medium, Access warns you when you open any unsigned database.

When you set security to High and attempt to open an unsigned database, Access displays the dialog box shown in Figure 30-19.

Figure 30-19.   Attempting to open an unsigned or untrusted database with macro security set to High.

Of course, macros cannot be disabled in an Access desktop database or project file, so it's the fact that the file is unsigned that's keeping you from opening it. When you have macro security set to High and you attempt to open a database that is digitally signed but the signature has not

Chapter 30

yet been trusted on your system, Access displays the dialog box shown in Figure 30-20.

In the sample dialog box shown in Figure 30-20, I signed the database with a certificate that I generated on my local machine, but I hadn't trusted the publisher of the signature yet. When you see this dialog box, it might tell you that the signature has been authenticated— Access was able to contact the certifying authority on the Internet and obtain a matching key for the signature. In either case, you can click the Details button to find out more about the signature. If you decide to trust the signature from this source, you can select the Always trust files from this publisher and open them automatically option, which makes the Open button available, and click the Open button to open the database.

I did not digitally sign any of the sample databases—they would become unsigned as soon as you changed any of the queries or sample code. If your company enforces High macro security for all workstations, you won't be able to open any of the sample databases. If you control your own macro security setting, I do not recommend that you change your macro security setting to Low unless you never open any database except ones that you create. If you have installed the JET service pack, you can leave your macro security setting at Medium and be assured that you can open most databases with very little risk. I have designed all the sample applications to run successfully in "sandbox" mode. You can click the Open button in the Security Warning dialog box to open and run any of the sample databases.

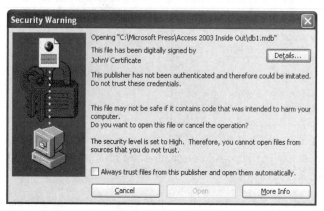

Figure 30-20. Opening a digitally signed database with High macro security settings, but you haven't trusted the publisher yet or the signature cannot be authenticated.

Understanding the macro security settings isn't all you need to know as a developer of Access applications that will be used by others. If you know that all your users are running with Low security, you don't need to do anything at all. If you have users who have selected Medium security, you can instruct them about the security warning that they'll see when they try to open your application. When you have users who must run with macro security set to High, then you must digitally sign your Visual Basic project with a signature that is trusted on those users' machines.

Your company might already have a public trusted signature that was issued by one of the recognized companies, such as VeriSign. (You can read about the trusted signature products from VeriSign at *http://www.verisign.com/products/microsoft/index.html*.) Contact your system administrator to find out if your company owns a public certificate that you can use to sign your projects. If your company owns a public certificate, you can sign your projects with that certificate and distribute your database application outside your company with confidence.

Your administrator might have created a trusted certificate that is registered on your domain server. You can use that certificate to sign the projects in database applications that you intend to distribute to other users within your company.

Microsoft Office 2003 also provides a Digital Certificate utility that allows you to create a local signature that you can use to sign projects on your local machine. This gives you an opportunity to test how signing a database works. To run this utility, click your Windows Start menu, choose All Programs, choose Microsoft Office, choose Microsoft Office Tools, and then click Digital Certificate for VBA Projects. The utility displays a window, as shown in Figure 30-21.

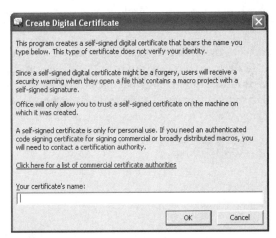

Figure 30-21.   The Digital Certificate for VBA Projects utility allows you to create a local signature.

The bad news is a local certificate works only on your machine. If you give your database application to another user, the user won't be able to trust you as a publisher on his or her machine. However, a local certificate is useful to test signing your database applications and to learn how certificates work with macro security.

To sign a database application, you must open any module in the Visual Basic Editor (VBE). The project should be fully compiled and saved before you attempt to sign it. Choose Digital Signature from the Tools menu to see the dialog box shown in Figure 30-22.

Figure 30-22. Using the Digital Signature facility in the Visual Basic Editor to digitally sign your project.

Click the Choose button to see a list of certificates available on your system, as shown in Figure 30-23.

You can select any certificate and click the View Certificate button to view the details about the certificate. In the Select Certificate dialog box, select the certificate you want and click OK to sign your project with that certificate. Keep in mind that once you sign a project, you should make no further design changes before you distribute the database application to others. If you make a design change, Access removes the signature from your project.

Figure 30-23. Viewing the list of available certificates on your machine.

You should now understand the issues surrounding security in both an Access desktop database and a project file. In the final chapter, you'll learn how to set up your application so that you can distribute it to others.

Chapter 31

Distributing Your Application

Although you can certainly use Microsoft Access to create database applications only for your personal use, most serious users of Access eventually end up building applications to be used by others. If you have created a stand-alone desktop database application, and your users all have the same version of Access installed on their machines, you can simply give them a copy of your database file to run. However, most database applications become really useful when the data is shared by multiple users.

In Chapter 6, "Importing and Linking Data," you learned about linking tables from another database and using the Linked Table Manager. In Chapter 29, "Upsizing a Desktop Application to a Project," you learned about some of the advantages of using a client-server architecture to allow multiple users running the same application to share data. In Chapter 30, "Securing Your Database," you learned about security issues that you should consider before giving an application that you have developed to others. All these topics help you understand how to design and secure a multi-user application. However, they don't provide you with the techniques you can employ in your application design to ensure that your application installs and runs smoothly and to ensure that your users can't tamper with your code. In this final chapter, you'll learn

- How to split a desktop database to use shared data on a server and linked tables on each client machine and create code that verifies and corrects linked table connection properties when your application starts.

- A technique to write code in a project file that verifies the connection to SQL Server when your application starts.

- The advantages of runtime mode and design considerations for using it.

- How to create an execute-only version of your application so that users can't tamper with your code.

- Techniques for creating application shortcuts to simplify starting your application.

- Tools you can use in the Microsoft Office Access 2003 Developer Extensions to distribute your application to users who don't have Access.

Using Linked Tables in a Desktop Database

Your first foray into the world of client-server applications will most likely involve creating a data-only .mdb file on a server and using linked tables in a desktop application that you install on multiple desktop machines that can link to the data server. Although you could place your entire desktop database application on a shared server and allow multiple users to open the application over the network, you would soon find that performance suffers significantly. Also, if your application needs to keep information about how each user works with the application, it would be more complicated to store this information in the database because all users share the same file.

The main advantage to splitting your database over simply sharing a single desktop database is that your application needs to retrieve only the data from the tables over the network. Because each user will have a local copy of the queries, forms, reports, data access pages, macros, and modules, Access running on each user workstation will be able to load these parts of your application quickly from the local hard drive. Using a local copy on each client machine also makes it easy to create local tables that save settings for each user. For example, the LawTrack Contacts application allows each user to set a preference to open a search dialog box for companies, contacts, and invoices or to display all records directly.

Taking Advantage of the Database Splitter Utility

You could split out the tables in your application into a separate file and link them into the database that contains all your queries, forms, reports, and modules "by hand" by first creating a new empty database (see Chapter 4, "Creating Your Database and Tables,"), and then importing all your tables into that database using the techniques described in Chapter 6. You could then go back to your original database and delete all the tables. Finally, you could move the data database (the one containing the tables) to a file server, and then link these tables into your original code database (the one containing all your queries, forms, reports, and modules), again using the techniques you'll find in Chapter 6.

Fortunately, there's an easier way to do this in one step using the Database Splitter utility. Open your original database, choose Database Utilities from the Tools menu, and then choose Database Splitter. The wizard displays the window shown in Figure 31-1.

When you click the Split Database button, the wizard opens a second window where you can define the name and location of the back-end, or data-only, database. Be sure to choose a location for this database on a network share that is available to all potential users of your application. Click the Split button in that window, and the wizard exports all your tables to the new data-only database, deletes the tables in your original database, and creates links to the moved tables in your original database. You can now give each user a copy of the code database—containing your queries, forms, reports, modules, and linked table objects pointing to the new data-only database—to enable them to run the application using a shared set of tables.

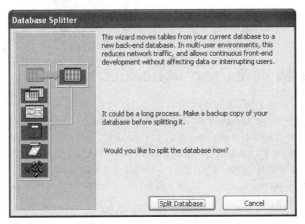

Figure 31-1. The Database Splitter Wizard.

One disadvantage to using the Database Splitter is that it splits out all tables that it finds in your original desktop database. If you take a look at the desktop database version of the Law-Track Contacts application (*Contacts.mdb*), you can see that the application also uses some local tables (tables that remain in the code database). For example, the ErrorLog table contains records about errors encountered when the user runs the application. If the error was caused by a failure in the link to the server, the code that writes the error record wouldn't be able to write to this table if the table were in the server database. The database also contains local copies of lookup tables that aren't likely to change frequently, such as the tlkpStates table that contains U.S. state codes and names and the ztblYears table that provides a list of years for the frmCalendar form. Access can fetch data from local tables faster than it can from ones linked to a database on a server, so providing local copies of these tables improves performance.

> **Note** The new data-only database you create using the Database Splitter is owned by the user ID that you used to log on to Access. Even if the code database is secured, the data-only database will not be. You must run the User-Level Security Wizard against the new data-only database to secure it. See Chapter 30 for details.

Particularly if you have secured your application, you should have each user log on to the same workgroup file that you copy to a network share. See "Creating an Application Short-cut," page 1215, for details about setting up a shortcut for each user that points not only to the local copy of the application but also specifies the location of the shared workgroup file.

Although splitting a database application makes it easier for multiple users to share your application, this technique works well only for applications containing a moderate amount of data (under 200 MB is a good guideline) with no more than 20 simultaneous users. Remember that Access is fundamentally a desktop database system. All the work—including solving complex queries—occurs on the client machine, even when you have placed all the data on a network share. Each copy of Access on each client machine uses the file sharing and locking mechanisms of the server operating system. Access sends many low-level file read, write, and lock commands (perhaps thousands to solve a single query) from each client machine to the file server rather than sending a single SQL request that the server solves. When too many users share the same application accessing large volumes of data, many simple tasks can start taking minutes instead of seconds to complete.

Creating Startup Code to Verify and Correct Linked Table Connections

If you were careful when you created your linked tables, you used a Universal Naming Convention (UNC) path name instead of a physical or logical drive letter. Unless the network share name is different on various client computers, this should work well to establish the links to the data file when the user opens your application. However, even "the best-laid schemes o' mice an' men gang aft aglee."[1] (Or, if you prefer, Murphy's Law is always in force.)

In Chapter 6, you learned how to use the Linked Table Manager to repair any broken connections. However, you can't expect your users to run this wizard if the linked table connections are broken. You should include code that runs when your startup form opens that verifies and corrects the links if necessary. Also, you might over time make changes to the structure of the data tables and issue an updated version of the client desktop database that works with the newer version of the tables. Your startup code can open and check a version table in the shared data database and warn the user if the versions don't match.

You can find sample code that accomplishes all these tasks in the desktop database version of the LawTrack Contacts database (*Contacts.mdb*). Open the database and then open the *modStartup* module. Select the ReConnect function, where you'll find the following code:

```
Public Function ReConnect()
Dim db As DAO.Database, tdf As DAO.TableDef
Dim rst As DAO.Recordset, rstV As DAO.Recordset
Dim strFile As String, varRet As Variant, frm As Form
Dim strPath As String, intI As Integer
' Called by frmSplash - the normal startup form for this application
    On Error Resume Next
    ' Point to the current database
    Set db = CurrentDb
    ' Turn on the hourglass - this may take a few secs.
    DoCmd.Hourglass True
    ' First, check linked table version
    Set rstV = db.OpenRecordset("ztblVersion")
    ' Got a failure - so try to reattach the tables
    If Err <> 0 Then GoTo Reattach
    ' Make sure we're on the first row
    rstV.MoveFirst
    ' Call the version checker
    If Not CheckVersion(rstV!Version) Then
        ' Tell caller that "reconnect" failed
        ReConnect = False
        ' Close the version recordset
        rstV.Close
        ' Clear the objects
        Set rstV = Nothing
```

---

1. Burns, Robert. "To a Mouse, On Turning Her Up in Her Nest With the Plough." 1785

```
        Set db = Nothing
        ' Done
        DoCmd.Hourglass False
        Exit Function
    End If
' Versions match - now verify all the other tables
' NOTE: We're leaving rstV open at this point for better efficiency
'    in a shared database environment.
'    JET will share the already established thread.
' Turn on the progress meter on the status bar
varRet = SysCmd(acSysCmdInitMeter, "Verifying data tables...", _
        db.TableDefs.Count)
' Loop through all TableDefs
For Each tdf In db.TableDefs
        ' Looking for attached tables
        If (tdf.Attributes And dbAttachedTable) Then
            ' Try to open the table
            Set rst = tdf.OpenRecordset()
            ' If you got an error - then try to relink
            If Err <> 0 Then GoTo Reattach
            ' This one is OK - close it
            rst.Close
            ' And clear the object
            Set rst = Nothing
        End If
        ' Update the progress counter
        intI = intI + 1
        varRet = SysCmd(acSysCmdUpdateMeter, intI)
Next tdf
' Got through them all - clear the progress meter
varRet = SysCmd(acSysCmdClearStatus)
' Turn off the hourglass
DoCmd.Hourglass False
' Set a good return
ReConnect = True
' Edit the Version table
rstV.Edit
' Update the open count - we check this on exit to recommend a backup
rstV!OpenCount = rstV!OpenCount + 1
' Update the row
rstV.Update
' Close and clear the objects
rstV.Close
Set rstV = Nothing
Set db = Nothing
' DONE!
Exit Function

Reattach:
    ' Clear the current error
    Err.Clear
    ' Set a new error trap
    On Error GoTo BadReconnect
    ' Turn off the hourglass for now
    DoCmd.Hourglass False
```

```
' ... and clear the status bar
varRet = SysCmd(acSysCmdClearStatus)
' Tell the user about the problem - about to show an open file dialog
MsgBox "There's a temporary problem connecting to the LawTrack data." & _
    " Please locate the LawTrack data file in the following dialog.", _
    vbInformation, "LawTrack Contacts Manager"
' Establish a new ComDlg object
With New ComDlg
    ' Set the title of the dialog
    .DialogTitle = "Locate LawTrack Contacts Data File"
    ' Set the default file name
    .FileName = "ContactsData.mdb"
    ' ... and start directory
    .Directory = CurrentProject.Path
    ' ... and file extension
    .Extension = "mdb"
    ' ... but show all mdb files just in case
    .Filter = "LawTrack File (*.mdb)|*.mdb"
    ' Default directory is where this file is located
    .Directory = CurrentProject.Path
    ' Tell the common dialog that the file and path must exist
    .ExistFlags = FileMustExist + PathMustExist
    If .ShowOpen Then
        strFile = .FileName
    Else
        Err.Raise 3999
    End If
End With
' Open the "info" form telling what we're doing
DoCmd.OpenForm "frmReconnect"
' ... and be sure it has the focus
Forms!frmReconnect.SetFocus
' Attempt to re-attach the Version table first and check it
Set tdf = db.TableDefs("ztblVersion")
tdf.Connect = ";DATABASE=" & strFile
tdf.RefreshLink
' OK, now check linked table version
Set rst = db.OpenRecordset("ztblVersion")
rst.MoveFirst
' Call the version checker
If Not CheckVersion(rst!Version) Then
    ' Tell the caller that we failed
    ReConnect = False
    ' Close the version recordset
    rst.Close
    ' ... and clear the object
    Set rst = Nothing
    ' Bail
    Exit Function
End If
' Passed version check - edit the version record
rst.Edit
' Update the open count - we check this on exit to recommend a backup
rst!OpenCount = rst!OpenCount + 1
' Write it back
```

```
    rst.Update
    ' Close the recordset
    rst.Close
    ' ... and clear the object
    Set rst = Nothing
    ' Now, reattach the other tables
    ' Strip out just the path name
    strPath = Left(strFile, InStrRev(strFile, "\") - 1)
    ' Call the generic re-attach function
    If AttachAgain(strPath) = 0 Then
        ' Oops - failed.  Raise an error
        Err.Raise 3999
    End If
    ' Close the information form
    DoCmd.Close acForm, "frmReconnect"
    ' Clear the db object
    Set db = Nothing
    ' Return a positive result
    ReConnect = True
    ' ... and exit
Connect_Exit:
    Exit Function
BadReconnect:
    ' Oops
    MsgBox "Reconnect to data failed.", vbCritical, _
      "LawTrack Contacts Manager"
    ' Indicate failure
    ReConnect = False
    ' Close the info form if it is open
    If IsFormLoaded("frmReconnect") Then DoCmd.Close acForm, "frmReconnect"
    ' Clear the progress meter
    varRet = SysCmd(acSysCmdClearStatus)
    ' ... and bail
    Resume Connect_Exit
End Function
```

The code begins by attempting to open the linked ztblVersionTable. If the open generates an error, the code immediately jumps to the Reattach label about halfway down the listing. If the version checking table opens successfully, the code next calls the CheckVersion function (not shown here) that compares the version value in the table with a public constant saved in the modGlobals module. If the versions don't match, that function displays an appropriate error message and returns a False value to this procedure. If the version check fails, this procedure returns a False value to the original calling procedure (in the frmSplash form's module) and exits.

If the versions do match, the code next loops through all the table definitions in the database and attempts to open a recordset on each one to verify the link. Note that the code leaves the recordset on the version checking table open. If it didn't do this, each subsequent open and close would need to establish a new network connection to the file server, and the checking of all tables would take minutes instead of seconds. Note also that the code uses the SysCmd system function to display a progress meter on the Access status bar.

If all linked tables open successfully, the procedure returns True to the calling procedure and exits. If opening any of the tables fails, the code immediately jumps to the Reattach label to attempt to fix all the links.

The code beginning at the Reattach label clears all errors, sets an error trap, and then displays a message informing the user that there's a problem. After the user clicks OK in the dialog box, the code creates a new instance of the ComDlg class module, sets its properties to establish an initial directory and ask for the correct file type, and uses the ShowOpen method of the class to display a Windows Open File dialog box. The class module returns a True value if the user successfully locates the file, and the code retrieves the class module's FileName property to find out the path and name of the file chosen by the user. If the ShowOpen failed, the code raises an error to be logged by the error-handling code at the end of the procedure.

Next, the code opens a form that is a dialog box informing the user that a reconnect is in progress. The code attempts to fix the link to the version-checking table using the path and file the user selected. Notice that the code sets the Connect property of the TableDef object and then uses the RefreshLink method to reestablish the connection. If the table isn't in the file the user selected, the RefreshLink method returns an error, and the code after the BadReconnect label near the end of the procedure executes because of the error trap.

After checking that the version of the code matches the version of the database, the code calls the AttachAgain function (not shown here) and passes it the path and file name. You can also find this function in the modStartup module. The function loops through all the TableDef objects, resets the Connect property for linked tables, and uses RefreshLink to fix the connection. Because this sample database also has some linked Excel worksheets, you'll find that code in the AttachAgain function checks the type of linked table and sets up the Connect property appropriately.

If you'd like to see how this code works, you can open the *Contacts.mdb* file and then use Windows Explorer to temporarily move the *ContactsData.mdb*, *FictitiousCompanies-Simple.xls*, and *FictitiousNamesSimple.xls* files to another folder. Open the frmSplash form, and you should see the code prompt you to identify where you moved the *ContactsData.mdb* file. The code in the AttachAgain procedure assumes that the two Excel files are in the same folder as the *ContactsData.mdb* file.

Verifying Server Connection in a Project File

As you can imagine, it's equally important to verify the connection to the SQL Server database in an Access project file (.adp). In some ways, checking the connection is much simpler than checking linked tables in an Access desktop database. If the project's IsConnected property is True, then the project thinks it has a good connection to some database. However, you should also verify that the connected database is the one required by the project.

When the project's IsConnected property is False, you have some more work to do. If you expect the project file to run with a local copy of SQL Server, the code must first attempt to start the server and connect to it. If the project uses an SQL Server running on another machine, the code must attempt to connect to that server. After establishing a connection, the code can query the master database to find out if the required database is on the server.

If it is, then the code can fix the ConnectionString property of the project's Connection object and attempt to reopen the connection.

If any of the above fails, the code can open the Data Link Properties dialog box to prompt the user to fix the connection. If you don't want to train your users on how to use the Data Link Properties dialog box, the code can also display an error message instructing the user to "contact your system administrator" and exit.

You can find code in the project file version of the LawTrack Contacts sample application (*Contacts.adp*) that performs the necessary tests in the *modStartup* module. Both the frm-Copyright and frmSplash forms call the OpenStartup function to perform the tests. The code for the OpenStartup function is as follows:

```
Function OpenStartup() As Boolean
On Error GoTo OpenStartup_Err
Dim intResponse As Integer, strMsg As String
    ' Set the server name
    strSrvrName = "(local)"
    ' Check if we're already connected
    If CurrentProject.IsConnected Then
        'check if we are connected to the expected db
        If CheckConnectedServer() Then
            OpenStartup = True
        Else
            ' Tell them they may need to link the sample
            strMsg = strNotThisServer1 & vbCrLf & vbCrLf & strSelectPrompt2
            intResponse = MsgBox(strMsg, vbOKCancel + vbInformation, _
              strSelectTitle)
            If intResponse <> vbCancel Then
                ' They want to try the connection dialog...
                DoCmd.RunCommand acCmdConnection
                ' See if that was successful
                If CurrentProject.IsConnected Then
                    ' Yes, verify we have the right database
                    If CheckConnectedServer() Then OpenStartup = True
                End If
            End If
        End If
    Else
        ' Attempt to autostart server
        Select Case StartSQLServer()
            Case 1   ' Started and connected OK
                OpenStartup = True
            Case 2   ' Started, but couldn't find database
                ' Tell them they may need to link the sample
                strMsg = strNotThisServer1 & vbCrLf & vbCrLf & _
                  strNotThisServer2
                intResponse = MsgBox(strMsg, vbOKCancel + vbInformation, _
                  strSelectTitle)
                If intResponse <> vbCancel Then
                    ' They want to try the connection dialog...
                    DoCmd.RunCommand acCmdConnection
                    ' See if that was successful
                    If CurrentProject.IsConnected Then
```

1211

```
                              ' Yes, verify we have the right database
                              If CheckConnectedServer() Then OpenStartup = True
                         End If
                    End If
               Case Else
                    ' Tell them they may need to install MSDE
                    strMsg = strSelectPrompt1 & vbCrLf & vbCrLf & strSelectPrompt2
                    intResponse = MsgBox(strMsg, vbOKCancel + vbInformation, _
                      strSelectTitle)
                    If intResponse <> vbCancel Then
                         ' They want to try the connection dialog...
                         DoCmd.RunCommand acCmdConnection
                         ' See if that was successful
                         If CurrentProject.IsConnected Then
                              ' Yes, verify we have the right database
                              If CheckConnectedServer() Then OpenStartup = True
                         End If
                    End If
          End Select
     End If
OpenStartup_Exit:
     Exit Function
OpenStartup_Err:
     MsgBox Err.Description
     Resume OpenStartup_Exit
End Function
```

Because this is a sample application that expects to find the ContactsSQL database on your local server, it sets a public variable to "(local)" to force the search on your machine in all functions in this module. When the IsConnected property of the CurrentProject object is True, the code calls the CheckConnectedServer function that you can find in this same module. That function verifies that the project is connected to ContactsSQL and changes the database name if it is not. If the CheckConnectedServer function fails, it returns False, so this code displays a message describing the problem and asking you if you want to fix the problem using the Data Link Properties dialog box. (The text of all messages is in constants defined at the beginning of the module.) If you click Yes in the message dialog box, the code uses RunCommand acCmdConnection to open Data Link Properties. This is the same as choosing Connection from the File menu. After the Data Link Properties dialog box closes (the code pauses while it is open), the code calls CheckConnectedServer again to see if you were successful.

If the project's IsConnected property is False, the code calls the StartSQLServer function to try to start your local server, find ContactsSQL on that server, and fix the connection properties. That function returns the value 1 if the server was started and the connection repaired, the value 2 if the server was started but the code couldn't find ContactsSQL on your server, or the value 3 if the server couldn't be started at all (MSDE is not installed). The Select Case code displays an appropriate error message and offers to open the Data Link Properties dialog box.

You will see these various error messages if you attempt to open the *Contacts.adp* project file before installing the Microsoft SQL Server Data Engine (MSDE) on your machine, if you haven't started your server, or if you haven't attached the *ContactsSQL.mdf* sample file to your server. See the Appendix, "Installing Microsoft Office," for instructions on installing MSDE. See Chapter 17, "Building Tables in an Access Project," and Chapter 18, "Building Queries in an Access Project," for details about using the Data Link Properties dialog box and running the supplied batch files to attach the sample database to your server.

You can study the other functions called by the OpenStartup function in the *modStartup* module on your own. I provided comments for every line of code to help you understand how the code works.

Understanding Runtime Mode

When Access starts in runtime mode, it does not allow the user to access the Database window or to use any of the built-in toolbars or menus. So, the user can only run your application, not edit any of the objects. As you might expect, many keystrokes are also disabled, such as pressing F11 to show the Database window or Ctrl+Break to halt Visual Basic code execution. If you also purchase the Microsoft Visual Studio Tools for the Microsoft Office System package, you'll obtain a license to distribute your database with the modules to execute in runtime mode to users who do not have Access installed on their system. For more information about the new Microsoft Visual Tools for Office, see *http://msdn.microsoft.com/vstudio /office/officetools.aspx.*

However, to execute successfully in runtime mode, your application must have the following:

- All features of the application must be implemented with forms and reports. The user will not have access to the Database window to execute queries or to open tables.

- The application must have a startup form or an Autoexec macro that opens a startup form.

- All forms and reports must have custom toolbars. No built-in toolbars are available in the runtime version. Forms and reports should also have custom menus because runtime mode provides very restricted built-in menus.

- All (or nearly all) code must be written in Visual Basic and must implement error trapping. Any untrapped errors cause the application to exit.

- The application should execute the Quit method of the Application object to terminate. If you simply close the final form, the user will be left staring at an empty Access workspace.

The primary sample databases, LawTrack Contacts (*Contacts.mdb*) and Housing Reservations (*Housing.mdb*), meet the above requirements except the startup form is set to *frmCopyright* to display important information each time you open one of the databases, and the Exit button on the main switchboard form merely closes the form and attempts to return to the Database window.

If you would like to see what runtime mode looks like, you must first install the runtime modules from your Microsoft Office 2003 installation CD. Insert the CD in your CD drive and cancel the setup program that starts. Open Windows Explorer and go to the \FILES\ACCRT subfolder. Double-click the ACCESSRT.MSI file to install the runtime modules.

After you install the runtime files, you can open the *Housing.mdb* desktop database, choose Startup from the Tools menu, and change the Display Form/Page setting from frmCopyright to frmSplash. The sample files include a shortcut, *Housing Runtime*, that opens this database in runtime mode. This shortcut should work as long as you installed Microsoft Office in the default folder (C:\Program Files\Microsoft Office\Office 11) and the sample files in the default folder (C:\Microsoft Press\Access 2003 Inside Out). If necessary, you can change the shortcut by right-clicking the shortcut and selecting Properties on the shortcut menu. The target setting in this shortcut is as follows:

```
"C:\Program Files\Microsoft Office\Office11\MSACCESS.EXE" "C:\Microsoft Press
\Access 2003 Inside Out\Housing.mdb" /runtime
```

After you change the Display Form/Page setting in the Startup properties of the database and correct any settings in the shortcut target, you can double-click the shortcut to start the application in runtime mode. Sign on as any employee of your choosing to see the main switchboard form. Try pressing F11 to see if anything happens—the Database window should not appear. You can move around in the application using the command buttons on the various switchboard forms. When you click Exit on the main switchboard, code in the form closes all open forms and then closes the switchboard. You'll be left looking at a blank Access workspace and a very limited menu bar. You can choose Close from the File menu to close this limited copy of Access.

Creating an Execute-Only Database

Even if you have secured your database, you might still want to be sure that no one can examine or change the Visual Basic procedures you created. After you have fully compiled your Visual Basic project, Access no longer needs the original text of your Visual Basic statements. You can create a special execute-only copy of your database by using one of the utilities supplied with Access. An additional advantage of an execute-only database is that it might be significantly smaller than a copy that contains all the code—particularly if you have written many Visual Basic procedures.

To create an execute-only copy of any completed database application, open that database and go to the Database window. Choose Database Utilities from the Tools menu, and then choose Make MDE File from the submenu for an Access .mdb desktop database, or choose Make ADE File from the submenu for an Access .adp project file. The Save As dialog box asks you for a location and name for your new database or project. It then makes sure the current database is fully compiled and saved, copies the database to a new file with the appropriate .mde or .ade extension, removes the Visual Basic source code, and compacts the new file.

If you open an .mde file (you can find a file called *Contacts.mde* on the companion CD), you'll find that you can't open any form or report module or any module object. You also won't be able to open a form or a report in Design view. (This is an additional benefit of an .mde file.) Figure 31-2 shows the Modules list in the *Contacts.mde* database file. Notice that the Run, Design, and New buttons are disabled, indicating that you can neither create a new module nor view the source code of an existing module, and that the only way to run code is through the database application's interface. You'll find that the Design and New buttons are also disabled for all forms and reports.

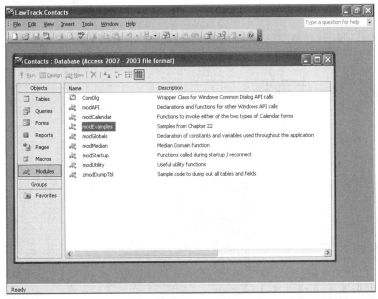

Figure 31-2. You can't edit any modules in the Contacts.mde database file.

Creating an Application Shortcut

When you're all done, you might need to create a way for users to easily start your application. If your users all have a copy of Access, you could give them your database application files and simply instruct them to open the appropriate file. But what if you've secured your database, requiring the user to be a member of a specific workgroup? What if the user doesn't have Access, so you have to set them up to execute your application with the runtime version of Access? What if you want to also define certain utility functions that the user might need to execute from time to time? The answer is to create a shortcut.

You use shortcuts all the time in Windows to start programs on your computer. When you install an application on your computer, the setup program usually creates a shortcut that it adds to your Start menu. Some setup programs also add a shortcut on your desktop. The icon for a shortcut on your desktop has a small white box in the lower left corner with an arrow in it. You can right-click a shortcut and choose Properties from the shortcut menu to see the definition of the shortcut.

To create a shortcut on your Windows desktop for your Access application, right-click the desktop, choose New from the shortcut menu, and then choose Shortcut. You can also create a shortcut in a folder by opening Windows Explorer, navigating to the folder you want, choosing New from the File menu, and then choosing Shortcut from the submenu. In either case, Windows opens the Create Shortcut dialog box to help you find the program you want the shortcut to open. Click the Browse button and find C:\Program Files\Microsoft Office\Office11\MSACCESS.EXE. Click OK to select the file and then click the Next button. Give your shortcut a name, such as the name of the database you plan to open with the shortcut, and then click Finish.

Right-click your new shortcut and choose Properties from the shortcut menu. You'll see a window similar to the one shown in Figure 31-3.

Figure 31-3. Modifying the Target setting in a Windows shortcut.

At the top of the Shortcut tab is the icon the shortcut displays and the name of the shortcut. You can click the General tab and enter a new name to rename your shortcut. Target type tells you that this shortcut starts an application. Target location displays the original location of the program that this shortcut starts. The Target box allows you to specify the program or file that you want to run. Note that at this point your new shortcut only starts the Access program—it doesn't specify a file to open or any parameters. You can specify the database file name and enter any parameters used by the program in this box.

Immediately following the name of the Access program in the Target box, enter a space followed by the database you want to open (with its full path). Follow the name of the database with the options you need to perform the task you want. For example, you might need to specify the location of the workgroup file your application requires.

Note You can also specify a database file name in the Target box in a shortcut, and Windows opens the program that can process this file (in this case, Access) when you double-click the shortcut. However, Access won't recognize any parameters that you include after the file name. You must specifically ask to open the Access program (msaccess.exe) and add the file name and parameters.

Table 31-1 summarizes the shortcut command-line options you can use. When you include multiple command-line options, separate each with a space.

Table 31-1. **Access Shortcut Command-Line Options**

Option	Description
<database>	Opens the specified database. If the path or file name contains blanks, you must enclose the string in double quotes. Must be the first option after the folder and file location for MSACCESS.EXE.
/cmd <command string>	Specifies a program parameter that can be retrieved by a Visual Basic procedure using the built-in Command function. Must be the last option on the command line.
/compact [<target>]	Compacts and repairs the specified database but does not open the database. If you omit the target file name, Access compacts the database into the original file name and location.
/convert <target>	Converts the specified version 8 or earlier database to version 9 (Access 2000) format and stores it in the target file.
/excl	Opens the specified database with exclusive access. Only one user at a time can use a database that is opened exclusively.
/nostartup	Opens the specified database without displaying the task pane.
/profile <userprofile>	Specifies the name of a user profile in the Windows registry. You can use a profile to override database engine settings and specify a custom application title, icon, or splash screen.
/pwd <password>	Specifies the password for the user named in the /user parameter. If the password contains the / or ; character, enter the character twice. For example, if the password is #ab/cd;de, enter **#ab//cd;;de**.
/repair	Repairs the specified database but does not open the database.
/ro	Opens the specified database in read-only mode.
/runtime	Specifies that Access will execute with runtime version options.
/user <userid>	Specifies the logon user ID.
/wrkgrp <workgroupfile>	Uses the specified workgroup file.
/x macroname	Runs the specified macro after opening the specified database.

For example, to open the *HousingSecured.mdb* database, to specifically use the Secured.mdw workgroup file, and to specify that Access uses runtime mode, enter the following on the Target line:

```
"C:\Program Files\Microsoft Office\OFFICE11\MSACCESS.EXE"
    "C:\Microsoft Press\Access 2003 Inside Out\HousingSecured.mdb" /wrkgroup
    "C:\Microsoft Press\Access 2003 Inside Out\Secured.mdw" /runtime
```

This text assumes you've installed the sample files in the default folders. In the **Start in** box, specify the starting folder for the application. In the **Shortcut key** box, you can enter a single letter or number that the user can press with Ctrl+Alt+ to run the shortcut. The shortcut key must be unique for all shortcuts on your system. In the Run drop-down list, you can choose to start the application in a normal-size window (the default), minimized as an icon on your taskbar, or maximized to fill your screen. In the Comment box, you can enter text that appears when the user pauses the mouse over the shortcut.

Click the Find Target button to verify that the target you entered is valid. Click the Change Icon button to select a different icon stored within the target program (MSACCESS.EXE has 64 available icons) or to locate an icon file on your hard disk. Click the Advanced button if you need to set up this shortcut to run under a specific Windows user ID.

On the Compatibility tab of the Properties dialog box, you can find an option to run the program in compatibility mode as though it's running on an older operating system such as Windows 95 or 98. You can also force your display to 256 colors, use 640×480 screen resolution, or disable Windows themes when this program runs. On the Security tab, you can allow or deny permissions to use this shortcut for specific Windows users or groups. The Security tab only appears if you are using an NTFS (rather than a FAT) drive.

After you have completed the settings you want, click OK to save your changes to the shortcut. You can now double-click the shortcut to run the program with the options you specified.

> **Note** To actually use the sample shortcut that you just created, you must first switch to the Secured.mdw workgroup, open *HousingSecured.mdb* and sign on as the HousingAdmin user, and change the startup form to *frmSplash*. See Chapter 30 for details.

Understanding the Visual Studio Tools for the Microsoft Office System

You can obtain additional tools and a license to freely distribute runtime versions of your applications by purchasing Microsoft Visual Studio Tools for the Microsoft Office System. This package includes the following:

- **Microsoft Office Access 2003 Developer Extensions.** This package includes the following tools for Access:
  - A royalty-free license to distribute the runtime modules for Microsoft Access. This allows you to provide your application to users who do not have Access.
  - A package and deploy wizard that helps you create installation files that include your database application, the runtime modules necessary to run your application, and any supporting files (such as ActiveX controls or icons). The wizard creates a standard Microsoft Windows Installer setup file (.msi).
  - A custom startup wizard that helps you create the Startup properties for your desktop database or project file.
  - A property scanner utility that lets you search all collections, objects, and properties in your desktop database or project file for a particular value.

- A source code database to help you discover how the wizards included with this package work.
- White papers on Access desktop database security, conditional formatting, normalization, and managing SQL Server security.

● **Microsoft Visual Basic .NET Standard Edition.** This package provides you with additional tools to allow you to use Microsoft Visual Basic .NET to write code for Microsoft Word and Microsoft Excel applications.

● **Microsoft SQL Server 2000 Developer Edition.** This includes a full desktop edition of SQL Server 2000 (not just MSDE) with all the tools you need to fully manage SQL Server on your desktop machine.

Appendix

Installing Microsoft Office

This book assumes you have installed Microsoft Access as part of Microsoft Office Professional Edition 2003. To install Microsoft Office and related software for a single user, you need a Microsoft Windows–compatible computer configured as follows:

- A Pentium 233 MHz or higher processor (Pentium III recommended as a minimum).

- Microsoft Windows 2000 Service Pack 3 or later, or Microsoft Windows XP (recommended). At least 64 megabytes (MB) of RAM (128 MB recommended) for the operating system, plus 16 MB of RAM for each application running simultaneously. Microsoft Access, Microsoft Outlook, and the Microsoft SQL Server Data Engine (MSDE) run best on machines with 256 MB or more of RAM.

- A hard drive with at least 245 MB of free space for a minimum installation when your network administrator has set up an install package for you on a server. When you perform a local installation, you might need up to 2 gigabytes (GB) during a full installation on your primary hard drive for the installation files and programs. At the end of the Office install, you have the option to leave some of the installation files on your hard drive, which requires up to an additional 240 MB of free space. You need an additional 44 MB of space to install MSDE.

- A CD-ROM drive. If you are installing over a network, no CD-ROM drive is required.

- A mouse or other pointing device.

- A Super VGA (800×600) or higher display.

Other options required to use all features include:

- A multimedia computer for sound and other multimedia effects.

- Dial-up or broadband Internet access.

- Microsoft Mail, Microsoft Exchange, Internet SMTP/POP3 service, or other MAPI-compliant messaging software for e-mail.

- Microsoft Exchange Server for advanced collaboration functions.

- Microsoft Internet Explorer 6.0 or later to run InfoPath. The examples in this book require version 5.01 or later.
- Connection to an Internet service provider with updated Microsoft FrontPage extensions for Web publishing features, or a local copy of Microsoft Internet Information Services (IIS) installed.

Installing Microsoft Office

Before you run the Office Setup program, be sure that no other applications are running on your computer and then start Windows.

If you're installing from the Microsoft Office Professional CD-ROM, insert the first CD-ROM. On most systems, Office Setup starts automatically. If Setup does not start automatically, choose the Run command from the Windows Start menu. In the Run dialog box, type **x:\setup.exe** (where *x* is the drive letter of your CD-ROM drive).

To install from a network drive, use Windows Explorer to connect to the folder in which your system manager has placed the Office setup files. Run Setup.exe in that folder by double-clicking it. If you're installing Office from a Master License Pack, choose Run from your Start menu and include a PIDKEY = parameter and the 25-character volume-license key in the Open box, as in:

```
x:\setup.exe PIDKEY=1234567890123456789012345
```

Note that the setup program might take several minutes after it displays its opening screen to examine your machine and determine what programs you currently have installed—be patient! If you didn't supply a license key on the command line, the setup program first asks for a valid product key. If you're installing from a CD, you can find the product key in the materials included with the Office 2003 installation CDs. Enter a valid key and click Next to go to the next screen. The setup program asks for your name and your company name. Then click Next, and Setup requires that you accept the license agreement. Click Next again, and the setup program shows you different options depending on whether you have programs from a previous version of Office installed on your machine.

Choosing Options When You Have No Previous Version of Office

When you have never installed any previous version of Microsoft Office on your machine (or you have deleted all previous versions), the setup program displays an initial set of options as shown in Figure A-1.

At the bottom of the window, you can see the Install to box with a default location chosen. You can enter a different program file location or click the Browse button to select a location on your hard drive. I recommend that you keep the default location. The fastest way to complete an install is to select Typical Install and click Next. You'll see a Summary screen confirming the products that the setup program will install and how much space is required and available on your hard drive. You can click Install to finish the installation.

The Typical Install option includes components that Microsoft considers most useful to the majority of users. You can see in Figure A-1 that you can also select Complete Install, Minimal Install, or Custom Install. The Complete Install option installs every available Windows component to your hard drive. The Minimal Install option includes only the basic parts of Word, Excel, PowerPoint, Outlook, Publisher, and InfoPath, but *does not* include any of Microsoft Access! (The installation program creates a shortcut to Access, but you'll be prompted to install it when you click the shortcut.) If you don't want to tailor the installation to your specific needs by choosing Custom Install, you can select Typical Install or Complete Install to include Access so that you can work through this book. Click Next, and the setup program displays the Summary window, as shown in Figure A-4 on page 1227.

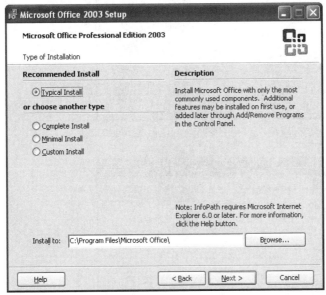

Figure A-1. Initial install options when you have no previous version of Office installed.

I personally like to choose Custom Install to pick the components I need. Custom Install also allows you to choose only some of the applications. When you select Custom Install and click Next, the setup program displays the first of the Custom Setup windows, as shown in Figure A-2 on the next page. The applications you see listed will depend on the Microsoft Office Edition you are installing. (You must have Microsoft Office Professional Edition 2003 to install Microsoft Access.)

By default, the setup program selects all the programs on your CD. You can clear the check box next to any program name that you don't want to install. You can also select the Choose advanced customization of applications option (shown selected in Figure A-2, but not selected by default in the setup program) to specifically tailor the options for each application. If you don't choose this option, Setup performs a Typical Install, but only for the programs you selected. Select this option and then click Next to see the Advanced Customization window, as shown in Figure A-3 on the next page.

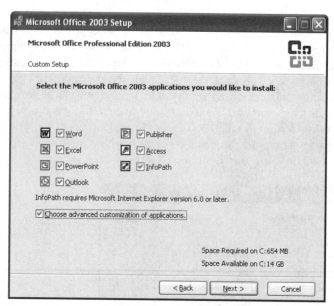

Figure A-2. Choosing programs to install in Custom Setup.

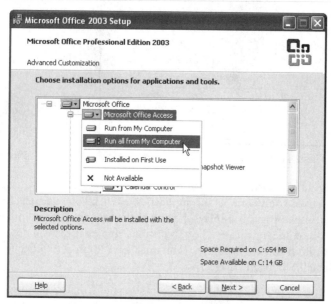

Figure A-3. Advanced Customization options.

The setup program shows you a hierarchical view of the available installation choices for all of Office and for each Office program. Click the plus sign next to any program to expand it and see its components and features arranged in subcategories. When you see a program, component, or feature that interests you, click the down arrow next to its disk drive icon to choose the installation option for the component and all subcomponents it might include.

To work through all the examples in this book, you should select the Run all from My Computer option for Microsoft Access, as shown in Figure A-3. Choosing this option selects the Run from My Computer option for all Access components. If you were to select Installed on First Use, the installation program creates a shortcut for the program on your Start menu, but you'd be prompted to install the application when you click the shortcut. Choosing Not Available causes the installation program to neither install the program nor provide a shortcut.

I personally like to begin by selecting the Run all from My Computer option for the top-level item, Microsoft Office. This is the same as choosing the Complete Install option earlier. I then go through each of the major components and selectively choose Run from My Computer, Installed on First Use, or Not Available for programs or features that I want to change from the default. For example, you might want to go to the Office Shared Features category and change the selections for Alternative User Input (Speech and Handwriting) or select or remove some of the extra fonts under International Support. Under Office Tools, you might want to remove the HTML Source Editing options if you plan to also install Microsoft FrontPage. If you're unsure about any option, you can click its title to see a brief description in the lower part of the window.

After you have finished making your selections, click Next to see the Summary window, as shown in Figure A-4.

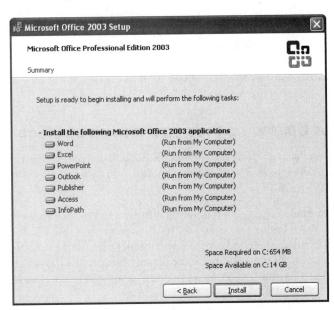

Figure A-4. The Summary window of the setup program.

You can verify the list of programs and click Install to proceed. If you're not sure, you can click Back to return through the various windows to verify the options you selected. When the setup program finishes, it shows you a Setup Completed window, shown in Figure A-5 on the next page.

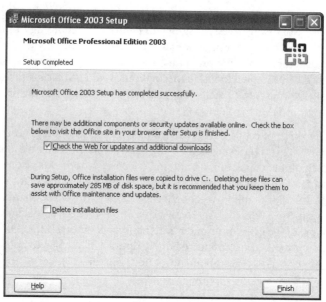

Figure A-5. The Setup Completed window in Microsoft Office 2003 Setup.

In this final window, you can select options to open your Web browser to check for additional updates. You can also select the Delete installation files option. If you set any options to Installed on First Use, you should leave the installation files on your hard drive unless your drive is running low on space. When you do this, you won't have to reinsert your installation CD if you later happen to choose an option in one of the Office programs that requires adding setup options.

Choosing Options to Upgrade a Previous Version of Office

When you have a previous version of any of the Microsoft Office programs installed on your computer, the setup program shows you different options after you accept the license agreement, as shown in Figure A-6.

At the bottom of the window, the setup program again offers an Install to box where you can enter a different location. In this case, it lists the location where you installed the previous version of Microsoft Office. The setup program will install Office 2003 in a subfolder at this location. Because I have multiple versions installed on my machine, I always choose a custom install location for each version. I recommend that you choose the location identified by the setup program.

Notice that the setup program offers an Upgrade option. When you select this option, Setup removes all previous versions and performs a Typical Install. If you select this option and click Next, Setup displays the Summary window shown in Figure A-4 on page 1127.

As a professional Microsoft Access developer, I keep several different versions of Access installed on my primary development machine so that I can continue to support older applications that I wrote. (I actually have Access 97, 2000, 2002, and 2003 installed!) You might also want to keep an older version of Excel, PowerPoint, or Word. To keep an older version, you must select one of the four options under or choose another type. These options all work the same as the options presented when you don't have an earlier Office version on your machine, but they give you the additional option of selecting which earlier versions to keep. When you select Custom Install and click Next, Setup shows you the Custom Setup window shown previously in Figure A-2 on page 1126 and, if you select Choose advanced customization of applications in this window, Setup next shows you the Advanced Customization window shown in Figure A-3 on page 1126. Refer back to those steps if you select these options, and then continue below.

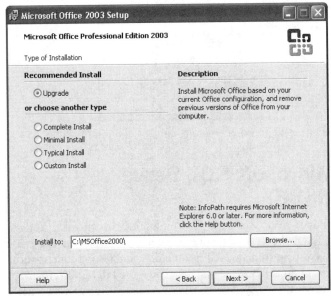

Figure A-6. Installation options when you have previous versions of Microsoft Office programs installed.

When you select any of the other three options, or after you complete the customization selections described above and click Next, Setup displays the Previous Version of Office window, as shown in Figure A-7 on the next page.

Notice that you cannot choose to keep a previous version of Microsoft Outlook if you have chosen to install the 2003 version of Outlook. You still have the choice at this point to remove all previous versions if you like, by selecting the first option. You can also choose the second option and clear all the check boxes (except for Outlook) to keep all the previous versions. I typically clear the Microsoft Access check box to keep all my earlier Access versions. Click Next to go to the Summary window shown in Figure A-4 on page 1127. After clicking Install, the setup program proceeds and displays the Setup Completed window in Figure A-5 on page 1128 when it is finished.

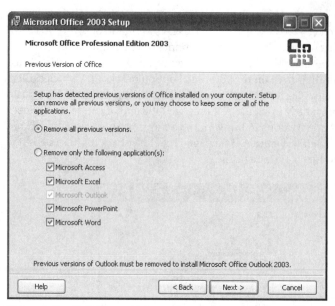

Figure A-7. Selecting which previous program versions you want to keep.

Installing the Microsoft SQL Server Data Engine (MSDE)

If you intend to build Microsoft Access projects (.adp files), which link directly to a database defined in Microsoft SQL Server, you should install the Microsoft SQL Server Data Engine (MSDE) on your desktop machine to facilitate building and testing your application. MSDE is a special version of Microsoft SQL Server 2000 configured to run on either operating system supported by Microsoft Office 2003—Windows 2000 SP3 or Windows XP. With MSDE installed, you can use a Microsoft Access project file to create databases and define tables, views, diagrams, and stored procedures that you can later move to SQL Server on a network. You normally install MSDE on your desktop machine. However, you can also install MSDE on a server. If you need to install MSDE on a server, you must install it from that server's console.

MSDE has its own Setup program—you can't install MSDE using Office 2003 Setup. To get ready to run MSDE Setup, insert the first of your Office 2003 Setup discs. If Office 2003 Setup starts, click Cancel. Choose Run from your Start menu, enter the following, and click OK.

```
x:\MSDE2000\MSDE2KS3.exe
```

where x is the drive letter of your CD-ROM drive.

This program doesn't install MSDE on your system—it merely unpacks and copies the files needed to install MSDE to your hard drive in a location that you specify. When you run this program, it shows you the license agreement that you must accept in order to unpack the installation files to your hard drive. After you accept the license agreement by clicking the I Agree button, the program displays a dialog box where you can specify the location for the installation files, as shown in Figure A-8.

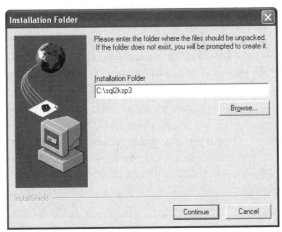

Figure A-8. Specifying the location for the MSDE Setup files on your hard drive.

You can accept the default location, or you can enter a specific drive and folder name or click the Browse button to navigate to a location on your hard drive. Click Continue to create the installation files on your hard drive. Be sure to remember the location because you will need it to start the actual installation program.

You will find the MSDE setup program in the MSDE subfolder of the location that you specified in Figure A-8. If you accept the default location, you will find the setup program at C:\sql2ksp3\MSDE\setup.exe. You cannot run this program directly from Windows Explorer because you must specify at least one parameter for the program to run successfully. You can find a complete description of all the parameters in section 3.7 of the sp3readme.htm file that you can find in the same folder as the setup program. Table A-1 lists the most common parameters that you should use.

Table A-1. Common Parameters for the MSDE Setup Program

Parameter	Description
BLANKSAPWD=1	You can install an unsecured copy of MSDE by including this parameter. The setup program allows the password of the sa (system administrator) user ID to be blank. If you do not supply this parameter, you must supply the SAPWD parameter. I strongly recommend that you do not install an unsecured copy.
INSTANCENAME=<name>	You can install multiple copies of MSDE on your machine, but each copy must have a unique instance name. If you plan to install only one copy, you can omit this parameter. The setup program assigns a default instance name of MSSQLSERVER to the copy you're installing.

Table A-1. Common Parameters for the MSDE Setup Program

Parameter	Description
password	that, you must supply the SAPWD parameter and specify a password, and you should remember this password and keep it in a safe place. If you also include the SECURITYMODE=SQL parameter, you will need this password to sign on to the server. Do not use the same password that you use to log on to Windows.
SECURITYMODE=SQL	Use this parameter if you do not want MSDE to use Windows user authentication. When you do not include this parameter, your server will be installed to use Windows user authentication, and the setup program adds the local Windows Administrators group with authorization to act as system administrator. You should be logged on to a Windows user ID that is a member of the Administrators group when you do not include this parameter.

I strongly recommend that you use Windows user authentication. When you do this, only Windows-authenticated users who have been granted permission on your server can gain access to it. (The members of the Administrators group on your machine automatically have permission.) If you use SQL Server security, anyone who discovers the password to the sa user ID can gain access to your server. So, you should not use the SECURITYMODE=SQL parameter, but you must supply the SAPWD parameter to successfully run the setup program. To run Setup, choose Run from the Start menu. In the Open box, enter

```
C:\sql2ksp3\MSDE\setup.exe SAPWD=somepassword
```

where C:\sql2ksp3 is the location you specified in Figure A-8, and *somepassword* is the password that you want to assign to the sa user ID. The password should be at least six characters and can be as long as 128 characters. A password should also contain some combination of letters, numbers, and symbols such as # or) to make it more difficult to guess. Note that you can include additional parameters on the command line, separated by spaces. Click the OK button in the Run window to execute the setup program.

The setup program displays a dialog box that shows you the progress and time remaining for the installation. On a fast machine, the installation should complete in two to three minutes. You can click Cancel in this dialog box at any time to cancel the installation.

After the installation completes, you should find a new Service Manager entry in your Windows Startup group (Start, All Programs, Startup) to start the SQL Server Service Manager. This program should start the next time you restart your machine, but you can select it from your Start menu after Setup completes to start the program for the first time. (If you don't find the program on your Start menu, you can also start it from C:\Program Files\Microsoft SQL Server\80\Tools\Binn\sqlmangr.exe.) The Service Manager presents options as shown in Figure A-9.

Figure A-9. The SQL Server Service Manager.

The Server drop-down list should show the name of your current machine. The Service Manager also scans your network for other SQL Servers. If you have administrative authority on other servers, you can select one from the drop-down list and control the services running on that machine. The Services drop-down list should display the SQL Server service. You can also find entries that allow you to start and stop the Distributed Transaction Coordinator (DTC) and SQL Server Agent. You need DTC only if you execute stored procedures that need to protect updates to databases on multiple servers within a transaction. The SQL Server Agent allows you to schedule automatic execution of tasks such as backing up or compacting your databases.

Select your server, the SQL Server service, and click the Start/Continue button to start your server. (You should see a small server icon with a green arrow inside a circle on your taskbar when your server is running.) You can click the Pause button to pause your server (still running but not accepting any new connections) or the Stop button to stop it. The icon on your taskbar changes to indicate the current status of your server. You should normally leave your server running, especially when you're developing project file applications in Access. You should leave the Auto-start service when OS starts option selected to restart your server each time you start Windows.

You can close the Service Manager program window, but the service continues to run. You can right-click the server icon on your taskbar to display a shortcut menu. From this menu, you can open the Service Manager window again, start or stop services on your machine, set options, or exit the Service Manager program.

Managing ODBC Connections

When you need to connect to your Microsoft Access database tables (in an .mdb or .mde file) from any Office application or on a Web server, you must first define an Open Database Connectivity (ODBC) Data Source Name (DSN) on the system from which you want to make the connection. You don't need to define a connection to your database for links from another Access database—Access uses its own internal drivers to make the connection.

If you want to use Microsoft Access to connect to SQL databases that support the ODBC standard, you must install both the ODBC driver for that database and define a connection in the Microsoft ODBC Data Source Administrator. The ODBC driver for Microsoft SQL Server is included with Access.

ODBC isolates applications from differences among database systems. If your application performs all its database processing through ODBC interfaces you can, in theory, change to a different database system without changing your application. When you create a DSN to point to a database, you can reference the DSN when linking to the database from Access or any other program that supports ODBC. If you move the data to another database (for example, move a FoxPro table to SQL Server), you need only update the DSN. You most likely will not need to change your application.

So, it really doesn't make sense to code the file name of your Access or SQL Server database—or specify the type of database—within your application. If you do and then later change the database system to some other product or change the database name, you'll have to change the connection information inside the application, and that would be counter to the design of ODBC.

You can create a DSN to define—once—the database's type, physical location, physical name, and any other configuration details. The application then references the DSN by name to connect to the database and doesn't need to know (or be configured with) all database-specific details.

There are three kinds of ODBC Data Source Names:

- **User** This type of DSN stores its information in the system registry on a user-by-user basis. User DSNs are available only when the corresponding user is logged on to the computer.

- **System** A System DSN also stores its information in the registry, but it's available no matter who's currently logged on (or even if no one is currently logged on). You should create a System DSN for Web servers.

- **File** Like a system DSN, a File DSN is available no matter who's currently logged in. A File DSN isn't stored in the system registry, though; it's stored in an ordinary text file. The advantage of a File DSN is that setting it up doesn't require physical use of the ODBC Data Source Administrator. If you know the format of the parameters for the kind of database file you'll be connecting to, you can create a File DSN with Notepad or any plain text editor. You can find a sample File DSN named *Housing.dsn* in the sample files included on your companion CD.

Creating an ODBC System Data Source Name for Microsoft Access

The most universal type of DSN is a System DSN. The ODBC Data Source Administrator creates registry entries for this type of DSN that can be used by all applications, no matter which user is signed on. You must use a System DSN, for example, to define the database connections on a Web server. You can create a System DSN for a Microsoft Access database by following these steps:

1 Log onto the computer whose applications require a connection to your database. If you're creating a System DSN on a Web server, you must be logged on at the Web server's console.

2 Open Windows Control Panel.

3 Double-click the Administrative Tools shortcut. In Administrative Tools, double-click the Data Sources (ODBC) shortcut.

4 The ODBC Data Source Administrator window opens, as shown in Figure A-10.

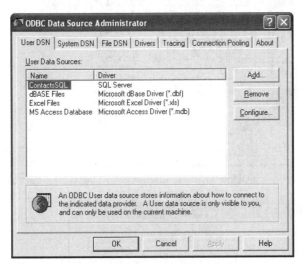

Figure A-10. ODBC Data Source Administrator dialog box.

Note New versions of the ODBC Data Source Administrator usually appear with each new version of any Microsoft database product, operating system, or Web server, and at other times as well. As a result, the screens on your computer might differ somewhat from those shown here.

5 To create a System DSN, first click the System DSN tab and then click the Add button.

6 When the dialog box shown in Figure A-11 appears, choose Microsoft Access Driver, and then click Finish.

7 The ODBC Microsoft Access Setup dialog box appears, shown in Figure A-12.

8 Make the following settings in the dialog box to configure the ODBC Microsoft Access Driver, shown in Figure A-12. Only the Data Source Name and Database entries are required; the others are optional. Click the Options button to see the additional settings.

   ■ **Data Source Name.** Give the data source a name that applications will use to identify it.

   ■ **Database.** Click the Select button, find the database that you want in the Select Database dialog box that appears, and click OK.

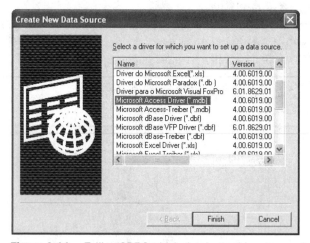

Figure A-11. Telling ODBC which database driver to use for a data source.

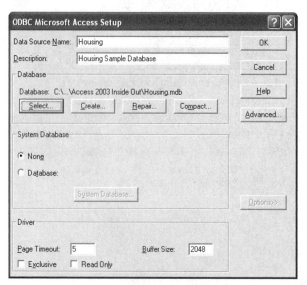

Figure A-12. Defining an ODBC Data Source Name for a Microsoft Access database.

If the database resides on another computer, be sure to specify its location in Universal Naming Convention (UNC) format. Network locations mapped to drive letters might change depending on who's logged in to the computer, and disappear completely when no one is logged in. A UNC file name has this form:

```
\\<server name>\<share name>\<folder path>\<filename>
```

> **Note** To specify a UNC name, you must enter the entire server, share, path, and file name in the Database Name field of the Select Database dialog box that appears when you click the Select button.

Entries in the remaining fields, described here, are optional:

- **Description.** Enter one line of documentation regarding the DSN.
- **System Database.** If your application uses a system database, click the Database option button and then use the System Database button to locate the database.
- **Page Timeout.** Specify a time limit for completing ODBC operations. The default value is normally adequate.
- **Buffer Size.** Specify the number of bytes available for ODBC buffering. The default value is normally adequate.
- **Exclusive.** Select this option if the application requires exclusive use of the database.
- **Read Only.** Select this option if the application requires read-only use of the database.
- **Advanced.** Click this button if using the database requires additional settings, such as a user name and password. Keep in mind that anyone authorized to use the system can also use this DSN. If your database is secured, you might not want to supply a user name and password here. ODBC prompts for any required user name and password when you don't define them in the DSN.

9 When all your entries are correct, click the OK button to create the System DSN.

If you have several applications that use the same database, you should use the same System DSN for all of them. That way, if you ever have to move, rename, or reconfigure the database, you only have one System DSN to update.

If you need to establish a System DSN on a Web server and you don't have access to your Web server's console, someone who does have access will need to set up the System DSN for you. On a corporate intranet, contact your departmental administrator or MIS department. For Internet service providers, contact the support staff or system administrator.

Using ODBC for Connecting to Microsoft SQL Server

Like Access, Microsoft SQL Server is an ODBC-compliant database. If SQL Server drivers are available on your PC, you can use ODBC for opening SQL Server databases in Access. If SQL Server drivers are available on your Web server, Microsoft Active Server Pages can read

SQL Server databases via ODBC. Here's the procedure for defining an ODBC System DSN for a SQL Server database:

1 Log onto the computer whose applications require a connection to your database. If you're creating a System DSN on a Web server, you must be logged on at the Web server's console.

2 Open Windows Control Panel.

3 Double-click the Administrative Tools shortcut. In Administrative Tools, double-click the Data Sources (ODBC) shortcut.

4 The ODBC Data Source Administrator dialog box opens, as shown previously in Figure A-10 on page 1235.

5 To create a System DSN, first click the System DSN tab and then click the Add button.

6 In the Create New Data Source dialog box (Figure A-11), scroll in the list to find and select SQL Server, and then click Finish. This starts the Create a New Data Source to SQL Server Wizard, the first window of which is shown in Figure A-13.

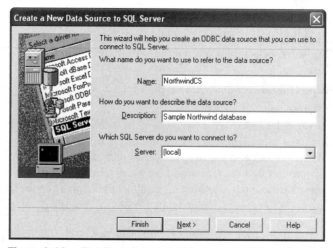

Figure A-13. The first step in defining an ODBC Data Source Name for SQL Server.

7 Enter the following fields. (The figure shows how to create a DSN for the Northwind sample database on the local MSDE server.)

■ **Name.** Give the data source a name that applications will use to identify it. This is the name that ultimately appears in the Name column of the ODBC Data Source Administrator window (Figure A-10).

■ **Description.** Specify one line of documentation regarding the DSN. This field is optional.

- **Server.** Specify the computer where the SQL Server software (or MSDE) is running. If the computer name doesn't appear in the drop-down list, type it in. Use (local) to point to the server on your machine.

8 Click Next to see the second window of the wizard, shown in Figure A-14.

You might need to ask your SQL Server administrator how to fill in these values, which are as follows:

- How should SQL Server verify the authenticity of the login ID? When your machine is running Windows 2000 or Windows XP, you should normally select With Windows NT authentication using the network login ID unless the database administrator has instructed you to use an SQL Server login ID and password. Select With SQL Server authentication using a login ID and password entered by the user if you're using SQL Server's built-in security.

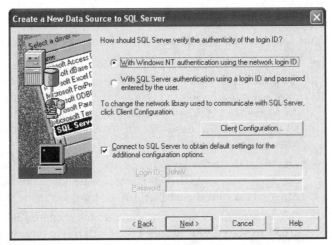

Figure A-14. Settings related to SQL Server communication and security.

- Client Configuration. Click this button to select the type of network library (protocol) that the server supports. You don't need to change the default settings for MSDE.

- Connect to SQL Server to obtain default settings for the additional configuration options. To obtain defaults from the server specified in the previous dialog box, select this check box. If the server uses SQL Server login IDs, you'll also need to supply a login ID that has administrative rights and a password. Click Next to continue.

9 The next window of the wizard, shown in Figure A-15, allows you to select a default database and options for the connection.

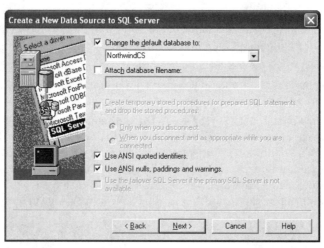

Figure A-15. Selecting a default database and connection options.

- **Change the default database to.** When you use Windows NT authentication, the default database for the user is typically the master catalog database. You must select this option and choose the actual database that you want from the drop-down list. When you use an SQL Server login ID, you can leave this option set to the default, and the user will have the option to select another database when using this DSN.

- **Attach database filename.** You can specify the path and location of an SQL Server data file (.mdf) that ODBC will attach when using this DSN. You can type the name to be used as the database name in the Change the default database to box.

- **Create temporary stored procedures for prepared SQL statements and drop the stored procedures.** The wizard makes these options available only when you are defining a connection to an earlier version of SQL Server. You can ignore these options for SQL Server 2000 (or MSDE).

- **Use ANSI quoted identifiers.** Selecting this option instructs ODBC to include a SET QUOTED IDENTIFIERS ON command in any command stream that it processes. This is handy when some of the objects in the database have names that include blanks or other special characters. When you select this option, you must enclose all string and date/time literals in single quotes in any command that you execute via this connection. Some products, such as Access and the Microsoft Query utility for Microsoft Excel, will generate errors if you do not select this option. The wizard selects this option by default.

- **Use ANSI nulls, paddings and warnings.** Setting this option asks the ODBC driver to set to ON the ANSI_NULLS, ANSI_PADDINGS, and ANSI_WARNINGS options. ANSI_NULLS requires that you use the ANSI tests for Null (IS NULL, IS NOT NULL) in predicates instead of the = Null syntax of Transact-SQL. ANSI_PADDINGS specifies that trailing blanks in varchar columns and trailing zeroes in varbinary columns are not trimmed before saving the value.

ANSI_WARNINGS causes SQL Server to return warning messages for conditions that violate ANSI rules. Access expects all three options to be set, and the wizard selects this option by default.

■ **Use the failover SQL Server if the primary SQL Server is not available.** The wizard makes this option available when you have selected a server that has a failover server defined. This option is not available when connecting to MSDE.

10 Click Next to go to the final window of the wizard. These final options seldom require configuration, so unless your SQL Server administrator has instructed you differently, click Finish to bypass them. For more information on the settings, click the Help button.

11 Next, ODBC displays the informational screen shown in the background of Figure A-16. Clicking the Test Data Source button causes ODBC to attempt to connect to the database using the settings you specified. If you see the message TESTS COMPLETED SUCCESSFULLY, your System DSN is ready to use. If you don't see the confirmation message, recheck your entries and perhaps consult your SQL Server administrator.

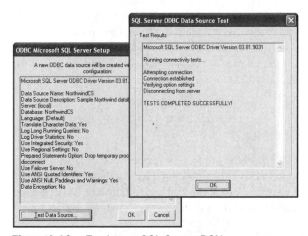

Figure A-16. Testing an SQL Server DSN.

Converting from a Previous Release of Microsoft Access

Microsoft Office Access 2003 (version 11 of Access) can work with the data and tables in a database file created by Access version 2, version 7 (Access for Windows 95) version 8 (Access 97), version 9 (Access 2000), and version 10 (Access 2002). Depending on the complexity of the application, you might be able to open and run a version 2, 7, or 8 database application with version 11, but you won't be able to modify any of the objects in the database. You can open a version 9 or version 10 database with version 11 and modify any of the objects in the database.

You can convert a version 2, version 7, or version 8 database file to either the Access 2000 format (version 9) or the Access 2002–2003 format (versions 10 and 11). First, make sure all

Appendix

Access Basic or VBA modules are compiled in your earlier version database. For version 2 databases, this means you must open each form and report module individually and compile and save the module. Start Access 2003, and choose Database Utilities from the Tools menu. Choose Convert Database from the submenu and then choose To Access 2000 File Format or To Access 2002–2003 File Format. (Access 2003 also includes a utility to convert a 2000 or 2002–2003 format database back to version 8.) In the Database to Convert From dialog box, select the earlier version file that you want to convert. Access opens the Convert Database Into dialog box. You must specify a different file name or location for your converted database because Access won't let you replace your previous version file directly.

Note In order to convert a version 2 database to Access 2000 or 2002–2003 format, you must install additional software. You can download the additional software from the Office Updates Web site. Open Microsoft Access and choose Check for Updates from the Help menu.

If you open a version 2, 7, or 8 database in Access 2003, you will see a dialog box offering to convert the database to the current version or attempt to modify the database for shared use between versions. For these versions, I recommend that you attempt to convert them rather than modify them for shared use. You can also convert an earlier version database by creating a new Access 2000 or 2002–2003 format database and then importing all the objects from the older version database.

Conversion Issues

Microsoft Access 2003 reports any objects or properties that it is unable to convert by creating a table called Convert Errors in your converted database. The most common problems you're likely to encounter are Visual Basic libraries that were available in a previous version but not in Access 2003 or obsolete code that you created in a user-defined function.

Other changes that might affect the conversion of your application code or how your converted application runs include the following:

- In versions 2 and earlier, you could use the fourth parameter in the Format function to test for a Null value in a string variable or field. In versions 7 and later, you must use the IIf function to test for the special Null case. The Format function can handle Null in both arithmetic and date values in all versions.

- In versions 7 and earlier, you had to use macros to construct custom menus. Access 2003 continues to support macros for custom menus, but you might want to rebuild custom menus using the custom command bar facility.

- As of version 8, DoMenuItem is no longer supported. The conversion utility replaces this command in all macros with the equivalent RunCommand action or method. The DoMenuItem method in Visual Basic code is still supported for backward compatibility, but you should locate and change these statements after converting your database.

- In version 8, you could create a formatted Windows dialog box with the MsgBox action or function, separating the sections of the message with the @ character. Versions 9 and later no longer support this feature. You should remove the @ character used in this way in code you wrote for version 8.

- Versions 7 and 8 supported the Microsoft DAO 2.5/3.*x* compatibility library for databases converted from previous versions. Versions 9 and later no longer support this library. You will need to change the reference to this library to DAO 3.6 after you convert the database, and you might need to change old Visual Basic statements that depended on the older version of DAO.

- If you convert a database by importing its objects, your new database might not compile or execute properly. The problem is most likely a reference to an obsolete Visual Basic code library. You can correct this by opening any module in the Visual Basic Editor and then choosing References from the Tools menu. Remove any libraries marked MISSING and attempt to compile the project.

- Unless you also have Office 2002 installed on your machine, you won't be able to edit any data access pages that you created in Access 2002.

Creating an Office Toolbar in Windows XP

Microsoft Office XP and earlier included a utility program, the Microsoft Office Shortcut Bar, that allowed you to add a toolbar to your Windows desktop to make it easy to start any Office program. You could also create shortcuts with this utility to open office documents; open a new task, appointment, contact, message, or note in Microsoft Outlook; or open any program installed on your computer.

Microsoft Office 2003 no longer includes this utility because the functionality is replaced by the Windows XP toolbar facility. Creating a Windows XP toolbar to replace the Office Shortcut Bar is easy. First, create a folder on your hard drive that will contain the shortcuts to your programs. You can copy most of the shortcuts that you need for Office programs from C:\Documents and Settings\All Users\Start Menu (New Office Document and Open Office Document) and C:\Documents and Settings\All Users\Start Menu\Programs\Microsoft Office (shortcuts to start Access, Excel, FrontPage, InfoPath, Outlook, PowerPoint, Publisher, and Word). Be sure to copy the shortcuts, not move them. If you move them they will disappear from your Start menu.

The Office Shortcut Bar also provided options to open new appointments, contacts, messages, notes, and tasks within Microsoft Outlook. Creating shortcuts to open new items within Outlook is somewhat more difficult. You must create new shortcuts that point to Outlook and include special command line switches depending on the task that you want Outlook to perform. (You cannot use the Start menu shortcut to Outlook because it is a special system shortcut that you cannot modify.)

You can create a new shortcut in your folder by selecting the folder in Windows Explorer, choosing New from the File menu, and then choosing Shortcut on the submenu. Windows starts a wizard that lets you choose the location of the file you want to run and name the shortcut. In the Type the location of the item box of the wizard, point to the Outlook program—usually C:\Program Files\Microsoft Office\Office11\Outlook.exe. Click Next and in the Type a name for this shortcut box enter **New Outlook appointment** and click Finish.

1243

Right-click the new shortcut and choose Properties from the shortcut menu. On the Target line, type a space at the end of the line and add the new appointment switch from Table A-2 to define a shortcut to create a new appointment in Outlook. Follow the same procedure to create additional shortcuts for Outlook as shown in Table A-2.

Table A-2. Command Line Switches for Microsoft Outlook

Switch	Usage
/c IPM.APPOINTMENT	New Outlook appointment
/c IPM.CONTACT	New Outlook contact
/c IPM.NOTE	New Outlook message
/c IPM.STICKYNOTE	New Outlook note
/c IPM.TASK	New Outlook task

After you have created all the shortcuts you want, you can turn the folder into a Windows XP toolbar. Right-click on a blank area in the Windows taskbar. Make sure that the Lock the Taskbar option in the shortcut menu is cleared. Choose Toolbars on the shortcut menu and then click New Toolbar. Windows XP opens the New Toolbar window, shown in Figure A-17.

Figure A-17. The New Toolbar window in Windows XP.

Click the plus sign next to My Computer to see all your hard drives. Navigate to the new folder that you created containing all the shortcuts and click OK. You'll see the new toolbar appear in the taskbar. You can grab the left end of the toolbar and resize it or drag it to a new location on your desktop. You can right-click the toolbar and choose the Show Text option to show the name of each shortcut and the Show Title option to show the name of the folder you used for all the shortcuts. If you've dragged the toolbar away from the taskbar into its own window, you can also choose the Always On Top option to keep the toolbar on top of other windows. If you've dragged the toolbar away from the taskbar and docked it to another edge of your screen, you can additionally choose the Auto-Hide option so that the toolbar closes when you move your mouse away from the edge of the screen (move back to the edge to reopen the toolbar). I have mine docked at the top of my desktop (as shown in Figure A-18) with the Always On Top and Auto-Hide options set so that the toolbar doesn't get in the way when I don't need it.

If you don't want to go to all the trouble to build this toolbar, but you installed all the Office programs in the default location, you can locate the *XPToolbar* folder that you'll find on the companion CD and use that in the Windows XP New Toolbar window.

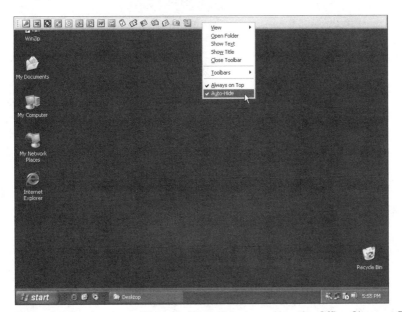

Figure A-18.   A custom Windows XP toolbar to replace the Office Shortcut Bar.

Appendix

Index to Troubleshooting Topics

Index to Troubleshooting Topics

Index

About the Author

John Viescas   Back in his home state of Texas after 16 years in the Pacific Northwest, John Viescas has been enjoying the winter sunshine and trying to figure out how to stay cool in July and August. If you hang out on the Web, you can find him answering questions about Microsoft Access in the newsgroups. John has been named a Microsoft MVP every year since 1993 for his continuing help to the Access users' community.

John got started in computing long before many of the current employees at Microsoft were "knee high to a grasshopper." It amazes him to think that the laptop he carries with him when he travels has more than 30,000 times the memory, has 1,000 times the disk space, and is many times faster than the first so-called mainframe computer he used to teach himself Autocoder (a computer language spoken by the ancients).

John has been working with database systems for most of his career. He began by designing and building a database application using Indexed Sequential Access Method files (ISAM—another ancient technology) for a magazine and paperback book distributing company in Illinois in 1968. He went on to build large database application systems for El Paso Natural Gas Company in his hometown in the early 1970s. From there he went to Applied Data Research in Dallas, where he managed the development of database and data dictionary systems for mainframe computers and became involved in the evolution of the SQL database language standard. Before forming his own company in 1993, he helped market and support NonStop SQL for Tandem Computers in California. Somewhere along the way (would you believe 1991?), he got involved in the early testing of a new Microsoft product that was code-named "Cirrus." The first edition of *Running Microsoft Access* was published in 1992. Since then, he has written four more editions of *Running*, coauthored the best-selling *SQL Queries for Mere Mortals*, and is pleased to be writing about Access from the "inside out" for this book.

In addition to working with Microsoft Access, John enjoys winging somewhere with his wife, Suzanne, just for fun. Between them, John and Suzanne have seven children and (at last count) eleven grandchildren. When they're not involved with their far-flung family, they like to spend at least part of their time in sunny places like Hawaii or romantic places like Paris (no, not Texas). Unless he's on vacation (and even then, sometimes), you can reach John via his Web site at *http://www.viescas.com*.

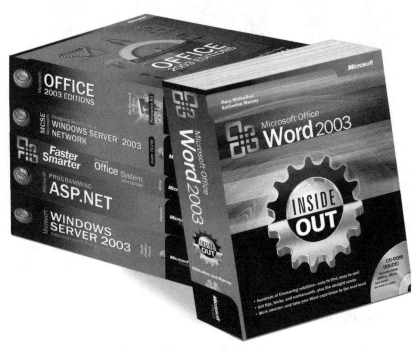